WORLD WAR II

AMERICA AT WAR
1941–1945

Norman Polmar
Thomas B. Allen

RANDOM HOUSE New York

WORLD WAR II

AMERICA AT WAR
1941–1945

For
Beverly and Scottie . . .
whose indulgence and patience,
like our love for them,
increase with time.

Cartoons on pages 442 and 534 copyright © 1944 by Bill Mauldin. Reprinted with permission of Bill Mauldin.

Drawing on page 317 from James P. O'Donnell *The Bunker: The History of the Reich Chancellery Group,* Houghton Mifflin Company, Boston, 1978.

Drawings on pages 89, 124, 125, 127, 152, 319, 373, 408, 486 courtesy of Salamander Books, London.

Library of Congress Cataloging-in-Publication Data

Polmar, Norman.
    World War II : America at war, 1941–1945 /
    Norman Polmar, Thomas B. Allen.
    p. cm.
    Includes bibliographical references and indexes.
    ISBN 0-394-58530-5
    1. World War, 1939–1945—Chronology. 2. World War, 1939–1945—
United States—Chronology. 3. World War, 1939–1945—Encyclopedias.
4. World War, 1939–1945—United States—Encyclopedias. I. Allen,
Thomas B. II. Title.
D743.5.P56 1991
940.53′02′02—dc20   91-16212 CIP

Project manager, Harriet Serenkin
Book design by Charlotte Staub
Manufactured in the United States of America
1 2 3 4 5 6 7 8 9

Contents

Abbreviations

AA	Antiaircraft	DE	Destroyer escort*
AAF	U.S. Army Air Forces	FBI	U.S. Federal Bureau of Investigation
AG	Miscellaneous auxiliary ship*	IX	Miscellaneous unclassified ship*
AP	Transport*	JCS	U.S. Joint Chiefs of Staff
APV	Aircraft transport*	LST	Landing ship, tank*
ASW	Antisubmarine Warfare	mm	millimeter
AVG	American Volunteer Group (Flying Tigers)	MTB	Motor Torpedo Boat
		OSS	U.S. Office of Strategic Services
BB	Battleship*	PCE(R)	Submarine chaser-escort (rescue)*
BBC	British Broadcasting Corp.	POW	Prisoner of War
CA	Heavy cruiser*	PT	Patrol-torpedo boat*
cal.	caliber	PTC	Patrol-torpedo boat chaser*
CinC	Commander in Chief	radar	Radio Detection And Ranging
CL	Light cruiser*	RAF	Royal Air Force
CLAA	Light antiaircraft cruiser*	SA	*Sturmabteilung* (Storm Detachment)
CV	Aircraft carrier*	SM	Submarine minelayer*
CVB	Large aircraft carrier*	sonar	Sound Navigation And Ranging
CVE	Escort aircraft carrier*	SS	*Schutzstaffel* (Elite Guard)
CVL	Light aircraft carrier*	SS	Submarine*
DD	Destroyer*		

*U.S. Navy ship designation.

About This Book

World War II: America at War 1941–1945 looks at World War II through American eyes. We wrote it from an American viewpoint not for patriotic reasons but because we believe that this viewpoint provides a way to see how the war touched and even shaped the American way of life, if not the American character. It was a world war. But to Americans who fought in it, who worked to win it, who waited and watched—and, now, to those who want to know about it—World War II was an American war.

When we say we look at the war through American eyes, we do not lose sight of the way the war came to America, and the way America came to war. That is, we recognize that the roots of America's involvement in the war go far deeper than Dec. 7, 1941, America's first official day at war. The United States became involved in war as a result of the sinking of the American gunboat *Panay* in 1937, the German Blitzkrieg across Poland in 1939, and the U-boat attacks on British merchant ships— sometimes escorted by U.S. warships—in the North Atlantic in 1940–1941. These events are discussed in the Prologue to War, which is where we suggest you begin reading. Then continue on to the War Chronology.

The War Chronology can serve as an appointment calendar or diary, a day-by-day listing of the events as they happened. As you read the War Chronology, you will see words in SMALL CAPITAL LETTERS. If you turn to those words in the War Guide, you will find another appointment, this time with a description of a person, or a place, or a weapon, or an event of the war. You can go through the war that way, reading about what happened on a certain day, then in the War Guide reading about the events and people who had a role in the happenings of that day.

The War Guide is an alphabetical listing of people, places, and events related to World War II. We hope you will browse through the War Guide, finding bits of the mosaic of the war and fitting them into your own sense of how it must have been. As you browse through the War Guide, you will also notice words in SMALL CAPITAL LETTERS. These words point you to other entries that will give you more information about the entry you're reading.

As you go through the War Guide, you will note that some of the people described there are not usually thought of in terms of World War II. These people include Lt. George Bush, Lt. Richard M. Nixon, Lt. Comdr. Lyndon B. Johnson, Lt. John F. Kennedy, and 1st Sgt. Joe Louis. They were far less important in the war than, say, Prime Minister Winston Churchill and Gen. Dwight D. Eisenhower. But looking through American eyes, we wanted to see what these young, future American leaders did during the war. Entries like these are in the War Guide because we find them interesting and hope you will. You will also read about civilians who walked onto the stage of war, such as Bob Hope and Tokyo Rose. The information provided about people in the war—as well as the subjects covered in the other entries—reflect our view of what was important in the war and what is important for an understanding of the war fifty years later.

The War Guide describes the important events of the war, such as the Allied landings at Normandy on D-Day, and some not so important but unusual events, such as history's last cavalry charge by Italian troops at Izbushensky in the Soviet Union. It describes the important weapons, such as the U.S. P-51 Mustang fighter, which saved the U.S. strategic bombing effort over Germany, and the Japanese M6A1 Seiran, a plane designed to be launched from a submarine to attack the Panama Canal.

It also talks about the absurd—Pumpkin Bombs and Rommel's Asparagus, neither of which were found at the corner grocery store—and German Superguns intended to shoot across the English Channel. And it presents the commonplace—the M1 Garand rifle and Carbine that armed most American troops.

The countries and military services that fought in the war are also described in the War Guide. Note that since they are so frequently mentioned, they are not set in SMALL CAPITALS. Each country's entry gives you an historic perspective that will fit the country into the world at war. Significant happenings on their soil—such as the invasion of Sicily and the battle of Bataan—are detailed as entries. The military services of each major participant in the war are found under the nation's entry. Thus, the entry for France is followed by entries for the French air force, army, and navy. There are separate entries for prominent and unusual military forces, such as Germany's Afrika Korps and Britain's Jewish Brigade. There are also entries to explain military formations, such as Corps, Division, Fleet, and Squadron.

Finally, the backdrop of battles and campaigns is presented in entries such as medicine, awards and decorations, and segregation. On the home front, the war years are portrayed with entries on songs, movies, and V-mail.

The war's major campaigns make up another element of the War Guide. They were neither places nor countries. They ranged over months and weeks (one, the Battle of the Atlantic, lasted almost six years), over countryside and city, across thousands of square miles of terrain or boundless seas.

A campaign is easily defined as a continuous series of military operations, but few histories of the war agree on what was and was not a campaign. The *United States Army in World War II,* the official Army history, has a list of campaigns, but only those involving the U.S. Army. The U.S. Marines have an official list of battles, as does the Navy. But they differ from the Army's list, even though there were many joint operations. (The appendixes U.S. Navy Battle Stars and U.S. Army and Air Forces Battle Streamers contain those services' official listings of actions in the war.)

Perhaps it is the historic approach and not the battles themselves that defines a campaign. We believe so. Therefore, for this book we created our own list of campaigns. They appear, like all entries, alphabetically in the War Guide and in small capitals in the text. The campaigns are listed here in chronological order:

Japanese Campaign in the Far East (1937–1943)
Polish Campaign (1939)
Battle of the Atlantic (1939–1945)
Denmark and Norway Campaign (1940)
France and Low Countries Campaign (1940)
Battle of Britain (1940)
North Africa-Middle East Campaign (1940–1943)
Balkans-Greece-Crete Campaign (1941)
Japan's China-Burma Campaign (1941–1943)
German Campaign in the Soviet Union (1941–1943)
Allied China-Burma-India Campaign (1941–1945)
Japanese Campaign in the Central Pacific (1942)
Northwest Africa Campaign (1942–1943)
U.S. Solomons–New Guinea Campaign (1942–1943)
U.S. Central Pacific Campaign (1943–1945)
Soviet Offensive Campaign (1943–1945)
Italian Campaign (1943–1945)
Allied Campaign in Europe (1944–1945)

Two campaigns described in this book are labeled as battles, but by their importance and subsequent fame, they rise to a higher strategic significance and to a greater remembrance. The Battle of the Atlantic and the Battle of Britain are names that ring so nobly in the minds of those who remember the war, they must be handed down intact to those who will know of World War II only by reading about them.

The Epilogue to War describes, in brief, the aftermath of the war. It discusses how the people and events of the conflict affected the postwar period—which only ended in the recent demise of the Soviet empire.

The book has two indexes—one listing all the personalities mentioned in the book and the other listing all code words.

NORMAN POLMAR
THOMAS B. ALLEN

Acknowledgments

We are in debt to many individuals and institutions for their assistance in compiling this history of America at war. In particular, Steven Llanso of the USNI Military Database and Peter Mersky of *Approach Magazine* provided invaluable assistance. Mr. Llanso prepared the first drafts of many of the personality entries; Mr. Mersky reviewed the multitude of aircraft entries.

Roger Macbride Allen, a distinguished author in his own right, provided invaluable assistance in preparing the manuscript.

Other individuals who helped in editorial matters include Janice McKenney and Hannah Zeidlik of the U.S. Army Historical Center and Dr. Dean Allard and Bernard F. Cavalcante of the U.S. Naval Historical Center. Laura Johnston assisted in preparing several of the campaign entries.

James Witte and Constance Allen Witte were most helpful in providing translations of German-language material. Linda Cullen and Mary Beth Straight of the U.S. Naval Institute, Paul Kemp of the Imperial War Museum, and Charles Haberline of the U.S. Naval Historical Center helped research photographs for this book. Malcolm Saunders of Mitchell Beazley International provided several useful reference works.

Our editor, Harriet Serenkin, gave us invaluable assistance and guidance in addition to her expert wielding of a copy pencil. We also appreciate the efforts of Jack Hornor, Ellen Lichtenstein, Gail Bradney, Charlotte Staub, Trumbull Rogers, Anita Mondello, Ursula Brennan, and Martha Solonche.

Finally, we appreciate the assistance provided by the staffs of the Naval Museum in Leningrad, the National Archives and the U.S. Army Library (Pentagon) in Washington, D.C., the Imperial War Museum in London, the *Bibliothek für Zeitgeschichte* in Stuttgart, and the U.S. Marine Corps History and Museums Branch, with special thanks to Col. F. Brooke Nihart.

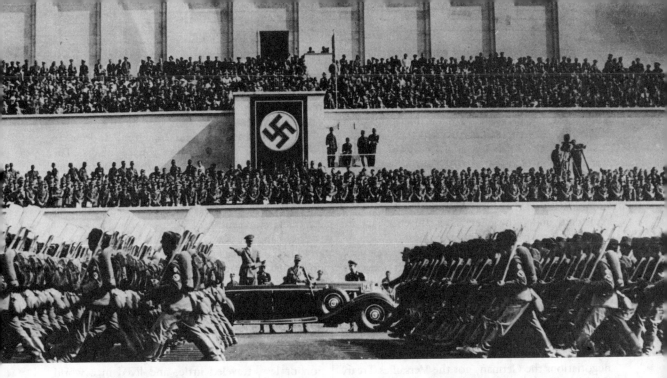

Prologue to War
1919–1941

For America, World War II began on Dec. 7, 1941, when Japanese planes bombed PEARL HARBOR. Americans who remember back to that Sunday can summon up the exact moment when they heard the news, which shattered a Sunday afternoon listening to a football game or a Sunday afternoon concert on the radio: *We interrupt this broadcast to bring you a special news bulletin. Pearl Harbor has been attacked by the Japanese.*

For many other Americans, the war had begun at other moments. For the crew of the U.S. gunboat *PANAY* (PR 5), war came in 1937, when Japanese planes attacked their ship on the Yangtze River. For the crewmen of the *REUBEN JAMES* (DD 245), the war began on Oct. 31, 1941, when a German U-BOAT sank their ship.

For Americans eager to fight as volunteers, the war had begun at other times. Some went into the ABRAHAM LINCOLN BRIGADE to fight the Fascists in the SPANISH CIVIL WAR of 1936–1939; others became pilots for the FLYING TIGERS to fight the Japanese invaders of China, the first country to fall victim to aggression in the war that would engulf the world.

For sentimental Americans who sang wistfully of "The Last Time I Saw Paris," the war began with the fall of PARIS in June 1940. In that year and the year before, impatient young American men, using

Pomp and pageantry were a tenet of the Nazi faith. A massive exhibition complex was built at Nuremberg for parades, processions, and paying tribute to the Führer. Here Adolf Hitler—standing in the car—salutes formations of the German labor service troops while Nazi Party officials and motion-picture cameras watch. *(Imperial War Museum)*

false names to avoid prosecution under U.S. NEU-TRALITY ACTS, went off to fight for England by joining the British Army or the all-American EAGLE SQUADRONS of the Royal Air Force.

For millions of other young American men, the war began on Oct. 29, 1940, when a blindfolded Secretary of War HENRY L. STIMSON reached into a ten-gallon glass bowl and started drawing the numbers assigned, by lottery, to those who had registered under the SELECTIVE SERVICE Act for America's first peacetime military draft.

The impersonal forces of history, however, look not to private moments but to the march of events, and, in search of the beginnings of World War II, history turns to April 1919. In that month, repre-sentatives of the WEIMAR REPUBLIC, the newborn democratic Germany, went to Versailles, France, under the assumption that they would negotiate as equals with the victors of World War I. Instead of negotiations the Germans got the Versailles Treaty thrust at them. It bankrupted Germany and made it a breeding ground for demagogues of the left and the right, including ADOLF HITLER. He took over an obscure political group and used it as a stepping-stone to power. His NATIONAL SOCIALIST GER-MAN WORKERS' PARTY, hailing him as *Der Führer,* gave him the legitimacy he needed to be installed as chancellor of an economically desperate Germany in 1933.

In BERLIN, Hitler's brown-shirted NAZI storm troopers beat up opponents, smashed the windows of Jewish shops, and made ANTI-SEMITISM official national policy. Few Americans reacted. But one who did was the feisty mayor of New York City, FIORELLO H. LA GUARDIA, who called Hitler a "brown-shirted fanatic." The German government protested, and on March 5, 1937, Secretary of State CORDELL HULL expressed U.S. regret at the mayor's intemperate words.

On that March day in 1937 the United States was neutral, ill-prepared for war, and concerned with its own problems. The 1920s had seen a drastic weak-ening of U.S. defenses. The size of the Army had fallen below that authorized by law, and the num-ber of Navy ships was less than that permitted by international armament agreements. When FRANK-LIN D. ROOSEVELT became President on March 4, 1933, the U.S. Army ranked seventeenth in the

world. When La Guardia took on Hitler, the mayor's New York City police force was larger than the U.S. Marine Corps.

Roosevelt, in his second Inaugural Address, in 1937, did not even mention foreign affairs. The United States, struggling through the Depression, had little concern with what was happening beyond its Atlantic and Pacific shores. Isolationism was symbolized by *The Chicago Tribune*'s editorial calls for the strengthening of U.S. coast ARTILLERY.

Hitler and the Nazis; *Il Duce* BENITO MUSSOLINI and his Italian Blackshirts invading Ethiopia, using poison gas and bombers against spears; the Japanese troops ravaging China and raping the women of NANKING—they were all far away and irrelevant. Americans were trying to find jobs, or trying to stave off foreclosure of their mortgaged farms, or living on food handed out by relief agencies. The average American adult had an eighth-grade educa-tion or less, traveled little, and lived in a world encompassed by family and community. Most Americans lived on farms or in towns with fewer than 10,000 people. Not many of them had a global view.

Isolationism, the driving force of the AMERICAN FIRST COMMITTEE, kept much of the country look-ing inward. After the Italian invasion of Ethiopia in 1935, an opinion poll asked Americans whether the United States should join with other nations to stop one nation from attacking another; 67 percent said no.

President Roosevelt and Cordell Hull, however, saw the spread of militarism and fascism through the world as a threat to international order and ultimately as a danger to the United States. Few Americans realized that U.S. interests had become global. American automobile and aircraft manufac-turers, along with cotton and tobacco farmers, had markets throughout the world.

From 1936 to 1938 the United States, producer of two thirds of the world's petroleum, was the leading exporting nation of the world and was sec-ond only to the UNITED KINGDOM as an importer. The United States needed rubber, primarily for au-tomobile tires, from Pacific plantations and tin from Malaya; other manufacturers imported vast amounts of raw materials, from asbestos to zinc; U.S. women wanted silk stockings, and the silk came from China; American families wanted coffee from Brazil, tea from India, and sugar from the Philippines.

Much of the nation's imports and exports was carried in ships flying the U.S. flag. The newly created U.S. Maritime Commission, with JOSEPH P. KENNEDY as its first chairman, reported in 1937 that the United States had 1,422 oceangoing merchant ships, warned that nearly all of them were obsolete, and called for a government-subsidized shipbuilding program. The first new cargo ship under the program was delivered in June 1939. By the end of the year there were sixteen U.S. shipyards building merchant ships and twenty-one more ships had been launched.

Whatever the U.S. stake in foreign matters, Americans were beginning to see and hear the world through their newspapers, which traditionally had given much more coverage to Main Street than to global affairs, and from their radios, which were beginning to recognize news as a commodity that sponsors would buy. Newspapers had awakened with the diplomats when the MUNICH PACT was signed. Sensing the importance of the pact, the Associated Press covered the events as a major news story, transmitting as many as 31,000 words a day to member newspapers.

The reality of the outer world was finding its way into the American consciousness. Schoolboys who had been trading baseball cards found WAR CARDS with their bubble gum and began collecting gruesome scenes of atrocities in China instead of pictures and batting averages of Lou Gehrig and Joe DiMaggio. Moviegoers were laughing at *The Great Dictator,* with Charlie Chaplin playing a strutting, mustachioed tyrant named Adenoid Hynkel. Hitler protested, but this time no one apologized.

Other anti-Nazi MOVIES came from both Hollywood and England, and the NEWSREELS, shown between feature films at movie theaters, brought Americans vivid images: the book burning by Nazi students at the University of Berlin in May 1933; the air raids on NANKING in 1937 and Barcelona in 1938; Hitler's snub of American black champion Jesse Owens, star of the 1936 Olympic Games in Berlin.

On the night that the books were burned—books that included the works of Jack London and Upton Sinclair—Nazi PROPAGANDA chief JOSEPH GOEBBELS, standing before the fire, said, "These flames not only illuminate the final end of an old era; they also light up the new."

It took more than four years for that era to be acknowledged by U.S. foreign policy. The change arrived suddenly, triggered by the Japanese invasion of China in the summer of 1937.

War in China had begun in 1931, when Japanese troops, claiming that Chinese troops were sabotaging a stretch of Japanese-owned railway, seized the Chinese city of Mukden (now Shenyang). The "Mukden incident" gave warning to the West of the rise of the military in Japan. Japan responded to the LEAGUE OF NATIONS censure by quitting the League. But the walkout inspired scarcely a harsh word from Western chancelleries. Japan's swift conquest of northeastern China was of little interest to any nation but prostrated China. Diplomatic and commercial business went on as usual, even when the Japanese set up the state of Manchoukuo and installed a Chinese puppet administration.

The full-scale Japanese invasion of China in 1937, however, alarmed the U.S. foreign affairs establishment. President Roosevelt's counselors told him that the Japanese aggression could not be ignored. As he well knew, however, there would be little concern about China on the part of the average American. Reaction would have to come from WASHINGTON and its policymakers, not from America's grass roots.

Events in Asia were much farther away than events in Europe. Millions of Americans were European immigrants, or sons and daughters and grandsons and granddaughters of European immigrants. They had ties to the map that Hitler wanted to change. Through immigration and through cultural heritage, the United States had a long relationship with Europe. China and Japan, however, were alien nations, a bias reflected in the U.S. immigration laws that discriminated against Asians.

Roosevelt, whose strength was in domestic politics, now felt compelled to test that strength by telling his nation that aggression in faraway Asia was linked to aggression in Europe, that this aggression could hurt the United States.

Japan's invasion of China, like Italy's invasion of Ethiopia and Germany's deploying of troops in the

Rhineland in 1936, had proved the impotence of the League of Nations. Roosevelt's foreign-policy advisers, led by Hull, realized that nations could not rely on international law as a keeper of the peace.

By the end of July 1937 Japanese troops had taken Peking and Tientsin. Soon all of eastern China would be under Japanese control. Roosevelt and Hull saw this as a breakdown of international order. In 1922, the United States, the British Empire, France, the Netherlands, Portugal, Italy, Belgium, China, and Japan, by signing the Nine-Power Treaty of Washington, had agreed to respect the sovereignty and borders of China. Japan had brazenly broken that treaty.

None of the other signatories would act. But at least one of them, the United States, would speak out. Cordell Hull, troubled by the moral consequences of aggression, warned that the world must run under rules of moral behavior. "If the world followed them," he said, "the world could live at peace forever. If the world ignored them, war would be eternal."

On Oct. 5, 1937, at the urging of Hull, Roosevelt went to Chicago, a stronghold of isolationism, and made a speech in which he compared war to a contagious disease that had to be quarantined. "The peace-loving nations," he said, "must make concerted effort in opposition to those violations of treaties and those ignorings of humane instincts which today are creating a state of international anarchy, international instability from which there is no escape through mere isolation or neutrality."

A kind of answer to Roosevelt came on Dec. 12, when Japanese warplanes bombed the *Panay*. Americans reacted with shock and anger. Japan apologized and offered indemnity, but there was no way to roll back the newsreels that brought the foundering *Panay* and wounded survivors into American movie theaters. The United States had been attacked. Americans had been killed. Faraway war no longer was something merely involving foreigners.

Roosevelt's quarantine speech and the sinking of the *Panay* alerted the nation to the rumblings of war. But the United States, unable and unwilling to plunge deeper into foreign affairs, was merely a bystander in the major international events of 1938: Germany's takeover of Austria; the Munich Pact

that handed Czechoslovakia over to Germany; Japan's announcement of a "new order"—the GREATER EAST ASIA CO-PROSPERITY SPHERE, which was to give Japan the RESOURCES of the lands now controlled by the colonial powers.

As American isolationists stepped up their warnings against U.S. involvement in other nations' wars, Nazi propagandists in the United States tried to stir up anti-British sentiment. The Nazis hoped to keep the United States neutral so that U.S. armaments did not reach British arsenals. Some of the propaganda was not subtle.

In April 1938, more than 3,500 Americans jammed a casino in the heavily German Yorkville section of New York City to celebrate Hitler's forty-ninth birthday. On Feb. 20, 1939, ostensibly to celebrate George Washington's birthday, 20,000 people showed up in New York's Madison Square Garden for a "Mass Demonstration for True Americanism" sponsored by the GERMAN-AMERICAN BUND. A brown-shirted Nazi Legion of 1,200 gave the stiff-armed Nazi salute to a speaker's platform on which a figure of George Washington was flanked by two black SWASTIKA flags. A Bund manual, made public in Jan. 1941 by the House Committee on Un-American Activities, said Bund members would "exterminate with all their power the stinking poison of red Jewish infection in America."

In the spring of 1939 the New York World's Fair opened and offered Americans a look at the "World of Tomorrow." ALBERT EINSTEIN, who had fled Hitler's Germany, dramatically switched on the fair's garish night illumination by pressing a button that was somehow connected with "cosmic rays." Lights flashed in salute to an elemental force that people dimly knew as atomic power. In August Einstein would write a letter to Roosevelt, launching the project that would create the ATOMIC BOMB.

In June, King GEORGE VI and Queen Mary of England, making the first royal visit to the United States in history, went to the World's Fair in the company of President and Mrs. Roosevelt. The visit, which included a highly publicized hotdogs-and-beer picnic at the Roosevelts' Hyde Park home, was more than a friendly meeting of royal family and American First Family. Roosevelt saw the visit as part of a campaign to turn the American people from isolationism to support of the British in the war that he believed was soon to come. For England and Europe, it was the last summer of peace.

In August, Germany and the Soviet Union, enemies in public but longtime military collaborators in private, stunned the world by announcing their NONAGGRESSION PACT, which set the stage for war. Hitler, planning to invade Poland, needed assurance that the Soviets would accommodate him. He and Soviet leader JOSEF STALIN also secretly agreed to a division of Poland and the Baltic states. The pact particularly shocked Japan, which three years before had allied itself with Germany against the Soviet Union through the ANTI-COMINTERN PACT. Baron Kiichiro Hiranuma resigned as prime minister, setting in motion a series of Cabinet shakeups that would ultimately strengthen the political power of the Japanese military.

On Aug. 31, Nazi SS troops in Polish Army uniforms staged an attack on a radio station at Gleiwitz on the German-Polish border. One of them grabbed a microphone and yelled, in Polish, a call to war. They riddled the building with shots, then fired into the bodies of German CONCENTRATION CAMP inmates who had been previously murdered with drugs and dressed in Polish uniforms (in an SS operation called Canned Goods). The next day, Hitler announced war against Poland, listing among the causes "the attack by regular Polish troops on the Gleiwitz transmitter."

On Sept. 1 a German BLITZKRIEG struck Poland. Hitler ordered his troops to "kill without pity or mercy all men, women, and children of the Polish race or language." At 2:50 A.M., according to a note that President Roosevelt scrawled at his bedside, he received news of the invasion via a telephone call from the U.S. ambassador in WARSAW to the U.S. ambassador in Paris. Roosevelt, assuming his role as Commander in Chief, ordered that "all Navy ships and Army commands be notified at once."

England and France started mobilizing and urged Hitler to withdraw to begin peace negotiations. When Hitler did not respond, the two nations, which had promised to come to Poland's aid, issued an ultimatum that was to expire at 11 A.M. on Sunday, Sept. 3. At 11:15, the British Prime Minister, NEVILLE CHAMBERLAIN, announced a state of war existed between Great Britain and Germany. Americans would call it the EUROPEAN WAR—the term

World War II would come later. Later that same day, a German U-boat torpedoed the *ATHENIA*, a British liner bound for Montreal; 112 people, including twenty-eight Americans, died.

In a classic pincer movement, German forces, led by PANZER armor units, struck Poland from north and south. The blitzkrieg rolled across Poland in a month. Meanwhile, the Soviet Union, acting under a secret clause in the Nonaggression Pact, invaded Poland from the east and occupied a vast region. Other secret clauses bestowed the Baltic republics of Lithuania, Estonia, and Latvia upon the Soviet Union, which took them over by the implied threat of military force in October 1939.

Finland, which was also expected to bow to Soviet will, resisted and asked for negotiations. The Soviet Union brushed aside the Finns' request for talks and, shamelessly claiming self-defense, invaded the little nation in November. The Red Army expected little resistance. But the Finns fought gallantly, winning the hearts—but not the help—of democratic nations. Finnish ski troops sometimes wiped out isolated Soviet units and even routed an entire division. A massive Soviet counteroffensive in Jan. 1940 finally crushed the Finns. A subsequent peace treaty shrank Finland back to the size it had been at the time of Peter the Great.

Elsewhere in Europe, by the spring of 1940, hardly anything of military significance had occurred on land since the invasion of Poland. At sea, U-boats and British merchant ships had begun the BATTLE OF THE ATLANTIC, the longest and in many ways the most important battle of the European War. But U.S. and British journalists, looking around in Europe, saw nothing happening there and called the lull the Phony War. The Germans called it the *Sitzkrieg,* and Chamberlain referred to it as the Twilight War.

At sea and in the air, however, there was real war. The Royal Air Force, although dropping only anti-Hitler propaganda pamphlets over Germany, lost planes to German antiaircraft defenses. And in the autumn of 1939 the Royal Navy suffered the loss of some 1,300 men in the sinking of the aircraft carrier *Courageous* and the battleship *Royal Oak.* In December the Royal Navy revenged its losses with the death of the German "pocket battleship" *ADMIRAL GRAF SPEE,* scuttled after being hunted down in the

Atlantic. Nor was it a Phony War for English merchant ships or German U-boats. The Battle of the Atlantic had begun on the day the war began and it would go on until Germany's SURRENDER.

America's response to the European War was spelled out immediately by President Roosevelt: "This nation will remain a neutral nation, but I cannot ask that every American remain neutral in thought as well." The President called Congress into special session and asked for still another change in the NEUTRALITY ACT, which governed U.S. conduct toward belligerent nations.

The new law, signed by Roosevelt on Nov. 4, 1939, allowed "cash-and-carry"—belligerents could buy arms as long as they paid cash and carried off their purchases in their own ships. Although the language of the act suggested that arms could be sold to any belligerent nation, the intent of the legislation was the legalizing of arms sales to England and France for their war against Germany.

U.S. neutrality already had been fading in the Pacific. In July 1939, trying to curb Japan's aggression through economic warfare, the United States told Japan that it planned to allow the commercial treaty between the two nations to expire in Jan. 1940. The U.S. decision had potentially disastrous consequences for Japan. Poor in resources, Japan had become extraordinarily dependent upon the United States, which supplied Japan with 66 percent of its oil, virtually all of its aviation fuel, 91 percent of its copper, and 90 percent of the metal scrap that Japan vitally needed in lieu of adequate iron deposits.

The Roosevelt administration also extended what had become known as the "moral embargo," begun in June 1938 to restrain arms manufacturers from exporting to belligerents aircraft, aircraft parts, and aerial BOMBS that could be used against civilian cities. The embargo, backed by moral principle but not by specific law, was urged in reaction to the March 1938 bombing of Barcelona by the German-aided Nationalists during the Spanish Civil War. In Dec. 1939 Roosevelt specifically aimed the moral embargo at Japan and expanded it to include the exporting of any technical information pertaining to the manufacture of aviation fuel.

The U.S. actions brought down another Japanese Cabinet and intensified the Roosevelt adminis-

tration's belief that economic pressure would restrain Japan. U.S. public opinion polls now backed a strong embargo. Hull, hoping that he could lure Japan to the negotiating table, said that U.S.-Japanese trade could continue without the treaty. But Japan began looking to another solution to its perennial shortage of resources: the colonial possessions of countries Germany was on the verge of defeating.

In the spring of 1940 Germany suddenly ended the Phony War with the DENMARK AND NORWAY CAMPAIGN, followed immediately by the FRANCE AND LOW COUNTRIES CAMPAIGN. On June 10, as Panzer units swept across France, Italy declared war against England and France. "The hand that held the dagger," said President Roosevelt, "has struck it into the back of its neighbor."

On June 14 Germans entered Paris and on June 22 France and Germany signed an armistice in the same railway carriage used for the German surrender in World War I. The new German blitzkriegs could also claim as a victim the government of Neville Chamberlain, who had been replaced as prime minister by WINSTON CHURCHILL on May 10.

When France surrendered, Churchill was ready with a secret operation—code-named Catapult—to neutralize the French Navy. French ships in British and Egyptian ports were boarded and captured with only minor incidents. Other ships that were in French North African ports were given an ultimatum: sail to British ports and fight against the Germans, submit to disarming and custody, or face destruction.

French naval officers vainly attempted to negotiate. Royal Navy warships bombarded and bombed several French ships in the port of Mers el-Kébir, near Oran, killing about 1,300 French sailors.

Soon after the fall of Paris, Roosevelt asked Congress for more defense appropriations, including enough money to build 50,000 warplanes a year. In August, the Selective Service Act, endorsed by Roosevelt, was passed by Congress. And that fall, extensive tests began on the B-17C FLYING FORTRESS heavy bomber and other new U.S. combat aircraft.

Hitler ordered the annihilation of the RAF as a prelude for SEA LION, the invasion of England. The BATTLE OF BRITAIN began. Hitler also set in motion the HOLOCAUST when, on Oct. 16, some 400,000 JEWS were herded into the WARSAW GHETTO. By then Mussolini was occupying British and French Somaliland, had troops in Egypt, and had invaded Greece.

American interest in the European War quickened. Radio, newspapers, and magazines stepped up coverage of the war. From LONDON, CBS correspondent EDWARD R. MURROW gave American radio listeners word portraits of the horrors and heroism of the BLITZ. Newsreels showed American moviegoers the bombing of Rotterdam, the German Panzer units roaring down French roads, the disaster at DUNKIRK.

Militant Japanese leaders, responding to German victories, overthrew moderate politicians and began rapidly moving toward alliance with what Benito Mussolini called the AXIS powers. On Sept. 27, 1940, Japan joined the Axis by signing the TRIPARTITE PACT, which called for each of the three nations to provide military assistance in case of attack by any nation not yet in the war—a nation that was unmistakably the United States.

By the time the pact was signed, the United States and England had made an agreement of their own, the DESTROYERS-FOR-BASES DEAL. Churchill on May 15, in his first message as prime minister to Roosevelt, had asked for "the loan of 40 or 50 of your older destroyers." In one of several subsequent appeals, Churchill said, "The fate of the war may be decided by this minor and easily remedied factor." Unable by law to *give* any aid to a belligerent, President Roosevelt, in the midst of his campaign for an unprecedented third term, made a deal, trading fifty aged destroyers for the rights to several British bases in the Western Hemisphere.

Japan, meanwhile, was seeking from the pro-Nazi VICHY FRANCE regime approval for what would become an occupation of French INDOCHINA, from which supplies had been flowing to China. Indochina would give Japan a base for further expansion and acquisition of Southeast Asia's oil, rubber, tin, quinine, and timber. As Japan set out on this new avenue of conquest, the United States imposed an embargo on aviation gasoline and scrap metal.

After the fall of France, the United States, reminding Vichy France and Germany about the Monroe Doctrine, said no changes would be toler-

ated in the status of Danish, Dutch, and French colonies in the Western Hemisphere. The United States was particularly anxious about the oil refineries in the Dutch West Indies. In the summer of 1940 Canadian and French troops were landed in Curaçao and Aruba to defend the refineries, among the largest in the world.

U.S. policymakers and military strategists, concerned about the large numbers of Nazi propaganda and ESPIONAGE agents in Latin American countries, took two steps to keep the Western Hemisphere out of German hands. The FEDERAL BUREAU OF INVESTIGATION extended its vigil against espionage and SABOTAGE into Latin America. And Hull worked to forge a strong united-hemisphere defense policy.

Foreign ministers of Latin American republics met and adopted the "Act of Havana," which said that nations of the Americas would temporarily take over any territory likely to fall under a conqueror's control. The agreement promised that the territory would revert to the parent nation's control after the war. (At a similar meeting in Rio de Janeiro in Jan. 1942, the foreign ministers developed a common hemisphere defense policy. By then most of the hemisphere's twenty-one republics had broken off relations with the Axis powers. Many declared war on the Axis. For the way the Latin American nations dealt with the war, see the individual country entries.)

Roosevelt, after winning his third term, got from Congress a LEND-LEASE law that authorized the president to sell, transfer, lend, lease, or dispose of, in any way, arms and supplies to any country "whose defense the President deems vital to the defense of the United States." No longer neutral, the United States was now giving England all help "short of war." That three-word phrase proved to be a flimsy definition in the months that led to Dec. 1941, for war now began to seem close.

In July, responding to Japan's invasion of southern Indochina, Roosevelt froze Japanese assets in the United States and cut off all oil exports to Japan. In August, Roosevelt met with Churchill in the first ATLANTIC CONFERENCE. The two leaders issued the ATLANTIC CHARTER, which made the United States an open ally in the British war against Germany.

In the Atlantic, an undeclared war against the United States had already begun. On Sept. 4, the U.S. destroyer GREER (DD 145) was attacked by a German U-boat while helping British-bound CONVOYS. Roosevelt immediately warned Germany and Italy that German or Italian warships that entered U.S.-patrolled waters would "do so at their own risk." On Oct. 17, a U-boat damaged the destroyer *Kearny* (DD 432), killing eleven of her crew, and on Oct. 31 the U.S. destroyer *REUBEN JAMES* (DD 245) was sunk about 600 miles off Ireland by another German submarine. Of her 160-man crew, only forty-five were saved.

In Japan, military officers favoring a tougher stand against the United States met in October and, urging that the nation "get ready for war," managed to bring down another Cabinet and install Gen. HIDEKI TOJO as the new prime minister.

Japan's leading naval strategist, Adm. ISOROKU YAMAMOTO, had long believed that he had an answer to Japan's needs: aircraft carriers that could extend the island nation's reach halfway across the Pacific. As proof of what carrier-based planes could do, he pointed to TARANTO. On Nov. 13, 1940, British carrier planes had caught the Italian fleet at anchor in the inner harbor of the Italian naval base at Taranto and had disabled three Italian battleships in the first major carrier strike in history.

For Taranto, Yamamoto substituted Pearl Harbor, where in 1940 the United States had permanently moved its Pacific Fleet, hoping to use its presence as a deterrence to Japanese aggression in the Far East. But the United States almost immediately began weakening its Pacific Fleet by transferring BATTLESHIPS, AIRCRAFT CARRIERS, CRUISERS, and destroyers to the Atlantic and the occasional shooting war against German U-boats.

Yamamoto, who had spent a significant amount of time in the United States, opposed war because he realized how great was the U.S. industrial potential. Still, with the Japanese government committed to conflict, he believed that his country could have one year to complete its conquests before the United States could mobilize its might. He felt that an aerial and submarine attack against the U.S. fleet at Pearl Harbor could insure that one year of operational freedom.

He began planning. By the fall of 1941 Yamamoto was playing war games and training fliers for an attack on Pearl Harbor.

On the diplomatic front, Tojo reiterated Japanese demands that the United States end aid to China, accept the Japanese seizure of Indochina, resume normal trade, and not reinforce bases in the Far East. He publicly maintained that the demands were not negotiable and set a deadline for U.S. acceptance. Unaware of U.S. success in MAGIC code-breaking, he told the Japanese Ambassador to the United States, KICHISABURO NOMURA, that negotiations were still possible.

Cordell Hull, clinging to this last hope for peace, met with Nomura (aided by special envoy SABURO KURUSU). But the two nations were at an impasse. On Nov. 26, 1941, Hull once more stated the U.S. position: Japan must withdraw from China and Indochina, recognize CHIANG KAI-SHEK as the legitimate ruler of China, abandon territorial expansion, and accept international standards of reciprocal trade.

Tojo saw Hull's statement as an "ultimatum" and began the countdown to war. On Dec. 2 he ordered a secretly assembled attack task force to begin its mission: attack Pearl Harbor on Dec. 8, Japan time, which was Sunday, Dec. 7, Hawaiian and Washington time.

At about 7:55 A.M. on Dec. 7, Lt. Cmdr. Logan Ramsey, operations officer of Patrol WING 2 at Pearl Harbor, saw what he thought was a barnstorming U.S. plane flying low. Then he saw "something black fall out of the plane" and heard an explosion. He ran into a radio room and ordered every operator to send the same message: *Air Raid, Pearl Harbor—This Is No Drill*.

At 12:30 P.M. on Dec. 8, 1941, President Roosevelt stood before a joint session of Congress and began, "Yesterday, December 7, 1941—a date which will live in infamy—the United States of America was suddenly and deliberately attacked by naval and air forces of the Empire of Japan. The United States was at peace with that Nation and, at the solicitation of Japan, was still in conversation with its Government and its Emperor looking toward the maintenance of peace in the Pacific. Indeed, one hour after Japanese air squadrons had commenced bombing in Oahu, the Japanese Ambassador to the United States and his colleague delivered to the Secretary of State a formal reply to a recent American message. . . .

"With confidence in our armed forces—with the unbounded determination of our people—we will gain the inevitable triumph—so help us God. I ask that the Congress declare that since the unprovoked and dastardly attack by Japan on Sunday, December 7, a state of war existed between the United States and the Japanese Empire."

At 1 P.M. the Senate unanimously adopted a resolution declaring war. At 1:10 P.M. the House voted for war, 388 to 1. The single dissenting vote was cast by Representative Jeannette Rankin of Montana, who had also voted against a declaration of war in 1917.

That night, Churchill later wrote, he "slept the sleep of the saved and the thankful." On Dec. 11 Hitler appeared before the Reichstag and, in a long, rambling speech that even included comparisons of his poverty—"the child of a small, poor family"—to Roosevelt's riches, declared war against the United States. Following, as ever, in Hitler's footsteps, Mussolini did the same on the same day.

America was at war.

WAR CHRONOLOGY

1941

Jan. 1 In the first military move toward the Japanese attack on PEARL HARBOR, Adm. ISOROKU YAMAMOTO, Commander in Chief of the Japanese Combined Fleet, orders Rear Adm. TAKIJIRO ONISHI, one of Japan's leading naval aviators, to prepare a preliminary study for an air raid on Pearl Harbor; Onishi is assisted by Comdr. MINORU GENDA. This attack will prevent the U.S. FLEET from interfering with the JAPANESE CAMPAIGN IN THE FAR EAST.

Jan. 6 President ROOSEVELT recommends the LEND-LEASE program to Congress and enunciates the FOUR FREEDOMS.

Jan. 10 LEND-LEASE bill introduced in the U.S. Congress.

Jan. 11 HITLER orders forces to be prepared to enter North Africa to assist the Italian effort, marking the establishment of the AFRIKA KORPS.

Jan. 20 President ROOSEVELT is inaugurated for his third term as president; Henry A. Wallace is his vice president.

Jan. 22 Italian forces surrender the port of TOBRUK to the British.

Jan. 23 Col. CHARLES A. LINDBERGH, testifying on the LEND-LEASE bill before the House Foreign Affairs Committee of Congress, suggests negotiations with HITLER to end the EUROPEAN WAR.

Jan. 29–March 29 U.S.-British military staff talks are held in WASHINGTON (code name ABC-1).

Feb. 1 The U.S. Navy organizes for war: the U.S. Atlantic FLEET is reestablished under Adm. ERNEST J. KING. This fleet, first constituted on Jan. 1, 1906, was abolished in 1922 when the U.S. Fleet organization was established in the place of separate ocean fleets.

Feb. 6 HITLER issues directive for economic war against Britain.

Feb. 16 British forces mine SINGAPORE waters in preparation for a Japanese assault.

March 1 Bulgaria joins the AXIS.

"There is great courage and a blind belief that Britain will survive. . . . And of the future, I think most of them would say, 'We shall live hard, but we shall live.'"

American radio broadcaster Edward R. Murrow describing the German Blitz against London in March 1941

March 11 Congress passes LEND-LEASE legislation, which is signed into law by President ROOSEVELT. The following day the president asks Congress for $7 billion to finance the program.

U.S. ARMY AIR CORPS Ferry Command is established; changed to AIR TRANSPORT COMMAND on March 20, 1942.

March 17 Two German U-BOAT aces are lost in a North Atlantic CONVOY battle: The submarine *U-100* commanded by Joachim Schepke is rammed and sunk by the British destroyer *Vanoc* (with Schepke lost), and the *U-99* commanded by OTTO KRETSCHMER is sunk by the British destroyer *Walker* (with Kretschmer taken prisoner).

March 25 President ROOSEVELT authorizes repairs to British warships in U.S. navy yards.

Yugoslavia joins the AXIS.

March 26 Italian MANNED TORPEDOES attack the British fleet at Suda Bay, CRETE, and use detachable warheads to sink the British cruiser *York* lying at anchor. This attack adds a new dimension to naval warfare.

> **"Battle of the Atlantic"**
>
> Term used by First Lord of the Admiralty A. V. Alexander on March 15, 1941, to describe the campaign against German U-boats

March 27 HITLER postpones assault on Soviet Union (Operation BARBAROSSA).

Yugoslav coup brings in a government friendly to the ALLIES.

March 28 In a naval engagement off Cape Matapan in the Mediterranean, a British battleship-carrier force under Adm. ANDREW BROWNE CUNNINGHAM completely surprises an Italian naval force, sinking three cruisers and two destroyers. The British lose one aircraft in the engagement, which occurred because of British code-breaking efforts.

March 30 German AFRIKA KORPS under Gen. ERWIN ROMMEL begins its first offensive against British forces in Libya.

March 31 President ROOSEVELT orders the U.S. Coast Guard to seize thirty AXIS and thirty-five Danish merchant ships in U.S. ports.

> **"The commander must try, above all, to establish personal and comradely contact with his men, but without giving away an inch of authority."**
>
> *Generalfeldmarschall* Erwin Rommel

April 3 Pro-German military government is established in Iraq.

April 6 German forces invade Greece and Yugoslavia.

April 8 German troops occupy Salonika.

April 9 The U.S. BATTLESHIP *North Carolina* (BB 55) is commissioned at the New York Navy Yard. She is the first U.S. dreadnought to be completed since the *West Virginia* (BB 48) in Dec. 1923.

U.S. and Danish governments sign agreement for U.S. forces to provide for the defense and supply of Greenland until Denmark regains its freedom from Germany.

April 10 The U.S. DESTROYER *Niblack* (DD 424), while collecting survivors from a torpedoed Dutch freighter in the North Atlantic, makes a DEPTH CHARGE attack against a German U-BOAT.

President ROOSEVELT extends the U.S. NEUTRALITY PATROL to longitude 25° west and removes the Red Sea from the list of combat areas forbidden to U.S. shipping.

April 13 German troops occupy Belgrade, capital of Yugoslavia.

Soviet Union and Japan conclude a nonaggression pact.

April 17 Yugoslavia surrenders to the Germans.

April 19 Germans launch their heaviest air raid to date against LONDON.
Britain sends troops to Iraq.

April 21 Britain decides to withdraw troops from Greece as the Greek government signs an armistice with Germany.

April 27 German troops occupy Athens, capital of Greece.

April 28 Col. CHARLES A. LINDBERGH resigns his reserve commission in the Army Air Corps in response to President ROOSEVELT's biting criticism of his pro-NAZI statements.

May 6 Comedian BOB HOPE leads a group of Hollywood performers to March Field, California, for his first USO show, which is broadcast on radio.

May 9 The German submarine *U-110* is captured at sea by the Royal Navy, revealing considerable ENIGMA material.

May 10 HITLER's deputy RUDOLF HESS flies to Scotland in an ME 110 aircraft.

An He 111 bomber flies over the East End of London on Sept. 7, 1940, the first day of heavy bombing of the Blitz. Britain had long believed in the axiom "the bomber always gets through," and with the fear of urban bombing and bombs carrying gas, there was great trepidation when the Blitz began. *(Luftwaffe via Imperial War Museum)*

May 10–11 LONDON undergoes the heaviest bombing raid of the BLITZ. Over 2,000 fires are started and 1,212 persons are killed and 1,769 are seriously injured.

May 15 U.S. government interns French merchant ships in American harbors.
A British JET-PROPELLED AIRCRAFT, a Gloster-Whittle E.28 Pioneer, makes its first flight; it lasts seventeen minutes.
British troops capture Sollum, Mosaid, and Halfaya Pass on the Egyptian-Libyan border.

May 16 Iceland secedes from Denmark.

May 19 President ROOSEVELT names New York Mayor FIORELLO LA GUARDIA to head U.S. CIVIL DEFENSE efforts.

May 20 German AIRBORNE troops begin assault of CRETE as part of the BALKANS-GREECE-CRETE CAMPAIGN. The island is held by British and New Zealand troops, mainly withdrawn from Greece, and irregular Greek units.

May 21 The U.S. freighter *Robin Moor* is sunk by the German submarine *U-69* in the South Atlantic while en route to South Africa. She is the first American merchant ship to be sunk by Germany.

May 24 The British battle cruiser *HOOD* explodes after being struck by shells from the German battleship *BISMARCK* and heavy cruiser *Prinz Eugen* as the German ships break into the Atlantic to attack British merchant shipping.

May 26 The German battleship *BISMARCK* is located about 550 miles west of Land's End, England, by a PBY CATALINA of RAF Coastal Command No. 209 Squadron. SWORDFISH TORPEDO planes from the carrier *ARK ROYAL* begin a series of attacks that will cripple the dreadnought.

May 27 The *BISMARCK* is sunk by British surface ships.

British warships begin the evacuation of CRETE. Through June 1, when the surviving British forces on Crete surrender, the warships take 17,000 troops off the island. This is the first time in history an island has been captured without the use of naval forces.

President ROOSEVELT broadcasts a declaration of Unlimited National Emergency—"The war is coming very close. . . . [I]t would be suicide to wait until they are in our front yard."—and proclaims a State of National Emergency.

May 29 The U.S. government arranges for training of 8,000 British pilots and navigators at American bases.

June 2 The USS *Long Island* (AVG-1, later CVE-1) is commissioned into the U.S. fleet. She is the first of 115 "jeep" or ESCORT CARRIERS converted or built by the U.S. and Royal Navies.

The VICHY FRENCH government grants the AXIS the use of the port of Bizerte in Tunisia for rations and clothing; it initially excludes the movement of troops, munitions, and war matériel.

June 6 U.S. government authorizes seizure of foreign ships in U.S. ports.

June 8 British and French troops enter Syria and Lebanon and engage VICHY FRENCH forces.

June 14 U.S. government freezes AXIS assets in the United States.

June 16 The U.S. government orders the closing of German and Italian consulates in the United States within thirty days.

June 17 President ROOSEVELT dedicates WASHINGTON National Airport.

June 18 German-Turkish friendship pact is signed.

June 20 U.S. Army Air Forces is established under Maj. Gen. HENRY H. ARNOLD, which replaces the ARMY AIR CORPS.

June 21 Gen. Sir Claude Auchinleck is appointed Commander in Chief of British forces in the Middle East, replacing Gen. Sir ARCHIBALD WAVELL, who became Commander in Chief in India.

FREE FRENCH forces occupy Damascus, Syria, after heavy fighting against VICHY FRENCH troops.

June 22 The GERMAN CAMPAIGN IN THE SOVIET UNION begins (Operation BARBAROSSA). The Germans employ the largest ground and air forces yet assembled in modern history for a single operation.

June 24 President ROOSEVELT releases Soviet credits and promises U.S. aid.

June 25 Finland declares war on the Soviet Union. Finland had been defeated by the Soviet Union in the "winter war" of 1939; it now enters the conflict against the Soviets as an ally of Germany.

Sweden allows the transit of one German division from Norway to Finland.

July 1 German troops enter Riga.

> *"Any man or state who fights on against Nazidom will have our aid. Any man or state who marches with Hitler is our foe."*
>
> **Prime Minister Winston Churchill** immediately following the German invasion of the Soviet Union on June 22, 1941

July 5 German troops reach the Dnieper River in the Soviet Union.

July 7 U.S. troops occupy Iceland.

July 8 In the first combat mission ever flown by the B-17 FLYING FORTRESS, twenty B-17C models flown by RAF Bomber Command bomb Wilhelmshaven. The British are not impressed with the aircraft.

July 12 VICHY FRENCH troops in Syria surrender to British and FREE FRENCH forces.

July 13 Britain and the Soviet Union sign a mutual aid pact. This provides the means for the British to transfer war matériel to the Soviet Union.

July 17 The U.S. government issues a "blacklist" of 1,800 Latin American firms with AXIS ties and freezes their assets in the United States.

July 21 France accepts Japanese demand for military control of Indochina. This will give Japan vital airfields to support the JAPANESE CAMPAIGN IN THE FAR EAST.
  Germans make first air raid on MOSCOW.

July 24 U.S. government denounces Japanese actions in Indochina.

July 25 U.S. government freezes Japanese and Chinese assets.

July 31 U.S. Army establishes Military Police Corps.

Aug. 1 U.S. government issues embargo on all exports of aviation fuel.
  First flight of the Grumman TBF AVENGER torpedo plane.

> *"With the Russians, as I was always at some pains to stress, we were dealing with strategic and political brains of high caliber and cunning."*
>
> *Generalleutnant* Reinhard Gehlen, head of German military intelligence for the Eastern Front, in his book *The Service*

Aug. 8 The Japanese government suggests meeting of Prime Minister Fumimaro Konoye and President ROOSEVELT in Honolulu.

Aug. 9–12 President ROOSEVELT and Prime Minister CHURCHILL meet at Placentia Bay, Newfoundland, arriving in the U.S. CRUISER *Augusta* (CA 31) and the British battleship *PRINCE OF WALES*, respectively. Newspapers will refer to their top-secret meeting as taking place "somewhere in the Atlantic."

Aug. 10 Britain and the Soviet Union promise aid to Turkey if it is attacked.

Aug. 12 Marshal HENRI PHILIPPE PÉTAIN announces full French collaboration with Germany.

Aug. 14 President ROOSEVELT and Prime Minister CHURCHILL announce the ATLANTIC CHARTER.

Aug. 17 President ROOSEVELT agrees to renew discussions with Japan.

Aug. 20 HITLER authorizes development of the V-2 MISSILE "up to operational readiness."

Aug. 25 British (including Indian) and Soviet troops enter Iran.

Aug. 27 Prime Minister Fumimaro Konoye issues an invitation for a meeting with President ROOSEVELT.

Aug. 28 The German submarine *U-570* is captured by the Royal Navy; she will be commissioned in British service as the *Graph*.

Sept. 4 German submarine *U-652* fires at the U.S. DESTROYER *GREER* (DD 145) off Iceland, beginning an undeclared shooting war.
  United States extends LEND-LEASE aid to Poland.

Sept. 5 U.S. Navy establishes the post of Assistant Secretary for Aeronautics, that office having been abolished in 1932 as an economy measure. Artemus L. Gates, a World War I naval aviator, is sworn in to the position.

Sept. 11 President ROOSEVELT declares that the United States will protect ships of any nationality "engaged in commerce in our defensive waters." This declaration becomes known as the "shoot first order."

Sept. 19 German troops occupy Kiev, USSR.

Sept. 23 Gen. CHARLES DE GAULLE forms the FREE FRENCH National Liberation Committee based in LONDON.

Sept. 27 The U.S. LIBERTY SHIP *Patrick Henry* is launched at Baltimore, Md., the first of over 2,700 of the cargo ships to be built in American yards during the war. With thirteen other merchant ships launched that day, Sept. 27 becomes Liberty Fleet Day.

Syria ceases to be a French mandate and becomes independent.

Sept. 29 United States and Britain send an economic mission to MOSCOW to determine Soviet defense needs.

Oct. 6 German troops renew their offensive against MOSCOW.

Oct. 9 President ROOSEVELT requests congressional approval for arming U.S. merchant ships.

Oct. 17 The Fumimaro Konoye ministry resigns in Japan and HIDEKI TOJO becomes prime minister and minister of war.

The U.S. DESTROYER *Kearney* (DD 432) is torpedoed by the submarine *U-568* in the North Atlantic. The U.S. warship is able to limp to Iceland for temporary repairs.

Oct. 20 German troops reach the approaches to MOSCOW.

Oct. 23 In a shake-up of the Red Army high command, Marshal GEORGI K. ZHUKOV, Chief of the Soviet General Staff, assumes command of central area operations in an effort to halt German advances.

Oct. 25 German troops capture KHARKOV and launch a new drive toward MOSCOW.

Oct. 30 President ROOSEVELT offers $1 billion in credits to the Soviet Union.

Oct. 31 The U.S. DESTROYER *Reuben James* (DD 245) is torpedoed and sunk by the German submarine *U-552* west of Iceland with the loss of 115 lives.

Nov. 1 The U.S. Coast Guard is directed by President ROOSEVELT to operate as part of the Navy.

Nov. 6 In the South Atlantic, the U.S. CRUISER *OMAHA* (CL 4) and a destroyer seize the German blockade runner *Odenwald,* carrying a cargo of rubber from Japan to Germany. Uncertain of the legality of his capture, Capt. T. E. Chandler of the *Omaha* reports that the *Odenwald* was stopped as a suspected "slave trader."

> *"If we should go to war against the United States we must recognize the fact that the armistice will have to be dictated [by the Japanese] from the White House."*
>
> Adm. Isoroku Yamamoto explaining the impossibility of a Japanese victory over the United States to a friend

Nov. 10 Prime Minister CHURCHILL announces that if Japan attacks the United States, Britain will declare war immediately.

Nov. 14 The British aircraft carrier *ARK ROYAL* is sunk by the German submarine *U-81* in the western Mediterranean.

Nov. 15 Japanese special envoys KICHISABURO NOMURA and SABURO KURUSU arrive in WASHINGTON to discuss peace initiatives with the U.S. government.

Nov. 16 German troops capture Kerch and with it the whole of the Crimea except for the fortress port of SEVASTOPOL.

Nov. 17 Congress revises the NEUTRALITY ACT to allow the arming of U.S. merchant ships.

Nov. 24 U.S. troops occupy Surinam, Dutch West Indies.
　　　　U.S. government grants LEND-LEASE aid to FREE FRENCH.

Nov. 25 The British battleship *Barham* is sunk by the *U-331* in the Mediterranean. Three TORPEDOES in a salvo of four strike the ship. This is the first sinking by a submarine of a battleship while under way; 862 men are lost.

Nov. 26 The Japanese carrier task force under Vice Adm. CHUICHI NAGUMO departs Hitokappu Bay in the KURIL ISLANDS en route to attack PEARL HARBOR. With radio silence strictly enforced, the Japanese warships take a northern route to evade detection by merchant shipping.
　　　　The U.S. government declares oil embargo on Japan.
　　　　Lebanon becomes independent from FREE FRENCH and British control (although French troops are not completely removed until 1946).

Nov. 27 President ROOSEVELT and Secretary of State CORDELL HULL confer with Japanese envoys amid reports that Japanese troops are massing in Indochina for a possible attack on Malaya and SINGAPORE.
　　　　Adm. HAROLD R. STARK, the U.S. Chief of Naval Operations, sends "war warning" message to the commanders of the Pacific and Asiatic Fleets.

Nov. 28 The U.S. AIRCRAFT CARRIER *ENTERPRISE* (CV 6) departs PEARL HARBOR to deliver Marine F4F WILDCAT fighters to WAKE ISLAND. Under the command of Vice Adm. WILLIAM F. HALSEY, she will be approaching Pearl Harbor on the morning of Dec. 7.

Dec. 2 The U.S. merchant ship *Dunboyne* receives the first U.S. naval ARMED GUARD, having been fitted with guns to fight off surfaced U-BOATS.
　　　　HITLER orders *Fliegerkorps* II with some 325 combat aircraft from the EASTERN FRONT to SICILY for operations in the Mediterranean area.

Dec. 4 The U.S. AIRCRAFT CARRIER *LEXINGTON* (CV 2) departs PEARL HARBOR to deliver Marine SB2U VINDICATOR dive bombers to MIDWAY Island. She will still be at sea on Dec. 7.

Dec. 6 President ROOSEVELT asks Japan to remove troops from Indochina.
　　　　Soviet Army launches a major counteroffensive in the central area of the EASTERN FRONT.

> *"Climb Mt. Niitaka 1208."*
>
> Coded message from Adm. Yamamoto to Japanese naval forces at 5 P.M. on Dec. 2, 1941, that operations against the United States would commence on Dec. 8 (Tokyo date)

The U.S. battleships *Tennessee* (BB 43) and the sunken *West Virginia* (BB 48) at Pearl Harbor. The specter and shock of the attack overshadowed the fact that such ships, with speeds of only 21 knots, would have limited use in the next war—mainly for shore bombardment. *(U.S. Navy)*

Dec. 7 Japanese carrier force attacks PEARL HARBOR. Almost simultaneously, Japanese land-based aircraft strike the Philippines, WAKE ISLAND, and GUAM, and Japanese troops conduct AMPHIBIOUS LANDINGS in Malaya and Thailand, and seize SHANGHAI (Dec. 8 in Far East).

The Japanese destroyers *Akebono* and *Ushio* bombard U.S. military facilities on MIDWAY.
Japan declares war on the United States and Great Britain.

Dec. 8 Japanese troops make an AMPHIBIOUS LANDING north of SINGAPORE on the Malay peninsula and enter Thailand.

United States and Britain declare war on Japan.
German offensive in the Soviet Union bogs down.

Dec. 9 China declares war on Japan, Germany, and Italy.
False air raid report alarms New York City.

Dec. 10 The British battleship *PRINCE OF WALES* and the World War I–era battle cruiser *HOOD* are sunk by Japanese bombers off the coast of MALAYA. They are the world's first capital ships to be sunk by air attack while at sea.

In the first U.S. bombing mission of the war, five B-17 FLYING FORTRESSES take off from Clark airfield in the Philippines, each carrying twenty 100-pound bombs, to attack a large Japanese CONVOY off Vigan.

Japanese troops land on Luzon, the northernmost of the Philippine Islands.
Japanese troops seize GUAM, the first U.S. territory to be occupied during the war.

Dec. 11 Germany and Italy declare war on the United States.
Japanese troops invade Burma.

Dec. 12 U.S. government takes over the French luxury liner *NOR-MANDIE* and thirteen other French merchant ships that are in American waters.

Dec. 13 British forces launch offensive in Libya.

Dec. 15 The U.S. SUBMARINE *SWORDFISH* (SS 193) sinks the Japanese merchant ship *Atsutasan Maru* off the coast of Indochina. This is the first ship sunk by a U.S. submarine in World War II.

Dec. 16 President ROOSEVELT appoints a commission headed by Associate Justice Owen J. Roberts to investigate the PEARL HARBOR attack.

Japanese troops invade British Borneo.

Dec. 17 Vice Adm. W. S. Pye temporarily relieves Adm. HUSBAND E. KIMMEL as Commander in Chief U.S. PACIFIC FLEET at PEARL HARBOR pending the arrival of Adm. CHESTER W. NIMITZ from WASHINGTON. Nimitz becomes CinC Pacific Fleet on board the SUBMARINE *Grayling* (SS 209) at Pearl Harbor on Dec. 31.

A squadron of Marine SB2U VINDICATOR dive bombers arrives on MIDWAY after an overwater flight of 1,137 miles from Hickam Field on Oahu. They are the first combat planes to be based on Midway. (A fighter squadron flying the F2A BUFFALO will arrive on Midway on Dec. 25, having flown off an AIRCRAFT CARRIER.)

Dec. 18 Japanese troops invade HONG KONG.

Dec. 19 HITLER takes personal command of the German Army.

Dec. 20 FLYING TIGERS enter combat against the Japanese over Kunming in southern China.

A Japanese submarine sinks the merchant ship *Medio* off Eureka, Calif. She is the first U.S. merchant ship to be sunk in the Pacific.

Dec. 22 Prime Minister CHURCHILL arrives in the United States for the first WASHINGTON CONFERENCE.

Japanese troops begin major AMPHIBIOUS LANDINGS along the coast of Lingayen Gulf on Luzon.

Dec. 23 Gen. DOUGLAS MACARTHUR decides to evacuate MANILA and withdraw his forces to the BATAAN peninsula.

WAKE ISLAND is captured by Japanese troops.

Dec. 25 The British garrison at HONG KONG surrenders to the Japanese.

Dec. 26 MANILA is declared an OPEN CITY. The Japanese heavily bomb the city the next day.

Automobile tire RATIONING begins in the United States.

Dec. 28 U.S. Navy authorizes first contingent of construction BATTALIONS (SEABEES).

> *"The only thing now to do is to lick the hell out of them."*
>
> Senator Burton K. Wheeler, Dec. 1941

> *"Enemy on island—issue in doubt."*
>
> One of the last messages sent by Comdr. Winfield S. Cunningham, commander of the U.S. Navy–Marine Corps garrison on Wake Island, Dec. 23, 1941

1942

Jan. 1 Representatives of twenty-six nations meeting in WASHINGTON sign the Declaration of the United Nations based on the ATLANTIC CHARTER, which had been agreed to by President ROOSEVELT and Prime Minister CHURCHILL in their meeting off Newfoundland in Aug. 1941.

Reinforcements of German bombers and TORPEDO planes begin to arrive in the Arctic to attack RUSSIAN CONVOYS; the bombers are based mainly at Stavanger and Kirkenes. Also, the number of U-BOATS based in Norway is increased from three to nine to attack the convoys.

British COMMANDOS stage a successful raid on the German-held Lofoten Islands off the coast of Norway.

U.S. OFFICE OF PRICE ADMINISTRATION bans the retail sale of new automobiles and trucks.

Jan. 2 In the Philippines, the city of MANILA and the U.S. naval base at Cavite fall to the Japanese.

The first U.S. AIRSHIP units, Navy Airship Patrol Group 1 and Air Ship Squadron 12, are established at Lakehurst, N.J., the Navy's principal "blimp" base.

Jan. 3 Gen. Sir ARCHIBALD WAVELL, Supreme Commander of the American-British-Dutch-Australian (ABDA) forces, is directed to hold the Malay Barrier, a line running through the Malay Peninsula, Sumatra, Java, and northern Australia, in an effort to check the Japanese southern advance.

> *"The U-boat attack was our worst evil. It would have been wise for the Germans to stake all upon it."*
>
> **Prime Minister Churchill** describing Allied shipping losses to U-boats in early 1942

Jan. 5 U.S. and Filipino troops complete withdrawal to a new defensive line along the base of the BATAAN peninsula. The rations of troops in Bataan and CORREGIDOR are cut in half.

Jan. 7 President ROOSEVELT submits a record budget of $58.9 billion to Congress, of which $52.7 billion is for the war effort. He also recommends $9 billion in new wartime taxes.

The Japanese open their assault on BATAAN.

Jan. 9 The Anglo-American COMBINED CHIEFS OF STAFF and the U.S. JOINT CHIEFS OF STAFF are established.

Jan. 10 Japanese submarine *I-6* torpedoes and damages the U.S. AIRCRAFT CARRIER *SARATOGA* (CV 3) steaming 500 miles southeast of Oahu. The submarine escapes. This is the only damage inflicted by the thirty Japanese fleet submarines and five MIDGET SUBMARINES that had participated in the PEARL HARBOR attack.

Jan. 11 Five German U-BOATS arrive off the U.S. East Coast to begin preying on unescorted American merchant ships in Operation *Paukenschlag* (Drumbeat).

Japanese troops invade the DUTCH EAST INDIES and Dutch Borneo.

Jan. 13 The Sikorsky R-4 helicopter makes its first flight at Bridgeport, Conn. It will be the only helicopter to enter U.S. military service during the war.

Representatives of the Allied nations meeting in LONDON declare that perpetrators of WAR CRIMES should be prosecuted. This lays the foundation for postwar trials of war criminals.

Jan. 14 The WASHINGTON CONFERENCE concludes with President ROOSEVELT and Prime Minister CHURCHILL agreeing that the COMBINED CHIEFS OF STAFF will direct the Anglo-

American war effort and that the Allied strategy will be to defeat Germany first, then Japan.

Jan. 15   The ABDA Command opens its headquarters on Java.

Jan. 15–17   Prime Minister CHURCHILL makes his first air crossing of the Atlantic after meeting with President ROOSEVELT. A Boeing flying boat of the British Overseas Airways Corporation flies him from Norfolk, Va., to Portsmouth via Bermuda.

Jan. 16   Japanese advance into Burma begins.

The German battleship *TIRPITZ*, the largest dreadnought in the Atlantic area, arrives at Trondheim, Norway, from the Baltic. She is ready to attack the RUSSIAN CONVOYS.

Jan. 18   The German-Japanese-Italian military convention is signed in BERLIN.

Jan. 19   Japanese troops capture North Borneo.

Jan. 20   The U.S. DESTROYER *Edsall* (DD 219) and three Australian minesweepers sink the large Japanese minelaying submarine *I-124* off Darwin, Australia.

NAZI officials meet in the Berlin suburb of WANNSEE to decide the "FINAL SOLUTION of the Jewish Question."

Jan. 21   Gen. ERWIN ROMMEL launches a counterattack in Libya.

Jan. 23   Maj. Gen. JOSEPH STILWELL is selected to become the senior U.S. officer in China and principal adviser to Generalissimo CHIANG KAI-SHEK.

Japanese troops capture RABAUL on NEW BRITAIN at the top of the SOLOMON ISLANDS and invade BOUGAINVILLE. Rabaul will become the major Japanese base in the area.

The U.S. JOINT CHIEFS OF STAFF meet for the first time as a body. The occasion is a conference with the British CHIEFS OF STAFF in WASHINGTON. The Americans are Gen. GEORGE C. MARSHALL, Chief of Staff of the Army; Adm. HAROLD R. STARK, Chief of Naval Operations; Adm. ERNEST J. KING, Commander in Chief U.S. FLEET; and Lt. Gen. HENRY H. ARNOLD, head of the Army Air Forces.

Jan. 23–24   In night action in the Makassar Strait, four U.S. DESTROYERS attack Japanese shipping off Balikpapan, Borneo. Four Japanese transports and one patrol craft are sunk. This is the first major U.S. Navy surface action since the Spanish-American War of 1898.

Jan. 25   Thailand, a Japanese puppet state, declares war on the United States.

The Japanese submarine *I-173* bombards MIDWAY.

Jan. 26   The first U.S. troops arrive in Northern Ireland.

Jan. 27   The USS *Gudgeon* (SS 211) becomes the first U.S. submarine to sink a Japanese warship, the submarine *I-173*. The attack comes about because of U.S. MAGIC code-breaking efforts.

Jan. 28   The U.S. Eighth AIR FORCE is activated at Savannah, Ga., under Brig. Gen. Asa N. Duncan. It will become the principal U.S. air command in Europe.

AFRIKA KORPS troops under Gen. ERWIN ROMMEL capture Benghazi, capital of Cyrenaica (Libya).

"Sturgeon *no longer virgin.*"

Message sent by Lt. Comdr. John L. Burnside, commanding officer of the U.S. submarine *Sturgeon* (SS 187), after firing a spread of torpedoes at a Japanese convoy in the Makassar Strait on the night of Jan. 22–23, 1942

Jan. 29   The Anglo-American high command establishes the ANZAC defense area covering the ocean expanses between Australia, New Zealand, and NEW CALEDONIA; Vice Adm. Herbert Leary (USN) is named commander.

Great Britain and the Soviet Union sign an alliance with Iran wherein Iran agrees to remain neutral. Soviet and British troops will occupy Iran to provide a route for Allied war supplies to reach the USSR.

The U.S. Navy successfully test-fires 5-inch PROXIMITY FUZE shells at the Dahlgren, Va., naval proving ground. The proximity fuze—which detonates a shell near the target and does not require a direct hit—will revolutionize antiaircraft gunnery.

Jan. 30   American movie star Carole Lombard and fifteen U.S. AAF ferry pilots are killed in a commercial airplane crash in the Nevada mountains near Las Vegas. She was returning to California from Indianapolis, where she had been entertaining troops.

Jan. 30–31   During the night, British and Commonwealth troops withdraw from the Malayan mainland into SINGAPORE island in the path of Japanese advances. The three-quarter-mile causeway to the island is blown up as the siege of Singapore begins.

Feb. 1   A puppet government under German control is established in Norway with VIDKUN QUISLING as premier.

A U.S. carrier task force with the U.S. carriers *Yorktown* (CV 5) and *Enterprise* (CV 6) under the command of Vice Adm. WILLIAM F. HALSEY strikes Japanese-held islands in the MARSHALL and GILBERT groups. This is the first U.S. carrier offensive operation of the war.

In Libya, Maj. Gen. Neil M. Ritchie orders a withdrawl of the British XIII Corps to the Gazala-Bir Hacheim line to avoid envelopment by the AFRIKA KORPS.

Feb. 2   Japanese troops land on Java, DUTCH EAST INDIES.

Feb. 4   A U.S.-Dutch naval force of four cruisers and seven destroyers under Rear Adm. Karel Doorman (Netherlands Navy) sets out to attack Japanese shipping off Balikpapan, Borneo. The force is detected and the U.S. CRUISERS *Houston* (CA 30) and *Marblehead* (CL 12) are heavily damaged.

Feb. 8–9   Japanese troops make a night landing on SINGAPORE island, immediately capturing one of the island's four airfields.

A Japanese submarine makes a night bombardment of MIDWAY.

Feb. 9   U.S. government imposes daylight saving time—called WAR TIME—for the duration of the conflict.

The former French luxury liner *NORMANDIE*, taken over by the U.S. Navy for conversion to the transport *Lafayette* (AP 53), catches fire and, on the morning of Feb. 10, she capsizes at a Manhattan pier.

Feb. 10   A Japanese submarine bombards MIDWAY. It is the fourth time Japanese ships have shelled the atoll since Dec. 7.

Feb. 11–12   In one of the most daring operations of the war, the German battleships *Gneisenau* and *Scharnhorst* and the heavy cruiser *Prinz Eugen* escape from the French port of Brest and sail up the English Channel to return to Germany. The British attack the German ships in their daylight sortie, which is hindered by bad weather. Both battleships suffer damage from MINES, but the German CHANNEL DASH is successful.

Feb. 14 Vice Adm. Conrad E. L. Helfrich (Netherlands Navy) succeeds Adm. THOMAS HART (USN) as commander of the ABDA naval striking force.

Japanese paratroopers land on Sumatra, DUTCH EAST INDIES.

Feb. 15 Following a Japanese attack from the landward side of the fortress city, SINGAPORE surrenders to the Japanese, ending the assault on Malaya. About 3,000 selected people are evacuated from Singapore by ship on Feb. 13–15, but nearly all are killed or captured.

Feb. 18 U-BOATS shell Aruba, Dutch West Indies, and Port of Spain, Trinidad, sinking a tanker and damaging two other ships.

Feb. 19 Japanese carriers launch 188 planes that join with fifty-four land-based bombers from Kendari in the CELEBES to attack Darwin in northern Australia. They destroy numerous aircraft on the ground and sink several ships, including the U.S. DESTROYER *Peary* (DD 226). This is the largest Japanese air strike since the PEARL HARBOR attack and the first of several on Darwin.

Japanese troops land on Bali.

Feb. 20 During an attempted strike by the U.S. AIRCRAFT CARRIER *LEXINGTON* (CV 2) against the Japanese naval-air bases at RABAUL, Lt. EDWARD O'HARE in a single aerial engagement becomes the first U.S. fighter ACE of the war.

U.S. government loans $1 billion to the Soviet Union.

Feb. 22 President ROOSEVELT orders Gen. DOUGLAS MACARTHUR to leave the Philippines. Additional messages are sent urging the general to escape to safety.

Feb. 23 Japanese submarine *I-17* shells the oil refinery at Ellwood near Santa Barbara, Calif., with her 5.5-inch deck gun. This is the first attack of the war on the U.S. mainland.

Feb. 24 A U.S. carrier task force centered on the USS *ENTERPRISE* (CV 6) under Vice Adm. WILLIAM F. HALSEY bombs and shells WAKE ISLAND. It is the first attack on Wake since it surrendered to the Japanese on Dec. 22.

Feb. 25 The ABDA command is dissolved and the defense of Java is left to Dutch forces.

Feb. 26 The first U.S. AIRCRAFT CARRIER, the USS *LANGLEY* (AV 3, formerly CV 1), is sunk seventy-four miles south of Java by Japanese land-based bombers. She carried crated fighter planes desperately needed by the Allied forces.

Feb. 27–28 In an RAF Bomber Command attack on Wilhelmshaven and Kiel, two direct bomb hits inflict severe damage on the battleship *Gneisenau*. She is taken out of service for the remainder of the war.

Feb. 27–March 1 The battle of the JAVA SEA between U.S. and Japanese surface forces is an overwhelming Japanese victory. The U.S. CRUISER *HOUSTON* (CA 30), the largest Allied warship in the Far East, is sunk by Japanese gunfire and TORPEDOES in Sunda Strait on the night of Feb. 28–March 1.

Feb. 28 The U.S. DESTROYER *Jacob Jones* (DD 130) is struck by two or three TORPEDOES off the Delaware Capes. Fired by the German submarine *U-578,* the torpedoes blow off the ship's bow and stern; her own DEPTH CHARGES explode as the stern section sinks, killing survivors in the water. Rough weather also takes a toll, and only eleven men of a crew of about 125 survive.

The U.S. government places wholesale price ceilings on canned goods.

March 1   The first German U-BOAT to be sunk by U.S. forces is the *U-656,* depth-charged southwest of Newfoundland by a Navy PBO Hudson patrol plane piloted by Ens. William (Bill) Tepuni.

March 3   First combat operation by the RAF LANCASTER four-engine bomber is a minelaying mission over the Heligoland Bight.

March 4   Two Japanese EMILY flying boats bomb Oahu, HAWAII, in the second Japanese air attack against PEARL HARBOR.

Aircraft from the USS *ENTERPRISE* (CV 6), in a task force commanded by Vice Adm. WILLIAM F. HALSEY, strike Marcus Island, less than 1,000 miles from Japan, the closest U.S. carriers have yet come to the Japanese homeland.

> ### "Sighted sub, sank same."
> Words put into the mouth of Chief Aviation Machinist's Mate Donald F. Mason by an anonymous U.S. Navy public relations officer. In fact, Mason, flying a Navy patrol bomber in Jan. 1942, did not sink a U-boat at this time. However, he *did* sink the *U-503* on March 15.

March 6   Five U.S. citizens of German ancestry are convicted of ESPIONAGE in the first U.S. spy trial of the war.

The German battleship *TIRPITZ* and destroyers sail from Trondheim, Norway, in the first attack against the RUSSIAN CONVOYS.

March 7   The British evacuate Rangoon, the capital of Burma, in the face of Japanese advances.

Japanese troops land at Salamaua and Lae on NEW GUINEA.

The first SPITFIRE fighter aircraft reach MALTA, with fifteen flown in from the British aircraft carriers *Argus* and *Eagle.*

March 8   The Dutch command on Java surrenders to the Japanese.

March 9   The U.S. Army is reorganized into three major commands: Army Ground Forces under Lt. Gen. LESLEY J. McNAIR, Army Air Forces (AAF) under Lt. Gen. HENRY H. ARNOLD, and Services of Supply (later Army Service Forces) under Maj. Gen. Brehon B. Somervell.

March 11   Gen. DOUGLAS MACARTHUR leaves CORREGIDOR in Manila Bay by PT-BOAT. Four U.S. PT-boats commanded by Lt. JOHN BULKELEY carry MacArthur, his wife, son, a family nurse, thirteen Army officers, a sergeant, and two Navy officers. (The master sergeant was a code specialist.) The boats transit the 560 miles to Mindanao in the central Philippines in thirty-five hours. From there MacArthur's party is flown in B-17 FLYING FORTRESS bombers to Australia, a distance of 1,580 miles.

Maj. Gen. JONATHAN WAINWRIGHT becomes commander of U.S. forces in the Philippines. He is promoted to lieutenant general on March 20.

March 12   The positions of Commander in Chief U.S. FLEET and Chief of Naval Operations are combined under Adm. ERNEST J. KING. Adm. HAROLD R. STARK, the Chief of Naval Operations at the time of the PEARL HARBOR attack, is reassigned as Commander U.S. Naval Forces in Europe, with offices in LONDON.

> ### ". . . I shall return."
> Statement by Gen. Douglas MacArthur from Australia following his escape from Corregidor in March 1942—MacArthur's symbol, which helped spark the Philippine resistance against the Japanese.

March 17   Japanese aircraft bomb targets at Port Darwin, Australia. Gen. MACARTHUR, flying from the Philippines to Australia, is diverted to Batchelor airfield, fifty miles from Darwin.

March 18 President ROOSEVELT appoints Gen. MACARTHUR commander of the Southwest Pacific theater.

March 23 Japanese troops invade the ANDAMAN ISLANDS in the Bay of Bengal without opposition.

March 24 The U.S. Pacific theater—a UNIFIED COMMAND—is established with Adm. CHESTER W. NIMITZ as Commander in Chief.

> *"Don't tell them anything. When it's over, tell them who won."*
>
> Adm. Ernest J. King when asked to state the Navy's policy toward public relations, 1942

March 25 The U.S. government seizes patents for the manufacture of synthetic rubber from the Standard Oil Co. and I. G. FARBEN of Germany.

March 26 In Canberra, Australia, Gen. DOUGLAS MACARTHUR is awarded the MEDAL OF HONOR. The medal is presented by the Australian prime minister.

March 27 An interservice squabble ends when the U.S. War and Navy Departments announce that the Navy will control all antisubmarine operations off the American coasts, including patrols by AAF aircraft.

> *"Bring Douglas MacArthur home. Place him at the very top. . . . Put him in supreme command of our armed forces under the President."*
>
> Republican party leader Wendell Willkie, 1942

U.S. JOINT CHIEFS OF STAFF issue proposals for cross-Channel invasions in 1942 and 1943.

March 28 British COMMANDOS carry out a successful raid on the giant dry dock at SAINT-NAZAIRE, France, to deny its use to German battleships. The destroyer *Campbeltown,* formerly the USS *Buchanan* (DD 131), is rammed into the dock gates and, while being examined by German officials, 4½ tons of explosives on board blow up.

March 30 The U.S. JOINT CHIEFS OF STAFF divide the Pacific region into the Pacific Ocean Area under Adm. CHESTER W. NIMITZ and the Southwest Pacific Area under Gen. DOUGLAS MAC-ARTHUR; Nimitz remains the Commander in Chief U.S. Pacific FLEET.

U.S. troops arrive on Ascension Island between South America and Africa to begin construction of an airfield that will prove invaluable in ferrying aircraft to Africa and Asia.

April 1 U.S. troops begin mass evacuation of JAPANESE-AMERICANS from Pacific Coast states.

Prime Minister CHURCHILL asks President ROOSEVELT to make the AIRCRAFT CARRIER *WASP* (CV 7) available to ferry fighter aircraft to the besieged island of MALTA in the Mediterranean. Roosevelt agrees. (See April 20, 1942.)

U.S. Navy begins a partial CONVOY system in Atlantic seaboard waters after German U-BOATS sink forty-eight merchant ships of 274,295 gross tons during March. However, losses to U-boats continue at a high rate in American waters.

April 2 Prime Minister CHURCHILL receives a letter from President ROOSEVELT saying that Gen. GEORGE C. MARSHALL, U.S. Army Chief of Staff, is en route to England with a plan for opening a SECOND FRONT in Europe. Roosevelt says he hopes that the plan "will be received with enthusiasm by Russia," which has been demanding an Anglo-American invasion of NAZI-held Europe. The plan was drawn up by Maj. Gen. DWIGHT D. EISENHOWER on Marshall's staff.

April 3   The Japanese begin all-out assault on U.S.-Filipino defenders of BATAAN.

April 4–9   The four aircraft carriers of the Japanese PEARL HARBOR striking force sail into the Indian Ocean, raiding British bases and ports. Japanese carrier planes sink the old carrier *Hermes,* completed in 1918, and two cruisers plus several lesser ships. The Japanese suffer virtually no losses.

> *"Whomsoever England allies herself with, she will see her allies stronger than she is at the end of this war."*
>
> Adolf Hitler in a speech before the Reichstag, April 1942

April 6   First U.S. troops arrive in Australia.

April 7   Soviets open rail link to besieged LENINGRAD.

April 8   Col. William D. Old (U.S. AAF) pilots the first transport flight over THE HUMP, the Himalayan air route between India and southern China.
U.S. Army Chief of Staff Gen. GEORGE C. MARSHALL and presidential adviser HARRY HOPKINS arrive in LONDON for talks with British military leaders.

April 8–9   RAF Bomber Command sends 272 bombers against HAMBURG at night in the largest bomber strike of the war until the THOUSAND-PLANE RAID on COLOGNE in May.

April 9   U.S. and Filipino troops on BATAAN peninsula in the Philippines, the last major combat forces in the islands, unconditionally surrender to the Japanese. Many soon become victims of the BATAAN DEATH MARCH.

April 12   Indian leader JAWAHARLAL NEHRU says that India will not help the British war effort but will attempt to fight on its own to preserve its territory from Japanese incursion.

April 16   The island of MALTA is awarded the George Cross in recognition of its heroism under attack. It is the first such award to any part of the BRITISH COMMONWEALTH. The island is undergoing almost daily attacks by German and Italian bombers, with some raids numbering 200 aircraft.

April 17   NAZI annihilation of the JEWS in the WARSAW GHETTO begins when fifty social workers are shot on the night of April 17–18.

April 18   The U.S. AIRCRAFT CARRIER *HORNET* (CV 8) launches sixteen U.S. Army B-25B MITCHELL bombers led by Lt. Col. JAMES DOOLITTLE from a position 800 miles east of TOKYO in the first bombing raid against Japan.

April 20   The besieged island of MALTA in the Mediterranean, under sustained German and Italian air attack, is reinforced by forty-seven SPITFIRE fighters flown off from the U.S. carrier *WASP* (CV 7), which is briefly sent into the "Med" to help the British. This is the first of two such missions for the *Wasp* during her brief career. A second *Wasp* operation on May 9 flies off forty-seven Spitfire fighters to Malta (one returned to the carrier and made a dramatic landing, without a carrier arresting hook). The British carrier *Eagle* flies off an additional seventeen Spitfires on May 9.
PIERRE LAVAL, premier of VICHY FRANCE, in a radio broadcast, establishes a policy of "true reconciliation with Germany."

April 21 U.S. government agrees to finance construction of the "BIG INCH," a pipeline to run from the oil fields of Texas to New York to compensate for oil lost in tanker sinkings by U-BOATS.

President ROOSEVELT orders the seizure of all U.S. patents owned by the AXIS powers.

April 24 SELECTIVE SERVICE registration begins for all American men between ages forty-five and sixty-four.

April 24–25 German planes bomb Exeter, England, at night, launching what NAZI radio calls "terror raids" on historic British towns. These are also known as BAEDEKER RAIDS.

The U.S. Office of CIVIL DEFENSE orders a "DIMOUT"—the extinguishing of bright lights—along the U.S. East Coast to prevent the silhouetting of ships and to cut down on U-BOAT night attacks.

The newly created U.S. OFFICE OF PRICE ADMINISTRATION freezes the store-shelf prices of most U.S. food items and stabilizes rents in 301 areas related to defense activity.

A B-25B Mitchell bomber revs its engines in anticipation of taking off from the pitching deck of the carrier *Hornet* (CV 8) for the first bombing raid on Japan. Flying the heavily laden B-25s from the ship in rough seas was a remarkable feat. *(U.S. Navy)*

April 29 Japanese soldiers take Lashio, Burma, the end of the BURMA ROAD, the vital ground supply link between China and India. Cut off from Western supplies except those delivered by air, the Nationalist Chinese are forced to withdraw from their forward positions confronting the Japanese. The Japanese conquest of central Burma is complete.

HITLER meets with BENITO MUSSOLINI and other Italian Fascist leaders at SALZBURG, Austria. The Russian winter and Soviet tenacity have stopped the German advances in the Soviet Union; Germany is beginning to suffer heavily from British bomber raids. The Italian leaders are frustrated as they see no end to the conflict.

May 1 Japanese troops occupy the town of Mandalay in Burma.

Retired Adm. WILLIAM D. LEAHY, U.S. ambassador to VICHY FRANCE, departs the city of Vichy for Portugal by train. He returns to the United States by ship, arriving on June 1.

May 2 Japanese troops land on Florida Island in the SOLOMON ISLANDS, and on nearby Tulagi, adjacent to GUADALCANAL, on May 3.

Maj. Gen. CARL SPAATZ is assigned as commander of the U.S. Eighth AIR FORCE in Britain. The first units of that command will arrive in England on May 12 to prepare for the STRATEGIC BOMBING offensive against Germany.

United States grants LEND-LEASE aid to Iran and Iraq.

May 3 Japanese troops capture the island of Tulagi in the SOLOMON ISLANDS.

May 4 The U.S. SUBMARINE *Spearfish* (SS 190) departs CORREGIDOR carrying to Australia and safety thirteen female nurses and twelve male officers. She is the last direct contact with the outside world for the dying fortress.

May 5 Japanese Imperial General Headquarters orders the Combined Fleet to prepare for the invasion of MIDWAY Island and the ALEUTIAN islands.

U.S. Lt. Gen. JOSEPH STILWELL, withdrawing his defeated American-British force from Burma, learns that the Japanese have cut a key railway line into China and is forced instead to lead his troops into India.

The use of steel is forbidden in more than 400 civilian products in the United States.

In the first Allied invasion of the war, British troops land on MADAGASCAR in the western Indian Ocean to prevent the VICHY FRENCH government on the island from providing support to Japanese naval forces.

> *"With broken heart and with head bowed in sadness but not in shame I report . . . that today I must arrange terms for the surrender of the fortified islands of Manila Bay— Corregidor, Fort Hughes, Fort Drum, and" [end of message].*
>
> Lt. Gen. Jonathan M. Wainwright in last message from Corregidor, May 6, 1942

May 6 The Japanese capture CORREGIDOR. Lt. Gen. JONATHAN M. WAINWRIGHT unconditionally surrenders the battered island fortress and all U.S. and Filipino forces in the Philippine islands.

May 7–8 In the battle of the CORAL SEA, a Japanese landing force en route to capture PORT MORESBY, New Guinea, is turned back by a U.S. task force in a major carrier engagement. It is the first military defeat suffered by the Japanese in the war and history's first naval battle fought entirely by aircraft with the opposing warships never sighting their opponents.

May 10 Prime Minister CHURCHILL warns Germany that if it uses poison gas on the Russian front, Britain will retaliate by using gas against German targets. Subsequently, on June 5, President ROOSEVELT issues a similar warning to the Japanese against continuing to use poison gas in China. (See CHEMICAL WARFARE.)

> *"Scratch one flattop!"*
>
> Radio message from Lt. Comdr. Robert Dixon, dive-bomber squadron commander from U.S.S. *Lexington* (CV 2), at the battle of Coral Sea, May 7, 1942, as the Japanese carrier *Shoho* sinks

May 12 The last organized U.S. troops in the Philippines surrender on Mindanao. However, numerous U.S. soldiers and sailors will continue to fight the Japanese with Filipino GUERRILLAS.

The Soviet Army launches its first major offensive of the war against German forces at KHARKOV in the eastern Ukraine. After five days of intensive fighting the Germans go over to the offensive and by May 25 the majority of the Soviet troops have been encircled and destroyed in a major defeat for the Red Army.

May 14 U.S. Women's Army Auxiliary Corps (WAAC) is created; later shortened to simply Women's Army Corps (WAC).

President MANUEL QUEZON establishes a Philippine government-in-exile in WASHINGTON.

May 15 Gasoline RATIONING goes into effect on the U.S. East Coast.

May 18 An agreement is signed between the United States and Panama for use of defense and air bases in Panama for the protection of the Panama Canal.

May 20 Japanese troops complete the conquest of Burma and reach the frontier of India.

May 21 Soviet Foreign Minister VYACHESLAV MOLOTOV asks Prime Minister CHURCHILL to open the SECOND FRONT in western Europe. Churchill says this is not possible in 1942. Nine days later, Molotov flies from Britain to the United States to meet with President ROOSEVELT. Molotov declares that a Second Front will pull some forty German divisions away from fighting the Soviets on the EASTERN FRONT.

May 22 Mexico declares war on Germany, Japan, and Italy.

May 23 Soviet troops withdraw from the Kerch peninsula in the Crimea, leaving the region to German forces.

May 26 The British and Soviet governments sign a twenty-year mutual assistance treaty.
    The U.S. AAF P-61 BLACK WIDOW night fighter makes its first flight.

May 27 Two Czechs, dropped by parachute from a British plane over Czechoslovakia, attempt to assassinate Nazi leader REINHARD HEYDRICH in Prague. Heydrich dies on June 4. (See ASSASSINATIONS.)
    Gen. ERWIN ROMMEL begins a major offensive in Libya with his AFRIKA KORPS, which includes three German and two Italian divisions, against the British Eighth Army. This thrust will take Rommel to TOBRUK and then into Egypt.

May 30–31 The first THOUSAND-PLANE RAID of the war is carried out by the RAF Bomber Command on the German city of COLOGNE when 1,047 are dispatched in Operation Millennium.

May 31 Three Japanese MIDGET SUBMARINES, launched from larger I-boats standing offshore, enter Sydney Harbor, Australia. No ships are sunk and all three midgets with their two-man crews are lost.

June 1 American LEND-LEASE to the Soviet Union begins, with war matériel being provided through Iran and Alaska.

June 3 Flight training begins for more than 200 U.S. Military Academy cadets at West Point. This is the first major elective offered in the history of the Military Academy. Training is given at Stewart Field, twelve miles north of West Point.
    Japanese carrier-based aircraft strafe and bomb DUTCH HARBOR on the island of Unalaska in the ALEUTIAN ISLANDS as a diversion at the outset of the battle of MIDWAY.

June 4 British Eighth Army counterattacks in Libya.

June 4–5 The Japanese are decisively defeated in the battle of MIDWAY, the second major carrier battle of the war.

June 5 The United States declares war on Bulgaria, Hungary, and Rumania.

June 7 The Japanese invade Attu and Kiska in the ALEUTIAN ISLANDS with a total 1,800 troops. They will retain the toehold on the Aleutians until U.S. soldiers retake them in mid-1943.

June 8 European Theater of Operations is established.

June 9 The Japanese high command announces that "The MIDWAY Occupation operations have been temporarily postponed."

The governments of the United States and Britain agree to pool their production of food and war matériel.

June 10 The Czech village of LIDICE is destroyed and all male inhabitants are murdered in retribution of the assassination of NAZI leader REINHARD HEYDRICH.

June 11 The United States and Soviet Union sign a mutual aid agreement.

June 12 Twelve U.S. AAF B-24 LIBERATOR bombers attack oil refineries at PLOESTI, Rumania. This is the first of several U.S. bomber attacks flown from North Africa against this vital source of petroleum for Germany.

June 13 In an attempt at SABOTAGE, four Germans intending to blow up American factories come ashore from a German U-BOAT in rubber landing craft off Amagansett Beach, Long Island, N.Y. A few days later, four others are landed from another U-boat at Ponte Vedra Beach, Fla.
  President ROOSEVELT creates the OFFICE OF STRATEGIC SERVICES (OSS) and names Brig. Gen. WILLIAM DONOVAN as director.

June 16 The OFFICE OF WAR INFORMATION is established by President ROOSEVELT with journalist-radio broadcaster ELMER DAVIS as director.

June 17 *YANK,* a weekly magazine for the U.S. armed services, begins publication.

June 18 MILTON EISENHOWER (brother of Army Maj. Gen. DWIGHT D. EISENHOWER), director of the newly created WAR RELOCATION AUTHORITY, writes to President ROOSEVELT about the need to intern JAPANESE-AMERICANS. More than 110,000 men, women, and children are put behind barbed wire in the Japanese internment.
  Prime Minister CHURCHILL arrives in WASHINGTON after crossing the Atlantic in a Boeing Clipper flying boat, which lands on the Potomac River after a twenty-seven-hour flight. He meets with President Roosevelt to decide on the invasion of French North Africa in late 1942.

June 19 Vice Adm. ROBERT L. GHORMLEY (USN) takes command of the South Pacific Area and South Pacific Forces, reporting to Adm. CHESTER W. NIMITZ, to coordinate U.S. military operations near the SOLOMON ISLANDS.

June 21 Gen. ERWIN ROMMEL's troops capture the vital port of TOBRUK, taking 28,000 British and Australian prisoners. HITLER promotes Rommel to *Generalfeldmarschall* for his success. On June 24 Rommel's troops cross the Egyptian border.

June 22 Japanese submarine shells Fort Stevens at the mouth of the Columbia River.
  Lt. Gen. JOSEPH STILWELL becomes commander of U.S. forces in the China-Burma-India (CBI) Theater.

June 24 Headquarters for the U.S. European Theater of Operations (ETO) is established in London under the command of Maj. Gen. DWIGHT D. EISENHOWER. "Ike," as he is becoming known, will be promoted to lieutenant general in July 1942.

June 25 President ROOSEVELT and Prime Minister CHURCHILL conclude their second wartime conference in WASHINGTON. Among the decisions reached is for a combined effort to develop the ATOMIC BOMB.

June 26 First flight of the Grumman F6F HELLCAT fighter.

June 27 CONVOY PQ 17 departs Iceland bound for MURMANSK and Archangel.

The Soviet port and fortress of SEVASTOPOL in the Crimea on the Black Sea falls to German and Rumanian troops after a four-week siege.

June 28 German troops launch an offensive to seize Soviet oil fields in the CAUCASUS and the key industrial city of STALINGRAD.

June 29 BENITO MUSSOLINI flies to Derna in Libya, expecting to lead a triumphal entry into Cairo at the head of the AFRIKA KORPS. He will return to Italy on July 20 following the failure of *Generalfeldmarschall* ERWIN ROMMEL's offensive.

July 1 First B-17 FLYING FORTRESS of the U.S. Eighth Air Force arrives in Great Britain.

German troops capture SEVASTOPOL.

July 4 *Generalfeldmarschall* ERWIN ROMMEL is compelled by British air and ground resistance to suspend his attacks against the defenses at El Alamein in Egypt.

Flying six borrowed RAF A-20 BOSTON light bombers, U.S. AAF pilots make their first bombing mission in Europe, taking part in an RAF raid against German airfields in Holland.

The FLYING TIGERS of the American Volunteer Group become part of the AAF Tenth AIR FORCE; the Flying Tigers' contract with the Chinese government is terminated.

July 5 CONVOY PQ 17—a RUSSIAN CONVOY—scatters upon command from British naval headquarters because of the feared threat of attack by German warships.

July 7 President ROOSEVELT asks retired Adm. WILLIAM D. LEAHY, former U.S. ambassador to VICHY FRANCE, to serve as his Chief of Staff and ex officio as Chairman of the JOINT CHIEFS OF STAFF. Leahy accepts and is recalled to active duty on July 20.

July 10 First flight of the Douglas A-26 INVADER attack-medium bomber.

Lt. Gen. CARL SPAATZ becomes head of the AAF in Europe.

July 11 RAF LANCASTER bombers fly the longest raid of the European War yet made, flying 1,750 miles to attack German shipyards at Danzig (now Gdansk), Poland.

July 17 Army Chief of Staff Gen. GEORGE C. MARSHALL, Navy Chief of Naval Operations ERNEST J. KING, and presidential adviser HARRY HOPKINS arrive in LONDON to urge British leaders to begin the SECOND FRONT with a cross-Channel attack into Western Europe.

July 18 The German ME 262 makes its first flight. In 1944 it will become the world's first JET-PROPELLED AIRCRAFT to enter service.

Rear Adm. RICHMOND KELLY TURNER becomes commander of the U.S. Amphibious Force South Pacific at Wellington, New Zealand. He will become the premier Navy commander of AMPHIBIOUS LANDINGS in the Pacific area.

July 19 German U-BOATS are withdrawn from off the U.S. Atlantic Coast because of the increasing efficiency of American antisubmarine measures, ending Operation *Paukenschlag* (Drumbeat).

July 20 First U.S. Army WAC training class begins at Fort Des Moines, Ind.

July 21 Japanese troops land near Gona on NEW GUINEA, beginning the Papua operation and forestalling the Allied operation Providence, which was to have secured the same area.

July 24 The Soviet city of ROSTOV is captured by German troops.

July 25 The COMBINED CHIEFS OF STAFF agree to establish the command structure for Operation Torch, the NORTH AFRICA INVASION.

July 30 Adm. WILLIAM D. LEAHY chairs his first JOINT CHIEFS OF STAFF meeting.

The U.S. women's naval reserve is established as the WAVES (Women Accepted for Volunteer Emergency Service).

July 31 The AIRCRAFT CARRIER *ESSEX* (CV 9) is launched at Newport News Shipbuilding & Dry Dock Co., Va., the first of seventeen fast carriers that will enter service during the war, forming the backbone of the U.S. Navy's fast carrier striking forces.

The U.S. Army establishes the Transportation Corps.

Aug. 1 The first German U-BOAT to be sunk by the U.S. Coast Guard is credited to Ens. Henry C. White, who sinks the *U-166* off the approaches to the Mississippi River while flying a J4F WIDGEON biplane.

Aug. 4 The British government charges that MOHANDAS GANDHI and his All-India Congress Party favor "appeasement" with Japan.

Aug. 5 The British government repudiates the MUNICH PACT.

Aug. 6 The city of Voronezh in the Soviet Union falls to German troops.

Aug. 7 The U.S. 1st Marine DIVISION under Lt. Gen. A. A. VANDEGRIFT lands on the islands of Tulagi and GUADALCANAL in the SOLOMON ISLANDS. This is the first U.S. AMPHIBIOUS LANDING of the war and the start of the lengthy U.S. SOLOMONS–NEW GUINEA CAMPAIGN.

Aug. 8 U.S. Marines capture the unfinished Japanese airfield on GUADALCANAL. The primitive base is named Henderson Field after the late Marine Maj. Lofton Henderson, a hero of the battle of MIDWAY.

The All-India Congress Party demands immediate British withdrawal from India.

Aug. 8–9 A force of U.S. and Australian warships off SAVO ISLAND, standing guard for the GUADALCANAL landing, are surprised in a night attack by Japanese cruisers and destroyers. Three U.S. heavy CRUISERS and the Australian cruiser *Canberra* are sunk, and three U.S. DESTROYERS are damaged.

Aug. 10 One of the most ambitious British attempts to reinforce the island of MALTA in the Mediterranean is begun as Operation Pedestal.

Aug. 11 The German submarine *U-73* attacks a MALTA-bound CONVOY and sinks the twenty-two-year-old British carrier *Eagle,* one of the world's first aircraft carriers.

Aug. 12 A paddle-wheel Great Lakes excursion ship is commissioned as the USS *Wolverine* (IX 64), having been converted to serve as a Navy pilot training carrier. Along with the USS *Sable* (IX 81), commissioned the following May, these ships train thousands of student pilots on the Great Lakes.

Prime Minister CHURCHILL arrives in MOSCOW for talks with STALIN.

The first U.S. aircraft to land on the newly completed Henderson Field on GUADALCANAL is a Navy PBY CATALINA flying boat. The first F4F WILDCAT fighter aircraft will arrive on Aug. 20.

Aug. 14 Lt. Gen. DWIGHT D. EISENHOWER is named Anglo-American commander for Operation Torch, the NORTH AFRICA INVASION.

Aug. 17 One hundred twenty-two U.S. Marine raiders under Lt. Col. EVANS F. CARLSON come ashore from the SUBMARINES *Argonaut* (SM 1) and *Nautilus* (SS 168) to raid MAKIN ISLAND in the GILBERT ISLANDS.

Twelve B-17E FLYING FORTRESS bombers of the Eighth AIR FORCE bomb rail marshaling yards at ROUEN, France, in the first U.S. AAF bomber raid of Europe. Another six B-17s fly a diversionary strike with both groups escorted by RAF SPITFIRE fighters. Brig. Gen. IRA EAKER flies on the strike, which does only token damage.

Aug. 18 Lt. Gen. BERNARD L. MONTGOMERY is named to replace Maj. Gen. N. M. Ritchie as commander of the British Eighth Army in Egypt.

Aug. 19 British and Canadian troops raid the German-held port of DIEPPE on the English Channel, the first major AMPHIBIOUS LANDING in Europe. The assault is a disaster.

Aug. 20 U.S. Twelfth AIR FORCE is activated at Bolling Field in WASHINGTON in preparation for the NORTH AFRICA INVASION.

Aug. 21 U.S. Marines turn back the first major Japanese ground attack on GUADALCANAL in the battle of Tenaru. Japanese ground, naval, and air attacks against the Marines will continue for several months.

Aug. 22 The light carrier *INDEPENDENCE* (CVL 22) is launched at the Camden shipbuilding yard in Philadelphia, Pa. She was one of nine light cruisers completed as fast light carriers.

Angered by the sinking of several of its merchant ships, Brazil declares war on Germany and Italy. Brazil will be the only South American nation to send combat troops to fight in Europe.

Aug. 23 Six hundred mounted Italian troops rout 2,000 Soviet troops at Izbushensky in history's last CAVALRY charge.

German troops begin an assault on the major Soviet industrial city of STALINGRAD.

Aug. 24 In the battle of the EASTERN SOLOMONS, the third carrier-versus-carrier battle of the war, U.S. naval forces defeat a Japanese force attempting to screen reinforcements for the GUADALCANAL fighting.

Aug. 29 American RED CROSS announces that Japan has refused to allow safe conduct for the passage of ships with supplies for U.S. PRISONERS OF WAR.

Aug. 30 U.S. troops land on Adak Island in the ALEUTIAN ISLANDS.

Sept. 4 Soviet planes bomb BUDAPEST in the war's first air raid on the Hungarian capital.

Sept. 5 U.S. OFFICE OF PRICE ADMINISTRATION imposes rent ceilings.

Sept. 6 German troops capture the Soviet port city of Novorossisk.

Sept. 8 The U.S. War Production Board shuts down GOLD mines to release labor for the war effort.

Sept. 9–10 The Japanese submarine *I-25* launches a floatplane piloted by Warrant Flying Officer Nobuo Fujita from a position off the coast of Oregon to drop incendiary BOMBS on U.S. forests near Brookings, Ore. Two fire-bombing missions are flown by the aircraft, each time carrying two 154-pound bombs. It is the only bombing of the continental United States during the war. News of the attack is voluntarily withheld by U.S. newspapers.

Sept. 12 The British liner *LACONIA* is sunk by the submarine *U-156,* leading to heavy losses among the Italian prisoners she is carrying and sparking a controversy on U-BOAT treatment of survivors.

Sept. 14 German troops begin a major frontal attack against Soviet troops holding STALINGRAD. Savage street fighting follows.

Sept. 15 Comdr. Takaichi Kinashi, commanding officer of the Japanese submarine *I-19,* fires what is probably the most effective TORPEDO salvo of the war. Operating south of the SOLOMON ISLANDS, he has two U.S. task forces within the 13,000-yard range of his Type 95 torpedoes. His six-torpedo salvo sinks the AIRCRAFT CARRIER *WASP* (CV 7), inflicts fatal damage on the DESTROYER *O'Brien* (DD 415), and causes damage to the BATTLESHIP *North Carolina* (BB 55), the only modern Allied battleship in the Pacific.

Sept. 16 The RAF announces that the three EAGLE SQUADRONS (Nos. 71, 171, and 133) comprised of U.S. volunteers will be incorporated into the AAF. American fighter pilots in the RAF had shot down seventy-three enemy aircraft.

Sept. 21 The Boeing B-29 SUPERFORTRESS makes its first flight at Seattle, Wash. It will be the largest bomber of any nation to enter operational service during the war.

Sept. 23 Brig. Gen. JAMES H. DOOLITTLE takes command of the U.S. Twelfth AIR FORCE in England; it will control AAF operations in the NORTH AFRICA INVASION from Nov. 1942 and, subsequently, in SICILY and Italy.

Sept. 25 In one of the most precise bombing strikes of the war, RAF MOSQUITO fighter-bombers attack GESTAPO headquarters in Oslo, Norway.

Sept. 28 Gen. HENRY H. ARNOLD, head of the AAF, gives "highest priority" to development of the very-long-range Northrop B-35 FLYING WING and the Consolidated B-36 PEACEMAKER. These planes are intended for trans-Atlantic bombing operations; neither plane will fly before the end of the war.

Oct. 1 The German attack on STALINGRAD comes to a complete halt.

Oct. 2 The British troop transport *QUEEN MARY* rams the British cruiser *Curacao* off the Irish coast. The cruiser sinks with the loss of 338 men.

Oct. 3 Germany conducts the first successful test flight of a V-2 MISSILE; the rocket-powered missile flies perfectly over a 118-mile course.

Oct. 11 The Japanese submarine *I-25* sinks the Soviet submarine *L-16* some 500 miles west of Seattle, Wash. Comdr. Meiji Tagami, the commanding officer, had mistaken the Soviet submarine for an American craft. The Soviet submarine was en route from Vladivostok to the Kola Peninsula via the Panama Canal.

Oct. 11–12 In the battle of CAPE ESPERANCE in the U.S. SOLOMONS–NEW GUINEA CAMPAIGN, U.S. CRUISERS and DESTROYERS decisively defeat a Japanese task force in a night surface encounter.

Oct. 13 U.S. soldiers of the 164th Infantry REGIMENT of the Americal DIVISION reinforce the 1st Marine Division on GUADALCANAL, the first Army troops to land on the island.

Oct. 14–15 The Japanese cruisers *Chokai* and *Kinsugasa* bombard Henderson Field on GUADALCANAL at night with 752 rounds of 8-inch ammunition. The next morning six Japanese transports unload troops at nearby Tassafaronga, screened by destroyers and aircraft. U.S. planes attack, forcing three transports to run aground; other Japanese ships are damaged.

Oct. 15–16 In another night bombardment of Henderson Field on GUADALCANAL, the Japanese cruisers *Maya* and *Myoko* fire 1,500 8-inch rounds at U.S. Marine positions.

Oct. 18 The first JET-PROPELLED AIRCRAFT to fly in the United States, the Bell P-59A AIRACOMET, makes its maiden flight at Muroc Dry Lake, Calif.

Vice Adm. WILLIAM F. HALSEY succeeds Vice Adm. ROBERT L. GHORMLEY as commander of the South Pacific Area, with responsibility for the naval aspects of the U.S. SOLOMONS–NEW GUINEA CAMPAIGN when Adm. CHESTER NIMITZ decides "the critical situation requires a more aggressive commander."

Oct. 19 The Japanese submarine *I-36* launches a floatplane for a one-way reconnaissance flight over PEARL HARBOR from a position some 300 miles south of Oahu. The pilot and crewmen report on the ships in the harbor, after which the aircraft is lost at sea.

Oct. 22 Maj. Gen. MARK W. CLARK and a small U.S. party land secretly from a submarine to confer with French officials in Algeria about the pending Anglo-American landings.

Oct. 23 CONVOYS depart Hampton Roads, Va., for the NORTH AFRICA INVASION.

Oct. 23–24 In a nighttime attack, the British Eighth Army under the command of Lt. Gen. BERNARD MONTGOMERY opens an offensive against ROMMEL'S AFRIKA KORPS. Breaking through German lines near the Qattara Depression, the British decisively smash Rommel's tanks in the battle of El Aqaqqir on Nov. 2, putting the Afrika Korps in full retreat. The British forces begin a 1,750-mile drive to join the Allied troops that will land in French North Africa in Nov. 1942.

Oct. 26 In the bitter and continuing struggle for GUADALCANAL, U.S. and Japanese warships clash in the battle of SANTA CRUZ. U.S. losses include the AIRCRAFT CARRIER *HORNET* (CV 8); Japanese losses are light.

Nov. 2 German forces are decisively defeated in a massive tank battle at El Aqqaqir. Retreat of German and Italian forces under *Generalfeldmarschall* ERWIN ROMMEL begins from the Egyptian border, although two days earlier HITLER had ordered Rommel to "hold at all costs."

Lt. Gen. DWIGHT D. EISENHOWER flies from England to GIBRALTAR to establish the Allied command post for the NORTH AFRICA INVASION.

Nov. 7 French Gen. HENRI GIRAUD is secretly brought out of VICHY FRANCE by the British submarine *Seraph* (under American command). After meeting with Gen. EISENHOWER at GIBRALTAR, he is flown to North Africa on Nov. 9.

Nov. 8 British and American troops under the overall command of Lt. Gen. DWIGHT D. EISENHOWER land at three points along the coast of North Africa—near Casablanca, Oran, and Algiers. There is light resistance by VICHY FRENCH troops. All three landing areas of Operation Torch are quickly in Allied hands.

VICHY FRANCE severs diplomatic relations with the United States.

HITLER reaffirms his intention of capturing STALINGRAD despite heavy losses.

Nov. 9 German troops invade Tunisia, the initial units being air landed at the Tunis airport without opposition from nearby French troops.

Nov. 10 Adm. JEAN DARLAN orders French forces in North Africa to cease resistance to the Anglo-American forces.

In response to the Allied landings in North Africa, German troops move into Tunis and Bizerte.

> *"Geronimo!"*
> Shout of U.S. paratroopers when jumping, first used in combat in the North African campaign, Nov. 1942

Nov. 11 German troops invade unoccupied VICHY FRANCE. At TOULON the French scuttle their warships rather than risk their being used by the Germans.

The limited VICHY FRENCH resistance in North Africa comes to an end.

British troops cross from Egypt into Libya as the AFRIKA KORPS withdraws westward.

Nov. 12 The Congress approves the drafting of men eighteen and nineteen years old.

U.S. Ninth AIR FORCE established in place of the Middle East Air Force (which had been created on April 8, 1942).

Third WASHINGTON CONFERENCE begins with Prime Minister CHURCHILL and President ROOSEVELT leading their respective delegations.

Nov. 13 Lt. Gen. DWIGHT D. EISENHOWER flies to Algeria to conclude an agreement with Adm. JEAN DARLAN.

British troops recapture TOBRUK.

The COMBINED CHIEFS OF STAFF approves plans for the invasion of SICILY after the defeat of German-Italian forces in North Africa.

Nov. 14–15 In a clash off GUADALCANAL, a Japanese naval force is defeated: the battleship *Hiei* is heavily damaged and scuttled by her crew, the first Japanese battleship to be lost in the war. U.S. losses include the CRUISER *Juneau* (CLAA 52), whose sinking takes the lives of the five SULLIVAN BROTHERS.

Nov. 15 Gen. HENRI GIRAUD is appointed French Commander in Chief in North Africa by Adm. JEAN DARLAN.

Nov. 16 German and Italian troops complete the occupation of Tunisia. FREE FRENCH forces begin fighting the Germans.

Nov. 19 Soviet troops take the offensive at STALINGRAD.

Nov. 20 The 1,525-mile ALCAN HIGHWAY between Dawson Creek, British Columbia, and Fairbanks in the Yukon Territory, is officially opened.

British troops retake Benghazi, capital of Libya.

First flight of the Vought-Sikorsky VS-173, a full-scale model of a fighter aircraft with an almost circular wing. A military version of this aircraft, the Navy's F5U, is later constructed, but never flown.

Nov. 22 Soviet troops complete encirclement of the German Sixth Army at STALINGRAD.

Nov. 23–24 Darwin, Australia, is attacked by Japanese aircraft.

Nov. 27 The French fleet in TOULON is scuttled to keep it from being taken over by the Germans.

Nov. 29 Coffee RATIONING goes into effect in the United States.

Dec. 1 A member of the British Parliament reports that the Nazis have killed more than 2,000,000 JEWS through Sept. 1942.

Dec. 2 Dr. ENRICO FERMI and a team of European-American scientists achieve the first true nuclear chain reaction at Stagg Field of the University of Chicago. This is a key event in the development of the ATOMIC BOMB.

Dec. 4 In the first U.S. bomber attack on the Italian mainland, twenty-four U.S. AAF B-24 LIBERATORS flying from North Africa attack Naples.

Dec. 9 Maj. Gen. ALEXANDER PATCH, commanding general of the U.S. Army's Americal DIVISION, relieves Maj. Gen. A. A. VANDEGRIFT, commanding general of the 1st Marine Division, as U.S. field commander on GUADALCANAL.

Dec. 14 The first American-built LANDING SHIP, TANK *(LST 1)* is completed at the Dravo Corp. in Pittsburgh, Pa.

Dec. 20–21 Japanese planes bomb Calcutta, India, in the city's first raid of the war. A second raid is flown on Dec. 22–23 and a third on Dec. 23–24. The British report that the three raids killed twenty-five persons and injured fewer than 100.

Dec. 24 Adm. JEAN DARLAN, the nominal leader of the VICHY FRENCH government in North Africa, is assassinated. Gen. HENRI GIRAUD succeeds him as High Commissioner of French North and West Africa.

Dec. 27 The Germans form the Smolensk Committee to enlist Soviet troops who have surrendered to fight against Soviet forces. Gen. ANDREI VLASOV will command the so-called Russian Army of Liberation.

Dec. 31 After a bloody five-month campaign, Emperor HIROHITO gives Japanese commanders permission to evacuate GUADALCANAL and accept the American victory.

The USS *ESSEX* (CV 9) is commissioned.

1943

Jan. 2 Allies capture Buna in NEW GUINEA.

Jan. 5 Allied Air Forces in Africa are activated under Maj. Gen. CARL SPAATZ.

Jan. 12 Soviet forces raise the siege of LENINGRAD.

Jan. 14 President ROOSEVELT and Prime Minister CHURCHILL begin the ten-day CASABLANCA CONFERENCE.

Jan. 15 British Eighth Army begins drive on Tripoli.

Jan. 22 Japanese forces at Sanananda on NEW GUINEA are defeated in a major Allied victory.

Jan. 27 Ninety-one B-17 FLYING FORTRESS and B-24 LIBERATOR bombers of the U.S. Eighth AIR FORCE based in England fly the first American bomber raid against Germany, striking the port of Wilhelmshaven; fifty-three of the aircraft reach the target. Only three aircraft are lost to enemy fighters in the daylight raid, which takes the defenders by surprise.

Jan. 30 German troops on the offensive break through U.S. and French lines in North Africa.

Grossadmiral KARL DÖNITZ becomes Commander in Chief of the German Navy, replacing ERICH RAEDER.

BERLIN is attacked for the first time in daylight by RAF MOSQUITO bombers.

> *"I don't mind being called tough, since I find in this racket it's the tough guys who lead the survivors."*
>
> Col. Curtis LeMay, 1943

Jan. 31 Soviet high command announces the destruction of the German Sixth Army at STALINGRAD and the capture of *Generalfeldmarschall* FRIEDRICH PAULUS.

Feb. 1 Maj. Gen. NATHAN F. TWINING and fourteen men come down at sea near the New Hebrides on a flight from GUADALCANAL and spend six days on a raft before being rescued.

Feb. 2 The last of German forces encircled at STALINGRAD are destroyed or surrender to Soviet troops.

Feb. 4 British Eighth Army crosses into Tunisia.

Feb. 7 Shoe RATIONING begins in the United States.

Feb. 8 The 77th Indian Brigade (CHINDITS) under Brig. ORDE WINGATE begins GUERRILLA operations behind Japanese lines in Burma.

Feb. 9 Organized Japanese resistance ends on GUADALCANAL.

Feb. 14 Soviet troops retake ROSTOV.

Feb. 20 Commanded by *Generalfeldmarschall* ERWIN ROMMEL, German troops break through KASSERINE PASS in Tunisia, defeating U.S. forces.

Feb. 23 *Generalfeldmarschall* ERWIN ROMMEL takes command of Army Group Africa, controlling all German-Italian troops in North Africa.

Feb. 25 U.S. Army II CORPS troops retake the KASSERINE PASS.

March 2–4 U.S. forces achieve victory over the Japanese in the battle of the BISMARCK SEA.

March 6 STALIN takes the rank of Marshal of the Soviet Union following the Soviet success at Smolensk.

March 9 *Generalfeldmarschall* ERWIN ROMMEL departs North Africa.

March 10 The U.S. Fourteenth AIR FORCE is activated in China under the command of Maj. Gen. CLAIRE CHENNAULT. The command initially consists entirely of fighter aircraft, with some pilots being former FLYING TIGERS. Medium and heavy bombers are gradually added.

March 16 Final Allied offensive in Tunisia begins.

March 20 The largest CONVOY battles of the BATTLE OF THE ATLANTIC are fought, marking the turning point in the U-BOAT war.

March 24 U.S. RATIONING regulations are announced for meat, butter, and cheese.

March 28 U.S. Army II CORPS opens drive in TUNISIA toward Gabès.

April 1 The U.S. government puts nationwide food rationing into effect.

April 7 U.S. and British patrols meet along the Gabès Road between Wadi Akarit and El Guettar near the Tunisian frontier, linking the British Eighth Army under Gen. BERNARD MONTGOMERY and Anglo-American forces under Gen. DWIGHT D. EISENHOWER. The two armies now form a single front against the German-Italian forces remaining in TUNISIA.

April 8 P-51 MUSTANG fighters fly their first combat mission over Europe.

April 9 Rank of commodore is reestablished in U.S. Navy.

April 18 Eighteen U.S. AAF P-38 LIGHTNING fighters from the 339th Fighter SQUADRON, led by Lt. Col. THOMAS G. LANPHIER, JR., shoot down the Japanese BETTY bomber carrying Adm. ISOROKU YAMAMOTO, just south of BOUGAINVILLE in the SOLOMON ISLANDS. The attack is possible because of U.S. code-breaking efforts.

April 21 President ROOSEVELT announces that several of the airmen in the DOOLITTLE RAID have been executed by the Japanese.

April 22 The Japanese government, hinting at more reprisals for future American bombings of Japan, states that captured fliers will be given "one-way tickets to hell."

May 2 Labor leader John L. Lewis calls a truce in the nationwide coal strike thirty minutes before President ROOSEVELT was to go on radio to denounce the strike as detrimental to the war effort.

May 7 Last major German strongholds in North Africa—Tunis and Bizerte—fall to Allied forces.

May 10 U.S. troops invade Attu in the ALEUTIAN ISLANDS, beginning the drive to expel Japanese forces from that area.

May 12 Third WASHINGTON CONFERENCE of Prime Minister CHURCHILL and President ROOSEVELT begins.

May 13 The last German and Italian troops in North Africa surrender at Cape Bon, Tunisia.

May 14 A Japanese submarine launches TORPEDOES at the Australian hospital ship *Centaur;* 299 persons die when she sinks.

May 16–17 Fifteen RAF LANCASTER aircraft bomb the Möhne and Eder dams on the Ruhr River. Major industrial areas are flooded as 1,500-pound UPKEEP BOMBS, designed especially for the mission, are released from heights of 100 feet or less to breach the massive dams.

May 22 STALIN abolishes the Comintern.

The Navy announces that all U.S. warships sunk at PEARL HARBOR have been returned to service except for the *ARIZONA* (BB 39), *Oklahoma* (BB 37), and *Utah* (AG 16).

May 24 *Grossadmiral* KARL DÖNITZ, Commander in Chief of the German Navy, informs HITLER that because of high losses the U-BOATS must be withdrawn from the Atlantic.

May 31 Capture of Attu by U.S. forces is completed, ending Japanese occupation of ALEUTIAN ISLANDS. (Japanese troops had been secretly evacuated from Adak.)

Responsibility for the construction of U-BOATS is transferred from the German Navy to the control of ALBERT SPEER, head of armament production.

June 3 French Committee of National Liberation—provisional government of the French Empire—is formed in Algeria.

June 10 COMBINED CHIEFS OF STAFF officially inaugurates the around-the-clock bomber offensive against Germany. (See STRATEGIC BOMBING.)

June 11 The Italian island of PANTELLERIA surrenders after heavy aerial bombardment as an Allied amphibious force prepares to land.

June 14 U.S. Supreme Court reverses a law that compels school children to salute the American flag.

> *"Battle is the most magnificent competition in which a human being can indulge. It brings out all that is best; it removes all that is base."*
>
> Lt. Gen. George S. Patton, Jr., on June 27, 1943, to officers of the 45th Infantry Division

June 15 The world's first jet-propelled bomber, Germany's Ardo AR 234 *BLITZ,* makes its first flight.

June 24 U.S. Army Lt. Col. W. R. Lovelace makes a record parachute jump from 42,200 feet.

July 4 German tank attack begins the battle of KURSK.

July 7 HITLER makes the V-2 MISSILE program a top priority in German armament planning.

July 8   Col. M. G. Grow, U.S. Eighth AIR FORCE surgeon, is given the Legion of Honor award for developing the flak vest for bomber crewmen.

Eight U.S. AAF B-24 LIBERATOR bombers flying from MIDWAY strike WAKE, the first attack on the Japanese-held island by U.S. land-based bombers. Air strikes will continue throughout the war, primarily as a training operation.

July 9   First Anglo-American troops land in SICILY; the AMPHIBIOUS LANDINGS begin on July 10. First use of DUKW amphibious truck in an assault.

> *"A landing against organized and highly trained opposition is probably the most difficult undertaking which military forces are called upon to face."*
>
> Gen. George C. Marshall during planning for the Sicily landings

July 18 The U.S. Navy AIRSHIP *K-74* is shot down by antiaircraft fire from the German submarine *U-134;* it is the only U.S. blimp lost to enemy action during the war.

July 19 The first air raid on ROME is made by 158 B-17 FLYING FORTRESS and 112 B-24 LIBERATOR bombers. The bombing was preceded by the dropping of warning leaflets. Although all of the planes were American, the U.S. and British governments took equal responsibility for the attack.

July 22 Palermo, SICILY, surrenders to U.S. Seventh ARMY.

July 25 Italian dictator MUSSOLINI is overthrown by a coup. Field Marshal PIETRO BADOGLIO takes command of the Italian Army and government.

The U.S. DESTROYER ESCORT *Harmon* (DE 678) is launched; this is the first U.S. ship to be named for a black. Leonard Roy Harmon was a mess attendant 3rd class who was killed on board a CRUISER while helping injured sailors during a night action off GUADALCANAL in Nov. 1942.

July 27 An embarrassed President ROOSEVELT reprimands the OFFICE OF WAR INFORMATION for referring to King Victor Emmanuel III of Italy as a "moronic little king" in a short-wave radio broadcast beamed to Europe.

Aug. 1   The second U.S. AAF attack against Rumanian oil refineries at PLOESTI is flown by 177 B-24 LIBERATOR bombers from bases in North Africa.

Aug. 1-2 As fifteen U.S. PT-BOATS try to block Blackett Strait south of Kolombangara Island in the SOLOMON ISLANDS, the *PT 109* commanded by Lt. JOHN F. KENNEDY is rammed and sunk by the Japanese destroyer *Amagiri.* Kennedy, towing an injured sailor, and other survivors swim for five hours to reach a small island.

Aug. 9   WOLFGANG LÜTH, high-scoring commander of the *U-43,* is the first member of the U-BOAT service to be awarded Diamonds, Oak Leaves, and Swords to the Knight's Cross of the IRON CROSS.

Aug. 14 Anglo-American QUEBEC CONFERENCE opens.

Aug. 17 The Allied forces complete the conquest of SICILY.

Aug. 17-18 RAF Bomber Command makes first major bombing raid against the German missile development facility at PEENEMÜNDE.

Aug. 23 Germans abandon KHARKOV.

Aug. 25 ALLIES complete occupation of NEW GEORGIA.

Aug. 26 United States recognizes the French Committee of National Liberation.

Sept. 3 British troops land in Italy, coming ashore at Calabria.

Field Marshal PIETRO BADOGLIO signs armistice with the ALLIES, which is not revealed until Sept. 8.

Sept. 4 Allied troops recapture Lae-Salamaua, NEW GUINEA.

Sept. 8 The Italian government surrenders unconditionally to the ALLIES.

Sept. 9 Anglo-American Fifth ARMY troops land at SALERNO, Italy; British troops land at TARANTO.

The Italian battleship *Roma* becomes the first major ship in history to be sunk by a GUIDED MISSILE—a single aircraft-launched German FRITZ-X guided bomb ignites fires that destroy the ship; 1,254 of her crew are lost.

Sept. 10 ROME seized by German forces.

Sept. 11 The Italian Fleet surrenders to the ALLIES at MALTA.

Sept. 13 Over 1,200 paratroopers are dropped at SALERNO, Italy, without the loss of a man or aircraft in a highly successful Allied AIRBORNE operation.

Sept. 16 A German FRITZ-X guided bomb strikes the British battleship *Warspite* in the Mediterranean; the warship is severely damaged and is out of action for the remainder of the war.

Sept. 23 A Fascist puppet government is established in northern Italy under MUSSOLINI.

Sept. 25 Soviet troops recapture SMOLENSK.

Sept. 29 Field Marshal PIETRO BADOGLIO and Lt. Gen. DWIGHT D. EISENHOWER sign surrender documents on board the British battle cruiser *Nelson* at MALTA.

Oct. 1 British troops enter Naples and occupy Foggia airfield.

Oct. 7 Approximately 100 U.S. PRISONERS OF WAR remaining on WAKE are executed on order of Rear Adm. Shigematsu Sakaibara, the Japanese island commander.

Oct. 12 U.S. Fifth ARMY troops begin assault crossing of Volturno River in Italy.

Oct. 13 Italy declares war on Germany.

Oct. 14 Two hundred ninety-one B-17 FLYING FORTRESS bombers of the U.S. Eighth AIR FORCE flying from England raid the SCHWEINFURT ball bearing plants. Losses are heavy, with sixty B-17s shot down and others damaged; 228 reach the target. As a result of these losses, daylight STRATEGIC BOMBING against targets deep in Germany are halted until fighter escorts become available.

Soviet troops reach Zaporozhye, the industrial center of the Ukraine.

Oct. 19 Allied foreign ministers begin conference in MOSCOW.

Oct. 26 Emperor HIROHITO tells the Japanese Diet that Japan's situation is "truly grave," in a rare admission of the plight of the country.

> *"Most of you know what it is to see a pile of one hundred or five hundred or a thousand bodies. To have stuck it out and . . . barring exceptions caused by human weakness, to have remained decent: This is what has made us tough. . . . This is a glorious page in our history which has not and never will be written."*
>
> *Reichsführer* Heinrich Himmler to SS officers in Posen (Poznań), Poland, Oct. 4, 1943

Nov. 1 Allied forces invade BOUGAINVILLE in the SOLOMON ISLANDS.

Nov. 3 In largest U.S. strike to date against Germany, over 500 Eighth AIR FORCE bombers attack Wilhelmshaven.

Nov. 5 U.S. Fifth ARMY begins attack on German Winter Line fortifications in Italy. The attack is fruitless.

Nov. 6 German troops withdraw from Kiev.

Nov. 7 British troops launch limited offensive along the coast of Burma.

Nov. 12 German troops invade Leros in the Aegean Sea.

Nov. 16 Adm. LOUIS MOUNTBATTEN activates the Southeast Asia Command.

Nov. 20 U.S. AMPHIBIOUS LANDINGS begin against MAKIN and TARAWA in the Central Pacific.

Nov. 22 President ROOSEVELT and Prime Minister CHURCHILL meet in Cairo. They will then fly to Tehran to meet with STALIN.

> *"Nobody can actually duplicate the strain that a commander is under in making a decision during combat."*
>
> Capt. Arleigh ("Thirty-one Knot") Burke, the U.S. Navy's leading destroyer commander of the war, Nov. 1943

Nov. 23 Organized Japanese resistance ends on TARAWA and MAKIN atolls.

Nov. 28 President ROOSEVELT and Prime Minister CHURCHILL arrive in Tehran to meet with STALIN in the first meeting of the BIG THREE.

Dec. 1 The Swedish exchange liner *Gripsholm* arrives in New York with 1,439 Americans and Canadians released from Japanese internment camps.

Dec. 2 President ROOSEVELT and Prime Minister CHURCHILL meet in Cairo with Generalissimo CHIANG KAI-SHEK.

Dec. 10 SELECTIVE SERVICE begins policy of not drafting men who were fathers before Dec. 7, 1941.

Dec. 13 Seven hundred ten U.S. Eighth AIR FORCE bombers attack Kiel, Germany. The strike is escorted to the target and back to bases in England for the first time by P-51 MUSTANG fighters. It is the largest daylight raid to date by the U.S. AAF.

Dec. 14 Soviet forces begin winter offensive.

Dec. 15 U.S. troops under Brig. Gen. Julian W. Cunningham make a preliminary landing on the Arawe Peninsula of NEW BRITAIN in the SOLOMON ISLANDS.

Dec. 18 Generalissimo CHIANG KAI-SHEK gives U.S. Gen. JOSEPH W. STILWELL command of Chinese troops in Burma and India.

Dec. 24 Gen. DWIGHT D. EISENHOWER is named to command the Allied cross-Channel NORMANDY INVASION of Europe, which is scheduled for May 1944.

Dec. 26 Main Allied assault of NEW BRITAIN begins with 1st Marine DIVISION coming ashore at Cape Gloucester.

In a sea battle near Bear Island, north of Norway, a British force led by the battleship *Duke of York* engages the German battleship *Scharnhorst,* attempting to intercept a CONVOY en route to MURMANSK. The battle was joined in darkness (4:15 P.M.) and the German dreadnought is sunk late that afternoon by British gunfire and TORPEDOES.

Dec. 27–29 U.S. Army takes over the operation of American railroads to forestall a strike.

1944

Jan. 1 United States activates U.S. Strategic Air Forces in Europe to coordinate STRATEGIC BOMBING operations.

Jan. 3 Soviet troops enter the German-held portion of Poland.

Jan. 4 U.S. aircraft begin massive air drops of supplies to GUERRILLA forces in Western Europe.

Jan. 9 First flight of the Lockheed XP-80 SHOOTING STAR, which will become the first operational U.S. jet-propelled fighter. It will not see combat in the war.

Jan. 11 Anglo-American bombers begin Operation Pointblank, the STRATEGIC BOMBING offensive against the German aircraft industry and Luftwaffe.

Jan. 15 Soviet forces open offensive to relieve the German siege of LENINGRAD.
U.S. Fifth ARMY successfully concludes operation against the Winter Line in Italy by the capture of Mount Trocchio.

Jan. 20 Allied forces begin unsuccessful operations to cross the Rapido River and seize CASSINO.

Jan. 21 Japan's Premier HIDEKI TOJO admits that there is only a "hair's breadth between final victory and defeat" in the Pacific War.

> *"Look at an infantry-man's eyes and you can see how much war he has seen."*
> Sgt. Bill Mauldin, cartoonist, in *Up Front*

Jan. 22 U.S. troops make an AMPHIBIOUS LANDING behind German lines at ANZIO, just south of ROME. The U.S. commander, Maj. Gen. JOHN P. LUCAS, proves too cautious and loses the opportunity to capture Rome with minimal German opposition.

Jan. 23 Randolph Churchill, member of Parliament and son of Prime Minister CHURCHILL, parachutes into the headquarters of Yugoslav GUERRILLA leader JOSEF TITO.

Jan. 26 Argentina breaks diplomatic relations with Germany and Japan.

Jan. 29 Eight hundred U.S. heavy bombers strike Frankfurt in the largest American raid yet made against Germany.
U.S. BATTLESHIP *MISSOURI* (BB 63) is launched at the Brooklyn Navy Yard, N.Y. She is christened by Miss Margaret Truman, the daughter of Senator HARRY S TRUMAN.

Jan. 31 U.S. troops make an AMPHIBIOUS LANDING on KWAJALEIN atoll in the MARSHALL ISLANDS.

Feb. 17 U.S. troops land on ENIWETOK atoll.

Feb. 18 U.S. carrier-based aircraft attack the Japanese base at TRUK in the CAROLINE ISLANDS.

> Gobbledygook: *"The way the users of Latin phrases and big words, the double-talkers and the long-winded writers were moving in on us like an invisible empire."*
> Texas Congressman Maury Maverick, 1944

Feb. 19 U.S. Eighth AIR FORCE and RAF Bomber Command commence "BIG WEEK" series of heavy bomber attacks against German aircraft production facilities.

Feb. 20 The destruction of RABAUL as an effective Japanese base is completed by U.S. land- and carrier-based aircraft as the Japanese abandon Rabaul's air bases.

Feb. 23 U.S. carrier-based aircraft begin air attacks against the MARIANA ISLANDS.

Feb. 24 U.S. forces (MERRILL'S MARAUDERS) begin ground campaign in northern Burma.

Feb. 26 SELECTIVE SERVICE reviews occupational draft deferments of 5,000,000 men in response to a shortfall of recruits.

March 4 Six hundred U.S. Eighth AIR FORCE bombers drop 1,600 tons of bombs on German targets. Although for the first time the primary target of U.S. bombers is BERLIN, only twenty-nine planes reach that target; those bombers are escorted all the way to Berlin by P-51 MUSTANG fighters. (The official U.S. AAF history called the massive effort "none too successful.")

March 5 Gen. ORDE WINGATE's long-range penetration groups begin landing behind Japanese lines in central Burma.

March 12 The JOINT CHIEFS OF STAFF issues orders for Gen. DOUGLAS MACARTHUR and Adm. CHESTER W. NIMITZ to begin a dual advance to the Luzon-Formosa area by Feb. 1945.

The British government halts travel between Britain and Ireland to help conceal invasion maneuvers. Later, telephone connections are also suspended.

March 17 U.S. Fifteenth AIR FORCE bombers make the first air attack on Vienna.

March 20 German troops occupy Hungary.

March 22 The British CHIEFS OF STAFF recommend that plans for the invasion of southern France (Operation Anvil) be dropped in favor of a greater effort in Italy; American military leaders reject the proposal.

> *"Overpaid. Oversexed. And over here!"*
>
> **British men complaining about the hundreds of thousands of U.S. troops in England during the buildup for the Normandy invasion**

April 1 U.S. planes accidentally bomb the Swiss town of Schaffhausen, killing at least fifty people and wounding another 150. (In 1949 the U.S. government will pay Switzerland 62,000,000 Swiss francs for the bombing of Schaffhausen and other violations of Swiss territory by U.S. aircraft during the war.)

April 3 Three hundred seventy-five U.S. B-17 FLYING FORTRESS and B-24 LIBERATOR heavy bombers make first major air attack on BUDAPEST.

April 8 Soviet troops open an offensive in the Crimea.

April 10 Soviet troops recapture Odessa.

April 12 U.S. Twentieth AIR FORCE is activated under the command of Gen. HENRY H. ARNOLD, head of the AAF, to direct STRATEGIC BOMBING operations against Japan. The principal components of the Air Force will be the XX Bomber COMMAND in China-India and the XXI Bomber Command in the MARIANAS.

April 16 Soviet troops take Yalta in the Crimea.

The last U.S. BATTLESHIP to be built, the *Wisconsin* (BB 64), is placed in commission.

April 17 Japanese troops begin their last offensive operation in China.

April 22 Allied troops land at Aitape and HOLLANDIA in NEW GUINEA.

April 28 Secretary of the Navy FRANK KNOX dies of a heart attack; he is succeeded by Under Secretary of the Navy JAMES V. FORRESTAL.

April 30 Gen. DOUGLAS MACARTHUR, secretly recruited by conservative Republicans for the presidential nomination, declares that he neither desires nor will accept the nomination.

May 3 U.S. OFFICE OF PRICE ADMINISTRATION ends most meat RATIONING.

May 9 Soviet troops retake the port city of SEVASTOPOL in the Crimea.

May 11 ALLIES open an offensive against the German Gustav Line in Italy with their goal the taking of ROME.

May 12 The German submarine *U-2501* is launched; she is the first of the revolutionary TYPE XXI U-BOATS.

May 18 Allied troops capture CASSINO.

May 21 LST explosion occurs in WEST LOCH of PEARL HARBOR.

May 23 U.S. Army VI CORPS launches offensive to break out of the ANZIO beachhead.

May 27 Allied troops land on Biak Island, NEW GUINEA.

June 2 U.S. Fourteenth AIR FORCE bombers begin SHUTTLE-BOMBING of Germany with the Italian-based bombers being refueled and rearmed at Soviet bases.

June 4 U.S. Fifth ARMY troops enter ROME.

The German submarine *U-505* is captured off the west coast of Africa by a U.S. TASK FORCE led by the ESCORT CARRIER *Guadalcanal* (CVE 60).

June 5 In the first combat mission by U.S. B-29 SUPERFORTRESS bombers, seventy-seven of the four-engine bombers flying from India strike Japanese railway facilities at Bangkok, Thailand. Five B-29s and seventeen crewmen are lost in the raid, none to Japanese action.

U.S. and British AIRBORNE troops land behind German coastal defenses in Normandy.

June 6 The largest AMPHIBIOUS LANDING in history lands U.S., British, and Canadian troops on the Normandy coast of France to begin the ALLIED CAMPAIGN IN EUROPE.

June 10 Prime Minister CHURCHILL and Allied military leaders visit the Normandy beachhead.

The U.S. Eighth ARMY is activated in Memphis, Tenn.

In Italy, the British V Corps pursues German forces up the Adriatic coast, with the Indian 4th Division taking Pescara and Chieti.

June 13 First German V-1 BUZZ BOMBS fall on England.

June 15 U.S. Marines land on SAIPAN in the first assault of the MARIANA ISLANDS.

U.S. Army VII CORPS seals off German forces in the Cotentin Peninsula in France; the German garrison at Cherbourg surrenders on June 27.

June 15–16 In the first bombing raid on Japan since the DOOLITTLE RAID in April 1942, forty-seven B-29 SUPERFORTRESS bombers strike the steelworks at Yawata. The planes, based in Bengal, India, refuel in China en route to Japan. Two of the B-29s crash, killing all on board, with the only combat loss being a B-29 that lands in China and is bombed by Japanese planes (the crew escaping). BOMB damage to the steelworks is officially assessed by the U.S. AAF as "unimportant."

> *"Soldiers, Sailors and Airmen of the Allied Expeditionary Forces! You are about to embark upon the Great Crusade toward which we have striven for these many months. The eyes of the world are upon you. . . . I have full confidence in your courage, devotion to duty and skill in battle. We will accept nothing less than full Victory!"*
>
> Gen. Dwight D. Eisenhower, Supreme Commander Allied Expeditionary Force, to troops of the Normandy invasion, June 6, 1944

American troops wade ashore at Utah Beach during the Normandy invasion. Casualties were heavy, but pre-assault naval bombardment and aerial bombings greatly reduced the Allied losses. *(U.S. Army)*

June 17 French troops land on the island of Elba in the Mediterranean.

June 19 U.S. carrier forces under Adm. RAYMOND A. SPRUANCE shatter the remaining Japanese carrier forces in the battle of the MARIANAS. The one-sided air battle is known as the "Marianas Turkey Shoot" as the Japanese lose about 220 planes in air combat while twenty American planes are lost to enemy action.

June 18 U.S. First ARMY units break through German lines on the Cotentin Peninsula and cut off the German-held port of Cherbourg.

June 22 President ROOSEVELT signs the GI BILL OF RIGHTS to provide broad benefits for veterans of the war.

June 23 In one of its largest air strikes of the war, the U.S. Fifteenth AIR FORCE sends 761 bombers against the Rumanian oil refineries at PLOESTI.

June 27 Organized German resistance ceases at Cherbourg.

July 1 Representatives of forty-four nations meet at BRETTON WOODS, N.H., to discuss international economic problems.

July 3 U.S. First ARMY opens general offensive to break out of the "hedgerow" area of the Normandy coast.

July 5 Soviet troops recapture the city of Minsk in the Ukraine.

July 7–8 Free French leader CHARLES DE GAULLE meets with President ROOSEVELT in WASHINGTON.

July 16 Soviet troops occupy Vilna.

July 17 *Generalfeldmarschall* ERWIN ROMMEL is wounded in an Allied fighter strafing attack in France.

July 18 U.S. troops capture Saint-Lô, France, ending the "battle of the hedgerows."
British and Canadian troops take Caen, France, after a five-week German effort to hold the city, a gateway to PARIS.

July 19 Leghorn, Italy, falls to the U.S. Fifth ARMY.
U.S. troops conduct an AMPHIBIOUS LANDING on GUAM in the MARIANAS.

July 20 An attempt is made at Rastenburg in East Prussia to assassinate HITLER. (See JULY 20 PLOT.)
U.S. First ARMY launches Operation Cobra from the Saint-Lô area to break through German defenses and escape from the Normandy beachhead.
President ROOSEVELT is nominated for an unprecedented fourth term at the Democratic convention in Chicago; Senator HARRY S TRUMAN is nominated as his running mate, ousting Vice President Henry A. Wallace.

July 23 Soviet troops take Lublin, Poland.

July 27 American troops complete the liberation of GUAM.
Soviet troops capture Lwów, Poland.

July 31 Soviets take Kovno (Kaunas), the capital of Lithuania.

Aug. 1 Polish underground begins uprising as Soviet offensive approaches WARSAW.
U.S. 12th ARMY GROUP under Gen. OMAR BRADLEY and U.S. Third ARMY under Gen. GEORGE PATTON become operational in France.

Aug. 4 U.S. explosive-laden, radio-controlled bombers are first used against German V-1 BUZZ BOMB sites under project APHRODITE.
First successful intercept of a V-1 buzz bomb is made by RAF Flying Officer T. D. Dean piloting a METEOR turbojet aircraft; his guns jam and he destroys the missile by tipping it over with his wing.
U.S. and British troops occupy Florence, Italy.

Aug. 7 German forces launch major counterattack against U.S. forces near Mortain, France.

Aug. 8 U.S. troops complete the capture of the MARIANA ISLANDS.

Aug. 12 Prime Minister CHURCHILL begins meetings with Yugoslav GUERRILLA leader JOSEF TITO and Yugoslav Prime Minister Ivan Šubašić in Naples.
Lt. JOSEPH P. KENNEDY, JR. (USN) dies when his bomber blows up over the English coast before he and his copilot can turn radio control of the plane over to another aircraft and bail out. (See APHRODITE.)

Aug. 15 American-British-French force conducts a major AMPHIBIOUS LANDING on the southern coast of France, between Toulon and Cannes, in Operation Anvil.

Aug. 19 Insurrection against Germans begins in PARIS.

Aug. 20 President ROOSEVELT and Prime Minister CHURCHILL appeal to STALIN to aid the WARSAW insurgents; however, the Soviet Army remains halted within sight of the city while German troops savagely put down the uprising.

U.S. and British forces close pincers on German units in the Falaise-Argentan pocket of France.

Aug. 21 Representatives of the BIG FOUR conduct the DUMBARTON OAKS CONFERENCE in WASHINGTON to discuss formation of what will be the UNITED NATIONS.

Aug. 23 King Michael of Rumania organizes a coup against his pro-German government and surrenders to Soviet forces.

Aug. 25 Troops of the U.S. Third ARMY cross the Seine River.

French and American troops liberate PARIS, with Gen. DWIGHT D. EISENHOWER ordering the French 2nd Armored Division to lead the Allied entry into the French capital.

Rumania declares war on Germany.

Aug. 28 German forces at Toulon and Marseilles surrender.

Aug. 30 PLOESTI, the center of the Rumanian oil industry, falls to Soviet troops.

Aug. 31 The British Eighth Army penetrates the German GOTHIC LINE in Italy.

Soviet troops enter the Rumanian capital of Bucharest.

> *"There is only one sort of discipline—*perfect discipline. *If you do not enforce and maintain discipline, you are potential murderers."*
>
> Gen. Patton to U.S. III Corps officers, 1944

Sept. 2 Troops of the U.S. First ARMY enter Belgium.

Sept. 3 British troops liberate Brussels.

U.S. Seventh ARMY units capture Lyons, France.

Sept. 4 A truce ends hostilities between Finland and the Soviet Union.

British troops liberate vital port city of Antwerp.

Sept. 5 First combat launching of V-2 MISSILES; the first missile is fired against PARIS.

The Soviet Union declares war against Bulgaria.

Sept. 8 The first German V-2 MISSILES are launched against Britain.

U.S. Ninth ARMY begins all-out assault against the port of Brest.

Sept. 9 The Soviet Union and Bulgaria agree to an armistice.

Sept. 10 U.S. First ARMY overruns Luxembourg; Third Army crosses the Moselle River below Metz.

Sept. 11 Patrols from U.S. First ARMY enter Germany near AACHEN.

The U.S. First ARMY liberates Luxembourg.

Sept. 12 The German garrison at Le Havre surrenders.

Rumania signs armistice with the ALLIES.

Sept. 12–16 President ROOSEVELT and Prime Minister CHURCHILL and their advisers begin the second QUEBEC CONFERENCE.

Sept. 15 Soviet troops and Yugoslav forces under JOSEF TITO meet.
U.S. forces begin landings on Morotai and the Palaus.

Sept. 16 Soviet troops enter Sofia, the capital of Bulgaria.

Sept. 17 The first Allied AIRBORNE ARMY launches Operation MARKET-GARDEN to secure a path of advance for the British Second Army through Holland. It is the largest AIRBORNE assault yet attempted.

Sept. 18 U.S. Ninth ARMY captures the port of Brest.
Finland signs armistice with ALLIES.

Sept. 20 British Eighth Army reaches Rimini Line in Italy.
Soviet troops cross the Danube River in force and push toward Belgrade.

Sept. 22 Soviet forces occupy Tallinn, the capital of Estonia.

Sept. 28 Canadian troops capture Calais, France.

Sept. 29 President ROOSEVELT rejects the MORGENTHAU PLAN for postwar Germany.

Oct. 1 U.S. First ARMY begins siege of AACHEN, Germany.
Germans suppress insurrection in WARSAW as Soviet troops delay advance.

Oct. 3 German troops evacuate Athens.

Oct. 9 Prime Minister CHURCHILL arrives in MOSCOW for a nine-day conference with STALIN.

Oct. 13 Soviet troops overrun Riga, the capital of Latvia.
Germans launch first V-2 MISSILE against the port of Antwerp.

Oct. 14 *Generalfeldmarschall* ERWIN ROMMEL, ordered to BERLIN as a suspected collaborator in the JULY 20 PLOT to assassinate HITLER, commits suicide.
British and Greek troops occupy Athens.

> *"Prejudice against innovation is a typical characteristic of an officer corps which has grown up in a well-tried and proven system."*
> *Generalfeldmarschall* Rommel

Oct. 16 Soviet troops enter East Prussia.
U.S. Army II CORPS launches offensive toward Bologna, Italy.

Oct. 17 Petsamo (Pechenga), in northern Finland, is taken by Soviet troops.

Oct. 18 Soviet forces enter Czechoslovakia.
Lt. Gen. JOSEPH STILWELL is recalled from China by President ROOSEVELT when Generalissimo CHIANG KAI-SHEK continues to complain about his meddling in Chinese affairs and his rivalry with Chiang's air force commander, Maj. Gen. CLAIRE CHENNAULT.
Fourteen B-29 SUPERFORTRESS bombers, flying their first combat mission from the MARIANA ISLANDS, attack the bypassed Japanese base at TRUK. There were no bomber losses in accomplishing "indifferent" damage to the base.

Oct. 20 Belgrade falls to Soviet and Yugoslav partisan forces.
U.S. Sixth ARMY troops land on LEYTE, the beginning of Gen. DOUGLAS MACARTHUR's return to the Philippines.
Last German troops in AACHEN surrender to the ALLIES after savage fighting that reduces the city to rubble.

Oct. 23 The United States, Great Britain, and Soviet Union recognize the French provisional government headed by Gen. CHARLES DE GAULLE.

Oct. 23–26 Battle for LEYTE GULF is an overwhelming U.S. victory over Japanese naval forces in a series of separate naval engagements.

Oct. 25 First Japanese KAMIKAZE attacks are made against U.S. warships.

Oct. 28 Bulgaria signs armistice with the ALLIES.
 The first B-29 SUPERFORTRESS bomber missions are flown from airfields in the MARIANA ISLANDS in a strike against the Japanese bases at TRUK.

Oct. 30 The Soviet Union, in an early sign of breaking from the ALLIES, declines to participate in the Chicago conference on postwar aviation. Representatives of fifty-two nations begin the meeting on Nov. 1.

Nov. 2 British troops capture Salonika, Greece.

Nov. 4 Gen. Sir John Dill, representative of the British CHIEFS OF STAFF, dies in WASHINGTON; he is buried in Arlington National Cemetery.

Nov. 7 President ROOSEVELT is reelected for an unprecedented fourth term.

Nov. 8 U.S. Third ARMY begins drive to breach the German WEST WALL and reach the Rhine.

> *"I would be a damn fool to pretend that individual kamikazes did not scare me; they scared me thoroughly and repeatedly. But the kamikaze conception did not scare me for a moment."*
>
> Adm. Halsey, Commander
> U.S. Third Fleet

Nov. 9 U.S. Third ARMY launches full-scale attack to take Metz.

Nov. 12 Twenty-one British LANCASTER bombers attack the battleship *TIRPITZ* in Tromso Fjord, Norway, sinking the anchored ship with three TALLBOY BOMBS.

Nov. 18 President ROOSEVELT informs Prime Minister CHURCHILL that U.S. troops will be withdrawn from Europe as soon as possible after the German defeat.

Nov. 21 Anglo-American differences cause impasse at Chicago aviation conference.

Nov. 24 Twenty-four U.S. B-29 SUPERFORTRESS bombers strike the Nakajima aircraft plant northwest of TOKYO in the first STRATEGIC BOMBING raid flown from bases in the MARIANA ISLANDS. Another seventeen planes abort en route to the target and six more cannot drop their BOMBS because of mechanical difficulties; no bombers are lost to enemy action. Few of the bombs strike the target.

Nov. 28 Port of Antwerp is opened to Allied shipping.

Dec. 1 EDWARD R. STETTINIUS, JR. succeeds CORDELL HULL as U.S. secretary of State.

Dec. 2 Gen. CHARLES DE GAULLE arrives in MOSCOW for four days of talks with STALIN.

Dec. 3 Civil war breaks out in Greece.
 U.S. troops penetrate the SIEGFRIED LINE near Saarlautern.

Dec. 4 U.S. Third ARMY troops cross the Saar River.

Dec. 5 Units of the U.S. Seventh ARMY begin attacks northward toward the MAGINOT LINE.

Dec. 10 Franco-Soviet agreement is signed in MOSCOW.

Dec. 13 U.S. First ARMY launches attack to capture Roer and Urft dams.

Dec. 14 FIVE-STAR RANK is established for the U.S. Army and Navy.

Dec. 15–21 Seven U.S. generals and admirals are promoted to FIVE-STAR RANK.

Dec. 16 German forces stage a surprise counterattack in the ARDENNES Forest of Belgium, beginning the battle of the Bulge.

Gen. MARK CLARK assumes command of the Allied armies in Italy (the 15th ARMY GROUP).

Dec. 17 U.S. AAF establishes the 509TH COMPOSITE GROUP to operate B-29 SUPERFORTRESS bombers to deliver the ATOMIC BOMB.

Dec. 21 Germans begin siege of U.S. troops in the Belgian town of BASTOGNE.

Dec. 22 German forces encircle U.S. troops at BASTOGNE; Brig. Gen. ANTHONY MCAULIFFE responds "Nuts!" to the German demand for surrender.

Dec. 27 U.S. Third ARMY raises the siege of BASTOGNE.

Soviet troops complete the encirclement of BUDAPEST.

Prime Minister CHURCHILL arrives in Athens for talks with Greek leaders in an effort to halt civil war.

Dec. 31 Hungarian provisional government asks armistice from ALLIES and declares war on Germany.

1945

Jan. 1 Germans launch attack toward Alsace.

Jan. 3 ALLIES launch counteroffensive in the ARDENNES.

The U.S. UNIFIED COMMANDS—Southwest Pacific Area (under Gen. of the Army DOUGLAS MACARTHUR) and Pacific Ocean Area (under Fleet Adm. CHESTER W. NIMITZ)—are abolished; MacArthur is placed in command of all U.S. ground forces in the Pacific and Nimitz all naval forces, in preparation for the final assaults against IWO JIMA, OKINAWA, and the Japanese home islands.

Jan. 9 U.S. Sixth ARMY lands on Luzon.

Jan. 11 Political truce is signed in Greece to halt civil war.

U.S. carrier-based planes strike Japanese bases in Indochina.

Jan. 12 Soviet forces open massive winter offensive across the Vistula River in southern Poland.

Jan. 15 Prime Minister CHURCHILL proposes that the independence of Iran be discussed at the next summit conference.

The U.S. JOINT CHIEFS OF STAFF decide that the XX Bomber COMMAND (B-29 SUPERFORTRESS bombers) will cease operations in the China-India area and transfer to the MARIANA ISLANDS.

Jan. 16 HITLER enters an underground bunker (*FÜHRERBUNKER*) in BERLIN, where he will remain for the rest of the war (105 days) with only brief, daytime trips outside of his lair.

U.S. First and Third ARMIES link up at Houffalize in Germany.

Jan. 17 WARSAW falls to Soviet troops.

Jan. 19 Soviets capture Lodz.

Jan. 20 Hungary signs armistice with the ALLIES.
    Maj. Gen. CURTIS E. LEMAY becomes commander of the XXI Bomber COMMAND in the MARIANA ISLANDS.

Jan. 23 Soviet forces reach the Oder River in Lower Silesia.

Jan. 26 First flight of the first U.S. Navy JET-PROPELLED AIRCRAFT, the McDonnell FD-1 Phantom.

Jan. 28 BURMA ROAD is reopened.

Jan. 29 U.S. Third ARMY launches attack on the German West Wall; the U.S. First ARMY joins the attack the following day.

Jan. 30–Feb. 2 President ROOSEVELT and Prime Minister CHURCHILL and their military staffs meet at MALTA in preparation for their subsequent meeting with STALIN.

Jan. 31 The first TYPE XXIII U-BOAT to go to sea, the *U-2324,* departs Kristiansund, Norway, to operate off the British coast on the first war patrol of this advanced submarine class.

Feb. 3 U.S. Sixth ARMY attacks Japanese troops in MANILA, the attack lasting until March 4.

Feb. 4 One thousand U.S. bombers attack BERLIN.
    Soviet troops enter Posen (Poznan), Poland.

Feb. 4–16 Allied leaders meet in the YALTA CONFERENCE, the second meeting of the BIG THREE.

Feb. 5–9 American and French troops destroy German forces in the Colmar pocket.

Feb. 13 Soviet Army completes capture of BUDAPEST.

Feb. 15 President ROOSEVELT meets with Prime Minister CHURCHILL at Alexandria, and then with King Farouk of Egypt, King Ibn Saud of Saudi Arabia, and Emperor HAILE SELASSIE of Ethiopia on board U.S. warships in the Middle East. It is the last meeting of Roosevelt and Churchill.

Feb. 13–14 The RAF Bomber Command devastates the German city of DRESDEN with night raids by 873 heavy bombers.

Feb. 14 U.S. troops breach the main SIEGFRIED LINE.

Feb. 14–15 U.S. Eighth AIR FORCE flies two daylight raids against DRESDEN with 521 heavy bombers.

Feb. 16 U.S. forces recapture BATAAN.

Feb. 18 The first operational German TYPE XXI U-BOAT, the *U-2511,* sails from Germany to Norway to prepare for deployment.

> *"The raising of that flag on Suribachi means a Marine Corps for the next fifty years."*
>
> Secretary of the Navy James V. Forrestal to Marine Lt. Gen. Holland M. Smith as the American flag was raised on Mt. Suribachi, Iwo Jima, Feb. 23, 1945

Feb. 19 U.S. Marines land on IWO JIMA.

Feb. 23 Turkey declares war on Germany and Japan to obtain a seat at the SAN FRANCISCO CONFERENCE.

Feb. 24 Egyptian Prime Minister Nahas Pasha is assassinated after reading the declaration of war against Germany and Japan. (See ASSASSINATIONS.)

Feb. 25 U.S. Fifth ARMY begins limited offensive in the Apennines, Italy.

Marines under fire crouch in the volcanic sands of Iwo Jima, which is dominated by the 550-foot-high Mount Suribachi. The battle for the 4½-by-2½-mile island was costly, but deemed necessary for an emergency base for B-29 Superfortress bombers flying from the Mariana Islands to bomb Japan. *(U.S. Navy)*

Feb. 26   1,200 U.S. bombers strike BERLIN.

March 1   U.S. SUBMARINE *Queenfish* (SS 393) sinks the Japanese merchant ship *AWA MARU* carrying supplies for Allied PRISONERS OF WAR although the ship had been granted safe passage by the U.S. government. The submarine's captain is court-martialed and the U.S. government accepts full responsibility, promising indemnity after the war.

March 2   U.S. AIRBORNE troops recapture CORREGIDOR in MANILA harbor.

March 6   U.S. Ninth ARMY completes drive to the Rhine.

March 7   COLOGNE, Germany's third largest city, falls to the U.S. First ARMY.
            U.S. First ARMY troops seize intact the LUDENDORFF RAILWAY BRIDGE at Remagen and make the first Allied RHINE CROSSINGS.

March 9–10   Two hundred seventy-nine B-29 SUPERFORTRESS bombers from the MARIANA ISLANDS carry out the first low-level incendiary bombing of TOKYO, burning out approximately fifteen square miles of the city. This assault, directed by Maj. Gen. CURTIS E. LeMAY, is in response to the failure of high-altitude bombing; antiaircraft guns bring down fourteen B-29s.

March 10   U.S. Eighth ARMY units land on Zamboanga Peninsula on Mindanao in the Philippines.

March 15   The VII CORPS of the First U.S. ARMY crosses the Rhine River in strength.

March 18   One thousand two hundred fifty bombers of the U.S. Eighth AIR FORCE, escorted by 670 fighters, make the heaviest air attack to date on BERLIN.
            U.S. Third ARMY takes Coblenz.

March 20   British troops liberate Mandalay.
            U.S. Seventh ARMY breaks through German West Wall defenses.

March 23 U.S. Third ARMY begins crossing the Rhine.

March 27 One hundred five B-29 SUPERFORTRESS bombers lay MINES in Japan's Shimonoseki Strait in an effort to halt Japanese shipping.

Argentina declares war against Germany and Japan.

March 30 Twenty-six B-29 SUPERFORTRESS bombers fly the final U.S. bomber mission from bases in India.

Soviet troops occupy Danzig, Poland, and enter Austria.

April 1 U.S. Tenth ARMY lands on OKINAWA in the final AMPHIBIOUS LANDING of the war.

U.S. First and Ninth ARMIES complete the encirclement of the Ruhr.

April 5 Soviet troops enter the suburbs of Vienna.

April 6 U.S. Army Forces Pacific is established under Gen. of the Army DOUGLAS MACARTHUR; the new command includes Army troops formerly assigned to U.S. Army Forces Far East (under MacArthur) and Pacific Ocean Area (under Fleet Adm. CHESTER W. NIMITZ).

April 7 First fighter-escorted mission is flown by B-29 SUPERFORTRESS bombers against Japan. The P-51 MUSTANG fighters are based on IWO JIMA.

U.S. carrier planes sink the super-battleship *YAMATO* and several of her escorts en route to attack U.S. amphibious shipping off OKINAWA.

April 9 The last Allied offensive in Italy begins.

Soviet troops enter the center of Vienna.

April 10 The last Luftwaffe wartime flight over Britain is made by an Arado AR 234B flying a reconnaissance mission from Norway.

German ME 262 jet fighters shoot down ten U.S. bombers near BERLIN.

April 11 The U.S. Ninth ARMY's 2nd Armored DIVISION reaches the Elbe River, south of Magdeburg and fifty miles from BERLIN.

April 12 President ROOSEVELT dies at Warm Springs, Ga.; HARRY S TRUMAN is sworn in as president in a somber White House ceremony.

U.S. troops cross the Elbe River and capture Weimar.

Soviet troops capture Königsberg.

April 13 Vienna falls to Soviet troops.

April 14 U.S. Fifth ARMY opens the final Allied offensive in the ITALIAN CAMPAIGN.

Canadian troops reach the Dutch coast on the North Sea east of Leeuwarden, completely cutting off the German troops remaining in Holland.

April 16 The German POCKET BATTLESHIP *Lützow,* moored at Swinemünde in the Baltic, is sunk by RAF bombers. She was the last German capital ship still afloat.

April 20 German military command divided between *Grossadmiral* KARL DÖNITZ, in northern area, and *Generalfeldmarschall* ALBERT KESSELRING in the south as Allied armies split Germany. HITLER remains in BERLIN.

The U.S. Seventh ARMY captures Nuremberg.

April 21 U.S. Fifth ARMY drives into Bologna, Italy.

April 23 Soviet troops enter BERLIN amidst heavy fighting.

Troops of the U.S. Fifth ARMY cross the Po River.

A U.S. Navy PB4Y-2 PRIVATEER bomber launches two BAT GUIDED MISSILES against Japanese ships in Balikpapan Harbor, Borneo. It marks the first Allied use of homing missiles during the Pacific War.

April 24–June 26 The formative UNITED NATIONS conference is held in San Francisco.

April 25 U.S. and Soviet patrols establish contact on the Elbe River, near Torgau. The troops are from the Ukrainian First Army and U.S. First ARMY.

April 28 BENITO MUSSOLINI, his mistress, and several other Fascist officials are executed by Italian GUERRILLAS near Lake Como. Their bodies are hung on display at a Milan gas station.

April 29 German forces in Italy SURRENDER at Caserta, to be effective on May 2.

U.S. soldiers free 32,000 surviving inmates of the DACHAU CONCENTRATION CAMP.

One of the last photos taken of Hitler shows the Führer awarding decorations to twenty German boys who fought against Soviet troops and tanks during the final assault on Berlin. Such children, brought up on the propaganda of the Third Reich, were willing to fight to the end. *(Imperial War Museum)*

April 30 HITLER and his wife, EVA BRAUN, commit suicide in the *FÜHRERBUNKER.* MARTIN BORMANN sends message to *Grossadmiral* KARL DÖNITZ in Plön informing him that Hitler has chosen him as his successor in place of *Reichsmarschall* HERMANN GÖRING.

The *U-2511* departs Norway on the first war cruise of a TYPE XXI U-BOAT.

U.S. Seventh ARMY clears the city of Munich of German defenders.

May 1 *Grossadmiral* KARL DÖNITZ announces HITLER's death to the German people and his appointment as the German leader's successor.

May 2 Soviet and British troops join hands for the first time near Wismar, Germany.

BERLIN falls to Soviet troops after twelve days of fierce, house-to-house fighting.

German troops in Italy cease fighting.

May 3 HAMBURG surrenders to British troops.

British troops recapture Rangoon.

> *"I am not a bit anxious about my battles. If I am anxious I don't fight them. I wait until I am ready."*
>
> Field Marshal Bernard L. Montgomery as quoted in the official publication *British Commanders*

May 4 *Grossadmiral* KARL DÖNITZ broadcasts to all U-BOATS at sea to cease hostilities and return to base. At the time there are forty-five U-boats in the Atlantic.

German forces in the northern area surrender to Field Marshal BERNARD MONTGOMERY at Lüneburg Heath.

May 5 Elsie Mitchell and five children are killed in Lake County, Ore., when they come across a Japanese BALLOON BOMB, which detonates when they examine it. They are the only combat casualties on the U.S. mainland during the war.

May 7 Germany unconditionally surrenders to the ALLIES at Gen. DWIGHT D. EISENHOWER's headquarters at Rheims, France, with *Generaloberst* ALFRED JODL signing for Germany. The surrender comes into force at midnight on May 8–9, ending the war in Europe. German troops continue fighting Soviet forces in Eastern Europe. (See SURRENDER, Germany.)

The submarine *U-320* becomes the last U-BOAT to be sunk in the war; she is heavily damaged by a PBY CATALINA from RAF Coastal Command and founders on May 9.

May 8 President TRUMAN and Prime Minister CHURCHILL announce Allied Victory in Europe (V-E DAY).

May 9 The Soviets hold a second SURRENDER ceremony in BERLIN.

May 10 German troops in Czechoslovakia cease fighting.

May 23 British troops arrest *Grossadmiral* KARL DÖNITZ and his cabinet at Flensburg. This marks the collapse of the central German government.

May 25 U.S. JOINT CHIEFS OF STAFF approve the directive for Operation Olympic, the invasion of the Japanese homeland, scheduled for Nov. 1, 1945. (See MAJESTIC.)

June 5 Britain, France, the Soviet Union, and the United States announce their assumption of supreme authority in occupied Germany.

June 9 Japanese Premier KANTARO SUZUKI declares that Japan will fight to the last rather than accept UNCONDITIONAL SURRENDER.

June 15 U.S. Third and Seventh ARMIES are designated for the occupation of Europe. Other U.S. forces are scheduled for the invasion of the Japanese home islands.

June 16–17 Six thousand Chicago truck drivers go on strike; 6,500 soldiers are assigned to operate the trucks with another 10,000 called in on June 20.

June 18 Organized Japanese resistance ends on Mindanao in the Philippines.

June 22 U.S. Tenth ARMY completes the capture of OKINAWA.

June 26 UNITED NATIONS charter is signed at SAN FRANCISCO CONFERENCE.

June 28 Gen. of the Army DOUGLAS MACARTHUR's headquarters announces the end of all organized Japanese resistance in the Philippines.

July 10 U.S. carrier-based aircraft begin sustained strikes against targets in Japan in preparation for AMPHIBIOUS LANDINGS.

July 11 SUPREME HEADQUARTERS ALLIED EXPEDITIONARY FORCE (SHAEF) is dissolved.

July 14 U.S. BATTLESHIPS and CRUISERS bombard the Japanese home islands for the first time.

July 16 Near ALAMOGORDO, N.M., the world's first ATOMIC BOMB is successfully detonated in the TRINITY test at 5:30 A.M.

Maj. Gen. CURTIS E. LeMAY becomes commander of the Twentieth AIR FORCE, directing

B-29 SUPERFORTRESS operations from the MARIANA ISLANDS. (He will be relieved on Aug. 2 by Lt. Gen. NATHAN F. TWINING.)

July 16–26 Allied leaders meet in the POTSDAM CONFERENCE, in a suburb of BERLIN.

July 26 Results of the British general election become known; CHURCHILL's government is defeated and the Labor Party has gained a large majority.

The U.S. CRUISER *INDIANAPOLIS* (CA 35) unloads the components for the Little Boy ATOMIC BOMB at TINIAN.

July 29 U.S. *INDIANAPOLIS* (CA 35) is sunk by the Japanese submarine *I-58* while en route to Leyte in the Philippines; 881 crewmen are lost as the ship sinks before a radio message can be sent out and the survivors are adrift for more than two days.

July 31 Assembly of the first ATOMIC BOMB for combat use is completed on TINIAN.

Aug. 1 U.S. AAF 509TH COMPOSITE GROUP becomes operational on TINIAN.

Aug. 6 The B-29 SUPERFORTRESS "Enola Gay" piloted by Col. PAUL TIBBETS drops an ATOMIC BOMB on HIROSHIMA.

Aug. 8 The Japanese ambassador in MOSCOW sees Foreign Minister VYACHESLAV MOLOTOV to seek Soviet mediation with the ALLIES; instead he is handed the Soviet declaration of war, effective that day.

Aug. 9 The Soviet Union enters the war against Japan.

The B-29 SUPERFORTRESS "Bockscar" piloted by Maj. CHARLES W. SWEENEY drops an ATOMIC BOMB on NAGASAKI.

Japanese Prime Minister KANTARO SUZUKI and Emperor HIROHITO decide on an immediate peace with the ALLIES.

Aug. 12 Chinese leader CHIANG KAI-SHEK criticizes "independent action" by Communist Chinese commanders in failing to accept direction from his government.

Aug. 14 Japanese government accepts UNCONDITIONAL SURRENDER.

Gen. of the Army DOUGLAS MACARTHUR is appointed Supreme Allied Commander Allied Powers for the occupation of Japan.

Aug. 16 Lt. Gen. JONATHAN WAINWRIGHT, who was taken prisoner by the Japanese on CORREGIDOR on May 6, 1942, is released by U.S. troops from a PRISONER OF WAR camp in Manchuria.

> *"Men, all I can say is, if I had been a better general, most of you would not be here."*
>
> Gen. Patton to wounded soldiers at Walter Reed Army Hospital, Washington, D.C., 1945

Aug. 18 Probably last combat action of any kind against the Japanese when a pair of B-32 DOMINATOR bombers on a photo mission over TOKYO are attacked by fighters.

Aug. 21 President TRUMAN cancels all contracts under the LEND-LEASE Act except when the Allied governments are prepared to pay or when completion of the contracts would be in the best interests of the United States.

Aug. 22 Soviet troops land at Port Arthur and Dairen on the Kwantung Peninsula in China, and in the KURIL ISLANDS.

Aug. 27 B-29 SUPERFORTRESS bombers begin dropping supplies to Allied PRISONER OF WAR camps in China.

Aug. 28 Chinese Communist leader MAO TSE-TUNG arrives in Chungking to confer with Nationalist leader CHIANG KAI-SHEK in a futile effort to avert civil war.

Aug. 29 Soviet fighters bring down a B-29 SUPERFORTRESS dropping supplies to PRISONERS OF WAR in Korea.

U.S. AIRBORNE troops are landed in transport planes at Atsugi airfield, southwest of TOKYO, to begin the occupation of Japan.

Sept. 2 Japanese government formally SURRENDERS to the ALLIES on board the U.S. BATTLESHIP *MISSOURI* (BB 63) in Tokyo Bay, witnessed by an armada of U.S. warships with 1,000 carrier-based aircraft flying overhead.

President TRUMAN proclaims V-J DAY.

Sept. 3 Gen. TOMOYUKI YAMASHITA, the Japanese commander in the Philippines, surrenders his forces to Lt. Gen. JONATHAN M. WAINWRIGHT at Baguio.

Sept. 4 U.S. flag is raised on WAKE ISLAND after the SURRENDER of the approximately 1,200 Japanese troops on the bypassed atoll.

Sept. 8 Gen. of the Army DOUGLAS MACARTHUR enters TOKYO to direct the occupation of Japan.

U.S. troops land at Jinsen near Seoul, the capital of Korea.

Sept. 9 Japanese troops in Korea surrender.

Sept. 20 First turbo-prop aircraft flies in England. The turbojet Gloster METEOR was refitted with Rolls-Royce Trent engines for the flight.

Sept. 22 Gen. GEORGE S. PATTON tells newsmen that he had "never seen the necessity of the de-Nazification program" and compared "this Nazi thing" to "a Democratic and Republican election fight." On Oct. 2 Gen. DWIGHT D. EISENHOWER will remove Patton as U.S. commander in Bavaria.

Sept. 27 Under Secretary of War ROBERT PATTERSON replaces HENRY STIMSON as secretary of War.

Oct. 1 All restrictions on fraternizing between Allied soldiers and German women are relaxed by the ALLIED CONTROL COUNCIL, except for certain bans on intermarriage.

Oct. 15 VICHY FRENCH Premier PIERRE LAVAL is executed by firing squad for his wartime collaboration with the Germans.

Oct. 24 Wartime Norwegian collaborator VIDKUN QUISLING is executed by firing squad.

Nov. 6 First landing by a jet-propelled aircraft takes place aboard the U.S. ESCORT CARRIER *Wake Island* (CVE 65) by a Ryan FR-1 FIREBALL piloted by Ens. Jake C. West. The Fireball, a combination piston-turbojet aircraft, suffered a reciprocating engine failure as it was about to come aboard.

Nov. 7 World speed record of 606.25 mph is set by RAF Group Capt. H. J. Wilson in a Gloster METEOR. (The previous record was 469.142 mph flown by German pilot Fritz Wendel in an ME (BF) 109R on April 26, 1939.)

Nov. 15 A joint congressional committee in WASHINGTON opens the major postwar investigation of the PEARL HARBOR attack.

Nov. 20 Gen. of the Army DWIGHT D. EISENHOWER is named Chief of Staff of the Army and Fleet Adm. CHESTER W. NIMITZ is appointed Chief of Naval Operations.

World nonstop, unrefueled distance record of 8,198 miles is achieved by a B-29 SUPERFORTRESS flying from GUAM to WASHINGTON in 35 hours, 5 minutes.

Nov. 23 RATIONING of meat and butter ends in the United States.

Dec. 3 First "pure" jet aircraft to land on board an aircraft carrier is made on the British *Ocean*; the aircraft is a de Havilland Vampire I flown by Lt. Comdr. Eric M. Brown.

Dec. 5 Five U.S. Navy TBM AVENGER torpedo planes, on a training flight from Fort Lauderdale, Fla., disappear over the Bermuda Triangle with fourteen crewmen on board.

Dec. 15 Gen. of the Army DOUGLAS MACARTHUR, head of the U.S. occupation forces, orders the end of Shinto as the state religion of Japan.

Dec. 19 Capt. Charles B. McVay, III, late commanding officer of the U.S. CRUISER *INDIANAPOLIS* (CA 35) is acquitted by a Navy court-martial, having been charged with not giving prompt orders to abandon the warship after she was torpedoed by a Japanese submarine.

WAR GUIDE

A

Japanese code name for the capture of RABAUL.

A-10 Missile

German design for a trans-Atlantic ballistic missile intended to attack the United States. Conceived in mid-1940—before Germany was at war with the United States—the ROCKET-powered A-10 was actually the first stage for a weapon with a range in excess of 3,000 miles, the precursor of the modern Intercontinental Ballistic Missile (ICBM). The second stage would be a V-2 MISSILE or the planned A-9, a lighter version of the winged variant of the V-2 (the A-4b). Launching weight for the two-stage weapon was 191,000 pounds, including 36,300 pounds for the second stage. With limited accuracy

and a payload of just under a ton of high explosives, it would be employed to attack American morale rather than specific targets. The project did not reach the detailed design point.

The A-10 concept, a product of the PEENE-MÜNDE missile team, was history's first attempt to develop an intercontinental missile.

A-20 Havoc/Boston

Highly effective U.S. attack/light bomber aircraft. The ubiquitous A-20 Havoc was developed from the Douglas DB-7 aircraft originally designed in 1937 for the French Air Force. The U.S. AAF and the British and Soviet air forces used these aircraft in most theaters of the war, primarily for low-level bombing. On July 4, 1942, American crews in

The prime architects of Allied victory against the Axis: Franklin D. Roosevelt and Winston S. Churchill, shown here on the deck of the British battleship *Prince of Wales* during their historic Aug. 1941 meeting at which they produced the Atlantic Charter. (*U.S. Navy*)

the European theater flew their first combat mission in British Boston III aircraft.

The A-20 was a mid-wing, twin-engine aircraft, which underwent several major modifications during its production run. The aircraft had a relatively narrow fuselage with a "stepped" cockpit. The bomber variants had a glazed nose occupied by the bombardier-navigator; the P-70 night fighter/intruder version had a solid nose fitted with air intercept RADAR and armed with four 20-mm cannon or six .50-cal. machine guns in underfuselage mountings; a camera version designated F-3 was also built. Several gun-turret variations were also tried in the aircraft.

Designed by the Douglas Airplane Co. for the French in 1937, the prototype was test-flown for the first time on Oct. 26, 1938; the French ordered 105 aircraft followed by a U.S. Army order for 206. However, with the fall of France in 1940 nearly 300 of the aircraft were delivered to the British, who called them Bostons and employed them in the western desert for strikes against the AFRIKA KORPS. Between 1940 and 1944 a total of 7,385 of these aircraft were produced, with a substantial number being transferred to Britain and the Soviet Union. Boeing as well as Douglas produced the A-20. Peak AAF strength of A-20s was just over 1,700 aircraft in Sept. 1944, with the A-20G being the principal variant. Production halted in 1944 when the superior A-26 INVADER became available. (Eight of the early A-20 aircraft went to the U.S. Navy with the designation BD-2.)

The A-20G could carry 2,600 pounds of BOMBS and was armed with eight .50-cal. machine guns. Maximum speed for that variant was 339 mph (10 mph faster than the P-70) and had a range of 1,000 miles. The A-20C variant, an attempt to merge British and American requirements, could carry a 2,000-pound aerial TORPEDO as an alternative to bombs. The normal crew was three for both the A-20 and P-70 aircraft.

A-22 Maryland

British reconnaissance bomber originally designed to a U.S. ARMY AIR CORPS requirement. After being rejected by the U.S. Army, 115 similar planes were ordered by the French Air Force, the first of which flew in Aug. 1939. Only a few were delivered before France surrendered. The remaining aircraft were diverted to the RAF and given the name Maryland. The British took some eighty French-ordered aircraft plus about 150 ordered outright from the Martin Co.

Almost all RAF Marylands served in the Middle East, with some flying reconnaissance missions from MALTA to gain intelligence on supplies being shipped to North Africa. One of these planes flew a reconnaissance mission over the port of TARANTO in preparation for the carrier strike against the Italian battle fleet in Nov. 1940. Subsequently many went to the South African Air Force and a few to the Royal Navy, the latter to tow aerial targets.

The prototype aircraft flew in Feb. 1939. With the designation XA-22 it was the Martin entry in the 1940 "light bomber" competition of the U.S. Army. It lost to the Douglas DB-7, which became the U.S. AAF A-20 HAVOC/BOSTON.

The twin-engine Maryland was a sleek-looking, low-wing aircraft with a "step" in the after fuselage, aft of the wing and BOMB bay. The main landing gear was retractable. Up to 2,000 pounds of bombs could be carried. It had an elongated glazed nose and fully retractable landing gear. Four .303-cal. machine guns were fitted in the wings, with a .303-cal. flexible gun in a retractable dorsal turret and one more in a flexible ventral position.

Maximum speed was 278 mph and range was 1,210 miles. The Maryland had a crew of three.

A-26 Invader

The U.S. Army Air Force's most advanced medium bomber. The AAF intended to replace the B-25 MITCHELL and B-26 MARAUDER medium bombers with the A-26 (whose designation indicated attack aircraft), but production delays limited the number of aircraft built before the war ended. Still, the A-26 was well liked by pilots and compiled a distinguished combat record in the last year of the war. The A-26 combat debut, in early 1944 in the Southwest Pacific, was marked by unfavorable reports. Combat sorties in Europe beginning in Sept. 1944 brought more positive accounts, and the plane's success story was assured.

Like its predecessors, the A-26 was a twin-engine, mid-wing aircraft. It was produced with both solid and Plexiglas noses, with a variety of gun installations being fitted in the former. While mostly machine gun batteries were fitted, one A-26C flew with a 37-mm and a 75-mm cannon in the nose. The FA-26C was a camera-fitted variant produced in small numbers.

The Douglas Aircraft Co. began designing the plane in Jan. 1941, building the new model on the best features of the B-7 and A-20 HAVOC/BOSTON, but with enhanced payload and range. The first XA-26 flew on July 10, 1942, and went into production in Sept. 1943. Almost 2,500 had been delivered by Aug. 1945. Just over 5,200 aircraft were canceled when the war ended.

The A-26C model had a maximum speed of 373 mph and a combat range of 1,400 miles. The A-26 payload was remarkable for a medium bomber, consisting of eighteen .50-cal. machine guns and up to 4,000 pounds of BOMBS in an internal bomb bay and another 2,000 pounds of bombs or sixteen 5-inch rockets on wing points.

A few A-26s were flown by the U.S. Navy during the war as target-tow aircraft with the designation JD. (The bomber aircraft were redesignated B-26 in 1947 and were used extensively in the Korean War with a few surviving to serve in Vietnam in the 1960s.)

A-28/A-29/B-34 Hudson

A highly versatile combat and support aircraft adapted from a Lockheed commercial design. The Hudson was highly successful in a number of military roles for U.S. and British services—bomber, photo-reconnaissance, night fighter, trainer, target tow, cargo, antisubmarine, and maritime patrol. The conversion of the twin-engine, twin-tail Lockheed transport to a military role was made expressly to meet British requirements for an RAF coastal reconnaissance bomber.

The U.S. AAF and Navy flew the Hudson in coastal patrols as did the RAF Coastal Command; some of the latter had submarine-hunting RADAR while U.S. Navy night fighters had air-intercept radar. An A-29 made the first successful attack on a U-BOAT by an AAF aircraft. The U.S. Army also flew the Hudson in the photo-reconnaissance role and procured them for use as trainers and target tows for air gunners, and to train navigators.

The U.S. Navy began flying the aircraft—with the designation PBO and name Ventura—in Oct. 1941. These aircraft, in turn, sank the first two U-boats destroyed by the U.S. Navy. Subsequent Navy production aircraft were designated PV (the Lockheed AIRCRAFT DESIGNATION letter having been changed from "O" to "V"); the RAF Coastal Command also flew the PV-1 as the Ventura IV and V. The Navy's need for land-based patrol aircraft led to development of an enlarged version of the aircraft, the PV-3 Harpoon. The U.S. Navy and Marine Corps also flew the PV-1 as a night fighter in the South Pacific area.

The first military model of the Lockheed commercial design originated with a contract for 250 planes. The contract was placed in June 1938 after a bomber mock-up had been produced for the British by Lockheed in a few days. The first military variant flew on Dec. 10, 1938. Some 1,500 Hudsons were purchased for British and Australian service before the aircraft was included in LEND-LEASE (at which time the plane received the U.S. AAF designation A-28; those with uprated engines were designated A-29 and 200 carried the designation B-34). Some of the early bombers could be fitted with benches for use as troop transports (designated C-63). Some of the original British order was withheld for U.S. AAF and Navy use.

When production ended in May 1943 a total of 2,522 Hudsons (including Navy PBO and foreign models) had been delivered plus 300 AT-18 training models. In addition to those flown by the RAF and RAAF, the A-29 was also flown by the Chinese Air Force. Production of naval variants continued through the war with 1,635 PV models being delivered.

The design was a twin-engine, twin-tail aircraft, fitted with tail wheel and fully retractable main landing gear. The nose was glazed in early models; most had a dorsal-power turret with two .50-cal. machine guns; various models had twin .50-cal. guns fitted in a turret under the nose and twin .30-cal. guns in a ventral or tunnel position, firing aft. Some U.S. Navy models had six or eight .50-cal. guns fitted in the nose for the night-fighter role. An internal bomb bay could carry 1,600 pounds of BOMBS (increased in later models to 4,000 pounds) or an aerial TORPEDO; some versions also had wing racks for up to two 1,000-pound bombs or DEPTH CHARGES.

Crew was four to six, depending on the guns fitted and the aircraft's role.

A-30 Baltimore

Never operational with U.S. forces, the Baltimore was designed in 1940 to an RAF requirement for a medium bomber to succeed the A-22 MARYLAND (which also never served with U.S. markings). Operational with the RAF beginning in Jan. 1942, the Baltimore flew both bombing and reconnaissance missions exclusively in the Mediterranean area, having a major role in North African operations. Subsequently, the Baltimore operated against AXIS targets in Italy until the end of the war.

The prototype Baltimore flew on June 14, 1941. The entire Martin production run of 1,575 aircraft was delivered to the RAF.

A twin-engine, mid-wing aircraft, the Baltimore was in many respects an enlarged Maryland. Although similar in appearance to the Maryland, the later aircraft was easily distinguished by a more pointed, glazed nose. The internal bomb bay could carry 2,000 pounds of BOMBS. It had four .30-cal. machine guns in the wings, two to four .303-cal. guns in a dorsal turret, and two more guns in the ventral position.

The maximum speed of the Baltimore II was 302 mph and 329 mph for the Baltimore V. Range was 950 miles. The crew numbered four.

A-31/A-35 Vengeance

Developed to a British order for a dive bomber, the Vengeance never achieved popularity in the RAF nor the U.S. AAF. Neither air force made extensive use of the aircraft (nor did the U.S. or Royal Navies, which took delivery of a few planes). The Vengeance demonstrated the U.S. and British opposition to dive-bombing techniques and represented a tremendous waste of resources.

Deliveries of the Vengeance to the RAF began in 1942 and many of the initial batch were passed on to the Royal Australian Air Force. The aircraft saw combat in RAF markings only in Burma. None of the aircraft provided to the AAF saw combat service.

Vultee Aircraft designed the Vengeance for the RAF in 1940 in response to the JU 87 *STUKA* that had gained success for the Germans in 1939–1940. It was the first RAF aircraft designed specifically for the dive-bomber role. The prototype flew in July 1941. With British production ongoing, Vultee and Northrop received AAF orders for 300 aircraft, designated A-31A. Most of these, however, went to Britain and the few retained by the AAF were used as target tugs. Most of the RAF aircraft were also used as target tugs. Additional aircraft were built for the AAF as the A-35, the principal difference from the A-31 being the substitution of .50-cal. machine guns for the British .303-cal. guns. A few aircraft went to the U.S. and Royal Navies (the former as TBV-1), but also were used in auxiliary duties. Production ended in Sept. 1944 with 1,528 planes being built of which 1,205 went to the RAF. Brazil received twenty-nine of the aircraft under LEND-LEASE.

A low-wing aircraft with a radial engine and long canopy, the Vengeance was distinguished by a straight-top tail fin, set forward of the horizontal tail surfaces.

The A-35A had a maximum speed of 273 mph with a range of 600 miles. The BOMB load was 2,000 pounds in an internal bomb bay. The aircraft had four .50-cal. guns in the wings (six in the A-35B), with another .50-cal. gun fired aft by the second crewman.

Aachen (Aix-la-Chapelle)

First German city captured by Allied forces. Despite orders from HITLER to hold the city at all costs, the German commander retreated from Aachen when U.S. troops reached German soil, near Trier, on Sept. 11, 1944. As the Americans began attacking the WEST WALL defenses around the city, they were not aware of the German withdrawal. While fighting raged at the outlying defenses and stalled the U.S. advance, German reinforcements poured into Aachen. By Oct. 16, U.S. troops had surrounded the city and began fighting street-by-street. German defenders, using the city sewer system to harass the U.S. invaders, held out until Oct. 21, when the Germans surrendered the heavily damaged city. Aachen Cathedral, where Charlemagne had been crowned, emerged unscathed.

ABC-1

Code name for the American-British military staff conferences held in WASHINGTON to develop joint military strategy from Jan. to March 1941. The conference agreed on a "Germany first" strategy wherein *if* the United States entered the war the Anglo-American military priority would be to defeat Germany first and that there would be "unity of command" in all theaters.

ABDA

American–British–Dutch–Australian command (1941–1942) for operations in Southeast Asian waters.

Abel, Rudolf Ivanovich (1903–1971)

Senior Soviet intelligence officer. Abel is believed to have been born at Polvolog, Russia, with the name Alexander Ivanovich Belov. He studied engineering and had a working knowledge of chemistry and nuclear physics. Fluent in English, German, Polish, and Yiddish as well as Russian, he worked as a language teacher until 1927 when he joined the OGPU (state security organization, later the NKVD and then KGB).

During the war Abel served on the German front as an intelligence officer and is reported to have penetrated the *ABWEHR,* using the name Johann Weiss. At the end of the war he was a major in the NKVD. He also appears to have used the name Martin Collins in this period.

Abel subsequently spied for the Soviet Union in France and in the United States, where he was arrested in 1957; he was exchanged for American U-2 pilot Francis Gary Powers in Feb. 1962.

Aberdeen

Code name for CHINDIT stronghold near Manhton, Burma.

Abraham Lincoln Brigade

Unit of American volunteers who fought on the Republican (Loyalist) side against the forces of Gen. FRANCISCO FRANCO during the SPANISH CIVIL WAR. Recruitment, by anti-Fascist groups as well as the Soviet-operated Comintern and the COMMUNIST PARTY OF THE UNITED STATES, produced about 3,000 volunteers. Recruitment and activities of the brigade had to be clandestine because participation in the war violated U.S. NEUTRALITY ACTS. The first group of about ninety sailed as "tourists" to Europe on the liner *NORMANDIE* from New York City in Dec. 1936. Although informa-

tion on the brigade remains scanty, recent historic studies indicate that about half of the volunteers died and that 30 to 46 percent of the Americans were JEWS, reacting to NAZI Germany's support of Franco. Many of them were sons of immigrants who had fled HITLER'S Germany or who knew relatives and friends still there.

Abrams, Lt. Col. Creighton W. (1914–1974)

U.S. armored force commander in Europe in 1944–1945. Abrams established a reputation for aggressive leadership as commander of the 37th Tank BATTALION (4th Armored Division).

In France in Sept. 1944, during a counterattack, he drove his TANKS deep into German-held territory, and in a single day he took 354 prisoners and captured or destroyed twelve tanks, eighty-five other vehicles, and five heavy guns; Abrams' losses were twelve dead and sixteen wounded, with no tanks lost. His battalion led the U.S. forces breaking the German siege of BASTOGNE during the battle of the Bulge in Dec. 1944. (See ARDENNES.)

Abrams was commander of the U.S. forces fighting in Vietnam from 1968 to 1972, and was U.S. Army Chief of Staff at the time of his death.

Abwehr

The foreign and counterintelligence arm of the German High Command from 1925 to 1945. A 1938 reorganization, which lasted for the next six years, gave the *Abwehr* the following major divisions: (1) ESPIONAGE—Subdivisions were designated by letters: G, false documents; H, Army West (Anglo-American intelligence); H *Ost,* Army East (Soviet intelligence); Ht, Army technical; i, communications; L, air force; M, naval; T/Lw, technical air force; Wi, economics; (2) SABOTAGE; and (3) Counterespionage.

The *Abwehr* was headed by Adm. WILHELM CANARIS from Jan. 2, 1935, to Feb. 18, 1944, when HITLER established a unified German Intelligence Service under HEINRICH HIMMLER but with ERNST KALTENBRUNNER in direct charge. The *Abwehr*'s duties were given to the REICH CENTRAL SECURITY OFFICE.

The *Abwehr* failed to effectively provide the German High Command with top-grade intelligence

Capt. David McCampbell was the U.S. Navy's leading fighter ace with thirty-four victories to his credit. He is shown here with thirty of them indicated on his plane. McCampbell flew the F6F Hellcat, an outstanding fighter aircraft. *(U.S. Navy)*

COUNTRY	NAME	VICTORIES
Australia	Group Capt. Clive R. Caldwell	28
Austria	Maj. Walter Nowotny	258
Belgium	Flight Lt. Vicki Ortmans	11
Canada	Squadron Leader George F. Buerling	31
Czechoslovakia	Sgt. Josef František	28
Denmark	Group Capt. Kaj Birksted	10
Finland	Flight Master E. I. Juutualainen	94
France	Squadron Leader Pierre H. Clostermann	19
Germany	Maj. Erich Hartmann	352
Hungary	2nd Lt. Dezjö Szentgyörgyi	43
Ireland	Wing Comdr. Brendan E. Finucane	32
Italy	Maj. Adriano Visconti	26
Japan	Chief Warrant Officer Hiroyoshi Nishizawa	103
Netherlands	Lt. Col. van Arkel (plus 12 V-1 BUZZ BOMBS)	5
New Zealand	Wing Comdr. Colin F. Gray	27
Norway	Flight Lt. Svein Heglund	16
Poland	Jan Poniatowski	36
Rumania	Capt. Prince Constantine Cantacuzino	60
South Africa	Squadron Leader M. T. St. J. Pattle	41
United Kingdom	Group Capt. James E. Johnson	38
United States	Maj. RICHARD I. BONG	40
USSR	Guards Col. Ivan N. Kozhedub	62

The United States had 1,214 fighter aces in World War II—688 Army, 350 Navy, 123 Marine Corps, twelve flying with the RAF, five shooting down five or more planes with the RAF and U.S. AAF, five with the Royal Canadian Air Force, twenty-four with the FLYING TIGERS (including Lt. Gen. CLAIRE CHENNAULT), and seven flying with the Flying Tigers and U.S. AAF.

Bong was credited as the top-ranking U.S. Army ace while the highest ranking Navy ace was Capt. DAVID MCCAMPBELL with thirty-four victories, and the top Marine was Maj. JOSEPH J. FOSS with twenty-six victories. However, research undertaken in the late 1980s indicated that some of the victories accredited to the top U.S. aces may in fact not have been their kills; this volume lists the official kill credits. Marine Lt. Col. GREGORY (Pappy) BOYINGTON shot down twenty-eight Japanese aircraft, six of which while he was with the Flying Tigers.

U.S. AAF fighter ace Albert J. Baumler is credited with shooting down eight enemy aircraft while flying for the Republican side in the SPANISH CIVIL

during the war. This was due in part to the pessimistic, anti-Hitler views of Canaris. The *Abwehr* was dissolved on June 1, 1944, and Canaris was subsequently arrested and executed.

Accolade

Proposed British attack on the Dodecanese Islands, 1941.

Ace

World War I term that originated in France and carried over into World War II for fighter pilots who shot down five or more aircraft. The term *ace* was also used to designate the top-scoring U-BOAT commanders during the war; however, there were no clear-cut criteria for the submarine aces.

The top fighter aces of World War II and their credited victories were:

WAR; he then shot down five additional planes in World War II flying with the Tenth AIR FORCE. (There was one other American ace in the Spanish Civil War: Frank G. Tinker, who also flew as a fighter pilot for the Republican side and was credited with shooting down eight enemy aircraft.)

(In World War I the U.S. Army had eighty-eight fighter aces, many of whom flew with the Lafayette Escadrille. The leading U.S. ace was Capt. EDWARD RICKENBACKER, with twenty-six confirmed aerial victories. However, the means of crediting victories in World War I was different from that used in World War II, and in some cases a combined kill by several pilots was counted as a victory for each pilot.)

Acheson, Dean G. (1893–1971)

U.S. government official. A World War I Navy ensign, Acheson became active in Maryland politics in the 1920s and was an early backer of FRANKLIN D. ROOSEVELT. Acheson briefly served the new President as under secretary of the Treasury in 1933. He left the Treasury after a disagreement over policy. A tireless public supporter of Roosevelt's prewar pro-British policies, Acheson returned to government in Feb. 1941 as assistant secretary of state.

Acheson, a dapper, sharp-tongued master of political repartee, was a WASHINGTON operator, skilled in back-channel manipulation of State Department responses to White House demands. He was the U.S. member and chairman of the council of the UNITED NATIONS RELIEF AND REHABILITATION ADMINISTRATION. He was also a key U.S. negotiator in the BRETTON WOODS CONFERENCE that set global postwar economic policies.

In Aug. 1945 he became under secretary of state to Secretary of State JAMES F. BYRNES. Acheson touched off a minor political controversy by publicly criticizing Gen. DOUGLAS MACARTHUR, saying that the United States government, not MacArthur's occupation force, would set policy for the governing of Japan. In a confidential report just after his appointment the British Embassy in Washington told the Foreign Office that Acheson "owes his appointment at least in part to the good opinion he has won as State Department liaison officer with Congress, where he has impressed many of the Pres-

ident's old friends. . . . He is, in addition, warmly disposed towards us."

In 1949 he succeeded GEORGE C. MARSHALL as secretary of State and became a close ally of President TRUMAN in the management of the Cold War and the diplomatic aspects of the Korean War. He remained secretary of State until 1953.

Achse (Axis)

German plan to disarm Italian armed forces upon Allied invasion of Italy, Sept. 1943; also known as *Alarich* and Constantin.

Ack-ack

Term for antiaircraft fire. The word traces to the World War I British phonetic alphabet that used *ack* for *A*. (See ANTIAIRCRAFT WEAPONS.)

Acrobat

Proposed British advance into Tripolitania (Libya), 1941.

Action Groups

SS *Einsatzgruppen* units of 800 to 3,000 men that followed the German Army during the initial advance of the GERMAN CAMPAIGN IN THE SOVIET UNION. The units rounded up civilians and shot them down in massive slaughters. The action groups were conceived by SS chief HEINRICH HIMMLER and REINHARD HEYDRICH, chief of the REICH CENTRAL SECURITY OFFICE.

Although "Bolshevik leaders" were supposedly the major target, most of the victims were JEWS. Other categories were "Asiatic inferiors," Gypsies, and "useless eaters," mainly mentally ill or terminally ill people. One of the action group's reports specifically mentions the killing of 6,400 Polish mental patients.

Historian John Toland, in his biography of HITLER, noted that many of the action group officers were professional men. "They included," he wrote, "a Protestant pastor, a physician, a professional opera singer, and numerous lawyers. The majority were intellectuals in their early thirties. . . . [T]hey brought to the brutal task their considerable skills and training and became, despite qualms, efficient executioners."

The extermination units, according to the

Nuremberg International Military Tribunal on WAR CRIMES, killed 2,000,000 men, women, and children in occupied countries. As the chief of one of the groups described the method, victims were rounded up and taken in trucks to the execution site, usually an antitank ditch. "Then they were shot, kneeling or standing, by firing squads in a military manner and the corpses thrown into the ditch." A witness told of seeing "a heap of shoes of about 800 to 1,000 pairs, great piles of under-linen and clothing" at one mass grave in the UKRAINE. "The pit," he said, "was already two-thirds full. I estimated that it contained about a thousand people."

After SS chief Heinrich Himmler, visiting an execution, was upset at the sight of women and children being killed in this way, another method was ordered for them: They were put in "gas vans . . . so constructed that at the start of the motor the [exhaust] gas was conducted into the van, causing death in ten to fifteen minutes."

Adak,

see ALEUTIAN ISLANDS.

Adler

German code name for a radio used for submarine-to-aircraft communications.

Adler-Tag (Eagle Day)

Start of main attacks by Luftwaffe in the BATTLE OF BRITAIN, Aug. 13, 1940.

Admiral Graf Spee

The first major German warship to be sunk in the war, in a battle off the Plate estuary between Argentina and Uruguay. According to CHURCHILL, "The effects of the action off the Plate gave intense joy to the British nation and enhanced our prestige throughout the world."

The *Admiral Graf Spee* was one of three armored cruisers built in the 1930s under the provisions of the Versailles Treaty. They were intended primarily to attack merchant shipping and were popularly referred to as "pocket battleships." The other ships in the class were the *Admiral Scheer* and *Deutschland* (renamed *Lützow* after the loss of the *Graf Spee* because HITLER feared the psychological impact on the German people of the loss of a ship with that name).

At the start of the war in Sept. 1939 the *Graf Spee* and *Deutschland* were in the Atlantic awaiting orders to attack British and French shipping. The *Graf Spee* sank nine merchant ships (50,089 gross tons) through early December 1939, when she was located by a British force of three smaller cruisers. The *Graf Spee* was damaged in a battle with those ships on Dec. 13, 1939 (as were two of the British ships). The German warship sought refuge in neutral Argentina to repair her damage. But the Argentine government declared that the ship could remain at the port of Montevideo for only seventy-two hours, an insufficient time to effect repairs.

Meanwhile, the British spread reports that a major task force, including an aircraft carrier, was awaiting the *Graf Spee* just over the horizon. Believing such reports to be true, on Dec. 16 a message endorsed by Hitler was sent to *Kapitän zur See* Hans Langsdorff, the *Graf Spee*'s commanding officer. He was told to attempt to extend the time in neutral waters, but if unable to do so to break through the British warships waiting offshore and reach Buenos Aires. Failing that, he was told to scuttle the ship.

On Dec. 17 more than 700 of the ship's crew were transferred to a German merchant ship in the harbor. Then, with large crowds watching, the pocket battleship got underway. When clear of the harbor, scuttling charges were detonated and the ship blew up and sank. Two days later Capt. Langsdorff shot himself.

Although ostensibly rated at 10,000 tons standard displacement, in fact the *Deutschland* displaced 11,700 tons. She was armed with a main battery of six 11-inch guns plus eight 5.9-inch guns. (The largest of the British cruisers that engaged the *Graf Spee* had a main armament of six 8-inch guns; the other two British ships each had eight 6-inch guns.) The *Graf Spee*'s maximum speed was 26 knots and she had a crew of 1,124 men.

Admiral Q

Code name for President ROOSEVELT at the CASABLANCA CONFERENCE, 1943.

Admiralty Islands

Islands in the Bismarck Sea and site of Operation Brewer AMPHIBIOUS LANDING in Feb. and March 1944. U.S. Army units landed at several islands, beginning with Los Negros on Feb. 29. Japanese defenders fought off the invaders until March 8, when the island was declared secured and supply ships safely entered Seeadler Harbor. The other major landing was on Manus Island on March 15. In fierce fighting that continued until March 25, U.S. troops used FLAMETHROWERS and tanks to quell most resistance. A naval base and air fields were built on Manus for use in the air assaults on RABAUL.

Aerial

Code name of evacuation of British troops from French ports (after the massive withdrawal from Dunkirk), June 1940.

Afrika Korps

German forces in North Africa. The Afrika Korps was established on Jan. 11, 1941, when HITLER stated that "for strategic, political and psychological reasons Germany must assist Italy in Africa." On Feb. 12, 1941, *Generalleutnant* ERWIN ROMMEL arrived in Africa to take charge of German troops in Libya. In theory, Italian Marshal ETTORE BASTICO was overall commander of AXIS forces in North Africa, with an Italian armored corps and Rommel's PANZER Group Africa under his command. Rommel, in turn, had command of the Afrika Korps and an Italian corps. In reality, Rommel directed all Axis combat operations in North Africa at the time.

The German troops were initially ill suited for living and operating in the desert environment but they rapidly adapted. In particular, the Afrika Korps became expert at CAMOUFLAGE and movement in the desert.

Under Rommel's direction, the two German panzer (tank) divisions and a light (infantry) division spearheaded the Axis offensive that reached as far east as EL ALAMEIN in Egypt in July 1942. However, the British Eighth Army subsequently went on the offensive at El Alamein in late Oct. 1942 and began to drive back the Afrika Korps. (Rommel was on sick leave in Germany when the British attacked; he immediately returned to North Africa.) The Germans were unable to effectively reinforce Rommel because of the demands of the RUSSIAN FRONT and the interdiction of shipping across the Mediterranean by British naval forces.

Rommel's retreat ended behind the MARETH LINE in Tunisia, where he regrouped. In Feb. 1943, he launched a spoiling attack to his west against British and American forces that had landed in North Africa on Nov. 8, 1942. The attack fell short and his troops were soon forced to retreat again when the British Eighth Army staged a flanking attack around the Mareth Line. Rommel flew out of Tunisia on March 9, 1943. Command of the Afrika Korps passed to *Generaloberst* Hans-Jürgen von Arnim, commander of the Fifth Panzer Army. But the Anglo-American drive could not be stopped, and on May 13 the surviving Afrika Korps troops in North Africa surrendered. Von Arnim and Italian Field Marshal GIOVANI MESSE, in overall command of Axis forces in North Africa, were captured along with 125,000 German and 115,000 Italian troops.

Rommel demanded that his soldiers in Africa conduct themselves strictly by the soldier's code. Accordingly, there were no reports of atrocities of any kind charged to his troops, and in the post–World War II period the Afrika Korps insignia—a palm tree—was the only wartime marking allowed to be worn by African veterans, albeit with the traditional SWASTIKA deleted.

Agent

Code name used for CHURCHILL.

A-Go

Japanese battle plan for the battle of the MARIANAS, June 1944.

Agouti

Code name for British scheme to inject air through a ship's propeller into the water around the propeller to reduce cavitation noise that interfered with the ship's ASDIC (SONAR) operation.

AGT,

see ARMY GENERAL CLASSIFICATION TEST.

Aida

Code word for German plan to take over Egypt and the Suez Canal, Jan. 1942.

Air Force

The largest combat command within the U.S. Army Air Forces. Comprised primarily of DIVI-

SIONS and COMMANDS, the so-called "numbered" air forces were normally commanded by a major general or lieutenant general. The numbered air force designations were properly spelled out, although they also appeared as numerals (e.g., 8th Air Force, 9th Air Force).

On Dec. 18, 1940, the ARMY AIR CORPS had established four area air districts within the United States. On Jan. 16, 1941, these were redesignated as numbered air forces to correspond with those of the four field ARMIES—the First, Second, Third, and Fourth Air Forces (AF). During the war the First and Fourth AF were assigned to the Army's continental East Coast and West Coast defense commands, respectively. The Second and Third AF were committed primarily to training missions.

During 1940–1942 the several air forces established overseas were designated by the region in which they operated. In 1942 they, too, were changed to numbered air forces:

The Fifth Air Force originated as the Philippine Department AF, activated in Sept. 1941 as the U.S. Army began its buildup in that area. It became the U.S. Air Forces Far East in Oct. 1941 and the Fifth AF in Feb. 1942.

The Sixth Air Force was formerly the Panama Canal AF, which was activated in Nov. 1940; it was changed to the Caribbean AF in Aug. 1941 and then to the Sixth AF in Feb. 1942.

The Seventh Air Force originated as the Hawaiian AF, activated in Nov. 1940. It became the Seventh in Feb. 1942. Initially charged with defense of the Hawaiian Islands and training, it became a major component of the Central Pacific actions after mid-1943.

The Eighth Air Force was activated as the VIII Bomber Command in the United States in Feb. 1942 but was immediately considered as the Eighth Air Force; technically it did not become the Eighth AF until Feb. 1944. A heavy bomber force based in England, the Eighth AF soon became the symbol of the AAF—waves of B-17 FLYING FORTRESS bombers striking targets in NAZI Germany in PRECISION BOMBING attacks. The Eighth AF was the only one to make use of air divisions; at the end of the war the Eighth contained the 1st, 2nd, and 3rd Air Divisions, the major subordinate organizations.

The headquarters for the Eighth AF moved to OKINAWA in July 1945 in anticipation of shifting to B-29 SUPERFORTRESS bombers for the war against Japan.

The Ninth Air Force was activated in Sept. 1941, initially as the V Air Support Command, but was changed to the Ninth AF in Apr. 1942. It was also known as the Middle East AF when it shifted to Egypt in Nov. 1942. It went to Britain in Oct. 1943 to operate over Western Europe in conjunction with the Eighth AF. The Ninth AF concentrated its heavy bombers in the IX Bomb Division, with its other (tactical) aircraft being assigned to its tactical air commands.

The Tenth Air Force was activated in the United States in Feb. 1942 and moved to India in March–May 1942.

The Eleventh Air Force was originally Alaskan AF, activated in Jan. 1942; a month later it was redesignated the Eleventh AF.

The Twelfth Air Force was activated in the United States on Aug. 20, 1942, and immediately began shifting to England. After the Anglo-American invasion of North Africa on Nov. 8, 1942, its aircraft and units were shifted to that area.

The Thirteenth Air Force was activated in NEW CALEDONIA in Jan. 1943.

The Fourteenth Air Force was activated in China in March 1943, tracing its origins to the American Volunteer Group (AVG) or FLYING TIGERS.

The Fifteenth Air Force was activated in Nov. 1943 with headquarters in Tunis. The AF shifted to Italy in Dec. 1943.

The Twentieth Air Force was activated in Apr. 1944. During the war the numbered air forces were assigned to UNIFIED COMMANDS except for the Twentieth AF, which directed B-29 Superfortress bomber operations in the Far East and Pacific areas. The Twentieth AF was established directly under the U.S. JOINT CHIEFS OF STAFF with Gen. H. H. ARNOLD, head of the AAF, as nominal Twentieth AF commander. Arnold's staff in WASHINGTON assumed dual assignments, but in fact this was unsuccessful because of the burden on the AAF staff. Arnold exercised his command chiefly through a special Chief of Staff, who was at the Twentieth AF base complex in the MARIANA ISLANDS. As a result of difficulties of command, the responsibilities for the B-29 operations were shifted to the U.S. Army Strategic Air Forces in the Pacific (see below).

The First Tactical Air Force (TAF) became operational early in Nov. 1944 in France to coordinate tactical air support of U.S. ground forces. The Third TAF was in the China-Burma-India area; it was comprised of both tactical aircraft and, after April 1944, troop transports, and had both U.S. and RAF units assigned. (The Second Tactical Air Force was an RAF organization that provided support to the British 21st ARMY GROUP in Europe.)

The operational U.S. air forces, and their commanders during the war period, were:

There were no sixteenth through nineteenth air forces.

The complexity of STRATEGIC BOMBING operations against Germany (including coordination with the RAF Bomber Command) and to a lesser degree against Japan, led the U.S. Joint Chiefs of Staff to establish the U.S. Strategic Air Forces in Europe and U.S. Strategic Air Forces in the Pacific. In Europe the command had administrative control of the Eighth and Ninth Air Forces based in England, and operational control of the Eighth Air Force and the Fifteenth Air Force flying from Mediterranean bases. Lt. Gen. Spaatz headed this organi-

EUROPE	Eighth Air Force	Maj. Gen. IRA C. EAKER	Feb. 1942–Dec. 1942
		Brig. Gen. Newton Longfellow	Dec. 1942–July 1943
		Maj. Gen. Frank L. Andrews	July 1943–Jan. 1944
		Lt. Gen. JAMES H. DOOLITTLE	Jan. 1944–May 1945
	Ninth Air Force	Brig. Gen Junius W. Jones	Sept. 1941–Nov. 1942
		Lt. Gen. LEWIS H. BRERETON	Nov. 1942–Aug. 1944
		Lt. Gen. HOYT S. VANDENBERG	Aug. 1944–May 1945
	Twelfth Air Force	Maj. Gen. James H. Doolittle	Sept. 1942–March 1943
		Lt. Gen. CARL SPAATZ	March 1943–Dec. 1943
		Lt. Gen. John K. Cannon	Dec. 1943–April 1945
		Maj. Gen. B. W. Chidlaw	April 1945–May 1945
		Brig. Gen. Charles T. Myers	May 1945–Aug. 1945
	Fifteenth Air Force	Maj. Gen. James H. Doolittle	Nov. 1943–Jan. 1944
		Maj. Gen. NATHAN F. TWINING	Jan. 1944–May 1945
	First Tactical Air Force	Maj. Gen. Ralph Royce	Nov. 1944–Feb. 1945
		Maj. Gen. Robert M. Webster	Feb. 1945–May 1945
PACIFIC	Fifth Air Force	Maj. Gen. Lewis H. Brereton	Oct. 1941–Feb. 1942
		Lt. Gen. George H. Brett	Feb. 1942–Sept. 1942
		Lt. Gen. GEORGE C. KENNEY	Sept. 1942–June 1944
		Lt. Gen. Ennis C. Whithead	June 1944–Sept. 1945
	Seventh Air Force	Maj. Gen. Frederick L. Martin	Nov. 1940–Dec. 1941
		Maj. Gen. Clarence L. Tinker	Dec. 1941–June 1942
		Brig. Gen. Howard C. Davidson	June 1942
		Maj. Gen. Willis H. Hale	June 1942–April 1944
		Maj. Gen. Robert W. Douglass	April 1944–June 1945
		Maj. Gen. Thomas D. White	June 1945–Oct. 1946
	Eleventh Air Force	Lt. Col. Everett S. Davis	Jan. 1942
		Col. Lionel H. Dunlap	Feb. 1942–March 1942
		Maj. Gen. William O. Butler	March 1942–Sept. 1943
		Maj. Gen. Davenport Johnson	Sept. 1943–May 1945
		Brig. Gen. Isaiah Davies	May 1945–June 1945
		Maj. Gen. John B. Brooks	June 1945–Sept. 1945
	Thirteenth Air Force	Maj. Gen. Nathan F. Twining	Jan. 1943–July 1943
		Brig. Gen. Ray L. Owens	July 1943–Jan. 1944
		Maj. Gen. Hubert R. Harmon	Jan. 1944–June 1944
		Maj. Gen. St. Clair Strett	June 1944–Feb. 1945
		Maj. Gen. Paul B. Wurtsmith	Feb. 1945–Sept. 1945

	Twentieth Air Force	Gen. H. H. ARNOLD	April 1944–July 1945
		Maj. Gen. CURTIS LEMAY	July 1945
		Lt. Gen. Nathan F. Twining	Aug. 1945–Sept. 1945
CHINA-INDIA-BURMA	Tenth Air Force	Col. Harry A. Halverson	Feb. 1942–March 1942
		Maj. Gen. Lewis H. Brereton	March 1942–June 1942
		Brig. Gen. Earl L. Naiden	June 1942–Aug. 1942
		Maj. Gen. Clayton L. Bissel	Aug. 1942–Aug. 1943
		Maj. Gen. Howard C. Davidson	Aug. 1943–Aug. 1945
		Maj. Gen. Albert F. Hegenberger	Aug. 1945–Sept. 1945
	Fourteenth Air Force	Maj. Gen. CLAIRE L. CHENNAULT	March 1943–Aug. 1945
		Maj. Gen. Charles B. Stone III	Aug. 1945–Sept. 1945
CARIBBEAN	Sixth Air Force	Maj. Gen. Davenport Johnson	Sept. 1941–Nov. 1942
		Maj. Gen. Hubert R. Harmon	Nov. 1942–Nov. 1943
		Brig. Gen. Ralph H. Wooten	Nov. 1943–May 1944
		Brig. Gen. Edgar P. Sorenson	May 1944–Sept. 1944
		Maj. Gen. William O. Butler	Sept. 1944–July 1945

zation from Jan. 1944 until June 1945, when he became commander of Army Strategic Air Forces in the Pacific with headquarters on GUAM. This arrangement gave AAF strategic bombing operations a high degree of independence from their respective unified commands.

The Twentieth Air Force, as reconstituted after the SURRENDER of Germany in May 1945, was to share the strategic bombing of Japan with the Eighth Air Force. After the Allied victory in Europe, Lt. Gen. Doolittle established headquarters for his Eighth Air Force on Okinawa. Together the two air forces were to have an estimated strength of 1,000 to 1,500 operational B-29 bombers plus fighter escorts. In addition, beginning in late 1945, the RAF had planned to move thirty-six SQUADRONS of LANCASTER and Lincoln bombers to the western Pacific to operate under the aegis of the Twentieth Air Force.

Air Transport Command

Established on March 20, 1941, as the Air Corps Ferrying Command, primarily to ferry aircraft from U.S. factories to England. It became the Air Transport Command (ATC) on June 20, 1942. During the war the ATC carried more than 4,000,000 people more than 8.5 billion passenger-miles.

Airacobra,

see P-39.

Airacomet,

see P-59A.

Airborne

Parachute and air-landed troops and equipment. The U.S. Army carried out extensive airborne operations during the war in Europe and, to a lesser extent, in the western Pacific and Burma.

The first U.S. combat airborne operations took place on Nov. 8, 1942, when the ALLIES invaded French North Africa to launch the NORTHWEST AFRICAN CAMPAIGN. One U.S. parachute BATTALION and a British parachute brigade (three battalions) were used to good effect in the campaign, although they were often dropped in small "packets" or landed by aircraft at French airfields.

The Allied AMPHIBIOUS LANDINGS and subsequent campaign in SICILY in June 1943 included the participation of U.S. parachute REGIMENTS from the 82nd Airborne DIVISION (as well as a British air-landing brigade). The American drops were not reached as scheduled, drops missed their landing zones, and Allied ships fired at U.S. transport planes. But once on the ground the paratroopers were highly successful in achieving their objectives. After the amphibious landings on the Italian mainland in Sept. 1943, on Sept. 15 portions of two U.S. parachute regiments were dropped at SALERNO to support the landings. That drop was undertaken with only a few hours' advance notice.

The next major Allied airborne landings were the night before the NORMANDY INVASION, when the U.S. 82nd and 101st Airborne Divisions were dropped behind German coastal defenses to interdict approach routes to the beaches where the landings would take place on June 6. In addition to the eighteen U.S. parachute battalions of the two U.S. airborne divisions, one Canadian and five British airborne battalions participated in the initial assaults. Again, the airborne troops were highly successful. In the subsequent U.S. amphibious landings in southern France in Aug. 1944, a provisional U.S. airborne force was parachuted to support the beach landings.

In the ill-fated MARKET-GARDEN operation of Sept. 1944 the U.S. 82nd and 101st divisions and the British 1st Airborne Division and 1st Polish Parachute Brigade were to be dropped into Holland to secure bridges in the path of the British XXX Corps. The paratroopers and GLIDER-landed troops were thus to pave the way for a rapid Allied advance of some 60 miles beyond German lines. While the U.S. divisions were able to secure their bridges at Zon, Veghel, and Groesbeek, the British-Polish drop at Arnhem encountered heavy German TANK forces. The lightly armed paratroopers were soon under heavy German fire. The slow advance of the British ground force caused the loss of 7,578 officers and men killed, wounded, or captured in the British-Polish units.

The largest Allied airborne operation of the war, scheduled for May 1, 1945, was to have been the first use of the Allied AIRBORNE ARMY. Six airborne and four air-landed divisions were selected for an airborne assault near Kassel in western Germany to attack the Ruhr area from the rear. Sufficient transport aircraft were not available for this operation.

Instead, in Operation Varsity, the U.S. 17th Airborne Division and a British airborne division were dropped across the Rhine in the largest mass drop of the war. A total of 1,285 transports and 2,290 gliders were used in the initial lift of 9,387 U.S. paratroopers and glider men and 4,976 British troops; several hundred bombers followed dropping supplies. The March 24, 1945, operation was highly successful.

An airborne assault on BERLIN was planned, but was not carried out. Given the code names TALIS-MAN and then ECLIPSE, two U.S. airborne divisions and one British brigade were to seize the airports. These troops would be reinforced and then seize German officials and documents as well as communications centers, and await the arrival of Allied ground troops. Planning for the Berlin drop continued until the end of the war. Airborne units were also prepared for drops on eleven PRISONER OF WAR camps. After the war the 82nd division did go to Berlin—as the U.S. occupation force.

Allied airborne troops were generally used as combat reserves when they were not engaged in operations. In this role, the 82nd and 101st divisions saw intense fighting during the battle of the BULGE.

In the Pacific, U.S. airborne units conducted regiment-size drops in New Guinea, several on the island of Luzon in the Philippines, and, on Feb. 16, 1945, the 503rd Airborne Regiment was parachuted onto CORREGIDOR island in Manila Bay. These drops were made on the island's golf course and parade field in one of the most difficult parachute assaults of the war. One of the most successful drops occurred on Feb. 23 when 412 paratroopers from the 11th Airborne Division dropped on the Japanese internment camp at Los Baños on Luzon, rescuing 2,147 civilian prisoners without loss of life among the troops or prisoners.

In the Burma campaign MERRILL'S MARAUDERS and other U.S. and British forces made extensive use of glider landings and parachute drops of supplies in 1943–1944.

The U.S. Marine Corps had pioneered U.S. military parachute operations. In 1927 a dozen Marines jumped from a low-flying transport over Anacostia Flats in WASHINGTON, D.C. The U.S. Army did not make its first experimental parachute jumps until the following year. The Marines maintained an active interest in parachute operations as well as glider development and in Oct. 1940 the Marine commandant decided that one battalion in each regiment would be "air-landed" troops, with one COMPANY in that battalion being parachutists. Instead, however, in May 1941 the 1st Marine Parachute Battalion was formed, followed by three more battalions; in April 1943 the 1st Parachute Regiment was established to direct these battalions. Beginning in Aug. 1942 these units all fought in the U.S.

SOLOMONS–NEW GUINEA CAMPAIGN—coming ashore in landing craft. Because the "para-Marines," as they were sometimes called, were not making parachute drops, on Dec. 30, 1943, the commandant ordered the abandonment of all parachute forces. The troops were integrated into regular Marine units. There were no Marine combat jumps during the war because of the shortage of transport aircraft and the long distances involved in the Pacific area.

The U.S. Army's first major airborne unit was the 501st Parachute Infantry Battalion created at Fort Benning, Ga., in the fall of 1940. Nine months later a second battalion was formed. The airborne forces were elevated to the regiment level in early 1942 and in Aug. 1942 the Army's 82nd Motorized (Infantry) Division was reorganized to form both the 82nd and 101st Airborne Divisions. Subsequently, three additional airborne divisions were established—the 11th, 13th, and 17th.

U.S. paratroopers received additional "jump" pay above their normal pay. This amounted to $50 per month for enlisted men and $100 for officers.

Germany also conducted extensive airborne operations during the early years of the war, staging parachute assaults in Denmark and Norway in 1940; glider attacks against Belgiam forts in 1940 paving the way for the invasion of France; and the air assault against CRETE in May 1941, the first time in history that an island was captured without the use of naval force. The Japanese and Soviets also employed airborne forces on a significant scale. Before the war the Soviets pioneered the development of large-scale airborne assaults dropping large numbers of troops as well as light tanks during airborne exercises.

Airborne Army

The First Airborne Army was an Anglo-American command established to control all Allied AIRBORNE forces in the European theater. It was the only organization of its size in history. The First Airborne Army was established on Aug. 2, 1944, under the command of U.S. Lt. Gen. LEWIS BRERETON, previously commanding general of the U.S. Ninth AIR FORCE.

By late 1944 the Army consisted of the British 1st and U.S. XVIII Airborne CORPS; they were as-

signed a total of five airborne DIVISIONS, one air transportable division, and one (Polish) airborne BRIGADE.

The First Airborne Army was not employed as a total force. The largest Allied airborne operation was MARKET-GARDEN, when three divisions and an airborne brigade were used in a series of airborne landings to capture bridges in Holland in Sept. 1944. In early 1945 Gen. Brereton conceived a plan to capture the Ruhr industrial region by a ten-division airborne assault, code-named Arena. That operation was undertaken, however, on a much smaller scale as Operation Varsity. Several plans were also developed for an airborne assault against BERLIN.

(See also KURT STUDENT.)

Aircraft Carriers

These ships replaced battleships as the "capital ship" of the U.S., British, and Japanese navies during the war. Their bomber aircraft were more flexible and had longer range than battleship guns.

When the war began the United States had seven aircraft carriers in commission. All escaped the Japanese attack on PEARL HARBOR on Dec. 7, 1941. Of three ships in the Pacific, the *LEXINGTON* (CV 2) and *ENTERPRISE* (CV 6) were ferrying Marine aircraft to MIDWAY and WAKE islands, respectively, and the *SARATOGA* (CV 3) was on the U.S. West Coast. These ships, reinforced by the *WASP* (CV 7) and *HORNET* (CV 8) from the Atlantic, fought defensive actions against the Japanese, raiding Japanese territory, carrying out the DOOLITTLE RAID against Japan, and fighting in the CORAL SEA and Midway carrier battles. The "Lex" was sunk at Coral Sea and the *Yorktown* at Midway. In this period the carriers were the U.S. Navy's only major striking force; no modern BATTLESHIPS were available and U.S. SUBMARINES were hampered by faulty TORPEDOES.

Subsequently, the vicious naval engagements in the GUADALCANAL-SOLOMONS area led to loss of the *Wasp* and *Hornet*. At one point in late 1942 the *Enterprise* was the only operational carrier in the war zone, and she was damaged.

In 1943 new carriers began joining the fleet: Thirteen of the large, 27,100-ton *ESSEX* (CV 9) class and nine of the 13,000-ton *INDEPENDENCE*

A row of *Essex* (CV 9)-class aircraft carriers at rest at Ulithi atoll between strikes at Japanese targets. Each *Essex* could carry up to 110 high-performance aircraft, such as these F6F Hellcats with their wings folded. *(U.S. Navy)*

(CVL 22) light carriers would be completed by mid-1945. These ships, carrying 110 and forty-five aircraft, respectively, carried the offensive to the Japanese. The carriers were able to make almost continuous raids against Japanese-held positions, support U.S. AMPHIBIOUS LANDINGS, and in the carrier battles of the MARIANAS and Philippine Sea defeat the surviving Japanese carrier forces. During the last few months of the war U.S. carriers struck Japan, hitting industrial targets and airfields, the latter to reduce interference with U.S. assaults on IWO JIMA and OKINAWA, and the planned invasion of Japan.

From the battle of Midway to the end of the war only one U.S. fast carrier was sunk, the light carrier *Princeton* (CVL 23), which was hit by Japanese BOMBS at LEYTE GULF in Oct. 1944. Several other carriers were damaged, some heavily, by Japanese bombers and KAMIKAZES. However, carrier aircraft always defeated land-based aircraft in the Pacific campaigns.

In the Atlantic the carrier *Wasp* worked briefly with the British Home Fleet and in April 1942 made two sorties into the Mediterranean to fly off SPITFIRE fighters to MALTA. The carrier *Ranger* (CV 4), unsuitable for operations in the Pacific because of slow speed (29.5 knots) and lack of torpedo planes, also worked with the British in the Atlantic. She participated, with three U.S. ESCORT CARRIERS, in the Nov. 1942 NORTH AFRICA INVASION.

When the war ended, the U.S. Navy had twenty-eight fast carriers in service—three prewar ships, seventeen of the *Essex* class, and eight *Independence*-class ships. (Theoretical aircraft capacity totaled almost 2,500 aircraft.) In addition to these fast (32- to 33-knot) carriers, the Navy also had large numbers of escort carriers for antisubmarine, close air support, aircraft ferrying, and training duties. Another seven of the *Essex* class were under construction as were two improved, light carriers (CVL) and three large or "battle" carriers (CVB) of 45,000 tons standard displacement, all of which would be completed after hostilities ended. (Several other, unfinished carriers were canceled in March 1945.)

Aircraft Designations

Each of the major belligerents in the war had a scheme for designating its military aircraft, except for Britain, which primarily assigned names to indicate major designs. Japan and the United States had different designation schemes for their respective army and naval aircraft.

In addition, some nations assigned popular names to their aircraft while the Allies gave Japanese aircraft code names, e.g., the Japanese G4M naval bomber was given the Allied code name Betty. Fighters and floatplanes were given boys' Christian names (Zeke, Nick, Dave) while most others received girls' names (Betty, Mavis, Gale). Code names were not used for German and Italian aircraft as the Allies had more detailed data on their designs and status than was available for Japanese warplanes.

German The German scheme indicated the manufacturer and the aircraft's sequence number. For example, JU 88 indicated the Junkers *Flugzeug und Motorenwerke* with the Air Ministry indication of the 88th aircraft design. Suffix letters indicated subtypes and series, as Ju 88A-5. The suffix letter *V* was used to indicated prototypes, as Ju 88V-3 for the third prototype.

Derivative aircraft were given prefix numbers, as the Ju 90 evolved into the JU 290 Ural bomber and the JU 390 trans-Atlantic bomber.

The major exception to the German designation scheme was the famed Bf 109 fighter, which initially carried that designation, indicating *Bayerische Flugzeugwerke* (BFW) and, subsequently, ME 109. (The later designation is used throughout this volume.)

British British aircraft names had suffix numerals to indicate variants. Thus the Fairey-built SWORDFISH reached Mark III while the Supermarine-produced SPITFIRE reached Roman designation XX, after which arabic numbers were used through 24.

A few aircraft had formal type designations; for example, the Swordfish began life as the Torpedo-Strike-Reconnaissance (TSR) aircraft Mark I. But names and mark numbers were almost invariably used.

Japanese The Japanese Army Air Force designated its aircraft by the manufacturer and a sequence number. Thus, the Kawasaki twin-engine bomber of the 1930s was the Ki-21 (given the Allied code name Sally).

The Japanese naval air force had a more complex scheme, similar to that of the U.S. Navy. The first letter indicated function, followed by the sequence of that type of aircraft in Japanese service, and the designation of the manufacturer. Suffix numbers indicated variants. The functional letters were:

A	carrier fighter	K	trainer
B	carrier attack	L	transport
C	carrier reconnaissance	M	special aircraft
D	carrier bomber	N	floatplane fighter
E	floatplane reconnaissance	P	land-based bomber
F	floatplane observation	Q	antisubmarine
G	medium/heavy bomber	R	land-based
H	flying boat		reconnaissance
J	land-based fighter	S	night fighter

Thus, the A6M2 Type 0 (ZERO) Zeke was a carrier-based fighter, the sixth such aircraft to enter Japanese naval service, produced by Mitsubishi, and the second model.

Soviet Until 1940 the Soviet Union employed a designation scheme with letters indicating the aircraft type followed by a sequential number. The type letters were:

ARK	arctic service	I	fighter
BB	short-range bomber	KOR	ship-based aircraft
DB	long-range bomber	PS	transport
SB	medium bomber	U	trainer
TB	heavy bomber	UT	trainer

Thus, the famed Polikarpov barrel-shaped fighter had the designation I-16.

In 1941 the designation scheme was changed to indicate the design bureau of the aircraft with a sequential number. Thus, the Mikoyan-Gurevich fighter originally designated I-61 became the MiG-1.

United States The U.S. Army Air Corps/Air Forces used a type designation with numbers indicating the sequence of the aircraft within the type. The type designations were:

A	attack	O	observation
AT	advanced trainer	OA	amphibian-
B	bomber		observation
BT	basic trainer	P	pursuit (fighter)
C	cargo/transport	PT	primary trainer
CG	cargo/transport glider	R	rotary wing
F	reconnaissance		(helicopter)
	("foto")	TG	glider trainer
L	liaison	UC	utility

The same aircraft configured for different roles were given different designations; accordingly, the B-29 SUPERFORTRESS bomber in the photo reconnaissance role was the F-13.

The U.S. Navy scheme identified the aircraft type, the aircraft of that type produced by the specific manufacturer, and the manufacturer, with suffixes indicating the variant and modification. Marine Corps aircraft used Navy designations. The type designations were:

B	bombing	O	observation
F	fighting	OS	observation-scout
G	utility/transport	P	patrol
H	rotary wing	PB	patrol bomber
	(helicopter)	R	transport
J	utility		(multi-engine)
L	glider	S	scouting
N	trainer	TB	torpedo bombing

Thus, the F4U-5N CORSAIR was the fourth fighting plane produced by Chance-Vought, the fifth variant, modified for night operation. Because of the large number of naval aircraft developed from the 1920s onward, some manufacturer letters were used more than once, and some were not the initial letter of the manufacturer (e.g., *B* indicated Beech, Boeing, and Budd Aviation, while Brewster was *A,* Grumman was *F,* North American was *J,* Chance-Vought was *U,* Consolidated was *Y*).

Planes of one U.S. service flown by the other were given new designations; thus, PBY CATALINA flying boats operated by the U.S. Army were OA-10 while B-25 MITCHELL bombers flown by the Marine Corps became PBJ.

See AIRSHIPS for designation scheme used for those craft.

Aircraft Warning Corps

U.S. civilian volunteers who served in filter and information centers operated by the Army Air Forces continental fighter commands. At its peak the corps had more than 600,000 members.

Airships

The U.S. Navy was the only service of any nation to operate airships (blimps) during the war. These blimps were employed mostly for coastal antisubmarine patrol and were highly effective in that role.

Blimps were intended to search for U-BOATS and guide in aircraft or surface ships to attack them. When the war began the Navy had ten blimps; there were 167 in service at the end of the war. Most of the patrols were flown by 134 K-type blimps. Although their appearance came after May 1943, when the U-boats had been largely defeated in the BATTLE OF THE ATLANTIC, no CONVOY suffered a ship sunk by enemy action while being escorted by a blimp.

Blimp flight crews flew missions of twenty hours or more from bases in the United States, the Caribbean, and North Africa. On May 29, 1944, a formation of Navy blimps departed South Weymouth, Mass., arriving at Port Lyautey (now Kenitra), French Morocco on June 1. This was the first crossing of the Atlantic by nonrigid airships; the blimps covered a distance of 3,145 nautical miles in fifty-eight hours (plus brief stopovers at Argentina, Newfoundland, and the Azores). By war's end on-board accommodations were provided, and one blimp, piloted by Comdr. J. R. Hunt, flew nonstop across the Atlantic to North Africa and returned, via the Caribbean—an unrefueled flight of more than eleven days!

By war's end the blimps had made some 55,900 operational flights totalling 550,000 flight hours.

The only U.S. airship to be destroyed by enemy action in the war was the *K-74* on the night of July 18, 1943. Her RADAR detected a surfaced submarine and the blimp attacked with machine guns. One of her two DEPTH CHARGES failed to release. The *K-74* was hit by three 88-mm rounds and some 200 rounds of 20-mm ammunition. She came down at sea and all but one of her crew were rescued. The submarine, the *U-134,* escaped although she was damaged. An RAF bomber subsequently sunk the U-boat in the Bay of Biscay as she was returning to a French port.

In addition to antisubmarine patrol, blimps rescued people at sea and dropped medical supplies to survivors.

The definitive K-type blimp *K-2* flew for the first time in Dec. 1938. There were many variations of the K-type, which had over 400,000 cubic feet of nonflammable helium for lift and two reciprocating engines for propulsion. The K-types had a cruising radius of some 1,500 nautical miles and a top speed of about 75 mph, and normally carried a crew of eight to ten. They were armed with a few depth charges and several machine guns.

The U.S. Navy had been a latecomer to the airship activity, trailing behind the other major powers and the U.S. Army. The Navy ordered its first blimp—a nonrigid airship designated *DN-1*—in 1915. By the end of World War I, in Nov. 1918, the Navy had a number of blimps in service, including several in Europe flying antisubmarine patrols. (Many sources contend that the British were responsible for the term *blimp,* derived from their Model B "limp" airship, but there was no such craft. More authoritative sources credit Lt. A. D. Cunningham, Royal Navy; after pressing his thumb into the gas bag of the airship *Sea Scout No. 12* on Dec. 5, 1915, a "blimp" sound resulted—and that sound rapidly became part of the airman's lexicon.)

A U.S. Army and Navy agreement in 1921 left the Army Air Service responsible for coastal patrol with blimps or nonrigid airships while the Navy concentrated on rigid airships for long-range scouting in support of the fleet. In the 1920s and 1930s the Navy constructed several large, rigid airships, some of which could carry protective fighters; in effect, these were "flying aircraft carriers." After two of these airships, the *Akron* and *Macon,* crashed at sea, the Navy ended its rigid airship program.

In 1937 the U.S. Army Air Corps transferred its blimps to the Navy, which then became the world's exclusive operator of military airships although the German *GRAF ZEPPELIN,* a civilian passenger airship, did fly electronic surveillance missions on the eve of World War II.

The U.S. Navy used the term Lighter-Than-Air (LTA) for both the blimps and rigid airships.

Alamo

Code for U.S. Sixth ARMY while operating as a ground task force under the Commander in Chief Southwest Pacific Area.

Alamogordo

A New Mexico town near the site of the explosion of the first ATOMIC BOMB. The Alamogordo Bombing and Testing Range, part of the Alamogordo air base, was being used for practice bombings by B-29 SUPERFORTRESS bombers in the spring of 1945 when scientists were searching for an atomic bomb test site.

Maj. Gen. LESLIE R. GROVES, in charge of the atomic bomb project, had ruled out LOS ALAMOS, the desolate area where the bombs were being built, as a test site, because he feared that a disastrous test would threaten the work being done there. He had also stipulated that the site not have any Indians living on it. As he later explained, "I wanted to avoid the impossible problems that would have been created by Secretary of the Interior HAROLD L. ICKES, who had jurisdiction over the Bureau of Indian Affairs. His curiosity and insatiable desire to have his own way in every detail would have caused difficulties and we already had too many."

Other desolate areas in California, Texas, and New Mexico had been considered. Alamogordo was selected for several reasons: It was far from any inhabited area; it was close enough to the laboratory at Los Alamos (about 160 miles away) so that scientists could travel between the two places; it was flat enough for widely scattered instruments to detect the blast from several directions; and it was far enough away from Los Alamos so that activities at the two sites would not be linked by inquisitive observers.

Test planners set up a camp at an 18-mile by 24-mile stretch of desert in a far corner of the range. Nearby ranchers were paid for their land and told to move out. Military policemen reportedly helped dislodge balky ranchers by puncturing water tanks and shooting stray cattle.

The test bomb was successfully detonated on July 16, 1945. (See TRINITY.)

Aland Islands,

see FINLAND.

Alarich,

see *ACHSE.*

Albacore

British TORPEDO bomber intended as a replacement for the SWORDFISH. The Albacore possessed many advantages over the Swordfish, but never replaced that aircraft. The Albacore entered service with Royal Navy squadrons in March 1940; for their first year they operated only from land bases.

The only occasion on which Albacores made torpedo attacks from carriers occurred in March 1941 when Albacores from the *Formidable* attacked the Italian fleet off Cape Matapan. Albacores were used primarily as bombers and antisubmarine aircraft.

The prototype Albacore flew on Dec. 12, 1938. Production ceased in 1943 after 803 aircraft had been produced. At its peak strength in mid-1942, the Albacore filled fifteen Navy squadrons.

Developed by Fairey Aviation, the Albacore was—like the Swordfish—a biplane with a fixed landing gear. However, the Albacore was faster, had a greater range, and had an enclosed cockpit (with electrical heating).

The aircraft had a top speed of 161 mph and a range of 930 miles. Six 250-pound or four 500-pound BOMBS, or an aerial torpedo could be carried externally. There were two fixed, forward-firing .303-cal. machine guns and a flexible .303-cal. gun fired by the radioman-gunner. Two or three crewmen flew the aircraft.

Albania

Capital: Tirana, pop. 1,063,000 (est. 1939). Albania, a Balkan nation on the Adriatic Sea, entered the war involuntarily on Good Friday, April 7, 1939, when Italy invaded the nation, violating a defense alliance. King Zog fled and his country became a kingdom under Italy.

On Oct. 28, 1940, Italy used Albania as a jumping-off point to invade Greece. The Greek Army forced the Italians back into Albania and occupied parts of the country, including Santi Quaranta (which BENITO MUSSOLINI had renamed Porto Edda, after his oldest daughter). Germany came to Italy's assistance and in April 1941, after defeating Yugoslavia, Germany drove the Greeks out of Albania, which Italian forces reoccupied. Many Albanians, organized under various leaders, continued to fight as GUERRILLAS.

After the Italian surrender in Sept. 1943, the Germans promised Albania that victory would bring a Greater Albania incorporating parts of Yugoslavia and Greece. But Albanian guerrillas, led by pro-Soviet Communist partisans, kept on fighting the Germans, with the aid of British advisers, arms, and ammunition. In Oct. 1944 British forces seized the port of Sarandë and on Nov. 18 Albanian partisans began the liberation of Tirana, the capital, which the Germans evacuated on Nov. 20.

Enver Hoxha, a schoolteacher who had led the Communist partisans, created a one-party government and began killing thousands of Albanians accused of collaboration with the Fascists or opposition to Hoxha's totalitarian rule. (He remained the hard-line leader of Albania until his death in 1985.)

Albemarle

A twin-engine British reconnaissance-bomber design that saw service only as a transport and GLIDER tug. Delays in production and numerous modifications led to the decision to employ the plane only in auxiliary roles. The first Albemarles were delivered to the RAF in Jan. 1943. As glider tugs these aircraft were used at SICILY and in the NORMANDY INVASION.

A total of 600 were built through Dec. 1944, with several aircraft going to the Soviet Union.

The Armstrong-Whitworth Albemarle had a bomber-like appearance, with a mid-wing configuration, twin radial engines, a glazed nose, dorsal power turret, and twin tail fins. It was the first British military aircraft to have a tricycle (nosewheel) undercarriage, with the main wheels only partially retracting into the engine nacelles.

The plane had a maximum speed of 265 mph and a range of 1,300 miles. The crew was four and several passengers could be carried. A power-turret carried four .303-cal. machine guns and there were two hand-held guns amidships in the fuselage.

Alberta

Section of the MANHATTAN PROJECT with responsibility for delivery of the ATOMIC BOMB as a practical air-dropped weapon. Alberta was organized in March 1945, taking over functions previously performed by the ordnance division of the Manhattan Project.

Alcan Highway

Popular name for the Alaska-Canada Highway, which ran from the railhead at Dawson Creek, British Columbia, to the Richardson Highway at Big Delta, 100 miles from Fairbanks. The highway, built to aid in the defense of the Territory of Alaska and to develop a supply route to the Soviet Union, went through 1,420 miles of wilderness, mountains, and muskeg swamps.

U.S. Army engineers and civilian workers began construction in the spring of 1942 under an agreement with Canada. The last stretch of road was completed on Oct. 25, 1942, when two bulldozers, one driven by a white engineer, the other by a black, broke through from two directions and met. Many of the highway builders were black troops, assigned as laborers in the Corps of Engineers because of SEGREGATION policies. It was officially opened on Nov. 20, 1942.

Aleutian Islands

Chain of islands running east 1,700 miles from the Alaskan mainland. Japanese strategists saw the conquest of the Aleutians as vital to protecting Japan's northern flank. Japanese carrier planes bombed the U.S. Navy air and SUBMARINE bases at DUTCH HARBOR, on Unalaska Island, on June 3, 1942. On June 7, Japanese troops occupied Attu, the westernmost island, neighboring Agattu, and Kiska, farther to the east.

The Aleutian operation had two purposes. It was tied to the Japanese attack on MIDWAY, as a diversionary move, and it protected Japan and the KURIL ISLANDS from Aleutian-launched U.S. air attacks. But the Aleutian operation failed in its primary purpose of drawing the U.S. fleet away from the defense of Midway. The U.S. Commander in Chief, CHESTER W. NIMITZ, was not fooled, thanks to successful MAGIC code-breaking efforts.

The Japanese lost several ships and submarines in the Aleutians campaign, along with several thousand men. Although these losses were relatively small, they were significant to a nation that had to fight an economical war. The occupation of the islands did not delay U.S. bomber raids against the Kurils because the U.S. AAF did not then have the resources to undertake such strikes.

Japanese seizure of the barren arctic islands offered no immediate threat to the United States. But to halt further penetration of the island chain, U.S. troops landed on Adak Island on Aug. 30 and set up an advance air base, putting the Japanese garrisons within bombing range. On Jan. 11, 1943, another U.S. force occupied Amchitka Island, 70 miles west of Kiska. A bombing campaign and U.S.

Navy patrols essentially besieged the Japanese garrisons—about 7,800 troops on Kiska and about 2,400 on Attu.

On March 26, 1943, two U.S. CRUISERS and four DESTROYERS patrolling around the KOMANDORSKIYE ISLANDS (Commander Islands), Soviet islands east of the Kamchatka Peninsula, came upon a Japanese convoy escorted by a heavy cruiser, two light cruisers, and eight destroyers. The convoy was carrying supplies and troop reinforcements for Japanese garrisons on Attu and Kiska. In the battle of Komandorskiye Islands, a force of U.S. cruisers and destroyers force drove off the Japanese convoy. After this defeat, the Japanese supplied their Aleutian troops by submarine.

On May 11, 1943, the U.S. 7th Infantry DIVISION landed on Attu. Five hours before the main assault, two U.S. submarines landed about 200 men of the Army's 7th Scouts. The submarines served as navigation beacons for the main landing force.

After eighteen days of fierce fighting, U.S. troops encircled the last Japanese defenders at Chichagof harbor. On May 31, the island was secured. All but thirty Japanese had been killed. After the defeat, the Japanese evacuated Kiska, first taking out some troops and civilians by submarine, then loading the remaining troops onto surface ships, without being observed by U.S. forces. When American and Canadian troops landed on Kiska on Aug. 15, 1943, the island was deserted.

The Aleutian air bases put Japan's Kuril Islands, north of the Japanese home islands, within bombing range. For the rest of the war, U.S. bombers attacked Japanese bases on these islands.

Alexander, Field Marshal Harold (1891–1969)

British army officer and hero of World War I, he led the British 1st Division into France in Sept. 1939 and in May 1940 organized the British evacuation of DUNKIRK. Subsequently, as Commander of the British Army in Burma, he was forced to retreat into India. On Aug. 18, 1942, he was made Commander in Chief of British Middle East forces and led the successful British drive against *Generalfeldmarschall* ERWIN ROMMEL'S AFRIKA KORPS.

In Feb. 1943 Gen. DWIGHT D. EISENHOWER

made Alexander his deputy and field commander of the ALLIES' North African forces. Alexander became a field marshal on June 4, 1944, and was later made Supreme Commander of the Mediterranean Theater. In May 1945 he accepted the surrender of German troops in northern Italy. He was made a viscount in 1946 and 1st Earl Alexander of Tunis in 1952.

Algeria

Capital: Algiers, pop. 7,234,684 (est. 1936). A governor-general appointed by the French government administered Algeria, which had no parliament and was considered an extension of metropolitan France. French colonists ruled the social and economic life of the country, where only one Moslem child out of eight went to school and natives were contemptuously called *pied-noirs,* "black feet," for their shoeless poverty.

As the EUROPEAN WAR loomed, France and Italy skirmished diplomatically over Italy's desire for a wider role in North Africa, inspiring France to beef up Algeria's defenses. France stationed more than 85,000 troops in Algiers, including Foreign Legionnaires and Arab cavalry. In 1939 the French began building a large army-naval base at Oran's port of Mers el-Kébir.

The fall of France in June 1940 put these bases, as well as the troops in Algeria, in the hands of the pro-German regime of VICHY FRANCE. On July 3, a British fleet appeared off Mers el-Kébir and gave the commander of the French warships in port there an ultimatum: go to the West Indies or scuttle the ships—or be destroyed. The British could not allow the ships to go into German service. The French refused to acknowledge the ultimatum and the British attacked them, sinking or damaging several French ships and killing about 1,300 French seamen.

Algeria was a key Allied objective in the NORTH AFRICA INVASION of Nov. 1942. Although Vichy forces initially fought the invaders, political negotiations quickly ended resistance. On Nov. 23, 1942, Gen. DWIGHT D. EISENHOWER, commander of the invasion forces, made Algiers his headquarters.

Gen. CHARLES DE GAULLE, leader of the anti-Vichy FREE FRENCH, in Dec. 1943 said that Al-

gerian natives and other natives in French colonies had so helped the ALLIES that they should be awarded civil rights. But before the Algerians could test French sincerity the French and Algerians clashed—ironically during celebrations over the end of the EUROPEAN WAR in May 1945. Nationalists killed eighty-eight French and, in retaliation, French security forces killed at least 1,500 Algerian Moslems. The massacre sowed the bitter seeds for what would be the long and bloody Algerian-French war of the 1950s.

Aliens

U.S. American politicians, diplomats, and lawmakers began grappling with the alien problem before America's entry into the war and were still struggling with it after the war was over. In prewar years, U.S. officials were confronted with questions about the admission of refugees from Nazi persecutions.

In 1938 President ROOSEVELT extended temporary visas for about 15,000 refugees who had already made their way to the United States. But that was about the extent of U.S. aid to refugees in the 1930s. In 1939, Congress rejected a Child Refugee Bill, which would have given sanctuary to 20,000 German children, most of them JEWS. On June 28, 1940, Congress passed the Alien Registration Act, which compelled all aliens over the age of fourteen to register and be fingerprinted (except for government officials and their families). More than 5,000,000 aliens registered.

When America entered the war, prejudices flared against Americans of German, Italian, and Japanese descent. But only JAPANESE-AMERICANS—two-thirds of them U.S. citizens—were singled out for mass internment.

Within days after the Japanese attack on PEARL HARBOR Roosevelt issued proclamations that prohibited enemy aliens from owning cameras, short-wave radios, or firearms. Enemy aliens were also forbidden to travel by airliner or to change residence or jobs without permission.

About 25 percent of the aliens in the United States became "enemy aliens" as soon as America entered the war. They included 703,000 Italians, 321,000 Germans, 118,000 Hungarians, and 93,000 Japanese. About 2,000 aliens from Germany and Italy were declared dangerous enough to be placed in internment camps, along with members of their families who volunteered and were cleared for admittance to the camps. Japanese-Americans got no such choice; men, women, and children were all interned. Italians were exempted from enemy alien laws in Oct. 1942.

Inspired apparently by the fact that CHINA was an ally, Congress in 1943 repealed the Chinese Exclusion Act, which dated to 1882, and set the annual immigration limit for Chinese at 105. When the war ended in Europe, the entry of DISPLACED PERSONS sparked new debates about immigration laws.

Allen, Maj. Gen. Terry de la Mesa (1888–1969)

Commander of the 1st Infantry DIVISION (the "Big Red One") during the NORTHWEST AFRICA CAMPAIGN. He and his executive officer, THEODORE ROOSEVELT, JR., cultivated an iconoclastic leadership style that amounted to "us" (any soldier in the 1st) against "them" (anyone else, including enemy forces, rear-echelon soldiers, even superior officers). Allen courted court-martial proceedings several times during his career.

Although the 1st Division in the Tunisian campaign was creditable, out of battle, the 1st gained a reputation for bad conduct that began at the top. Allen, independent and moody, refused to respond to demands that he shape up his soldiers. So insubordinate was the 1st that Gen. DWIGHT D. EISENHOWER nearly dropped it from the landing forces for the invasion of SICILY. But the 1st was restored to the landing force and Allen was retained as its commander.

Allen's troops fought well in the first days, but after a lackluster performance in attacks in early August, Lt. Gen. OMAR N. BRADLEY relieved both Allen and Roosevelt. Remarkably, Allen commanded another division later in the war, the only U.S. general to do so. He trained the new 104th Division and commanded it in northwest Europe from Sept. 1944 to the end of the war.

Allied Campaign in Europe (1944–1945)

The Allied invasion of France and ultimate liberation of Europe hinged on the ALLIES' ability to assemble the resources for a massive AMPHIBIOUS LANDING and on the German high command's failure to predict and decisively counter the impending assault. Formal planning for the NORMANDY INVASION, code-named Operation Overlord, began in March 1943 under the supervision of British Lt. Gen. Frederick Morgan. President ROOSEVELT and Prime Minister CHURCHILL later appointed Gen. DWIGHT D. EISENHOWER as supreme commander of the ALLIED EXPEDITIONARY FORCE. His chief opponent, *Generalfeldmarschall* GERD VON RUNDSTEDT, commanded the forces dug in along HITLER'S ATLANTIC WALL, a network of fortifications that stretched along the entire Channel coast and deep inside France.

Just before D-DAY, Allied deception efforts convinced the German high command that an assault force under Gen. GEORGE S. PATTON was being readied in England to cross the Channel to the Pas de Calais. The deception, code-named Operation Fortitude, kept the Germans guessing about further Allied landings during and even weeks after the assault. (See also CAMOUFLAGE.)

Early on the gloomy morning of June 6, 1944, German troops manning the Atlantic Wall along the Normandy coast awakened to a fierce naval and aerial bombardment. Before them stretched an Allied armada of more than 5,000 warships and landing ships. The sky thundered with the power of 11,000 aircraft. Allied air forces controlled the skies over the 50-mile front. By day's end, close to 150,000 Allied troops and their vehicles and supplies were ashore in France, all landed in open beaches.

Meanwhile, Hitler was launching a new type of air war: On June 13, Germany launched its first V-1 BUZZ BOMBS at London. These vengeance weapons, as Hitler called them, could have devastated the invasion fleet had they been used a short time earlier and had more accuracy. But deployment of the V-1s had been delayed by intensive Allied bombing of the V-1 launching areas along the French coast.

Not until June 27 did U.S. troops capture Cherbourg, which had been well defended by both Germans and terrain. The formidable HEDGEROWS of the *bocage* afforded German troops the ultimate in battlefield protection and natural camouflage. By June 30, the Allies had control of the Cotentin Peninsula.

British and Canadian forces occupied Caen on July 9, and Gen. BERNARD L. MONTGOMERY launched Operation Goodwood nine days later in an attempt to break through German defensive positions on the Bourguebus Ridge. The operation, which ended on July 21, cost the British more than 5,000 casualties and several hundred tanks.

The Allied capture of Saint Lô on July 19 allowed elements of Gen. OMAR N. BRADLEY's First ARMY to break out of Normandy on July 25 and begin a rapid sweep (code-named Operation Cobra) across France. Bradley's forces reached Avranches by July 30. During the carpet bombing (see STRATEGIC BOMBING) that aided the breakout, Lt. Gen. LESLEY J. MCNAIR was killed when an American BOMB fell short.

By Aug. 6 Patton's *real* force—the Third Army—had charged south and cut off the Brittany Peninsula. The Allies' attempt to encircle the retreating German Army in Normandy bogged down, and the "Falaise Pocket" was not sealed until August 20. More than 40,000 German soldiers escaped the trap—among them *Generalfeldmarschall* Günther von Kluge, who had replaced von Rundstedt as Commander in Chief in the west. The Germans surged toward the Seine to fight again, but the battle signaled the ruin of Hitler's efforts to shore up his crumbling "Fortress Europe."

Eisenhower later wrote: "The battlefield at Falaise was unquestionably one of the greatest 'killing grounds' of any of the war areas. . . . Forty-eight hours after the closing of the gap . . . it was literally possible to walk for hundreds of yards at a time, stepping on nothing but dead and decaying flesh."

The original plans for the Allied campaign called for an invasion of the French Riviera, Operation Anvil-Dragoon, at the same time as the Normandy invasion. But the southern France operation was postponed in order to devote full attention to Normandy.

The delayed invasion began on Aug. 15, when U.S. and FREE FRENCH forces landed on the French Mediterranean coast between Cannes and Toulon. Within days, the Allied invaders secured 40 miles of beach and the southern ports that would prove vital to the movement of men and material for the Allied drive into Germany. By Aug. 28, aided by French GUERRILLAS, the Allies had liberated Toulon and Marseilles. Nice fell by the end of the month. In a maneuver that inflicted heavy casualties on the Germans, Allied forces cut off Germans who were retreating up the Rhône Valley.

On Sept. 15 the U.S. and French troops coming up from the south linked up with Patton's forces.

French soldiers and U.S. First Army troops, meanwhile, had liberated German-occupied PARIS on Aug. 25. American forces hardly paused, moving eastward, crossing the Moselle River and approaching AACHEN on the German border, while British and Canadian troops rolled into Belgium and freed Brussels and Antwerp on Sept. 4. In twenty-one days Patton's Third Army sped from Avranches to the Seine. The RED BALL EXPRESS barreled along French highways, carrying tons of supplies to the fast-moving forces, but supply shortages and stiffening resistance slowed down the drive to the German border.

Soon after the U.S. First Army crossed the German border on Sept. 12, the Allies executed MARKET-GARDEN in northern Holland, the largest AIRBORNE operation ever attempted. On Sept. 17 more than 4,000 Allied transport planes and GLIDERS dropped three airborne DIVISIONS along a 60-mile route to secure and hold the bridges spanning the Rhine River area to be relieved by British ground troops. Although U.S. forces achieved some success, Operation Market-Garden was called off on Sept. 25 when German forces overwhelmed the British paratroopers holding a fragile foothold on a bridge at ARNHEM. The defeat crushed Allied hopes of establishing a corridor for an offensive into Germany before year's end.

In Dec. 1944, the Germans launched a surprise offensive, Operation *Greif,* against a weak spot in the American line in the ARDENNES in Luxembourg and southern Belgium; the sudden German advance created a bulge in the line, giving a name to the epic battle. Hitler himself planned the attack to capture Antwerp and divide the Allied armies. The battle began on Dec. 16, when three German divisions advanced 50 miles on a 50-mile-long front. When asked to surrender, the commander of the U.S. 101st Airborne Division barely holding BASTOGNE replied, "Nuts!" The American troops rallied after better weather permitted an Allied air bombardment. The brilliant drive of Patton's Third Army to

Bastogne ended the offensive, and in Jan. 1945 the Germans began a slow retreat, flattening the bulge in the Allies' line to what it had been in December.

The Allied offensive in February cleared the west banks of the Rhine of enemy troops. After capturing COLOGNE, the First Army advanced on Remagen and began the RHINE CROSSINGS (see LUDENDORFF RAILWAY BRIDGE). Days later, the Third Army crossed the Rhine to the South and three Allied armies crossed to the north, eventually trapping more than 300,000 German soldiers in the Ruhr Valley around April 1. At this point, no significant German forces stood between Allied armies and BERLIN.

Allied armies rapidly closed in on the Germans from all directions. Soviet armies rolled toward Berlin from the east; Canadian troops liberated the Netherlands; the British Second Army headed for Bremen; in the north, Bradley's four armies raced eastward to the Elbe River to meet the Red Army; and to the south, Allied Armies rolled toward Austria and Czechoslovakia. On April 25 U.S. First Army and Red Army units met at Torgau, on the Elbe River. Three days later, Italian partisans captured and executed BENITO MUSSOLINI; the German forces in Italy surrendered on May 2.

Along the way, Allied forces liberated several CONCENTRATION CAMPS. The liberators discovered appalling evidence of mass torture and murder and freed many camp survivors who lingered close to death. More than 6,000,000 men, women, and children, most of them JEWS, perished in the camps.

Hitler did not live to see NAZI Germany's defeat. He and his *FÜHRERBUNKER* bride, EVA BRAUN, committed suicide on April 30. On May 2, Berlin fell to the Soviets. Germany's unconditional SURRENDER signed in Reims, France, on May 7 marked an end to more than five years and eight months of fighting. On May 8, V-E DAY, the Allies celebrated the end of the European phase of World War II.

Berlin lay in ruins, its population devastated—victims of Allied STRATEGIC BOMBING and the Soviet assault on the city, which killed an estimated 100,000 Berliners.

Allied China-Burma-India Campaign (1944–1945)

The China-Burma-India theater (CBI) was as much a political theater as a military one. Powerful players stepped on stage not only to defeat the Japanese but also to perform political acts that would influence the postwar world.

Strategy in the CBI was shaped by such considerations as one advanced by Gen. ALAN F. BROOKE, chief of the Imperial General Staff: If England were to have any future influence in the Far East, a British Army must retake Burma. But a Chinese army, commanded by an American, Lt. Gen. JOSEPH STILWELL, early in 1944 was already in Burma.

Stilwell, cantankerous and far more a general than a diplomat, was deputy commander to Adm. LOUIS MOUNTBATTEN and still Chief of Staff to CHIANG KAI-SHEK. Caught up in the geopolitical demands of two other countries, Stilwell struggled to make military decisions that would win battles and satisfy his global-thinking masters.

Mountbatten had been put at the head of the newly created Southeast Asia Command by Prime Minister CHURCHILL and President ROOSEVELT during their QUEBEC CONFERENCE of Aug. 1943. His interest was in defending British interests both by retaking Burma and by defending India. In 1947 he would become the last viceroy of India, reigning over its troubled independence.

Geopolitics had little to do with the military reality: The liberation of Burma and the preservation of India were strategically linked. In order to defend India the Allies had to go on the offensive into Burma.

The first move, in Jan. 1944 under Gen. Sir WILLIAM SLIM, was down the Arakan coast of Burma, where the British had been mauled in the spring of 1943. Slim's troops met a strong Japanese advance. The Japanese surrounded two British divisions, which were supplied by air through a three-week siege. British reinforcements from the north then trapped the Japanese, cracking them against the earlier British arrivals.

The Arakan advance was a sideshow to the major Japanese offensive, called the "March on Delhi," on the Plain of Imphal. Here was the center of the massive British buildup for the offensive into Burma. In mid-March the Japanese launched Operation *U-Go*, hurling 100,000 troops across the Chindwin River at several points. A large force pushed toward Kohima, a small hill station on the only all-weather road along the Burma-India frontier. From there they planned to take Imphal and, ultimately, as much of India as they could seize.

The Japanese were counting on support in India. Nationalist leader MOHANDAS GANDHI, after threatening mass civil disobedience, had been jailed in Aug. 1942. Hindu supporters of Gandhi had destroyed railroad stations and cut communications lines to Assam. Another nationalist, Subhas Chandra Bose, initially operating in Germany (see PROPAGANDA), fostered FIFTH COLUMN subversive activities in India.

Shifting to Japanese-occupied Malaya and Burma, he recruited about 7,000 Indian PRISONERS OF WAR for what he called the Indian National Army. Bose's ragtag army joined Japanese troops in the March on Delhi.

Japanese infantry battalions—weapons and supplies on trains of mules, elephants, and oxen—pressed through the jungle and on the night of April 6 struck Kohima. A hastily assembled force of Imperial troops, some of them recovering from wounds, defended Kohima. There were about 3,000 of them, huddled in what an officer called a jungle STALINGRAD. Against a Japanese division of 18,000 men, the defenders of Kohima held out, day after day. A series of battles swarmed around Kohima until July, when the Japanese finally fell back, starving and in tatters, deep into Burma.

To the rear of the Japanese in Burma Maj. Gen. ORDE WINGATE led an airborne assault of 10,000 CHINDITS, who would be supplied by air. The British and U.S. air forces and Burmese GUERRILLAS were also harassing the Japanese. An American irregular unit similar to the Chindits, MERRILL'S MARAUDERS, fought with Stilwell as he was advancing his Chinese troops down the Hukawng Valley.

Stilwell's Chinese were fighting while U.S. Army engineers were building the LEDO ROAD, from Assam across the Patkai Range through the Hukawng Valley to Myitkyina and Bhamo and then on to the BURMA ROAD. By the beginning of 1945 Stilwell's forces had reached the Burma Road. But Stilwell, recalled to WASHINGTON in Oct. 1944, was no longer with them.

At Mandalay, Slim, by a brilliant maneuver that brought his army down on unsuspecting Japanese forces, hurtled southward to free Rangoon. It was taken on May 3 by a seaborne assault from Arakan.

The disintegrating Japanese forces ceased to exist as an army.

One of the most grisly events of the Pacific War occurred on the night of Feb. 19–20, 1945, when about 1,000 Japanese soldiers retreated into impassable swamps on Ramree Island, off the west coast of Burma in the Bay of Bengal. The British, pursuing in canvas boats with mortars and machine guns mounted on railroad ties, cut the Japanese off in the shallows between the island and the mainland and began shelling.

"The din of the barrage," a British eyewitness wrote, "had caused all crocodiles within miles to slide into the water," drawn by the scent and taste of blood from wounded Japanese. As the tide ebbed, the Japanese, mired knee-deep in the muck of the swamp, were attacked by the crocodiles. Twenty Japanese survived.

"Some . . . perhaps died of yet other causes," says Roger A. Caras in *Dangerous to Man,* "but there can be little doubt that this [was] one of the most deliberate and wholesale attacks upon man by any large animals at any time that is on record and fully authenticated."

As the war in Burma flickered out, China was fighting its own war with American supplies but not American ground forces. In late 1943 the first substantial U.S. air offensive was being prepared when hundreds of thousands of Chinese were put to work building airfields in China for B-29 SUPERFORTRESS bombers. Long-range attacks against Japan began with a raid on Yawata on June 15, 1944.

Japan reacted with a swift and largely successful offensive throughout Southeast China. As U.S. air power began to operate from the MARIANA ISLANDS and U.S. interest in Chinese bases declined, heavy Chinese losses defending these bases could be seen as virtually pointless. That is the way Chiang Kai-shek saw it.

China was in the midst of a large-scale offensive when the ATOMIC BOMB ended the war in Aug. 1945. But Chiang's major interest was in fighting MAO TSE-TUNG and his Communist Army. Unfortunately for Chiang, the conservative view he applied to military matters extended to his domestic policies as well. Against them, Mao's message of shared sacrifice and shared power became more and more effective.

U.S. disenchantment with Chiang grew in the

later war years, as the perceived need for Chinese action against Japan declined. Nevertheless, the carefully fostered view of Chiang as a heroic resister of tyranny survived and was even augmented by his defeat by the Communists in 1949.

Allied Commands,

See UNIFIED COMMANDS.

Allied Conferences

Strategy-setting meetings among Allied leaders. Even before the U.S. entrance into the war, President ROOSEVELT and British Prime Minister CHURCHILL began the practice of meeting regularly to discuss strategy. These early conferences evolved into ones involving other major-power leaders, who were usually referred to in the press as the Big Two, BIG THREE, or the BIG FOUR, depending on how many were meeting. (The word *summit* was not used for these wartime conferences. Churchill first used the term in 1950, when he suggested a "parley at the summit.")

The Big Two conferences between Roosevelt and Churchill were ATLANTIC, Aug. 9–12, 1941; WASHINGTON (also known as Arcadia Conference or United Nations Conference), Dec. 22, 1941–Jan. 14, 1942; Washington, June 25–27, 1942; CASABLANCA, Jan. 15–23, 1943; Washington (code-named Trident), May 11–17, 1943; QUEBEC (code-named Quadrant), Aug. 10–24, 1943, and Sept. 12–16, 1944 (code-named Octagon); EGYPT, Feb. 15, 1945.

Other conferences were: U.S. Secretary of State CORDELL HULL, British Foreign Minister ANTHONY EDEN, and Soviet Foreign Minister VYACHESLAV M. MOLOTOV: MOSCOW, Oct. 18–Nov. 1, 1943; CAIRO (code-named Sextant), Nov. 22–26, 1943. Roosevelt, Churchill, and Generalissimo CHIANG KAI-SHEK of China: TEHRAN, Nov. 28–Dec. 1, 1943. Roosevelt, Churchill, and Soviet leader STALIN: BRETTON WOODS, July, 1944. Representatives of Allied nations: DUMBARTON OAKS, Aug. 21–Oct. 7, 1944. Roosevelt, Churchill, and Stalin: YALTA (code-named Argonaut), Feb. 4–11, 1945. Representatives of Allied Nations: SAN FRANCISCO, April 25–June 26, 1945. President TRUMAN, Stalin, and Churchill (later replaced by Prime Minister CLEMENT ATTLEE): POTSDAM, July 17–Aug. 2, 1945.

Allied Control Council

Organization of Allied nations occupying postwar Germany. The BERLIN-based council administered the occupation of Germany, which was divided into four zones: U.S., British, French, and Soviet. The council's tasks included the disbanding of the German military establishment, the administration of a wage and price policy, and the return of PRISONERS OF WAR. The council, established by the Allied Control Commission, dealt with matters affecting all of Germany through military governors for each zone. But the three Western powers could not get agreement from the Soviet Union, which advocated dismantling of Ruhr industries for war reparations. In March 1948, as the Western power prepared to coordinate policy for the creation of what would be West Germany, the Soviet member of the Control Council walked out.

Allied Expeditionary Force

Allied air, ground, and naval forces assembled for the NORMANDY INVASION and ALLIED CAMPAIGN IN EUROPE. The SUPREME HEADQUARTERS ALLIED EXPEDITIONARY FORCE (SHAEF) was established in June 1942 near London. Gen. DWIGHT D. EISENHOWER took command at SHAEF in Jan. 1944.

The principal subordinate commands were the Allied Expeditionary Air Force and Allied Expeditionary Naval Force. All Allied ground forces were initially under the 21st ARMY GROUP headquarters but, following the Normandy landings, the U.S. 12th Army Group was established under Lt. Gen. OMAR N. BRADLEY after which there was no overall ground commander for the campaign.

Allied Military Government

Civil affairs organization used to administer liberated territory not yet under civilian control. The Allied Military Government (AMG) worked in several phases, beginning with the providing of basic services immediately after liberation and continuing through formal occupation of former AXIS territory. In the U.S. zone of occupied Germany, AMG representatives focused on purging NAZIS from government and key businesses. Of 1,456,467 persons investigated, 373,762 were disqualified from holding any government position or any job higher than laborer. (In a similar screening of "ultranationalists" in Japan, 186,000 Japanese were removed from government posts.)

By the end of the war more than 7,000 specially trained civil affairs officers were on duty in occupied territory in Europe, Japan, and Korea. Another 23,-000 officers and enlisted personnel were assigned to civil affairs. Many of the military officials were replaced by civilians as Allied efforts shifted from occupation to restoration of civil government.

AMG investigators launched the search for perpetrators of WAR CRIMES, with forty-nine major war criminals being put on trial in Nuremberg and Tokyo. In the U.S. zone of Germany, more than 16,000 Germans were arrested as suspects or material witnesses in investigations of crimes against U.S. nationals. In these 504 AMG-supervised trials there were 457 convictions. AMG officers were also responsible for the postwar repatriation of PRISONERS OF WAR.

Military government experts included officers whose civilian professions were put to military use. Art historians and curators tracked down looted treasures. Newspapermen set up newspapers purged of Nazi editors. Agronomists, public health workers, bankers, and teachers were also in the AMG ranks.

Allies

Nations that fought Germany, Japan, and Italy (the AXIS) in World War II. The ALLIES, a term that carried over from World War I, numbered twenty-six nations by Jan. 2, 1942, when their representatives assembled in WASHINGTON to agree on war aims and sign the ATLANTIC CHARTER. The UNITED KINGDOM, which included England, Scotland, Wales, and Northern Island, was considered one nation and was usually referred to as "England" or "Great Britain." Other nations in the BRITISH COMMONWEALTH, such as Australia and India, entered the war with varying degrees of independence. (For information on declarations of war, see entries on each country.)

The UNITED NATIONS CONFERENCE introduced the new phrase UNITED NATIONS, but *Allies* would persist as a more popular collective name for the nations fighting the Axis. *Allied* would also be used for joint military actions and for joint political units, such as the ALLIED CONTROL COUNCIL.

As the war went on, other nations joined the Allied side, and most became members of the United Nations. By the end of the war there were forty-nine Allied nations. They were (with the date they entered the war):

Argentina (1945)	El Salvador (1941)	Norway (1940)
Australia (1939)	Ethiopia (1942)	Panama (1941)
Belgium (1940)	France (1939)	Paraguay (1945)
Bolivia (1943)	Greece (1940)	Peru (1945)
Brazil (1942)	Guatemala (1941)	Poland (1939)
Canada (1939)	Haiti (1941)	San Marino (1944)
Chile (1945)	Honduras (1941)	Saudi Arabia (1945)
China (1941)	India (1939)	South Africa (1939)
Colombia (1943)	Iran (1941)	Turkey (1945)
Costa Rica (1941)	Iraq (1943)	Union of Soviet
Cuba (1941)	Lebanon (1945)	Socialist Republics
Czechoslovakia	Liberia (1944)	(1941)
(1941)	Luxembourg (1940)	United Kingdom
Denmark (1940)	Mexico (1942)	(1939)
Dominican Republic	Mongolia (1945)	United States (1941)
(1941)	Netherlands (1940)	Uruguay (1945)
Ecuador (1945)	New Zealand (1939)	Venezuela (1945)
Egypt (1945)	Nicaragua (1941)	Yugoslavia (1941)

Alpha

(1) Plans to defend Kunming and Chungking against Japanese forces; (2) U.S. 3rd DIVISION force organized for operations in southern France.

Alsos mission

Mission that followed U.S. combat troops in Europe to examine newly occupied areas for signs of German progress on the ATOMIC BOMB. Alsos was a cooperative effort of the MANHATTAN PROJECT, under Maj. Gen. LESLIE GROVES, the OFFICE OF SCIENTIFIC RESEARCH AND DEVELOPMENT, Army intelligence staff (G-2), and the Navy. (The Navy subsequently left the mission, having established its own intelligence mission in Europe.)

The Alsos mission was headed by Lt. Col. Boris T. Pash, an Army intelligence officer, and consisted of scientific and military personnel. Armed with a letter from Secretary of War HENRY L. STIMSON directing all U.S. forces to accord the mission "every facility and assistance," Pash led his group to Italy in 1943 and examined institutes and university laboratories in France, Belgium, and Germany in 1944–1945. The mission performed poorly in Italy, but did obtain considerable information later on German nuclear weapon efforts, and helped to capture several German atomic scientists who subsequently worked in the West. (Soviet troops had stripped the Kaiser-Wilhelm Institute in BERLIN, the center of German atomic research, before U.S. troops reached the city. The Alsos mission found that a U.S. intelligence command was using the building as headquarters and had dumped the few remaining pieces of equipment and material in the backyard, unaware of its importance.)

The code name *Alsos,* chosen by Gen. Groves, was the Greek word for "grove."

Altmark

German supply ship that entered a fjord of neutral Norway when pursued by ROYAL NAVY destroyers. On the night of Feb. 16–17, 1940, a boarding party from the British destroyer *Cossack* forced the *Altmark* aground and—with the call "The Navy's here!"—rescued 299 British seaman who had been captured by the *ADMIRAL GRAF SPEE* during her attacks on merchant ships in the Atlantic. The order to violate Norway's neutrality came from the First Lord of the Admiralty, WINSTON CHURCHILL.

Ambrosio, Marshal Vittorio (1879–1958)

Chief of the Italian Armed Forces from Feb. 1943 until Sept. 1943. After Italy entered the war he commanded the Italian Second Army in Yugoslavia and in 1942 became Chief of Staff of the Army General Staff. He was appointed Chief of Staff of the Armed Forces *(Commando Supremo)* by BENITO MUSSOLINI to replace a more moderate officer in the senior Italian military post when Ambrosio first began consideration of defecting from the AXIS. After the Italian capitulation in Sept. 1943 Ambrosio was appointed Inspector General in the government of PIETRO BADOGLIO.

America

Flagship of the U.S. merchant fleet, she sailed as the troop transport *West Point* (AP 23) during the war. Built as a luxury liner, the *America* entered service with the United States Lines in August 1940. Because of the war in Europe, she sailed on the New York–West Indies cruise route instead of the tran-Atlantic route.

She was acquired by the Navy in June 1941, renamed, and quickly converted to a troop ship. All passenger accommodations and salon furniture

were stripped away; steel plates were placed on bulkheads to protect murals and pipe-framed berths were placed everywhere, including the swimming pool. Up to 8,000 troops could be carried. For self-defense she was fitted with 5-inch, 3-inch, and lighter antiaircraft guns.

Her first voyage as the *West Point,* in July 1941, was to transport 137 Italian and 327 German diplomatic personnel and their families from the United States to Lisbon. She returned to the United States with American and Chinese diplomatic personnel. Next she carried 5,443 British troops and 100 U.S. troops from Halifax to Bombay, India, in the first of numerous worldwide troop-carrying voyages. Japanese planes attacked the *West Point* several times in the Far East during Jan. 1942, but she suffered only light shrapnel damage while docked at SINGAPORE.

After the war she participated in Operation MAGIC CARPET, bringing U.S. troops home from Europe and the Pacific.

She was decommissioned on Feb. 28, 1946, and returned to the Maritime Commission. She had carried over 350,000 troops during her naval career. On one voyage she embarked 9,305 men (including the ship's crew).

The ship was reconfigured as a luxury liner and, as the SS *America,* was returned to the United States Lines on Oct. 31, 1946. She then began her intended trans-Atlantic passenger service.

A large, graceful ship, the *America* had twin funnels, identical in shape and size, but the forward stack was a dummy, provided for aesthetic reasons. The ship was 723 feet long and, as a transport, displaced 35,400 tons. Steam turbines propelled her at 17.5 knots, relatively slow for a liner of that time. The ship, launched on Aug. 31, 1939, was christened by ELEANOR ROOSEVELT, wife of the President.

American First Committee

U.S. organization devoted to stopping American involvement in the war. The committee, though inspired by U.S. isolationism, was primarily anti-British and anti-ROOSEVELT. The group aimed its fervent rhetoric at the war in Europe, not the Sino-Japanese war, which had drawn relatively scant American attention. The committee, which at its height had about 60,000 members, used CHARLES A. LINDBERGH as its chief spokesman. But the ANTI-SEMITISM preached by him and others affiliated with the committee hurt its cause. The chairman of the committee, founded in Sept. 1940, was Robert E. Wood, a retired U.S. Army general and chairman of Sears, Roebuck. The committee showed its lack of grass-roots support in March 1941 when Congress overwhelmingly voted for LEND-LEASE legislation that gave direct aid to Great Britain. The committee dissolved after the Japanese attack on PEARL HARBOR.

American Volunteer Group,
see FLYING TIGERS.

Americide
The accidental killing of Americans by Americans. From the day that the United States entered the war, on numerous occasions U.S. forces fired on friendly forces.

On the morning of Dec. 7, 1941, during the Japanese air attack on PEARL HARBOR, several SBD DAUNTLESS scout bombers from the AIRCRAFT CARRIER *Enterprise* (CV 6) attempting to land on FORD ISLAND, in the center of Pearl Harbor, were fired on by anxious U.S. Army gunners (as well as Japanese fighters).

There were more fatal incidents of Americide during the war. The most senior U.S. officer killed by "friendly fire" in the war was Lt. Gen. LESLEY J. MCNAIR, former commander of Army Ground Forces, who was preparing to take command of an ARMY GROUP. McNair went to the front in France in July 1944 to observe Operation Cobra, the planned breakout from the Normandy beachhead.

AAF bombers, intending to bomb German lines ahead of U.S. troops, "bombed short." The BOMB salvoes that fell on July 24 killed sixteen American soldiers and injured four times that number. Even worse, on the next day the AAF bombs killed 102 soldiers and wounded 380. Among the dead was McNair. A search of the cratered area produced a portion of his finger with his West Point class ring, his only identifiable remains. (For security reasons McNair's death was kept a secret and only a few general officers attended his funeral.)

More Americans were killed by friendly fire dur-

ing the invasion of SICILY. On the night of July 11, 1943, the Army's 504th Parachute Infantry REGIMENT of the 82nd Airborne DIVISION boarded 144 C-47 SKYTRAIN transports in North Africa. Their destination was an airfield already in friendly hands, three miles east of Gela. As the transports approached the coast of Sicily a line of tracer shells arched up toward the transports. Suddenly other antiaircraft guns on U.S. warships and ashore opened fire. One after another, planes were hit, some staggering on to drop their paratroopers wherever they could, others diving toward the sea in flames. Although ships and units ashore had been warned of the parachute drop, for several days the Luftwaffe had pounded the ships and beaches, and gunners were nervous.

Of the 144 transports, twenty-three were shot down and thirty-seven others badly damaged. Of their human cargo, ninety-seven paratroopers were killed and some 400 were injured.

Americide occurred at sea as well. On Sept. 21, 1944, the U.S. SUBMARINE *Seawolf* (SS 197) stood out from Brisbane, Australia, to begin her fifteenth war patrol against Japanese shipping. She was last contacted on Oct. 3 in the area of Morotai Island in the Indonesian chain. A few days later a Japanese submarine attacked U.S. ships in the area. Although the attack took place in a "sub safe" area, where U.S. submarines were allowed to transit and no antisubmarine attacks were to be made by U.S. forces, both Navy planes and DESTROYER ESCORTS attacked a submarine contact there on Oct. 7. Their target was undoubtedly the *Seawolf,* with some sixty-five men on board. The submarine was never heard from again.

Even U.S. surface ships were not immune to attack by friendly forces. On Jan. 24, 1945, the U.S. salvage ship *Extractor* (ARS 15) was steaming from GUAM to the Philippines. Through mistaken identification the submarine *Guardfish* (SS 217) fired a single TORPEDO, which struck and sank the small, 1,089-ton ship within five minutes. Six crewmen were lost, the others being rescued by the submarine.

More tragic, U.S. submarines operating against the Japanese merchant marine sank a number of ships carrying Allied PRISONERS OF WAR; at least several hundred American POWs are believed to have been killed in such sinkings. And, a technical failure led to the loss of the high-scoring submarine *Tang* (SS 306) on Oct. 24, 1944. As her last torpedo was fired at a Japanese ship, it began a "circular run" and turned back to hit the launching submarine. The submarine sank to the bottom in 180 feet of water; Japanese ships DEPTH CHARGED the craft, but the survivors were able to escape to the surface. Nine were rescued by the Japanese ships and survived the war in a POW camp; sixty men died in the sinking.

There were many incidents of Americide during the war—sometimes because of personnel error, sometimes because of the "fog of war."

Amphibious Landings

Landings on hostile beaches were carried out in most theaters by all of the major belligerents. For long-range operations specialized AMPHIBIOUS SHIPS were to carry troops, vehicles, and equipment across seas for amphibious landings, with LANDING CRAFT and AMPHIBIOUS TRACTORS carrying the assault troops and material to the beach. Amphibious landings were highly complex, requiring the close coordination of air, naval, and ground forces. The amphibious ships and assault troops were extremely vulnerable to hostile fire during the landing. Japanese and U.S. amphibious landings were often coordinated with AIRBORNE assaults.

Japan The first amphibious landings of the war were carried out by Japan in China as part of the JAPANESE CAMPAIGN IN THE FAR EAST. For those landings the Japanese Army developed specialized amphibious ships and landing craft. In the fall of 1941, as Japan moved closer to war with the United States and Britain, the Japanese developed a highly ambitious plan: simultaneous air strikes against U.S. forces at PEARL HARBOR and in the Philippines, to be followed by landings in the Philippines, on WAKE, MALAYA, GUAM in the MARIANA ISLANDS, Borneo, and in the DUTCH EAST INDIES.

The Japanese had considered an amphibious landing on Oahu in the Hawaiian Islands to follow the Pearl Harbor air strike. That proposal was quickly discarded because of the shortage of shipping and the need for the carrier striking force to transmit rapidly on the stormy northern route to

Hawaii for maximum secrecy, a transit impossible for troop ships.

In May 1942 the Japanese sent an amphibious force to capture PORT MORESBY on NEW GUINEA, to establish air bases for strikes against Australia. Subsequent amphibious landings on the northern coast of Australia were contemplated. But the defeat of the supporting Japanese carriers in the battle of CORAL SEA led to a temporary delay in Japanese plans until an airfield could be established on GUADALCANAL and a seaplane base at Tulagi in the SOLOMON ISLANDS.

In June 1942 the Japanese sent a large invasion force to capture MIDWAY Island, as a staging base for further operations against Pearl Harbor and to force the U.S. Pacific FLEET into a decisive engagement. That landing was aborted after the Japanese defeat in the carrier battle. However, in a diversion for the Midway operation and to prevent American use of the ALEUTIAN ISLANDS for bomber bases, Japanese troops landed on Attu and Kiska in the Aleutian Islands as part of the JAPANESE CAMPAIGN IN THE CENTRAL PACIFIC.

The Japanese landings on Guadalcanal and Tulagi in July 1942 to establish bases for air support of a new advance against Port Moresby led to the U.S. landings on Guadalcanal in Aug. 1942.

Japanese amphibious landings were carried out mostly by Army troops, with some by marines of the Special Naval Landing Force.

United States The first U.S. amphibious assault of the war took place at Guadalcanal on Aug. 7, 1942, when the 1st Marine DIVISION landed to seize the airfield under construction by the Japanese. This was the start of the lengthy U.S. SOLOMONS–NEW GUINEA CAMPAIGN, which included a series of landings, mostly by Army troops, on Japanese-held NEW GEORGIA, NEW BRITAIN, BOUGAINVILLE, and New Ireland. A planned assault against RABAUL—with twenty-three Allied ground divisions and forty-five air GROUPS—was called off and that heavily defended Japanese base was isolated by air and naval attacks.

With the availability of large numbers of AIRCRAFT CARRIERS and amphibious ships and their escorting ships, and BATTLESHIPS for shore bombardment, a massive amphibious offensive was undertaken by U.S. forces in the U.S. CENTRAL

PACIFIC CAMPAIGN. Soldiers and Marines were landed—at high cost in casualties—on the almost barren atolls of TARAWA, MAKIN, ENIWETOK, and against the islands of the Mariana Islands, and Palaus. The Marianas were wanted for bases to enable B-29 SUPERFORTRESS bombers to strike Japan.

The dual U.S. thrusts in the Pacific came together for the recapture of the Philippines, the massive assaults against the islands of Leyte and then Mindoro and Luzon that began in Oct. 1944.

With the Philippines partially secured, in anticipation of eventual landings in Japan, in February 1945 U.S. Marines assaulted IWO JIMA. Only 660 miles from Japan, Iwo Jima would provide bases to support B-29 and fighter operations against Japan. Next, on March 1, 1945, Marines and soldiers struck OKINAWA, only 350 miles from the Japanese homeland. Okinawa would be important for naval and air bases for the final assaults of the war.

The planned invasion of Japan was to involve close to 5 million Allied soldiers, sailors, airmen, and marines. Operation Olympic was to have twenty U.S. Army and Marine ground divisions and one airborne division, supported by fifty-three air groups. U.S. troops were to land on Kyushu under direction of the U.S. Sixth ARMY. Expected U.S. casualties were estimated at 30,000 to 50,000 dead and wounded, although later statements—after the ATOMIC BOMBS were dropped on Japan—cited potential casualties of 1 million men. Olympic was scheduled for Nov. 1, 1945.

Subsequently, Operation Coronet would land Allied troops on the Kato Plain, 50 miles east of TOKYO. This assault, by the U.S. First and Eighth Armies, was to have been the largest amphibious assault in history, although firm details had not been worked out when Japan capitulated in Aug. 1945. (See MAJESIC.)

While all major amphibious landings were carried out from surface ships, U.S. and British SUBMARINES regularly landed small raiding parties on enemy coasts. Two U.S. submarines put 221 Marine raiders ashore on Makin for a two-day rampage in Aug. 1942. (Some U.S. military officers later expressed the opinion that the Makin landing alerted the Japanese to U.S. interest in the area and led to the fortification of Makin and Tarawa.)

With a need to commit Allied troops to a SECOND FRONT in Europe, but not strong enough to land in German-held Europe, on Nov. 8, 1942, Anglo-American forces landed at three points on the North African coast in Operation Torch, the beginning of the NORTHWEST AFRICA CAMPAIGN. One of the landings, on the Atlantic coast of Morocco, was carried out entirely by U.S. troops, while Anglo-American forces landed at Oran and Algiers.

By May 1943 the vaunted German AFRIKA KORPS, caught between Allied pincer movements from the east and west, surrendered as did the remaining Italian troops in North Africa. Then, using North Africa as a jumping-off point, in Aug. 1943 the Allies invaded SICILY and, the following month, Anglo-American forces landed in Italy (see ITALIAN CAMPAIGN). Amphibious landings were a key component of Allied successes in the Mediterranean area, and although the British wished to undertake more landings in the Aegean area, they were vetoed by the U.S. leadership as distracting resources from the principal objective, the invasion of northwestern Europe.

The NORMANDY INVASION of June 6, 1944, was the largest amphibious landing in history. Coming ashore on open beaches, the assault force of Operation Overlord consisted of three American, one Canadian, and two British divisions; three airborne divisions were landed the night before behind German lines.

Swarms of landing craft approach Iwo Jima, which is dominated by the 550-foot-high Mount Suribachi. *(U.S. Navy)*

The Allies had earlier planned a simultaneous landing on the southern (Mediterranean) coast of France. Commitments in the Mediterranean and the shortage of LANDING SHIPS, TANK (LSTs) led to a delay in Operation Anvil-Dragoon until Aug. 15, 1944. On that date a FREE FRENCH division and a U.S. division came ashore. (The day before a multinational COMMANDO group had come ashore to block key roads to the assault beaches.)

The U.S. Army conducted more amphibious landings than did the Marines during the war. The Marines, however, certainly carried out the most difficult and bloodiest landings, at Tarawa, Eniwetok, and Iwo Jima.

Germany   Germany began the DENMARK AND NORWAY CAMPAIGN with amphibious landings in Norway, coordinated with airborne assaults. In this instance, the German troops were landed at several coastal ports by merchant ships disguised as innocent freighters and by warships.

After the fall of France in June 1940 the German high command planned an invasion of England, given the code name *Seelöwe* or SEA LION. The German Army looked at the operation as a "gigantic river crossing." Large numbers of coastal and river craft were assembled, and plans begun to land an assault wave of two motorized and eleven infantry divisions, and drops by two Luftwaffe parachute divisions. This initial wave would land 90,000 combat troops with 650 tanks. Against the lightly armed British army, smarting from the evacuation of DUNKIRK, the German assault force and massive follow-on effort—a total commitment of forty-one divisions—could have met with success. However, the Luftwaffe had first to gain control of the air over Britain and this could not be done. After several delays, on Sept. 17, 1941, HITLER postponed Sea Lion indefinitely.

Great Britain   Immediately after the fall of France in May 1941, the British began commando raids against the French coast and Norway. These were intended primarily for psychological reasons, and to gain experience in what the British called "COMBINED OPERATIONS."

A large amphibious landing was undertaken on Aug. 19, 1942, at DIEPPE, a German-held French port seventy miles from England. The assault force consisted of 6,000 Canadian and British troops, and a token addition of sixty U.S. Army RANGERS. The landing—which Prime Minister CHURCHILL later labeled a "reconnaissance in force"—was unsuccessful and suffered high casualties. Still, the landing at a port convinced the German high command that when the ALLIES eventually landed in Western Europe it would be at a port, and not on open beaches as occurred at Normandy in June 1944.

Subsequently, British forces had major roles in the North African, Sicilian, Italian, and Normandy landings.

Soviet Union   There does not appear to have been a specialized Soviet amphibious force from the Bolshevik Revolution of 1917 until 1939, when the 1st Separate Naval Infantry Brigade was established in the Baltic Fleet to fight in the war with Finland (1939–1940). But the large numbers of naval infantry units fought as ground troops and were not used in landing operations.

There were several significant amphibious operations during the war. The approximately 100,000 naval troops remaining under fleet and flotilla control were used to defend naval bases and islands as well as to carry out amphibious landings, often in concert with army troops. The Soviet Navy conducted 114 amphibious landings during the war, in the GERMAN CAMPAIGN IN THE SOVIET UNION and the SOVIET OFFENSIVE CAMPAIGN. Some Soviet landings were quite small—essentially raids of platoon size. But four of the landings—two at Kerch-Feodosiya and one at Novorossisk on the Black Sea, and one at Moon Sound in the Baltic—each involved several thousand troops.

According to Soviet sources, of the 114 landings, sixty-one were planned and organized in less than twenty-four hours! In all, the Navy landed some 330,000 troops during the war, soldiers as well as marines. Most of the landings were short-range operations, across straits, bays, and large rivers, and several were made in coordination with parachute landings, especially those along the North Korean coast in Aug. 1945 during the brief Soviet campaign against the Japanese.

Several important postwar Soviet officials were associated with amphibious operations during the war. Adm. S. G. GORSHKOV, Commander in Chief of the Soviet Navy from 1956 until 1985, had directed landings in the Black Sea-Azov-Danube campaigns, and LEONID BREZHNEV, head of the Soviet government from 1964 until his death in 1982, was a political officer with the 18th Assault Army during landings on the Black Sea coast, where he received a minor wound.

Amphibious Ships

Specialized ships for AMPHIBIOUS LANDINGS and supporting troops on hostile beaches. The first U.S. war-era amphibious ships were high-speed transports (designated APD). Beginning in 1936 the U.S. Navy converted older DESTROYERS to carry 120 troops; the ships had davits installed for carrying four LCVP-type LANDING CRAFT. In all, thirty-six older destroyers (DD) and more than 100 of the newer DESTROYER ESCORTS (DE) were converted by the Navy into high-speed transports.

Other large, "non-beaching" U.S. amphibious ships included merchant ship hulls converted to attack transports (APA) and attack cargo ships (AKA), followed by large numbers of ships built specifically for these roles. More than 300 ships were built specifically as APAs and AKAs and would carry the bulk of the troops and cargoes for amphibious assaults. These ships differed from "straight" cargo ships and troop transports because they were not pier-to-pier carriers; they unloaded troops and equipment into landing craft in the assault area. Both types had davits and booms for unloading landing craft. But they could not accommodate enough landing craft and AMPHIBIOUS TRACTORS (LVT) for the numbers of troops and amount of cargo needed in large-scale invasions.

The solution was the docking-well ship. These ships used the floating dry dock concept: they could flood ballast tanks, be lowered into the water, and have landing craft float in or out. The landing ship dock (LSD) was a large, non-beaching amphibious ship displacing 8,700 tons full load, with a docking well 252 feet long and 44 feet wide. These ships could each transport two or three loaded LCTs or thirty-six loaded LCM(3)s in the docking well, plus cargo and troops internally, and vehicles could be carried on a removable super deck fitted above the docking well. Alternatively, an LSD could carry ninety amphibious tractors or about 110 of the wheeled DUKW amphibious trucks.

The U.S. Navy also built six large ships with the designation landing ship vehicle (LSV). These ships, just over 450-feet long, displaced some 8,100 to 9,000 tons full load and an internal ramp system for carrying LVTs and DUKWs, which were unloaded over a stern ramp. Each LSV could accommodate some fifty vehicles and had accommodations for 800 troops. Although a successful design, these ships lacked the flexibility of the docking-well ships and were very expensive as troop ships in comparison to the APA types.

The NORTH AFRICA CAMPAIGN landings of Nov. 1942 demonstrated the need for specialized flagships to command AMPHIBIOUS OPERATIONS. Fifteen merchant ships being built under contract to the Maritime Commission were selected for conversion to amphibious force flagships (AGC). But to meet the flagship need while the ex-merchant ships were being completed, a large, 14,150-ton Army-operated passenger ship was taken in hand for conversion to an AGC. This ship was followed by a seaplane tender and six large Coast Guard cutters that could be spared from antisubmarine work because of the large number of destroyer escorts becoming available for CONVOY escort. (The Coast Guard ships remained in that service and carried their previous gunboat designations while serving as AGCs.) The fifteen large 12,800-ton merchant-hull command ships had staff accommodations for approximately fifty-five officers and 580 enlisted men in addition to their crews, but they could embark more men when necessary.

Better known were the large number of landing ships that could "beach"—run aground—to unload their troops and vehicles. The most important was the LANDING SHIP, TANK (LST), built in large numbers by the United States and Britain. The U.S. LSTs were 328 feet long and could carry 2,100 tons of cargo—tanks, trucks, munitions—although for beaching, 500 tons was a more feasible load. U.S. shipyards built 1,052 LSTs during the war.

In addition, 558 smaller LST-type ships were built with the designation LSM for landing ship medium. These 203-foot ships, with open tank decks, were widely used in the Pacific, while the larger LSTs were employed in all theaters from 1943 onward. The flexibility of the LSM design was demonstrated when twelve LSMs were converted to

LSM(R) ROCKET ships, with a 5-inch gun installed aft and up to eighty-five rocket launchers fitted. Subsequently, an improved LSM(R) was built with the hull and propulsion of the LSM, but with the superstructure aft and twenty automatic-loading 5-inch rocket launchers fitted forward, supplemented by a 5-inch gun mount and four 4.2-inch mortars.

The landing craft infantry (large) or LCI(L) was 158½ feet long, displaced 380 tons, and was fitted with catwalks on both sides of the bow that could be lowered into the surf to unload troops. This was an ocean-going craft that carried 200 troops or 75 tons of cargo. More than a thousand of these craft were ordered. Of those, 164 were modified to provide close-in fire support for landings. These LCI(G) gunboats had one or two 40-mm BOFORS guns, several 20-mm guns, and small rocket launchers; the LCI(M) mortar craft had 40-mm and 20-mm guns plus three 4.2-inch (105-mm) mortars, the largest in U.S. service; and the LCI(R) rocket craft had six 5-inch rocket launchers plus the guns.

Another 130 LCI(L)s were more extensively converted to support craft and redesignated LCS(L). They had a 3-inch or twin 40-mm gun mount fitted forward, a second twin 40 forward of the bridge, and a third twin 40 aft, plus 20-mm guns and small rocket launchers. Small and relatively maneuverable, the LCI/LCS craft could steam up to the beaches with the troop-carrying craft, providing truly close-in support.

By the end of the war the U.S. Navy had almost 3,000 of the ocean-going amphibious and large landing ships described above.

Specialized amphibious ships were also built and converted by the Japanese and British navies.

Amphibious Tractors

Tracked landing vehicles capable of operating on land and water. The first operational use of Landing Vehicles, Tracked (LVT) was in the Marine landings at GUADALCANAL on Aug. 7, 1942. However, the LVTs—called "alligators" and "amtracs" by the Marines—were not considered reliable enough to land the assault troops. All of the initial landings at Guadalcanal and the adjacent islands were made from LANDING CRAFT, mostly LCVPs with bow

ramps, with the LVTs being used to bring ashore the follow-up supplies.

In the Marine landing at TARAWA on Nov. 20, 1943, LVTs were used in the assault waves for the first time because of offshore obstructions, including the reef at Betio Atoll. These LVTs, some fitted by the Marines with armor plate to provide additional protection from small arms fire, were highly successful at Tarawa. Thereafter LVTs were accepted as the preferred method of landing troops on hostile beaches, because they could carry troops beyond the surf line and easily unload them and their equipment, including JEEPS and light artillery, over a rear ramp directly onto the beach.

In the June 1944 landing at SAIPAN some 700 LVTs were used in the assault waves to bring ashore 8,000 Marines.

In addition to the troop-carrying LVTs, the Marines also employed armored amphibious tractors designated LVT(A). These were essentially amphibious tanks, armed with a 75-mm howitzer, which provided fire support as they waddled to shore with the LVTs. The LVT(A)s were generally called "Buffalos."

LVT development began in the 1930s when Donald Roebling developed a tracked amphibious vehicle for rescue work in the Everglades of central Florida. A photo of the Roebling craft in *Life* magazine caught the eye of an admiral, who passed it on to the Marine general commanding the Atlantic Fleet Marine Force. After looking at the swamp vehicle, the Marines took steps to evaluate a military version. The first production contract was awarded in 1940, with the first vehicle coming off the assembly line in July 1941.

The early LVTs had cleated tracks that could move them on land at 15 mph and in water at 4 knots. They could carry twenty fully equipped troops or two tons of cargo. Development of the LVT(A) began as early as 1940. They were first fitted with a 37-mm cannon, which was soon discarded in favor of the 75-mm howitzer. One or two machine guns were fitted to all vehicles. During the war there were improvements in reliability, horsepower, speed, and cargo capacity.

The Marine Corps procured 18,620 amphibious tractors of various models, including the LVT(A)s, during the war.

Anakim

Allied plans for the recapture of Burma, 1944.

Andaman Islands

Group of islands in the Bay of Bengal captured by the Japanese in March 1942. An Allied plan to retake the islands, code-named Buccaneer, was called off for lack of LANDING CRAFT. The Japanese evacuated the Andamans late in 1944 and they were reoccupied by British forces in Jan. 1945.

Anderson, Gen. Sir Kenneth (1891–1959)

Commander of the British 3rd Division during the FRANCE AND LOW COUNTRIES CAMPAIGN in 1940; the 3rd was evacuated from DUNKIRK in June 1940. He commanded the Eastern Task Force, landing in Algiers, Algeria, in the NORTHWEST AFRICA CAMPAIGN's invasion of North Africa. Anderson, cautious and hesitant, did not exploit opportunities. Gen. DWIGHT D. EISENHOWER, who found it difficult to speak ill of any Allied officer, characterized Anderson as "a gallant Scot, devoted to duty, and absolutely selfless. Honest and straightforward, he was blunt, sometimes to the point of rudeness, and this trait, curiously enough, seemed to bring him into conflict with his British confreres more than it did with the Americans." Gen. OMAR BRADLEY thought that "as an army commander, Anderson was in over his head." In part, Anderson was the victim of the very rawness of the Anglo-American team in North Africa. But his bluntness offended many of his peers, especially as it was coupled with so little apparent talent for leadership.

Anfa

Code name for participants at the CASABLANCA CONFERENCE, Jan. 1943.

Anger

British code name for the submarine *H-43* landing and then carrying off an officer from the island of Guernsey to determine the state of German defenses.

Anklet

Code name for British naval operation to cut German communications in northern Norway, Dec. 1941.

Anschluss,

see AUSTRIA.

Anson

Widely flown British reconnaissance and training aircraft. The twin-engine Anson, which first flew in 1935, performed invaluable service throughout the war. Production continued until 1952—total Avro production was 8,138 aircraft with another 2,882 being built in Canada. The Anson also was employed as a light transport and ambulance; in the bomber training role it could carry small BOMBS under each wing and had a power gun-turret with two .303-cal. machine guns for gunnery training.

ANT-6

Outstanding Soviet heavy bomber, also known as the TB-3. Perhaps the plane's most glowing tribute in the West came from aviation historian Bill Gunston: "The only aircraft that could rival it at the end of the 1930s was the Boeing B-17B [FLYING FORTRESS], which entered service in mid-1939. The American bomber could fly slightly higher and much faster, but it carried much less than half the bomb load. The very fact that it is reasonable to compare the TB-3 with the B-17 underlines the greatness of the TB-3's designers back in the 1920s."

The ANT-6 was the largest land plane in the world when it entered service in 1933–1934; when production ceased in late 1937 a total of 818 of the several models of the ANT-6 had been manufactured. This quantity was remarkable for a four-engine aircraft in the between-war period. These planes formed the backbone of Soviet strategic aviation into World War II, flying bombing missions against Japanese forces in Manchuria and against Finland, and finally against the Germans, including night attacks on BERLIN.

Designed by Andrei N. Tupolev (hence ANT),

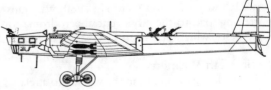

ANT-6 bomber.

the doyen of Soviet aircraft designers, this was an all-metal monoplane with a corrugated aluminum covering or skin, and four engines fitted to the leading edges of the wing. The original version of the aircraft had a wingspan of 132 feet, a length of 79⅓ feet, and a maximum take-off weight of 36,360 pounds. The later models of the ANT-6 could reach a speed of 276 mph, carrying up to 5 tons of bombs for short distances. The ANT-6 had a large, fixed undercarriage and was fitted with wheels that were replaceable by skis for operations from snow-covered airfields and arctic ice. Extensive instrumentation in the ANT-6 permitted routine night flights, a necessity in the northern latitudes of the Soviet Union. The ANT-6's normal combat crew was nine and there was space for twelve troops. The planes were often pressed into service as transports, especially for dropping "sticks" of paratroopers. They could also carry small tanks, slung under the fuselage, in these operations. In exercises, while skimming some *3 feet* above the water, an ANT-6 could release amphibious tanks without a parachute—doing so on the final test with a crew inside the tank!

In addition to defensive machine guns, in exercises ANT-6s repeatedly took off carrying four fighters, two mounted above its wings and two suspended under its wings, all of which could be launched in flight. It could carry a fifth fighter atop the fuselage, but the problems involved in loading that fighter made it operationally impractical. A further "parasite" fighter concept in 1934–1935 involved *landing* a fighter by hooking onto a retractable hook-and-trapeze fitted to the underside of the bomber's fuselage. The fighter could be carried by the bomber until hostile interceptors were encountered. It then would be released to engage the enemy and return to base. When war came the concept was actually used, with light bombers being carried by the ANT-6s.

The prototype ANT-6 was assembled at Moscow's Fili works and on Oct. 31, 1930, was transported by road to the city's central aerodrome for flight tests, which began on Dec. 22 that year.

Antiaircraft Weapons

The wide use of aircraft in the war led to a related development in antiaircraft weapons. Antiaircraft guns were called AA by U.S. forces, ACK-ACK by the British (and many journalists), and FLAK by the Germans (as well as journalists and Allied bomber pilots—who "took flak" and wore "flak vests").

On land, antiaircraft guns ranged from light machine guns up to German twin-barrel 128-mm Flak 40, the heaviest AA gun used in the war, which were mounted on massive FLAK TOWERS in several European cities. Ground troops often fired at aircraft—ineffectively—with rifle, pistols, and any other weapon at hand; such efforts were mainly for the psychological benefit of the troops being bombed and strafed. U.S. ground troops had five dedicated AA weapons; the rounds per minute given below is cyclic, not necessarily the sustained firing rate:

WEAPON	MOUNTING	EFFECTIVE CEILING	RPM
quad .50-cal. machine guns	towed or half-track	low-flying aircraft	2,300
37-mm	towed	10,500 feet	120
40-mm BOFORS	towed	11,000 feet	120
3-inch (76-mm)	towed	27,900 feet	25
90-mm	towed	33,800 feet	15–25
120-mm	towed	56,000 feet	

The towed guns, except for the "quad 50s," were fired after being detached from the towing truck, their wheels jacked up or removed, and outriggers extended to stabilize the gun. The "quad 50s" were mounted on a four-wheel trailer, or in a half-track.

Sometimes the 37-mm AA gun was comounted with two .50-cal. machine guns, as the ballistics of the two weapons were almost identical. All of these weapons except the 120-mm guns could be used for direct fire against enemy troops and vehicles—*in extremis.* The "quad 50s" were particularly effective as close-in weapons against enemy troops. The 120-mm guns were used mainly for city or homeland defense and were not considered "tactical" weapons.

U.S. tanks, half-tracks, and certain other vehicles mounted .30-cal. or .50-cal. machine guns for air defense, and some 6×6 TRUCKS had ring mounts above the cabs for mounting machine guns.

When the war began the U.S. Army made extensive use of sound locators and searchlights to detect aircraft. However, by the time U.S. forces landed in North Africa in late 1942 these systems had largely been discarded, although searchlights did reappear from time to time.

The U.S. Navy had seven principal AA guns in ships, in addition to .30-cal. and .50-cal. machine guns in smaller units and SUBMARINES. For multiple mounts the rounds per minute in this table is per barrel except for the 1.1-inch quad:

WEAPON	MOUNTING	EFFECTIVE CEILING	RPM
1.1-inch	quad	16,000 feet	550–600
20-mm OERLIKON	single, twin, quad	10,000 feet	450–480
37-mm	single	10,500 feet	120
40-mm Bofors	single, twin, quad	11,000 feet	120
3-inch (76-mm)	single	29,800 feet	20
5-inch (127-mm)	single (25-cal.)	27,400 feet	15–20
5-inch (127-mm)	single, twin (38-cal.)	37,200 feet	15–22

All of these guns were considered cannon and not machine guns, i.e., they fired explosive shells. The quad 1.1-inch gun mounts, installed in U.S. warships from 1935, suffered from mechanical breakdown and the 1.1-inch shell was too small to stop an aircraft. As soon as the 20-mm and 40-mm guns became available the 1.1s were discarded.

Numerous 20-mm Oerlikon guns were placed on the larger warships from 1941, the single and twin mounts being simply "bolted on" wherever room could be found. They were sometimes the main gun battery of smaller ships. A quad 20-mm mount was developed for PT-BOATS and five BATTLESHIPS each received one quad 20-mm mount.

The 37-mm guns were Army weapons, adapted for use in certain LANDING CRAFT and PT-boats. The 40-mm Bofors, late in arriving in the fleet, was the most widely used gun in U.S. ships and in many respects the most effective AA gun available. The 5-inch/.38-cal. gun was the principal gun armament of U.S. DESTROYERS and AIRCRAFT CARRIERS, and the secondary gun battery of CRUISERS and battleships. They were dual-purpose guns, intended for use against both surface and air targets. When TORPEDO bombers attacked warships the ships often used their larger caliber guns to fire in the path of the approaching bombers in the hope that the shell splashes would catch and destroy the attackers.

Prior to 1943 the 3-inch and larger ammunition could have an altitude preset at which the shell would detonate in the hope that the explosion damaged a nearby enemy aircraft; gunners no longer had to attempt to hit the aircraft, but they had to estimate the altitude of the attacking aircraft.

In 1943 the PROXIMITY FUZE or VT entered service. It detonated an antiaircraft shell at the closest point to an enemy aircraft. Also called an influence fuze or Variable-Time (VT) fuze, the proximity fuze greatly increased the probability that a round would destroy an enemy aircraft. Proximity-fuzed ammunition could be fired from 3-inch and larger guns.

Aboard ship, guns of 40-mm and larger size could be linked to RADAR directors that gave accurate estimates of an approaching aircraft's range, speed, and altitude, and could direct effective AA fire in darkness and through clouds.

The Germans, in addition to antiaircraft guns (flak), were engaged in the development of several antiaircraft GUIDED MISSILES when the war ended. The missile development effort began in late 1942 in response to the growing Anglo-American STRATEGIC BOMBING effort against German cities. Led by WERNHER VON BRAUN, a German team initiated the *WASSERFALL* (Waterfall) project. This produced an unmanned, vertically launched rocket designed to intercept Allied bombers. A number of other AA missiles were in various stages of development when the war ended—the *Schmetterling* (Butterfly) and *Taifun* (Typhoon) among others; another missile, the *Gentian* (gentian flower) was an unmanned version of the ME 163 *KOMET* with a 700-pound warhead fitted in place of a pilot.

Although flight tests of these weapons were carried out, none became operational. One plan called for AA missiles to protect seventy cities in Germany.

The most unusual AA weapons in the war were undoubtedly some of the British gadgets. Several rocket launchers were developed and fitted to merchant ships—the Pillar Box, Strength through Joy, and Harvey projectors. Although the last did have some success against German aircraft attacking merchant ships, none was a truly suitable AA weapon.

More diabolical, and more successful, was the

ingenious RAF device called the Parachute And Cable, generally shortened to PAC. This was a powerful rocket that carried a steel cable, which had a parachute attached to one end, up to an altitude of 500 feet. The cable was expected to catch on the wings and propellers of low-flying bombers. These devices were used from 1940 onward, ashore and at sea. (After firing the cable could be retracted back aboard the ship.)

During the BATTLE OF BRITAIN at least one German bomber blew up after snagging a PAC that tore off its port wing. More German bombers were downed by this device, and others returned to base with gashes in their wings. This success led to the "aerial MINE" in which an explosive charge was attached to the wire. This device, as well as the Type J PAC—which required a rocket powerful enough to carry up a five-ton cable—were not successful. By 1943 the seagoing PACs were credited with destroying nine German aircraft and at least thirty-five ships claimed to have been saved from BOMB hits when their attackers avoided the cables spiraling skyward.

Even in wartime there was some humor: Gerald Pawle, in his account of secret British weapons research entitled *The Secret War,* recounted how a merchant ship armed with PAC "was flying from her main topmast the usual barrage BALLOON. A gust of wind blew the cover off the spare binnacle, and this fell on the lanyard connected to the PAC projector. The rocket fired, and the PAC scored a direct hit on the balloon, which burst into flames. Its cable, falling over the stern, became wound round the propeller, and this immediately acted as a winch. Before the master realized what had happened the topmast was pulled out of the ship!"

Anti-Comintern Pact

Anti-Communist agreement between Japan and Germany, signed on Nov. 25, 1936. The two nations agreed that in the event of an unprovoked attack by the Soviet Union on either Japan or Germany, they would move "to safeguard their common interests" and "take no measures which would tend to ease the situation of the Soviet Union."

The pact was a response to the seventh congress of the Communist International (the Comintern), which in July 1935 had reiterated its anticapitalist, antiimperialism philosophy. HITLER said that the pact would help defend Western civilization from the threat of worldwide communism presented by the Comintern.

Italy signed the pact in 1937 and Hungary and Spain, in 1939. The Soviet-German NONAGGRESSION PACT of 1939, which surprised Japan, invalidated the Anti-Comintern Pact. When Soviet leader STALIN made the Nonaggression Pact with Germany, he shrugged off the Anti-Comintern Pact as something that had "frightened principally the City of London [the British financial center] and the English shopkeepers." But the Nonaggression Pact was in turn invalidated by the German invasion of the Soviet Union in June 1941, after which the Anti-Comintern Pact was renewed for five years in Nov. 1941.

Stalin dissolved the Comintern on May 22, 1943, in a show of comradeship with the other ALLIES, assuring them that his nation was no longer leading a worldwide campaign against capitalism. On March 15, 1944, in another public relations move, "The Internationale," which Communists and Communist sympathizers throughout the world had sung in shows of fraternal harmony, was dropped as the Soviet national anthem.

Anti-Semitism

Theories or actions directed against JEWS. Although prejudice against Jews is deeply rooted in the history of many countries, the term dates to 1880, when two German schoolteachers circulated an "Anti-Semites' Petition" asking for "the emancipation of the German people from a form of alien domination which it cannot endure for any length of time."

HITLER used the term frequently in his speeches and writings. He tried to make a distinction between "irrational" anti-Semitism, giving Russian pogroms as an example, and "rational" anti-Semitism, which he described in a 1919 letter as "a systemic and legal struggle against, and eradication of, what privileges the Jews enjoy over foreigners. . . . Its final objective, however, must be the total removal of all Jews from our midst." Such statements, which riddle his book *Mein Kampf* and other writings, are the foundation for the FINAL SOLUTION—the eradication of Jews.

"Anti-Semitism" entered the English language soon after it appeared in Germany and was used to describe anti-Jewish activities in the United States. Anti-Semitism was particularly strong in the AMERICAN FIRST COMMITTEE, many of whose members equated going to war with somehow playing into the hands of "Zionists" and "international Jews." Anti-Semitic PROPAGANDA, much of it AXIS inspired, circulated throughout the war. Some of the most frequently heard tales were that President ROOSEVELT was himself a Jew (or at least was controlled by Jews) and that American Jews were draft dodgers. In reality, the number of Jews in the armed forces was in proportion to that of Jews in the U.S. population.

Anton

German code name for the occupation of VICHY FRANCE, Nov. 1942.

Anvil

Early code name for Dragoon.

ANZAC

Acronym for the Australian and New Zealand Corps formed in Dec. 1914. The Corps fought with distinction in the abortive landings at Gallipoli in 1915. Subsequently, the term *Anzac* was used to describe any member of the Australian or New Zealand armed forces.

Anzio

Site, about 35 miles south of ROME, of Allied AMPHIBIOUS LANDING in the ITALIAN CAMPAIGN. The landing was a two-division assault to put pressure on the GUSTAV LINE, the German defenses blocking the advance of Allied forces that had landed at SALERNO on Sept. 9, 1943. British Prime Minister CHURCHILL had promoted the landing to hasten the fall of ROME and perhaps even expedite the ending of the EUROPEAN WAR.

On the night of Jan. 22, 1944, in an initial landing called Operation Shingle, RANGER-led U.S. and British forces landed at this town on the Tyrrhenian Sea. There was no active opposition to the landing, and prospects for fulfilling the mission of the landing looked promising.

The commander of the invasion troops, U.S. Maj. Gen. JOHN P. LUCAS, should have been elated. His 36,000 troops and their 3,000 vehicles had landed without casualty and the immediate objective, the Alban Hills, stood only about 20 miles away. There were virtually no German troops between the beach and the hills or beyond them to the ultimate objective: Rome.

The Anzio landing was timed to follow an Allied thrust across the Rapido and Garigliano Rivers, *Generalfeldmarschall* ALBERT KESSELRING sent reserve divisions against the threat to the Gustav Line, leaving the troops landing at Anzio with little opposition. But the attempted river crossings ended in failure and substantial American losses; the Germans were able to shift forces to Anzio.

Lucas, overly cautious, delayed an advance inland until he built up more supplies. After a week there were 69,000 U.S. and British troops and their equipment ashore, the beachheads had been secured, and supplies continued to pour ashore. Still, Lucas delayed. "I am far too tenderhearted ever to be a success at my chosen profession," he once had confided to his diary.

On the day following the landings the Germans had begun intensive air attacks on the troop concentrations. Then they moved up major ground forces to block the invaders and force them back into the sea. Under the pounding of German artillery the Allied troops began a bloody four-month struggle to hold onto the beachhead and a few square miles beyond it.

During the battle of Anzio, U.S. forces suffered more than 72,000 casualties. In comparison, about 15,000 fell in the NORMANDY INVASION.

Artist BILL MAULDIN, who made some of his Willie and Joe cartoons on the beachhead, wrote of the German artillery: "Their 88mm. is the terror of every dogface. It can do everything but throw shells around corners, and sometimes we think it has even done that." The "kraut who is twisting the controls on the 88 a couple of mountains away doesn't see what he is shooting at, and so his shell is just as likely to hit the good soldier who is under cover as the dumb one who is standing on top of a knoll." Also shelling the beachhead were the "Anzio Annie" and the "Anzio Express," two 280-mm railroad guns that emerged from a railroad tunnel and hurled 562-pound projectiles.

HITLER called the beachhead "an abscess." AXIS SALLY, the American woman who made PROPAGANDA broadcasts for the Germans, taunted the troops by dubbing the beachhead "the largest self-supporting PRISONER OF WAR camp in the world." Churchill telegraphed Soviet leader STALIN: "Although the landing was a brilliant piece of work and achieved complete surprise, the advantage was lost and now it is a question of hard slogging." To others, he bitterly said, "I had hoped that we were hurling a wildcat onto the shore, but all we had got was a stranded whale."

The men on the beachhead fought valiantly while decisions were made about Lucas. He was finally replaced on Feb. 23 by Maj. Gen. LUCIAN K. TRUSCOTT, JR. He staged a breakout on May 23, following the cracking of the Gustav Line. Two days later Truscott's forces made contact with the advancing ALLIES.

Aphrodite

Allied code name for the use of radio-controlled bombers against German targets in Europe such as SUBMARINE PENS and V-2 MISSILE launching sites. War-weary heavy bombers—B-17 FLYING FORTRESSES and B-24 LIBERATORS—were loaded with 20,000 pounds or more of explosives or NAPALM (jellied gasoline) and taken aloft by pilots who bailed out of the aircraft before they reached the English coast. At that point a control aircraft would take over to direct the drone or—as AAF documents referred to them—"robot" aircraft to its target by radio with forward-looking television being used to guide the aircraft to the target. The control aircraft were also B-17 and B-24 bombers, with photographic aircraft and escorting fighters also accompanying the drones.

The Aphrodite missions, conducted by the Eighth AIR FORCE, began in Aug. 1944, their targets being German missile launch sites near the Pas de Calais in France. The first mission was flown on Aug. 4 with a succession of four B-17G bombers: a control failure lost the first aircraft 15 miles from the target; the second impacted successfully and detonated about 500 feet from its target; one spun to earth in England; and the fourth struck about 1,500 feet from its target.

Two days later, on Aug. 6, two more B-17G

drones were sent against missile sites; both crashed into the sea. The official Aphrodite project report reads: "The results of the six missions flown were not satisfactory as far as damage to enemy installations is concerned. However, these missions were in the nature of experimental missions, and have proved the value and serviceability of the weapon and equipment." Still, the decision was made not to fly additional drone missions until better control equipment became available.

Meanwhile, a Navy detachment attached to the Eighth Air Force began drone missions, using naval (PB4Y-1) variants of the B-24 Liberator bomber, with PV-1 Ventura bombers as the control aircraft. On the first Navy mission, on Aug. 12, a premature explosion destroyed the plane over England. The two Navy pilots were killed before they could bail out—Lt. JOSEPH P. KENNEDY, JR., and Lt. Wilford J. Willy.

The second PB4Y-1 was launched against a V-2 missile site at Heligoland on Sept. 3, 1944. Because of controller error, the plane crashed and exploded into a nearby barracks area.

Aphrodite strikes were resumed by the AAF—with improved control gear—in mid-Sept. 1944. In this phase the drone bombers were sent against U-BOAT submarine pens at Heligoland and oil refineries at Heide-Hemmingstedt. Most of the eight B-17s launched between Sept. 11 and 30 blew up in flight or were lost; relatively little damage was inflicted. (One drone pilot was killed when he bailed out over England and his parachute failed to open.)

Subsequently, in late Oct. 1944 the decision was made to shift drone targets for the next phase to industrial objectives in German-held Europe, as far inland as possible. Also, if primary targets could not be hit, the drones were to be crashed "as a last resort [into] any German city."

On Dec. 5 two drone B-17s were sent toward the railroad marshalling yards in the German city of Hereford. Control problems again plagued the robot bombers: one exploded over a wooded area and the second made an uncontrolled belly landing. The latter plane did not explode and was relatively intact, giving the Germans full access to the Aphrodite control system (faulty though it was).

The final Aphrodite missions of the war were flown on Jan. 1, 1945, against thermal power stations at Oldenburg, Germany. One crashed and exploded in the town, the second struck three miles from its target.

The Aphrodite experiment was over. Its successes were few, but its cost was also low. More practical would be air-launched guided bombs and missiles. (See GUIDED MISSILES.)

Ar 196

A highly successful catapult floatplane flown by the German Navy. The Ardo-built Ar 196 was an agile aircraft flown from German warships and shore bases in reconnaissance, bombing, coastal patrol, and antisubmarine roles. The Ar 196A-1 variant entered service in late 1939, with up to four aircraft being carried on board German heavy cruisers, battleships, and POCKET BATTLESHIPS. The plane was first seen on the ill-fated pocket battleship *ADMIRAL GRAF SPEE.* The aircraft also flew from land bases, two land-based Ar 196s being responsible for the capture of the British submarine *Seal* in the Kattegat in 1940.

The plane could operate from the water or be catapulted from surface ships. A total of 598 aircraft were produced by Ardo and other firms, including a few by the French SNCA factory in SAINT-NA-ZAIRE and the Fokker factory in the Netherlands.

Unlike U.S. and Japanese floatplanes, the Ar 196 had twin floats (although four aircraft did evaluate a single-float arrangement). The Ar 196 was a single-engine, low-wing aircraft with a large glazed cockpit; the observer-gunner, however, was only partially enclosed by the canopy. The aircraft had a maximum speed of 193 mph with a range of 665 miles in the recce role. One 110-pound BOMB or a DEPTH CHARGE could be carried under each wing. Two 20-mm cannon were fitted in the wings and there was a flexible twin 7.9-mm machine gun mount firing aft.

Ar 232

German cargo aircraft whose limited service and numbers were eclipsed by the JU 52 aircraft. The Ar 232A had twin radial engines of 2,000 horsepower each while the almost identical Ar 232B had four 690-horsepower engines. The aircraft, with a long, single tail boom and twin tail fin, could carry some 10,000 pounds of cargo with a maximum speed (for the Ar 232B) of 211 mph. Only forty aircraft were built. The subsequent Ar 432 project was similar, but constructed of wood and metal instead of being all metal.

Ar 234 *Blitz* (Lightning)

The world's first jet-propelled bomber. This high-performance aircraft, like several other German JET-PROPELLED AIRCRAFT, arrived on the scene too late to have an impact on the war. The twin-engine Ar 234B-2 production variant had a maximum speed of 461 mph, an operational ceiling of 36,000 feet, and a range of more than 950 miles (while carrying a 2,205-pound BOMB load to half that distance). The improved, four-engine Ar 234 could reach 546 mph.

The Ar 234B-1 reconnaissance version was first flown operationally over France in July 1944; it could carry various combinations of cameras. Later recce flights were flown over Britain. The Ar 234B-2 bomber version became operational in 1945 with bombs carried under the engine nacelles with a maximum load of 4,410 pounds. The first bombing raids were made during the battle of the BULGE in Dec. 1944. Limited by fuel shortages, sporadic bomber missions continued, and in early March intensive Ar 234 strikes were flown against the bridge at REMAGEN. Ar 234 sorties virtually ceased by the end of that month.

The Ardo-built bomber was developed in response to an Air Ministry requirement for a high-speed reconnaissance aircraft. It first flew on June 15, 1943, and entered production the following June. The sixth prototype (Ar 234V-6), which flew on April 8, 1944, had four turbojet engines. There were continuous problems with the jet engines, which had a normal service life of only twenty-five hours.

Several night-fighter variants of the Ar 234 were developed, with two or three crewmen and air-intercept RADAR provided; the Ar 234C was configured to carry and launch a V-1 BUZZ BOMB. In another development, Ar 234s were fitted with a *Deichsels-chlepp* (air trailer) to carry additional fuel.

The basic Ar 234 was a single-place aircraft, with a streamlined fuselage and a high-mounted wing with underslung engine nacelles. The early aircraft were launched with jettisonable trolleys and landed on skids (grass fields being the optimum for landing); subsequently, a nosewheel tricycle landing gear was fitted. Most production aircraft were pressurized for high-altitude flight and had ejection seats for the crew; all aircraft had braking parachutes. The bomber variants had an autopilot so that the pilot could swing the control column clear to use the aircraft's bomb sight.

Some variants had a pair of rear-firing 20-mm cannon to "brush off" chasing fighters. The night fighters were armed with one or two 20-mm forward-firing cannon and some with a ventral pack containing two 30-mm guns.

Ar 240

Developed in Germany as a high-altitude fighter and bomber, the Ar 240 encountered numerous development difficulties. During its six years of development there were several prototypes and evaluation aircraft built, and only some of those fifteen aircraft became operational. The plane was evaluated in the two-seat "heavy" fighter or *Zerstörer* (destroyer) role, night-fighter, high-speed bomber configuration, and as a reconnaissance aircraft.

The first Ardo-built prototype flew in June 1940. When the war ended the plane was still under development, with four prototypes of the still more improved Ar 440 with in-line engines being tested. No series production of either aircraft was ordered.

The Ar 240 was a twin-engine, mid-wing aircraft, with a large glazed canopy for the two-man crew; it had a long, streamlined fuselage with a twin-tail configuration.

Maximum speed for the Ar 240C subseries was 454 mph at 36,700 feet. The planned armament varied considerably: up to eight machine guns or six cannon in fighter variants, with a 4,000-pound BOMB load for the bomber variants.

A.R.4 Guided Missile

This was an Italian attempt to produce a radio-controlled GUIDED MISSILE for attacking heavily defended targets. The A.R. (*Assalto Radioguidato*) was a simple wooden monoplane that was to be taken off by a pilot who would jettison the undercarriage, set the missile on course, and, after radio control was taken over by an accompanying plane, bail out.

(In this regard the project was similar to the U.S. APHRODITE operation.)

Resembling a conventional aircraft, the A.R.4 was powered by a radial engine. It was to be fitted with two 2,205-pound BOMBS, giving the missile a loaded weight of 13,227 pounds. After the undercarriage was dropped, the missile was to achieve a speed of 225 mph.

The first manned test flight was on June 13, 1943. Four additional missiles were completed at the time of the Italian capitulation in Sept. 1943. They were never used in combat.

Arcadia

Code name for U.S.-British WASHINGTON CONFERENCE, Dec. 1941–Jan. 1942.

Arcadia Conference,

see UNITED NATIONS CONFERENCE.

Archangel

Soviet White Sea port that was used as one of the destinations of Allied convoys to the Soviet Union. When Archangel froze over, convoys headed for MURMANSK.

Archery

Code name for British naval raid against Stadlandet, Norway, Dec. 1941.

Ardennes

A wild, craggy plateau in northern France that was the site of major battles in World War I and World War II. In May 1940 German armies launched the major thrust of their FRANCE AND LOW COUNTRIES CAMPAIGN from the Ardennes. And in Dec. 1944, in the last German offensive of the war, troops attacking from the Belgiam region of the Ardennes broke through U.S. lines in the Battle of the Bulge.

The Bulge got its name from the German maneuver that launched the costly battle. German troops and tanks, secretly massed in the Eifel region of western Germany, ripped open the American defensive line and poured through, creating a "bulge" and a potential division of Allied forces.

The battle of the Bulge was the largest fought on the Western Front and the largest ever fought by

American soldiers execute three German "spies"—ages 21, 23, and 24. They were commandos captured during the battle of the Bulge which followed the German Ardennes Offensive. They were wearing U.S. Army uniforms. These were the first of many Germans captured, tried, and executed for that crime. *(U.S. Army via Imperial War Museum)*

the U.S. Army. "Of the 600,000 GIs involved," wrote historian Stephen E. Ambrose in an article on the battle, "almost 20,000 were killed, another 20,000 were captured, and 40,000 were wounded. . . . Two U.S. infantry DIVISIONS were annihilated; in one of them, the 106th, 7,500 men surrendered, the largest mass surrender in the war against Germany."

The battle began on Dec. 16 as warming weather drew a dense mist from the snow that covered a hilly, 50-mile front between Monschau, Germany, and Echternach, Luxembourg—the thinnest edge of the Allied line. Through the fog-drenched forest came the spearhead of fourteen German infantry divisions, backed by five PANZER divisions, including a unit that used U.S. tanks and vehicles to confuse and panic U.S. soldiers.

Many isolated U.S. units were overwhelmed; others began falling back in disorderly retreats. The fog that had helped spring the surprise on the ground also prevented Allied planes from attacking the German columns jamming the narrow roads leading west.

The U.S. forces' confusion in the Ardennes slowly proceeded up the chain of command until it reached Gen. DWIGHT D. EISENHOWER'S headquarters near PARIS. At first Gen. OMAR N. BRADLEY, U.S. 12th ARMY GROUP commander, belittled the German offensive as a "spoiling attack" to slow down the ALLIES' eastward drive for the Rhine and victory in Europe. Others, including Eisenhower, were inclined to take the attack more seriously. British officers, mindful of the 1940 Ardennes breakout, speculated that the Germans had begun a daring attempt to retake Liége and Antwerp, splitting Allied forces and disrupting their supply lines.

Eisenhower ordered reinforcements to the breakthrough point and started looking at more epic moves, for by noon on Dec. 17, his intelligence officers had counted and identified twenty-four German divisions in the Ardennes. "Where in hell has this son-of-a-bitch gotten all his strength?" an incredulous Bradley later asked. The answer was teenagers; an overwhelming number of the German troops slain in the battle were fifteen or sixteen years old, according to historian Ambrose, who checked the grave markers of the Germans who were killed in the battle.

English-speaking Germans, wearing U.S. uniforms and U.S. DOG TAGS, cut telephone wires to disrupt Allied communications. Rumors spread about German hoaxes (including a purported plot to kill Eisenhower). Bewildered GIs suddenly could not trust everyone in a U.S. uniform. The plan to use fake GIs and captured U.S. equipment had been hatched by OTTO SKORZENY, a German officer who specialized in COMMANDO-like operations. The operation was code-named *Greif* (griffin).

Small American units, cut off and attacked by strong German forces, fought gallantly. Cooks, bakers, and clerks grabbed rifles and many, for the first time in their army careers, shot at the enemy. On a ridge that lay athwart the German advance, U.S. infantrymen, outnumbered five to one, turned the Germans southward. The initial 50-mile bulge was shrinking.

But the main line of the breakthrough pressed eastward. One of the German objectives was BASTOGNE, a Belgian town that both Germans and Americans saw as a key road junction. Eisenhower sent the U.S. 101st AIRBORNE DIVISION to Bastogne and the 82nd Airborne Division to Saint-Vith on the northern shoulder of the bulge. To draw on further reinforcements, Eisenhower would have to pull British forces out of the line. Such a move would mean a demand from Field Marshal BERNARD L. MONTGOMERY for control of the Ardennes front.

Bradley, in command of all U.S. ground forces in northwestern Europe, insisted that his own forces could stop the German advance. When Eisenhower agreed to temporarily put two of Bradley's three ARMIES under Montgomery's command, Bradley threatened to resign, a threat he did not carry out.

Soon after the U.S. airborne troops reached Bastogne it was surrounded. Eisenhower, sensing that the German offensive was weakening, wanted a counterattack that was focused on Bastogne. Gen. GEORGE S. PATTON'S Third Army was along the Moselle River, poised for a long-scheduled attack. Eisenhower asked Patton how long it would take him to wheel some 250,000 men and their armor 90 degrees to relieve Bastogne. "Forty-eight hours," Patton replied. He did not reveal that he had already worked out the plans for the incredibly complex maneuver. He needed only to issue the order by telephone to get his troops moving. He did so in a maneuver reminiscent of his dramatic advance in the Army's 1941 LOUISIANA MANUEVERS.

On Dec. 19 word reached Eisenhower that at least 7,500 U.S. troops, cut off from their headquarters, had surrendered. Stragglers entered Bastogne, where, in answer to a demand for surrender, Brig. Gen. ANTHONY C. MCAULIFFE, acting commander of the 101st, uttered the memorable reply, "Nuts!"

Fighting raged in snow and fog along the edge of the bulge. SS troops massacred captured U.S. soldiers at MALMÉDY. U.S. desertions under fire increased to such an extent that Eisenhower set an example for would-be deserters by ordering the execution of Pvt. EDDIE SLOVIK, the first American soldier executed for desertion since the Civil War.

The battle of the Bulge was turning into a nightmare that seemed to have no ending. Some people wondered if Paris would fall or if the Germans would break through to the coast. Then on the night of Dec. 22 clearing weather allowed U.S. planes to bomb and strafe German positions, and drop food and ammunition to besieged Bastogne. Patton's forces raised the siege on Dec 26.

The tide of battle had turned. Eisenhower pressed Montgomery for a counterattack in the north, but Montgomery stalled until he had "tidied up the lines"—his way of saying that he was pulling back U.S. forces that had dented the northern shoulder of the bulge. He finally got a counterattack moving on Jan. 3, flattening the bulge.

The battle ended officially with a Jan. 7 press conference conducted by an arrogant Montgomery, who took full credit for "straightening out" the American problem and winning "possibly one of the most interesting and tricky battles I have ever handled." The GIs, he said, fought well enough—as long as they had good leadership. An infuriated Eisenhower telephoned Prime Minister CHURCHILL, who tried to ease U.S. anger by lavishly praising his U.S. allies for "the greatest American battle of the war."

Bradley sulked, and Patton would not be mollified. If Montgomery had moved quickly enough, Patton said, "We could have bagged the whole German army. I wish Ike were more of a gambler, but he is certainly a lion compared to Monty, and Bradley is better than Ike as far as nerve is concerned. Monty is a tired little fart. War requires taking risks, and he won't take them."

The Ardennes offensive was indeed an American victory—some 30,000 Germans killed, 40,000 wounded, 30,000 PRISONERS OF WAR. It was also a personal defeat for ADOLF HITLER, who had ordered the attack, startling his top commanders. ALBERT SPEER, Minister of Armaments and War Production, heard about the proposed offensive in Oct. 1944. Speer quoted Hitler as saying, "You'll see! It will lead to collapse and panic among the Americans. We'll drive right through their middle and take Antwerp." In reality, Speer wrote, "The failure of the Ardennes offensive meant that the war was over."

Arena

Code name for Allied plan to capture the Ruhr industrial region by a ten-DIVISION AIRBORNE assault, 1945.

Argentina

Capital: Buenos Aires, pop. 12,762,000 (est. 1938). When the European War began, Argentina declared its neutrality while simultaneously anticipating problems stemming from the fact that Germany under diplomatic cover had been organizing Argentina's sizeable German population—about 60,000 Germans and 110,000 people of German descent. Adding to the concern was the existence of a large local Fascist party based on NAZI principles. There were also about 780,000 Argentineans of Italian birth and another 2,200,000 of Italian descent.

A test of Argentina's neutrality came in Dec. 1939 when the German POCKET BATTLESHIP *ADMIRAL GRAF SPEE* was scuttled in Montevideo, Uruguay, where she fled after a running battle with the Royal Navy. Many of the *Graf Spee's* officers and men escaped to Argentina, which interned them only to see most of them escape because of suspiciously lax supervision.

Argentina managed to maintain neutrality while joining the United States in developing Western Hemisphere defenses, keeping England as the leading customer for Argentine beef, negotiating a trade treaty with Japan, and combatting German propaganda.

In 1941 a congressional committee discovered that the local Nazi party, although supposedly dissolved in 1939, was still in existence, formed under German supervision as a military organization, with about 60,000 Nazis living around Buenos Aires. Through Nazi assessments on German residents, the German government was financing a potential subversive threat to the Argentine government. Congress voted to expel the German ambassador but the president of Argentina refused to carry out the resolution.

Argentina's neutrality policy was strained in 1942 by German U-BOAT attacks on two Argentine ships and by the U.S. public assertion that Argentina and Chile, the only Latin American nations that had not broken off relations with the AXIS powers, were serving as ESPIONAGE centers for the Axis. Argentina asked for the evidence, which was provided through the FEDERAL BUREAU OF INVESTIGATION, and thirty-eight persons were subsequently arrested for espionage.

When Chile broke off relations with the Axis on Jan. 1943, Argentina stood alone and U.S. pressure intensified. The emergence of strongman Juan Perón and a Fascist government strained U.S.-Argentine relations, and when the Argentine government arrested people in Buenos Aires celebrating the liberation of PARIS in Aug. 1944, relations reached their nadir. On Sept. 29 President ROOSEVELT denounced Argentina's pro-Axis policy.

Isolated by all members of the UNITED NATIONS and the Pan-American Union, Argentina finally declared war on Germany and Japan on March 27, 1945, and in early April Argentina began rounding up known Axis agents and confiscating Axis properties. U.S. officials privately questioned these eleventh-hour moves, but publicly Argentina was being accepted. The new administration of HARRY S TRUMAN, in contention with the Soviet Union over U.N. membership for Soviet republics, supported Argentina, which finally ratified the U.N. charter on Sept. 8, 1945 and became a somewhat belated U.N. member.

Argonaut

Code name for Allied conferences held at MALTA and YALTA, Jan.–Feb. 1945.

Argument

Code name for U.S. AAF plan for bombing of German factories producing fighter aircraft, Feb. 20–25, 1944; the actual operation was referred to as "Big Week."

Arizona (BB 39)

U.S. BATTLESHIP destroyed in the Japanese attack on PEARL HARBOR. Symbolic of the disaster that befell U.S. forces on Dec. 7, 1941, she was one of seven battleships moored along the eastern side of FORD ISLAND in the center of Pearl Harbor. (The eighth battleship at the base was in a dry dock of the nearby navy yard.)

The *Arizona* was moored alongside the repair ship *Vestal* (AR 4) when the Japanese carrier-based bombers struck. About 8:10 A.M. a 1,760-pound armor-piercing BOMB, released by Petty Officer Noburo Kanai in a B5N KATE bomber, struck near the *Arizona*'s No. 2 14-inch gun turret, penetrated to the magazine beneath the turret, and detonated. The forward portion of the ship exploded, killing 1,104 Navy and Marine officers and enlisted men, including Rear Adm. Isaac C. Kidd, Commander Battleship DIVISION 1, and the ship's commanding officer, Capt. F. Van Valkenburgh (both of whom were posthumously awarded the MEDAL OF HONOR as was the senior surviving officer of the ship, Lt. Comdr. S. G. Fuqua).

The ship may also have been struck by one or two aerial TORPEDOES and several other bombs. She was a total loss. Her destruction—with the highest death toll of any single warship loss in U.S. naval history—became a rallying cry for Americans in World War II.

The sunken ship's superstructure and gun turrets were later cut away, and a memorial has been erected above her remains. Hundreds of bodies are still interred within her twisted steel hull. Every day the national colors are raised, as if the *Arizona* were still in commission.

The *Arizona* had been launched on June 19, 1915, and placed in commission the following year.

The ship remained in U.S. waters during World War I. Subsequently, during two decades of peacetime cruising she sailed to Europe, the Mediterranean, and Caribbean, and carried out exercises off both the U.S. Atlantic and Pacific coasts. She was permanently assigned to Pearl Harbor in April 1941.

With a standard displacement of 32,600 tons and an overall length of 608 feet, the *Arizona* had a main battery of twelve 14-inch guns. Steam turbines could drive her at 21 knots. The ship was rebuilt and modernized in 1929–1931.

(The repair ship *Vestal*, moored alongside the *Arizona*, suffered two bomb hits early in the attack and a torpedo passed under her to detonate against the battleship. When the *Arizona* exploded, men were blown off the decks of the *Vestal*, including her commanding officer, who immediately swam back aboard. The repair ship got underway and survived the damage, and the war.)

Ark Royal

The most famous British aircraft carrier of the war, the *Ark Royal* had a brief but eventful career. She was the first British carrier of "modern" (post–World War I) design, joining the fleet in 1938.

When the EUROPEAN WAR began in Sept. 1939, the *Ark Royal* was sent out on antisubmarine patrol to hunt U-BOATS, but after the sinking of the carrier *Courageous* the "Ark" was withdrawn from that role. During the next two years the carrier operated in the Norwegian Sea, sped to the South Atlantic in search of the German POCKET BATTLESHIP *ADMIRAL GRAF SPEE,* and then operated again in British and Norwegian waters. Off Norway in April 1941 she opposed the German landings of the DENMARK AND NORWAY CAMPAIGN. Her SKUA fighter-bombers, flying from an airfield at Scapa Flow in the Orkney Islands, flew a 660-mile round trip to sink the German light cruiser *Königsberg* in Norwegian waters. On several occasions the Luftwaffe reported to have sunk the "Ark."

In June 1941 the *Ark Royal* entered the Mediterranean and took part in the attacks on French warships in North Africa. Afterwards, the ship operated against the Italian Navy and Air Force, and escorted CONVOYS to MALTA. On the morning of Nov. 13, 1941, while returning to "Gib" after flying off RAF

HURRICANE fighters for Malta, the carrier was struck by one of three TORPEDOES fired by the German *U-81*.

Soon the carrier was able to recover her electrical power, control the flooding, and set course for Gibraltar. Only one man had been killed in the explosion, but most of her crew was taken off by escorting ships. Unseen by her skeleton crew, water was pushing into the ship through bulkheads and joints weakened by the torpedo explosion. Electric power and steam were lost again and the ship started to settle. Efforts to save the ship failed and early the next morning, as her remaining crew members were taken off, the carrier sank, just 25 miles from Gibraltar and safety.

The *Ark Royal* had been launched in 1937. She displaced 22,000 tons at standard displacement, was 800 feet long, and had steam turbines that could propel her at 31.5 knots. Unlike later British fleet carriers, the *Ark Royal* did not have armor. She normally embarked some sixty aircraft; when war began in Sept. 1939 the *Ark Royal* was assigned eighteen Skua fighter-bombers and forty-two SWORDFISH torpedo planes.

By contemporary standards she had a heavy antiaircraft armament: sixteen 4.5-inch guns, six 8-barrel "pom-poms," and thirty-two .50-cal. machine guns. At the start of the European War it was British practice when threatened by enemy aircraft to stow all planes below deck, in the hangar, and rely on antiaircraft guns for defense.

Armed Guards

U.S. Navy personnel placed on board merchant ships to man defensive guns; also called Naval Armed Guards. This protective measure was authorized by Congress on Nov. 17, 1941. The guns, it was hoped, would deter German U-BOATS, which normally attacked unescorted merchant ships on the surface, where they had maximum speed and maneuverability. Even after CONVOYS were established, the large number of merchant ships sailing independently—all those capable of speeds of 14.5 knots or more—required defensive armament.

The first ship to be so protected was the SS *Dunboyne*, which was provided with several .50-cal. machine guns and a seven-man Navy detachment under command of a petty officer. She sailed for MURMANSK in early Dec. 1941. By the end of the year the Navy had provided fourteen merchant ships with Armed Guard crews. In early 1942 the Navy decided to provide Armed Guards to British transports carrying American troops.

By the end of 1942 there were Armed Guards on 1,000 U.S. merchant ships and a few foreign ships, mostly American-owned flying the flag of Panama. More foreign-flag ships followed as they increasingly carried a large burden of the matériel being sent to the fighting fronts.

Most Armed Guard crews were commanded by a lieutenant or ensign in the naval reserve and consisted of twelve to fifteen sailors; later this was increased to as many as twenty-seven men as more guns were provided. Few of the enlisted men or officers had been to sea before they reported to their ship, as experienced sailors were needed for warships. In some ships, merchant seamen assisted in manning the guns, usually by passing ammunition. Runs to Murmansk and other Soviet ports and to the Mediterranean often required the Armed Guards to remain at their guns around the clock for two, three, or even four days at a time.

There was frequent friction between the sailors and merchant seamen. The civilians received considerably more pay for making the same voyage and being exposed to the same dangers; but there was also teamwork and good feeling. Many merchant skippers sent heartfelt letters of appreciation to the Navy after their gunners had brought them through an air or submarine attack.

A variety of guns were fitted to merchant ships: 5-inch guns for use against surface ships, 3-inch and the standard 20-mm OERLIKON cannon for use against aircraft, as well as .50-cal. machine guns until there were enough of the "20s" to go around.

Army

Military combat organization (field army) comprised of several CORPS and DIVISIONS plus headquarters and supporting units. A U.S. army was nominally commanded by a lieutenant general or full general.

During World War II the U.S. Army had nine field armies in war theaters; those armies and their commanders were:

EUROPE	First Army	Lt. Gen. George Grunert	Oct. 1943–Mar. 1944
		Gen. OMAR N. BRADLEY	Mar. 1944–Aug. 1944
		Gen. COURTNEY HODGES	Aug. 1944–May 1945
	Third Army	Lt. Gen. Courtney Hodges	Feb. 1943–Mar. 1944
		Gen. GEORGE S. PATTON	Mar. 1944–May 1945
	Fifth Army	Lt. Gen. MARK W. CLARK	Jan. 1944–Dec. 1944
		Lt. Gen. LUCIAN K. TRUSCOTT	Dec. 1944–May 1945
	Seventh Army	Lt. Gen. George S. Patton	July 1943–Jan. 1944
		Lt. Gen. Mark W. Clark	Jan. 1944–Mar. 1944
		Lt. Gen. ALEXANDER M. PATCH	Mar. 1944–May 1945
	Ninth Army	Lt. Gen. WILLIAM H. SIMPSON	May 1944–May 1945
	Fifteenth Army	Maj. Gen. Ray E. Porter	Jan. 1945
		Lt. Gen. Leonard T. Gerow	Jan. 1945–May 1945
PACIFIC	Sixth Army	Gen. WALTER E. KRUEGER	Feb. 1943–Sept. 1945
	Eighth Army	Lt. Gen. ROBERT L. EICHELBERGER	Sept. 1944–Sept. 1945
	Tenth Army	Lt. Gen. SIMON B. BUCKNER*	June 1944–June 1945
		Gen. JOSEPH W. STILWELL	June 1945–Sept. 1945

*Killed in action on June 18, 1945.

At the time of the NORMANDY INVASION in June 1944, Gen. Bradley entered France as commander of the U.S. First Army. On Aug. 1, 1944, Bradley's 1st ARMY GROUP was activated in France and immediately redesignated as the U.S. 12th Army Group to control (under Bradley) all U.S. ground forces in northwestern Europe. Also on Aug. 1 the Third Army became operational under Gen. Patton. (Command of the First Army passed to Gen. Hodges.)

In addition, there was an Anglo-American AIRBORNE ARMY.

(See also UNITED STATES, ARMY.)

Army Air Corps

Designation of U.S. Army's aviation component from 1926 to 1941. The Army Air Forces (AAF) was established on June 20, 1941. Maj. Gen. H. H. (HAP) ARNOLD was named chief, Army Air Forces, reporting to the Army's Chief of Staff, Gen. GEORGE C. MARSHALL. (See UNITED STATES, AIR FORCE.)

Army General Classification Test

The basic aptitude test given to inductees and Army enlistees. The GCT, as it was generally known, replaced the "Army alpha" of World War I and was given to literate inductees beginning in Oct. 1940. (Recruits were initially given a literacy test and a visual classification test. At first, SELEC-TIVE SERVICE rejected illiterates.) Although usually thought of as an intelligence test, the AGCT examined general learning, covering vocabulary, arithmetic, and block-arrangement reckoning. Recruits were classified into five groups according to test results; the higher the group assigned, the better chance the recruit had to receive specialized or technical training. The highest possible score was 163; candidates for officer training had to score at least 110. The test glaringly revealed the educational variance between whites and blacks. In one sampling, for example, 77.8 percent of the black inductees made low-group scores, compared to 29.1 percent of the white inductees. (See also SEGREGATION.)

Army Group

U.S. Army command established in Europe for controlling large troop formations. Army Groups directed ARMIES and separate units and were used by the U.S. Army only in World War II.

The first U.S. force to serve within an Army Group was the II CORPS under Lt. Gen. GEORGE S. PATTON in the Tunisian aspect of the NORTH AFRICA CAMPAIGN. In Jan. 1943 the Allied forces commander, Lt. Gen. DWIGHT D. EISENHOWER, placed all Allied ground forces in the drive against surviving German and Italian forces in Tunisia under the British 18th Army Group commanded by Lt. Gen. KENNETH ANDERSON.

Eisenhower in Feb. 1943 directed Gen. HAROLD

ALEXANDER, who had succeeded Anderson as commander of the 18th Army Group that month, to plan and coordinate the subsequent Allied invasion of SICILY. That designation was changed to 15th Army Group shortly before the landings—the new designation derived from adding the U.S. Seventh Army to the British Eighth Army.

Following the Allied landings in Italy in Sept. 1943, the 15th Army Group under Alexander commanded Anglo-American ground forces until Dec. 1944, when U.S. Gen. MARK W. CLARK took command of the Army Group (with Alexander replacing Gen. Dwight D. Eisenhower as theater commander in the Mediterranean).

In the fall of 1943, Lt. Gen. OMAR N. BRADLEY was directed to establish both the 1st U.S. Army Group (FUSAG) and the First U.S. Army in England. Their headquarters were separate, with the planning staff for the Army Group located at Bryanston Square, LONDON, and for the Army at Clifton College, Bristol. From Dec. 1943 through the NORMANDY INVASION all Allied ground forces were commanded by the British 21st Army Group under Gen. BERNARD MONTGOMERY who was designated as the overall Allied ground forces commander until a U.S. Army Group was established in France. Bradley entered France in June 1944 as commander of the U.S. First Army. On Aug. 1, 1944, Bradley's 1st Army Group was activated but immediately redesignated as the U.S. 12th Army Group as he took command of all U.S. ground forces in northwestern Europe. (Significantly large American forces, however, would serve under the 21st Army Group at various times because of the British manpower shortage.)

The 1st U.S. Army Group continued to exist as a diversionary force in England to make the Germans believe that a further Allied landing would take place in Europe. The "paper" 1st Army Group was commanded by Gen. LESLEY J. MCNAIR until his accidental death in France from an Allied bombing attack on July 25, 1944; he was replaced by Lt. Gen. John L. DeWitt, although the 1st Army Group was abolished a short time later.

For the Allied landings in southern France in Aug. 1944 the U.S. 6th Army Group was established under U.S. Gen. JACOB L. DEVERS.

The size of the staffs and headquarters of Army Groups varied greatly; at the end of the war the headquarters of Bradley's 12th Army Group had more than 900 officers assigned (more officers than in a U.S. DIVISION) plus many hundreds of enlisted men. At that time the 12th Army Group consisted of four Armies with ten corps and forty-three divisions. With more than 1.25 million men, it was the largest U.S. field combat organization in history.

The British, German, and Soviet armies also had Army Groups, the last being designated as *fronts*.

Principal Army Group components were:

ARMY GROUP	LOCATION	MAJOR COMPONENTS
6th Army Group	France (1944–1945)	U.S. Seventh Army French First Army
12th Army Group	France-Germany (1944–1945)	U.S. First Army U.S. Third Army U.S. Ninth Army U.S. Fifteenth Army
15th Army Group	Sicily (1943)	U.S. Seventh Army British Eighth Army
	Italy (1943–1945)	U.S. Fifth Army British Eighth Army
18th Army Group	Tunisia (1943)	British First Army British Eighth Army U.S. II Corps
21st Army Group	France-Holland-Germany (1944–1945)	U.S. Third Army* British Second Army Canadian First Army

*Assigned to the U.S. 12th Army Group when that organization was established in France on Aug. 1, 1944.

Arnhem

A Dutch town with bridges over the Rhine River, objectives of the British 1st AIRBORNE DIVISION in Sept. 1944 in Operation MARKET-GARDEN. The plan was conceived by Field Marshal BERNARD L. MONTGOMERY, who saw it as a way to make "a powerful full-blooded thrust to the heart of Germany."

The plan depended upon the seizure of several bridges by airborne forces. The problems began as soon as parachute troops and GLIDERS began landing at Arnhem on Sept. 17. Delays in dropping their equipment hindered them, as did mistakes in locating the dropping zones and faulty intelligence about German forces.

Poor weather and bad communications added to

the confusion as the British troops fought their way to the bridges. German defenders destroyed the railroad bridge and held the southern end of the road bridge. The British troops battled to hold the northern end, but overwhelming German forces forced them to give way.

Maj. Gen. R. E. Urquhart, the division commander, sent a message to Montgomery: "All will be ordered to break out rather than surrender." On Sept. 25, when it was clear that no relief could reach them, the breakout toward Allied lines began. About 10,300 British and Polish airborne troops fought at Arnhem; fewer than 2,900 escaped death, wounds, or capture.

In a speech in the House of Commons commemorating the paratroopers' courage, Prime Minister CHURCHILL said, " 'Not in vain' may be the pride of those who survived and the epitaph of those who fell."

Claims were made in postwar accounts of Market-Garden that Christiaan Lindemans, a Dutch resistance leader, betrayed the operation and alerted the Germans to the parachute drop at Arnhem. Although Lindemans did turn out to be a double agent working for the Germans, "he was never in a position to betray Arnhem, even if he might have wanted to, or even if he thought he actually had." That is the conclusion in *A Thread of Deceit,* an analysis of wartime ESPIONAGE myths written by Rupert Allason, a Conservative Member of Parliament and authority on British intelligence who writes under the pseudonym Nigel West. (Lindemans, known as "King Kong" because of his size, committed suicide in July 1946 while in Dutch custody.)

Arnhem was liberated on April 15, 1945.

Arnold, Gen. of the Army Henry H. (1886–1950)

Chief of the U.S. ARMY AIR CORPS from Sept. 1938 to June 1941, and subsequently Chief of the Army Air Forces until the end of the war.

"Hap" Arnold was one of the first pilots in the U.S. Signal Corps, getting his wings in 1911 after being personally instructed by one of the Wright brothers. During World War I he directed Army aviation training. Between the world wars Arnold became a convert to Gen. William (Billy) Mitchell's belief in the need for an independent strategic bomber force that would reduce or eliminate the need for ground forces. Arnold, however, managed to avoid the opprobrium that Mitchell's public statements eventually earned him. This typified Arnold's style, whose genial demeanor did not denote either inefficiency or political naiveté.

Soon after his appointment as chief of the Air Corps with the rank of major general, Arnold began cajoling U.S. aircraft manufacturers into increasing production, and civilian flying schools into expanding their facilities on the strength of his assurance that funding would soon be available. In the spring of 1941 Arnold went to England to exchange airpower ideas with senior British air officers.

With the creation of the Army Air Forces in 1941 the U.S. military air service's independence became more pronounced. In 1942 Arnold, a lieutenant general and subordinate to the Army's Chief of Staff, Gen. GEORGE C. MARSHALL, was accorded a seat on the U.S. JOINT CHIEFS OF STAFF so that he could equate to Britain's Chief of Air Staff, further enhancing the status and semi-independence of the AAF. Arnold formed alliances with leading RAF officers, notably those who favored STRATEGIC BOMBING independent of the ground force campaigns. Arnold was less successful in his relations with the U.S. Navy and Royal Navy, which had operational control of the RAF Coastal Command, as those services competed with the AAF for four-engine bomber production, principally the B-24 LIBERATOR, which was a highly effective antisubmarine aircraft.

The effects of Arnold's view of air power, especially the degree to which strategic bombing helped to win the war in Europe, remain the subject of debate. For the strategic bombing offensive against Japan, Arnold created the Twentieth AIR FORCE, which was directly answerable to him; they flew new B-29 SUPERFORTRESS bombers. Arnold planned to demonstrate unequivocally the power of strategic bombing to end a war without a ground invasion. The Japanese SURRENDER after the TOKYO fire raids and the dropping of the ATOMIC BOMB were cited by air-power advocates as proof of Arnold's theory. Whatever the ultimate worth of air power in World War II, Arnold's direction of the AAF and his advocacy of a separate air arm made the establishment of the postwar separate Air Force unstoppable.

Arnold retired in March 1946 and was commissioned a five-star general of the Air Force in 1949. (He had been one of seven U.S. officers given FIVE-STAR RANK during the war—general of the Army; when the separate U.S. Air Force was established after the war its leaders felt that their founding father should be given a distinctive air service rank—the only five-star rank in that service's history.)

Arrow,

see G-50.

Artificial Harbors

Protective breakwaters and piers erected at the NORMANDY INVASION to permit the rapid unloading of vehicles and supplies. The size of the Allied invasion force and the quantity of vehicles, munitions, and provisions for this force in sustained conflict were considerable.

Anglo-American invasion planners expected that it would be at least several weeks before a major port could be captured. Proposals for simple causeways and pontoon-type piers were impractical because of the exceptional spring tides—as much as 24 feet—and expected storms for that time of year. In addition, any scheme for piers and breakwaters had to be mobile, so that the components could be towed from England to the beachheads, easily assembled in a short time, and able to withstand heavy weather. Further, in view of the size of the assault, each of the two planned harbors would be about the size of Gibraltar.

After considering and evaluating a variety of concepts, the Royal Navy developed the Mulberry harbor concept as designed by Commo. John Hughes-Hallett, who had been involved with earlier AMPHIBIOUS LANDINGS. (WINSTON CHURCHILL had expressed specific ideas on this problem during World War I and again early in World War II.) Of the scheme, the official U.S. Army history said, "While their solution was in a sense an obvious one, it was at the same time as unconventional and daring in its conception as any in the annals of military operations."

Each Mulberry harbor had breakwaters consisting of sunken merchant ships and huge concrete caissons, dubbed Phoenix units. After being towed to their proper position the ships and concrete caissons were flooded and sunk. Floating piers several hundred yards long—called Whales—were then installed for ships to come alongside to unload, with trucks carrying their cargo ashore. These floating Whales were on fixed "legs," to permit them to rise and fall with the tides. Mulberry A was installed at St. Laurent to support the American beachhead and Mulberry B at Arromanches for the British landings.

Another sixty unneeded ships were sunk to provide shallow-water shelters to protect the smaller landing craft from rough seas while they were unloading larger ships, and when they were at rest. The old British battleship *Centurion,* the French battleship *Courbet,* the British cruiser *Durban,* the Dutch cruiser *Sumatra,* and a number of merchant ships were sunk as the blockships for these harbors. The ships were given the code name Corncobs and a complete harbor was labeled Gooseberry.

Some of the components of the Mulberry and Gooseberry projects began their tow from British ports six days before the invasion. By June 18, less than two weeks after the assault, the daily cargo moving across Mulberry A onto the OMAHA-UTAH beaches was averaging about 14,500 tons. That night, the Normandy beachhead was struck by a major storm that lasted until June 22. The winds and high seas destroyed Mulberry A off Omaha beach and damaged the British Mulberry. Scores of ships and hundreds of landing craft were sunk or damaged, and an American DIVISION that was forced to wait out the storm aboard ship eventually came ashore sick and exhausted. Loss of the Mulberry harbors temporarily disrupted the flow of supplies. The wrecked American Mulberry was abandoned. The British one was repaired with components from Mulberry A, and material continued to come across the beaches at increasing rates.

Artillery

Artillery was—with infantry and armored forces—one of the three principal combat arms of ground forces during the war. The U.S. Army and Marine Corps had field artillery, antiaircraft artillery, and coastal artillery units during the war.

The basic artillery unit was the firing BATTERY, consisting normally of four or six guns or howitzers. Three or four firing batteries formed a BATTALION. In addition, battalions had a headquarters and service battery. Three or four artillery battalions were usually assigned to each Army and Marine DIVISION. Additional artillery battalions were provided at the CORPS and ARMY levels, to reinforce divisional artillery as required.

Field Artillery U.S. Army infantry divisions had four field artillery battalions: three with 105-mm towed howitzers (twelve or, after 1943, eighteen guns per battalion) and one with 155-mm towed howitzers (twelve guns); armored divisions had three battalions of 105-mm self-propelled howitzers (eighteen guns per battalion); and an AIRBORNE division had one parachute artillery battalion with 75-mm pack howitzers (sixteen guns) and one or two GLIDER artillery battalions with 75-mm howitzers (twelve each). Within Army divisions the artillery was grouped as "divarty," and not structured in a REGIMENT or BRIGADE, as in other armies.

Antitank guns, ANTIAIRCRAFT WEAPONS, and ROCKET launchers were in separate units, apart from the artillery battalions.

Marine Corps divisions did have an artillery regiment with four battalions: two with 75-mm pack howitzers and two with 105-mm towed howitzers. Marines—and Army units in AMPHIBIOUS LANDINGS—usually had warships standing offshore to provide initial gunfire support.

When working together, Army and Marine units in the Pacific in 1944–1945 were able to easily coordinate and even exchange artillery. For example, within a week of landing on OKINAWA five battalions of Marine corps-level 155-mm howitzers and guns were assigned to the Army's XXIV Corps. Similarly, later in the battle for Okinawa 105-mm and 155-mm howitzers of the Army's 27th Infantry Division were under the operational control of the Marine's III Amphibious Corps. On one occasion in the battle the 1st Marine Division had twenty-two battalions of artillery ranging from 75-mm pack howitzers to 8-inch howitzers under its control.

The 75-mm pack howitzer was the smallest howitzer in regular Army and Marine service. It was highly accurate but fired a small shell—14.6 pounds with a maximum range of 9,760 yards. The "75,"

however, could be easily manhandled, broken down to be carried in pieces, and could be easily brought ashore in LANDING CRAFT, AMPHIBIOUS TRACTORS, or DUKW amphibious trucks.

The 105-mm howitzer was the most widely used U.S. artillery piece. It was rugged, could be towed by a variety of trucks, and fired a 33-pound shell with a range of 12,500 yards.

The largest artillery piece normally found in Army divisions was the 155-mm towed howitzer. This weapon fired a 95-pound shell with a maximum range of 12,300 yards, increased to 16,000 yards in later models.

At the corps level were 8-inch howitzers (200-pound shell, 18,500 yards), 8-inch guns (240-pound shell, 35,000 yards), and 240-mm howitzers (360-pound shell, 25,170 yards). There were self-propelled (tracked) versions of the 75-mm, 105-mm, and 155-mm howitzers, which were used by U.S. forces.

In combat, U.S. artillery was generally highly effective. American military historian Russell F. Weigley wrote, "From the time American divisions first entered the Second World War against Germany in 1942, the same Germans who disparaged American infantry consistently praised American artillery." In his classic volume *Eisenhower's Lieutenants,* Weigley explained: "Part of the reason for a good artillery showing from the beginning was that battlefield experience counts less among the guns than in infantry or armor. Artillerymen largely do the same thing in combat that they have done all through their training—laying down fire on targets they do not see. In addition, exceptional communications equipment permitted American artillerymen to excel in the ability of a single forward observer—often flying in a Piper or Stinson liaison plane—to request and receive the fires of all the batteries within range of a target in a single concentrated barrage. The American guns specialized in 'TOT'—time on target—concentrations of multiple batteries, or even of numerous battalions, upon designated targets for designated periods of time."

The major problem of U.S. artillery during the war was movement—there were never sufficient trucks or "prime movers" to move the big guns, and never enough trucks to keep up with the demands for moving ammunition. Also, in the first six months after the NORMANDY INVASION there were insufficient port facilities to unload the massive amounts of ammunition required by the Allied armies. To overcome ammunition shortages, in the Oct. 1944 fighting around the city of Metz, the Army's XX Corps used captured 155-mm German ammunition as well as captured 88-mm and 105-mm howitzers, and even 76.2-mm guns that the Germans had captured earlier from the Soviets. At one point ammunition was so critical in the XX Corps that the corps artillery commander forbade the use of artillery except for repelling attacks that endangered U.S. positions, counterbattery fire against active enemy guns, and observed fire against the most important German targets. U.S. Third Army records report that from Oct. 11 to Nov. 7, 1944, total expenditure of all artillery was 76,325 rounds—less than that command would fire in a *single day* in the battle of the BULGE in Dec. 1944.

U.S. commanders also employed TANK and TANK DESTROYER guns to compensate for artillery shortfalls, especially in Marine units fighting on Pacific islands.

Foreign military forces used larger artillery during the war. The largest gun ever built was the German KARL GUSTAV of 800-mm (31.5-inch) diameter; the longest-range guns to see action were the German SUPER GUNS.

Coast Artillery The Army and Marine Corps both operated coast artillery guns during the war. The Army had a Coast Artillery branch (which survived until 1950, when it was merged with field artillery). The Army weapons were for the most part permanently emplaced, at coastal fortifications along the U.S. coast, in HAWAII, and in Manila Bay in the Philippines. The last included an impressive array of artillery on the island of CORREGIDOR and adjacent islands:

12	14-inch guns
10	12-inch guns
2	10-inch guns
6	6-inch guns
24	155-mm howitzers
48	75-mm rapid-fire guns
various	antiaircraft guns

Most of these weapons were on Corregidor, with the 14-inch guns on the islands of Carabao, Caballo, and Fort Drum.

Some of these weapons dated back to before World War I. The most effective were the four 12-inch guns on Corregidor; they fired a 700-pound shell with a range of 29,500 yards. The guns could fire upon ships entering Manila Harbor or troops approaching the bay from the land side. Unfortunately, virtually all of these guns were highly vulnerable to air attack.

Adjacent to Corregidor was Fort Drum, a rock that had been encased in concrete to resemble a stationary BATTLESHIP. (A ship-like cage mast was also fitted.) Fort Drum mounted four 14-inch guns, in two ship-like revolving steel turrets, plus four 6-inch guns in casements. With the tide moving past Fort Drum giving the illusion of movement, it often looked like a real "concrete battleship," as it was promptly dubbed.

While these weapons cost the attacking Japanese many casualties, they soon fell silent under heavy Japanese air attack and fire from Japanese batteries on the mainland.

At two other locations U.S. coastal defense artillery engaged the Japanese early in the war. These were Marine batteries, operated by Marine Defense Battalions. At WAKE Island in the mid-Pacific the Marines had six 5-inch coastal defense guns (plus twelve 3-inch antiaircraft guns, plus machine guns). The guns came into action on Dec. 11, 1941, as a Japanese landing force approached the atoll. Well-laid fire from the guns sank the Japanese destroyer *Hayate* and damaged several other ships, including a light cruiser. The unfortunate *Hayate* was the first Japanese warship (other than minesweepers) to be sunk in the war. But the defenders were too few, and too poorly armed, and the Japanese overran the sandspit on Dec. 23.

Midway Island had also been fortified by the Marines prior to the Japanese attack on PEARL HARBOR. Here the Marine 6th Defense Battalion and other Marine and Navy defenders were taken under fire on the night of Dec. 7, 1941, by a pair of Japanese destroyers. The Marines responded with 5-inch gunfire and are believed to have heavily damaged one of the destroyers, which was able to withdraw. During the war Midway was shelled by Japanese submarines, but never again by surface ships (although such a bombardment was planned for early June 1942, in preparation for a major Japanese landing; see battle of MIDWAY.)

Antiaircraft Artillery See ANTIAIRCRAFT WEAPONS.

Asdic

British term for acoustic detection equipment (see SONAR). The British Admiralty coined the term "asdic" during World War I. The first known reference appeared in a report dated July 6, 1918.

There is considerable confusion over the origins of this term. After WINSTON CHURCHILL used the term in the House of Commons in Dec. 1939, the Admiralty advised that the word was an acronym for *A*llied *S*ubmarine *D*etection *I*nvestigation Committee, "a body which was formed during the war of 1914–1918, and which organized much research and experiment for the detection of submarines." However, no committee bearing this name has been found in the Admiralty archives. The term has also been cited as indicating *A*nti-*S*ubmarine *D*ivision, the Admiralty department that sponsored antisubmarine research in World War II.

Ashcan

(1) slang for DEPTH CHARGE; (2) code name for Allied detention centers for senior German officials.

Ashworth, Comdr. Frederick L. (1912—)

Weapons officer for the ATOMIC BOMB dropped on NAGASAKI. A 1933 graduate of the Naval Academy, Ashworth served in surface ships before becoming a Navy pilot. In 1942 he went to the South Pacific to command a TBF AVENGER bomber SQUADRON flying combat missions against Japanese ships from the airstrip at GUADALCANAL. In Aug. 1943 he became aviation staff officer for amphibious planners in the Central Pacific until mid-1944.

After serving briefly in Navy ordnance projects, in Nov. 1944 he was assigned to the LOS ALAMOS laboratory to work on the development of the atomic bomb. After working on the bomb, he was sent to TINIAN as a representative of Maj. Gen. LESLEY GROVES and on Aug. 9, 1945, flew as the weapons officer in the B-29 SUPERFORTRESS carrying the Nagasaki bomb.

Ashworth was responsible for arming the weapon after the plane took off from Tinian. When the primary target, Kokura, was found closed in by weather, he participated in the decision to attack Nagasaki. Ashworth was awarded the Legion of Merit by the AAF and the Silver Star by the Navy for his role in that attack.

After the war he participated in the 1946 ATOMIC BOMB TESTS at Bikini and was a senior U.S. nuclear weapons planner. He also commanded the second Navy squadron capable of delivering nuclear weapons. Later, he commanded an aircraft carrier. Ashworth retired in 1968 with the rank of vice admiral.

Aspidistra

Secret British communications station in England.

Assassinations

Deliberate killing of key military and political leaders was relatively rare during the war. While several assassinations were contemplated or even plotted, few succeeded. Two major assassinations that were successfully carried out:

REINHARD HEYDRICH, chief of the REICH CENTRAL SECURITY OFFICE, deputy protector of Czechoslovakia, was attacked by two Czech agents trained and equipped in England. On May 27, 1942, the agents ambushed Heydrich's car, firing at him and his bodyguard and rolling a bomb under the car. The bomb may have contained germs in an attempt at "biological assassination." Heydrich died, apparently of infection, on June 4. His death set off such a spasm of retribution that it may have lessened Allied interest in assassination attempts on NAZI leaders. (See LIDICE.)

Adm. ISOROKU YAMAMOTO, Commander in Chief of the Japanese Combined FLEET, who conceived the attack on PEARL HARBOR, was killed on April 18, 1943. While Yamamoto was on a tour of forward bases in the Pacific, U.S. intelligence decoded a report of his itinerary. A flight of U.S. AAF P-38 LIGHTNING fighters intercepted the bomber in which he was flying and shot it down. Despite reports that Yamamoto's assassination had been approved by President ROOSEVELT or Secretary of the Navy FRANK KNOX, there is absolutely no evidence that the issue was raised in WASHINGTON. Rather, the decision was made at Pearl Harbor by Adm. CHESTER W. NIMITZ, Commander in Chief Pacific Fleet.

Other assassinations of the era:

- King Boris III, Czar of Bulgaria and friend of HITLER, was shot by an anti-Nazi, pro-Soviet gunman on Aug. 28, 1943.
- President of Bolivia, pro-AXIS Lt. Col. Germán Busch, died of gunshot wounds in Aug. 1939, in a death officially reported to be suicide.
- Rumanian Prime Minister Armand Călinescu, on a Bucharest street on Sept. 21, 1939, by the Fascist Iron Guard.
- French Adm. JEAN DARLAN, commander of FREE FRENCH forces in North Africa, on Dec. 24, 1942, by a young gunman, Bonnier de la Chapelle, long afterward identified as a monarchist and a supporter of Gen. CHARLES DE GAULLE.
- Egyptian Prime Minister Ahmed Maher Pasha, on Feb. 24, 1945, after announcing Egypt's declaration of war on Germany, by a young pro-Fascist.
- ERNST RÖHM, early supporter of HITLER and organizer of the SA storm troopers. On the night of June 30, 1934—the Night of the Long Knives, as it came to be called by the Nazis—Hitler launched the Blood Purge in which Röhm was assassinated, along with the leadership of the SA.
- Syrian leader Abdur-rahman Shahbandar killed in July 1940 by religious zealots.
- Iraq's Kurdish Gen. Bekr Sidqi, who seized power by military revolt in 1936, shot on Aug. 16, 1937, by a fellow Kurd.

Anti-Hitler cliques, primarily in the senior military leadership, planned several attempts on Hitler's life. But only one, a bombing, came close to succeeding. (See JULY 20 PLOT.)

There is evidence that Gen. DWIGHT D. EISENHOWER was targeted for assassination. Although never definitively confirmed, reports in Dec. 1944—during the battle of the BULGE—teams of fifty English-speaking Germans, in U.S. uniforms, parachuted into the PARIS area on a mission to assassinate Eisenhower and other high-ranking Allied officers. Extra security was ordered. The plan, which apparently was never carried out, was attributed to OTTO SKORZENY, the leader of several COMMANDO-type operations (such as the rescue of BENITO MUSSOLINI). The code name of the operation was reportedly *Greif.*

In Libya on Nov. 17, 1941, Lt. Col. GEOFFREY KEYES led a British commando raid on the headquarters of Gen. ERWIN ROMMEL in the hopes of killing him. Rommel was at a birthday party elsewhere. Keyes, killed in the poorly planned raid, was posthumously awarded the VICTORIA CROSS.

Assassination was always a possible solution to political problems in Japan as military and nonmilitary politicians jockeyed for position. Japanese Premier Yuko Hamaguchi was shot in a TOKYO railroad station by a member of the right-wing Love of Country Association, in Nov. 1930. In mid-1940 a branch of the Japanese secret police plotted to kill political officials who favored friendship with the United States. And, according to some Japanese sources, Isoroku Yamamoto was made Commander in Chief of the Combined Fleet to remove him from Tokyo and keep him safe from assassination at that time.

Aster

German code name for withdrawal of troops from Baltic states.

ASWORG

The U.S. Navy's Anti-Submarine Warfare OPERATIONS RESEARCH Group was established within the National Defense Research Committee on April 1, 1942, to analyze the effectiveness of antisubmarine tactics, sensors, and weapons. Their analysis provided the operating forces with data on such problems as the most effective size of CONVOYS, attack tactics, the use of different weapons and sensors, etc. ASWORG analysis, for example, demonstrated that a ship's chance of being sunk in a ninety-ship convoy with nine escorts was about one tenth that of being sunk in a thirty-ship convoy with three escorts.

The ASWORG provided about 100 civilian scientists to serve as the analytical staff of the U.S. Tenth FLEET.

ASWORG was directed throughout the war by P. M. Morse, formerly with the Massachusetts Institute of Technology. It was the idea of Capt. Wilder D. Baker, on the staff of Adm. ERNEST J. KING, Commander in Chief U.S. Fleet and Chief of Naval Operations.

AT-6 Texan

The most widely flown U.S. advanced trainer and a highly versatile aircraft. The aircraft served from

1938 in the RAF as the Harvard, and from 1941 in the U.S. Army and Navy (designated SNJ in the latter service). It remained in service throughout the war.

The North American–built AT-6 evolved from the firm's BC-1 basic combat trainer produced for the U.S. ARMY AIR CORPS in 1937. That aircraft had a fixed undercarriage, but was otherwise similar to the AT-6. BC-1 production totaled 272 aircraft plus three similar BC-2S and one BC-3. The AT-6 was produced in greater numbers than any other specialized trainer in history. Including 1,800 aircraft built in Canada by Noorduyn, total AT-6 production was on the order of 15,000 aircraft of which 5,068 went to the U.S. Navy. A few Navy SNJs were fitted with arresting hooks for carrier operation. A planned Navy SN2J of 1946 did not go into production.

The AT-6 was a low-wing monoplane that resembled a fighter-type aircraft, with a radial engine, clean lines, and a fully retractable main undercarriage. The student and instructor sat in tandem, under a long glazed canopy. One fixed forward-firing .30-cal. machine gun was fitted, and gunnery training aircraft had a flexible .30-cal. gun at the after end of the cockpit. BOMB racks could be fitted as could cameras for reconnaissance training, and the plane could tow target sleeves.

The AT-6A variant had a top speed of 210 mph and the aircraft was credited with a range of 630 miles.

After the war the aircraft served in a large number of air forces as a trainer and ground-attack aircraft. In 1948 the remaining U.S. AAF aircraft were redesignated T-6. Several were modified to serve as spotting aircraft behind enemy lines in the Korean War, being designated LT-6.

AT-10 Wichita

Twin-engine advanced trainer flown in large numbers by the U.S. AAF at the start of the war. The aircraft was designed in 1941 in an effort to conserve strategic materials and was made largely of plywood. It was used as a "transition trainer" to multiengine aircraft.

Designed by Beech, it was a straightforward, low-wing aircraft with two radial engines and a "snub nose." There was space for one instructor and three student pilots. A total of 2,371 aircraft were built. They were unarmed.

Athenia

The first ship to be sunk in the EUROPEAN WAR. On Sept. 3, 1939, the passenger ship *Athenia* was 250 miles northwest of Ireland when she was torpedoed and sunk by the submarine *U-30*. The U-BOAT'S commanding officer, *Leutnant* J. Lemp, sighting the ship in the evening, thought she was an armed British merchant cruiser, and attacked without warning. One hundred twelve lives were lost, among them twenty-eight Americans.

Because Lemp had made no report of the sinking, when the British protested the sinking the German PROPAGANDA spokesmen announced that the ship had been sunk by a British mine or submarine, and the act was probably instigated by WINSTON CHURCHILL, First Lord of the Admiralty.

The *Athenia* had a gross tonnage of 13,465, was 526 feet long, and had steam turbines providing a speed of 15.5 knots. She was completed in 1923 and could carry more than 1,500 passengers.

Athletic

British code name for carrier-based air strikes in Bodo and Lodingen areas of Norway, Oct. 1944.

Atlantic, Battle of,

see BATTLE OF THE ATLANTIC.

Atlantic Charter

Declaration of U.S. and British war aims. The charter, drawn up at the ATLANTIC CONFERENCE of Aug. 1941, proclaimed that the two nations were fighting the AXIS "to ensure life, liberty, independence and religious freedom and to preserve the rights of man and justice." Each country agreed not to sue for a separate peace; not to seek to gain territory or make border changes without the consent of the people involved; to support self-government for every nation; to give all nations, "great or small, victor or vanquished" access to raw materials and trade; to cooperate with all nations in assuring economic and social security; to support freedom of the sea; and to "aid and encourage" postwar general disarmament. The charter's principles, ratified by the twenty-six Allied nations at the UNITED NA-

TIONS CONFERENCE of Jan. 1942, laid the foundation for the UNITED NATIONS.

Atlantic Conference

Meeting between President ROOSEVELT and Prime Minister CHURCHILL "to make known certain common principles in the national policies of their respective countries on which they base their hopes for a better future for the world." The conference took place on Aug. 9–12, 1941, at Placentia Bay, Newfoundland. Roosevelt and Churchill alternated their sessions between the U.S. CRUISER *Augusta* (CA 31) and the British BATTLESHIP *PRINCE OF WALES*. The common principles they agreed on were incorporated into the ATLANTIC CHARTER, the foundation of the UNITED NATIONS.

Atlantic Wall

An array of German fortification that stretched along the entire Channel coast and, in places, extended deep into France. By HITLER'S description the Wall was "a belt of strongpoints and gigantic fortifications" running from Norway to the Pyrenees, a defense "impregnable against every enemy." In reality, the Wall, much of it built by SLAVE LABOR, was strong in places and weak in others and never extended as far as Hitler had envisioned.

The Wall, parts of which were built from fortifications taken from France's MAGINOT LINE, was dotted by massive reinforced-concrete pillboxes that protected crews manning artillery, machine guns, and antitank weapons. On the beach were antitank obstacles and minefields. Offshore were submerged obstacles to hang up LANDING CRAFT. Beyond the beach were more minefields and weapons ranging from machine guns to railroad guns.

Both *Generalfeldmarschall* ERWIN ROMMEL and *Generalfeldmarschall* GERD VON RUNDSTEDT scoffed at the wall. Rundstedt, who had overcome the Maginot Line in 1940 simply by outflanking it, mistrusted static defenses. He called the wall an "enormous bluff" built "more for the German people than for the enemy."

For the NORMANDY INVASION the Atlantic Wall proved formidable but not impassable. The British created a special unit, the 79th Armoured DIVISION, to crack the Atlantic Wall along its assault beaches in the Normandy invasion. The division's vehicles included tanks with mine-clearing flails, tanks that carried demolition charges that could be placed against obstacles, and recovery vehicles that could rescue vehicles stranded in the surf. The troops also employed special cliff-scaling devices. The division's men trained against replicas of German obstacles built from photographs and descriptions obtained in COMMANDO raids on the Wall's beaches.

Atomic Bomb

The weapon that ended the war against Japan and became the centerpiece of U.S. defense strategy for the next forty-five years. There were three major aspects to the atomic bomb in World War II: its scientific development, the program for building it, and the system for delivering it to targets.

Development

Through the late 1920s and early 1930s a handful of physicists, most of them in Europe, worked on theories about ways to release the power locked in the structure of the atom. Leo Szilard, a Hungarian physicist who fled to England from NAZI Germany in 1933, believed that an element could be found that, when split by neutrons, would emit two neutrons while absorbing one. "In certain circumstances," he said, "it might be possible to set up a nuclear chain reaction, liberate energy on an industrial scale and construct atomic bombs." He urged British officials to investigate such a weapon.

In the wake of experiments in 1938 by German chemist Otto Hahn and Austrian physicist Lise Meitner at the Kaiser Wilhelm Institute outside BERLIN, efforts focused on achieving a controlled chain reaction using the radioactive element URANIUM. Meitner (who also fled Germany because, though a baptized Protestant, she was a JEW under Nazi law) was one of the first scientists outside of Germany to perceive the potential of what physicists already were calling nuclear fission.

In Copenhagen, she and Otto Frisch, another scientific refugee from the Nazis, passed word of the experiments to Danish physicist NIELS BOHR, who was about to leave for the United States. In Jan. 1939 at the Institute for Advanced Study in Princeton he discussed the atomic discoveries with still

another German refugee physicist, ALBERT EIN-
STEIN. Winner of the 1921 Nobel Prize for physics,
Einstein was world renowned. Szilard (by then at
Columbia University) and refugee physicists ED-
WARD TELLER and Eugene Wigner realized that
Einstein's fame would help to get a message about
the military potential of the atom directly to Presi-
dent ROOSEVELT. Responding to the physicists'
pleas, Einstein signed a letter to Roosevelt in Aug.
1939, less than a month before the beginning of the
EUROPEAN WAR.

"Some recent work," the letter said, ". . . leads me
to expect that the element uranium may be turned
into a new and important source of energy in the
immediate future and it is conceivable . . . that
extremely powerful bombs of a new type may thus
be constructed." Roosevelt, absorbed with international affairs since the outbreak of war, did not hear
of the message until October. He responded by
setting up the Advisory Committee on Uranium,
the element that held the secret to unlocking the
atom.

In both Germany and Japan, physicists and chem-
ists working on atomic research were also aware that
atomic energy could be used to make a bomb. Ultimately, however, neither country came close to
making the weapon. Both governments failed to
make an all-out attempt to build a bomb; in addition, British-Norwegian COMMANDO raids would
destroy a Norwegian heavy-water facility that Germans hoped to use for bomb making. But in 1939
it appeared that Germany and perhaps Japan were
in a bomb-building race with England. British
atomic scientists, in a government-sponsored secret
group, were exploring systems for the production
of weapons-grade fissionable material. (The Soviet
Union also had an atomic bomb program; see
below.)

The official U.S. effort soon bogged down, due
primarily to government and military disinterest.
Not until the Japanese attack on PEARL HARBOR
plunged America into the war did the building of
the bomb receive intensive attention.

On June 17, 1942, in a report to Roosevelt,
VANNEVAR BUSH, head of the OFFICE OF SCIEN-
TIFIC RESEARCH AND DEVELOPMENT, said that an
atomic weapon was feasible. From then on, the
MANHATTAN PROJECT, as it was code-named, oper-

ated on the highest national priority. To build the
bomb, Bush would pull together some 30,000 people—engineers and scientists, WASHINGTON
bureaucrats, and Cabinet-members—and erect an
immense, industrial-scale base for the building of
the bomb.

One of the leaders in the quest for a chain reaction was Nobel laureate ENRICO FERMI, an Italian
physicist who had left Fascist Italy with his Jewish
wife and children. Working with teams of physicists
first at Columbia and then at the University of Chicago, Fermi conceived of what he called a "pile"—
the first nuclear reactor: stacks of graphite bricks
and cylinders or spheres of uranium, with neutron-
absorbing cadmium rods that controlled the nuclear reactions.

Fermi and his team of scientists worked in what
had been a squash court under the stands of the
football stadium at the University of Chicago. After
building a pile consisting of 771,000 pounds of
graphite, 80,590 pounds of uranium oxide, and
12,400 pounds of uranium metal, on Dec. 2, 1942,
Fermi supervised the movement of the control rods
until his pile achieved the world's first self-sustaining nuclear chain reaction.

(Uranium, in its abundant form as the element
U-238, did not fission readily; U-235, an isotope of
U-238, did. The graphite slowed down neutrons
spontaneously produced by the uranium. The neutrons, after losing some momentum bouncing into
the graphite, reacted with U-235 atoms, creating
nuclear fission and a chain reaction.)

Fermi's pile—a kind of slow-motion version of
the bomb—proved that a self-sustaining chain reaction could be produced. But for a bomb some
method had to be found to separate the U-235
isotope from U-238 uranium. Another way toward
a fissionable element was the transmuting of U-238
into plutonium. The latter operation, scientists believed, could be done in a number of expensive,
tedious ways.

Vast facilities, supported by new towns, were established at Oak Ridge, Tenn., and Hanford,
Wash., to try all methods. The officer in overall
charge of building and operating the facilities of the
Manhattan Project was Maj. Gen. LESLIE M.
GROVES, whose previous assignment had been the
building of the PENTAGON.

Construction

Groves decided that a central laboratory was needed to design the bomb. His idea was endorsed by J. ROBERT OPPENHEIMER, a professor of physics at the University of California and the California Institute of Technology. Oppenheimer was put in charge of "Site Y," as the laboratory was known until its actual location was chosen by Groves and Oppenheimer: LOS ALAMOS, a boys' school in a wilderness atop a New Mexico mesa.

Oppenheimer quickly recruited a cadre of scientists for Los Alamos, which in April 1943 began work on "the gadget," as the bomb was usually called. By the end of the war several thousand men and women were working at Los Alamos, among them British and Canadian scientists under a special agreement for cooperation on atomic research. One of the British workers was KLAUS FUCHS, a German refugee who had fled to England. Fuchs was also a Soviet spy. (See ESPIONAGE.)

The laboratory designed two completely different bombs, dubbed "Little Boy" and "Fat Man." Little Boy, 10½ feet long, 29 inches in diameter, and 9,700 pounds, was essentially a gun with a U-235 bullet that was fired at a U-235 target; when the two U-235 components met, the chain reaction and explosion occurred. Fat Man, 10 feet 8 inches long, 5 feet in diameter, and 10,000 pounds, was more complex—and more powerful. It was built around two hemispheres containing plutonium. Conventional explosives, arranged as "lenses" to produce a tightly focused implosion, drove the two hemispheres together, doubling the plutonium's density and producing the supercritical mass. The resultant chain reaction would produce an atomic explosion.

In a test, code-named TRINITY, in the New Mexico wilderness on July 16, 1945, a teardrop-shaped Fat Man–style bomb was cradled in cables atop a 103-foot steel tower. Some test observers wondered whether the bomb would set off a chain reaction that would burn up the atmosphere or even shake the earth on its axis. Shortly before dawn, electrical charges detonated the explosives, and the bomb produced a blinding explosion equivalent in force to 18,600 tons of TNT.

Components of a Little Boy–style bomb were already on their way to war. Except for the U-235 target element, the bomb parts went by truck from Los Alamos to nearby Kirkland Air Force Base, then by plane to San Francisco, where they were taken to Hunter's Point Naval Shipyard for loading aboard the cruiser *INDIANAPOLIS* (CA 35). She would take them to TINIAN ISLAND, the Pacific base for the B-29 SUPERFORTRESS bomber that would carry the bomb to HIROSHIMA.

Delivery

The B-29, which became operational in 1943, was the only U.S. bomber capable of carrying a 10,000-pound bomb. Modification of the first B-29 began in Nov. 1943, under the cover of preparing the plane for transporting Roosevelt and Prime Minister CHURCHILL on overseas trips. In Aug. 1944 modification of seventeen other B-29s began and Lt. Col. PAUL W. TIBBETS was assigned to command the atomic-bomb delivery organization, the 509TH COMPOSITE GROUP.

A Little Boy atomic bomb, the type detonated over Hiroshima. (*U.S. Army Air Forces*)

A Fat Man atomic bomb, the type detonated over Nagasaki. (*U.S. Army Air Forces*)

In April 1945, a Target Committee consisting of scientists under the aegis of military officers, began discussing likely cities for the first atomic bomb. Groves had set several conditions, among them targets not yet damaged by air raids and "of such size that the damage would be confined within it, so that we could more definitely determine the power of the bomb." One of the earliest candidates was Hiroshima.

At the same time, Secretary of War HENRY L. STIMSON set up the INTERIM COMMITTEE to advise President TRUMAN on the use of the bomb. On June 1, Truman received from Secretary of State-designate JAMES BYRNES, a member of the committee, a recommendation that the bomb should be used against Japan as soon as possible and without prior warning. By accepting that commendation, Truman authorized the dropping of the bomb.

On July 26, when the *Indianapolis* arrived at Tinian, five C-54 transports of the AIR TRANSPORT COMMAND left Kirkland; three carried components of Little Boy and two carried components of Fat Man.

From Tinian, Tibbets' planes flew to Japanese-held islands and dropped PUMPKIN BOMBS, practice bombs of the same weight and shape as atomic bombs but containing conventional explosives. On Aug. 5, Little Boy was loaded into Tibbets' plane, on which he ordered the painting of his mother's name, "ENOLA GAY."

Early the next day, Tibbets' crew, along with U.S. Navy Capt. WILLIAM S. (Deke) PARSONS from Los Alamos, the weaponeer, took off, flew to Hiroshima, and dropped the bomb. At 8:16 A.M., local time, it detonated 1,900 feet above a hospital. Its force was equivalent to 12,500 tons of TNT. The city was instantly destroyed; at least 140,000 people were killed or would be dead by the end of the year.

On Aug. 9, "BOCKSCAR," a B-29 named after Frederick Bock but piloted on this day by Maj. CHARLES W. SWEENEY, took off from Tinian carrying a Fat Man bomb and headed for the city of Kokura, Japan. Cloud and smoke swathed the city and FLAK bursts erupted around the plane. So Sweeney opted for the alternate city on the target list, Nagasaki. The bombardier found a hole in the clouds and dropped the bomb. It detonated at 11:02 A.M. 1,650 feet above the city with a force

equivalent to about 22,000 tons of TNT. Hemmed in by the hills around the impact point, the explosion caused less damage than the Hiroshima bomb. But in the instant of explosion thousands died; by the end of the year an estimated 70,000 had died.

After dropping the Nagasaki bomb, Sweeney's B-29, low on fuel because of the target diversion, made an emergency landing on OKINAWA with only a few gallons of fuel remaining. After refueling the plane flew back to Tinian, arriving late that night. Neither of the bombers nor the several weather-reporting and photographic B-29s on the two atomic bombing raids were damaged.

Groves estimated that a second Fat Man would be "ready for delivery" after Aug. 17 or 18. But it was not needed, for the SURRENDER of Japan came on Aug. 14. Additional fissionable material was being produced but with the end of hostilities no additional bombs were fabricated.

In the months following the end of the war about 23,000 U.S. servicemen went into Hiroshima and Nagasaki. None of them had been warned about radioactivity. Hundreds died prematurely and others lived for years suffering from cancer and blood diseases. In 1988 Congress authorized aid to veterans who could prove that they had been in the bombed cities and had certain types of cancer linked to atomic-bomb radiation.

America had not been alone in working on the atomic bomb:

Great Britain Britain began major research into atomic energy in 1939 and by mid-1941 a government committee reported that there was a reasonable chance that an atomic bomb could be developed in the next few years. The CHIEFS OF STAFF recommended immediate action. However, on Oct. 11, 1941 President Roosevelt wrote to Churchill proposing a combined atomic bomb effort. Subsequently, Britain pooled all resources and scientists working on the atomic bomb (under the British code name Tube Alloys) with the U.S. effort.

Soviet Union The Soviet Union was the only other nation to have a viable atomic bomb program during the war. Atomic research was underway in the Soviet Union as early as 1932. In 1939 or 1940, the USSR Academy of Sciences established a senior research committee to address the "uranium problem," which included the potential results of nuclear fission.

The German invasion of the Soviet Union in June 1941 curtailed nuclear research efforts if not interest, with the major laboratories conducting research into nuclear physics, in LENINGRAD and Kharkov, being evacuated eastward from the war zone.

Early in the war academicians I. V. Kurchatov and A. P. Aleksandrov, the leading Soviet nuclear scientists of the 1940s, worked primarily on the protection of ships against magnetic mines. Late in 1942, however, they were reassigned to the development of nuclear weapons. There is ample evidence that the Soviets were by then aware of nuclear developments in the United States as well as in Germany. The Soviets correctly concluded that the United States was making an atomic bomb when American physics journals ceased publishing material about uranium fission and chain reactions; similar indications from Germany were confirmed by a notebook containing calculations related to nuclear weapons taken from the body of a dead German officer. The Soviets were also aided by an atomic espionage ring in the United States and Canada.

By late 1942 the Soviet State Defense Committee had established a military nuclear program, only a few months after the U.S. Manhattan Project to develop the atomic bomb had been initiated in the United States. In early 1943 research was resumed in MOSCOW under the leadership of Kurchatov, with scientists and engineers being recalled from the front, other research institutes, and industry to develop the atomic bomb. This wartime effort was under the overall direction of LAVRENTY BERIA, the head of state security (including the NKVD) and one of STALIN's principal lieutenants.

Immediately after the U.S. atomic bombings of Japan the Central Committee of the Communist Party "outlined the primary state task—to eliminate in the shortest period of time the monopoly of the United States in nuclear weapons. . . ."

The secret Laboratory No. 2 of the Academy of Sciences in Moscow was the focus for basic scientific research into nuclear weapons. The scale of the Soviet laboratory effort was, however, much smaller than the analogous U.S. activity at Los Alamos, New Mexico. The first Soviet atomic reactor, the F-1 (Physics-1) was started up on Dec. 25, 1946, and the first Soviet atomic bomb was detonated in Aug. 1949—several years before U.S. scientists had predicted that such an event would occur.

Atomic Bomb Tests

The fourth and fifth detonations of ATOMIC BOMBS. The two tests, called Operation Crossroads, were conducted by a joint U.S. Army-Navy task force at Bikini atoll in the MARSHALL ISLANDS in July 1946. Bikini was selected because it was isolated from currents and was outside the range of most prevailing winds. The targets at Crossroads were ninety-three U.S., German, and Japanese ships, along with weapons, equipment, aircraft, and animals lashed to their decks.

The idea for the tests came from the U.S. Navy, which in Sept. 1945 suggested that the effects of a bomb on a warship be determined by exploding an atomic bomb over the captured Japanese battleship *Nagato,* the sole surviving capital ship of the Imperial Fleet. The Navy proposal evolved into a mammoth operation entailing the creation of a test task force of 150 ships, seventy-five aircraft, and 40,000 men. The 167 natives who lived on Bikini (and were familiar with the Bible) were told they were like the "children of Israel" and had to live in another place. The Navy moved them to Rongerik atoll north of KWAJALEIN in the Marshalls.

Thousands of test animals were tethered to various places on the ships as proxies for crewmen. The use of animals outraged many citizens. "Why don't you put Japs on these ships instead?" one American asked the Crossroads planners. Another suggested that prison convicts replace the animals.

The *Nagato,* which had been bombed in the battle of LEYTE GULF but was still afloat at the end of the war, was towed to the site like some prize prisoner being paraded in chains. The former German heavy CRUISER *Prinz Eugen* arrived at the atoll under her own power, as did a Japanese light cruiser. Other target ships included the BATTLESHIPS *Arkansas* (BB 33), *New York* (BB 34), *Pennsylvania* (BB 38), and *Nevada* (BB 36); the latter two ships survivors of the Japanese attack on PEARL HARBOR; and the CRUISERS *Salt Lake City* (CA 25) *Pensacola* (CA 24), plus DESTROYERS, SUBMARINES, and AMPHIBIOUS SHIPS.

Three bomb tests were originally scheduled. They were given the phonetic labels Able, Baker, Charlie. The Able bomb was dropped by the B29 SUPERFORTRESS "Dave's Dream" on July 1, 1946. The target was the *Nevada,* painted bright orange and in the center of an array of ships. The bomb exploded over the ships, missing its target by 2,000 yards. Up from the lagoon rose a ball of fire about three miles in diameter and then a mushroom-shape cloud that rose to a height of about five miles.

The bomb sank a destroyer and two transports, capsized another destroyer, mortally damaged the Japanese cruiser, and wrecked the carrier *INDEPENDENCE* (CVL 22) and a submarine. (The carrier became a radiological research facility.) The *Nevada, Arkansas, Pensacola,* and all other ships within three-fourths of a mile of the bomb's explosion were badly damaged. Examination of the animals showed that radiation would have killed nearly everyone on board the ships centered under the air burst and for varying distances beyond.

In the Baker test on July 25, a bomb suspended from a LANDING CRAFT was exploded about ninety feet below the surface. The explosion produced a column of water about 2,200 feet in diameter and 7,000 feet high under a gigantic cloud. The awesome spectacle, captured by still and movie cameras, became an enduring symbol of the destructive power of an atomic bomb. The target ships around it look like doomed toys. So powerful was the water column that at first observers thought they saw on its edge the 26,000-ton *Arkansas,* her bow pointed skyward and about to be sucked into the cloud. It was a shadow, not the battleship. In reality, the Baker bomb created 90-foot waves that capsized the *Arkansas,* which plunged 110 feet to the bottom, her superstructure hammered into the seafloor. The waves lifted up the massive aircraft carrier *SARATOGA* (CV 3) and slapped her down. She sank about seven hours later. Divers who have seen the *Saratoga* in her grave say SB2C HELLDIVER bombers—and light bulbs—on her hangar deck are still intact.

The two tests destroyed twenty-one ships, and members of Congress asked whether the atomic bomb had made the Navy obsolete. The test results were examined by two boards, one appointed by the JOINT CHIEFS OF STAFF, the other by President TRUMAN. "To us who have witnessed the devastating effects of these tests," the President's Evaluation Board reported, "it is evident that if there is to be any security or safety in the world, war must be eliminated as a means of settling differences among nations."

Test Charlie, which was to have exploded a bomb even deeper than the Baker bomb, was canceled, apparently because of the immense amount of radioactivity spewed by Baker. Spray rained down on some of the ships and many of the crewmen in the test-observation fleet. (Long after the war many men who were at Crossroads joined the 15,000-member National Association of Atomic Veterans. Members of the association say that many of them have cancers induced by exposure to Crossroads radiation. The U.S. government has not accepted the claims.)

In later years, twenty-two more atomic and hydrogen weapons were tested at Bikini. The natives never returned.

Attila

Early code name for German occupation of VICHY FRANCE.

Attlee, Clement R. (1883–1967)

British prime minister. Attlee, leader of the Labor Party, was deputy leader of the House of Commons and deputy prime minister in Prime Minister CHURCHILL'S wartime coalition cabinet. When Labor won the 1945 general election, Attlee became prime minister and replaced Churchill in the midst of the POTSDAM CONFERENCE. Churchill once called him "a sheep in sheep's clothing."

Attu,

see ALEUTIAN ISLANDS.

Audacity

The first Allied ESCORT CARRIER to see action. The diminutive *Audacity* had a short but eventful career escorting British CONVOYS. She was too small to have a hangar, and her six fighters had to be parked and maintained on her open flight deck.

In her first operation, escorting a convoy from Britain to GIBRALTAR in Sept. 1941, her Martlet (F4F-3 WILDCAT) fighters helped guide convoy escorts to U-BOATS and shot down an FW 200 CON-DOR bomber that had attacked a merchant ship. On Oct. 2 she departed "Gib" with another convoy headed back to Britain. She departed again for Gibraltar on the 29th, this time with eight fighters on board. On Dec. 14 she left with another Britain-bound convoy, her last. Only four Martlet fighters were available.

The convoy was quickly engaged by U-boats, with the *Audacity*'s Martlets giving reports to the convoy escorts and strafing one, but another submarine shot down a Martlet with its deck guns. (But the U-boat stayed on the surface too long by doing so and was sunk by the escorts.) More U-boats attacked and late on the night of Dec. 21 the submarine *U-751* fired a torpedo into the *Audacity*. The carrier stopped, and two more "fish" struck her. The escort carrier plunged to the bottom, taking with her seventy-five officers and ratings, including her commanding officer, Comdr. D. W. McKendrick. In all, twelve U-boats had attacked the convoy with five being sunk (the convoy also suffered one destroyer sunk, three escort ships damaged, and two merchant ships sunk).

Kontradmiral KARL DÖNITZ, head of the submarine force, wrote in his official report: "The worst feature [of the convoy] was the presence of the aircraft carrier. Small, fast, maneuverable aircraft circled the convoy continuously, so that when it was sighted the [U-]boats were repeatedly forced to submerge or withdraw. The presence of enemy aircraft also prevented any protracted shadowing or homing procedure by German aircraft. The sinking of the aircraft carrier is therefore of particular importance, not only in this case but also in every future convoy action."

The *Audacity* was converted from the German banana boat *Hannover,* launched in 1939. She was captured by the British in the West Indies in Feb. 1941 and hastily converted to an escort carrier, and placed in commission in June 1941. The *Audacity* had a gross tonnage of 5,537 tons and was 475 feet long. Diesel engines could propel her at 15 knots.

Auschwitz

Site, in German-occupied Poland, of a CONCEN-TRATION CAMP that became a DEATH CAMP where 3,000,000 people, most of them JEWS, died. Until 1941 the camp had about 9,000 prisoners. But, with the invasion of the Soviet Union, room was needed for tens of thousands of Soviet PRISONERS OF WAR. Of 12,000 Soviet POWs sent there in Dec. 1941 to expand the camp, only 150 survived the winter.

The expansion added to Auschwitz a camp area called Birkenau after the birch woods that had stood there. This would be the killing camp for Auschwitz, making it, in the words of *SS-Hauptsturmführer* RUDOLF HÖSS, the commandant, "the greatest extermination center of all time." By his account, more than 2,500,000 people were killed by mass executions or in gas chambers; 500,000 other starved to death. Höss, describing his "pioneer" work as a death-camp commandant, said that at Auschwitz, unlike other death camps, "We tried to fool the victims into believing that they were going through a delousing process. . . . Frequently, women would hide their children under their clothes, but we found them and we sent the children to be exterminated."

Victims arrived expecting to be forced to work, at worst imprisoned, but not killed. Some were handed postcards to mail to relatives. A printed message on the postcard said: *We are doing very well here. We have work and we are well treated. We await your arrival.*

New arrivals, stumbling out of jammed freight cars, walked before the camp physician, Dr. JOSEF MENGELE, who called out "Right!" for work squads or "Left!" for the gas chambers, which were disguised as bathhouses. Sometimes, while the selection went on an inmate orchestra of pretty young girls, in white blouses and navy-blue skirts, played music from "The Merry Widow."

A survivor, testifying at the Nuremberg WAR CRIMES trials, told of Mengele experiments on ways to sterilize Jewish women. Some women arrived pregnant. After they gave birth, she said, "the babies were drowned in a bucket of water. After a while, another doctor arrived, and for two months they did not kill the Jewish babies. But one day an order came from Berlin saying that again they had to be done away with. Then the mothers and their babies were called to the infirmary. They were put in a lorry and taken away for the gas chamber."

Arriving men, women, and teenaged children

able to work were sent to nearby factories built for Siemens, I. G. FARBEN, and KRUPP. They lived in filthy, disease-ridden SLAVE LABOR barracks, starved, and worked until they died.

Bodies were burned in open pits. When they overflowed and their stench began disturbing people who lived near the camp, Höss installed six crematorium–gas chamber complexes. The two large ones, by his methodical accounting, had a killing capacity of 2,000 people at a time; the smaller ones, up to 1,500 each. "The killing itself took the least time," he later told war crimes investigators. "You could dispose of 2,000 head in a half hour, but it was the burning that took all the time." The ashes of the dead went to nearby farmers to enrich their soil.

Among the victims of Auschwitz were more than 17,500 Gypsies, declared "enemies of the THIRD REICH." A "camp" of Gypsies, totaling about 4,000 people, was wiped out in one day, Aug. 1, 1944. An unknown number of Gypsy men served in the German Army, returned home on leave and, without explanation, were sent to Auschwitz or other death camps.

Australia

Capital: Canberra, pop. 7,200,000 (1940). As a member of the BRITISH COMMONWEALTH, Australia automatically joined with the UNITED KINGDOM in its declaration of war against Germany on Sept. 3, 1939. Although Australia's constitution prohibited compulsory service overseas, Prime Minister R. G. Menzies announced that volunteers could be sent to aid England. The effect was two armies: the all-volunteer Australian Imperial Force, whose troops fought under British command in North Africa, Greece, Crete, and the Middle East; and the militia, which could not be sent beyond Australia and its territories, including northeast NEW GUINEA and Papua. In Jan. 1940 compulsory military training was introduced for home defense, and the two-army system continued. But by the end of 1944, all of the men in the naval and air forces as well as 95 percent of the army combat troops were officially volunteers and thus eligible for battle beyond Australia's shores. Ultimately, 859,000 Australians were in uniform during the war.

Australia, which had a restrictive, whites-only immigration policy, carried this into the war by barring "non-Europeans" from compulsory service. But about 23,000 Aborigines and "part-Aborigines" did get into uniform, along with about 8,750 natives of the Torres Strait Islands, which lie between the tip of Australia's Cape York and the southern shore of Papua.

The Japanese attack on PEARL HARBOR and the fall of SINGAPORE turned Australia to its own defense. In what was called "Australia's Pearl Harbor," Japanese carrier-based aircraft bombed Darwin on Feb. 19, 1942, sinking twelve ships, including the U.S. DESTROYER *Peary.* (DD 226).

Early in 1942 most Australian troops in the British Eighth Army were sent back to their homeland. But, expecting scant aid from England, Menzies' successor, Prime Minister John Curtin, said his nation "looks to America free of any pangs as to our traditional links of kinship with the United Kingdom." The first American troops reached Australia on Dec. 22, 1941. And on March 17, 1942, Gen. DOUGLAS MACARTHUR, escaping from the Philippines, arrived in Darwin to become Supreme Commander of Allied forces in the Southwest Pacific. Until 1944, most of the ground troops serving under him were Australians.

Nearly 1,000,000 Americans would be stationed in, or would pass through, Australia during the war. The peak of the U.S. presence came in May 1944, when there were more than 500,000 Americans in Australia and New Guinea. "Australian girls seem to have lost their heads over American servicemen," an archbishop complained in 1943, and both countries contemplated the banning of American-Australian marriages. But about 12,000 Americans (including some nurses and WACs) married Australian spouses.

Austria

Capital: Vienna, pop. 6,600,000 (est. 1939). The collapse of the Austro-Hungarian monarchy in World War I created Austria, a German-speaking country but not part of Germany. Eying Austria as his first conquest, ADOLF HITLER pledged to annex it. In 1934 Germany secretly fomented a civil war that led to annexation. That tactic failed, and in 1936 Hitler, stalling for time, recognized Austria's independence while secretly working to undermine its government. After Austrian officials discovered evidence of German subversion, Austria protested. This led to a showdown between Austrian Chancellor Kurt von Schuschnigg and Hitler, who met at BERCHTESGADEN, Hitler's mountain redoubt, on Feb. 12, 1938. Hitler gave Schuschnigg a series of ultimatums, including the appointment of a NAZI as minister of police and a general amnesty for all Nazi convicts. Schuschnigg signed and Hitler said he believed this meant "peace for five years."

Hitler kept pressing Schuschnigg, who decided on a general plebiscite to see whether the Austrian people wanted their nation to remain independent of Germany. Furious, Hitler ordered cancellation of the plebiscite and resignation of the Austrian government. Schuschnigg did resign, but the military occupation of Austria was already under way. On March 12, German troops marched into Austria and met no resistance. Hitler, proclaiming Austria a nameless part of Germany, said *Anschluss* (union) had been achieved.

The Germans hunted down anti-Nazis, including Schuschnigg, and sent them to prison or CONCENTRATION CAMPS. Trade unions and hundreds of other "political" organizations were dismantled and their properties confiscated. Catholic schools were closed, Nazi commissioners took over the financial affairs of major monasteries, and Nazi personnel officials approved all matters pertaining to the Catholic clergy. ANTI-SEMITISM came with *Anschluss*, beginning with Nazi plundering of Jewish property. The killing of Jews began. Thousands fled, including Sigmund Freud. Baron Louis Rothschild, whose fortune had been confiscated, paid a ransom of $12,000,000 to the GESTAPO and was allowed to leave for Switzerland. By July 1, 1939, about 135,000 Jews remained in Austria of the 290,000 who had lived there before the Nazis came.

Vienna saw little of the war until the city was heavily bombed by Allied air forces in the fall of 1943. Soviet troops turned much of Austria into a battlefield during the Red Army drive on BERLIN in the spring of 1945. Vienna was devastated in savage house-to-house fighting.

Automobiles

The U.S. government, acting under the WAR POWERS ACT and girding for government-controlled WAR PRODUCTION, in July 1941 cut back on the manufacture of automobiles. Soon after U.S. entry into the war, the government ordered total conversion of the automobile industry to war production. Sales of new motor vehicles were banned after Jan. 1, 1942, and all new, used, or unsold 1942 models were put in a pool for specific sale to doctors, veterinarians, and others doing essential work. After the surrender of Germany in May 1945, some passenger-car production was allowed and on July 1, 1945, all restrictions were lifted.

Because of the RATIONING of gasoline and tires, automobile driving was drastically curtailed. War workers shared rides, other owners put their cars up on blocks in the garage, and advertising posters sternly asked, "Is this trip necessary?" Before the war, the average American car was driven about 9,000 miles a year; during the war, the average dropped to 5,500 miles.

Avalanche

Code name for Allied landing at SALERNO, Sept. 9, 1943.

Avenger,

see TBF/TBM.

Avery, Sewell L. (1874–1960)

Director of Montgomery Ward & Co. and a longtime foe of the New Deal, who defied President ROOSEVELT and the War Labor Board (WLB). On April 26, 1944, after Montgomery Ward refused to obey a WLB order to extend an expired union contract, U.S. troops took possession of the firm's Chicago plant. When Avery refused to leave, two soldiers carried him out in what became a famous wartime photograph. In Dec. 1944 Avery again defied a WLB order and the Army seized seven plants. Avery's resistance became a symbol of civilian defiance of wartime regulations. A federal judge ruled in Jan. 1945 that the government's seizure of the Chicago plant was illegal and in April Avery was reelected Montgomery Ward chairman.

Awa Maru

A Japanese passenger-cargo ship that was sailing under a guarantee of safe conduct when she was torpedoed by a U.S. SUBMARINE. The *Awa Maru* was one of two Japanese ships designated by the international RED CROSS to carry relief supplies to Allied PRISONERS OF WAR.

The lengthy arrangements for the relief operation were made through neutral Switzerland by the United States. The Japanese, whose merchant fleet had been nearly wiped out, accepted the proposal— but not for humanitarian reasons. The Japanese saw the ships as a means for getting supplies to their own troops in Southeast Asia and for bringing back to Japan important officials and selected technicians considered vital to the war effort.

The United States delivered about 2,000 tons of supplies to a port in Siberia. The *Hoshi Maru* left Japan on Jan. 8, 1945, loaded 275 tons of supplies, and transported the cargo to SHANGHAI without incident. The much bigger *Awa Maru,* which had a normal cargo capacity of 11,269 tons, sailed next, but by a far more complicated route, which was reported to the United States through Sweden: Leave Japan on Feb. 17 and stop at Taiwan, HONG KONG, Saigon, SINGAPORE, Indonesia, and return to Japan via Singapore and the Taiwan Strait.

Under the agreement, the *Awa Maru* would have white crosses painted on her hull, funnels, and hatch covers. She was to illuminate the crosses at night and run with all navigational lights lit. A description of the *Awa Maru* and her course was sent in plain language three times a night for three consecutive nights to all U.S. submarines in the Pacific. The message began: *Let pass safely the Awa Maru carrying prisoner of war supplies.*

Secretly, the Japanese were planning another cargo for the *Awa Maru:* forty boxes of GOLD believed to have amounted to about 375 pounds. The United States routinely intercepted and decoded the diplomatic messages regarding the Japanese secret plans for the ship. (Other messages revealed that the *Hoshi Maru* had carried from Shanghai to Japan six boxes of confiscated opium, nineteen boxes of whiskey, and fifty-two boxes whose contents were not described.)

The *Awa Maru,* it is now known, dropped the gold in Singapore and went on to Indonesian ports, where she loaded tons of desperately needed rubber and tin and hundreds of people.

About 10:00 on the night of April 1, the U.S.

submarine *Queenfish* (SS 393) made RADAR contact with a ship traveling at a high speed at a range of 17,000 yards. The captain of the *Queenfish,* two-time Navy Cross winner Comdr. Charles E. Loughlin, assumed the ship to be a Japanese warship, presumably a destroyer. He fired a spread of four TORPEDOES. Within two minutes he heard four explosions.

Following procedure, Loughlin headed for the target to pick up survivors for intelligence purposes. He found one, who told him that he had sunk a relief ship guaranteed safe passage. The survivor was the only person alive of the 2,004 people who had been on the *Awa Maru.* The sinking was one of the worst maritime disasters in history.

When Adm. ERNEST J. KING, Commander in Chief U.S. Fleet, learned of what happened, he ordered Loughlin relieved of command and court-martialed. He was charged with negligence in obeying orders, disobeying an order, and inefficiency in the performance of duty.

The safe-passage messages, it turned out, had been received and not seen by Loughlin. The intercepted messages about the gold were not introduced at the trial. Loughlin was convicted on the charge of negligence in obeying orders. For his punishment he received a letter of admonition. He retired from the Navy in 1961 as a rear admiral.

On the day of Japan's SURRENDER, Japan asked the United States for reparations of $52,500,000 for the loss of the ship, her cargo, crew, and passengers. No mention was made of gold and no reparation was paid.

(A novel inspired by the incident, *Ship of Gold,* was written by the authors of this book.)

Awards and Decorations

The U.S. military services presented millions of individual decorations for gallantry and meritorious service during the war. They were presented to men and women for combat action as well as to those who organized and managed the war. Service medals were awarded to individuals (and units) for service in various campaigns and theaters; the Army (including the AAF) and Navy (including the Marine Corps and Coast Guard) generally awarded different medals. In addition, units—including ships—were given awards for accomplishments in combat.

The principal U.S. decorations were:

Medal of Honor   The highest U.S. military decoration, it is awarded to members of the Army and Navy who distinguished themselves conspicuously by gallantry and intrepidity at the risk of life, above and beyond the call of duty, in action involving actual combat with the enemy. See MEDAL OF HONOR.

Distinguished Service Cross   The second highest award given by the Army-AAF, presented for exceptional heroism in combat. The award was established in 1918.

Navy Cross   Also given for exceptional heroism in combat, this is the second ranking Navy–Marine Corps award. It was established in 1919.

Distinguished Service Medal   Usually awarded to senior officers, this medal is presented by the Army, Navy, and Marine Corps for exceptional meritorious service in a position of great responsibility. The Army established the medal in 1918 and the Navy the following year.

Silver Star   Given by both services for gallantry in action. Established in 1932.

Legion of Merit   Normally awarded to officers for exceptionally meritorious service. It was established in 1942 for both services. (The Medal for Merit was also authorized in 1942 to be awarded to civilians who distinguished themselves by exceptional conduct in the performance of outstanding services; it was the civilian counterpart of the Legion of Merit.)

Distinguished Flying Cross   Given for heroism or extraordinary achievement in flight, this award was established in 1926.

Soldier's Medal   An Army award for heroism not involving conflict with the enemy. Established in 1926.

Navy and Marine Corps Medal   Since 1942 given for heroism not involving conflict with the enemy.

Bronze Star   For heroic or meritorious achievement during military operations by members of all the armed services. Established in 1944.

Air Medal   Presented for meritorious achievement in flight to members of all the armed services. Established in 1942.

Commendation Medal   Meritorious service in peace or war; established for the Navy in 1944 and the Army in 1945.

Purple Heart   Reinstituted for the Army in 1932 and in 1942 for the Navy–Marine Corps, this medal was awarded to service personnel wounded or killed in combat. The Purple Heart was originally established by Gen. George Washington in 1782 for meritorious action or service performed; soon after the Revolutionary War it fell into disuse and no further awards were made until 1932—the 200th anniversary of George Washington's birth. To qualify for the awarding of the medal, a wound must necessitate treatment by a medical officer.

In addition to these awards and decorations, Army infantrymen could qualify for the Combat Infantryman Badge, awarded for ground combat in an infantry unit; a Medical Badge was also issued to Army medical personnel assigned during combat to medical detachments of infantry BATTALIONS or REGIMENTS. The services presented flight wings to pilots and other air crewmen, "dolphin" badges to Navy submariners when they qualified in submarines; and special badges to men who qualified as parachutists, GLIDER crewmen, and divers.

Badges were also awarded to personnel of all services for qualification in various individual weapons (pistols, rifles, etc.), with marksman, sharpshooter, and expert levels of qualification.

See also HERO OF THE SOVIET UNION, IRON CROSS, VICTORIA CROSS.

Axiom

Code name for U.S. mission sent by Southeast Asia Command to WASHINGTON and LONDON in Feb. 1944 to discuss Operation Culverin.

Axis

Term describing enemies of the ALLIES. Italian Premier BENITO MUSSOLINI coined the term, originally referring to the alliance of Italy and Germany, officially forged by the PACT OF STEEL in 1939. On Sept. 27, 1940, Germany, Italy, and Japan signed a TRIPARTITE PACT that called for each to provide military assistance in case of attack by any nation not yet in the war, and Japan became a member of the Axis, implying opponents as tightly knit as the Allies. The Axis nations did not coordinate their strategies, but there was operational cooperation between Japan and Germany, whose U-BOATS in the Indian Ocean used the Japanese submarine bases at SINGAPORE and Penang off MALAYA.

The term *Axis* was given greater currency after Prime Minister CHURCHILL used it in Parliament—"the soft underbelly of the Axis"—on Nov. 11, 1942, referring to SICILY and Italy. *Axis* was also used in the Declaration on Liberated Europe issued after the YALTA CONFERENCE by the United States, England, and the Soviet Union.

Other nations that joined the Axis were Albania, Bulgaria, Hungary, Rumania, Yugoslavia, and Thailand. The UNITED KINGDOM, but not the United States, declared war on Finland, which fought for a short time on the side of Germany against the Soviet Union. Finland was considered an Axis nation, as was Spain, which, although officially neutral, aided Germany in many ways and recruited the BLUE DIVISION to fight with German forces on the EASTERN FRONT.

Axis Sally

An American woman who broadcast PROPAGANDA for the Germans. Mildred E. Gillars, a native of Portland, Me., and a former Ohio Wesleyan student, went to Germany in the 1920s and worked as a singer. When the war began, she left a job teaching English to broadcast propaganda from a BERLIN radio station. In broadcasts aimed at American troops in Europe, she taunted soldiers with tales of unfaithful wives and girlfriends back home. The troops dubbed her Axis Sally and scoffed at her while enjoying her jazz records and her frequent playing of "Lili Marlene," one of the hit SONGS of the war. Arrested after the war, she was convicted of TREASON in 1949 and sentenced to twelve years in prison. She was paroled in 1961.

Azon Guided Bomb,
see GUIDED MISSILES.

B-17 Flying Fortress

The most famous Allied bomber of World War II. The B-17 was not the fastest bomber, nor did it have the largest bomb capacity, nor the longest range, nor was it produced in the greatest numbers. Rather, its popular fame came from an effective U.S. AAF public relations program and its wide use. From the combat viewpoint, the B-17 was able to sustain considerable damage and still fly and had a heavier defensive gun armament than any aircraft except for the U.S. B-29 SUPERFORTRESS.

The first combat mission to be flown by the Flying Fortress took place on July 8, 1941, when twenty B-17C models flown by RAF Bomber Command attacked the German port of Wilhelmshaven.

The British were not impressed with the aircraft. When the Japanese attacked PEARL HARBOR on Dec. 7, 1941, there were twelve B-17s at Hickam Field, adjacent to the naval base; six were being used for training and the other six were undergoing repair. Another twelve B-17s began landing at Hickam during the raid, flying in from California. Several of these B-17s were destroyed in the Japanese raid.

Of thirty-five B-17s in the Philippines, Japanese planes destroyed sixteen on the ground at Clark Field near MANILA on the first day of war. (The seventeenth plane at Clark Field, suffering generator troubles, was late getting off for the preattack warning and was still airborne when the other six-

B-17 Flying Fortress bombers of the U.S. Eighth Air Force drop their bombs over a target in German-held Europe. Although out-performed by other Allied and Axis bombers, the B-17's reputation benefitted from an active AAF public relations campaign and the plane's impressive ability to continue flying after suffering considerable damage. *(U.S. AAF via Imperial War Museum)*

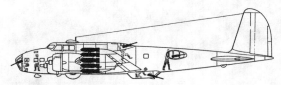

B-17D Flying Fortress.

teen had landed at Clark Field and were caught by Japanese bombers.) On Dec. 10 the surviving B-17s began the first U.S. offensive action of the war with attacks against Japanese shipping. By the end of the year the few remaining B-17s were withdrawn to Australia. Several new B-17E models were sent to Java in the desperate attempt to stop the Japanese assault on the DUTCH EAST INDIES.

Subsequently, the B-17 became one of the two U.S. AAF heavy bombers in the Southwest Pacific and European theater. The first B-17E arrived in England on July 1, 1942, assigned to the Eighth AIR FORCE; the first U.S. B-17 bombing mission was against ROUEN on Aug. 17. Eighth Air Force B-17s were deployed to North Africa from the fall of 1942 following the Allied landings in early Nov. 1942. The peak AAF inventory for B-17s was 6,043 aircraft in Sept. 1943. At that time there were thirty-three B-17 GROUPS overseas (compared to forty-five-and-a-half groups of B-24 LIBERATOR bombers at the time). U.S. B-17 Flying Fortresses dropped 640,036 tons of bombs on European targets from 1942–1945 compared to 452,508 tons from B-24s. However, B-24s continued in service in the Pacific after the end of the war in Europe.

In 1941 the RAF received twenty B-17C aircraft under LEND-LEASE. The British flew only a few combat missions with the B-17 and were not impressed with its performance in the frigid skies over Europe.

The surviving aircraft were used for antisubmarine operations and a few were used in the Middle East in 1942.

The B-17 was a four-engine, mid-wing aircraft with a tail wheel, easily recognized by its circular-section fuselage with a stepped cockpit, four engines, and large tail fin. Early models carried defensive .30-cal. machine guns in blisters; beginning with the B-17E, a manually operated tail-gun turret and power-operated dorsal and ventral ("belly") turrets were introduced, all with twin .50-cal. machine

guns, in addition to several hand-operated guns. The B-17G added a "chin" turret with twin .50-cal. guns giving that plane a total of thirteen guns, justifying the term "flying fortress." Despite this defensive armament, losses to German fighters and, to a lesser extent, antiaircraft fire were high, with some of the B-17 raids over Germany suffering losses of 16 percent.

An XB-40 was a more heavily gunned B-17 developed in an effort to provide a long-range escort for bombers. That plane was too heavy to keep up with the bombers, and the desperate need to escort B-17s flying daylight raids was met by the P-51 MUSTANG fighter. Other variants included radio-controlled, bomb-laden aircraft to strike German missile sites (BQ-7); reconnaissance (F-9); search-and-rescue (SB-17); and cargo conversions (C-108). Older aircraft used to fly VIPs were known by the designations CB-17 and VB-17, with a few special training aircraft known as TB-17. The single B-38 was a B-17E with upgraded engines.

The U.S. Navy acquired several B-17s toward the end of the war and, with the designation of PB-1W, used them to develop the concept of airborne RADAR picket aircraft to provide early warning of Japanese air attacks against the fleet.

Boeing engineers initiated design work on a four-engine bomber in June 1934. Known as Boeing Model 299, it embodied features of the Boeing 247 twin-engine, high-performance airliner and the firm's experimental XB-15 four-engine bomber. The first prototype Model 299—with the Boeing trade name Flying Fortress and the military designation XB-17—flew on July 28, 1935. This aircraft flew 2,000 miles nonstop from Boeing's plant in Seattle, Wash., to Wright Field in Ohio at the impressive speed of 252 mph. The last of thirteen Y1B-17 aircraft development aircraft was delivered in Aug. 1937. The aircraft was ordered into production in 1938 as the B-17B. This would be the first model assigned to combat units.

A total of 12,731 aircraft were built by Boeing, Douglas, and Lockheed before the war ended. (All were stricken almost immediately after the war; when the U.S. Strategic Air Command was established in 1946 no B-17s were listed among its tactical aircraft.)

The standard bomb load for the B-17 was 4,000

to 6,000 pounds. The B-17G had a top speed of 287 mph, with a range of 2,000 miles when carrying 6,000 pounds of bombs. The aircraft was credited with an effective combat range of 1,600 miles. The B-17E and later planes were flown by a crew of ten: pilot, copilot, bombardier, navigator, engineer/top gunner, radioman/gunner, belly gunner, two waist gunners, and the tail gunner.

B-24 Liberator

U.S. heavy bomber. Produced in larger numbers than any other U.S. military aircraft in history, the B-24 Liberator heavy bomber was one of the most effective aircraft of the war. While flown primarily as a long-range bomber, B-24 variants flew effectively as antisubmarine, reconnaissance, and cargo aircraft.

In the bomber role the B-24 was flown by the U.S. AAF in the European, North African, Mediterranean, and South Pacific theaters. Just before the Japanese attack on PEARL HARBOR two B-24s were modified to be flown to the Philippines for subsequent (peacetime) reconnaissance flights over Japanese bases in the CAROLINE and MARSHALL islands; one of these planes was destroyed at Hickam Field, adjacent to Pearl Harbor, on Dec. 7, 1941. The first American B-24s to see combat were dispatched to Java where, on Jan. 16, 1942, five Liberators bombed Japanese airfields and shipping in a frustrated effort to halt Japanese advances in the DUTCH EAST INDIES.

The B-24 first gained public attention for the dramatic low-level bombing attack by twelve B-24D aircraft against the PLOESTI oil refineries in Rumania on June 12, 1942. That was the first of several B-24 attacks flown from North Africa, a 2,400-mile round trip against this vital source of petroleum for Germany. While the B-17 FLYING FORTRESS received more publicity, B-24s based in England also participated in the STRATEGIC BOMBING of Europe and—operated by the U.S. AAF and

Navy and the RAF Coastal Command—were highly effective in antisubmarine operations in the Atlantic. Flying antisubmarine patrols up to twenty hours' duration, the B-24s were in many respects the most effective land-based aircraft flown in that role. The U.S. Navy received 977 B-24s (designated PB4Y-1) in addition to the specialized PB4Y-2 PRIVATEER variants for long-range patrol and reconnaissance missions. (After the war some of the Navy PB4Y-1 aircraft were flown by the Coast Guard in the search-and-rescue role.)

The B-24 was developed by Consolidated Aircraft in response to an AAF request of early 1939 for a new long-range bomber. Drawing heavily on the Boeing Company's experience with the B-15 and B-17 bombers as well as Consolidated's own P4Y flying boat (precursor of the PBY CATALINA), the four-engine Consolidated XB-24 flew for the first time on Dec. 29, 1939. By that time service test models were already on order for the AAF. As soon as the prototype flew, France ordered sixty of the four-engine bombers; the British took over that contract (with the designation LB-30), and when the United States entered the war fifteen of these planes nearly ready for delivery went to the AAF.

The B-24 underwent almost continuous modification during production, with increases in bomb load and defensive gun armament. The B-24 was distinguished by its large fuselage, which provided a commodious bomb bay, high wing, and twin tail, making it much less attractive than the B-17. The B-24N had a single tail, but was not directly related to the Navy's PB4Y-2.

Production deliveries began in 1941 at Consolidated plants, with B-24 production also being undertaken by the Douglas Airplane Co. and Ford Motor Co. The first Liberators provided to Britain were flown across the Atlantic in March 1941. Several were employed as unarmed transports to ferry pilots and other personnel across the Atlantic. RADAR-equipped Liberator I antisubmarine aircraft entered service with the RAF Coastal Command in September 1941; the plane's range and payload made one of the best sub-hunting aircraft to fly during the war. The RAF began using Liberators as bombers from June 1942 in the Middle East and then in the Indian Ocean area.

Between 1940 and the end of the war 18,190

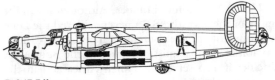

B-24J Liberator.

B-24s were produced. The AAF had a peak inventory of 6,043 planes in Sept. 1944 (24 percent greater than the peak B-17 force—a total of forty-five-and-a-half bomber GROUPS flew the B-24 compared to a maximum B-17 force of thirty-three groups). When the war in Europe ended, orders for 5,168 B-24N models were canceled.

The RAF took delivery of about 1,900 bomber and cargo models of these aircraft and several hundred more planes went to the U.S. Navy. One British LB-30 Liberator transport had its guns deleted and was modified—and later lengthened and fitted with a single tail fin—to become the "Commando" (the personal transport of Prime Minister CHURCHILL).

Major U.S. variants included the C-87 and C-109 cargo aircraft, F-7 photo-reconnaissance model, and AT-22/TB-24 trainer. One B-24D was modified to an XB-41 "destroyer," intended to fly as a gunship escort for other B-24s, but this modification was impractical. (The Navy PB4Y-2 Privateer is listed separately.)

The production B-24s could carry up to 8,800 pounds of BOMBS with a defensive armament of ten .50-cal. machine guns. Maximum speed was 300 mph with a combat range of just over 2,000 miles for most models (2,850 miles for the B-24D). A crew of ten was carried in the bomber role, and eight or more in the RAF antisubmarine aircraft.

B-25 Mitchell

U.S. medium bomber named for aviation iconoclast William (Billy) Mitchell. The B-25 and the contemporary B-26 MARAUDER were the U.S. AAF's medium bombers for most of the war. The B-25's most famous action was the April 1942 raid on Japan led by Lt. Col. JAMES DOOLITTLE from the aircraft carrier HORNET (CV 8). Subsequently,

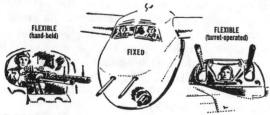

B-25 Mitchell armament.

the aircraft was flown on virtually every battle front of the war, including antisubmarine patrols and antishipping strikes.

(Prior to the Doolittle raid, on Feb. 2, 1942, two B-25s were flown off of the carrier *Hornet* in the Atlantic to demonstrate the feasibility of such an operation; later, in Nov. 1944, the Navy flight-tested a Marine PBJ-1H fitted with an arresting hook for carrier operation.)

The B-25 was a twin-engine, mid-wing aircraft with a distinctive twin-tail configuration. The aircraft was well liked by pilots (in contrast to the unpopular B-26). While the standard B-25 models had a glazed nose, the "gunship" version had a solid nose with several machine guns and, in some models, a 75-mm cannon. Dorsal, tail, and waist turrets added another six .50-cal. machine guns, giving the B-25H solid-nose aircraft a total of fourteen guns in addition to the cannon.

North American Aviation began development of the B-25 in early 1938 and a company prototype aircraft flew in January 1939. In Sept. 1939 a production contract was awarded. Thus, there was no XB-25 experimental prototype and the first flight of a B-25 occurred on Aug. 19, 1940. Despite the B-25 production of 9,816 aircraft, during the war AAF squadrons reached a peak of only 2,656 aircraft (July 1944) because of the large numbers of B-25s flown by the U.S. Marine Corps (with the designation PBJ-1) and by foreign air forces, especially Britain and the Soviet Union. B-25 production ended in Aug. 1945 in favor of the A-26 INVADER.

The standard B-25 crew was six men (the Doolittle planes had five). Later model B-25s carried up to 3,200 pounds of BOMBS; the B-25H model could also carry an aerial TORPEDO. The B-25J (PBJ-1J), the major production model, had a maximum speed of 275 mph and a range of 1,275 miles with full bomb load.

B-26 Marauder

U.S. AAF medium bomber. Although flown for most of the war, the B-26 never achieved the fame or popularity of the contemporary B-25 MITCHELL. Its initial combat missions were in the Southwest Pacific; it also served in North Africa and in the European theater.

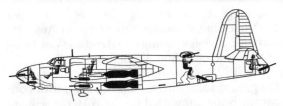

B-26B Marauder.

The B-26 was not popular with AAF pilots and was promptly dubbed "Widow Maker" because of its high accident rate and the difficulty of bailing out of the aircraft. (A larger wing resulted from one accident-investigation board's findings.) There were several production delays and serious consideration was given to scrapping the aircraft in 1942 but Lt. Gen. GEORGE C. KENNEY, on the basis of combat experience in the Southwest Pacific, recommended the aircraft.

The B-26 was a twin-engine, mid-wing bomber with a distinctive, almost pointed glazed nose and a tall tail fin. It was the first American bomber designed with a powered gun turret.

The Glenn L. Martin Co. designed the B-26 in 1938–1939, and the AAF contracted for the aircraft directly from the drawing board. The first production aircraft—there being no experimental prototype—flew on Nov. 25, 1940. Martin produced 2,656 B-26s through April 1945; the peak AAF strength was 1,931 aircraft in March 1944. Several foreign nations flew the B-26 during the war and a few TB-26G target-tow aircraft went to the U.S. Navy with the designation JM.

The B-26 normally had a crew of six. The B-26G had a maximum speed of 283 mph and a combat range of 1,100 miles. The aircraft mounted up to twelve 50-cal. machine guns, with twin-gun dorsal and tail turrets, and fuselage pods carrying additional forward-firing guns. The internal bomb bay could hold 4,000 pounds of BOMBS; some models could carry a TORPEDO.

B-29 Superfortress

The most advanced bomber to see combat in World War II. The Boeing-designed B-29 carried out intensive attacks against Japanese industrial and urban targets in 1944–1945, and B-29s dropped the ATOMIC BOMBS on HIROSHIMA and NAGASAKI in August 1945. The B-29 was a four-engine, streamlined bomber, with pressurized compartments for the flight crew. It was also the first U.S. bomber with a RADAR bombing system, the AN/APQ-13, which replaced the NORDEN BOMBSIGHT. With a maximum takeoff weight of 135,000 pounds, the B-29 was the largest bomber of the war. (The B-29 and the B-32 DOMINATOR were the only *very* heavy bombers of the war.)

The first XB-29 flew on Sept. 21, 1942, and the first B-29 bombing mission was flown against Bangkok from airfields in India (using landing fields in China as staging bases) on June 5, 1944. Meanwhile, the Navy and Marine Corps were recapturing the MARIANA ISLANDS to provide B-29 bases some 1,500 miles from TOKYO. The first strike from the Marianas was flown on Oct. 28, 1944, against the Japanese submarine base at TRUK. Subsequently, heavy B-29 raids began against Japan from the Marianas, a thirteen-hour round-trip flight. These were initially high-altitude, daylight strikes that had limited success. Although designed for daylight PRECISION BOMBING from 30,000 feet or more, the B-29 proved more effective in night area bombing raids with incendiaries at an altitude of 5,000 feet. A fire-bomb raid against Tokyo in March 1945 by 279 B-29s killed 83,783 persons.

The largest B-29 raid of the war came on Aug. 1, 1945, when 836 aircraft were launched from the Marianas with 784 reaching their targets in Japan. In addition to dropping almost 170,000 tons of BOMBS during fourteen months of war, B-29s dropped over 12,000 aerial mines in Japanese and Korean waters to halt coastal shipping. Combat losses during those sorties totaled 147 to Japanese fighters and/or antiaircraft fire. In return, several hundred Japanese fighters were shot down (B-29 gunners claimed over 2,000 kills during the war). When the war ended the AAF had forty GROUPS of B-29s, of which twenty-one groups totaling almost 1,500 aircraft reached advanced bases in the Pacific by the end of the war.

Total B-29 production was 3,996 aircraft by the Boeing, Bell, and Martin companies, with all but 230 delivered by Aug. 1945 (another 5,000 B-29s were canceled at the end of the war). Variants included 117 F-13 photo aircraft. Maximum speed was 358 mph and maximum bomb load was 20,000 pounds. Defensive armament was eight or ten .50-

cal. machine guns in four remote-control turrets, plus a tail turret mounting two machine guns and one 20-mm cannon. The crew normally consisted of eleven men: pilot, copilot, bombardier, navigator, flight engineer, radio and radar operators, and four gunners.

The single B-39 was a YB-29 refitted with liquid-cooled engines. The B-44 was a B-29A with upgraded engines; it was to be produced as the B-29D, but instead was given the designation B-50 and limited production followed. After the war the U.S. Navy flew four specialized B-29s with the designation P2B while the RAF flew eighty-nine bomber aircraft with the name Washington. U.S. Air Force B-29s were used in the Korean War. The aircraft was copied and produced by the Soviet Union as the Tu-4 and given the NATO code name Bull.

See also 509TH COMPOSITE GROUP and AIR FORCE.

B-32 Dominator

U.S. very heavy bomber developed as insurance against possible failure of the B-29 SUPERFORTRESS long-range bomber. (The B-32 and B-29 were the only *very* heavy bombers of the war.) The success of the B-29 meant the failure of the B-32 to achieve wartime fame, and only fifteen of the aircraft saw combat in the Pacific before the end of the war. The first B-32 combat mission was flown by two aircraft on May 29, 1945, flying from a base in the Philippines against the nearby Japanese-occupied town of Antatet in the Cagayan Valley. More bombing missions in the Philippines followed as well as small strikes against Japanese targets on Formosa and, flying from OKINAWA, against Japan on the night of Aug. 14–15. Following the end of hostilities, B-32s flew photo missions over Japan.

What may have been the last combat action of any kind *against the Japanese* in World War II occurred on Aug. 18 when a pair of B-32s on a photo mission over Tokyo were attacked by an estimated fourteen Japanese fighters—ZEROES and TOJOS. One B-32 was damaged, but both bombers returned safely to Okinawa; the B-32 gunners claimed two fighters destroyed and two probables. (The last attack on a U.S. aircraft in the war zone occurred when Soviet Yak fighters fired on and forced down a B-29 dropping supplies to PRISONERS OF WAR near

Hamhung, Korea, on Aug. 29, 1945.) The last B-32 operational mission was flown on Aug. 28, with one aircraft crashing on takeoff and one being lost because of technical problems.

The B-32 was developed by Consolidated Aircraft Corp. in tandem with the Boeing B-29, with both aircraft being contracted by the AAF on Sept. 6, 1940. Both planes were test-flown for the first time in Sept. 1942, the first XB-32 on Sept. 7 and B-29 on Sept. 21. However, delays in getting the B-32 into production and the superior performance of the B-29 led to the latter aircraft being produced in much larger numbers. Also, because of weight problems, the production B-32s dispensed with the pressurized cabins and remote-control gun turrets, both of which were key features of the B-29.

The four-engine, high-wing B-32 took advantage of the Consolidated experience with the B-24 LIBERATOR heavy bomber. The first two XB-32s had the Liberator's twin-tail configuration and other features. XB-32 flight tests revealed aerodynamic problems and after redesign the third XB-32 emerged as the standard single-tail aircraft. During 1943–1944 the AAF placed production orders for just under 2,000 aircraft. The B-32 program continued to encounter delays and not until Aug. 1944 did the B-32 begin service tests. Not including the three XB-32s, only 115 planes were delivered by the end of Aug. 1945, including forty TB-32 crew trainers. Almost 1,600 additional planes were canceled and immediately after the war the existing planes were discarded.

The B-32 had a defensive armament of ten .50-cal. machine guns in five power-operated turrets; up to 20,000 pounds of BOMBS could be carried, the plane having a range of 3,600 miles while carrying 8,000 pounds of bombs. The plane had a maximum speed of 364 mph at its ceiling of 30,000 feet.

B-35 Flying Wing

Radical long-range bomber design. In early 1941, with the possibility that Germany could conquer Britain, the U.S. AAF initiated a program to develop trans-Atlantic bombers. This effort produced the B-36 PEACEMAKER and the B-35 Flying Wing.

The Northrop-design for the B-35 was a tailless flying wing. The design was so radical that priority was given to other aircraft projects, but the design was still pursued because, according to the official AAF history, the B-35 showed "considerably more promise in performance and bomb range on the basis of gross weight" than the B-36. In Sept. 1941 Northrop received a contract to build a prototype aircraft. On Sept. 28, 1942—although Britain was obviously safe from invasion—the head of the AAF, Gen. H. H. ARNOLD, gave the two bombers the "highest priority."

Development of the B-35 continued to lag, but in all fifteen aircraft were ordered for development and evaluation. The first XB-35 flew on June 25, 1946. Series production was canceled in favor of the B-36. (Two of the YB-35B models, powered by four piston engines driving "pusher" contrarotating propellers, were converted to YB-49s with four turbojet engines. These aircraft formed the origins of the Northrop B-2 "stealth bomber" that first flew in 1989.)

B-36 Peacemaker

A trans-Atlantic bomber developed to bomb Europe from bases in the United States. By the spring of 1941 the U.S. War Department believed that the United States would likely be drawn into the war and that all of Europe—including England—could be under AXIS control. The B-36 was developed to bomb targets in Europe from bases in North America. In the spring of 1943 when it appeared that China might collapse under Japanese attack, the B-36 was considered for operations in the Pacific because of problems in the B-29 SUPERFORTRESS and B-32 DOMINATOR programs. Despite a high priority for its development, the first XB-36 did not fly until Aug. 8, 1946, almost five years after the prototype was ordered. (Also developed under this transoceanic bomber program was the Northrop B-35 FLYING WING bomber, an early precursor to that firm's B-2 "stealth" bomber.)

Built too late to participate in the war, a total of 446 B-36s were produced by Consolidated Aircraft Corp. through 1954. They served in the U.S. Strategic Air Command as bombers and reconnaissance aircraft until 1959. None ever dropped a bomb in anger.

The B-36 was the largest combat plane ever built with a 162-foot length and a 230-foot wingspan. Maximum bomb load was 43 tons with a gross weight of 328,000 pounds. The aircraft was propelled by six large piston-pusher engines (later supplemented by four turbojets in underwing pods). Defensive armament consisted of up to twelve 20-mm cannon in retractable twin turrets. A C-99 cargo version was developed to carry 400 fully equipped troops; only one was built.

Ba 349

Desperation rocket-powered fighter aircraft. The Germans developed the concept that a rocket-propelled aircraft could be launched vertically against approaching Allied bomber formations. The pilot was to make a single firing pass, launching twenty-four 73-mm or thirty-three 55-mm short-range rockets against the bombers. He would then bail out.

The idea of a vertically launched rocket interceptor was first voiced by Dr. WERNHER VON BRAUN in 1939. The concept was then taken on by Erich Bachem, then technical director of the Gerhard Fieseler aircraft works, who prepared a series of designs under the generic designation Fi 166. These evolved into the *Natter* (adder) design, which subsequently received the official designation Ba 349.

The Ba 349 was successfully flight-tested—both manned and unmanned—before the war ended. A small interceptor unit became operational near Stuttgart in April 1945 but did not see combat. The potential effectiveness of this aircraft was even less than the rocket-propelled ME 163, which did become operational.

The Ba 349B had a maximum speed of 620 mph at 16,400 feet and a cruising speed of 495 mph. Endurance was 4.36 minutes at 9,840 feet or 3.15 minutes at 29,530 feet. Takeoff weight was 4,920 pounds with rocket boosters; the actual "aircraft"— without fuel or boosters—weighed 1,940 pounds. There were proposals to fit the aircraft with two 30-mm cannon. The aircraft was launched from an 80-foot vertical ramp.

Babington-Smith, Flight Officer Constance

British aviation writer who was one of the leading Allied photo interpreters during World War II. An officer in the Women's Auxiliary Air Force of the RAF for six years, she became an expert in aerial photographic interpretation and was in charge of the aircraft section of the Central Interpretation Unit.

She is credited with being the first analyst to identify the German V-1 BUZZ BOMBS at the PEENE-MÜNDE missile test site on the Baltic Sea in May 1943. In 1945 she was assigned to U.S. AAF intelligence in WASHINGTON to work on photographic interpretation for the Pacific theater. She was awarded the Legion of Merit by the U.S. AAF and the M.B.E. by the British government.

After the war she was a researcher for *Life* magazine and wrote several books on aviation and intelligence.

Backbone

British plan for operations against Spanish Morocco.

Backhander

Code name for U.S. task force operations on Cape Gloucester, NEW BRITAIN.

Bacteriological Warfare,

see BIOLOGICAL WARFARE.

Bader, Group Capt. Douglas (1910–1982)

British fighter pilot who flew combat missions after losing both legs. Bader lost his legs in a flying accident in Dec. 1931, about one year after joining the RAF. He was invalided out of the service in 1933. He rejoined the RAF in 1939, having been fitted with artificial legs. Bader refused a desk job and was posted to an RAF fighter unit and subsequently commanded No. 242 squadron, flying HURRICANE fighters during the BATTLE OF BRITAIN. After being promoted to wing commander his fighter collided with a German ME 109 over France on Aug. 9, 1941, and he came down in German territory. He escaped from a German hospital, but was recaptured and spent the remainder of the war as PRISONER OF WAR. The RAF dropped a replacement leg to him while a POW.

After the war Bader was awarded the Order of the British Empire.

Badoglio, Marshal Pietro (1871–1956)

Chief of the Italian General Staff and head of government when Italy surrendered. Although Ba-doglio disliked fascism, he nonetheless served it and led the Italian invasion of Ethiopia in 1935. But when Italy entered the war as Germany's ally, he resigned as Chief of Staff. In July 1943, after the Allied invasion of SICILY, the Fascist Grand Council deposed BENITO MUSSOLINI and Badoglio took over the government. On Sept. 3, after secret negotiations, he signed a conditional SURRENDER with the ALLIES. On Oct. 13 he declared war on Germany, thereby guaranteeing Italy postwar status as an ally. After the capture of ROME he resigned to pave the way for the formation of a new government.

Baedeker Raids

German bomber attacks on historic British towns and cities, selected, the Germans said, from the Baedeker tourist guides. The attacks were also known as the "cathedral raids" because most of the towns had famous cathedrals. Karl Baedeker was a nineteenth-century German printer who produced a series of widely known guide books. His successors continued publishing the guides, which were translated into English and French. They were well known to British travelers. The Baedekers rated worthwhile tourist sites and hotels by labeling them with one or more stars.

The raids began on the night of April 24–25 with the bombing of Exeter and continued into May on cities of England marked with two stars in the Baedeker guides. The German radio said the "terror raids" were in reprisal for RAF strikes against Rostock on the Baltic, site of a Heinkel aircraft factory. Those raids, on four nights from April 23–28, destroyed much of the city.

Bagration

Code name for the massive Soviet attack against the German Army Group Center, June 1944.

Bailey Bridge

Sectional steel panel bridge used by Allied troops to replace destroyed bridges. The bridge, named for Sir Donald Coleman Bailey of the British Ministry of Supply, was preferred by U.S. Army combat engineers because it was lighter and more easily assembled than U.S. collapsible bridges.

The Bailey bridge came in segments 10 feet long. They could be bolted three across. A 100-foot section able to support 30-ton tanks could be assembled by combat engineers in three hours. Bailey bridges spanned distances as great as 240 feet.

Baka

The MXY-7 *Ohka* (Cherry Blossom) was a manned flying bomb, developed as a KAMIKAZE weapon. The Allied code name Baka—which was Japanese for "fool"—was considered by many Americans as more appropriate for this desperation weapon. Bomber-type aircraft ("mother" planes) were to take off with the Baka attached to their belly, fly to the vicinity of U.S. warships, and then release the suicider to crash into a ship.

The first Baka attack took place on March 21, 1945, with sixteen G4M2 BETTY aircraft carrying the Baka bombs flying from Japan against U.S. ships off OKINAWA. Despite an escort of thirty fighters, attacks by U.S. carrier fighters forced the bombers to jettison the Bakas (their pilots remained in the mother planes). All of the bombers were shot down. Another Baka attack on April 1 was also unproductive, although the Japanese claim a Baka damaged the BATTLESHIP *West Virginia* (BB 48). Evidence shows that the minor damage inflicted on the rehabilitated PEARL HARBOR veteran was from a bomb-carrying suicide plane.

The first Bakas seen by U.S. naval forces were the first to score a kill. On April 12 suicide aircraft were again attacking the U.S. warships off Okinawa. The clear day brought out an estimated 185 kamikazes plus almost 200 conventional attackers against the U.S. warships in RADAR picket duties off the embattled island. An A6M ZERO smashed into the DESTROYER *Mannert L. Abele* (DD 733), breaking the ship's keel and leaving her dead in the water. One minute later she was hit by a Baka—and she sank in less than five minutes. Seventy-nine of her crew were dead or missing. The same day another Baka hit the destroyer *Stanly* (DD 478), smashing through her bow before exploding on the other side of the ship. She was hurt, but kept moving and shooting. Within ten minutes a second Baka zoomed toward her, ripped the national ensign off the gaff, and hit the water 2,000 yards away. A Zero then dived on the ship, was hit by 40-mm gunfire, and broke apart over the ship, the fuselage and bomb falling 15 yards off.

The Bakas returned periodically to plague the U.S. ships off Okinawa. But their effectiveness was limited, in large part because of the vulnerability of the mother planes while en route to the attack area. Too often the Bakas were jettisoned or the bombers shot down far short of their targets; more dangerous were the single-engine fighters and dive bombers pressed into the kamikazes and Army Air Force *taiatari* (suicide) role.

Design of the Baka is credited to Ens. Mitsuo Ohta, a Navy pilot who, with the help of the Aeronautical Research Institute of Tokyo University, drafted preliminary plans that were submitted to the Navy in Aug. 1944. Unpowered prototypes were designed and constructed within a few weeks and flight trials began in Oct. 1944 with powered trials in November. Large-scale production had already been ordered and 755 of the *Ohka* Model 11 bombs were delivered between Sept. 1944 and March 1945.

The *Ohka* Model 22 was a smaller version, intended to be carried into combat by the Navy P1Y FRANCES medium bomber; this Baka had a smaller wingspan and a warhead of only 600 pounds of high explosive (compared to 2,646 pounds in the Model 11). Fifty of these Bakas were produced. The subsequent Model 33 was a "mid-size" Baka intended to be carried by the G8N RITA four-engine bomber, having a warhead of 1,764 pounds. But the low priority given to the G8N led to cancellation of the Model 33 as well as the Model 43, which was to have been catapulted from surfaced submarines. A two-seat unarmed, powered training variant, designated Model 43 K-1 KAI *Wakazarura* (Young Cherry), was developed but only two were built. Thus, a total of 807 powered Bakas were produced.

The Baka was mostly fuselage, with stub wings, a glazed canopy over the cockpit, and a small twin-fin tail. The entire forward portion of the fuselage was taken up with the warhead. The Baka was carried aloft by a "mother" aircraft, usually a naval G4M2 Betty; the Baka pilot could enter the bomb while in flight. After release he would ignite the Baka's battery of three rockets, which provided a combined thrust of 1,764 pounds for 8 to 10 seconds. The weapon had an effective range of about 25 miles from the launching aircraft. Maximum powered speed was 403 mph, with higher velocities being reached in the terminal dive.

Balkans-Greece-Crete Campaign (1941)

ADOLF HITLER saw the Balkans as the crossroads of Europe, a region rich in food and oil that could be transported overland to offset the British blockade of German ports. Hitler also needed to tame the Balkans to protect his southern flank before he could launch Barbarossa, the GERMAN CAMPAIGN IN THE SOVIET UNION.

He began his takeover of the Balkans early in 1941 by neutralizing oil-rich Rumania and placing some 680,000 troops there in response to the Soviet seizure of Bessarabia and northern Bucovina in June 1940. Germany also appropriated some Rumanian territory but instead of occupying it forced Rumania to hand over land to Hungary and Bulgaria. All three nations, together with Yugoslavia, became members of the AXIS. But Yugoslavians would balk, overthrowing the government that made the deal with Hitler.

While Hitler was planning his Balkan strategy, Italy's dictator, BENITO MUSSOLINI, decided on his own to invade Greece—without informing his Axis partner, Hitler. On Oct. 28, 1940, Italy sent the first of 200,000 troops into Greece from Italian-controlled Albania. The Italians met unexpectedly stiff resistance and not only were repelled but were driven back into Albania by Greek troops.

Personally outraged at Yugoslavia's shift from potential puppet to potential enemy, Hitler on March 27, 1941, hastily summoned his military leaders and ordered an "unmerciful" invasion of Yugoslavia. Hitler's pique would produce more than an invasion of Yugoslavia. It would force a postponement in Operation Barbarossa, the invasion of the Soviet Union. The four-week delay would change the German timetable of conquest, trapping German troops in the snows and freezing cold of the Russian winter. (Historian WILLIAM SHIRER called the postponement of Barbarossa "probably the most catastrophic single decision in Hitler's career.")

On April 6, 1941, a German BLITZKRIEG crossed the borders of Bulgaria, Hungary, and Austria, striking Yugoslavia—and Greece, where Mussolini had asked for help. Belgrade, on Hitler's specific orders, was destroyed in what he called "Operation Punishment." Yugoslavia surrendered on April 17,

but a widespread GUERRILLA war soon began against the occupiers.

In Greece, the Germans were initially stopped by the Metaxas Line, a complex of fortresses along the Greek-Bulgarian border. But the German success in Yugoslavia added a front to Greek defenses and resistance quickly crumbled. Augmented by forces originally intended for Barbarossa, the Germans overran the Peloponnesus Peninsula and took Athens on April 27. BRITISH COMMONWEALTH forces, rushed to Greece just before the invasion, were evacuated by sea to CRETE under heavy German air attacks.

Of the more than 57,000 British, Australian, and New Zealand troops sent to Greece, 43,000 were evacuated, 27,000 to Crete and the rest to Egypt. To safeguard their conquest of Greece and secure the Aegean Sea, the Germans next had to capture Crete, the island that traditionally protected the eastern Mediterranean. In a massive AIRBORNE assault, the Germans took the island, forcing another evacuation of British-led forces and establishing a natural "aircraft carrier" for launching air attacks against Allied shipping in the eastern Mediterranean. But, primarily because of the imminent demands of the Barbarossa campaign, Germany could not fulfill the strategic potential of Crete.

Balloon Bombs

At intervals during 1944–1945 the Japanese launched paper balloons carrying incendiary BOMBS to set fires in U.S. forests. The balloons were blown eastward from Japan at altitudes of 30,000 to 50,000 feet at speeds of 20 to 150 knots. The balloons reached the United States and Canada from three to five days after launching.

The first remains of incendiary balloons were found in the northwestern United States in Nov. 1944. By March 1945 there were confirmed reports of 100 per month crossing the North Pacific, but the numbers then declined, probably because the velocity of the winds across the North Pacific decreases as summer approaches.

The effects of the balloon warfare were nil, according to U.S. intelligence reports. However, on May 5, 1945, Elsie Mitchell and five children were killed while fishing in Lake County, Ore. They found a Japanese balloon bomb that detonated when they examined it. (They were the only casualties to enemy action on the U.S. mainland during the war.)

Balloon bomb envelopes were made of four or five plies of mulberry paper about the thickness of cigarette paper and bonded with cellulose cement to produce an excellent balloon covering. The hydrogen-filled balloons were spherical, 33 feet in diameter, with a lifting capacity of about one-half ton at sea level and about 300 pounds at 30,000 feet. A metal valve with a rubber diaphragm maintained a pressure of about one ounce per square inch and prevented the balloon from exploding should it rise above pressure height. The incendiary payload consisted of four bombs of about ten pounds each and one bomb, either incendiary or high-explosive antipersonnel, of about 30 pounds.

An ingenious electrical device using a wet-cell, two-volt battery was used to release sand-bag ballast to help keep the balloon aloft until it reached its target area and then ignite fuses when the balloon began to descend. The remains of some 200 balloons of this type were found in the United States and Canada; one, without bombs, was found as far east as Grand Rapids, Mich.

The destruction of the balloons was relatively easy when they were sighted. Aircraft could easily shoot them down; a U.S. pilot downed one when he dived on it and his slipstream forced the balloon down. In Montana a sheriff downed one with a rifle.

Balloons

Used as both defensive and offensive weapons during the war. Several nations employed BARRAGE BALLOONS to deter low-flying aircraft. The Japanese used BALLOON BOMBS for attacks on the northwestern United States and Canada.

Balsam

British code name for strikes flown over southern Malaya and Sumatra by carrier-based aircraft.

Baltic States,

see ESTONIA, FINLAND, LATVIA, LITHUANIA.

Baltimore,

see A-30.

Bangalore Torpedo

Allied explosive device, developed by the British, to cut through barbed wire. A metal tube packed with high explosives, it was also used to blow up railway tracks, detonate buried mines, and as an element in booby traps.

Banzai Charge

A wild, frontal Japanese attack aimed at killing as many enemy as possible while dying in battle. The charge, usually a desperate final act when facing certain defeat, got its name from the battle cry *Tenno heika banzai!* ("Long live the Emperor!") The largest charge against U.S. forces was on SAIPAN. Banzai charges were also made in many other Pacific battles.

BAR,

see BROWNING AUTOMATIC RIFLE.

Bär, *Oberstleutnant* Heinrich (1913–1957)

Leading jet fighter ACE of the war. Flying a jet-propelled ME 262 *Sturmvogel* in the closing months of the war, "Heinz" Bär destroyed at least sixteen Allied aircraft, mostly B-17 FLYING FORTRESS bombers. His total aerial kills in the war was 220, with 124 against British and American aircraft.

Some sources cited Bär as the first jet ace of the war, but this can be contested by several Me 262 pilots.

Barbarossa

Code name for German offensive against the Soviet Union, June 1941. The plan was originally called Fritz and then Directive 21. HITLER, on Dec. 18, 1940, issued the directive and renamed it Barbarossa, surname of Frederick I (1121–1190). Legend had it that Frederick would rise from his deathlike sleep and restore Germany to power again.

Barbey, Vice Adm. Daniel E. (1889–1969)

Barbey ended the war as the U.S. Navy's most experienced amphibious force commander. Barely known outside the Southwest Pacific area, Barbey skillfully labored under equipment shortages to land more than 1,000,000 men and 1,500,000 tons of supplies in the two years that he served as the amphibious force commander for Gen. DOUGLAS MACARTHUR.

Barbey served in surface ships prior to the war, commanding a destroyer, destroyer division, and the battleship *New York* (BB 34). His distinctive contributions to AMPHIBIOUS LANDINGS began in 1941 with his appointment as a captain to the position of Chief of Staff to the Service Force and Amphibious Force, Atlantic Fleet. He fostered the development of the DUKW amphibious truck and several of the specialized landing ships used by the ALLIES during the war.

As a rear admiral, in June 1943 he reported to Australia as Commander Amphibious Force, Southwest Pacific—Gen. MacArthur's amphibious commander. His force, which included an Army Engineer Amphibious BRIGADE, carried out fifty-six landings along the NEW GUINEA coast and in the Philippine archipelago. (See: battle of LEYTE GULF.) His force grew from ad hoc assemblies with few specialized landing ships to a full-fledged fleet with three task groups in 1945. Barbey, a vice admiral when the war ended, did not always agree with Gen. MacArthur, and thought the March 1944 landing on Los Negros Island in the ADMIRALTIES was an unnecessary risk.

In Nov. 1945 he became commander of the Seventh FLEET, being responsible for the landing of U.S. occupation troops in Korea and North China.

Barracuda

This awkward-looking plane was another effort by the British to develop a successor to the SWORDFISH TORPEDO bomber. The aircraft were six years from the start of design (1937) by Fairey Aviation until service entry. Their first action was at the SALERNO landings in Sept. 1943, with a single squadron flying from the carrier *Illustrious*. Then, beginning on April 3, 1944, with a strike by forty Barracudas from the carriers *Furious* and *Victorious*, the aircraft were used in a series of strikes against the German battleship *TIRPITZ* in Norwegian waters. The dreadnought suffered fourteen direct BOMB hits and several near-misses (the fjords prevented a torpedo attack). These and subsequent Barracuda strikes put the *Tirpitz* out of action for several months until, in Sept. 1944, the warship was sunk by RAF LANCASTER four-engine bombers.

The Barracuda did not demonstrate the versatility of the Swordfish as a reconnaissance and antisubmarine aircraft, although the Barracuda Mk III did have a surface-search RADAR beneath the rear fuselage.

The prototype Barracuda flew on Dec. 7, 1940. Production delays were caused by priority being given to other aircraft types. Still, 2,582 Barracudas were produced during the war.

It was the first British monoplane torpedo bomber, entering service far later than Japanese and U.S. monoplanes in that role. The aircraft had a "shoulder" wing, with the horizontal tail surface mounted high on the fin. The awkward appearance of the aircraft became ridiculous when the wings were folded (each "breaking" twice as they swung upward).

The Mk II had a maximum speed of 228 mph and a range of 685 miles. It could carry a single aerial torpedo under the fuselage or four 500-pound bombs. For the short-range *Tirpitz* attacks armor-piercing 1,600-pound bombs as well as 500-pound bombs were carried by the Barracudas; the bombers, however, attacked from below about 3,000 feet, which prevented the armor-piercing bombs from achieving their full potential. The Barracuda's defensive armament consisted of a twin .303-cal. machine gun mount firing from the rear cockpit. A three-man crew flew the Barracuda.

Barrage Balloon

Unmanned, small-scale BLIMP used in air defense. Borrowing an idea from World War I, British air-defense officials moored hydrogen-filled balloons to protect areas from low-level bombers. Tethered to fixed points on land or from ships, the balloons often had suspended steel cables; the tethers and cables were to foul the propellers and wings of attacking aircraft. Their effectiveness was difficult to assess, but their relative cost was cheap compared to antiaircraft guns and fighter aircraft.

Barrage balloons, which in America became a symbol of the BATTLE OF BRITAIN in 1940, were also effective in 1944 against V-1 BUZZ BOMB attacks. More than 200 of these missiles were snared by the cables. Barrage balloons were also used during some AMPHIBIOUS LANDINGS.

There were experiments by the British in suspending explosive devices from barrage balloons to detonate when enemy aircraft struck the cables. The concept was quickly discarded as too dangerous to those handling the balloons and others on the ground.

Barrister

Code word for the Anglo-French capture of DAKAR; formerly Black and Picador.

Baruch, Bernard M. (1870–1965)

Adviser to President Wilson in World War I and President ROOSEVELT in World War II. Baruch, a prominent Wall Street financier who had served as an adviser to President Roosevelt since 1934, during the war additionally became an adviser, on industrial production and postwar reconversion, to JAMES F. BYRNES, director of economic stabilization and director of war mobilization. After the war, President TRUMAN appointed Baruch U.S. delegate to the United Nations Atomic Energy Commission. His "Baruch Plan," which called for international control of atomic energy, was vetoed by the Soviet Union. Baruch is credited with being the first person to use the term *Cold War* to describe U.S.-Soviet relations.

Bastico, Marshal Ettore (1876–1972)

Italian commander in North Africa from 1941 to 1943. Bastico was a veteran of the Italian-Turkish War (1911–1912), World War I, the war in Ethiopia, and the SPANISH CIVIL WAR. In 1940 he became commander of the Dodecanese Islands and July 1941 was named governor of Libya and commander of the Italian forces in North Africa. Gen. ERWIN ROMMEL'S AFRIKA KORPS was under his command, with the two generals often disagreeing on the conduct of the campaign against the British.

When HITLER promoted Rommel to *Generalfeldmarschall* in June 1942, BENITO MUSSOLINI promoted Bastico to marshal. Subsequently, Rommel was placed under the Chief of Staff of the Italian Armed Forces *(Commando Supremo),* Marshal UGO CAVALLERO, taking Bastico out of the chain of command.

Bastico returned to Italy in Feb. 1943 as the Allied armies defeated the last German and Italian troops in North Africa. He served in Italy until retiring in 1947 and wrote the multivolume *Evolution of the Art of War.*

Bastogne

A key objective in the German ARDENNES offensive that launched the Battle of the Bulge in Dec. 1944. The U.S. 101st AIRBORNE DIVISION occupied the Belgian town early in the battle and held it against strong German assaults. Stragglers from other battered U.S. units made their way to Bastogne. These forces fought on as food, ammunition, and medical supplies dwindled. Clouds and snow kept Allied aircraft from attacking the Germans or dropping supplies.

The Germans wanted Bastogne because it was a road junction in a rugged region of few roads. Capture of the town would prolong the offensive and perhaps enable the Germans to thrust to Antwerp.

On Dec. 20 German troops surrounded the town and two days later demanded that the outnumbered U.S. troops surrender. Brig. Gen. ANTHONY C. MCAULIFFE, acting commander of the 101st, replied with a memorable single word: "Nuts!"

Gen. GEORGE S. PATTON'S Third ARMY troops fought their way to Bastogne and broke through to relieve the defenders on Dec. 26. The next day U.S. trucks and ambulances rolled into the town, ending the siege.

Bat Bombs

Proposed weapon using bats fitted with incendiary BOMBS and dropped from aircraft. The bat bombs were to be used on the wood-and-paper homes of the Japanese. The idea came from Dr. Lytle S. Adams, a Pennsylvania dental surgeon who was inspired after a visit to Carlsbad Caverns, N.M., home of millions of bats. Adams wrote the White House, which passed the idea to the Army CHEMICAL WARFARE Service (CWS). According to the CWS's official history, "President ROOSEVELT OK'd it and the project was on."

After experimenting with several species, Adams and a team of naturalists selected the Mexican freetailed *(Tadarida brasiliensis),* which was the species Adams had seen at Carlsbad. The freetails, which weigh up to half an ounce, could carry a 1-ounce bomb and still fly. The task of making a weapon system out of the bats fell to the Army Air Forces, which turned to Dr. L. F. Fisser of the National Defense Research Committee.

Fisser designed two bombs for the bats. One, weighing just over half an ounce, would burn for four minutes; the other, a 2-ouncer, burned for six minutes. The bombs were filled with jellylike kerosene and set off when a chemical corroded a spring-held wire that propelled a firing pin to the bomb's igniter head.

The bomb was attached by string and a surgical clip to loose skin on the bat's chest. The armed bats were loaded, about 180 at a time, in cardboard containers set to open at about 1,000 feet. The bats, according to the CWS history, were to "fly into hiding in dwellings or other structures, gnaw through the string, and leave the bombs behind."

The bats' first test missions, using dummy bombs, were flown in May 1943 aboard a B-25 MITCHELL bomber. In the bat drop, many disappeared and many fell to earth. More than 6,000 bats were used and a hangar and general's car set afire before the AAF decided in Aug. 1943 to give the project to the Navy, which called it Project X-Ray and soon passed it to the Marines. The bat bombs were still being tested in Aug. 1944 when the project was canceled. About $2,000,000 and an unknown number of bats had been lost on the project.

Bat Missile

GUIDED MISSILE used by the U.S. Navy in the final stages of the Pacific war. It was the most sophisticated winged (guided) missile flown in the war. Three Navy patrol bomber SQUADRONS (VPB) flying the PB4Y-2 PRIVATEER were equipped with Bat glide bombs, carrying one missile under each wing. The Bat's range and speed depended upon the altitude of the launch aircraft, with maximum range being about 20 miles; its terminal speed was 300 mph.

Bats were first used in combat on April 23, 1945, when Privateers from VPB-109, flying from Palawan in the Philippines, launched Bat missiles against Japanese shipping in Balikpapan Harbor, Borneo. Two small freighters were hit and sunk or damaged, and an oil-storage tank ashore was destroyed. But their principal target, a Japanese transport, escaped unscathed. Surrounding land interfered with the missile's RADAR signals.

Subsequently, VPB-109 was transferred to OKINAWA, followed by the two other Bat squadrons. They made several attacks against Japanese warships and merchantmen, but they apparently only damaged several ships, scoring no kills. Modified Bats were also used against bridges in Japanese-controlled areas of Burma. (Some sources contend that Bats sank a Japanese destroyer; there is no evidence to support this claim.)

The harbinger of the Bat was the Dragon missile developed in 1941 by RCA; that was an air-launched, television-guided TORPEDO for use against surface ships. That weapon became the Pelican, with a DEPTH CHARGE as warhead and then a 2,000-pound bomb. The final iteration of this concept was the Bat, developed by the Navy's Bureau of Ordnance and Massachusetts Institute of Technology in collaboration with Western Electric.

Western Electric produced 300 Bats in 1944 and 2,800 in 1945, together with eighty-two control systems for the launching aircraft. The Bat itself had a self-contained, active homing radar, the missile being named for the flying mammal that could see in the dark by sending out high-pitched screams and listening for the sound waves to bounce back from walls and other obstacles. While being carried on an aircraft, the missile was fed target data collected by the aircraft's radar. When an enemy ship was selected, the Bat's radar was locked onto the target's echo signal and the missile was released, the aircraft remaining outside the range of the target's defensive guns. The missile's guidance then controlled the tail plane and wing elevons to guide the missile to its target. The payload of the Bat was a 1,000-pound bomb; the total weapon weighed 1,880 pounds.

In addition to the Privateer, the Bat was considered for carrying by the Navy's F7F TIGERCAT, a twin-engine, carrier-based fighter. An SB2C-1C HELLDIVER was launched by catapult from a carrier with a Bat to demonstrate the feasibility of employing the missiles from carriers, but further trials were halted in favor of the Privateer.

The Bat was originally designated bomb Mk 57 and went to war as the Mk 9 SWOD (Special Weapon Ordnance Device); after the war the Bat was given the Air-to-Surface Missile (Navy) designation ASM-N-2.

Bataan

A rugged, mountainous peninsula in the Philippines and the site of a gallant but hopeless battle early in the JAPANESE CAMPAIGN IN THE FAR EAST. After the Japanese invasion of the Philippines in Dec. 1941, Gen. DOUGLAS MACARTHUR, commander of both U.S. and Filipino forces in the Philippines—totaling about eleven divisions—withdrew to the Bataan Peninsula. MacArthur had believed that he could defend against and even defeat a Japanese invasion. Withdrawal to Bataan was part of his plan. But the strategy depended upon the arrival of reinforcements who would help him fight back up the peninsula. But the U.S. Navy, devastated by the PEARL HARBOR attack, could not help the Philippines.

Gen. MASAHARU HOMMA, commander of the Japanese invasion force, had been given fifty days and two divisions to take Luzon, the main island of the Philippines and site of its capital city MANILA. In planning his strategy, he assumed that MacArthur's forces would stand and fight rather than to lose Manila.

When MacArthur withdrew to Bataan, Homma decided not to change his "Manila First" plan. Not until Jan. 9, 1942, after first occupying Manila, did Homma turn to Bataan. Following a heavy ARTILLERY barrage, Homma sent his men across the Calaguiman River to within 150 yards of the defense line and then hit the defender with a suicidal BANZAI charge. Homma drove MacArthur's troops farther and farther down the peninsula, but their valiant defense denied Homma the swift victory he wanted.

MacArthur, under orders from President ROOSEVELT, in March left the Philippines for Australia, leaving command to newly promoted Lt. Gen. JONATHAN WAINWRIGHT. By then the defenders included some 500 U.S. sailors and their officers, evacuated from bombed-out naval facilities, who formed the Provisional Naval Battalion. They dyed their white uniforms with coffee grounds, hoping for khaki but getting yellow instead. A startled Japanese officer wrote in his diary that he had seen "a new type of suicide squad dressed in brightly colored uniforms."

With a reinforced army, Homma on April 3 hit the weak U.S.-Filipino lines hard. "Waves of shock troops have attacked almost continuously, without regard to casualties, which have been heavy on both sides," said a WAR DEPARTMENT communiqué. "American and Filipino troops, including naval and Marine contingents, have stubbornly resisted. . . ." The next communiqué announced the "complete physical exhaustion of the troops" and "the probability that the defenders on Bataan have been overcome."

On April 9 Bataan's defenders surrendered. When MacArthur heard the news, he issued an emotional statement: "The Bataan force went out as it would have wished, fighting to the end of its flickering, forlorn hope. No army has ever done so much with so little. . . . To the weeping mothers of its dead I can only say that the sacrifice and halo of Jesus of Nazareth has descended upon their sons and God will take them unto Himself." The starving survivors, taken as PRISONERS OF WAR, were forced on a barbaric 60-mile BATAAN DEATH MARCH.

From Bataan about 2,000 men and a few nurses made it to the fortified island of CORREGIDOR, which would surrender on May 6. On June 9 Homma, who had failed to keep to his fifty-day schedule, was relieved of his command.

Bataan Death March

The 60-mile movement of some 76,000 PRISONERS OF WAR—12,000 of them Americans, the rest Filipino troops—under barbaric conditions after the U.S.-Filipino surrender of BATAAN to Japanese forces in April 1942. Word of the atrocity came three years later, when three American officers escaped from the Japanese and brought out the story of what quickly became known as the Bataan Death March.

It began on April 10, 1942, when thousands of prisoners were assembled, searched, and stripped of all belongings. Some were beheaded, allegedly for having Japanese money. Then, in groups of 500 to 1,000, the prisoners were marched off, without food or water, toward a camp being built at San Fernando in Pampanga Province.

"A Japanese soldier took my canteen, gave the water to a horse, and threw the canteen away," one of the escapees reported. "We passed a Filipino prisoner of war who had been bayoneted. Men recently killed were lying along the roadside; many had been run over and flattened by Japanese trucks. . . . The night of the 11th we again were searched and then the march resumed. . . . The stronger were not permitted to help the weaker. We then would hear shots behind us."

On April 12, the Japanese gave the prisoners "the sun treatment." They were made to sit in the open sun, without water. "Many of us went crazy and several died. The Japanese dragged out the sick and delirious. Three Filipino and three American soldiers were buried while still alive."

For some, the march lasted six days; for others, twelve. A U.S. WAR DEPARTMENT report estimated that 5,200 Americans died on the march. But the dying went on at the prison camp, where the death rate went as high as 550 men a day.

After the war blame for the death march centered on Gen. MASAHARU HOMMA, who was convicted and executed in postwar WAR CRIMES trials.

Batfish (SS 310)

U.S. SUBMARINE that sank three Japanese undersea craft—the world's only submarine to sink that number of enemy submarines.

The *Batfish* undertook six war patrols between Dec. 1943 and the end of the war. In Feb. 1945 U.S. intercepts of Japanese radio transmissions (see MAGIC) indicated that several Japanese submarines had been ordered to Luzon to evacuate stranded pilots to Japan, where trained pilots were desperately needed. The *Batfish* was one of several U.S. submarines ordered to form a barrier to intercept the Japanese undersea craft.

The *Batfish* was operating off the northern Philippine island of Luzon late on Feb. 9, 1945, when she torpedoed and sank the surfaced Japanese submarine *RO-55*. (Although a U.S. DESTROYER ESCORT reported attacking the surfaced *RO-55* late on the night of Feb. 7–8, and was initially given credit for sinking the submarine, it appears more likely that in fact the *Batfish* destroyed the *RO-55*.) Two days later the *Batfish* detected and sank the *RO-112* off Camiguin Island, and two days after that the U.S. submarine sank the *RO-113* off Babuyan Island.

All three *Batfish* successes came through the de-

tection of RADAR emissions from the Japanese submarines. The Japanese submarines were apparently using their air-search radars because they feared U.S. nocturnal air attacks.

In addition to the three submarines, the *Batfish* sank three other Japanese ships, a minesweeper, and two merchant ships; her six victims totaled 8,543 tons. (The *Batfish* was also credited with having TORPEDOED a destroyer, which was stranded and under salvage when the torpedo apparently broke her in two.) The submarine earned the Presidential Unit Citation and nine BATTLE STARS for her war patrols.

After the war the *Batfish* was decommissioned and placed in "mothballs" from April 1946 until March 1952, when she was recommissioned for antisubmarine training; from 1960 to 1969 she served as an immobilized training ship, being stricken in 1969, and then became a memorial at Muskogee, Okla.

A *Balao* (SS 285)–class submarine, the *Batfish* was built at the Portsmouth Navy Yard (N.H.). She was launched on May 5, 1943, and commissioned that August. The submarine displaced 1,525 tons surfaced and 2,425 tons submerged, and was 311½ feet long. Her armament consisted of ten 21-inch (533-mm) torpedo tubes—six bow and four stern, and she carried twenty-four torpedoes. For use against small surface ships the *Batfish* had a 5-inch (127-mm) deck gun and lighter antiaircraft weapons and machine guns. Her crew numbered eighty-five.

Battalion

A military unit, usually of ground forces, consisting of three or four COMPANIES or (if artillery) BATTERIES. Infantry, artillery, and armored battalions are normally subordinate to REGIMENTS or DIVISIONS, although these and special-purpose battalions (e.g., signal, reconnaissance) can be attached to higher formations or can be independent units. Battalions are normally commanded by lieutenant colonels.

In the 1943 U.S. Army tables of organization an infantry battalion provided for 871 officers and enlisted men, a tank battalion 729 men, an armored infantry battalion 1,000 men, and an infantry (airborne) parachute battalion 530 men.

Artillery battalions also varied considerably in

size. In 1943 an armored artillery battalion (105-mm howitzers) had an authorized strength of 534 men, a light artillery battalion (105-mm howitzers) had 509 men, a medium artillery battalion (155-mm howitzers) 519 men, and an airborne antiair/antitank battalion (57-mm guns and .50-cal. machine guns) 641 men.

The specialized battalions of an infantry division in 1943 were the medical battalion with an authorized strength of 465 men and the engineer battalion with 647 men; the 1943 armored division had an engineer battalion of 693 men, a medical battalion of 417 men, and an ordnance (maintenance) battalion of 762 men.

Battery

ARTILLERY unit usually consisting of several sections including four or six firing sections that each manned one howitzer or gun. Batteries were subordinate to artillery BATTALIONS and were the smallest artillery organization that provided mess, supply, and other support functions to troops. (In most other branches the term COMPANY was used in place of battery while certain CAVALRY and reconnaissance organizations used the term *TROOP*.) Batteries were normally commanded by captains.

In the 1943 U.S. Army tables of organization medium artillery batteries had 109 officers and enlisted men (with four 155-mm howitzers) and light artillery batteries had 100 (with four 105-mm howitzers). Armored artillery batteries were larger, normally with six 105-mm self-propelled howitzers.

There were artillery batteries that fired larger weapons, while various headquarters and service batteries were assigned to artillery battalions and BRIGADES.

Within infantry units (divisions, regiments, battalions), specialized weapon, cannon, and antitank units were called companies and not batteries as they were part of the infantry branch and not artillery.

Battle of the Atlantic

The longest and in several respects most vital and complex battle of the war. The Atlantic was a vital route for Britain to bring in supplies to survive and for the United States to take the war to Germany. In 1940 Prime Minister CHURCHILL stipulated that about 120,000 tons of cargo—at least twenty ships—had to arrive at British ports each day for the country to survive and defeat Germany.

The German Navy and the Luftwaffe sought to deny that ocean to the ALLIES. The German Navy had planned to primarily use surface ships to attack Allied CONVOYS. However, the heavy German naval losses in the invasion of Norway in 1940 left the burden of the war at sea on submarines. Thus the U-BOAT would be the principal German weapon used in the battle, although aircraft, surface ships, and MINES played a significant but limited role.

First Phase (Sept. 1939–Dec. 1941)

The battle began on the day Britain and France declared war against Germany, Sept. 3, 1939, when the submarine *U-30* sank the 13,851-ton British liner *Athenia* carrying over 1,100 passengers. One hundred and twelve lives were lost, of whom twenty-eight were Americans.

When the EUROPEAN WAR began the German Navy had only fifty-seven U-boats in commission, of which twenty-six were large enough to operate in the Atlantic. The average number of submarines at sea, in the Atlantic and North Sea, during Sept. 1939 was twenty-three. The U-boats suffered from faulty TORPEDOES and the lack of naval aircraft to fly reconnaissance over the Atlantic to locate merchant convoys.

Despite the small number of German submarines, they inflicted significant damage on British shipping and naval forces. Two weeks after the war began the *U-29* sank the carrier *Courageous* while on antisubmarine patrol, with 519 officers and men going down with the ship; the carrier *ARK ROYAL* had a close escape from a U-boat's torpedoes, and the Royal Navy was forced to realize that using carriers and the few available destroyers in U-boat hunting groups was both fruitless and dangerous. Rather, the grouping of merchant ships in convoys was quickly adopted as the best means of protecting merchant ships. Still, by the end of the first month of the war the U-boats had sunk forty-one merchant ships (153,000 gross tons—the measurement of carrying capacity).

The following month was worse, although the average number at sea declined to ten as the boats on patrol when the war began had to return to port for supplies and torpedoes. But in Oct. 1939 the *U-29* (now commanded by U-boat ACE GÜNTHER PRIEN) sank the battleship *Royal Oak* within the British base of Scapa Flow in the Orkney Islands of Scotland. The dreadnought went down with her admiral and 785 crewmen. The destruction of merchant shipping was more significant as the monthly tonnage grew during 1939–1940.

The fall of France greatly increased U-boat effectiveness as the French coast provided more direct access for submarines to reach the shipping lanes (see SUBMARINE PENS). The *U-30* arrived at Lorient on July 7, 1940, the first U-boat to reach a French port to refuel, take on provisions, and rearm.

As the number of U-boats increased, *Kontradmiral* KARL DÖNITZ, head of the U-boat arm, was able to implement the "WOLF PACK" tactic that he had developed in the late 1930s. The first wolf pack had been tried in mid-Oct. 1939 when four U-boats attacked a convoy sailing from GIBRALTAR to Britain. In rapid succession, three submarines sank three merchant ships and the convoy scattered. That should have made them more vulnerable to attack as the few escort ships could not effectively protect them, but on that occasion there were no further losses.

During this period Dönitz's plans for the battle were continually hampered by the shortage of U-boats. The number of submarines available for Atlantic operations fell, from losses, and also from the need for boats to return to dockyards for overhauls after months at sea. Long-range U-boat strength reached a nadir of twenty-two units in Feb. 1941. At any given time about one third of the available submarines were actually on patrol.

Second Phase (Jan. 1942–May 1943)

The entry of the United States into the war clarified the situation for U-boat commanders with respect to U.S. warships. Since the NEUTRALITY PATROL had begun in Sept. 1939 American warships had been assisting British convoy escorts. Now American ships were fair game and the first few months of 1942 became known as the *Paukenschlag* (Drumbeat) as U-boats attacked U.S. merchant shipping off the U.S. East Coast and in the Caribbean with impunity. Despite the British experience—which was shared with the United States—

U.S. antisubmarine efforts were ineffective, convoys nonexistent, and the Navy and Army Air Force leaders fought over the allocation of long-range aircraft that were needed for hunting submarines. The first U-boat success by Americans occurred when a Navy PBO Ventura (see A-28 HUDSON) sank the *U-656* off Newfoundland on March 1, 1942.

By mid-1942 the U-boat command was approaching its goal of severing Britain from the United States. In June the Allies lost a total of 173 ships (834,196 tons) to U-boats, most in the western Atlantic. New U-boats were being delivered at the rate of thirty *each month* (against losses of twenty-one submarines in the first *six months* of 1942). However, despite their successes—due in part to periodically being able to read Allied convoy codes (see *B-DIENST*)—the Germans completely missed several convoys sailing from the United States and Britain for the NORTH AFRICA INVASION. During Nov. 1942, 1,065 Allied ships made passages from Britain and the United States to North Africa, many entering the western Mediterranean; U-boats sank only twenty-three of those ships.

After those Nov. 1942 landings, HITLER demanded that U-boats be sent into the Mediterranean, a move that reduced the effectiveness of the Atlantic campaign. Also, Hitler regularly demanded naval reinforcements for Norway, including U-boats, because of his fear of an Allied invasion there. Although no landings were forthcoming, those U-boats were effective against the RUSSIAN CONVOYS.

While these diversions were significant, Allied shipping loss in the Atlantic continued to climb as the U-boat fleet grew. By March 1, 1943, there were 400 U-boats in service, of which 222 were front-line, ocean-going submarines; of those, 114 were at sea in the Atlantic. There were several major convoy battles in March: In the first three weeks Convoy SC 121 lost thirteen ships, HX 228 lost four, HX 229 also thirteen, and SC 122 another nine—in all thirty-nine. Official Royal Navy historian S. W. Roskill would later record, ". . . the Germans never came so near to disrupting communication between the New World and the Old as in the first twenty days of March, 1943." By the end of the month U-boats had sunk eighty-two ships in the North Atlantic, with another thirty-eight sunk in other areas. With such losses there could not be a matériel buildup in England for a cross-Channel invasion; indeed, such losses could threaten the survival of Britain. Further, with nearly two thirds of the ships sunk having been in convoys, a British Naval Staff appreciation noted: "It appeared possible that we should not be able to continue [to consider] convoy as an effective system of defence." Roskill added that convoys had been the "lynch pin" of British maritime strategy for three-and-a-half years. "Where could the Admiralty turn if the convoy system had lost its effectiveness? They did not know; but they must have felt, though no one admitted it, that defeat stared them in the face."

And, more U-boats were going to sea. Suddenly, however, merchant ship losses declined and U-boat sinkings increased. For example, although Convoy SC 130 sailing in mid-May 1943 was attacked by a total of thirty-three U-boats, not a single merchant ship was lost while five submarines succumbed to antisubmarine efforts. From then on U-boat losses were regularly exceeding merchant ships sunk.

New Allied antisubmarine weapons long in production were coming into the battle in decisive numbers. Large numbers of convoy escorts were at sea and fitted with the highly effective 10-centimeter RADAR; long-range bombers, especially the B-24 LIBERATOR, were available in greater numbers; new ESCORT CARRIERS could provide aircraft to close the "gap" between the land-based aircraft; and Allied code-breaking efforts (ULTRA) were increasingly successful in giving the Allies information on U-boat activity.

Third Phase (May 1943–May 1945)

After the losses in May 1943 Dönitz withdrew his U-boats from the North Atlantic convoy routes. He acknowledged that Germany had suffered a serious defeat. But he was confident that the withdrawal was only temporary, that German technology would soon provide countermeasures against the Allied advantages, especially radar and the consequent danger of surprise air attacks.

Acoustic homing torpedoes (GNAT) were introduced to U-boats; they would be fired to home onto the sounds of an escort ship's propellers (but they were quickly countered by FOXER). When U-boats leaving French ports were regularly located

on the surface at night by radar-equipped aircraft, Dönitz had his submarines travel on the surface in daylight, giving them a heavy antiaircraft armament to shoot down those planes (and traveling submerged in darkness). But Allied planes were soon able to outgun (and ROCKET) the U-boats. By then Dönitz had outfitted several of his U-boats with SNORKELS that permitted his submarines to remain submerged indefinitely, but impeded their speed. When Dönitz attempted to keep his submarines away from port by refueling and resupplying them with food and torpedoes at sea, Allied code-breaking permitted the rapid eradication of the MILCH COW supply submarines.

At every turn the U-boat effort was frustrated, albeit not without continued losses to Allied merchant ships. The snorkel and heavy antiaircraft gun batteries had been interim measures until new submarines would be available, the TYPE XXI long-range submarine and TYPE XXIII coastal submarine. These craft were truly revolutionary, but they were too late. Allied STRATEGIC BOMBING had at last contributed to the U-boat campaign by damaging shipyards and blasting submarines in fitting-out basins. More significant, RAF fighter aircraft attacking with rockets and bombers laying mines made it impossible for U-boats to carry out trials and training in the Baltic.

When the war ended in early May 1945 only six of the Type XXIII submarines had been on patrol and only one Type XXI was fully operational, with hundreds of both designs in various stages of construction and working up to combat readiness. But they came too late. The Battle of the Atlantic had been won by the Allies, albeit at great cost.

In all theaters U-boats sank over 3,500 merchant ships totaling 18,300,000 tons (British records 2,603 ships aggregating 13,500,000 tons), of which 2,452 ships of 12,800,000 tons sunk in the Atlantic. In addition, U-boats sank 175 naval warships armed auxiliaries. Tens of thousands of British, American, and other Allied merchant seamen and sailors had died in those burning and sinking ships.

It was also a close battle: "The only thing that ever really frightened me during the war was the U-boat peril . . . ," wrote Prime Minister Churchill. "I was even more anxious about this battle that I had been about the glorious air fight called the BATTLE OF BRITAIN."

Battle of Britain

The air war over Britain from Aug. 13 to Oct. 31, 1940. After the capitulation of France in June 1940 the German Army and Luftwaffe were poised on the coast of the English Channel. Beyond the 20-odd miles of water lay England, virtually defenseless except for the relatively few fighter and bomber squadrons of the Royal Air Force. HITLER, having succeeded in the FRANCE AND LOW COUNTRIES CAMPAIGN beyond his own hopes and the plans of his generals, now awaited the entreaties from England for peace negotiations.

But the British were not forthcoming to entreat with German diplomats and, almost reluctantly, Hitler began plans for Operation SEA LION (See-löwe), the invasion of England. First the Luftwaffe would have to sweep the RAF from the skies—not merely win aerial superiority, but destroy the fighters and bombers that could impede the assault.

After the assault on France and the Low Countries, which had come on the heels of the battle for Norway, the Luftwaffe required rest, rearming, and the movement of its support establishment, BOMBS, ammunition, and fuel to bases in France. Thus, even if the decision were made immediately after the DUNKIRK evacuation in early June, the Luftwaffe could not have effectively attacked England.

But the Luftwaffe did begin probing flights over England, and bombers began attacking British shipping offshore and laying mines in coastal waters. In this phase of the air battle—from July 10 through Aug. 10, 1940—the Luftwaffe lost 227 aircraft while the RAF lost only ninety-six. And many of the RAF pilots were able to parachute to safety, a possibility denied to German pilots shot down over England. More important, this period permitted a buildup of RAF fighters and the development of intercept tactics at a low level of combat intensity. The British were also able to discover the German bomber navigation system, which was based on electronic beams sent out from the continent and crossing over the bombers' target.

The main phase of the Battle of Britain began on Aug. 13—*Adler-Tag* or Eagle Day. The Luftwaffe had six weeks to destroy the RAF in preparation for the Sea Lion assault. On Eagle Day the RAF Fighter Command could muster 909 first-line SPITFIRE and HURRICANE fighters plus eighty-four older aircraft. Arrayed against this defensive force, the Luftwaffe had over 2,800 fighters and bombers disposed in three air fleets for the coming battle: *Luftflotte* 2 under *Generalfeldmarschall* ALBERT KESSELRING in Belgium, Holland, and northeastern France; *Luftflotte* 3 under *Generalfeldmarschall* Hugo Sperrle in northwestern France; and *Luftflotte* 5 under *Generaloberst* Hans-Jürgen Stumpff in Norway and Denmark. (Sperrle had commanded the Condor Legion in the SPANISH CIVIL WAR.) Overall command of the air attack was vested by Hitler in his most-trusted lieutenant, *Reichsmarschall* Göring.

Luftflotte 5 would have a small (and disastrous) role in the coming battle because of the distance to targets in Britain. Francis K. Mason in his hallmark *Battle Over Britain* lists Luftwaffe strength at the end of July as:

	LUFTFLOTTE 2 & 3	LUFTFLOTTE 5
Bombers		
(DO 17, HE 111, JU 88)	1,200	115
Dive bombers (JU 87)	280	—
Single-engine fighters		
(ME/BF 109)	760	30
Zerstörer		
(ME/BF 110, JU 88C)	220	45
Long-range reconnaissance	50	30
Short-range reconnaissance	90	—
	2,600	220

The massive German raids that began on Eagle Day were intended to destroy British air defenses: killing fighters in the air and at their bases, destroying airfields, and knocking out the Chain Home RADAR stations that could give warning of German air attacks. The Eagle Day raids began in the morning and continued through the day, formation after formation of bombers escorted by waves of fighters.

But the day got off to a bad start for the Luftwaffe, as the first bomber raids droned on toward their targets unaware that last-minute weather reports had caused Göring to delay the raids until afternoon, the recall order only getting through to most of the escorting fighters. Warned by radar,

RAF fighters were waiting for the bombers. More bombers—with fighter escorts—came in the afternoon. Soon the defending fighters were simply overwhelmed by the stream of German aircraft.

When the day was over, the Luftwaffe had lost forty-six aircraft; many more were damaged. The RAF had lost thirteen fighters in aerial combat; another forty-seven aircraft were destroyed on airfields, but only one was a fighter. Most significant for the RAF, the Germans had knocked out one of the radar stations on the Isle of Wight and damaged five others.

The loss of the radar stations would have been disastrous, for without radar guidance (working through sector control stations) the RAF fighters would have been unable to scramble in time to meet German attackers, and would have too little information on their location to mount successful intercepts. (Antiaircraft guns—which did not yet have PROXIMITY-FUZE ammunition—were a secondary means of stopping air attacks.)

But here Göring made a major error as, on Aug. 15, at a conference of the three air fleet commanders he concluded, "It is doubtful whether there is any point in continuing the attacks on radar sites, in view of the fact that not one of those attacked has so far been put out of operation."

Operation Sea Lion historian Peter Fleming has astutely observed: "Here, early in the battle, we get a glimpse of fuddled thinking at the highest level in the German camp. The radar stations were an Achilles heel, or something very like one. The fact must have been recognised up to a point, or they would not have been singled out on the first day. By the fourth day it was believed, erroneously, that the attacks had been wholly ineffective; yet no effort had been made to improve on the first day's results. Finally (most singular of all) the commander-in-chief of an air force, confidently committed to depriving the British Isles—in six weeks—of both the will and the means to resist, was prepared to accept as indestructible a number of flimsy and conspicuous installations sited on the most readily accessible parts of enemy territory."

Day after day the Luftwaffe came. Aug. 15 also marked the first and last major daylight strike by *Luftflotte* 5 flying from bases in Norway and Denmark. The approaching aircraft were easily detected and intercepted; the Luftwaffe high command had thought that Fighter Command would be too busy over western England to adequately defend Scotland. But as the bombers and long-range fighters approached the Firth of Forth they were fallen on by Hurricanes and "Spits." Of about 100 aircraft sent out by *Luftflotte* 5, eight bombers and seven fighters were destroyed, several more heavily damaged, and many bombers were forced to jettison their bombs into the sea. None of the intercepting fighters was lost. (Some of the air fleet's planes were then sent to France to operate against Britain.)

Ju 87 *Stuka* dive bombers, which had done so well against ground forces in the benign conditions of Poland and France, were easily blasted out of the skies by RAF fighters. Of the eighty-five Ju 87s attacking targets in Britain on Aug. 17, twenty-six were shot down and another fourteen were damaged. They were withdrawn from the battle on Aug. 19. Still, there were plenty of Luftwaffe bombers, and they kept coming.

RAF Fighter Command was hard pressed. For thirteen days—from Aug. 24 through Sept. 6—there were an average of 1,000 German aircraft over England. Although the Luftwaffe was losing more planes per day than the RAF, the Hurricanes (which carried the brunt of the battle) and Spitfires were being worn out as well as shot down. And so were their pilots. Two or three fighter scrambles a day were normal; six or seven sorties per day were not uncommon. On Aug. 30 for the first time Fighter Command flew more than 1,000 sorties in a single day; fighter pilots fell asleep as soon as their aircraft stopped taxiing when they landed—ground crews had to turn off the engines—and the pilots slept while their planes were rearmed and refueled. Although the Navy's Fleet Air Arm and RAF Bomber Command contributed some pilots to Fighter Command, the defenses were still wearing thin. And, the training of new pilots was becoming more difficult because of the need for experienced pilots to fly missions rather than teach.

The British leadership, never quite certain at that stage of how strong the Luftwaffe really was and how many new fighters and bombers were being turned out each day by German factories, was beginning to realize by late Aug. 1940 that within a few weeks Fighter Command would be exhausted.

Then, German fighters and bombers could destroy the British bomber forces and clear the way for Sea Lion.

Meanwhile, the Luftwaffe was experiencing frustration if not fear of defeat. The air fleets had concentrated their attacks on forward airfields and aircraft factors from Eagle Day through Aug. 24. RAF Fighter Command had not been knocked out (although it would be a close thing had the existing Luftwaffe schedule continued). On Aug. 24 Göring shifted battle strategy; the new target was the sector control stations, which took the information provided by radar, plotted the incoming raids, and vectored the defending fighters. The stations, manned mostly by the RAF Women's Auxiliary Air Force, became the focus of intensive strikes.

Through Sept. 6 the Luftwaffe inflicted grievous damage on these sector centers. The RAF defenders lost 277 fighters in this two-week phase of the battle, against Luftwaffe losses of 378 aircraft; the 5-to-7 ratio, however, was the best that the Germans achieved during the battle. In that same period Fighter Command lost 103 pilots killed and 128 seriously wounded—out of a fighter pilot strength of about 1,000, almost one quarter had been lost in just two weeks. (Fighter Command lost a total of 375 pilots in the battle.)

"In the fighting between Aug. 24 and Sept. 6, the scales had tilted against Fighter Command," Prime Minister CHURCHILL would write afterwards. The fighter bases and sector stations were hit hard: "If the enemy had persisted in heavy attacks against the adjacent sectors and damaged their operations rooms or telephone communications, the whole intricate organisation of Fighter Command might have been broken down."

Then, suddenly, on Sept. 7, there was another change in Luftwaffe strategy. The morning was quiet, an "enigmatic lull for six hours," writes Mason. Late in the afternoon German bombers began the first concentrated attack on LONDON. All through the night, until just before dawn on the 8th, relays of Luftwaffe aircraft spewed high-explosive and incendiary bombs over the sprawling capital city. Bombers were thereafter over London for fifty-seven consecutive nights. The sector stations and fighter airfields were reprieved by the start of the BLITZ.

Wrote Churchill: "It was therefore with a sense of relief that Fighter Command felt the German attack turn on to London on Sept. 7. . . . Göring should certainly have persevered against the airfields, on whose organisation and combination the whole fighting power of our air force at this moment depended."

This is not to say that the pressure on Fighter Command was fully released. On Sept. 7 the RAF lost forty-one Spitfires and Hurricanes, and one BLENHEIM; the Germans lost sixty-three aircraft. The air battle continued, much of it now at night, when defensive antiaircraft guns, guided by probing searchlight beams, engaged German bombers as the few RAF night fighters also took to the skies.

The Luftwaffe had failed to defeat the RAF. Air Chief Marshal HUGH DOWDING, who had since 1936 led the buildup of Fighter Command, had triumphed despite the RAF leadership that had long considered defensive fighters as a stepchild to bomber and long-range escort development. (See: UNITED KINGDOM, AIR FORCE.) The air battle continued, by day as well as by night, in daylight almost entirely by fighter bombers, the Me (Bf) 109s and Me (Bf) 110s. On Sept. 17 Hitler postponed Operation Sea Lion indefinitely. On Oct. 4, meeting with Italian leader BENITO MUSSOLINI at BRENNER PASS, Hitler declared that only the lack of five consecutive days of good flying weather had prevented the Luftwaffe from gaining aerial superiority over Britain.

From July 10 through the end of October, the RAF lost 915 fighters (plus fighters and other planes destroyed on airfields); the Luftwaffe lost 1,733 aircraft to British fighters and antiaircraft guns, with much higher total loss.

Even before the battle was ended or even decided, Churchill, ever professing optimism during the worst adversity, paid the ultimate and lasting accolade to the RAF Fighter command. His words, spoken in the House of Commons on Aug. 20, were a tribute to not only the Spitfire and Hurricane pilots, but those who maintained, refueled, and rearmed them, the officers and "girls" in the sector stations, the technicians working the Chain Home radars, and Hugh Dowding and his lieutenants:

"Never in the field of human conflict was so much owed by so many to so few."

Battle Pennant,

see BATTLE STREAMERS.

Battle Stars

The U.S. Navy awarded battle stars to ships and units that participated in combat operations. The stars were emblazoned on campaign ribbons painted, at times, on the ships' superstructure. Battle stars were also worn on personnel campaign ribbons. (See Appendix for complete listing.)

Battle Streamers

U.S. Army and AAF battle streamers—bunting attached to unit flags—were awarded to units that served in World War II. Stars for participation in these actions were worn on personnel campaign ribbons. (See Appendix for complete listing.)

Battleaxe

Code name for the failed British offensive in the western desert, North Africa, Nov. 1941.

Battleships

When the Japanese struck at PEARL HARBOR on Dec. 7, 1941, the U.S. Navy had seventeen battleships in service—fifteen completed from 1912 to 1923, and two modern ships, the *North Carolina* (BB 55) and *Washington* (BB 56), both completed in 1941. At the time of the Pearl Harbor attack nine of the older ships were in the Pacific Fleet; of the eight at Pearl Harbor, Japanese planes destroyed two, the *ARIZONA* (BB 39) and *Oklahoma* (BB 37), and inflicted heavy damage on five others, sinking two and forcing one to run aground so she didn't block the channel. Those five ships were later rebuilt and served in the war. One Pacific Fleet battleship was at Bremerton, Wash., at the time of the attack. On Dec. 7 six of the older battleships and the two new ships were in the Atlantic.

Eight additional battleships were delivered to the fleet during the war: four ships of the *IOWA* (BB 61) class and four of the *South Dakota* (BB 57) class. All ten of the modern ships were armed with nine 16-inch guns plus lesser weapons. The four *Iowa*s were the largest and most heavily armed battleships built by any nation except for the Japanese *YAMATO* and *Musashi* (both were sunk by aircraft from U.S. AIR-

CRAFT CARRIERS). The U.S. Navy had planned a larger class of battleships, the 58,000-ton *Montana* (BB 67) class, to have been armed with twelve 16-inch guns; that program was canceled in 1943 before any units had been laid down.

In addition to battleships, the U.S. Navy completed two large cruisers during the war, the *Alaska* (CB 1) and *Guam* (CB 2), both commissioned in 1944. They were generally referred to as battle cruisers, although they were more heavily armored than the famed ships of that type of the World War I era, such as the British *REPULSE*. The U.S. ships each carried a main battery of nine 12-inch guns.

During the war there were two battleship-versus-battleship engagements off GUADALCANAL in 1942. In one the new *Washington* (BB 56) sank a Japanese battle cruiser (while suffering no damage, although an accompanying U.S. battleship was severely damaged by cruiser and destroyer fire). Six old U.S. battleships—four of them survivors of the Japanese attack on Pearl Harbor—fought a night battle with Japanese ships in Oct. 1944 in Surigao Strait during the battle for LEYTE GULF in the Philippines; the U.S. battleships and other warships ambushed and sank two Japanese battleships. In the Atlantic, two old U.S. battleships engaged the unfinished French battleship *Jean Bart* during the Nov. 1942 landings at Casablanca at the start of the NORTHWEST AFRICA CAMPAIGN. On occasions during the war, U.S. battleships served with the British Home Fleet to provide distant covering forces for the RUSSIAN CONVOYS and other northern operations, but those ships did not see action.

The principal roles of U.S. battleships during the war, however, were providing antiaircraft defense for carrier task forces and shore bombardment in preparation of amphibious landings. Beginning on July 14, 1945, U.S. battleships bombarded coastal targets in Japan (in conjunction with carrier air strikes). On that date, three battleships, two CRUISERS, and nine destroyers bombarded the steel and iron works at Kamaishi with 802 rounds from the 16-inch guns plus lesser caliber guns.

No U.S. battleships were sunk by enemy action after the Pearl Harbor attack. Thus, at the time of the Japanese surrender on board the U.S. battleship *MISSOURI* (BB 63) in Tokyo Bay on Sept. 2, 1945, the Navy had in service ten modern battleships, two battle cruisers, and thirteen older battleships.

Batty,

see APHRODITE.

Baytown

Code name for (1) Allied crossing of the Straits of Messina, Sept. 3, 1943; (2) U.S. plans to open a port on the coast of China to supply Nationalist forces.

Bazooka

A light, shoulder-held ROCKET launcher for use against tanks. The U.S. weapon was invented during the war to provide an infantry weapon to counter German tanks. Gen. DWIGHT D. EISENHOWER credited the bazooka as one of the four weapons that helped most to win the war (the others being the C-47 SKYTRAIN/DAKOTA TRANSPORT, JEEP, and ATOMIC BOMB).

The smooth-bore, electrically fired bazooka launched a rocket projectile with an effective range of about 300 feet. The tube-like device was 54

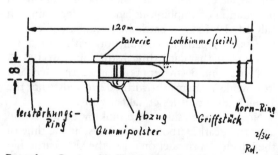

Bazooka—German intelligence sketch.

inches long with a diameter of 2.36 inches; the rocket projectile weighed 3½ pounds. The tube folded in half for carrying or stowage. Normally one soldier fired the bazooka and a second served as loader.

Introduced in 1942, the bazooka was only marginally effective against German PANTHER vice Panzer and TIGER tanks when fired at their armored frontal areas; however, it proved to be effective against their tracks and some spots where the armor was weak. Almost a half-million bazookas were produced. A U.S. infantry division in July 1943 was authorized to have 557 bazookas, and the smaller airborne division 567 of them. It remained in U.S. service into the Korean War.

The bazooka was named for a musical device invented by American comedian Bob Burns. He, in turn, had adapted his device from a funnel-ended farming instrument used for hand-planting.

B-Dienst

German Navy cryptoanalytical service during the war. *B-Dienst* (the abbreviation for *Beobachtungdienst* or "observation service") was highly effective in decoding Allied radio traffic to permit the guiding of U-BOATS to CONVOY positions. *B-Dienst* was particularly important because of the lack of other intelligence sources on Allied convoy movements.

The service traced its origins to 1919 when members of the Imperial German Navy's World War I code-breaking organization were recalled to service. *B-Dienst* had several successes against British naval codes in the 1920s and 1930s, and by the eve of World War II was having successes with other foreign codes.

Some British naval codes were read through the critical convoy battle of March 1943; U.S. Navy codes could not be read with any frequency. Then, in April 1942, even this meager code-breaking success stopped because the U.S. Navy put a new machine cipher into service. In addition to breaking the British codes through analysis, *B-Dienst* was helped when the British destroyer *Sikh* was sunk in shallow water off TOBRUK in Sept. 1942 and her codebook was recovered.

Breaking the British codes permitted U-BOATS to be vectored to intercept convoys. Thus, *B-Dienst* made a major contribution to the German successes in the BATTLE OF THE ATLANTIC.

The code broken in Sept. 1942 went out of use in April 1943, after which *B-Dienst*'s successes declined. Many of the service's files—and hence its effectiveness—were destroyed in an Allied air raid on BERLIN in Nov. 1943. Allied coding efficiency also continued to reduce the ability of *B-Dienst* to read codes as the war progressed. Still, according to intelligence historian David Kahn, *B-Dienst* compiled "a record unmatched by any other intelligence agency of the THIRD REICH."

During the war the *B-Dienst* staff grew to some 5,000 men and women, of whom about 1,100 were in Berlin. After the Nov. 1943 bombing, *B-Dienst* operations were moved from Berlin to Eberswalde, some 25 miles northeast of the capital. In 1943 the organization was intercepting about 8,500 messages *per day,* although some were duplicates and certainly not all could be deciphered.

Bearcat,

see F8F.

Beaufighter

Highly effective British night fighter and antishipping aircraft developed from the BEAUFORT bomber and reconnaissance aircraft. The nightfighter variants began reaching the RAF Fighter Command in Sept. 1940 and with air-intercept RADAR and four 20-mm cannon in the nose and six .303-cal. machine guns in the wings was a deadly threat to German aircraft in daylight as well as at night.

The Mk IC entered service with RAF Coastal Command in early 1941, armed with eight ROCK-ETS and capable of carrying an aerial torpedo. Coastal Command versions had surface-search radar, making them effective against surfaced U-BOATS as well as surface craft.

Four U.S. AAF night-fighter squadrons in the Middle East received Beaufighters in mid-1943; they were flown until the end of the war (no U.S. designation was assigned).

The Bristol-developed Beaufighter prototype flew on July 17, 1939, shortly after 300 fighter variants had been ordered. Total British and Australian production was 5,962 aircraft, which served

through the end of the EUROPEAN WAR. A few saw service against the Japanese in the Pacific.

The Beaufighter had a conventional, twin-engine configuration, with a shortened, solid nose compared to the glazed nose of the Beaufort. In addition to the forward-firing guns, a single .303-cal. machine gun was fired from a manually operated dorsal position. The antishipping variants could carry two 500-pound BOMBS in lieu of a torpedo. The Mk X variants had a top speed of 320 mph and a range of 1,400 miles with a torpedo, or 1,750 with torpedo and additional fuel tanks.

Beaufort

British torpedo and reconnaissance aircraft. The RAF employed the twin-engine Beaufort primarily as a land-based torpedo bomber. In that role it was unable to prevent the escape of the German battleships *Gneisenau* and *Scharnhorst,* and the heavy cruiser *Prinz Eugen* during the CHANNEL DASH in Feb. 1942. From 1943 they were superseded in the torpedo attack role by the more-capable BEAU-FIGHTER.

The Bristol Beaufort was a twin-engine aircraft that first flew on Oct. 15, 1938. Production aircraft entered service with the Coastal Command in Dec. 1939. A total of 1,120 aircraft were built.

The Mk I had a maximum speed of 265 mph, and could carry up to 1,500 pounds of BOMBS in an internal bomb bay, or a semirecessed aerial torpedo. Two .303-cal. machine guns were mounted in the nose and another pair in a dorsal power turret. The crew numbered four.

Beaverbrook, Lord (1879–1964)

British publisher and politician. Lord (William Maxwell Aitken) Beaverbrook had an erratic career in Prime Minister CHURCHILL's wartime government. Removed in less than a year as minister of aircraft production, he later became minister of production, serving only fifteen days. He used his considerable influence as a close adviser to Churchill to champion military aid to the Soviet Union and the opening of a SECOND FRONT.

Beck, Gen. Ludwig (1880–1944)

Chief of the German General Staff from 1935 to 1938 and a leader of abortive conspiracies against

HITLER. As Chief of the General Staff, Beck opposed Hitler's plans for conquest and resigned his post in protest in 1938, hoping to impress his fellow officers.

After the EUROPEAN WAR began, Beck secretly continued his opposition and became a leader in the resistance against Hitler. He would probably have been the provisional leader of a post-Hitler Germany if the JULY 20 PLOT against Hitler had succeeded in 1944. Beck was at Army headquarters in BERLIN helping to continue what he thought was a successful plot when he learned that it had failed. He was handed his pistol by an officer loyal to Hitler. Beck tried twice to kill himself. A sergeant, following Beck's dying request, fired a fatal shot from Beck's pistol into his head.

Begonia

British code name for minelaying operations by carrier-based aircraft in Aaramsund, Norway, Sept. 1944.

Belgium

Capital: Brussels, pop. 8,386,553 (est. 1938). Germany, which had violated Belgium's neutrality by invading the nation in World War I, repeated the act on May 10, 1940, launching a BLITZKRIEG that ended with Belgium's surrender on May 28. King Leopold III, Commander in Chief of his beaten army, considered himself a prisoner of war. Members of the Belgian Cabinet, some of whom had escaped via Spain, established a government-in-exile in London. It declared war against the AXIS powers and established control over troops in its major African colony, the Belgian Congo. (Congo troops aided British troops in the liberation of Ethiopia in 1941 and of French West Africa in 1942.)

Germany annexed Eupen and Malmédy, making those regions part of the THIRD REICH. Drawing from Fascist movements in Flemish and French-speaking parts of the country, the Germans set up a collaborationist regime, established a Belgian HITLER YOUTH organization, and recruited a Belgian Fascist military unit that fought for Germany on the EASTERN FRONT. But the Belgian underground so harassed the conquerors that in July 1944 German control was tightened and more retaliatory power given the SS.

The German pillage of Belgium began immediately after surrender. The Germans exported such vast amounts of food to Germany that by the fall of 1940 an estimated one fifth of the Belgian population was starving. King Leopold went to BERCHTESGADEN and won from HITLER a cutback in food exports. When the Germans began deporting tens of thousands of Belgians for work in Germany, the king won exemptions for women, young girls, war orphans, and the children of PRISONERS OF WAR. Thousands of other Belgians, suspected of acts against the occupation authorities, were sent to German CONCENTRATION CAMPS and DEATH CAMPS. On June 7, 1944, the SS arrested the king. Both he and other members of the royal family were taken to Germany.

Allied troops liberated Belgium in Sept. 1944 during the ALLIED CAMPAIGN IN EUROPE, and the government-in-exile returned to Brussels. But for Belgium, the war was not over. Stubborn German forces on islands at the mouth of the Scheldt River kept Antwerp under fire, preventing Allied use of the port until Nov. 28. On Dec. 16 Gen. GERD VON RUNDSTEDT launched an offensive in the Belgian ARDENNES and German V-1 BUZZ BOMBS and V-2 MISSILES fell on Antwerp and Liège. The Ardennes offensive produced the Battle of the Bulge, which temporarily put some of Belgium back under the Germans' control until the Allies again drove them out in Jan. 1945. U.S. troops freed King Leopold and his family near Strobl, Austria, shortly before V-E DAY.

Bellows

British code name for reinforcement of MALTA, Aug. 1942; part of Operation Pedestal.

Belsen,

see CONCENTRATION CAMPS.

Beneš, Eduard (1884–1948)

President of Czechoslovakia from 1935 until 1938, when he resigned as a protest of the MUNICH PACT, which began the dismantling of his country by Germany. He then went to the United States, where he lectured at the University of Chicago. When the EUROPEAN WAR began, he founded the Czech National Committee in France. After the fall of France in June 1940, he moved to London and set up a provisional government, which the ALLIES recognized. He organized GUERRILLA resistance and negotiated a Czech-Soviet mutual friendship treaty.

Following the liberation of Czechoslovakia in May 1945 he set up a provisional government in Prague. He authorized the forcible expulsion of Germans and Hungarians from what had become again Czech territory, and nationalized banks, coal mines, and major industries. He was elected president in 1946 and served until 1948, when he resigned after Soviet-backed Communists took over the government.

Beowulf

German code name for occupation of Baltic islands.

Berchtesgaden

Site of HITLER's mountaintop retreat, also known as Eagle's Nest, in the Alps of southern Bavaria, near SALZBURG. Berchtesgaden was for a time the headquarters for the German Army High Command and the site of diplomatic meetings. Hitler's self-designed house, "Berghof" ("mountain court"), sat atop a 6,000-foot mountain and was virtually impregnable. A 10-mile, switchback road ended at a mountain wall that opened to a long tunnel carved in the living rock. The tunnel led to an elevator that rose 370 feet to Berghof. A French diplomat who visited here wrote, "Was this edifice the work of a normal mind or of one tormented by megalomania and haunted by visions of domination and solitude?"

Bergen-Belsen,

see CONCENTRATION CAMPS.

Berghof,

see BERCHTESGADEN.

Beria, Lavrenti Pavlovich (1899–1953)

Notorious head of Commissariat for Internal Affairs (NKVD) under JOSEF STALIN from 1938 until his execution in 1953. Beria had been a close associate of Stalin, head of the secret police in the dictator's native Georgia, and a methodical policeman

and intelligence collector. Soon after his appointment in Dec. 1938, Beria was made a candidate (nonvoting) member of the ruling Politburo, the first chief of the secret police to join that ruling body.

Beria was already infamous in the Soviet Union as a policeman and as a lecher. He regularly picked up young girls on the street and took them to his office, where he forced them to commit sodomy and then raped them. The threat of arrest of their families was usually a sufficient inducement for them to suffer in silence, although some are reported to have committed suicide in shame. One of his victims, a young girl who had voluntarily come to Beria's office to plead for her arrested brother, was held for several days and raped repeatedly. Beria then decided to "keep her" by marrying her. The change in his marital status did not end his perversions with young girls and with women employed by the NKVD, sometimes in his own home as well as in his office.

Beria was the acme of the secret policeman, at least in the Stalinist sense. He increased surveillance in foreign countries of the few remaining old Bolsheviks, among them Leon Trotsky, who had been Stalin's rival to succeed Lenin. (A Beria agent "executed" Trotsky in Mexico in Aug. 1940.) Many thousands more fell to the pistols of Beria's executioners as Stalin's purges continued until the Soviet Union and Germany went to war in June 1941.

With the outbreak of war, Beria became one of Stalin's most important lieutenants. Beria, a deputy premier since Feb. 1941, was made a member of the State Defense Committee by Stalin during the war. He was promoted to Marshal of the Soviet Union in 1945 and made a full member of the Politburo (later Presidium) in 1946.

During the war the secret police had increased responsibilities—to protect the Kremlin leadership and to ensure the loyalty of the armies fighting the Germans. The latter role included the establishment of NKVD fighting formations. (See SMERSH.) Beria also became involved with foreign intelligence. Soviet diplomatic delegations to Britain, Canada, and the United States were assigned NKVD operatives to seek out military information that could be of value to the Kremlin. In addition, a Soviet purchasing commission was established in the United States to speed the transfer of arms to the Soviet Union. With more than one thousand employees, the commission—under Beria—became a collection point for secrets.

Stalin put Beria in charge of ATOMIC BOMB development and gave him responsibility for copying the three U.S. B-29 SUPERFORTRESS bombers that had landed in Siberia so that the Soviets would have an atomic bomb delivery system.

Beria continued in his various roles after the war, envisioning himself as Stalin's successor. When Stalin died on March 5, 1953, Beria shared the ruling of the Soviet Union with Georgi Malenkov and NIKITA KHRUSHCHEV. However, Beria survived only until June 26, 1953, when he went to the Kremlin for a meeting of the leadership. In a joint plot of the collective leadership and the military, Beria was arrested and tried. He was probably executed in Dec. 1953.

Berlin

The capital city of Germany. Berlin was severely damaged by Allied STRATEGIC BOMBING during the war and was the only AXIS capital that became a battleground, with street-by-street fighting as Soviet troops captured the city in April–May 1945.

Berlin was the capital of the THIRD REICH and an important industrial center. At the beginning of the war (1939) the city's population numbered some 4,300,000. The first bombing raid occurred on the night of Aug. 25–26, 1940, after Prime Minister CHURCHILL directed RAF Bomber Command to strike the German capital in retaliation for an accidental German bombing of central LONDON on Aug. 24. Forty-three twin-engine bombers took off for the 600-mile flight to Berlin. Only twenty-nine actually reached the city. Their bombs inflicted no meaningful damage. It was the first of four British raids against Berlin in a ten-day period. Sporadic RAF raids against Berlin followed. American correspondent WILLIAM L. SHIRER reported after the first raid, "Berliners were stunned. They did not think it could happen. When this war began, [HERMANN] GÖRING had assured them it couldn't. He had boasted that no enemy planes could ever break through the outer and inner rings of the capital's antiaircraft defense."

The second Ally to attack Berlin was the Soviet

Union. On the night of Aug. 7–8, 1941, five Soviet Navy IL-4 twin-engine bombers, flying from a base in Estonia, made a token strike against the city. A more impressive strike occurred on the night of Aug. 11 by twelve four-engine PE-8 bombers of the Soviet Air Force. The loss of the Baltic states to German troops later in 1941 prevented the Soviets from flying additional raids.

While Berlin continued to be a target for RAF bombers, it was not given the highest priority until Air Chief Marshal ARTHUR HARRIS, head of BOMBER COMMAND, sent a memorandum to Churchill on Nov. 3, 1943, declaring: "We can wreck Berlin from end to end if the USAAF will come in on it. It may cost us 400–500 aircraft. It will cost Germany the war." Churchill could not resist such a proposal to use technology to rapidly defeat the enemy and gave his approval.

Massive RAF night bombing raids followed during the long winter nights. The U.S. AAF was unable to participate because of its heavy losses in daylight, PRECISION BOMBING raids during the preceding months. There were four heavy RAF night raids on Berlin in Nov. and four in Dec. with a total loss of 180 bombers (a loss rate of 4.5 percent). The first two night raids in Jan. 1944, however, cost the RAF bombers 7 percent losses as German night-fighter defenses improved. RAF losses continued to increase in night raids over Berlin and other cities. Between Nov. 18, 1943, and March 31, 1944, the RAF flew thirty-five major attacks against German cities and lost 1,047 aircraft, with more than that number damaged. The German night fighters had triumphed; despite the devastation from bombing, Berlin and the other cities were still very much in the war.

American bombers of the Eighth AIR FORCE, after several delays because of bad weather, conducted their first raid on Berlin on March 4, 1944. Of fourteen bomber wings that took off from Britain, only one—twenty-nine B-17 FLYING FORTRESS aircraft escorted by P-51 MUSTANG fighters—managed to strike the Berlin suburb of Klein Machnow. Little damage was inflicted on the target or to the bombers on that historic strike.

U.S. bombers returned to Berlin three more times in March—on March 6 a total of 660 bombers hit Berlin, encountering heavy opposition with sixty-nine bombers shot down; on March 8 a total of 590 bombers struck with thirty-seven lost; and on March 22 a total of 664 bombers reached the target with only twelve lost. The two latter raids inflicted major damage on their targets; the low losses were due to the large number of escorting fighters available.

In April the Allied bombers—British and American—were diverted to support the NORMANDY INVASION planned for early June 1944. Bombing raids against Berlin were later resumed while on the ground Soviet troops advanced westward.

The Soviet drive for Berlin was in two thrusts, one of which would go through Poznan, Poland, and the other through Breslau, on the River Oder, in Germany. The final advance on Berlin was begun on April 16, accompanied by massive artillery barrages. On April 21 Soviet troops entered the suburbs of the besieged city—the First Belorussian Front, under Marshal IVAN KONEV, from the north and the First Ukrainian Front, under Marshal GEORGI ZHUKOV, from the south. The Russians outnumbered the German defenders in troops, tanks, guns, and tactical aircraft.

As Soviet troops approached the city, HITLER decided, against the advice of his senior generals, to remain in the city, making the *FÜHRERBUNKER* his home and command post, although it was ill equipped for the latter role. Soviet forces completed encirclement of the city on April 25. Hitler and his just-married mistress, EVA BRAUN, committed suicide in the bunker on April 30. The city was surrendered to the Soviets on the morning of May 2.

Anglo-American forces halted at the Elbe River on orders of Gen. DWIGHT D. EISENHOWER's and made no effort to beat the Soviet troops to Berlin. Gen. OMAR BRADLEY had estimated that the Anglo-American forces would incur 100,000 casualties if they had to fight their way to Berlin. As early as Nov. 1944 the First Allied AIRBORNE ARMY had begun planning an AIRBORNE assault on Berlin if German collapse seemed imminent (Operation Eclipse). The plan provided for an initial assault by two American airborne DIVISIONS and a British BRIGADE. A key objective would be Berlin's Tempelhof airfield to permit the air landing of massive reinforcements. The operation was never carried out.

Allied bombing had totally destroyed about one sixth of the city and damaged most of the remainder. By the end of the war the city's population had dropped to 2.8 million. The city at surrender was rubble. The heart of Berlin was gutted and more than 80 percent of its dwellings destroyed. What buildings survived were looted in a frenzy of booty-hunting by riotous Soviet troops. For several days, until Red officers were able to get them under control, the conquerors robbed and raped women, young and old.

In the weeks following the German surrender the surviving factories in Berlin and other areas held by Soviets troops were stripped of their machinery, which was shipped to the Soviet Union. American and British troops entered Berlin in July and French troops in August. The city (like Germany as a whole) was divided into four zones administered by the occupying powers. The Allies established a four-power council to govern the city. (A mayor was elected on Oct. 20, 1946, in the city's first free elections since 1933. He was, however, unacceptable to the Soviets and the deputy mayor became the de facto chief executive of the city.)

Berlin (Operations)

(1) German code name for the breakout of the battleships *Gneisenau* and *Scharnhorst* into the Atlantic CONVOY lanes in Jan.–March 1941; (2) British code name for the escape of British and Polish paratroopers encircled at ARNHEM during Operation MARKET-GARDEN in Sept. 1944.

Bernadotte, Count Folke (1895–1948)

Swedish RED CROSS official who acted as a contact between German and Allied officials during the war. Bernadotte, a diplomat and vice president of the Swedish Red Cross, helped to arrange an exchange of disabled British and German PRISONERS OF WAR, and in the final months of the EUROPEAN WAR worked to aid the plight of CONCENTRATION CAMP victims. He succeeded in keeping 423 Danish JEWS alive through much of the war by persuading the Germans to keep them in the so-called "model ghetto" at Theresienstadt, Czechoslovakia. He then got them returned to Denmark just before the war ended.

In other negotiations, Bernadotte worked with SS chief HEINRICH HIMMLER, who, hoping to negotiate an end to the war, doled out concessions that saved the lives of many prisoners. In April 1945, Bernadotte carried a SURRENDER offer from Himmler to Allied officials, who turned it down.

On Sept. 17, 1948, Bernadotte was assassinated by Jewish terrorists in Palestine while working as a mediator for the UNITED NATIONS.

Bernhard

German code name for the secret operation that produced more than £100,000,000 in counterfeit English notes in an effort to undermine the British economy. The effort was unsuccessful, with most of the notes being produced in 1945 and hidden when Germany was about to capitulate.

Betio,

see TARAWA.

Bettelstab (Beggar's Staff)

German code name for proposed operations against the Oranienbaum pocket in the Soviet Union, summer 1942.

Betty

One of the best-known Japanese aircraft of the war, the twin-engine G4M Type 1 medium bomber (Allied code name Betty) performed in ways that rivaled many four-engine bombers. Almost 200 were in service at the time of the PEARL HARBOR attack, and they operated wherever land bases were available to the Japanese. Twenty-six of these planes joined with G3M NELL bombers to sink the *PRINCE OF WALES* and *REPULSE.* These aircraft flew against land and naval targets throughout the Pacific area, and near the end of the war were modified to carry BAKA suicide aircraft.

The Mitsubishi G4M was designed as the successor to the G3M Nell; the prototype flew in Oct. 1939 and it was put into production that same month as the G6M1 long-range escort fighter. That

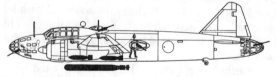

Betty (G4M1) bomber.

project, however, was quickly abandoned with the thirty units completed being employed as transports and trainers. In April 1941 the bomber version entered production. The much-improved G4M2 prototype flew in Nov. 1942. Total Betty production was 2,416 aircraft—more than any other Japanese bomber. These included sixty G4M3 variants with more protection, a fire extinguishing system, and more powerful engines, but U.S. bombing raids disrupted production of these advanced aircraft. Late-production aircraft also had a surface-search RADAR.

The mid-wing Betty had a rounded appearance, with glazed nose and tail positions; it was a mid-wing aircraft with twin radial engines and a large tail fin. The aircraft was fitted with an internal BOMB bay that could carry an aerial TORPEDO or up to 2,200 pounds of bombs. The excellent performance of the Betty was achieved at the expense of armor for the crew and fuel tanks, making the aircraft highly vulnerable to attack.

The G4M2a variant could reach 272 mph and was credited with a range of 2,260 miles. Defensive armament in the G4M2a variant consisted of four 20-mm cannon and one 7.7-mm machine gun, all in flexible mounts. The crew numbered seven.

Bf 109,

see ME 109.

Biak Island

One of the objectives on Gen. DOUGLAS MACARTHUR's "leap-frogging" campaign against Japanese forces in western NEW GUINEA to establish air bases for his invasion of the Philippines. He used the leap-frogging technique to isolate units of the Japanese forces without major assaults.

The AMPHIBIOUS LANDING at Biak turned out to be much more of an operation than expected. MAGIC intercepts of Japanese communications indicated that a major force defended the island. But MacArthur believed otherwise. When his men landed on June 15, 1944, they were unopposed. As they moved in from the beachhead, however, they ran into ferocious resistance.

The U.S. forces had to turn back Japanese attempts to reinforce the island and fight until July to secure the islands and its airstrips. About 450 U.S.

soldiers and about 6,000 Japanese were killed before fighting ended on July 22. (See also NOEMFOR and HOLLANDIA.)

Big Four

The name journalists and headline writers gave the combination of President ROOSEVELT, Prime Minister CHURCHILL, Soviet leader STALIN, and Chinese leader CHIANG KAI-SHEK. The Big Four never met together, primarily because Stalin refused to recognize Chiang, who was fighting Soviet-backed Chinese Communists. Roosevelt and Churchill met four months before PEARL HARBOR at the ATLANTIC CONFERENCE and several other times during the war. Roosevelt, Churchill, and Chiang met at the CAIRO CONFERENCE of Nov. 1943. (See ALLIED CONFERENCES and BIG THREE.)

"Big Four" was also used, mostly after the war, to label the four occupying powers of Germany: the United States, England, the Soviet Union, and France.

Big Inch

Pipeline from the oilfields of Texas to the Midwest and New York. The 24-inch-diameter pipeline was built in 1942 with government funds but operated by oil companies working cooperatively. The pipeline, which carried 335,000 barrels of oil per day, was initially built to get crude oil to areas threatened by shortages of petroleum because of the sinking of coastal tankers by German U-BOATS.

The "Little Big Inch," also built with government funds, was a 20-inch pipeline that in March 1944 began carrying up to 235,000 barrels of gasoline a day from refineries in the Southwest to terminals near New York Harbor.

Big Three

The name journalists and headline writers gave the combination of President ROOSEVELT, Prime Minister CHURCHILL, and Soviet leader STALIN. The three met at the TEHRAN CONFERENCE, Nov. 28–Dec. 1, 1943, and the YALTA CONFERENCE, Feb. 1945. At the POTSDAM CONFERENCE, July 17–Aug. 2, 1945, Stalin met President TRUMAN for the first time and Churchill was replaced by his successor, Prime Minister CLEMENT ATTLEE. (See ALLIED CONFERENCES and BIG THREE.)

Big Week

Code name for massive U.S. AAF STRATEGIC BOMBING effort against German factories producing fighter aircraft, Feb. 1944.

Bigot

Code word name for access to top-secret Allied planning at various headquarters in England for the NORMANDY INVASION.

Bikini,

see ENIWETOK.

Bingo

Code name U.S. AAF air attacks against electrical power transformers in areas of Italy controlled by German troops, Nov. 1944.

Biological Warfare

Bacteriological or (later) Biological Warfare (BW) was considered but never used during the war. Although under the 1925 Geneva Protocol most nations agreed to abstain from the use of "bacteriological methods of warfare" (as well as gases), several nations conducted research in offensive or defensive BW. Some German leaders did advocate its use during the war.

Germany Scientists in Germany had an active BW research program in World War I and took credit for successful operations in Rumania and the United States. (The Germans claimed to have infected with glanders bacilli all of the U.S. Army horses on one transport en route to England and that the horses had to be thrown overboard.)

The first formal NAZI-era German interest in BW occurred in 1939 when the chief medical officer of the SS wrote a memorandum on the practicality of employing biological agents as weapons. While the memo concluded that BW was impractical, HITLER apparently saw the document and issued an order forbidding preparations for offensive BW. Still, in 1940, after German intelligence discovered French research on BW, an informal BW working committee of representatives from various German military and scientific agencies was established.

In May 1942 the Army High Command reminded the committee and German scientists of

Hitler's dictum, but encouraged work on BW defensive measures. The following March, Hitler ordered intensive study of all forms of defense, including the conduct of experiments to gain knowledge of possible enemy schemes.

SS leader HEINRICH HIMMLER, however, subsequently ordered a study of offensive BW and offered scientists the full support of the SS, including CONCENTRATION CAMP inmates and facilities. Apparently, BW experiments were not carried out in concentration camps because of the crowded conditions; a separate BW laboratory was built, which would have used concentration camp inmates as guinea pigs, but it was not yet in use when the war ended.

German scientists investigated a variety of BW weapons, including BOMBS, aircraft spraying anthrax spores, aircraft dropping dead rodents infected with plague bacilli, and submarines releasing live, infected rats off of enemy coasts. (The swimming ability of rats was tested on a Berlin lake.) Typhus-infected lice were rejected as being too complex an operation. Various BW agents were also considered for sabotage.

The German scientific community did develop serums and vaccines to counter possible Allied use of anthrax and plague. Ointments, aerosols, and other methods were evaluated.

The German High Command believed that BW agents were used against their troops in France, Poland, and the Soviet Union. In occupied France sabotage was suspected when, in January 1942, 600 German soldiers contracted typhoid in a soldiers' club in Paris. In one area in the Soviet Union, 3,044 cases of typhus were reported between Jan. and July 1943; the Germans attributed the typhus to "planned sabotage" by GUERRILLAS.

So far as is known, no German BW weapons were used in the war. Himmler expressed the wish in 1944 that Germany had biological weapons to delay the anticipated Allied invasion of France.

Japan By the late 1930s the Japanese Army had begun a biological warfare research program centered at what was known as the 731 Unit located in the suburbs of Harbin, Manchuria. Given the cover name of Epidemic Prevention and Potable Water Supply Unit, the 731 Unit was commanded by Lt. Gen. Ishii Shiro, a medical officer.

The 731 Unit's research included ways to spread plague, cholera, and typhoid, and how to cause frostbite and gas gangrene among enemy troops. The unit also developed a defoliation bacilli bomb that could clear an area of 50 square kilometers. In unconfirmed reports, in 1940 Chinese sources claimed that Japanese aircraft dropped plague-infected fleas in sacks of grain.

Human beings were used for experiments by the 731 Unit under the project code name Maruta. Reportedly, some 3,000 Chinese, Koreans, and Manchurians were used in biological and frostbite experiments. British sources contend that some of the U.S. survivors of the 1942 BATAAN DEATH MARCH were also used in the experiments, along with some Australian prisoners and Japanese petty criminals.

When the war ended in Aug. 1945 efforts were made to destroy all traces of the 731 Unit, including destruction of surviving human guinea pigs. Japanese personnel of the unit were given the highest priority for evacuation back to Japan before Soviet troops entered the area.

United Kingdom British scientists secretly developed a biological weapon from the spore-forming bacterium of anthrax, a cattle and sheep disease transmittable to human beings. The poison, designed to be loaded into bombs and dropped on German cities, primarily infected the lungs. The anthrax project was usually referred to in memos as "N."

British scientists believed that "50 percent of the inhabitants who were exposed to the cloud of anthrax might be killed by inhalation, while many more might die through subsequent contamination of the skin." Another report said, "Half a dozen LANCASTERS [bombers] could apparently carry enough, if spread evenly, to kill anyone found within a square mile and to render it uninhabitable thereafter."

United States The U.S. Army conducted a BW research program during World War II, although virtually no details are publicly available. The principal U.S. weapon secretly developed during the war was brucellosis, which caused not widespread death (the fatality rate was expected to be only 2 percent) but debilitating disorders: "chills and undulating fever, headache, loss of appetite, mental depression, extreme exhaustion, aching joints and sweating."

According to an official statement, "The Biological Warfare policy during this period was first to deter BW use against the United States and its forces, and secondly, to retaliate if deterrence failed. From its inception, the program was characterized by continuing in-depth review and participation by the most eminent scientists, medical consultants, industrial experts, and government officials."

Soviet Union The Soviet Union is known to have had an interest in biological agents and protective measures since the 1930s.

See also CHEMICAL WARFARE.

Birch, John (1918–1945)

"First victim of the Cold War." An American missionary in China when America entered the war, Birch became an assistant chaplain in the FLYING TIGERS and then a U.S. Army second lieutenant serving as a liaison between Chinese and U.S. forces in China. On Aug. 25, 1945—eleven days after the war ended—he was killed, for no apparent reason, by Chinese Communists near Qingdao. (Robert Welch, the well-known anti-Communist of the 1950s, singled Birch out as the first casualty of the cold war and named his organization the John Birch Society.)

Birke (Birch Tree)

Code name for German evacuation of Finland, Aug. 1944.

Birkhahn (Blackcock)

Code name for German evacuation of Norway, 1945.

Bismarck

One of Germany's two largest warships during the war. The battleship *Bismarck* had a brief but highly eventful career. The chase and sinking of the *Bismarck* was one of the most exhilarating episodes of the war.

The *Bismarck* was the penultimate battleship to be built in Germany, followed by the slightly larger *TIRPITZ*. Commissioned in August 1940, she was at that time the most powerful battleship in the world. After the ship's lengthy working-up period in the

Baltic, HITLER visited the battleship at Gotenhafen (Gdynia) as she was being prepared for operations against Allied merchant shipping in the Atlantic.

In late May 1941 the *Bismarck,* accompanied by the heavy cruiser *Prinz Eugen,* sailed to Bergen, Norway, for their first—and only—operational sortie. They were sighted by British reconnaissance aircraft, but the German warships, taking advantage of bad weather, steamed westward, to enter the Atlantic through the Denmark Strait, between Iceland and Greenland.

In the Denmark Strait the Germans were sighted and tracked by a British cruiser employing RADAR. Although the *Bismarck* actually evaded the "shadower," the ship used her radio to advise naval high command of her situation and thus revealed her position to the Royal Navy. Subsequently, on May 24 the British battle cruiser *HOOD* and new battleship *PRINCE OF WALES* intercepted the German ships just south of the Denmark Strait (the *Prince of Wales* still had workmen on board). In a brief but furious engagement, the *Hood* was hit by gunfire from both German ships. A magazine blew up, and she sank with but three survivors from a crew of 1,350.

The *Bismarck* received minor damage in the brief battle, and was then struck by a torpedo from a British carrier plane. Damage was slight and although the *Bismarck* eluded the searching British ships, she was leaking fuel oil and her admiral decided he would put into the French port of Brest for repairs. (The *Prinz Eugen* was detached to operate independently and soon entered the German-held port of Brest.) The German commander, *Vizeadmiral* GÜNTHER LÜTJENS, not realizing he had escaped his pursuers, sent a lengthy radio message that the British were able to detect and from it determine the *Bismarck*'s location.

Several British warships steamed toward the *Bismarck,* among them the aircraft carrier *ARK ROYAL.* A combination of British direction finding and code-breaking (see ULTRA) gave indications of the *Bismarck*'s location and probable track; an RAF PBY CATALINA flying boat then sighted the *Bismarck* some 700 miles west of Brest at 10:30 A.M. on May 26. The trap tightened. That night SWORDFISH torpedo planes from the carrier *Ark Royal* attacked. An aerial torpedo hit on the *Bismarck*'s stern and disabled her rudder. She was crippled, able only to steam in circles. Too far from France to be aided by German aircraft, and with no effective U-BOATS in the area, she was at the mercy of the rapidly closing British warships. Gunfire from the battleship *King George V* and battle cruiser *Rodney* soon reduced the German battleship to a blazing hulk; she was then torpedoed and at 10:36 A.M. on May 27 she sunk beneath the waves. There were 110 survivors from a crew of some 1,900.

The loss of the *Bismarck* marked the end of German surface ship operations in the Atlantic. The *Bismarck* displaced 50,900 tons full load and was armed with a main battery of eight 15-inch guns. (The *King George V* and *Prince of Wales* each had ten 14-inch guns.) The *Bismarck*'s maximum speed was 30 knots.

Bismarck Sea

Western Pacific area encompassed by the Bismarck Archipelago, which includes the islands of NEW BRITAIN, New Ireland, and the ADMIRALTY ISLANDS. The battle of the Bismarck Sea was fought between land-based Allied aircraft and a Japanese CONVOY from the stronghold of RABAUL. On March 1, 1943, a convoy of sixteen Japanese ships was spotted en route to Lae on the northeast coast of NEW GUINEA. The convoy was carrying reinforcements to Japanese garrisons in New Guinea.

The following morning, U.S. AAF B-17 FLYING FORTRESS bombers attacked the ships, sinking one transport. Two Japanese destroyers, rescuing soldiers from the transport, were later attacked by more U.S. B-17s as well as Australian BEAUFORT bombers and U.S. A-20 HAVOC attack planes and B-25 MITCHELL medium bombers. The A-20s and B-25s, using new, low-level tactics, bombed and strafed at low altitudes. The two destroyers were sunk as was a third trying to join in the rescue. One of the destroyers, in her death throes, rammed another Japanese ship, which also sunk. A second Allied air attack in the afternoon sank a fourth destroyer. About 3,000 troops and sailors were lost in the sinkings.

From March 1 to 4 a total of 174 planes from the U.S. Fifth AIR FORCE and the Royal Australian Air Force dropped 213 tons of BOMBS on the Japanese ships.

"Bitch of Buchenwald,"

see KARL KOCH.

Black

Early code name for the capture of DAKAR; later Picador and Barrister.

Black Book

Name given by the British to *Sonderfahndungsliste G.B.* (Special Search List Great Britain), compiled by the REICH CENTRAL SECURITY OFFICE as part of the SEA LION invasion plan. The 2,820 people on the list were British subjects and European exiles who were to be arrested and "taken into protective custody" by the GESTAPO following the German invasion of England. The list was in alphabetical form. But when existence of the Black Book became known after the war, people on the list proudly proclaimed their "ranking" as an indication of their importance as enemies of the Nazis.

On the list were leading politicians, such as Prime Minister CHURCHILL and Foreign Secretary ANTHONY EDEN, along with authors H. G. Wells, Noel Coward, Virginia Woolf, E. M. Forster, Rebecca West, C. P. Snow, and Aldous Huxley (who had emigrated to the United States in 1936). Sigmund Freud was also on the list, though he had died on Sept. 23, 1939.

Others included Lord Baden-Powell, founder of the Boy Scouts, who had been involved in British intelligence; cartoonist DAVID LOW, and Lady Astor. Among the Americans inexplicably on the list were BERNARD BARUCH and Paul Robeson. Among the missing was George Bernard Shaw, who, apparently, was seen by the Germans as a potential friend because, a month after the war had begun, he had written a propeace essay.

The man who was to head the roundup of the enemies was an SS officer, Frank Six, a former dean of the economic faculty at the University of Berlin. Documents named him as commander of proposed ACTION GROUPS—the designation for SS units that committed mass murders in Europe. Six, convicted of WAR CRIMES, was sentenced to twenty years in 1948 and released in 1952.

Black Eagles

The all-black 99th Fighter Squadron. The U.S. Army Air Forces initially resisted intense political pressure to admit blacks, especially to flight training. Using as a yardstick the percentage of young black males in the U.S. population, the Army set 10.6 percent as the proper proportion. Supposedly, the proportion would continue through assignment to Army and Army Air Forces units. But the highest percentage achieved by the Army Air Forces was 6.1 percent in Nov. 1943. Nearly all of the black airmen were assigned to low-level base maintenance tasks.

Facing suit for SEGREGATION from a Howard University student, the AAF in Nov. 1941 set up a pilot training center for blacks at the Tuskegee Institute in Alabama, a black school founded by Booker T. Washington. The training site was a field built under the Civilian Pilot Training Program, established in 1939 to create a pool of pilots who, with combat instruction, could serve in event of war. Throughout the war Tuskegee was the only place where black pilots—some 1,000 "Tuskegee Airmen," as they were sometimes called—were trained for combat.

Black officers were barred from the officers' club at the nearby Maxwell air base. Black soldiers and officers rode on segregated trains, and when they were filled with white soldiers, the blacks sat on trunks in the baggage cars. Black pilots gave themselves two names: "Black Eagles" and, bitterly, "Lonely Eagles." A member of the 99th recalled decades later: "We fought two wars: one with the enemy and the other back home in the U.S.A.— HITLER and Jim Crow."

The first class graduated on March 7, 1942, but the pilots were kept at Tuskegee, going through additional training, while the Army decided what to do with them. As an Army Air Forces general put it, the consensus of officers he had talked to believed that "the negro type has not the proper reflexes to make a first-class fighter pilot." Finally, knowing that even the White House was getting impatient, the AAF designated the 99th Pursuit (later Fighter) Squadron as the first all-black AAF unit, and on April 25, 1943, sent the squadron to North Africa. Their commanding officer was then-Lt. Col. BENJAMIN O. DAVIS, JR.

Black Eagles kept coming from Tuskegee for the rest of the war. Three more all-black squadrons were added to the 99th and formed into the 332nd Fighter Group, which became part of the 15th AIR FORCE. The 332nd, which flew ground-support missions over ANZIO and escorted bombers on missions over southern Italy, was the only group that never lost a bomber to enemy fighters. Tuskegee airmen shot down an estimated 111 enemy planes.

Late in 1943 the AAF began training bombardiers, navigators, radio operators, and gunners for an all-black bombardment group. But by the time the 477th Medium Bombardment Group was deemed ready to go overseas, the war was nearly over and the 477th never left the United States.

Black Market

The illegal source of scare and rationed wartime goods. U.S. black market goods were sold in violation of laws regulating prices and rationing. The term came from Europe, where a black market was a secret market where scarce goods were sold. In the United States the term came to mean "under the counter" trading activities that were illegal (a butcher who sold meat without asking for RATIONING stamps) or unethical (a butcher who dutifully collected the stamps but sold only to favored customers). Most black market deals in the United States involved gasoline or meat.

The OFFICE OF PRICE ADMINISTRATION (OPA), which directed rationing, combatted black markets through an enforcement section that included lawyers, accountants, and special law-enforcement agents augmented by others drawn from the FEDERAL BUREAU OF INVESTIGATION, the Treasury Department, and state and local police forces. Some cases were settled by civil actions, with violators paying treble damages for price gouging and losing their OPA licenses. More serious cases—such as the theft or counterfeiting of ration stamps—were handed over to prosecutors for criminal trials. Cases reaching civil or criminal courts averaged 4,500 a month.

In Europe following the NORMANDY INVASION, U.S. soldiers set up black markets in American goods, including cigarettes, penicillin, and other drugs. Truckloads of supplies were sold by drivers on the RED BALL EXPRESS. The black market launched by occupying forces was so widespread that in 1946 special currency that could not be converted into dollars was issued to U.S. forces.

Black Shirts,

see SS.

Black Thursday

Code name for night of Dec. 16, 1943, when RAF Bomber Command aircraft returning from a raid on BERLIN found their bases blanketed with impenetrable fog causing numerous crashes.

Black Widow,

see P-61.

Blackcock

Code name for British XII Corps operations to clear German salient between the Meuse and Roer-Wurm rivers from Roermond southward, Nov. 1944.

Blackout

The darkening of a city or area to thwart enemy bombers. In the months of crisis leading up to the EUROPEAN WAR, England, France, Germany, and other prospective belligerents prepared their civilian populations for air raids. One of the typical civil defenses was the blackout.

When the United States went to war, the federal CIVIL DEFENSE organization stepped up its recruitment of volunteers and introduced blackout drills in many cities. In HAWAII, a strict, military-enforced blackout started immediately after the attack on PEARL HARBOR and continued throughout much of the war.

However, the naivete of the United States was seen when the East Coast was not blacked out for the first four months of the war—well into the U-BOAT campaign against merchant ships in the Atlantic. Historian SAMUEL ELIOT MORISON wrote, "One of the most reprehensible failures on our part was the neglect of the local communities to dim their waterfront lights, *or of the military authorities to require them to do so,* until three months after the [German] submarine offensive started. When this obvious defense measure was first proposed, squawks went up all the way from Atlantic City to southern Florida that the 'tourist season would be ruined.' Miami and its luxurious suburbs threw up six miles of neon-light glow" which silhouetted merchant ships for the U-boats. (See DIMOUT.)

An air attack on the United States was unlikely, but the blackouts went on for psychological reasons. Civilians felt they were doing something to help the war effort when they learned to put up blackout curtains and walk in cities lit by dimmed street lights.

During drills, air raid wardens in glow-in-the-dark arm bands and white helmets patrolled the streets, warning violators that light was peeking through darkened windows or scolding smokers who lit up out of doors. Few people complained beyond mutterings about pompous wardens. Some people worried about crime and safety on darkened streets. Railroad executives, for example, feared that blackouts would cause accidents at darkened stations and yards, but the railroads' wartime safety record was remarkably good.

Blackpool

Code name for CHINDIT roadblock on railroad near Namkwin, Burma.

Blacks,

see SEGREGATION.

Blau (Blue)

Code name for German offensives at Voronezh, Soviet Union, June 1942.

Blenheim

The Blenheim was developed as a high-speed bomber for the RAF. When it took to the air it was some 40 mph faster than the fighters then in service. But its performance in the war was lackluster and it was replaced in 1942 by the far more capable A-20 BOSTON and MOSQUITO. The improved, "long-nose" Mk IV did have considerable success, however, against German shipping.

A twin-engine aircraft, the Blenheim was ordered "off the drawing board" from the Bristol firm without the benefit of a prototype. The first aircraft flew on June 25, 1936, with the RAF taking delivery of operational aircraft early the following year. In addition to their bomber role, the Blenheim pioneered the night-fighter role during the BATTLE OF BRITAIN, being one of the first aircraft fitted with air-intercept RADAR. They were phased out of the Bomber Command in 1942, although they continued in service in the Middle East and Far East. Production totaled 1,134 of earlier models and 3,297 of the Mk IV.

The Blenheim Mk IV had a maximum speed of 266 mph and was credited with a range of 1,460 miles. An internal BOMB bay could carry 1,000 pounds of bombs and small bombs could be carried under the wings. The aircraft had three forward-firing .303-cal. machine guns and twin .303-cal. guns in a dorsal power turret. The crew was three.

Bletchley Park

An ugly Victorian mansion in Bedfordshire, about 40 miles north of London, that housed England's Government Code and Cipher School. The British government's code-breakers, some of them veterans of such work in World War I, moved into Bletchley in Aug.–Sept. 1939.

During the war it was the center for British ENIGMA code-breaking activities. By the end of the war about 10,000 men and women were at Bletchley Park, most of them housed in rows of wooden barracks hastily constructed in the estate's gardens.

When British traitor WILLIAM JOYCE (Lord Haw-Haw) hinted of a secret operation at Bletchley, the British Broadcasting Company put out a story that the antennas around the town were for local radio stations. After the U.S. entry into the war, many Americans worked at Bletchley. The activities at Bletchley remained state secrets for nearly thirty years.

Bleucher

German code name for assault against Kerch Strait between the Black Sea and the Sea of Azov, Aug. 1942.

Blimps,

see AIRSHIPS.

Blissful

Code name for landing by U.S. 2nd Marine Parachute BATTALION on Choiseul Island in the SOLOMONS, Oct. 1943.

Blitz

The intensive German bombing of LONDON from Sept. 1940 through May 1941. The city's first

air raid of the war sounded a short time before noon on Sunday, Sept. 3, 1939, minutes after Prime Minister NEVILLE CHAMBERLAIN had broadcast that a state of war existed with Germany. Thousands of Londoners hurried to take shelter, but no Luftwaffe bombers appeared over the city. It was also the first false alarm.

But the threat of the much-publicized Luftwaffe bombers had led to a recruitment of air-raid wardens, the buildup of the fire-fighting service, and the preparation of shelters. Soon after war was declared, some 600,000 nonessential workers and children were evacuated from the city. But no bombers came.

The prelude to the Blitz began in June 1940, just after the fall of France. While aerial combat was fought daily over the city of London, no BOMBS were dropped and citizens stood in the open, shielding their eyes against the sunlight as they watched fighter contrails twisting in the summer sky. This changed late on the afternoon of Sept. 7, 1940, when the first of several hundred German bombers to strike the capital city that night released their bombs. It was the first of fifty-seven consecutive nights of bombing, and the start of attacks that would last until the following May.

"The Blitz was a confession of inadequacy," wrote British historian Peter Fleming in *Operation Sea Lion,* "a gamble on terror undertaken because other weapons had failed to produce the swift decision that was required and expected of them; and strangely enough it was begun because of a comparatively trivial blunder unwittingly committed by a few German aircraft a fortnight earlier."

The Luftwaffe had failed to defeat the RAF in the BATTLE OF BRITAIN. Without air supremacy there could be no invasion. Now, perhaps, judged *Reichsmarschall* HERMANN GÖRING, head of the Luftwaffe, the British could be cowered into submission without invasion. The first bombs to fall on the City of London struck on Aug. 24, 1940, when German bombers making a night attack against aircraft factories and oil-storage tanks near the capital inadvertently struck the city. It is not known whether inexperience on the part of the bomber crews or problems in their beam-riding navigation system caused the mistake. (The same night, the

Luftwaffe bombed Birmingham, Bristol, Liverpool, and targets in southern Wales.)

Prime Minister CHURCHILL responded immediately. On the night of Aug. 25–26 a force of eighty-one RAF bombers attacked BERLIN, although only forty-three found their targets through the dense fog. Heretofore RAF raids on the German capital had dropped only PROPAGANDA leaflets. On every night that weather conditions permitted, the RAF returned to strike Berlin. HITLER reacted immediately and vigorously. On Sept. 4 the German dictator declared that reprisals against the British would be devastating. He expected the bombing of London to "cause the population to flee the city and block the roads." Thus, late on the afternoon of Sept. 7 some 320 bombers escorted by over 600 fighters of *Luftflotten* 2 and 3 began the Blitz. Hitler's order saved the RAF Fighter Command from likely defeat in the Battle of Britain. But the cost to the capital of the BRITISH COMMONWEALTH was horrendous.

The opening blows on Sept. 7 fell on several areas of London, including the City, Westminster, and Kensington. The heaviest blows fell on the docks and the East End of London, where an area of about one-and-a-half square miles between North Woolrich Road and the Thames River were totally destroyed. The second wave—of some 250 bombers—came over that night, with planes attacking until early the next morning.

When dawn came on Sunday, Sept. 8, there were 430 persons dead and 1,600 seriously injured. Power, railway, water, and telephone services were disrupted. That night, as firefighters continued to fight the conflagrations, the bombers returned, as they would for every night for almost two months.

RAF night fighters and more than 1,300 antiaircraft guns (firing 3-inch and larger shells) brought the attackers under fire as they crossed the British skies. The Luftwaffe suffered, but London (and other British cities) were smashed. The Luftwaffe attacks continued through the winter of 1940–1941 and into the spring.

The heaviest raid against London came on the night of May 10–11, 1941. Over 2,000 fires were started. That night German bombs killed 1,212 persons and seriously injured another 1,769. About 2,000 fires were ignited and the House of Com-

mons was severely damaged. But this would be the last heavy raid on London for nearly three years. The Germans saw 10 percent of their attacking planes destroyed and even more damaged on that night. (The same night the RAF Bomber Command attacked HAMBURG with 110 aircraft.)

Warehouse basements and Underground (subway) stations were used as bomb shelters. By the end of Sept. 1940 it was estimated that 177,000 people were sleeping nightly in London's underground stations. Living conditions were primitive, with poor sanitation and no privacy. Additional toilets were installed and bunks were fitted where possible. Canteens provided hot food and drinks. Ingenious means of shelters were provided—the Anderson Shelter was a corrugated iron structure

The German aerial Blitz on London failed to break the will or back of the British people. The nightly raids forced hundreds of Londoners into underground stations, where they slept on makeshift beds on the stone floors or benches. This was the scene at the Elephant and Castle station on the night of Nov. 11–12, 1940. *(Imperial War Museum)*

that was partially buried in a backyard; for those without yards, the Morrison Shelter was an open steel box in which to hide or sleep, able to withstand even a building falling onto it (although few of these were available during the Blitz). By mid-October an estimated 250,000 Londoners had been bombed out of their homes, and the Luftwaffe bombers kept coming. Most bombed-out Londoners moved in with family or friends, or crammed into those public buildings that had space. Again, living conditions were primitive for many until the end of the war, but London continued to function as a city and as a capital.

After May 10–11 the Luftwaffe shifted its strikes to RAF airfields and other cities, but even those attacks soon petered out as the German legions and the Luftwaffe air fleets were already fighting in Greece and the Balkans, to be followed by the massive German assault against the Soviet Union. (The Norway-based *Fliegerkorps* X had already been transferred to the Mediterranean in late 1940, reflecting the shift in German priorities.)

While the Blitz had centered on London, there were heavy, continuous bombing raids in that period against the port cities of southern England, the industrial cities of the northern part of the country, and the cities along the Clyde in Scotland. After the Blitz was over the Germans periodically flew bomber strikes over England. And, of course, beginning in mid-1944 London again became the focus of German attacks with the V-1 BUZZ BOMB and the V-2 MISSILE attacks.

The Blitz against London lasted eight months. London survived; the cost: 40,553 killed—18,629 men, 16,201 women, 5,028 children, and 695 whose charred remains were "unclassified." Another 46,850 were seriously injured. Block after block of homes, offices, warehouses, and shops were rubble. Possessions of a lifetime were gone. But London and Britain had survived—perhaps best expressed by chalked words found on thousands of boarded-up shop windows during the Blitz: *Business as Usual.*

Blitzkrieg

Germany's "lightning war" tactic that combined swiftly moving ground forces and devastating air attacks. Germany tested elements of the tactic, particularly air-ground coordination, in the 1936–1939 SPANISH CIVIL WAR, a laboratory for German weapons and tactics.

The first blitzkrieg launched the POLISH CAMPAIGN in Sept. 1939, beginning the EUROPEAN WAR. The blitzkrieg began with a surprise ground and air attack, using air forces to destroy the enemy's own air forces. On the ground, fast, motorized infantry, motorcycle infantry, and tanks smashed through enemy defenses. Dive bombers broke up or panicked enemy troop concentrations.

The next blitzkrieg, this time with the addition of seaborne and AIRBORNE assault troops, brought Germany a quick victory again in the DENMARK AND NORWAY CAMPAIGN of April 1940. In the FRANCE AND LOW COUNTRIES CAMPAIGN that swiftly followed, the blitzkrieg once more rolled across the enemy. In less than four months of actual ground-air combat, the blitzkrieg had completely conquered Poland, Norway, Denmark, Belgium, the Netherlands, and France. It had routed the British Army, and only the English Channel had saved England from falling victim in the summer of 1940.

In his planning for the GERMAN CAMPAIGN IN THE SOVIET UNION, HITLER directed "daring operations led by deeply penetrating armored spearheads"—again, the blitzkrieg. At first, it seemed that the blitzkrieg into the Soviet Union was running smoothly and swiftly against the understrength, ill-prepared, and shocked Red Army. ("We are being fired on," a Soviet front-line unit radioed its headquarters. "What shall we do?") But long supply lines, the Russian winter, and massive Soviet resistance all combined to blunt the effect of the blitzkrieg. In that disastrous campaign, the blitzkrieg was shown to be a tactic that did not work everywhere every time.

As a young officer, Gen. CHARLES DE GAULLE had advocated blitzkrieg-style tactics, as had British military analyst BASIL LIDDELL HART. But neither French nor British military planners had accepted the idea of lightning warfare.

Allied military doctrine was changed by the blitzkrieg, which stimulated the mechanization of the U.S. and British armies. (Although constructed of two German words—*Blitz* for lightning and *Krieg* for war—blitzkrieg was coined by British newsmen.)

Blockbuster

Code name for Canadian 2nd Corps offensive in Calcar-Udem-Xanten area. (See also BOMBS.)

Blomberg, *Generalfeldmarschall* Werner von (1878–1946)

Minister of Defense who played a key role in HITLER's move from elected chancellor to dictator in Aug. 1934. As minister of Defense and a distinguished soldier, it was crucial that Blomberg accept the NAZI-created law that gave Chancellor Hitler the title Führer and Commander in Chief of the armed forces. Blomberg also approved the new oath of allegiance that every German serviceman had to take from then on: "I swear by God . . . that I will render unconditional obedience to Adolf Hitler . . ." Blomberg was made supreme commander of the Wehrmacht, the combined armed services created by Hitler in 1935.

When Hitler began planning his march of conquest, Blomberg and *Generaloberst* Baron Werner Freiherr von Fritsch, chief of the High Command of the German Army, voiced opposition. The Nazi SS, with the endorsement of HERMANN GÖRING, sought a way to remove both generals.

For Blomberg, the Nazis found a scandal: He had married a prostitute—shaming both the proud officers corps and Hitler and Göring, who had attended the wedding. Blomberg was forced to resign from the Army on Feb. 4, 1938. Von Fritsch resigned the same day on charges that he had had homosexual relations with HITLER YOUTH members. The charges were dismissed at a subsequent court-martial and he was recalled to active duty when the EUROPEAN WAR began. Witnesses said that he chose death on the battlefield by walking toward Polish guns in combat near WARSAW in Sept. 1939.

Blue Division

Spanish military unit that fought on the side of Germany on the EASTERN FRONT from late in 1941 to April 1944. The division, which numbered about 20,000 men, was ostensibly disbanded under Allied pressure on Spain, which was supposedly neutral. But Spanish troops in a "Blue Legion" unacknowledged by Spain continued to fight for Germany.

Blues

British code name for carrier-based air attacks on southern Norway, June 1944.

Bluestone

Code name for the British submarine *Unbeaten* landing special agents near Vigo, Spain, Oct.–Nov. 1942. (Shortly after this successful operation, on Nov. 11, the *Unbeaten* was apparently sunk in error by a British aircraft.)

Blume (Flower)

German code name for alert of an Allied invasion of Western Europe.

"Bockscar"

Name of B-29 SUPERFORTRESS bomber that delivered the ATOMIC BOMB on NAGASAKI on Aug. 9, 1945. The aircraft was flown by Maj. CHARLES SWEENEY, but was named for its assigned pilot, Capt. Fred Bock.

Bodenplatte (Base Plate)

Code name for Luftwaffe attacks by some 750 planes against Allied airfields in Belgium, Holland, and Luxembourg, Jan. 1, 1945.

Bodyguard

Code name for Allied cover and deception operation to mask the NORMANDY INVASION. Originally given the code name JAEL, it was apparently changed after a remark by Prime Minister CHURCHILL: "In wartime, truth is so precious that she should always be attended by a bodyguard of lies." There were two parts to the deception effort; these were given the code names Cockade and Zeppelin. (See also CAMOUFLAGE.)

Bofors 40-mm Gun

The Swedish-design, rapid-fire 40-mm Bofors was the most widely used antiaircraft gun of the war. It was in the arsenal of most Allied and AXIS nations, and in all theaters of the war. The U.S. Army had a large number of them and they were the U.S.

U.S. sailors on a surfaced submarine blast Japanese small craft. Torpedoes were expensive and, when the submarines were in no danger of counterattack, they would attack on the surface with gunfire. In the foreground is a 40-mm Bofors rapid-fire cannon, its ammunition in four-round clips; behind it crewmen fire a 5-inch gun. (*U.S. Navy*)

Navy's most widely used gun aboard ship. In their report on antiaircraft guns, military writers Peter Chamberlain and Terry Gander concisely described the Bofors: "It was reliable, efficient and available, and gunners on both sides could ask no more of any gun."

The 40-mm Bofors was first produced in 1930 and was first delivered to the Swedish Navy in 1932. Foreign orders came quickly and by the outbreak of the EUROPEAN WAR in 1939 it was used by eighteen nations with licensed production by several. Beyond countries that bought and produced the guns, hundreds were captured by Germany from British and Dutch forces in 1940, while the Japanese obtained Bofors when they conquered the DUTCH EAST INDIES in 1942.

In the United States there was initially little interest in the Bofors because of the domestic 37-mm gun M1. However, in early 1941 the 40-mm Bofors was adopted by the U.S. Army because it was lighter than the M1, fired a heavier shell, and

fired ammunition common with British guns. But American production lines did not begin turning out Bofors until 1943. Tens of thousands were produced for the Army and Navy, with others going to Allies.

The U.S. Army used thousands of single-barrel 40-mm Bofors, usually on four-wheel towed carriages. During AMPHIBIOUS LANDINGS the soldiers would sometimes set them up on AMPHIBIOUS SHIPS to add their fire to shipboard batteries, and in coastal operations the British used barges fitted with a pair of 40-mm Bofors for antiaircraft protection of the landing area (calling these craft landing barge, flak, or LBF).

The U.S. Navy procured the gun in single, twin, and quad mounts, and beginning in mid-1942 installed them aboard ships ranging in size from BATTLESHIPS and AIRCRAFT CARRIERS to PT-BOATS. By the end of the war the standard armament of an *IOWA* (BB 61)-class battleship included eighty 40-mm guns (all quad mounts) while the *ESSEX* (CV 9)-class carriers normally had seventy-two 40-mm guns (quad and twin mounts). At one point the venerable carrier *SARATOGA* (CV 3) had 100 40-mm guns (all quad mounts). DESTROYERS and DESTROYER ESCORTS had several mounts, as did lesser warships, landing ships, and auxiliary ships. Many U.S. submarines had one or two "wet mount" 40-mm guns on deck.

The 40-mm Bofors had a cyclic rate of fire of 120 rounds per minute in Army guns and 160 in naval guns; however, because it was manually loaded, a 60 to 90 rounds-per-minute rate was realistic. The 40-mm/56-cal. Bofors was fired by two gunners and several loaders, plus either a radio talker or pointer to point out approaching aircraft to the gunner. The Army gun had a simple open sight; the naval guns had open sights or RADAR directors.

Weights of the gun mounts varied. The single gun, on a towed carriage, weighed some 5,500 pounds. The Army guns were air-cooled, the naval twin-barrel and quad weapons had water cooling jackets. Ammunition was hand loaded in 4-round clips. The armor-piercing round, the heaviest, weighed 2 pounds. Maximum altitude at 90° elevation was 7,600 yards, while maximum range at 42° elevation was 11,000 yards.

Bohr, Niels (1885–1962)

Danish physicist who worked on the ATOMIC BOMB. Bohr was awarded the 1922 Nobel Prize in physics for work that showed how totally the physical characteristics of the atom underlaid chemical reactions. ALBERT EINSTEIN said of Bohr's ability, "This is the highest form of musicality in the sphere of thought."

Germany's invasion of Denmark in April 1940 was followed by an agreement that Denmark could retain its government. That atmosphere allowed Bohr, one of Denmark's most distinguished citizens, to continue working. But Danish SABOTAGE and other anti-NAZI activities by the Danish resistance movement brought German reaction in Aug. 1943: occupation and the arrest of Danish JEWS.

Bohr helped the resistance smuggle some Jews out and then, as he himself was about to be arrested, got his family safely to Sweden. Then he appealed directly to King Gustav of Sweden for Sweden to give asylum to Denmark's Jews. The Swedes did so, and within two months 7,220 Jews reached safety in Sweden—thanks to the Swedish coast guard and Bohr.

After working with British physicists on atomic bomb research (code-named Tube Alloys), Bohr was invited to the United States to join the teams of physicists who were developing the bomb at LOS ALAMOS. He and his son, Aage, also a physicist, were given the code names Nicholas and James Baker. At Los Alamos they were called Uncle Nick and Jim.

J. ROBERT OPPENHEIMER, scientific director of the Los Alamos effort, said Bohr at Los Alamos brought both his technical brilliance and psychological inspiration. Reminiscing about Bohr after the war, Oppenheimer said, "Bohr spoke with contempt of Hitler, who with a few hundred tanks and planes had tried to enslave Europe for a millennium. He said nothing like that would ever happen again."

During the war Bohr met with both President ROOSEVELT and Prime Minister CHURCHILL in a fruitless attempt to get the leaders to work on international control of the bomb, with Soviet cooperation. Churchill coldly rejected the idea; Roosevelt seemed interested. But Churchill convinced him that the idea was naive and possibly dangerous. After the war Bohr continued to work for international controls through the UNITED NATIONS.

Bolero

Code name for buildup of U.S. forces and supplies in Britain for the cross-Channel invasion.

Bolivia

Capital: La Paz, pop. 3,426,296 (est. 1938). Politically unstable, with a large German community, Bolivia in June 1941 was feared to be on the brink of a coup engineered by local NAZIS and a German diplomat. Under strong U.S. pressure, the Bolivian government expelled the diplomat and arrested supporters of the rumored coup. The United States had reason to worry. Both Germany and Japan wanted Bolivia's tin and tungsten, much of which was going to the United States under a 1940 trade agreement.

Bolivia made another tungsten-purchase agreement with the United States in 1941 even though the Japanese offered a higher price. After the Japanese attack on PEARL HARBOR, Bolivia moved closer to U.S. policy. Due to internal unrest and anti-American feelings, Bolivia delayed declaration of war on the AXIS until April 7, 1943.

Bomb Disposal

Technique of disarming or destroying unexploded BOMBS, which were known as UXB in British jargon. Unexploded bombs were those that failed to detonate as intended, or that had delay fuzes, to explode after a specific amount of time to impede clearing a damaged area, repairing runways, or doing other work around the site.

All nations practiced some form of bomb disposal in combat areas. The best-known bomb disposal operations were by the British Army's Royal Engineers in Britain, especially after the Luftwaffe began using large numbers of delayed-action bombs. The Royal Navy was responsible for disarming German MINES that were dropped by parachute in Britain. Early in the German air attacks on Britain civilians helped in the effort. One bomb disposal team consisted of the Earl of Suffolk, his female secretary, and his elderly chauffeur, who referred to themselves as the "Holy Trinity." The trinity dealt successfully with thirty-four UXBs; the thirty-fifth one "claimed its forfeit," wrote WINSTON CHURCHILL.

He later wrote about the UXB teams: "Somehow or other their faces seemed different from those of ordinary men, however brave and faithful. They were gaunt, they were haggard, their faces had a bluish look, with bright gleaming eyes and exceptional compression of the lips; withal a perfect demeanour. In writing about our hard times, we are apt to overuse the word 'grim.' It should have been reserved for the UXB disposal squads."

DRAPER KAUFFMAN, a U.S. naval officer who worked in bomb disposal in Britain, helped institute bomb disposal activities in the U.S. military services.

Allied and AXIS bomb disposal specialists worked in virtually every combat area to disarm unexploded bombs and ARTILLERY shells. Their efforts continued after the war, and into the 1980s as unexploded ordnance was discovered.

Bomba

High-speed calculating machine developed by Polish military intelligence before the war to perform the calculations necessary for using a German ENIGMA encryption machine without knowledge of the specific rotor settings. The Bomba had portions of six Enigma machines wired into its circuits.

In July 1939 British and French code specialists met with their Polish counterparts in the Pyry Forest near WARSAW, Poland. Along with other matériel, the technical drawings of the Bomba were turned over to the ALLIES. Subsequently, in 1940 the Bomba concept was transformed into the British-built BOMBE super-calculating machines. (The term *Bombe* was also applied, apparently retroactively, to the original Polish machine.)

The Bomba was primarily the product of Polish mathematician-cryptanalyst Marian Rejewski.

Bombardon

Breakwater section of reinforced concrete that could be towed across the English Channel and then sunk as part of the ARTIFICIAL HARBORS built by the ALLIES during the NORMANDY INVASION.

The Bombardons were some 200 feet long and 25 feet wide and resembled a Maltese cross when viewed end-on. Afloat, with the top half of the vertical arm being hollow to serve as buoyancy chambers, they had a draft of 19 feet. Ninety-six Bombardons were used in the two artificial harbors off the Normandy beaches.

Bombe

Series of high-speed calculating machines assembled by the British code-breaking team at BLETCHLEY PARK to determine German ENIGMA machine code settings. The British Bombes were developed from the Polish BOMBA.

There were several versions of the Bombe, which were electro-mechanical (not electronic) devices that could rapidly test the possible daily rotor settings for Enigma machines. As Ronald Lewin explained in his *Ultra Goes to War,* since " . . . the order of placing the wheels [rotors] in the Enigma could be varied in sixty different ways, and for each order 17,576 possible settings for the individual wheels had to be checked, no human brain could conceivably compete with the electromagnetic bombe in reaching, and very consistently reaching, an answer to questions of such magnitude."

The first Bombe was assembled at Bletchley Park in early 1940. The device, some 8 feet high and having a similar depth, was a mass of lights, plugs, and wires. Additional Bombes were constructed to permit simultaneous attacks on the various codes used by the German armed forces and the GESTAPO. From mid-1943 the U.S. military intelligence services were operating Bombes in the United States to help break AXIS codes.

The Bombes were operated and serviced (they were continually spewing forth printed paper) by Wrens—female Royal Navy sailors.

See also COLOSSUS.

Bombs

Aircraft bombs were a principal weapon in World War II, being used against ships and ground targets. The U.S. AAF and Navy used a variety of bombs with high-explosive, fragmentation, chemical, and incendiary warheads. Some bombs were fitted with parachutes to retard their fall so that low-flying bombers could escape their blast.

The standard U.S. high-explosive bombs came in 100-, 300-, 600-, 1,000-, 2,000-, and 4,000-pound sizes, although the last was rarely used. An experi-

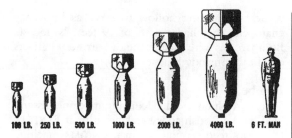

Bombs.

100 LB.   250 LB.   500 LB.   1000 LB.   2000 LB.   4000 LB.   6 FT. MAN

mental 42,000-pound high-explosive bomb was developed by the U.S. AAF in 1945, but was not used in combat. A small number of PUMPKIN BOMBS of 5,000 pounds, armed with high explosives, were produced for use by B-29 SUPERFORTRESS bombers practicing to use ATOMIC BOMBS.

Fragmentation or antipersonnel bombs came in 20-pound, 23-pound, and 30-pound sizes and were dropped on enemy troop formations.

Chemical bombs containing mustard gas were not used in the war. (See CHEMICAL WARFARE.) Other bombs filled with phosphorus and titanium tetrachloride were used to produce dense white smoke. Bombs were also considered a means to deliver BIOLOGICAL WARFARE agents, but those weapons were never developed.

Incendiary bombs generally weighed up to 50 pounds and were packaged in clusters to break apart over their target, each to ignite a fire. Often bombers would release demolition bombs to smash the roofs of buildings and expose the flammable interior walls and furnishings to incendiary bombs. These weapons were filled with thermite compositions and later magnesium hexagon, and caused mass destruction of many German and Japanese cities. The U.S. STRATEGIC BOMBING SURVEY estimated that ton for ton, incendiaries were four to five times as destructive as high explosive bombs against European cities; the ratio was much higher against Japanese cities with lightly built structures. The Japanese also launched incendiaries against the United States and Canada in BALLOON BOMBS.

The smallest bomb used by U.S. aircraft was a 100-pound practice bomb with a 5-pound charge of black powder; these bombs were usually dropped on land targets that had bull's-eyes or warship outlines.

U.S. air forces also used bombs filled with jellied gasoline or NAPALM and antisubmarine DEPTH CHARGES.

Three atomic bombs were detonated during the war—at the ALAMOGORDO test site in New Mexico and over the Japanese cities of HIROSHIMA and NAGASAKI.

The British also introduced the first practical 4,000-pound bomb, dubbed "blockbuster" because a single bomb of that size was capable of devastating an entire city block. A WELLINGTON bomber dropped the first 4,000-pound "blockbuster" during a strike on Emden on April 1, 1941. These bombs were later assembled in multiples to form 8,000- and 12,000-pound blockbusters. The largest conventional bombs used in the war were the British "earthquake" bombs designed by Barnes Wallis, the 12,000-pound TALLBOY and 22,000-pound GRAND SLAM. The Tallboy was used to sink the German battleship *TIRPITZ* after the dreadnought survived lesser bomb hits, and was used with effect against German SUBMARINE PENS and other heavily reinforced concrete structures. Among the most unusual bombs produced during the war were the UPKEEP and HIGHBALL "bouncing bombs," also a Barnes Wallis design, intended to destroy dams in the Ruhr Valley and attack enemy warships, respectively. These Wallis bombs could only be carried in specially modified LANCASTER bombers, except the Highball weapons—never used in combat—which were carried in MOSQUITO light bombers.

The British also developed an armor-piercing 4,500-pound bomb, which had a large ROCKET in the tail, to increase the downward velocity of the bomb for attacking German submarine pens.

The largest AXIS bomb used in the war was the German 5,511-pound SB 2500 "Max," with an explosive charge of 3,748 pounds. Few were used. The Germans did experiment with a 17.7-ton bomb (see ME 323). Both the Germans and British employed naval MINES as bombs against ground targets.

See also BAKA, GUIDED MISSILES, and JOHNNY WALKER.

Bong, Maj. Richard I. (1920–1945)

The leading U.S. fighter ACE of the war. An AAF pilot, "Dick" Bong flew the P-38 LIGHTNING to achieve his forty confirmed victories against Japanese aircraft in the Southwest Pacific and the Philippines. He flew two combat tours, in 1944, interrupted by an assignment at an AAF gunnery school in the United States.

Bong was a strong supporter of teamwork in fighter tactics; his wingman, Lt. Col. Thomas J. Lynch, scored twenty kills while supporting Bong's moves, the two forming a remarkable team. Fighter ace historians Raymond F. Toliver and Trevor J. Constable wrote: "Bong and Lynch would trade the leadership position during a rhubarb with such perfection and precision, it was as though each of them was intuitively flying the other's aircraft as well as his own. They were like two men constantly able to read each other's thoughts. In battle, one was always in firing position on the enemy, while the other kept the shooting aircraft's tail clear."

One of Bong's aerial victories was achieved with a bomb. Upon sighting two Japanese planes below them, Bong and his wingman jettisoned their 500-pound bombs and dived—in time to see Bong's bomb smash through the tail of a Japanese plane, which went spinning downward.

For "voluntarily and at his own request" flying repeated combat missions, Bong was awarded the MEDAL OF HONOR after his 38th victory, presented by Gen. DOUGLAS MACARTHUR on Dec. 12, 1944, as well as numerous other decorations. He was killed on Aug. 6, 1945, while flight-testing the P-80 SHOOTING STAR.

Boniface

Code word employed by Prime Minister CHURCHILL for ULTRA intelligence. He used it on the theory that should the enemy learn the code name they would assume that he was relying on a secret agent.

Bonus

Original code name for British assault of MADAGASCAR in the Indian Ocean; changed to Ironclad.

Booby Trap

Named for the "boob" who would set one off, these were hidden MINES, GRENADES, ARTILLERY shells, and explosive charges rigged to explode when an unsuspecting soldier moved an innocent-looking object, or tripped a wire, or opened a door. The German BOUNCING BETTY was often used in this way. In some instances, BOMBS with delay fuzes that were dropped on an enemy target were bobby-trapped to prevent their being disarmed. (See BOMB DISPOSAL.)

As Allied armies advanced, both the Germans and Japanese would often booby-trap discarded pistols, swords, and other objects that would make an appealing souvenir to a soldier or Marine.

Boomerang

The only Australian-designed aircraft to see combat in the war. The CA-12 Boomerang was a ground-attack fighter that served in five squadrons of the Royal Australian Air Force. Although frequently in action against Japanese aircraft, it failed to destroy a single enemy in the air!

The first aircraft was flown on May 29, 1942. A total of 250 were built by the Commonwealth aviation firm through 1944. One CA-12 was provided with a turbo-supercharger in an effort to increase performance at altitude; that plane became the CA-14A, but no production followed as more-capable U.S. fighter aircraft were becoming available in large numbers.

A low-wing monoplane with a large radial engine, the Boomerang had a traditional fighter design. Top speed was 296 mph. The single-seat aircraft had two 20-mm cannon and four .303-cal. machine guns and could carry a single 500-pound BOMB.

Bormann, Martin (1900–1945?)

Nazi Party leader. An early member of the NAZI Party, Bormann became Chief of Staff to RUDOLF HESS, the deputy führer. Soon after Hess' flight to Scotland in 1941, Bormann became a confidant to HITLER and his deputy for party affairs. He wielded great power, although he often appeared to be hardly more than a wily bureaucrat. Minister of Propaganda JOSEPH GOEBBELS, who was frequently frustrated by Bormann, wrote in his diary, "Bormann has turned the Party Chancellery into a paper factory."

Many of the papers would form the damning record that would convict Nazis brought before the Nuremberg trials for WAR CRIMES after the war.

Bormann served as secretary at secret meetings where Hitler harangued about the persecution of Eastern European JEWS and the running of SLAVE LABOR camps. In a record dutifully set down by Bormann, for example, Hitler says he will "eradicate everyone who opposes us." Another Bormann memo says that "all representatives of the Polish intelligentsia are to be exterminated."

A German intelligence officer summed up Bormann as "the evil genius behind the Führer's commands." Indicted for war crimes, he was the only one of the twenty-two senior Nazis who was not present at the Nuremberg trials. After being convicted by the words in his own memos and the testimony of fellow Nazis, he was sentenced to death in absentia. Survivors of Hitler's last days in the FÜHRERBUNKER claimed that Bormann was killed during an attempt to escape from Soviet-encircled BERLIN. But reports persisted in postwar years that he was alive in South America, having possibly been taken there in a U-BOAT. A skull tentatively identified as his was found in Berlin in 1973 and a West German court declared him officially dead.

Boston,

see A-20.

Bougainville

Largest of the SOLOMON ISLANDS, invaded by U.S. Marines in Nov. 1943 as part of an Allied plan—Operation Cartwheel—to get rid of RABAUL, the big, heavily defended Japanese base on the eastern end of NEW BRITAIN Island. From an airfield on Bougainville, U.S. fighters would be close enough to the Japanese base—about 200 miles—to provide escort for Rabaul-bound bombers.

Debate about dealing with Rabaul split U.S. strategists. Gen. DOUGLAS MACARTHUR wanted to invade and overpower Rabaul. The JOINT CHIEFS OF STAFF (JCS), believing that too many U.S. troops would die in an AMPHIBIOUS LANDING, wanted to neutralize the base with continual bombing raids. At the QUEBEC CONFERENCE of Aug. 1943 President ROOSEVELT and Prime Minister CHURCHILL established the strategy for the U.S. CENTRAL PACIFIC CAMPAIGN and made the decision about Rabaul by siding with the JCS.

The Bougainville operation, code-named Good-

time, began on Nov. 1, 1943, when the I Marine Amphibious CORPS, under Lt. Gen. A. A. VANDEGRIFT, landed at Torokina on Bougainville's western coast against Japanese ARTILLERY that U.S. naval gunfire had done little to silence. By nightfall, however, about 14,000 Marines, along with 6,200 tons of supplies, were ashore.

The next day the Marines began slogging inland through swamp and jungle. On the night of Nov. 6 the Japanese landed about 475 men on the now-vacant Marine beachhead. The Japanese counterinvaders were wiped out.

During one night's action, members of a Marine patrol, trapped on a river bank, were rescued by a LANDING CRAFT escorted by two PT-BOATS, one of which was commanded by Lt. JOHN F. KENNEDY, back in action after the loss of his not-yet-famous *PT 109*. (Kennedy's future secretary of Agriculture, Lt. Orville Freeman, was wounded on Bougainville.)

As Marines began staking out the area chosen for the airfield, Japanese resistance increased. The field was built under first, and by Jan. 1944 bombers with fighter escorts were flying to Rabaul. In March a large Japanese force attacked U.S. soldiers and Marines. For two weeks, again and again the Japanese troops were hurled back, each time suffering large losses. That was the last major Japanese action, but skirmishing continued until the end of the war.

Bouncing Betty

Allied nickname for a German antipersonnel land MINE that was detonated by trip wires when troops disturbed an object that was wired to the mine (see BOOBY TRAP) or tripped over the wire strung between trees or rubble. Known by the German designation *Schützenminen,* these weapons were loathed by Allied troops.

The mines could be left on the ground (simply covered over) or buried. They exploded 3 to 6 feet above the ground and each showered some 300 steel balls with the effect of shrapnel over a radius of several hundred feet. The explosive charge was 1¼ pounds.

Bouncing Bombs,

see HIGHBALL and UPKEEP BOMBS.

Bowery

British code name for reinforcement of MALTA, May 1942; included U.S. AIRCRAFT CARRIER *WASP* (CV 7).

Bowspirit

Allied code word devised to notify U.S. invasion forces of a twenty-four-hour delay in the NORMANDY INVASION.

Boyington, Lt. Col. Gregory (1912–1987)

A leading U.S. Marine Corps fighter ACE, "Pappy" Boyington shot down more Japanese aircraft than the top Marine ace, Maj. JOSEPH FOSS; however, Boyington's first six aerial victories were achieved while flying with the FLYING TIGERS (1941–1942).

Subsequently entering the Marine Corps, Boyington flew F4U CORSAIRS in the SOLOMON ISLANDS area. He took command of Marine Fighter SQUADRON (VMF) 214—called the "Black Sheep" squadron—in Sept. 1943. Its nickname came from many of its pilots having been rejected from other units. He was shot down during a fighter sweep over the Japanese base of RABAUL on Jan. 3, 1944, but not before he shot down three aircraft that day.

He was a PRISONER OF WAR for twenty months. Upon his release he was awarded the MEDAL OF HONOR as well as the Navy Cross. Boyington—called Pappy because he was the oldest pilot in VMF-214—was "Unsurpassed by any other American fighter ace for sheer color, flamboyance and fighting skill . . . ," wrote fighter ace historians Raymond F. Toliver and Trevor J. Constable.

B.R.20 *Cicogna* (Stork)

Italian twin-engine bomber that flew for the Nationalists in the SPANISH CIVIL WAR and, in small numbers, was supplied to Japan before the EUROPEAN WAR. The first major B.R.20 operation in World War II occurred in Oct. 1940 when seventy-five of the bombers were flown to Brussels, from which they made several night raids against targets in Britain. They were withdrawn three months later to support the Italian invasion of Greece. In the fall of 1942 a B.R.20 force was sent to the EASTERN FRONT, while others were employed against anti-Fascist GUERRILLAS in the Balkans. Few B.R.20s remained at the time of Italy's SURRENDER in Sept. 1943.

The Fiat B.R.20, which first flew in 1936, was intended as a fast, easily produced medium bomber. A total of some 625 aircraft were produced, including the seventy-five for Japan and a few for Spain and Venezuela. It had a maximum speed of 255 mph and a range of 1,860 miles; it could carry up to 3,528 pounds of BOMBS and had four 7.7-mm machine guns for self-defense.

Bradley, Gen. of the Army Omar N. (1893–1981)

The highest-ranking American field commander in the European theater. Like his World War II sponsor, Gen. GEORGE C. MARSHALL, Bradley did not see action in France in World War I. But in the interwar years, especially as commandant of the Army's Infantry School at Fort Benning, Ga., his competence and imagination caught Marshall's attention and Bradley became the first of his West Point class (1915) to be promoted to brigadier general; he had never been a full colonel.

In Feb. 1943 Bradley was promoted to major general and became Eisenhower's "eyes and ears" in the NORTH AFRICA CAMPAIGN, which had begun in Nov. 1942. In March Bradley was appointed deputy commander of Gen. GEORGE S. PATTON's II CORPS. When Patton moved up to plan the invasion of SICILY as Seventh ARMY commander in April 1943, Bradley assumed command of II Corps, leading it through the last month of the North Africa campaign and the conquest of Sicily.

Bradley demonstrated a tactical competence and an awareness of the demands of logistics. These virtues, plus his combat experience (the most of any corps commander) led Gen. DWIGHT D. EISENHOWER to direct Bradley to establish both the 1st Army Group (FUSAG) and the First U.S. Army in England. Bradley led the First Army in the NORMANDY INVASION. On Aug. 1, Bradley's 1st Army Group was activated (but immediately redesignated the U.S. 12th Army Group) as Bradley took command of all U.S. ground forces in northwestern Europe.

As Eisenhower's highest-ranking American field commander, Bradley followed in the tradition established by Gen. John J. Pershing in World War I by maintaining control of U.S. forces. Eisenhower backed him by resisting attempts of Bradley's British counterpart—Field Marshal BERNARD MONTGOMERY, Commander of 21st Army Group—to garner more U.S. forces. At times large numbers of U.S. troops did operate under British control. (See MARKET-GARDEN.)

Bradley threatened to resign during the battle of the Bulge when Eisenhower agreed to temporarily put two of Bradley's three field armies under Montgomery's command. Eisenhower faced Bradley down and there was no resignation.

From the Normandy invasion, the breakout from Saint Lô, the sweep across France and into Germany, and during the ALLIED CAMPAIGN IN EUROPE, Bradley demonstrated a readiness to convert setbacks into defensive stands. But he was criticized, not least by Patton, for his caution. If he temporized, perhaps it was because of Bradley's understanding of the rifleman's view: "The rifleman trudges into battle knowing that statistics are stacked against his survival. He fights without promise of either reward or relief. Behind every river, there's another hill—and behind that hill, another river. . . . Sooner or later, unless victory comes, the chase must end on the litter or in the grave."

Bradley served as commander of the 12th ARMY GROUP—the largest U.S. field command in World War II—until the end of the war in Europe.

Bradley was given the temporary rank of full general on March 13, 1945. In June President TRUMAN appointed him administrator of veterans' affairs. On Sept. 22, 1950, he was promoted to the FIVE-STAR RANK of general of the Army and became the first chairman of the JOINT CHIEFS OF STAFF, serving until his retirement in Aug. 1953.

Braid

Code name for Gen. GEORGE C. MARSHALL.

Brassard

Code name for Allied operations against the island of Elba.

Brauchitsch, *Generalfeldmarschall* Walther von (1881–1948)

Commander in Chief of the German Army from 1938 to 1941. A member of an old Prussian military family, Brauchitsch served as an artillery captain in World War I and was awarded the IRON CROSS, First Class.

In 1938 HITLER's men engineered the removal of Commander in Chief Werner Freiherr von Fritsch on trumped-up charges of homosexuality. Brauchitsch succeeded von Fritsch and became a supporter of Hitler, despite *Der Führer*'s meddlesome handling of generals. By taking a NAZI activist as his second wife, Brauchitsch also helped win acceptance from Hitler while losing respect from many fellow officers.

Promoted to *Generalfeldmarschall* in 1940, Brauchitsch helped plan Operation BARBAROSSA, the invasion of the Soviet Union. As the German Army began to crack under Red Army pressure after the invasion, so did Brauchitsch. In failing health and losing influence with Hitler, Brauchitsch retired in Dec. 1941—coincidentally after telling Hitler that MOSCOW could not be taken and recommending that the German Army in the Soviet Union go on the defensive. Hitler himself took over as Supreme Commander.

For Brauchitsch, the war was over. He was still awaiting trial by the ALLIES for WAR CRIMES when he died.

Braun, Eva (1912–1945)

HITLER's mistress and, on the last days of their lives, his wife. Hitler, nationally known and rising in power, met Eva, a seventeen-year-old clerk in a Munich photo shop in 1929, when he was forty. As she later told her sister, she was on a ladder reaching for files when she saw "a man with a funny mustache" admiring her legs.

When Hitler met Eva he was still carrying on a romance with his niece Geli Raubal, who was nineteen years his junior. In 1931 Geli killed herself with a gun after a quarrel with Hitler.

Eva lived at first in a flat Hitler maintained in Munich and was a habitual resident at Hitler's mountain retreat at BERCHTESGADEN, usually arriving a few hours after Hitler, in company with his secretaries. The car with the women was never in the official motorcade. "The secretaries also served the function of disguising the mistress's presence," said ALBERT SPEER, a frequent guest at Hitler's mountain home. "I could only wonder at the way Hitler and Eva Braun avoided anything that might suggest an intimate relationship—only to go upstairs to the bedrooms together late at night. It has always remained incomprehensible to me why this needless, forced practice of keeping their distance was continued even in this inner circle."

Around 1939, according to Speer, Eva "was assigned a bedroom" in Hitler's BERLIN residence, which she entered by "stealing into the building through a side entrance and going up a rear staircase." Gossips wondered if they would ever marry. Eva doubted it, for Hitler believed that his destiny did not include marriage. Besides, he was uncomfortable with shows of affection. Friends were surprised when he held her hand in public.

She told Speer that Hitler, who was always worried about his health, expected to die before he was fifty. "I'll soon have to give you your freedom," he said one day. "Why should you be tied to an old man?" Their relationship was stormy and frustrating for Eva, the classic back-alley mistress. She twice attempted suicide. Apparently to keep her under close control, Hitler in 1939 installed her in a suite in the Chancellery. She occupied former Chancellor PAUL VON HINDENBURG's bedroom and slipped in and out through a servant's entrance.

She had no interest in politics, and, unlike many other women in Hitler's entourage, she did not display any personal power. But when, late in the war, Hitler wanted to ban permanent waves and end the production of cosmetics, she tried to persuade him to reverse the order. He modified the order only slightly, telling Speer to stop producing hair dyes and "repairs upon apparatus for producing permanent waves."

In Jan. 1945 Hitler entered the underground *FÜHRERBUNKER* in embattled Berlin and, except for a few above-ground daytime occasions, stayed in it for the rest of his life. In April, with the city battered by bombings and the barrages of the approaching Red Army, Eva unexpectedly arrived in Berlin and joined Hitler in the bunker.

She had her own bedroom in Hitler's suite, which she filled with furniture from her suite in the Chancellery, which was above the bunker. On a chest was an inlay of a four-leaf clover entwined with her initials. She lived in cramped luxury. When Speer visited her, he wrote, "The orderly brought in a bottle of Moet et Chandon, cake, and sweets."

Shortly before midnight on April 28 Eva and Hitler were married in the bunker by a Berlin municipal councilor who was found in a unit of the *Volkssturm* (People's Army or home guard) fighting near the *Führerbunker*. They filled out a marriage certificate that said they had "no hereditary disease" and were "of complete Aryan descent." The bride wore black. Hitler wore a uniform.

Hitler dictated a will that said Eva Braun would "go to her death with me at her own wish as my wife. This will compensate us both for what we lost through my work in the service of my people."

Around 2:20 A.M. on April 30 Eva and Hitler retired to his private quarters, where he shot himself in the right temple and she took poison, most likely one or more of the cyanide capsules available in the bunker. Their bodies were taken to the Chancellery garden, drenched with gasoline, and set afire.

Braun, Wernher von (1912–1977)

German rocket expert. As technical director of the rocket research facility at PEENEMÜNDE, he helped to develop the V-2 MISSILE. By the time the Soviets occupied the coveted research site in 1945, von Braun had surrendered to Allied troops. He was quickly whisked to the United States in Operation Paper Clip. He helped to produce the U.S. Jupiter-C rocket and Saturn rockets. In 1960 he became director of the Marshall Space Flight Center in Huntsville, Ala. Von Braun was the only scientist who received high awards for weapons research from both NAZI Germany and the United States.

Braunschweig (Brunswick)

Code name for German offensive toward STALINGRAD and the Caucasus, July 1942; formerly Operation *Blau*.

Brawn

British code name for abortive operation to attack the German battleship *TIRPITZ* in Altenfjord with carrier-based aircraft, May 1944.

Brazil

Capital: Rio de Janeiro (now Brasilia), pop. 41,500,- 000 (est. 1940). When the war began, Brazil declared itself officially neutral but with a bias toward the Allied side. The U.S. entry into the war led Brazil to break off relations with the AXIS powers.

After German U-BOATS sank five Brazilian ships off her coast in Aug. 1942, she declared war against Germany and Italy.

Allied antisubmarine patrols operated out of Brazilian bases and the Brazilian air force assumed the leading role in air defense of the South Atlantic. In July 1944 a BRAZILIAN EXPEDITIONARY FORCE fought in Italy under U.S. command.

Brazilian Expeditionary Force

The only Latin American ground force to see combat in the war. The 25,000-man force arrived in Italy late in 1944 and served until the end of the war. More than 2,000 were wounded and 451 were killed.

Bremen

German port continually attacked by British and U.S. bombers during the EUROPEAN WAR. The site of a naval and U-BOAT base and submarine building facilities, Bremen was virtually destroyed. By Sept. 13, 1942, it had been bombed 100 times. Yet, when the city was captured by British troops in April 1945, they found about forty U-boats being built or under repair.

Bren Light Machine Gun

Widely used British .303-cal. light machine gun. It was considered one of the best weapons of its type in the war, with a reputation for accuracy and reliability. During the war its role in the British Army was similar to that of the BROWNING AUTOMATIC RIFLE (BAR) in the U.S. Army and Marine Corps. (Improved versions of the Bren guns firing NATO 7.62-mm ammunition were still in use with the British armed forces in the 1990s.)

Developed from the Czech 7.92-mm ZB26 machine gun, the Bren was put into production at Enfield, England, in 1937. The ZB26 was considered one of the best machine guns of the prewar period (and was in production in China into the 1950s).

The Bren was a gas-operated, air-cooled weapon. It weighed 19.14 pounds and was fed by a 30-round "banana" magazine fitted in the top of the weapon. The gun had a cyclic firing rate of 520 rounds per minute (although magazines could not be reloaded fast enough to maintain that rate of fire). The

weapon had a rifle-like shoulder butt, a pistol grip, carrying handle, and a bipod was fitted.

The name is derived from the first two letters of the Czech city of Brno (also Brünn) and the first two letters of Enfield.

Brenner Pass

Pass between Austria and Italy. After Germany's acquisition of Austria in 1938, the pass was established as the boundary between Germany and Italy. The lowest of the major Alpine passes, the Brenner was also the railroad route for German coal sent to Italy, which was unable to get coal by sea because of a British blockade. The pass was the traditional route for Teutonic invaders of Italy. Here German *Führer* HITLER, probably aware of the history, suggested a meeting with Italy's *Il Duce* BENITO MUSSOLINI on March 18, 1940.

U.S. Under Secretary of State SUMNER WELLES, on a fact-finding mission for President ROOSEVELT, had just been in ROME and Hitler wanted to know what was discussed. But, as COUNT GALEAZZO CIANO, Mussolini's foreign minister and son-in-law, noted in his diary Hitler made it "more a monologue than anything else."

The two dictators met again at the pass on Oct. 4, 1940, just before German troops moved into Rumania. "Hitler put at least some of his cards on the table," Ciano wrote, telling Mussolini that Germany's planned invasion of England was called off.

The next time they met, on June 2, 1941, Hitler and Mussolini met again at the pass. This time Hitler did *not* tell his friend about an invasion: Operation BARBAROSSA, the invasion of the Soviet Union, would be launched in nineteen days. Mussolini had already told Hitler that such an invasion would be unwise. For that reason—and for security reasons—Hitler refrained from talking about Barbarossa. He spent most of the meeting telling *Il Duce* about current events and the recent flight of RUDOLF HESS to England.

Brereton, Lt. Gen. Lewis H. (1890–1967)

Leading U.S. AAF commander. Brereton was appointed to command the U.S. Far East (Tenth) AIR FORCE in Oct. 1941 under Gen. DOUGLAS MACARTHUR. When the Japanese attacked the Philippines on Dec. 8, most of his B-17 FLYING FORTRESS heavy bombers were caught on the ground by the attacking Japanese, depriving MacArthur of his principal air weapon. After attempting to delay the Japanese with his few surviving aircraft, Brereton left the Philippines to take command of the newly formed Tenth Air Force at New Delhi, India, to direct air operations in the China-India-Burma theater. He held that command from March to June 1942.

In mid-1942, Brereton traveled from India to Cairo to command the U.S. Middle East Air Forces, which became the Ninth Air Force. His achievements included support to Allies fighting in North Africa and the low-level PLOESTI bombing raids. In late 1943 the Ninth Air Force was reestablished in England; promoted to lieutenant general in April 1944, Brereton led the Ninth Air Force in providing tactical support in the NORMANDY INVASION.

In Aug. 1944 he took command of the First Allied AIRBORNE ARMY consisting of U.S., British, and Polish AIRBORNE units. These were army formations (which Brereton and AAF commanding general H. H. ARNOLD believed should be part of the Army Air Forces). Brereton commanded that force during its massive assault in northern Holland (Operation MARKET-GARDEN) and in subsequent smaller but more successful airborne operations.

Bretton Woods Conference

International meeting that laid out a program for postwar trade and international monetary stability. The UNITED NATIONS Monetary and Financial Conference, usually called the Bretton Woods Conference after its New Hampshire site, was held in July 1944 to work out ways to finance long-term rehabilitation of war-ravaged countries and maintain international monetary cooperation. Representatives of Allied nations set up plans for the International Monetary Fund and the International Bank for Reconstruction and Development (World Bank), which both came into being in Dec. 1945.

Brevity

Code name for British offensive in the western desert, May 1941.

Brewer

Code name for Allied operations in the ADMIRALTY ISLANDS.

Brezhnev, Leonid (1906–1982)

Soviet political officer who served in the CAUCASUS, the Black Sea area, and the UKRAINE, rising in rank to major general. In 1964 he became first secretary of the Soviet Communist Party, replacing NIKITA KHRUSHCHEV. He was chairman of the presidium and president from 1977 until his death.

Brigade

Major army formation. Prior to the war the U.S. Army's DIVISIONS were based on the "square" or rectangular principal, with the infantry component organized into two brigades, each composed of two REGIMENTS. The divisions were changed to a triangular structure on the eve of war, with the brigades abolished and the division's principal infantry components becoming three regiments.

Similarly, the U.S. Army abolished ARTILLERY and CAVALRY brigades as formal organizations. In their place, brigade headquarters were created as required, consisting of small headquarters units to which BATTALIONS of engineers, artillery, TANK DESTROYER, or other specialized units could be assigned as necessary. The U.S. Army also had one AIRBORNE brigade. This arrangement led to considerable flexibility in the assignment of specialized units. In many instances, however, specialized battalions were assigned directly to CORPS and ARMY headquarters.

The armies and marine corps of several countries retained the brigade structures throughout the war.

A brigade was commanded by a brigadier general or colonel.

Brimstone

Code name for planned Allied assault of Sardinia in 1944.

Britain, Battle of,

see BATTLE OF BRITAIN.

British Commonwealth

Overall designation for the nations that were united by the British Crown during the war. In 1917, at a conference of nations known to the world as the "British Empire," the Crown abandoned that term and officially replaced it with "British Commonwealth of Nations." The Commonwealth bestowed dominion status on the United Kingdom (British Isles), Canada, Australia, New Zealand, the Union of South Africa, and Ireland (Eire). But India and Burma were still considered below dominion status, as were GIBRALTAR, MALTA, and the scattered British colonial holdings in Africa, Central America, the West Indies, and the Pacific. When the war began, about 500 million people, occupying about one fourth of the world's habitable lands, were under some form of Commonwealth status. The British Empire remained a popular term until postwar liberation movements brought the British flag down throughout the world.

Broadway

Code name for airborne drop site for CHINDITS, about 50 miles northwest of Indaw, Burma.

Brooke, Gen. Alan F. (1883–1963)

Brooke (later Field Marshal Viscount Alan-brooke), as Chief of the Imperial General Staff (CIGS) from Dec. 1941 to June 1946, was Gen. GEORGE C. MARSHALL's British counterpart for much of World War II and certainly his equal in terms of his influence on his political master. He was Prime Minister CHURCHILL's principal military adviser, an exhausting and at times thoroughly frustrating role to play. He thus played a crucial role in the Allied strategy and planning of the war.

Although his relationships with most American commanders was cordial, Brooke profoundly disagreed with the principal U.S. strategy for prosecuting the EUROPEAN WAR. Brooke's basic vision included an appreciation that the Soviet Army would always be by far the largest land force opposing HITLER. Because U.S. and British forces would have to stage an amphibious assault to invade the continent, Brooke argued, what mattered most was dispersion of German effort away from the coast of Western Europe. To this end, he strongly backed the invasions of SICILY and Italy, delaying the NORMANDY INVASION until 1944.

Brooke's unswerving opinion of Gen. DWIGHT D. EISENHOWER was that he had "a most attractive personality and, at the same time, a very, very limited brain from a strategic point of view." He did,

however, concede that Eisenhower could rise to the occasion in a crisis.

For the British, Brooke holds much the same place as Gen. Marshall does for Americans—his part in winning the war not as well known as some of the field commanders, but nonetheless indispensable. His strategic vision remained consistent and was clearly argued throughout his term as CIGS.

Brown Shirts,

see SA.

Browning Automatic Rifle

SQUAD assault weapon usually known by the acronym BAR. This potent infantry weapon was widely used by the Army and Marine Corps. In service since World War I, the M1918 BAR could be fired while standing or from a prone position; a bipod was fitted to the M1918A1 model (adopted in 1937) for steadying the weapon in the latter mode. The BAR was a .30-cal. weapon, firing the same ammunition as the 1903 SPRINGFIELD and M1 GARAND rifles.

One to three BARs were assigned to U.S. Army and Marine Corps squads.

A gas-operated, fully automatic-only weapon, the BAR weighed 21 1/2 pounds loaded. Ammunition was fed from a 20-round, detachable box magazine. Effective range was approximately 875 yards with a maximum range of 3,500 yards; the rate of fire was 550 rounds per minute.

The BAR was invented in 1917 by John Browning.

Browning Machine Guns

Weapons used by the Allies. During the war the United States and Britain produced a variety of Browning-design machine guns for aircraft, ground, and shipboard use. The guns were in fixed or on flexible mountings. All were recoil-operated weapons firing belt-fed ammunition (initially fabric and later metal-link belts that disintegrated as the rounds were fired).

When the war began U.S. aircraft carried primarily .30-cal. Browning M2 machine guns (i.e., barrels 3/10 inch in diameter). This caliber was soon increased to .50-cal. as a standard for U.S. aircraft. Ground vehicles and ground troops employed both

.30- and .50-cal. guns throughout the war, as did naval ships and craft.

The standard aircraft .30-cal. M2 machine gun had a barrel length of 24 inches, weighed 21.5 to 23 pounds, and could fire at a theoretical rate of 1,000 to 1,350 rounds per minute. The .50-cal. M2 and M3 guns for aircraft had a barrel length of 36 inches, weighed 61 to 69 pounds, and had rates of fire of 750 to 850 rounds per minute (M2) and 1,150 to 1,250 (M3). Aircraft guns were air-cooled.

Ground and naval machine guns could be air- or water-cooled, the latter having large "jackets" around the barrel. The weapons had rates of fire of 400 to 500 rounds per minute for .30-cal. weapons and 500 to 650 rounds per minute for .50-cal. weapons. Vehicle and naval machine gun mounts sometimes had twin barrels, and a four-barrel, air-cooled .50-cal. mounting was developed for antiaircraft defense of ground units. The quad mounting, which could be fixed or mounted on a vehicle, was also useful against lightly armored ground targets (troops and vehicles). The air-cooled weapons were lighter and more flexible for ground use, and hence were produced in larger numbers.

The following table shows the number of machine guns in U.S. Army DIVISIONS in 1945; this does not include guns fitted in tanks:

	.30-CAL. MG	.50-CAL. MG
Infantry division	211	237
Armored division	433	385
Airborne division	284	165

John Moses Browning (1855–1926) was one of America's most prolific gun inventors. After making his first gun from scrap metal at the age of thirteen, he went on to design pistols, rifles, and machine guns. The U.S. Army began adopting his machine guns as its standard automatic weapons in 1890. Browning also developed the BROWNING AUTOMATIC RIFLE (BAR).

Bruce, David K. E. (1898–1977)

Head of the Office of Strategic Services in London and director of OSS European operations. Bruce was chief representative of the American RED CROSS in London when WILLIAM DONOVAN, head of the OSS, picked him to be the chief of the Secret Intelligence Branch of the OSS. Operating out of London, Bruce became the OSS chief for Europe, a position that called on diplomatic as well as espionage skills, for OSS frequently clashed with the British intelligence agency MI6.

After the war he became the U.S. ambassador to France (1949–1952), West Germany (1957–1958), and England (1961–1969), the only person ever to hold three major ambassadorships. In 1970 he was the chief U.S. negotiator at the Paris peace talks.

Brückenschlag (Bridging)

German code name for planned offensive to close the Toropets bulge in the Soviet Union, 1942.

Buccaneer

Code name for proposed Allied AMPHIBIOUS LANDING in the Andaman Islands in 1944.

Buckner, Lt. Gen. Simon Bolivar, Jr. (1886–1945)

The highest ranking U.S. officer to be killed by enemy fire during the war. Buckner, who began the war as commander of the U.S. Alaska Defense Command, directed the retaking of the ALEUTIAN ISLANDS from the Japanese in the spring of 1943. Buckner left the Alaska Command in March 1944 and in June began forming the Tenth ARMY, which was composed of the Army XXIV CORPS (four DIVISIONS) and the Marine Corps' III Amphibious Corps (three divisions). His assignment was to plan the capture of the island of OKINAWA.

The Tenth Army landed on Okinawa on April 1, 1945, and took all but the southern quarter in three weeks, well ahead of schedule. As U.S. forces inched south, suffering heavy losses, Buckner went forward to check on operations of the 8th Marine REGIMENT. On June 18, five Japanese artillery rounds struck nearby. Buckner was fatally wounded and died within a few minutes. Okinawa was conquered three days later with Buckner's opponent, Lt. Gen. Mitsuru Ushijima, commander of the 32nd Army, committing suicide before dawn on June 21.

(Lt. Gen. LESLEY J. MCNAIR, killed in France in 1944, was senior to Buckner, but he was killed in a U.S. bombing attack.)

Budapest

City that endured one of the most sustained sieges of the war. The capital of Hungary, it became a battleground in Oct. 1944 when the SOVIET OFFENSIVE CAMPAIGN, having swept through Poland and the Balkans, ran into stubborn German resistance. Repulsed on a drive for Budapest, the Soviets in December began encircling the city. The siege would last fifty-two days.

HITLER had ordered a to-the-last-man defense of Hungary, presumably with the aid of the Hungarians. But the nation, long allied with Germany, had no heart for the war and looked on the Soviets as liberators. And the Hungarian Army, devastated by its losses on the EASTERN FRONT, was an unreliable partner at this stage of the war.

The Germans transformed the beautiful ancient city into a fortress, defending first Buda on the east side of the Danube and then, blowing up all seven bridges, withdrawing to Pest on the west side of the river. The Germans made the Parliament building, department stores, the university, and banks into strong points connected by underground passages. Commercial buildings were emptied to make room for gun emplacements and munitions. The contents of the buildings were used for barricades. One street was blocked by an immense pile of smashed pianos thrown out of a musical-instruments warehouse.

Shelled by Soviet artillery and bombed in incessant raids, much of the city was slowly reduced to rubble as the Soviets closed in late in December driving the Germans from Pest. By mid-January the Red Army held more than three fourths of the city's buildings. But the fighting went on, block by block, and in some buildings floor by floor.

On Dec. 6 a Hungarian provisional government had declared war on Germany and on Jan. 20, 1945, signed an armistice. But still the fighting in Buda went on. Hitler refused requests for permission to surrender. On Feb. 11, the Germans, nearly out of ammunition, tried to break out of the city. Only a few hundred made it. On Feb. 12 the remnants of the garrison, about 33,000 men, surrendered. More than 159,000 German and Hungarian troops were killed or captured in the fight for the city.

Buffalo

(1) Code name for Allied operations to break out from the beachhead at ANZIO, Italy; (2) see F2A.

Büffel-Bewegung (Buffalo Stampede)

Code name for German operations on the Soviet central front, 1943.

Bugle

Code name for Allied air attacks against German oil and communications targets in the Ruhr area, March 1945.

Buick

Code name for U.S. AAF mass drop of supplies to the French Marquis by 192 B-17 FLYING FORTRESS bombers dropping 2,281 parachute containers, Aug. 1, 1944; part of Operation Carpetbagger.

Bulgaria

Capital: Sofia, pop. 6,370,000 (est. 1940). When the war began, Bulgaria declared neutrality. But, in reaction to early German success, Bulgaria, under land-hungry King Boris III, developed a pro-NAZI policy. In Feb. 1941 Bulgaria, at German urging, signed an agreement of friendship with Turkey so that country would not react when German troops marched through Bulgaria to invade Greece and Yugoslavia. On March 2 Bulgarian officials flew to Vienna and signed the TRIPARTITE PACT, aligning their country with the AXIS; on the same day, German troops entered Bulgaria from Rumania.

Bulgarian troops marched into prosperous territories taken from Greece and Yugoslavia. The Bulgarians, exploiting and persecuting the conquered peoples, were benefiting from their pro-German policy. But the Germans wanted payment: aid in the war against the Soviet Union.

Although Bulgaria declared war on the United States and the United Kingdom on Dec. 12, 1941, there was widespread support among Bulgarians for Germany's other enemy, the Soviet Union. (Russia in 1878 had helped to free Bulgaria from Turkish rule, and the deed was never forgotten.) While King Boris worked to get Bulgarian troops to aid the Germans on the EASTERN FRONT, a pro-Soviet underground began a terror campaign. Assassins killed more than 100 pro-Nazi officials. King Boris died on Aug. 28, 1943, without an announced cause of death; almost certainly it was an ASSASSINATION.

Allied planes bombed Sofia in Jan. and March 1944. By then Bulgaria was on the verge of revolution. The government declared neutrality, but the ALLIES refused to recognize it. On Sept. 1, 1944, the government resigned. In the next eight days the Soviet Union declared war on Bulgaria, the underground rose and seized government offices, Bulgaria declared war on Germany, and the Soviet Union declared a truce.

The Bulgarian Army did go to war—with the Red Army, fighting against Germans in Hungary, Austria, and Yugoslavia. On Oct. 28 Bulgaria signed an armistice with the Allies. In trials that began on Dec. 24, three royal regents, eight royal advisers, twenty-two ministers, and sixty-eight members of parliament were executed. After other trials the following spring, 2,600 more death sentences were decreed. Bulgaria's Communist government set up more than eighty "labor camps," where thousands died and were buried in mass graves. (Not until the emergence of freedom in Bulgaria in 1990 would the mass graves be found.)

For Bulgaria and other Eastern European countries, the YALTA CONFERENCE in Feb. 1945 pledged free elections after the creation of interim governments "broadly representative of all democratic elements." But in reality Bulgaria would become one of the Soviet satellite states of Eastern Europe.

Bulge,

see ARDENNES.

Bulkeley, Comdr. John D. (1911—)

As a Navy lieutenant, Bulkeley was commander of the U.S. Navy's PT-BOAT SQUADRON in the Philippines at the start of World War II. After his six boats ineffectually attacked Japanese warships assaulting the Philippines, he personally led the four boats that carried Gen. DOUGLAS MACARTHUR and his party from the besieged island of CORREGIDOR in March 1942 to the southern Philippines, from where MacArthur was able to fly on to Australia.

When the order came for MacArthur to break away, Bulkeley and his four battle-worn craft were chosen for the mission. Running at half their designed speed, the boats suffered breakdowns, near-encounters with enemy warships, and rough seas, but *PT 41* (Bulkeley's boat) and *PT 34* delivered their passengers to Mindanao after thirty-five hours at sea. He was awarded the MEDAL OF HONOR for his Philippine exploits.

In Feb. 1943 Bulkeley took Motor Torpedo Boat (MTB) Squadron 7 to NEW GUINEA, operating against Japanese shipping in the area until Sept. 1943. He led MTB Squadron 2 to England in March 1944 in preparation for special operations in the English Channel. His PT-boats entered the waters off the Normandy coast to bring back samples of sand from the beaches that would be assaulted on D-DAY. He then commanded MTB Squadron 102 through the NORMANDY INVASION. To divert German attention from the actual sites of the Aug. 1944 Anglo-American landings in southern France, a task force under Bulkeley's command composed of British gunboats, the U.S. destroyer *Endicott* (DD 495), and twenty-two PT-boats staged a noisy simulated bombardment up the coast. When challenged by two German corvettes, *Endicott*'s crew and two PT-boats sank both of them. Bulkeley ended the war as the *Endicott*'s commanding officer and went on to have a long postwar career, retiring in 1974 as a rear admiral but remaining on active duty at the request of the secretary of the Navy until 1988.

A 1942 book based on Bulkeley's adventure, *They Were Expendable* by W. L. White, was one of America's great war stories. The title came from a remark by Bulkeley to the effect that PT men and boats were considered expendable. The book was made into a 1945 MOVIE of the same name, in which Robert Montgomery, who was a U.S. Navy captain in the war, and John Wayne both played PT-boat officers.

Bullfrog

Code name for projected Allied attack on Akyab, Burma, Jan. 1945.

Bundles for Britain

U.S. volunteer organization founded in Dec. 1939 to send food, clothing, and medical supplies to British civilians. Launched by Natalie Wales Latham and other upper-class Anglophiles in New York City, the organization spread to grass-roots America, especially after the BATTLE OF BRITAIN began late in the summer of 1940. The wife of Prime Minister CHURCHILL became honorary sponsor of the organization. Bundles for Britain, a well-publicized demonstration of American support for England, anticipated LEND-LEASE, the U.S. government-to-government aid to England. When Lend-Lease went into effect in March 1941, it was sometimes waggishly referred to as "Bundles for Britain."

Bunghole

Code name for joint U.S.-British operation to parachute American specialists into the Balkans to assist GUERRILLA operations, Feb. 1944.

Buritone

British code name for reinforcement of MALTA, Aug. 1942.

Burke, Commo. Arleigh A. (1901—)

A leading U.S. DESTROYER commander in World War II. Burke, who earned the sobriquet "31-knot Burke" for his high-speed destroyer tactics, was also a tactician and strategist for the Navy's fast carrier force.

Most of Burke's prewar career was spent in ordnance work and in destroyers. He was an ordnance inspector at the WASHINGTON (D.C.) Navy Yard from Aug. 1940 to Jan. 1943, when he took command of a destroyer DIVISION in the SOLOMONS area. His ships were engaged in heavy fighting, and he was wounded in one firefight with Japanese ships. He took command of a destroyer SQUADRON in Aug. 1943, and two months later became Commander Destroyer Squadron 23, which was known as the "Little Beavers" after their insignia, based on the COMIC strip Red Ryder.

During intensive fighting in the South Pacific area, the "Little Beavers" under Burke's leadership sank one Japanese cruiser, nine destroyers, one submarine, and several smaller ships; they were also credited with thirty planes shot down. None of his ships was lost.

In March 1944 Burke because the Chief of Staff to Vice Adm. MARC A. MITSCHER, the Navy's fast

carrier force commander (TASK FORCE 38) and was promoted to acting commodore. In that role he participated in carrier operations against HOLLANDIA and SAIPAN, and in the battles of the Philippine Sea and LEYTE GULF. Subsequently TF 38 operated against IWO JIMA, OKINAWA, and the Japanese home islands. During this period Adm. Mitscher's health began to fail and he increasingly relied on Burke.

Burke was detached from TF 38 to head an antiKAMIKAZE development unit in July–Aug. 1945, after which he returned to research work in ordnance. (Burke again served as Chief of Staff to Mitscher when the latter commanded the Eighth FLEET and then the Atlantic Fleet in 1946–1947).

In the postwar years Burke became a top U.S. Navy planner and periodically held major surface ship commands. In 1955 he was appointed Chief of Naval Operations (CNO); he was promoted to the top Navy post at age fifty-three over eighty-seven more senior active admirals. Burke was CNO for an unprecedented six years before retiring in 1961.

Burma

Capital: Rangoon, pop. 16,823,798 (1941). Under the Government of India Act of 1935, the British detached Burma from India and made the country a Crown Colony with its own constitution and parliament, but with a governor appointed by the British Crown. Nationalists were not satisfied with colonial status and some allied themselves with Japanese agents who in the late 1930s plotted to bring Burma under Japanese control. The agents recruited a pro-Japanese FIFTH COLUMN—Burmese secretly working for Japan—and tried to stop the construction of the BURMA ROAD by inciting labor troubles and Hindu-Moslem rioting. But the road was completed and until Dec. 1941 Burma remained a British colony isolated from the EUROPEAN WAR.

Peace ended on Dec. 8, 1941, when Japanese troops landed unopposed at Victoria Point, at the southern tip of Burma, launching the Burma phase of JAPAN'S CHINA-BURMA CAMPAIGN. Two weeks later, the Japanese attacked farther up the peninsula and bombed Rangoon. Accompanying the Japanese Army was a ragtag unit of Burmese traitors who styled themselves as the Burma Independence Army. In heavy fighting, British forces pulled back, soon losing Rangoon and, on April 29, 1942, Lashio, the Burmese end of the Burma Road. When Mandalay fell on May 2, 1942, Japan held all of central Burma. The Chinese were cut off from Western supplies except those delivered by air via THE HUMP over the Himalayas.

U.S. Army Lt. Gen. JOSEPH W. STILWELL withdrew his defeated American-British force from Burma into India, and the Japanese occupation of Burma began. The Japanese picked puppet administrators from the ranks of the Burma Independence Army and the political party that supported it. Japan tried to draw Burma into an alliance of Pacific countries called the GREATER EAST ASIA CO-PROSPERITY SPHERE. Thousands of Burmese GUERRILLAS, however, took to the mountains and harassed the Japanese throughout the war.

Burma again became a battlefield in 1943 when the ALLIED CHINA-BURMA-INDIA CAMPAIGN began with CHINDITS, a brigade of specially trained GURKHAS, Burmese, and British forces, raiding Japanese supply lines. Meanwhile, in Aug. 1943 the Japanese, following a pattern used in other conquered territory, granted ostensible independence to Burma; on the same day, Burma declared war on the ALLIES. Japanese became the second language, envoys were sent to other Co-prosperity Sphere nations, and the sons of many influential Burmese families were sent to Japan to complete their education.

Guerrillas and a rehabilitated Burma National Army aided the Allies in their campaign to take back Burma. As the Allies neared Rangoon in the spring of 1945, the puppet government fled to Japan. The British occupied Burma until a civil government was in place in 1946. On Oct. 17, 1947, under a treaty with Great Britain, Burma became an independent republic. (It is now known as Myanmar.)

Burma Road

A 717-mile road from Lashio in Burma to Kunming in Yunnan, an industrial center in southwest China. The road, opened in Dec. 1938, coursed through a mountainous, malaria-plagued wilderness, climbing to 8,500 feet in places. Much of the one-lane road was built by hand in eight months by an army of 150,000 men, women, and children, organized in families or clans. The road generally followed an ancient caravan route between China and Burma.

U.S. and British loans paid for the trucks that used the road and financed most of its construction in China; Burma paid for its section of the road, over strenuous Japanese objections. The road was a lifeline for China, which, cut off from the sea by Japanese coastal conquests, needed an overland route to get supplies from the outside world. (After the fall of France in June 1940, Japanese took over French INDOCHINA in a move to cut off China's other major road, which ran from Yunnan to Indochina and was connected by rail with the port of Hanoi.)

When the Japanese conquered Burma in April 1942, they seized the Burma terminus of the road. Allied planners lashed together a complicated alternative route: by rail from Calcutta, India northeastward to Sadiya, on the India-Burma border; by plane from there for 200 miles to Myitkyina, Burma; by river barge to Bhamo, Burma; from there, via a branch road, to the stretch of the Burma Road still in Chinese hands. But the Japanese seized the area around the Myitkyina airport and plans shifted to an airlift over the Himalayas known as THE HUMP.

Although the airlift partially eased China's logistical crisis, a land link still was needed. So in Dec. 1942 U.S. Army engineers began building the LEDO ROAD in Assam, India (a terminus of The Hump) across the Patkai Range through the Hukawng Valley to Myitkyina and Bhamo and then on to the Burma Road.

Burp-gun

Best-known individual Soviet weapon of the war. The submachine gun was widely used by Soviet soldiers and sailors during the latter stages of the war. Officially designated PPSh M1941, it was popularly known as the "burp-gun" for its staccato firing sound.

The 7.62-mm weapon could be set for single-shot or fully automatic fire. Its distinctive look came from the large wooden stock, large perforations in the barrel jacket that acted as a muzzle brake during firing, and the 71-round, drum-type magazine. (A

35-round box magazine could also be used.) Operation was by the blow-back principle.

The PPSh weighed 11½ pounds with its drum-type magazine. Effective range was rated at 100 yards and on fully automatic its firing rate was 90 to 100 rounds per minute. It was a relatively simple and rugged weapon.

Bush, Lt. George (1924—)

Reputed to be the youngest pilot in the U.S. Navy during the war. His plane was hit by FLAK as he flew over Japan's Bonin Islands near OKINAWA on Sept. 2, 1944. He was flying a TBM AVENGER off the AIRCRAFT CARRIER *San Jacinto* (CVL 30). He and his two crewmen bailed out after the plane was hit. The crewmen were lost. Bush was in the water about an hour and a half when he saw something coming toward him. It was the American SUBMARINE *Finback* (SS 230), which picked him up. Bush was awarded the Distinguished Flying Cross. After the war he went to Yale University, entered the oil business and then politics, becoming President of the United States in 1989.

Bush, Vannevar (1890–1974)

Director of the OFFICE OF SCIENTIFIC RESEARCH AND DEVELOPMENT (OSRD), which initiated the U.S. efforts to build the ATOMIC BOMB. In June 1941, President ROOSEVELT made Bush, then chairman of the National Defense Research Council, director of the OSRD—an agency Bush had invented and urged on Roosevelt. A distinguished scientist and engineer, Bush had been president of the Carnegie Institution and vice president of the Massachusetts Institute of Technology.

Bush had a rare ability to bring scientists together to pool their talents on a project. He himself foresaw the problems of an atomic-weapons arms race. But he put the needs of the war above his own doubts. He infused that same thinking into his work not only with scientists but also with military officers and government officials. One of his most valuable assets was his ability to make a team of both scientists and military officers by allaying their traditional suspicions of each other.

Buttress

Code name for British assault against Reggio, Italy, Sept. 1943.

Buzz Bombs,

see V-1.

Bv 138

Principal German naval flying boat during the war. The large, three-engine Bv 138 was a distinctive aircraft employed in long-range reconnaissance, cargo, antisubmarine, and minesweeping roles during the war. They flew mostly from Norwegian and Baltic-area airfields.

After a lengthy development period the prototype flew in 1937 but was extensively modified before entering service; two of the early aircraft were used in the invasion of Norway in April 1940. In addition to traditional flying-boat roles, some Bv 138s were converted to aerial minesweepers, being fitted with a large dural loop and electric generating equipment that would detonate magnetic mines by flying low over the water. Some antisubmarine aircraft had FuG 200 surface-search RADAR sets.

A total of 279 aircraft were delivered between 1937 and 1943.

The aircraft's distinctive design provided a short hull—dubbed the "shoe box"—with a high wing carrying fixed floats and twin in-line *diesel* engines that were faired back into twin tail booms; a third engine was mounted atop the wing. Some aircraft were modified for catapult launching from auxiliary ships and all could use ROCKET-assistance for difficult water takeoffs. The aircraft had a top speed of 171 mph and a range of 3,105 miles in the reconnaissance role.

The principal production model, the Bv 138C-1, had two 20-mm cannon, one 13-mm machine gun, and one 7.9-mm machine gun. Up to four 330-pound BOMBS or DEPTH CHARGES could be carried under the wings. The Bv 138's crew was normally six and up to ten passengers could be carried.

Bv 222 *Wiking* (Viking)

Designed before the war as a trans-Atlantic flying boat, this six-engine aircraft served Germany as a transport and cargo aircraft. The aircraft flew with a crew of eleven and could carry 110 armed troops or cargo. Following the first flight on Sept. 7, 1940, a total of seven prototypes and seven Bv 222C production aircraft entered Luftwaffe service. Their loaded takeoff weight was 101,390 pounds;

maximum speed was 242 mph and, with judicious handling, endurance was twenty-eight hours with a maximum range of 3,790 miles.

A larger Bv 238 version was developed, having a maximum weight of 198,460 pounds in the reconnaissance version and 209,439 pounds in the planned bomber version. Only a prototype was completed, which flew in April 1944. It was sunk at its moorings by strafings by U.S. P-51 MUSTANG fighters.

Byrnes, James F. (1879–1972)

Director of U.S. OFFICE OF WAR MOBILIZATION and presidential adviser. Byrnes was one of the few American politicians who served in all branches of government. A South Carolina Democrat, he was a member of the House of Representatives and later the Senate. President ROOSEVELT appointed him to the Supreme Court in June 1941, but in Oct. 1942 he left the bench to become what Roosevelt called "assistant president," advising the President and serving first as director of the Office of Economic Stabilization and then as director of the Office of War Mobilization. Some observers said that while Roosevelt ran the war Byrnes ran the country.

Byrnes switched to foreign affairs when he served as a member of the U.S. delegation to the YALTA CONFERENCE in Feb. 1945. He resigned from his mobilization post in April, saying that looming victory in Europe had essentially ended his wartime labors. But in June 1945 President HARRY TRUMAN made him secretary of state and brought him to the POTSDAM CONFERENCE as a key adviser. Byrnes was a shrewd and effective politician who greatly influenced Truman. Distrustful of the Soviet Union since his Yalta experience, Byrnes bided his time until the war ended. After the war he became an advocate of a hard line against the Soviets and is considered one of the American architects of the cold war.

C

C-46 Commando

U.S. transport aircraft second only to the C-47 SKYTRAIN/DAKOTA in numbers and popularity. The C-46 was used mostly in the Pacific area and gained notoriety for flying THE HUMP.

Unlike the C-47, which was based on the successful DC-3 transport, the C-46 was a military version of an as-yet-unproved commercial transport. The aircraft, much larger and heavier than the C-47, had engineering problems, which delayed introduction until 1944. It was used to carry cargo, tow GLIDERS, and drop paratroopers.

A twin-engine, low-wing aircraft, the C-46 was a "tail sitter" with a fixed tail wheel, the main wheels retracting partially into the engine nacelles. Its fuselage was more rounded than that of the C-47. The C-46 had a large cargo loading door on the port side and folding seats along the walls for forty troops.

The design originated in 1937 as a thirty-six-passenger commercial transport advertised as offering a new level of luxury and performance. The first flight was in March 1940. The U.S. Army immediately placed an order for twenty-five aircraft with the Curtiss firm. In 1941 the prototype was purchased by the AAF and evaluated with the designation C-55; it was subsequently transferred to Britain under LEND-LEASE.

Large-scale production followed at several firms, but only 3,144 entered AAF service by August 1945. Several hundred more were canceled at the end of the war. Modifications reached the C-46G variant, with a few TC-46 trainers being flown in

The most disastrous convoy of the war was PQ 17, which fell victim to German bombers and U-boats after being ordered to scatter to avoid the German battleship *Tirpitz*. The slaughter was extensive, including this freighter—flying a barrage balloon to deter low-flying bombers—sunk by submarine torpedoes. *(German Navy)*

the postwar period. The Marine Corps flew about 150 Commandos with the designation R5C.

The production aircraft had a crew of four and carried up to fifty troops or thirty-three litters or 10,000 pounds of cargo. Maximum speed was 269 mph and range was 1,200 miles. (All of these characteristics were superior to those of the C-47, except for range.)

C-47 Skytrain/Dakota

The most widely used transport aircraft of the war. The C-47 transport was known by U.S. pilots as the Skytrain and by other air forces as the Dakota. The official U.S. AAF history observed, "A steady and proven aircraft, the C-47 earned for itself a reputation hardly eclipsed even by the more glamorous combat planes." Also known as the "Gooney Bird," the C-47 was cited by Gen. DWIGHT D. EISENHOWER as one of the four weapons that helped most to win the war (the others being the BAZOOKA, JEEP, and ATOMIC BOMB). The C-47 was employed in every theater, as a cargo and troop transport, and in combat for parachute operations. The only other transport aircraft that approached the C-47 in fame and popularity was the German JU 52.

Among the more famous C-47 operations were the Allied parachute assaults in the NORTH AFRICA INVASION, SICILY, the NORMANDY INVASION, against the Dutch bridges in Operation MARKET-GARDEN, and numerous Pacific AIRBORNE drops, and flying over THE HUMP from India to China. By the time of the Normandy invasion in June 1944 there were over 1,200 U.S. AAF C-47s available to carry paratroops in England, plus a small number flown by the RAF. Additional C-47s were arriving on a daily basis. At Normandy 13,000 paratroopers of the U.S. 82nd and 101st Airborne DIVISIONS were dropped or airlanded by GLIDERS behind German lines on the eve of the AMPHIBIOUS LANDING by 822 C-47s; other transports and C-47s dropped the British 6th Airborne Division.

A twin-engine, low-wing aircraft, the C-47 was a "tail sitter" with a fixed tail wheel and the main wheels retracting partially into the engine nacelles. A single C-47 was fitted with twin floats, each of which contained retractable wheels; this design proved too difficult for loading and unloading

cargo. (The floats contained retractable wheels and fuel tanks.)

The C-47 was the military cargo version of the Douglas DC-3 commercial aircraft, which first flew on Dec. 15, 1935. From then until 1940 a total of 430 DC-3s were delivered to U.S. and foreign airlines. The U.S. Army ordered modifications to the aircraft, including stronger cabin floors, large loading doors, and more powerful engines. A single aircraft was completed with the designation C-41, followed by large orders for the C-47 and C-53, entering service on Jan. 1942 and Oct. 1941, respectively. The C-53 Skytrooper was an AAF version of the DC-3 fitted to carry personnel only. Engines were removed from one C-47 and it was used in glider experiments (designated CG-17).

Before the war was over the AAF had accepted 10,123 C-47s and C-53s, which was nearly one half of the transport aircraft acquired from 1940 to 1945, and the U.S. Navy flew several hundred more with total production of the DC-3 type reaching 10,926 aircraft. (The Navy designation was R4D; after the war upgraded Navy and Air Force models were designated C-117.) The approximately 200 DC-3s taken from commercial service by the AAF were designated C-48 through C-52, C-68, and C-84.

The standard C-47 could carry twenty-seven troops or eighteen to twenty-four litters. The C-47 usually flew with a crew of three, or up to five when carrying paratroopers. Maximum speed was 230 mph and range was 1,600 miles.

In Jan. 1947 the U.S. Navy flew six ski-fitted C-47s from an AIRCRAFT CARRIER. Fitted with jet-assistance bottles, the C-47s were flown to Antarctica for use by Rear Adm. Richard E. Byrd in his explorations. The C-47/R4D/C-117 remained in U.S. military service through the 1970s, and when this book went to press was still flown by several other air forces. Unusual configurations included the gunship, electronic warfare, and maritime patrol variants.

C-54 Skymaster

The outstanding four-engine transport of the war. The C-54 was the military version of the commercial Douglas DC-4. It was flown by the U.S. AAF AIR TRANSPORT COMMAND and NAVAL AIR

TRANSPORT SERVICE (as the R5D) on long-distance hauls. Strictly a troop transport and cargo plane, it was not adapted for parachute drops. Many were fitted to evacuate wounded from forward areas and several flew in the VIP configuration, some having several berths.

The most famous VIP aircraft was the "Sacred Cow," a C-54 adapted for use by President ROOSEVELT. It was first used by him in Feb. 1945 to fly from MALTA to Saki airfield in the Crimea for the YALTA CONFERENCE. The plane—the first ever assigned to a president on a permanent basis—had an elevator and other features to handle the president's wheelchair, a conference room, and four staterooms with accommodations for fourteen staff members. (This VC-54C, later used by President TRUMAN, was retired to a museum in 1961.) One C-54B was transferred to Britain for use by Prime Minister CHURCHILL, and Gen. DOUGLAS MACARTHUR had his personal C-54 named "Bataan."

The prototype DC-4 had flown on June 21, 1938, having been developed by the Douglas Aircraft Co. in close collaboration with U.S. airlines. (That plane was larger than the subsequent DC-4/C-54 production aircraft and had a triple-tail configuration.) The commercial aircraft was to seat forty-two passengers in a high degree of comfort. Early in 1942 the AAF commandeered the DC-4 production line; the first of these planes flew on March 26, 1942. Series production followed at two Douglas plants as the basic aircraft was modified with a strengthened floor, a large door, and boom hoist for handling heavy items, including JEEPS. More fuel tanks were provided, and normal seating was for fifty. The cabins were convertible for passengers, troops, cargo, and wounded evacuees. Wartime improvements reached the C-54E variant, a very-long-range aircraft; only one was built.

More than 1,000 C-54s were delivered by the end of the war. They flew a total of 79,642 ocean crossings up to V-J DAY with only three C-54s lost. Regular routes were established across the Atlantic and Pacific; there was also a Ceylon-to-Australia route, a 3,100-mile flight. The C-54 was also a veteran of flights over THE HUMP.

The military aircraft C-54 had a six-man crew and seats for fifty passengers or up to seven tons of cargo. Maximum range in the passenger role was 3,900 miles and maximum speed was 265 mph.

C-56/C-57 Lodestar

A small twin-engine transport that saw varied service in the war. The C-56 and its variants flew as an ambulance, cargo carrier, GLIDER tug, paratroop transport, and VIP transport. The U.S. AAF acquired a large number of Lockheed Lodestar commercial airliners and procured several new aircraft using mainly the designations C-56 and C-57, with a few designated C-59, C-60, C-66, and C-111.

The basic Lockheed Model 18 was a seventeen-passenger developed from the Electra series. Powered by two Wright Cyclone engines, the Lodestar proved to be one of the world's fastest aircraft in its class. First flown in Feb. 1940, many were in commercial service when the United States entered the war in Dec. 1941 and the AAF requisitioned more than 100 of the planes. Subsequently, ten C-59s and fifteen C-60s were procured for other countries, principally Britain (the designations indicating different engines than the C-56). Later another 346 C-60s were ordered for the AAF. One C-66 was purchased for foreign transfer while three smaller Model 14 aircraft were acquired in 1944 and designated C-111. The U.S. Navy, Coast Guard, and Marine Corps also took over commercial Lodestars and procured new aircraft, all given the naval designation R50. Most were VIP or staff transports with four to fourteen seats, but thirty-five R50-6 variants were eighteen-seat paratroop transports for the Marines (as were several AAF C-60A variants).

The basic C-56 was a mid-wing aircraft with a twin-tail configuration, resembling the Lockheed-built bombers that also evolved from the Electra line. (See A-28/A-29/B-34 HUDSON.) The main undercarriage retracted almost completely into the twin engine nacelles; the tail wheel did not retract. Flown by a two-man crew, most C-56s had seventeen seats, but one, the C-66, was an eleven-passenger plane and two, designated C-56E, had twenty-two seats.

Top speed of the C-56 was 253 mph, with range rated at 1,600 miles.

C-69 Constellation

In many respects the C-69 Constellation was the most advanced transport aircraft of the war era, presenting a graceful, futuristic appearance that became synonymous with trans-ocean flight in the postwar period. During the war "Connies" flew as transports with the U.S. AAF AIR TRANSPORT COMMAND and the Navy.

The first military versions were taken over on the production line, having been the commercial Lockheed Model 49 aircraft ordered by T.W.A. Designated C-69, the first AAF aircraft flew in Jan. 1943. The four-engine aircraft was the largest (82,000 pounds maximum) and fastest (330 mph) transport built to date for the AAF. A total of twenty-two C-69s were built for the AAF before contracts were terminated on V-J DAY. The Navy took title to several Model 49s in 1945; they were given the designation R7O and were initially flown by Patrol Bomber SQUADRON (VPB) 101, not the NAVAL AIR TRANSPORT SERVICE.

(After the war the U.S. Air Force and Navy acquired large numbers of the Model 749 Constellation; designated C-121 and naval R7V/PO/WV, these became transports, VIP aircraft, research, and RADAR early-warning aircraft.)

The C-69 was a graceful, four-engine, low-wing aircraft. It had a distinctive, streamlined "turtleback" fuselage and triple-tail configuration. It stood high on a tricycle landing gear. The standard C-69 carried sixty troops; the single C-69C had a VIP configuration for forty-three passengers. The canceled AAF aircraft included a C-69B with bench seats for ninety-four troops.

The C-69 was credited with a range of 2,400 miles.

C.200 *Saetta* (Lightning)

The C.200 was a fast, highly maneuverable Italian fighter that evolved from a racing seaplane design (as did the RAF SPITFIRE). However, the Italian aircraft was underpowered, a common shortfall of Italian fighters, and it was lackluster in service. These fighters served on all Italian fronts with later models having their wings strengthened to carry two small (352-pound) BOMBS.

Designed by Mario Castoldi and produced by Aeronautica Macchi, the C.200 prototype flew in 1937 and was immediately ordered into production. A total of 156 had been delivered by the time Italy entered the EUROPEAN WAR in 1940. About 1,000 were built.

A short, low-wing aircraft, with a small tail fin, the early C.200 aircraft had an enclosed cockpit; the

canopy was discarded in the later aircraft. The Fiat radial engine was rated at only 840 horsepower. A German DB 601 in-line (liquid-cooled) engine was fitted in a C.200 airframe and was a harbinger of the C.202 fighter. The C.200 had a pair of 12.7-mm machine guns and was badly undergunned by contemporary fighter standards.

C.202 *Folgore* (Thunderbolt)

An attempt to improve Italian aircraft performance through the use of German engines, the C.202 was still not a total success. The C.202 entered squadron service in 1941 and saw service throughout the war in the Mediterranean and on the EASTERN FRONT. While more successful than earlier Italian fighters, it failed to reach the performance and achievements of contemporary British and German aircraft.

The C.200 *SAETTA* fitted with a DB 601 in-line engine flew in Aug. 1940 and, with the Daimler-Benz being built under license in Italy, production was initiated. The first Aeronautica Macchi–built C.202s entered squadron service in 1941. A total of some 1,500 aircraft were built.

Similar in appearance to the C.200 but two feet longer with an in-line engine, the C.202 had an enclosed cockpit. One C.202 airframe was then fitted with the DB 605 engine, leading to the C.205 fighter. The C.202 had a top speed of 369 mph and was credited with a range of 475 miles. Armament in later models consisted of two 12.7-mm and two 7.7-mm machine guns; one production batch had two 20-mm cannon in underwing pods in an effort to compensate for the aircraft's shortfall in firepower. Two small BOMBS could be carried under the wings.

C.205V *Veltro* (Greyhound)

The ultimate in the development of the C.200 *SAETTA* and C.202 *FOLGORE* fighter designs, the C.205V was an excellent aircraft but entered service in mid-1943, too late to have an impact on Italian air operations. A C.205 fitted with the uprated engine first flew on April 19, 1942. Using the same basic airframe of its predecessors, the Aeronautica Macchi aircraft had a German DB 605A in-line engine that was built in Italy. The plane was noted for its maneuverability and ease of handling.

Sixty-six planes were in service at the time of the

Italian SURRENDER in Sept. 1943, of which about one half were operational. Limited production continued with a total of 262 planes being produced. A few improved prototypes were also flown.

The C.205V could reach 399 mph at optimum altitude. Early planes had two machine guns, but most were fitted with two 20-mm cannon and two 12.7-mm machine guns, and could carry two 330-pound BOMBS in the fighter-bomber role.

C rations,

see RATIONS.

Cabinet War Rooms

The suite of rooms beneath the New Public Offices in LONDON where Prime Minister CHURCHILL, his War Cabinet, and CHIEFS OF STAFF met during the war.

More than 100 Cabinet meetings were held in the Cabinet War Rooms, which opened in Oct. 1939. By the spring of 1940 it had expanded to a sixteen-room suite centered around the Map Room, where information about the war in all parts of the world was funneled. The first prime minister to make use of the accommodations was NEVILLE CHAMBERLAIN. Churchill, who succeeded Chamberlain on May 10, 1940, was soon taken to the rooms. Shortly later, he was shown the rooms and he said, "This is the room from which I'll run the war."

Because Churchill was both prime minister and minister of defense, he presided over not only policy but also day-to-day conduct of the war. He did much of his presiding in the underground rooms, especially after the BATTLE OF BRITAIN began in the late summer of 1940. Churchill vetoed a move to a safer place, and the Cabinet War Rooms were made more bombproof.

Churchill had a bedroom in the suite but rarely slept there. He preferred the ground floor, in apartment "No. 10 Downing Street Annexe," which had been provided for the Churchills and their staff. He made several radio broadcasts from the underground command post.

In a cubbyhole called the Transatlantic Telephone Room he conversed with President ROOSEVELT. Conversations were kept secret by a scrambler device developed by Bell Telephone and named

SIGSALY by the U.S. Army Signal Corps. It was sent to London on the QUEEN ELIZABETH in May 1943 but not put in the rooms because it was so big. It was installed in Selfridge's department store and, through an intermediate scrambler, linked to the War Rooms by underground cable.

Cactus

U.S. code name for GUADALCANAL. U.S. combat aircraft operating from Guadalcanal were referred to as the Cactus Air Force.

Cadillac

(1) Code name for mass drop by 322 U.S. AAF B-17 FLYING FORTRESS bombers of 3,780 supply containers to the French Marquis, July 14, 1944 (part of Operation Carpetbagger); (2) U.S. Navy project to develop airborne RADAR warning aircraft, employing TBM AVENGER and B-17 FLYING FORTRESS bombers.

Caesar

British code word to initiate certain defensive actions in the event of a German invasion; changed to Cromwell on June 5, 1940.

Cairo Conference

Meeting of President ROOSEVELT, Prime Minister CHURCHILL, and Generalissimo CHIANG KAISHEK of China. At meetings in Cairo on Nov. 22–26, 1943, the three leaders agreed that "Japan shall be stripped of all the islands in the Pacific which she has seized or occupied" since World War I along with all occupied Chinese territory. They also called for independence for Korea and agreed that UNCONDITIONAL SURRENDER would be demanded of Japan. During the conference, Roosevelt and Churchill met President İsmet İnönü of Turkey to ask the nation to enter the war against Germany. From Cairo, Roosevelt and Churchill continued on to the TEHRAN CONFERENCE with Soviet leader JOSEF STALIN.

Calendar

British code name for reinforcement of MALTA, April 1942; the U.S. AIRCRAFT CARRIER WASP (CV 7) participated in this operation.

Caliph

Code name for possible Allied landings in the Bordeaux region as an alternate to the invasion of southern France.

Callboy

British code name for reinforcement of MALTA, Oct. 1941.

Camel

Code name for U.S. 36th Infantry DIVISION force for operations in southern France.

Camouflage

The art of concealment, practiced since ancient times, had a new set of eyes to outwit in World War II: aerial photography. Stereoscopic cameras produced images in three dimensions; infrared photographs could detect the difference between real and counterfeit shrubbery.

Camoufleurs countered with nets that covered trucks, tanks, and guns, hiding them from aerial view or making them look like haystacks. The roofs of factories were painted so that from the air they appeared to be a farm landscape. Or, in England, fake factories were built of wood and cardboard. From the air, with their given fake, smoldering smokestacks, they looked real enough to draw German bombers from real targets.

The U.S. Army created fake divisions—including one supposedly commanded by Gen. GEORGE S. PATTON during the preparations for the NORMANDY INVASION. When the *National Geographic Magazine* wanted to publish a collection of the insignia and decorations of the U.S. armed forces in 1944, the Army obliged, but added twenty-one shoulder sleeve insignia for nonexistent U.S. units. They belonged to a fake Fourteenth ARMY with two fictional CORPS and nineteen nonexistent divisions.

The most elaborate camouflage tactics were developed by the 23rd Headquarters Special Troops, a unit organized for deception operations in the European theater. Recruited into the unit were painters, illustrators, theatrical set designers, and future fashion designer Bill Blass.

From mid-1944 to early 1945 the 23rd pretended to be actual armored or infantry DIVISIONS. While

Camouflage—"ghost" division insignia.

the real Fifth Armored Division or 90th Infantry Division was about to pull out of an area to head for a new position, the 23rd would slip in, assuming the identity of the vacating unit.

The 23rd, whose audio tricksters could produce the radio communications and sound effects of a division, could visibly imitate a division with the addition of a few tanks, antiaircraft batteries, and other tactical equipment. In a typical operation, units of the 23rd would move into an area being vacated at nightfall, inflate a fleet of rubber tanks, trucks, artillery pieces, and jeeps, and then carry on as if it were a division. Men wearing the shoulder patches of the imitated unit would make themselves known in the area. They would send details to supply dumps, chat with civilians, and drive around in trucks, with two men sitting near the rear and the canopy down so that no one would know whether the truck carried twelve men or two.

The 23rd opened its bag of tricks especially wide during the RHINE CROSSINGS in a deception plan code-named Exploit. In March 1945, the U.S. Army had crossed the Rhine via the LUDENDORFF RAILWAY BRIDGE at Remagen. The Ninth Army was attempting to cross at Viersen, near the Dutch border.

To make the Germans believe that two divisions were assembling near the village of Viersen, the 23th set up false radio nets, built roads to sites where crossings were not to take place, and arrayed real antiaircraft BATTERIES around fake command posts—to discourage German reconnaissance planes from getting close enough to see that the tanks and trucks were dummies.

The men restricted civilians from a wide area—to simultaneously keep them from seeing the dummy and to follow standard procedure for assembling units. Men of the 23rd even put out washing near partly concealed tents. Meanwhile, the real movement went on in what military deception experts describe as concealing the real while displaying the false. An Army critique of the operation called it "a model of deception."

Canada

Capital: Ottawa, pop. 10,376,766 (est. 1939). At the beginning of the EUROPEAN WAR Canada, a British dominion, was concerned about a reenactment of a World War I crisis: the refusal of French-speaking citizens to join the war effort. In World War I, French Canadians had rioted over attempts to conscript them into the armed forces. They called themselves *les Canadiens* and, while willing to fight for Canada as Canadians, they had no such loyalty for England.

When the UNITED KINGDOM declared war on Germany on Sept. 3, 1939, Canada did not immediately follow suit. To show its independence to both the world and its own *les Canadiens,* the Canadian government, under Prime Minister W. L. Mackenzie King, did not declare war but referred the matter to the Canadian parliament. With a few dissenting votes, it declared war on Sept. 10.

At that moment Canada had a navy of 1,774 men, an army of about 4,500, and an air force of 4,060. While Canada hastily began building up the armed services and establishing a war-production program, military officials conferred with British officials about Canada's role in BRITISH COMMONWEALTH defenses. Canada was assigned the mission of protecting British America: Canada itself, the British West Indies, Newfoundland, Labrador, and the French islands of St. Pierre et Miquelon off Newfoundland. (England in 1933 had removed Newfoundland from the dominion because of its extreme poverty and had made it a colony.)

The fall of France in June 1940 eased the *les Canadiens* issue, for the French Canadians realized that Canada was now a bastion of FREE FRENCH culture. In a dramatic demonstration of this, on Dec. 24, 1941, French Vice Adm. Émile Muselier seized the islands of St. Pierre et Miquelon in the name of the Free French to keep them out of the hands of the German collaborationist VICHY FRANCE regime.

A few anticonscription *les Canadiens* leaders were interned, but there was no repeat of World War I

rioting. The question of conscription was settled through compromise. Men could be drafted only for home defense; only volunteers would be sent overseas. This was known as the two-army policy.

The controversy over conscription, however, would not go away. To change the conscription law so that draftees could be sent overseas, King's Liberal government, in April 1942, staged an extraordinary plebiscite asking the voters to release the Liberal Party from its no-draftees-overseas pledge. The nation overwhelmingly voted in favor of removing the restriction. But voters in the French-speaking Province of Quebec rejected it three to one. King, though now able to change the two-army policy, kept it to calm *les Canadiens.*

Once again, however, the issue flared up. In late 1944, Col. James L. Ralston, the minister of national defense, returned from a tour of combat zones and reported that the Canadian Army overseas could not be sustained by volunteers alone, even though the turnout of volunteers was impressive. Both the Royal Canadian Navy and the Royal Canadian Air Force had all the men they needed. The 875,000 Canadians who had *volunteered* up to that time were statistically in proportion to the number of men who had been *drafted* in the United States.

But the Canadian draft law was so lenient that of the 150,000 draftees called up in the first five years of the war, 60,000 had refused to "go active" and so were assigned to guard duties and other jobs on Canadian soil. Of the volunteers, the French-speaking areas were supplying men at half the rate of other provinces. Ralston insisted that with figures like these it was obvious that Canadian Army forces in combat in Europe in need of replacements could not depend upon volunteers.

When King did not respond with overseas conscription, Ralston resigned, causing a political uproar that King tried to still by ordering overseas a group of 16,000 men who had enlisted for service in Canada only. In protest, the associate minister of national defense, who represented a Quebec constituency, resigned. Army officers who spoke against the two-army policy were threatened with court-martial. Some home army troops talked of mutiny.

The political war got so heated that demands for

a general election in June 1945 could not be ignored. King's party, emphasizing its war record and playing down conscription, was returned with a small minority.

Canada had become an arsenal and training ground for the British Empire. Canada established more than 150 major air and ground schools, with more than 200 supplementary units; they trained 113,553 airmen. So many pilots were trained in Canada that President ROOSEVELT called the nation "the aerodrome of democracy." The army grew to six divisions, the navy to 939 vessels, of which 378 were combat ships, more than 100 of which took part in the NORMANDY INVASION. The air force increased to 222,550 men and nearly 17,000 women. Three women's military services were formed: the Royal Canadian Air Force women's division (the WDs), the Canadian Women's Army Corps (the CWACs, pronounced "quacks"), and the Women's Royal Canadian Naval Service (the Wrens).

Canada and the United States worked together long before the U.S. entry into the war. On Aug. 18, 1938, President Roosevelt, speaking at Queens University in Kingston, Ontario, pledged assistance to Canada in case of invasion by a foreign power. In April 1941, the two nations completed a joint strategic military and naval plan. In the same year, under LEND-LEASE, the United States opened bases in Newfoundland. Canada agreed on U.S. construction of the ALCAN HIGHWAY through Canada and helped build and expand airfields for defense of Alaska. The two countries jointly developed oil refinery and pipelines, established a system of weather observation posts, and set up organizations for the joint allocation of food, RESOURCES, and production facilities.

Canaris, Adm. Wilhelm (1887–1945)

Chief of German Military Intelligence (*ABWEHR*) from 1935 to 1944, Adm. Canaris had doubtful loyalty to ADOLF HITLER, placing the German military and nation above *der Führer* and his sycophants.

A professional naval officer, Canaris served in several shipboard and shore assignments, including the cruiser *Dressler* in the South Pacific at the start of World War I. After her sinking in 1915 he was able to return to Germany in disguise—via England. Canaris was engaged in intelligence work in Spain and Italy from 1916 to 1918, when he took command of a submarine. His intelligence mentor was Col. Walter Nicolai, fabled head of German military intelligence in the war.

After the war Canaris remained in the Navy and served in shore assignments and at sea, commanding the old battleship *Schlesien* in 1932–1933. Initially he was a supporter of Hitler because of his opposition to the Versailles Treaty and communism. Canaris was made chief of military intelligence on Jan. 1, 1935, with the rank of *Konteradmiral*. When Germany sent aid to the Nationalist side in the SPANISH CIVIL WAR, he organized German naval assistance.

During World War II he held tight control of the *Abwehr*, which was not particularly effective. However, it is difficult to determine if this was because of Canaris' ineptitude or his anti-Hitler viewpoint. To protect some anti-Hitler conspirators, he took them into the *Abwehr*. In Feb. 1944, after being investigated by the SS, Canaris was dismissed from the *Abwehr* and appointed chief of the Office for Commercial and Economic Warfare. He was arrested on July 20, 1944, immediately following the abortive JULY 20 PLOT against Hitler.

Canaris was held at Flossenbürg CONCENTRATION CAMP until he was tried on April 8, 1945; he was executed early the next morning. He was hanged twice because the first time he did not die; his body was incinerated.

It has been reported that Canaris had met during World War I with Mata Hari in Spain, and possibly with WILLIAM J. DONOVAN, head of the U.S. OFFICE OF STRATEGIC SERVICES, in Switzerland during World War II. Canaris and Hari, however, were in Madrid at the same time only once and it is unlikely that they met; similarly, the possibility of Canaris' having met the head of the OSS was also highly unlikely.

Canned Goods

German code name for an SS operation to throw the blame for the invasion of Poland onto the Polish Army, Aug. 31, 1939.

Cannibal

Allied code name for planned Chinese offensive into Burma to capture Akyab and the line of the Chindwin River.

Cape Esperance

During the battle for GUADALCANAL Cape Esperance, on the northwest coast of the island, was the landing point for Japanese transports and barges that landed supplies and men. When the Japanese evacuated the island in Feb. 1943, they slipped away from beaches on the cape.

On Oct. 11–12, 1942, a force of U.S. CRUISERS and DESTROYERS detected, with RADAR, Japanese ships heading for Guadalcanal. In the ensuing naval battle off the cape U.S. ships fired upon each other while performing complex maneuvering. The U.S. Navy at first believed that four Japanese cruisers and four destroyers were sunk. In reality, a Japanese cruiser was badly damaged, as were two U.S. destroyers.

Capital

Code name for Allied plan to attack across the Chindwin River to Mandalay to recapture northern Burma, 1944.

Capital Ships

Term for battleships and battle cruisers. By the end of the war it could also be applied to aircraft carriers.

Carbine

Lightweight rifle. More U.S. soldiers carried carbines during the war than any other individual weapon. The M1 carbine was a .30-cal. lightweight weapon issued to officers, artillerymen, and technicians in the Army and Marine Corps. Resembling a small rifle, the M1A1 model had a folding wire stock for use by paratroopers. It was not as accurate as the M1903 SPRINGFIELD or M1 GARAND rifles.

The M1 Carbine was a gas-operated, semiautomatic weapon weighing 6 pounds with a 15-round magazine; it could also be fitted with a 30-round magazine. The later M2 model had a fully automatic firing mode. Effective range was approximately 300 yards with a 40-rounds-per-minute rate of fire.

More than 6 million carbines of all marks were produced.

Carbonado

Code name for revised Operation Beta.

Cargo

Code name for President ROOSEVELT.

Carlson, Lt. Col. Evans F. (1896–1947)

Commander of the U.S. Marine Corps' 2nd Raider BATTALION, better known as CARLSON'S RAIDERS. An Army second lieutenant who switched to the Marine Corps, Carlson got to know President ROOSEVELT as a member of the President's personal guard at Warm Springs, Ga. Through Roosevelt's influence, Carlson was sent as an observer with MAO TSE-TUNG's Eighth Route Army in 1937. Carlson developed a great admiration for the "spiritual strength" of the Communist forces and carefully studied their effective style of GUERRILLA warfare.

He resigned from the Marines in 1939 to lecture and write about the Chinese and the foolishness of selling scrap steel to the Japanese. In May 1941 he returned to the Marine Corps, was promoted to lieutenant colonel, and in early 1942 was assigned to command one of the two new Marine raider battalions with Maj. JAMES ROOSEVELT, the President's son, as his executive officer. In Aug. 1942 Carlson led a force of Marine raiders in an assault on Japanese-held MAKIN in the GILBERT ISLANDS; subsequently he served with his battalion on GUADALCANAL.

Afterwards Carlson contracted malaria and was out of action. He later served on TARAWA and was wounded on SAIPAN. His nearly mystical faith in the Chinese method of leadership and of combat did not sit well with most Marine leaders. He retired as a brigadier general in 1946 and continued his idealistic advocacy of the Chinese Communists.

Carlson's Raiders

U.S. Marine 2nd Raider BATTALION, commanded by Lt. Col. EVANS F. CARLSON. The Raiders, whose executive officer was Maj. JAMES ROOSEVELT, the President's son, consciously emulated the Chinese Communist style of leadership and tactics, represented by "ethical indoctrination," relatively democratic leadership, and the battle cry "Gung Ho!"—Carlson's variant of a Chinese phrase meaning "Work Together."

The Raiders' first action was a landing on MAKIN Atoll in the GILBERT ISLANDS on Aug. 17, 1942, ten days after the Marine landings on GUADALCANAL and Tulagi. Coming ashore from the submarines *Nautilus* (SS 168) and *Argonaut* (APS 1), thirteen officers and 198 men paddled to the beach in rubber boats. Although they wiped out the eighty-five-man Japanese garrison, only seven of nineteen boats managed to return to the submarines the following day, and twenty-one Marines were lost. Nine captured Marines were later beheaded by the Japanese.

The raid's outcome was comparable to that of the DOOLITTLE RAID on Tokyo: militarily insignificant, but an American morale builder (and the subject of a war MOVIE, "Gung Ho"). However, the raid may have been counterproductive by leading to the Japanese reinforcement of Makin and Betio Atolls, on which a Marine landing encountered fierce resistance in Nov. 1943.

The Raiders next were sent to Guadalcanal where, still acting as an independent raiding force, they began a thirty-day, 150-mile harassment of the Japanese in classic GUERRILLA style. The Marines had minimal resupply or even radio contact with the main Marine forces. Twelve times they ambushed enemy columns by sending a contact patrol to engage the enemy, drawing Japanese reinforcements into the fire fight, and attacking them from the flanks. Over 500 Japanese were slain; Carlson's losses were twenty-one dead and fourteen wounded.

The 2nd Raider Battalion was disbanded on Feb. 1, 1944, as the Marine Corps converted all raider battalions (and 1st Raider REGIMENT) into the 4th Marine Regiment. (The raiders were abolished because of the changing conditions of the Pacific campaigns and the use of regular Marine units in assault and COMMANDO-type operations.)

Caroline Islands

An archipelago in the western Pacific northeast of New Guinea. Part of the JAPANESE MANDATED ISLANDS holdings, the Carolines in 1935 were closed to foreigners as the Japanese began fortifying them. The Carolines' island group of TRUK became a major Japanese naval and air base complex and the headquarters of the Japanese Combined Fleet.

Carpet Bombing,

see STRATEGIC BOMBING.

Carpetbagger

Code name for Allied air operations from Britain to drop supplies to patriot forces in Western Europe, 1943–1944.

Cartwheel

Code name for converging drives on RABAUL by U.S. forces.

Casablanca Conference

Meeting of Allied leaders on war aims. On Jan. 14 to 23, 1943, President ROOSEVELT and Prime Minister CHURCHILL met at Casablanca, Morocco, with the COMBINED CHIEFS OF STAFF following the success of the NORTH AFRICA INVASION. (Stalin turned down an invitation.) It was the first time a President had left American soil while the country was at war. Roosevelt, in a statement with far-reaching consequences, announced that the war could end only by the UNCONDITIONAL SURRENDER of Germany, Japan, and Italy. Churchill concurred. But officials on both sides privately criticized the decision for possibly stiffening enemy resistance and prolonging the war.

The "Big Two" also agreed to give top priority to the campaign against U-BOATS in the Atlantic and to launch a combined bombing offensive against the German war machine (see STRATEGIC BOMBING). Gen. CHARLES DE GAULLE and Gen. HENRI GIRAUD also participated in the conference, which called for the unification of the French in the war against the AXIS.

The meeting was kept secret until Jan. 27, when the principals had departed. Newspapers, accepting voluntary CENSORSHIP, had held a sealed communiqué about the conference since Jan. 24. German intelligence had believed that "Casablanca" was a code word and that the conference actually had taken place in WASHINGTON.

Casanova

Code name for U.S. 95th Infantry DIVISION diversionary action during operations against Mertz.

Case Code Names,

see *FALL* CODE NAMES.

Casey, William J. (1913–1987)

Aide to the chief of the LONDON headquarters of the OFFICE OF STRATEGIC SERVICES (OSS), forerunner of the Central Intelligence Agency. A New York lawyer before the war, "Bill" Casey joined the Navy and was assigned to the fledgling OSS. In 1943 he became a staff officer under Maj. Gen. WILLIAM J. DONOVAN, founder of the OSS, and DAVID BRUCE, director of OSS European operations out of London.

Of his arrival in London, Casey later wrote, "I surely contributed to the impression that moved Malcolm Muggeridge [a British writer and wartime intelligence officer] to comment: 'Ah, those first OSS arrivals in London. How well I remember them, arriving like *jeunes filles en fleur* straight from a finishing school, all fresh and innocent, to start work in our frowsy old intelligence brothel.'"

But Casey and the other OSS arrivals soon broke from their British tutors and began operations of their own. Casey, as chief of Secret Intelligence in Europe, sent OSS JEDBURGH agents into German-controlled areas of France to work with the FRENCH RESISTANCE. Casey also infiltrated agents, many of them recruited from German PRISONERS OF WAR, into Germany on intelligence-gathering missions during the latter phases of the EUROPEAN WAR.

After the war, Casey returned to the world of law and finance. He became president of the Export-Import Bank. President RICHARD M. NIXON appointed Casey chairman of the Securities and Exchange Commission. After serving as the manager of Ronald Reagan's successful presidential campaign in 1980, Casey was appointed director of Central Intelligence in 1981. He remained in that post until 1987, when he suffered a fatal stroke. Teamed up with Reagan, Casey injected the CIA into U.S. foreign policy. CIA operatives were involved in diverting to the Nicaraguan contras funds from the sale of arms to Iran. Casey's personal involvement in the Iran-Contra scandal was still an unresolved issue when he died.

Cassino

Town near the Rapido River in central Italy and a key position in the German Gustav Line. Looming over the town was 1,715-foot Monte Cassino, on which was an abbey that traced its roots to a structure built by St. Benedict in 529 A.D. The abbey, a center of Christian monasticism, was filled with irreplaceable treasures.

The long and ferociously fought ITALIAN CAMPAIGN made this ancient town a battleground, and the height with its treasure became Hill 516, simply another one of the heights that were observation points for the German defenders manning the Gustav Line.

Allied forces poised to take it in Feb. 1944 asked for artillery and air support. When troops began fighting their way up Monastery Hill, the bomb safety line—a line far enough in front of troops to keep them out of the bombing zone—originally included the abbey. But Gen. Sir Bernard Freyberg, commanding officer of the New Zealand Corps advancing on Cassino, wanted closer and heavier support. He got 147 B-17 FLYING FORTRESS and eighty-two B-25 MITCHELL bombers.

Freyberg, a veteran of Gallipoli and nine times wounded in World War I, had fought on CRETE and in Africa. The air officer who set the line, U.S. Army Capt. George Walton, had to give in under Freyberg's orders. "The first stick of our bombs," he later said, "fell squarely on the New Zealanders."

Waves of bombers pulverized the ancient abbey on Mount Cassino, which was assumed to be occupied by Germans. *The New York Times* told how the abbey "crumbled slowly into ruins beneath vast clouds of smoke as German soldiers who had violated all civilized codes by employing the sanctuary for military purposes met their day of wrath." The *Times* reflected the Allied conviction of the time. Not known then was that the bombing had killed a bishop and several Benedictine monks; that *Generalfeldmarschall* ALBERT KESSELRING had formally told the Vatican he would not occupy the abbey; and that German soldiers were kept beyond a zone extending 300 meters around the abbey.

When the smoke cleared, German opposition on the mountain did not lessen because that was not where the Germans were. But the rubble—produced by 576 tons of BOMBS and massive ARTILLERY barrages—gave the Germans the raw materials of a defensive position that was better than the abbey itself.

Freyberg's New Zealand Corps and an Indian division failed in attempts to take the mountain. Still stalled before the town of Cassino on the Ides of March, the Allies pounded it with more artillery and air attacks. Bomb craters on the approaches to the town were so large that the troops had to build bridges across some of them to advance.

In May a Polish corps was sent against the heights. The first assault was repulsed with heavy casualties, but on the second attempt, on May 18, the Poles took Mount Cassino and raised their country's flag.

A papal investigation later confirmed that the Germans had not used the abbey as an observation post and, when it seemed likely that the building was going to be bombed, German troops had helped the Benedictines remove many of the art treasures.

Castor,

see APHRODITE.

Casualties

The exact number of people killed or maimed in World War II will never be known. In this TOTAL WAR, civilians died by the millions in the CONCENTRATION CAMPS and DEATH CAMPS of Germany, by the tens of thousands in the many prisons and internment camps of Japan and Germany, by the thousands in Allied air raids in Europe and Japan. Many thousands of others were starved and worked to death when SLAVE LABOR was forced on conquered peoples by both Germany and Japan. NAZI mass murders by category—JEWS, Poles, Gypsies, mentally ill, chronically ill, among others—added between 5,000,000 and 6,000,000 more to the unknown toll.

A neutral compilation by several international agencies and released by the Vatican in 1946 estimated that the casualties, military and civilian, in World War II were 22,060,000 dead and 34,400,000 wounded. But accurate nation-by-nation figures on war casualties are difficult to compile because of inadequate information and differences in the ways various nations compiled figures.

The U.S. STRATEGIC BOMBING SURVEY, for example, reported in Dec. 1945 that Allied bombing had killed about 500,000 German civilians, but the figure derived from an official German report, issued in Oct. 1946, puts German civilian deaths at 4,150,000; using figures from another study, the German civilian toll becomes 3,450,000. Also clouding casualty figures was the failure of the Soviet Union to release information about captives. (See PRISONERS OF WAR.)

Battle deaths among U.S. forces amounted to about one out of every 450 Americans, based on the U.S. population in 1940. Official U.S. casualty figures for the period between Dec. 7, 1941, and Dec. 31, 1946, are:

SERVICE	NUMBER SERVING	BATTLE DEATHS	OTHER DEATHS	WOUNDS NONMORTAL
Army*	11,260,000	234,874	83,400	565,861
Navy	4,183,466	39,950	25,664	37,778
Marines	669,100	19,773	4,778	67,207
Total	16,112,566	294,597	113,842	670,846

(In 1946, the United States officially declared dead all personnel previously declared missing in action in World War II.)
*Including Army Air Forces.

Casualty figures for other belligerents, reported immediately after the war, still included "missing" combatants. In some cases, the missing were prisoners of war still not accounted for. Definitive figures on German and Japanese prisoners of the Soviet Union would still be in dispute in 1991. Deaths of military personnel reported by the major belligerents:

ALLIES

British Commonwealth:
    544,596 killed or missing, including
        United Kingdom 397,762
        Canada 39,319
        Australia 29,395
        New Zealand 12,262
        South Africa 8,681
        India 36,092
Union of Soviet Socialist Republics: 7,500,000
France: 210,671
China: 2,200,000 (from 1937, not including losses
    during Japanese incursions beginning in 1931)

AXIS

Germany: 3,250,000
Italy: 300,000
Japan: 1,506,000 (1937–1945)

Catalina,

see PBY.

Catapult

Code name for British attack on French warships in North African ports to prevent their future use by Germany, July 1940.

Catchpole

Code name for U.S. operations against ENIWE-TOK and Ujelang atolls in the MARSHALL ISLANDS, early 1944.

Catherine

Code name for proposal by First Lord of the Admiralty WINSTON CHURCHILL in 1939 to modify British R-class battleships for operations in the Baltic Sea.

Caucasus

Soviet region between the Black and Caspian Seas. The Caucasus, rich in RESOURCES, was the objective of the 1942 offensive in the GERMAN CAMPAIGN IN SOVIET UNION. The Germans' drive to the oil fields of the Caucasus began in the summer of 1942, inspired by a severe shortage of oil in Germany. Like the UKRAINE, the Caucasus was also coveted by Germany as a source of food. The Caucasus and the Ukraine produced half of the Soviet Union's wheat and pork.

"If I do not get the oil of Maikop and Grozny, then I must end the war," HITLER told *Generaloberst* FRIEDRICH PAULUS, commander of the German Sixth Army on June 1, 1942, a month before the German summer offensive began. Maikop is an industrial city in the center of the oil field; Grozny, where oil was discovered in 1893, was second only to Baku as an oil producer.

The Sixth Army took the Maikop oil fields in Aug. 1942 and raised the SWASTIKA atop Mount Elborus (18,481 feet), the highest peak in the Caucasus Mountains. But Grozny was beyond the Germans' grasp and had not been captured when the great retreat from the Caucasus began in the winter of 1943.

Cavallero, Marshal Ugo (1880–1943)

Chief of Staff of the Italian Armed Forces from Nov. 1940 until Feb. 1943. Cavallero became head of the *Commando Supremo* when the Italian Army became bogged down in Greece (see BALKANS-GREECE-CRETE CAMPAIGN). He soon gained a reputation as an aggressive and effective administrator. Although Cavallero was strongly nationalistic he worked well with *Generalfeldmarschall* ALBERT KESSELRING when he arrived in Italy as Germany's Commander in Chief South. Cavallero had several angry meetings with *Generalfeldmarschall* ERWIN ROMMEL, the German commander in North Africa; Rommel was placed by Cavallero directly under his own command. BENITO MUSSOLINI, both fearing that Cavallero was engaged in a plot against him but also wishing for a more moderate officer as relations between Italy and Germany deteriorated, relieved Cavallero in Feb. 1943.

In Aug. 1943 Cavallero was arrested for an alleged plot, although he was soon released. He committed suicide shortly thereafter. After his death it was revealed that Cavallero had indeed plotted to oust Mussolini.

Cavalry

The cavalry was traditionally a military force that went into battle on horses. In World War II the term was expanded to cover motorized forces. But horses and pack animals were still used extensively in the war.

When the EUROPEAN WAR began with the German invasion of Poland on Sept. 1, 1939, each side had large numbers of horses in its army. Typically, a German infantry division had 5,375 horses, compared to some 940 vehicles. Horses pulled artillery and hauled supplies, usually from railheads. The Germans continued to use horses for these purposes throughout the war. The Polish army included a cavalry division and twelve cavalry brigades.

One of the poignant images of the invasion is a gallant Polish cavalry charge against the German BLITZKREIG. Officers of Poland's Pomorske Cavalry Brigade, white-gloved, riding white horses, and carrying sabers and lances, charged into the tanks of a German armored corps—and were slaughtered.

Speaking of the Polish cavalry, a U.S. Army general told Congress in March 1940: "Had Poland's cavalry possessed modern armament in every respect and been united in one big cavalry command with adequate mechanized forces included, and supported by adequate aviation, the German light and mechanized forces might have been defeated."

The U.S. Army's 1st Cavalry DIVISION, which was to have been a combined horse and motorized unit, saw combat in the Southwest Pacific as dismounted infantry. Its authorized strength was 12,724 men. The U.S. Army's 2nd Cavalry Division was sent to North Africa in early 1944 but was inactivated in May 1944, with its troops being assigned to support units.

That was the last hurrah for the U.S. cavalry, though not for Army steeds and other four-legged animals. The U.S. Army's 10th Light Infantry DIVISION, which fought in the ITALIAN CAMPAIGN, had 6,152 horses and mules.

The Italian Army laid claim to the last cavalry charge in history. The charge occurred during the GERMAN CAMPAIGN IN SOVIET UNION, when Italian units fought side by side with their German allies. On Aug. 23, 1942, at Izbushensky, on the great bend of the Don River, the 600 mounted men of the Italian Savoy Cavalry charged 2,000 Soviet troops armed with machine guns and mortars. The charge was a desperate move to seal an opening between the German Sixth Army and the Italians. Wielding sabers and pitching hand grenades, the Italians put the Soviets to flight. It was a temporary, costly, but celebrated victory for the Italian cavalry.

The Soviet Union was the only great power to retain horse cavalry during the war. The hard-riding, dreaded Cossacks of the Czar were officially forgiven for their opposition to the Bolshevik cause during and even after the civil war of 1917–1920. In 1937 Cossack units, mainly cavalry, again appeared in the Red Army.

In 1941 the Soviets had thirty cavalry divisions, some of which were organized into cavalry corps, and a number of independent cavalry brigades. A cavalry division numbered only 7,000 men, in three or four horse cavalry regiments, sometimes with a tank regiment and a horse artillery regiment. The Soviets envisioned the cavalry as a mobile force to exploit breakthroughs of enemy defenses.

Celebes

A large island in what were the DUTCH EAST INDIES. Celebes was taken by the Japanese in Jan.–Feb. 1942 during the launching of the JAPANESE CAMPAIGN in the FAR EAST. Frequently bombed by U.S. aircraft, the island's Japanese garrison surrendered to Australian forces in Sept. 1945. Celebes is now known as the Indonesian island of Sulawesi.

Celestes

Code name for Generalissimo CHIANG KAI-SHEK at the 1943 Cairo conference.

Cemeteries

By the end of the war the U.S. Army had established several hundred temporary burial grounds on battlefields. In 1947, the secretary of the Army and the American Battle Monuments Commission (ABMC), which had been created after World War I, selected fourteen sites in foreign countries to become permanent burial sites for the Americans who fell in battle overseas.

The ABMC was given jurisdiction over the permanent sites after the American Graves Registration Service made the interments. All temporary burial sites were "disestablished" and the remains were disposed of in accordance with the desires of the next of kin. Some directed that the isolated burials be left undisturbed; most chose to have their dead buried in hometown or military cemeteries.

Each grave in the ABMC cemeteries in foreign countries is marked by a marble headstone surmounted by a Cross or Star of David. On the headstones of servicemen who could not be identified is inscribed the phrase used for the UNKNOWN SOLDIER: "Here rests in honored glory a comrade in arms known only to God." (This reflected the fact that in World War I, when the phrase was "an American soldier," only a soldier died on a battlefield. In World War II, when an unknown person might be a sailor or airman, the phrase was changed to "comrade in arms.")

The question of where to bury American dead in Europe arose soon after U.S. troops began arriving in UNITED KINGDOM in Jan. 1942. Gen. John J. Pershing, hero of World War I, was then chairman of the ABMC. He authorized the burial of Americans who died in England in a U.S. cemetery established at Brookwood in Surrey, England, after World War I. The first burials were made in April 1942.

A new question arose when the first of several Americans convicted of capital crimes in England was scheduled to be executed. (See JUSTICE, MILITARY.) After the first execution, in March 1943, a "Plot X" was designated in a forest at the edge of the Brookwood cemetery. By the end of the war there were nineteen graves in Plot X.

After the war, the American dead at Brookwood were transferred to an American cemetery that had been opened at Cambridge in Dec. 1943. But the remains of the executed soldiers were transferred to PLOT E, a "dishonored" area of the U.S. military cemetery at Oise-Aisne in France, where the Army had buried Pvt. EDDIE SLOVIK, the only U.S. soldier executed for desertion in World War II.

Censorship

U.S. censorship efforts during World War II were relatively mild. Communications entering or leaving the country were examined; internally, press and radio censorship were essentially voluntary. The key to the conduct of wartime censorship was President ROOSEVELT'S decision to establish the Office of Censorship as a U.S. civilian agency that controlled wartime news. The agency was opposed by the Army and Navy, which had plans for military control of information.

In theaters of war and in HAWAII, a U.S. territory, the military did establish strict censorship. Although in Hawaii enlisted men were often recruited to handle the volume of mail, the practice in the armed services was for officers to censor outgoing mail. The dispatches of WAR CORRESPONDENTS were also censored.

Censorship was legalized by the first WAR POWERS ACT, enacted on Dec. 18, 1941. The act authorized the president to censor all communications entering and leaving the country. The next day the president appointed Byron Price, executive news director of the Associated Press, director of censorship. Although Congress gave Price extreme powers to restrict and withhold news, he chose to make censorship voluntary. Newspapers and radio stations cooperated, even to the extent of limiting the

dissemination of weather forecasts (a restriction removed in October 1943). Voluntary censorship worked remarkably well. Many secrets, such as the development of the atomic bomb and the travel schedules of President Roosevelt, circulated among editors and reporters, who did not print what they knew.

In the only serious incident, the government in 1942 impaneled a federal grand jury to look into an alleged security breach by the *Chicago Tribune,* which had said that U.S. code-breaking had contributed to the victory at the battle of MIDWAY. No indictment was returned. Nor was anyone punished for breaking an official embargo about the German surrender by publishing a premature news bulletin about V-E DAY.

Much of the work of the 14,000 employees of the Office of Censorship focused on the control of overseas communications, including radiograms, mail, and telephone calls. Censors even read mail going to and coming from prisoners of war. Some spies were caught when suspicious censors passed questionable mail to counterintelligence officers.

Publications considered subversive were banned from the mails. One of these was *Social Justice,* which was published by Father Charles E. Coughlin, the "radio priest," who, despite censuring by the Catholic hierarchy, preached ANTI-SEMITISM and had a large pro-NAZI following.

"Girlie" magazines flourished, especially among servicemen, and in the atmosphere of wartime censorship, the Post Office sought the power to bar them from the mails. In what would become a landmark case, the Postmaster General chose *Esquire* as an example of a lewd, lascivious, and obscene magazine. *Esquire,* well known for its drawings of luscious, lightly clothed "pinup girls" (see LANGUAGE and NOSE ART), also published leading American authors, a fact the Post Office chose to ignore.

In a case that dragged through the courts from 1943 to 1946, the Post Office tried to keep the magazine out of the mails—and from servicemen; thousands of special editions on lightweight paper were mailed to military hospitals and bases "with compliments of *Esquire* for the exclusive use of the armed forces."

Post Office censors scrutinized each page of the 1943 issues, stamping with tiny pink fingers the drawings, cartoons, or saucy verse considered offensive. When the courts did not see enough to bar the magazine as obscene, the Post Office shifted to the argument that *Esquire* did not make a contribution to the public good and was therefore unworthy of second-class mailing privileges. The U.S. Supreme Court ultimately ruled, however, that giving the Post Office such power was "abhorrent to our traditions."

Cerberus

Code name for breakout of German battleships from the port of Brest in the CHANNEL DASH, Feb. 1942.

CG-4 Waco

The principal U.S. troop-carrying GLIDER of the war. The aircraft entered combat for the first time—rather disastrously—in the Allied invasion of SICILY in July 1943. But the CG-4, often called by its manufacturer's name, the Waco, was sound. More success was achieved with the glider in operations by Gen. ORDE WINGATE'S CHINDITS in Burma in March 1944.

The gliders were used extensively in the NORMANDY INVASION in June 1944, the landings in southern France in Aug. 1944, and the later RHINE CROSSINGS. In 1943 two British variants were towed across the Atlantic by C-47 DAKOTA transports; each glider carried 1½ tons of cargo during the experimental flight, which was flown in stages with actual flight time being twenty-eight hours for the 3,500-mile operation.

The CG-4 was the winner of a U.S. Army four-company glider design competition held in 1941. The Waco design was test-flown as the XCG-4 in May–June 1942, with series production following as 12,393 of the unpowered aircraft were delivered from sixteen assembly lines (the Waco firm itself built only 1,074). Thirteen of the CG-4A variants were acquired by the U.S. Navy and Marine Corps in 1943 (designated LWR-1). The British took a number of Wacos, which, given the name Hadrian, were used in the Sicily assault; the British did not use the glider in further operations, although a number were being readied in Southeast Asia for operations against the Japanese when the war ended in Aug. 1945.

The CG-4 was made of wood and metal and was mostly fabric covered. A high-wing glider, it had a hinged nose portion that swung upward for loading and unloading; the hinged section contained the cockpit with dual controls for the pilot and copilot. The fuselage could accommodate thirteen troops or a ¼-ton JEEP or 75-mm pack howitzer and crew. Troops could also enter and exit through side doors. The preferable tow aircraft was the C-47 Dakota, although a variety of British bomber-type aircraft were also employed as glider tugs for the Waco.

There were several experimental variants, including a twin-engine model (XPG-1) that was to be towed to its target and after the assault take off and return to base under its own power.

The CG-4 could be towed at speeds up to 150 mph, although 125 mph was a normal maximum. Its stalling speed was 44 mph.

CG-13 Waco

Development of a U.S. troop-carrying GLIDER with twice the capacity of the widely used CG-4 WACO began in 1942. The result was the thirty-seat CG-13, which did not see operational service in the war. The CG-13 was the largest glider produced for the Allies during the war. (The only larger military glider was the single XCG-16, which had a gross weight of 19,580 pounds compared to the CG-13's 18,900 pounds.)

Waco-designed prototypes built by Ford and Northwest were flown from March 1943, followed by orders to the firms for 400 gliders. However, only 132 were delivered. The aircraft were generally referred to as the Waco (as was the CG-4).

The CG-13 was a high-wing, heavy glider. Like the CG-4, the larger aircraft had an upward-hinging nose to permit rapid loading and unloading of a ¼-ton JEEP or 75-mm pack howitzer. Side doors were fitted for troops to embark; a rear door could be used to release parachute cargo containers ("parapacks") while the glider was in flight.

The maximum towing speed was 209 mph, although 135 mph was considered a more feasible maximum. Stalling speed was 79 mph.

Chaff,

see ELECTRONIC COUNTERMEASURES.

Chamberlain, Neville (1869–1940)

British prime minister at the outbreak of the EUROPEAN WAR. Chamberlain, who became prime minister in 1937, is best remembered for his policy of appeasement toward HITLER. Chamberlain initiated negotiations with Hitler ("a gentleman," as Chamberlain once described him) over Czechoslovakia and convinced French Premier ÉDOUARD DALADIER to accept the concessions given to Hitler in the MUNICH PACT. On Sept. 30, 1938, after returning from Munich Chamberlain said, "I believe it is peace for our time." For decades, Chamberlain's words (along with his inevitable umbrella) would be symbols of appeasement. Politicians who opposed an international agreement would denounce it as "another Munich."

Following Germany's invasion of Poland on Sept. 1, 1939, Chamberlain issued an ultimatum to Hitler, telling him that if Germany did not withdraw from Poland, England and France would go to war against Germany. At 11:15 A.M. on Sunday, Sept. 3, Chamberlain announced that a state of war existed between the two countries.

He remained prime minister until Germany launched the DENMARK AND NORWAY CAMPAIGN in May 1940. Norway's fall led directly to the fall of Chamberlain. In a dramatic confrontation in Parliament, one of his own supporters turned to the prime minister and, drawing his words from another British crisis, quoted Oliver Cromwell: "Depart, I say, and let us have done with you! In the name of God, Go!" Opposition backbenchers, chanting "Go! Go! Go!" drove him from the House. Two days later, on May 10, KING GEORGE VI asked WINSTON CHURCHILL, then First Lord of the Admiralty, to form a government. Chamberlain remained in the new government as lord president of the council until ill health forced him to resign on Sept. 30, 1940. He died on Nov. 9.

Champion

Code name for Allied plans for a general offensive in Burma, late 1943.

Channel Dash

Dramatic escape of German warships from the French port of Brest up the English Channel to German ports. The German battleships *Gneisenau* and *Scharnhorst* had been at Brest since March 22, 1941, as was the heavy cruiser *Prinz Eugen,* which had been there since she had taken part in the BISMARCK sortie in May 1941. At Brest the ships were subjected to regular British bombings, and were periodically damaged.

Although the British kept careful watch on Brest with aircraft and submarines to prevent their escape, in a carefully planned *daylight* sortie the three warships successfully raced north through the English Channel. The escape—Operation Cerberus—began late on the night of Feb. 11, 1942, under the command of *Vizadmiral* Otto Ciliax. By chance, the departure was masked by a British air raid and defensive smoke screen. The three major German warships, screened by six destroyers and twenty-one torpedo boats, sped north through the darkness. Beginning at dawn, relays of German fighters provided protective air cover, with German fighter ace ADOLF GALLAND having some 250 fighters under his command for the operation. A fighter direction officer was in the German flagship *Scharnhorst* and, for once, Luftwaffe-Navy coordination was excellent.

Not until the afternoon of Feb. 12 did the British Admiralty know definitely that the German squadron was at sea. British coastal gun batteries opened fire, followed by almost continuous RAF attacks, with a Royal Navy SWORDFISH squadron joining in. Subsequently, British motor torpedo boats and destroyers sought to intercept the squadron, all without inflicting any damage. Off the Scheldt the *Scharnhorst* hit a mine; she stopped, but within a half hour was under way again. During the night of Feb. 12–13 both the *Scharnhorst* and *Gneisenau* were slightly damaged by mines near Terschelling. The German ships continued northward and reached port safely on Feb. 13.

The Germans did lose a destroyer and minesweeper to mines during the preparations for the breakout; during the actual Channel Dash one German torpedo boat and seventeen aircraft were lost. The RAF lost forty aircraft to enemy fire (plus two SPITFIRES that collided during the operation), and six Navy Swordfish were shot down. The Channel Dash was a major British defeat on their own front steps but, more important, it marked the end of German surface warship operations in the Atlantic.

The *Scharnhorst* was repaired and sailed north to operate from northern Norway with the *Tirpitz* against the RUSSIAN CONVOYS. She was sunk by British warships in the arctic in Dec. 1944. While the *Gneisenau* was in dock undergoing repairs she was hit by a bomb and severely damaged; she was decommissioned at Gdynia and in 1945 was scuttled just before Soviet troops reached the port. The *Prinz Eugen* survived the war and was taken over by the U.S. Navy. The cruiser was brought to the United States and, after careful examination of her several advanced features, was used as a target ship in the ATOMIC BOMB TESTS at BIKINI in July 1946.

Channel Islands

British islands ten to thirty miles off the French coast. After bombing and strafing the long-demilitarized islands of Jersey and Guernsey, German troops invaded on June 30, 1940. In 1942 the Germans deported about 2,000 residents of the islands to internment camps in Germany and brought in workers to build roads and fortifications. The islands—the only British possessions occupied by Germany during the war—were liberated on May 9, 1945, when the 30,000-man German garrison surrendered.

Chaplains

The U.S. Army and Navy both had chaplain corps during the war to bring spiritual guidance and minister to the needs of the armed forces. In both services clergymen of the Jewish, Protestant, and Roman Catholic faith were given commissions (with the Protestant chaplains drawn from a number of different denominations).

The Army provided chaplains to the Army Air Forces, and the Navy to the Marine Corps and Coast Guard. They saw front-line service with combat troops, assisted draftees in adjusting to military life, and counseled all men—regardless of faith—to help them solve their problems. Several chaplains died in action, among them the FOUR CHAPLAINS who died when a troop transport sank.

A Navy chaplain, Comdr. Joseph T. O'Callahan, won the MEDAL OF HONOR for his work aboard the AIRCRAFT CARRIER *Franklin* (CV 13) when she was devastated by fire and explosions after being struck by Japanese BOMBS while operating off the coast of Japan in March 1945. (See *ESSEX.*)

Chariot

British code name for raid against German-held port of SAINT-NAZAIRE on the French coast.

Charnwood

British code name for offensive near Caen, Normandy, July 1944.

Chastise

British attack on German dams by LANCASTER bombers using the UPKEEP "bouncing bombs," May 1943.

Chattanooga Choo Choo

Code name for Allied air operations against German train movements in France and Germany.

Cheadles

Code name for RAF nuisance raids against Luftwaffe airfields in France.

Cheese

Code name for FREE FRENCH submarine *Minerve,* operating from Britain, landing agents and resistance stores in Norway, Aug. 1942.

Chemical Warfare

A practice in warfare as old as poison-tipped arrows. "Chemical warfare" in modern times is usually synonymous with poison gas, which was first used in modern times by the German Army in World War I in violation of the Hague Conventions on war. The French and British retaliated with their own hastily manufactured gas.

Although it is frequently said that no poison gas was used in World War II, the assertion ignores the fact that millions of people were killed by poison gas in the DEATH CAMPS of the NAZIS during HITLER's war on JEWS, Gypsies, and others deemed unworthy of life. The lethal chemical was usually ZYKLON-B.

Germany developed two chemicals for possible combat use in the war: tabun, a "nerve gas" that evolved from research into insecticides, and sarin, a more powerful nerve agent. Research into a third nerve agent, soman, was going on as the war ended. Soviet scientists are believed to have obtained the formula for soman.

By 1942, Germany was producing nerve gas in vast quantities in a large secret factory in a forest in Silesia. Engineers worked on experimental weapons—a machine gun that fired gas-filled bullets at tanks, gas mines, gas grenades, even gas-filled rockets to fire at LONDON.

Luftwaffe pilots swooped over German soldiers and sprayed them with substitutes for aerosol gases. Some "condemned" prisoners were victims of tests, as CONCENTRATION CAMP prisoners probably were. Near the end of the war, Germany tried to wipe out all traces of such experiments by destroying records.

In 1943, with nerve-gas production going on in some twenty factories, German strategists began contemplating the use of gas to counteract losses in battle. But Germany never used poison gas on the battlefield.

Allied possession of poison gases was proved by the dispersal of mustard gas in explosions following a surprise German air attack on the congested port of Bari, Italy, on Dec. 2, 1943. Among the sixteen ships sunk in the raid was the merchant ship *John Harvey,* which exploded, spewing a mixture of oil and mustard gas around the harbor. Hospitals were unaware that among the casualties from the attack were 600 victims of mustard gas, eighty-three of whom died.

During the planning for the NORMANDY INVASION Allied officers weighed the possibility of a German gas attack that would be met by Allied use of gas. Gen. OMAR BRADLEY, in *A Soldier's Story,* wrote, "even a light sprinkling of persistent gas on Omaha Beach could have cost us our footing there."

The United States, Britain, and Germany all worked on poison gases and contemplated their use. When the war started, both Germany and Britain told neutral Switzerland that they would not use poison gas or BIOLOGICAL WARFARE. But the British had already distributed gas masks to civilians and would manufacture 70,000,000 masks. On July 6, 1944, in a "Most Secret" memorandum to his CHIEFS OF STAFF, Prime Minister CHURCHILL said that he might someday "ask you to drench Germany with poison gas."

A Sikh in British service and his mule both wear gas masks—a common accoutrement of soldiers in World War II. Several nations had chemical weapons available, but only the Japanese and Italians are known to have used them. Neither used them against American forces. *(Imperial War Museum)*

Chennault, Maj. Gen. Claire L. (1890–1958)

U.S. airman, leader of the famed FLYING TIGERS, and controversial Allied air commander in China. A pilot since 1919 and a specialist in fighter tactics, Chennault ran afoul of the bomber advocates who led the U.S. ARMY AIR CORPS in the 1930s. He retired from the Army in 1937 because of deafness.

Col. Chennault subsequently accepted an offer to train fighter pilots for the Chinese Air Force. He returned to the United States in early 1941 to recruit American pilots (which was done with the U.S. government's permission, although Americans were forbidden by law to fly for the British). These pilots formed the American Volunteer Group (Flying Tigers), which began flying against the Japanese on Dec. 20, 1941, when their P-40B Tomahawks inflicted heavy damage on Japanese bombers attempting to attack Kunming. Chennault's Flying Tigers downed an estimated 286 Japanese aircraft at the cost of eight American pilots killed in air action, plus four pilots missing and three men killed on the ground.

In April 1942 Chennault was recalled to active U.S. service, promoted to brigadier general, and given command of U.S. AAF units in China. These were consolidated as the Fourteenth AIR FORCE in March 1943.

Subsequently promoted to major general, Chennault came into conflict with Gen. JOSEPH STILWELL of the U.S. Army, who was Chief of Staff to Chinese leader CHIANG KAI-SHEK and an advocate of the large-scale use of Chinese ground forces. Although Chiang supported Chennault, the difficulty of moving fuel and munitions into China to support a large air force prevented the proposed buildup. The U.S. B-29 SUPERFORTRESS bombing effort from China was ineffective and placed a heavy burden on Allied supply routes (B-29s generally had to fly their own bombs and ammunition to bases in China). Further, a Japanese offensive in 1944–1945 resulted in the loss of several air bases.

Although Chiang had supported Chennault and Stilwell had left the China area in late 1944, Chennault would not continue in his command as the war came to an end; he resigned his command on July 6, 1945.

Cherryblossom

Code name for U.S. 3rd Marine DIVISION landing on BOUGAINVILLE, Nov. 1, 1943.

Chiang Kai-shek (1886–1975)

Leader of wartime non-Communist China. Through both Chinese and American PROPAGANDA efforts, Chiang Kai-shek was depicted as the valiant, besieged leader of the Chinese people, holding out against rapacious Japanese armies. He was seen by many as the Asian equivalent of Ethiopia's HAILE SELASSIE—defeated by superior machines and greater numbers, but prevailing by strength of will and character.

By virtue of his country's size, he was accorded status as one of the BIG FOUR, when in fact he only met two of the BIG THREE: President ROOSEVELT and Prime Minister CHURCHILL; Soviet leader JOSEPH STALIN declined. Roosevelt and Churchill thought little of Chiang, but tolerated him as someone representing an ally.

Not until after the war did Chiang emerge as a man of limited intelligence, a petty tyrant who had been far less interested in fighting the Japanese than in crippling the Chinese Communists under MAO TSE-TUNG. Chiang, his wife, and his brother-in-law T. V. Soong had manipulated American public

opinion while doing little to draw Japanese strength away from other fronts.

Chiang can best be seen against the background of the protracted struggle for control that followed the Chinese revolution in 1911. (See CHINA.) Chiang's rise to power was first aided by his experiences in the Soviet Union during a 1923 military mission sent by Sun Yat-sen, the "father of the Chinese revolution." During the shifting conflicts among Sun's successors, Chiang assumed command of the Kuomintang Party Army in 1925.

Chiang's goals were relatively simple: expand his power, suppress rivals, attack communism because it challenged his basis of power. Chiang's resistance to the 1931 Japanese invasion of Manchuria and the 1937 attack on China itself was premised on his desire to maintain control of the internal Chinese struggle.

Chiang did not ally himself with the Japanese, but he did not throw all of his weight against them. When Anglo-American advisers such as Gen. JOSEPH STILWELL sought to create a modern, well-trained Chinese Army of thirty divisions, Chiang resisted, seeing such a force as a source of rival power. (Stilwell privately called Chiang "the Peanut.") Chiang wanted control of U.S. LEND-LEASE aid, but would promise little in return.

Unfortunately for Chiang, he applied his conservative, short-sighted view to his domestic policies as well. Against them, Mao's message of shared sacrifice and shared power became more and more effective. U.S. disenchantment with Chiang grew in the latter war years as the perceived need for Chinese action against Japan declined. Nevertheless, the carefully fostered view of Chiang as a heroic resister of tyranny survived and was even augmented by his defeat by the Communists in 1949. This image greatly influenced U.S. Asian policy almost until Chiang's death.

Chiefs of Staff

British military executive for the conduct of the war comprised of the service chiefs. The COS was created in 1924 as the Chiefs of Staff sub-committee of the Committee of Imperial Defence (CID). The Chairman of the CID—the prime minister—was the ex officio chairman with the other members being the three service chiefs of staff. Normally the

COS met with one of its own number being designated by the prime minister as chairman. Thus, the British COS predated its American counterpart, the JOINT CHIEFS OF STAFF, by seventeen years.

In 1936 the position of Minister for the Co-ordination of Defence was established, who could convene the Chiefs of Staff when he felt necessary, with himself in the chair. The situation, however, changed under the pressure of the EUROPEAN WAR, with Prime Minister NEVILLE CHAMBERLAIN in April 1940 appointing the First Lord of the Admiralty, WINSTON CHURCHILL, who would be responsible for and chair the COS committee. Mr. Churchill, of course, succeeded to prime minister and minister of defence.

The Combined Chiefs of Staff during the war consisted of:

- Adm. of the Fleet DUDLEY POUND, First Sea Lord (1939–1943)
- Adm. of the Fleet Sir ANDREW CUNNINGHAM, First Sea Lord (1943–1946)
- Gen. Sir John Dill, chief of the Imperial General Staff (1940–1941)
- Gen. Sir ALAN BROOKE, chief of the Imperial General Staff (1941–1945)
- Air Chief Marshal Sir Charles Portal, chief of the Air Staff (1940–1945)

When meeting with the U.S. Joint Chiefs of Staff, the two bodies became the COMBINED CHIEFS OF STAFF.

Children

The war's impact fell heavily on children. Even before the war began, Britain started evacuating the first of at least 1,000,000 children from London and other potential urban targets to rural areas. About 5,000 of the children left the British Isles for refuge in the United States, Canada, Australia, New Zealand, and South Africa. Unknown numbers of British children remained behind. Air raids killed or orphaned an unknown number. (Pioneering research on orphaned children during the war laid the foundation for modern studies of posttrauma stress disorder in children.)

Through much of the war German children suffered little, for the harvests of conquered nations fed Germany well and children, like workers in heavy industry, were allotted extra rations. Although Germany ordered some evacuations of children, the image of civilian flight did not sit well with HITLER and his propagandists. Thus, when Anglo-American bombing began reducing German cities to rubble, Germany's nonevacuation policy doomed urban children, who died by the thousands.

Evacuation of children from Japanese cities did not occur until after the devastating B-29 SUPERFORTRESS raids began in 1944. In one raid on TOKYO alone, at least 30,000 children died.

The cost of World War II, usually expressed in military and civilian casualty statistics, was focused on children in a report of the Child Study Association of America published in 1947. The report focused on the suffering of children in occupied countries, where invaders "systematically removed food, livestock, fuel and clothing in such quantities that most of the population suffered serious privations, which came especially hard upon the children." Only about 10 percent of the JEWS who survived the HOLOCAUST were children, the report said, adding that by 1946 "there were practically no children between the ages of six and twelve years among the displaced Jews in Germany."

The toll of children in occupied countries was:

Belgium   90,000 children sent to internment or concentration camps, 170,000 abandoned or orphaned; 87 percent of the victims of tuberculosis were children.

China   Of 13,000,000 displaced children, a huge number died of starvation and disease. "Starvation and sickness," said the report, "killed more children and then left the survivors more enfeebled in China than in any other invaded country." About 2,000,000 orphans wandered the country after the war.

Czechoslovakia   300,000 children displaced, many to forced-labor camps; 60,000 to 70,000 were sent to concentration camps.

Denmark   A large number of children of Jewish parents sent to camps in Germany.

France   300,000 children forcibly evacuated, with 200,000 being deported for work in Germany; 50,000 children in French colonies became refugees. Nearly all children in Paris tested positive for tuberculosis; their death rate increased 51 percent in 1942.

Greece About 10 percent of the total population—including some 250,000 children—starved to death. Thousands more were killed in mass executions. About 50,000 children became refugees.

Netherlands 300,000 children homeless; unknown number put in concentration camps or sent to forced labor in Germany.

Norway Tens of thousands of children forced to leave their homes or had them burned down in reprisals. Unknown number of others sent to forced labor in Germany.

Poland About 1,100,000 children were killed in the Nazi campaign that "exterminated" 10 percent of the Polish population. Some 2,800,000 children were "uprooted and left destitute"; an unknown number were sent to forced labor in Germany. At the end of the war there were 1,200,000 orphans.

Soviet Union When Germany invaded the Soviet Union, 14,000,000 children were evacuated from war zones to thousands of "mother and child centers" in the countryside. The war created at least 1,000,000 orphans and left 3,000,000 separated from their families. By the end of the war at least 8,500,000 children were without shelter.

Although spared the death and starvation that stalked children in war zones, American children also felt the shock of war. Two terms—"door-key children" and "juvenile delinquent"—spoke to the plight of children whose parents were absent much of the time. The door-key youngsters usually had a mother and father working at defense plants; others had a father in uniform and a mother working to support the family. (More than 1,000,000 American fathers were taken into the armed services through SELECTIVE SERVICE.) Juvenile court cases, predominantly concerned with girls 8 to 14, rose 56 percent.

Chile
Capital: Santiago, pop. 4,626,508 (est. 1938). In the mid-1930s the Nacista Party, based on NAZI principles, frequently clashed with government security forces. The turmoil culminated with rioting in May 1937, when the government arrested leading local Nazis and banned mass meetings and the wearing of uniforms or insignias by political organizations. But the Nacistas, aided by a former Chilean

president, gathered strength, and in Sept. 1938 seized public buildings, plotted the ASSASSINATION of leading politicians, and incited riots that killed sixty-two people. The leader of the Nacistas was arrested and jailed, only to be released by the incoming president in Dec. 1938.

When the EUROPEAN WAR began in Sept. 1939 Chile declared its neutrality and later showed it by expelling a German for distributing ANTI-SEMITIC literature and an Englishman for distributing anti-Nazi literature. The Nacistas reorganized as the Popular Socialist Vanguard in an attempt to portray it as free of Nazi affiliation. Rumors of a pro-German coup spread in late 1941 when caches of arms were found in areas where thousands of Germans lived. Chilean government police arrested scores of Germans and claimed that as many as 200,000 local Nazis, many of them of German descent, were plotting to overthrow the government. Chile banned radio propaganda or mass meetings in favor of any belligerents and shut down all foreign educational institutions in a move aimed at closing German schools.

Chile finally broke off relations with the AXIS powers on Jan. 20, 1943. (This made Argentina the only Latin American nation that still had relations with the Axis.) In March Chile signed a LEND-LEASE agreement with the United States. Chile became a member of the UNITED NATIONS in Feb. 1945 and declared war on Japan on April 11, 1945.

Chilli
Code name for series of low-level flights by B-24 LIBERATOR bombers of the RAF Coastal Command into the Baltic Feb.–March 1945; the planes inflicted no serious damage on U-BOATS and no aircraft were lost.

China
Capital: Nanking (1928–1937), Chungking (1938–1945); pop. 457,835,475 (est. 1936). World War II began along a stretch of railroad track near the northeastern Chinese city of Mukden (now Shenyang). There, on Sept. 18, 1931, Japanese troops, claiming that Chinese saboteurs were tampering with the roadbed of the Japanese-owned South Manchuria Railway, seized Mukden. This bogus "Mukden incident" launched a swift con-

quest of northeastern China, where the Japanese set up the state of Manchukuo ("the state of Manchu"). They installed as their puppet emperor Henry P'u-i, who had been forced to abdicate in 1912 as China's last emperor.

China in 1931, bankrupt and torn by civil war, did not immediately react to Japan's aggression. Generalissimo CHIANG KAI-SHEK, the militaristic leader of China, was forced to choose between going to war with Japan or fighting the Chinese Communist Party for his own political survival in a protracted struggle for control of China. Chiang chose to devote his strength to the civil war. Internal warfare had begun soon after Chinese nationalists had overthrown the ancient Manchu dynasty and proclaimed the Chinese Republic on Oct. 10, 1911.

By 1926 Chiang had taken over both the National People's Party (known in the West as the Kuomintang) and the Kuomintang Party Army. Combining forces with the Soviet-backed Chinese Communist Party, Chiang wrested control of vast areas of China from powerful despots known as the warlords. Paving the way for Chiang's military success were Communist PROPAGANDA agents, among them MAO TSE-TUNG, working in his native Hunan Province. With their promise of an "agrarian revolution" to break with the feudal past, the Communists appealed to landless peasants and tenant farmers.

The climax of Chiang's military campaign was the capture of SHANGHAI, China's commercial capital, where the Communist Party had been leading uprisings against employers and foreign rule. Victory at Shanghai was a turning point for Chiang and the right-wing forces in the Kuomintang. Moving swiftly, he attacked Shanghai labor leaders and Communists, killing about 300. In a later purge in Canton (now Guangzhou), 6,000 Communists were killed by Chiang's troops.

By Oct. 1928 Chiang's Kuomintang was in control of much of China. The nation, which for centuries had been subject to foreign interference, set her own tariffs, reformed the tax laws, and, from the new capital of NANKING (now Nanjing), began running a new China. Chiang maintained an army of 5,000,000 men and spent up to 80 percent of the central government's revenue on the military. The urban-based, banker-backed Kuomintang did little

to help the peasants, who, exploited by landowners and victims of frequent famines, turned increasingly to the promises of the Communists.

Chiang unsuccessfully tried to counter Communist ideology with the New Life Movement, which combined the traditional Confucian moral code with modern hygienic practices. Kuomintang officials told peasants that by keeping clean and well disciplined they could build a strong new China. But the peasants turned to the Communists, who continued their conquests of Chinese soil and souls. Their power was concentrated in four contiguous southern provinces—Fukien (today Fujian), Kiangsi (Jiangxi), Hunan, and Hupeh (Hubei)— where Mao and a former Shanghai Communist leader, CHOU EN-LAI, recruited peasants for the Communist Red Army and trained it in GUERRILLA tactics.

Between 1930 and 1934 Chiang tried five times to encircle the Communist Army. Finally, in 1934, Chiang followed the advice of his military adviser, former Commander in Chief of the German Army, Gen. Hans von Seeckt: amass 700,000 troops against the Communists, press them into pockets through the use of fortified strongpoints and control of highways, encircle the enemy troops, and annihilate them. At first, the strategy worked; the Communists were surrounded and were slowly being strangled. Then, in Oct. 1934, Mao made a bold and desperate move by withdrawing some 90,000 encircled followers in five separate groups, joined them up, and began a military epic, the Long March.

Mao's people, living off the land and fighting at least fifteen battles and numerous skirmishes, in a little over a year trekked 6,000 miles from Fukien to the mountains of Yenan in northern Shensi (Shaanxi). They fought their way across twenty-four rivers and eighteen mountain ranges, through swamps and jungles. Of the 368 days of the Long March, 235 were spent walking by day, eighteen walking by night.

Safe in the caves of Yenan, Mao Tse-tung and Chou En-lai built both a stronghold and an ideology: peasant-based communism. Chiang, meanwhile, continued to ignore the Japanese, who were readying a full-scale assault on China. In Dec. 1936 a group of anti-Japanese, pro-Communist officers arrested him and attempted a coup. Chiang was released through the negotiations of Chou En-lai, who extracted from Chiang a dual promise: The Kuomintang would join with the Communists and take a hard line toward Japan. (Behind the scenes was the Soviet Union, which had reacted to the Japan-Germany ANTI-COMITERN PACT by stepping up aid to the Chinese Communists and pushing an "anti-imperialist" party line.)

Since 1931 Japanese forces had been flowing into what Japan declared an "autonomous regime" around Peking (Beijing) as the prelude to a plan for occupying China's five northern provinces and creating from them a puppet state similar to Manchukuo. As in 1931, the Japanese faked an incident, this time, on July 7, 1937, claiming that Chinese troops attacked Japanese troops on maneuvers at the Marco Polo Bridge near Peking. Using the clash there as an excuse, Japan poured troops into China, Japanese warships bombarded Shanghai, and Japanese warplanes bombed Chinese cities.

President ROOSEVELT reacted to Japan's undeclared war by calling on other nations to "quarantine the aggressors." He won little support because of widespread U.S. isolationist sentiment, led by the AMERICA FIRST COMMITTEE.

The Japanese swiftly seized Peking and the port of Tientsin (Tianjin) and, in an AMPHIBIOUS LANDING, took Shanghai on Nov. 11. They next launched a fierce attack on the nearby Kuomintang capital of Nanking. Anticipating the fall of the city, Chiang's government withdrew to Chungking (Chongqing), a river town in isolated Szechwan (Sichuan) Province. The Chinese chose it because its location—hemmed by mountains at the confluence of two rivers—made it a redoubt that could defy a siege. Its many caves sheltered an ever-growing population (by 1942, about 1,000,000) from frequent Japanese air raids.

Japanese air raids on Nanking sank the U.S. Navy gunboat *PANAY* (PR 45) and brought the distant war home to Americans. More than 50,000 civilians were slaughtered and 20,000 cases of rape were later documented. The Japanese occupation of the capital shocked the West. The "rape of Nanking," as it was branded, rallied Western sentiment against Japan.

At the time the EUROPEAN WAR began in Sept.

1939, a war all but forgotten by the West was raging across China. By 1939, between 2,000,000 and 2,500,000 Chinese had been killed. Japan, declaring China virtually conquered and a mainstay of Japan's GREATER EAST ASIA CO-PROSPERITY SPHERE, occupied more than 900,000 square miles, held all major ports and cities, and had set up a provisional government in Peking and a regional puppet government in Nanking.

Most of China's defensive operations were conducted by Mao's guerrillas, who set up village self-defense units to harass the Japanese. The Kuomintang distrusted the Communist guerrillas and sent the Kuomintang Army into large-scale battles.

Cut off from the sea, China depended upon the BURMA ROAD for supplies. The Japanese continually bombed the road's China terminus at Kunming. Air raids on Chungking were killing as many as 5,000 people a month. The LEAGUE OF NATIONS, which had been characteristically ineffective when Japan invaded China, charged in 1939 that the Japanese were encouraging the opium habit in Japanese-controlled territories. The increase in addiction was so great, said a League investigator, that "enormous quantities of Iranian opium had to be imported to supply the demand."

The shaky agreement between Chiang Kai-shek's Kuomintang and the Communists was breaking down. The Kuomintang dominated the southwest, the Communists the northwest, and Chiang frequently used his troops not against the Japanese but to check Communist advances.

The JAPANESE CAMPAIGN IN THE FAR EAST, beginning with the attack on PEARL HARBOR, opened a new phase of the "China Incident," as Japan persistently called the war against China. The Japanese invasion of Burma shut down the Burma Road and, through the acquiescence of pro-German VICHY FRANCE, Japan won control of French INDOCHINA, cutting off more Chinese supply lines.

Before the U.S. entry into the war the FLYING TIGERS had arrived in China; in Nov. 1941 there were eighty-four pilots ready for combat. The U.S. and British declarations of war on Japan in Dec. 1941 meant new aid to China. The U.S.-built LEDO ROAD and a U.S. airlift over THE HUMP brought vital supplies into China, including LEND-LEASE deliveries.

Chiang Kai-shek clashed with U.S. Army Gen. JOSEPH STILWELL and other Anglo-American advisers over how to run his war. Chiang saw the ALLIED CHINA-BURMA-INDIA CAMPAIGN as less important to China than the U.S. CENTRAL PACIFIC CAMPAIGN of 1943–1945, which drew from China Japanese troops who were sent to fight U.S. troops island-hopping toward Japan. But the Japanese withdrawals created vacuums into which Mao's Communists entered. Soon Chiang's war against Japan shifted to an all-out war against Mao's Communist armies.

U.S. disenchantment with Chiang grew in the latter war years as the perceived need for Chinese action against Japan declined. U.S. Ambassador PATRICK J. HURLEY attempted to mediate between Chiang and Mao, but his consistent pro-Chiang stance undercut his efforts. Also unsuccessful was his successor, Gen. of the Army GEORGE C. MARSHALL, who served as President TRUMAN'S special representative in China from Nov. 1945 to Jan. 1947.

On Aug. 8, 1945, two days after the ATOMIC BOMB was dropped on HIROSHIMA, the Soviet Union, ignoring a neutrality pact still in effect, declared war on Japan and swiftly invaded Manchukuo, which once more became Manchuria. By the Japanese SURRENDER on Aug. 14, Soviet troops held all of Manchuria's major cities. Under agreements made at the YALTA CONFERENCE, the Soviet Union got joint control with China of Port Arthur and possession of Manchurian railroads—essentially getting back Chinese rights that czarist Russia had lost to Japan following their 1904–1905 war.

Soviet troops methodically looted Manchuria of whole factories and other booty and remained in occupation until April 1946. By then Manchuria was one of the major battlefields of the Chinese civil war, which in 1949 ended in a Communist victory. The People's Republic of China was proclaimed in Peking on Sept. 21, 1949, by Mao. Chiang Kai-shek moved his Kuomintang government to the island of Formosa (Taiwan), ninety miles off mainland China, on Dec. 8, 1949. The United States continued to recognize Formosa as the true China until 1972, when President RICHARD M. NIXON took the first major steps toward recognition of the People's Republic.

China, Army

China had a large force available during the war which had a very limited capability. When CHIANG KAI-SHEK gained control of China's Kuomintang or Nationalist government in 1925 there were two major armies and numerous smaller, warlord-led forces in China. Chiang collaborated with the Communist Party in 1926–1928 and their combined armies checked the power of several warlords south of the Yangtze River. But the two political entities soon broke and there were major battles between the Kuomintang and Communists in the early 1930s, with the Kuomintang fielding a 700,000-man army with German advisers. This campaign reduced the Communists to essentially GUERRILLA forces. In the face of conflict with Japan, the two Chinese forces signed an uneasy truce in 1937 that lasted until 1945.

During this period, despite its anti-Communist stance, the Kuomintang government had Soviet military advisers, and received Soviet military equipment. (Chiang had studied military matters in the Soviet Union in 1923.)

The Japanese successfully carried out military aggression in Manchuria and China, and then initiated a major assault on China in the late 1930s. At the time full-scale war broke out in 1937 the Chinese armed forces numbered over 2,000,000 men organized in 182 infantry divisions, forty-six separate brigades, nine CAVALRY divisions, six cavalry brigades, four artillery brigades, and twenty artillery regiments. However, the Kuomintang Army was continuously defeated by the better-trained and better-armed Japanese.

By the end of 1938 the Japanese controlled most of eastern (coastal) China. Only the vastness of China and, after 1941, other campaigns undertaken by the Japan that demanded troops, ships, and aircraft saved the Chinese Army from overwhelming defeat. Similarly, the Chinese Air Force was continually outfought by the Japanese, who had support from both land- and carrier-based aircraft in the theater. At any time the Chinese had a couple of hundred aircraft—early in 1941 the Soviets provided 100 bombers and 148 fighters—but they were invariably inferior to Japanese planes.

The United States gave military assistance to

China from early 1941, including air defense of the BURMA ROAD, being built to provide a land route for Allied supplies going to China. This requirement led to the establishment of the American Volunteer Group of fighter pilots, better known as the FLYING TIGERS. A former U.S. Army pilot, CLAIRE LEE CHENNAULT, led the Flying Tigers and became air adviser to Chiang. After the United States entry into the war the Fourteenth AIR FORCE was established in China with Chennault, recalled to U.S. service, in command.

In March 1942 Gen. JOSEPH STILWELL of the U.S. Army was sent to China as Chief of Staff to Chiang and commander of U.S. forces in the China-Burma-India theater. He and Chennault quarreled over whether to emphasize air or ground forces. Chiang tended to support Chennault's position and Stilwell was recalled in late 1944.

With the large quantities of matériel and training provided to China by the United States, the Chinese succeeded in tying down large numbers of Japanese troops but were unable to be decisive. The poor leadership and corruption of the Chinese Army became evident after the war, when the Communist forces were able to easily and decisively defeat the Kuomintang Army.

The Chinese had a small naval force, that primarily laid MINES in rivers and coastal areas, while a small marine force conducted missions along the coast and on land.

China-Burma India Theater,
see ALLIED CHINA-BURMA-INDIAN CAMPAIGN.

Chindits
A brigade of specially trained GURKHAS, Burmese, and British troops that fought behind Japanese lines during the ALLIED CHINA-BURMA-INDIA CAMPAIGN. The Chindits, who took their name from a Hindu myth, stealthily penetrated Japanese-held areas, attacked supply lines, and disrupted communications. There were two units, called Long Range Penetration Groups; one had 2,200 men and 850 mules, the other 1,000 men and 250 mules. Once in the bush they broke into smaller forces and were entirely supplied by air.

The first Chindits, the 3,000-man 77th Indian Infantry Brigade, was made up of men drawn from British, Ghurkha, and Burmese battalions. They went into action in Feb. 1943 in Burma. A few weeks later, after blowing up railway bridges and ambushing Japanese outposts, 2,182 made it back to British lines. By the end of 1943, the force had grown to three brigades supplied by their own Air COMMANDO Force, which used GLIDERS to land some Chindit units.

The Chindits were invented, trained, and commanded by Brig. ORDE C. WINGATE, whose faith in unconventional warfare was based on his experiences in Palestine and Ethiopia. Writing about the Chindits after the war, a Japanese historian said Wingate's hit-and-run warriors "reduced the Japanese power to wage war on the four Burma fronts and so fatally affected the balance."

Choltitz, Gen. Dietrich (1894–1966)
German commanding officer and military commander of PARIS who disobeyed HITLER's orders to destroy the NAZI-occupied city rather than let it fall unscathed to Allied forces. Although there was fighting in the city, Choltitz agreed to a truce with FRENCH RESISTANCE leaders that helped to avert serious damage.

During a military staff meeting at the WOLF'S LAIR in Rastenburg, on Aug. 25, 1944, Hitler learned that U.S. and French forces had entered the city. He asked, *"Brennt Paris?"* ("Is Paris burning?") When he learned that the city was being handed over unscarred, he flew into one of his characteristic rages.

Choltitz, responding to what he later called Hitler's contempt for "the fundamental laws of morality and dignity," had refused to carry out the order to burn Paris. The French imprisoned Choltitz, but soon released him.

Chou En-lai (1898–1976)
Cofounder with MAO TSE-TUNG of the Chinese Communist Party. As a student he was imprisoned in 1919–1920 for his radical activities. When he was released he went to France and became a leader of Chinese Communists in exile. He returned to China in 1924. As chief of the Whampoa military academy, he served under CHIANG KAI-SHEK. When Chiang's Nationalists moved against the Commu-

nists, Chou fled and helped to organize the Chinese Communist Army.

In 1936 a powerful warlord kidnaped Chiang; Chou negotiated and won Chiang's release by getting a promise of a united Nationalist-Communist alliance against the threat of Japan. Again Chou became a military adviser to Chiang, but once more the two leaders split, this time permanently.

Chou, second to MAO TSE-TUNG in the Communist hierarchy, was the chief Communist negotiator in the many attempts to bring the Nationalists and Communists together during and immediately after the war. With the establishment of the Communist Party as the government of China in 1949, Chou became premier and foreign secretary.

Christophorus

German code name for program to secure vehicles from the civilian sector for operations in the Soviet Union, Jan. 1942.

Chuikov, Gen. Vasily I. (1900–1982)

Soviet commander responsible for the defense of STALINGRAD and commander of the forces attacking BERLIN. Chuikov entered the Red Army in 1919 and commanded a regiment during the Russian Civil War. He subsequently specialized in tank tactics, commanding a mechanized brigade in 1937 and then a rifle corps in 1938–1940.

He served as Soviet military attaché in China and adviser to CHIANG KAI-SHEK from 1941 to mid-1942, when he returned to the Soviet Union to command the Sixty-Second Army. He was in charge of the Soviet defense of Stalingrad (after which his command was renamed the Eighth Guards Army), and led the final assault on Berlin (under the direction of Marshal GEORGI ZHUKOV). His command was in almost continuous combat, leading Chuikov to write: "The Eighth Guards Army was like a boxer who has been called on to go from one ring to another without a break and fight opponents of varying weights; before the last fight there had not even been time enough to take a deep breath and wipe the sweat away."

Promoted to marshal, he commanded the Soviet occupation forces in Germany from 1946 to 1953, was head of the Kiev Military District from 1953 to 1960, and deputy minister of defense and com-

mander of Soviet Ground Forces from 1960 to 1965. He then became chief of civil defense, a military post. He was twice awarded the HERO OF THE SOVIET UNION.

Churchill, Winston S. (1874–1965)

British prime minister and minister for defense, was the most experienced leader of a major nation in World War II. He first reached cabinet rank in 1908 and at one time or another prior to the EUROPEAN WAR was home secretary, First Lord of the Admiralty, Minister of Munitions, secretary of state for War and Air, colonial secretary, and chancellor of the Exchequer.

Even when he was out of government in the 1930s Churchill managed to receive a steady stream of intelligence on the German military buildup. But in that period he remained out of favor for his insistent warnings that HITLER had to be confronted by the Western democracies before his brazen arms buildup made war inevitable.

He was also the most literate of any national leader and had a technical understanding of military strategy and tactics—a circumstance that, combined with an apparently inexhaustible energy, plagued his military advisers throughout the war. From the moment of his becoming prime minister he demanded "offensive" operations—COMMANDOS and parachute raids, the development of landing craft, and the like—never seeming to understand the dimensions of Britain's shortage of men and equipment. Naval historian S. W. Roskill observed in his *Churchill and the Admirals,* "Fortunately, although he could be stubborn and obstinate to a degree, he could be deflected from such purposes if stood up to resolutely enough." Still, Roskill, and others, cited "his erroneous strategic concepts, such as his blindness to the threat from Japan and his share in the responsibilities for the disasters in Greece and CRETE in 1941, [which] brought very serious consequences in their train."

In 1939, Churchill was again appointed First Lord of the Admiralty—the position he held at the beginning of World War I (which prompted the Royal Navy to display "Winston's back!" on many signal halyards). He almost immediately began a private correspondence with President ROOSEVELT with an eye to ensuring eventual U.S. entry into the war. When Hitler invaded France in May 1940, NEVILLE CHAMBERLAIN's government fell and Churchill was reluctantly chosen prime minister. His history of inconstant party loyalty and the dislike most other British politicians held for him quickly faded. For, with his inspiring rhetoric, he aroused his people in their struggle against the loathsome enemy he always pronounced as "Nahzees."

Recognizing Britain's inability to defeat Germany on her own, Churchill prayed, begged, and connived for the United States to enter the war against Germany. His deepening relationship with Roosevelt during Britain's dark days of 1940 yielded the DESTROYERS-FOR-BASES DEAL of Sept. 1940, and then the LEND-LEASE act signed in March 1941. When Hitler invaded the Soviet Union in June 1941, Churchill knew his island was now safe from invasion as Germany had a two-front conflict. When Japan attacked PEARL HARBOR, Churchill noted America's involvement in the war with the remark, "So we had won after all!"

Despite his gratitude for the immense American contribution and the immediate American reaffirmation of a Germany First strategy, Churchill put himself at odds with U.S. European strategy from the start. He and his military advisers consistently opposed a landing in northwest Europe, advocating instead attacks along the periphery, together with the STRATEGIC BOMBING of Germany. Churchill also suspected his Soviet ally of unsavory ambitions for most of Eastern Europe and persistently offered a Balkan invasion alternative to both the NORMANDY INVASION and the invasion of southern France. Some observers saw the dark motive of imperial preservation, others agreed that the Anglo-American armies would not soon be ready to confront directly the veteran German forces.

Because Churchill was correct about Anglo-American unreadiness to invade Europe in 1942, he succeeded in making the first Anglo-American military effort the NORTH AFRICA INVASION. He then persuaded the United States to continue a Mediterranean liberation by invading SICILY in July 1943 and Italy in Sept. 1943. By that time, however, the U.S. material and troop-strength predominance forced Churchill to accede to the invasion of France in June 1944.

In the Pacific–Far East area, Churchill was less insistent (except about India's domestic policies) as he recognized the relatively small contribution Britain could make once her Asian colonies had fallen to the Japanese.

Churchill largely conducted the war from his CABINET WAR ROOMS, sitting before a huge map of the world, his military and civilian aides arrayed before him. He traveled extensively, to meet with his own military leaders in the field as well as to have talks with Roosevelt, STALIN, and CHIANG KAI-SHEK.

During the course of the war, Churchill was militant England incarnate. He hectored his civilian and military subordinates, peppering them with recommendations, sometimes wise and sometimes dubious. He daily reviewed ULTRA intercepts, and demanded landings and attacks that backfired on several occasions. His energy or interest never flagged. Throughout the war his V-for-Victory wave, his bulldog tenacity, and always-present cigar became symbols of Britain's determination.

In a sense, though, Churchill's wartime England—patriotic, romantic, and imperialistic—was anachronistic. By 1945, another England—worn, tired, and looking inward—had become a majority and Churchill was voted out. He returned as prime minister in 1951, but enjoyed far less success and retired in 1955.

Probably the most prolific writer of any national leader in history, Churchill received the Nobel Prize for Literature in 1953. The last of his six-volume *History of the English-Speaking Peoples* was published in 1958. His six-volume *History of the Second World War* gave posterity a magnificent overview of the war. It remained for another historian, A. J. P. Taylor, to summarize Churchill's dominant role in the twentieth century: "The savior of his country." Churchill "mobilized the English language and sent it into battle," said EDWARD R. MURROW, who broadcast to America the horrors and the triumphs of the Battle of Britain. Some of Churchill's most memorable wartime words:

"I have nothing to offer but blood, toil, tears, and sweat."—his first statement to the House of Commons as prime minister, May 13, 1940. (He liked the phrase well enough to use it or variations on it at least five other times.)

Victory at all costs, victory in spite of all terror, victory however long and hard the road may be; for without victory there is no survival.

In the same House of Commons speech:

We shall not flag or fail. We shall go on to the end. We shall fight in France, we shall fight on the seas and oceans, we shall fight with growing confidence and growing strength in the air, we shall fight on the beaches, we shall fight on the landing grounds, we shall fight in the fields and in the streets, we shall fight in the hills; we shall never surrender.

Speech to the House of Commons, June 4, 1940, following the evacuation of British troops from DUNKIRK.

We would rather see London laid in ruins and ashes than that it should be tamely and abjectly enslaved.

Radio broadcast on July 14, 1940, during the BATTLE OF BRITAIN.

Never in the field of human conflict was so much owed by so many to so few.

Speech to the House of Commons, Aug. 20, 1940, honoring the RAF Fighter Command.

We are waiting for the long-promised invasion. [A long pause.] So are the fishes.

Radio broadcast to the people of France, Oct. 21, 1940, after German's failure to launch Operation SEA LION, the planned invasion of England.

Never give in, never give in, never, never, never, never—in nothing, great or small, large or petty—never give in except to convictions of honor and good sense.

Speech at Harrow School, Oct. 29, 1941.

Now this is not the end. It is not even the beginning of the end. But it is, perhaps, the end of the beginning.

Speech on Nov. 10, 1942, two days after the Allied North Africa invasion.

Ciano, Count Galeazzo (1903–1944)

Italian foreign minister. Son of an early supporter of the Italian Fascist movement, Ciano won his title of nobility through his father, who was minister of communications and president of the Fascist Chamber of Deputies. Soon after graduation from the University of ROME Ciano joined the Italian Diplomatic Service.

In 1930 Ciano became the son-in-law of Italian *Il Duce* BENITO MUSSOLINI when he married the dictator's daughter Edda and began a rapid rise in the Mussolini government. After a stint as Mussolini's press chief, in 1934 he became under secretary of state for PROPAGANDA and a member of the Fascist Grand Council. In 1935, just turning thirty-three, he was appointed minister for foreign affairs. Except for a short stint commanding a bomber squadron during the Italian invasion of Ethiopia in 1935, he remained foreign minister until Feb. 1943, when Mussolini, distrustful of Ciano's anti-war attitude, removed him.

U.S. Under Secretary of State SUMNER WELLES called Ciano "the amoral product of a wholly decadent period in Italian and, for that matter in European, history." But Welles also found him charming, even though he was, like his father, financially corrupt (with a personal fortune estimated at some $60,000,000) and probably responsible for several political ASSASSINATIONS.

Welles, like many students of European history, was fascinated by Ciano's greatest treasure—his diary, which he began in 1939. Welles described the diary as "one of the most valuable historical documents of our times."

Ciano's diary provided historians with invaluable insights into Italian-German dealings during World War II. For example, he wrote of Germany's attitude toward Italy: "We were treated never like partners, but always as slaves. . . . Only the base cowardice of Mussolini could, without reaction, tolerate this and pretend not to see it." Ciano also deftly observed leaders of the times:

ADOLF HITLER: "He sleeps very little. Always less. And he spends a great part of the night surrounded by collaborators and friends. . . . It is always Hitler who talks! He can be Führer as much as he likes, but he always repeats himself, and bores his guests."

German Foreign Minister JOACHIM VON RIBBENTROP: He "says nothing new and nothing original. He is the exaggerated echo of Hitler." At dinner, just before the German invasion of the Soviet

Union, Ribbentrop told Ciano: "If we attack them, the Russia of STALIN will be erased from the map within eight weeks."

Mussolini was deposed on July 25, 1943, by a group that included Ciano. The next month the Germans took Ciano into custody. He was released only to fear that he was the target of a conspiracy. He fled north, where Mussolini, having been rescued by the Germans, had set up a puppet regime. In Jan. 1944 Mussolini ordered a show trial of Ciano and four other former Fascist Grand Council members who had voted to depose Mussolini. They were sentenced to death and shot by an Italian firing squad on Jan. 11.

On Dec. 23, 1943, condemned to death, Ciano furtively continued writing. On that day, in Cell 27 of the Verona Jail, he set down the last words in his diary, calling it "an honest testimonial of the truth in this sad world." His wife, Edda—"a wildcat," JOSEPH GOEBBELS once called her—managed to smuggle the diary out of Italy when, disguised as a peasant, she slipped over the border to Switzerland with their children.

Cicero

German code name for Elyesa Bazna, a German spy who got his information by serving as valet of the British ambassador to Turkey, Sir Hughe Knatchbull-Hugessen. Among the secrets this ESPIONAGE garnered for Germany: information about the CASABLANCA CONFERENCE of President ROOSEVELT and Prime Minister CHURCHILL; details of Allied bomber operations; the code word, Overlord, for the NORMANDY INVASION.

The spy saga surfaced in 1950 in *Operation Cicero* by Ludwig Moyzisch and in a 1952 movie, *Five Fingers* with James Mason. Confronted with the story, British Foreign Secretary Ernest Bevin admitted in the House of Commons that "the Ambassador's valet succeeded in photographing a number of highly secret documents in the Embassy and selling the films to the Germans." Moyzisch, who claimed to be the intelligence officer who ran "Cicero," did not reveal Bazna's name.

Bazna did this himself in his book *I Was Cicero,* published in 1962. Bazna wrote that the Germans had paid him £300,000 for spying. He was paid in British currency, which turned out to be counterfeited. He served a prison sentence for spending some of the money.

Bazna, an Albanian, worked at first as chauffeur for the British first secretary and was later promoted to valet, a post he held from Oct. 1943 to April 1944, when a secretary at the German Embassy in Ankara, who had knowledge of Cicero, defected to the British and Bazna left.

Another possible explanation for Bazna's exit was a discovery by ALLEN DULLES, the OFFICE OF STRATEGIC SERVICES spy chief who was running German agents out of Bern. Among the documents Dulles received was the copy of a cable in which the German Ambassador in Turkey, FRANZ VON PAPEN, boasted about the acquisition of top-secret documents from the British Embassy in Ankara. Dulles passed the information to British intelligence officers, who began an investigation.

But, by some accounts, the British security officials confined their probe to employees in the embassy. Bazna worked in the ambassador's residence, where he had easy access to carelessly handled top-secret documents.

Cigarette Camps,

see NORMANDY INVASION.

Circus

British term for RAF fighter sweeps over France to draw Luftwaffe aircraft into SPITFIRE "traps," from June 1941.

Citadel,

see ZITADELLE.

Civil Air Patrol

U.S. volunteer organization of civilian pilots and mechanics. Members of the Civil Air Patrol, using their own planes, aided in border and coastal patrols, took part in search-and-rescue missions for downed military pilots, towed targets, and aided in the training of ground observers. Formed on Dec. 1, 1941, the CAP originally was under the Office of Civilian Defense. In April 1943 the CAP was transferred to the Army Air Forces, which used the civilian aircraft as auxiliaries, chiefly on antisubmarine patrol along the Atlantic Coast. Some CAP planes carried depth charges or small bombs. The CAP was credited with sinking or damaging two U-BOATS.

Civil Defense

Protection of the American homefront by civilian volunteers. Radio, NEWSREEL, and newspaper reports about air raids in Europe inspired Americans to voluntarily establish state-level civil defense organizations during 1939 and 1940. These efforts were watched over by the Council of National Defense until another federal agency, the Office of Civilian Defense (OCD), took over the task. The OCD was created by President ROOSEVELT on May 20, 1941. Roosevelt named FIORELLO H. LA GUARDIA, mayor of New York City, the first director of civil defense.

After the United States declared war on the AXIS, the United States stepped up civilian defense activities, which were patterned after those of the British. A major lesson learned from the BATTLE OF BRITAIN was the need for civilian volunteers. Experience in England had shown that neither the military services nor fire and police services could provide sufficient aid to civilians threatened by air attack.

(Military defense of cities was limited. Because of fears of SABOTAGE, soldiers patrolled bridges in some areas, especially on the West Coast and in WASHINGTON, D.C., during America's early months of war. On the Pacific Coast, for a time, BARRAGE BALLOONS were hoisted over shipyards and sandbags were piled around telephone exchanges. In Los Angeles, antiaircraft guns on at least one occasion fired at nonexistent Japanese warplanes.)

About 1,500 local defense councils were already established when La Guardia took over the new federal agency; by the end of the year there were 6,000. When the Japanese attacked PEARL HARBOR, there were about 1,000,000 volunteers; after the attack, the total quickly grew to 5,000,000.

Volunteer air raid wardens were assigned in every neighborhood. BLACKOUTS darkened many communities, especially coastal cities. These cities in particular staged drills that sent residents scurrying to shelters in cellars or in the basements of office buildings. Utility workers worked on ways to deliver gas, water, and electricity if facilities were damaged by bombs or SABOTAGE. Neighboring communities developed mutual-aid plans so that public-safety agencies in one could help another in case of emergency.

Senior Boy Scouts and Girl Scouts were organized into auxiliary civil defense units to act as messengers and serve as "victims" for first-aid classes. Other volunteers learned to identify enemy aircraft through silhouettes and joined the AIRCRAFT WARNING CORPS. Eventually, when it became obvious that the United States was not going to be bombed, the air-raid precautions faded away. But the OCD provided the foundation for a succession of agencies, including the current Federal Emergency Management Agency.

Clarion

Code name for U.S. AAF attacks against German communications, Feb. 22–23, 1945.

Clark, Gen. Mark Wayne (1896–1984)

Mark Clark (whose associates called him "Wayne") was the youngest general to command a U.S. ARMY and ARMY GROUP in World War II. He is, however, remembered as much for his ambition and vanity as he is for his intelligence, competence, and great success as a military leader.

Clark, wounded and decorated in World War I, arrived in England in July 1942 to take command of the nascent Army Ground Forces in Europe. In Oct. 1942 he was appointed deputy commander in chief of Allied Forces in Northwest Africa in preparation for the forthcoming NORTH AFRICA INVASION. One of his first assignments was to meet clandestinely with French military leaders in North Africa to gain their cooperation for the landings. It was a risky, nearly lethal mission that demonstrated Clark's coolness and personal bravery.

His relations with French leaders after the landings further reinforced Gen. DWIGHT D. EISENHOWER'S respect for Clark, who began campaigning for an independent command. Eisenhower named him commander of the Fifth Army in Jan. 1943 and secured his promotion to lieutenant general. Given a chance to temporarily lead the Army's II CORPS in combat in Feb. 1943, Clark turned it down as too junior a posting. So, when his forces made ready to invade Italy in Sept. 1943, Lt. Gen. OMAR N. BRADLEY noted, Clark "had not yet commanded large-scale forces in combat in World War II. Moreover, I had some serious reservations about him personally. He seemed false somehow, too eager to impress, too hungry for the limelight, promotions, and personal publicity."

His first major combat operation in Sept. 1943 did not quell all doubts. He decided to forgo naval bombardment of SALERNO to avoid tipping his hand to the German defenders during the invasion of Italy. While the lack of a bombardment may have produced a slowing down of German *strategic* reaction, the decision meant that little was done to cut down the local defenders, who so assailed the American landing beaches that Clark contemplated pulling the U.S. forces off and shifting them into the British sector.

Clark made slow progress up the Italian peninsula, suffering heavy casualties and igniting controversy about his ability. The failure of a river crossing later led to a Senate committee investigation; a decision to destroy the treasured monastery at CASSINO haunted subsequent victories. These events and his decision to take ROME colored the perception that Clark should be held responsible for lengthening the long and bloody ITALIAN CAMPAIGN. But Clark soldiered on, month after month. He was appointed 15th Army Group commander in Dec. 1944 (at age forty-eight) and oversaw the Italian campaign until its end in May 1945.

Clark's ability to command a polyglot international army, maintain relatively smooth relations, and keep pressing ahead in a forlorn secondary theater demonstrated that if he was vain and did overreach, he nonetheless possessed real leadership abilities beneath the slick veneer.

Claude

The Japanese A5M carrier-based fighter flown in the 1930s and used in the air war over China. The Claude was a single-seat, open-cockpit aircraft with fixed landing gear. The prototype flew in 1935. Almost 1,000 were produced through 1940 and, although it was not flown against U.S. forces in the Pacific, it did see extensive combat over China.

Clausewitz

Variation of *Blau*.

Clay, Gen. Lucius D. (1897–1978)

After service in the Corps of Engineers, soon after America's entry into the war he became deputy chief of staff for requirements and resources. Later he became assistant chief of staff for matériel. He gave his staff simple instructions: "Find out what the Army needs and get it."

In March 1945 Clay became a civil affairs deputy to Gen. DWIGHT D. EISENHOWER, Supreme Allied Commander. Clay, promoted to lieutenant general in April, headed the U.S. section of the ALLIED CONTROL COUNCIL for Germany and became military governor of Germany.

Before becoming military governor, he asked the Department of State what American policy was for Germany. "Told that we had none, he proceeded unabashed to govern Germany on his own, deciding the most important thing was simply to govern Germany on his own," Theodore H. White wrote in *In Search of History*. Clay, White says, had "an army engineer's quick answer to the quick question of how to get the Germans back to work: You let them run their own country, but under strict controls."

Clay was among the few U.S. officials who immediately saw the need to react firmly to the Soviet Union's 1948 BERLIN blockade. (See the Epilogue.) "If we mean to hold Europe against communism," he told President TRUMAN'S advisers, "we must not budge." He ran the Berlin airlift that defied the blockade.

Clay helped to create the Republic of West Germany, beginning the process with a 1948 memo that ordered the German states in the Western occupation zone: "be advised that a constituent assembly will be held not later than 1 September 1948 to prepare a constitution for ratification. . . ."

After the war he urged his old boss to run for President in 1952 and worked in Eisenhower's political campaign.

Claymore

Code name for British COMMANDO raid on Lofoten Islands, March 1941.

Cleanslate

Code name for U.S. Army and Marine landings in the RUSSELL ISLANDS, Feb. 1943.

Clipper

Code name for British XXX Corps offensive to reduce the German salient at Gelsenkirchen.

Coastwatchers

Volunteers, most of them Australians and New Zealanders, who hid out in the SOLOMON ISLANDS and Bismarck Islands to report on Japanese ship and aircraft movements. Sheltered by anti-Japanese natives, the coastwatchers radioed reports of Japanese aircraft takeoffs, alerting Allied fighter control centers. They were especially valuable in reporting Japanese planes flying down THE SLOT from RABAUL to GUADALCANAL. Vice Adm. WILLIAM F. HALSEY said after Guadalcanal was secured, "The coastwatchers saved Guadalcanal and Guadalcanal saved the Pacific." Coastwatchers also were scattered along the coast of NEW GUINEA.

James Michener wrote of coastwatchers in *Tales of the South Pacific,* but the most famous exploit involving coastwatchers was the rescue of JOHN F. KENNEDY in the Solomons. It was a coastwatcher who learned that Kennedy and the crew of his PT-BOAT were in danger and arranged for their deliverance into safe hands.

The Australian Navy originated the idea and began training coastwatchers before the war. Typically, a coastwatcher was a solitary man: a planter, missionary, or colonial bureaucrat who volunteered to live an extremely dangerous double life.

In April 1944 a coastwatcher recovered papers from the body of Vice Adm. MINEICHI KOGA, CinC of the Combined Fleet, after his plane crashed off the Philippines island of Cebu, killing all on board. Some of the papers had to do with *Sho-Go,* the Japanese plan for defense of the Philippines. (See LEYTE GULF.)

Civilians also served as coastwatchers on isolated islands in the Philippines. These coastwatchers, however, did not operate as independently as the Australian-trained variety. The Philippines coastwatchers were armed, and many worked with Filipino GUERRILLA forces—which is not what a coastwatcher was to do. "If your watcher gets involved in something like guerrilla warfare," a U.S. Navy intelligence officer wrote after the war, "he quickly spoils his usefulness as an observer and as a reporter."

There were coastwatchers in other areas during the war, the most notable being Norwegians, who informed the British of German shipments.

Cobra

Code name for U.S. First ARMY operation to break out of the NORMANDY beachhead and penetrate German defenses west of Saint-Lô, France, July 1944.

Cochran, Jacqueline (1910—)

First director of WASP (Women's Air Force Service Pilots). When the EUROPEAN WAR began, Cochran, a famed racing pilot, recruited American women to serve in England's Air Transport Auxiliary, which ferried aircraft from factories to RAF bases. She wrote to ELEANOR ROOSEVELT, wife of the President, suggesting a similar U.S. organization.

After U.S. entry into the war, another woman aviator, Nancy Harkness Love, convinced the Army that its Ferrying Command should use women pilots. Love's organization was called the Women's Auxiliary Ferrying Squadron. Love's squadron and WASP operated separately until Nov. 1942 when they merged under Cochran's direction, with Love in charge of ferrying missions.

Cochran won the Bendix Transcontinental Air Race in 1938. She was at that time a businesswoman who headed a chain of beauty parlors.

Cockade

Code name for Allied diversionary operations to pin down German forces in the west, 1943.

Colditz

Reputedly escape-proof German prison fortress for Allied officers who had escaped from other German PRISONER OF WAR camps. Yet prisoners did escape. They got out in many ways. They dug tunnels and burrowed out. They dressed themselves in self-made German uniforms and, with counterfeited German currency, identity cards, and other documents in their pockets, walked out.

Colditz was a castle in a town of the same name in Saxony. The prison was officially known as Oflag IVC. At various times the prison held British, U.S., French, Dutch, Polish, and Belgian officers. About

130 prisoners escaped; some thirty of them eluded recapture and made it across frontiers.

One of the prisoners described what escape planners were up against: "The garrison manning the camp outnumbered the prisoners at all times. The Castle was floodlit at night from every angle, in spite of the BLACKOUT. Notwithstanding the clear drops of a hundred feet or so on the outside from barred windows, there were sentries all around the camp, within a palisade of barbed wire. Beyond the palisade were precipices of varying depth."

The man who wrote that, P. R. Reid, a British army officer, escaped, was captured, and returned—to escape again. In his book *The Colditz Story,* Reid tells of the many brazen schemes that he supervised as "escape officer." He had been given the designation escape officer, which was an actual role in the secret structure prisoners set up for planning and executing escapes.

When Colditz was liberated by U.S. forces in April 1945, some of the prisoners were working on what would have been the grandest escape: in a glider painstakingly built and hidden in the ceiling of the chapel.

Collar

British code word for CONVOY to MALTA, Nov. 1940.

Collins, Lt. Gen. Joseph L. (1882–1963)

Commander of the 25th Infantry DIVISION at GUADALCANAL and NEW GEORGIA and commander of the U.S. Seventh CORPS in the NORMANDY INVASION. Collins got his nickname, "Lightning Joe," from the "Tropic Lightning" nickname of the 25th.

A hard-driving leader, he admired and emulated Gen. OMAR BRADLEY and, like him, was considered a soldier's soldier. He was sometimes called the "GI's General." Collins took the Seventh Corps from Utah Beach at Normandy to the breakout at Saint Lô, across France to the ARDENNES and to the linkup with the Red Army at the Elbe River. (See ALLIED CAMPAIGN IN EUROPE.)

He was Army Chief of Staff from 1949 to 1953 and later served his wartime boss by becoming President DWIGHT D. EISENHOWER'S personal representative in South Vietnam.

Cologne

Heavily bombed German city that was the target of the war's first THOUSAND-PLANE RAID. On May 30–31, 1942, the RAF Bomber Command launched Operation Millennium, sending 1,158 bombers against Cologne. During the three-hour night raid 1,455 tons of BOMBS, most of them incendiary, were dropped. The raid devastated more than 600 acres of the city and destroyed an estimated 13,000 homes. The Germans reported 469 dead and more than 4,000 injured. The British lost forty bombers during this first major attack as part of a STRATEGIC BOMBING campaign to destroy German industry with "area bombing" rather than PRECISION BOMBING.

Colombia

Capital: Bogota, pop. 8,730,000 (est. 1938). When the EUROPEAN WAR began in Sept. 1939 Colombia announced that planes of the German-managed airline Scadta would henceforth carry Colombian air force copilots; in June 1941 German employees were told to leave the airline. A few hours after the United States declared war on Japan, Colombia broke off relations with Japan, with Germany and Italy on Dec. 19, and with VICHY FRANCE on Nov. 26, 1942. Colombia declared war on Germany on Nov. 26, 1943, interned "dangerous" Germans, and confiscated some German property.

Colombia joined with the U.S. Navy in coastal patrols, but the nation's most valuable contribution to the U.S. war effort was the increased export of cinchona bark used for the manufacture of quinine for prevention of malaria.

Colonel Warden

British code name for Prime Minister CHURCHILL.

Colorado

British code name for CRETE.

Colossus, Code Name

Code name for British effort to use COMMANDOS dropped by parachute to destroy southern Italy's water supply by attacking the aqueduct at Tragino Campagna; the Feb. 1941 effort was a failure.

Colossus

A more advanced electro-mechanical computer than the BOMBE, the Colossus was used by British code-breakers at BLETCHLEY PARK to determine German ENIGMA machine code settings. The Colossus, first used in Feb. 1944, was comparable to the electronic computers of the early 1950s, being capable of reading some 25,000 bytes per second. By the end of the war there were ten Colossus machines in use at Bletchley Park.

Combat Command

Principal component of U.S. Army armored DIVISIONS after Sept. 1943. Within those divisions all TANK, armored ARTILLERY, and armored infantry BATTALIONS were administratively self-contained and interchangeable, and thus could be assigned to either of a division's principal combat commands (designated "A" and "B") or the reserve combat command.

Normally one combat command was commanded by the deputy division commander (a brigadier general) and the others by colonels.

Combat Teams

Ground combat units formed into temporary groupings for specific operations. Teams based on a reinforced BATTALION were called battalion combat teams and those on REGIMENTS were known as regimental combat teams. They were sometimes known by the name of their commander.

Combined Chiefs of Staff

The British CHIEFS OF STAFF and the U.S. JOINT CHIEFS OF STAFF acting together in meetings or through representatives to advise the prime minister and President on military policy.

The Combined Chiefs of Staff was conceived during the ARCADIA CONFERENCE in WASHINGTON, and established on Jan. 14, 1942. The headquarters was in Washington, with the heads of the British Joint Mission Staff in Washington representing their respective service chiefs in their absence.

Two bodies to support the Combined Chiefs of Staff were also established, the Combined Staff Planners, to undertake studies and draft plans, and the Combined Secretariat, to maintain records, and prepare and distribute staff papers.

Combined Operations

A British command that supervised the use of two or more armed services in a single operation. The Combined Operations Command was the official name of the organization. Originally, a combined operation was an AMPHIBIOUS LANDING in which the fighting services took part together.

The Combined Operations Command's primary mission was to train officers and enlisted men of the Royal Navy, the Royal Marines, the Army, and the Royal Air Force in the conduct of amphibious warfare. The command was also charged with the task of planning and executing hit-and-run raids. These were carried out by men popularly known as the COMMANDOS. Admiral of the Fleet Sir ROGER KEYES, as the first director of the combined operations staff, initially commanded the commandos; in Oct. 1941 he was succeeded by Adm. Lord LOUIS MOUNTBATTEN.

Comet

Allied Code name for the proposed AIRBORNE capture of the Rhine River bridges at Arnhem, Holland, by the British 1st Airborne Division and the Polish 1st Parachute Brigade in Aug. 1944. The operation was delayed and then replaced, in Sept. 1944, by Operation MARKET-GARDEN.

Comics

Several comic strips were born during the war and others developed wartime motifs. Many young comic readers first learned such words of war as *AXIS* and *SABOTAGE* by reading the wartime adventures of Dick Tracy and Little Orphan Annie. They, along with most comic strip heroes and heroines, spent the war tracking down German and Jap (rarely *Japanese*) saboteurs. Another war phrase, *GI Joe,* appeared in a strip by Lt. Dave Berger in *YANK* Magazine for the first time in June 1942.

Milt Caniff, who had begun "Terry and the Pirates" in 1934, enlisted Terry, the young hero of the strip, in the Army Air Forces. One Sunday strip, in which Lt. Col. Flip Corkin gives patriotic advice and extols the AAF, was the only comic strip ever inserted in full in the *Congressional Record*. The character Corkin was inspired by Col. Philip Cochrane, commanding officer of the First Air Commando GROUP in the China-Burma-India theater.

By the time Caniff introduced Steve Canyon to newspaper readers in 1947, the U.S. Air Force was a leading Caniff fan. Air Force public relations made Canyon a semireal person by providing him with a service record that showed him winning his wings in 1942 and holding a Distinguished Flying Cross and twenty-one other medals and ribbons. Canyon was officially retired in April 1989.

Command

The principal U.S. Army Air Force organizational structure within numbered AIR FORCES. The commands grouped all aircraft or services of a given type (e. g., fighter, bomber, service) for administrative and operational purposes. Within the AAF operational structure, commands ranked with air divisions between numbered air forces and WINGS.

Initially commands were given Roman number designations corresponding with their respective air force; thus, the Seventh Air Force (headquarters on Oahu, Hawaii) contained the VII Fighter Command, the VII Bomber Command, and the VII Air Force Service Command. However, this assignment scheme was not maintained; for example, in 1945 the Twentieth Air Force's fighter aircraft were assigned to the VII Fighter Command based on IWO JIMA.

Also, the planned structure for the Twentieth Air Force's STRATEGIC BOMBING operations against Japan in 1946 provided that the Air Force staff in WASHINGTON would control the XXI Bomber Command based in the MARIANA ISLANDS; the XXII Bomber Command in the Philippines, FORMOSA, or OKINAWA; and possibly the XXIII Bomber Command flying from Alaska. The Eighth Air Force, after returning to the United States from Europe to convert to B-29 SUPERFORTRESS bombers, was to deploy to the Marianas and absorb the XX Bomber Command for strikes against Japan.

The AAF also had administrative commands within the United States with responsibility for administrative, research and development, and training functions. These commands were: Training, I Troop Carrier, Materiel, Air Service, and Proving Ground. In addition, the AIR TRANSPORT COMMAND was responsible for ferrying aircraft from factories to operational commands, and delivering personnel and supplies throughout the world.

Commando,

see C-46.

Commandos

An all-volunteer British organization founded in 1940 to conduct raids against German-occupied areas. Commandos, trained and controlled by the COMBINED OPERATIONS Command, were best known for their cross-Channel raids, such as those at DIEPPE, their first large-scale assault, and smaller raids at SAINT-NAZAIRE, on the German-held CHANNEL ISLANDS, and along the Norwegian coast. Commandos also operated in Libya, CRETE, North Africa, Italy, SICILY, Burma, and MADAGASCAR. Two brigades went ashore on the first day of the NORMANDY INVASION.

Small raids began in June 1940 with ten commando units, each with about 500 men. The commando organization was built around the specifics of British LANDING CRAFT and the structure of the Royal Navy. A commando platoon consisted of the number of men who could fit aboard the assault landing craft (ALC); a troop filled two ALCs. A battalion-size unit was called a "commando," so the word had two meanings: the individual soldier and a battalion-size group of commandos. The name had been used by hit-and-run Boer GUERRILLA groups that harried British forces during the Boer War (1899–1902).

Commandos were given rigorous training, ranging from parachute jumps to mountain climbing. A unit in training might be forced to march 60 miles in twenty-four hours. One unit marched 130 miles in five days, covering the first 42 miles in nineteen hours. During the war some 25,000 volunteers—RANGERS, Frenchmen, Norwegians, Poles, Belgians, Dutchmen—went through the rugged commando training course at Achnacarry Castle in Scotland.

The commandos' *Handbook of Irregular Warfare* reminded them that "the days when we could practice the rules of sportsmanship are over. For the time being every soldier must be a potential gangster. . . . The vulnerable parts of the enemy are the heart, spine, and privates. Kick him or knee him as hard as you can in the fork. . . . Remember you are out to kill."

Among the Americans who trained and fought with the commandos was U.S. Army Col. LUCIAN K. TRUSCOTT, who applied what he learned to the establishment of the U.S. Army Rangers.

Communist Party of the U.S.

A tiny political organization, the Communist Party of the United States (CPUS) was closely watched by the FEDERAL BUREAU OF INVESTIGATION and Congressional investigators. But American Communists had no power and little influence on the war effort.

From the beginning of the EUROPEAN WAR until June 1941 the CPUS campaigned against the U.S. defense buildup. The policy reflected what was then the international Communist Party line, which took its cue from the NONAGGRESSION PACT between Germany and the Soviet Union. Although Germany was a Fascist state, the American Communists ignored the ideological problem.

The party line drastically changed in June 1941 when Germany invaded the Soviet Union. From that time on, the CPUS vigorously supported a strong U.S. defense policy and LEND-LEASE (especially when the Soviet Union was added to the aid list). American Communists also added their voices to the Soviet demands for a SECOND FRONT that would force the transfer of some German forces from the Soviet Union.

American Communists, which claimed a membership of 100,000 (one third in New York State), tried to shuck its old revolutionary image. On May 22, 1944, it changed its name to the Communist Political Association, and Earl Browder, its president, addressed the delegates to its convention as "ladies and gentlemen" instead of "comrades."

When World War II ended and the Cold War began, the American Communists changed again. Browder was ousted as a dangerous right-wing deviate, his "association" dissolved, and, in July 1945 the Communist Party of the United States returned, once more following the political line dictated from the Soviet Union.

Company

Military unit, usually of ground forces, consisting of three or four PLATOONS. Combat companies were normally subordinate to BATTALIONS and were the smallest military organization that provided mess, supply, and other support functions to troops. (In ARTILLERY units the term *BATTERY* was used in place of company while certain CAVALRY and reconnaissance organizations used the term TROOP.) There were also numerous types of support companies. Companies were normally commanded by captains.

In the 1943 U.S. Army tables of organization, an infantry provided for 193 officers and enlisted men; other combat companies (heavy weapons, cannon, tank, etc.) were smaller, as were most support companies (service, maintenance, truck, etc.), as well as headquarters companies for battalions, REGIMENTS, and DIVISIONS. An infantry division's signal company in 1943 was authorized 226 men and the quartermaster company had 193. AIRBORNE rifle companies were smaller—127 officers and enlisted men in 1942, increased to 176 in 1944—in part because support functions were provided by support units. (The airborne division's signal company numbered 285 and ordnance quartermaster company totaled 208).

The nine "line" or rifle and three weapon companies within a regiment were identified by letter—*A, B, C,* etc., usually known by their code names, Able, Baker, Charlie, etc.

Compass

Code name for British counteroffensive against Italian forces in Egypt, Dec. 1940.

Concentration Camps

Camps for the imprisonment of men, women, and children by NAZI Germany. The term came from prisoner centers used by the British for the internment of Boer civilians during the 1899–1902 Boer War. The German camps were part of a system that included nearby factories for SLAVE LABOR by prisoners and DEATH CAMPS for the systematic extermination of JEWS, Gypsies, and others deemed undesirable. The first camps were considered internment and education centers or labor camps by Germans who accepted Nazi PROPAGANDA.

HITLER opened the first of about 100 camps soon after he became chancellor of Germany in 1933. He said they would be used to make "antisocial" Germans into "useful members" of Nazi soci-

Nordhausen was a German concentration camp—not a death camp—that provided slave labor for the underground V-1 buzz bomb and V-2 missile factories. But beatings, malnutrition, and lack of medical care took their ghastly toll. These bodies were found when Allied troops captured the area. *(Imperial War Museum)*

ety. The earliest camps were DACHAU, near Munich; Sachsenhausen, near Kassel; and Buchenwald, near Weimar, capital of the democracy that the Nazis destroyed. A women's concentration camp, Ravensbrück, fifty miles north of Berlin, was established in 1938.

Theresienstadt, a concentration camp disguised as a "model ghetto," was located in Czechoslovakia, about forty miles from Prague. It opened in late 1941. Among the inmates were prominent Jews, decorated Jewish veterans of World War I, Danish Jews, and elderly Jews who paid for the privilege after being ordered to make a "transfer of residence."

Theresienstadt, administered like other ghettos by a *Judenrat* or a cruelly intimidated Council of Jews, was laid out like a town, and was periodically scrubbed up to impress visiting foreigners, who were impressed by its schools, concerts, and artist organizations. But it was still a place of death, from disease, malnutrition, and, occasionally, execution. Beginning in Jan. 1942, Theresienstadt was, for most people, a stopover on the way to the death camp at AUSCHWITZ. Of the 140,000 Jews sent to Theresienstadt, only 14,000

survived. Some 15,000 children passed through; about 100 survived.

The Germans forced talented Jews in the camp to make a PROPAGANDA film, "Hitler Presents a Town to the Jews." The Jews who made it so exaggerated the kindness and sweetness of the Nazis that the Germans did not release it and sent the creators of the movie to Auschwitz.

The "state security" law authorizing the concentration camps was enforced by the GESTAPO; the guarding of the camps was entrusted to the SS, which assigned the task to Death-Head detachments, whose members wore skull-and-crossbones insignia on their black tunics and caps.

The first prisoners were enemies of the state and the party. To this category were soon added violators of racial-purity laws, including Jews, "Aryans" who had had sexual relations with Jews, and homosexuals ("sinful deviants"). Others included "workshy" citizens (beggars, prostitutes, Gypsies, drunkards), conscientious objectors, Jehovah's Witnesses, and Germans who had served in the French Foreign Legion (charged with serving a foreign power).

In some camps, identification numbers were tattooed on the arms of prisoners. They were usually dressed in vertically striped uniforms with triangular insignias designating their category: red for political prisoners, yellow for Jews, pink for homosexuals, black for asocial or "work-shy" prisoners, purple for Jehovah's Witnesses, green for criminals; prisoners included in a second or third category wore extra triangles. At Auschwitz, Jews later wore a red triangle with a second yellow triangle to form a Star of David. This was later changed to a yellow bar above the triangle.

Pregnant women were rarely allowed to survive or give birth, although this did happen. A pregnancy unit was set up at the Kaufering concentration camp in Dec. 1944; the seven mothers and the children born to them survived the war.

More torture chamber than prison, the typical concentration camp was run mercilessly. Psychiatrist Bruno Bettelheim, who was a prisoner at both Dachau and Buchenwald, observed that "it was left pretty much up to the individual guard's fancy whether he wanted to torture a prisoner; if he felt like shooting one, he could always do so and claim self-defense or prevention of an escape." At one camp any inmate contemplating suicide was asked to aid authorities in identifying him by first writing his or her identification number on a slip of paper and putting it in the mouth before hanging.

Medical officers in the camps, Bettelheim wrote, sometimes showed self-serving mercy. "For instance, on one terribly cold winter night the prisoners had to stand at attention for many hours. Many of them died of exposure, while several hundred had their limbs frozen." The medical officer, Bettelheim continued, "insisted that the commander either shoot the prisoners or send them back to the barracks, because, as he put it, he could not be bothered the next day with hundreds of amputations. . . ." Bettelheim calculated that on a diet of fewer than 1,800 calories per day the prisoners had to perform work that required 3,000 to 3,300 calories. Death by starvation or disease was always more likely than survival.

Although the overall operation varied little from camp to camp, each had its own special horrors, and each became a death camp, if not by strict SS definition. Among the major concentration camps were:

Mauthausen   Among the first inmates of this Austrian camp were 10,000 left-wing veterans of the SPANISH CIVIL WAR, interned in France when that war ended in 1939 and turned over to the Germans by the VICHY FRANCE regime. About 1,500 survived. Many workers died in the granite quarry, owned by Vienna for the mining of paving stones. Here, toward the end of the war, at least forty-seven Allied airmen died after sadistically being forced to carry heavier and heavier loads of stone up and down the quarry's 148 carved steps. The camp was liberated by Gen. GEORGE PATTON'S advance units on May 3, 1945. One of his officers later wrote that "the smell, the odor . . . burn in the nostrils and memory. I will always smell Mauthausen." Although technically not a death camp, Mauthausen was the site of 36,318 deaths, according to its meticulously kept Death Book.

Ohrdruf   Gen. DWIGHT D. EISENHOWER'S first view of a camp came on April 12, 1945 when he inspected the small "work camp" at Ohrdruf, near Buchenwald. In the cellar of one building was a row of gallows; any prisoner who had been caught trying to escape was sentenced to a lingering death: He had a piano-wire noose looped around his neck and was suspended so that his toes just brushed the floor. At liberation, about 3,200 bodies lay about; some had fresh head wounds. They were prisoners shot as the U.S. troops neared the camp. Neighbors claimed they knew nothing about the camp. Eisenhower ordered that every man, woman, and child from nearby towns be marched through the camp at bayonet point. Then he had them bury the dead. As he was leaving he turned to one of his soldiers and asked, "Still having trouble hating them?"

Buchenwald   Built near Weimar, capital of the short-lived WEIMAR REPUBLIC, the camp served a nearby munitions plant. Unknown numbers of Jews, mentally ill patients, and others rounded up in "euthanasia" actions, were killed at Buchenwald, although it was not technically a death camp. When U.S. troops liberated the camp on April 10, 1945, CBS correspondent EDWARD R. MURROW was with them. In one of his most memorable reports, he told of walking into what had been a stable for eighty horses. "There were 1,200 men in it, five to a bunk. The stink was beyond all description. . . . I asked how many men had died in that building during the last month. . . . They totaled 242

. . . out of 1,200 in one month. In another part of the camp they showed me the children, hundreds of them. Some were only six. One rolled up his sleeves, showed me his number. It was tattooed on his arm . . . B-6030, it was."

Dachau During the liberation of the camp by American forces on April 29, 1945, on a railway siding was a train of fifty cars—"all full of terribly emaciated dead bodies, piled up like the twisted branches of cut-down trees," a witness wrote. Several SS camp guards reportedly fired on the prisoners as U.S. soldiers arrived. In the ensuing firefight, prisoners seized abandoned German weapons and joined incensed GIs in killing every guard. An estimated 27,000 inmates, liberated but hopelessly ill, died within a few days after being freed. One of the surviving inmates was the courageous Pastor MARTIN NIEMÖLLER, an early critic of Nazism.

Bergen-Belsen Located near Hanover, Belsen was opened in July 1943 as a PRISONER OF WAR camp. Later the Germans pressed it into service for civilian prisoners being evacuated from camps in the path of the Allied advance. Here ANNE FRANK died in March 1945; her diary survived to inspire the world. When British forces liberated the camp on April 14, 1945, they found nearly 10,000 unburied corpses and hundreds of others in mass graves. About 6,000 emaciated survivors were taken to Sweden, under the direction of Count FOLKE BERNADOTTE, president of the Swedish RED CROSS. Some 14,000 who received medical attention in the camp nevertheless died within a few days after liberation. Belsen was made into a DISPLACED PERSONS camp. An estimated 50,000 people died in the camp.

Condor,

see FW 200.

Condor Legion,

see SPANISH CIVIL WAR.

Congressmen

Many of the men who voted to declare war had to decide how to serve in that war. Some, including Texas Congressman LYNDON B. JOHNSON, were members of the Naval Reserve; others, such as Senator Henry Cabot Lodge of Massachusetts, were in the Army Reserve. Some enlisted, interrupting or ending their political careers.

Many were well above the draft age; SELECTIVE SERVICE did not call up men over forty-four. Senator HARRY S TRUMAN of Missouri, a World I Army veteran who had retained his reserve commission, requested a call to active duty from Gen. GEORGE C. MARSHALL, Army Chief of Staff. Truman later said that Marshall had told the senator he was "too damned old."

Lodge served on a special tour of duty with a U.S. tank unit attached to British forces in Libya in 1942. Following his reelection later in 1942, Lodge decided not to complete his term. He resigned his Senate seat in 1944 and went on active duty. Fluent in French, he served as the Sixth Army GROUP'S liaison officer with the First French Army.

The question of whether members of Congress should be exempt from war service was finally settled on July 9, 1942, when President ROOSEVELT ordered all congressmen in the armed services to return to Congress. Eight members of Congress were then on active duty. Four resigned from Congress and remained in the armed services; one of them would be killed in action. Four, including Johnson, resigned from the armed forces.

Coningham, Air Marshal Sir Arthur (1895–1948)

Air vice marshal and commander, No. 4 Group Bomber Command at the start of the war, Coningham, as Commander, Western Desert Air Force, first achieved special prominence as an exponent of air cooperation with army operations during Operation Crusader near the Egyptian border in Nov. 1941.

Although not as intimate as later American practice would become, such cooperation was a major step and contributed to Gen. BERNARD MONTGOMERY'S victories in Egypt and the pursuit of *Generalfeldmarschall* ERWIN ROMMEL in the NORTHWEST AFRICA CAMPAIGN. When the British 8th Army and the Anglo-American forces linked up in Tunisia, Coningham took command of all tactical air units.

Coningham believed that Montgomery claimed more credit for British successes than was due him.

Coningham could be acidulous in his criticism, as when he disingenuously expressed the hope that Gen. GEORGE PATTON'S II CORPS wasn't adopting the "discredited practice of using air force as an alibi for lack of success on the ground." Patton predictably seethed with rage.

Following the NORMANDY INVASION, Coningham soon established a reputation for effective close-air support, in large part because there was virtually no German Air Force opposition. The "shuttle service" of "cab ranks" of fighters and fighter bombers strafing hapless German columns in the Falaise pocket became a famous image of air power.

Conquer

Signal code name for U.S. Ninth ARMY, 1944–1945.

Conscription,

see SELECTIVE SERVICE.

Convoy

Merchant ships were usually organized into convoys by all nations during the war. Ships were grouped in convoys primarily to concentrate defenses—surface ships and aircraft, and, on occasion, submarines. Since it was impossible to provide an escort for every individual merchant ship at sea, the grouping of merchant ships permitted a few escorts to convoy a large number of merchants.

A secondary—but highly significant—advantage of the convoy was the reduction in the number of "units" that enemy submarines could contact, since, for sighting, the convoy becomes one unit (albeit a large one), the same as a single merchant ship.

In the Atlantic, the Allies sailed merchant ships independently that had a sustained speed over 15 knots (briefly lowered to 13 knots). It was believed—correctly—that even if sighted by a U-BOAT, the ship's speed would prevent a submarine from gaining an attack position. In the BATTLE OF THE ATLANTIC in 1941–1942, the larger the convoy, the fewer relative number of ships sunk per attack; the number of ships sunk *per U-boat* in the attack remained about the same. In the following table on convoy operations, note that the ratio of escorts to merchant ships declined rapidly with convoy size.

MERCHANT SHIPS (average)	ESCORT SHIPS (average)	WOLF PACK ATTACKS	SHIPS SUNK PER ATTACK	SHIPS SUNK PER U-BOAT
11.0	4.0	1	7.0	1.8
20.4	6.5	8	4.8	0.7
29.7	6.8	11	5.6	1.1
38.5	6.1	13	6.1	1.1
48.3	6.5	7	4.9	0.9
62.5	8.0	2	9.0	1.2

Thus, convoys proved an effective counter to U-boat attacks in the Atlantic. Only one convoy was turned back by U-boats alone (some were turned back by weather); Convoy SC 52 en route to England in Nov. 1941 returned to Halifax because of losses despite a heavy escort (two destroyers and seven CORVETTES). Still, convoys proved effective until March 1943, when it appeared that even the convoy effort could not defeat the U-boats. But the convoy system did prevail (along with other improvements in Allied antisubmarine efforts, see BATTLE OF THE ATLANTIC).

Convoys were also used by German shipping in the Baltic, Italian shipping in the Mediterranean, and Japanese shipping in the Far East. In all areas convoying—with adequate escorts—generally proved an effective defense against aircraft and submarine attacks.

Allied convoys were given designations based on a series of code letters. These codes addressed the route, whether a fast or slow convoy, and on some routes the day of the week it sailed. The major convoy route codes were:

GUS	North Africa–USA
HG	Gibraltar–UK
HX	New York/Halifax–UK
OB	Liverpool–Western Approaches (England)
OG	UK–Gibraltar
ON	UK–North America
ONS	UK–North America (slow)
OS	UK–West Africa
PQ	UK–Northern USSR
QP	North USSR–UK
SC	Halifax–UK
SL	West Africa–UK
UGS	USA–North Africa

Sometimes suffix letters were added: F for fast, M for medium speed, and S for slow.

Convoy PQ 17

The worst CONVOY disaster of World War II. PQ 17 was a RUSSIAN CONVOY, departing Iceland on

June 27, 1942, bound for the Soviet port of ARCH-ANGEL. The thirty-five Allied merchant ships of the convoy carried vital war material for the Red Army. It was escorted by six destroyers, four corvettes, and nine lesser antisubmarine craft. In addition, there were two distant covering forces, an Anglo-American cruiser-destroyer force and, farther off, an Anglo-American battleship-carrier force, which included the USS *Washington* (BB 56).

The German threat to the convoy included a surface group centered on the new battleship *TIRPITZ*, U-BOATS, and land-based aircraft, all flying from bases in Norway. When the British Admiralty learned through ENIGMA that the *Tirpitz* had put to sea, the order was given on July 4 for the convoy to "scatter" to make attacking the individual merchant ships more difficult for the battleship.

But the *Tirpitz* did not attack. Instead, the scattered merchant ships, with their escorts relatively ineffective, were attacked beginning on July 2 by HE 111 and HE 115 bombers and several submarines. When the battle was over on July 15, PQ 17 had lost twenty-four merchant ships—69 percent of the convoy's merchant ships—of 143,977 tons. Lost in those ships were 430 tanks, 3,350 military vehicles, and 210 aircraft, plus almost 100,000 tons of other war equipment.

One of the few clever actions on the part of the Royal Navy in this action occurred when Lt. Leo Gradwell, commanding officer of the antisubmarine trawler *Ayrshire*, collected three merchant ships and shepherded them to the ice pack, when he had the starboard sides of the ships painted white to CAMOUFLAGE them from German reconnaissance. Those four ships safely reached Archangel.

The German losses were five aircraft.

Co-prosperity Sphere,

see GREATER EAST ASIA CO-PROSPERITY SPHERE.

Coral Sea

Site of the first naval battle in which the participating warships did not fire upon their opponents. It was the first naval battle to be fought entirely by carrier aircraft. And it was the first Japanese setback of World War II.

The Coral Sea is between Queensland, Australia, on the west and the New Hebrides and NEW CALEDONIA on the east. To the north it is bound by Papua and the SOLOMON ISLANDS. The battle of the Coral Sea was set up by the Japanese plan, known as operation *Mo,* to take PORT MORESBY in NEW GUINEA. The capture would endanger Australia and end the threat of Allied air attacks against Japanese bases at RABAUL and in the Solomon Islands.

For the operation the Japanese mustered seventy ships, including two large aircraft carriers, a small carrier, cruisers, destroyers, and transports to carry the troops who were to invade New Guinea. The deployment of the Japanese ships was known to the U.S. Navy, which had been breaking the Japanese naval code.

To counter the Japanese thrust, the U.S. Navy had only the AIRCRAFT CARRIERS *LEXINGTON* (CV 2) and *Yorktown* (CV 5) and some DESTROYERS and CRUISERS. They were formed into a TASK FORCE under Rear Adm. FRANK J. FLETCHER.

On May 3 the Japanese landed some troops at Tulagi, off GUADALCANAL in the Solomons. Aircraft from the *Yorktown,* hunting for the main Japanese force, found only minor Japanese ships off Tulagi. The American aircraft sank three minesweepers, fatally struck a destroyer, and damaged several other ships.

The two fleets searched for each other, the Japanese finding only an oiler and a destroyer, both of which were sunk. The Americans on May 7 found what a garbled message called two Japanese carriers and four heavy cruisers; the message should have read two heavy cruisers and two destroyers. While ninety-three U.S. aircraft roared off in search of the misidentified Japanese carriers, Japanese reconnaissance planes were looking for the U.S. carriers.

What the U.S. aircraft did find was the light carrier *SHOHO* and her cruiser-destroyer escort. The ninety-three planes headed for the carrier and within minutes she went down, hit by thirteen BOMBS and seven TORPEDOES. As the *Shoho* sunk, Lt. Comdr. ROBERT E. DIXON of the *Lexington* radioed back the message "Scratch one flattop!" probably coining the term that became synonymous with aircraft carrier.

Poor weather hampered the Japanese planes searching for the U.S. carriers. They jettisoned their bombs and torpedoes and headed back toward their carriers. U.S. fighters spotted them and shot down ten planes while losing two. The melee ended

The first U.S. aircraft carrier to be sunk in the war was the *Lexington* (CV 2), shown here in flames during the battle of the Coral Sea. Although her loss was a severe blow to the Navy, the May 1942 battle was an American victory as the Japanese were forced to turn back their transports en route to capture Port Moresby. *(U.S. Navy)*

well past sunset. Some of the Japanese planes then stumbled across the *Yorktown* and, in the darkness, mistook her for one of their own. Several planes prepared to land on the carrier when the pilot of the lead plane discovered his error and frantically gave his plane full power and started climbing amidst a barrage of antiaircraft fire. The surviving planes finally found their carriers, which turned on searchlights to guide the battered warriors home.

On May 8, with most of the U.S. carrier aircraft heading for the Japanese carriers, sixty-nine Japanese planes located the *Lexington* and the *Yorktown.* Torpedo planes streaked for both sides of the *Lexington.* Two torpedoes hit her on the port side. Five bombs also struck her but did relatively little damage. The *Yorktown* was also hit by a bomb that pierced her flight deck and went through to the fourth deck before exploding.

Internal explosions racked the *Lexington,* and not quite five hours after she was attacked, orders were given to abandon ship. After her 2,735 officers and men were evacuated, she was torpedoed by a U.S. destroyer.

Meanwhile, aircraft from the *Yorktown* sighted the two Japanese carriers. In a coordinated torpedo and bombing run, the U.S. planes attacked the *Shokaku.* The torpedoes all either missed or, if any hit, failed to explode. Only two bombs hit. *Lexington* planes in a subsequent strike again failed in a torpedo attack but did hit the *Shokaku* with one bomb.

By the tally of ship losses, the U.S. Navy ap-

peared to have lost the battle of the Coral Sea. But the battle was an Allied victory because it turned back the Japanese expedition against Port Moresby and prevented air attacks on Australia. Several months later the Japanese would attempt to take Port Moresby by an overland route and would be decisively defeated. The damage to the *Shokaku* and the substantial loss of pilots and planes would prove fatal to the Japanese in the next carrier battle at MIDWAY.

Corkscrew

Code name for Allied occupation of the island of Pantelleria, June 11, 1943.

Cormorant,

see *KORMORAN.*

Corncobs

Code name for blockships used in constructing the Allied ARTIFICIAL HARBORS at Normandy.

Corncrake

Code name for operation in which the British submarine *Seadog* was to embark agents from the Norwegian coast, June 1943.

Corona

Operation Corona was the successful British use of "ghost controllers"—German-speaking persons at a radio station in Britain—to interfere with German ground controller sending instructions to night fighter pilots over Germany.

Coronado,

see PB2Y.

Coronet

Code name for planned Allied AMPHIBIOUS LANDINGS on Honshu, Japan, March 1946.

Corps

Intermediate command headquarters in the U.S. Army and Marine Corps, normally controlling three to six DIVISIONS. In the Army the corps was conceived as essentially a commander with a handful of staff officers to control combat operations. The assigned units varied with the tactical situation. In addition to divisions, corps were usually assigned a variety of specialized COMPANIES, BATTALIONS, and REGIMENTS, among them infantry, TANK, ARTILLERY, air defense, engineer, signal, military police, truck transport, maintenance, and medical. For example, in mid-1944 the Army's VII Corps, the largest in Normandy at the time, had assigned four infantry and two armored divisions plus twenty separate artillery battalions, five tank battalions, seven tank-destroyer battalions, eleven antiaircraft battalions, and numerous support units.

The authorized strength of a corps headquarters of the U.S. Army varied from 234 men in 1942 to 185 in 1945. The associated corps headquarters company (which provided personnel such as drivers, radio operators, and clerks) totaled 137 men in 1942 but only ninety-five in 1945. Separate combat and support units would boost the corps to many thousand men beyond the troop strength of its assigned divisions.

Army corps were commanded by a major general or lieutenant general and were assigned Roman numeral designations (e.g., II, V, X Corps).

The first U.S. Army corps to see combat as a full element was the II Corps, under Maj. Gen. GEORGE S. PATTON, for the March 1942 Allied offensive in the NORTHWEST AFRICA CAMPAIGN.

The corps-level organization of the U.S. Marine Corps was the amphibious corps, which had both operational and administration functions for AMPHIBIOUS LANDINGS. The Marine's I Amphibious Corps was activated in Nov. 1942 but did not plan and carry out a landing until the BOUGAINVILLE operation starting on Nov. 1, 1943. The I Amphibious Corps was subsequently redesignated III because it was to work primarily with the Navy's Third Fleet. The V Amphibious Corps—to work with the Fifth Fleet—was organized on Aug. 30, 1943. Both corps worked together in the June 1944 landings of the MARIANA ISLANDS, where the two amphibious corps jointly commanded three Marine and two Army divisions, and one Marine BRIGADE plus supporting units.

(As a result of command problems in the Marianas, in July 1944 Fleet Marine Force Pacific was established at PEARL HARBOR as the top-echelon Marine command in the Pacific area.) Marine amphibious corps were commanded by a major general or lieutenant general.

Corregidor

Fortified island at the entrance to MANILA Bay in the Philippines. Corregidor, the largest of fortified islands in the bay, had been equipped early in the twentieth century for harbor defense; most of its gun emplacement could face only westward, toward the sea.

After the Japanese invasion of the Philippines in Dec. 1941, Gen. DOUGLAS MACARTHUR, commander of both U.S. and Filipino forces in the Philippines, withdrew to the BATAAN peninsula. Under heavy Japanese assaults, the defenders were driven down the peninsula. MacArthur was ordered out of the Philippines and turned command over to newly promoted Lt. Gen. JONATHAN WAINWRIGHT. Starving and demoralized, they surrendered on April 9. From Bataan about 2,000 men and a few nurses made it to Corregidor, which lay about 3,500 yards off the tip of Bataan.

The Japanese had been bombing Corregidor steadily since December. Even before the surrender of Bataan, the invaders moved up heavy artillery to bombard the island; more guns arrived after the Bataan surrender. Many of the fortress guns could not turn to fire at the Japanese.

In Jan. 1942 the Corregidor garrison went on half-RATIONS. The arrival of Bataan survivors added to the plight of the fortress. Japanese bombers and guns pounded the island day and night, but the inhabitants, huddled in the rock-hewn tunnels of Corregidor, survived. A WAR CORRESPONDENT leaving the island told Wainwright he should leave, too. Wainwright reportedly replied, "I have been one of the 'battling bastards of Bataan' and I'll play the same role on The Rock as long as it is humanly possible."

The crescendo of bombs and shells increased on April 29, the birthday of Emperor HIROHITO and the launching of a preinvasion barrage. The Japanese landed on the island on the night of May 5.

Still Corregidor fought. Many of the defenders, untrained in combat, grabbed pistols or rifles and held off the invaders through the night. In the morning the Japanese brought in tanks and artillery, and Wainwright surrendered. He and 11,500 Americans and Filipinos on Corregidor became prisoners of war. He would survive the war. Many others would not, for the survivors of Corregidor and Bataan (see BATAAN DEATH MARCH) were among the most cruelly treated prisoners of the war.

After sustained air attacks and sea bombardment, Army AIRBORNE troops parachuted onto Corregidor in Feb. 1945 during the liberation of the Philippines. MacArthur returned to the island on March 2, 1945.

Corsair,
see F4U.

Corvettes
Highly effective British CONVOY escort ships. The corvettes were unglamorous workhorses of the BATTLE OF THE ATLANTIC. In the words of Chief Artificer Watts in NICHOLAS MONSARRAT's classic novel *The Cruel Sea,* "Whoever designed that ship must have been piss-arse drunk." (Monsarrat, who served in corvettes during the war, also told about these ships in his novel *Three Corvettes,* as well as in other works.)

These antisubmarine ships—primarily of the "Flower" class—were simple and quick to build. British and Canadian shipyards produced 159 of this class during the war, and from May 1940 onward they were the backbone of many convoy escort groups in the Atlantic. Thirty-five corvettes—22 percent of the class—were lost during the war to enemy attacks and collisions, some while under foreign flags. British naval historian S. W. Roskill

wrote about the corvettes, "It is hard to see how Britain could have survived without them." The Flower-class ships sank thirty-nine U-BOATS and three Italian submarines, and prevented many more U-boats from attacking convoys.

While most of these ships served in the Royal Navy, Canada sailed several and twenty-three went to other navies, most representing defeated countries operating from Britain—nine being manned by FREE FRENCH, one by Dutch, six by Norwegians, four by Greeks, one by Yugoslavs, and two by New Zealanders. Another ten British-built Flowers were acquired by the U.S. Navy in early 1942 under a "reverse" LEND-LEASE program in response to the German U-boat successes off the U.S. Atlantic coast, and eight more Canadian-built units entered U.S. service in 1943. (The latter were ordered by the U.S. Navy as were seven that, instead, were provided to Britain under Lend-Lease, further confusing those who keep track of warships.)

The first Flower-class corvette, the *Gladiolus,* was launched on Jan. 24, 1940, and placed in commission in April that year. The early ships had a standard displacement of 925 tons and were 205 feet long. They had reciprocating steam engines with the British-built ships burning coal and Canadian ships using oil. The maximum speed of these single-screw ships was 16 knots. Armament consisted of a single 4-inch gun, light antiaircraft weapons, and depth charges. Some ships were additionally fitted for minesweeping. The normal complement was eighty-five officers and ratings. The later Flower-class units were slightly larger (1,015 tons, 193 feet).

A subsequent forty-four corvettes of the "Castle" class were built. Their characteristics compensated for Flower-class shortfalls, the latter ships being longer (for better seakeeping), with more range, and larger crews. These ships were 1,060 to 1,100 tons, 252 feet long, and were manned by ninety-nine and later up to 120 officers and men.

After the war the surviving corvettes served in several Third World navies.

Costa Rica
Capital: San Jose, pop. 656,129 (1940). This republic was so pro-American that it declared war on Japan a few hours *before* the United States did, on

Dec. 8, 1941, following up with seizure of Japanese fishermen in Costa Rican territory and then declarations against Germany and Italy on Dec. 11. Costa Rica ended relations with Hungary and Rumania on May 15, 1942. One of the nation's most significant contributions to the war effort was its leaasing of land to the United States for the growing of cinchona trees, whose bark was used in the manufacture of quinine for prevention of malaria.

Cottage

Code name for U.S. invasion of Kiska, 1943.

Coventry

A British industrial city of about 125,000 people and a symbol of massive urban bombing. On the moonlit night of Nov. 14–15, 1940, a flight of 449 German bombers dropped 150,000 incendiary BOMBS and 503 tons of high explosives (1,400 bombs), and 130 parachute mines on Coventry. More than 550 people were killed and 1,000 injured; 50,749 houses were destroyed or damaged. The ruins of Coventry's St. Michael's Cathedral became a symbol of German ruthlessness. The destruction inspired the word *coventryize,* meaning reduce a city to rubble.

Given the concept of STRATEGIC BOMBING, Coventry was a potential target. Prime Minister CHURCHILL once said that more war matériel was produced per square yard in Coventry than in any other city in England. But the Germans admitted that the heavy raid, code-named Moonlight Sonata, was in retaliation for an RAF bombing of Munich on Nov. 8.

Because the Royal Air Force had advance knowledge of a raid that night, several postwar accounts of the bombing suggested that Churchill, aware that Coventry was to be attacked, had to make an agonizing decision: He could inform Coventry officials so that at least a partial evacuation could be made. But that would reveal the existence of ULTRA, the super-secret decoding of German communications. So, the story went, Churchill decided to preserve the secret of Ultra at the cost of sacrificing Coventry.

The story was based on postwar revelations about the RAF's ability to detect and understand a German navigational system known as *Knickebein*

(crooked leg). A transmitter in Europe sent out a continuous, narrow-beam signal that served as a pathway for Luftwaffe bombers. A signal from a second site crossed the first at the place that was the target. The beams thus produced electronic cross hairs for the bombers.

RAF intelligence analysts could read the cross hairs and anticipate the site of a raid. Once the continually changing frequencies of the *Knickebein* were determined, they could be jammed or mimicked, sending the bombers off course. As Nigel West explains it in *A Thread of Deceit,* his authoritative book on "ESPIONAGE myths" of the war, by about 3 P.M. on Nov. 14 RAF intelligence knew that the two beams were intersecting over Coventry. Other intelligence sources, however, indicated that LONDON or a nearby area was the target.

Churchill, according to West, was told that the raid was "probably in the vicinity of London, but if further information indicates Coventry, Birmingham or elsewhere, we hope to get instructions out in time."

The jammers were confident that they could deflect the bombers. Churchill, West writes, "had good reason to believe that adequate counter-measures were available: so far as he knew, the German bombs would fall, but on empty fields."

But the wrong frequency was given and the jamming, unknown to RAF intelligence at the time, did not work. The raid went on as planned. As for Ultra, the word *Coventry* never appeared on an interception.

Crabb, Lt. Comdr. Lionel (1910–1956)

One of the Royal Navy's best-known underwater SABOTAGE experts and divers. Known by the nickname "Buster," when the war began he was a merchant seaman. In 1940 he joined the Royal Navy Patrol Service and was given a commission in 1941. His health, however, prevented him from going to sea. He was then assigned to BOMB DISPOSAL and while at GIBRALTAR in 1942 he began working with divers against Italian frogmen and HUMAN TORPEDOES attempting to attack British ships.

He left the Navy in 1948 but returned to active duty in diving work from 1952 to 1955. Reportedly in April 1956, on a secret mission for MI6, Crabb dived into Portsmouth Harbor to spy on the Soviet light cruiser *Ordzhonikidze,* which had brought NIKITA KHRUSHCHEV and N. A. Bulganin to England. His headless body was later found floating in the harbor.

Crete

A mountainous Greek island, 160 miles long and 6 to 35 miles wide, 60 miles southeast of the Greek mainland. After the German conquest of mainland Greece in the BALKANS-GREECE-CRETE CAMPAIGN of 1941, Crete became the next objective. About 27,000 British, Australian, and New Zealand troops, with little equipment, were evacuated from Greece to Crete in April 1941 under heavy Luftwaffe air attack. These BRITISH COMMONWEALTH forces supplemented about 28,000 British troops already on Crete.

The Germans controlled the air but not the sea. Unwilling to risk a major AMPHIBIOUS LANDING, German strategists accepted the idea of *Generaloberst* KURT STUDENT, commander of German AIRBORNE forces. Student's plan called for a paratroop-and-GLIDER operation code-named *Merkur* (Mercury). It would be history's first airborne assault without land or sea support.

For three weeks more than 700 Greece-based German fighters and bombers, flying up to 300 sorties a day, strafed and bombed Crete's three airfields. After this intensive aerial bombardment, on the morning of May 20, 1941, in a three-pronged airborne assault, 2,000 to 3,000 German paratroopers were dropped on each airfield. Most of the first wave of paratroops were killed as they descended or on the ground as they attempted to assemble against a ferocious defense. Paratroopers at Máleme airfield in western Crete were pinned down and threatened with annihilation when Student sent in his last airborne units to take the airfield.

The British commander at the Máleme airfield withdrew his men and sent them to fight a nearby pocket of invaders. The break in defense at the airfield gave the Germans the chance to land reinforcements both at the airfield and, by gliders, on a nearby beach. The Germans took the airfield and in a week landed most of a mountain division and the rest of a parachute division, putting all of 22,750 men into the battle. Aided by an intense aerial bom-

bardment, the Germans mounted a determined assault on the northern coast port of Canea on Suda Bay, inflicting heavy casualties.

The British-led forces retreated over the mountains to the south coast port of Sfakia, where 18,-000 troops were evacuated; about 13,000 were captured. During the battle the Royal Navy fought to keep German troops from reaching the island by ship or landing craft. German JU 87 *STUKA* dive bombers badly damaged the aircraft carrier *Formidable* (see HANS GEISLER). The Royal Navy lost three cruisers and six destroyers off Crete, and other ships were damaged during the battle and the evacuation that followed.

The Germans suffered nearly 4,000 dead and 2,600 wounded; 170 transport aircraft and most of the German gliders were destroyed, along with a few combat aircraft. More than 3,000 of the German dead and 2,000 of the wounded were from the parachute division and support units. The loss in specialized airborne personnel was so great that the Luftwaffe would never again stage a major airborne assault.

Cricket

Code name for Malta portion of the ARGONAUT Conference.

Cromwell

Code name for British alarm signal for the German invasion of Britain in 1940 (formerly the code name was Caesar). A Cromwell alert was issued by the headquarters of the British Home Forces on the night of Sept. 7, 1940, during the BATTLE OF BRITAIN. The decision to bring British defensive forces to a higher state of alert was made at a meeting of the CHIEFS OF STAFF at which Prime Minister CHURCHILL presided. It followed a heavy German bombing raid and sightings of German craft off Calais. The alert remained in force until Sept. 19.

Crossbow

Code name for RAF operations against German V-weapons, 1944.

Crossroads,

see ATOMIC BOMB TESTS.

Crossword,

see SUNRISE.

Cruisers

When the Japanese struck at PEARL HARBOR on Dec. 7, 1941, the U.S. Navy had eighteen heavy cruisers (CA) armed with 8-inch guns and nine light cruisers (CL) with 6-inch guns, all of relatively modern design. In addition, there were ten older scout cruisers (CL) with 6-inch guns. Several additional cruisers were under construction.

Cruisers were in most theaters where U.S. naval forces saw action. Their roles included screening AIRCRAFT CARRIERS and BATTLESHIPS, independent cruiser-destroyer operations, and shore bombardment. On Dec. 24, 1941, the Navy commissioned the first antiaircraft cruiser, the *Atlanta* (CLAA 51). That ship was smaller than contemporary cruisers, displacing 6,000 tons standard with a length of 541 feet. Her main armament was sixteen 5-inch dual-purpose guns in twin mounts, which were highly effective for the antiaircraft defense of surface ships.

The largest U.S. warships in the Far East when the war began were the heavy cruiser *HOUSTON* (CA 30) and the scout cruiser *Marblehead* (CL 12). The *Houston* was sunk by the Japanese in the battle of JAVA SEA on Feb. 28, 1942. The *Marblehead*, although damaged, survived the Japanese onslaught; because the Japanese controlled Far Eastern waters, the *Marblehead* was forced to sail westward, making an around-the-world cruise to return to the United States.

The worst night of the war for U.S. cruisers occurred on the night of Aug. 8–9, 1942, in the battle of SAVO ISLAND in the SOLOMON ISLANDS when a Japanese cruiser-destroyer force sank three U.S. heavy cruisers with heavy loss of life, as well as a U.S. destroyer and an Australian cruiser. The last cruiser sunk was the *INDIANAPOLIS* (CA 35), which was torpedoed by a Japanese submarine on July 30, 1945, after delivering components for the ATOMIC BOMB to TINIAN.

Total U.S. cruiser losses during the war were seven of the prewar "heavies" (CA) and one light cruiser (CL). Two of the antiaircraft cruisers were also sunk, the *Atlanta* and *Juneau* (CLAA 52), both going down in the Solomons in Nov. 1942, the latter with the five SULLIVAN BROTHERS on board. No war-built heavy or light cruisers were sunk during the war other than these two CLAAs. From 1942 through 1945 U.S. shipyards delivered thirteen heavy cruisers, twenty-five light cruisers, and eight antiaircraft ships. (Two "large" or battle cruisers were also completed; see BATTLESHIPS). Thus, at the end of the war the Navy had in service seventy cruisers of the CA-CL-CLAA categories.

Crusader

Code name for British offensive in the western desert, North Africa, Nov. 1941.

Crux III

British code name for the transfer of agents and supplies from the submarine *Seanymph* to a Norwegian fishing vessel for landing on the Norwegian coast, Jan. 1944.

Cryptography

All the major belligerents tried to protect their communications by encoding or enciphering them. In the cryptography war within the war itself, the ALLIES clearly won.

Both ULTRA and MAGIC, the principal Allied code-breaking achievements, "were undoubtedly responsible for major, even crucial strategic success," historian John Keegan writes in *The Second World War*. He cites MIDWAY, EL ALAMEIN, and the entire ALLIED CAMPAIGN IN EUROPE as the most important examples of victory through code-breaking. "Twenty years after the war was over, when their German opponents discovered that their most secret correspondence had been read daily by the British and Americans," Keegan writes, "they were struck speechless."

In the BATTLE OF THE ATLANTIC both sides used cryptography as a weapon. The Germans' *Beobachtung-Dienst* (Observer Service) was reading much of the Royal Navy's radio traffic until the British Admiralty adopted the cipher machine used by the U.S. and Canadian Navies. The British, through the Government Code and Cipher School at BLETCHLEY PARK'S use of ENIGMA machines, were able to read some German traffic, though an additional "Shark" code key used by U-BOATS took extra cracking.

RAF Group Capt. F. W. Winterbotham, who was in charge of the security and dissemination of the Ultra signal intercepts, noted in *The Ultra Secret* that code-breaking did more than reveal the enemy's intentions. "Over the years of reading the signals of HITLER, RUNDSTEDT, ROMMEL, KESSELRING, and other German commanders in Europe, most of us who were closely connected with this miracle source, as WINSTON CHURCHILL called it, obtained a fairly complete insight into the way their minds worked, of the attitudes of the various generals toward Hitler, and of the reasons behind their various appreciations . . . as to when and where we were going to operate. These latter gave us the priceless opportunities to mis-guide them about our operations with our deception plans."

Cuba

Capital: Havana pop. 4,778,583 (1943). Strongman Fulgencio Batista, chief of the Cuban Army and leader of the "sergeants' revolt" of 1933, emerged from behind the throne and became president in 1940. He immediately legalized a pro-Fascist organization linked with Generalissimo FRANCISCO FRANCO of Spain. But fears of pro-German leanings were dispelled when the governor of Havana dissolved the Cuban NAZI party and when Cuba shipped a substantial gift of sugar to British civilians.

In Feb. 1941 Cuba ordered all German and Italian consular officials out of the country. Cuba declared war on Japan on Dec. 8, 1941, on Germany and Italy on Dec. 11, and, following the U.S. lead, ended relations with VICHY FRANCE on Nov. 10, 1942.

Cuba signed a military agreement with the United States, allowing the use of airfields for U.S. warplanes, and signed a mutual defense pact with Mexico for defense against U-BOATS. U.S. officials suspected that German U-boats were using remote Cuban bays as bases and rendezvous. But, according to historian SAMUEL ELIOT MORISON, Cuba, "which had a small fleet of gunboats and patrol craft, was the most cooperative and helpful of all the Caribbean states. The Cuban Navy took care of its

own coastal shipping and participated in escorting the seatrains from port Everglades [Fla.] to Havana."

Rumors persisted throughout the war, and afterward, that U-boats refueled and took on supplies in secluded coves. In reality, the lack of such bases in Latin America forced the German Navy to develop supply submarines, the MILCH COWS.

Cudgel

Code name for plan for small-scale landing on Arakan coast, Burma.

Culverin

Code name for planned Allied operations against western Sumatra and Malaya, 1944.

Cunningham, Adm. of the Fleet Andrew Browne (1883–1963)

One of Britain's most distinguished naval officers in the war and served effectively as naval deputy to Gen. DWIGHT D. EISENHOWER. Adm. Cunningham (Viscount Cunningham of Hyndhope) was Commander in Chief Mediterranean when the war began in Europe.

His triumphs as CinC Mediterranean included the carrier-based air attack on TARANTO on Nov. 11, 1940, that sank or damaged three Italian battleships and the battle of Cape Matapan in March 1941 in which three Italian cruisers were sunk and the Italian fleet demoralized for the rest of the war. The most trying times for Cunningham were the two-year-long siege of MALTA and the evacuations of Greece and CRETE in April and May of 1941, respectively. Of the high cost in lost ships and men off Crete, Cunningham told his staff: "It takes the Navy three years to build a ship. It would take three hundred years to build a new reputation. The evacuation will continue."

In Nov. 1942 he was appointed Naval Commander in Chief Allied Expeditionary Force, North Africa and Mediterranean—in effect naval deputy to Gen. Eisenhower—a post he held through the NORTH AFRICA INVASION, the invasion of SICILY, and the launching of the ITALIAN CAMPAIGN. Cunningham proved successful as a partner in the Anglo-American coalition in the Mediterranean.

He and Gen. Eisenhower appear to have had a genuinely warm regard for each other. Cunningham, reputed to have had a temper like a squall line, was also known for a broad sense of humor. When Adm. Sir James Somerville was invested in his second chivalric order, Cunningham signaled: "Congratulations. Fancy twice a Knight at your age." Angry about bad intelligence he had been given, he once signaled, "Drive a long hat pin into the stern of the officer responsible for reporting merchant shipping movements."

In Oct. 1943 he was appointed First Sea Lord and Chief of Naval Staff, the senior officer of the Royal Navy, a post he held until June 1946. As First Sea Lord he directed the Royal Navy in fighting the German U-BOATS in the Atlantic as well as providing forces to combat the Japanese Navy in the Pacific, while on another level combating WINSTON CHURCHILL, that "former naval person" who took a strong, personal interest in Royal Navy matters.

Adm. Cunningham supported his subordinates, junior officers, and men in a manner that attracted reverent loyalty from virtually all. He is said to have had few peers as a shiphandler, whether a single ship or an entire fleet.

Cunningham, Adm. of the Fleet Sir John D. (1885–1962)

British naval officer who succeeded Adm. A. B. Cunningham (no relation) as Commander in Chief Mediterranean.

Cunningham in July 1940 led the British naval forces supporting the attempt of Gen. CHARLES DE GAULLE to assault the VICHY FRANCE naval base at DAKAR in West Africa. Although the operation failed, Prime Minister CHURCHILL was pleasantly surprised when Cunningham argued for carrying out the operation even after several French cruisers eluded British forces and reinforced Dakar. Commenting on Cunningham's "evident zeal," Churchill said: "It was very rare at this stage of the war for commanders on the spot to press for audacious courses."

Cunningham later moved to the Admiralty, becoming Fourth Sea Lord. After two years of staff duty, he was appointed Commander in Chief Levant (Eastern Mediterranean) in late 1942 and then became CinC of the Mediterranean Fleet in Sept. 1943. Adm. A. B. Cunningham, whom Sir John replaced, commented that his successor was "the only man I ever met whose memory compared with Winston's [Churchill]."

When Cunningham took command the Mediterranean Fleet was supporting ground forces in Italy and prosecuting the antisubmarine campaign. In one of his first tasks, he gave naval support for the reoccupation of the Dodecanese Islands in the Aegean Sea in Oct.–Nov. 1943, a campaign that ultimately failed. Much later, an associate believed that Cunningham's participation in the defeats in Norway, Dakar, and the Dodecanese made him "very cautious, cynical and suspicious of adventure."

Cunningham was dubious about the AMPHIBIOUS LANDING at ANZIO in Jan. 1944. The logistics two weeks after the landing required 21,940 vehicles (including 380 tanks)—or 315 LANDING SHIPS, TANK (LST) loads—on the compact and congested beaches to support 70,000 men. But he gave unflinching support at Anzio and to other Allied requirements during his tenure.

Cutthroat

U.S. code name for intensive, three-day attack by AAF fighters and medium bombers against the Shaggy Ridge area of NEW BRITAIN in support of Australian ground troops, Jan. 18–20, 1944.

Cycle

Code name for evacuation of British and French troops from Havre, France, June 1940.

Cyclone

Code name for Allied task force for Noemfoor Island, in Southwest Pacific, June 1944.

Czechoslovakia

Capital: Prague, pop. 15,167,800 (1937). Created in World War I from territory of the Austro-Hungarian monarchy, Czechoslovakia in the prelude to World War II became the victim of the 1938 MUNICH PACT and a lasting symbol of appeasement to HITLER'S territorial demands. Czechoslovakia lost to Germany, as a result of the pact, about 11,000 square miles, the Sudetenland, where some 3,000,000 ethnic Germans lived. Also taken, by German estimates, were 66 percent of Czechoslovakia's coal, 86 percent of its chemicals, 70 percent of its iron and steel, and 70 percent of its electric power.

Czechoslovakia kept on losing territory—to Poland, to Hungary, and finally, once more to Germany. On March 15, 1939, after Germany threatened an air raid on Prague, Czechoslovakia agreed to hand over the two western provinces of Bohemia and Moravia, which, under German pressure, seceded from Czechoslovakia to form what the Germans called the Protectorate of Bohemia and Moravia. Subsequently forced to grant autonomy to Slovakia and the Carpathian Ukraine, Czechoslovakia ceased to exist as a country. Czech army officers and enlisted men slipped into Poland, where a Czech and Slovak Legion fought the Germans on Polish soil when the EUROPEAN WAR began on Sept. 1, 1939.

The German puppet state of Slovakia was established with Father Josef Tiso, a Roman Catholic priest and a Czech NAZI, as head of state. The Slovakia government enacted the most severe laws against JEWS of any country except Germany. About 70,000 Slovakian Jews died, many in CONCENTRATION CAMPS in Poland and Germany.

A Reich protector was appointed over Bohemia and Moravia, the remaining Czech army was disarmed and demobilized, and Germany began a systematic transformation of the country into a German state. Czech national monuments were taken down, the names of historic marketplaces were changed to HERMANN GÖRING and Adolf Hitler Squares; the singing of traditional Czech songs was forbidden.

Czechs reacted with demonstrations, underground resistance, and student uprisings. The Nazis arrested hundreds, executed uprising leaders, closed universities, and appointed REINHARD HEYDRICH, chief of the REICH CENTRAL SECURITY OFFICE, as deputy protector. Unleashing GESTAPO agents, he began a reign of terror that was only intensified after his ASSASSINATION. (See LIDICE.)

In April 1944, when word reached underground leaders that Soviet forces were nearing the Carpathian Ukraine border, GUERRILLAS intensified their SABOTAGE and harassment of German occupiers. In October the Soviet troops, with Free Czech units among them, reached Bohemia from the east while U.S. and British forces approached from the west. (See ALLIED CAMPAIGN IN EUROPE.) On May 4, resistance fighters in Prague rose and with the aid of a onetime German unit under turncoat Soviet Lt. Gen. ANDREI A. VLASOV, drove the Germans from the city.

With the liberating troops came Czech civilian administrators dispatched by the government in exile in London. EDUARD BENEŠ, who had resigned as president of Czechoslovakia after the Munich Pact, returned to Prague in May 1945 and began organizing a postwar government. Beneš authorized the expulsion of Germans from what had been the Sudetenland and Hungarians from what had been Slovakia. Hundreds of thousands died as they fled or were forcibly driven to the British occupation zone in Germany.

The YALTA CONFERENCE had promised that liberated Czechoslovakia would get an interim government that was "broadly representative of all democratic elements" and pledged to free elections. But Czechoslovakia became a Soviet satellite state and, after the selection of Beneš in 1946 there would be no free elections until the peaceful overthrow of Communist governments in 1989.

Dachau

A CONCENTRATION CAMP in Bavaria, ten miles from Munich (and like all concentration camps and DEATH CAMPS named for the nearest town). The SS considered Dachau a model for those that followed. Founded in March 1933 by SS chief HEINRICH HIMMLER, it became a training ground for SS officers and men assigned to other camps. Among Dachau's prisoners were Polish priests, who were seen to be obstacles to the conversion of Poland to a German fiefdom. About 850 priests died there.

Dachau was also the site of sadistic and usually lethal "medical experiments" on prisoners (see DOCTORS TRIAL) and what were called "leather inspections" of dead prisoners to see whether their skin was worth tanning. According to testimony at the WAR CRIMES trials at Nuremberg, the bodies were flayed, the skin "chemically treated, and placed in the sun to dry. After that it was cut into various sizes for use as saddles, riding breeches, gloves, house slippers, and ladies' handbags. Tattooed skin was especially valued by SS men."

The Czech doctor who testified said that when there were not enough bodies for good leather, an order would be given for more bodies. "The next day," he went on, "we would receive twenty or thirty bodies of young people. They would have been shot in the neck or struck on the head so that the skin would be uninjured."

The crematorium at Dachau was reopened after the war to cremate the bodies of the ten major NAZI war criminals found guilty and hanged at Nurem-

Sailors aboard the carrier *Hornet* (CV 8) cheer as another B-25B Mitchell bomber takes off for the Doolittle Raid against Japanese cities. The April 1942 raid—announced to the press by President Roosevelt—had an important psychological impact on an American public weary of reports of defeats. *(U.S. Navy)*

berg, along with the body of HERMANN GÖRING, who killed himself on the eve of his execution.

Dakar

Capital of French West Africa and an important port, equidistant from Brazil and Europe. Because France's African colonies were under the control of VICHY FRANCE, some Allied strategists saw Dakar as a potential German U-BOAT base. Soon after France surrendered in June 1940, the Royal Navy attacked and seriously damaged the French battleship *Richelieu* in Dakar. On Sept. 23, 1940, in Operation Menace, Royal Navy warships escorted ships carrying Gen. CHARLES DE GAULLE, the leader of the FREE FRENCH, and about 2,500 Free French troops for a landing at Dakar. But the operation was a debacle. The Royal Navy at GIBRALTAR had failed to intercept French warships that sailed from Toulon and entered Dakar harbor. Several British warships were damaged in exchanges of gunfire with shore batteries aided by the guns of the damaged *Richelieu*. The landing operation was abandoned on Sept. 25.

Dakota,

see C-47 SKYTRAIN/DAKOTA.

Daladier, Édouard (1884–1970)

French statesman. Twice a short-term premier of France (ten months in 1933, a few days in 1934) and minister of defense, he formed a shaky government in April 1938 and took part in the negotiations leading to French-British appeasement of Germany and the MUNICH PACT, which the two countries signed with Germany and Italy on Sept. 28, 1938. In the face of criticism, Daladier said that he signed the pact unwillingly. His wartime Cabinet, formed in Sept. 1939, fell on March 20, 1940, but he stayed on as minister of war.

Arrested by the collaborationist VICHY FRANCE regime, he was turned over to the Germans. After the war he testified in the trial of Marshal HENRI PHILIPPE PÉTAIN, charging that collaborationists had been plotting with NAZIS since 1934.

Dampfhammer (Steam Hammer)

Variation of *Blau*.

Darlan, Adm. Jean François (1881–1942)

French naval officer and politician. When the EUROPEAN WAR began, Adm. Darlan was Commander in Chief of the French Navy. At the time of France's surrender, he hinted that he would order the French fleet to British ports, leading British Prime Minister CHURCHILL later to say, "If I could meet Darlan, much as I hate him, I would cheerfully crawl on my hands and knees for a mile if by doing so I could get him to bring that fleet of his into the circle of Allied forces." But Darlan became Navy Minister in the VICHY FRANCE regime, collaborated with France's German conquerors, and sent most of the French fleet to French North Africa, where the Royal Navy later attacked them.

Darlan was commander of all Vichy French military forces when Anglo-American forces launched the NORTH AFRICA INVASION on Nov. 8, 1942. On that day, unknown to the Allied leadership, Darlan happened to be in Algiers visiting his critically ill son. The Anglo-American allies had been counting on French Gen. HENRI-HONORÉ GIRAUD to aid them with the French authorities in North Africa, but when Lt. Gen. DWIGHT D. EISENHOWER learned of Darlan's presence, he had U.S. diplomat ROBERT D. MURPHY and Maj. Gen. MARK CLARK begin negotiating with Darlan, while virtually placing him under house arrest.

After vacillating between cooperating with the Allies and heeding orders from Vichy, on Nov. 13 he finally signed a cease-fire agreement and was rewarded with the title of French governor in Africa. Allied negotiations with a collaborationist touched off an uproar in the United States and England. President ROOSEVELT attempted to put down the protests by quoting a Russian proverb: "My children, it is permitted you in time of grave danger to walk with the devil until you have crossed the bridge."

A young gunman, Bonnier de la Chapelle, long afterward identified as a follower of Gen. CHARLES DE GAULLE and a monarchist, killed Darlan on Dec. 24, 1942. De la Chapelle was quickly tried and executed under orders of Darlan's successor, Gen. Giraud. In 1945 the Gaullist government "annulled" the conviction, posthumously clearing de la

Chapelle's name, but leaving the circumstances of the ASSASSINATION still unrevealed.

Dauntless,
see SBD.

Davis, Brig. Gen. Benjamin O. (1877–1970)

First black general officer in the U.S. armed forces. Davis served as a lieutenant of Volunteers in 1898–1899, after which he enlisted in the U.S. Army. He was subsequently commissioned and in 1911–1912 was U.S. military attaché in Liberia. Davis subsequently served mainly in instructor positions. He was promoted to brigadier general in Oct. 1940 and in 1941 was assigned as an assistant to the inspector general of the Army.

The first black general officer in the U.S. armed forces was Benjamin O. Davis, who served on Gen. Dwight D. Eisenhower's staff as his adviser for "Negro troops." Davis helped to provide black soldiers to combat units that were desperately short of riflemen in the fighting in northwestern Europe in 1944–1945. (*U.S. Army*)

In 1942 Davis was sent to England where he became the special adviser and coordinator on black (then called Negro) troops to the theater commander, Gen. DWIGHT D. EISENHOWER. Davis' role was particularly important after the ARDENNES battle because of the dire shortage of infantrymen in U.S. Army units in Europe and the need for black combat troops. (See SEGREGATION.)

Davis, Lt. Col. Benjamin O., Jr. (1912—)

Commanding officer, of the 99th Pursuit (later Fighter) SQUADRON, the first all-black unit in the Army Air Forces. (See SEGREGATION.) Davis, who in 1936 was the first black graduate of the U.S. Military Academy in nearly fifty years, was the son of an officer who in 1940 would, as a brigadier general, become the U.S. Army's highest ranking black officer.

The younger Davis was one of the BLACK EAGLES in a wartime black airman training program at the Tuskegee Institute in Alabama, a black school founded by Booker T. Washington. As a lieutenant colonel Davis took the squadron to North Africa in April 1943. He returned to the United States to supervise the training of the 332nd Fighter Group. On March 24, 1945, the 332nd, with Col. Davis leading, flew cover for Fifteenth Air Force B-17 FLYING FORTRESS bombers during a 1,600-mile round-trip attack on BERLIN.

Davis won the Distinguished Flying Cross during the war. After the war he became the nation's first black major general in 1959 and the first black lieutenant general in 1965, serving as deputy commander in chief of the U.S. Strike Command when he retired in 1970.

Davis, Elmer (1890–1958)

Director of the OFFICE OF WAR INFORMATION (OWI). President ROOSEVELT appointed Davis, a popular radio commentator and writer, director of the OWI on June 13, 1942. The move clearly put control of war news and PROPAGANDA in the hands of a civilian and a journalist.

Davis was a well-known figure in the relatively new medium of radio journalism. After twenty years on *The New York Times,* in 1924 Davis had become a free-lance journalist. In 1939 he became a commentator for the Columbia Broadcasting Corporation.

Davis' mandate gave him control over dissemination of official news within the United States and all other parts of the world except Latin America. That was the exclusive realm of Nelson A. Rockefeller, Coordinator of Inter-American Affairs.

Davis struggled with the military over the issue of news management. He followed his instinct, honed by a long journalistic career, to keep government out of the news business. As a result, news CENSORSHIP was essentially voluntary; WAR CORRESPONDENTS, while under military control on the battlefield, wrote freely; government-inspired PROPAGANDA was minimal.

Even a little propaganda was too much for many people, and Davis often was at odds with Congressmen who suspected he was a New Deal propagandist posing as a wartime patriot. During one of his battles with Congress he remarked that JOSEPH GOEBBELS, Germany's propaganda chief, at least did not have to go to the Reichstag for funds.

President TRUMAN abolished the OWI on Aug. 31, 1945, handing its mission over to the State Department. Davis resigned Sept. 12 and soon resumed his career as a radio commentator.

Daylight Saving Time,

see WAR TIME.

D-Day

Day designated as the start of an Allied military operation. The most famous D-Day was the NORMANDY INVASION on June 6, 1944.

de Gaulle, Gen. Charles (1890–1970)

French Army officer who emerged from France's defeat as her supreme statesman. An infantry officer who was decorated and captured in World War I, he became a student of war, developing new doctrines that clashed with military articles of faith. One of his books, *The Army of the Future,* recommended dynamic, offensive strategies and swift-moving mechanized forces. At the time, France was building the expensive MAGINOT LINE, and his ideas were rejected by both military men and French politicians.

The tall, patrician de Gaulle never underestimated himself. When he was a student at the *Ecole de Guerre* military college, a classmate said to him, "I have a curious feeling that you are intended for a very great destiny."

"Yes," de Gaulle replied. "So have I."

When the EUROPEAN WAR began in Sept. 1939 with Germany's BLITZKRIEG smashing through Poland, de Gaulle was theoretically commander of tanks in the French Fifth Army, but under the army command structure, the operational use of the tanks was outside of his authority. After Germany's swift and victorious POLAND CAMPAIGN, de Gaulle's superiors partially accepted his recommendations and put him in command of an armored division. At forty-nine he was the youngest general in the French Army. His division launched one of the few offensives against Germany's FRANCE AND LOW COUNTRIES CAMPAIGN.

On June 6, 1940, two days after the massive Allied evacuation at DUNKIRK, de Gaulle became under secretary of state to the minister of national defense and war. By then Marshal HENRI PÉTAIN, de Gaulle's idol and mentor since World War I, had succeeded PAUL REYNAUD as French Premier. On June 9 de Gaulle went to LONDON to confer with Prime Minister CHURCHILL about coordinating the strategy of the two countries' armies. When de Gaulle returned to PARIS, the government was leaving. He pleaded that Pétain stand and fight in France or evacuate French troops to French North Africa and fight on from there.

But Pétain was on the verge of surrendering and the French Army was collapsing. De Gaulle returned to London and on June 18, in a stirring speech broadcast to France by BBC, insisted that "France is not alone!" De Gaulle was charged with TREASON and condemned to death by the VICHY FRANCE, the collaborationist regime. Acting on his own, infuriating Churchill, de Gaulle became a power unto himself. "I am France!" he proclaimed and created an exile force, the FREE FRENCH movement, which evolved into the Free French National Council.

Another movement arose in French North Africa, where, after the NORTH AFRICA INVASION and the ASSASSINATION of Adm. JEAN DARLAN, de Gaulle negotiated a power-sharing arrangement with Gen. HENRI GIRAUD. They became the co-presidents of the a new organization, the French Committee of National Liberation. Some deft maneuvering produced Giraud's ouster and de Gaulle became the leader of both the Free French in North Africa and the FRENCH RESISTANCE in German-occupied France.

As the NORMANDY INVASION was about to be launched, de Gaulle demanded that his provisional government be declared the government of all liberated areas in France. Gen. DWIGHT D. EISENHOWER settled the controversy by promising not to accept any political entity except de Gaulle's, and de Gaulle was made Supreme Commander of the French Armed Forces. On Aug. 26, 1944, de Gaulle entered Paris in triumph behind French and American troops.

After Germany's defeat, de Gaulle was elected interim president of the provisional government by a newly elected constitutional assembly. He tried to make France a major participant in Allied postwar planning. But Churchill, President ROOSEVELT, and Soviet leader JOSEF STALIN did not invite de Gaulle to the YALTA CONFERENCE.

De Gaulle resigned as provisional president on Jan. 20, 1946. He returned to politics in 1958 and became president of France, remaining in that post until 1969 when, over a trivial political matter, he resigned. He died the following year and President George Pompidou said, "France is a widow."

de Lattre de Tassigny, Gen. Jean-Marie (1889–1952)

Senior FREE FRENCH field commander. A CAVALRY officer in World War I, de Lattre changed to infantry after the war and saw combat in Morocco before becoming a staff officer. During the May–June 1940 FRANCE AND LOW COUNTRIES CAMPAIGN he commanded first a brigade and then the 14th Infantry Division, which fought successfully against Gen. HEINZ GUDERIAN'S PANZERS.

After the French capitulation de Lattre was given a command in the small VICHY FRENCH forces. In Nov. 1942 he attempted to stop the German occupation of Vichy France, but was arrested. He escaped and reached North Africa in the fall of 1943. Offering his services to Gen. CHARLES DE GAULLE, he was given command of the First French Army,

numbering some 250,000 men in mid-1945. He led the Army in the Aug. 15, 1944, invasion of southern France and then fought through the remainder of the ALLIED CAMPAIGN IN EUROPE. He signed the German SURRENDER documents on behalf of France on May 8, 1945.

After the war de Lattre held senior French and NATO posts, and was high commissioner and CinC of French forces in Indochina in 1950–1952. Illness forced his retirement shortly before his death in Jan. 1952. He was posthumously promoted to marshal of France.

de Seversky, Maj. Alexander P. (1894–1974)

Leading advocate of air power in the war period. De Seversky was a Russian fighter pilot with thirteen aerial victories in World War I as well as an author, test pilot, aircraft designer, and inventor.

Born in Russia, he attended the Naval Academy and trained as a pilot. On his first mission against the Germans in World War I his plane was hit by enemy fire, apparently causing a BOMB to become "hung up" on his aircraft; when he brought the plane down at sea the bomb exploded. Although he lost a leg in the accident, de Seversky was allowed to return to flying duty. He subsequently shot down thirteen German aircraft in aerial combat.

Late in the war he was assigned to the Russian Embassy in WASHINGTON and after the 1917 Revolution he chose to remain in the United States. Befriending Brig. Gen. William (Billy) Mitchell and other air power advocates, he became a leading spokesman for military aviation. De Seversky also helped to develop in-flight refueling techniques and gyroscopically stabilized aircraft instruments and bombsights. In the 1930s he organized the Seversky Aircraft Corp., which later became Republic Aviation; he test-flew his own prototype aircraft, setting speed records and in 1937 winning the coveted Bendix Cup in a transcontinental race and in 1938 and 1939 the Harmon Trophy, the latter presented to him by President ROOSEVELT.

His book *Victory Through Air Power,* published in 1942, urged America to concentrate on aviation to defeat the AXIS. It also called for a separate U.S. air force and a unified high command after the war. Walt Disney made the book into a movie, and a print was flown to the QUEBEC CONFERENCE in 1943 at Prime Minister CHURCHILL'S request for viewing by President Roosevelt and the COMBINED CHIEFS OF STAFF.

Late in the war he became a personal consultant to Secretary of War ROBERT P. PATTERSON and was his representative at the ATOMIC BOMB TESTS for Bikini in 1946. After the war, de Seversky lectured at war colleges and seminars in the United States and abroad, preaching the dogma of air power.

In the 1950s de Seversky warned that the Soviet Union was outstripping the United States in space activities, while his books *Air Power, Key to Survival* (1950) and *America—Too Young to Die!* (1961) continued to advocate the use of aviation (and space) for America's first line of defense.

de Valera, Eamon (1882–1975)

New York–born Irish politician. De Valera, an Irish revolutionary, in 1916 survived the abortive Easter Week Rising against British control of Ireland. Sentenced to life imprisonment, he was released in a year and was soon arrested for again fomenting revolution. He escaped to the United States, where he raised funds as the elected president of the unrecognized Irish Republic. He resigned as president when the Irish Parliament (the Dáil Eiraenn) accepted the Anglo-Irish Treaty of London in 1921, ending the revolt against the British but touching off a civil war. Republicans, allied with the terrorists of the Irish Republic Army, opposed any agreement that allowed the six northern counties to remain under British control. (These counties form what became the United Kingdom's Northern Ireland.)

De Valera returned to power in 1932 and introduced a constitution that abolished the Irish Free State and created the Republic of Eire (Ireland). He served as president of the executive council and minister for external affairs from 1932 to 1937. He became prime minister in 1937 and remained in that office, through many crises brought about by his policy of Irish neutrality, until 1948. He was president of Ireland from 1959 to 1973.

Deadlight

Allied code name for the scuttling of German U-BOATS in the Atlantic after the war.

Death Camps

Several sites where the NAZIS carried out the FINAL SOLUTION—the attempt to exterminate all JEWS. CONCENTRATION CAMPS, built for holding prisoners, were not death camps by design, although millions died in them of starvation, disease, torture, and execution. Death camps were specifically intended for the systematic mass murder of Jews, along with another detested minority—Gypsies—and thousands of non-Jews, including homosexuals. The Nazis called the camps *Vernichtungslager*, extermination camps. At least 5,000,000 people were killed in the camps.

The largest death camp was AUSCHWITZ, in southern Poland, near the town of that name, where as many as 6,000 men, women, children, and infants were killed each day, beginning in the summer of 1941. Other death camps were at TREBLINKA, Maidenek, Sobibor, Belsec, and Chelmno. The camps were all in Poland, where the largest concentrations of European Jews were found and where a good rail system provided for efficient transportation of victims. Experts in the mass murders of the "euthanasia" program (see DOCTORS TRIAL) were assigned to aid the SS at the death camps.

At Belsec, about 600,000 people, nearly all of them Jews, were killed in about a year. Carbon monoxide was piped into the death chamber. An SS official's report described the gassing of 600 to 700 victims jammed into a 270-square-foot chamber: "Inside, the people were still standing erect, like pillars of basalt, since there had not been an inch of space for them to fall or even lean. Families could still be seen holding hands, even in death. It was a tough job to separate them as the chambers were emptied to make way for the next batch. The bodies were tossed out, blue, wet with sweat and urine, the legs soiled with feces and menstrual blood." Later, ZKYLON B, the chemical used to produce much more efficient poison gas, was introduced at Auschwitz.

Maidenek, like Treblinka, was built as a concentration camp and converted into a death camp. Many of the 500,000 Jews killed at Maidenek were murdered by gunfire.

Chelmno was near Lodz, a major armaments-manufacturing center. Exhaust gases were piped into sealed railroad cars. Killings, reaching up to 1,000 a day, went on until Jan. 1945. Total deaths there were estimated to be 340,000. The victims' clothing was usually sent off to Winterhilfe, a German relief organization. Such possessions as clocks, scissors, and flashlights were cleaned and priced by SS bureaucrats and sold to German soldiers; eyeglasses went to the Public Health Office, which sold them. Other merchandise was sometimes distributed to department stores.

Human fat was sometimes rendered into soap; body parts, skulls, and skeletons were sent to scientific institutes. Women's hair, cut off in what the Germans called "beauty salons," was also salvaged. Hair from Treblinka was used to make mattresses and felt slippers for U-BOAT crews. Cash, gold fillings, wedding rings, gold watches, silverware, jewels, and other loot from victims were put in the "Max Heilger Deposit Account" of the Reichsbank. The account belonged to the SS.

In Nov. 1944 Himmler, with a vague hope of negotiating a peace, ordered the end of the killing at the death camps. Dismantling of the gas chambers and crematoria began, but mass deaths continued until the camps were liberated by Allied troops. Methodically kept records at many camps helped Allied prosecutors develop evidence for WAR CRIMES trials.

Decker

Code name for small British incendiary BOMB used early in the war.

Decorations,

see AWARDS AND DECORATIONS.

Defiant

This British aircraft introduced a new concept to fighter design, having no forward-firing guns but being fitted with a four-gun power turret aft of the cockpit.

Entering service with the RAF in Dec. 1939, the Defiant first flew combat missions on May 12, 1940. Defiants initially had considerable success against German aircraft over France and by the end of the month the Defiant was credited with shooting down sixty-five enemy planes, mainly German bombers attacking British and French troops at DUNKIRK. But the German ME 109 soon took a toll of Defiants. In Aug. 1941 all were reassigned as night fighters. Fitted with air-intercept RADAR, the Defiants were highly successful in this role. By early 1942 they were relegated to target-tow, gunnery training, and air-sea rescue duties, having been replaced in combat roles by more advanced fighters. Between 1942 and 1945 the Royal Navy flew a large number of the aircraft as target tugs. Produced by the Boulton Paul firm, the prototype Defiant flew on Aug. 11, 1937. Through Feb. 1943 a total of 1,060 aircraft were built.

A low-wing monoplane with an in-line engine, the aircraft had a fully retractable main landing gear. The pilot's cockpit was faired back into the powered gun turret, which had four .303-cal. machine guns; there were no forward-firing guns. The Rolls-Royce Merlin engine gave the aircraft a relatively high speed.

Maximum speed was 303 mph for the Mk I variant while the Mk II, delivered from Feb. 1941, could reach 315 mph. The plane had a two-man crew.

Delta

Code name for U.S. 45th DIVISION force for operations in southern France.

Demon

Code name for the British evacuation of Greece, April 24–May 1, 1941.

Dempsey, Gen. Sir Miles C. (1896–1969)

One of the least known of Allied Army commanders, in large part because he had so little interest in self-promotion. (He did not publish any postwar memoirs.) A veteran of World War I, he was a brigade commander when war broke out in Europe. Sent to France, after the German breakthroughs his troops fought a rearguard action in support of the DUNKIRK evacuation and were finally taken off themselves.

In Nov. 1942 he took command of the XIII Corps under Gen. BERNARD MONTGOMERY's Eighth Army fighting in North Africa and then led the corps in the invasion of SICILY in July 1943, where it constituted the right side of Montgomery's line. In Sept. 1943 Dempsey's XIII Corps crossed the Strait of Messina to Italy's "toe," then drove northward to meet Gen. MARK CLARK's forces landing at SALERNO, advancing 300 miles in seventeen days.

His quiet competence made Dempsey a logical choice for command of the Second Army, which led British forces ashore at the NORMANDY INVASION in June 1944. Dempsey subsequently led the Second Army across the Rhine in late March 1945 and swept northeastward, taking HAMBURG, BREMEN, and Kiel, and reaching the Danish border by the time of the German SURRENDER in May 1945. (See ALLIED CAMPAIGN IN EUROPE.)

Denmark

Capital: Copenhagen, pop. 3,777,000 (est. 1938). Neutral in World War I and hoping to remain so in World War II, the monarchy of Denmark signed a nonaggression pact with Germany on May 31, 1939. On April 9, 1940, Germany broke the pact by launching the DENMARK AND NORWAY CAMPAIGN. Denmark, swiftly overrun, surrendered and became an occupied country.

At first the German occupation was relatively undemanding. King Christian X remained on his throne and the parliament continued to function. But in the fall of 1942 the Germans began an attempt to make Denmark into a German possession. A GUERRILLA movement arose and, urged on by Denmark officials in exile in London, harassed the Germans with hundreds of acts of SABOTAGE, from derailing trains to blowing up factories. On Aug. 28, 1943, the German occupation authorities reacted with a demand that the Danish government declare an emergency and authorize the death penalty and the taking of hostages. The government refused.

The Germans occupied Copenhagen and other cities, disarmed the Danish army, and sent the SS into Denmark. The Danish Navy scuttled several ships; others fled to Sweden. Thousands of Danes were arrested. Saboteurs were summarily killed, along with what a German report called "compensatory murders in a proportion of at least five to one." The royal family was interned. The sabotage and the general strikes went on.

In Sept. 1944 the Germans began rounding up all Danish policemen, taking 2,000 of them to CON-CENTRATION CAMPS in Germany. But the resistance continued and a united underground formed the Council of Liberty, which would reform a postwar government.

Denmark, unlike other occupied countries, resisted German attempts to impose laws and actions against JEWS. When Germans attempted to round up Denmark's Jews, thousands of Jews were ferried to Sweden in an operation that involved both Danish officials and ordinary citizens. Some 400 Jews who failed to escape were deported to the "model camp" of Theresienstadt. The Danes put such pressure on the Germans that none of the Danish Jews were sent on to AUSCHWITZ. All but fifty-one of the Theresienstadt Danes survived.

The SURRENDER of Germany on May 7, 1945, touched off some skirmishes between resistance groups and German sympathizers. A German garrison on the island of Bornholm in the Baltic Sea held out until May 9 when Soviet forces temporarily took control of the island.

Denmark and Norway Campaign (1940)

Germany's campaign against Denmark and Norway was undertaken to safeguard the vitally needed iron ore shipments from Sweden and to provide the German Navy with safe passage through Norwegian coastal waters out into the North Atlantic.

The German BLITZKRIEG of Poland in Sept. 1939 had ended with an uneasy truce over Europe. Although Britain and France had declared war on Germany—and that war was being violently fought at sea in the BATTLE OF THE ATLANTIC—there was no war on land. To many in Europe and the United States, the lack of obvious war became known as the Phony War.

But Hitler and the German High command were not inactive. Plans were being drawn up for the next German conquest—the Scandinavian peninsula. Besides gaining its strategic objectives, Germany would get Scandinavian fish and dairy products, needed to feed Germany in the face of the Anglo-French naval blockade of German ports.

Weserübung (Weser Exercise), the code name for the invasion of Norway *(Nord)* and Denmark *(Sud)*, was a major operation for the German Navy. Naval groups were to land forces along the Norwegian coast on April 9, 1940, while AIRBORNE units were dropped on Norway and Denmark, primarily to seize airfields.

Norway learned of Exercise Weser, on April 8, when Norwegians in Kristiansund picked up 122 survivors from a German transport that had been torpedoed by a Polish submarine. The Germans admitted that they were part of an invasion force, but the Norwegian Cabinet made no move to set up defenses. The assault would begin on April 9, 1939. Even as the Germans were planning the operation, so were the British and French beginning operations against Norway. On April 8, England's First Lord of the Admiralty, WINSTON CHURCHILL, had flagrantly violated international law by ordering the laying of mines in Norwegian waters to harass the iron-ore trade between Germany and neutral Norway.

Germany's invasion of Norway and Denmark the next day appeared to be an incredibly rapid counter to the British mining. It was not known at the time that the Germans were not reacting; they were carrying out Weser, developed some two months before.

In a dazzling display of blitzkrieg, German troops crossed the Danish border early on the morning of April 9, overwhelming the Danes, who quickly surrendered. At the same time, German troops emerged from cargo ships in Norwegian ports. At the same moment, German aircraft overflew Norwegian airfields disgorging parachutists. These were followed by German destroyers that steamed up key fjords to unload more troops and provide gunfire support to the assault.

The Norwegians defended their territory valiantly. British troops were landed, along with RAF fighters, in a vain effort to halt the German advances. But all failed as the German Army and Luftwaffe demonstrated the unstoppable tactics they had perfected in Poland.

At sea, however, the Allies were more successful. The first German losses were at the hands of the Norwegian defenders of Oslo Fjord, opening fire with coastal defense batteries at point-blank range. The Norwegian defenders had no orders for dealing with an undeclared act of war and the decision to open fire was taken by a junior officer on his own initiative. Those batteries, on the morning of the war, sank the heavy cruiser *Blücher* with heavy casu-

alties, including several hundred troops and civilians who were to be occupation officials. At Bergen two elderly Norwegian coastal defense ships similarly opened fire damaging another cruiser, and at Oslo Fjord gunners knocked out a German torpedo boat.

Although the Germans took their revenge on the Norwegian defenders, sinking two Norwegian coastal defense ships and capturing two others, German losses were heavy: British naval aircraft flying from the Orkney Islands sank a light cruiser, while British destroyer guns and torpedoes sank ten German destroyers. Also in the Norwegian campaign, both operational German battleships, the *Scharnhorst* and *Gneisenau,* were damaged. The British and French suffered several destroyers sunk, as well as the carrier *Glorious* during naval actions that continued into June.

By late May the British and French troops had established a favorable position near Narvik, but the military collapse in northern France and the Low Countries necessitated the abandoning of the Norwegian campaign. During the first week of June the Allies successfully evacuated 27,000 men, almost without loss, as well as King Haakon and the officials who would become the government-in-exile. (See also DENMARK and NORWAY.)

Depth Charges

The principal antisubmarine weapon of the war, popularly known as the "ash can" because of its shape. Depth charges were developed and first used in World War I. The depth charge was a cylinder filled with explosives (initially TNT and later Torpex) and fitted with a hydrostatic fuze to detonate the depth charge at a depth set immediately before release of the weapon.

Depth charges were launched from surface ships or dropped from aircraft and AIRSHIPS. Surface ships had depth charge racks for rolling depth charges over the stern. Beginning in 1941 U.S. destroyers and some smaller antisubmarine ships used "K" and "Y" guns; these were depth charge projectors whose shape resembled those letters. The K-gun fired a single depth charge to one side of the ship while the Y-gun fired a charge to both sides. These projectors, combined with rolling depth charges over the stern, produced a pattern that would, as they descended into the depths, encompass the target submarine.

The standard U.S. depth charges through most of the war were the 600-pound Mk 7, which was rolled from racks, and the 300-pound Mk 6, which was fired from projectors. The weights refer to the explosive charge; the actual depth charges were heavier: 720 and 420 pounds, respectively. During the war a teardrop-shaped, lightweight 200-pound Mk 8 (total weight 340 pounds) was developed; it sank at a faster rate to reduce the interval between the time that the weapon was released and when it reached the predicted depth of the submarine.

The early wartime depth charges were designed for a maximum setting of 300 feet, but as intelligence indicated that German U-BOATS could dive significantly deeper, the depth was increased to 600 feet. (The British had depth charges that could reach greater depths; the British Mk X depth charge was a 10-foot-long cylinder containing 2,000 pounds of explosive, fired from a shipboard TORPEDO tube. See also SQUID.)

Antisubmarine aircraft and airships could also carry depth charges that were BOMB shaped as well as cylindrical, the former sinking at a much faster rate. The standard U.S. aircraft depth charge was the 325-pound Mk 17.

The number of depth charges needed to sink a submarine—if it was sunk at all—varied considerably. For example, on June 30, 1942, some 130 miles off Bermuda, a U.S. Navy PBM MARINER surprised the *U-158* on the surface; two depth charges were dropped, one was a near miss and the other struck the submarine and exploded alongside as she dived. That was the end of the *U-158*. In contrast, when the *U-238* was attacked by the British 2nd Escort Group on Feb. 1, 1944, the U-boat evaded her attackers for eight hours. Finally, after a HEDGEHOG barrage and the expenditure of *66* depth charges, the U-boat succumbed to the tenacious hunters under Capt. F. J. WALKER. Both depth charge expenditures were unusual.

Derfflinger

German code name for planned Ninth Army drive from Rzhev to Ostashkov in the Soviet Union, mid-1942.

Desert Rats

Nickname of the British 7th Armoured Division, which gained accolades for its performance in North Africa against German and Italian forces. The division's insignia included the jerboa, a North African rodent, and the division was cited for its "darting and biting" tactics.

Destroyer Escorts

Antisubmarine ships built to counter the shortfall in DESTROYERS in the U.S. and Royal Navies. The destroyer escort or DE had its origins in U.S. Navy studies in 1939 of wartime mass production of destroyers. Several "austere" destroyer designs were developed, although it was generally felt by the Navy's leadership that such ships sacrificed capability for little if any cost savings. British wartime experience soon influenced the U.S. designs (such as the primary mission being antisubmarine warfare) and the British asked for fifty DEs. They were approved by President ROOSEVELT on Aug. 15, 1941, with the first contracts awarded on Nov. 1, 1941. In Jan. 1942—with the United States in the war—the U.S. Navy ordered another 250 DEs, to be followed by hundreds more. The DE program was considered a "pool," from which either Navy could take ships as needed and available.

Although many of the British ships were laid down in naval shipyards, most of the more than 550 war-built DEs were constructed in civilian yards, most of which had never built a warship as large as a destroyer. Sections were prefabricated in factories throughout the United States and the ships built at seventeen yards throughout the country. Using mass production techniques, they were built rapidly—the record reported as fifty-four days from keel-laying to completion.

The first DE went to Britain in Jan. 1943, followed by five more of the original order, but forty-four went to the U.S. Navy. In all, seventy-eight ships went to Britain (called Captain-class frigates) and six to the FREE FRENCH; during 1944, six of the U.S. ships were transferred to Brazil. The other 460 served under the American flag. (Beginning in 1943, with the U-BOATS on the defensive, additional DE construction was canceled in favor of LANDING CRAFT.)

At sea the DEs proved invaluable antisubmarine ships, operating in the Atlantic and Pacific areas. In the Pacific the USS ENGLAND (DE 635) sank six Japanese submarines in May 1944, the single-ship record for any nation. While intended to hunt submarines, in the Oct. 1944 Battle of LEYTE GULF off the Philippines a force of eighteen ESCORT CARRIERS was screened by nine destroyers and fourteen DEs. Without warning, the U.S. ships were attacked by a Japanese battleship force. The U.S. warships—armed with no gun larger than 5-inch (127-mm)—were confronted by the super-battleship YAMATO with 18.1-inch (460-mm) guns and other major Japanese warships. In the ensuing battle, the destroyers and DEs used their guns, TORPEDOES, and smoke to deter the attacking warships. Two destroyers and one DE were sunk and others damaged before the Japanese force turned away.

Surprisingly, only nine U.S. DEs were sunk during the war—four by U-boats, two by Japanese submarines, one by Japanese gunfire, one by a Japanese KAITEN suicide submarine, and one by a German mine (in the NORMANDY INVASION); two others were damaged beyond repair. The British lost ten.

The original DE design was a 1,150-ton ship, 289½ feet long, with diesel-electric propulsion for 18 knots. These ships were armed with three 3-inch (76-mm) guns—considered almost useless by friend and foe because of their short range and slow rate of fire. Ninety-seven of these "short-hull" ships were built (thirty-two going to Britain).

The design was improved for the "long-hull" design—displacement increased to between 1,100 and 1,450 tons with a length of 306 feet. A variety of turbo-electric, diesel-electric, and diesel power plants were used, providing speeds of 21 to 24 knots. The variety of plants were used in these ships to avoid the delay of producing the gearing needed for conventional steam turbine propulsion. Most long-hull DEs also had three 3-inch guns, but the last 150 or so had two 5-inch guns. All of these ships had three 21-inch (533-mm) antiship torpedo tubes, and all carried several BOFORS 40-MM and OERLIKON 20-MM antiaircraft guns plus a large number of DEPTH CHARGES and, in many ships, HEDGEHOGS.

At the end of the war several DEs were being converted to RADAR picket ships (DER) to provide amphibious landing areas with early warning of enemy air attacks.

Beginning in 1943, with the submarine threat declining, fifty ships under construction were completed as high-speed transports (APD) and another forty-five were converted from existing DEs. These were used for AMPHIBIOUS LANDINGS, to carry UNDERWATER DEMOLITION TEAMS (frogmen), COMMANDOS, and special troops. The APDs were all long-hull ships, fitted with a single 5-inch gun forward, with one depth charge rack and SONAR retained to provide a minimal antisubmarine capability, and provided with davits for four landing craft. Each could carry 160 troops. Only one of these ships was lost during the war, hit by a KAMIKAZE off OKINAWA, but two others were so heavily damaged that they were not returned to service.

Destroyers

Versatile surface warships widely used in the war. JOHN STEINBECK wrote, "A destroyer is a lovely ship, probably the nicest fighting ship of all. . . . In the beautiful clean lines of her, in her speed and roughness, in curious gallantry, she is completely a ship, in the old sense."

Known as "tin cans" because of their thin skin as well as "greyhounds" because of their high speed, at the start of the war U.S. destroyers were intended primarily to screen the battle fleet. In that role they would lay smoke screens and intercept attacking enemy destroyers; they would also seek out enemy warships and attack with TORPEDOES, hoping to damage them for subsequent destruction by U.S. BATTLESHIPS and CRUISERS.

On Dec. 7, 1941, the Navy had 171 destroyers in service: seventy-one were flush-deck, four-stack ships built during and just after World War I, and 100 were relatively modern destroyers built from 1934 onward. All had "banks" of 21-inch torpedo tubes for attacking enemy ships; the newer destroyers had several 5-inch guns for use against surface ships and aircraft. All destroyers also had SONAR for locating and DEPTH CHARGES for attacking SUBMARINES, and a few machine guns for defense against aircraft. (In addition to these ships, at the start of the war another forty-seven older destroyers were serving as light minelayers, high-speed minesweepers, and transports.)

U.S. destroyers were in action in all theaters of the war, beginning with the *Ward* (DD 139), which sank a Japanese MIDGET SUBMARINE in the approaches to PEARL HARBOR just before the air attack of Dec. 7, 1941. In addition to antiship and antisubmarine operations, during the war destroyers provided antiaircraft defense for task forces and performed shore bombardment in support of AMPHIBIOUS LANDINGS.

During the war U.S. shipyards delivered some 390 destroyers to the Navy (twelve had their torpedo tubes replaced by mine rails and another twelve by minesweeping gear).

Seventy-one destroyers were lost during the war, more than any other U.S. warship type. Most were lost in action, but three were sunk in accidental collisions and two went down in a typhoon off Luzon. The latter losses provided the setting for Herman Wouk's play and novel *The Caine Mutiny*. Many more destroyers were damaged, especially in the KAMIKAZE attacks of 1944–1945. (Suicide planes sank nine destroyers.) The three destroyers that had been wrecked in the Japanese attack at Pearl Harbor were totally rebuilt and were not counted in the seventy-one ships lost.

Destroyers-for-Bases Deal

In one of the most unusual "swaps" in history, in Sept. 1940 the United States transferred fifty overage DESTROYERS to Britain in exchange for naval and air bases in the Western Hemisphere. Britain, beset by U-BOAT attacks against its shipping, required more antisubmarine ships. Prime Minister CHURCHILL offered to the United States ninety-nine-year leases—without payment—on sites in the British colonies.

Churchill had asked President ROOSEVELT for the destroyers in May and June 1940. In the latter appeal Churchill wrote: "It has now become most urgent for you to let us have the destroyers. . . . Mr. President, with great respect I must tell you that in the long history of the world this is a thing to do *now.*" Churchill expected that British construction programs would provide sufficient antisubmarine ships in 1941, but with the French coast now available for U-boat bases, he was desperate.

Roosevelt was opposed in providing such assistance by many members of Congress as well as U.S.

Navy officials who felt the United States needed those ships. Still, Roosevelt persevered and the historic Anglo-American deal was agreed in principle on July 24, 1940, with formal agreement on Sept. 2, 1940. The first eight destroyers were given over to British crews at Halifax on Sept. 9—three days after the Luftwaffe began all-out air attacks on LONDON. (See BATTLE OF BRITAIN.) The other ships followed rapidly. All were crammed with provisions—including many items no longer seen in wartime Britain—and many things not known to British sailors, including bunks instead of hammocks for the ratings or enlisted men.

In return, Britain ceded sovereign rights to bases in Antigua, the Bahamas, British Guiana, Jamaica, St. Lucia, and Trinidad. Bases were also granted at the same time in Argentina (Newfoundland) and Bermuda, but they were outright "gifts" and were not part of the destroyer deal. The bases would be invaluable for U.S. defense of the Panama Canal and Caribbean area in the event of war with Germany. Naval historian SAMUEL ELIOT MORISON wrote, "This destroyer-naval base deal of 1940 was the first definite reaction by the Roosevelt Administration to a precarious situation which the American people in general were not yet willing to face." (See also LEND-LEASE.)

The fifty overage destroyers, which had been completed in 1917, were flush-deck, four-stack ships armed with four 4-inch (102-mm) guns and twelve 21-inch (533-mm) TORPEDO tubes. DEPTH CHARGES were their only weapon against a submerged U-boat. Steam turbines could drive the ships at up to 365 knots, an important factor in hunting submarines. However, the ships, some 1,150 tons standard displacement and 314⅓ feet long, were "lively" in rough seas and had too great a turning circle to engage surfaced U-boats in close-in combat.

Upon arrival in British ports they had to have British ASDIC (SONAR) fitted, messing arrangements changed, and other modifications. British antisubmarine expert DONALD MACINTYRE observed: "That most of them performed splendid service in filling a critical gap in our convoy defenses will not be denied. At the same time it has to be recorded that to their new British owners they seemed vile little ships."

Of the fifty ships, seven were manned by Canadian crews. On May 30, 1944, nine of the destroyers were turned over to the Soviet Navy. One of the British ships was blown up in a daring COMMANDO raid on the giant dry dock at SAINT-NAZAIRE, France; eight others were lost during the war.

Detachment

(1) Part of a military unit or force separated from the main organization, usually to undertake a specific mission or assignment; (2) U.S. code name for the invasion of IWO JIMA, Feb. 1945; it was one of the least-used code words of any created in the war.

Devastator,

see TBD.

Devereux, Maj. James P. S. (1903–1988)

Commander of the U.S. Marines on WAKE ISLAND at the time of the Japanese attack. Devereux enlisted in the Marines in 1923, was commissioned two years later, and served in Nicaragua, Cuba, and China.

At the time he was ordered to Wake he was executive officer of the Marine 1st Defense BATTALION. Devereux arrived on the island on Oct. 15, 1941, to command the Marines being placed there to protect the island for use as a U.S. staging base for U.S. aircraft going to the Southwest Pacific. Additionally he served as island commander until Navy Comdr. Winfield S. Cunningham arrived on Nov. 29 to become island commander.

When the Japanese attacked on Dec. 8 (Dec. 7 Hawaiian time) there were 388 Marines on Wake from the defense battalion and from Marine Fighter SQUADRON 211, whose twelve fighters flew into Wake from the USS ENTERPRISE (CV 6) on Dec. 4.

Devereux directed the gallant but futile defense of the small atoll against massive Japanese air, naval, and, finally, ground attack. Wake fell to the Japanese on Dec. 27 and Devereux and the other Marine and Navy survivors became PRISONERS OF WAR; they were shipped back to Japan for the duration. Forty-nine of his Marines had died defending the island.

Released after World War II, Devereux retired from the Marine Corps in 1950 as a brigadier general. He was elected to the U.S. House of Representatives from Maryland, serving from 1951 to 1959.

Devers, Gen. Jacob L. (1887–1979)

Devers was one of only three U.S. generals to command an ARMY GROUP in the European theater in World War II (OMAR N. BRADLEY and MARK CLARK being the others). Yet his fame has been the most fleeting of the three.

In May 1943, as a lieutenant general, Devers became the senior American officer in England and was responsible for the logistical and planning buildup to Overlord—the June 1944 NORMANDY INVASION. As such, he and Gen. DWIGHT D. EISENHOWER (then Allied commander in the Mediterranean) argued over heavy bomber allocations. When Eisenhower arrived in England in Jan. 1944 he sent Devers to North Africa as deputy allied commander, giving as his reason that Devers "had a reputation as a very fine administrator" and in Africa "his lack of battle experience would not be crucial."

Bradley had a different reason, based in part on his Sept. 1943 assessment of Devers: "I found him to be overly garrulous (saying little of importance), egotistical, shallow, intolerant, not very smart, and much too inclined to rush off half-cocked."

Devers performed effectively in his new post and, when it was decided to keep Clark in Italy, Devers was named to command the Sixth Army Group invading Southern France on Aug. 15, 1944. Although many strategists believed the invasion to have been unnecessary (see ALLIED CAMPAIGN IN EUROPE), the landings were nonetheless well executed and the pursuit of the withdrawing German forces up the Rhône Valley vigorous.

Postwar historians often write quite glowingly of Devers's character and abilities. He is usually described as firm, yet fair minded. But most assessments acknowledge the impulsive streak that so irritated Bradley. When combined with the nearly ungovernable FREE FRENCH Army on his right flank, Devers's inaccurate estimates of enemy intentions could lead to embarrassments.

In the end, however, Devers maintained control of the 1st French Army, possibly to a degree attainable by no other American. He executed his mission successfully and was promoted to general in May

1945. He subsequently served as commander of Army Ground Forces until his retirement in 1949.

Devil's Brigade

Translation of German nickname for the First Special Service Force. The force, consisting of men from U.S. and Canadian units, was suggested by Geoffrey N. Pyke, a wartime adviser to Adm. LOUIS MOUNTBATTEN. Pyke conceived of a COMMANDO-style unit that would travel in armored snow vehicles against such targets as Norwegian hydroelectric plants. The force was never used for that purpose. But, under Brig. Gen. Robert T. Frederick, the force fought through the ITALIAN CAMPAIGN and earned a reputation as tough, often savage fighters. In rear areas they had another reputation as disciplinary problems. Some of the men entered the force as "volunteers" evicted from Army correction stockades.

Dewey, Thomas E. (1902–1971)

Republican candidate for President in 1944. Dewey, who became famous as a mob-fighting New York City District Attorney in the 1930s, ran for the Republican presidential candidacy in 1940, losing to WENDELL L. WILLKIE. In 1944 he won the nomination on the first ballot but lost the election to President ROOSEVELT, who was running for an unprecedented fourth term, which became an issue in the campaign. In 1948, Dewey, heavily favored to win, ran against President HARRY S TRUMAN and lost again.

Dexterity

Code name for Allied operations against Cape Gloucester, NEW BRITAIN, Dec. 1943.

DFS 230

Small German transport GLIDER. This small, unpowered aircraft was a key factor in the German capture of the "impregnable" Fort Eben Emael in Belgium on May 10, 1940, in the FRANCE AND LOW COUNTRIES CAMPAIGN, permitting the German blitzkrieg into the west, and was used in the dramatic removal of BENITO MUSSOLINI from Gran Sasso on Sept. 16, 1944.

The *Deutsches Forschungsinstitut für Segelflug* glider was developed to prevent the normal dispersal of AIRBORNE troops landing by parachute on small objectives. The German goal was to have a ten-place glider cost 7,500 Deutsche marks—the equivalent cost of manufacturing ten parachutes. Developed in great secrecy, the DFS 230 began flight tests in 1937. In addition to the pilot and nine armed troops, some 600 pounds of cargo could be carried.

For the capture of Eben Emael—Operation Granite—the Germans used eleven gliders carrying eighty-five troops (including pilots) plus a considerable amount of explosives, six machine guns, and four flame throwers. In all, forty-one of the DFS 230 gliders were committed to the May 10 assault in the West, the others landing troops to capture key bridges needed by German ground forces along the Belgian-Dutch frontier.

During the fall of 1938 a glider-borne COMMANDO force was formed and DFS 230 production was increased, with more than 1,500 of the gliders being produced by 1943.

The high-wing DFS 230 was fabricated of a steel tube framework covered with canvas. The two-wheel trolley was jettisoned after takeoff and the glider landed on a central, plywood ski-like skid. It could be towed by a variety of twin-engine combat aircraft as well as the ubiquitous three-engine JU 52 transport. (In trials DFS 230s were towed by five small He 72 *Kadett* training biplanes.) Some gliders were fitted with braking ROCKETS to bring them to a halt in very short distances (as required at Gran Sasso). Towing speed was 130 mph and in descent the gliders could maneuver at speeds up to 180 mph.

Diadem

Code name for Allied plan to capture ROME, 1944.

Dieppe

French Channel port. On Aug. 19, 1942, in the first major European AMPHIBIOUS LANDING of the war, British and Canadian troops raided German-held Dieppe. The landing force of 5,000 Canadian troops, 1,000 British troops, plus a token force of sixty U.S. Army RANGERS, encountered heavy German opposition. The Allies lost more than 3,000 men killed or captured in this operation, code-named Jubilee.

The landing was inspired by a belief among Britain's leaders something had to be done in Europe to counter Germany's continued successes since launching the BLITZKRIEG into Poland in Sept. 1939. An assault, even a small one somewhere along the French coast, could demonstrate to the people of the occupied countries that they were not forgotten and that help—and eventually liberation—would come. Also, there was a buildup of Canadian troops in Britain who were impatient for action. Military leaders decided that even a hit-and-run assault would provide needed experience in modern landing techniques.

Dieppe was chosen as the most suitable target because wide beaches adjacent to the town provided good prospects for landing troops. German defenses, however, were formidable: coastal defense guns, an offshore minefield, and nearby airfields and troops to reinforce the town's garrison. But Dieppe could be reached by fighter aircraft based in England, a vital consideration.

Operation Jubilee hit its first snag at 3:47 A.M. when five armed German trawlers discovered the approaching assault boats and opened fire. Surprise was lost, and the Germans established a deadly crossfire in the predawn darkness.

By nine, after the carnage on the beaches brought the realization of failure, the British commanders decided to withdraw the surviving troops. The destroyers formed a line to escort the rescue boats in. The evacuation took three hours under murderous German fire.

By early afternoon, the battered remnants of the Dieppe raiders were headed back to England, leaving twenty-four officers and 3,164 men behind—killed or as prisoners. Of the 5,000 Canadian troops, some 900 were dead and almost 2,000 were captured. All the vehicles they had dragged off the crafts to the beaches also remained behind.

Dieppe—which Prime Minister CHURCHILL later termed a "reconnaissance in force"—is rationalized by some historians as providing invaluable experience for future assaults. But it is debatable as to the extent that there was a direct impact of the lessons of Dieppe on the subsequent North African and later Allied landings. The specialized amphibious ships that were being built and numerous other factors greatly changed the nature of the NORTH AFRICA INVASION only three months later.

There was one major benefit to the Allies from Dieppe. As astutely observed by British naval historian S. W. Roskill: "The Germans decided that the Dieppe raid indicated that, when the time came for the Allies to invade the European continent in earnest, their initial thrust would be aimed at capturing a large port. It is likely that this false deduction contributed greatly to the successful landing on the Normandy beaches in June 1944."

Dime

Code name for the Scoglitti assault in the invasion of SICILY, consisting of the U.S. 47th Infantry DIVISION and the 753rd TANK BATTALION.

Dimout

Dimming of lights along the U.S. East Coast to prevent the silhouetting of ships, thus making them harder for German U-BOATS to sight. The dimout was ordered as a CIVIL DEFENSE measure on April 26, 1942. In New York City, Times Square's spectacular advertising signs were blacked out, along with lights in the upper stories of skyscrapers.

Dinah

The Ki-46 Type 100 reconnaissance aircraft "has proven one of the most successful Japanese designs, and is still one of the Nips' fastest aircraft," read a U.S. intelligence evaluation of mid-1945. The high-speed Dinah could pull away from pursuing U.S. P-38 LIGHTNINGS. Its overall excellence led a German technical mission to consider licensed production of the aircraft—a reversal of the usual policy of trading German technology and aircraft to the Japanese in return for strategic raw materials. The Dinah was unusual in being flown by the Japanese naval air arm although it was primarily an Army aircraft. The Dinah flew throughout the Pacific war, being used late in the conflict to overfly the U.S. B-29 SUPER-FORTRESS bomber bases in the MARIANA ISLANDS.

The Mitsubishi high-performance aircraft first flew in Nov. 1939; its performance (reaching 312 mph) was soon improved with upgraded engines. The Ki-46-II was the principal production variant (611 were built), with a II-KAI three-seat operational trainer also being produced. A further improved Ki-46-III appeared in 1943 (654 built). A Ki-46-IVa recce version was built (four units) but a planned IVb ground-attack plane was never completed. Production totaled 1,742. Some III aircraft were modified to a fighter configuration with two 20-mm cannon in the aircraft's solid nose and others with an additional, oblique-mounted 37-mm cannon.

A twin, radial-engine aircraft, the low-wing Dinah had a streamlined shape with foreshortened nose and a streamlined dorsal hump containing cockpits for the pilot and second crewman. In some aircraft the latter fired a flexible 7.7-mm machine gun.

Top speed of the Ki-46-II was 375 mph with a maximum range of 1,535 miles. The III variant was rated at 391 mph with a range of 2,485 miles!

Director

Code name for the Allied TASK FORCE for the invasion of Arawe, NEW BRITAIN.

Displaced Persons

Designation for people uprooted by the war in Europe. The Allied Military Government classified as "displaced persons" people driven outside their countries by war, and "refugees" as people who were temporarily homeless in their own countries. (Another category was "displaced persecutees," for survivors of concentration camps.)

SUPREME HEADQUARTERS ALLIED EXPEDITIONARY FORCE (SHAEF) assumed responsibility for the DPs, as they were called. The basic cause of the massive displacements of people was the German practice of shipping conquered peoples to Germany for SLAVE LABOR in war industries. A May 1944 study by SHAEF, based on reports from intelligence sources and governments-in-exile, gave the following estimates on DPs; the countries listed are the countries of origin:

France	2,320,000
Soviet Union	1,840,000
Poland	1,403,000
Belgium	559,000
Netherlands	402,000
Czechoslovakia	350,000
Yugoslavia	328,000
Italy	195,000
Latvia, Estonia, Lithuania	100,000
Hungary	65,000
Denmark	45,000
Germany	40,000
Luxembourg	30,000
Bulgaria	25,000
Rumania	14,000
Greece	12,000
Norway	10,000
Total	7,738,000

As liberation forces moved across France at the start of the ALLIED CAMPAIGN IN EUROPE, they found more than 1,000,000 refugees of France, Belgium, and the Netherlands to care for. ALLIED MILITARY GOVERNMENT officers, aided by representatives of the UNITED NATIONS RELIEF AND REHABILITATION ADMINISTRATION, set up "assembly centers"—many of them more accurately called DP camps—to process the refugees, who, for the most part, needed only temporary help while they awaited the passage of combat from their home areas.

A new phase of the DP problem came when the Allied campaign pushed into Germany. Retreating German commanders sent tens of thousands of DPs forward in attempts to clog the roads and impede the Allied advance. In March 1945 the Allies had 200,000 people on their hands. By May, when the German Army collapsed, the number had risen to more than 6,000,000.

About 2,000,000 French, Dutch, and Belgian DPs were rapidly repatriated. But DP officials in the British, French, and British occupation zones of Germany found that an overwhelming number of the remaining DPs did not want to return to Soviet-controlled homelands. There were about 300,000 "persecutees," many of whom had to remain in the horror of the concentration camps while the Allies worked on ways to help them. German PRISONERS OF WAR were conscripted to clean up the camps, and military hospital units were set up. Special care was given for survivors suffering from malnutrition.

Still, thousands died. (See CONCENTRATION CAMPS.)

About 800 DP camps, some in commandeered German schools and other public buildings, housed the millions still without homes. They were allotted at first 2,000 calories a day; this was later increased to 2,300, with persecutees getting 2,500. At the time, the typical German was living on 1,000 to 1,500 calories a day.

As of Sept. 30, 1946, the Western Allies reported that repatriation was "unlikely" for about 575,000 DPs; these included 200,000 Poles and 120,000 JEWS, many of whom would migrate to Israel when it was founded in 1948. The U.S. Displaced Persons Acts of 1948 and 1950 essentially ended the saga of the DPs by admitting 405,000 of them to the United States.

Diver

Code name for British defense against and attacks on German V-WEAPONS, 1944.

Division

The largest ground combat formation that normally includes infantry, ARTILLERY, and armored components. Divisions are usually commanded by a major general. The types of divisions in various armies included infantry/rifle, armored/TANK, artillery, AIRBORNE/parachute, mountain, CAVALRY, defense/fortress, and marine.

(Navy ship divisions were administrative organizations, usually for four ships of the same type, e.g., BATTLESHIPS, CRUISERS, SUBMARINES.)

The REGIMENT or BRIGADE was the principal troop component of a division; in World War II divisions were generally rectangular (with four regiments) or triangular (with three regiments). On Oct. 1, 1940, the nine regular U.S. infantry divisions were reorganized as triangular divisions with three infantry regiments and with their artillery regiment broken up into four artillery BATTALIONS. U.S. armored divisions had combat commands (designated A, B, and Reserve) that consisted of tank and infantry battalions. In some armies, the division's artillery was organized as a brigade or an additional regiment (the latter in the U.S. Marine Corps), while the U.S. Army grouped artillery bat-

talions within the division as simply the "division artillery" (with the slang term "divarty" being used).

The U.S. Army had a peak strength of eighty-nine divisions during World War II—sixty-seven infantry, sixteen armored, five airborne, and one cavalry. There were, briefly, ninety divisions, but the 2nd Cavalry Division was inactivated in May 1944 (see below).

There were three "light" infantry divisions formed in 1943 to evaluate specialized organizations: the 10th Light Division (Pack, Alpine), 71st Light Division (Pack, Jungle), and 89th Light Division (Truck). After exercises to demonstrate their capabilities, the 71st and 89th reverted to standard infantry divisions. The 10th, however, was successfully employed as a "mountain" division in the ITALIAN CAMPAIGN in 1945.

The size of divisions varied during the war. Under the tables of organization in June 1941 a U.S. infantry division had 15,514 officers and enlisted men; by July 1943 the number was reduced to 13,746 men; in Jan. 1945 an infantry division was authorized 14,037 men.

On March 1, 1942, the U.S. armored division consisted of 14,620 officers and men (with 252 medium and 158 light tanks); in the Sept. 1943 reorganization, armored divisions were authorized 10,937 men (with 186 medium and seventy-seven light tanks). The June 1945 organization for an armored division authorized 10,670 men (with 195 medium and seventy-seven light tanks).

U.S. airborne division as conceived in 1942 had only 8,505 officers and enlisted men. The need to provide rear-echelon security, maintenance, and support troops at the embarkation airfields, and for having a forward and rear command element, led to an increase in division strength to 12,979 before the end of the war. The airborne divisions normally had two parachute infantry regiments and one GLIDER infantry regiment.

The U.S. 1st Cavalry Division—which was to have been a combined horse and motorized unit—saw combat in the Southwest Pacific as dismounted infantry. Its authorized strength was 12,724 men. The U.S. 2nd Cavalry Division was sent to North Africa in early 1944 but was inactivated in May 1944, with its troops being assigned to support units.

The 10th Light Division—in its "mountain" configuration—in late 1944 had an authorized strength of 14,101 officers and men, plus 6,152 horses and mules.

All U.S. Army and Marine Corps divisions had numerical designations except for the Americal Division, its name derived from *Ameri*can and New *Cal*edonia, the division having been activated at NEW CALEDONIA in May 1942. (In 1954 the Americal Division was redesignated as the 23rd Infantry Division.)

The U.S. Marine Corps had six divisions at the end of the war, the first having been established in Feb. 1941. Each of these divisions had approximately 20,000 officers and enlisted men.

The first U.S. division to enter combat in World War II was the 1st Marine Division, which made an AMPHIBIOUS LANDING on GUADALCANAL and Tulagi in the SOLOMON ISLANDS on Aug. 8, 1942. The first U.S. Army divisions in combat were the 2nd Armored, 3rd Infantry, and 9th Infantry Divisions, which participated in the NORTH AFRICA INVASION on Nov. 8, 1942, against resistance from VICHY FRENCH forces.

The Army's 12th Infantry Division—known as the Philippine Division—was in the Philippines at the beginning of the war. The division fought with distinction and great heroism until the fall of CORREGIDOR on May 6, 1942, when the division ceased to exist as an entity. (It continued to be carried on Army rolls, however, and was redesignated as the 12th Infantry Division [Philippine Scouts] in March 1946.)

(Some historians credit France with employing the first troop formations known as divisions in the late eighteenth century. Napoleon Bonaparte made extensive use of such divisions in his campaigns.)

Several divisions were established but not fully formed nor committed to action during the war; those are indicated in the table by double asterisks (**). The U.S. divisions listed in the table participated in World War II; NATIONAL GUARD (NG) and Army Reserve (AR) divisions are indicated.

Divisions, Air

U.S. Army Air Forces organizational structure for heavy bomber aircraft. See AIR FORCES.

DIVISION	TYPE	CAMPAIGNS	NICKNAME
1st	Infantry	Algeria, Morocco, Tunisia, Sicily, Normandy, Northern France, Rhineland, Ardennes-Alsace, Central Europe	Big Red 1
2nd	Infantry	Normandy, Northern France, Rhineland, Ardennes-Alsace, Central Europe	Indian Head
3rd	Infantry	Algeria–French Morocco, Tunisia, Sicily, Naples-Foggia, Anzio, Rome-Arno, Southern France, Rhineland, Ardennes-Alsace, Central Europe	Marne
4th	Infantry	Normandy, Northern France, Rhineland, Ardennes-Alsace, Central Europe	Ivy
5th	Infantry	Normandy, Northern France, Ardennes-Alsace, Rhineland, Central Europe	Red Diamond
6th	Infantry	New Guinea, Luzon	Sightseeing Sixth
7th	Infantry	Aleutian Islands, Eastern Mandates, Leyte, Ryukyus	Bayonet
8th	Infantry	Normandy, Northern France, Rhineland, Central Europe	Pathfinder
9th	Infantry	Tunisia, Sicily, Normandy, Northern France, Rhineland, Central Europe	The Varsity
10th	Mountain	North Apennines, Po Valley	Mountaineers
11th	Airborne	New Guinea, Leyte, Luzon	Angels
12th	Infantry	(Philippine Islands—see above)	The Plymouth Division
13th	Airborne	Central Europe	——
14th	Infantry	**	Wolverine
17th	Airborne	Rhineland, Ardennes-Alsace, Central Europe	Golden Talon
18th	Infantry	**	Cactus Division
19th	Infantry	**	——

DIVISION	TYPE	CAMPAIGNS	NICKNAME
24th	Infantry	Central Pacific, New Guinea, Leyte, Luzon, Southern Philippines	Victory
25th	Infantry	Northern Solomons, Central Pacific, Luzon, Guadalcanal	Tropical Lightning
26th	Infantry (NG)	Northern France, Rhineland, Ardennes-Alsace, Central Europe	Yankee
27th	Infantry (NG)	Central Pacific, Western Pacific, Ryukyus	New York
28th	Infantry (NG)	Normandy, Northern France, Rhineland, Ardennes-Alsace, Central Europe	Keystone
29th	Infantry (NG)	Normandy, Northern France, Rhineland, Central Europe	Blue and Gray
30th	Infantry (NG)	Normandy, Northern France, Rhineland, Ardennes-Alsace, Central Europe	Old Hickory
31st	Infantry (NG)	New Guinea, Southern Philippines, Western Pacific	Dixie
32nd	Infantry (NG)	New Guinea, Papua, Leyte, Luzon	Red Arrow
33rd	Infantry (NG)	New Guinea, Luzon	Prairie
34th	Infantry (NG)	Tunisia, Naples-Foggia, Anzio, Rome-Arno, North Apennines, Po Valley	Red Bull
35th	Infantry (NG)	Normandy, Northern France, Ardennes-Alsace, Rhineland, Central Europe	Santa Fe
36th	Infantry (NG)	Naples-Foggia, Anzio, Rome-Arno, Southern France, Rhineland, Ardennes-Alsace, Central Europe	Texas
37th	Infantry (NG)	Northern Solomons, Luzon	Buckeye
38th	Infantry (NG)	New Guinea, Luzon, Leyte	Cyclone
40th	Infantry (NG)	Bismarck Archipelago, Luzon	Grizzly
41st	Infantry (NG)	New Guinea, Luzon, Southern Philippines	Sunset
42nd	Infantry (NG)	Rhineland, Ardennes-Alsace, Central Europe	Rainbow
43rd	Infantry (NG)	New Guinea, Northern Solomons, Guadalcanal, Luzon	Winged Victory
44th	Infantry (NG)	Northern France, Rhineland, Ardennes-Alsace, Central Europe	Jersey Blues
45th	Infantry (NG)	Sicily, Naples-Foggia, Anzio, Rome-Arno, Southern France, Rhineland, Ardennes-Alsace, Central Europe	Thunderbird
46th	Infantry	**	Iron Fist
47th	Infantry	**	Viking
48th	Infantry	**	——
49th	Infantry	**	Argonaut
51st	Infantry	**	Rattlesnake
63rd	Infantry (AR)	Rhineland, Central Europe	Blood and Fire
65th	Infantry	Rhineland, Central Europe	Battle Axe
66th	Infantry	Northern France	Black Panther
69th	Infantry	Rhineland, Central Europe	Fighting 69th
70th	Infantry	Rhineland, Ardennes-Alsace, Central Europe	Trailblazers
71st	Infantry	Rhineland, Central Europe	Red Circle
75th	Infantry	Rhineland, Ardennes-Alsace, Central Europe	——
76th	Infantry (AR)	Rhineland, Ardennes-Alsace, Central Europe	Onaway
77th	Infantry (AR)	Western Pacific, Leyte	Statue of Liberty
78th	Infantry (AR)	Ardennes-Alsace, Rhineland, Central Europe	Lightning
79th	Infantry (AR)	Normandy, Northern France, Rhineland, Ardennes-Alsace, Central Europe	Cross of Lorraine
80th	Infantry (AR)	Northern France, Rhineland, Ardennes-Alsace, Central Europe	Blue Ridge
81st	Infantry (AR)	Western Pacific, Southern Philippines	Wildcat
82nd	Airborne	Sicily, Naples-Foggia, Normandy, Ardennes-Alsace, Rhineland, Central Europe	All America
83rd	Infantry (AR)	Normandy, Northern France, Ardennes-Alsace, Rhineland, Central Europe	Thunderbolt

DIVISION	TYPE	CAMPAIGNS	NICKNAME
84th	Infantry (AR)	Rhineland, Ardennes-Alsace, Central Europe	Railsplitters
85th	Infantry (AR)	Rome-Arno, North Apennines, Po Valley	Custer
86th	Infantry (AR)	Central Europe	Blackhawk
87th	Infantry (AR)	Rhineland, Ardennes-Alsace, Central Europe	Golden Acorn
88th	Infantry (AR)	Rome-Arno, North Apennines, Po Valley	Blue Devil
89th	Infantry (AR)	Rhineland, Central Europe	Rolling W
90th	Infantry (AR)	Normandy, Northern France, Rhineland, Ardennes-Alsace	Tough "Ombres"
91st	Infantry (AR)	Rome-Arno, North Apennines, Po Valley	Powder River Division
92nd	Infantry	Rome-Arno, North Apennines, Po Valley	Buffalo
93rd	Infantry	New Guinea, Northern Solomons	Bloody Hand
94th	Infantry (AR)	Northern France, Rhineland, Ardennes-Alsace, Central Europe	NeufCats
95th	Infantry (AR)	Northern France, Rhineland, Central Europe	Victory
96th	Infantry (AR)	Leyte, Ryukyus	Deadeye
97th	Infantry (AR)	Central Europe	Trident
98th	Infantry (AR)	Asiatic-Pacific	Iroquois
99th	Infantry (AR)	Rhineland, Ardennes-Alsace, Central Europe	Checkerboard
100th	Infantry (AR)	Rhineland, Ardennes-Alsace, Central Europe	Century
101st	Airborne	Normandy, Ardennes-Alsace, Rhineland, Central Europe	Screaming Eagle
102nd	Infantry (AR)	Rhineland, Central Europe	Ozark
103rd	Infantry (AR)	Rhineland, Ardennes-Alsace, Central Europe	Cactus
104th	Infantry (AR)	Northern France, Rhineland, Central Europe	Timberwolf
106th	Infantry (AR)	Rhineland, Ardennes-Alsace, Central Europe	Golden Lion
Americal	Infantry	Guadalcanal, Northern Solomons, Southern Philippines, Leyte	Miracle
1st	Cavalry	Leyte, New Guinea, Bismarck Archipelago, Luzon	The 1st Team
2nd	Cavalry	(inactivated in North Africa, May 1944)	——
1st	Armored	Tunisia, Naples-Foggia, Anzio, Rome-Arno, North Apennines, Po Valley	Old Ironsides
2nd	Armored	Algeria–French Morocco, Sicily, Normandy, Northern France, Rhineland, Ardennes-Alsace, Central Europe	Hell on Wheels
3rd	Armored	Normandy, Northern France, Rhineland, Ardennes-Alsace, Central Europe	Spearhead
4th	Armored	Normandy, Northern France, Rhineland, Ardennes-Alsace, Central Europe	——
5th	Armored	Normandy, Northern France, Rhineland, Ardennes-Alsace, Central Europe	Victory
6th	Armored	Normandy, Northern France, Rhineland, Ardennes-Alsace, Central Europe	Super Sixth
7th	Armored	Northern France, Ardennes-Alsace, Rhineland, Central Europe	Lucky Seventh
8th	Armored	Rhineland, Ardennes-Alsace, Central Europe	Thundering Herd
9th	Armored	Rhineland, Ardennes-Alsace, Central Europe	Phantom
10th	Armored	Rhineland, Ardennes-Alsace, Central Europe	Tiger
11th	Armored	Rhineland, Central Europe	Thunderbolt
12th	Armored	Rhineland, Ardennes-Alsace, Central Europe	Hellcat
13th	Armored	Rhineland, Central Europe	Black Cat
14th	Armored	Rhineland, Ardennes-Alsace, Central Europe	Liberator
16th	Armored	Central Europe	——
20th	Armored	Central Europe	——

Dixie

Code name for U.S. mission to observe Chinese Communist forces.

Dixon, Chief Aviation Machinist's Mate Harold

U.S. Navy pilot and leader of heroic raft odyssey. Dixon and his two-man air crew, petty officers 2nd class Gene Aldrich and 3rd class Tony Pastula, took off from the U.S. AIRCRAFT CARRIER *ENTERPRISE* (CV 6) in the Pacific on Jan. 16, 1942, flying a TBD DEVASTATOR bomber. The aircraft missed its rendezvous with the carrier and the plane, out of gas, came down at sea. With only the contents of their pockets, the three men spent thirty-four days adrift in an open rubber life raft. The fliers were burned raw by the sun and swamped by heavy seas; they survived by drinking rainwater and eating raw fish and birds they could catch by hand, drifting coconuts, and marine growth on floating stumps. They finally reached the island of Pukapuka, some 750 miles from where their plane went down, and were rescued by a U.S. warship. (They had actually drifted about 1,000 miles.)

Dixon was awarded the Navy Cross for his "extraordinary heroism, exceptional determination, resourcefulness, skilled seamanship, excellent judgment and highest quality of leadership."

Dixon, Comdr. Robert E. (1906—)

U.S. Navy dive bomber leader. During the Battle of CORAL SEA, on May 7, 1942, he led the SBD DAUNTLESS dive bombers of Scouting SQUADRON 2 from the carrier *LEXINGTON* (CV 2) against the Japanese carrier *SHOHO*. As planes from the "Lex" and *Yorktown* (CV 5) smashed the Japanese warship, Dixon radioed back to his own carrier, "Scratch one flattop!"

Dixon retired in 1960 as a rear admiral.

Do 17/Do 215

German medium bomber, reconnaissance, and night-fighter aircraft. This Dornier design was known as the "Flying Pencil" or "Eversharp" because of its long, narrow fuselage. Originally developed as a commercial mail-carrying aircraft, the Do 17 was rejected for that role but was adopted by the Luftwaffe as a high-speed bomber in 1935.

The first two production models—the Do 17E and F—saw combat in the SPANISH CIVIL WAR as bombers. They were followed by specialized PATHFINDER and photo-reconnaissance variants, with bomber versions continuing to be improved. A night-fighter version was evaluated, being a Do 17Z-3 with the nose of a JU 88 fighter, but that hybrid was abandoned for a specialized night-fighter configuration of the Do 17, of which only nine were completed; a small number of Do 215 night-fighter/intruder aircraft were also built.

The invasion of Poland began with an attack on the Dirschau railroad bridge by a squadron of Do 17s on Sept. 1, 1939. Thereafter the planes were in the forefront of German assaults throughout Europe and in the BATTLE OF BRITAIN. By mid-1941 the DO 217 had replaced the earlier plane, with the improved Do 215 serving into 1942.

Production of the Do 17 totaled some 1,700 aircraft; the Do 215 production run was smaller. The latter designation was derived from a Do 17Z demonstration aircraft sent to Yugoslavia in 1937, with Do 217 then being applied to improved models. No aircraft were purchased by Yugoslavia although the Soviet Union did procure several aircraft before Germany attacked that country.

A streamlined, twin-engine, high-wing aircraft, the Do 17 first flew in 1934. The original single tail fin was replaced by a twin-tail configuration. The main landing gear fully retracted into the radial engine nacelles. The maximum speed of the Do 17 was 255 mph and was credited with a tactical radius of 205 miles in the bomber role.

An internal BOMB load of 2,205 pounds was carried and defensive armament for the bomber variants was up to eight 7.9-mm machine guns. The Do 17Z-10 night fighter had two 20-mm cannon and four 7.9-mm guns in a solid nose (the bomber variants having a glazed nose). The bomber crew was four or five, depending upon the number of guns fitted.

Do 18

German flying boat employed in reconnaissance and search-and-rescue roles. The high-wing aircraft, resembling the U.S. PBY CATALINA, had two in-line diesel engines housed in a single nacelle mounted above the wing. The Dornier design originated as a trans-Atlantic mail carrier, which first flew in 1935, and entered Luftwaffe service in 1936. When production ended in 1940, the Luftwaffe had accepted ninety-four aircraft with civil-military production totaling about 160 units.

Do 24

This three-engine flying boat was designed by the German firm Dornier for the Dutch government. It was in production jointly by Aviolanda and De Schelde in Holland and was taken over by Germany after the 1940 invasion of Holland. Meanwhile, two German-built prototypes were used by the Luftwaffe in the 1940 invasion of Norway.

When Germany invaded the Netherlands the Dutch firms had completed twenty-five aircraft, some of which were already in the Far East. Those saw extensive combat during the effort to slow the Japanese advances of 1941–1942. Six of the Do 24K aircraft that reached Australia were taken over by the Royal Australian Air Force.

Meanwhile, Germany took over the aircraft in Holland and employed them for search-and-rescue. Production was continued in Holland under German aegis as well as in France. These Do 24s were also employed in the transport and reconnaissance roles by the Luftwaffe. (Those French-built aircraft not yet delivered to the Luftwaffe after the NORMANDY INVASION were later taken over by the French Navy; a transport flotilla flying the Do 24 was organized in Dec. 1944.) The Germans also transferred Do 24s to Spain and one, which landed in Sweden, was given to that nation and flown until 1951 when, under the wartime Allied agreements, it was transferred to the Soviet Union! Also, the Germans transferred twelve aircraft to Spain to enable that nation to carry out search-and-rescue operations in areas of interest to Germany.

The German-built prototype Do 24 flew on July 3, 1937. In all, thirty-seven aircraft were built in Germany, 195 in the Netherlands, and forty-eight in France—a total of 280, a relatively large production run.

The Do 24 was a three-engine flying boat, with the wing mounted above the fuselage on heavy struts, bearing some resemblance to the U.S. PBY CATALINA; three radial engines were mounted in the wing; a tall, twin tail was fitted. Large hull sponsons were fitted for lateral stability on the water, alleviating the need for wing floats.

The Do 24T model had a maximum speed of 211 mph with a maximum range of 2,950 miles. A hydraulically powered dorsal turret had a single 20-mm cannon and single 7.9-mm machine guns were mounted in the nose and tail. In the attack role twelve 110-pound bombs could be carried under the wings. The plane's crew numbered five or six.

Do 217

A development of the DO 17/215 medium bomber, this Dornier aircraft was a more versatile aircraft. Entering service in 1940, the Do 217 was employed as a bomber, night fighter, torpedo, anti-shipping and photo-reconnaissance aircraft, and GUIDED MISSILE carrier.

They were flown extensively in most combat areas. The aircraft were used to attack CONVOYS in the North Atlantic and Arctic with conventional BOMBS, and beginning in 1943 they were employed with guided missiles to attack warships. The first operational sorties came in Aug. 1943 when Do 217s carrying the Hs 293A missile—a guided bomb—attacked a British submarine on the surface in the Bay of Biscay; that craft escaped, but two days later the British corvette *Egret* was sunk and a Canadian destroyer damaged by these weapons. The corvette was the first warship to ever be sunk by a guided weapon, i.e., one whose direction could be changed after being launched.

On Sept. 9 a Do 217 launched a FRITZ-X guided missile against the Italian battleship *ROMA,* en route to MALTA to surrender to the Allies. Two hits by guided missiles sank the warship with 1,255 of her crew being lost. Subsequent Do 217/Fritz X attacks severely damaged the Italian battleship *Italia,* the British battleship *Warspite,* the British cruiser *Uganda,* and the U.S. CRUISER *Savannah* (CL 42). In the ANZIO landings in Jan. 1945 strikes by Do 217s using guided missiles sank a British cruiser and destroyer. The Hs 293A guided missile was also carried by Do 217 variants.

The first Do 217 flew in Aug. 1938 and crashed a month later, killing both crewmen. The first production variants entered service in 1940. Production totaled 1,730 aircraft, including a small number of Do 217J models supplied to Italy.

The Do 217 was a mid-wing, twin-engine aircraft with a streamlined fuselage and twin tail. The main undercarriage fully retracted into the engine nacelles (radial and in-line engines were provided). The Do 217E-2 model had a maximum speed of 320 mph, increased in the Do 217M-1 model to 348 mph. The Do 217E aircraft could internally carry 4,410 pounds of bombs; alternatively, two aerial TORPEDOES could be carried under the wings. Defensive armament for that model was one 15-mm cannon and five 7.9-mm machine guns. The Do 217 night fighters had four 20-mm cannon plus four 7.9-mm machine guns in a solid nose, with some aircraft also having upward-firing fixed 20-mm cannon. The night fighters had no bomb bays and were fitted with air-intercept RADAR.

Doctors Trial

The Nuremberg WAR CRIMES trial of twenty-three SS physicians and scientists, held before a U.S. Military Tribunal from Dec. 1946 to Aug. 1947. Charges against the defendants went back to the "euthanasia" work early in the NAZI era and continued into murderous experiments in CONCENTRATION CAMPS and DEATH CAMPS. The trial revealed that the SS had authorized the use of prisoners for experiments, medical and SS participation in racial-purity and eugenics research.

Although the trial focused on SS doctors, it reached into the German health and medical establishment, as represented by such SS doctors as Karl Brandt, HITLER's personal physician and Reich Commissioner for Health and Sanitation.

Brandt endorsed Hitler's belief that the way toward a master Aryan race began with medically supervised eugenic murders. A euthanasia document found by U.S. war crimes investigators showed that the killers wanted to keep their work secret: "Thirty thousand attended to," it said. "Another hundred thousand to one hundred and twenty thousand waiting. Keep the circle of those in the know as small as possible."

The document referred to work done by the Generation Foundation for Welfare and Institutional Care, known as T-4 because it was located at Tiergartenstrasse 4 in Berlin. The program put into practice what Hitler had urged in *Mein Kampf*: the master race needed to eliminate "all who are in any way visibly sick or who have inherited a disease and can therefore pass it on." The Reich Committee for Scientific Research of Hereditary and Severe Constitutional Diseases, administrator of the program, required midwives and physicians to require the registration of any children suffering from congenital malformation or mental retardation. About 5,000 physically or mentally disabled children were killed between 1939 and 1944. A total of about 70,000 were killed through this program. A form letter told the next of kin that the person had died of pneumonia or a heart attack or other disease and that the body had been cremated because of fears of contagious disease.

The Public-Benefit Patient Transportation Society took mentally ill adult patients from asylums to killing centers in vans sometimes called "murder boxes." This was also handled by the SS. A few were killed by ZYKLON-B, the gas later used in death camps, but most were killed in fake shower rooms by carbon monoxide gas. About 80,000 to 100,000 were killed. Next of kin got letters similar to those sent to the victims of the "research" program.

At the Dachau concentration center, the Luftwaffe set up a pressure chamber for experiments on oxygen deprivation, related to the effects of high-altitude flight. An unknown number of inmates were put in the chamber and died horribly as air was withdrawn and they gasped for breath in a near-vacuum. In experiments to determine how a downed Luftwaffe airman could survive in the sea, soaking wet inmates were placed in subzero chambers. "Some lived," a research aide reported, "but most of them died."

Four of the Doctors Trial defendants were acquitted, seven were sentenced to death, including Brandt, who was hanged on June 2, 1948. SS Dr. Karl Clauberg, who performed grisly research in Experimental Block 10 at the death camp at AUSCHWITZ, died in 1955 before standing trial, after his release by the Soviets. (The most notorious Auschwitz physician was JOSEF MENGELE.) Clauberg experimented on women inmates, trying to develop high-speed sterilization techniques. He injected irritating chemicals into his subject's uterus, causing intense pain and, frequently, death. He began his work at the women's concentration camp in Ravensbrück.

Dog Tags

Slang for identity disks or tags worn by U.S. soldiers, sailors, and airmen on a chain around the neck. Servicemen and women had two identical, rounded oblong metal tags that gave name, date of birth, religious preference, and blood type. When a soldier was injured the tag was used to identify blood for transfusion; in case of death, one tag was usually shoved between the corpse's teeth as permanent identification and the other kept by the unit's commander or administrative officer.

Some armed forces used tags that also listed the individual's parent military unit; some discs were designed to be broken in half to provide two parts.

Dominator,

see B-32.

Dominican Republic

Capital: Ciudad Trujillo, pop. 1,656,219 (1939). Early in 1939 Generalissimo Rafael Trujillo, the strongman leader of the Dominican Republic, offered colonization for up to 100,000 JEWS fleeing Eastern Europe. Before the end of 1940 about 500 immigrants, most of them German Jews, arrived and were given well over 50,000 acres of land. U.S. experts soon arrived to develop electrical and sanitary facilities.

The nation declared war on Japan on Dec. 8, 1941, on Germany and Italy on Dec. 11, and, following the U.S. lead, ended relations with VICHY FRANCE on Nov. 9, 1942. The Dominican Republic's principal contribution to the war was the establishing of coastal patrols that watched for U-BOATS attempting to use remote bays as hideouts.

Dönitz, *Grossadmiral* Karl (1891–1980)

Commander of the German U-BOAT force and ADOLF HITLER's successor as head of the THIRD REICH. Dönitz began his naval career as a cadet in 1910. During World War I he served on a German light cruiser loaned to the Turkish Navy and then commanded a small submarine, which was sunk, causing his capture by the British in Oct. 1918.

Between the wars Dönitz served ashore and afloat and became an early member of the NAZI party and admirer of Hitler. In 1936 he was named com-

mander of the fledgling German submarine force. In the prewar period he helped build the U-boat force and developed WOLF PACK tactics. Although he requested assignment to another part of the Navy, he was kept in command of the undersea force. After *Kapitänleutnant* GÜNTHER PRIEN's sinking of the British battleship *Royal Oak* in Oct. 1939, Dönitz was promoted to *Kontradmiral*; he was promoted to *Vizeadmiral* a year later and to full admiral in 1942.

In Jan. 1943, when ERICH RAEDER resigned as CinC of the Navy, Hitler appointed Dönitz although he was not Raeder's first choice as a successor. Hitler undoubtedly appointed Dönitz—and promoted him to *Grossadmiral*—because the U-boats were the only element of the German armed forces still on the offensive. Ironically, Raeder had resigned because Hitler demanded that all surface warships be retired. But upon becoming CinC Dönitz, too, argued for keeping the surface ships in active service, primarily for use against the RUSSIAN CONVOYS.

In 1943–1945 Dönitz presided over a series of defeats of the German Navy in the Atlantic, Arctic, Baltic, and Black Sea areas. He attempted to continue the U-boat war, but after May 1943 the issue was never in doubt—the British and U.S. Navies had won the BATTLE OF THE ATLANTIC, although there were periodic successes for the U-boats.

Dönitz, unlike Raeder, was a fervent Nazi. In addition to military decorations, in Jan. 1944 his loyalty to National Socialism was recognized by the award of the coveted Golden Party Badge.

As the Allied armies cut Germany in half in mid-April 1945, Hitler gave Dönitz command of forces in the northern sector; on April 22 he established his headquarters at Ploen (Plön), near Kiel, on the Baltic. On the night of April 30 Dönitz was informed that Hitler had appointed him as his successor as president of the Reich and Supreme Commander of the Armed Forces (in place of HERMANN GÖRING). On the morning of May 1 Dönitz received word from the *FÜHRERBUNKER* that he was to replace Hitler, although word of Hitler's suicide was temporarily kept secret from him.

Dönitz led the crumbling Third Reich for twenty-three days from his headquarters in Flensburg-Mürwik, attempting to continue the war on the EASTERN FRONT, to delay the Soviet advances as some 2,000,000 German troops and civilian refugees fled to British and American lines. Finally, he sent his representatives to sign the German SURRENDERS to Field Marshal BERNARD MONTGOMERY on May 4, to Gen. of the Army DWIGHT D. EISENHOWER on May 7, and to the Soviets on May 9.

The British arrested Dönitz and his Cabinet on May 23 and he was held to be tried for WAR CRIMES at Nuremberg. Although the U.S. CinC in the Pacific during the war, Adm. CHESTER W. NIMITZ, testified that the U.S. Navy had practiced unrestricted submarine warfare in the Pacific, Dönitz was found guilty of war crimes and sentenced to ten years in Spandau prison—the lightest sentence given to any of the defendants. Peter Padfield, a British naval historian, observed that the Nuremberg tribunal censured Dönitz although the evidence at the trial did "not establish with the certainty required that Dönitz deliberately ordered the killing of shipwrecked survivors." But Padfield contended in *Dönitz, The Last Führer* that Dönitz "had

incited his men to kill survivors, the 'ambiguities' in his orders had been criminal, and he bore prime responsibility for the murder of the crew of the [steamer] *Peleus*—to take one proven instance."

He was imprisoned until 1956. After his release Dönitz wrote three books and, briefly, lectured to high school students on the Nazi movement and submarine warfare.

Both of his sons died in the war, one in a U-boat and one on a torpedo boat; his daughter's husband also died in a submarine.

Donnerschlag

Code name for planned breakout of German Sixth Army from STALINGRAD, Dec. 1942. Also given code name *Wintergewitter* (Winter Storm).

Donovan, Maj. Gen. William J. (1883–1959)

Director of the U.S. OFFICE OF STRATEGIC SERVICES (OSS) during the war. "Wild Bill" Donovan established and directed the U.S. clandestine intelli-

The end of the Third Reich. Hitler's successor, *Grossadmiral* Karl Dönitz is arrested in Flensburg, Germany, on May 24, 1945. He is shown at the time of his arrest flanked by the brilliant Albert Speer, Hitler's architect and minister for munitions production, and *Generaloberst* Alfred Jodl, acting commander in chief of the German Army. *(Imperial War Museum)*

gence and special operations organization from its establishment in 1941. His OSS was the precursor of the Central Intelligence Agency (CIA).

When World War I began, Donovan, a prominent and prosperous New York lawyer, went to Europe to help Herbert Hoover in famine relief efforts. He was recalled to the United States in 1916 for active Army duty and saw action fighting Pancho Villa's raiders on the Mexican-U.S. border. In World War I he was a BATTALION commander in France, where he was wounded and awarded the Distinguished Service Cross and the MEDAL OF HONOR.

Donovan's faith in the black arts of intelligence began in the years following World War I, when State Department officials sent him on a mission to revolt-torn Russia. He recommended that the United States use covert operations, rather than troops, against Russian Communists.

Donovan later served in the Justice Department, then opened a law firm. In the immediate prewar years he was a special ambassador for President ROOSEVELT, traveling throughout Europe and the Middle East. In the summer of 1941 Roosevelt made Donovan "Coordinator of Information," a vague title for a vague job, which Donovan attempted to define with a memo calling for the establishment of "an effective service for analyzing, comprehending, and appraising" information about "the intentions of potential enemies and the limit of the economic and military RESOURCES of those enemies."

Roosevelt wrote *OK* on the memo. But a bureaucratic war began. The new intelligence agency was formidably opposed by J. EDGAR HOOVER, director of the FEDERAL BUREAU OF INVESTIGATION, the Army's military intelligence organization, and the Office of Naval Intelligence. The Army, however, was convinced by Brig. Gen. WALTER BEDELL SMITH that since Donovan had easy access to the White House and important Roosevelt administration officials, it would be a good idea to tuck his new organization under the JOINT CHIEFS OF STAFF. Donovan's organization on June 13, 1942, became the OSS under JCS jurisdiction. (Smith in 1950 would become director of Central Intelligence.)

Donovan almost lost his fledgling OSS in July 1942 when he authorized monthly burglaries of the Spanish Embassy in WASHINGTON to gather diplomatic messages needed as part of the intelligence-gathering for the NORTH AFRICA INVASION. The FBI came close to exposing the operation. Intervention by the JCS saved Donovan and the OSS.

Donovan spent much of his time fighting off resistance from a host of critics, ranging from British intelligence officials who opposed him as a rival in Europe to Gen. DOUGLAS MACARTHUR, who barred the OSS from the Pacific theater. Donovan, however, was a man hard to stop. He knew when to be tough and when to be smooth. One of his European operatives, WILLIAM CASEY (another future director of Central Intelligence) described him as "a roly-poly man, soft of voice and manner belying the sobriquet 'Wild Bill' he had never been able to shake."

During the NORMANDY INVASION Donovan was pinned down on a Normandy beach by German machine-gun fire. He turned to another OSS officer and said, "We know too much." He drew a pistol and added, "If we are going to get captured, I'll shoot you first. Then myself. After all, I'm the commanding officer."

After the war Donovan served briefly as associate prosecutor at the Nuremberg WAR CRIMES trials of Nazi leaders.

Doolittle, Lt. Gen. James (1896—)

Leader of the first air raid on Japan. Before the war "Jimmie" Doolittle, who had been an Army flight instructor in World War I, was already famous in aviation circles for his exploits as a test pilot and racing pilot, who won the Schneider Trophy for the U.S. Army in 1925. Recalled to active duty in 1940, he initially worked with automotive executives on plans for conversion to WAR PRODUCTION. In early 1942, as an Army Air Forces lieutenant colonel, Doolittle was directed to train volunteer flight crews for a carrier-launched raid on Japan. He personally led the raid against Japan on April 18, 1942, after which his plane crash-landed in China. (See DOOLITTLE RAID.)

Doolittle made his way out of China and returned to the United States. Awarded the MEDAL OF HONOR for leading the raid, he was also promoted to brigadier general (one of only two U.S.

AAF officers to skip the rank of colonel during the war).

He was assigned to command the Twelfth AIR FORCE in England in Sept. 1942, which was deployed to North Africa after the NORTH AFRICA INVASION in Nov. 1942. In Feb. 1943 Doolittle assumed command of the Anglo-American Strategic Air Force in North Africa. This was followed by command of the Fifteenth Air Force, which covered the central Mediterranean area. In Jan. 1944 he took command of the Eighth Air Force in England flying heavy bombers against European targets (he was promoted to lieutenant general after taking command). He held that position until May 1945, when he began moving part of his command to the Pacific in preparation for operations against Japan. He left active duty in Jan. 1946. In 1985, Congress promoted Doolittle to full general.

Doolittle Raid

First bombing raid on Japan. Conceived by a naval officer as a means of raising U.S. morale in the dark days of early 1942, a plan to bomb Japan was embraced by the Navy and Army Air Forces. The strike force of sixteen B-25B MITCHELL bombers was trained and led by Lt. Col. JAMES (JIMMIE) DOOLITTLE.

AAF pilots conducted extensive training on ground mockups of a carrier deck, learning to take off with a run of only 450 feet compared to the normal runway takeoff of 1,200 to 1,500 feet (there would, however, be considerable wind over the carrier's deck). The volunteer crews flew their planes across country to be loaded by crane on the deck of the U.S. AIRCRAFT CARRIER *HORNET* (CV 8) in late March 1942 at Alameda, near San Francisco. The ship then rendezvoused with a Navy carrier task force commanded by Vice Adm. WILLIAM F. HALSEY. Centered on the carrier *ENTERPRISE* (CV 6), the force also contained four CRUISERS, eight DESTROYERS, and two oilers. The plan was to launch the bombers when the *Hornet* was 400 miles east of TOKYO.

Japanese picket boats sighted the carrier force before reaching the bomber launching position. The pickets were sunk by cruiser gunfire *after* they had broadcast a warning to Japan. But the Japanese high command believed that the carriers would have to come closer to Japan before launching conventional carrier aircraft.

The *Hornet* began launching the sixteen Army bombers from a position 800 miles east of Tokyo on April 18 in history's first bombing raid against Japan. Doolittle's planes bombed Tokyo, Kobe, Nagoya, and Yokohama without opposition. Thirteen planes struck Tokyo beginning at 12:15 P.M. Most planes carried an incendiary cluster and three 500-pound BOMBS; the pilots had specific orders not to bomb the Imperial Palace. The bombers arrived immediately after a scheduled air raid drill and most of those in Tokyo who saw the bombers and antiaircraft fire thought they were part of the exercise.

Because of bad weather and the longer-than-expected flight due to the early launch following detection by picket boats, fifteen of the planes crash-landed in China and one landed at a Soviet base at Primorsky in Siberia. Of the seventy-five fliers who crashed in China, three died accidentally and eight were captured by the Japanese. After trials of the Doolittle "criminals," the Japanese executed three men and one died in prison. The fliers in China, plus the five-man crew detained in the Soviet Union eventually returned to the United States. The four survivors in Japan were liberated at the end of the war.

When asked where the bombers came from, President ROOSEVELT replied "SHANGRI-LA," referring to the mythical Asian kingdom in James Hilton's novel *Lost Horizon*. The U.S. Navy promptly named an aircraft carrier under construction the *Shangri-La* (CV 38).

The Doolittle raid inflicted little damage but had important psychological impact for the United States and Japan. The raid also forced the Japanese to push forward the planned assault on MIDWAY atoll to help prevent further carrier attacks against Japan. Because of this speedup, two Japanese carriers were unable to join the striking force. This gave the U.S. Navy better odds in the decisive carrier battle (four Japanese carriers to three U.S. carriers).

Dornberger, *Generalmajor* Walter (1895–1980)

Military head of the German V-2 MISSILE program. An ARTILLERY officer in World War I, Dornberger was placed in charge of the German military ROCKET program in 1930. He established a test center near BERLIN, with one of his assistants being WERNHER VON BRAUN.

The rocket program was moved to PEENEMÜNDE on the Baltic coast in 1937. There Dornberger, as commanding officer of the Peenemünde Rocket Research Institute, and von Braun led the V-2 development effort, with the first successful test flight occurring on Oct. 3, 1942. As that first ballistic missile rose skyward, Dornberger later wrote in his autobiographical *V-2*, "I am not ashamed to admit that I wept with joy. I couldn't speak for a moment; my emotion was too great. I could see that Colonel Zanssen was in the same state. He was standing there laughing. His eyes were moist. He stretched out his hands to me. I grasped them. Then our emotions ran away with us. We yelled and embraced each other like excited boys. . . . everyone was shouting, laughing, leaping, dancing, and shaking hands."

The first operational missiles were fired against PARIS on Sept. 6, 1944; two days later, two V-2s struck England; more than a thousand were launched against England as well as ROTTERDAM during the next six months. Allied bombing, vacillation of German leadership, and technical problems had delayed the introduction of the V-2 into combat until Sept. 1944.

In May 1945, when Germany capitulated, Dornberger surrendered to the Americans. He was imprisoned in England for two years but was not tried for WAR CRIMES. He emigrated to the United States and in 1947 became a missile consultant to the newly established U.S. Air Force. In 1950 he joined the Bell Aircraft Corp. where he worked on a variety of spacecraft projects.

Double Cross,
see XX COMMITTEE.

Dowding, Air Chief Marshal Sir Hugh (1882–1970)
Commander of the Royal Air Force Fighter Command during the BATTLE OF BRITAIN. A veteran of the World War I Royal Flying Corps, Dowding laid the foundation for the aerial defense of England.

During the 1930s, as research coordinator for the RAF he worked on the development of the SPITFIRE and HURRICANE fighters and successfully urged the erection of RADAR installations along the coasts. In 1936 he became Air Officer Commanding in Chief of Fighter Command.

From the time the EUROPEAN WAR began in Sept. 1939 to the German sweep across France in May–June 1940, Dowding was under pressure to commit substantial numbers of Fighter Command aircraft to the Continent. But he stubbornly resisted, fending off even demands from Prime Minister CHURCHILL. Fighter Command did provide vital cover for the British withdrawal from DUNKIRK, but Dowding essentially won his argument: His fighters' prime mission was the direct defense of Britain.

An austere, solitary man who earned the nickname "Stuffy," Dowding made few friends and, when the chances of a German invasion of England faded in the fall of 1940, he was succeeded by Air Marshal Sir Sholto Douglas. Dowding retired in 1942. He became a baron and won a memorial in Westminster Abbey that says: "He Led the Few in the Battle of Britain."

Downfall
U.S. code name for the overall assault on Japan, 1945–1946; see MAJESTIC.

DPs,
see DISPLACED PERSONS.

Dracula
Code name for planned Allied AMPHIBIOUS LANDING at Rangoon, May 1945.

Draft,
see SELECTIVE SERVICE.

Dragon Teeth
Term for extensive German TANK barriers that made up part of the SIEGFRIED LINE (West Wall) along the western frontier of Germany. The "teeth" were rows of reinforced concrete blocks that resembled rows of giant teeth.

Dragoon
Code name for Allied invasion of southern France, Aug. 1944; later changed to Anvil.

Dresden

German city devastated by Anglo-American bombers. Shortly after 10 on the night of Feb. 13–14, 1945, the RAF Bomber Command carried out one of the heaviest raids of the European air war, with 873 RAF bombers dropping thousands of incendiaries and high-explosive bombs up to 4 tons on Dresden. They set the city on fire and started a firestorm as the rising column of intense heat sucked up oxygen and burned it, creating hurricane-like winds and temperatures up to 1,000° F or higher. On Feb. 14, beginning at noon, 311 B-17 FLYING FORTRESS bombers released 771 tons of bombs on the flaming city, and on the following day 210 B-17s dropped another 461 tons. The firestorm raged for four days and could be seen for 200 miles.

The raid destroyed 1,600 acres in the center of the city, about three times the area destroyed in LONDON during the more than two months of sustained bombing in the 1940 BLITZ. In Dresden people in air raid shelters suffocated or were baked alive. German sources estimated that 135,000 persons were killed, including thousands of refugees fleeing from advancing Soviet troops. The city was heavily bombed again on March 12 and April 17. Soviet troops captured the city on May 8.

American novelist Kurt Vonnegut, Jr., a PRISONER OF WAR in Dresden during the bombing, described it in a terrifying scene in *Slaughterhouse Five:* "There were sounds like giant footsteps above. Those were sticks of high-explosive bombs. The giants walked and walked." (The novel's title names the place, two stories under a cattle slaughterhouse, where Vonnegut and other American prisoners endured the firestorm.)

The first raid was planned by Allied strategists to break German morale and paralyze Dresden, an important rail-communications center for German forces on the EASTERN FRONT. Writing in his diary about the bombing of Dresden a month later, Minister of Propaganda JOSEPH GOEBBELS said, "The morale of the German people, both at home and at the front, is sinking ever lower."

Prime Minister CHURCHILL, responding to moral questions raised by the bombing, called for a review of "the question of bombing of German cities simply for the sake of increasing terror, though under other pretext." Dresden became a symbol of the horrors of modern war, and Air Chief Marshal Sir ARTHUR HARRIS, Commander in Chief of the RAF Bomber Command, became inextricably linked with it. But the U.S. Eighth AIR FORCE generally escaped criticism for its role in the city's destruction.

Duck

Code name for British destroyers bombarding the German airfield at Stavanger, Norway, April 1940.

DUKW Amphibious Truck

Known invariably as the "duck," the DUKW amphibious truck was widely used by U.S. and British forces in the war. First employed during Operation Husky, the invasion of SICILY in July 1943, the American-developed DUKW was a six-wheel vehicle that could travel through the water (using a small propeller and rudder) as well as on land.

The U.S. Army operated the DUKW extensively in AMPHIBIOUS LANDINGS, liking the land mobility of the vehicle. The U.S. Marine Corps initially used the vehicle sparingly, preferring the LVT AMPHIBIOUS TRACTOR, which afforded light protection for its troops, had a rear ramp that facilitated unloading troops and vehicles, and could crawl over coral reefs and other obstacles. Also, LVTs were more mobile in jungles, where they could crush through the undergrowth and traverse swamps. But the DUKW did not chew up telephone wires laid on the ground or destroy roads the way tracked vehicles did. The DUKWs were carried into the assault area in LST and LSM AMPHIBIOUS SHIPS.

Officially rated as a 2½-ton, 6×6 amphibian

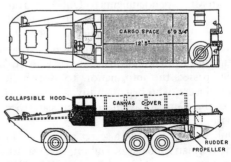

DUKW amphibious truck.

truck, the "duck" could carry twenty-five troops or twelve litters, or 5,000 pounds of cargo, including a 105-mm howitzer. Maximum speed was 50 mph on land and 5.5 knots in water. At a speed of 35 mph the vehicle had a land range of some 400 miles. The cargo-troop hold of the DUKW was open, but could be fitted with a canvas cover. The Army armed some DUKWs with ROCKETS in an effort to provide a fire support weapon for troops ashore, but it was of dubious value.

Dulles, Allen (1893–1969)

Chief of the OFFICE OF STRATEGIC SERVICES office in Bern. Dulles' chief accomplishment was the contacts he made with anti-HITLER Germans seeking ways to end the war with Germany.

Hans B. Gisevius, the German vice consul in Zürich from 1940 to 1944, got Dulles in touch with the small German resistance movement. When the JULY 20 PLOT to kill Hitler failed, Gisevius fled to Switzerland and continued to work from there to bring about a negotiated peace between the ALLIES and Germany. The U.S. State Department, pursuing the UNCONDITIONAL SURRENDER policy of President ROOSEVELT, showed scant interest in Dulles' surrender-seeking efforts.

Dulles was able, however, to help arrange Operation Sunrise, the secret surrender of German forces in northern Italy (see SURRENDER, GERMANY). Dulles met with *SS-Obergruppenführer* Karl Wolff, HEINRICH HIMMLER's former adjutant, who was German military governor of northern Italy. Wolff sent out peace feelers in Feb. 1945, but Allied political hesitation about a "conditional" capitulation delayed Wolff's surrender until April 29.

Fritz Kolbe (code-named George Wood), one of Dulles' agents, delivered more than 2,000 German Foreign Ministry documents to Dulles at great risk. Among them was the copy of a cable in which the German Ambassador in Turkey, FRANZ VON PAPEN, boasted about the acquisition of top-secret documents from the British Embassy in Ankara. Dulles passed the information to British intelligence officers, who began an investigation that inspired the German agent to disappear. (See CICERO.)

Dulles also learned of a secret radio transmitter, in the German Embassy in Dublin, that was used to direct U-BOATS to Allied ships.

Dulles, who had worked at the Versailles Peace Conference after World War I with his brother, John Foster Dulles (a future secretary of state), throughout his life shuttled between private practice as a lawyer and government service. He helped to organize the Central Intelligence Agency in 1947, became its deputy director in 1951 and its director in 1953.

Dumbarton Oaks Conference

Wartime meeting that led to the founding of the UNITED NATIONS. Representatives of the United States, the United Kingdom, the Soviet Union, and China met at Dumbarton Oaks, an estate in WASHINGTON, D.C., to begin planning the creation of a world organization. From Aug. 21 to Sept. 28, 1944, U.S., Soviet, and British officials met. From then until Oct. 7, the Soviet Union left the talks and China entered (because at this time the Soviet Union was not at war against Japan). An agreement was reached by all four participating nations. They essentially agreed on the outline of the UN. But political details were not worked out. This would be the work of the SAN FRANCISCO CONFERENCE.

Dumbo

American slang for PBY CATALINA flying boats used in the search-and-rescue role; named for cartoonist Walt Disney's flying elephant.

Dunkirk

The French Channel port used by British troops for their evacuation from the continent as German forces completed their FRANCE AND LOW COUNTRIES CAMPAIGN with the conquest of France. The epic cross-Channel evacuation, known as Operation Dynamo, involved more than a thousand vessels, from Royal Navy destroyers to fishing craft, yachts, and pleasure boats, sailed by gallant civilians. (The smallest vessel was the *Tamzine,* a 14-foot fishing boat, which took troops from the beach to evacuation ships.)

British officials estimated that only 50,000 men, under merciless air attacks, might escape capture by the encircling Germans. But by June 3, 1940—the ninth day of the evacuation—338,226 troops, including about 100,000 French soldiers, had reached England. Most of the troops' weapons and all heavy guns and vehicles were abandoned. The

British were wont to hail Dunkirk as a victory, but Prime Minister CHURCHILL told Parliament that this was "a deliverance" and "wars are not won by evacuations."

Dunlop

British code name for the reinforcement of MALTA, April 1941.

Dutch East Indies

Oil-rich islands conquered by Japan early in the war. Japan's need for oil mandated the taking of these islands at any cost. The cost turned out to be little because the Japanese easily defeated the ABDA (American-British-Dutch-Australian) forces attempting to halt the southward advances of the JAPANESE CAMPAIGN IN THE FAR EAST.

The invasion began with landings on Borneo and Island of CELEBES on Jan. 11, 1942, and Sumatra on Feb. 14–16, using troops landed from transports and paratroopers. Japanese forces completed the swift takeover on March 1, with landings on Java. Allied losses included the U.S. aircraft transport *LANGLEY* (AV 3), the U.S. CRUISER *HOUSTON* (CA 35), and the Australian cruiser *Perth*. Organized resistance, primarily by Dutch forces, ended on March 8.

Dutch Harbor

Site of a U.S. Naval Base on the ALEUTIAN island of Unalaska. The island was attacked by Japanese carrier aircraft on June 3, 1942, as a diversion at the outset of the battle of MIDWAY.

The Japanese sent the carriers *Junyo* and *Ryujo,* with two heavy cruisers, three destroyers, and an oiler to Dutch Harbor under cover of fog. Twelve aircraft bombed and strafed the port, killing about twenty-five U.S. servicemen and shooting down a PBY CATALINA.

The next day the carriers again launched strikes at Dutch Harbor, blowing up fuel tanks and killing a score of men. U.S. Army bombers made futile attacks on the two Japanese carriers. On June 7, in a separate action, Japanese troops made unopposed landings on the islands of Kiska and Attu.

On June 3 a Japanese pilot had radioed his carrier to say his ZERO was damaged and he was making an emergency landing on Akutan Island, where he wanted a submarine to pick him up. His wheels caught in the boggy terrain and the plane flipped over on its back. The pilot was killed, apparently as a result of a broken neck.

In July, a U.S. Navy patrol plane spotted the downed Zero and a salvage party was dispatched from Dutch Harbor. A freighter carried it—the first Zero to fall into U.S. hands—to the naval air station at North Island, San Diego, where it was repaired and flown to develop tactics against Zeros.

Dynamo

Code name for British evacuation of DUNKIRK, May–June 1940.

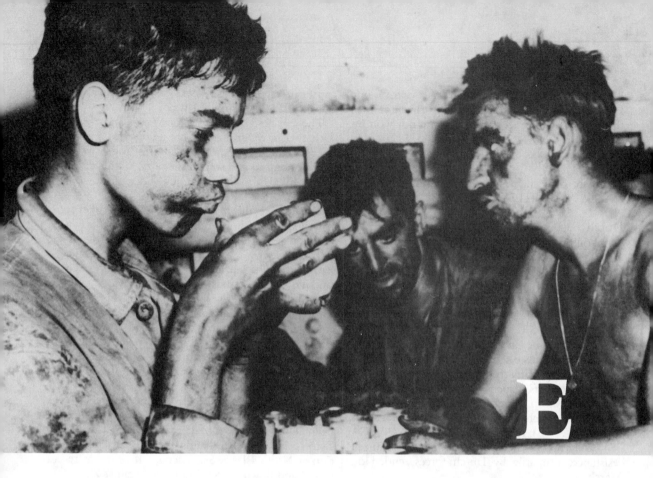

E

88-mm Flak

One of the most effective and versatile guns of World War II. The German 88-mm Flak (short for *Fliegerabwehrkanonen* or antiaircraft guns) was used in all land theaters.

The 88-mm Flak was introduced into service in 1933 and first saw action in the SPANISH CIVIL WAR. When World War II began in Europe in the fall of 1939 the Luftwaffe had almost one million men or nearly two-thirds of its strength serving in antiaircraft units, many armed with 88-mm flak guns. The guns were employed in the antitank role during the invasion of France in May 1940 (although once or twice they were used in that role in Spain). Subsequently, the AFRIKA KORPS in North Africa and German troops in the Soviet Union employed the weapon in both the antitank and antiair-

craft roles. It remained the backbone of Germany's air defense throughout the war.

The gun was generally mounted on a towed carriage with four two-tire bogeys; the wheels were removed and four outriggers were extended for firing. It had a practical rate of fire of 15 rounds per minute, firing a shell weighing 19.8 pounds with a muzzle velocity of 2,690 feet per second. This provided an effective ceiling of 26,250 feet when used against aircraft while maximum range in the antitank role was about 52,500 feet. A hollow-charge shell developed for the antitank role was effective at that range, although the gun's effective killing range was generally considered some 6,000 feet. Maximum gun elevation was 85°.

The initial service version was the 88-mm Flak 18. Several modifications followed, the Flak 36 having

Battle-weary Marines down cups of coffee on a Navy transport after two days and nights of savage fighting on Eniwetok. *(U.S. Coast Guard)*

an improved mounting, and the Flak 37 dials and fittings for use with a remote fire-control system. The Flak 41, which entered service in 1943, had a longer and stronger barrel, with a muzzle velocity of 3,110 feet per second, a range of 35,000 feet, and rate of fire of 20 rounds per minute. The Flak 18 weighed 15,432 pounds in travelling position while the Flak 36/37 were 18,078 pounds.

The gun had a firing crew of ten, reduced during the war to seven men.

Eagle

(1) Code name for Gen. MARK W. CLARK; (2) signal code name for the First U.S. ARMY GROUP, 1944–1945; the name *Eagle Tac* was used to indicate the Group's *tac*tical headquarters.

Eagle Day,

see *ADLER-TAG*.

Eagle Squadrons

RAF fighter units with U.S. pilots. When the war began in Europe several hundred Americans volunteered for service with the RAF although the U.S. NEUTRALITY ACTS made them liable to prosecution if they served in the RAF. (Although by 1941 American pilots were being urged by the U.S. government to fight in China with the FLYING TIGERS.)

Seven Americans are known to have served as pilots in RAF fighter squadrons in the BATTLE OF BRITAIN beginning in July 1940; others, with false identities, may also have served. One of the seven, Pilot Officer William M. (Billy) Fiske, shot down a German JU 88 bomber but two days later his HURRICANE fighter was damaged and he crash-landed with fatal wounds; five of the other seven were killed later in the war.

By Oct. 1940 there were enough American fliers entering the RAF to form No. 71 Squadron, the first of the all-American Eagle Squadrons. Two more Eagle Squadrons followed, No. 133 and 171. After the battle of Britain, these fighter squadrons flew combat missions over German-occupied France.

On Sept. 16, 1942, the British government announced that the RAF's three Eagle Squadrons would be incorporated into the U.S. AAF. In British service the American fighter pilots are credited with having shot down seventy-three German aircraft. (Other Americans served in the RAF in Bomber Command and other units.)

Eagle's Nest,

see BERCHTESGADEN.

Eaker, Lt. Gen. Ira C. (1896–1987)

Commanding general of U.S. Eighth AIR FORCE. Before America's entry into the war, Eaker, then a colonel, was stationed in England as an observer with the Royal Air Force. Promoted to brigadier general in Jan. 1942, he supervised the arrival in England of the first elements of the Eighth Air Force the following month. In April 1942 he was made chief of the U.S. Army Bomber Command in the European theater and, against British opposition, was a leading advocate of daylight PRECISION BOMBING. He participated in the first B-17 FLYING FORTRESS bombing mission, against the rail yards of ROUEN, on Aug. 17, 1942. A combined U.S.-British STRATEGIC BOMBING offensive, launched in January 1943, was known as the Eaker Plan. He served as commanding general of the Eighth Air Force from Dec. 1, 1942, to Jan. 1, 1944, when, as a lieutenant general, he assumed command of Allied air forces in the Mediterranean. In April 1944 he became deputy commander of the Army Air Forces and chief of the air staff in WASHINGTON, positions he held until his retirement in June 1947.

Earthquake Bombs,

see GRAND SLAM and TALLBOY BOMBS.

Eastern Front

Term for the German-Russian front from June 1941 until May 1945.

Eastern Solomons

The area, off GUADALCANAL, where a major naval battle took place on Aug. 23–25, 1942. The battle began when COASTWATCHERS in the SOLOMON ISLANDS spotted a Japanese reinforcement fleet heading for Guadalcanal, where U.S. Marines had landed on Aug. 7.

The Japanese force consisted of five transports that were to land 1,500 men under a covering force of four heavy cruisers, a light cruiser, and five destroyers. Supporting the landing would be three aircraft carriers, seven heavy cruisers, three light cruisers, twenty-two destroyers, and a seaplane carrier.

Three U.S. carriers were about 100 miles east of Guadalcanal, outside the Solomon chain, when the Japanese fleet was spotted. In the air and sea battle that followed, the U.S. carrier ENTERPRISE (CV 6) was badly damaged but the Japanese lost a light carrier, a destroyer, a transport, and sixty-one aircraft. The surviving Japanese troops were reloaded into destroyers, and landed without their heavy equipment three days later.

E-Boats

German motor torpedo boats that were highly effective in coastal waters of Europe. In addition to attacking Allied warships and merchant ships with TORPEDOES, the E-boats laid MINES.

The term *E-boat* originated with the Royal Navy, probably indicating "enemy" motor torpedo boat. The German designation was S-boat, for *Schnellboot* (fast boat). The first S-boat of the World War II era was completed in 1930. When the war began the German Navy had eighteen E-boats in service.

Typical of these craft was the *S-26,* which became the standard design for wartime production. This 92½-ton craft was 115 feet long, had diesel propulsion, and could reach 39 knots. Armament normally consisted of two 21-inch (533-mm) torpedo tubes and two 20-mm cannon, with a total of four or six torpedoes carried. During the war 37-mm and BOFORS 40-MM GUNS were also fitted to E-boats; some also carried mines. A crew of twenty-one manned the craft. Construction of E-boats continued through the war with more than 500 completed through early 1945.

E-boats were audacious in their operations, attacking in day or night. Until the loss of German bases on the French and Dutch coasts, they would sortie across the English Channel to strike at shipping along the English coast. On April 28, 1944, as the Allied navies prepared for the NORMANDY INVASION, a group of E-boats sailed from Cherbourg and fell on American LANDING SHIPS, TANK conducting an amphibious exercise off the coast of Devon (Operation Tiger). The torpedo boats

struck savagely at the unescorted LSTs, sinking the *LST 507* and *LST 531.* In the confusion that followed, 749 U.S. soldiers were killed and others injured. The E-boats escaped unscathed.

The E-boats and U-BOATS were the only effective German naval units when the war in Europe ended. About 100 E-boats were still in service (and were subsequently divided among the ALLIES).

Eclipse

Code name for the planned Allied AIRBORNE assault on BERLIN.

Ecuador

Capital: Quito, pop. 3,011,062 (1941). Ecuador declared its neutrality when the EUROPEAN WAR began in Sept. 1939 but soon reacted against German and Italian PROPAGANDA efforts by expelling the Italian military mission and deporting Germans who were pilots for a German-controlled airline. Later, Japanese agents in the guise of "oil explorers" were also expelled.

Ecuador showed its support for the United States by ending relations with Japan, Germany, and Italy on Jan. 29, 1942, selling its entire rubber crops to the United States, and authorizing U.S. air and naval bases on the mainland and on islands of the Galápagos. Ecuador, still technically neutral, became one of the ALLIES on Feb. 15, 1945, by signing the UNITED NATIONS agreement and announcing that a state of war had existed with Japan since Dec. 7, 1941.

Edelweiss (edelweiss)

German code name for advance into Caucasus area, July–Nov. 1942.

Eden, Anthony (1897–1977)

British statesman and wartime foreign secretary. When NEVILLE CHAMBERLAIN accelerated HITLER negotiations that led to the MUNICH PACT, his foreign secretary, Anthony Eden, resigned in protest in Feb. 1938. After England declared war on Sept. 3, 1939, Eden reentered the Chamberlain Cabinet as dominions minister. Chamberlain's fall in May 1940 brought WINSTON CHURCHILL in as prime minister, and Churchill made Eden, long a political ally, first war minister and then foreign secretary.

Eden took part in all major ALLIED CONFER-
ENCES and was designated by Churchill to be his
successor if Churchill should die in office. Eden, the
earl of Avon, was tied to Churchill's fortunes, going
out of office with Churchill in 1945 and returning
as foreign secretary with Churchill's return as Prime
minister in 1951. Eden became prime minister in
1955.

Egypt

Capital: Cairo, pop. 15,904,525 (est. 1937). Although Egypt was an independent kingdom under
young King Farouk when the EUROPEAN WAR
began in Sept. 1939, she had still not fully emerged
from British rule. Under a 1936 treaty, British
troops still were garrisoned in Egypt, primarily to
protect the Suez Canal, and the Royal Navy operated major bases at Alexandria and Port Said. Egypt
ended diplomatic relations with Germany Sept. 3,
1939, and imposed martial law, but did not join
England in declaring war on Germany.

War came to Egypt on June 11, 1940, when
Italy, a day after declaring war on France and England, crossed into Egypt from Libya, which Italy
had taken over in 1939. Egypt still refrained from
declaring war, touching off a bitter internal government debate. The move seemed to have pleased the
British, who were not anxious to equip the Egyptian Army. They also saw an advantage in having
Cairo as an OPEN CITY where diplomatic and ESPIO-
NAGE work could go on uninterrupted. German
and Italian agents conducted virulent anti-British
PROPAGANDA campaigns in Egypt, but, by buying
Egypt's entire 1940 cotton crop, England won a
round in the propaganda war.

In the shooting war, the Italian Army launched
a major offensive into Egypt on Sept. 13, 1940,
from Cyrenaica, the eastern province of Libya. A
British force, outnumbered three-to-one, drove the
Italians back into Libya, wiping out ten Italian divisions and taking 130,000 PRISONERS OF WAR. But
the British victory was a prelude to two years of
desert warfare as the NORTH AFRICA CAMPAIGN
churned across Egypt, with German troops reaching within forty miles of Alexandria.

When the British decisively defeated the German
AFRIKA KORPS at EL ALAMEIN in Nov. 1942, the
Egyptian government, deciding that for Egypt the

war was over, turned its attention to the issues of
Arab unity, Zionist claims to Palestine, and the expulsion of British forces from the Middle East. But
when the YALTA CONFERENCE in Feb. 1945 made
declaration of war against the AXIS a condition for
membership in the UNITED NATIONS of victors,
Egypt belatedly succumbed to reality and on Feb.
24 declared war on Japan and Germany.

Egypt Conference

Meetings of President ROOSEVELT with Middle
East leaders and then with Prime Minister
CHURCHILL in Feb. 1945 following the YALTA
CONFERENCE. President Roosevelt met with King
Farouk of Egypt, King Ibn Saud of Saudi Arabia,
and Emperor HAILE SELASSIE of Ethiopia. After
this meeting, Churchill went aboard the U.S.S.
Quincy (CA 71) "for what was to be my last talk
with the President. . . . The President seemed placid
and frail. I felt that he had a slender contact with
life." Later, Churchill met with the president of
Syria, Farouk, and Ibn Saud (who had previously
met with the President on board a U.S. DE-
STROYER). Churchill and Ibn Saud discussed the use
of shipping routes to keep supplies moving to Allied
nations. Saudi Arabia was officially neutral during
the war.

Eiche (Oak)

German code name for the removal of BENITO
MUSSOLINI in an operation led by OTTO
SKORZENY, Sept. 13, 1943.

Eichelberger, Lt. Gen. Robert L. (1886–1961)

Awareness of Gen. Eichelberger's great skill and
success as an American Army commander has been
muted by two limitations: He *did not* serve in
Europe and he *did* serve under Gen. DOUGLAS
MACARTHUR. Eichelberger occasionally bridled
under the near-total news blackout of non-MacAr-
thur generals. He diverted his resentment into a
series of letters home to his wife, in which MacArthur was inevitably described as "Sarah" (for Ed-
wardian-era actress Sarah Bernhardt). As Eichelberger once wryly wrote to her: "We have difficulty
in following the satellites of MacArthur, for like

those of Jupiter, we cannot see the moons on account of the brilliance of the planet."

Eichelberger had served in the 1930s as secretary to the Army's General Staff (when MacArthur was its chief) and as superintendent of the Military Academy at West Point. When MacArthur's offensive in Buna on NEW GUINEA bogged down in Dec. 1942, he appointed Eichelberger to command the 32nd Infantry DIVISION: "Bob, take Buna or don't come back alive." Eichelberger raised morale, impelled his forces to take charge of the campaign, and he took Buna. Promoted to command MacArthur's I CORPS, Eichelberger leap-frogged along the northern coast of New Guinea in concert with other Army units, a drive that included the daring capture of HOLLANDIA in April 1944. When the campaign in BIAK stalled in June 1944, Eichelberger was brought in to restart it—and did.

By Nov. 1944 Eichelberger had been promoted to lieutenant general and given command of the U.S. Eighth ARMY, which completed the conquest of New Guinea in midmonth. After Christmas 1944, his forces were unleashed in a series of fifty-eight landings throughout the Philippine archipelago. After the SURRENDER of Japan, Eichelberger's Eighth Army oversaw the military aspects of Japanese demobilization.

In his *Reminiscences,* MacArthur wrote of Eichelberger, "He proved himself a commander of the first order, fearless in battle, and especially popular with the Australians."

Eichmann, Adolf (1906–1962)

NAZI functionary who officiated over the FINAL SOLUTION, killing millions of JEWS in the HOLOCAUST. Eichmann, who spent his youth in HITLER's hometown of Linz, Austria, became a Nazi in Austria and, under the wing of Austrian Nazi chief ERNST KALTENBRUNNER (who would be second in command of the SS), became a self-taught SS authority on Jews.

In 1937 he went to Palestine to talk to Arab leaders, apparently about Jews and Zionism in the Middle East. He was expelled by the British authorities in Palestine.

Back in Germany, he rose quickly to the rank of SS-*Obersturmbannführer* and became chief of Subsection IV-B-4 (the Reich Central Office of Jewish

Emigration) of the REICH CENTRAL SECURITY OFFICE (known by its German initials, RSHA). In 1940 he was asked to develop a plan for the evacuation of 4,000,000 Jews to MADAGASCAR, which some German leaders looked upon as a place to deport Jews (the island being controlled by VICHY FRANCE). On Jan. 20, 1942, as the Nazi expert on Jews, Eichmann attended the WANNSEE CONFERENCE on the "Final Solution of the Jewish Question." His notes on the meeting, known as the Wannsee Protocol, survived the war and became part of the evidence at the Nuremberg WAR CRIMES trial. The minutes showed that the Nazis, with Eichmann as a key and fanatically committed operative, had methodically planned genocide against the Jews.

After German occupying forces entered Hungary in March 1944, Eichmann arrived and set in motion mass deportations of Hungarian Jews to AUSCHWITZ. This was a typical duty for Eichmann, who also supervised the SS ACTION GROUPS that massacred Jews in conquered territory.

As the war was ending, Eichmann was arrested, along with many other Nazis. He seemed to expect to be tried for his crimes. One of his associates told authorities that as Germany was nearing defeat Eichmann said he would "leap laughing into the grave because the feeling that he had five million people on his conscience would be for him a source of extraordinary satisfaction."

But Eichmann did not wait to accept his fate. He slipped out of U.S. custody and disappeared.

Soon after the founding of Israel in 1948 the new state set up a Nazi-hunting unit in its secret service, the Mossad. Eichmann's name was high on the list. The Israelis suspected that Eichmann had been aided in his escapes by the ODESSA, a secret organization of ex-SS officers. Odessa provided escaping SS with false identities and arranged passage out of Germany at the end of the war.

The Mossad believed that the South American end of the Odessa escape route was Buenos Aires. Argentina had harbored thousands of Nazi PROPAGANDA and ESPIONAGE agents before and during the war. (Argentina did not declare war on Germany and Japan until March 27, 1945.) Thus the Israelis' hunt for Eichmann centered on Argentina.

They found him there in May 1960, kidnapped

him, and secretly flew him to Israel. He was charged with crimes against humanity, crimes against the Jewish people, and crimes in violation of international laws on the conduct of war. In a trial that lasted from April 11 to Aug. 14, 1961, Israeli prosecutors extracted another long chapter in the well-documented Nazi war against the Jews.

Eichmann pleaded that he was only following orders. "Why me?" he asked at his trial. "Why not the local policemen, thousands of them? They would have been shot if they had refused to round up the Jews for the death camps. Why not hang them for not wanting to be shot? Why me? Everybody killed the Jews."

But the court found that it was Eichmann who had been the bureaucratic murderer of millions of Jews. He was found guilty and sentenced to death. He was hanged on May 31, 1962.

Eicke, Theodor (1892–1943)

Inspector of CONCENTRATION CAMPS and SS Death-Head detachments. A WEIMAR REPUBLIC police official sacked for his pro-NAZI views, Eicke joined the street-brawling SA, the Nazi paramilitary organization. In 1930 he became a member of the SS (the *Schutzstaffel*—"protection detachment"), but after a quarrel with SS superiors, he was put in a psychiatric clinic as "a dangerous lunatic." After a short stay, he resumed his SS career and in 1933 was appointed commandant of the new concentration camp at DACHAU. He installed as guards SS Death-Head troops and established Dachau as a model camp. Among the regulations he proclaimed was hanging for several kinds of "agitators," including anyone who "collects true or false information" about the camp and tried to get it to the outside world. In 1943, as an SS general of the *WAFFEN* SS, the military arm of the SS, he was killed on the EASTERN FRONT.

Einsatzgruppen,

see ACTION GROUPS.

Einstein, Albert (1879–1955)

German-born physicist who played an important role in the U.S. government's decision to build the ATOMIC BOMB. Einstein was enlisted by other physicists to lend his prestige to their plan for alerting President ROOSEVELT to the need to build the bomb.

Einstein, director of the Kaiser Wilhelm Physical Institute in BERLIN in 1914, was awarded the 1921 Nobel Prize for his contribution to theoretical physics. He went to the Institute for Advanced Study at Princeton in 1933 as the NAZIS took control in Germany. As a JEW he knew he could not work in Germany, which subsequently confiscated his property. He remained in the United States and became an American citizen.

Einstein authorized and signed a letter that had been written by physicist Leo Szilard in the summer of 1939. The "Einstein letter" was finally delivered to the President on Oct. 11 by Alexander Sachs, a New Deal supporter and longtime friend of Roosevelt.

The letter said that "extremely powerful bombs of a new type might be constructed" and that such a bomb carried by ship into a port "might very well destroy the whole port together with some of the surrounding territory." The letter also said that Germany was believed to have "stopped the sale of URANIUM from the Czechoslovakian mines which she has taken over." After reading the letter the President launched what would soon become the MANHATTAN PROJECT to build the bomb.

Although Einstein is credited with getting the United States started on the development of the bomb, he himself did not work on it, apparently because he was considered a potential security risk. As VANNEVAR BUSH, director of the OFFICE OF SCIENTIFIC RESEARCH AND DEVELOPMENT, explained to another scientist, "I wish very much that I could place the whole thing before him . . . but this is utterly impossible in view of the attitude of people here in WASHINGTON who have studied into his whole history." This vague remark probably referred to Einstein's outspoken pacifism and support of Zionism.

Eisenhower, Gen. of the Army Dwight David (1890–1969)

More than any other single person, Eisenhower determined the course of the Western Allies' war in Europe from 1942 to 1945. From the NORTH AFRICA INVASION through the invasion of SICILY and the ITALIAN CAMPAIGN, to the NORMANDY INVASION and the ALLIED CAMPAIGN IN EUROPE, Eisenhower grew to be the indispensable coalition general, a peerless coordinator and commander of Allied operations. No other military leader in World War II had so much influence on the conduct of the war.

At the beginning of World War II, "Lt. Colonel Eisenhaur" (as he was identified in a Feb. 1942 White House appointment book) would have not believed any of the above would describe his war career. But Eisenhower's rise from obscurity as a staff officer was not based on luck. He had solid experience behind him, including path-breaking armor studies with GEORGE PATTON in the early 1920s and service with the assistant secretary of war. When Army Chief of Staff DOUGLAS MACARTHUR evaluated Eisenhower in the mid-1930s, he stated that "this officer has no superior of his time in the Army." Eisenhower served with MacArthur for seven years—four in the Philippines where he later was quoted as saying he "studied dramatics" under MacArthur.

Gen. of the Army Dwight D. Eisenhower—or Ike as he was invariably called by his colleagues and front-line troops—was an outstanding coalition commander and strategist. *(U.S. Army via Imperial War Museum)*

As Chief of Staff of the Third ARMY he planned the winning battle plan during the LOUISIANA MANEUVERS in 1941 and shortly thereafter came under Army Chief of Staff GEORGE MARSHALL's direct supervision, being made the Army's deputy chief of the War Plans Division four days after the attack on PEARL HARBOR. By this time, his peers and superiors regarded him as brilliant and possessing the rare ability to boil down reams of proposals and recommendations into clear, concise prose.

Eisenhower's first task was to recommend the U.S. response to the invasion of the Philippines. His response—hold Australia to keep the supply lines open, but don't try to rescue U.S. forces in the archipelago—was adopted. He fully supported the "Germany First" grand strategy already agreed to by President ROOSEVELT and Prime Minister CHURCHILL.

One of Eisenhower's greatest talents was his ability to fall in line with a final decision and execute it with energy, intelligence, and a genuine amiability that quickly endeared him to the press and to the public. Ike, as the press and public came to know him, was especially noted for his easy affinity with troops. At higher levels, Eisenhower rigorously enforced a policy of Allied unity from the moment he became Supreme Commander of the North Africa invasion. His policy often annoyed field commanders in all of the subject armies. He persevered nonetheless, and once relieved an American officer because he called an annoying associate "a *British* son-of-a-bitch." Through most of the war in Europe, Eisenhower's air deputy was British Air Marshal ARTHUR TEDDER and his naval chief was a British admiral.

Eisenhower also demonstrated a sensitivity to the political and diplomatic tempests that often swirled around his Allied command. His two most controversial decisions—appointing the VICHY FRANCE Adm. JEAN FRANÇOIS DARLAN as Commander in Chief of French Forces in North Africa in Nov. 1942 and notifying Soviet leader STALIN in 1945 that U.S. forces would not be advancing to BERLIN—have at least arguable justifications for them. His refusal to move on Berlin has been cited as an example of his narrow view of strategic aims; it can be argued with equal force that absorbing casualties to take German territory that was to be given to the

Soviets and a city that was due to be divided among the victors would have been callous and unwise.

His lack of experience in command in the field (a career shortcoming he often lamented before the war) affected judgment of him, particularly in the debate over his conduct of the battlefield war in Europe. Eisenhower's immediate subordinates Gen. OMAR N. BRADLEY and Patton occasionally believed that Ike either was being swayed by the last person to talk to him or had become more British than the British. But more often than not Eisenhower's British commanders disparaged his military competence.

However, Eisenhower was strongly aided by his own burgeoning confidence—and by the unswerving support of Marshall. And even his critics saluted his ability to rise to a crisis firmly in control of himself and his coalition army. In deciding not to postpone the Normandy landings another day, in correctly interpreting the scale and purpose of the German counteroffensive in the battle of the BULGE in Dec. 1944, and in insisting on the double envelopment of the RUHR in 1945, Eisenhower demonstrated his willingness to accept the responsibility that fell to the Supreme Commander.

He ended the war in Europe in command of an immense host—sixty U.S., thirteen British, seven French, three Canadian, and one Polish divisions—that was relatively well integrated and smoothly operated. No other coalition commander achieved so complete a military and political success.

At the end of the war Ike was the stalwart man of D-DAY, the general with the grin and the natty jacket that bore his name. He was less glamorous than Patton, less imperial than MacArthur, but he was a trusted, well-tempered leader. It was this quality that in 1952 brought him the Republican nomination for president, the vote of the people in that year, and his reelection in 1956.

Eisenhower, Milton (1899–1985)

Director of the War Relocation Authority (WRA), the federal agency responsible for the removal of 120,000 JAPANESE-AMERICANS from the West Coast to internment camps in isolated areas of the West.

As Eisenhower described the action in a report to Roosevelt: the federal government would "take all

people of Japanese descent into custody, surround them with troops, prevent them from buying land, and return them to their former homes at the close of the war."

The youngest of six Eisenhower brothers, Milton was quite close to his brother DWIGHT EISENHOWER. In 1927, when Maj. Dwight Eisenhower was in WASHINGTON working on a guide to the European battlefields of World War I, Milton helped him with the writing. By then Milton was on his way to becoming a government bureaucrat.

He had been a high-ranking aide to successive Republicans who held the post of secretary of Agriculture. When the New Deal arrived in Washington in 1933, President ROOSEVELT's secretary of Agriculture, Henry A. Wallace, kept Eisenhower on. After the war started, Milton Eisenhower spent some six months as head of the WRA and then became associate director of the OFFICE OF WAR INFORMATION. In May 1943 he left Washington to become president of Kansas State College. He moved on to Pennsylvania State University in 1950 and in 1956 became president of Johns Hopkins University.

Eisenhower Jacket

Also known as the "Ike jacket," this was a short, olive-drab color dress jacket issued to U.S. Army personnel later in the war. It somewhat resembled the British battledress blouse.

El Alamein

Coastal village about 65 miles west of Alexandria and the site of the deepest German penetration into Egypt. Two crucial battles were fought at El Alamein. In the first, July 2, 1942, the British fought off newly promoted *Generalfeldmarschall* ERWIN ROMMEL, and in the second, Oct. 23–Nov. 4, the British sent Rommel heading back to Libya in full retreat.

The town itself was the seaward end of the El Alamein Line, a 35-mile-wide defensive complex of which the southern flanks were guarded by the 700-foot dip of the vast Qattara Depression, 7,000 square miles of impassable terrain.

In June 1942 Rommel, having taken TOBRUK, rolled into Egypt but was hampered by his overextension of men and supplies. On July 1 he hit the El Alamein Line, but not hard enough to even dent it.

Both sides paused to regroup. In the interval, Lt. Gen. BERNARD L. MONTGOMERY took over the British Eighth Army and predicted that El Alamein would be the turning point in the desert war.

On Oct. 23, with a four-hour artillery barrage, Montgomery sprang a broad offensive code-named Lightfoot. Rommel's defenses were five miles deep, a complex of minefields, dug-in antitank guns, and well-positioned infantry and armored forces. Against this the British had three armored divisions and the equivalent of seven infantry divisions. The British also had Montgomery. But the Germans did not have Rommel.

Rommel, ill from liver and blood-pressure ailments, was at a mountain resort in Austria. He would reach the battlefield of this second battle of El Alamein two days after it started.

Montgomery's plan called for two corridors to be cut through the defenses. After two days of heavy fighting, little progress was made. To the north, however, Australian troops had made a deep thrust, and Montgomery shifted his attention there. On Nov. 2, in a breakthrough attack code-named Supercharge, he punched through. "Then," wrote WINSTON CHURCHILL, "came the last clash of armour in the battle. All the remaining enemy tanks attacked our salient on each flank, and were repulsed."

British aerial reconnaissance showed the first sign of enemy retreat. But a direct order came from HITLER to Rommel: no retreat. "As to your troops," *Der Führer* said, "you can show them no other road than that to victory or death."

Rommel did send some forces forward, inflicting damage and prolonging the battle. In response, the British increased the pressure, breaking the front. As Churchill says, "The battle was now won." On Nov. 4, disobeying Hitler, Rommel began a full retreat, and the expulsion of AXIS forces from North Africa had begun. "Up to Alamein we survived," Churchill wrote. "After Alamein we conquered."

El Salvador

Capital: San Salvador, pop. 1,744,535 (est. 1939). German influence was strong in El Salvador, where Germans owned prosperous coffee and sugar plantations. The German consul general was also the manager of the major mortgage bank and a German headed the Salvadorean military academy. But this smallest of Central American states stayed firmly on the side of the United States. El Salvador declared war on Japan on Dec. 8, 1941, on Germany and Italy on Dec. 12, and, following the U.S. lead, ended relations with VICHY FRANCE on Nov. 13, 1942.

Electro Submarine

Term for the German TYPE XXI U-BOAT, being a reference to the submarine's large battery capacity, which gave the Type XXI an unprecedented high underwater speed and endurance.

Electronic Countermeasures

The extensive use of electronic systems—radio, RADAR, and SONAR (ASDIC)—in the war led to intensive countermeasures development, especially in Britain and the United States.

Among the earliest Electronic Countermeasures (ECM) were those developed by the British to counter the German *X-Gerät* (X-device) and *Knickenbein* (crooked leg), which were beam-guidance devices used by German bombers. In brief, directional radio waves (beams) were projected toward England and made to cross over the specific target, providing accurate navigation "fixes" at night and in bad weather.

In 1940—in time for the BATTLE OF BRITAIN—the British countered these beams by transmitting "mush" or noise on the frequencies used for the beams, to conceal the patterns of dot and dashes from Luftwaffe pilots. British jamming devices were fitted in "jamming" aircraft and at ground positions, this effort being known as Operation Headache, with the jamming devices called Aspirin and Bromide. Sometimes jamming worked, other times—as in the Nov. 14, 1940, Luftwaffe strike on COVENTRY—they did not, in part because more sophisticated German aircraft receivers could distinguish the beam signals even with jamming.

The Germans were familiar with the British "Chain" radar installations, their 240-foot towers being readily identifiable. (The Germans also used the airship GRAF ZEPPELIN in an attempt to determine British radar frequencies—a "ferret" mission.) Early air attacks in the Battle of Britain attempted to destroy the radar installations, but the Luftwaffe shifted targets before fatal damage was inflicted and no ECM efforts were undertaken during the remainder of the battle.

But the Germans did use jamming to conceal the CHANNEL DASH by the battleships *Gneisenau* and *Scharnhorst,* and the cruiser *Prinz Eugen* up the English Channel in Feb. 1942. German jamming of British coastal radars had been previously ineffective. Then, each day the jamming became a little more effective, and the British suspected nothing until, on the day of the escape, British sea-watching radar was completely useless.

When British bombers began using electronic navigation systems for the night bombing of Germany, the Germans similarly developed radar detection devices and countermeasures.

British ECM efforts were aided by equipment taken from crashed German aircraft; subsequently, British COMMANDOS landed in France and dismantled German radars (see JACK NISSENTHAL). As Allied aircraft began bombing occupied France and Germany, it became vital to jam German air-defense radars. One scheme—called Moonshine by the British—received the pulses from German *Freya* radars, amplified them, and sent them back, thus jamming the set. The same technology permitted a British aircraft to simulate several aircraft on a German radar screen, thus luring German fighters away from the real objective. More advanced devices of this type were called Mandrel.

But in the electron war of "measure and countermeasure," German fighters would home in on Mandrel-equipped bombers, forcing them to transmit for two minutes and then keep silent for two minutes; but that reduced their effectiveness. And, German radars were improved to overcome brute-force jamming.

Other devices were also used to confuse or jam German radars, with the most widely used called "Window." In the summer of 1941 an RAF WELLINGTON fitted with special radio aerials found that it was always fired on by German gunners, even when other planes were about. The crew correctly deduced that the aerials caused an exaggerated echo on German radar. During their next attack on the Libyan city of Benghazi the plane's crew dropped packets of aluminum strips cut 18 inches long and 1 inch wide—the size of the aircraft's special aerials. The Window had no effect; the plane was still a primary target for whatever reason. The strips were used once more and then the idea was dropped.

However, the idea was resurrected a year later and, after experiments, a bundle of 240 aluminum strips were found to produce a radar echo similar to that from a BLENHEIM bomber. Ten such clouds of Window released over a mile would make it virtually impossible for a radar to pick out an aircraft's real echo. RAF Bomber Command and then the U.S. bomber forces based in England began using Window on a regular basis as they approached defended German targets.

The AAF called Window "chaff," as it resembled wheat chaff flying in the wind. By 1944 every AAF bomber in the lead WING of a strike would carry 144 chaff packages; dropped at intervals of four seconds, each plane could lay a chaff lane of about 20 miles in length to jam German ground radars.

RAF bombers were also fitted with tail-mounted radar receivers that warned of approaching German night fighters using radar and ground based antiaircraft radar. These devices—called Boozer (passive) and Monica (active)—had limited effectiveness, as some night fighters flew without radar, and ground-based radars were almost continuously detected in a target area. And, of course, these devices fell into German hands when RAF bombers were shut down, leading to another round of measure and countermeasure.

As the Allied high command planned the NORMANDY INVASION, a special effort was made to prevent German coastal radars from detecting the invasion fleets. Beginning in March 1944 RAF fighter-bombers armed with ROCKETS began intensive attacks on known *Mammut* and *Wassermann* early-warning radars. The Second Tactical AIR FORCE flew almost 2,000 sorties against these radars, often with losses; by D-DAY all but sixteen of these ninety-two narrow-beam radars were destroyed.

Meanwhile, new Window strips were developed, these being nearly 6 feet long that folded when carried in an aircraft and extended when dropped. A carefully calculated Window drop pattern was developed and on D-Day RAF aircraft dropped massive clouds of this Window to give the illusion of two invasion fleets farther north in the English Channel than the actual Allied ships.

Also, more than 200 ships of the invasion fleet carried tactical radar jammers. And twenty-nine RAF bombers made a special diversionary raid, away from the invasion beaches, releasing streams of Window to indicate a larger force—possibly transports carrying troops. They also dropped special fireworks to resemble a ground battle in progress, and parachuted a few men of the SPECIAL AIR SERVICE to further contribute to the Germans' confusion. Only one German coastal radar, near Caen, actually detected the approaching invasion force but its reports were ignored by plotting centers because they could not be confirmed by other radars! The entire ECM effort at Normandy was a British show.

German and British electronic specialists also fought a deadly conflict under the sea. Radar made a major contribution to the Allied victory in the BATTLE OF THE ATLANTIC, depriving the U-BOATS of their ability to operate on the surface at night, to maneuver at high speed, and to recharge their batteries. As more effective radar became available to antisubmarine forces, the Germans installed radar detectors in their submarines. However, the Germans were unaware that the British were using centimeter radar. When their submarines could not detect Allied radar emissions (while radar could detect the surfaced U-boats), the Germans believed that their own detectors were giving off emissions that the British and American aircraft could detect. Hence, potentially useful radar detectors were not used, while work continued on more efficient detectors.

The U-boats also carried balloons, to which metal strips could be attached to float just over the water and fox Allied radars, and submarines (and SNORKEL heads) were coated with radar-absorbing anechoic materials. But the final solution to Allied radar at sea was not in specific countermeasures, but in development of the snorkel breathing tube and then the TYPE XXI and later U-boats, which would permit a submarine to remain submerged during an entire war patrol.

As Allied antisubmarine methods improved, the Germans introduced acoustic homing TORPEDOES to attack escort ships (see also GNAT). These were countered by Allied escort ships towing noisemakers known as FOXERS to distract the homing torpedoes. Other schemes were also used to reduce the acoustic signatures of the escort ships. At the same time, the U-boats attempted various means of disguising their location, such as ejecting bubbles that would jam an escort ship's sonar and launching noisemaking decoys to give an escort ship's sonar operator a moment or two of indecision as to which was the real submarine.

Electronic countermeasures had less impact in the Pacific War because of the limited Japanese development and use of radar. Since the Japanese were on the offensive for the first eight months of the war, not until the Marines landed on GUADALCANAL in the SOLOMON ISLANDS on Aug. 7, 1942, did Americans get a good look at Japanese radars. A damaged early-warning radar set was found at the unfinished airfield. A U.S. Navy officer who examined the set wrote: ". . . I remember being impressed at how crude it was compared with our own early sets. Goodness knows, our first generation . . . sets were crude enough! Nearly all the tubes in the Japanese equipment appeared to be copies of the types made by General Electric."

The Guadalcanal radar led to an intensive U.S. effort to find out more about Japanese radars; the submarine *Drum* (SS 228) was fitted with a radar intercept receiver in Sept. 1942 for a forthcoming patrol into Japanese home waters; a month later an AAF B-17E FLYING FORTRESS based in the Southwest Pacific was similarly outfitted. But neither of these ferret efforts detected radar emissions. More radar receivers were fitted in submarines, surface ships, and Navy as well as AAF aircraft. U.S. warships were also fitted with radar jammers.

The Japanese did have radar, but it was primitive by U.S. standards and easily avoided or jammed. When B-29 SUPERFORTRESS bombers began pounding the Japanese home islands in 1944, there was concern for the large number of air-defense radars. Accordingly, several B-29s as well as B-24 LIBERATOR photo planes were fitted for the radar ferret mission in addition to their primary bombing or photo roles, with an ECM officer also carried.

The data they brought back led to the fitting of

radar jammers in B-29 bombers beginning in April 1945, with chaff—a variety called "Rope"—also being used to defeat Japanese radars.

See also HIGH-FREQUENCY/DIRECTION FINDING.

Elefant (Elephant)

German code name for program to obtain trucks from the civilian sector in the Soviet Union, Jan. 1942.

Elkton

Code name for Allied plan for the seizure of NEW BRITAIN, NEW GUINEA, and New Ireland, 1943.

Ellis, Lt. Col. Earl H. (1880–1923)

In the 1920s the leading proponent of U.S. development of capability for AMPHIBIOUS LANDINGS. Immediately after World War I, "Pete" Ellis began lecturing on the role of the Marine Corps in seizing bases in the Pacific in time of war for the U.S. fleet and to deny them to the Japanese. His 50,000-word plan, submitted to the commandant of the Marine Corps in July 1921, was a blueprint for a Marine advance across the Pacific. It began, "In order to impose our will upon Japan, it will be necessary for us to project our fleet and land forces across the Pacific and wage war in Japanese waters." His assault targets in the 1921 plan included the MARSHALL, CAROLINE, PELELIU, and Ryukyu Islands (including OKINAWA)—most sites of World War II amphibious assaults. He listed specific atolls to be captured, the troop requirements, as well as the weapons, reef-crossing vehicles, and tactics to be used.

Ellis concluded: "To effect such a landing under the sea and shore conditions obtaining and in the face of enemy resistance requires careful training and preparation, to say the least; and this along Marine Corps lines. It is not enough that the troops be skilled infantry men and jungle men or artillery men of high morale; they must be skilled water men and jungle men who know it can be done—Marines with Marine training."

In Aug. 1921 Ellis began an extensive tour of the Pacific. At several stops he became ill. In 1922 in Yokohama, Japan, he was admitted to the U.S. naval hospital and diagnosed as suffering from alcoholism. After being hospitalized a second time at Yokohama, he sailed for SAIPAN and then the Marshall Islands. He was again hospitalized but continued his tour of Japanese-held islands. Ellis died mysteriously while visiting the Japanese-held Palau Islands in May 1923. His impact on the development of U.S. Marine amphibious doctrine in the 1920s and 1930s was considerable.

Emily

The H8K or Type 2 flying boat is described by aviation historian William Green as "undoubtedly one of the finest Japanese warplanes to see operational service" during the war, and "one of the most formidable flying boats employed by any of the combatants." It was designed for use as a reconnaissance aircraft, bomber, TORPEDO plane, or antisubmarine aircraft. Given the Allied code name Emily, the plane made its combat debut in an attack on Oahu, Hawaii, on the night of March 4–5, 1942—the second attack on PEARL HARBOR (Operation K). The Emily was widely used in the Pacific War despite the small number built, and it earned the respect of U.S. fighter pilots as being a difficult plane to attack and shoot down.

The prototype H8K1 made its maiden flight in Jan. 1941. Production totaled only 167 aircraft, including thirty-six H8K2-L transports and two improved H8K3 variants.

The Emily was a high-wing aircraft with a deep, stepped fuselage; four radial engines were fitted in the wings and the aircraft had large, fixed stabilizing floats. The improved H8K2 had upgraded engines, fully protected fuel tanks, armor protection for the crew, and surface search RADAR. The H8K2-L *Seiku* (Clear Sky) was a transport variant that could be configured to carry up to sixty-four passengers. The experimental H8K3 variant had retractable wing-tip floats and a retractable dorsal gun turret.

The H8K2 had a maximum speed of 290 mph with a maximum range of 4,445 miles. Offensive payloads, carried under the wings, consisted of either two 1,764-pound aerial torpedoes or eight 551-pound BOMBS or DEPTH CHARGES. The standard gun armament in the H8K2 and H8K3 aircraft was one 20-mm cannon in nose, dorsal, and tail turrets as well as in side blisters, plus single 7.7-mm machine guns in side hatches and ventral positions—an impressive eight defensive guns. The crew normally numbered ten.

End Run

Code name for Allied task force for Operation Galahad survivors used in drive on Myitkyina, Burma.

England (DE 635)

The highest scoring antisubmarine ship of any navy in the war. The USS *England*, a DESTROYER ESCORT, was commissioned on Dec. 10, 1943, under the command of Comdr. W. B. Pendleton.

In May 1944, in anticipation of a U.S. Navy-Marine thrust into the Western Pacific, the Japanese naval command stationed thirteen submarines east and north of the ADMIRALTY ISLANDS and off the northern coast of NEW GUINEA. These submarines were to provide early warning of an American approach to the Admiralty Islands or the Philippines. U.S. intelligence intercepted and decrypted the Japanese communications about the operation and three U.S. destroyer escorts were vectored to the Japanese patrol line. The escorts were armed with HEDGEHOGS and DEPTH CHARGES.

On May 19, the three escorts found, and the *England* sank, the submarine *I-16*, which had just departed TRUK with a cargo of supplies to be taken to BOUGAINVILLE.

The antisubmarine ships began to overrun the Japanese picket line on May 22. That day the *England* sank the submarine *RO-106* and the next day the *RO-104*. The three escorts were encountering Japanese submarines at roughly 30-mile intervals. The trio missed the next boat in line, but the *England* sank the *RO-116* on May 24 and the *RO-108* on May 26. On May 31 the two other escorts located and attacked the *RO-105*, but not until the *England* joined the attack was that submarine sunk.

The U.S. ships reported their successes, and some of those messages, reportedly intercepted and decoded by the Japanese, caused the other submarines on the Admiralty picket line to change positions and escape the trio of submarine hunters.

By sinking six submarines (in twelve days) the *England* became the top-scoring antisubmarine ship of any navy in either world war.

Near the end of the war the *England* was con-verted to a high-speed troop transport (redesignated APD 41).

The *England,* launched on Sept. 26, 1943, had a standard displacement of 1,400 tons and had a length of 306 feet. Turbo-electric drive could propel the ship at 24 knots. In addition to antisubmarine weapons, the *England* had three single 3-inch (76-mm) guns plus light antiaircraft guns and three large, 21-inch (533-mm) TORPEDO tubes. Her crew numbered about 200.

The *England* was named for a Navy ensign killed on the BATTLESHIP *Oklahoma* (BB 37) during the Japanese air attack on PEARL HARBOR.

Enigma

Complex code machine used by the German armed forces and ministries during the war. The Allies were able to decipher many of the Enigma codes during the war through an effort generally known (incorrectly) as ULTRA. The ability to read German, Japanese, and Italian military and diplomatic codes was a major cause of several Allied successes.

Enigma encryptions, when the machines were used properly and there were no other compromises, were unbreakable. For example, the German naval ciphers given the Allied code names Barracuda and Pike, among others, were never once broken during the war.

The Enigma machine was about the size of a portable typewriter with a standard typewriter-style keyboard; it provided electro-mechanical enciphering through nonrepeating ciphers. Three (later four and five) interchangeable rotors and numerous plug connectors provided up to *200 quintillion* permutations. The rotor settings could be rapidly changed—up to several times per day.

The machine was invented by the German engineers Arthur Scerbuis and Boris Hagelin for use by commercial firms to keep business secrets in their communications. The machine was first exhibited in 1923. Enigma was the manufacturer's name for the machine, reportedly based on the intricate Enigma Variations of Sir Edward Elgar, composer of "Pomp and Circumstance."

Enigma machines were simple to operate and suitable for field and shipboard use. The German Navy began using the Enigma machines in 1926,

A major factor in several Allied victories in the war was the Anglo-American ability to read coded messages processed through the German Enigma system. At left can be seen the Enigma machine in the command vehicle of armored warfare expert Hans Guderian during his highly successful operations in France in June 1940. *(German Army via Imperial War Museum)*

followed by the Army in 1928, and the Air Force in 1933. By 1939 there were more than 20,000 machines of different models in German military and diplomatic use. The Japanese began using an Enigma variant in 1934.

In the 1930s the Polish and French intelligence services began to attack the Enigma codes, the latter with the clandestine aid of Hans-Thilo Schmidt who worked for the German Cryptographic Agency. Several Enigma machines, constructed by Polish technicians who had worked in the Enigma factory, were provided to France and Britain in 1939 (and subsequently to the United States). Because of the rapid cipher changes possible with the Enigma—and periodic changes to the machine's rotors and plug arrangement—simply having the machines was not enough for code-breaking. Mere

possession of the machine did not provide continuous access to the messages being transmitted (which first had to be "captured" by radio intercept).

Before the fall of Poland in 1939, the Poles also built the BOMBE, an electromechanical device that could rapidly move through rotor permutations to find a "key" within a reasonable amount of time. After the fall of Poland (1939) and France (1940), the British were able to improve their reading of Enigma messages though the use of refined Bombe devices, the work of thousands of mathematicians and cryptologists at BLETCHLEY PARK, and carelessness by German radio operators. The salvage of a sunken German U-BOAT, and the capture of several German weather reporting trawlers and the submarines *U-110* and *U-505,* the latter by the U.S. Navy, provided the Allies with Enigma machines, rotors, and settings. (The German high command believed that even if an Enigma machine was captured, the myriad of possible settings made the possession of a machine of no value; the German leaders did not realize the depth of the cryptographic activity in Britain and the United States.)

Toward the end of the war against Germany the Enigma was of limited value, especially in the battle of the BULGE because the Germans were using more secure land-lines for communications.

Eniwetok

Atoll in the northwestern segment of the MARSHALL ISLANDS and one of the objectives of Operation Granite in the U.S. CENTRAL PACIFIC CAMPAIGN. A combined force of U.S. Marines and U.S. Army soldiers made AMPHIBIOUS LANDINGS on Feb. 18, 1944, moving inland behind carefully orchestrated aircraft strikes, ARTILLERY barrages, and naval gunfire. BATTLESHIPS came within 1,500 yards of the beach to blast Japanese defenses.

The atoll was secured by Feb. 23. Most of the 3,500 Japanese defenders were killed, as were 348 U.S. soldiers and Marines.

From the former Japanese airfield at Engebi on Eniwetok and from airfields taken elsewhere in the Marshalls, Marine aircraft bombed Japanese outposts on other atolls, making further landings unnecessary.

In 1947 Eniwetok (now Enewetak) became a testing ground for nuclear weapons; in 1952 the

United States exploded the first hydrogen bomb there.

"Enola Gay"

Name of B-29 SUPERFORTRESS bomber that delivered the ATOMIC BOMB on HIROSHIMA on Aug. 2, 1945. The aircraft was flown by Col. PAUL W. TIBBETS and was named for his mother.

Enterprise (CV 6)

The U.S. Navy's most decorated AIRCRAFT CARRIER of the war—she escaped destruction so often and so narrowly that she was known to some as the "Galloping Ghost." Commissioned in 1938, the "Big E," as she was usually called, shifted to the Pacific the following year.

At the time of the Japanese attack on PEARL HARBOR on Dec. 7, 1941, she was at sea, returning to Pearl after delivering twelve Marine F4F WILDCAT fighters to WAKE ISLAND. Vice Adm. WILLIAM F. HALSEY, who flew his flag in the *Enterprise,* had ordered the carrier and her escorting CRUISERS and DESTROYERS on full war alert when the ships had sailed for Wake in view of the deteriorating political situation.

His planes were already flying searches for Japanese ships when news of the alert came. Some of his planes arrived over Pearl Harbor during the attack—and were shot at by both U.S. Army gunners as well as Japanese planes. After a hasty refueling at Pearl, the *Enterprise* continued to search for the Japanese carriers. Her first action did not come until early Feb. 1942 when her planes struck Japanese installations and shipping in the MARSHALL ISLANDS. The next month her planes attacked Wake and March islands. She then accompanied the carrier *HORNET* (CV 8) on the DOOLITTLE RAID in April 1942.

At the Battle of MIDWAY the following month SBD DAUNTLESS dive bombers from the "Big E" and the *Yorktown* (CV 5) sank four Japanese carriers. Subsequently, the "Big E" fought in most carrier actions of the Pacific War, from the landings on GUADALCANAL in Aug. 1942 to the OKINAWA landings in May 1945; part of the time she had a night-operating air GROUP. In the fall of 1942 she was, for a while, the only U.S. carrier operational in the Western Pacific. The *Enterprise* was hit several times by Japanese BOMBS and KAMIKAZES, the last time off Okinawa on May 14. She was repaired in a U.S. shipyard. But her next mission was lifting 1,100 troops from Pearl Harbor to the United States as part of Operation MAGIC CARPET. She then sailed to Europe to bring home more troops.

During the war her pilots claimed to have shot down 911 Japanese planes and sunk seventy-one enemy ships. The *Enterprise* earned twenty BATTLE STARS for her service in addition to the Presidential Unit Citation. She was decommissioned in Feb. 1947.

The *Enterprise* had a standard displacement of 19,900 tons and was 809½ feet long. Steam turbines could drive her at 34 knots. When the war began her air group numbered seventy-two planes; as a night carrier in 1945 she operated eighteen RADAR-equipped F6F HELLCATS and twenty-seven TBM-3 AVENGERS.

Epsom

Code name for British offensive near Caen, Normandy, July 1944.

Escort Carriers

Escort or "jeep" carriers were developed early in the war to provide antisubmarine aircraft to help protect CONVOYS. These ships proved highly effective in hunting German U-BOATS but were also invaluable in providing close air support of ground troops during AMPHIBIOUS LANDINGS, ferrying short-range aircraft overseas, and training carrier pilots.

Both the U.S. and British navies had studied the possibility of converting merchant ships to auxiliary aircraft carriers in the 1930s. (Several merchant ships had been converted to aircraft carriers and seaplane tenders during World War I.) As German air attacks from bases in France began in 1940, the Royal Navy resurrected the merchant carrier idea and the captured German banana boat *Hannover* was converted in Jan. 1941 to an escort carrier. As HMS *AUDACITY* she had a brief but eventful career escorting GIBRALTAR convoys.

While the U.S. Navy had little interest in escort carriers, after President ROOSEVELT and Prime Minister CHURCHILL exchanged views on the subject, in March 1941 the U.S. Maritime Commission handed over to the Navy two unfinished merchant hulls for conversion to escort carriers. The first became the USS *Long Island,* commissioned in June 1941, and the second HMS *Archer,* commissioned in Nov. 1941. The 7,886-ton, 492-foot *Long Island* was a true "flattop," initially completed without an island superstructure. She had a hangar deck below the flight deck, connected by a single elevator; she could operate twenty-one aircraft. (U.S. escort carriers were originally designated as AVG—aircraft escort vessel; then ACV—auxiliary aircraft carrier; and on July 15, 1943, the designation was changed to CVE—escort aircraft carrier; the *Long Island* became CVE 1.)

The *Long Island* was followed by fifty similar conversions in 1941–1944, of which twelve went to the Royal Navy. Then, with the U.S. Navy still opposing the concept, industrialist HENRY J. KAISER built fifty more with his famed mass production techniques, the last commissioned on July 8, 1944, exactly a year after the first. Subsequently, the Navy ordered a series of large CVEs—23,875-ton, 553-foot escort carriers that could operate thirty-five aircraft. Ten of these ships were finished before the end of the war, bringing the U.S. escort carrier program to a remarkable 115 ships.

Following the *Audacity* operations the first major escort carrier mission was the British *Avenger* escorting CONVOY PQ 18 to the Soviet port of ARCHANGEL in Sept. 1942. In that operation the *Avenger* embarked twelve HURRICANE fighters and three SWORDFISH bombers; although not fully successful, the *Avenger* did make a significant contribution to the convoys' defenses. (The *Avenger* was a primary target for German bombers, but she escaped their efforts unscathed.)

The first major operation for U.S. escort carriers was the NORTH AFRICA INVASION in Nov. 1942 when three American and three British CVEs provided antisubmarine and close air support for the landings; one other American CVE carried seventy-eight Army P-40F WARHAWK fighters that were flown ashore as soon as bases were available. British and American CVEs later provided support for several Mediterranean landings.

The most important contribution of the escort carriers was in the BATTLE OF THE ATLANTIC. These ships were able to "close the gap" in the ocean areas between land-based British and American antisubmarine aircraft flying from bases in Britain, Iceland, Greenland, Canada, and the United States. In that area German submarines could often move freely on the surface, outrunning convoys to gain attack positions. By Sept. 1944, when the loss of submarine bases on the French coast forced a virtual halt to long-range U-boat operations, four British and nine U.S. escort carriers had sunk thirty-three submarines and shared credit with surface ships or land-based aircraft for twelve others in the Atlantic. Two of the U.S. ships, the *Bogue* (CVE 9) and *Card* (CVE 11), each sank eight U-boats, with the *Bogue* assisting in two others. And the *Guadalcanal* (CVE 60) helped to capture the submarine *U-505.*

In addition to the *Audacity,* two other British escort carriers were sunk in the Atlantic: the *Avenger* by a U-boat with most of her crew lost, while the *Dasher* blew up in a gasoline explosion losing 378 crewmen; another British ship badly damaged by a U-boat limped to port, but was not repaired. The U.S. Navy lost only one CVE in the Atlantic, the *Block Island* (CVE 21), sunk by a U-boat's TORPEDOES.

In the Pacific, U.S. escort carriers provided close air support in numerous amphibious assaults against Japanese-held islands. The "jeeps"—flying Navy aircraft—were indispensable in that role. Few were attacked. The *Liscome Bay* (CVE 56) was torpedoed by a Japanese submarine off TARAWA in Nov. 1943 with heavy loss of life. Then, on Oct. 25, 1944, off the coast of Leyte in the Philippines, a force of eighteen escort carriers and their escorts of DESTROYERS and DESTROYER ESCORTS were suddenly attacked by a massive Japanese task force. The battleship *YAMATO*—the world's largest—three other battleships, eight cruisers, and thirteen destroyers fell on the hapless escort carriers. The carriers had no armor-piercing BOMBS, their planes being assigned to support troops ashore. For more than two hours the Japanese fired on the unarmored U.S. ships. Several CVEs were hit, some many times, but they kept steaming and launching planes. The *Gambier Bay* (CVE 73) capsized and sank, taking with her about 100 of her crew. Two destroyers and one destroyer escort were also sunk by gunfire at LEYTE GULF as the escort ships and carrier planes finally forced the Japanese ships to break off.

While under the Japanese guns, the escort carriers were attacked by the first organized KAMIKAZE raid of the war. The *St. Lô* (CVE 63) was sunk with some 100 of her crew. Other carriers were damaged—six suffered major damage that day. Kamikazes sank the *Ommaney Bay* (CVE 79) off the Philippines in Jan. 1945 and the suiciders damaged several more escort carriers before the end of the war.

Considering their lack of armor and damage control features, and their slow speed (most 18 or 19 knots), it is surprising that more of the escort carriers weren't sunk as they were prime targets for U-boats in the Atlantic and kamikazes in the Pacific. Their role was vital.

Espionage

Spying, the second oldest profession, sustained many people and inspired many tales during World War II. What consequences, if any, espionage had on the war itself is extremely hard to judge.

"The very nature of espionage makes it a difficult subject to research and it is often well-nigh impossible to establish exactly what took place during a particular event," according to *A Thread of Deceit*, a book on "espionage myths of World War II" written by Rupert Allason, a Conservative Member of Parliament and authority on British intelligence, who writes under the pseudonym Nigel West.

"In wartime," he continued, "intelligence operations are shrouded necessarily with a further layer of secrecy, which conspires to confuse and deceive. Whenever books come to be written about celebrated (or notorious) incidents, errors creep in and history becomes distorted. Confronted by an official reluctance to set the record straight, authors tend to rely on each other's material and in so doing compound previous errors." He also pointed out that the coauthors of the official *British Intelligence in the Second World War* were all former intelligence officers.

Given the admonitions about the unreliability of espionage, few spies or intelligence incidents during World War II (1) stand up to common standards of historical research and (2) had an impact on the war. Some that did, published as entries in this book, are CICERO, LUCY SPY RING, MINCEMEAT, RED ORCHESTRA, DUSKO POPOV, RICHARD

SORGE, SPECIAL OPERATIONS EXECUTIVE (SOE), and XX COMMITTEE. (Three nonespionage entries in this book—ARNHEM, COVENTRY, and DIEPPE—had "spy story" aspects to them. New information about these stories is based on discoveries recounted in *A Thread of Deceit*.)

The second point, regarding the influence of espionage on the war, can be easily summed up in terms of spying *against* the United States: No significant effect. (See FEDERAL BUREAU OF INVESTIGATION.)

CRYPTOGRAPHY, an important aspect of espionage, did play an extremely important role in the war. (See also ENIGMA, WILLIAM F. FRIEDMAN, EDWIN T. LAYTON, MAGIC, PURPLE, JOSEPH J. ROCHEFORT, and ULTRA.) The importance of intelligence agencies varied. (See *ABWEHR*, GESTAPO, MI5, MI6, NKVD, and SMERSH.)

The manipulation of agents in another country is the most difficult aspect of espionage to analyze and accredit. British military historian John Keegan in *The Second World War*, looking at Allied-sponsored GUERRILLA, SABOTAGE, and espionage activities in German-occupied countries, pronounced them "costly and misguided."

He distinguished spontaneous partisan actions in Yugoslavia from that aided by the British SOE and the American OSS because in Yugoslavia military units still had weapons and discipline that gave operations there a chance against the German Army. But of allied calls for espionage and sabotage in France, Poland, and Czechoslovakia, he wrote, "All failed at the price of very great suffering to the brave patriots involved but at trifling cost to the German forces that put them down."

Essen

Heavily bombed German industrial city. Essen was the site of the KRUPP works, an industrial complex covering 800 acres in Essen. In forty minutes during one March 1943 raid, RAF bombers dropped 150 of the 4,000-pound bombs the British called blockbusters. In a year of steady raids beginning in Aug. 1942 the RAF dropped 6,926 tons of bombs on Essen.

Much of Krupp's production depended upon the use of SLAVE LABOR. A tattered, starving legion of prisoners lived in abominable camps around the city. One of the camps was a former dog kennel. French PRISONERS OF WAR slept five to a pen. Each pen was 3 feet high, 9 feet long, and 6 feet wide.

When American troops entered Essen in April 1945, they were disgusted by what they saw and smelled at the camps. In *The Arms of Krupp* William Manchester described the scene: "GIs waving M1's forced *Hausfrauen* to empty their pantries for freed prisoners, officers paraded Kruppianer [Krupp workers] through the foulest camps, knocking down the arms of those who tried to hold their noses. . . ."

Essex (CV 9)

Lead ship for the AIRCRAFT CARRIER class that spearheaded U.S. striking forces in the Pacific in 1943–1945. The *Essex* was commissioned on the last day of 1942 and sixteen sister ships were in service before the war ended.

After training operations in the Atlantic, the *Essex* shifted to the Pacific in May 1943. She departed PEARL HARBOR for her first actions against the Japanese, flying strikes against Marcus Island on Aug. 31 and against WAKE ISLAND on Oct. 5–6. The *Essex* and sister carriers then supported U.S. AMPHIBIOUS LANDINGS at TARAWA in Nov. 1943. *Essex*-class carriers and the smaller *INDEPENDENCE* (CVL 22)–class carriers subsequently participated in all major U.S. amphibious landings in the Pacific.

At the battle of the MARIANAS—the largest carrier battle in history—the U.S. carrier force (TASK FORCE 58) contained six *Essex*-class carriers plus the older *ENTERPRISE* (CV 6), and eight *Independence*-class light carriers. The 564 aircraft on the decks of the six *Essex*es at the start of the battle represented 63 percent of the 900 aircraft on the fifteen carriers. They had a key role in the overwhelming U.S. victory over the Japanese forces.

By the end of the war the U.S. fast carrier forces (TF 38/58) generally had up to ten carriers of the *Essex* class. Because of the threat from Japanese KAMIKAZE attacks, the mix of aircraft on the *Essex*-class carriers was changed to emphasize fighters. At the Marianas battle the typical *Essex* had about ninety-five aircraft: forty to forty-five F6F HELLCAT fighters, thirty to thirty-five SBD DAUNTLESS or SB2C HELLDIVER dive bombers, and fifteen to twenty TBF/TBM AVENGER TORPEDO planes; by the end of the war the *Essex* aircraft numbered just over 100, with an average of seventy-three fighters (F6F and F4U CORSAIR), only fifteen dive bombers, and fifteen torpedo planes per ship.

The Japanese singled out the carriers for their submarine and air attacks throughout the war. However, the *Essex* class proved particularly lucky and resilient, until the kamikazes entered the war. The *Intrepid* (CV 11) was hit by a torpedo from a Japanese KATE in Feb. 1944 during carrier strikes on TRUK. The carrier was damaged, lost eleven dead and seventeen injured, but steamed away under her own power and was rapidly repaired. During the war several other ships were damaged by BOMBS and kamikazes.

Two ships were devastated: On March 19, 1945, during strikes against the Japanese home islands, a Japanese plane struck the carrier *Franklin* (CV 13) with two small bombs. The bombs exploded in the hangar deck, killing all personnel in the area and igniting fires that quickly enveloped armed and fueled aircraft. For five hours the ship rocked with explosions as bombs and ammunition continually detonated. A huge cloud of smoke rose from the ship as crewmen fought the fires, pushed armed planes over the side, and jettisoned red-hot bombs. Internal communications were lost. The carrier could still steam at 16 knots, but the engine rooms then had to be abandoned because of heat, and the carrier was briefly taken in tow. She was only 55 miles off the coast of Japan, but she was saved. Her dead numbered 832 and 270 were injured. She returned to Pearl Harbor and then the United States under her own power and was rebuilt (although she did not return to combat).

On May 11, 1945, a kamikaze smashed into the *Bunker Hill* (CV 17) while operating between OKINAWA and Japan. A ZERO crashed into the ship, followed moments later by a JUDY dive bomber, which released a bomb that struck the *Bunker Hill;* the plane then crashed into the carrier. The ship shuddered under explosions and fire. For several hours her crew fought fires and exploding bombs. She, too, survived. Casualties numbered 389 dead and missing, and 264 injured. Vice Adm. MARC MITSCHER, TF 58 commander, was in the *Bunker Hill;* uninjured, he transferred to another carrier.

The *Bunker Hill* also returned to the United States for repairs (but did not see further action).

Typhoons also damaged the big carriers. In a June 1945 storm the forward flight decks of the *Hornet* (CV 12) and *Bennington* (CV 20) were smashed, and other carriers received lesser damage.

When the war ended there were seventeen *Essex*-class carriers in the fleet. Another seven were still under construction, and they were completed through 1950. Eight other *Essex*es being built or on order were canceled and never finished. Many of the twenty-four ships that were finished fought in the Korean and Vietnam Wars, and took part in U.S. naval operations during the Cold War era. The *Lexington* (CV 16) of this class served as a training carrier into the 1990s.

The *Essex* design was an improvement over the U.S. carriers built in the late 1930s. The *Essex*es were considered the most capable carriers of the war except that they lacked an armored flight deck, as found in British carriers. The ships had a standard displacement of 27,100 tons; thirteen ships were 872 feet long, the later, "long-hull" *Essex*es, 888 feet. Steam turbines gave them a speed of 32.7 knots. A heavy gun armament was provided—twelve 5-inch (127-mm) dual-purpose weapons, and toward the end of the war some seventy-two 40-mm BOFORS and fifty-two 20-mm OERLIKON antiaircraft guns. Each *Essex* had a crew of some 3,450 officers and enlisted men, including flight crews and maintenance personnel.

Estonia

Capital: Tallinn, pop. 1,131,000 (est. 1939). Independent from 1918, when Germany annexed Memel, Lithuania, to March 1939, Estonia tried to protect itself from Germany by signing a nonaggression pact. Estonia had a similar pact with the Soviet Union, and thus lived in uneasy balance between two powerful neighbors. When those neighbors announced their NONAGGRESSION PACT on Aug. 23, 1939, Estonia was doomed, for a secret protocol of the pact put Estonia in the Soviet "sphere of influence," giving the Soviets the right to move against Estonia without German interference.

On Sept. 28, 1939, the Soviet Union forced Estonia to accept "mutual assistance" that gave air and naval bases to the Soviets. Soon afterward, NAZI officials convinced about 15,000 German-speaking Estonians to migrate to Germany. Soviet troops entered Estonia, but no move was made against the government until June 16, 1940, when Soviet tanks rolled into Tallinn and the Soviets staged a mock election that put a slate of collaborating Estonians into office. In its first act the new legislature voted to incorporate Estonia into the Soviet Union; the Kremlin accepted the "request" on Aug. 6.

In the swift and savage takeover that followed, the Soviets rounded up well-known clergymen, politicians, and intellectuals, along with their wives and children, and deported them to prison camps. Some 60,000 Estonians were killed, imprisoned in Estonia, or deported to the Soviet Union to all but certain death. (Soviet documents made public in 1990 indicated that the thousands of Polish officers slaughtered in the KATYN MASSACRE were slain to make room for deportees from Estonia and the other Baltic states, Latvia, and Lithuania, which were similarly taken over.)

When German troops invaded the Soviet Union in June 1941, they easily took Estonia, which was then absorbed into Germany as the new province of Ostland. Estonia remained under German occupation until Feb. 1944 when Soviet troops entered the country on their sweep eastward against retreating Germans. The defenders in Estonia included not only Germans but also about 65,000 Estonian conscripts. With the fall of Tallinn on Sept. 22, 1944, these Estonians and thousands of others faced another round of Soviet persecution, this time by vengeful occupation forces. About 30,000 Estonians fled to Sweden and 50,000 to Germany, never to return.

Once again thousands of Estonians were deported to the Soviet Union. This time, however, they were replaced by settlers from the Soviet Union. (The United States continues to recognize Estonia as an independent state.)

Ethiopia (Abyssinia)

Capital: Addis Ababa, pop. 10,000,000 (est. 1939). In Dec. 1934 Ethiopian and Italian soldiers clashed in a dispute about water wells on the border with Italian Somaliland. Unsatisfied with a LEAGUE OF NATIONS finding of mutual responsibility for the incident, Italy on Oct. 3, 1935, invaded Ethiopia

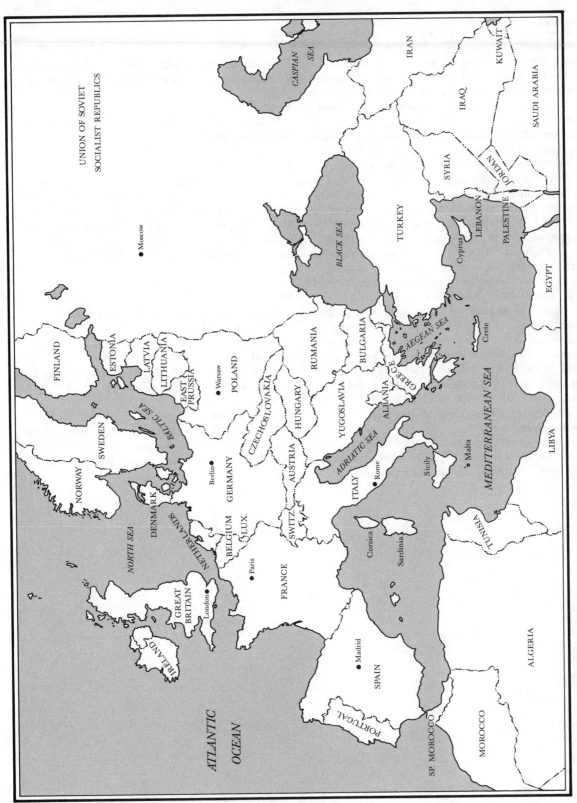

Europe at the start of the European War.

from Somaliland and Eritrea, another Italian colony. The invasion—Italian warplanes and poison gas against spear-brandishing Ethiopians—graphically portrayed fascism and aggression. The United States reacted by declaring a "moral quarantine" against selling oil to Italy. The League of Nations condemned the invasion; Italy quit the League.

After fierce resistance by the Ethiopian Army, the Italian forces captured Addis Ababa on May 5, 1936. Emperor HAILE SELASSIE, a symbol of resistance to aggression, escaped. He appeared before the League of Nations in Geneva and, in a memorable scene, pleaded in vain for help for his country.

In Ethiopia, GUERRILLAS kept on fighting. But Italy annexed the country on June 1, making it, with Eritrea and Italian Somaliland, a colonial territory called Italian East Africa.

Tens of thousands of Italians migrated to Ethiopia to work on roads and other Italian-financed public works. A repressive occupation built up anti-Italian feeling, which Haile Selassie stoked from his exile in the Sudan. A British East African offensive in 1941 drove the Italians out of Eritrea and Ethiopia; Addis Ababa was liberated and on May 5, 1941, Haile Selassie left the Sudan to return to his throne in triumph.

Under the PEACE TREATIES after the war, Italy gave up any claim to Ethiopia. In 1950 the UNITED NATIONS made Eritrea "an autonomous unit" of Ethiopia. Italian Somaliland and British Somaliland joined in 1960 and became the republic of Somalia.

Eureka

Code name for the TEHRAN CONFERENCE, Nov.–Dec. 1943.

European War

(1) An American term referring to the period of World War II that began on Sept. 1, 1939, when Germany invaded Poland, and ended on Dec. 11, 1941, when Germany and Italy declared war on the United States; (2) a general term for warfare in Europe until the SURRENDER of Germany on May 7, 1945.

Excess

British code name for a major CONVOY to MALTA, Jan. 1941.

Exploit

Code name for U.S. Army deception plan for RHINE CROSSINGS, 1944.

Extended Capital

Code name for modification of the plan for the British Fourteenth Army attack across the Chindwin River to Mandalay to recapture northern Burma, 1945.

.45-caliber Pistol

Principal sidearm of the U.S. military during the war. The M1911 pistol or "45" was a powerful weapon: a single hit anywhere on the body would usually stop a person. However, the gun was not accurate and it had considerable recoil.

The pistol was recoil-operated and fed by a seven-round magazine that fit in the grip; an eighth round could be loaded in the breech. It weighed 2.5 pounds loaded and was carried in a distinctive russet leather holster carried on a web belt. (Military policemen wore it on a leather "Sam Browne" belt.)

The M1911 was based on a John Browning design of 1900 and produced by the Colt arms company (which led to the pistol also being referred to as the "Colt .45"). It was selected by the U.S. gov-

ernment in 1911 because of the need to provide a more powerful hand gun than had been available to the U.S. Army during the counterinsurgent operations in the Philippines. The .45 was a particularly rugged and reliable weapon.

A .455-caliber model was produced for the RAF.

509th Composite Group

U.S. AAF unit that flew ATOMIC BOMB missions against Japan. The 509th Composite GROUP was established on Dec. 17, 1944, at Wendover Field in Utah under the command of Col. PAUL W. TIBBETS. The group had only one SQUADRON, the 393rd Bombardment Squadron, commanded by Maj. CHARLES SWEENEY. The squadron flew specially modified B-29 SUPERFOR-

Sailors watch helplessly as ships and aircraft explode during the Japanese attack on Pearl Harbor. This was the scene from Ford Island, in the center of the harbor, inundated with large PBY Catalina flying boats and smaller floatplanes from battleships and cruisers. *(U.S. Navy)*

TRESS bombers with fifteen production B-29s being built at the Martin-Nebraska plant modified to carry the atomic bomb.

The group deployed from the United States to TINIAN in May–June 1945 and was based at the island's North Field. The unit was nominally under the XXI Bomber Command of the Twentieth AIR FORCE, but actual direction was from the president through the secretary of war, HENRY L. STIMSON, and the head of the atomic bomb project, Maj. Gen. LESLIE GROVES.

The 509th flew training flights from Tinian, some with bombs being dropped on bypassed Japanese-held islands. During July the unit flew twelve strikes of two to six planes against Japan, both for training and to accustom the Japanese to seeing small bomber formations. The planes used conventional bombs and PUMPKIN BOMBS.

B-29s piloted by Tibbets and Sweeney dropped atomic bombs on HIROSHIMA and NAGASAKI, respectively, in Aug. 1945.

F2A Buffalo

A lackluster carrier-based fighter, the F2A did have the distinction of being the U.S. Navy's first monoplane fighter. When the war began there were twenty-one F2A Buffalos in the AIRCRAFT CARRIER *LEXINGTON* (CV 2), seven in the ESCORT CARRIER *Long Island* (CVE 1), and fourteen assigned to a single Marine fighter SQUADRON. Small numbers at various U.S. bases brought the total in service to 107; the F2As previously embarked in the carrier *SARATOGA* (CV 3) had already been replaced by the F4F WILDCAT.

The only F2As that saw combat were Marine-piloted aircraft at MIDWAY. Marine Fighter Squadron (VMF) 221's F2As had been flown into Midway on Dec. 25, 1941, from the carrier *Saratoga*. At the time of the June 1942 battle there were twenty F2As and six or seven F4F Wildcats in VMF-221. They were ineffective in stopping the waves of Japanese bombers attacking Midway, although Marine sources credit them with shooting down eighteen A6M ZERO fighters and twenty-five D3A VAL dive bombers, undoubtedly inflated figures. The Marines lost thirteen of the F2As and two F4Fs in the battle plus others damaged. The last F2As were discarded by the Marines in Sept. 1942.

The prototype Brewster XF2A-1 flew in Dec. 1937 and after Navy trials production was ordered in June 1938. The first production F2A was completed in June 1939, and Brewster produced 503 through the end of 1939. Of those, 163 went to the Navy and Marines, and 340 to ALLIES—Britain, Finland, and the DUTCH EAST INDIES. The Finnish planes were used with success against the Soviets in the 1941–1944 war, but the plane proved ineffective against the Japanese. (Most of the British Buffalos had been shipped to Singapore and Rangoon.)

The "bullet"-shaped F2A was characterized by its short, stubby fuselage, stalk-like inward retracting main landing gear, and retractable tail wheel. The large radial engine had a prominent spinner. The improved F2A-3 had increased armor for pilot and fuel tanks, but added weight that further reduced the plane's performance.

The F2A-1 had a maximum speed of 300 mph and was credited with a range of some 1,100 miles; speed was increased to 323 mph in the F2A-2. Armament consisted of two .50-cal. machine guns in the upper cowling and two in the wings; two 100-pound BOMBS could be carried under the wings. The F2A was a single-seat aircraft.

F4F Wildcat

The principal U.S. Navy carrier fighter when the United States entered the war. Although the F4F was inferior in performance to the Japanese A6M ZERO fighter, American pilots often outfought their opponents. Aviation historian William Green called the Wildcat "the first really successful western shipboard fighter monoplane . . . [but] an undistinguished warplane from the performance aspect." The F4F also served in large numbers in the Royal Navy as the Martlet (called Wildcat after March 1944).

Beginning in 1943 the Wildcat, having been the only U.S. Navy and Marine fighter in the Pacific War during 1942, was replaced on larger U.S. carriers by the F6F HELLCAT. The Wildcat's battle honors included WAKE, MIDWAY, CORAL SEA, GUADALCANAL, the SOLOMONS, and the BATTLE OF THE ATLANTIC. During the ill-fated American defense of Wake atoll in Dec. 1941 the Wildcats were effective in attacking Japanese ships as well as intercepting Japanese bombers.

In 1942 the F4F kill-to-loss ratio for air combat was 5.9:1 and for the whole war the F4F/FM ratio was 6.9:1, in many respects reflecting the superior U.S. and British pilots. The Navy's first fighter ACE, EDWARD (BUTCH) O'HARE, scored his five victories in Feb. 1942 flying an F4F. The Wildcat continued in U.S. and British naval service until the end of the war with the General Motors–built FM variant flown from almost all jeep or ESCORT CARRIERS.

Development of the XF4F-1 began at Grumman Corp. in 1935 as a biplane fighter, but the prototype was not completed and instead the Navy ordered the XF4F-2 monoplane fighter in July 1936. The first flight occurred on Sept. 2, 1937, but the prototype lost to the Brewster F2A BUFFALO in Navy competition. Subsequently, the F4F design was modified and a more powerful engine fitted to produce the XF4F-3, which first flew on Feb. 12, 1939. The potential of the aircraft was evident and series production was ordered. Export orders were placed by France and Britain, with the former delivered to the Royal Navy after the fall of France. By Dec. 1941 seven of the eight U.S. Navy carrier-based fighter squadrons and three of the four U.S. Marine fighter squadrons flew the F4F (the two others had the F2A Buffalo).

The F4F had a short, stubby fuselage with short, square-tip wings. The F4F-4 and later aircraft had folding wings for carrier stowage. There were camera-equipped variants, including the twenty unarmed F4F-7 (range was over 3,500 miles!), and one aircraft was evaluated with twin floats (making its first flight in Feb. 1943).

During the war production of the Wildcat was undertaken by Eastern Aircraft with the designation FM, which produced 5,280 of the Wildcat/Martlet total of 7,251 aircraft (including prototypes that reached the XF4F-8 model). The FM-2 variant—similar to the F4F-4 model—became the standard fighter on board U.S. and British escort carriers. The F4F-4 had a maximum speed of 318 mph and a combat range of 770 miles. It was armed with six .50-cal. machine guns; the FM-2 had four guns, but had wing racks for two 250-pound BOMBS or six 5-inch (127-mm) ROCKETS for attacking submarines. All Wildcats were single-seat aircraft.

F4U Corsair

U.S. Navy carrier-based fighter in continuous production longer than any other World War II–era aircraft. The F4U Corsair was a large, powerful fighter. Flying from AIRCRAFT CARRIERS and land bases, the F4U had an overall 11:1 kill-to-loss ratio over Japanese aircraft with an estimated 1,400 enemy planes of all types destroyed by F4Us in the Pacific.

The Vought Corp. began development of the F4U in early 1938, designing the smallest possible airframe around the most powerful engine available, the Pratt & Whitney XR-2800 Double Wasp. To accommodate the engine without overly long landing gear struts, the plane had an inverted gull wing with the main legs of the landing gear located at the wing knuckles. (The wings folded upward for carrier stowage.)

The prototype XF4U-1 made its first flight on May 29, 1940, and by the end of the year it had flown 404 mph, faster than any U.S. fighter then flying. Contracts for production were not forthcoming for more than a year and production deliveries of the F4U began to Navy squadrons in Oct. 1942. However, because of poor cockpit visibility and other problems the aircraft "flunked" its initial carrier trials. The F4U was rejected by the Navy for carrier service, and most war-built aircraft went to the Marine Corps for land use. However, with the KAMIKAZE threat developing in late Dec. 1944, Marine F4U squadrons were assigned to carriers.

The British and New Zealand navies also flew the F4U, the latter from carriers, the plane's first carrier operation being the April 3, 1944, strikes from the carrier *Victorious* against the German battleship *TIRPITZ*. Subsequently, a few U.S. Navy squadrons flew the modified F4U-1A from carriers, and soon small numbers of the F4U-2 with AI-type RADAR for use as a night fighter and the F4U-1P camera plane were being put on most of the Navy's larger carriers. (The F4U-2 was the first single-seat night fighter to enter service with any country.)

A total of 12,570 Corsairs were built, with the designations F4U (Vought), FG (Goodyear), F3A (Brewster), and AU (Vought attack model) being used. The final Corsairs were AU-1 models intended for the fighter-bomber role, the last coming off the Chance Vought production lines in late December 1952. These were the last propeller fighters built by the United States.

The improved F4U-4 variant had a maximum speed of 446 mph and a combat range of 1,000 miles. These aircraft carried six .50-cal. machine guns and could carry two 1,000-pound BOMBS; the F4U-5 and AU-1 (formerly F4U-7) models had instead four 20-mm cannon and the latter could deliver four 1,000-pound bombs. The F4U was a single-seat aircraft.

After the war the F4U was flown from French carriers in the Indochina conflict and in the 1956 Suez invasion. In 1952—during the Korean War—an F4U shot down a Soviet-built MiG-15 turbojet fighter.

F5F Skyrocket

First twin-engine U.S. naval fighter. Developed by the Grumman Corp., it first flew in 1941 as the XF5F-1 (that same year a variant flew as the U.S. Army's XP-50). Although not accepted for production by either service, the F5F gained wide notoriety as the aircraft flown in the COMIC strip "Blackhawk." Only one prototype was built.

The large radial engine nacelles protruded past the rounded nose; the single-seat aircraft had a twin-tail configuration; the undercarriage fully retracted into the nacelles. The plane had a carrier hook fitted although it is not believed to have ever flown from a carrier.

The F5F was credited with a top speed of 358 mph. As a warplane it was to carry several machine guns in the nose.

F6F Hellcat

The first U.S. Navy carrier-based fighter that could defeat the Japanese A6M ZERO fighter under virtually all conditions. According to aviation historian William Green, "the appearance of the Hellcat in the late summer of 1943 changed the [combat] situation virtually overnight." The F6F was credited with 4,947 of the 6,477 enemy aircraft destroyed in the air by U.S. Navy carrier pilots. The principal fighter on the larger U.S. AIRCRAFT CARRIERS from 1943 to 1945, the F6F was predominant in the carrier battles of the MARIANAS and LEYTE GULF.

The aircraft was also flown in large numbers from British carriers.

Work on the F6F began in 1941 at the Grumman Corp., which took advantage of pilot experience with the Navy's first monoplane fighters (F4F WILDCAT and F2A BUFFALO) and air combat in Europe. The Navy ordered the first XF6F-1 on June 30, 1941, although significant changes were made before that aircraft flew as the XF6F-3 on June 26, 1942. Large production orders for the F6F-3 had already been placed in May 1942 and deliveries to the fleet began early in 1943, possibly a record from the prototype to combat squadron acceptance. (Despite the prewar beginnings of the Hellcat, many stories survive that the fighter was designed on the basis of a wrecked Zero found in the ALEUTIANS in June 1942.)

The first action for the F6F occurred with aircraft from the carriers *Essex* (CV 9) and *Yorktown* (CV 10) during a strike on Marcus Island on Aug. 31, 1943. By the end of the war all U.S. large (CV) and light (CVL) carriers had the F6F in their fighter squadrons, as did British carriers. (The British initially called the aircraft Gannet, but soon changed it to Hellcat.)

Developed from the F4F Wildcat, the later aircraft was larger and had cleaner lines, but retained the square wing tips and other appearance features of the F4F/FM series. There were several night-fighter versions with wing-pod mounted radar (and after the war there were camera variants).

Production totaled 12,274 aircraft through Nov. 1945, all from Grumman. The definitive F6F-5 had a top speed of 380 mph and a combat range of 945 miles. Armament consisted of six .50-cal. machine guns or two 20-mm cannon and four machine guns. Air-to-ground ROCKETS were sometimes carried, but rarely did they carry BOMBS. The single-seat F6F was flown in relatively small numbers by the Marine Corps, mostly in the F6F-3N and F6F-5N night-fighter models operating from land bases.

While myth had it that the F6F was based on secrets learned from a Zero that had crashed in the Aleutians on June 3, 1942, that aircraft was not returned to the United States, repaired, and reassembled for flight until Oct. 1942. The prototype F6F had flown some months earlier.

(While the F6F was phased out of the fleet before

the Korea War began in 1950, several attacks were launched against targets in North Korea with radio-controlled, explosive-laden F6F-5K aircraft; some F6F-5D aircraft were used to control the drones. The French Navy flew F6Fs in their Indochina war.)

F7F Tigercat

U.S. Navy twin-engine fighter intended for operations on the large AIRCRAFT CARRIERS of the large *Midway* (CV 41) class. A Grumman aircraft developed specifically as a carrier night fighter, the F7F-1N was a single-seat aircraft while the -2N and -3N models were two-seaters; the "straight" F7F-1 was intended to operate in the ground support role.

The first of two XF7F-1 prototypes flew in Dec. 1943, with the Marine Corps ordering 500 to support AMPHIBIOUS LANDINGS in the Pacific. Deliveries began in April 1944, but production became defused with ground-attack, night-fighter, and photo-reconnaissance variants. It was also considered as a launch platform for BAT GUIDED MISSILES. None saw combat in the war. The 364 aircraft that were produced through late 1946 by Grumman served mostly in Marine units until 1954. They saw combat in the Korean War, but were not normally based aboard carriers.

The Tigercat bore little resemblance to the previous Grumman twin-engine naval fighter, the F5F SKYROCKET. The F7F was a graceful-looking aircraft, with a long, narrow fuselage, large nacelles, and a fully retractable tricycle landing gear. The night fighters had a lengthened nose to house an air-intercept RADAR.

The aircraft had a maximum speed of 435 mph and was credited with a 1,200-mile range as a fighter. The standard fighter armament was four 20-mm guns in the nose; in the attack role two 1,000-pound BOMBS could be carried under the wings or an aerial TORPEDO under the fuselage.

F8F Bearcat

The penultimate piston-engine fighter delivered to the U.S. Navy and an outstanding fighter aircraft. The F8F Bearcat was a relatively lightweight fighter with an outstanding rate of climb and speed, but at the cost of range. The F8F entered service too late to be used by the U.S. Navy in World War II, but it had an important role in service with the French *l'Armée de l'Air* in the Indochina War.

Work began at Grumman in 1943 on the Bearcat, a successor to the firm's highly successful F4F WILDCAT and F6F HELLCAT. The Hellcat's Pratt & Whitney R-2800 radial engine was fitted in a lighter aircraft. The first XF8F-1 flew on Aug. 21, 1944. Production contracts followed in the fall—2,023 to be built by Grumman, followed by 1,876 more ordered from General Motors as the F3M-1. The first production aircraft reached the fleet on May 21, 1945, too late to see combat against the Japanese. With V-J DAY came production cancellations, but deliveries totaled 1,263 through May 1949. (The only piston fighter delivered to the Navy after that date was the F4U CORSAIR, the last of which was completed in late 1952.) F8Fs remained in U.S. Navy service until Jan. 1953. They were also flown by France and Thailand.

A low-wing aircraft, the F8F had a "bubble"-style canopy that provided excellent pilot visibility. The outer wing panels folded upward for carrier stowage. The main landing gear and tail wheel fully retracted.

The maximum speed of the F8F-1 was 421 mph and the aircraft was credited with a range of 1,100 miles. The original armament of four .50-cal. machine guns was upgraded in the F8F-2 to four 20-mm cannon. A dozen F8F-2N night fighters had only two cannon and were fitted with an air-intercept RADAR pod; the sixty F8F-2P photo-reconnaissance planes also had only two cannon. Wing racks could hold two 1,000-pound BOMBS or two drop tanks. The F8F was flown by a single pilot.

Fabius

Code name for AMPHIBIOUS LANDING exercises for the NORMANDY INVASION, May 1944.

Fall Blau (Case Blue)

German code name for Luftwaffe operations against Britain, 1938–1939.

Fall Gelb (Case Yellow)

German code name for planned invasion of Belgium, France, and Holland, May 1940.

Fall Grün (Case Green)

German code word for a proposed attack on Czechoslovakia, 1938.

Fall Weiss (Case White)

Code name for German invasion of Poland, Sept. 1, 1939.

Far Eastern Commission

Organization created by the ALLIES for the occupation of Japan. After the surrender of Japan, the Allies decided not to set up occupation zones, as was done in Germany. Instead, Gen. of the Army DOUGLAS MACARTHUR was appointed the virtual ruler of the nation, with the formal title of Supreme Commander of the Allied Powers in Japan (SCAP). He reported to the Far Eastern Commission consisting of representatives of the United States, England, China, France, the Netherlands, Canada, Australia, New Zealand, India, the Soviet Union, and the Philippines.

Fat Man,

see ATOMIC BOMB.

Federal Bureau of Investigation

Principal U.S. government agency for enforcement of ESPIONAGE laws and investigation of reports of SABOTAGE. The FBI's mandate extended to Latin America, where its Special Intelligence Service helped to gather information that led to many arrests of German agents by Argentina and other Latin American nations.

The FBI got jurisdiction over sabotage and espionage in 1936, but J. EDGAR HOOVER, director of the FBI, kept the focus on the highly publicized pursuit of gangsters by his "G-men." Hoover showed little interest in sabotage and espionage until the eve of the EUROPEAN WAR. Within days after the war began in Europe, President ROOSEVELT gave the FBI a more specific mandate to investigate not only espionage but also NEUTRALITY ACT violations. In fiscal year 1939 the FBI handled 1,651 cases under this mandate, compared to 250 the year before.

Despite the high numbers supplied to Congress by the statistics-minded Hoover, neither espionage

nor sabotage had any real effect on the U.S. war effort. The only German saboteurs known to reach the U.S. were quickly caught after they arrived by U-BOATS. The FBI apprehended them after an informer among them called the FBI—twice; the first time he was ignored.

In another case, on Nov. 29, 1944, U-boat *U-1230* landed William C. Colepaugh, a twenty-six-year-old American, and Erich Gimpel, a thirty-four-year-old German, on an isolated beach in Frenchman Bay near Bar Harbor, Me. The agents were to get information on U.S. rocket, aircraft, and ship-building activities and send it back to Germany via MICRODOTS in letters sent to mail drops in neutral countries.

Again, an informer—Colepaugh—tipped off the FBI, which, after a massive manhunt, found Gimpel. They both were tried by a military court under a previous order from President Roosevelt giving the military jurisdiction over espionage and sabotage cases. They were found guilty and sentenced to death. President TRUMAN later commuted the sentences.

FBI agents joined Army security agents in keeping watch on key scientists working on the ATOMIC BOMB. But it was not until after the war that investigators discovered the full extent of espionage, not by Germany and Japan but by one of the ALLIES—the Soviet Union. The FBI also worked with Canadian security officials in tracking down Soviet spies used during the war to obtain secret scientific military information about atomic energy, RADAR, SONAR, explosives, and the PROXIMITY FUZE.

A little-known interest of the FBI during the war was black (then called Negro) newspapers because of suspected subversive, antiwar, and Communist sympathies. The suspicions stemmed from editorial complaints about SEGREGATION in the armed services and discrimination practices in war industries. Hoover tried to get black papers indicted under the Espionage Act, but Attorney General Francis Biddle blocked the move.

During the war, at Hoover's direction the FBI had been investigating American Communists and Communist sympathizers, lengthening its watch list to include writers JOHN STEINBECK and ERNEST HEMINGWAY among others. After the war, the FBI extended the wartime mandate of investigating threats to national security to continue investigations of Communists.

Felix

Code name for German plan to occupy GIBRALTAR, late 1940.

Fermi, Enrico (1901–1954)

Italian-born physicist whose research established the theory behind the ATOMIC BOMB. Fermi was awarded the 1938 Nobel Prize in physics for research on radioactive particles. He left Italy that year for the United States with his wife, who was Jewish; he feared that the ANTI-SEMITISM of Fascist Germany would soon spread to Fascist Italy.

Soon after Fermi arrived in the United States he learned that two German physicists had discovered that the bombardment of uranium with neutrons splits the uranium nucleus, releasing enormous amounts of energy. He vividly envisioned the consequences of that discovery—an atomic bomb. He later said that he looked out the window of a New York building and thought about the implications. "A little bomb like that," he said to himself, cupping his hands as if he held a ball, "and it would all disappear."

A controlled chain reaction would show beyond a doubt that a bomb was possible. Fermi, working in New York and at the University of Chicago, put together a device that could produce a chain reaction: a pile, he called it—layers of graphite impregnated with bits of uranium. The pile was built in a squash court beneath the stands of Stagg Field on Chicago's South Side.

On the afternoon of Dec. 2, 1942, Fermi stood on a balcony and ordered that a control rod be withdrawn, inch by inch, from the pile. At 3:49 the pile "went critical": Fermi had achieved the first self-sustaining nuclear chain reaction.

That was the beginning of the enormous effort to build the atomic bomb. Fermi was a leading worker on the bomb, from this beginning to the day of Trinity, the code name for the test of the first bomb, on July 16, 1945 at ALAMOGORDO. He was a man of precise figures and simple solutions. Characteristically, he used swirling scraps of paper to determine the amount of energy liberated by the world's first nuclear explosion. He dropped the papers as a blast of air hit from the explosion. "The shift was about 2½ meters," he later wrote, "which, at the time, I estimated to correspond to the blast that would be produced by ten thousand tons of T.N.T." (He was off by 8,600 tons.)

After the war Fermi resumed teaching at the University of Chicago. Shortly before he died of cancer in Nov. 1954 his biographer, Emilio Segrè, visited Fermi in the hospital. "In typical fashion," Segrè wrote, "he was measuring the flow of nutrients [from a feeding tube] by counting drops and timing them with his stopwatch."

Feuerzauber (Fire Magic)

Original name for *Nordlicht*.

Fi 156 *Storch* (Stork)

Popular, widely used German liaison aircraft. Capable of short-run takeoffs and landings, the Fi 156 was used to transport VIPs, for reconnaissance, as an ambulance, and for artillery observation. It was flown in all combat areas that the Germans fought, and was extensively used by Field Marshal ERWIN ROMMEL in North Africa for his frequent visits to the front lines. An Fi 156 was used to fly BENITO MUSSOLINI out of the Italian mountains after his dramatic rescue by OTTO SKORZENY. (On that occasion the Fi 156 took off with an overload of several hundred pounds—the pilot, Mussolini, and Skorzeny.) At the end of the war the Fi 156 was among the last aircraft to reach the besieged capital of BERLIN, as several VIPs paid their final visits to HITLER. Those planes landed on the East-West Axis, the great boulevard in the center of Berlin, often under Soviet artillery fire.

The Fi 156 first flew in 1936. The Fieseler-designed aircraft was built by Morane Saulnier factories France and the Mraz firm in Czechoslovakia as the Fieseler factories were employed mainly to produce combat aircraft. Wartime production was more than 2,500 aircraft.

A single-engine, high-wing aircraft with a large glazed cockpit and elongated main landing gear, the Fi 156 was reliable and easy to fly. Experiments were conducted with skis and a caterpillar landing gear, the latter for rough terrain. Maximum speed was 109 mph and range was 236 miles. A 7.9-mm machine gun could be fitted in the rear of the cabin for self-defense. Normally the Fi 156 carried one pilot plus one passenger or litter. (An enlarged Fi 256 with space for five persons was developed but not produced.)

Fido Torpedo

U.S. air-dropped antisubmarine TORPEDO that had acoustic guidance for homing in on the propeller noises of submarines. First employed in Atlantic antisubmarine operations from U.S Navy TBF/ TBM AVENGER torpedo planes based on ESCORT CARRIERS, the weapon was highly effective against submerged U-BOATS. It was also used by land-based aircraft, especially the B-24 LIBERATOR and PBY CATALINA.

The Fido's combat debut occurred in the Atlantic in May 1943 when a Liberator from the RAF Coastal Command heavily damaged the *U-456,* which surfaced and was soon destroyed by CONVOY escort ships. The next day an RAF Liberator sank the submarine *U-266* with a Fido. During 1943–1945 some 340 Fido torpedoes were used against U-boats; they sank sixty-eight submarines and damaged another thirty-three, a very high success rate for an antisubmarine weapon. Allied aircraft using depth charges against U-boats achieved a 9.5 percent kill rate compared to 22 percent for Fido torpedoes.

The Fido was designated as the Mark 24 mine to disguise its true capabilities. The existence of Fido was unknown to the German Navy until after the war had ended.

Fido's guidance was based on four passive hydrophones. When dropped into the water from an aircraft the Fido dived to a preset depth and began an acoustic search for the submarine, the torpedo's effective detection range being approximately 1,500 yards. If no propeller sounds were detected the torpedo would begin a circular search, which it could maintain for ten to fifteen minutes. At least one submarine, the *U-296,* was sunk by a Fido after a run of thirteen minutes. On another occasion, against the *U-1107,* a Fido entered the water only eighty yards from the submarine but ran for three minutes before exploding, apparently having not made initial detection of the submarine but had gone into a circular search pattern before finding its target.

The weapon was 84 inches long and 19 inches in diameter, and weighed 680 pounds. It had electric propulsion with a battery as the power source. The warhead was 92 pounds of HBX-1, known as Torpex, with a contact fuze that detonated when it struck the submarine's hull. Maximum speed was 12 knots.

Development of the Fido had begun in 1940 by a team headed by the Western Electric Co. Approximately 4,000 of these torpedoes were produced during the war. They remained in U.S. Navy service until 1948.

Fifth Column

Applied to efforts by citizens who spy for or sympathize with the invading or occupying enemy. The term came into use in the SPANISH CIVIL WAR during the siege of Madrid, when Gen. Emilio Mola, a pro-FRANCO (Nationalist) officer, boasted that he had four columns of troops marching against the city and a fifth column of sympathizers inside the city. "Fifth columnists" was picked up by the British to describe NAZI sympathizers in Southwest Africa at the beginning of the war. The phrase was established in the United States by ERNEST HEMINGWAY, an anti-Franco war correspondent who wrote a play about that war entitled *Fifth Column.*

Final Solution

The code term *(Die Endlösung)* used by Germans carrying out the extermination of JEWS. One of the earliest uses of the term came on July 31, 1941, little more than a month after the invasion of the Soviet Union, when HERMANN GÖRING ordered REINHARD HEYDRICH, chief of the REICH CENTRAL SECURITY OFFICE, to prepare a plan "showing the measures for organization and action necessary to carry out the final solution of the Jewish question." (On Oct. 10, 1941, Heydrich added Gypsies to the extermination orders. That winter several German officials discussed the possibility of drowning 30,000 Gypsies by sending them out in ships in the Mediterranean and bombing the ships.) In Jan. 1942 Heydrich and his aide, ADOLF EICHMANN, conducted the WANNSEE CONFERENCE, whose agenda was "the final solution of the European Jewish Question."

Finland

Capital: Helsinki, pop. 3,834,662 (est. 1939). A Grand Duchy of Czarist Russia, Finland emerged from the Bolshevik Revolution as an independent republic. A rugged, lake-laced land that prospered on lumbering, Finland kept an uneasy eye on her giant neighbor, the Soviet Union. Early in 1939, when she and Sweden were negotiating the fortification of islands they shared in the Gulf of Bothnia, the Soviets began bullying Finland. Pressure increased as the months passed. On Aug. 23, 1939, the Soviet Union and Germany stunned the world with their NONAGGRESSION PACT. A secret protocol to the pact put Finland and the other Baltic states in the Soviet "sphere of influence" and the Soviets began planning to take over Finland, Estonia, Latvia, and Lithuania.

The first move was aimed at Finland, on Sept. 24, 1939, when the Soviets prohibited Finnish ships from passing through Leningrad via the Neva River. On Oct. 5, the Soviet Union summoned a Finnish delegation to Moscow and insisted on the removal of some Finnish fortifications supposedly threatening LENINGRAD. The Soviets also demanded several pieces of Finnish territory and the right to establish a naval base in the port of Hanko. Finland stalled, and futile talks went on until Nov. 13.

On Nov. 30, after claiming that Finnish guns had opened fired on Soviet troops, Red Army forces poured over the border and Soviet planes bombed Helsinki and four other cities. Then, to the astonishment of the Soviets and the Western world, the Finns beat back the invaders. Finnish ski troops wiped out isolated Soviet units and even routed an entire division. The white-clad Finns fighting in the snow became symbols of David fighting Goliath. President ROOSEVELT condemned the invasion and extended $10,000,000 in credit to a nation hailed as the only one to pay all its World War I debt to the United States.

On Jan. 20, 1940, Prime Minister CHURCHILL said Finland "had exposed, for all the world to see, the military incapacity of the Red Army." But by then the Soviets had regrouped. They sent in massive reinforcements and launched a sustained bombing campaign against Finnish cities. In March, exhausted by fighting against overwhelming odds, Finland opened negotiations and, as the price for peace, lost the Karelian Isthmus—the land bridge to Leningrad—and other border territories. The Soviet-Finnish border was essentially restored to the boundary set by Peter the Great in 1721.

Later in 1940, Finland, technically neutral but anti-Soviet, allowed German troops to pass through Finland for the German occupation of Norway. Many Germans remained on Finnish soil and, when Germany attacked the Soviet Union in June 1941, Finland, "for the liberty of the fatherland," joined forces with Germany and its "genial leader." Britain declared war on Finland on Dec. 6, 1941, and the American government, supporting Britain, seized six Finnish ships in U.S. ports.

To people in nations fighting the Germans, Finland turned from that gallant little nation to that opportunistic little nuisance. Luftwaffe planes flew from Finnish air bases to bomb the Soviet ports of Murmansk and Archangel and to attack the RUSSIAN CONVOYS. There was heavy fighting there between Germans and Soviet soldiers. Without directly fighting the ALLIES, Finland was clearly on the side of Germany.

U.S. Secretary of State CORDELL HULL on Feb. 8, 1944, warned Finland of serious consequences if the nation continued to support Germany. The Soviets punctuated the warning with a bombing attack on Helsinki. In June the United States broke off relations with Finland but still did not declare war. Finally, on Sept. 2, 1944, Finland surrendered to Soviet forces sweeping eastward. In a peace treaty signed seventeen days later, Finland agreed to give up once more to the Soviet Union essentially what it had yielded up in 1940. On March 3, 1945, Finland declared war on Germany.

Fire Team

U.S. Army and Marine Corps team of three or four riflemen within a SQUAD armed with M1 rifles and one BROWNING AUTOMATIC RIFLE. The fire team provided close-in fire support for other squad members.

Firebrand

Code name for Allied invasion of Corsica, Sept.–Oct. 1943.

Firefly

The final British two-seat carrier fighter of the piston-engine era. The Firefly combined the powerful Griffon engine and elliptical wing shape (as in the SPITFIRE). The first Fairey Aviation–built Firefly flew on Dec. 22, 1941, with production following. The aircraft received high marks in the night-fighter, photo-reconnaissance, and strike roles, the last against Japanese targets in the DUTCH EAST INDIES. In addition to its armament of four 20-mm cannon, the Firefly could carry two 1,000-pound BOMBS or eight large ROCKETS. Top speed was 316 mph and range was more than 1,000 miles. The Royal Navy took delivery of only 658 Fireflies during the war; production of a postwar antisubmarine variant continued until 1951.

Fireflies served into the 1950s, seeing combat in the Korean War and against insurgents in Malaya.

Firestorm

Description of the conflagration produced when many fires, caused by bombings, combine, sucking up oxygen and creating a hurricane-like thermal column with temperatures of more than 1,400° F. The term was first used by German firefighters in the four-day July 1943 bombing of HAMBURG by U.S. and British bombers in what Allied planners called Operation Gomorrah. The firestorm burned out about eight square miles of Hamburg and killed about 45,000 people. Similar firestorms destroyed COLOGNE and DRESDEN.

First U.S. Army Group

Fake army unit created as part of a plan to deceive the Germans about the landing points for the invasion of Europe. (See CAMOUFLAGE.)

Fischreiher (Heron)

German code name for the attack on STALINGRAD by Army Group B, July–Nov. 1942.

Five-star Rank

Highest U.S. military rank. Five-star rank was established for the U.S. Army and Navy on Dec. 14, 1944. Previously the most senior military ranks were four-star, general in the Army and Marine Corps, and admiral in the Navy. The five-star offi-

cers and the order of their date of rank and hence precedence were:

FLEET ADMIRAL

Dec. 15 WILLIAM D. LEAHY, Chief of Staff to President ROOSEVELT
Dec. 17 ERNEST J. KING, Commander in Chief U.S. Fleet and Chief of Naval Operations
Dec. 19 CHESTER W. NIMITZ, Commander in Chief Pacific Ocean Area

GENERAL OF THE ARMY

Dec. 16 GEORGE C. MARSHALL, Chief of Staff U.S. Army
Dec. 18 DOUGLAS MACARTHUR, Commander in Chief Southwest Pacific Area
Dec. 20 DWIGHT D. EISENHOWER, Supreme Allied Commander Europe
Dec. 21 HENRY H. ARNOLD, Commander U.S. Army Air Forces

A fourth fleet admiral was established, but the rank was not awarded until Dec. 11, 1945, when it was given to WILLIAM HALSEY. The delay occurred when Navy's leadership was unable to decide whether to assign the rank to Halsey or to Adm. RAYMOND A. SPRUANCE. In the event, it went to Halsey. Spruance, however, was compensated with the same benefits given to the five-star officers, i.e., full pay and allowances for the rest of his life.

After the war and following his retirement, Gen. Arnold's five-star rank was changed to General of the Air Force, reflecting the establishment of the Air Force as a separate military service.

The only other American to hold five-star rank during his lifetime was Gen. OMAR N. BRADLEY, who was promoted to General of the Army when he became the first chairman of the JOINT CHIEFS OF STAFF on Sept. 20, 1950.

The insignia for five-star rank was a cluster of five stars, smaller than those standard for general and flag officers. The naval officers' sleeve insignia was one wide and four narrow gold stripes.

(Gen. John J. Pershing, commander of U.S. forces in Europe in World War I, held the rank of General of the Armies, but he wore only four stars.)

Flak

German antiaircraft forces. Germany deployed a massive air-defense system centered on fighter aircraft and antiaircraft guns or flak (short for *Fliegerabwehrkanonen*). German air defenses were part of the Luftwaffe which, at the start of the war, had almost 1 million men or nearly one third of the Air Force's strength. By the fall of 1944 the Luftwaffe flak arm had a peak strength of more than 1.2 million men and women. By 1944 the Luftwaffe flak units had large numbers of young boys, old men, and women manning the guns as the able-bodied men were conscripted for ground combat forces. In some areas the manpower shortage was so critical that foreign volunteers and even PRISONERS OF WAR were used to serve the guns.

ALBERT SPEER, head of German armaments production, wrote that the Allied STRATEGIC BOMBING of Germany was "the greatest lost battle on the German side. The losses from the retreats in Russia or from the surrender of STALINGRAD were considerably less. Moreover, the nearly 20,000 antiaircraft guns stationed in the homeland could have almost doubled the antitank defenses on the EASTERN FRONT. In the territory of the Reich those guns were virtually useless. Over the attacked cities they did little more than provide a kind of reassuring fireworks display for the population. By that time bombers were operating from such high altitudes that the shells of the 8.8-centimeter flak guns reached the planes at too slow a speed."

Speer's numbers support a British intelligence estimate of Jan. 1944 that reported 20,625 antiaircraft guns and 6,880 searchlights in Germany and Western Europe, with another 9,569 antiaircraft guns and 960 searchlights on other fronts.

The German Army and Navy also had flak components for the air defense of ground forces and naval bases, respectively, but they were comparatively small. Luftwaffe units also provided air defense to ground troops.

The most used German antiaircraft gun was the 88-MM FLAK, which was used in all theaters where Germans fought. Heavier antiaircraft guns were the 105-mm Flak 38 and 128-mm Flak 40, the latter comprised of twin barrels installed about 3 feet apart on a common mounting—the heaviest antiaircraft gun mount used in the war. The larger weapons were mounted on the ground and, in larger cities, also in FLAK TOWERS. Several thousand guns of these calibers were produced (with the 88-mm Flak also being used extensively as an antitank weapon).

The Germans used a variety of lighter antiaircraft guns, of both indigenous production and captured foreign weapons.

The larger antiaircraft guns were supported by excellent optical fire-control devices, searchlights, and RADAR for aircraft detection and gunfire control.

Flak towers

Massive towers for ANTIAIRCRAFT guns. The Germans constructed concrete Flak towers in Berlin, Hamburg, Vienna, and other cities to provide antiaircraft defenses in heavily populated areas.

The towers were several hundred feet tall to permit clear fields of fire in built-up areas. They were constructed in pairs: the larger tower mounted four heavy antiaircraft guns or *Fliegerabwehrkanonen*—105-mm, 128-mm, or paired 128-mm weapons; the smaller tower had the radar and fire-control systems for the guns. Both tower types additionally mounted several smaller, 20-mm antiaircraft guns. The lower levels of the towers contained ammunition storage and barracks, and provided air-raid shelters for civilians and control centers for civil defense activities.

Flamethrowers

Flame-spurting weapon first introduced by German troops in World War I and used extensively in World War II by German, Japanese, Soviet, and U.S. troops. Flamethrowers were particularly effective against bunkers and other fortifications, and

Flak tower.

were highly valued by U.S. Marines in the Pacific area when attacking Japanese defensive positions.

Flamethrowers were carried with the fuel tanks carried on the user's back and the flame directed by a hand-held hose, or fitted in tanks, with the flame usually projected through the gun barrel.

The standard M1 flamethrower used by U.S. troops had two fuel tanks (holding 4 gallons of fuel) and a pressure tank that was strapped onto a man's back; it weighed about 70 pounds and projected a stream of flame some 25 to 30 yards. The stream of fire from the 75-mm gun barrel of a SHERMAN TANK could reach 100 yards. This larger flamethrower sometimes was called a Ronson, after the cigarette lighter.

Flasher (SS 249)

U.S. SUBMARINE that sank the most enemy tonnage in World War II, being credited with 100,231 tons of Japanese ships. (The U.S. submarine that sank the most enemy ships was the *TAUTOG* (SS 199).)

The *Flasher* entered the Pacific conflict when she sailed from PEARL HARBOR on Jan. 6, 1944, on her first war patrol, to the Philippines area. On Jan. 18 she sank a 2,900-ton Japanese gunboat, followed by three merchant ships before she entered Fremantle, Australia, to replenish and rearm. On her fifth war patrol off the coast of Indochina, in Dec. 1944 the *Flasher,* under Lt. Comdr. G. W. Grider, became the "tonnage king" of the submarine force by sinking two Japanese destroyers and four tankers for 42,868 tons. At the time the Japanese were desperately short of tankers.

She carried out six war patrols, sinking one light cruiser, one ex-light cruiser, two destroyers, two gunboats, five tankers, and ten other merchant ships for a total of twenty-one ships of 100,231 tons. The submarine received the Presidential Unit Citation and six BATTLE STARS for her six wartime patrols.

At the end of the war she was ordered to New London, Conn., where she was decommissioned on March 16, 1946, and placed in "mothballs." The ship was stricken in 1959 and scrapped.

A *Gato* (SS 212)–class submarine, the *Flasher* was built at the Electric Boat Co., in Groton, Conn. She was launched on June 20, 1943, and commis-

sioned that September. The submarine displaced 1,525 tons surfaced and 2,425 tons submerged, and was 311¾ feet long. Her armament consisted of ten 21-inch (533-mm) TORPEDO tubes—six bow and four stern, with twenty-four torpedoes being carried. For use against small surface ships the *Flasher* had a 3-inch (76-mm) deck gun and machine guns. Her crew numbered eighty-five.

Flashlamp

Code name for RAF operation to attack German coastal gun batteries at the beginning of the NORMANDY INVASION.

Flax

Code name for Allied air operations to interdict German transport aircraft flying between Tunisia, Italy, and SICILY, 1943.

Fleet

The largest naval formation. When the war began the operating forces of the U.S. Navy were organized into the Pacific Fleet (based at PEARL HARBOR), the Atlantic Fleet, and the Asiatic Fleet. On Dec. 31, 1941, the overall position of Commander In Chief U.S. Fleet (ComInCh) was established in WASHINGTON; Adm. ERNEST J. KING held that position throughout the war (also becoming Chief of Naval Operations in March 1942).

The U.S. Asiatic Fleet survived until Feb. 4, 1942. Forced from the Philippines, having sustained major losses, and the surviving ships mostly assigned to the ABDA (American-British-Dutch-Australian) naval command, the Asiatic Fleet was abolished on that date.

During the war the Pacific Fleet was commanded by Adm. CHESTER W. NIMITZ (who also headed the U.S. UNIFIED COMMAND Pacific Ocean Area); the Atlantic Fleet was under Adm. Royal E. Ingersoll (Jan. 1941–Nov. 1944) and Adm. Jonas H. Ingram (Nov. 1944–Sept. 1946).

After the outbreak of war several numbered fleets were established within the U.S. Atlantic and Pacific Fleets. Those in the Atlantic-Mediterranean area were given even numbers; those in the Pacific area received odd numbers. The U.S. numbered fleets were:

Third Fleet   The Third Fleet generally shared the same naval forces with the Fifth Fleet; while one fleet commander and his staff were at sea operating against the Japanese, the other commander and staff would be ashore at PEARL HARBOR planning the next operation.

The III Marine Amphibious CORPS was assigned to the Third Fleet as the amphibious command and planning staff.

Adm. WILLIAM F. HALSEY commanded the Third Fleet from June 1944 until Nov. 1945.

Fourth Fleet   The U.S. South Atlantic Force as renamed on March 15, 1943.

Commanded by Vice Adm. Jonas H. Ingram until Nov. 1944, and then Rear Adm. William R. Munroe until late in 1945.

Fifth Fleet   The Fifth Fleet operated against the Japanese.

The V Marine Amphibious CORPS was assigned to the Fifth Fleet as the amphibious command and planning staff.

Adm. RAYMOND A. SPRUANCE was Commander Fifth Fleet from March 1944 until Nov. 1945.

Seventh Fleet   Called "MacArthur's Navy," the Seventh Fleet was formed to provide naval support to operations by Gen. DOUGLAS MACARTHUR. This fleet did not have fast AIRCRAFT CARRIERS, but was assigned ESCORT CARRIERS.

The Seventh Fleet was commanded by Vice Adm. THOMAS C. KINKAID from Nov. 1943 until Nov. 1945.

Eighth Fleet   Established to conduct the AMPHIBIOUS LANDINGS at SICILY and SALERNO, the Fleet then carried out landings in southern France.

Vice Adm. H. KENT HEWITT commanded the fleet from Feb. 1943 until April 1945.

Tenth Fleet   "Paper" fleet established in the NAVY DEPARTMENT to coordinate antisubmarine warfare. The Tenth Fleet was belatedly established on May 20, 1943, under the direct command of the Chief of Naval Operations, Adm. ERNEST J. KING, with day-to-day operations directed by Rear Adm. Francis S. Low, the Chief of Staff.

The BATTLE OF THE ATLANTIC was essentially won in May 1943, almost simultaneous with setting up the Tenth Fleet. The delay was caused largely by Adm. King wishing to keep direct control of the antisubmarine campaign and bitter controversy between the Army Air Forces and the Navy over the control of land-based antisubmarine aircraft.

Twelfth Fleet   This fleet, with headquarters in LONDON, was primarily the U.S. Navy's planning staff for European operations. It was commanded by Adm. HAROLD R. STARK (Oct. 1943–Aug. 1945), who had been CinC U.S. Naval Forces Europe in April 1942, a position he continued to hold until Aug. 1945.

Fleming, Ian (1908–1964)

British intelligence officer and author who created the fictional superspy James Bond. Ian Lancaster Fleming was educated in England, Germany, and Switzerland. Fleming was a journalist in MOSCOW in 1929–1933, and then a banker and stockbroker in England until he entered the Royal Navy in 1939.

During World War II Lt. Comdr. Fleming served in naval intelligence. After the war he served as foreign manager of the London *Sunday Times* and created the superspy James Bond. He wrote more than a dozen novels, the first, *Casino Royale,* which was published in 1953. His wartime experience gave Fleming a rich background in intelligence and high-tech devices that he applied to master-spy James Bond.

Fletcher, Vice Adm. Frank Jack (1885–1973)

One of the early U.S. carrier commanders in the Pacific War, his wartime service was somewhat controversial. Fletcher was a surface ship officer, he won the MEDAL OF HONOR at Vera Cruz, Mexico, in 1914 and was awarded the Navy Cross in 1918 while commanding a DESTROYER. He later commanded a BATTLESHIP, and as a rear admiral in 1939 took command of a cruiser DIVISION. He was at sea off PEARL HARBOR when the Japanese attacked on Dec. 7, 1941.

He immediately took command of the abortive relief expedition to WAKE ISLAND, and shortly thereafter took command of a carrier TASK FORCE centered on the USS *Yorktown* (CV 5). His force raided Japanese positions in the GILBERT and MARSHALL ISLANDS, and on NEW GUINEA during the next few months. He then commanded the carrier force at the Battle of CORAL SEA in May 1942, and was senior U.S. commander at sea in the Battle of MIDWAY in June 1942, where his flagship *Yorktown* was sunk.

Fletcher was promoted to vice admiral late in June and, with the carrier *SARATOGA* (CV 3) as his flagship, commanded U.S. naval forces in the GUADALCANAL landing in Aug. 1942. There his early withdrawal of naval forces—because of the fear of Japanese air attack—led to severe criticism by U.S. Marine commanders. U.S. naval forces were heavily engaged during the month and, following major U.S. ship losses, Fletcher was reassigned.

Fletcher served most of the next two years in shore assignments in the United States. In April 1944 he took command of the Navy's Alaska Sea Frontier and also commanded the small North Pacific Force, which carried out bombardments of the Kuril Islands in 1944–1945, and helped occupy northern Japanese ports in Sept. 1945.

After the war, as a full admiral, Fletcher became a member and the chairman of the Navy's policy-making General Board. He retired in May 1947.

Flight

Two or more aircraft organized for tactical purposes. The flight was a subdivision of an aircraft SQUADRON.

Flintlock

Code name for U.S. operations in the MARSHALL ISLANDS, Jan. 31–Feb. 7, 1944.

Floating Chrysanthemums,

see *KIKUSUI.*

Fluckey, Comdr. Eugene B. (1913—)

U.S. SUBMARINE ACE who sank more Japanese tonnage in the Pacific War than any other submarine commander. After graduating from the Naval Academy in 1935, Fluckey served briefly in surface ships before entering the submarine service in 1938. From June 1941 until Aug. 1942 he served in the submarine *Bonita* (SS 165), which carried out five war patrols on the Pacific side of the Panama Canal (no enemy ships were encountered).

He made one patrol in the submarine *Barb* (SS 220) in Japanese waters in early 1944 before becoming commanding officer of that submarine. From April 1944 until Aug. 1945 the *Barb* undertook five war patrols, during which she sank fourteen Japanese merchant ships (75,000 tons) plus the small carrier *Unyo* and a frigate. Their total tonnage—over 95,000—was the highest of any single commanding officer in the Pacific. During the summer of 1945 the *Barb* joined other U.S. submarines in firing at Japanese coastal targets with their deck guns, with the *Barb* additionally firing ROCKETS into Japanese shore targets.

After the war Fluckey held additional submarine commands, was commanding officer of a submarine tender, an amphibious group, commanded all U.S. submarines in the Pacific, was director of naval intelligence, and head of the NATO Iberian Atlantic Command before retiring as a rear admiral in 1972.

Flying Fortress,

see B-17.

Flying Tigers

An American fighter force that flew in China with the Nationalist forces of CHIANG KAI-SHEK against the Japanese. The American Volunteer Group (AVG) pilots painted tiger shark faces on their aircraft to intimidate Japanese fliers, but they were soon labeled as Flying Tigers.

After the U.S. government decided in 1941 to provide direct military assistance to China, a decision was made to provide air defense for the BURMA ROAD, being built to provide a land route for Allied supplies going to China. CLAIRE LEE CHENNAULT, a retired U.S. Army Air Corps officer, was given the task of creating a fighter force while Chinese pilots were being trained. Accordingly, 100 American pilots were hired on one-year contracts, as were some 200 ground crewmen. They began arriving in China in the late summer of 1941. One hundred P-40B TOMAHAWK fighters, rejected by the U.S. and British air forces as being obsolescent, were released to Chennault. The fighters reached Rangoon in Sept. 1941 and training began there, the British territory at the time being safe from Japanese attacks.

By Nov. 1941 the AVG strength stood at only forty-three fighters and eighty-four pilots ready for combat. After Britain and America went to war with

Japan in December, AVG squadrons were moved to Mingaladon and Kunming to protect cities in southwest China and to patrol the Burma Road. Their first combat occurred on Dec. 20 when the P-40s inflicted heavy damage on Japanese bombers attempting to attack Kunming. Three days later they inflicted considerable damage on Japanese planes attacking Rangoon.

During the existence of the AVG the Flying Tiger pilots were credited with destroying 286 Japanese aircraft at the cost of eight American pilots killed in air action, plus four pilots missing and two pilots and one crew chief killed on the ground. Capt. Robert H. Neale, credited with shooting down fifteen-and-a-half Japanese aircraft, was the highest scoring AVG pilot. The AVG began receiving the improved P-40E in mid-1942 and was merged into the U.S. Fourteenth AIR FORCE on July 4, 1942. The Flying Tigers formed the China Air Task Force, remaining under Chennault, ending the brief but colorful career of the Flying Tigers.

Flying Wing,
see B-35.

Forager
Code name for U.S. invasion of the MARIANA ISLANDS, June 1944.

Force H
British naval force based on GIBRALTAR that had a major role in naval operations in the eastern Atlantic and Mediterranean areas. Established on June 28, 1940, Force H initially consisted of the aircraft carrier *ARK ROYAL,* two battleships, a battle cruiser, a light cruiser, and several destroyers.

Commanded by Vice Adm. Sir James Sommerville, the first task of Force H was to observe and then attack the French warships in North African waters to prevent them from being used by the Germans. (See FRANCE, NAVY.) Subsequent operations included escorting CONVOYS to MALTA, escorting the ill-fated amphibious assault on Dakar, and, in May 1941, speeding out into the Atlantic to help search for the German battleship *BISMARCK.* A SWORDFISH from the *Ark Royal* struck the *Bismarck* with a TORPEDO that jammed the dreadnought's rudder, making it possible for British surface forces

to catch up with and sink the ship. The *Ark Royal* was sunk by a U-BOAT in Nov. 1941 leaving Force H without a carrier.

Force H continued to operate in the Atlantic as well as the Mediterranean, and supported the Allied landings in SICILY and on the Italian mainland in 1943 before being "folded in" to other Allied naval commands as the U.S. and British naval forces dominated the Mediterranean.

Ford, Gerald R. (1913—)
Naval officer who served as assistant navigation officer and director of physical education aboard the carrier *Monterey* (CVL 26), seeing action in the South Pacific. Lt. Comdr. Ford was discharged in 1946, resumed his war-interrupted legal career, and entered politics. He became president on Aug. 9, 1974, following the resignation of RICHARD M. NIXON.

Ford Island
Site of a U.S. naval air station in the center of PEARL HARBOR and the berthing area for BATTLE-SHIPS. On Dec. 7, 1941, there were seven battleships moored along the southeast side of the island in two rows, five on the inside, two on the outside. (The eighth battleship at Pearl Harbor was in dry dock at the nearby navy yard.)

During the two-wave Japanese air attack on "battleship row," Japanese planes also strafed and bombed the air station—"NAS Pearl," as it was known throughout the Pacific Fleet—and the usual northeast winds blew billowing black clouds over the 1¼-mile-long island.

Later that day, as the log of NAS Pearl recorded: "Air raid alarm sounded. Six ENTERPRISE (CV 6) planes attempting to land on Ford Island were fired upon by all units in Pearl Harbor; four planes were lost."

Foremost
Code name for British submarine *Sealion* transferring money and supplies to fishing vessels for delivery to the French RESISTANCE, Sept. 1941.

Former Naval Person
Pseudonym used by WINSTON CHURCHILL in his correspondence with President ROOSEVELT.

Formosa,

see CHINA.

Forrestal, James V. (1892–1949)

Secretary of the Navy. A Wall Street banker, Forrestal succeeded W. FRANKLIN KNOX as secretary of the Navy on May 19, 1944, a few days after the latter's death. Forrestal had enlisted in the Naval Reserve in 1917 and was commissioned a short time later and assigned to the NAVY DEPARTMENT in WASHINGTON. Promoted to lieutenant (j.g.) in 1918, he resigned the following year.

With Dillion, Read, and Co., briefly before the war, he reentered the firm, becoming president in 1937. In June 1940 he became administrative assistant to President ROOSEVELT, specializing in Latin-American affairs. Forrestal was the first under secretary of the Navy, appointed when that position was created on Aug. 22, 1940. He was primarily responsible for procurement of the wartime navy.

After the war he helped President TRUMAN plan the establishment of a unified defense establishment, and served as the first secretary of Defense from Sept. 1947 to March 1949. He resigned from that post because of mental and physical exhaustion caused by the strain of his position. He was diagnosed as being paranoid for believing, among other things, that Israeli secret agents were following him. Several weeks after he was hospitalized at the Bethesda Naval Hospital near Washington, on the morning of May 22, 1949, he committed suicide by leaping to his death from the nineteenth floor. (Years later, Israeli sources admitted that agents had been following him to discover whether he was secretly negotiating against Israel with representatives of Arab countries.)

Fortitude

Code name for cover operations to conceal the NORMANDY INVASION.

Foss, Maj. Joseph J. (1915–)

Leading U.S. Marine fighter ACE. Foss was the first American to break the 1918 aerial record of EDDIE RICKENBACKER with twenty-five German planes shot down.

"Joe" Foss entered combat as executive officer of Marine Fighter SQUADRON (VMF) 121 when it arrived on GUADALCANAL in Oct. 1942. Flying the F4F WILDCAT, for more than a month Foss and other pilots of VMF-121 engaged almost daily in aerial combat against Japanese planes attacking U.S. Marines on the island. Foss was credited with twenty-three enemy planes shot down in this period.

After one engagement—in which Foss shot down three Japanese aircraft—his damaged F4F was forced down at sea. His canopy slammed shut upon impact with the water and the plane began to sink. With the cockpit filling with water, he managed to get the canopy open, escaped the plane, and swam to shore.

The squadron was taken out of combat from Nov. 20 until Jan. 1943, when it returned to Guadalcanal. On Jan. 15 he shot down three more Japanese planes to raise his score to twenty-six, more than were destroyed by any other Marine pilot. (The squadron was in combat through Jan. 29—in 122 days at Guadalcanal VMF-121 pilots were credited with shooting down 164 Japanese planes for the loss of twenty Marine pilots.)

Foss was awarded the MEDAL OF HONOR in May 1943 for his skill as a pilot and combat leader in addition to his record score. He returned to the United States to serve in a training assignment. He returned to the Pacific war zone in Feb. 1944 but did not add to his score of aerial victories.

After the war Foss served as governor of South Dakota and was a brigadier general in the Air NATIONAL GUARD.

See also GREGORY BOYINGTON.

Four Chaplains

Heroes of a ship disaster. In one of the war's most famous acts of heroism, four Army chaplains—Reverend George L. Fox, Rabbi Alexander D. Goode, Reverend Clark V. Poling, and Father John P. Washington—gave their life preservers to soldiers when the Army transport *Dorchester* was sunk in the predawn darkness of Feb. 2, 1943, by the German submarine *U-456*. The chaplains went down with the *Dorchester*.

The transport, which was carrying Army troops to GREENLAND, did not transmit a distress signal and was unable to launch about half of her lifeboats. Of the 906 men on board, only 229 were saved.

Four Freedoms

Democratic principles that became identified with U.S. war aims. President ROOSEVELT, in his State of the Union message of Jan. 6, 1941, said, "In the future days, which we seek to make secure, we look forward to a world founded upon four essential human freedoms": freedom of speech, freedom of "every person to worship God in his own way," freedom from want, securing "to every nation a healthy peacetime life for its inhabitants," and freedom from fear, "which, translated into world terms, means a world-wide reduction of armaments to such a point and in such a thorough fashion that no nation will be in a position to commit an act of physical aggression against any neighbor—anywhere in the world." Envisioned in highly popular paintings by Norman Rockwell, the Four Freedoms became the symbols of what the war was about.

Foxer

Code name for Allied antitorpedo device. The term was used for both a specific device to decoy TORPEDOES fired from U-BOATS to explode harmlessly at a distance from antisubmarine escort ships, and, subsequently, as a generic term for all such devices.

Alerted by intelligence sources—mostly interviews with German PRISONERS OF WAR—that the German Navy was developing an acoustic homing torpedo for use against escort ships, the Allied navies were ready with the Foxer when German Naval Acoustic Torpedoes (GNAT) made their appearance in Sept. 1943. The device was highly successful after initial high losses to the GNATs. According to the official British intelligence history, no ship towing a Foxer was ever hit by an acoustic torpedo. While noted German historian Jürgen Rohwer claimed that eight ships towing decoys were hit by acoustic homing torpedoes, even that number is a very small percentage of the Allied warships that were attacked while towing Foxers.

The Foxer was a towed noisemaker that distracted the acoustic-homing torpedo away from the noises generated by the warship's propellers. The device, however, could not be used at speeds above 15 knots, limiting a destroyer or frigate's maneuverability. It also interfered with the surface ship's

SONAR operation. But the benefits of decoying the GNAT—employed primarily against CONVOY escort ships—compensated for these limitations.

Several improved Foxer devices were developed. The Canadian-produced version, called the Cat, had a screeching noise, something akin to that produced by an electric saw. The screeching had a distinct psychological effect on U-boat crews.

(Other Allied efforts to counter GNATs included injecting oil and then, more successfully, air bubbles around ship propellers to reduce noise. Explosive "popcorn" and other devices were also used by Allied surface ships in attempts to confuse more-advanced GNAT guidance.)

Foxhole

A hole in the ground dug by a soldier or Marine. The idea—a place that simultaneously provides safety and a firing position—goes back to the origins of war. The term itself can be found in the *Domesday Book* and was used in World War I.

For Americans on the homefront in World War II, foxhole was a word loaded with meaning as a result of a quotation: "There are no atheists in the foxholes." The statement produced an arresting emotional image in the early days of the war. The quotation was attributed to Father William T. Cummings, a CHAPLAIN, in a sermon given at BATAAN early in 1942. Father Cummings died a PRISONER OF WAR. (President JOHN F. KENNEDY picked up the idea in 1963 in a message to Congress on a civil rights bill: "There are no 'white' or 'colored' signs on the foxholes or graveyards of battle.")

U.S. soldiers and Marines fighting in the Pacific called Japanese-style foxholes "spider webs" because the typical Japanese firing position was a large hole, covered with camouflage netting, from which tunnels radiated.

FR-1 Fireball

The first U.S. Navy aircraft to make a jet-propelled landing on an AIRCRAFT CARRIER. The plane was actually a composite aircraft with both a piston engine and turbojet. This conservative approach was due to the long take-off and landing runs required by early JET-PROPELLED AIRCRAFT. The FR-1 Fireball was a high-performance fighter aircraft, but arrived too late to see combat in the Pacific War.

The FR-1 reached an operational Navy squadron in March 1945 and carrier trials began on May 1, 1945. An FR-1 piloted by Ens. Jake C. West made history's first landing by a jet-propelled aircraft on a carrier on Nov. 6, 1945, aboard the U.S. ESCORT CARRIER *Wake Island* (CVE 65). West's Fireball suffered a reciprocating engine failure as it was about to come aboard and he made an all-jet landing. (The first "pure" jet aircraft landing on board an aircraft carrier was made on the British *Ocean* on Dec. 3, 1945; it was a de Havilland Vampire I flown by Lt. Comdr. Eric M. Brown.)

The FR-1 was designed by the Ryan Aeronautical Corp., which had never built naval aircraft or a combat aircraft. Still, the design proceeded rapidly and the first flight of an XFR-1 prototype occurred on June 25, 1944, just sixteen months after Ryan was authorized to proceed with three prototypes. Production contracts for 700 aircraft followed, but with V-J DAY cancellations, only sixty-six FR-1s were delivered in 1945. They were discarded by the U.S. Navy in 1947 after a brief operational career.

A low-wing, high-speed fighter, the FR-1 had a "bubble" canopy; a radial engine was fitted in the nose with a General Electric I-16 turbojet in the rear fuselage. The wings folded upward for carrier stowage and the tricycle landing gear was fully retractable.

The aircraft had a maximum speed of 404 mph and was credited with a range of 1,620 miles. Armament consisted of four wing-mounted .50-cal. machine guns, relatively light firepower for a contemporary fighter. Drop tanks could be carried but there were no provisions for bombs.

France

Capital: PARIS, pop. 41,907,056 (metropolitan France, 1936). France long confronted a Germany envious of French resources and strategic importance. In World War I, the confrontation ended with much of the country devastated and 1,400,000 Frenchmen killed in the trenches that scarred her soil. In the uneasy 1930s, again facing the menace of a rising Germany, France invested against another war by shielding her troops and protecting her borders with a sleekly modern defense, the MAGINOT LINE. The line—actually a zone 10 to 50 miles deep—guarded the French border from Lux-

embourg to Switzerland and gave France a false sense of security.

HITLER'S march into the Rhineland on March 7, 1936, did not change France's faith in her static strategy. Proposals to extend the Maginot Line up to the Meuse River were again rejected, for, as World War I hero Marshal HENRI PHILIPPE PÉTAIN had said, the rough terrain of the Ardennes "would make any attempted invasion in that sector impossible."

Overseas, France controlled a vast empire, with possessions in Asia, Africa, the Pacific, and on islands of the Atlantic. The colonial empire had a population of more than 70,000,000 and covered 4,600,000 square miles. (For French colonies that figured prominently in World War II, such as Indochina and Tunisia, see separate country entries.)

In Sept. 1938 French Premier ÉDOUARD DALADIER reluctantly joined British Prime Minister NEVILLE CHAMBERLAIN in negotiations leading to the signing of the MUNICH PACT (along with Hitler, and Italian leader BENITO MUSSOLINI). Daladier said he was unhappy about the pact, but he generally went along with England in the appeasement of Hitler. On Dec. 6, 1938, France and Germany signed a treaty accepting the French-German border and agreeing to "consult mutually in case subsequent developments create the possibility of leading to international disturbances."

The disturbances came the following August when Germany and the Soviet Union signed their NONAGGRESSION PACT, permitting the invasion of Poland on Sept. 1, 1939. France mobilized and on Sept. 3 declared war on Germany. For France, the war would have five distinct periods.

Sept. 1939 to May 1940 During these months of what was called the "phony war," French troops, joined by the British Army Expeditionary Force, manned defensive lines and awaited attack. In April 1940 a German BLITZKRIEG rolled over Denmark and Norway, and foreshadowed the French invasion. Internally, France was politically unstable. Communist organizations were dissolved; a vote of no confidence resulted in a Cabinet shuffle. Daladier stepped down to become minister for war; PAUL REYNAUD became premier.

May to July 1940 On May 10 Germany simultaneously invaded the Netherlands, Belgium, and

Luxembourg, and the phony war ended as lightning war began. The Netherlands, Luxembourg, and Belgium fell quickly, and French and British troops pulled back before the onslaught of Germany's FRANCE AND LOW COUNTRIES CAMPAIGN. On May 13 the Germans established a bridgehead at Sedan, the gateway into France, and the Battle of France began. On the morning of May 15 Reynaud called Prime Minister CHURCHILL in London and, speaking in English, said, "We have been defeated." Stunned, Churchill asked, "Surely it can't have happened so soon?" It had. The Germans had outflanked the Maginot Line and had sped through the Ardennes, doing what Pétain had said was impossible.

On June 10 the government evacuated Paris, moving first to Tours and then, on June 14, to Bordeaux. Two days later Reynaud resigned. His successor, Marshal Pétain, surrendered his retreating army. The Germans agreed to what was called an armistice, which was signed on June 22 at Compiègne in the same railway car in which a defeated Germany had signed the 1918 armistice. On June 28 Gen. CHARLES DE GAULLE, who had fled to England, was recognized by the British government as the "leader of all Free Frenchmen." De Gaulle set up the FREE FRENCH movement, an anti-Vichy government in London. The Vichy regime tried de Gaulle in absentia—for desertion—and sentenced him to death.

Germany took over the Alsace-Lorraine area of France as renewed parts of Germany and occupied northern and western France as a conquered territory, putting it under the military governor of Belgium. The rest of France was left unoccupied and was administered, along with French colonies, by a collaborationist government that would become known as VICHY FRANCE after its seat of government at Vichy, 200 miles southeast of Paris.

France was "fined" about $120,000,000 and was assessed "occupation costs" of about $2 billion a year (the equivalent of about four times the annual reparations Germany paid the victors in World War I). The Bank of France also had to extend enormous "credits" to Germany. Some 140 railroad *cars* of looted art—including works of Rembrandt and Rubens—rolled out of France into Germany.

July 1940 to Nov. 1942 In Paris and elsewhere in occupied France, the Germans imposed a tough, swaggering conquest. The Germans killed 100 French hostages for every German killed by the French underground—mostly GUERRILLA units known as the *Maquis*. The Germans are known to have killed 29,660 French hostages; another 40,000 French men and women perished in German custody; others were taken away and never heard from again, killed and "turned into mist" under the *Nacht und Nebel Erlass,* Night and Fog Decree, carried out by the SD. Thousands were deported to Germany to work in war factories.

Fine wines and seats on public transit were set aside for the conquerors, as German officers enjoyed the pleasures of Paris, usually on the arm of women who chose collaboration over resistance. (After liberation the collaborating women were paraded around with shaved heads as a mark of their shame.)

In Vichy, the life was less harsh because there were no occupying troops. But a French-run organization, the *Milice,* worked for Vichy as an antiresist-

A French partisan poses with his British-provided .303-cal. Bren machine gun while two youngsters look on. The French *Maquis* and other guerrilla units within German-occupied countries caused the Germans major problems, although there was far less trouble than has been shown on popular American television shows. These groups also provided valuable intelligence to the Allies. *(Imperial War Museum)*

ance corps. Joseph Darnand, a celebrated hero of the French army during World War I and World War II, ran the *Milice*, transforming it into a Vichy SS that fought the resistance with treachery and murder. (He later joined the French unit of the *WAFFEN* SS and in 1944, when France was liberated, went to Germany where he worked for HEINRICH HIMMLER. He was executed for treason in 1945.)

Life changed dramatically on Nov. 10, 1942, when, responding to the Allied NORTH AFRICA INVASION two days before, Germany invaded Vichy France, in violation of the armistice of 1940. On Nov. 27 German troops, in another violation, attacked TOULON, where the French fleet had been since the armistice. Italian troops occupied Corsica and Germany flew troops to take the French colony of Tunisia. All of France was occupied.

Nov. 1942 to June 1944   Anglo-American successes in the NORTH AFRICA CAMPAIGN, in which some French colonial forces saw action against the Germans, raised French morale and stepped up *Maquis* activities against the Germans. As the FRENCH RESISTANCE in France and the Free French in exile evolved into a political force, the collaborationists and the occupiers faced two challenges: the distant de Gaulle and, ever nearby, the Resistance. Countless members of the Resistance were arrested and executed, but the movement endured and, while united to fight the Germans militarily, increasingly quarreled among themselves over who would rule France after liberation. In an attempt to end the debate, in May 1944, anticipating the NORMANDY INVASION in June, de Gaulle's French Committee of National Liberation announced that it was the provisional government of France.

June 1944 to May 1945   French commandos went ashore in the Normandy invasion on June 6 and major French units made the Aug. 13 landing in southern France a U.S.-French operation. As the ALLIED CAMPAIGN IN EUROPE surged across France, the Resistance's military arm, the French Forces of the Interior (FFI), went beyond guerrilla sabotage actions. Well armed and well organized, FFI units created diversions that harassed or pinned down German forces, keeping them from Allied armies. The Free French took over the governing of liberated areas as Allied forces advanced.

Because of the number of Communists in the ranks of the Resistance, de Gaulle had found it necessary to support the Soviet Union's demands for a SECOND FRONT; reciprocating, Soviet Marshal STALIN backed de Gaulle and announced that Fighting France (the name changed in July 1942) was the only French movement that had the right to govern France. In Dec. 1944 de Gaulle signed a mutual aid treaty with the Soviet Union.

As the Allies neared Paris, the Communist wing of French Resistance rose against the Germans. This unexpected event, plus pressure from de Gaulle, forced Gen. DWIGHT D. EISENHOWER to change his strategy and move to liberate the city earlier than planned. De Gaulle, who had been in France for a short time after the Normandy invasion, hastily returned from his Free French headquarters in Algeria and entered Paris in triumph on Aug. 26, 1944, behind French and American troops.

While the war continued, de Gaulle's provisional government began rebuilding a country that had been fighting both the Germans and itself. The Gaullists proclaimed that the Vichy France state had never legally existed and set up the machinery for a postwar election in which women would be given the right to vote. The election brought in a new constitution and a new legislative body that elected de Gaulle interim president. But, denied the mandate he desired, he resigned on Jan. 20, 1946, and France's postwar political turmoil began.

France, Air Force

The *l'Armée de l'Air* of the 1920s and early 1930s was one of the largest and most modern in Europe. Indeed, in 1923 a British government report—described by naval historian S. W. Roskill as being "exaggerated to the point of being alarmist"—stressed the threat from the 940 military aircraft in France; in response, there were proposals to build up an RAF fighter force of 600 aircraft to protect Britain from air attack.

But by the early 1930s the French government ceased its interest in military aviation. WINSTON CHURCHILL wrote: "Money was grudged; the productive capacity of the factories was allowed to dwindle; modern types were not developed." Although with the rise of ADOLF HITLER the French Popular Front government of 1936 began major measures to increase the war-fighting capabilities of the French Army and Navy, no corresponding actions were taken with regard to the Air Force.

Not until the summer of 1938 was a program begun to rebuild the Air Force. When Germany began the FRANCE AND LOW COUNTRIES CAMPAIGN in May 1940 the French Air Force had 552 fighters and a small bomber force. The French planes—and some of the British fighter aircraft that had been sent to France—were outclassed by the German Messerschmitt ME (BF) 109; the best French fighter, the Morane 406, was 50 mph slower than the contemporary variant of the Me 109 and barely able to catch up with the faster German bombers. Indeed, many of the first-line French aircraft were obsolete, including ninety-eight American-built Curtis Hawk 75A fighters (see P-36).

Further, because of the backwardness of French production techniques, each Morane required some 18,000 man hours of labor compared to only 5,000 for the Messerschmitt, with French workers having a forty-hour work week while Germans were working double shifts (even without mobilization). After delivery to front-line units French aircraft were found to have major defects.

There was also a shortfall in ANTIAIRCRAFT WEAPONS in France. In 1939, when the Luftwaffe had seventy-two antiaircraft regiments, France had only five.

When the "phony war" ended on May 10, 1940, with the German assault on France and the Low Countries, the Luftwaffe rapidly gained control of the skies over the battlefield. The German air attacks were devastating, especially the attacks by JU 87 STUKA dive bombers. In *To Lose a Battle, France 1940,* Alistair Horne wrote of the effect on the morale of the French soldiers; quoting a soldier's account, "This bombing has tired even the toughest. What can one do with light machine-guns against 150 bombers?" Finally, the soldier concluded: "Not to see the enemy face to face, to have no means of defence, not to see the shadow of a French or Allied plane during the hours of bombing, this was one of the prime reasons for the loss of our faith in victory."

The successes of the British and French aircraft in the campaign were few. However, the first Allied aircraft to BOMB the German capital of BERLIN in the war was a French four-engine aircraft, a Farman F.2234, one of three similar trans-Atlantic aircraft taken over by the French Navy. The aircraft—completed in 1939 and named "Jules Verne"—attacked Berlin on the night of June 7–8, 1940, shortly before the French capitulation. The plane, with a range of 3,100 miles and a 4,409-pound bomb load, flew from a base in France northward, to then turn south and approach Berlin from an unexpected direction. The thirteen-and-a-half-hour flight had propaganda value but inflicted no damage. The French Air Force flew strikes against other targets in Germany as well as Italy before the surrender.

In the battle for France and the Low Countries the Luftwaffe lost an estimated 1,284 planes. RAF losses totaled 931, of which 477 were invaluable fighters. Data on French losses are less precise; one reasonable French figure is 560 aircraft lost. The French Air Force had failed; while the Luftwaffe losses were high, aircraft were rapidly replaced.

After the surrender some French pilots flew with the RAF and, later, with the U.S. Twelfth AIR FORCE in North Africa and the Eighth Air Force in England. Shortly after the NORMANDY INVASION, by June 14, 1944, two French squadrons were operating from Allied airfields in Normandy. (FREE FRENCH aircraft had opposed U.S. forces in the NORTH AFRICA INVASION.)

During the war French fliers in the Soviet Union formed the Normandie Squadron, a highly celebrated fighter unit that fought against the Germans. The squadron entered combat in the Smolensk region in March 1943, flying YAK-1 fighters as part of the Soviet 303rd Fighter Division of the 1st Air Army. During July 1943 the squadron changed to the more-capable YAK-9 and in 1944 the YAK-3. In those three years the French pilots flew a reported 5,240 missions and were credited with 273 aerial victories. Forty-two of the squadron's pilots were killed or missing, and four were awarded the HERO OF THE SOVIET UNION.

France and Low Countries Campaign (1940)

After Germany's two-week BLITZKRIEG shattered Poland in the first few days of Sept. 1939, France braced for invasion. A British Expeditionary Force arrived in France. For months the land forces waited, and people began talking about "the phony war." German U-BOATS, however, were keeping the war very real at sea, and Royal Navy sailors and merchant marine sailors were dying in the BATTLE OF THE ATLANTIC.

All was quiet along the MAGINOT LINE while Germany sent out peace feelers and neutral Holland and Belgium tried in vain to mediate between the warring powers. Then, with ferocious swiftness, Germany ended the phony war. In April 1940, Denmark and Norway were invaded. On May 10 came *Fall Gelb* (Case Yellow)—the invasion of Belgium, France, Holland, and Luxembourg. (See entries on these countries and Prologue to War.)

On the day the offensive began, British Prime Minister NEVILLE CHAMBERLAIN's government fell and WINSTON CHURCHILL replaced him. Three days later he told the House of Commons:

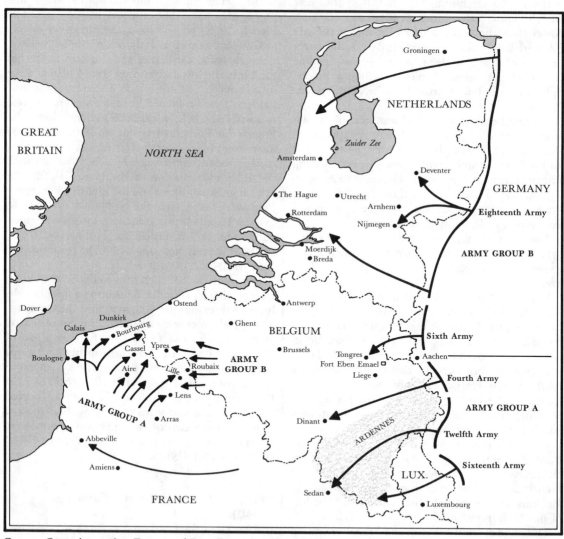

German Campaign against France and Low Countries, May 1940.

"I have nothing to offer but blood, toil, tears, and sweat."

Luxembourg, which had no defensive forces, could offer no resistance. The Dutch could resist. Their strategy assumed that aid would come from French and British troops reaching Holland via Belgium. The Dutch set up three lines of defense—dikes, mined canals, and trenches. To delay the invaders the Dutch blew up bridges across the Maas and Yssel Rivers and opened water gates in a network of dikes, flooding vast areas in western and eastern Holland.

But events were moving at blitzkrieg speed, and conventional defense was in vain. On May 14 the Germans bombed Rotterdam, killing 814 persons and making 78,000 homeless. The next day, the Dutch, to spare The Hague and other cities from bombing, surrendered.

Belgium defended herself behind the Albert Canal, whose centerpiece was Fort Eben Emael, which guarded the junction of the canal and the Meuse River. German AIRBORNE troops got to the canal's bridges before the Belgians could destroy them. To take the seemingly impregnable fortress, GLIDER-carried troops landed on its roof. They carried explosive charges to blast open gun turrets and drop into observation slits. On May 27 Belgium asked for an armistice.

To the south, German panzer units skirted the Maginot Line and defied French military doctrine by roaring through the hills and woods of the ARDENNES in two days. German infantry poured into the "Panzer Corridor" to hold it while the armor crossed the Meuse River at Sedan. On May 13 the Germans held Meuse bridgeheads from Sedan to Namur. The panzers thrust toward the Channel ports. French forces threw only one substantial counterattack at the Germans; it was made by the 4th Armored DIVISION, commanded by France's youngest general, CHARLES DE GAULLE.

As the German panzers on the coast turned northward to attack the ports of Boulogne, Calais, and DUNKIRK, the German high command ordered a halt so that infantrymen could sweep into the land in the armor units' wake. During the forty-eight hours that the panzers were halted Allied forces had a chance to throw defenses around Dunkirk and plan operation Dynamo, the epic evacuation of 338,226 troops, including about 100,000 French soldiers.

Meanwhile, remnants of the French Army, beaten and dispirited, pulled back mile after mile. On June 14 German troops entered PARIS and, outflanking the Maginot Line, forced the surrender of 400,000 troops. World War I hero HENRI PHILIPPE PÉTAIN, newly installed as prime minister, asked that the guns fall silent. On June 22 France signed a humiliating armistice in the same railway carriage at Compiègne where Germany had surrendered in Nov. 1918. ADOLF HITLER had conquered Western Europe, and he now could invade England. He began planning the landing operation, code-named SEA LION.

France, Army

When the EUROPEAN WAR began the French Army was unsure of its role. After the lengthy stalemate of trench warfare of World War I, the French had constructed the MAGINOT LINE of fortifications along the border with Germany. There the French would hold their borders intact while the German Army beat itself to pieces against the French defenses. Such a campaign would not in itself give France a "victory"; for that the French government counted on the French Navy to blockade Germany, causing an economic strangulation and forcing a negotiated peace.

The rise of ADOLF HITLER led France to begin rearming. In 1935 military service was extended to two years, new TANKS and guns were ordered into production, and armored divisions were created. In *To Lose a Battle*, Alistair Horne wrote of this rearming, ". . . it was desperately slow in getting off the ground. . . . hesitancy on the part of the [French] High Command, lack of coordination between the army and the arms manufacturers, added to the in-built hostility of the [Popular Front government] towards rearmament of any kind, plus the consequences of the strikes and the 40-hour week, resulted in the first orders for even the necessary machine tools not being given until the year after the launching of the new armament programme."

Germany was out-producing the French. While some French weapons, especially the heavy "B" tank and medium Somua, and 47-mm antitank gun were superior to their German counterparts, the French lacked both numbers and an employment strategy. Those officers—including CHARLES DE GAULLE—who foresaw the revolutionary role of tanks and aircraft, were largely ignored by the French leadership. Even the lessons of the SPANISH CIVIL WAR were largely ignored as the French put their faith on the Maginot Line to smash a German assault.

Britain and France had pledged to come to the defense of Poland should the Germans attack that country. But when the Germans did strike on Sept. 1, 1939, the French were unable to provide any assistance although a plan was developed to send arms to Poland through neutral countries. But across the Franco-German border there was an uneasy truce—what journalists labeled the "sitskrieg." Immediately upon the outbreak of the European War the British Expeditionary Army—five regular and five territorial (reserve) divisions—had moved to France along with RAF SQUADRONS.

On the eve of the German assault the French Army had some 120 divisions of which 100 were on the frontiers with Germany and Belgium; there were fourteen fortress divisions, six armored divisions, five partially mechanized CAVALRY divisions, and seventy-five infantry divisions. Added to these were ten British divisions. (The other French divisions were held in reserve.)

On May 10 the Germans attacked. The BLITZ-KRIEG came through the ARDENNES, the "impenetrable" area, and through Belgium and Holland, bypassing the Maginot Line. The German assault force was smaller—ninety-four divisions, but ten were PANZER and five motorized; further, the ground forces were coordinated with the Luftwaffe, and the Germans had been battle tested in Poland and Norway.

The German Army and Luftwaffe defeated the British and French armies in six weeks. (Italy had declared war on Britain and France on June 10; an attempt by Italy to march into southern France was easily repulsed by the French.)

Much of the French Army fled to Britain, evacuated from DUNKIRK and other ports. On June 18, in a dramatic broadcast over BBC radio, Gen. Charles de Gaulle announced that a battle had been lost but not the war. Ably supported by WINSTON CHURCHILL, de Gaulle established himself as the head of the FREE FRENCH armed forces based in England. By July 1940 the Free French Army-in-

exile had only 7,000 volunteers. Undaunted by this small response, and the British assault on the French fleet (see FRANCE, NAVY), de Gaulle persevered. He convinced Churchill to support an Anglo-Free French expedition to capture the French naval base at Dakar in French West Africa (Operation Menace). The assault force, carried mainly in British ships, consisted of 4,200 British soldiers and 2,700 Free French troops. Problems in command relationships, the placing of the amphibious commander in a warship, the lack of LANDING CRAFT, and lack of sufficient air support (the carrier *ARK ROYAL* did participate), doomed the Sept. 1940 expedition.

Meanwhile, in North Africa, Free French troops under Maj. Gen. JACQUES PHILIPPE LECLERC captured Kufra in southern Libya, and distinguished themselves in action against Germans and Italians on the Egyptian border, and in Ethiopia and French Somaliland. In June 1941 a force of 6,000 Free French soldiers joined with British troops in defeating VICHY FRENCH troops in Syria. After an armistice, several thousand Vichy troops joined the Free French Army. In the NORTH AFRICA CAMPAIGN Free French troops under Gen. MARIE-PIERRE KOENIG fought with the British Eighth Army. (Their name was changed to Fighting French in June 1942, but Free French was invariably used until the end of the war.)

The Allied NORTH AFRICA INVASION in Nov. 1942 complicated the Free French position. Gen. HENRI GIRAUD was chosen by the ALLIES to administer the occupied North African areas. De Gaulle was forced by ROOSEVELT and Churchill at the CASABLANCA CONFERENCE in Jan. 1943 to meet with Giraud, but there was no reconciliation. Not until June could the Allied leaders get the two French factions to jointly establish the Committee of National Liberation. But de Gaulle quickly assumed leadership. Hundreds of thousands of former Vichy soldiers now joined the Free French Army.

Beginning in the fall of 1943, 120,000 Free French troops joined the Allied forces fighting in Italy. De Gaulle landed in France a week after the NORMANDY INVASION began on June 6, 1944.

Several Free French units were landed early in the invasion, including Gen. Leclerc's 2nd Armored Division. It was this unit that Lt. Gen. OMAR N.

lined fuselage and fully retractable undercarriage. There was a glazed nose and fully glazed canopy over the tandem-seat cockpit. Later bomber variants had an air/sea search RADAR, while the P1Y2-S had an air-intercept radar.

The Frances had an impressive top speed of 340 mph for the P1Y1 aircraft with a range of 1,190 miles, capable of being extended to 3,340 miles at overload. As a bomber, the P1Y1 could internally carry an aerial torpedo or up to 2,205 pounds of bombs. Armament varied considerably with the standard P1Y1 being armed with a single flexible 20-mm cannon in the nose and another rear-firing gun at the after end of the cockpit. The abortive P1Y2-S night fighter had two upward-firing 20-mm guns plus the flexible rear-firing gun. Some sub-types had twin 13-mm machine guns in a dorsal turret in place of the after flexible gun. The Frances had a three-man crew.

Franco, Gen. Francisco (1892–1975)

Dictator of Spain. Commander of the Nationalists in the SPANISH CIVIL WAR, Franco took over Spain after his forces, aided by Germany and Italy, won the three-year war in 1939. He styled himself *Caudillo,* "leader" in imitation of his fellow dictators *Der Führer* HITLER of Germany and *Il Duce* BENITO MUSSOLINI of Italy.

After the fall of France in June 1940 Franco told Hitler that Spain would join the AXIS if given lavish foreign aid from Germany—along with being handed France's North African colonies. Hitler dickered over the deal and at a meeting with Franco on the French-Spanish border in Oct. 1940 added a German price for Spain's entry into the war: a Spanish-aided attack on the British stronghold of GIBRALTAR. The two dictators talked for nine hours and got nowhere. "Rather than go through that again," Hitler said later, "I would prefer to have three or four teeth yanked out."

When the ALLIES began winning the war, Franco hastily tried to change sides, even claiming that Spain was not really a dictatorship. But his bid for UNITED NATIONS membership for Spain was turned down. Spain finally entered the UN in 1955. Although he did initiate some reforms in his declining years, Franco remained *Caudillo* until his death.

Frank

The Ki-84 Type 4 *Hayate* (Gale) was "the most outstanding Jap Army fighter and far ahead of the OSCAR, TONY and TOJO . . . potentially the most dangerous Japanese army fighter plane," according to a mid-1945 U.S. AAF evaluation. The Frank was one of the most formidable Japanese aircraft of the war, being able to outclimb and outmaneuver both the U.S. P-47N THUNDERBOLT and P-51H MUSTANG fighters. It was also employed as a fighter-bomber.

The Frank made its combat debut in Aug. 1944 against AAF aircraft over Hankow, China. The aircraft was also flown extensively in the 1944–1945 Philippines campaigns, and in the OKINAWA operation.

The plane was initiated during a period of "easy victories," according to aviation historian William Green, because the Japanese Army Air Force "was sufficiently realistic to see that its ascendancy could not be maintained indefinitely unless superior warplanes were introduced." The Nakajima prototype flew in April 1943, fifteen months after design had been started. The first production model, the Ki-84-I, totaled 3,510 aircraft, including 100 built by the Manchurian Aircraft Manufacturing Co. U.S. air attacks against the engine and airframe plants severely reduced production, but it continued until almost the end of the war. A variety of advanced models were developed, most with improved engines, but they were developed too late to go into production.

The Frank, which resembled the Oscar, was a low-wing monoplane with bubble canopy. The aircraft was well liked and simple to fly, although taxiing and ground handling were generally poor. The Ki-106 was an effort to produce the Frank largely of wood. Flown for the first time in July 1945, the plane was heavier and more sluggish than the metal Ki-84. Only three prototypes were built.

The Ki-84-Ia was capable of 388 mph and had a maximum range of 1,025 miles with internal fuel and 1,815 miles with drop tanks. Armament of the Ia consisted of two 20-mm cannon and two 12.7-mm machine guns; the Ic had two 20-mm and two 30-mm cannon. In the fighter-bomber role two 551-pound BOMBS could be carried on wing racks.

Frank, Anne (1929–1945)

A young Jewish girl who died in a CONCENTRATION CAMP after keeping a diary that keeps her memory alive. Anne Frank was born in Germany, from which she and her family emigrated to Amsterdam in 1933. Soon after Germany invaded Holland in May 1940, the Germans invoked their laws against JEWS.

When the roundup of Dutch Jews began in Feb. 1941, friends saved the Frank family from a concentration camp by hiding them. The Franks and four others were put in a secret "annex" in what had been a warehouse. The friends did this at great risk, for NAZI authorities were also moving against Dutch Christians who opposed the anti-Jewish laws. Some 20,000 Dutch Christians were sent to concentration camps.

"Who has inflicted this upon us?" Anne asked in her diary. ". . . It is God that has made us as we are, but it will be God, too, who will raise us up again. If we bear all this suffering and if there are still Jews left, when it is over, then Jews, instead of being doomed, will be held up as an example."

Many of the diary's pages reflected her love of life and her hopes for the future: "In spite of everything I still believe that people are good at heart. . . . I can feel the sufferings of millions and yet, if I look up into the heavens, I think that it will all come right, that this cruelty too will end, and that peace and tranquility will return again."

On Aug. 4, 1944, GESTAPO agents, tipped off by a Dutch informer, burst into the annex and arrested everyone. The agents looted the rooms but tossed aside Anne's diary. The family disappeared into the nightmare world of concentration camps. Anne's mother died at AUSCHWITZ. Anne and her older sister Margot won a reprieve from the death camp and were sent to the camp at Bergen-Belsen. By early 1945 the camp, built for 10,000 prisoners, had 41,000. Most of them were dying from malnutrition, disease, and brutality. In March 1945, about 20,000 inmates of Bergen-Belsen died, including Anne and Margot. British forces liberated the camp on April 14, 1945.

The girls' father, Otto, alone survived. When he returned to Amsterdam after the war, he found Anne's diary still on the floor. Published as *Diary of a Young Girl,* Anne's book won the hearts of much

of the world. It has been published in thirty-two languages and made into a play and a movie. The secret annex has become an Amsterdam shrine.

Frank, Hans (1900–1946)

NAZI governor general of Poland. A lawyer who served as HITLER'S legal adviser, Frank began his Nazi career as an SA storm trooper, then switched to law when he passed the state bar examinations in 1926. Frank became head of the Nazi Party's legal office in 1929, defending Hitler in many cases. After the surrender of Poland, Hitler appointed Frank governor-general over that central portion of Poland that was not annexed by Germany or the Soviet Union. Frank, ensconced in Poland's old royal palace, ruled ruthlessly. He looted Poland of its treasures, stripping cathedrals, castles, and the national museums at WARSAW and Cracow of so much priceless art that he published a catalogue for Nazi leaders to peruse for selections. He proclaimed Germany the official language, made the Poles into "the slaves of the Greater German Empire," and, in a speech on Dec. 16, 1941, declared, "We must destroy the Jews." Within a year he had sent 85 percent of Poland's JEWS to concentration camps secretly designated as DEATH CAMPS. On trial at Nuremberg for WAR CRIMES, he confessed his guilt and begged for forgiveness. Convicted of both war crimes and crimes against humanity, he was hanged at Nuremberg on Oct. 16, 1946.

Frankton

Code word for British submarine *Tuna* landing Royal Marine COMMANDOS to destroy German shipping at the French ports of Bordeaux and Bassens, Dec. 1942.

Franklin (CV 13)

see ESSEX (CV 9).

Frantic

Code name for U.S. shuttle bombing missions from Britain and Italy that made use of stopover bases in the Soviet Union.

Fraser, Adm. of the Fleet Sir Bruce (1888–1981)

Soon after he took command of the British Home Fleet in 1943 Fraser declined promotion to

First Sea Lord in favor of Adm. A. B. CUNNINGHAM, saying "I believe I have the confidence of my own Fleet; Cunningham has that of the whole Navy."

Fraser (1st Baron Fraser of North Cape) did have a great rapport with the officers and ratings of his fleet, and he knew how to put them to work. During his thirteen-month tenure in the Home Fleet he commanded more ships than any other British admiral had since the Battle of Jutland in 1916. His men sank the German battleship *Scharnhorst* off Norway's North Cape in Dec. 1943 as the latter sortied to attack a MURMANSK-bound RUSSIAN CONVOY and attacked the German battleship *TIRPITZ,* then holed up in a Norwegian fjord.

In Aug. 1944 Fraser was named commander of the British Eastern Fleet based in Ceylon. (In Nov. 1944, it was renamed the British Pacific Fleet.) After operations against Sumatra, a portion of the Pacific Fleet—designated TASK FORCE 57 and typically consisting of four or five carriers and two battleships plus cruisers and destroyers—went into action with the U.S. Navy's Fifth FLEET off OKINAWA in Feb. 1945. Task Force 57 served with the U.S. Navy through the end of the war and took part in the Japanese SURRENDER ceremonies in Tokyo Bay on Sept. 2, 1945. Other British naval units under Fraser's command supported operations in Malaya and Burma.

After the war, Fraser served as First Sea Lord from 1948 to 1951 (the post he had declined in 1943).

Fredendall, Lt. Gen. Lloyd R. (1884–1963)

Commander of the U.S. 1st DIVISION in the NORTH AFRICA INVASION. Fredendall's command was the Center Task Force, which took Oran in the invasion. In the subsequent NORTH AFRICA CAMPAIGN Fredendall led the II CORPS and was defeated by ERWIN ROMMEL at Sidi Bou Zid and the KASSERINE PASS. Fredendall was not well liked by Gen. DWIGHT D. EISENHOWER, the Allied Commander in Chief, or fellow British and French officers. Eisenhower relieved Fredendall after the near-rout at the Kasserine Pass. He was given a training post in the United States.

Promoted to lieutenant general, Fredendall commanded the Central Defense Command until it was merged with the Eastern Defense Command early in 1944.

Free French

An anti-German, anti-VICHY FRANCE movement founded by Gen. CHARLES DE GAULLE. Fleeing Vichy France (where he had been condemned to death), de Gaulle set up the Free French, a government-to-be, in London, the site of many governments in exile. By creating a Vichy government submissive to Germany, France's government was illegitimate in the eyes of the ALLIES. So France's representation in London was different from that of other conquered countries: de Gaulle was recognized by the British government as the "leader of all Free Frenchmen" and the British gave financial support to the Free French. The British seized several ships of the French Navy, including two battleships, in British ports and sank or damaged others in French ports in North and West Africa.

On Dec. 24, 1941, while President ROOSEVELT and Prime Minister CHURCHILL were conferring in Washington, French Vice Adm. Émile Muselier, the Free French naval commissioner and a rival of de Gaulle, seized the French islands of St. Pierre et Miquelon off Newfoundland in the name of the Free French. On the agenda of the Roosevelt-Churchill UNITED NATIONS CONFERENCE (also known as the Arcadia Conference) was the fate of the islands, which could fall into Vichy hands, as French INDOCHINA, with German permission, had fallen into Japanese hands. Muselier's unilateral action established the arrogantly independent reputation of the Free French, a reputation that de Gaulle would personify.

The Free French evolved from the French National Committee, which de Gaulle had formed in June 1940 to provide a base for the many forces that made up the FRENCH RESISTANCE. French colonies in India and the Pacific, along with African colonies—including the Ivory Coast, Chad, and Cameroun—joined the Free French. From volunteers who made their way to England de Gaulle built up a FREE FRENCH ARMY and manned small navy and air force units. Their emblem was the Cross of Lorraine.

In June 1943 the London and African Free French under Gen. HENRI GIRAUD, together with Resistance forces, formed the French Committee of

National Liberation, the basis for a postwar French government. (In July 1942, in an effort to accommodate Communist resistance groups who saw the Free French as prospective Fascists, de Gaulle changed the name to Fighting French; the British and Americans usually still continued to refer to the movement as Free French.)

The Free French envisioned the creation of a political entity in occupied France itself. The idea was built into a PROPAGANDA campaign, with BBC broadcasts asserting: "In Europe, three countries are resisting: Greece, Yugoslavia, and the Haute-Savoie." This referred to an isolated French department (comparable to a U.S. state) in the French Alps. The Free French in London hoped to seize the area, occupy it—as partisan forces had done in Greece and Yugoslavia—and proclaim it Free France. Although GUERRILLAS in France once tried to wrest a part of Haute-Savoie from the Germans, the attempt failed. But, in the name of the Free French, de Gaulle would in 1944 set up a provisional postliberation government.

Free French Army,
see FRANCE, ARMY.

Freedom
Signal code name for Allied Force Headquarters in Algiers, North Africa.

Freighters
British code name for the Q-SHIP project, 1939–1940.

Fremede Heere Ost (Foreign Armies East)
Intelligence branch of the German General Staff concernced with the Soviet Union and the EASTERN FRONT. From April 1, 1942, until the end of the war, *Fremede Heere Ost* was headed by REINHARD GEHLEN.

French Forces of the Interior,
see FRENCH RESISTANCE.

French Indochina,
see INDOCHINA.

French Resistance
The overall name for well-organized French GUERRILLAS who, through acts of SABOTAGE and military actions, harassed the German occupiers of conquered France. Gen. DWIGHT D. EISENHOWER said the Resistance, which was estimated to total as many as 300,000 men and women, had been worth fifteen additional DIVISIONS to him.

Many French guerrilla units were known simply as the *MAQUIS,* which means "scrub" or "scrubland." The word conjures up a romantic countryside where bands of men and women in black berets strike at NAZI trains and garrisons. Twice, though, the *Maquis* fought the Germans in major pitched battles.

In March 1944, at a high plateau in the Haute-Savoie region of the French Alps, a band of about 400 *Maquis,* defending a parachute drop zone, were overwhelmed by 7,000 Germans and 1,000 VICHY FRANCE troops. About 150 *Maquis* were killed in battle or executed and 180 were taken prisoner. (When a memorial was placed on the plateau in 1973, the number of Germans had grown to 20,000.) In May, in mountainous terrain near Grenoble, south of the earlier battle, some 4,000 *Maquis* gathered to seize a plateau where FREE FRENCH paratroopers were expected to land and proclaim the Free French Republic of Vercors. The paratroopers did not arrive, but about 10,000 Germans, including GLIDER-delivered troops, did. They surrounded the Resistance men (and eleven Americans from the OFFICE OF STRATEGIC SERVICES). The Germans killed more than 600 in the Resistance and executed a number of wounded, many of whom while they still lay on stretchers.

Shortly after the NORMANDY INVASION, Eisenhower received word that the *Maquis* lacked supplies, preventing them from having a major role in the battle for France. A conservative estimate at the time placed the number of armed *Maquis* at 16,000 and the number ready to receive weapons at almost 32,000 more. Potential recruits—if arms were available—might raise the total to 100,000. Accordingly, the U.S. AAF undertook Operation Cadillac (part of Operation Carpetbagger) to drop arms to the *Maquis.*

The valiant success of the Resistance set in motion one of the worst atrocities of the war. In July 1944, the SS, infuriated because French guerrillas were harassing German units, selected Ouradour-sur-Glâne, a village in southwestern France, as a place to make an example. The SS machine-gunned 190 men of the village, herded 245 women and 207 children into a church and machine-gunned anyone attempting to escape as the SS troops burned the church to the ground. They then leveled the village. Ten people survived to later testify about the massacre. The ruins of Ouradour-sur-Glâne are maintained as a memorial.

The Resistance's military arm, the French Forces of the Interior (FFI), went beyond guerrilla sabotage and hit-and-run military actions. Well armed and well organized, the FFI aided the ALLIED CAMPAIGN IN EUROPE as it rolled across France. FFI units created diversions that harassed or pinned down German forces, keeping them from Allied armies, and then in many places took over the country behind the advancing Allied troops. Communist Resistance units in PARIS led an uprising in the city in Aug. 1944, hoping to gain control of postwar France by seizing the city. The uprising did not succeed, but the revolt changed Allied strategy and made the Communists a force to reckon with in postoccupation politics.

Some Resistance fighters went into the FREE FRENCH ARMY; others, disarmed, returned to peacetime lives as the Germans withdrew. Resistance leaders executed about 10,000 collaborators, jailed thousands of others, and replaced Vichy politicians.

Freshman

British AIRBORNE operation to destroy a German heavy water plant in Norway, Nov. 1942.

Fridericus

German code name for a series of operations east of the Donets River in the Soviet Union, 1942.

Friedman, William F. (1891–1969)

American cryptologist who broke the Japanese PURPLE code in 1940. The son of a Russian Jewish family that emigrated to the United States in 1892, Friedman was cited as "unquestionably one of the greatest cryptanalysts of all time," by David Kahn, World War II historian of code-breaking.

He was hired in 1921 by the Army Signal Corps to serve as a chief cryptographer. Friedman was made civilian head of the Army's Signal Intelligence Service in 1929, with six assistants to help him. (In 1935 an Army officer was assigned as military head of the group.)

Friedman began attacking the top-level Japanese Purple codes late in 1938. In August of 1940, after twenty months of work, he and his colleagues had solved their first Purple message. While breaking the Purple code did help U.S. military activities in the Pacific, its primary value was in deciphering communications from Japanese diplomatic and military missions in Nazi Germany to Japan. In 1941 he visited BLETCHLEY PARK to facilitate the exchange of Anglo-American code-breaking knowledge.

Friedman continued his code-breaking work during the war and in 1952 he became the first cryptologist to join the new National Security Agency.

Fritz

Early German code name for the invasion of the Soviet Union. (See BARBAROSSA.)

Fritz-X

Highly effective German antiship GUIDED MISSILE. A glide bomb that could be radio controlled by the launching aircraft, the Fritz-X was introduced into combat by the Luftwaffe on Sept. 9, 1943, with devastating results.

On that date the surviving warships of the Italian Navy were at sea, steaming toward MALTA where they would be surrendered to the ALLIES. The Italian ships were attacked by Dornier DO 217 bombers of *Kampfgeschwader* (bomber group) No. 100 carrying the Fritz-X missile.

The 35,000-ton battleship *ROMA* was struck by two of the guided bombs. A Fritz-X, with a 704-pound armor-piercing bomb as warhead, penetrated the *Roma*'s armor and exploded. Inrushing sea water and the rupture of electric cables caused fires. As the *Roma* fell out of formation, a second Fritz-X struck her, causing more fires and flooding. Moments after the second hit the magazine of a 381-mm (15-inch) gun turret detonated, and the ship rapidly capsized, broke in two, and sank. There were 595 survivors from her crew of 1,849.

The same day her sister ship *Italia* (ex-*Littorio*) was also struck by a Fritz-X, but survived. Subsequently Do 217/Fritz-X attacks inflicted heavy damage on British battleship *Warspite* and cruiser *Uganda,* and the U.S. CRUISER *Savannah* (CL 42). The *Warspite,* hit on Sept. 16, was so heavily damaged by two guided bombs that she had to be towed to port; the damage was extensive but, miraculously, only nine men were killed in the battleship. Her repairs required nine months.

The USS *Savannah* was hit by a single Fritz-X on Sept. 11. The bomb went through a gun turret, exploding deep in the ship. Only water rushing into the ship from holes caused by the explosion probably prevented a magazine detonation and loss of the 9,700-ton ship. Two hundred and six men were killed in the attack.

The Fritz-X bomber wing was unable to undertake further effective attacks from Italy because of the increase in Allied fighter forces. However, on April 30, 1944, operating from a base in France, Do 217s from *Kampfgeschwader* 100 attacked Britain for the first and only time; fifteen Do 217s attacked shipping at Plymouth but no important targets were hit.

Total Fritz-X production from April 1943 until Dec. 1944 was 1,386 missiles, of which 602 were expended in tests. The overall weight of the bomb was 3,454 pounds; its length was 10¾ feet. When dropped from an altitude of 26,240 feet it had a range of 5½ miles, declining as the launch aircraft released the missile from lower altitudes. Flares on the missile's fins permitted the controller in the Do 217 to track and guide the weapon toward its target. Several more advanced versions of the missile were under development, but none are believed to have been used in combat.

The Fritz-X was developed by Dr. Max Kramer and was officially designated X-1.

The Hs 293 antiship guided bomb was also employed by the Luftwaffe, with a second bomber wing being established, *Kampfgeschwader* 40, flying Heinkel HE 177s and, later Focke-Wulf FW 200 CONDORs in the missile strike role. Although that weapon was used to damage several ships, and sink the British sloop *Egret* on Aug. 27, 1944 (the first ship sunk by a guided missile), and the cruiser *Spar-*

tan on Jan. 22, 1944, the missiles had little effect on the war.

The basic Hs 293 had a total weight of 2,304 pounds with a warhead weight of 649 pounds; it was 11¾ feet long.

British historian Alfred Price, writing in the magazine *Flight International,* observed: "Like so many promising German weapons, the X-1 and Hs 293 arrived on the scene too late; had they been available just one year earlier—in time to combat the Malta CONVOYS—the course of the war in the MEDITERRANEAN would certainly have been changed, perhaps decisively. In the event the weapons between them sank or damaged some 440,000 tons of Allied shipping—not a very large score if one considers the scale of effort involved and the revolutionary nature of the missiles."

Frogmen,
see UNDERWATER DEMOLITION TEAMS.

Fry
Code name for Allied occupation of four islands in Lake Comacchio, Italy.

Fuchida, Capt. Mitsuo (1902–1976)

Air strike leader of the Japanese carrier force that attacked PEARL HARBOR. Fuchida gained combat experience during air operations over China in the late 1930s. He was considered one of Japan's most skilled fliers.

At 6 A.M. on Dec. 7, 1941, Comdr. Fuchida took off from the carrier-flagship *Akagi* to lead the 183 planes of the first attack wave against the U.S. FLEET at Pearl Harbor. Moments before the first BOMBS fell he transmitted the radio message *Tora . . . Tora . . . Tora . . . (Tiger . . . Tiger . . . Tiger . . .),* the code signal to Japanese commanders that the attack was a surprise.

Fuchida continued to serve as senior air commander with the fast carrier striking force, leading air attacks on the DUTCH EAST INDIES and against British bases and ships in the eastern Indian Ocean in early 1942. He was on board the *Akagi* at the battle of MIDWAY. Injured in the air attack, he was saved from the sinking carrier; upon returning to Japan he was immediately ordered to the Naval War

College as an instructor and directed to prepare a highly secret report on the battle.

Promoted to captain, he was the fleet air staff officer at the battle of the MARIANAS in June 1944, which marked the end of an effective Japanese carrier force.

After the war he became a rice farmer and, after converting to Christianity, became a nondenominational preacher. In the late 1960s he became an American citizen.

Fuchs, Emil Julius Klaus (1911–1988)

Scientist in Britain's atomic research program accused of giving American atomic information to the Soviets in 1945 and British atomic secrets to them in 1947. "Probably the most dangerous spy of all, since it was he who gave the Russians the secret of the bomb's manufacture," wrote British intelligence specialist H. Montgomery Hyde in *The Atom Bomb Spies.* Fuchs' Soviet cover name was "Golia."

Born in Germany, Fuchs was raised as a Quaker but later gave up Christian beliefs and turned to atheism. An anti-Nazi, he became a Communist in 1932. The following year he secretly left Germany for England. There he earned doctorate degrees in both mathematical physics and theoretical physics. Suspected of being an enemy alien, in 1940 he was sent to Canada but in May 1941 began work on the British nuclear effort and was soon passing information to Soviets. Fuchs went to the United States in Nov. 1943 and worked at the LOS ALAMOS nuclear laboratory. "Fuchs was popular at Los Alamos," wrote his scientific colleague Edward Teller, "because he was kind, helpful, and much interested in the works of others. But his exceptional intelligence was combined with exceptional reticence." He was also credited with having an excellent memory.

After the war he returned to Britain to become head of the theoretical physics division at the Harwell atomic research facility. The Canadian government began investigations in 1949 based on infor-

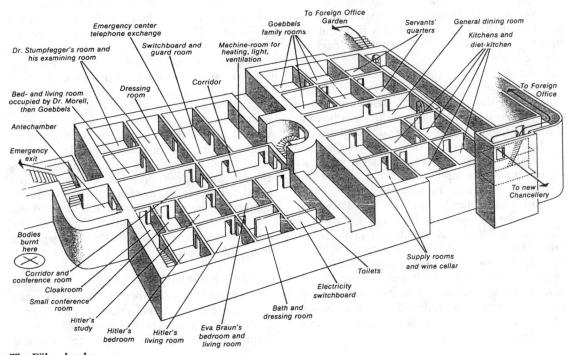

The Führerbunker.

mation provided by the U.S. FEDERAL BUREAU OF INVESTIGATION. He was arrested on Feb. 2, 1950, at the time he was the deputy chief scientific officer at Harwell.

Fuchs confessed, and his testimony was instrumental in the prosecution of HARRY GOLD, DAVID GREENGLASS, and ETHEL and JULIUS ROSENBERG. Fuchs was tried in March 1950 and sentenced to fourteen years in prison. He was released in 1959 and went to East Germany.

Führerbunker

HITLER's refuge during the final months of the THIRD REICH. A command post dedicated to Hitler's use, the *Führerbunker* was under the garden of New Reich Chancellery in BERLIN. The buried concrete roof was 16 feet thick, with exterior walls 6 feet wide. The main level was 55 feet below ground. Construction started late in 1944 and the bunker, which had its own electric generator, grew to thirty-odd small rooms connected by dank narrow passages. The bunker was never completed.

The *Führerbunker* was incorporated into an adjacent upper bunker that had been begun in 1936, the year German rearmament began. Spiral steps led down from the upper bunker to a bulkhead and steel door that sealed off the *Führerbunker* from the outside world.

Hitler entered the Chancellery area, never to leave, on Jan. 16, 1945, and spent almost all of his time in the *Führerbunker*. On a few occasions, when there were no Allied air raids, he briefly came out in the daytime. On Feb. 25 he addressed a secret meeting of *Gauleiters* (NAZI Party district leaders) just outside of Berlin and on March 15 he made a 60-mile, four-hour trip to the EASTERN FRONT, returning to the bunker before sundown.

Until Hitler's death on April 30, 1945, few slept in the bunker with him and his consort, EVA BRAUN; those who did included Hitler's valet, Heinze Linge; Hitler's physician, Dr. Theo Morell; and cook Konstanze Manzialy. He married Eva, then killed himself and his bride in the bunker. He also killed Blondi, his German shepherd, a dog that, according to ALBERT SPEER, "meant more to his master than the Führer's closest associates."

In the final days, Propaganda Minister JOSEPH GOEBBELS read aloud one of Hitler's favorite books, Carlyle's *Frederick the Great*. In his diary Goebbels later wrote that "tears stood in the Führer's eyes" when he heard that the unexpected death of Czarina Elizabeth led to Russia's withdrawal from the alliance against Frederick—a death that Frederick saw as a miracle that saved his cause. A few days after Goebbels read this passage to Hitler, President ROOSEVELT died, and Hitler thought this would lead to another similar miracle.

Goebbels also committed suicide in the bunker, along with his wife Magda, after murdering their six young children.

Full House

One of three phases of U.S. Eighth and Ninth AIR FORCES' strikes against German trains, supply dumps, airfields, and targets of opportunity past the immediate NORMANDY INVASION areas, June 1944.

Fulmar

British two-seat carrier fighter that introduced eight-gun fighter armament to the Fleet Air Arm. The Fulmar, developed by Fairey Aviation, first flew on Jan. 4, 1940, and immediately was ordered into production, entering service that June. Soon found on most British aircraft carriers, the Fulmar established a reputation in roles as a defensive and escort fighter, reconnaissance, and convoy protection (i.e., spotting surface U-BOATS and intercepting German recce aircraft). Beyond its armament of eight .303-cal. machine guns, the Fulmar received high marks for maneuverability and its 800-mile range. (Some aircraft had a .303-cal. gun firing from the after cockpit; no BOMBS or ROCKETS were carried.) However, the imposition of a second crewman increased weight, giving it a top speed of only 280 mph. Still, some of the 602 Fulmars delivered to the Navy through early 1943 were in service at the end of the war.

Fw 189 *Uhu* (Owl)

A German reconnaissance aircraft, used extensively on the Soviet front, although also flown in other theaters. It had a central nacelle with a glazed cockpit; the twin engines were mounted in nacelles that tapered into twin tail booms (akin to the U.S. P-38 LIGHTNING). With a top speed of only 221 mph the Focke-Wulf aircraft was not particularly survivable over hostile territory in the reconnaissance role. Entering service in late 1940, production totaled 846 by the end of the war.

Fw 190

The best piston-engine fighter to be flown by the Luftwaffe. "No combat aircraft has ever achieved perfection, but at the time of its debut the Fw 190 probably came as near to this elusive goal as any fighter," wrote aviation historian William Green. When the Focke-Wulf 190 entered action over France in the fall of 1941 it was the most advanced fighter operational in any air force and for the first time provided German pilots with a fighter superior to the British SPITFIRE. (A year later this superiority was largely erased with RAF introduction of the Spitfire IX.)

The Fw 190, which succeeded the venerable ME 109, was noted for its speed and maneuverability (the latter assisted by an electric tail-trimming device). Other features included four rapid-firing 20-mm cannon, a canopy jettisoned by explosive bolts, and heavy armor protection for the pilot. Fw 190s were employed primarily as daylight interceptors and ground-attack aircraft, but were also used on a limited basis as night fighters (sans radar), making use of light from ground searchlights and flares to locate Allied bombers. The late-model Fw 190G was a fighter-bomber variant

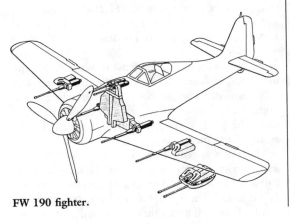

FW 190 fighter.

carrying one 1,100-pound or 2,200-pound BOMB under the fuselage.

In the fall of 1937 the German Air Ministry placed an order with Focke-Wulf Flugzeugbau for the design of a new single-seat fighter to supplement the Messerschmitt Bf 109—a second "iron in the fire." Under the direction of designer Kurt Tank, two proposals were made, one for an in-line and one for a radial-engine fighter. The latter was chosen by the Luftwaffe despite the drag imposed by the radial engine configuration. The first prototype was flown on June 1, 1939. The aircraft was eminently successful, attaining 370 mph in level flight. After the few faults were corrected, a preproduction batch was followed in mid-1944 by a series order for 100 Fw 190A-1 fighters. By mid-1944 production reached 1,000 per month with 20,000 being delivered by the end of the war.

The Fw 190 was a relatively small, low-wing monoplane with a large radial engine; the wide undercarriage was fully retractable. The first production aircraft, the Fw 190A-1, had four 7.9-mm machine guns; later variants had two machine guns and two 20-mm cannon or four 20-mm cannon. Prototypes included tank-killing models with seven 30-mm cannon (each with a single round) and another one with six 77-mm cannon (firing sabots containing a 45-mm armor-piercing round); another variant provided for upward-firing 30-mm guns triggered by a photo-electric cell as the fighter passed under an Allied bomber. Several planes were also modified to carry wire-guided air-to-air missiles. The ultimate operational model of the Fw 190 was the TA 152.

The Fw 190A-8 model had a top speed of 408 mph; the Fw 190D-12 with a power-boost in the engine could reach 453 mph at 37,000 feet. Normal range was on the order of 500 miles.

A few two-seat trainers were conversions from single-seat aircraft.

Fw 200 Condor

The Luftwaffe's long-range maritime patrol aircraft. Despite small numbers, the Condor achieved a respectable record for attacking Allied ships on the high seas and for searching out CONVOYS for U-BOAT attack. The Focke-Wulf Condor was an adaption of a four-engine commercial airliner. Called "Focke-Wolves" by WINSTON CHURCHILL, the planes flew great patrol loops over the eastern Atlantic, from France to Norway and then returning. The Condors were assigned to *Kampfgeschwader* (bomber group) 40, based at Bordeaux-Mérignac, France, from July 1940 to mid-1944.

The first Condor maritime mission to search for British shipping was flown over the North Sea on April 8, 1940. In 1940–1941 the aircraft had considerable success, sinking 363,000 tons of British shipping from Aug. 1940 through Jan. 1941. Although configured for maritime missions, they were sometimes employed as transports in emergency situations, as in the Mediterranean and at STALINGRAD. A few Fw 200s were also used to drop mines off British ports.

In an effort to counter the Fw 200 the Royal Navy put HURRICANE fighters to sea on merchant ships. The fighters were catapulted off to intercept the Fw 200, after which the pilot would parachute into the sea and hoped to be picked up by his convoy. More effective against the German planes were fighters launched from ESCORT CARRIERS. Royal Navy Martlet (F4F WILDCAT) fighters from the first British escort carrier, the *Audacity,* shot down several Condors in late 1941. (The *Audacity* was sunk by a U-boat on the night of Dec. 21, 1941.)

In Jan. 1943, eighteen of the maritime Condors were flown to southern Russia to help fly supplies to the besieged German garrison at Stalingrad. In 1943–1944 several Condors were modified to carry two Hs-293 GUIDED MISSILES for attacking shipping. No successes were recorded for Condors using this weapon and by mid-1944 the Condors were withdrawn from maritime service because the Allies overran their bases in France and because of fuel shortages. The surviving Fw 200s were then employed as transports.

The last scheduled flight by a Lufthansa Condor occurred on April 14, 1945, when an airliner flew from Barcelona to BERLIN. (The aircraft crashed a week later while attempting a return flight to Spain.)

The Fw 200 was a low-wing, four-engine monoplane with fully retractable undercarriage. It was an all-metal aircraft except for fabric-covered control surfaces. Accommodations were provided for twenty-six passengers. In the maritime reconnaissance/strike role the Fw 200 carried bombs under the wings. A lengthened ventral gondola was provided for gun positions, with a 20-mm cannon firing forward and a machine gun firing aft; there were also two dorsal machine-gun positions. These aircraft had strengthened fuselages and were fitted with FuG 200 surface search RADAR. Significant modifications were made to the design during the limited production run, primarily with updated engines.

The Fw 200 was designed in 1936 by Kurt Tank as a trans-Atlantic airliner for Lufthansa. The prototype flew on July 27, 1937. Several aircraft were placed in commercial service—four with Lufthansa, two in Denmark, and two in Brazil. One of the German aircraft flew to Japan in late 1938. It so impressed the Japanese that five commercial and one military variant were ordered, but all were delivered to the German Air Force.

The lack of effective long-range maritime patrol aircraft forced the German Air Force to adopt the Fw 200 for the maritime patrol role. Designated Fw 200C, the first ten military aircraft were delivered in Sept. 1939—four as unarmed transports and the rest as maritime patrol aircraft.

With maritime activities being given low priority by HERMANN GÖRING, head of the Air Force, Condor production was limited with only 252 aircraft delivered from 1940–1944. Thus, a total of only 274 Fw 200s of all types were produced.

Four Condor aircraft were configured as VIP transports including one for HITLER (named *Immelmann III*) and one for SS leader HEINRICH HIMMLER. Shortly before his death, Hitler's plane was made ready for a possible flight to Japan. Himmler's aircraft was later made available for the use of *Grossadmiral* KARL DÖNITZ; that plane was fully armed. The planes of both Hitler and Himmler had armored seats, which could be ejected from the aircraft and parachuted to earth in the event of an emergency.

Maximum speed of the Condor was 224 mph with maximum continuous cruise being 172 mph. Patrol range was 2,210 miles and with fuel overload 2,760 miles. The Fw 200C had a defensive armament of one 20-mm cannon forward in the gondola, one 13-mm machine gun aft in the gondola, and two 13-mm guns in two dorsal positions; two 13-mm guns could be mounted at beam hatches if extra crewmen were carried—a total of six gun positions. Nominal bomb load was four 551-pound bombs although the aircraft had a theoretical bomb capacity of over 11,000 pounds, or almost as much as a LANCASTER bomber. In the minelaying role two 2,200-pound mines were carried.

The standard Condor crew was five: pilot, copilot, navigator/radio operator/gunner, flight engineer/gunner, and rear dorsal gunner.

Gen. Charles de Gaulle (shown here in Normandy at Gen. Eisenhower's headquarters) courageously took command of the Free French forces after the fall of France in June 1940. A constant thorn in the sides of Churchill and then Ike, de Gaulle demanded equality with Britain and the United States in the direction of the European War. *(Imperial War Museum)*

G.50 *Freccia* (Arrow)

Italian fighter aircraft. The G.50 single-seat fighter flew for the Nationalist side in the SPANISH CIVIL WAR and, after modifications based on that testing ground, was produced for use by the Italian Air Force. It never matched the performance of wartime Allied or German fighters.

The Fiat-designed G.50 first flew on Feb. 26, 1937, and some 730 aircraft were produced (with thirty-five going to Finland) plus 100 two-seat trainers designated G.50B. The aircraft had a low, forward-mounted wing, giving the appearance of a racing plane. However, its speed was only 293 mph and armament consisted of only two 12.7-mm machine guns.

A prototype two-seat ground attack version was flown in 1942; this G.50 *bis*-A reached a speed of 329 mph but did not enter production.

Galahad

Code name for U.S. long-range penetration groups in Burma (i.e., MERRILL'S MARAUDERS).

Galland, *Generalleutnant* Adolf (1912—)

German fighter ACE and commander of the Luftwaffe Fighter Arm. At twenty-nine, he became the youngest general in the German armed forces.

Galland flew some 300 missions with Germany's Condor Legion in the SPANISH CIVIL WAR, 1936–1938. His World War II service began with the

A British Horsa glider—carrying U.S. airborne troops—is pulled aloft early on June 6, 1944, as part of the Allied D-day assault into Normandy. The C-47 Skytrain/Dakota "tug" and the glider both have "invasion stripes" painted on their wings and fuselage to provide recognition and immunity to friendly fire during the massive Normandy invasion. The C-47 was produced in larger numbers than any military transport in the war. (*U.S. Army Air Forces*)

POLISH CAMPAIGN in Sept. 1939. In June 1940 he became commander of *Jagdgeschwader* (fighter group) 26 and led it through the BATTLE OF BRITAIN. He is credited with downing 103 enemy aircraft. His decorations kept pace with his score as an ace; he received the IRON CROSS after seventeen victories, and, by the time he had ninety-four victories he also had the Iron Cross with Oak Leaves and Swords and Diamonds.

After the death of *Oberst* WERNER MÖLDERS in Nov. 1941, Galland was put in charge of fighters. He was promoted to *Generalleutnant* the next year. As the ALLIES began battering the Luftwaffe, Galland asked for the resources to build a stronger fighter force, but *Reischmarschall* HERMANN GÖRING, head of the Luftwaffe, continually rebuffed him. The Allies were winning control of the air and Galland was losing his confrontations with Göring.

In Jan. 1945 Göring relieved him of command, but he was allowed to resume combat flying. He took command of a fighter unit equipped with jet-powered ME 262 fighters. On April 26 he was shot down near Munich by a U.S. P-51 MUSTANG.

After the war Galland went to Argentina, where he was an adviser to the Air Force. Later, he returned to Germany and became a consultant to German aerospace companies.

Gallery, Capt. Daniel V., Jr. (1901–1977)

Commander of a highly effective U.S. antisubmarine group in the Atlantic. His "hunter-killer" group captured a German U-BOAT, the first enemy warship to be captured by the U.S. Navy on the high seas since the War of 1812.

After service in surface warships, in 1927 he underwent flight training and subsequently served in and commanded aircraft SQUADRONS. In Jan. 1941 he became the assistant U.S. naval attaché for air in LONDON. A year later he took command of a Navy patrol plane detachment in Iceland, participating in the BATTLE OF THE ATLANTIC.

In May 1943, as a captain, he was ordered to command the new ESCORT CARRIER *Guadalcanal* (CVE 60), which was placed in commission on Sept. 25, 1943. The carrier was the center of an antisubmarine group that included five DESTROYER ESCORTS. Gallery trained his men hard, and after their first successes against a U-boat emphasized

techniques for capturing code machines and documents from a damaged submarine that surfaced. His group sank the *U-544* in Jan. 1944, and the *U-68* and *U-515* in April.

The group detected the *U-505* operating submerged some 150 miles off the coast of French West Africa on the morning of June 4, 1944. Taken by surprise when one of the destroyer escorts depth-charged the U-boat, her captain brought the submarine to the surface and ordered his men to abandon ship.

One of the escort ship's crew, well trained under Gallery's guidance, boarded the abandoned submarine. While two sailors raced to the U-boat's radio room to remove cryptographic equipment, other American sailors disconnected the demolition charges the Germans had set and shut off an open waterline. The U-boat was taken in tow by the *Guadalcanal* and brought to Bermuda. The capture contributed greatly to the Allies' reading of ENIGMA communications. (The British had previously captured three U-boats at sea.)

In Sept. 1944, Gallery reported for staff duty in WASHINGTON. In Aug. 1945 he took command of the *Hancock* (CV 19), then operating off the Japanese coast.

Gallery was promoted to rear admiral in Dec. 1945 and, after a number of other ship and shore assignments, he retired in late 1960. He was a prolific writer, producing nine books and several articles—fact, fancy, and fiction about the Navy.

Galvanic

Code name for U.S. AMPHIBIOUS LANDINGS in the GILBERT ISLANDS, late 1943.

Gandhi, Mohandas (1869–1948)

Indian Hindu nationalist leader. Hailed as *Mahatma* (great-souled) by his followers, Gandhi was taking India toward freedom from British rule when the war began. He asked the British for independence as a condition for Indian cooperation. The British refused, and peace-preaching Ghandi contended that even if the Japanese invaded, civil disobedience would ultimately preserve India.

When Gandhi and his Indian Congress Party resisted British war preparations, British authorities arrested him and other party leaders. He was freed in May 1944. After the war he continued to work for independence, but despaired over the savage Hindu-Moslem fighting that led to the partitioning of India. A militant Hindu assassinated him on Jan. 30, 1948.

Garand,

see M1 GARAND.

Garbo

British code name for a Spaniard hired by the Germans to spy on the British. Garbo instead went to Lisbon and sent false reports of British CONVOYS and, subsequently, to Britain where he continued his deception activities.

Garbo worked against the Germans because of his dislike of Spanish dictator FRANCISCO FRANCO. He believed that only an Allied victory in the war could depose Franco. He first attempted to offer his services to British intelligence but was rejected. Garbo then offered his services to the German *ABWEHR,* which accepted him, and in July 1941 he began writing reports about British naval and shipping matters, which he made up, purporting to the Germans that he was in Britain when in fact he was in Lisbon.

In Feb. 1942 he met with British intelligence and offered himself as a double agent. In April 1942 he went to England where he remained for the rest of the war, operating as a double agent under British control. (See DOUBLE CROSS.) He established a paper network of agents, which improved his credibility with the Germans. At the same time, Garbo's activities forced the Germans to reveal several of their real agents to British intelligence.

He was decorated by the Germans (in absentia) with the IRON CROSS for his information on the NORMANDY landings *and* by the British government with the Member of the British Empire (M.B.E.) for sending the same phony information to the Germans by British-controlled radio.

His German code name was "Rufus."

Garden

Code name for British land operation to fight through Dutch bridges to ARNHEM in conjunction with the AIRBORNE operation code name Market. (See MARKET-GARDEN.)

Gardening

British term for planting MINES in German coastal areas, channels, and canals; the individual areas mined were given code names derived from fish, flowers, trees, and specific vegetables; e.g., the Kiel Canal was given the code name Lettuce and the port of Brest was Jellyfish.

Gavin, Maj. Gen. James M. (1908–1990)

U.S. paratroop commander famed for his heroism and dedication to airborne tactics. "Jumpin' Jim," as his men and the press called him, twice won the Distinguished Service Cross for valor in parachute operations. On July 9, 1943, spearheading the invasion of SICILY, he commanded the elite 82nd AIRBORNE DIVISION'S 505th Parachute Infantry REGIMENT and jumped with his troops. On Sept. 14, when the Allied invasion of SALERNO was stopped on the beaches, he and his men parachuted onto the beach in an unprecedented maneuver. A few days later Gavin was promoted to brigadier general and became assistant division commander of the 82nd. In the invasion of NORMANDY, Gavin led three regiments in a drop behind German lines. Completely surrounded, the 82nd kept German reinforcements from reaching the Allied beachhead. On Aug. 15, 1944, he became commander of the 82nd, which fought across Europe from the Netherlands to BERLIN. In 1944 Gavin was the Army's youngest division commander.

A critic of the Army's interest in advanced weapons over soldiering, he retired in 1958, as a lieutenant general, though admirers said he was in line for promotion to four stars. In civilian life he was U.S. ambassador to France, an architect of the Peace Corps, and a critic of the Vietnam War, which he called "a tragedy."

GCT,

see ARMY GENERAL CLASSIFICATION TEST.

Gehlen, *Generalmajor* Reinhard (1902–1979)

Head of German military intelligence for the EASTERN FRONT. Gehlen served in various Army positions, mostly in artillery. He was a liaison officer for senior commanders during the May 1940 campaign in France. He was assigned to the General Staff as an adjutant in July 1940 and subsequently became involved with the Eastern Front. In April 1942, with the rank of *Oberstleutnant*, he became the senior intelligence officer on the General Staff dealing with the Eastern Front—head of General Staff's Foreign Armies East Branch. In 1944 he was promoted to *Generalmajor*.

Gehlen surrendered himself, his principal assistants, and files to U.S. forces on May 22, 1945. The following year he established the Gehlen organization to make use of his intelligence net in Soviet-controlled areas to help the United States; in 1956 he became head of West German intelligence.

Geiger, Maj. Gen. Roy S. (1885–1947)

U.S. Marine aviator and field commander. An early Marine aviator, on Sept. 3, 1942, he arrived on GUADALCANAL to command the "Cactus Air Force," the various Navy and Marine planes flying from the still-contested island. His planes, redesignated as the 1st Marine Aircraft WING, supported Marines on the island and in subsequent U.S. operations in the SOLOMON ISLANDS.

As a major general, Geiger relieved Lt. Gen. A. A. VANDEGRIFT in Nov. 1943 as commandeer of the I Marine Amphibious CORPS, then fighting on BOUGAINVILLE. He subsequently led the Marine AMPHIBIOUS LANDINGS on GUAM, PELELIU, and OKINAWA in 1944–1945 (his command having been redesignated as the III Marine Amphibious Corps in 1944). When Army Lt. Gen. SIMON B. BUCKNER was killed on Okinawa in June 1945, Geiger briefly took command of the Tenth ARMY.

At the end of the war he became commanding general Fleet Marine Force Pacific—the senior Marine in the Pacific—and was the only U.S. Marine at the Japanese SURRENDER ceremonies on the BATTLESHIP *MISSOURI* (BB 63) on Sept. 2, 1945.

Geisler, *General der Flieger* Hans Ferdinand (1891–1966)

Commander of *Fliegerkorps* X, a Luftwaffe air corps that specialized in attacking British shipping. A naval officer, Geisler transferred to the Luftwaffe in 1935 and four years later organized the special-ized air corps to meet German Navy demands for Luftwaffe air units to fulfill naval requirements.

In Sept. 1939, when the EUROPEAN WAR began, HE 111 and JU 88 bombers from Geisler's command attacked the British carrier *ARK ROYAL* operating off the Norwegian coast. After one of his pilots filed his report stating that he *believed* he had made a direct hit on the ship, the German PROPAGANDA machine announced that the British carrier had been sunk, and the pilot was duly decorated. The *Ark Royal* was undamaged, and the German failure became a propaganda victory for the British.

Geisler's command played a key role in the April 1940 DENMARK AND NORWAY CAMPAIGN. After continued operations against British ships in northern waters in Dec. 1940, Geisler led the 226 aircraft of *Fliegerkorps* X to bases in SICILY (where forty fighters were added to his force of bombers and fighter-bombers). The command then played a major role in the Mediterranean battles of 1941–1942. His JU 87 *STUKA* dive bombers devastated the carrier *Illustrious* on Jan. 10, 1941, sending her limping into MALTA for emergency repairs (and later to the United States for permanent repairs). The Luftwaffe planes then plastered Malta and attacked other British shipping. In preparation for the German assault on CRETE, in May 1941 many of Geisler's aircraft were shifted to Greece. In that battle his Ju 87s smashed the British carrier *Formidable*. When Crete was captured, it became a base for *Fliegerkorps* X operations in North Africa. Many of Geisler's planes flew from bases in North Africa in support of the AFRIKA KORPS. Geisler commanded the air corps until Aug. 1942.

Genda, Capt. Minoru (1904–1989)

Japanese naval aviator who, with Rear Adm. TAKIJIRO ONISHI, planned the Japanese carrier attack on PEARL HARBOR. Genda was air operations officer for the Japanese carrier force in 1941–1942, serving on board the flagship *Akaga*. After staff duties ashore at RABAUL and Naval General Staff Headquarters in TOKYO, in 1944–1945 he directed naval air defense of the home islands.

After the war he rose to the rank of general and was Chief of Staff of the Japanese Air Defense Force and, subsequently, served in the Diet.

George

Japanese naval fighter developed late in the war, the Kawanishi N1K1-J *Shiden-Kai* (Violet Lightning) was based on the N1K1 REX floatplane, an unusual aircraft development cycle. After several teething problems, the George entered service in early 1944 and proved to be an excellent combat aircraft. A contemporary U.S. AAF handbook described the George as "one of Japan's newest and most dangerous aircraft."

Although some George variants were able to operate from aircraft carriers, the aircraft was flown only from land bases, initially flown in combat from bases in the Philippines. However, the Japanese fighters were easily brushed aside by the overwhelming numbers of U.S. carrier-based fighters that struck at the Japanese-occupied areas in 1944–1945. Also, the Japanese plane was plagued with engine and undercarriage problems, limited maintenance personnel, and spare-parts shortages.

In late 1941, while design work on the N1K1 Rex floatplane fighter was underway, the Kawanishi design team proposed a land-based version of the aircraft. The first N1K1-J prototype flew on Dec. 27, 1942 (less than eight months after the maiden flight of the Rex). The plane suffered problems with early engines and the undercarriage, but when aloft the plane demonstrated excellent maneuverability. Rushed into production, the Kawanishi and Himeji firms combined to produce 1,007 aircraft. Simultaneously, the aircraft was redesigned and simplified; the N1K2-J model—dubbed George 21 by the AAF—used many N1K1 components and was almost 500 pounds lighter. The first of these *Shindu-Kai* models flew on Dec. 31, 1944, but despite several production facilities sharing this project, raids by B-29 SUPERFORTRESS bombers disrupted the program and only 428 of the *Shiden-Kai* models were completed. A few N1K2-K two-seat trainers were also produced.

The N1K1-J was the first mid-wing Japanese fighter aircraft that, with its large engine, bore some resemblance to U.S. fighters. It was the first Japanese naval aircraft to have "adequate" fuel and pilot armor, according to U.S. estimates. The powerful engine led to an exceptionally long undercarriage, which caused problems and the pilot had poor visibility when taxiing. The revised N1N2-J was a low-wing aircraft, with a more streamlined fuselage and reshaped fin and rudder.

There were several armament "packages" for these aircraft: the N1K1-J had two 20-mm wing cannon and two 7.7-mm fuselage-mounted machine guns; the N1K1-Ja/b models had only the four wing cannon as did the N1K2-J, with differing arrangements. When employed as a fighter-bomber the aircraft could be fitted with racks for two 551-pound bombs.

Maximum speed of the N1K1-J was 363 mph, increased to 369 mph in the N1K2-J; maximum range was 1,580 miles for the first design, reduced to 1,490 miles in the upgraded aircraft.

George VI (1895–1952)

Wartime king of the UNITED KINGDOM and emperor of India. When Edward VIII abdicated in 1936—for "the woman I love," American divorcée Wallis Warfield Simpson—Edward's younger brother Bertie was a stuttering, physically frail man. But as King George VI he became a royal symbol of faith and courage during the BATTLE OF BRITAIN. He embodied the advice he had given his subjects in a grave radio broadcast on Sept. 3, 1939: "Stand firm and calm." While children and elders streamed out of London in a massive evacuation, the Royal Family remained. And like many Londoners, the king and queen and their two young daughters lived through the bombing of their home, Buckingham Palace.

Historians of might-have-been speculate about what would have happened if Edward VIII had reigned during the war. German Foreign Minister JOACHIM VON RIBBENTROP, who had met Edward when Ribbentrop was German ambassador to England, believed that Edward would have pressed for a separate peace with Germany. Documents that surfaced in the 1980s show intense German interest in gaining influence over Edward, who after his abdication became the Duke of Windsor. George VI, aware of his brother's sympathy for "good Germans," ordered him out of Portugal, where he had gone in 1940—and where German operatives hoped to detain him for use after German conquest of England. King George put his brother out of harm's way during the war by appointing him governor of the Bahamas.

King George visited the home fleet frequently and also journeyed to the fronts in North Africa and Italy.

George (Operation)

German code name for the Eighteenth Army's role in Operation *Nordlicht*.

German-American Bund

Pro-NAZI organization formed of Americans of German stock and extremists who supported Nazi-style fascism in the United States. The *Deutschamerikanische Volksbund* so turned Americans against the Germans that HITLER disavowed its claim that German-Americans should show their allegiance to Nazi Germany. In 1939, one of the earliest U.S. war MOVIES, *Confessions of a Nazi Spy,* linked the Bund with ESPIONAGE. But the Bund, which had about 8,000 members at its height, was fundamentally a PROPAGANDA organization. Fritz Kuhn, the head of the Bund in 1939 was indicted for embezzling its funds. His successor, Gerhard W. Kunze, was sentenced on Aug. 21, 1942, to fifteen years in prison for conspiracy against the United States.

Another American pro-Nazi organization was the SILVER SHIRTS. Its leader, William Dudley Pelley, was convicted of sedition in Aug. 1942 and sentenced to fifteen years in prison.

German Campaign in the Soviet Union (1941–1943)

ADOLF HITLER invaded the Soviet Union on June 22, 1941 to obtain the grain-growing areas of the UKRAINE, the oil fields of the CAUCASUS area, and SLAVE LABOR for German industry. These economic reasons far overshadowed the philosophical anti-Soviet views he had espoused in the 1920s and 1930s, which culminated in the ANTI-COMINTERN PACT of 1936.

The invasion of the Soviet Union was originally scheduled to begin on May 15, 1941, to provide for a lengthy campaign before winter inhibited troop movement. Indeed, some German commanders envisioned a ten-week campaign—and planned accordingly. The Italian fiasco in invading Greece in Oct. 1940, however, forced German intervention in Greece and, because of Soviet-Yugoslav negotiations, to also intervene in Yugoslavia to protect the southern flank of German operations in the Soviet Union. Thus the invasion of the Soviet Union did not begin until June 22, 1941.

The Soviet government had ample warning of the pending German invasion from Soviet as well as British intelligence sources. But Soviet leader JOSEF STALIN refused to permit his commanders to prepare for the assault, believing that if he did not provoke Hitler the German assault could be delayed.

Following a massive (and obvious) buildup on the western borders with the Soviet Union, beginning at 3 A.M. the border was crossed at numerous places along a front over 1,500 miles, from the Arctic Sea to the Black Sea. Overhead the Luftwaffe attacked Soviet airfields, shooting down about 400 Soviet aircraft and destroying another 800 on the ground as German aircraft struck a reported sixty-six Soviet airfields. German sources list only thirty-five of their planes lost on that first day.

The massive German thrust into the Soviet Union had three axes: Army Group North, attacking from Finland as well as Poland, was to assault the Baltic Republics and LENINGRAD (with a smaller assault from Finnish territory toward MURMANSK); Army Group Center was to move from East Prussia and Poland eastward to envelope Minsk and then Smolensk; and Army Group South, moving from Czechoslovakia, would assault the Ukraine and move toward the Caucasus.

The assault force, totaling some 3,050,000 men, was the largest army ever assembled for a single operation. There were 148 divisions of the German field strength allocated to the invasion—Operation Barbarossa: nineteen PANZER (tank), fifteen motorized infantry, and 114 infantry—plus 67,000 troops in four divisions from the German Army in Norway; another 500,000 men came from Finland (fourteen divisions and three brigades) and 150,000 from Rumania (fourteen divisions and three brigades), all of the Rumanian units being understrength.

German ARTILLERY was excellent, although most of the 7,200 pieces were drawn by horses and not

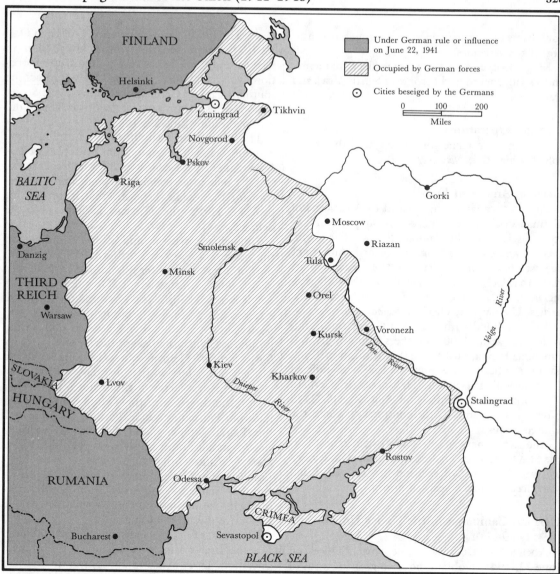

German Campaign in the Soviet Union, 1941–1943.

trucks or tractors. (Horses, however, could better traverse some Soviet roads, did not require tires and gasoline, and were frequently more reliable than motor vehicles.) The 3,350 German tanks were generally superior to Soviet vehicles, but some were obsolete. There were 600,000 other motor vehicles and 625,000 horses. The training and motivation of the German soldier was far superior to those of his Soviet counterpart. And, the Soviet military

leadership was generally poor, decimated by Stalin's purges of the 1930s, forced to gain approval by unit commissars for all major decisions, and unable to inspire the troops. Each of the three Army Groups was supported by a Luftwaffe air fleet with a total of 2,770 first-line aircraft assigned to Barbarossa.

The German forces smashed through the Soviet lines. There was some resistance, but with control of the air and a generally friendly population (especially in the Baltic Republics and the Ukraine), the German advances were rapid. Such defensive lines as the Soviets could establish were quickly destroyed by combination air-tank assaults—the unstoppable BLITZKRIEG. Minsk fell to the Germans on June 28; Smolensk on July 10. Kiev, the capital of the Ukraine, fell on Sept. 27. In a radio broadcast on Oct. 2 Hitler declared: "The enemy is broken and will never be in a position to rise again."

The Germans had bagged more than 1,500,000 prisoners in less than three months; another 663,000 surrendered when Army Group Center's Thirteenth Army took Vyazma, 125 miles west of MOSCOW, closing a trap on Oct. 6, 1941. But that night it snowed. The following morning the snow quickly melted and the roads and countryside dissolved into mud. The German commanders inquired to BERLIN about winter clothing—which might be needed if the advance was slowed. And, it was slowed. Although there were no major Soviet combat forces between the German lines and Moscow, the mud slowed German movement.

Another factor would also complicate the German advance: on Oct. 10 Marshal S. K. Timoshenko was relieved as commander of the western strategic sector by Marshal GEORGI ZHUKOV. Edward McCarthy wrote in *War in the East:* "In retrospect it was a move of supreme importance. At the time it was greeted with monumental indifference by the Germans." Zhukov had, in Sept. 1941, organized the defense of Leningrad; now he commanded the defense of Moscow.

In Moscow government papers were being burned, diplomats were being evacuated, factories were being relocated to the east, and Lenin's coffin was removed from the mausoleum in Red Square. Some sources contend that Stalin was paralyzed—and may have even left the city. Some 2,000,000 Muscovites were evacuated or abandoned the city. NKVD troops fired on panicky crowds trying to flee the city before the official evacuation began.

Zhukov planned his strategy and tactics; mud and the poor Russian roads—his greatest assets—were joined on the night of Nov. 6 by temperatures dropping and then remaining below freezing. The initial German reaction to the arrival of winter was joy, for they could escape the mud. But the troops had no winter clothes, heating devices, or lubricating oils.

The Germans were slowed to a crawl, attacked now by formations of the new Soviet T-34 TANKS and even cavalry. The Germans attempted to push on until, on Nov. 30, combat engineers came within 10 miles of the outskirts of Moscow (the main force was some 60 miles from the capital). But General Winter had won, and on Dec. 4 the extended German forces began pulling back.

Similarly, to the southeast, three Soviet armies launched a counteroffensive at ROSTOV and retook the city, which Army Group South had taken a month earlier. And, on Dec. 20 Zhukov launched a counteroffensive to push back the German front from Moscow. The Red Army was rejuvenated morally as Stalin reinstated gold-threaded epaulets for officers, created new decorations, reduced political commissars to political officers *(zampolit),* and ceased religious persecutions. And, fresh divisions were being brought to the front from Central Asia and Siberia.

Although many Russians had welcomed the German armies as liberators from Stalin's repressive dictatorship, and there were some indications that the Baltic States and Ukraine would be made semi-independent, the SS troops that followed the combat units soon inflicted a new brand of terrorism on the people. Communist leaders, Jews, and others were arrested and many were summarily executed; all food and goods were taken by the Army. The new repression alienated the inhabitants of the conquered areas, denying their help while encouraging them to support the GUERRILLA forces that were being organized behind the German lines.

To the north, Leningrad was surrounded, and laid to siege; that former capital of czarist Russia would withstand a 900-day ordeal of privation, and artillery and aerial bombardment. To the south the Germans had more success. The Ukraine fell, Sevastopol in the Crimea held out briefly, the Sea of Azov was outflanked, and the industrial center of Rostov was taken, while German troops also crossed the Kerch Straits. By Nov. 1942 German troops were on the outskirts of STALINGRAD, the large industrial city some 250 miles northwest of Rostov on the Volga River.

It fell to the Sixth Army under *Generaloberst* FRIEDRICH PAULUS to take Stalingrad and open the way to the oil fields of the Trans-Caucasus and, just possibly, a route to the Middle East and even a possible linkup with Japanese forces in India. But Paulus was hampered, by the bends of the Don that enabled Soviet forces to hold pockets on the western side of the river; by his army being stretched over a large area preventing concentration; by many of his troops being Italians and Rumanians, not the highest quality of fighters; and by his opponent, Gen. V. I. CHUIKOV, who held on to the rubble of Stalingrad with great tenacity. The first German effort to take the city came on Aug. 19. The Sixth Army fought in the ruins of the city for three months. By late Nov. 1942 the Sixth Army was trapped at Stalingrad and the SOVIET OFFENSIVE CAMPAIGN begun.

Germany

Capital: BERLIN, pop. 86,170,000 (1939). In April 1919 the WEIMAR REPUBLIC, a shaky new democracy born of Germany's postwar chaos, sent a delegation to the postwar conference at Versailles, France, under the assumption that Germans would negotiate a treaty with the Allies. There were no negotiations. The Germans were handed the Versailles Treaty, which stripped Germany of more than 27,000 square miles (roughly, the combined size of Delaware and West Virginia) and about 6,470,000 people.

The republic seemed doomed. A sullen, desperate society again was ready for politicians who would promise a better tomorrow—with or without a democracy. The visionaries came from both left and right. Germany's tattered industrialists and bankers, ever fearful of the Bolshevik menace that had toppled the Russian czar, looked to rescue from the right.

The unlikely savior was ADOLF HITLER, the founder of the NATIONAL SOCIALIST GERMAN WORKERS' PARTY, better known as the NAZI Party. But Hitler, a Socialist with the soul of a Fascist, proved to be adaptable. In April 1932, Hitler, running against eighty-four-year-old President PAUL VON HINDENBURG, a World War I hero, received 13,417,460 votes. Hindenburg, with 19,359,642 votes, won. But his days were numbered.

In July's legislative elections, the Nazis, now the most powerful party in Germany, won 230 seats in the German parliament, the Reichstag. On Jan. 30, 1933, Hindenburg, bowing to the demands of a growing lobby of conservatives and industrialists, made Hitler chancellor in a coalition Cabinet that shared power between Hitler and a conservative faction headed by Vice Chancellor FRANZ VON PAPEN.

"That evening," eyewitness historian WILLIAM L. SHIRER wrote, "from dusk until far past midnight the delirious Nazi storm troopers marched in a massive torchlight parade" through Berlin, "their bands blaring the old martial airs to the thunderous beating of the drums, their voices bawling the new Horst Wessel song and other tunes that were as old as Germany, their jack boots beating a mighty rhythm on the pavement. . . ." (Horst Wessel was an SA storm trooper killed in 1930, allegedly by a Communist. A marching song he wrote, the "Horst Wessel Lied," became an unofficial national anthem.)

The Hitler–von Papen alliance was shaky. Elections on March 5, 1933, would decide whether the Nazis had grown strong enough to gain a clear parliamentary majority. The German Communist Party, the largest in Europe outside of the Soviet Union, was expected to win about 100 of the 647 seats; the Nazis had to roll back the Communists to win control of the Reichstag. To do that, Hitler needed proof that the Communists were plotting a revolution.

The proof, dubious as it later proved to be, came on Feb. 27, when the huge, glass-domed Reichstag building went up in flames. While the flames still raged, Hitler's longtime political adjutant HERMANN GÖRING stood among the firefighters and said, "This is the beginning of a Communist uprising!" Göring's political police reported finding a mentally deranged Dutch Communist, stripped to the waist, in the building. Police arrested him and all the Communist members of the Reichstag, along with several Social Democrats.

German historians still debate whether Nazis set the fire and found a handy scapegoat. Whatever the truth, the Nazi PROPAGANDA machine convinced the public that the Communists had burned down the Reichstag as a signal for a revolution Hitler thwarted. The Nazis received only 44 percent of the vote in the elections, not enough for a governing majority. But Hitler had no further use for the trappings of democracy.

Immediately after the fire he had convinced von Hindenburg to sign an emergency decree giving Hitler essentially unlimited powers of arrest. On March 5 the Nazis kept opponents in jail cells during the parliamentary vote on the "Law for Removing the Distress of People and Reich." The sweeping enabling act passed 441 to 84. It dissolved parliament, suspended civil liberties, outlawed all parties except the Nazi Party, ended the Weimar Republic, and made Hitler dictator.

He proclaimed the THIRD REICH, a German empire that he promised would live for 1,000 years. When von Hindenburg died on Aug. 2, 1934, Hitler gave himself the title he would be known as for the rest of his life: *Der Führer*, the leader. The Nazi SWASTIKA became the national emblem. *"Ein Volk, ein Reich, ein Führer"*—one people, one empire, one leader—became the national slogan.

"It wasn't as if one day you lived under the Weimar Republic and the next day under Fascism," recalled a woman who was a child in 1933. But she remembered a steady improvement in her family's standard of living. Slums came down and new apartments went up. Men who had not worked in years had jobs. All able-bodied citizens were required to work.

All capable men between the ages of eighteen and twenty-five had to enroll in work battalions of the *Arbeitsdienst*, the Labor Service. They did manual labor, working on highways and farms. Women who entered the service worked in farmers' homes to free men to work in the fields. The biggest public works project was the building of the *Autobahnen* system, a highway network unprecedented anywhere in the world. (The 2,000-mile system was near completion in 1937 when the first major U.S. highway, the Pennsylvania Turnpike, was just being authorized.)

Germans lived in a climate of fear. Under *Sippengesetz*, the law of collective family responsibility, an entire family could be held responsible and punished for any transgression—particularly, an act of resistance—performed by any member of the family. "If the GESTAPO wanted to question you and they couldn't find you, they got hold of your wife or your father or mother or any of your relatives," a German woman of that era recalled. "And that puts a very effective stop to any kind of revolutionary activity. If you know perfectly well that whatever you've done somebody else might have to suffer for, you don't do very much. . . . I think that was possibly the worst thing to live with. You arrived at a state when you couldn't trust your best friend."

A Nazi-inspired book-burning by university students on May 10, 1933, symbolized the barbarism that was raging in the land of Goethe and Beethoven. Among the "disruptive authors" whose books were tossed onto a bonfire were Thomas Mann and Maxim Gorky. Mann left Germany, as did Arthur Koestler, Erich Maria Remarque, Bertholt Brecht, and many other writers. Ordinary people, some carrying only what they could clutch in their hands, fled after learning about the rapidly filling CONCENTRATION CAMPS and the purges of anti-Nazis in every walk of life. Thousands, Jews and Christians, intellectuals and scientists, migrated to new lives in new countries. ALBERT EINSTEIN went to the United States, Sigmund Freud to England.

At the beginning of each school day, teachers and children would raise their right hands in the Nazi salute. Religious education classes became instruction in Nazi history, Hitler's life, and Nazi Party philosophy. Students wrote essays based on quotations from Hitler or Nazi literature. Traditional history books gave way to Nazi books that showed "forward-looking emperors" anticipating Hitler's policy of *Lebensraum*. Children sang the Horst Wessel song in school music classes. Through HITLER YOUTH, the Nazis fostered what Hitler called a "violently active, dominating, brutal youth. . . . indifferent to pain"—and well indoctrinated for military service.

On March 16, 1935, Hitler repudiated the Versailles Treaty and inaugurated compulsory military service. At the same time he began an immense rearmament program. Six months later, a Nazi congress at Nuremberg enacted the Law for the Protection of German Blood and German Honor, which made Nazi ANTI-SEMITISM legal. Jews already had been barred from public office, the civil service, and journalism. The Nuremberg Laws, as they became known, stripped Jews of German citizenship and forbade marriage or extramarital relations between Jews and non-Jews. The laws, Hitler said, attempted to "regulate by law a problem that, in the event of repeated failure, would have to be transferred by law to the National Socialist Party for final solution." Those words—FINAL SOLUTION—would become the Nazi code for the killing of 6,000,000 Jews.

The Nazis built a huge stadium in Berlin for the 1936 Olympic Games, halted for three weeks the official campaign against the Jews, and put on a show to convince the world that the Third Reich was a civilized society. But Nazi theories of racial purity nevertheless made headlines because Hitler snubbed the star of the Games, Jesse Owens, a U.S. black athlete who won four gold medals in track events.

Hitler's lust for *Lebensraum* quickly expanded German borders and dramatically increased the German population. The Saar, after a plebiscite, was returned to Germany in 1935, adding 864,000 Germans to the population. The takeover of Austria in 1938 added 7,008,000 more. Next came the Sudetenland (2,945,000), handed over by the MUNICH PACT in 1938. The next year German troops annexed Bohemia and Moravia (6,805,000) from Czechoslovakia and seized Memel (153,000) from Lithuania.

On March 7, 1936, German troops marched into the formerly demilitarized Rhineland, showing the world that Germany no longer lived under the Versailles Treaty. The Luftwaffe by 1935 had more than 1,800 planes. That same year Hitler made membership compulsory in the Hitler Youth, a training organization for military service. Readying his country for war, on Nov. 5, 1937, at a secret meeting with Nazi and military officials, Hitler outlined his plans. *Oberst* Friedrich Hossbach, Hitler's military aide, wrote what became known as the Hossbach Memorandum, a key document in the WAR CRIMES trials at Nuremberg. Hossbach quoted Hitler as saying that "to make secure and to preserve the . . . German racial community," Germany had to go to war.

The German invasion of Poland on Sept. 1, 1939, began the EUROPEAN WAR and continued Germany's expansion. After a swift conquest, Hitler restored to Germany the Polish regions of Posen, Silesia, and the Polish Corridor, 90 miles long and 20 to 25 miles wide. Germany renamed the port Danzig.

After the Polish conquest the German DEATH CAMP system exterminated tens of thousands of Poles; others were moved from annexed lands considered Germany to regions of Poland not made part of Germany. German-speaking peoples by the tens of thousands were transported from Estonia, Latvia, and Lithuania and resettled in the Germanized region of Poland.

Following the conquest of France in June 1940, Germany occupied the northern three-fifths of the country and, designating the remainder "unoccupied," put it under the control of a collaborationist regime, VICHY FRANCE. Germany expelled tens of thousands of French families from Lorraine and Alcace, banned the French language there, incorporated the regions into the Third Reich, and resettled them with Germans.

Hitler realized his vision of a pan-European German empire with conquests of Denmark, Norway, the Netherlands, Belgium, and Luxembourg, along with domination of Hungary, Rumania, Bulgaria, Yugoslavia, and Greece. The invasion of the Soviet Union in June 1941 added still more territory to the Reich.

World War II, however, devastated Germany. More than 4,000,000 German servicemen were killed in the war. Allied bombers turned Germany's major cities and industrial centers to rubble. An estimated 593,000 civilians died in air raids and perhaps 1,000,000 in flight or forced migration when Soviet armies surged eastward across Germany—a total of over 5,000,000 plus many millions crippled and wounded.

The ALLIES, carrying out decisions made at the YALTA CONFERENCE in Feb. 1945 and the POTSDAM CONFERENCE in July 1945, authorized the "transfer to Germany of Germans remaining in Poland, Czechoslovakia, and Hungary." Unknown numbers of German PRISONERS OF WAR died in Soviet and U.S. prisoner-of-war camps. Thousands of other men were taken from Soviet-held territory and put to work in the Soviet Union, never to return. According to historian John Keegan, the German population of Europe east of the Elbe was reduced by death, flight, migration, and expulsion from a peak of 17,000,000 to 2,600,000.

The Allies gave Germany's East Prussian lands to Poland and the Soviet Union and established zones

German-controlled Europe, June 1941.

that put U.S., British, and French occupation forces in what had been western Germany and Soviet forces in eastern Germany, with the Western Allies retaining rights to Berlin, which was in the middle of the Soviet zone.

In May 1949 the Federal Republic of Germany (West Germany) was proclaimed; the Soviets quickly ushered in the German Democratic Republic (East Germany) in Oct. 1949. Divided Berlin became an espionage and propaganda battlefield of the Cold War. East Germany built the Berlin Wall in 1961, and extended a network of barriers the length of the border of the two Germanys to stop the hemorrhage of freedom-seeking East Germans who were fed up with the Communist regime. In 1989, the wall crumbled under the pressure of economic failure in East Germany. In Sept. 1990, the four wartime Allies gave up their rights over the conquered country and, on Oct. 4, 1990, the two Germanys became one, finally ending the long postwar era.

Germany, Air Force

"The bomber will always get through . . . ," Prime Minister Stanley Baldwin told the House of Commons on Nov. 10, 1932. Those words—ably abetted by novelists and movie-makers of the 1930s—struck a chord of fear in the hearts of Europeans. Germany, denied an air force by the Versailles Treaty, clandestinely established an air arm even before HITLER came to power: GLIDER clubs in Germany, cooperative aircraft training and industrial ventures in the Soviet Union, and secret planning staffs in Germany.

The clandestine Luftwaffe was revealed to the world in March 1935. Growth was rapid, as was innovation—especially the development of dive-bombing tactics (personified in the Junkers JU 87 STUKA dive bomber), AIRBORNE operations, and HELICOPTERS. The dive bombers would be a vital component of the BLITZKRIEG operation. Luftwaffe equipment and tactics were practiced in the SPANISH CIVIL WAR, which began in July 1936 when Hitler loaned the Nationalist forces under Gen. FRANCISCO FRANCO a squadron of Junkers Ju 87 transports to fly troops from North Africa to Spain. Soon the Condor Legion—a balanced force of fighters, bombers, and transports—was supporting

the Nationalist forces, and training German airmen in aerial terror tactics.

On the eve of the EUROPEAN WAR the Luftwaffe numbered some 1,500 bombers, 1,100 fighters, and numerous transport and support aircraft. But the major limitation of the Luftwaffe was *Reichsmarschall* HERMANN GÖRING, Commander in Chief of the Air Force and state minister for Air, and second in command to Hitler. Göring failed to make correct decisions concerning training, procurement, and weapons development, and prevented his able subordinates from doing so.

Thus, when Germany attacked Poland on Sept. 1, 1939, plunging Europe into war, the Luftwaffe could boast some of the most capable aircraft aloft, especially the Messerschmitt ME (BF) 109 and ME 110 fighters; while superior aircraft were in development and on the drawing boards. While the Luftwaffe was a completely independent service, it ignored strategic bomber development and concentrated on fighters and light bombers; while these were the ideal weapons for the blitzkrieg campaigns of 1939–1940, the Luftwaffe failed in the BLITZ and the BATTLE OF BRITAIN (1940) and the GERMAN CAMPAIGN IN THE SOVIET UNION (1941–1943). And, with its strength diverted to the EASTERN FRONT, the Luftwaffe was unable to defend the Reich from the Allied STRATEGIC BOMBING efforts. Eventually Germany would have been defeated by the ALLIES, but the shortcomings of the Luftwaffe accelerated the fall.

Göring's dictum "all that flies is mine" also prevented the establishment of a viable naval air arm. Although the German carrier program was of dubious potential (see *GRAF ZEPPELIN*), the shortage of naval reconnaissance aircraft, and the delays in developing effective Navy-Luftwaffe cooperation severely hindered U-BOAT operations. (When Adm. ERICH RAEDER was replaced by *Grossadmiral* KARL DÖNITZ as CinC of the Navy in Jan. 1943, Raeder appealed to Hitler to protect his successor from Göring and the Luftwaffe.)

Airborne forces were part of the Luftwaffe—the troops, GLIDERS, and transport aircraft. Under *Generaloberst* KURT STUDENT, the airborne assaults on the Belgium forts in 1940 and against CRETE the following year, as well as several lesser operations, were the paradigm of successful airborne operations. But the cost of taking on Crete was too great, and although the parachute force continued to expand during the war, it was employed only as ground troops.

As the war turned against Germany and more ground forces were needed, the Luftwaffe assembled its own army—from late 1942 some twenty Luftwaffe field (infantry) divisions were formed as well as the Hermann Göring Division, a PANZER formation. They fought with varying degrees of effectiveness. Also, the German antiaircraft forces (see FLAK) was a massive force during the war, mustering some 1,200,000 men and women at its peak.

As the war reached its dramatic crescendo, Hitler screamed out about the "wonder weapons" that would reverse the course of the war. Many of these were Luftwaffe weapons, some truly revolutionary. These included the Luftwaffe's V-1 BUZZ BOMB, GUIDED MISSILES, JET-PROPELLED AIRCRAFT, and ROCKET-powered fighters. But they came too few in number and too late to affect the war.

Germany, Army

Germany had the best trained, organized, and motivated army in the world when the war began. Its equipment was good, but certainly not the best available with the possible exceptions of small arms and artillery. (Most artillery, however, was horse drawn throughout the war.)

Under the Versailles Treaty the German Army had been limited to 100,000 men, with no realistic reserves. On the eve of the EUROPEAN WAR the Army contained almost 2,000,000 men, including thirty-nine infantry divisions, six PANZER (tank) divisions, three mountain divisions, four "light" divisions, and one CAVALRY brigade. (The light divisions were fast, mobile, semimechanized units—a modern version of the old cavalry concept.) German ANTIAIRCRAFT WEAPONS and AIRBORNE units were part of the Luftwaffe, and not the Army.

This Army teamed with the Luftwaffe for the highly successful BLITZKRIEG of Poland in Sept. 1939. Another forty-four divisions were raised within a few months of the POLISH CAMPAIGN, with the former light divisions converting to panzer units and the lone cavalry brigade being enlarged to a division.

Success followed success, as the Army-Luftwaffe

blitzkrieg struck in the DENMARK AND NORWAY CAMPAIGN (ably assisted by airborne and naval forces), and in the FRANCE AND LOW COUNTRIES CAMPAIGN. Finally stopped at the English Channel, the assault on Britain was delayed and then postponed indefinitely because the Luftwaffe was unable to gain control of the air and the Navy was incapable of undertaking an amphibious operation of that magnitude. (See SEA LION.)

Turning to the east, HITLER first flung the German Army into Greece and Yugoslavia, with relative success, and then undertook his long-planned assault on the Soviet Union. The size and sweep of the German Army at that point can be seen by the commitment of more than 3,000,000 troops (152 divisions) with 3,350 tanks for the invasion of the Soviet Union in June 1941. (See GERMAN CAMPAIGN IN THE SOVIET UNION.) Only the Soviet assault against Germany in 1944–1945 would see more men and tanks put in the field.

Immensely successful at first, Hitler and the Army's senior commanders had failed to understand the complexities and difficulties of such a campaign. By Dec. 1941 the German legions were halted short of their major objectives, and the fall successes turned to winter frustration. Hitler, in Dec. 1941, took personal command of the Army, with the headquarters of the *Wehrmacht* (armed forces) assuming responsibility for the direction of ground operations and with the Army's general staff being subordinate for operations only on the Eastern Front. (The German Army was *das Herr.*)

As the Army became bogged down on the Eastern Front, as reinforcements were needed in North Africa and then Italy, and as the hour approached for the Allied invasion of France, more divisions were needed. (Hitler believed that the British would someday invade Norway, hence a large force was maintained in that country.) A total of some 300 divisions were raised during the war, although many of those were Luftwaffe field divisions, Luftwaffe airborne divisions, the Luftwaffe panzer division "Hermann Göring," and *Volksgrenadier* or "people's" rifle divisions raised by HEINRICH HIMMLER from Sept. 1944 as Soviet armies approached Germany's borders.

As new divisions were formed they were smaller and had fewer tanks and less artillery (while Allied divisions were increasing in firepower). For example, the table of organization for a panzer division in 1940 called for 328 tanks while a panzer division of 1944—if at full strength—had but 159 tanks, albeit more capable ones. There were also numerous separate battalions, with the TIGER TANKS only assigned to such units and not to divisions.

(The lone cavalry division, partially mechanized for the campaign in France, late in 1941 was converted to the 24th Panzer Division; the SS also formed cavalry divisions.)

The German Army generally fought with bravery and valor, but was poorly served by Hitler and many of its generals. Still, HEINZ GUDERIAN, ERWIN ROMMEL, and KURT STUDENT can be listed among the dozen most capable field commanders of all nations fighting in the war.

Germany, Navy

The Versailles Treaty of 1919 precluded Germany from having an effective Navy, limiting it to a few surface ships—the largest to be six 10,000-ton warships armed with 11-inch (280-mm) guns. No submarines or naval air arm was permitted.

Although U-BOATS had almost defeated Britain in 1917, when German naval rearmament began in the 1920s—mostly in secret—the emphasis was on the construction of surface warships, which, it was believed, could be effective in a future war against Poland, France, or the Soviet Union. Conflict against England was not envisioned; indeed, *Grossadmiral* ERICH RAEDER, who became CinC of the German Navy in 1928, even prohibited war games with Britain as the opponent. Secretly, in the 1920s German designers and engineers did begin work on submarines under the cover of a Dutch firm, with German-designed submarines being built in several countries.

In 1929—as permitted by the Versailles Treaty—the keel was laid for the first of a class of 10,000-ton armored ships or *Panzerschiff*, soon called POCKET BATTLESHIPS. Lesser warships were also started, while the clandestine weapon programs were accelerated.

When HITLER took control of the German government in 1933, the naval buildup became more overt, with the construction of small, 250-ton Type I submarines beginning in 1935. That year an Anglo-German naval agreement was signed that replaced the provisions of the Versailles Treaty. The German fleet was now limited to 35 percent of the Royal Navy in all categories except for submarines, where 45 percent was permitted. By giving special notice, Germany could build up to 100 percent in submarines. As a concession to Britain, the agreement stated that in the event of war German submarines would observe the rules of international law: no merchant ships would be sunk without warning.

The first post-Versailles German warships would be the battleships *Gneisenau* and *Scharnhorst*, 31,800-ton ships with nine 11-inch guns. They were faster than any other European battleships, being capable of 32 knots. (While these characteristics were those of battle cruisers, they were generally referred to as battleships.)

Next Germany laid down the largest warships in Europe, the 41,700-ton *BISMARCK* and 42,900-ton *TIRPITZ*, each carrying eight 15-inch (381-mm) guns. Plans were prepared for larger, 56,200-ton battleships. (Only the British HOOD displaced more than the *Bismarck* but not the *Tirpitz*.)

In 1938 Hitler informed Adm. Raeder that Britain should be included as a potential enemy. Raeder and his staff immediately drew up a massive construction plan—known as the Z PLAN—for a fleet that by 1948 would provide Germany with twenty-two battleships, four aircraft carriers, eight pocket battleships and heavy cruisers, and large numbers of cruisers, destroyers, and submarines. In April 1939, Hitler abrogated the naval treaty with Britain that had restricted the size of the German Navy. Still, he told Raeder that "for my political aims I shall not need the Fleet before 1946!"

When the EUROPEAN WAR did begin in Sept. 1939 Germany had in service:

 2 battleships (11-inch guns)
 3 pocket battleships (11-inch guns)
 2 heavy cruisers (8-inch guns)
 6 light cruisers (5.9-inch guns)
34 destroyers and large torpedo boats
56 submarines (of which only 26 were suitable for operation in the Atlantic)

Under construction were the *Bismarck* and *Tirpitz*, the aircraft carrier *GRAF ZEPPELIN*, and several lesser warships, but only thirteen U-boats. Beyond the relatively small number of warships available to confront the British and French fleets, the German Navy was hampered by the fact that the Luftwaffe had control of all German military aircraft. The Navy was allowed to direct the operation of Luftwaffe air reconnaissance over the sea as well as tactical air operations during contract with enemy naval forces. This lack of a naval air arm would continually hamper German surface and U-boat operations; when Adm. KARL DÖNITZ relieved Adm. Raeder as CinC in Jan. 1943, Raeder's one request to Hitler was for him to protect Dönitz from the head of the Luftwaffe, *Reichsmarschall* HERMANN GÖRING.

In Aug. 1939 the German Navy had sent to sea several surface warships and submarines. When the war started, they immediately began to prey on British merchant ships. The BATTLE OF THE ATLANTIC—the campaign against Allied merchant shipping—was the longest and in some respects the most important battle or campaign of the war. While surface raiders were relatively successful in sinking merchant ships, after the loss of the pocket battleship *ADMIRAL GRAF SPEE* on Dec. 17, 1939, Hitler became overly cautious about the use of surface ships when there was a danger of interception by major British warships. Their few sorties into the Atlantic ended in May 1941 when the *Bismarck* was sunk in a series of furious engagements before she could attack any convoys. Subsequently, only U-boats were able to operate in the Atlantic.

The German Navy then concentrated exclusively on a submarine campaign in the Atlantic. Only in the Arctic, operating against the RUSSIAN CONVOYS, were German surface warships a factor for another few months. The sinking of the *Scharnhorst* by British warships off Norway's North Cape on Dec. 26, 1943, marked the end of major German surface ship operations, except in the Baltic.

Hitler periodically interfered with naval operations, although far less than he did with operations of the German Army. But he did demand that the battleships *Gneisenau* and *Scharnhorst* escape from the French port of Brest through the English Channel to reach German ports, resulting in the highly successful CHANNEL DASH.

Most important in the war were the U-boats, which came close, in the spring of 1943, to winning the Battle of the Atlantic. Second only to the undersea craft were German small combatants, especially the torpedo boats, that had major successes in coastal waters, especially in the English Channel and Mediterranean areas. While several successful AMPHIBIOUS LANDINGS were carried out in coastal waters by the German Navy, the Navy was incapable of carrying out the crossing of the English Channel planned for the fall of 1940. (See SEA LION.)

While the *Bismarck* and *Tirpitz* were completed after the start of the war, all other major warship construction halted; the carrier *Graf Zeppelin* was never finished.

When the war ended the German Navy had been thoroughly defeated, although the large numbers of TYPE XXI U-boats about to become operational could have cost the Allies a delay of the war had they gone to sea a few months earlier.

A senior German naval officer and leading postwar historian, Vice Adm. Friedrich Ruge, wrote: "The German Navy continually called attention to . . . shortcomings, but was powerless against the traditional continental outlook of the high authorities. Hence the Navy got no air force of its own, nor did it receive timely support for the expansion of the U-boat arm. It was not until defeat threatened that support was forthcoming, but by then the U-boat arm had been technically outstripped by the enemy, and two irretrievable years had been lost."

The largest warship to survive the war intact was the heavy cruiser *Prinz Eugen;* she was transferred to the United States and then sunk as a target ship in ATOMIC BOMB TESTS at Bikini in July 1946. The other surviving German warships—including U-boats—were allocated to the Allied navies, with the Type XXI submarine having considerable influence on U.S. and Soviet postwar submarine development.

Gerow, Lt. Gen. Leonard T. (1888–1972)

One of the few senior U.S. Army commanders not to graduate from West Point, Gerow (like Gen. GEORGE C. MARSHALL) graduated from Virginia Military Institute. Gerow was head of the Army's War Plans Division when the United States entered the war. In Oct. 1942 Gerow took the 29th Infantry DIVISION to England. He was promoted to command of the Army's V CORPS in July 1943 and led it in the NORMANDY INVASION in June 1944.

Gen. OMAR BRADLEY, commander of the 12th ARMY GROUP, considered Gerow "an outstanding gentleman and soldier—cool, hard-working, intelligent, well-organized, competitive—clearly destined for high rank and responsibility." Other observers were skeptical of Gerow's ability to command a corps. He was seen as meticulous, but detached; some even called him cold and unresponsive with little personality.

Gerow directed his V Corps capably from the hotly contested landings on Omaha Beach through the hedgerow battles and the drive across France, becoming the first American general to enter PARIS. He reacted quickly and decisively to the German Ardennes counteroffensive that produced the battle of the BULGE in Dec. 1944. His V Corps stiffened the northern shoulder of the salient and funnelled the German attack, providing a key early frustration of German plans.

In Jan. 1945 Gerow, as a lieutenant general, was appointed commander of the Fifteenth ARMY, which secured the rear areas created by the rapid final offensive of the EUROPEAN WAR. The Fifteenth Army was also responsible for providing occupation forces in Germany.

Gertrud

Code name for German plan to invade Turkey in the event that Turkey joined the ALLIES.

Gestapo

Acronym for *Geheime Staatspolizei* (secret state police), which ruthlessly annihilated all opposition, real or suspected, to the NAZI party. Founded in 1933 to replace the Prussian secret police, the Gestapo operated throughout Germany and the occupied countries and became a law unto itself. The Gestapo had absolute power over the lives of people believed to be acting against the state. Victims went to CONCENTRATION CAMPS or were tortured and slain. Sometimes, in a sham of legality, the accused were brought before the Gestapo-controlled People's Courts, whose judges were notorious for their unremitting stream of death verdicts.

REINHARD HEYDRICH, the chief deputy of HEINRICH HIMMLER, head of the SS, was the chief of the SD (security service). When Heydrich was additionally appointed chief of the REICH CENTRAL SECURITY OFFICE, the main Nazi security organization in 1939, he included the Gestapo under his command. The Gestapo was the political police, separated from the regular rural constabulary and municipal police. (See also SD.)

Ghormley, Vice Adm. Robert L. (1883–1958)

Principally known for his command of the South Pacific Forces and Area from April 1942 to Oct. 1942, Ghormley was responsible for the overall invasion of GUADALCANAL and Tulagi, which began on Aug. 7, 1942. He was able to deliver his forces to the beaches with remarkably few snags. The Guadalcanal invasion, which preceded the NORTH AFRICA INVASION by three months, was the first major U.S. AMPHIBIOUS LANDING in any combat theater.

After the landings, Ghormley's resources were stretched so thin that any loss was critical. The Japanese raid on the Allied fleet off SAVO ISLAND two days after the landings sank four Allied CRUISERS and infused the entire command echelon with caution. Severe damage to the AIRCRAFT CARRIER *ENTERPRISE* (CV 6) during the later battle of the EASTERN SOLOMONS led Ghormley to order U.S. carriers to remain south of the 10° South parallel unless in pursuit of enemy ships.

By Sept. 1942 Ghormley was tired and anxious. Visitors noted that he seldom left his stuffy cabin on the command ship *Argonne* (AG 31). His caution was degenerating into indecision. Continued losses, including the carrier *WASP* (CV 7) sunk and the carrier *SARATOGA* (CV 3) and BATTLESHIP *North Carolina* (BB 55) damaged by submarine torpedoes, drained him further. (Abscessed teeth may have had a debilitating effect on him as well.)

Adm. CHESTER W. NIMITZ, convinced that Ghormley was "too immersed in detail and not sufficiently bold and aggressive at the right time," replaced him with the more aggressive Vice Adm. WILLIAM F. HALSEY. The change of command came on Oct. 18, following the battle of CAPE ESPERANCE. When Ghormley asked Nimitz why he was being replaced. Nimitz replied with a question: "I had to pick from the whole Navy the man best fitted to handle that situation. Were you that man?" Ghormley replied, "No. If you put it that way, I guess I wasn't."

From Feb. 1943 to late 1944, Ghormley commanded the Hawaiian Sea Frontier and the 14th Naval District. He oversaw the demobilization of German naval units after the war.

GI Bill of Rights

Popular name for the Servicemen's Readjustment Act, which President ROOSEVELT signed on June 22, 1944. The act bestowed a number of benefits, including a free college education, upon veterans of World War II. The law's benefits were granted to any serviceman or servicewoman discharged under conditions other than dishonorable after ninety or more days of service or anyone discharged from an armed service because of an injury or disability incurred in the line of duty.

The act covered three basic kinds of benefits:

Jobs Veterans were given preferential treatment in hiring. Those who could not find jobs got unemployment allowances at $20 per week for up to fifty-two weeks. (Veterans receiving this benefit were called members of the "52-20 Club.") Another law provided for $300 mustering-out pay to those serving sixty or more days.

Housing The law authorized federal support to banks and other lending institutions that loaned money to veterans for housing or the purchase of farms. But housing was in short supply because of a lack of labor and materials. Congress in 1946 passed the Veterans Emergency Housing Act, which created a federal office that gave priority to veterans in allocation of housing materials and spurred the use of new techniques and materials (such as preassembled roof trusses and plastics) and stepped up financing of prefabricated houses.

Education Originally the law authorized fees up to $500 and subsistence allowances for $50 a month for a single veteran and $75 a month for a married veteran; the allotments were later raised to $65 and $90 a month, respectively. About 1,000,-000 veterans were enrolled in institutions of higher education from 1946 to 1948; veterans made up between 40 percent and 50 percent of total enrollment in U.S. colleges and universities.

Of the 15,000,000 veterans ultimately eligible for education and training benefits, about 50 percent participated. So many veterans swamped colleges and universities that they could not provide enough classrooms or housing. Congress reacted in Aug. 1946 by appropriating $75,000,000 to the Federal Works Agency for disassembling and transporting surplus military buildings to colleges, and campuses soon began sprouting QUONSET HUTS and GI barracks.

Under the law, the period of training or education was at least partially determined by length of service, with the maximum duration of benefits set at four years. Education facilities ranged from technical schools and business colleges to universities. Veterans were also given payments for on-the-job apprenticeships and vocational courses.

Robert M. Hutchins, president of the University of Chicago, dourly predicted in Dec. 1944 that the GI Bill would turn colleges and universities "into educational hobo jungles" because veterans, "unable to get work," would find themselves "educational hobos." Education, Hutchins warned, "is not a device for coping with mass unemployment."

In fact, both in the short term and the long term the GI Bill was a phenomenally successful program. A *Fortune* magazine study of the U.S. colleges' class of 1947 showed that veterans made up 70 percent of the class and that, as a whole, the graduates were the most mature, most responsible, and "most self-disciplined group" of college students in history. And widespread unemployment did not haunt the ranks of veterans.

A long-range study by the Joint Economic Committee of Congress showed that by 1987 those who had attended college under the GI Bill of Rights earned an average of $19,000 more a year than veterans who did not attend. Most of the veterans who went to college were the first members of their families ever to do so.

"The total gain in the nation's output of goods and services between 1952 and 1987 resulting from the government's education spending under the GI Bill amounted to almost $148 billion in constant dollars," according to the committee's economist. He estimated that the nation got back between $5 and $12.50 in benefits for each $1 spent for veterans' education.

The bill was to continue in force for five years after the end of the war. But variations of the original bill were extended to apply to veterans of the Korean War and the Vietnam War.

Gibraltar

Called "Gib" or "the Rock," Gibraltar was a major British colony and base on the coast of Spain, overlooking the strait between the Mediterranean Sea and Atlantic Ocean. In 1940 the British evacuated almost 17,000 men and women, fearing a German assault would be carried out through Spain. Only troops and important support personnel remained.

Gibraltar provided an invaluable harbor and air base to the ALLIES in the war; its harbor sheltered merchant ships en route to MALTA and the British battle force (FORCE H) that operated in the western Mediterranean; its airfield was a vital staging base for planes flying to Malta and, in early Nov. 1942, supporting the Anglo-American AMPHIBIOUS LANDINGS in North Africa. For those landings, the Allied Commander in Chief, Gen. DWIGHT D. EISENHOWER, flew from Britain to Gibraltar and used a subterranean command post from Nov. 5 until Nov. 13, when he went on to Algiers. According to Eisenhower, "Britain's Gibraltar made possible the invasion of northwest Africa. Without it the vital air cover would not have been quickly established on the North African airfields."

The Germans were able to keep watch on Gibraltar from Spanish territory, and an Italian CHARIOT unit—MANNED TORPEDOES—was based in a hulk on the Spanish coast and carried out attacks against British shipping in Gibraltar's harbor.

Gibson Girl

Slang for a portable, watertight radio transmitter carried in life rafts of some Allied aircraft. When operated by the turning of a crank it automatically sent a distress signal. The name was derived from the hourglass shape of the transmitter.

Gilbert Islands

West Pacific stepping-stones to the MARSHALL ISLANDS during the U.S. CENTRAL PACIFIC CAMPAIGN. Chosen for the Nov. 1943 AMPHIBIOUS LANDINGS of the Gilbert operation, code-named

Galvanic, were TARAWA, MAKIN ISLAND, and Apamama.

The islands lay south of the JAPANESE MANDATED ISLANDS and athwart the direct Hawaii-Australia air route. The islands were under U.S.-British administration when Japan seized them on Dec. 9, 1941. The Japanese ignored the adjacent, British-administered Ellice Islands. Allied forces later took advantage of this by occupying Funafuti, one of the Ellice Islands, and making it a base for operations against the Gilberts.

Some of the Gilberts and Ellices became the Republic of Kiribati in 1979. Another cluster became Tuvalu.

Gilmore, Comdr. Howard W. (1902–1943)

U.S. SUBMARINE commander who gave his life to help save his ship. Gilmore enlisted in the Navy in 1920 and, after later attending the Naval Academy, served in surface ships from 1926 to 1930. He then trained in submarines and, after peacetime service in several, in 1941 took command of the fleet submarine *Shark* (SS 174).

The day after the Japanese attack on PEARL HARBOR, Gilmore transferred to the new *Growler* (SS 215). During three war patrols he sank several Japanese ships and was twice awarded the Navy Cross. The submarine continued scoring against merchant ships on her four patrols, sinking a 6,000-ton passenger-cargo ship on Jan. 16, 1943, the *Growler*'s sixth confirmed sinking. On the night of Feb. 7, 1943, as the *Growler* was on the surface charging batteries, she sighted a small Japanese ship. The target suddenly changed course and, too late to take evasive action, the *Growler* rammed the 900-ton supply ship.

According to official Navy reports: "In the terrific fire of the sinking gunboat's [*sic*] heavy machine guns, Comdr. Gilmore calmly gave the order to clear the [submarine's] bridge, and refusing safety for himself, remained on deck while the men preceded him below. Struck down by the fusillade of bullets and having done his utmost against the enemy, in his final living moments Comdr. Gilmore gave his last order to the Officer of the Deck, 'Take her down!'" An officer and a lookout were also killed by the enemy gunfire.

The *Growler* dived and, although severely damaged, escaped the area and returned to port. Gilmore was posthumously awarded the MEDAL OF HONOR, the first U.S. submariner to receive the nation's highest award.

Giraud, Gen. Henri-Honoré (1879–1949)

French Army general who for a time shared leadership of the FREE FRENCH with Gen. CHARLES DE GAULLE. In June 1940, while fighting German invaders during the FRANCE AND LOW COUNTRIES CAMPAIGN, Giraud was captured and imprisoned. In April 1942, Giraud escaped from his prison (as he had done as a younger man in World War I) and made his way to VICHY FRANCE, where he promised to support the collaborationist regime of Marshal PHILIPPE PÉTAIN. But Giraud immediately began trying to organize a French anti-German army, looking primarily to Americans for assistance. He believed that he should be supreme commander of any offensive to liberate France, commenting, "We don't want the Americans to free us; we want them to help us free ourselves. . . ."

The Anglo-American ALLIES extracted him from France by submarine and flying boat in Nov. 1942, just before the NORTH AFRICA INVASION, which stunned Giraud. Taken to GIBRALTAR to meet with Gen. DWIGHT D. EISENHOWER, Giraud expected to be given supreme command of the North Africa landing and a subsequent invasion of southern France.

Eisenhower, overall commander of the invasion, appointed Giraud the Commander in Chief of French forces in French North Africa, but most of his fellow generals and admirals, as Vichy officers, had little use for him. In "a terrific blow to our expectations," Eisenhower later wrote, Giraud "was completely ignored."

For civil administration of French North Africa, the Allies relied on Adm. JEAN FRANÇOIS DARLAN. After Darlan's ASSASSINATION in Dec. 1942, Giraud was briefly appointed High Commissioner. Although he gave ambiguous support to Vichy France, he and French Gen. Charles de Gaulle were co-presidents of the French National Committee. Giraud, unable to compete with de Gaulle's growing prestige, resigned in Nov. 1943. (During this time Giraud's daughter and her four children were captured by the Germans in Tunisia and spirited off to Germany; his daughter died there in 1944.)

Gisela

Code name for German plan for the occupation of Spain and Portugal, 1942.

Gladiator

British biplane fighter flown by both the RAF and Royal Navy. While few were operational when the EUROPEAN WAR began, at the time twelve Sea Gladiators were flown by one of the two British carriers that embarked fighters (the other carriers carried only SWORDFISH torpedo bombers).

One squadron of naval Sea Gladiators (and one of FULMAR fighters), based in Scotland, fought with the RAF in the BATTLE OF BRITAIN. Four Sea Gladiators on loan to the RAF gained immortality as the defenders of MALTA, three being named "Faith," "Hope," and "Charity."

The Gloster-built Gladiator was the last biplane fighter to serve with the RAF. It began as a private venture and first flew in Sept. 1934. Production was ordered the following year, with a total of 311 ordered for the two British services plus 216 ordered for other countries, including China and Finland. A single-seat fighter, the Gladiator was highly maneuverable and easy to fly. It had a top speed of 253 mph and was armed with four .303-cal. machine guns.

Glen

This was the only Japanese aircraft to drop BOMBS on the U.S. mainland during the war. The E14Y1 floatplane—given the Allied code name Glen—was intended from the outset for operations from submarines.

Delivered to the fleet late in the summer of 1941, the plane flew its first operational sortie on Dec. 17, 1941, when a Glen launched from the submarine I-7 flew a reconnaissance mission over PEARL HARBOR, ten days after the Japanese air attack. In Aug. 1942 the submarine I-25 arrived off Cape Blanco, Ore. In darkness, the submarine surfaced and the Glen was extracted from the submarine's hangar and assembled. A pair of 167½-pound incendiary bombs were attached to wing racks and Warrant Flying Officer Nobuo Fujita and Petty Officer Shoji

Okuda climbed into the cockpit and were catapulted into the dawn sky. The floatplane flew inland some 50 miles and the fliers released the two fire-bombs on a forest area. The plane returned to the submarine and came down safely alongside. A second fire-bombing mission was also flown. (After attacking several U.S. ships, on Oct. 11 the *I-25* sank the Soviet submarine *L-16,* believing her to be an American undersea craft.)

The Glen was also flown from submarines in reconnaissance missions over the ALEUTIANS and MADAGASCAR, and over coastal areas of Africa, Australia, and New Zealand. One aircraft was aboard the submarine *I-8* when it visited Germany during the war.

The aircraft, designed at the Yokosuka naval arsenal, first flew in 1940. It had a welded-steel tube fuselage covered forward with light metal and aft with fabric and metal on the underside. The low-wing monoplane had large, twin floats. The wings and floats were fitted after the aircraft was taken out of the hangar. The plane could only be operated with smooth seas.

The aircraft had a maximum speed of 153 mph and was credited with a range of 550 miles. It would normally carry two 110-pound bombs and had a single 7.7-mm machine gun in the rear cockpit for self-defense. A two-man crew flew the aircraft.

Gliders

Unpowered, gliding aircraft used in several major AIRBORNE operations. Gliders were used in the 1920s when Germany, forbidden by the Versailles Treaty to have an air force, established "gliding clubs" as a means of allowing former military pilots to "keep their hand in" flying and to begin training new pilots. From this base of enthusiasm came an interest in scientific and military gliders in Germany. Military gliders had advantages over parachute landings because an entire SQUAD or PLATOON could be landed together, along with small vehicles and artillery ready to use.

The first significant military glider effort was undertaken by the *Deutsches Forschungsinstitut für Segelflug* (DFS), an affiliate of the Rhoen Research Institute. This was the DFS 230, a small troop-carrying glider (nine troops) that began flight tests in late 1937. During the fall of 1938 a glider-borne COM-MANDO force was formed and DFS 230 production was increased, with more than 1,500 of the gliders being produced by 1943. At the outset of the FRANCE AND LOW COUNTRIES CAMPAIGN in May 1940 the Germans used several DFS 230s to capture Fort Eben Emael on the Belgian border.

German emphasis on airborne forces (see KURT STUDENT) led to large numbers of the DFS 230 being built as well as the larger Gotha GO 242 (twenty-one troops) along with some 200 of the leviathan Messerschmitt ME 321 *GIGANT.* One of the largest aircraft of the war, the Me 321 was primarily a cargo glider (or 130 troops) that was envisioned for the airborne assault during the invasion of Britain (see SEA LION) after the German conquest of the Soviet Union, i.e., in 1942–1943.

The German invasion of CRETE in 1941 was one of the most impressive uses of airborne forces during the war, but also one of the most costly. After Crete gliders were used by the Germans primarily for carrying cargo and troops, especially to support besieged "pockets" in the Soviet Union. The DFS 230 was also used in the dramatic removal of BENITO MUSSOLINI from Gran Sasso on Sept. 16, 1944.

The Germans considered gliders as combat aircraft and they were often armed with defensive machine guns, the only armed gliders in the world (with a few possible Soviet exceptions). The DFS 230 was usually fitted with one gun, the Me 321 two or more, and the Go 242 up to eight.

The U.S. Army Air Forces paid little attention to gliders until the Germans demonstrated their effectiveness in 1940–1941 airborne assaults. The AAF began studying glider designs in February 1941, followed by a competition for cargo- and troop-carrying gliders resulting in the mass production of the Waco-designed CG-4A (thirteen troops) and CG-13 (thirty troops), with more than 14,000 of these gliders being produced. At one point the U.S. Army planned to produce 36,000 gliders, including the larger CG-16 that could carry two 105-mm howitzers or forty-two troops.

The U.S. Army employed gliders for the first time in the 1943 assault on SICILY, followed by their massive employment in the NORMANDY INVASION and Operation MARKET-GARDEN of 1944 and the RHINE CROSSINGS of 1945. They were also used extensively in the ALLIED CHINA-BURMA-INDIA CAMPAIGN.

(The U.S. Marine Corps planned a glider force but, like Marine paratroopers, the concept was not pursued because of the vast distances between bases and objectives in the Pacific, and the shortage of transport aircraft.)

The British also employed gliders for airborne assault, with the Airspeed-designed HORSA (twenty-five troops) being the workhorse of the glider force. That glider was also flown by the AAF.

The Soviet Union also used gliders during the war, primarily to supply GUERRILLA operations behind German lines. But while the Soviet Union had developed a massive airborne assault capability in the 1930s, it was not employed as a major force in the war. The Soviets did design a glider-bomber, the PB *(Planer Bombardirovshchik),* that could carry supply containers or bombs. But that aircraft was not produced.

The Japanese initiated glider development in 1937 but few were produced except possibly for the Ku-8, a cargo glider (or eighteen troops) based on a transport aircraft with engines removed. Some reports cite production of some 700 of the improved Ku-8-II model, but little is known of their operational use. Several were found on Luzon when the U.S. Army landed there in 1944.

GNAT

Allied acronym for German Naval Acoustic Torpedo. The GNAT was an advanced torpedo used by U-BOATS against Allied antisubmarine ships. The acoustic-homing torpedo, called *Zaunkönig* (Wren) and designated T5 by the German Navy, had acoustic guidance to search out the cavitation noises made by a ship's propellers. The GNAT, developed specifically for submarine use against CONVOY escort ships, was referred to as an "anti-DESTROYER" torpedo.

The first use of the GNAT was on Sept. 20, 1943, when U-boats attacking convoy ON 202 damaged a frigate with an acoustic torpedo, requiring the ship to be taken in tow. In three days the GNATs were used to sink a destroyer, frigate, and CORVETTE, and cause major damage to two other escort ships. The three-day action involved two adjacent convoys with a total of sixty-nine merchant

ships, which were attacked by twenty-one U-boats; six merchant ships and three U-boats were sunk.

The British had learned of GNAT development prior to its use through PRISONER OF WAR interrogations and ULTRA. Forewarned, the British quickly developed the FOXER devices to decoy the torpedoes away from warships. These were put into service only eighteen days after the convoy action described above. The Foxers totally defeated the acoustic torpedoes. Several hundred GNATs were used by German submarines.

Go 242

German twin-boom GLIDER developed by the Gotha firm as a result of success with the DFS 230 in the German blitzkrieg in the May 1940 invasion of FRANCE AND THE LOW COUNTRIES. The Go 242 was a highly original concept, providing for an uninterrupted cargo hold with direct access for loading near ground level by having a high-wing configuration with twin tail booms. The glider could carry twenty-one armed troops or cargo in addition to the two-man crew. The first Go 242 was accepted by the Luftwaffe in Aug. 1941, and a total of 1,528 were produced. The gliders were used extensively on the EASTERN FRONT.

The GO 244 was a powered version of the glider, with 133 of the unpowered versions being converted to that configuration (see below).

Go 244

Powered version of the German GO 242 GLIDER. Twin radial engines were easily mounted on the wing of the glider model, at the head of the twin tail booms (a configuration similar to postwar cargo aircraft, including the U.S. C-82 Packet and C-119 Flying Boxcar). Shortcomings of the aircraft on the EASTERN FRONT led to only forty-one powered aircraft being built, in addition to 133 glider conversions, before production facilities reverted to the glider version.

Goblet

Code name for planned Allied invasion of Cotrone, Italy.

Goebbels, Joseph (1897–1945)

Chief of NAZI Party PROPAGANDA. The image-maker of Nazism, Goebbels focused all German media on the needs of ADOLF HITLER and the THIRD REICH. A slight, pale man who limped, Goebbels had a doctorate in literature from Heidelberg and wrote plays and poetry before switching to politics. He joined the Nazi Party in 1925 and soon began writing the party's leaflets and other propaganda documents.

In 1926 Hitler made him *Gauleiter* (district leader) in BERLIN. He quickly displayed his talent for orchestrating demonstrations so that they turned into brawls that pitted Communists against Nazis or riots that sent party thugs rampaging against JEWS.

As Hitler's political manager, he dazzled German voters with a multimedia campaign, employing loudspeaker trucks, plastering streets with posters, distributing documentary films, and staging rallies of the faithful, who massed amid spectacular displays of the party's SWASTIKA emblem.

In March 1933, a few weeks after he became chancellor, Hitler made Goebbels minister of Propaganda and Public Enlightenment with the task of providing the "spiritual direction of the nation." Goebbels established the Reich Chamber of Culture, the fountainhead of all that the Nazis wanted Germans to see, hear, and know. Every library, every theater was under the control of Goebbels.

He shut down all non-Nazi publications and established hundreds of Nazi journals and newspapers. One of his decrees licensed journalists and made all editors party officials responsible for the party line in their publications. With loudspeakers and radios he wired Germany for one voice: the party's. He put loudspeakers on street corners and in factories and public places and distributed cheap radios, unable to receive foreign broadcasts. Germany led the world in radios per household.

He took over the German film industry, which turned out propaganda in the form of feature films, documentaries, and NEWSREELS filmed by German Army cameramen. As a fringe benefit, he bedded starlets and carried on numerous affairs. His romance with Lida Baarova, a Czech film star, displeased Hitler nearly as much as Frau Goebbels, who walked out on him, taking their children with her. Hitler ended the affair by having the actress banished from Germany, and Frau Goebbels went back to Goebbels.

Like his rival HERMANN GÖRING, Goebbels lived lavishly. But his wife Magda and their children maintained a relatively simple life, reflecting the propaganda chief's image of a basic German family.

When the EUROPEAN WAR began, Goebbels stepped up his propaganda campaign. "During a war," he said, "news should be given out for instruction rather than for information." He set up a vast organization to spread Nazi propaganda beyond Germany's borders, aiming broadcasts at specific countries. The star of the German broadcasts to England was WILLIAM JOYCE, a British traitor derided by his listeners as "Lord Haw-Haw."

Goebbels' fanatic support of Hitler was rewarded in 1944 when, after the JULY 20 PLOT on Hitler's life, Goebbels was made Reich Trustee for TOTAL WAR. He carried the doctrine of total war into the *FÜHRERBUNKER* in Hitler's last days, endorsing Hitler's desire for all of Germany to go down with him. If Hitler and Goebbels had had their way, in a final fulfillment of the SCORCHED EARTH POLICY, Germany would have been destroyed.

Huddled with Hitler in the *Führerbunker,* Goebbels read to him from one of Hitler's favorite books, Carlyle's *Frederick the Great,* and gave Hitler adoration at a time when others were plotting to end the war and get out of the bunker. Like her husband, Magda Goebbels saw the bunker as the fitting place for the saga of Nazism to end. She brought her six children into the bunker to live and die with their father and their führer.

Just before the end Magda tearfully spoke to HANNA REITSCH, an aviatrix who was about to leave. "My dear Hanna," she said, "when the end comes you must help me if I become weak about the children. . . . They belong to the Third Reich and to the Führer, and if these two cease to exist there can be no further place for them."

But when Reitsch flew out of Berlin and the end came there was no one to help Magda kill her children—Hela 12, Hilda, 11, Helmut 9, Holda, 7, Hedda, 5, and Heide, 3. On May 1, 1945, she had a dentist inject the children with morphine. As they fell into sleep, she placed potassium cyanide in each child's mouth. Then she and her husband walked up to the Chancellery garden, where the bodies of Hitler and his bride Eva had burned the day before. Goebbels ordered an SS orderly to shoot them. He killed them with shots to the backs of their heads. Their bodies were doused with gasoline and set afire. That night, the *Führerbunker* was burned and became a crematorium for the Goebbels children.

Goetz von Berlichingen

German code name for Luftwaffe attacks against Soviet naval forces at LENINGRAD, April 1942.

Gold (Operation)

Allied code name for Asnelles beach at the NORMANDY INVASION.

Gold

As the German BLITZKREIG overran France in May–June 1940, President ROOSEVELT directed the U.S. Navy CRUISER *Vincennes* (CA 44) on a secret mission to Morocco, where French officials had assembled ingots of gold from banks in southern and southwestern France. The *Vincennes,* reportedly selected by the president because of her French name, loaded $252,000,000 worth of French gold, and carried it to New York City. The gold was subsequently taken to the U.S. Gold Bullion Depository at Fort Knox, Ky., where it spent the war.

The *Vincennes* mission illustrates the flight of gold, both the gold of nations and the gold of individuals, from European war zones to neutral— and safe—United States. As Germany marched across Europe, so did gold, fleeing beyond the conqueror's grasp.

The flight began in the early 1930s, when threats of war, along with a reduction in the official valuation of the dollar, brought nearly $4 billion in gold into the United States. Beginning in Sept. and Oct. 1938, spurred by the MUNICH PACT, European gold cascaded into U.S. vaults. By April 1939, "Munich" gold worth $1.6 billion had reached the United States; by 1945, the total reached $18.7 billion. The United States held 60 percent of all the gold reserves in the world.

As Poland was being overrun, Polish gold reserves went from Poland through Rumania to a British ship in Istanbul. Other Polish gold remained for the war in the National Bank of Rumania.

Facing German invasion themselves, British of-ficials chose Canada as the safe place for British gold holdings. Gold and securities from the Bank of England and other British banks were dispatched to Canada in 1940 on board the cruiser *Emerald*. Similarly, in Dec. 1941 a U.S. Navy ammunition ship slipped through the Japanese blockade of CORREGIDOR in the Philippines carrying 2,925 pounds of Filipino gold to the United States.

In late Jan. 1942, with the situation in the Philippines becoming desperate, the U.S. SUBMARINE *Trout* (SS 202) arrived at Corregidor with 3,500 rounds of 3-inch (76-mm) antiaircraft ammunition. Needing ballast before escaping back to sea, in addition to several TORPEDOES, the *Trout* took on 2 tons of gold bars and 18 tons of silver pesos, plus stacks of negotiable securities.

Gold also moved in wartime because it was stolen by Germany and by Japan. The Swiss National Bank purchased German stolen gold during the war, ignoring its possible origin in conquered countries' treasuries. Hungary after the war claimed 30 tons of gold had been taken by Germany. Albania made similar claims. Japan took gold from all of the places it conquered and toward the end of the war tried to get some gold out of the country. (See also *AWA MARU.*)

NAZI-looted gold was found in several caches by Allied armies at the end of the war, but its postwar restoration was entangled in hundreds of competing claims. Not until 1981 did the United States and Czechoslovakia settle on claims growing out of Czech gold that was looted by Germany. The claims were complicated by attempts by U.S. nationals to receive compensation for property that Czechoslovakia confiscated between 1945 and 1981.

Beginning with the BRETTON WOODS CONFERENCE in July 1944, gold invariably played a role in plans for regulating and stabilizing the international monetary system after the war. Gold was seen both as a currency standard and as a reserve backing up the currencies of capitalist countries, particularly the United States, whose dollar was fully convertible to gold. (Rapid postwar recovery, gold's increasing commercial use, and private acquisition of gold reduced the effectiveness of the gold-based monetary system and it was phased out beginning in the early 1970s.)

Gold, Harry (1910-1972)

American chemist and Ethel Rosenberg's brother who conspired with Soviet atomic spy KLAUS FUCHS. Gold, born Heinrich Goldodnitsky in Switzerland, moved with his family to the United States in 1914. He became a U.S. citizen in 1922. Gold studied chemical engineering at the University of Pennsylvania and also attended Drexel Institute of Technology and Xavier University.

He worked for Soviet intelligence, apparently from 1934 to 1945. Gold passed to the Soviets secret data on the U.S. ATOMIC BOMB program received from British scientist Klaus Fuchs and from DAVID GREENGLASS, a machinist at the LOS ALAMOS atomic laboratory. Gold was dropped by Soviets for a breach in security in 1946. He was arrested May 22, 1950, on espionage charges. He confessed to U.S. officials and named Greenglass, Morton Sobell, and JULIUS AND ETHEL ROSENBERG, who were all arrested. Gold received a thirty-year prison sentence on Dec. 9, 1950. He was released on parole in 1965.

Gold's code name was "Raymond." He was awarded the Order of the Red Star by the Soviet Union.

Goldflake

Code name for movement of Canadian I Corps from Italy to Western Europe.

Goliath

(1) Code name for German radio station that transmitted to U-BOATS; (2) German "miniature" TANK that carried 150 pounds of high explosives that could be steered and detonated by remote control (cable) to destroy obstacles.

Gomorrah

Code name for sustained Allied bombing attack against HAMBURG, July 1943.

Goodtime

Code word for landing on the Treasury Islands in the SOLOMONS by the 8th New Zealand BRIGADE, Oct. 1943.

Goodwood

Code name for British armored offensive east of Caen, July 1944; this was a preliminary to Operation Cobra.

Gooseberry

Code name for the ARTIFICIAL HARBORS constructed for the NORMANDY INVASION to protect Allied shipping; part of the Mulberry system.

Göring, *Reichsmarschall* Hermann (1893-1946)

A fighter ACE in World War I, with a total of twenty-two kills, Göring was an early supporter of HITLER, working in Munich as head of the SA. He was at Hitler's side in the abortive 1923 "beer hall putsch" and was wounded in the fusillade when police fired into the NAZI mob.

He was not arrested with Hitler and other Nazis because, with the aid of his wife, Göring got out of Munich and to Austria, where he was hospitalized. Morphine given to him at that time introduced him to drugs, and he became an addict. Although confinement to a mental institution detoxified him in 1926, he later used paracodeine, a morphine derivative, and seesawed between addiction and withdrawal. He went into self-exile in Italy until 1927, when, taking advantage of an amnesty, he returned to Germany and resumed a career in aviation.

A close political ally of Hitler, Göring was smoother and more cultured than typical Nazis. He had an easy, cordial way with industrialists and financiers who wanted to support Hitler but were apprehensive about the Nazis' thuggish ways. Göring, exploiting his war-hero fame and business contacts, was a BERLIN representative for the Bavarian Motor Works (BMW); when he ran for the Reichstag national legislature in 1928, he was simultaneously serving as a lobbyist for Lufthansa airline.

Göring represented Bavaria, as did his perennial political rival, JOSEPH GOEBBELS, and in 1932 was elected president of the Reichstag. When Hitler became chancellor in 1933, he made Göring commissioner for aviation and the minister of the interior for Prussia. Göring transformed Prussia into a miniature version of the Germany soon to come. The political police became the *Geheime Staatspolizei* (secret state police), quickly known by the acronym GESTAPO. He set up auxiliary police organizations under SS and SA men and built CONCENTRATION CAMPS for enemies of the state.

Göring later handed the concentration camps and Gestapo over to HEINRICH HIMMLER. Death and torture were too coarse and nasty for Göring's regal style. When Hitler and the Nazi Party needed him to plot the downfall of others, however, he proved himself as vicious as the lowliest SA thug. He backed Hitler's extermination of JEWS. The WANNSEE CONFERENCE on the FINAL SOLUTION was instigated by an order from Göring to REINHARD HEYDRICH, head of the REICH CENTRAL SECURITY OFFICE. He was an avid supporter of Nazi racial policy, once referring to Czechs as a "vile race of dwarfs without any culture."

His culture included countless works of art looted from the museums and private collections of conquered countries. He lived in lavish elegance, choosing between two castles, a richly appointed apartment in Berlin, a private train, and the country estate he named Karinhall after his wife, who had died in 1931. On the 100,000 acres of Karinhall he assumed the role of Master of the German Hunt. For every role he had an extravagant costume, usually a uniform heavily laden with medals and decorations. When he became *Reichsmarschall* in 1940, he created a coat of arms showing a mailed fist clutching a club. A more realistic image would have been a chubby, ring-encrusted fist gripping a champagne goblet.

Göring married an actress, Emmy Sonnemann, in 1935. They had one child, Edda, born in 1938. Göring, entertaining diplomats and visiting celebrities, was the social front of the Nazi Party in the prewar years. He cultivated friendships with the Duke of Windsor and other British notables and showed off Germany's growing air power to CHARLES LINDBERGH, the U.S. air hero who became a leading isolationist and supporter of the AMERICAN FIRST COMMITTEE.

Because of the restrictions of the Versailles Treaty, Germany was not allowed to have a military air force. Under the cover of commissioner for aviation, Göring secretly began the Luftwaffe. His work in creating Nazi air power was well hidden. Some diplomats even thought him to be an advocate of

peace. In fact, he was an advocate of a powerful THIRD REICH that would dominate Europe by force of arms.

Göring believed that Germany would not be ready for war at least until 1942 and tried to persuade Hitler to hold back until Germany was better prepared. Although he might whisper of hopes of peace to susceptible diplomats, Göring yearned for war to prove the value of his Luftwaffe.

He gloated over the success of the Luftwaffe as part of the BLITZKRIEG that launched the POLISH CAMPAIGN and rode high with the world's largest air force until the BATTLE OF BRITAIN, STALINGRAD, and THOUSAND-PLANE RAIDS proved the Luftwaffe's inadequacies. As the Luftwaffe's performance slipped so did Göring's relationship with Hitler.

In April 1945, as Germany's defeat seemed inevitable to all but Hitler and a handful of sycophants, Göring saw himself eclipsed by Goebbels and others and sulked in Bavaria while Hitler and Goebbels huddled in the *FÜHRERBUNKER* in doomed Berlin. In spite of this, Göring was, officially at least, Hitler's successor.

In the bunker, however, Hitler, preparing for his suicide, wrote a last will and "Political Testament" in which he expelled Göring from the Nazi Party and stripped him of all rights, including the 1941 order that named him as successor. SS chief Heinrich Himmler received the same fate, for the same reasons: for "disloyalty to me," for "secretly negotiating with the enemy without my knowledge and against my will," and for "illegally attempting to seize control of the State." (See SURRENDER, GERMANY.)

Hitler was right. Göring had been planning to make peace. On April 23, on the basis of a radio message from Bormann and eyewitness accounts of Hitler's worsening mental condition, Göring had sent a telegram to Hitler (intercepted by ULTRA). In it he asked if he should take over the Reich if Hitler were unable to act. Outraged, Hitler, from a Berlin already surrounded by Soviet forces, ordered Göring arrested for TREASON.

Shortly later Göring was taken into custody by U.S. soldiers and indicted for WAR CRIMES. At his trial in Nuremberg he strutted and shouted, defending Hitler, playing his last role—Nazi martyr. He was found guilty of conspiracy to wage war, crimes against peace, war crimes, and crimes against humanity. He was sentenced to death. On Oct. 15, 1946, two hours before he was to be taken to the gallows, he swallowed a vial of potassium cyanide he had kept hidden from his guards. The other ten condemned were hanged on schedule. Göring's body was taken with the others to DACHAU, where the bodies were cremated in the concentration camp's crematorium. The ashes were dumped into a brook in Munich.

Gorshkov, Vice Adm. Sergei G. (1910–1988)

Soviet commander of naval flotillas on the Sea of Azov and Danube River. When Germany invaded the Soviet Union in June 1941, Gorshkov was a captain commanding a cruiser division in the Black Sea. After leading cruiser attacks against the coast of Rumania, Gorshkov was promoted to rear admiral and given command of the flotilla of small craft on the enclosed Sea of Azov, which helped support Red Army operations as German forces advanced into the region. In Nov. 1942, after the Germans gained control of the sea's coastlines, the flotilla was abolished.

Gorshkov then served as naval deputy for the Soviet 47th Army fighting in the Novorossisk area. During this period he served with several future Soviet defense leaders and met LEONID BREZHNEV and NIKITA KHRUSHCHEV, both political officers. When the Soviet armies went on the offensive and again reached the Sea of Azov, Gorshkov again became commander of the Azov flotilla in 1943–1944; as Soviet forces moved westward, in 1944 he established the Danube River flotilla. Here, too, he successfully supported ground operations and worked closely with major Soviet military commanders.

In late 1944 he was promoted to vice admiral and at the end of the year was given command of an *eskadra* (squadron) in the Black Sea Fleet. After the war Gorshkov went on to command the Black Sea Fleet and then served an unprecedented twenty-nine years as Commander in Chief of the Soviet Navy and a deputy minister of defense (1955–1985).

Gotenkopf (Goth's Head)

German code name for the bridgehead on the Taman Peninsula, on the eastern side of the Kerch Strait in the USSR, 1943.

Gothic Line

A German defense line across Italy north of Florence from Pisa on the Ligurian Sea to Pesaro on the Adriatic Sea. It was finally cracked in Sept. 1944 by U.S. and British armies. The line, built early in 1944, was a deep system of dug-in defenses and fortified towns, including Leghorn and Siena to the southeast. The French troops assigned to capture Siena were instructed not to damage the walled town, a shrine of medieval art. Siena was also a rallying point for Italian GUERRILLAS, who aided the ALLIES as fighting continued in the north.

Goumiers

French infantrymen from Morocco. The colonial soldiers served in French-led units called *Goums*. They served in Italy and in the liberation of France.

Grace

This large carrier-based attack plane was delivered to the Japanese Navy too late and in numbers too few to be effective. Designated B7A *Ryusei* (Shooting Star) by the Japanese, it was given the Allied code name Grace. The B7A was one of the first aircraft that could carry out level, dive-bombing, and TORPEDO attacks. It was also unusual for a Japanese carrier aircraft in having an internal BOMB bay, which could accommodate two 551-pound bombs. A 1,764-pound aerial torpedo or additional bombs could be carried externally.

The B7A flight test, which began in May 1942, was plagued with engine problems. A change of engine was required for the aircraft and hence production lagged. The aircraft reached fleet squadrons late in 1944, with only 114 produced through Aug. 1945. None is known to have operated from aircraft carriers.

The low-wing aircraft had a large radial engine, and a long glazed-cover cockpit. The main landing gear, with "spats" coverings, was fully retractable and the wings folded for carrier stowage.

The aircraft was capable of a speed of 352 mph

and was to have a combat range of 1,150 miles, with a search range of 1,900 miles. Defense armament consisted of two wing-mounted 20-mm cannon and a flexible 13-mm machine gun in the rear cockpit. The B7A had a two-man crew.

Graf Spee,

see *ADMIRAL GRAF SPEE.*

Graf Zeppelin (Airship)

German passenger airship, employed in 1939 for electronic surveillance of British RADAR installations. The *Graf Zeppelin* was completed in 1928 and was employed in commercial passenger service for eleven years before being retired.

She was placed in service for the Luftwaffe in the spring of 1939 to measure the wavelength of British radars and to pinpoint the location of the radar sites—what were known as "ferret" missions. The airship was used because existing airplanes lacked the endurance and space for electronic equipment necessary for such work.

Based at Frankfurt, Germany, the *Graf Zeppelin* made the first surveillance flight in late May 1939. However, no useful data were acquired because of problems with the equipment in the airship. The second flight, in early Aug. 1939, also failed to acquire useful information.

While the *Graf Zeppelin* was traced by British radar on her first flight, she escaped unnoticed on the second. But the airship was sighted visually and after the LONDON *Daily Telegraph* newspaper revealed the flight, the German government denied that the aircraft had left Germany or approached the coast of England. After the outbreak of the EUROPEAN WAR, in 1940 the *Graf Zeppelin* was dismantled.

The *Graf Zeppelin* was a rigid airship, launched in 1928. Her first long-range flight was across the Atlantic to the United States, a flight of 112 hours. The airship subsequently flew around the world in 1929, a journey—with numerous stops and extensive flights over Siberia—that took just over twenty-one days (with seven days spent at ports). That same year the craft surveyed the Arctic and in 1930 pioneered regular German airship service to South America.

The airship was 775 feet long, 100 feet in diameter, and five engines could drive her at a maximum speed of 80 mph. In commercial service the *Graf Zeppelin* could carry twenty passengers in relative luxury, with double cabins, a large saloon that served as dining room and lounge, and an excellent catering staff.

Graf Zeppelin (Ship)

German aircraft carrier. The *Graf Zeppelin* was one of four aircraft carriers that the German Navy intended to construct under the Z PLAN of 1938. The *Graf Zeppelin* was laid down at Kiel on Dec. 28, 1936, with HITLER attending the ship's launching on Dec. 8, 1938. The carrier's name honored the famous airship designer of World War I. (His daughter, Countess Hella von Brandenstein-Zeppelin, christened the ship.)

In July of 1939 the German naval staff expected the *Graf Zeppelin* to be completed by mid-1940 and be ready for service with her aircraft squadrons before the end of 1941. However, in April 1940 construction of the ship was halted after the Commander in Chief of the German Navy recorded, "The Führer is of the opinion that, considering the probable developments in aircraft carriers, carriers with planes with internal combustion engines will not be usable anymore in this war."

Hitler changed his mind in the spring of 1942 (after the success of Japanese carriers in the Pacific); the ship could not be completed until late 1943. There was no resumption of work and the ship was never completed; her 5.9-inch (150-mm) guns were removed for use as shore batteries in Norway, her galley equipment taken out for use at a submarine school, and other gear was installed in other ships. Soviet troops took possession of the carrier, in the Oder River, in early May 1945. Reportedly, the carrier was loaded with machinery and other booty to be towed across the Baltic Sea to LENINGRAD. However, she sank, possibly in a storm, while under tow in 1947.

The *Graf Zeppelin* was to have had a standard displacement of 23,200 tons and was 862¾ feet long. Steam turbines were to drive the ship at 33.8 knots. Her defensive armament was to consist of sixteen 5.9-inch guns plus numerous antiaircraft guns. (At one point consideration was given to installing 8-inch guns.) The ship was to operate some forty aircraft—ME 109 fighters and JU 87 *STUKA* dive bombers.

Material for a second carrier was assembled at Kiel, but she was never laid down. The German Navy also began the conversion of several merchant ships and the heavy cruiser *Seydlitz* to aircraft carriers, but none was finished when the war ended.

Grand Slam Bomb

The largest conventional BOMB used in the war. The 22,000-pound Grand Slam and the smaller, 12,000-pound TALLBOY BOMB were so-called "earthquake bombs," designed by Barnes Wallis of Vickers-Armstrong (Aircraft) to destroy subterranean targets such as bridge and viaduct foundations, with the bombs creating shock waves. For example, a miss of 60 feet was sufficient to create a shock wave to collapse a railroad bridge at Bad Oeynhausen in Germany. They were less successful against SUBMARINE PENS, which had 23-foot reinforced concrete roofs, although some successes were achieved by shock waves.

Grand Slam bombs were manufactured in both the United States and Britain, although they could be carried only by modified British LANCASTER four-engine bombers. (The Grand Slam bombers of RAF squadrons No. 8 and 617 had Merlin 24 engines with some of their guns and armor deleted; some planes also had their radios and operators taken off to increase payload weight.)

The Grand Slam was first used on March 14, 1945, against concrete viaducts at Bielefeld, Germany. During the final weeks of the war it was used against other viaducts and bridges as well as submarine pens in Germany.

The bomb was 25⁵/₁₂ feet long and had a diameter of 46 inches. Its warhead consisted of 9,135 pounds of the explosive Torpex.

Granite

(1) German code name for the GLIDER assault on Fort Eben Emael, Belgium, in May 1940; (2) code name for plan for Allied operations in the Pacific, 1944.

Grant Tank

First U.S. medium TANK. The M3 General Grant—generally known as just the Grant—was hastily developed in response to events in Europe by the U.S. Army's Ordnance Department. The prototype T5 tank was rushed into production in 1940 to carry a 75-mm short-barrel (low-velocity) gun.

Because of the difficulty of mounting a gun that large in a revolving turret, the Grant had the 75-mm gun mounted in a sponson on the right side; the tank's turret had only a 37-mm gun. This arrangement limited the traverse of the gun, while the tank's high silhouette with the main gun placed relatively low imposed tactical limitations as much of its bulk had to be exposed before opening fire. Still, the Grant put an Allied tank in the field with a 75-mm gun.

The Grant was introduced to combat in the M3A5 variant by the British. Large numbers of the tanks were shipped to the British Eighth Army in Egypt in the spring of 1941 for the NORTH AFRICA CAMPAIGN. Each British tank regiment in that campaign was provided with one or two squadrons of Grants as soon as possible. The Grant was the first Allied tank in North Africa that could compete with the German Pzkw IV on approximately equal terms. The American tank was subsequently used by U.S. armored units in the Nov. 8, 1942, NORTH AFRICA INVASION. The first U.S. tank-versus-tank engagements occurred that month against German forces in Tunisia.

In 1943 the Grant was succeeded in U.S. Army and Marine units by the more capable M4 SHERMAN medium tank.

The M3A5 Grant weighed 28.8 tons and, in addition to the 75-mm and 37-mm guns, carried three or four .30-cal. machine guns. The tank, propelled by a 400-horsepower gasoline engine, had a road speed of 25 mph and was protected by 57-mm armor over vital locations. The Grant's crew numbered six: commander, two gunners, two loaders, and driver.

Some models of the M3 were named General Lee in an effort to be evenhanded in the naming of tanks for generals in the American Civil War.

Grasp

Code name for British seizure of French ships in ports in England, GIBRALTAR, MALTA, and SINGAPORE, July 1940.

Grasshopper,

see L-SERIES.

Grease Gun

The M3 submachine gun developed for use by U.S. tank crewmen and other soldiers and Marines who could not carry a CARBINE or M1 rifle. The .45-cal. M3, of simple, stamped-metal construction, resembled the British STEN gun in concept.

The grease gun was a blowback-operated, fully automatic weapon, although an experienced soldier could squeeze off one shot at a time. It weighed 10¼ pounds and was fed from a 30-round magazine that served as a forward handle. An extending metal stock was fitted. Maximum range was about 100 yards with a rate of fire of 350–450 rounds per minute. It fired the same .45-cal. cartridge as the M1911 .45-CAL. PISTOL but could be adapted to fire 9-mm Parabellum ammunition.

The M3 grease gun was a simple, rugged, reliable weapon, although it was not accurate. And it lacked the artistic lines of the U.S. THOMPSON and German MP-38 submachine guns. The M3 was introduced to U.S. service in 1942. About 646,000 guns were produced during the war.

The M3 was called grease gun because of its resemblance to the automotive tool.

Great Patriotic War

Soviet term for the war with Germany, June 1941–May 1945. See UNION OF SOVIET SOCIALIST REPUBLICS.

Greater East Asia Co-prosperity Sphere

Japan's plan for a "new order" in East Asia—the creation of an empire that would provide both RESOURCES and a defensive perimeter around the home islands. The Co-prosperity Sphere would give Japan access to the riches of Asia: iron ore, oil, tin, rubber, and coal, which the Japan home islands lacked. Conquests in Manchuria, Korea, and China also provided industrial centers for the Co-prosperity Sphere.

The major Japanese war aim was tied to the Co-prosperity Sphere concept: After swift conquests of the Philippines, Burma, Malaya, Thailand, and the Dutch East Indies, Japan would begin negotiating a peace settlement. Safely behind her ring of conquered lands, she would agree to stop warfare in exchange for the right to maintain her empire and engage in profitable trade. But the strategy did not take into account the U.S. and British doctrine of UNCONDITIONAL SURRENDER or the impairment of Japanese ability to transport goods around her Sphere by merchant ship. U.S. AIRCRAFT CARRIERS and SUBMARINES so effectively destroyed the Japanese merchant fleet that by mid-1944 oil imports were cut in half and 50 percent of Japan's dry-cargo fleet had been sunk. By then, the Sphere was shattered and loss of the war was inevitable.

Greece

Capital: Athens, pop. 7,196,900 (1938). When the war began, Greece was a former kingdom being ruled by a dictator, Gen. Ioannis Metaxas. He tried to keep his nation neutral—but prepared. When Italian troops and Albanian irregulars invaded Greece on Oct. 28, 1940, a tough Greek Army not only repulsed the invasion but also swept into Italian-occupied Albania. Italy was both defeated and humiliated. After an Italian counteroffensive failed in the spring of 1941, Italian leader BENITO MUSSOLINI had to ask for German help.

On April 6, 1941, a strong Germany force invaded Greece from Bulgaria and was stopped by the "Metaxas Line," a complex of fortresses along the Greek-Bulgarian border. A German invasion from Yugoslavia outflanked Greek defenses and turned the tide of the battle. German ground troops and parachutists swept across the Peloponnesus Peninsula and entered Athens on April 27. This German offensive caused the fatal delay of Operation BARBAROSSA, the German invasion of the Soviet Union, which was postponed until June.

British and Australian troops, who had arrived from North Africa in March 1941, had to fight their way out of Greece, evacuating from Peloponnesus ports under heavy air attack. Thousands were captured there and on CRETE, where German airborne and paratroop forces landed on May 2. Eleven days later the last British forces left Crete in a desperate evacuation.

During the German-Italian-Bulgarian occupation of Greece, most of the country's harvests were seized by the conquerors, producing widespread famine. Underground resistance movements quickly formed. The two major GUERRILLA organizations, the Communists' National Liberation Front and the National Democratic Army, joined forces, under the prodding of British advisers who tried to harness guerrilla energy against the Germans instead of each other. The umbrella organization was known as EAM/ELAS, the initials of the two forces. For a while the powerful EAM/ELAS attacked other guerrilla groups, but the British imposed a shaky truce.

During the war the Soviet Union supported the Greek Communist guerrillas, who were aligning themselves against insurgents backed by the British. As the Germans retreated from Greece in the fall of 1944, a bloody civil war ravaged the war-weakened country. To strengthen their hold on the country, the Communist-led guerrillas wiped out opposition by killing thousands of Greeks for alleged wartime collaboration.

By the time Greece was liberated in the fall of 1944, British troops were fighting Communist-backed Greeks. As World War II ended, the civil war pitted the Communist insurgents against government troops and the U.S.-backed postwar government. In an early struggle of the cold war, President HARRY TRUMAN reacted to the Soviet intrusion in the civil war by pouring U.S. military aid into Greece.

Greenglass, Tech. Cpl. David (1922—)

The LOS ALAMOS contact for Soviet atomic spy HARRY GOLD, brother of Ethel Rosenberg. Greenglass entered the U.S. Army in 1943 and, after technical training, was assigned to the Los Alamos nuclear laboratory in a minor post related to building the ATOMIC BOMB. He provided the Soviets with plans of the Los Alamos laboratory complex as well as a rough sketch of the bomb dropped on NAGASAKI.

He was arrested on June 16, 1950, on espionage charges, having been linked to a Soviet spy ring by Harry Gold who, in turn, was also collecting secret material from KLAUS FUCHS. In addition, a Soviet intelligence message intercepted in 1944 that was decrypted in 1950 narrowed the search to Greenglass. He was tried and sentenced to a fifteen-year prison term. He gave evidence against ETHEL AND JULIUS ROSENBERG, apparently to have his own sentence reduced. He was released in 1960.

Greenland

Capital: Godthaab (now Nuuk), pop. 17,000 (est. 1938). The world's largest island and a Danish pos-

session, it became an American protectorate by agreement with the government-in-exile of German-occupied Denmark and an act of the U.S. Congress on April 9, 1941. The United States promised to provide for the defense of Greenland and keep it supplied for as long as Denmark remained under German occupation. U.S. troops landed there on July 7, relieving a British garrison for combat.

Greenland was strategically important for its cryolite, an ore needed for the manufacture of aluminum; as a site for reporting on weather affecting Europe; and for bases for Atlantic sea and air patrols. Germany quickly saw the significance of Greenland meteorological observations and set them up along the east coast. The weather information that established the date for the NORMANDY INVASION came mostly from weather stations in Greenland.

Germany also planned to establish an air base that would be supplied by U-BOATS. But U.S. vigilance, and occasional clashes with German weather units, kept Greenland in American hands.

A British diplomat in Washington early in the war noticed that on a White House map Greenland, Iceland, and Alaska all were colored green. He reported this ominous fact to the British Foreign Ministry, and wondered about the long-term intentions of the United States. He need not have worried; the United States relinquished its control when the war ended.

Greer (DD 145)

U.S. DESTROYER that made the first attack on a German U-BOAT in World War II. U.S. naval historian SAMUEL ELIOT MORISON wrote, "From the date of the *Greer* incident, Sept. 4, 1941, the United States was engaged in a *de facto* naval war with Germany on the Atlantic Ocean."

The *Greer* was steaming alone toward Iceland three months before the PEARL HARBOR attack when a British aircraft alerted the destroyer that a German U-boat lay some 10 miles ahead. The destroyer went to battle stations and caught up with the submarine, the *U-652*. For several hours, with the help of the British plane, the destroyer maintained SONAR contact with the submarine.

The aircraft dropped its DEPTH CHARGES at random when it had to return to base. The U-boat apparently believed that the *Greer* had attacked and turned on the destroyer, firing a single TORPEDO. The *Greer* counterattacked with depth charges and the U-boat fired a second torpedo at the destroyer. Both ships then broke off contact.

President ROOSEVELT called the German attack "piracy."

The *Greer* was one of the 267 flush-deck, four-stack destroyers built for the U.S. Navy during World War I, none of which entered service before the 1918 armistice. The ships displaced 1,150 to 1,340 tons fully loaded, were 314⅓ feet long, and were armed with four 4-inch (102–mm) guns and twelve 21-inch (533–mm) torpedo tubes. In World War II these ships served in the U.S., British, and Soviet navies (seven of the British ships being manned by Canadians).

Greif (Griffin)

German code name (literally, griffin, the mythical eagle-lion, but translated as "snatch" for the beast's kidnaping habits). The *Greif* unit was created for the battle of the BULGE in Dec. 1944. Some 3,500 German troops, under the command of COMMANDO *Oberst* OTTO SKORZENY, were to dress in U.S. uniforms and, using captured American vehicles and equipment, sow confusion behind American lines while also capturing bridges over the Meuse River. About 150 English-speaking German soldiers were mustered for the operation, but its only effect was the intensifying of U.S. security measures. After capture, many of the Germans, legally considered spies under U.S. JUSTICE, were summarily executed. (See also ASSASSINATIONS.)

Grenade

Code name for U.S. Ninth ARMY and First Canadian Army offensive in the Rhine, Feb. 1945.

Grenades

Hand and rifle grenades were used by the troops of all belligerents in all theaters of the war. Grenades—with high explosive or chemical fillings—were small, light, and could be hurled by a soldier, or fired from a simple attachment to a rifle. In most armies infantrymen carried grenades in addition to their individual weapons.

The standard hand grenades used by the U.S. Army and Marine Corps were the M2A1 and M3A fragmentation grenades. The M2A1 resembled a small pineapple with a sectional outer casing that broke apart when it exploded; it weighed 1.3 pounds. The M3A had a smooth, cylindrical casing and weighed only .84 pound. Both grenades had a ring-shaped safety pin and handle; after pulling the pin (*not* with one's teeth, as done in war MOVIES), the grenade was safe so long as the handle was depressed. Once the handle flew off the grenade had a four- or five-second fuze. The pin arrangement made the grenades useful for BOOBY TRAPS, with the trip wire being tied to the ring.

U.S. troops also had smoke, colored marking smoke, incendiary, and rifle grenades.

The most distinctive foreign grenades were the German "stick" or "potato masher," grenades, so called for their shape. The long handle, which contained the safety device, made the stick grenades easier to throw than an American grenade, and easier for a soldier to stick in his belt to carry. The Germans also used egg-shaped grenades (similar to the U.S. M3A). The Japanese had both stick- and egg-type grenades. When wounded or in an inescapable position, Japanese soldiers often used their grenades to commit *seppuku*.

Grew, Joseph C. (1880–1965)

U.S. ambassador to Japan. Grew, a U.S. diplomat since the early 1900s, was made U.S. Ambassador to Japan by President Hoover in 1932. He was a cordial diplomat toward Japan until the late 1930s when the expansionist policy of the GREATER ASIA CO-PROSPERITY SPHERE produced a U.S. counter-policy aimed at curbing Japanese actions, especially in China.

As the United States increased economic pressure on Japan, Grew became increasingly convinced that the United States was on a collision course with Japan. In his diary, writing of talks with President ROOSEVELT during Grew's visit to the United States in Oct. 1939, Grew said, "I brought out clearly my views that if we once start sanctions against Japan we must see them through to the end, and the end may conceivably be war."

On Jan. 27, 1941, Grew cabled the State Department that he had heard that Japan had "planned, in the event of trouble with the United States, to attempt a surprise mass attack at PEARL HARBOR." Grew's warning was shrugged off by the Office of Naval Intelligence, which concluded that "no move against Pearl Harbor appears imminent or planned in the foreseeable future."

After the attack did come on Dec. 7, Grew was interned. He returned to the United States on the diplomatic exchange ship *Gripsholm* in the summer of 1942 and immediately wrote and lectured against the popular belief that the United States, after defeating Germany, would "mop up the Japs."

After frequently hearing that phrase, Grew felt compelled to say: "At this very moment, the Japanese feel themselves, man for man, superior to you and me and to any of our peoples. They admire our technology, they may have a lurking dread of our ultimate superiority of RESOURCES, but all too many of them have contempt for us as human beings. . . . The Japanese *do* think that they can and will win."

Grew, renamed under secretary of state, a post he had held in the 1920s, became the principal Japanese adviser in the government. He served for a time as acting secretary of state. But his influence waned as he counseled a liberal economic policy for postwar Japan—in contrast to what a British observer called "universal 'exterminationist' anti-Japanese feeling."

By the time JAMES BYRNES became secretary of state in June 1945, Grew had lost whatever influence he had. He played hardly any role in the events leading to the end of the war and resigned immediatley after Emperor HIROHITO announced Japan's SURRENDER. Grew, against great opposition, had held that the Emperor should be kept on the throne despite the U.S. policy of UNCONDITIONAL SURRENDER. In the end, Grew's views were vindicated.

Gromyko, Andrei A. (1909–1989)

Soviet ambassador to WASHINGTON. The most experienced international negotiator for the Soviet Union, Gromyko served as ambassador to the United States from 1943 until 1946. He then served as Soviet delegate to the UNITED NATIONS security council.

He became Soviet foreign minister (under NIKITA KHRUSHCHEV) in 1957 and gained enduring distinction by lying to President JOHN F. KENNEDY during the Cuban missile crisis of 1962. He held the foreign ministry portfolio until 1985.

A Russian woman who knew Gromyko recalled that he was "cold . . . ugly in looks and personality."

Ground Observer Corps

U.S. civilian volunteers who operated thousands of coastal observation posts. The posts were manned twenty-four hours a day, from America's entry into the war until Oct. 4, 1943, when, with the threat of attack on U.S. shores diminished, the posts were operated only for tests and training. (See also COASTWATCHERS.)

Group

Principal U.S. Army Air Forces aircraft unit for administrative and operational purposes. Roughly comparable to an Army REGIMENT, AAF groups were comprised of a single type of aircraft. Groups were designated by Arabic numerals (e.g., 332nd Fighter Group, 374th Troop Carrier Group) and were normally commanded by lieutenant colonels or full colonels.

Within the AAF operational structure, groups ranked between WINGS and SQUADRONS.

There were several types of fighter and bombardment groups, but all were normally referred to as simply fighter or bomber groups. The fighter groups normally had three squadrons and the bomber groups four.

The normal allocations of aircraft and personnel to AAF groups in Feb. 1945 were:

TYPE OF GROUP	AIRCRAFT TYPES	AIRCRAFT	PERSONNEL
Very Heavy Bombardment	B-29	45	2,078
Heavy Bombardment	B-17 B-24	72	2,261
Medium Bombardment	B-25 B-26	96	1,759
Light Bombardment	A-20 A-26	96	1,304
Single-engine Fighter	P-47 P-51	111–126	994
Twin-engine Fighter	P-38	111–126	1,081
Troop Carrier	C-47	80–110	1,837
Combat Cargo	C-46 C-47	125	883

There were several other, specialized groups in the AAF, including air commando, air depot, air service, emergency rescue, glider, observation, photo-reconnaissance, and service. The 509TH COMPOSITE GROUP operated the B-29 SUPERFORTRESS bombers that dropped the ATOMIC BOMBS on Japan.

The U.S. Marine Corps also operated aircraft groups based on a single type of aircraft as the principal components of Marine aircraft wings. Navy squadrons on board an AIRCRAFT CARRIER were designated as an air group.

Groves, Maj. Gen. Leslie R. (1896–1970)

Director of the MANHATTAN PROJECT for the building of the ATOMIC BOMB. Groves was a military engineer with a knowledge about how both machinery and people worked. He was single-minded about his job. No matter what the problem, including the weather on the TRINITY test of the bomb, Groves ordered it solved.

Groves, deputy chief of construction of the Army Corps of Engineers, had just about finished building the PENTAGON when he was told he had a new assignment. "If you do the job right," Groves' superior told him, "it will win the war."

Groves carried that sense of purpose with him as he waded into the incredibly complex and widespread project. He had to locate URANIUM; recruit hundreds of scientists without quite telling most of them what he wanted them to do; build facilities from Tennessee to Washington state for a process that had not yet been invented; set up an elaborate security system; keep track of nuclear developments in Germany and Japan; establish the system for delivering a bomb that might never exist; select the target cities—and keep happy, despite security checks and isolation, and a "collection of crackpots."

That is what he is said to have called the small army of scientists he assembled at LOS ALAMOS, the desolate New Mexican site for most of the bomb development work. There is no doubt that he viewed many of his scientists with the enthusiasm a drill sergeant reserves for fresh recruits. But he did learn to get along with them well enough to get all the work out of them that he wanted and they could give.

Both VANNEVAR BUSH, director of the OFFICE OF SCIENTIFIC RESEARCH AND DEVELOPMENT, and Secretary of War HENRY L. STIMSON were reluctant to have the blunt, rough-hewn Groves as the director of the Manhattan Project. But they came around to seeing him as the ideal man for the post.

Groves was at first no enthusiast for J. ROBERT OPPENHEIMER, a brilliant but politically wooly physicist who was not the type to throw a crisp salute to a glowering brigadier general. But Groves picked him, and when his loyalty was questioned because he had wandered into some left-wing events, Groves dictated a characteristically terse memo that said the clearance was to be given immediately, "irrespective of the information which you have." The reason was simple: "He is absolutely essential to the project."

Groves' father had been an Army chaplain and his son was at West Point when Groves got the Manhattan Project assignment. He was thoroughly Army. He also had an impressive academic record. He had graduated from the University of Washington, studied for two years at the Massachusetts Institute of Technology, and then had gone to the U.S. Military Academy, where he graduated in 1918 fourth in his class.

Once, while visiting the Berkeley Radiation Laboratory, he began goading the eminent physicist Ernest Lawrence. "Your reputation is at stake here," he told Lawrence.

"You know, general," Lawrence replied, "my reputation has been made. But yours is at stake here."

His reputation was made when the test bomb was successfully set off at ALAMOGORDO and when HIROSHIMA and NAGASAKI were demolished. To a great extent, the bomb was the creation of both science and Groves. He was in charge. As he wrote in *Now It Can Be Told,* there "was never the slightest doubt in the mind of anyone . . . about to whom he should look for direction or assistance."

GRU *(Glavnoye Razvedyvatelnoye Upravlenie)*

Soviet military intelligence directorate, formally known as the Chief Intelligence Directorate of the General Staff. Also known as the Fourth Bureau of the Soviet General Staff, the GRU collected intelligence from agents or *illegals* in foreign countries and served as an intelligence staff for the Red Army. During the late 1930s the GRU directed all effective ESPIONAGE in the United States.

Like other Soviet political and military institutions, the GRU entered the war after losing much of its leadership in JOSEF STALIN's purges of the late 1930s. In 1937 the acting head of the GRU was arrested and shot by the NKVD, the state security apparatus. NKVD agents also went into other countries to murder GRU illegals as well as GRU and NKVD intelligence officers who had refused to return to the Soviet Union. In a second wave of terror against the GRU in the summer of 1938, the head of the GRU was executed, as was the NKVD officer then appointed to direct the GRU. (Throughout most of its history the GRU was headed by secret police officers or military officers subject to their influence.)

The GRU performed well during World War II. Its agents penetrated the German General Staff, successfully ran the operations of master spy RICHARD SORGE in Japan, and GRU agents stole secrets of the U.S. ATOMIC BOMB project. On an operational level, the GRU was generally able to provide Soviet military commanders with useful information about German forces and operations.

The head of the GRU in June 1941, when Germany invaded the Soviet Union, was Lt. Gen. Filipp Golikov. Although the GRU saw indications that Germany was about to invade the Soviet Union and duly informed Stalin, the Soviet dictator refused to take heed. Golikov was not executed or imprisoned, as were other military officers who "failed" at the start of the war. In the fall of 1941 he went to England and then the United States as head of a Soviet delegation seeking weapons; he may also have been renewing the Soviet intelligence networks in those countries. In Oct. 1941 he was appointed commander of the Tenth Army and went on to become Stalin's deputy for military personnel, attaining the rank of Marshal of the Soviet Union.

Lt. Gen. A. P. Paniflov succeeded Golikov as head of the GRU from 1941–1942, followed by Lt. Gen. I. I. Ilichev in 1942–1943, and Lt. Gen. F. F. Kuznetsov from 1943 until the end of the war.

Gruenther, Gen. Alfred M. (1899—)

An officer known for his brilliant staff work, Gruenther was sometimes called "the brain of the Army." He graduated from the U.S. Military Academy in 1917 and soon found his niche as a staff officer. Like many other officers who led the Army during the war, he was singled out for his work in the LOUISIANA MANEUVERS of 1941.

That year he became Chief of Staff of the Third ARMY, succeeding Brig. Gen. DWIGHT D. EISEN-HOWER in that post. He later served as deputy chief of staff to Eisenhower for the NORTHWEST AFRICA CAMPAIGN. In 1943, as the youngest major general in the U.S. Army, he became the Chief of Staff of the Fifth Army. He was one of the planners of the AMPHIBIOUS LANDINGS at SICILY, SALERNO, and ANZIO in the ITALIAN CAMPAIGN. When Gen. MARK W. CLARK moved up from commanding officer of the Fifth Army to commanding officer of the 15th Army GROUP in Dec. 1944, Gruenther continued to be Clark's Chief of Staff.

During the long, multinational campaign in Italy Gruenther often worked as a mediator between Clark and other Allied officers. Like Eisenhower, Gruenther liked to play bridge, and he was known as an expert in bridge circles.

After the war Gruenther was Chief of Staff and then, from 1953 until his retirement in 1956, Supreme Allied Commander in Europe, the top military post in the North Atlantic Treaty Organization (NATO).

G-Staff

General term for U.S. military staff officers. During the war there were up to six staff sections in headquarters for BATTALION and larger units:

G-1 Personnel
G-2 Intelligence
G-3 Operations
G-4 Supply
G-5 Civil Affairs or Military Government
G-6 Public Relations and Psychological Warfare

The G-5 and G-6 sections were used only at the highest headquarters, e.g., SUPREME HEADQUARTERS ALLIED EXPEDITIONARY FORCE (SHAEF).

The Army Air Forces used A-1, A-2, A-3, and A-4 to denote staff sections, while the Navy used N-1, N-2, N-3, and N-4.

The G-series of staff designations originated with the French Army in the late 1800s, with several staff bureaus being designated for various functions.

Guadalcanal

One of the SOLOMON ISLANDS and a principal objective of the U.S. SOLOMONS–NEW GUINEA CAMPAIGN. The U.S. invasion of Guadalcanal, Operation Watchtower, on Aug. 7, 1942, opened the first U.S. offensive of the war.

The first landings hit Florida and Tulagi Islands to the north of Guadalcanal, with accompanying assaults on nearby Tanambogo and Gavutu Islands. The Marines landing on these secondary islands ran into much more opposition than the Marines who walked ashore at Guadalcanal itself. The landings were a complete surprise to the Japanese, whose scouting aircraft had been grounded by bad weather.

When the Japanese on Guadalcanal finally realized the island had been invaded, twenty-four hours had passed and 11,145 Marines had landed (plus 6,805 more on the other islands). The first Japanese reaction was an ineffective air attack launched from RABAUL, about 600 miles away.

The Marines moved inland, toward their main goal, the airfield the Japanese were building. The Guadalcanal field was a key to the Japanese plan to take PORT MORESBY at the southern end of New Guinea, paving the way for air strikes and a possible landing in Australia. The small Japanese force on the island withdrew from the airfield, which was quickly taken and named Henderson Field in honor of Maj. Lofton R. Henderson, a Marine pilot who had been killed in the battle of MIDWAY the previous June.

But the battle had hardly begun. The Japanese, through actions at sea, were able to pour men and supplies onto the island, landing them by barges and transports from CAPE ESPERANCE. The naval battles in the waters off Guadalcanal—see Cape Esperance, SAVO ISLAND, EASTERN SOLOMONS, SANTA CRUZ—would determine whether the Marines could take the island.

Following the Japanese victory off Savo Island—four Allied cruisers sunk, minor damage to the Japanese ships—the Japanese began sending reinforcements to Guadalcanal. Believing that fewer than 1,000 U.S. troops had landed on Aug. 7, the Japanese landed a small detachment, which was promptly wiped out. The next reinforcement attempt would be more ambitious: 1,500 men in five well-protected transports. But, because the U.S. Navy was victorious in the battle of the Eastern Solomons, most of the Japanese were killed or deprived of their heavy weapons.

The Marines on the ground were defeating all the Japanese they could find in fierce fighting. But the Marines were constantly harassed from the sea and from the air. Almost every night a single bomber flew over to harass the Marines around Henderson. The bomber was cursed as "Washing Machine Charlie."

If the Japanese had bombed the Marines' dwindling supplies, they would have hurt the Marines far more. Before this could happen, however, Brig. Gen. ROY S. GEIGER arrived to take command of the "Cactus Air Force," the various Navy and Marine planes flying from Henderson. And on Sept. 18 more Marines came ashore with tanks, ammunition, and other vitally needed supplies.

The first MEDAL OF HONOR awarded to a Marine went to Sgt. John Basilone, who killed so many Japanese in an Oct. 24 battle that he had to send out Marines to clear his field of fire. The recommendation for his medal said he had "contributed materially to the defeat and virtually the annihilation of a Japanese regiment."

The Japanese depended upon the night landing of reinforcements from ships, called the TOKYO EXPRESS. But again and again, the Marines defeated the Japanese in chance encounters and in large-scale battles, while Navy and Marine planes flying from Henderson Field bombed and strafed the ships. The biggest reinforcement operation—an attempt to land 10,000 men in mid-November—ended in still another naval battle and the loss of six troop transports; a seventh, damaged, turned back. Four other transports were deliberately run aground to unload their troops. Planes from Henderson and naval gunfire pounded the stranded ships. The relatively few Japanese who reached the safety of the jungle were tired, groggy from constant shelling and bombing, hungry, and without most of their weapons. They were more a liability than an asset to their comrades.

"We've got the bastards licked!" Adm. WILLIAM F. HALSEY declared.

By the beginning of Dec. 1942 the Japanese were contemplating an evacuation of the island. Emperor HIROHITO had to give Japanese troops permission to evacuate Guadalcanal. But not until Feb. 1943 did the undetected withdrawal take place. The operation was so secret that the Marines did not realize it had happened until empty boats and abandoned Japanese supplies were found on the beaches of Cape Esperance.

More than 25,000 Japanese died on Guadalcanal, including about 9,000 from disease and starvation.

U.S. forces suffered about 1,500 dead and 4,800 wounded. And, scores of Japanese ships and hundreds of aircraft had been lost.

Guam

Largest of the MARIANA ISLANDS (30 miles long, average of 7 miles wide) and a major objective in the battle of the Marianas. Guam, ceded to the United States by Spain after the Spanish-American War, was a Pan-American China Clipper stop. Hours after the Japanese attack on PEARL HARBOR, Japanese bombers from SAIPAN made their first raid on Guam, whose defenses consisted of a few machine guns and small arms. After initial resistance against a Japanese invasion force of some 6,000 troops, Guam's defenders—about 500 Marines, sailors, and volunteer militiamen—surrendered on Dec. 10, 1941.

Guam was liberated on July 21, 1944, when Marines, with the Army in reserve, came ashore. The assault troops ran into intense artillery and mortar fire, as well as machine guns, situated on the cliffs above the beaches. The Marines struggled up from the beach all day. The next two days saw the Americans fighting inland against savage opposition. On the night of July 25–26, the Japanese made a massive charge with 5,000 troops, many drunk with saki, storming across the Marine lines and engaging the Marines in fierce hand-to-hand combat. The Japanese fell back, leaving half their original number dead and dying.

Marines and Army troops swept northward, supported by naval gunfire, air, and artillery, and on Aug. 10 the Marines declared Guam secure. Sporadic resistance continued while SEABEES built a massive base, from which the final stage of the Pacific War was directed. Even after the war Japanese survivors who had escaped into jungles and caves sniped at Americans. Incredibly, a few Japanese continued to fight their own private war, the last finally surrendering in the early 1970s.

Guatemala

Capital: Guatemala City, pop. 3,044,490 (1938). Even before the beginning of the EUROPEAN WAR the United States took particular diplomatic interest in Guatemala because it had an influential German minority and had developed animosity toward England over the border with British Honduras. These two factors raised fear that this northernmost Central American nation would become a center for German PROPAGANDA efforts in the Western Hemisphere. Although Germans were relatively few, their economic power was great; they controlled more than half of the coffee plantations.

In 1939 Guatemala responded to U.S. concerns by outlawing NAZI organizations and warning operators of German radio stations that no propaganda would be tolerated. Guatemala declared war on Japan on Dec. 7, 1941, on Germany and Italy on Dec. 11, froze German assets, took over German coffee plantations, and set aside its dispute with England until the end of the war.

Guderian, Heinz (1888–1954)

German master of the BLITZKRIEG. He led the swift German victories in the POLISH CAMPAIGN and the FRANCE AND LOW COUNTRIES CAMPAIGN. The fast-paced campaigns vividly demonstrated the mechanized warfare that Guderian did much to create. His 1937 book *Achtung Panzer!* was a blueprint of what was to blaze across Europe in the years soon to come.

Guderian caught HITLER's eye after the Polish Campaign and he was promoted over other officers, catapulting to the Army General Staff as general in charge of motorized troops in Nov. 1938. His fast-moving military career reached its peak during the GERMAN CAMPAIGN IN THE SOVIET UNION. When his panzer forces bogged down and began losing to the Russian winter, he lost favor with Hitler, who dismissed him in Dec. 1941.

He was kept idle until he became inspector general of the armored forces in Feb. 1943. By then he was becoming disillusioned with Hitler's generalship and was approached about removing *Der Führer*. Guderian did not join in the plans; nor did he inform on the conspirators.

The day after the failed JULY 20 PLOT to kill Hitler in 1944, Hitler made Guderian chief of the general staff of the *Oberkommando der Wehrmacht* (Army High Command). Hitler appointed Guderian, along with *Generalfeldmarschalls* WILHELM KEITEL and GERD VON RUNDSTEDT, to the Court of Honor that investigated the officers accused of being in the conspiracy. The Honor Court expelled hundreds of officers and doomed them by handing them over to the notorious People's Court for execution.

Guderian had shown his loyalty to Hitler as *Der Führer,* but he continued to oppose Hitler the general. Early in 1945 he began talking to others about the need to save the German Army by arranging an armistice. Hitler dismissed him in March.

Guerrillas

In both Europe and Southeast Asia, pro-Allied guerrillas engaged in SABOTAGE, killing occupying troops, and attacking communications and transportation centers. Their greatest value was in pinning down troops who otherwise would be fighting Allied armies. The irregulars engaged the invaders in numerous nameless engagements, actions that reflected the original meaning of the Spanish word: *guerrilla,* or "little war."

The invaders' swift regional conquests worked to the advantage of the guerrillas, for the conquered territory was usually lightly garrisoned; neither the Germans nor the Japanese wanted to tie up major units on occupation duties. Concentrating forces on key positions or communications centers, the occupiers had to police vast areas with small patrols or unreliable local militia.

The Germans themselves developed a kind of guerrilla warfare, secretly recruiting sympathizers in countries targeted for conquest. These subversive groups—the FIFTH COLUMN, as they were often called—were to rise up and aid the invader. But, as one definition puts it, a true guerrilla is "a native of the country in which he [or she] is fighting, who has spontaneously taken up arms against the foreign invader or oppressor." And these fighting patriots were the war's true guerrillas.

Some guerrilla units were hardly more than bands of patriots resisting the invaders as best they could with hunting rifles and homemade bombs. Other guerrillas were fully organized and under central control; these were significant military threats to occupying armies and, for ambitious guerrilla leaders, potent political assets after the war.

Unknown numbers of guerrillas were killed, along with thousands of men, women, and children, massacred in reprisals for guerrilla operations against occupying forces. Casualty counting, a routine element in conventional warfare, was impossible in hit-and-run guerrilla encounters. And statistics were rarely kept on atrocities against civilians who were supporting guerrillas.

But the Germans sometimes published notices of hostage killings in newspapers and posters, frequently announcing a ratio of 100 hostages killed for every German killed. From such evidence, estimates of hostage deaths put the figures at 29,660 in France (plus 40,000 deaths in prison), 2,000 in the Netherlands, and 8,000 in Poland. Thousands of others disappeared, killed under what was called the "Night and Fog Decree," a Nazi secret police order, under which prisoners were to "vanish without a trace."

Guerrilla activity was extensive and significant in most of the countries invaded by Axis forces. The Netherlands Interior Force, as the Dutch underground was called, helped downed Allied airmen elude German hunters, and the Polish Home Army, particularly in the closing days of the war, mounted strong resistance against the Germans. In Australia, spear-carrying Aborigines were organized into the Northern Territory's Special Reconnaissance Unit. They scouted for Japanese invaders, served as COASTWATCHERS, and rescued many Allied airmen downed in jungles.

Major guerrilla activity occurred in the following countries. (See also country entries by name.)

China Plagued by internal political strife, China was a country divided when the long war against Japan began in 1937. Nationalists in control of southwestern China distrusted peasants, particularly armed peasants, and so resisted any widespread formation of guerrilla units to fight the Japanese. But, for the Communists, in control of the northwest, the rise of militant peasants was ideological doctrine. Communist-led guerrillas attacked Japanese garrisons, wrecked trains, assassinated Japanese military officers, and disrupted Japanese supply lines. The Communists fielded mobile, radio-controlled striking forces armed with captured Japanese weapons and sustained in part by seized Japanese supplies. In the subsequent civil war, the Communist guerrillas formed the cadre of the triumphant Communist Army.

France The German conquest of France spawned two movements: FREE FRANCE, organized and headed by Gen. CHARLES DE GAULLE in exile in London, and the FRENCH RESISTANCE (the *Maquis*), in France itself. Supplied by parachute drops and encouraged by Free French broadcasts on the BBC, the French underground rapidly proliferated into competing factions. Seeking a central authority, de Gaulle inspired the creation of *Conseil National de la Résistance,* which was made up of representatives of the separate French Resistance groups. These included young men who escaped forced labor in Germany, veterans who had fought against FRANCO in the SPANISH CIVIL WAR, independent French Communist guerrilla groups, and Secret Army units loyal to de Gaulle.

Greece   As soon as German occupation began, many Greek Army officers went underground to organize resistance movements, particularly in isolated mountainous areas. The Greek Communist Party formed its own guerrilla units, which became the Greek Popular Liberation Army. Its principal rival was the National Democratic Army. They eventually united in an umbrella organization known as EAM/ELAS, the initials of the two forces. British Army officers slipped into Greece and led many of the guerrilla actions against German and Italian forces.

Italy   Italian Resistance leaders set up a secret committee of national liberation, which fought the monarchy and Italian Fascism as much as the Germans. By some estimates, more than 50,000 Italian guerrillas were killed in skirmishes with German and Italian troops. In a documented incident, avenging Germans killed 382 men, women, and children in the Ardeatine Caves after an attack in which thirty-five German soldiers were killed.

Guerrillas were especially effective in aiding Allied troops in northern Italy during the ITALIAN CAMPAIGN. By mid-1944, at least eight of the twenty-six German divisions in Italy were immobilized by the guerrillas (who styled themselves as "partisans," in semantic sympathy with their left-wing comrades in Yugoslavia).

By the end of the war, partisans held Venice, Genoa, and Milan. British and U.S. officials, concerned about a postwar Communist revolution, ordered the disbanding of the partisans. But, supported by the Soviet Union, the partisans gave the Italian Communist Party a patriotic aura that helped the Communists gain postwar political power.

Philippines   An extensive resistance organization was formed in the wake of the American withdrawal. As a U.S. Army officer described guerrilla activity, it "varied from one Moro swinging his bolo at a Jap neck to engagements involving hundreds of troops."

The guerrillas maintained contact with the headquarters of Gen. DOUGLAS A. MACARTHUR, who before leaving BATAAN sent groups of officers into the jungles to organize guerrilla units. Their primary mission was to gather intelligence information and transmit it to Allied commands. They did this extremely well, while simultaneously harassing Japanese occupation troops. U.S. submarines delivered radios and weapons to the guerrillas. Among the supplies were chocolate bars whose labels said: "I shall return—MacArthur."

Filipinos set up a "shadow government," ran an officers' training school, and even printed "guerrilla currency." The Philippines were divided into four guerrilla areas, with a military commander and a highly efficient recruitment system. Guerrilla groups, many made up of tribesmen, numbered in the thousands, with two or three U.S. officers. A U.S. Army colonel who escaped from Bataan commanded 8,000 guerrillas in northern Luzon. The total number of guerrillas may have been as high as 180,000.

Soviet Union   During the fighting against German invaders, as many as 250,000 Soviet guerrillas maintained a sustained threat to the Germans' rear areas. Guerrillas included bypassed Soviet Army units that had avoided capture; Jewish escapees from the Sobibór DEATH CAMP; troops in civilian clothes, assigned to organize partisan units; and civilians, especially Communist Party members, who banded together either for self-protection or in obedience to Soviet leader STALIN's directive. On July 3, 1941, eleven days after the German invasion, he ordered the partisans to make the occupied areas "unbearable for the enemy and his associates. They must be hounded and annihilated at every step . . . ." Many of the Soviet units were well equipped by both supportive residents and the Soviet military supply apparatus. Major German forces were diverted from the front to cope with the guerrillas, who concentrated on disruption of their long supply lines through the occupied regions.

Yugoslavia After the German invasion, two rival groups emerged: the National Liberation Partisan Detachments under Josef Brozovich, called TITO, and the Cetniks, a resistance movement formed by Col. Draža Mihajlović, a veteran of the Serbian Army in World War I. Tito's partisans quickly emerged as the most effective guerrillas. In Feb. 1944, British Prime Minister CHURCHILL credited Tito's well-organized partisans—150,000 of them, by Tito's count—with holding in check fourteen of the twenty German divisions in the Balkans.

Guidance

British code name for use of MIDGET SUBMARINES to attack a German floating dry dock in a Norwegian fjord, April 1944.

Guided Bombs,

see GUIDED MISSILES.

Guided Missiles

BOMBS and unmanned aircraft that could be controlled by radio signals from a nearby aircraft were extensively used in the war with varying degrees of success. In addition, the Germans developed guided missiles as ANTIAIRCRAFT WEAPONS.

United States The major U.S. guided missile program was the employment of worn-out bombers, packed with high explosives or NAPALM (jellied gasoline) to attack German SUBMARINE PENS, V-2 MISSILE launching sites, and oil refineries. These operations, conducted by the AAF and Navy in late 1944, had very little success. (See Project APHRODITE.)

In 1945 the AAF search for a powered bomb turned to using fighters. The P-38 LIGHTNING and P-47 THUNDERBOLT, laden with bombs, were considered. They would be taken off and flown to their targets under radio control from an accompanying aircraft, and then crashed into their targets. The end of the war in Europe came before the project reached the developmental stage.

The AAF and Navy also developed specialized guided missiles during the war. The AAF effort consisted primarily of the Azon (Azimuth-only) and Razon weapons, which came out of an earlier Army aviation interest in fitting bombs with wings or controllable fins. Ranges of up to 30 miles were envisioned. Several GB (Glide Bombs) were developed based on the 2,000-pound bomb. On May 25, 1944, bombers flying from England dropped 116 of the GB-1s against COLOGNE, but the results were unimpressive and no more attacks were undertaken. Improved GB-series weapons were tested in Europe but without success.

The AAF also developed a series of VB (Vertical Bomb) weapons. The Azon (VB-1) was a 1,000-pound bomb with moveable control surfaces in the tail that could be adjusted by radio signals from the launching aircraft to control the azimuth of the bomb. These weapons were used on several occasions against German targets in Europe and the Mediterranean area in 1944–1945, and against Japanese bridges in Burma in 1944–1945. In Burma the results were impressive with twenty-seven bridges reported to have been dropped with the use of 459 Azon bombs.

The Razon was an improved version, with control of the tail surfaces also being able to change the distance the bomb glided toward the target.

The Navy's BAT MISSILE was a sophisticated winged missile for use against heavily armed enemy warships. This weapon was employed in the closing months of the war with some success, although the scarcity of shipping targets and interference from surrounding land limited its effectiveness. Both the Navy and AAF also had some interest in glide bombs carrying aerial TORPEDOES (a concept that was pursued after the war by the U.S. and several other navies).

The U.S. Army and Navy also had considerable interest in the German V-1 BUZZ BOMB and both services planned to use the missile against Japan. Parts of V-1s that fell on England were rushed back to the United States and, within three weeks, in Aug. 1944 a "Chinese copy" was test-flown. The AAF immediately ordered 1,000 of these missiles (designated JB-2) with the first test-flown in Oct. 1944. Impressed with the weapon, the head of the AAF, Gen. H. H. ARNOLD, ordered mass production with a goal of launching 1,000 missiles per month—later raised to 500 per day for the assaults on Germany and Japan. But the Army high command cut the program back to 1,000 per month because of the impact the higher number would have on bomb and artillery production, and the shipping space that would be required.

The Navy, calling the Americanized V-1 the Loon, prepared plans for arming ESCORT CARRIERS with hundreds of the weapons for the bombardment of Japan. (The concept of SUBMARINE-launched Loons was also pursued.) But none of these schemes was ready before the Japanese capitulation in Aug. 1945.

The AAF also had contracted with the Northrop Corporation to produce a flying bomb based on the firm's flying-wing designs. (See B-35 FLYING WING.) Designated JB-1 (for Jet Bomb), the weapon encountered development problems. Also underway at the end of the war was the AAF JB-3, an air-to-air missile.

In Feb. 1944 the U.S. Army Ground Forces also began to look into the feasibility of guided missiles as antiaircraft weapons; in July the requirement was broadened to include a family of guided missiles to replace conventional field ARTILLERY. But little was accomplished in these areas during the war.

Germany   The V-1 buzz bomb was the first guided missile in history to be launched in large numbers against an enemy. The German Air Force began launching the V-1s against LONDON on June 13, 1944, exactly one week after the D-DAY landings at Normandy. (V-1 indicated *Vergeltungswaffe* or reprisal weapon; the Fieseler-developed missile was also designated Fi 103, and to disguise its real purpose it was also referred to as the FZG 76 for *Flakzielgerät* or long-range aiming device.)

Britains referred to them as "doodlebugs" or "buzz bombs." The 1,870-pound high-explosive warhead detonated just above the ground, inflicting considerable damage. During an eighty-day period the V-1s wrecked or damaged more than 1,000,000 buildings in England, killed 6,184 persons, and seriously injured 17,981 others. The port of Antwerp, important for the supply of Allied armies in Western Europe, was also a target for the V-1s.

German records indicate that 8,564 of the missiles were launched against England and Antwerp; about 43 percent failed, or were diverted or destroyed by fighters, antiaircraft fire, or BARRAGE BALLOONS. Fighters—especially the jet-propelled

METEOR—could intercept the missiles. The most effective way to destroy the V-1s was to bomb launch sites and production facilities (Operation Crossbow).

From July 1944 some 1,200 of the missiles were air-launched from HE 111H twin-engine bombers. Also, a scheme was developed for the AR 234B *BLITZ* jet-propelled bomber to tow a V-1 for air launching. A proposed *piloted* version of the V-1 was flight-tested but never used operationally.

The Luftwaffe also employed guided bombs against Allied ships. The principal weapon was the FRITZ-X or Kramer X-1, carrying a 1,300-pound armor-piercing bomb as warhead. On Sept. 9, 1943, the Luftwaffe attacked the Italian battleship *ROMA* in the Mediterranean, sinking the ship with heavy loss of life with a single Fritz-X. Air attacks using guided bombs also damaged her sister ship *Italia,* the British battleship *Warspite* and cruiser *Uganda,* and the U.S. CRUISER *Savannah* (CL 42). The *Roma* was the first major warship in history to be sunk by a guided weapon. On April 30, 1944, the Luftwaffe made a large attack with Fritz-X missiles against Plymouth, England, but no important targets were hit.

Also used against Allied ships by the Luftwaffe was the smaller Henschel Hs 293, which had a 1,100-pound warhead. On Aug. 25, 1943, they were used to damage a British CORVETTE in the Bay of Biscay. Two days later an Hs 293 sank the sloop *Egret* in the Bay. During the ANZIO landings in Jan. 1945 Luftwaffe attacks with this missile sank the British cruiser *Spartan* and a destroyer.

The Germans also developed guided missiles to defeat Allied heavy bombers. (See ANTIAIRCRAFT WEAPONS.)

Japan   The Japanese Air Force also developed an antiship guided missile, but it did not become operational before Japan capitulated. (See I-GO-1A GUIDED MISSILE.)

Gurkhas

Legendary Nepalese soldiers who fought alongside British forces in North Africa, Italy, and the China-Burma-India theater.

The Gurkhas had a reputation for savagery—their favorite weapon was the *kukri,* a short, slightly curved sword with a broad, razor-sharp blade. Stories are told about how they slit the throats of sleeping Germans, slipping in and out of bivouacs without being heard. But the stories are based on their ability to fight and their enthusiasm for fighting.

A Ghurkha PLATOON leader during the war complained that new men in his unit had arrived too late to fight and were "very annoyed that the war is finished." Lachhiman Gurung, badly wounded by two Japanese grenades in a battle near Pegu, Burma, fired and reloaded his rifle with one good hand, sighted with his one good eye, and held off a Japanese attack on his position for four hours. At dawn, when the Japanese broke off the attack, there were thirty-one dead Japanese in front of his trench.

When he learned that he was to get the VICTORIA CROSS, Lachhiman thought there had been a mistake. Byron Farwell, the author of a study of the Gurkhas, quotes Lachhiman as saying, "I was not brave. I saw all my friends wounded and then I looked at my hand and I was very, very angry."

British forces discovered the Gurkhas in the eighteenth century during clashes over British attempts to establish trade between Tibet and India. The Gurkhas, a Nepalese tribe that had subdued all their neighbors, blocked Indo-Tibetan trade through Nepal and fought ferociously. "I never saw more steadiness in my life," a British officer reported. "Run they would not, and of death they seemed to have no fear." When the fighting ended, the British enlisted the Ghurkhas into the British Army and they have been there ever since.

Gustav Gun

The largest gun ever built. The German 800-mm (31.5-inch) Gustav dwarfed the German "Paris Gun" of World War I (officially the 210-mm Kaiser Wilhelm Geschutz) and the Japanese 460-mm (18.1-inch) guns of the *YAMATO*-class battleships, the largest naval guns ever mounted. Despite its size and capability, "Undoubtedly the effectiveness of the cannon bore no real relation to all the effort and expense that had gone into making it," wrote German *Generalfeldmarschall* Erich von Manstein.

The Gustav was initially conceived in 1937 as a means of destroying the French MAGINOT LINE defenses. The 800-mm diameter barrel was complete and proof-tested in early 1941, and the completed gun was delivered to the German Army in

The 800-mm (31.5-inch) Gustav gun was the largest gun ever to fire in action. The massive German weapon was used during the war but then disappeared, as had the Paris Gun and the two German 210-mm Super Guns of World War II. The Gustav may have been captured by Soviet troops. *(Imperial War Museum)*

1942. It was sent to the Crimea to bombard SEVAS-
TOPOL during the siege of that Soviet port city. It
fired between thirty and forty rounds at that target.
Subsequently, the Gustav was shifted to the siege of
LENINGRAD, but the rapid advance of the Soviet
Army prevented its use. The gun was used briefly
near WARSAW in Sept. 1944, firing about thirty
rounds into the city during the Warsaw uprising.
The gun then disappeared—as had the Paris Gun
and the two 210-mm SUPER GUNS of World War II.
The Gustav may have been captured by Soviet
troops.

The size of the Gustav, which was railway
mounted, necessitated that it be transported in sections on special trains. The barrel itself was moved
in two sections. When the gun arrived at a firing
site, four parallel tracks would be laid down—two
for the gun (which had eighty wheels) and two
outer tracks for the traveling crane used to assemble
the gun. The process of laying the firing tracks and
assembling the gun took at least three weeks and the
efforts of some 1,420 men. The firing operation
required 500 men.

The Gustav weighed 1,329 tons in firing position. The barrel, 106½ feet long, fired an antipersonnel round that weighed 4.7 tons at a muzzle
velocity of 2,330 feet per second to a maximum
range of 29 miles. A 7-ton concrete-piercing round
had a range of 23 miles. A 2-ton "Arrow Shell" was

developed for the gun, to have a range of 95 miles,
but it was never fired.

The Krupp-built Gustav was given that name to
honor its designer, Karl Gustav. Because the soldiers who assembled and fired the gun sometimes
called it "Dora," there is confusion over whether
there was one or two guns. According to Master
Gunner Ian Hogg of Britain's Royal Artillery,
Dora, the second gun did exist but never left the
firing range at Rugenwalde. But if that gun in fact
existed, it too disappeared completely and Allied
troops found only a spare barrel and ammunition at
the end of the war. More likely, Dora was the spare
barrel.

Gustav Line

One of the German defense lines south of ROME.
It ran across the Italian peninsula from the Tyrrhenian Sea to the Adriatic and had CASSINO as its
hub. Studded with pillboxes, rock-sheltered gun
emplacements, and minefields, the line also used
the natural barriers of the Rapido, Garigliano, and
Sangro Rivers. In intense fighting across the rivers,
through the mountains, and along the coast, Allied
armies breached the line in May 1944.

Gymnast

Early Anglo-American code name for Torch.

H

Ha

Japanese code name for operations in Burma, near the Indian border, Feb. 1944.

Habforce

Code name for British operation in Iraq, May 1941.

Habicht (Hawk)

German code name for the proposed crossing of the Donets River in the Chuguyev-Kupyansk area of the USSR, March 1943.

Habkkuk

British plan to construct large aircraft carriers of artificial ice or "Pykrete." Named for the British scientist Geoffrey Pyke, Pykrete was manufactured from a mixture of sea water and sawdust frozen together. As Pykrete melted the fibrous content quickly formed a furry outer surface that acted as an insulator and greatly reduced the melting process. The material was considerably stronger than normal ice.

A scale model of a Pykrete carrier—given the code name Habkkuk—was built and tested in Canada. A full-size carrier was expected to have a displacement of one million tons, to be self-propelled, and be fitted with repair shops, accommodations, and antiaircraft guns. It was to serve primarily as a refueling base for carrier-based aircraft from other ships.

Prime Minister CHURCHILL was very interested

Adolf Hitler at Nuremberg exhibiting the assertive style that helped him capture the minds and emotions of the German people. Coupled with his early political and military successes, his charisma caused the overwhelming majority of the German people to follow him until his death, despite his callous disregard for them after they "failed" him in the string of defeats that began at Stalingrad. *(Imperial War Museum)*

in the project. During a demonstration of Pykrete for the COMBINED CHIEFS OF STAFF a revolver was used to fire into the material to demonstrate its hardness. A ricocheting bullet almost caused the first "combat" casualty among the chiefs.

The availability of long-range fighters caused the project to be dropped from consideration for the invasion of Europe. Subsequently, Churchill had Habkkuk studied for possible use in the invasions of Norway or Sumatra. However, the full-scale Pykrete carrier did not progress beyond the planning stage.

Haifisch (Shark)

Code name for German deception plan for Operation BARBAROSSA, 1941.

Haile Selassie (1892–1975)

Emperor of Ethiopia. In the 1930s Haile Selassie was a symbol of the weak power crushed by the aggressor. Ethiopians, with stone-age weapons, gallantly fought against the modern Italian army and air force that invaded the small desert nation in 1937. At least 30,000 civilians were massacred in Addis Ababa following the Italian conquest. The emperor went into exile in the Sudan and returned in triumph in 1940 after liberation by British-aided Ethiopian forces.

Haiti

Capital: Port-au-Prince, pop. 2,650,000 (est. 1937). Haiti's principal contribution to the war effort involved, with U.S. financial and technical aid, the growing of cryptostegia, a rubber-producing vine. This attempt to solve the American rubber shortage ended when U.S. scientists found ways to produce synthetic rubber. But the United States still had to pay another $9,600,000 in development funds to make up for Haiti's losses from the abortive rubber experiment.

Haiti declared war on Japan on Dec. 8, 1941, on Germany and Italy on Dec. 12, and Bulgaria, Hungary, and Rumania on Dec. 24. Following the U.S. lead, Haiti ended relations with VICHY FRANCE on Nov. 10, 1942.

Halberd

Code name for a British CONVOY to reinforce MALTA, Sept. 1941.

Halder, Franz (1884–1972)

Chief of the German Army General Staff from 1938 to 1942. Halder, who succeeded Gen. LUDWIG BECK as Chief of Staff, secretly opposed HITLER and probably would have attempted to overthrow him if Hitler had invaded Czechoslovakia in 1938. After Hitler won that country through the MUNICH PACT, Halder tempered his opposition, but he often questioned Hitler's political and military plans.

When Hitler promoted twelve generals to field marshal in July 1940, Halder was pointedly not included. Halder persisted in questioning Hitler's strategy, particularly after the June 1941 invasion of the Soviet Union. Hitler angrily dismissed him in Sept. 1942 when Halder disagreed with Hitler's disastrous decisions about the battle of STALINGRAD.

Halder retired to Bavaria. After the JULY 20 PLOT against Hitler's life, Halder, his wife, and daughter were arrested. He was not one of the plotters, although he knew and sympathized with many of them. He was taken to the Flossenbürg CONCENTRATION CAMP and expected to be executed. He languished there, in solitary confinement, until April 1945, when German troops released him and other notable prisoners. They then gave themselves up to American troops.

Half-track

Versatile U.S. Army combat vehicle. Produced in large quantities as personnel and gun carriers, the Army's half-track was exactly that—forward it had wheels and in the rear short tank-like tracks, making a robust, rough-terrain vehicle. It had lightly armored sides with an open top, armored engine covering and windshield screen, and was able to accommodate up to ten troops plus a crew of two or, if a machine gun was mounted, three crewmen. Access to the cargo compartment was through rear doors. A roller or winch fitted on the front bumper helped the half-track overcome obstacles.

The basic M2 half-track had provisions for one .50-cal. and one .30-cal. machine gun. However, the vehicle could be fitted with a variety of weapons, including a quad .50-cal. machine gun mount (for use against ground or air targets), 75-mm pack howitzers, and MORTARS.

Loaded combat weight was 20,000 pounds. The six-cylinder, water-cooled engine provided a maximum road speed of 45 mph and a cruising range of 150 miles.

The T14 half-track personnel carrier entered production in the late 1930s. Redesignated M2, it became the Army's standard half-track vehicle.

Halifax

The second of the British four-engine heavy bombers, entering service only a few months after the STIRLING. Built in large numbers, the Halifax was the first RAF four-engine bomber to drop BOMBS on Germany, in a raid on HAMBURG on the night of March 12–13, 1941. Along with the LANCASTER, the Halifax shared the bomber offensive against Germany from 1941 to 1945 (75,532 sorties dropping 227,612 tons of bombs). The Halifax was the only British four-engine bomber to be used in the Middle East during the war. In addition to bombing, the Halifax also served as a maritime reconnaissance aircraft, parachute troop carrier, dropping arms and agents to GUERRILLAS and other resistance fighters, and GLIDER tug.

The first prototype Halifax flew on Oct. 25, 1939; the first production aircraft flew a year later. The first Halifax operational sortie was flown by six aircraft against Le Havre on the night of March 11–12, 1941. Both daylight and night raids against German targets in Europe were flown until Dec. 1941, when the RAF switched to night attacks only. The Handley Page firm and several others manufactured the Halifax, with production continuing after the war, although most of the 6,176 planes were delivered before the war was over.

Powered by four Rolls-Royce Merlin in-line engines, the large Halifax had a glazed nose topped by a power gun turret, dorsal- and tail-gun turrets, and a twin-tail configuration. The Halifax Mk III had a top speed of 282 mph and a range of 1,030 miles. Up to 13,000 pounds of bombs could be carried with two .303-cal. machine guns in the nose turret, and four guns in the dorsal and tail turrets; some aircraft had a single .303-cal. or .50-cal. ventral gun position. A RADAR dome was fitted in the ventral position in some aircraft. The Halifax was flown by a crew of seven.

Halsey, Fleet Adm. William F. (1882–1959)

After serving in DESTROYERS in European waters in World War I, Halsey continued to serve in surface ships until 1935 when, a captain at the age of fifty-three, he earned his naval aviator's wings, then took command of the AIRCRAFT CARRIER *SARATOGA* (CV 3). He quickly developed an understanding of the offensive potential of carriers and by the time of the attack on PEARL HARBOR, Vice Adm. Halsey was commander of the Pacific Fleet's carriers.

In the first four months of 1942, Halsey conducted several raids on the GILBERT ISLANDS and MARSHALL ISLANDS, as well as supporting the American reinforcement of Samoa. His TASK FORCE

Adm. William F. ("Bill") Halsey was an impulsive and aggressive commander. In that regard and in his admiration for the American fighting man he was comparable to Gen. George Patton. However, Halsey stayed clear of political issues (easier for a fleet commander). *(U.S. Navy)*

carried the sixteen B-25 MITCHELL bombers for the DOOLITTLE RAID on Japan in April 1942. With these raids "Bill" Halsey ("Bull" was a journalistic nickname that none of his associates used) was on his way to becoming the best-known American admiral of World War II.

His carrier force was not in position to participate in the battle of the CORAL SEA in May 1942 and a severe bout of dermatitis put him in the hospital just before the battle of MIDWAY in June 1942. By Oct. 1942 Halsey had recovered sufficiently for Adm. CHESTER W. NIMITZ to appoint him commander, South Pacific in relief of the exhausted Vice Adm. ROBERT L. GHORMLEY. Halsey was promoted to full admiral in Nov. 1942. Together, Halsey and GEN. DOUGLAS MACARTHUR coordinated the taking of the SOLOMON ISLANDS and NEW GUINEA from Nov. 1942 to June 1944, when Halsey was assigned to command the Central Pacific Force.

From Aug. 1944 to Aug. 1945 Halsey and Adm. RAYMOND SPRUANCE alternated as commanders of the U.S. Navy's main striking force in the Pacific. Under Halsey, the force was known as the Third FLEET, under Spruance as the Fifth Fleet. One of his first acts as Third Fleet commander was to suggest a change in plans, moving the landings on Leyte Island in the Philippines from Dec. 20 to Oct. 20. Halsey's opinion that Spruance had let an opportunity slip away during the June 1944 battle of the MARIANA ISLANDS prompted him to make the most controversial move of his career during the battle of LEYTE GULF in Oct. 1944. Confident that his forces had driven back Japan's central fleet, Halsey headed north with his fast carriers and BATTLE-SHIPS to attack the northern force. Although his carrier aircraft sank all four Japanese carriers, that success was overshadowed by the near-disaster wrought on the ESCORT CARRIERS by the Japanese central fleet, which had doubled back. Halsey later commented that it might have been better had he led the Philippine Sea battle and Spruance the battle of Leyte Gulf.

Halsey supported MacArthur's recapture of the Philippines through the end of Jan. 1945, when he turned over command, as planned, to Spruance. Halsey's fleet had suffered significant damage from a typhoon in Dec. 1944, and his failure to take proper precautions was regarded as a principal rea-

son, although he was only mildly reprimanded. A similar lapse during a June 1945 typhoon was less favorably viewed and he was nearly relieved of command.

Halsey regained command of the Third Fleet in May 1945 and led it on a series of carrier raids against Japan until the war's end.

Halsey was known for his willingness to delegate responsibility, consider suggestions made by his subordinates, share credit, and assume blame—qualities that inspired near-absolute loyalty. His invigorating optimism and aggressiveness during the early months of the war is considered by many to have been his greatest contribution to the U.S. war effort. Halsey looked like a fighter and made fighting statements. He ordained a slogan for his fleet: "Kill Japs. Kill Japs. Kill More Japs." At times his flair for publicity embarrassed the Navy and his staff. But Halsey's own charisma appears to have insulated him to a useful degree against the overpowering presence of Gen. MacArthur.

Although Halsey was to pronounce himself entirely won over after their first meeting, the admiral was able to hold his ground against MacArthur in several confrontations. He also owed much to unstinting support from Nimitz, who was less enamored of MacArthur.

In late 1944 the Navy's leadership was unable to agree whether Halsey or Spruance should be given one of the four FIVE-STAR RANKS allocated to the Navy. In the event, the rank was not awarded until Dec. 1945 when it was belatedly given to Halsey.

Halcyon

Code name for Y-day, which denoted when Allied forces for Europe would be ready for the NORMANDY INVASION. Halcyon was June 1, 1944; thus, D-DAY was Halcyon + 5 (i.e., June 6, 1944).

Hamburg

German city bombed more than 180 times during the war. The RAF Bomber Command designated the systematic attacks on the city as the Battle of Hamburg; its code name was Operation Gomorrah. In the most destructive raid, 791 RAF bombers attacked the city on the night of July 24, 1943, aided for the first time by WINDOW, metal foil strips that confused German RADAR. U.S. B-17S followed up with daylight raids on July 25 and 26, then the RAF struck again, this time with more incendiary BOMBS than were dropped on July 24.

The massive fires created the war's first FIRE-STORM, which burned out about eight square miles of the city and killed about 45,000 people. Many died horribly. "Women and children were so charred as to be unrecognizable," a survivor recalled. "Their brains had tumbled from their burst temples and their insides from the soft parts under the ribs. . . . The smallest children lay like fried eels on the pavement." In these and subsequent raids more than 9,000 tons of bombs were dropped on the city.

Hammer

Code name for planned British capture of Trondheim, Norway, April 1940.

Hamp

Allied code name for a Japanese fighter aircraft originally given the code name HAP. Changed to Hamp but then identified as the A6M3 variant of the Japanese Navy's ZERO fighter (Allied type Zeke 32).

Hampden

British medium bomber that, despite several shortcomings, performed valuable service as a bomber and, subsequently, as a minelayer and TOR-PEDO bomber. The aircraft first flew on June 21, 1936, and, after several modifications, production was quickly initiated. The plane entered RAF service in 1938 and when the EUROPEAN WAR began was initially employed in daylight raids. However, heavy losses led to a switch to night operations. Twelve Hampdens were among the forty-three RAF bombers that made the first strike against BERLIN on Aug. 25–26, 1940. A few Hampdens participated in the THOUSAND-PLANE RAID against Cologne in May 1942, but the surviving Hampdens were returned from Bomber Command by the end of the year. Subsequently, it served in Coastal Command into 1944.

The twin-engine Hampden, developed by Handley Page, was actually built by several firms; 1,272 were built in Britain and another 160 in Canada. The plane, flown by a crew of four, had a top speed of 265 mph with a range of 1,990 miles. An internal BOMB bay could carry up to 4,000 pounds of bombs or, with modification, an aerial torpedo.

Hangman

Code name for clandestine British organization in Norway to report movement of German warships.

Hannover

German code name for operations against the Soviet pocket west of Vyazma, May–June 1942.

Hap

Allied code name given to a Japanese fighter; after Gen. H. H. (HAP) ARNOLD objected to his nickname being so used, the code was changed to HAMP. It was actually the A6M3 variant of the ZERO (Allied type Zeke 32).

Harpoon

(1) Code name for British CONVOY to MALTA, June 1942; (2) see A-28/A-29/B-34 HUDSON.

Harriman, W. Averell (1891–1986)

Wartime U.S. ambassador to the Soviet Union. Harriman, an early member of President ROOSE-VELT's bureaucratic coterie, began his war service in March 1941 as the President's England-based representative of the U.S. LEND-LEASE program. He also headed the American delegation for a U.S.-British mission to Moscow in Sept. 1941 launching what would be a long career as an adviser on U.S. dealings with STALIN. Harriman took part in all major wartime CONFERENCES. In Oct. 1943 he became the U.S. ambassador to the Soviet Union, a post he held until Feb. 1946.

Harris, Arthur (1892–1984)

Commander in Chief of the RAF Bomber Command. Air Chief Marshal Sir Arthur "Bomber" Harris, an early advocate of STRATEGIC BOMBING, took over Bomber Command in Feb. 1942 and within a month he had begun his bombing assault on the German war machine. He had little faith in either the British Army or Royal Navy as war winners, and made no secret of it. His belief in massive bombing was summed up in what he wrote to CHURCHILL in

Nov. 1943: "We can wreck Berlin from end to end if the USAAF will come in on it. It will cost us between 400–500 aircraft. It will cost Germany the war."

Harris loathed what he termed "panacea" targets or any offensive directed at specific economic targets, such as synthetic oil plants or transportation networks. His strategy led to massive, nighttime raids against German cities. For the most part, he left daylight PRECISION BOMBING to the Americans and ordered the Bomber Command to conduct intensive raids that "focused on the morale of the enemy civil population and in particular of the industrial workers."

Although he was willing to support the U.S. Eighth AIR FORCE'S precision bombing premise, he did not believe the Americans would be able to stand the losses or wreak the necessary damage. Ironically, Bomber Command losses in early 1944 began to soar just as the introduction of long-range fighter escorts was beginning to reduce the Americans' high-loss rate.

Harris' policy was dramatically carried out in the THOUSAND-PLANE RAID on COLOGNE in May 1942, the four-day demolition of HAMBURG in July 1943, and the devastating bombing of DRESDEN in February 1945. Probably because of the immediate postwar repugnance for the Dresden bombing, Harris was consigned to obscurity and Churchill effectively abandoned him at the end of the war, dissociating himself from Harris and failing to secure him any recognition. Harris retired from the RAF in 1945 and lived in South Africa for the rest of his life. He received a baronetcy in 1953, which most consider as falling well short of his due. Unlike virtually all major British wartime leaders, Harris was not honored with a knighthood.

Hart, Adm. Thomas C. (1877–1971)

Hart, a graduate of the U.S. Naval Academy's Class of 1897, was one of the oldest serving officers in the U.S. Navy at the beginning of World War II. He had been a midshipman on the *Massachusetts* at the Battle of Santiago Harbor in the Spanish-American War.

By the time the EUROPEAN WAR began, Hart had had a variety of commands, from BATTLESHIPS to all U.S. SUBMARINES. In July 1940 he took command

of the pitifully small U.S. Asiatic FLEET, which was scattered around the Western Pacific. Hart sent home 2,000 dependents, consolidated his fleet in MANILA Bay, and began training in anticipation of the Japanese attack he was sure would come soon. He responded to a war warning issued on Nov. 27, 1941, by sending his surface forces south and planning to use Manila as a base of operations for his submarines, which he thought of as too big and too full of gadgets.

The aging and ill-trained U.S. naval forces had no real chance against the Japanese, a fact Hart readily recognized. The Japanese devastation of Manila and the sinking of the British *PRINCE OF WALES* and *REPULSE* on Dec. 10 soon persuaded Hart that the Philippines were indefensible. He sailed to Surabaya in Indonesia by submarine on December 26. There he assumed command of the American-British-Dutch-Australian (ABDA) fleet, a collection of ill-matched cruisers and destroyers.

The ABDA fleet's attempt to hold the "Malay Barrier" failed in part because of inexperience and caution and because the four national forces had four different goals they wished to pursue. Moreover, the fleet was simply too small and undergunned to prevent the Japanese conquest, although a more coordinated strategy might have slowed it down. On Feb. 12, 1942, Hart was relieved of command at his own request; his replacement—Vice Adm. Conrad E. L. Helfrich of the Royal Netherlands Navy—fared no better. Hart retired as a full admiral in June 1942, but was recalled to serve on the Navy's General Board.

In 1944, Secretary of the Navy FRANK KNOX assigned Hart the task of collecting testimony from naval officers to be used in the courts-martial of the two principal commanders at PEARL HARBOR during the Dec. 7 attack—Adm. HUSBAND KIMMEL and Gen. WALTER SHORT. His selection was widely accepted both because of his experience as commander of the Asiatic Fleet and because of his intelligence and fairness. He retired again in Feb. 1945 after being named to fill a vacant U.S. Senate seat. He was the only admiral to serve in the Senate.

Hartmann, Maj. Erich (1922—)

World's top-scoring fighter ACE. A seventeen-year-old schoolboy when the war began in Europe,

Hartmann was not posted to his first operational Luftwaffe unit until Oct. 10, 1942. He joined *Jagdgeschwader* 52, a fighter group flying ME 109 fighters in the UKRAINE. Hartmann's entry into combat was not particularly distinguished; he scored his seventh victory in April 1943 when he flew his 100th combat mission.

By then, having perfected his flying and killing techniques, his victory score increased rapidly. On Sept. 20, 1943, he destroyed his 100th Soviet aircraft. He was shot down and captured, but quickly escaped. His successes continued and on Aug. 24, 1944, he shot down eleven enemy aircraft, bringing his score to 301 victories—the first of only two fighter pilots to exceed 300 kills. (This achievement brought Hartmann the Diamonds award to his Knights Cross of the IRON CROSS.) His final score was 352 enemy aircraft destroyed, including five U.S. AAF P-51 MUSTANG fighters that he shot down over Rumania.

Hartmann surrendered to U.S. forces in Czechoslovakia in May 1945 and was handed over to the Soviet government. He stood trial as a war criminal and was sentenced to ten years' imprisonment. He returned to West Germany in 1955 and rejoined the Luftwaffe.

Hartz Mountains,

see NATIONAL REDOUBT.

Haruna

Japanese battleship reportedly sunk in the opening days of the war in a suicide attack by one of America's first war heroes. On Dec. 10, 1941, one of the few surviving B-17 FLYING FORTRESS bombers in the Philippines attacked Japanese landing forces at Aparri in Northern Luzon.

One of those aircraft, piloted by U.S. Army Capt. COLIN KELLY, after bombing a ship several miles offshore, crashed near Clark Field. Based on survivors reports of the B-17 strike, Kelly was reported by newspapers to have crashed into the battleship *Haruna* steaming off the coast, sinking the Japanese dreadnought. Kelly became one of America's first war heroes—although the *Haruna* was at the time lying at anchor off Hiroshima in the Japanese home islands.

Subsequently, the *Haruna* participated in Japa-

nese operations in the South Pacific and was part of the attacking force at the battle of MIDWAY. During the intensive fighting on GUADALCANAL, on the night of Oct. 13–14, 1942, the *Haruna* and her sister ship *Kongo* bombarded the U.S. airfield and troops on the island with their 14-inch (380-mm) guns. The eighty-minute attack with fragmentation and incendiary shells smashed some fifty U.S. planes, killed forty-one men, and severely damaged airfield facilities.

The battleship saw little further action until the Oct. 1944 battle for LEYTE GULF. She was part of the First Diversion Attack Force that attempted to break up the U.S. AMPHIBIOUS LANDING off the eastern coast of the Philippines. The force was mauled by U.S. carrier planes on Oct. 23; the superbattleship *Musashi* was sunk and the *Haruna* damaged by near-misses. But on Oct. 25 the *Haruna* was among the Japanese ships that fell on the U.S. ESCORT CARRIER force, inflicting considerable damage before withdrawing.

The *Haruna* was finally sunk in shallow water while at anchor near Kure, Japan, on July 28, 1945, after being hit by twelve BOMBS in raids by U.S. carrier planes on the 24th and 28th.

The *Haruna* was one of the four *Kongo*-class ships built as battle cruisers (the three other ships were sunk during the war). She was completed in 1915 and was extensively rebuilt in 1926–1930, being reclassified as a battleship. During World War II she had a displacement of 27,613 tons, was 704 feet long, and had a 30-knot speed. Her main armament was eight 14-inch guns, with a secondary battery of fourteen 6-inch (152-mm) guns plus an antiaircraft battery.

Hats

British code word for CONVOY to MALTA, Aug.–Sept. 1940.

Havoc,

see A-20.

Hawaii

On Dec. 7, 1941, when the Japanese attacked PEARL HARBOR, many Americans were unaware of Hawaii's status as a U.S. territory. A 1936 study of clippings from mainland newspapers had shown that 89 percent of them referred to Hawaii as a possession, a colony, or a foreign country. Statehood advocates launched a public relations program that reduced this misinformation level to 39 percent by 1938, but on the eve of the war Hawaii was still a political orphan. In a *Fortune* magazine poll conducted in 1939, Americans were asked if they would want to go to war if an enemy attacked Hawaii; 17 percent said they would not.

In 1940 about 80 percent of Hawaii's 423,300 residents were U.S. citizens. The figure did not include thousands of U.S. Army, Navy, and Marine personnel. The most numerous of Hawaii's other races were about 150,000 Japanese or JAPANESE-AMERICANS; 40,000 Japanese children, some of them U.S. citizens, attended Japanese-language schools.

Following the Japanese attack, U.S. authorities treated Hawaii as a war zone, an imminent target of invasion, and a refuge for potential enemies: the Japanese and AJA (Americans of Japanese Ancestry) populations. On the day of the attack the territorial governor suspended the writ of habeas corpus (the Constitutionally protected right against false imprisonment and illegal detention) and signed a martial-law declaration prepared by the Army. Lt. Gen. WALTER C. SHORT, head of the U.S. Army's Hawaiian Department and Army commander on Oahu, declaring himself "military governor." Short was relieved of command on Dec. 17, but martial law—the harshest Americans had lived under since the Civil War—continued until Oct. 24, 1944.

On the mainland, Japanese-Americans were put into internment camps under civil law. In Hawaii, 1,441 were interned under martial law, and 980 spent the war in captivity. All Japanese-language schools were shut down. Thousands of Japanese-Americans, fearing accusations of disloyalty or even ESPIONAGE, burned Japanese books and pictures of Emperor HIROHITO and Americanized their names. AJAs in the National Guard were discharged as potential security risks; about 150 of them volunteered to do manual labor for the Army. In Jan. 1943, after AJAs were allowed to join the armed services, 9,500 volunteered and 2,700 were accepted.

The Act of Congress that had made Hawaii a territory allowed declaration of martial law in case of imminent threat of invasion. Acting under the martial-law declaration, the military ordered a strictly enforced nightly BLACKOUT, ordering the arrest of anyone carrying lighted cigarettes, cigars, or pipes during the blackout; people were also arrested when authorities saw through windows the glow of a radio dial or a kitchen stove's lighted burner. The military set a 6 P.M. to 6 A.M. curfew for anyone not on official business and drew up intelligence reports on 450,000 Hawaiians.

The Army took over the islands. Military officials appropriated more than 300,000 acres of land, from pineapple plantations to school buildings and campuses. CENSORSHIP, unknown in the United States, was clamped down on Hawaii. All outgoing mail was read by military censors and long-distance telephone calls had to be in English so that eavesdropping censors could listen in. Letters that could not be censored simply by scissors or black-ink blocks were returned to the correspondents for rewriting.

To prevent Japanese invaders from disrupting U.S. currency, Hawaiians were ordered to turn in all U.S. paper money, which was destroyed and replaced by bills with *HAWAII* overprinted on them. Hawaiians were forbidden to make bank withdrawals of more than $200 in cash a month and no one could possess more than $200 in cash. To keep track of civilians, the military required that everyone over the age of six carry an identification card. Anyone caught without a card was subject to arrest.

Military courts tried thousands of cases, whether or not they had anything to do with wartime security. People accused of a crime went before a military judge, who listened to the charges, usually made without the presence of a lawyer. The judge then issued a sentence, which could be reversed only by a "pardon" from the military governor. There could be no appeals because there were no civilian courts, including appellate courts.

Civil liberties champions in Hawaii fought the sustained martial law. In 1944, a federal judge, rejecting testimony from high-ranking military officers—including Adm. CHESTER W. NIMITZ, CinC of the Pacific Area—ruled that military governing of Hawaii was no longer valid. The military ignored the ruling and President ROOSEVELT had to step in; he announced in Oct. 1944 the suspension of martial law and the restoration of habeas corpus.

In 1946 the U.S. Supreme Court, hearing appeals from Hawaiians arrested during the war, declared that the writ of habeas corpus should not have been suspended and that declaration of martial law did not allow the military to take over civilian courts, even in wartime.

Hawaii (Code Name)

Japanese code name for the air attack on PEARL HARBOR, Dec. 7, 1941.

He 111

Principal German bomber during the 1940 BATTLE OF BRITAIN. The He 111, described by aviation historian William Green as "elegant, well-built, well-planned," was the first modern bomber to be acquired by the German Air Force in the 1930s. The He 111 was an outstanding and versatile medium bomber when first produced. However, by the summer of 1940 it was highly vulnerable to modern fighters, such as the British HURRICANE and SPITFIRE.

Like many German warplanes of the 1930s, the He 111 was first revealed to the world in the civilian livery of Lufthansa. It was publicly displayed for the first time on Jan. 10, 1936, at Tempelhof Airport in BERLIN as a ten-passenger transport, labeled "the fastest machine in civil aviation" by German publicists. The few ostensibly civil aircraft were in fact the prototypes for high-speed medium bombers. In 1937 He 111B aircraft were sent to Spain for the CONDOR LEGION; their first combat mission was bombing Republican airfields at Alcalá and Madrid-Barajas on March 9, 1937. The He 111 was able to evade Republican fighters by virtue of its speed.

From the earliest days of the war the He 111 was employed in attacks against French and British shipping. Subsequently, the He 111 served as the principal bomber in the Battle of Britain in 1940. British defenses inflicted grievous losses on the He 111s.

The aircraft remained in service throughout the war. In Sept. 1944 the He 111 was employed to launch FZG-76 guided BOMBS against LONDON from over the North Sea. Through Jan. 14, 1945, these planes launched more than 1,200 missiles against London and other cities. The He 111 was also used extensively on the RUSSIAN FRONT as a bomber and antishipping aircraft, with TORPEDO aircraft sinking numerous ships in the RUSSIAN CONVOYS, including ten Allied merchant ships in CONVOY PQ 18 in Sept. 1942 alone.

The He 111 had a conventional albeit streamlined bomber design with a low wing mounting two in-line engines. The long, slim nose had a glazed bombardier's position. A ventral "dustbin" was soon fitted as well as an open dorsal position for defensive guns (later replaced by a streamlined gondola). The bombardier also fired a gun in the nose position. The early aircraft had a "stepped" cockpit; the first He 111P, completed late in 1938, introduced the pilot's position faired into the nose of the aircraft. The aircraft's bomb bay consisted of eight individual cells, four on each side of a gangway; the cells carried 551-pound bombs in a *nose-up* position. The He 111P was the main variant used in the 1940 raids, although a number of He 111F models still remained in service at that time. (The series-produced He 111H followed.)

Recognizing the vulnerability of the He 111, early in the war a pair of machine guns were mounted to fire from side windows and another gun was fitted in the ventral gondola to fire forward; some aircraft also had a 20-mm cannon fitted in the nose and a few had a remote-control machine gun fitted in the tail.

The Heinkel firm began developing the He 111 in early 1934 and finished the first prototype late that year. It flew for the first time early in 1935. A speed of 214 mph—equal to that of many fighters—was reached early in the test program. The speed of development can be seen with delivery of the first production bomber aircraft in late 1936. (Only a few civil aircraft were flown; they were found to be not suitable for airline use.) During 1942 production of the He 111 was to run down in favor of producing the HE 177 heavy bomber and

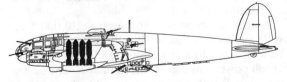

He 111 bomber.

Ju 288 medium bomber; however, failure of both types necessitated continued manufacture of the He 111. When German production finally ended after nine years in the fall of 1944, Heinkel plants had produced more than 7,300 of these aircraft. (License production continued in Spain into the 1950s.) The aircraft was also flown by China, Spain, and Turkey.

Some of the more unusual variants that flew were the He 111Z *Zwilling* (Twin)—essentially two aircraft connected at the wings with a fifth engine mounted—for use as a tug for large gliders and a saboteur transport that carried eight parachutists in place of bombs.

The He 111H had a speed of 258 mph at 16,400 feet; range with maximum bomb load was 760 miles, with a maximum range of 1,740 miles. Defense armament for the He 111H totaled one 20-mm cannon and six 7.9-mm machine guns. An internal bomb load of 4,408 pounds could be carried, or an external load of 5,510 pounds of bombs or a torpedo. The normal crew was five or six, depending upon the number of guns fitted.

He 115

German maritime reconnaissance and antishipping aircraft. The twin-engine He 115 was a floatplane and was effective in attacking Allied CONVOYS with BOMBS and aerial TORPEDOES, reconnaissance, and in laying naval MINES. The aircraft was also flown in the search-and-rescue role. It had a reputation for good handling in the air and on the water, also for being highly reliable and able to fly on one engine with a significant load.

The He 115 was the first German aircraft fitted to lay magnetic mines, an operation that began on the night of Nov. 20–21, 1939, when several planes laid mines by parachute off Harwich and at the mouth of the Thames River. The planes subsequently participated in the invasion of Norway in 1940. From late 1941 the planes attacked shipping in the arctic, including the doomed CONVOY PQ 17.

The prototype He 115 flew in 1936. Early models set a number of seaplane records, including a speed of 204.93 mph. The aircraft entered operational service in 1939 and served through the end of 1944; about 500 were delivered.

The mid-wing He 115 had two radial engines and

differed from most twin-engine seaplanes in having floats rather than being a flying boat. Production aircraft had a glazed nose and long, glazed cockpit. The He 115B could reach 196 mph and had a range of 1,300 miles. An internal weapons bay could carry up to four 551-pound bombs or a torpedo. Early models had two flexible 7.9-mm machine guns, with the He 115D having a forward-firing 20-mm cannon; later a chin-mounted 20-mm gun was added to most aircraft. The crew numbered three or four.

He 162 *Volksjäger* (People's Fighter)

A "tool of desperation" in the words of a wartime British intelligence report, this JET-PROPELLED AIRCRAFT was part of the German effort to turn the remaining aviation industry to producing fighters to intercept the Allied bomber formations that were devastating Germany in 1944–1945. The He 162 was a small, simple, jet-propelled aircraft that was to be flown by pilots (including teenagers) who had received rudimentary flight training on gliders! But the aircraft were considered "hot" to handle, and experienced pilots were needed.

A requirement for the *Volksjäger* was formally issued on Sept. 8, 1944, and twelve days later the Heinkel firm began construction of prototype aircraft. The first aircraft flew on Dec. 6, 1944—ninety days after conception of the aircraft. (Four days later the aircraft crashed, killing the pilot.) Production had totaled only 116 aircraft when Germany capitulated. Several He 162 units were formed, but combat was forbidden as they were not combat ready. There were some encounters with Allied fighters, but no actual combat is know to have occurred.

The He 162 design was simple, with a high wing and the turbojet engine mounted atop the fuselage; the wings had turned-down tips to prevent excessive side-slip; the tail assembly had twin fins. A ROCKET canister could be attached for take-off assistance. The nosewheel landing gear was fully retractable.

Maximum speed was 562 mph at 20,000 feet, with flight endurance at that altitude at full power being forty-eight minutes; at 36,000 feet endurance at full power was eighty-three minutes. The single-seat aircraft was armed with two 20-mm cannon.

The aircraft was also called "Salamander" by the Germans.

He 177 *Greif* (Griffin)

The Luftwaffe's principal "heavy bomber" and candidate to carry the German ATOMIC BOMB. The He 177 was developed as a heavy bomber, primarily to attack enemy shipping. The aircraft was plagued by technical problems, entered production before many were solved, and was thoroughly disliked by its crews; several early accidents gave it the appellation "Flaming Coffin." Added to the technical problems was the fact that the Luftwaffe had no strategic-bombing doctrine for the employment of the He 177.

The problems that delayed the service entry of the He 177 were pushed aside in Jan. 1943 when the first operational planes were pressed into cargo service to aid the beleaguered German garrison at STALINGRAD. More in line with the plane's original purpose, in 1943 several planes were modified to launch Hs 293A or FRITZ-X GUIDED MISSILES against Allied shipping. Attacks against CONVOYS began in Nov. 1943 with the former missile. Beginning on Jan. 21, 1944, several He 177s joined in the resumption of Luftwaffe bombing raids against Britain. The attacks (Operation Steinbock) continued into May 1944. The planes were also used in large numbers on the Soviet front.

Subsequently, Allied STRATEGIC BOMBING of German cities led to the conversion of several He 177s in 1944 to the fighter-interceptor role! Following prototype trials, five planes had their BOMB bays replaced by thirty-three upward-firing ROCKET tubes to fire air-to-air rockets; no actual intercept efforts were recorded. Among several other unusual modifications, an He 177 was flown to the Letov works near Prague in 1942 for modification to carry an atomic bomb when that weapon became available. Apparently several aircraft were taken in hand for that project, but modification work stopped in Aug. 1944 and the planes were badly damaged in a U.S. bombing raid on March 25, 1945.

One He 177A-1 was readied for a high-altitude flight across the Soviet Union to Japan to provide a prototype for production for the Japanese Navy. That project was also abandoned because the Japanese did not wish to violate their neutrality pact with the Soviet Union by the overflight. This aircraft and some others were, reportedly, considered for one-way (suicide) attacks against targets in the United States.

The Air Ministry requirement for a bomber able to carry 4,410 pounds of bombs to a target 1,000 miles from base led to the Heinkel firm developing the He 177. The first prototype flew on Nov. 19, 1939; several of the early aircraft crashed—as did a number of later planes. More than 1,000 aircraft were built with just over half that number being the He 177A-5 variant.

The He 177 was a mid-wing aircraft powered by two *double* engines in twin, radial nacelles. The unusual arrangement was adopted because 2,000-horsepower engines were not available for a standard twin-engine configuration. The aircraft had a large, twin-wheel undercarriage and small tail wheel, large wingspan, and single tail fin. (The few He 177B-5 models had a twin-tail arrangement.) The He 177A-5 had a maximum speed of 303 mph, a ceiling of only 8,000 feet, and with two Hs 293A missiles a range of 3,420 miles.

The standard bomb load was four 551-pound or two 1,102-pound bombs in the weapon bay, or two TORPEDOES or guided missiles under the wing. Heavier payloads could be carried for short distances. Defensive armament varied, with the original design providing for remote-control 20-mm gun turrets, which were never provided. The He 177A-5 production aircraft had two 20-mm cannon, three to five 130-mm machine guns, and one 7.9-mm machine gun. The crew numbered six.

Headache

British code name for countermeasures to Luftwaffe navigation beams projected over England; see ELECTRONIC COUNTERMEASURES.

Heckle

British code name for use of MIDGET SUBMARINES to attack a German floating dry dock at Bergen, Norway, Sept. 1944

Hedgehog

Highly effective antisubmarine spigot-MORTAR on Allied warships. The hedgehog consisted of twenty-four fixed spigots in six rows, aimed to fire over the bow of a ship; the spigots were slightly angled, so that the 70-pound projectiles, fired in salvo, would hit the sea some 230 yards ahead of the ship in a circular pattern about 130 feet in diameter. Each projectile was 7.2 inches (183 mm) in diameter with tail fins for stability in flight, and was filled with 30 pounds of the explosive Torpex. The launchers were reloaded by hand.

The hedgehog was a highly accurate weapon and, because it fired ahead, had the advantage that the attacking ship did not have to pass over the target U-BOAT, as the ship did when using DEPTH CHARGES, thus losing SONAR contact immediately before the attack. Unlike the depth charge, the hedgehog projectiles did not detonate at a preset depth, but only upon contact with a U-boat. This meant less interference with sonar but a near miss would do no damage. A single hit, however, could inflict fatal damage on a U-boat. On the other side of the coin, the effect of nearby—and sometimes even distant—depth-charge explosions certainly had a debilitating effect on a U-boat crew, especially when the attacks were sometimes kept up for several hours.

Early hedgehogs had problems. One exploded prematurely, heavily damaging a British ship. On occasion a projectile would not fire, presenting a potential danger for crewmen trying to remove it. Problems delayed its widespread installation in U.S. and British antisubmarine ships until 1943. A single hedgehog salvo had a 20 percent chance of sinking a U-boat, based on British 1943–1945 experience in the Atlantic. But, the USS *ENGLAND* (DE 635) in the Pacific sank six Japanese submarines with only twelve hedgehog salvoes—a 50 percent effectiveness.

The SQUID was a heavier version of the hedgehog. A lighter version, for use in smaller antisubmarine craft, was used by the U.S. Navy. This weapon—called "mousetrap"—fired a pattern from four or eight projectors.

In the U.S. Navy the hedgehog was used mostly in DESTROYER ESCORTS; the hedgehog was too large for destroyers because installation would displace guns. After the evaluation of mousetraps in twelve destroyers, the weapons were removed from all but one; destroyers continued to use depth charges as their only weapon against submerged submarines.

Hedgehog Obstacle

TANK obstacle made up of three crossed iron bars. Usually used on land, in preparation for the NORMANDY INVASION, the German Army set up hedgehogs in shallow water to tear the bottoms out of Allied LANDING CRAFT.

Heinrich

German code name for large antipartisan operation conducted west of Nevel in the western Soviet Union (near the Latvian border), Nov. 1943.

Helen

The Ki-49 Type 100 *Donryu* (Storm Dragon) failed to prove in combat the extravagant claims that were made for it at the time of its introduction into the Japanese Army Air Force (Allied code name was Helen). Like the more successful Japanese P1Y FRANCES, the Helen was developed as a high-speed heavy bomber, a type long neglected in Japanese service. The Helen was to operate without fighter escort, relying for protection on its speed and heavy gun armament.

The aircraft entered operational service in Aug. 1941, first seeing combat over China, and then in the Southwest Pacific area, including bombing raids on Australia. When the ALLIES invaded the Philippines, the Helens were heavily engaged; from Dec. 1944 many of the survivors were employed in suicide attacks against U.S. ships. Helens were also employed as transports and, heavily modified, in night-fighter and antisubmarine roles. An escort fighter version was developed (Ki-58), heavily armed and armored and intended to escort other Helens on long-range strikes; none was built as long-range Army fighters became available. Also, a bomber formation leader configuration (Ki-80) was developed, but only two were built.

The aircraft was criticized by its pilots as being underpowered (and hence too slow) and difficult to fly; however, the aircraft had armor and self-sealing fuel tanks, important factors in aerial combat, and its armament further enhanced chances of survival against Allied fighters.

The first prototype Nakajima Ki-49 flew in Aug. 1939. The early aircraft flew extensive trials, with engines being upgraded for the production models, but still not meeting performance requirements.

Through Dec. 1944 a total of 819 Helens were produced.

The Helen bore a superficial resemblance to the larger Navy G4M BETTY, both being twin-engine, mid-wing bombers with glazed nose and tail positions, the Helen being the first Army bomber with a tail gun position. The tail-sitting aircraft had a relatively tall tail fin.

Top speed for the Ki-49-II major production variant was 306 mph with a range of 1,245 miles and—in overload condition—1,835 miles. An internal BOMB bay could hold up to 2,205 pounds of bombs. Defense armament in the bomber role was one 20-mm cannon in the dorsal position, and flexible 12.7-mm machine guns in the nose, ventral, tail, and side positions—a total of six guns.

The planned Ki-58 was to have five 20-mm cannon and three 12.7-mm machine guns (no bombs carried). The abortive night-fighter effort provided for two-plane teams, one with a searchlight to locate the enemy bomber and one with a 75-mm cannon to destroy it. A crew of eight flew the bomber variants.

Helicopters

Germany, Britain, Japan, and the United States made use of rotary-wing aircraft—autogiros and helicopters—in the war. Autogiros had an unpowered rotor whose movement through the air served as a lifting surface (i.e., wing) while a conventional aircraft propeller provided forward thrust; autogiros could take off and land in very short distances but could not hover. Helicopters had a powered rotor that provided both lift and forward (or backward) thrust; they could take off and land vertically, and hover in flight.

Germany   Germany had the largest helicopter program during the war. Anton Flettner developed a series of successful helicopter designs with his Fl 265, which first flew in May 1939, demonstrating the efficiency of helicopters in support of military operations. During trials Fl 265s recovered an engine from a downed aircraft, lifted a cannon carriage weighing 496 pounds, and conducted shipboard landings and takeoffs. In flight tests ME 109 and FW 190 fighters maneuvered with an Fl 265 for twenty minutes with the gun camera film indicating that neither one of the fighters was able to gain a firing position on the helicopter!

This led Flettner to develop the Fl 282 *Kolibri* (Humming Bird), which first flew in 1940 and entered service as an antisubmarine aircraft in 1942. Only twenty-nine operational prototypes were built, but the single-seat helicopter was used aboard ship to search for submarines in the Baltic and Mediterranean; one landing was reported to have been made on the deck of a surfaced, moving submarine. Allied bombings aborted plans to produce 1,000 for the Army and Navy.

Probably the only other German helicopter to actually become operational was the Focke-Achgelis Fa 330 "automotive kite." This helicopter had a steel tubular construction with a conventional aircraft tail assembly that could be folded and disassembled to fit into a submarine. A submarine running into the wind could launch an Fa 330 tethered on a cable 200 to 500 feet in length, permitting the pilot to keep a lookout for Allied CONVOYS. A telephone line was imbedded in the steel cable for communication with the submarine, and in an emergency the pilot could parachute from the kite—and hope that the submarine would pick him up. About 200 of these devices were built with some being used at sea. (A powered version with a 60-horsepower engine was proposed, but never built.)

A Luftwaffe transport helicopter, the Fa 223, could carry four troops or, on an external sling, some 2,000 pounds of cargo. It first flew in 1940 and only ten were built before Allied bombing brought a halt to production—which was planned to reach 400 units per month. A few missions may have been flown, probably rescue operations.

A number of other German helicopters were test-flown and proposed. Most impressive was the Fa 284, a twin-engine helicopter that was to have been able to lift almost eight tons by sling, including armored vehicles and trucks. This aircraft did not fly.

Great Britain   The only British rotary-wing aircraft to see service in the war was the C.30A Rota, an autogiro designed by Juan de la Cierva. It first flew and entered RAF service in 1934 (with British-built variants being tested from an Italian cruiser as well as a British aircraft carrier).

These autogiros, flown by the RAF throughout the war, were used mainly as RADAR calibration targets. Twelve C.30As were built for the RAF and more than that number were taken over from civilian sources for military use.

Japan The Japanese Army sponsored development of the Kayaba Ka-1 autogiro, based on the American Kellett autogiro flown by the U.S. Army as the YG-1. About 240 were produced for the Japanese Army. Entering service in 1942 and intended primarily for antisubmarine work, they were also used ashore for artillery spotting and liaison.

The two-place Ka-1 was flown from land bases to hunt submarines, and from the small aircraft carrier *Akitsu Maru,* converted from a merchant ship, until she was sunk by a U.S. SUBMARINE in Nov. 1944.

USSR The Soviet Union experimented with several helicopter and autogiro designs before the war. Although it did not become operational, the TsAGI-designed A-15 autogiro that first flew in 1937 was a true military aircraft, having a radio, three machine guns, and an aerial camera.

United States In America the emphasis in the 1930s was on autogiro development with the Army, Navy, and Marine Corps testing these rotary-wing craft. The Navy flew a Pitcairn XOP-1 from the AIRCRAFT CARRIER *LANGLEY* (CV 1) in 1931 and tested one without a pilot, it being radio controlled. The Marines flew one during counter-GUERRILLA operations in Nicaragua. The Army's Kellet G-1 autogiro first flew and became operational in 1936. The Army flew several to evaluate the aircraft's potential to support military operations.

But the major development in this field was the work of Igor Sikorsky, who had developed the world's first four-engine aircraft in Russia on the eve of World War I. Sikorsky's first successful rotary-wing aircraft flew in 1940 and immediately attracted the attention of the U.S. Army and Navy. Although contemporary German helicopters were easier to fly and required less maintenance, Sikorsky VS-300 was the progenitor of the American helicopter program. The Army R-4 version and the Navy HNS-1 variant began flying in 1942 and entered service in 1943, with the Coast Guard operating the aircraft for the Navy.

The R-4 could carry a pilot and observer at speeds up to 75 mph with a range of 130 miles. Sikorsky produced 206, including prototypes, of which 103 went to the RAF and Royal Navy and one to Canada. They were used mainly for rescue operations, but in 1944 an R-4 flew an agent of the OFFICE OF STRATEGIC SERVICES into the Balkans on a clandestine mission. The Army and Coast Guard both conducted flight tests from ships and the Coast Guard cutter *Cobb* (WPG 181) operated two R-4s on a trans-Atlantic crossing.

The improved Sikorsky R-5 and R-6 (Navy HOS) also entered service during the war.

The Platt LePage R-1, a futuristic-looking single-engine, twin-rotor helicopter, and the equally streamlined Kellett R-8 helicopter with intermeshing, contra-rotating rotors were also evaluated during the war, but did not enter service.

Hellcat,
   see F6F.

Helldiver,
   see SB2C.

Heller, Joseph (1923—)

In his novel *Catch-22* (1955) Heller drew from the reality of life in the U.S. Army Air Forces the surrealism of a time and place during World War II. A character explains what Catch-22 was: If a pilot were crazy, he could be grounded. "All he had to do was ask; and as soon as he did, he would no longer be crazy and would have to fly more missions. . . . If he flew them he was crazy and didn't have to; but if he didn't want to he was sane and had to. . . ."

After hearing this, the book's hero, Yossarian, observes, "That's some catch, that Catch-22."

Hemingway, Ernest (1899–1961)

Writer and WAR CORRESPONDENT. Hemingway, an ambulance driver and casualty in World War I, went to war again in the SPANISH CIVIL WAR, which he covered from the Nationalist (Loyalist), anti-FRANCO side. His novel *For Whom the Bell Tolls,* a best-seller published in 1940, brought the war to the American public. The book's hero, Robert Jordan, died a martyr, believing "If we win here we will win everywhere." Jordan personified the anti-NAZI, idealistic young Americans who joined the ABRAHAM LINCOLN BRIGADE, made up of American volunteers.

During World War II Hemingway occasionally covered the war as a correspondent, in China and in France. He lived much of the time in Cuba, where, as he later told it, he "worked under Naval Intelligence," using his 40-foot cabin cruiser *Pilar* as a raider against U-BOATS believed to be using Cuban bays as sanctuaries. Hemingway never captured a U-boat, but he said he was "credited by Naval Intelligence with locating several Nazi subs which were later bombed out by Navy depth charges and presumed sunk."

No records bear out any of his claims. No private vessel was used as a "raider." As for U-boats in Cuban "sanctuaries," U.S. officials considered Cuba one of the most helpful of Caribbean countries working with the United States in the U-boat war.

The FEDERAL BUREAU OF INVESTIGATION opened a file on Hemingway, apparently because J. EDGAR HOOVER, director of the FBI, was annoyed by Hemingway's freelance anti-ESPIONAGE activity. The FBI had jurisdiction over espionage in Latin America. "Hemingway's investigations," an FBI report said, "began to show a marked hostility to the Cuban Police and in a lesser degree to the FBI."

Henderson, Leon (1885–1986)

Chief of the OFFICE OF PRICE ADMINISTRATION (OPA). President ROOSEVELT appointed Henderson, an economist, to the National Defense Advisory Commission in May 1940. In April 1941, when the Office of Price Administration and Civilian Supply (soon reorganized as the OPA) was established, Henderson was made its administrator. Henderson, often called the "price czar" in newspaper headlines, was described by newsman David Brinkley as "an economist who could not control his weight, his shirttail, his hair, his shoelaces or his temper. . . . His daily habit was to find the tenderest toes in Washington and step on them." Henderson was succeeded in Jan. 1943 by Prentiss M. Brown, a former Democratic senator from Michigan who lasted until Oct. He was followed by Chester Bowles, a former advertising executive, who took the OPA into its postwar years.

Herbstnebel (Autumn Fog)

(1) Early German code name for the ARDENNES offensive (see: *WACHT AM RHEIN*); (2) German code name for the evacuation of the Po area in Italy, 1944.

Herbstreise (Autumn Journey)

German code name for deception plan for Operation SEA LION in which, two days before the planned cross-Channel landings, four cruisers and four troopships (including the former liners *Bremen* and *Europa*) would feint a landing on the British coast between Aberdeen and Newcastle.

Hercules

Code name for plan for the Allied assault on Rhodes, early 1944.

Herkules

Code name for German plan for the invasion of MALTA, 1942.

Hero of the Soviet Union

The highest Soviet decoration awarded for heroism in the face of danger. During the World War II period the decoration was awarded for three different conflicts: the conflict with the Japanese at Khalkhin-Gol in Mongolia, 1937–1939; the war with Finland in 1939–1940; and the Great Patriotic War, 1941–1945.

The award was made to men and WOMEN of all ranks, from marshal to private. Multiple awards were made for heroism in different actions. For example, the two top-scoring Soviet fighter ACES, I. N. KOZHEDUB with sixty-two kills and A. I. Pokryshkin with fifty-nine kills, were three-time Heroes of the Soviet Union.

Massive numbers of the award were made in some operations. For example, in the crossing under fire of the Dnepr River in Sept. 1943—where Soviet forces attempted to prevent the Germans from making a defensive stand—some 2,000 awards of Hero of the Soviet Union were made to the first troops across.

Fliers and sailors also received the award in large numbers. The award meant a life pension and public recognition—a life-size bust of the recipient was to be displayed in his home town.

The award originated with Soviet flights into the Arctic to rescue the expedition under Dr. Otto Schmidt when their research ship, the *Chelyushkin*, became trapped in ice and sank in Feb. 1934. The rescue flights, in March and April, won seven of the fliers the first awards of the Hero of the Soviet Union.

Hersey, John (1914—)

WAR CORRESPONDENT and Pulitzer Prize–winning author of several books related to World War II. Born in China, he lived there until his family returned to the United States when he was a child. He studied at Yale and Cambridge and worked for a time as Sinclair Lewis's secretary. As a correspondent for *Life* magazine, he covered the Pacific. His first book, *Man on Bataan* (1942) won him little renown. But his second, *Into the Valley* (1943), written after he went ashore at GUADALCANAL and wrote about a skirmish there, established his reputation as a solid reporter and sensitive writer. His third book, *A Bell for Adano* (1944), a novel that takes place during the ITALIAN CAMPAIGN, won him the Pulitzer Prize for fiction.

While moving about the Pacific, he discovered PT-BOATS and wrote about them for *Life*. Later, in New York, he met Navy Lt. JOHN F. KENNEDY, who casually told Hersey a harrowing story about *PT 109*. Hersey interviewed survivors of the PT-boat's crew and wrote an article for *Life*, which turned it down. Hersey submitted it to the *New Yorker*, which published it in June 1944 and allowed the *Reader's Digest* to republish it. The account of Kennedy's heroism would become part of the legend of Kennedy, the candidate for President.

Hersey also wrote *The Wall* (1950), about the WARSAW GHETTO. His world-famous *HIROSHIMA* (1946) was the first comprehensive account of the ATOM BOMB attack as described by survivors.

Hershey, Maj. Gen. Lewis B. (1893–1977)

A veteran of Mexican border skirmishes and World War I, Hershey in 1937 was appointed executive secretary to the Joint Army and Navy SELECTIVE SERVICE Committee. For the rest of his Army career he would be the man in charge of the draft. Hershey set up the machinery for registering and calling up young men well before Congress passed the 1940 legislation authorizing the nation's first peacetime draft. He was appointed director of Selective Service on July 31, 1941. He continued in the post through the Korean War and much of the Vietnam War. Never before in his career had he personally been subjected to antidraft protests. He endured them stoically and stepped down in 1969

to become President RICHARD M. NIXON's adviser on manpower.

Hess, Rudolf (1894–1987)

Confidential aide to ADOLF HITLER and deputy führer who fled to England. Hess, who was wounded in World War I, was an officer in the same infantry regiment that Hitler served in as a corporal. Hess ended the war as a flier but did not fly in combat. After the war, believing that "great questions are always decided by blood and iron," he joined the NAZI Party.

Arrested after the abortive Nazi "beer-hall putsch" in Munich in 1923, Hess went to prison with Hitler and transcribed much of Hitler's book, *Mein Kampf*. He rose from private secretary to Hitler's principal—and doting—aide. Soon after Hitler became chancellor in 1933, he made Hess his deputy führer. In 1939, on the eve of the EUROPEAN WAR, Hess became a member of the Ministerial Council for the Defense of Germany and No. 3 man in government, after HERMANN GÖRING. "Hitler," Hess said, "is simply pure reason incarnate" and "the greatest son whom my nation has brought forth in the thousand years of its history."

During the Olympic Games held in BERLIN in 1936 Hess met a British aristocrat, the future duke of Hamilton. When the war began, Hess, apparently without Hitler's knowledge, wrote the duke a letter containing a peace feeler. The duke, on the instructions of the British government, ignored the letter.

Hess, with the help of Willy Messerschmitt, learned to fly an ME 110 fighter. On May 10, 1941, Hess took off from Ausburg in an unarmed Me 110 and headed for the Duke of Hamilton's estate. Off course, he bailed out over Scotland. He was baffled by England's lack of interest in his self-invented peace mission: He believed that when Germany invaded the Soviet Union the following month England could be persuaded to take Germany's side against communism.

He was said to have left a note to Hitler saying that if the mission failed Hitler could say that Hess had gone mad. That was just what Hitler did—in a rage. He purged Hess from the party and replaced him with MARTIN BORMANN. Although the Germans were as baffled as the British (who treated

Hess as a mental case), Hitler confidant ALBERT SPEER observed: "Hess was probably trying, after so many years of being kept in the background, to win prestige and some success. For he did not have the qualities necessary for survival in the midst of a swamp of intrigues and struggles for power."

The British put Hess in the Tower of LONDON and held him for the rest of the war. During the Nuremberg WAR CRIMES trials he feigned amnesia, but the tribunal found him guilty of conspiracy to commit crimes and crimes against humanity. Ignoring the Soviet prosecutors' call for a death sentence, the tribunal sentenced him to life in prison. He was sent, with six other convicted Nazis, to Spandau prison in the western sector of Berlin. He saw the others die or leave and after 1966 he became the sole prisoner. After he died in 1987 the prison was torn down and a supermarket was built on the site.

Hewitt, Adm. Henry K. (1887–1972)

The foremost U.S. practitioner of amphibious operations in the Atlantic-Mediterranean areas. In April 1942, after commanding naval forces in the western Atlantic as part of the U.S. NEUTRALITY PATROL, Hewitt was named commander of the Atlantic FLEET's Amphibious Force. During the next two and a half years he became one of the most experienced practitioners of large AMPHIBIOUS LANDINGS in any navy.

Hewitt began his "amphib" work with a difficult task, that of convoying the American forces from the U.S. East Coast to Morocco in Nov. 1942 for the NORTH AFRICA INVASION. Although the landing craft wastage was high and there was some opposition from French forces, the landings were remarkably well executed. In Feb. 1943, Hewitt was promoted to vice admiral and named commander of the U.S. Eighth Fleet. In July 1943 he commanded the Western Naval Task Force that carried out the landing of U.S. troops in SICILY. He then commanded all naval forces supporting the Allied landings at SALERNO and elsewhere in Italy. Gen. GEORGE S. PATTON's drive to Palermo and thence to Messina along the Sicilian coast was closely supported by Hewitt's ships.

In the Southern France landings of Aug. 1944 his Eighth Fleet's competence was at its peak, carrying out its tasks with dispatch and little loss. Hewitt

was in command of over 1,000 ships and responsible for 400,000 soldiers and sailors.

In April 1945 Hewitt was promoted to admiral and in August he was given command of the Twelfth Fleet—U.S. naval forces in Europe, a post he held until Sept. 1946. During this time the Navy began the peacetime deployment of warships to the Mediterranean that would later evolve into the permanently deployed Sixth Fleet.

Heydrich, Reinhard (1904–1942)

Chief of the REICH CENTRAL SECURITY OFFICE and one of the principal planners of Germany's FINAL SOLUTION for JEWS. Heydrich had been forced to resign from the German Navy in 1931 for "conduct unbecoming to an officer and gentlemen" after seducing a young girl. But that did not hurt his career as a NAZI. That same year he joined the Nazi Party and subsequently the SS. He was the first chief of the SD, *Sicherheitsdienst*, the intelligence-gathering and ESPIONAGE section of the SS.

After swiftly and mercilessly carrying out the "Blood Purge" of SA leader ERNST RÖHM, Heydrich became a *Brigadeführer* and a close associate of SS chief HEINRICH HIMMLER, who in 1936 gave Heydrich command of the GESTAPO. He issued the secret orders for the "spontaneous demonstrations" for *KRISTALLNACHT,* the 1938 assault on German Jews. Using blackmail and intelligence gathered by a huge network of informers, he manufactured the evidence that purged Gen. WERNER VON BLOMBERG and Gen. Werner Freiherr von Fritsch, chief of the High Command of the German Army.

Heydrich also engineered the fake incident, code-named Canned Goods, which gave Hitler a trumped-up reason to invade Poland: On Aug. 31, 1939, the eve of the scheduled invasion, Heydrich crafted a Polish "raid" on a German border radio station. The raiders were SS men dressed in Polish uniforms. For proof, he supplied bodies in Polish uniforms. The victims were German CONCENTRATION CAMP prisoners, killed by fatal injection, and then shot at the scene. Similar deceptions, using other similarly murdered prisoners, were staged elsewhere under his direction. (SS men who took part were later "put out of the way," a Nazi testified at the Nuremberg WAR CRIMES trial.)

When the war began, Heydrich launched Operation Reinhard, the plan for the systematic extermination of the Jews of Poland. The "Blond Beast," as Heydrich was called, became Deputy Reich Protector of Bohemia and Moravia (as Germany designated western Czechoslovakia) in Sept. 1941 and continued mass executions there. In Jan. 1942 he called the WANNSEE CONFERENCE, whose agenda was "the final solution of the European Jewish Question."

On May 27, 1942, two Czech agents, trained in England, parachuted into Czechoslovakia, ambushed Heydrich's car, fired at him and his bodyguard, and rolled a bomb under the car. There is some evidence that the British experts who constructed the bomb added a vial of deadly germs. Wounded but quickly treated, Heydrich nevertheless died, apparently of infection, on June 4.

In an orgy of bloody reprisals, SS men razed the Czech village of LIDICE and killed its male inhabitants; more than 1,000 Czechs elsewhere were sentenced to death; and 3,000 inmates of the Theresienstadt camp for Jews were sent to their deaths.

H-hour

Hour on D-DAY designated as the start of an Allied military operation.

Higgins, Andrew J. (1886–1952)

American shipbuilder who developed innovative LANDING CRAFT used by U.S. forces in World War II. He began building boats at the age of twelve and by 1926 had built a highly successful shallow-draft boat called the *Eureka* for use on the lower Mississippi River and along the Gulf Coast. This craft was the predecessor for a highly successful series of World War II–era landing craft.

Higgins' aircraft venture was less successful. According to the official U.S. AAF history, his Higgins Aircraft Co. of New Orleans was "one of the AAF's more expensive failures." The plant, erected at a cost of more than $23 million, produced only two C-46 COMMANDO transport aircraft before the end of the war (contracts for 498 more planes were canceled).

Highball Bomb

"Bouncing" BOMB intended to attack enemy ships in protected harbors. They were never used in combat. A design of Barnes Wallis, who conceived the UPKEEP and "earthquake bombs," the Highball bombs were spherical and two could be carried by a MOSQUITO light bomber. Prior to release the bombs were spun backwards at 700 to 900 revolutions per minute. The planes would release the bombs from an altitude of only 60 feet while flying at 360 mph. The bombs were to skip across the water and then detonate at a depth of 30 feet alongside the target ships.

RAF squadron No. 618 was formed on April 1, 1943, to deliver the Highball bombs, their principal target being the battleship *TIRPITZ*, normally anchored in a Norwegian fjord. However, the movement of the German battleship to a northern fjord placed the ship beyond the range of Mosquitos based in Britain; thus, the squadron was disbanded in Sept. 1943 and the modified Mosquitos were put in storage. In mid-1944 the decision was made to employ the Highball bombs against Japanese warships. Twenty-nine of the modified Mosquitos were returned to service with squadron No. 618, but with *Navy* pilots under RAF Wing Comdr. F. E. Hutchinson, and with the planes being further modified to operate from jeep or ESCORT CARRIERS. In Oct. 1944 two British escort carriers embarked twenty-eight Mosquitos (twenty-five Highball bombers and three photo-reconnaissance aircraft) and set course for the Far East. These were the first twin-engine aircraft to be regularly assigned to an aircraft carrier.

However, when the ships and No. 618 squadron arrived in the Far East there were continual delays in employing the Highball bombs and, finally, in June 1945 the squadron was again disbanded and the 150 bombs aboard the carriers were destroyed.

The Highball bombs weighed 1,280 pounds and carried 600 pounds of explosives. The Highball was developed simultaneously with Wallis' Upkeep bomb.

High-Frequency/Direction Finding

HF/DF or "Huff-Duff" was the means of locating U-BOATS by their radio transmissions. German submarine tactics, especially when "WOLF PACKS" were used, required that the submarine detecting a CONVOY broadcast the position to attract other U-boats.

The Royal Navy was the first navy to adopt Huff-Duff, employing both land-based and shipboard intercept systems. The British had begun the establishment of listening stations—primarily to intercept radio transmissions for code-breaking activities—in the late 1920s. The efforts were accelerated in the late 1930s because of the Abyssinian crisis and the SPANISH CIVIL WAR. In particular, during the Spanish conflict it became important to identify the "pirate" (Italian) submarines attacking merchant ships carrying supplies to the Republican forces.

The Royal Navy began deploying Huff-Duff systems in warships in the late 1930s. Subsequently, the Canadians developed a device that automatically recorded the bearings of the transmission. As a further improvement, employing the services of French research scientists who had fled the NAZIS, the U.S. Navy developed a device that automatically plotted the bearings to the transmitting U-boat as visual images on a screen. This device helped in making an attack on the U-boat by continuing to indicate the bearings of even a brief radio signal after transmission had ceased. The prototype version of this Huff-Duff system was tested at sea in a DESTROYER in March 1940, and was rapidly followed by improved models.

While shore-based stations were valuable for both the detection and recording of U-boat transmissions (for decoding under ULTRA) and rerouting of convoys, the availability of Huff-Duff on convoy escort ships provided the location of "shadowing" submarines to permit attacks by escorts or accompanying aircraft. When a convoy escort intercepted a U-boat transmission it generally meant the submarine was not more than 15 to 20 miles away (this was the "ground bounce" phenomena of high-frequency transmissions). As the intercept provided a bearing, it was possible to dispatch an escort or aircraft out to hunt for the U-boat. Even if the escort failed to sink the submarine, by forcing the submarine to submerge and cease broadcasting, the convoy could radically alter course and probably escape.

During the war the German submarine command consistently underestimated the vulnerability of U-boat operations to Huff-Duff detection.

Himmler, Heinrich (1900–1945)

Reichsführer-SS (leader of the SS, the NAZI secret police) and overseer of CONCENTRATION CAMPS. An army veteran of World War I, Himmler was an early Nazi official, handling party jobs while running a Bavarian chicken farm. His pince-nez and diffident manner cloaked the ruthless personality of a Nazi who was an architect of horror and terror, but never the practitioner.

An early follower of ADOLF HITLER, Himmler worked himself up from commander of political police in Bavaria to a place of power that ultimately was second only to Hitler's. Among his first acts as SS chief was the establishment in 1933 of DACHAU as a "model" concentration camp for dissidents. In 1934 he engineered the Night of the Long Knives, the Blood Purge against ERNST RÖHM, whose SA police apparatus was thus destroyed, assuring the rise of Himmler's SS (*Schutzstaffel*—"protection detachment"). Himmler put SS men in charge at Dachau, establishing the precedent that the SS would run concentration camps and carry out Hitler's orders to murder perceived enemies of the state.

When Germany went to war in 1939, Hitler made Himmler the Commissar for Consolidation of German Nationhood, which translated into the mass murder of JEWS and others whose genealogy or beliefs were contrary to Nazi beliefs. He set up Nazi stud farms where unwed "German women and girls of good blood" could bear the children "of soldiers setting off to battle." He supervised the forced eviction of Poles to the east to make room for ethnic Germans. He ordered the systematic killing of concentration camp inmates at AUSCHWITZ and oversaw the massacre of the WARSAW GHETTO.

Under his guidance, the Nazi "euthanasia action" killed more than 50,000 Germans judged mentally or chronically ill or otherwise unfit for work. (See WAR CRIMES.) "There is no more living proof of hereditary and racial laws than in a concentration camp," he once said. "You find there hydrocephalics, squinters, deformed individuals, semi-Jews: a considerable number of inferior people."

The war also gave Himmler the opportunity to transform his SS into a military force, the *WAFFEN SS*, which carried out on the battlefield—and in civilian enclaves behind the lines—the instructions that he gave a group of SS officers in Oct. 1943: "Whether or not 10,000 Russian WOMEN collapse from exhaustion while digging a tank ditch interests me only insofar as the TANK ditch is completed for Germany. . . . We Germans, who are the only people in the world who have a decent attitude to animals, will also adopt a decent attitude to these human animals. But it is a crime against our own blood to worry about them. . . ."

Appointed minister of the Interior in Aug. 1943, he became the administrator of concentration camps, organized conquered peoples for slave labor in war plants, and approved barbaric "medical experiments" in the camps. He also established the *Einsatzgruppen* (ACTION GROUPS) sent into occupied countries to exterminate Jews. (See REICH CENTRAL SECURITY OFFICE.)

In 1944 Himmler's SS swiftly rounded up and doomed the conspirators of the JULY 20 PLOT against Hitler, who rewarded Himmler with command of the reserve army that was to make Germany's last-ditch stand. Himmler was at the peak of his power.

But, as Germany crumbled in the spring of 1945, Himmler desperately attempted to negotiate a peace settlement through the Swedish Red Cross. Hitler learned of the talks and, in the political testament that contains his last words, expelled Himmler from the party. When the war ended, Himmler, in disguise, was captured near BREMEN by British troops. On May 23, 1945, he killed himself by swallowing a vial of poison.

Hindenburg, Paul von (1847–1934)

Germany's president from 1925 to 1934. A field marshal in World War I, Hindenburg was the second president of the WEIMAR REPUBLIC. When he ran for reelection in 1932, he defeated ADOLF HITLER, whom the aristocratic Hindenburg dismissed as "the Bohemian corporal." But, as Hitler rose to power, Hindenburg had to deal with him and made him chancellor on Jan. 30, 1933. When Hindenburg died, Hitler assumed the title and duties of president.

Hirohito (1901–1989)

Emperor of Japan from 1926 until his death. Japanese tradition made him a god, aloof from politics and the business of running a country. But law made him the Commander in Chief of the armed forces, and during his long reign Hirohito had to deal with the realities of peace and war.

The outside world first took note of him in 1921 when he toured Europe, becoming the first Japanese crown prince to visit the West. He seemed attracted by British culture and tradition and was especially interested in the ideals of a constitutional monarchy as exemplified by King George V. When Hirohito ascended to the throne in 1926 he chose for the name of his era *Showa,* "peace and enlightenment."

But his nation, under strong military leadership, soon was marching toward war. Hirohito remained aloof from most day-to-day political and military decisions. He did, however, approve such major Japanese Cabinet decisions as the invasion of China in 1937 and the attack on PEARL HARBOR. In an unusual oral-history memoir published a year after his death, the Emperor is quoted as saying that if he had tried to stop the attack, "it would have led to a coup d'état," his ASSASSINATION, and war with the United States, which he viewed as inevitable no matter what he did.

Hirohito pointed out in the memo that he ruled as a constitutional monarch and thus it was impossible for him "to do anything but give approval" to Cabinet decisions. Hirohito's culpability for WAR CRIMES continues to be debated. Evidence discovered by Western biographers shows that he was aware of the BATAAN DEATH MARCH and the execution of several U.S. fliers captured after the DOOLITTLE RAID in April 1942.

During the war Americans viewed Hirohito as well as his Prime Minister HIDEKI TOJO as symbols of Japanese perfidy. After the war Hirohito was expected to be one of the defendants in war crimes trials. But, because both the Japanese and the American conquerors wanted him to remain a steadying political influence, he was not tried or even interrogated. Nor did war crimes investigators question members of the imperial family, many of whom had been high-ranking military officers. Although the official myth held that the emperor bore no responsibility for the war, in a public-opinion poll conducted in Japan soon after his death, 52 percent of the respondents disagreed with the myth.

Accounts of Japan's final days in the war agree that Hirohito did play a decisive role in Japan's SURRENDER. A translation of the oral-history memoir quotes him as saying, "I was told that even TOKYO cannot be defended. I thought that the Japanese race will be destroyed if the war continued." A condition of that surrender was his continuance as emperor.

Gen. of the Army DOUGLAS MACARTHUR, the Supreme Allied Commander, abolished Shintoism as a state religion and ordered Hirohito to disclaim his divinity. Hirohito did so and continued to cooperate with MacArthur, who met privately with Hirohito at least eleven times during the occupation.

After the war Hirohito became a powerless symbol of an imperial past. His nation, though, mourned him with an outpouring of tribute when he died. Buried with him were some of his favorite possessions, including a microscope and a Mickey Mouse watch he had been given during a trip to the United States in 1975.

Hiroshima

Japanese port city that was the target of the first ATOMIC BOMB attack. For some time prior to Aug. 6, 1945, people in Hiroshima expected an air raid. Leaflets had showered down on them. There were frequent warnings. Then, just after midnight on Aug. 6, the red warning came. An all-clear sounded at 2:10 A.M. A yellow warning was sounded a 7:09 . . . the all-clear again at 7:31.

Before the people in Hiroshima could figure out what was happening, at 8:15 a blinding light blazed across the sky and people and buildings vanished. A tremendous explosion rocked the earth. Sheets of flames shot everywhere. A dark gray cloud spread for 3 miles in every direction across the city. Out of the center of the cloud rose a white billowing pillar. This image of vaporized wood and steel and flesh and bone became known as the mushroom-shaped cloud.

An atomic bomb had just been dropped from a B-29 SUPERFORTRESS named "Enola Gay," piloted by Col. PAUL TIBBETS, commanding officer of the 509TH COMPOSITE GROUP. At 2:45 Tibbets had

taken off from TINIAN Island and flown to Hiroshima. The city, spread across the delta of the Ota River, had a concentration of military installations, including the largest army base in western Japan. With distant mountains on three sides, Hiroshima was also a good site for observing the effects of the atomic bomb.

The 9,000-pound bomb, called Little Boy, was dropped from a height of 31,600 feet and exploded about 1,900 feet above Shima Hospital, near the center of Hiroshima. Within about eight-tenths of a mile around the center of the explosion everything combustible ignited spontaneously. People vaporized. The surfaces of granite stones melted or split into thin layers. On some stones were imprinted the shadows of the vaporized.

A woman about a mile from the blast center remembered seeing people stark naked, their clothes in rags. "Their hair was stiff, ruffled out and burnt short," she said. "Their hands were so severely burned that they could not move them. They were therefore forced to flee with their hands held out before them."

In his book *Hiroshima*, JOHN HERSEY describes a group of about twenty men: ". . . they were all in exactly the same nightmarish state: their faces were wholly burned, their eyesockets were hollow, the fluid from their melted eyes had run down their cheeks. (They must have had their faces upturned when the bomb went off; perhaps they were antiaircraft personnel.)"

No one knows how many people died that day or, burned and saturated with lethal radiation, started to die. The official Japanese estimate was 140,000 up to Dec. 1945, a death rate of 54 percent. Of the 76,000 buildings in the city, 70,000 were damaged or totally destroyed. Ninety percent of the doctors, nurses, and other medical personnel were killed or seriously injured and unable to care for the survivors.

Hiss, Alger (1904—)

A U.S. State Department official, he was secretary general at the 1945 San Francisco meeting at which the UNITED NATIONS was founded. Accused in 1948 of transmitting confidential State Department documents to the Soviet Union, he denied the charges. He later was accused of perjury before a congressional committee. Convicted of perjury in 1950, he was sentenced to five years in prison and was released in 1954.

Hitler, Adolf (1889–1945)

For the people of Allied and conquered countries, Hitler embodied the evil of Nazism. Germany was the enemy nation, but Hitler was the real enemy, the strutting, shouting dictator who had to be stopped before he and his diabolic philosophy engulfed the world. Topple Hitler and the evil would end.

That may have been a simplistic view of a complex war, but it was a view ratified by history. As John Toland concludes in *Adolf Hitler,* "To the surprise of the world, Hitler's death brought an abrupt, absolute end to National Socialism. Without its only true leader, it burst like a bubble. . . . No other leader's death since Napoleon had so completely obliterated a regime."

Hitler had a vision while under treatment for temporary blindness from mustard gas in the Western Front trenches of World War I. What he saw in his blinded mind was a command from fate. He seemed to see himself as an Aryan hero selected by the Teutonic gods to bestow upon Germany what he called the "Thousand-Year Reich." Out of the vision came a miracle—the restoration of his sight—and a summons to destiny. At that moment, he later said, he willed that he would abandon his quest for a career in art and enter politics to save Germany.

Germany had a mystic hold on Hitler, who looked upon it as his rightful native land even though he was born in the Austrian border town of Braunau am Inn. At the age of thirteen, after the death of his father, Hitler's mother moved the family to the Austrian town of Linz, which he would look upon as his hometown (see HITLERZENTRUM). He would chose Austria as his first conquest, making it rightfully part of Germany, uniting the "racial comrades" of the two countries.

Hitler loved his mother as much as he had feared his father, whose birth name was Aloys Schicklgruber. In later years, when Adolf Hitler became infamous, Schicklgruber was often used as a comic name for Hitler, but its origin was not well known. It was the maiden name of his paternal grandmother who was unmarried when Aloys was born. She later married a man named Hiedler. When Aloys grew up he took as his name Alois Hitler.

Adolf Hitler's beloved mother died in 1907. Grieving over her death in 1907, he lived an aimless life in Vienna and Munich, vaguely trying to transform a small talent for art into a career as an artist or architect. When World War I began, he avoided service in the Austrian Army to volunteer for a Bavarian infantry regiment. A frontline dispatch runner, he won the IRON CROSS, First Class, and left the Army as corporal. Still aimless but now summoned by destiny, he joined the rebellious veterans and jobless workers who were turning the streets of BERLIN and Munich into battlefields between the forces fighting to seize Germany's future. Some were Communists, some were Socialists, some were Social Democrats, some were veterans, and a few were in the German Workers' Party, which he joined in 1919.

Out of this evolved the NATIONAL SOCIALIST GERMAN WORKERS' PARTY, better known as the NAZI Party, which Hitler, an enthralling, heart-stirring speaker, took over in 1921. Two years later, exaggerating his own magnetism and the strength of his frenzied but weak party, he planned a putsch—a revolutionary thrust for power.

He set the start of the revolution for Nov. 11, 1923, the fifth anniversary of Germany's surrender. He planned to seize railroad, telegraph, and police stations, take over local governments throughout Bavaria, arrest Communists and labor leaders, and proclaim a provisional government and the start of a new Germany. The revolution was to be launched from a Munich beer hall, where the commissioner of Bavaria was holding a mass "patriotic demonstration" on Nov. 8.

The party's brown-shirted thugs (SA) and other armed Nazis surrounded the beer hall. At the appointed moment, Hitler entered, brandishing a pistol and leading an armed group to the speakers' platform. He fired the pistol toward the ceiling, shouted for quiet, and began haranguing the crowd, which acted more baffled than aroused to revolt. Throughout the night, amid confusing rhetoric, revolutionary rivals so dampened the revolutionary fervor that it appeared the Nazi uprising would die out before it was born.

The following day, under the party's SWASTIKA banners, Hitler led 3,000 followers in a march on the center of Munich. Police fired on the mob and in the rioting three policemen and sixteen party members were killed. One of the several Nazis wounded in the firefight was HERMANN GÖRING, who was spirited away by his wife. Hitler and nine others were arrested and tried for high TREASON. Hitler, the star of the widely publicized trial, made it his political launching site, a far better one than the beer hall. His accusers were the traitors; he said: "I feel myself the best of Germans who wanted the best for the German people." During one of the trial's twenty-four days he spoke for four hours. The obscure leader of an obscure party became a national figure—to some a menace, to others a hero.

Hitler, who could have been sentenced to life imprisonment, was handed a five-year sentence in Landsberg am Lech, a Bavarian prison known for its gentle incarceration policies (beer and wine at moderate prices, virtually unlimited visitation hours). Hitler served only nine months there and spent the time writing and polishing his rhetoric. "Before we saw the last of him," recalled a prison guard, "everyone here, from the governor to the furnace man, had become a convinced believer in his ideas."

In his cell, with editing and secretarial help from RUDOLF HESS, a devoted disciple, Hitler wrote his autobiography. He wanted to title it "Four and a Half Years of Struggle Against Lies, Stupidity and Cowardice," but a wise publisher suggested "My Struggle" (Mein Kampf). When he gained power, every household in Germany had to have a copy of Mein Kampf.

Mein Kampf became the testament of Nazism just as the Munich putsch became a revered myth of martyrdom. In later years each SS regiment would carry an eagle-topped standard dedicated by Hitler, who touched it with the "Blood Flag" borne by those who fell in the martyrdom at Munich in 1923.

Those who bothered to read Hitler's book would learn all they had to know about him and Nazism: "I understood the infamous spiritual terror which this movement exerts, particularly on the bourgeoisie, which is neither morally nor mentally equal to such attacks. . . . I achieved an equal understanding of the importance of physical terror toward the individual and the masses.

"The power which has always started the greatest religious and political avalanches in history rolling has from time immemorial been the magic power of the spoken word, and that alone."

"A majority can never replace the man. . . . Just as a hundred fools do not make one wise man, an heroic decision is not likely to come from a hundred cowards."

Hitler invented a strange mixture of Christianity and Teutonic paganism as a religious underpinning for Nazism. "I am now convinced," he said in Mein Kampf, "that I am acting as an agent of our Creator by fighting off the JEWS. I am doing the Lord's work."

Hitler had to twist through theology to explain why Jesus was not a Jew. Misinterpreting Catholic dogma, Hitler held that Jesus's mother, Mary, was conceived without physical intercourse. And, since Jesus' father was God, Jesus was therefore not Jewish through either of his parents. But Hitler could not get around the fact that Mary's parents had to be Jewish. So, by Nazi doctrine, that made Jesus a Mischling, a nonpracticing half-Jew.

Linked to his perversion of Christianity was a mystic belief in the Teutonic gods and goddesses of the operas of Richard Wagner, a fellow anti-Semite. From Wagner's Parsifal, for example, Hitler said he learned that "you can serve God only as a hero." He revered Wagner, and made frequent visits to the composer's family, leading romantic Germans to expect that he would marry Winifred Wagner, widow of Richard Wagner's son Siegfried.

But Hitler avoided marriage. When a newly married secretary once joshed him about urging marriage on everyone but himself, he said that he did not want to be a father. He added that "the children of a genius have a hard time in this world. One expects such a child to be a replica of his famous father and doesn't forgive him for being average."

Speculation about his furtive romantic life invariably surrounded his relationship with his niece Geli Raubal, nineteen years his junior. He was seen with her frequently and was proud to show off her blonde beauty. But the romance ended with a bullet in 1931, when, after quarrels that seemed to be inspired by Hitler's jealousy, she killed herself with a gun in his large Munich apartment where she lived with her mother, who was Hitler's half-sister (and housekeeper), and her sister.

Two years before, Hitler had met EVA BRAUN, a seventeen-year-old Munich shop girl who would become his mistress and, on the last day of his life, his wife.

By 1929 Hitler was the head of a legal party and promising to ever-growing crowds that he and his Nazi Party would defeat all of Germany's enemies, especially the Marxist Jews. In the party he was already *Der Führer,* the leader whose orders were never to be questioned. Around him were assembling the hard core of Nazis whose names would be linked with his and with the dark deeds of Nazism: Göring and Hess, MARTIN BORMANN, JOSEPH GOEBBELS and HEINRICH HIMMLER, ALBERT SPEER, and ERNST RÖHM, the chief of the SA, the street toughs who enforced Nazi edicts.

Röhm would not last as long as the others. After Hitler became chancellor in 1933 (see GERMANY), Röhm and scores of other SA leaders were murdered. The Nazis called the SA massacre the Blood Purge or the Night of the Long Knives. It grimly symbolized how the party, legal under WEIMAR REPUBLIC law, became lawless after Hitler was elected to power. As the Nazis made the Reichstag, the German parliament, just another organ of the party, *Der Führer* became not only Hitler's party title but his legal title as absolute ruler of his THIRD REICH.

He discarded the Versailles Treaty that limited Germany's armed forces and took Germany out of the LEAGUE OF NATIONS in 1933. He began a massive buildup of the German Army, Navy, and Air Force (Luftwaffe). In March 1935 he restored universal military service. The democracies did not react, and Britain even concluded a naval agreement with Germany in 1935 that accepted a greater German naval strength than what had been allowed by the Versailles Treaty, including the previously forbidden U-BOATS.

In 1936 Hitler sent troops into the demilitarized Rhineland. By then he had begun his militarizing of the nation, building a war machine and enlisting the citizenry into a martial society of HITLER YOUTH movements, state-run lives, and CONCEN-TRATION CAMPS for those doomed without trial as enemies of the Reich.

Commander in Chief of the armed forces under a 1934 edict, Hitler showed this was not an empty title when he forced the resignation of *Generalfeldmarschall* WERNER VON BLOMBERG, minister of defense, for marrying an exprostitute, and *Generaloberst* Baron Freiherr Werner von Fritsch, chief of the High Command of the German Army, for homosexual relations with Hitler Youth members (charges dismissed at a subsequent court-martial). He also sacked sixteen generals and reassigned forty-four others.

He was preparing for war, but he conquered first with words and threats, depending upon oratory and PROPAGANDA to get what he wanted to expand the Reich's *Lebensraum* (Living Space)—Austria and Czechoslovakia. When he finally had to win by force of arms, his panzers rolled across Poland in a BLITZKRIEG that stunned the world and began the EUROPEAN WAR.

He was his own foreign ministry and his own general staff, a former corporal snapping at proud Prussian generals, building resentment that would foster plots to overthrow him or to kill him. Luck and bungles saved his life several times. The JULY 20 PLOT in 1944, the most elaborate, used a bomb that exploded and left him dazed and with slight injuries. But he was able to organize a quick, vicious vengeance and, that very day, meet fellow dictator, BENITO MUSSOLINI of Italy, who hailed Hitler's survival as a miracle. To another well-wisher he said, "More proof that fate has selected me for my mission."

Whatever his luck in escaping ASSASSINATIONS, he also seethed with real and imagined illnesses. His hypochondria greatly influenced history, for he believed that he would die young and had to accomplish the triumph of the Third Reich as rapidly as possible. His stomach pains, chronic illnesses, and anxiety over failing health all contributed to his demand for swift solutions to political dilemmas and quick conclusions of military campaigns.

He saw himself as a military genius, but his decisions frequently produced disasters—the invasion of the Soviet Union, his faith in such "miracle weapons" as the V-1 BUZZ BOMB, his frequent underestimation of Allied power and fortitude. As he saw

Germany facing defeat early in 1945, he blamed not himself but his officers and his people for failing him.

In Jan. 1945 he secretly entered his *FÜHRER-BUNKER* in the rubble of Berlin. His people did not know that, during the final days of the Third Reich, their leader was huddling in the bunker ordering the destruction of their nation—a SCORCHED EARTH POLICY on German soil, a *Götterdämerung* worthy of a Wagnerian opera.

On March 18, when Albert Speer, minister for Armaments and War Production, protested the policy, Hitler said, "If the war is lost, the people will be lost also. It is not necessary to worry about what the German people will need for elemental survival. On the contrary, it is best for us to destroy even these things. For the nation has proved to be the weaker" in comparison to the Soviet Union. "In any case only those who are inferior will remain after this struggle, for the good have already been killed."

Hitler's closest aides had urged him to flee Berlin for BERCHTESGADEN, the site of his mountain retreat in Bavaria. But Hitler remained in his bunker, giving orders to an army that barely existed, launching counterattacks that took place only in his mind. He ordered Göring's arrest for treason after Göring, believing this was what Hitler wanted, moved to succeed him. Word also reached Hitler of Himmler's attempt to negotiate with the British and Americans. (See SURRENDER, GERMANY.) In a fit of rage, Hitler ordered the death of Eva's brother-in-law Otto Fegelein, Himmler's liaison officer to the *Führerbunker*. Fegelein was taken up to the Chancellery garden and shot.

Hitler moved now to perform the two acts that would precede his suicide: marrying Eva and dictating his will.

The marriage ceremony was performed on April 28 by a Berlin municipal councilor, snatched from a unit of the *Volkssturm* (People's Army or home guard) fighting near the *Führerbunker*. Both Hitler and Eva swore that they had "no hereditary disease" and were "of complete Aryan descent." There were a few champagne toasts and a short, somber party. During the party Hitler periodically disappeared to supervise the typing of his will and "Political Testament."

The testament reviews his life ("More than thirty years have passed since I made my modest contribu-

tion as a volunteer in the First World War . . . ") and warps history—"It is untrue that I or anybody else in Germany wanted war in 1939." The "people whom we have to thank for all this: international Jewry and its helpers." The testament, whose executor was Bormann, also named *Grossadmiral* KARL DÖNITZ, commander in chief of the German Navy, as his successor and Reich president and Supreme Commander of the Armed Forces.

Hitler died hating Jews. In the last sentence of his will, written on the eve of his suicide, Hitler charged the leaders of a dying Germany to continue a "scrupulous observance of the laws of race" and "merciless opposition" to "international Jewry."

He reiterated his decision to remain in Berlin "and there to choose death voluntarily. . . . I die with a joyful heart." Goebbels and Bormann signed as witnesses. So did two general officers, as a last touch of Hitlerian irony, for the testament reproached German Army officers for choosing surrender rather than death.

In the will he said that Eva Braun would "go to her death with me at her own wish as my wife. This will compensate us both for what we lost through my work in the service of my people." Goebbels also chose to die, along with his wife and six children.

As Hitler was preparing for his own death, he learned of the ignominious death of Mussolini and his mistress. Hitler ordered the poisoning of Blondi, his German Shepherd, a dog that, according to Albert Speer, "meant more to his master than the Führer's closest associates." He also had two other dogs in the bunker shot.

Around 2:20 A.M. on April 30 he said good-bye to his two secretaries and about twenty others. By then the Soviets held most of Berlin and artillery shells were smashing the adjacent Chancellery building. He retired to his private quarters with Eva and emerged, alone, later in the day for lunch. ERICH KEMPKA, his chauffeur, was sent to fetch gasoline from the Chancellery garage. Hitler and Eva returned to his private quarters. He shot himself in the right temple. She took poison, most likely one or more of the cyanide capsules available in the bunker. Kempka and others carried the bodies to the Chancellery garden and, during a furious Red Army barrage, drenched the bodies with gasoline and set them afire.

Hitler Youth

A military-style German organization for boys, compulsory after 1939. Girls belonged to *Bund Deutscher Mädchen,* the League of German Girls, which was also compulsory. The organizations embodied a tenet of HITLER's philosophy: "This new Reich will give its youth to no one." Soon after he became chancellor in 1933 Hitler said in a speech, "When an opponent declares, 'I will not come over to your side,' I calmly say, 'Your child belongs to us already. . . . What are you? You will pass on. Your descendants, however, now stand in the new camp. In a short time they will know nothing else but this new community'."

When the boys' and girls' organizations were formed in 1933, all other youth clubs were abolished. Children entered the youth movements at the age of six. At the age of ten, boys took an oath, swearing to devote "all my energies and my strength" to Hitler and "to give up my life for him, so help me God." The boys wore uniforms, drilled with rifles, and formed military units similar to those of the SS. The boys and girls marched to songs that indoctrinated them with NAZI philosophy. One song said: "Yes, when the Jewish blood splashes from the knives, things will go twice as well."

Although some parents managed to keep their children out of the organizations, those who defied the compulsory-membership law risked losing their sons and daughters to state orphanages. Boys and girls remained in the youth organization until eighteen, when they entered the work battalions of the *Arbeitsdienst,* the state's compulsory Labor Service. Boys went from the Labor Service to the armed forces. Some, though, were selected at twelve for six years of special Nazi training at one of the Adolf Hitler Schools. Other eligible boys and girls might be assigned to elite schools run by the SS.

The girls, who wore a schoolgirls' uniform with army-style shoes, began their service to the state by carrying buckets of water at mass meetings, reviving those who had fainted in the hysteria that often followed a Hitler speech. At eighteen girls became eligible for Faith and Beauty, a branch of the league that trained girls to become ideal mothers. Many did become mothers out of wedlock, but this was seen more as a patriotic accomplishment than a moral transgression. (German mothers received a bronze Honor Cross for having more than four children, a silver one for more than six, and a gold one for more than eight.)

Hitler Youth units, pathetically armed and trained, fought in the last days of the war, particularly during the defense of BERLIN.

Baldur von Schirach, leader of Hitler Youth Movement, was sentenced to twenty years imprisonment at the Nuremberg WAR CRIMES trials.

Hitlerzentrum

Name for the planned reconstruction of Linz, Austria, by ADOLF HITLER. Born in the nearby town of Braunnau, Hitler began school in Linz in 1900 (age eleven) and moved there with his mother after his father died in 1903. At age fifteen he was asked to leave school in Linz and attended classes in Steyr, about 15 miles away. Subsequently, while a student he designed a new Linz, including a new town hall and "a large bridge across the Danube that would have disfigured the lovely countryside," wrote British journalists David Roxan and Ken Wanstall in their book *The Rape of Art.*

After becoming *Der Führer,* Hitler sent scores of architects, city planners, and sociologists to Linz, who amassed volumes of detailed drawings and data on Linz. Hitler planned to rebuild the city—to be renamed "Hitlerzentrum"—to make it a showplace of Austro-Bavarian culture and to counter the degenerate sophistication of Vienna. In his inimitable manner, Hitler planned broad boulevards and a huge square (for ceremonies to welcome Hitler) flanked by massive cultural buildings, which would contain art masterpieces stolen from museums and cities in conquered countries.

Hitlerzentrum was to have a gigantic tower, 528-feet tall, which Hitler declared would "right a wrong" that had been earlier done to the bishop of Linz when he planned a church tower that would be higher than the steeple of St. Stephen's Cathedral in Vienna. The bishop was told that his steeple would have to be some six feet lower than Vienna's. (The Vienna cathedral was heavily damaged by Allied bombers during the war.)

The war interferred with Hitler's grandiose plans for Linz and the town remained much the same as it had before Hitler's vision for it—except for the heavy damage inflicted by Allied bombings during the war.

Ho Chi Minh (1890–1969)

Organizer and leader of the anti-Japanese Communist Viet Minh (Independence League) in INDOCHINA during the war. Born Nguyen That Thanh, Ho Chi Minh ("He Who Enlightens"), he spent some time in the United States during World War I and went to the Versailles peace conference to plead for independence for Vietnam. He remained in PARIS, helped found the French Communist Party, and studied in MOSCOW.

When the EUROPEAN WAR began, he returned to Vietnam under his assumed name and resumed his revolutionary activities. When the Japanese, with VICHY FRANCE and German approval, began taking over Indochina, he organized a resistance movement. His followers helped rescue downed U.S. fliers and did some intelligence gathering for the OFFICE OF STRATEGIC SERVICES.

At the end of the war, he proclaimed an independent Republic of Vietnam and began a GUERRILLA war against the French as they attempted to resume control of Indochina. When the French lost in battle to Ho Chi Minh in 1954, he installed, as president, his People's Democratic Republic of (North) Vietnam. He also established a Viet Cong guerrilla movement in southern Vietnam and by 1964 was at war against the armies of South Vietnam and the United States.

Hobby, Col. Oveta Culp (1905—)

First director of the U.S. WAC (Women's Army Corps). A former assistant city attorney of Houston and the wife of the publisher of the *Houston Post,* she was chief of the WOMEN's interests section of the WAR DEPARTMENT's public relations bureau when Gen. GEORGE C. MARSHALL, U.S. Chief of Staff, selected her to head the WAC. She was the first member of the U.S. Women's Army Auxiliary Corps, as the WAC was known at its founding in 1942. She served as director with the rank of colonel until she resigned in 1945 to return to the *Post;* she later was named publisher. In 1953 she became the first secretary of the Department of Health, Education and Welfare.

Hodges, Gen. Courtney H. (1887–1966)

Hodges, who received a commission from the ranks and won the Distinguished Service Cross in World War I, was in command of the Infantry School at Fort Benning when OMAR BRADLEY regarded him as "an august figure." Bradley said that Gen. GEORGE C. MARSHALL "had enormous regard for Hodges."

Marshall proved this in 1944 when, suggesting to Gen. DWIGHT D. EISENHOWER whom to pick as the U.S. ARMY GROUP commander for the battles of France and Germany, commented that Hodges was "exactly the same class of man as Bradley in practically every respect. [W]onderful shot, great hunter, quiet, self-effacing. Thorough understanding of ground fighting." Although leadership of the 12th Army Group went to Bradley, Hodges was given command of the First ARMY, which would lead the assault.

Once in command of the 12th Army Group, Bradley had a less glowing opinion of Hodges than before. Bradley believed Hodges seemed "indecisive and overly conservative," though he made no blunders during the NORMANDY INVASION and the subsequent fighting in the hedgerows. In the drive to the German border, Hodges' rate of progress was equal to that of Gen. GEORGE S. PATTON's, but Hodges' personality was so colorless that few ever heard of his accomplishments.

During this time, many of his peers and subordinates thought Hodges too reticent, too restrained. Under stress, Hodges could be querulous and brittle. When the Allied offensive stalled in September, Hodges made several attempts to revive it, including the disastrous HÜRTGEN FOREST attack in late October and early November. The German ARDENNES counteroffensive in December brought Hodges' First Army under Field Marshal BERNARD MONTGOMERY, who thought Hodges close to a breakdown. Eisenhower wrote a correction to this opinion: "I know you realize that Hodges is the quiet, reticent type and does not appear as aggressive as he really is. Unless he becomes exhausted he will always wage a good fight." Hodges did wage a good fight, stabilizing the northern shoulder and beginning a counterattack.

After the war in Europe ended, Hodges took his

First Army headquarters to the Far East for the expected invasion of Japan, and, when they were not needed, returned to Governor's Island in New York.

Holland,

see NETHERLANDS.

Hollandia

Capital of prewar Netherlands NEW GUINEA, on Humboldt Bay, about 25 miles west of the British New Guinea boundary. On April 22, 1944, U.S. forces made simultaneous AMPHIBIOUS LANDINGS at Hollandia and two other points on the coast. The operation, preceded by devastating bombings, was code-named Reckless. The Japanese garrison, which had held Hollandia since April 1942, had no air cover and offered little resistance. Hollandia became a major Allied base and was the headquarters of Gen. DOUGLAS MACARTHUR from Sept. 8, 1944, until his assault on the Philippines in Oct. 1944.

Hollywood Canteen,

see STAGE-DOOR CANTEEN.

Holocaust

The word that has become the term universally recognized for the killing of nearly 6,000,000 JEWS by NAZI Germany. Implied in the word is the image of DEATH CAMP crematoria where the bodies of Jews were burned. (In the original Greek the word described a sacrifice wholly consumed by fire.) *Genocide*—the murder of a people—was coined in 1944 to define the Nazi policy against European Jews. (See also ANTI-SEMITISM, FINAL SOLUTION, JEWS.)

Home Guard

Volunteers organized for defense of Britain. Armed with whatever arms that could be found—including relics from museums and war memorials—some 1,000,000 volunteers stood ready to defend their island from invasion. The original name, Local Defense Volunteers, was changed to Home Guard on the orders of Prime Minister CHURCHILL in 1940.

Homma, Gen. Masaharu (1887–1946)

Masaharu Homma, the "Poet General" and amateur playwright, has been described by men who knew him as being "emotional, sensitive, easily hurt, and with a deep need to be loved." In every assignment, he impressed his fellow officers with his brilliant intellect, calm, even remote demeanor, courage, and natural leadership abilities. Having spent from 1918 to 1925 with British Army units, he was leader of a pro-Western faction within the Japanese Army.

This is not a likely portrait of the general held responsible and executed for the BATAAN DEATH MARCH, a horrific procession into captivity of American and Filipino PRISONERS OF WAR in April 1942. How could the same man who permitted this atrocity make the stinging report condemning the "Rape of NANKING" in 1937?

The answer is complex. Homma's personality inclined him toward introspection and a sense of living just beyond reality. He was an imaginative military thinker, but was inclined to let his subordinates worry about the details. At another level, Homma's distaste for the fanatical nationalism that infected much of the Japanese military in the 1930s caused him repeatedly to fall out of favor with senior Army leadership.

His disaffection resulted in his being exiled to China in 1940, shifted to command of the Tientsin Defense Army, and transferred to command of the Army on Formosa (Taiwan). He continued opposing a Japanese war against Great Britain and the United States, believing that Japan had no chance against such an alliance. He also felt little respect for and less confidence in Gen. HIDEKI TOJO, who became prime minister in Oct. 1941.

In Nov. 1941, Lt. Gen. Homma received his assignment in the war that he opposed. He was to take Luzon, the main island of the Philippines and home to its capital city MANILA, in fifty days with two divisions. Homma protested, but was told that no discussion would be permitted. The assumption was that the American and Filipino forces would stand and fight rather than lose the city and would not withdraw into the BATAAN Peninsula.

Unfortunately for Homma's timetable, his enemy

did begin pulling back into Bataan. He was unwilling to deviate from the "Manila First" essence of his orders, a decision that cost him months of grim combat and, eventually, his life. He occupied Manila on Jan. 2, 1942, but did not receive the surrender of Bataan until April 9, after which Homma concentrated on reducing the fortress of CORREGIDOR. Lt. Gen. JONATHAN WAINWRIGHT's surrender came on May 6.

On June 9 Homma was relieved of his command and sent home to Japan, where he remained for the rest of the war. Although considered one of Japan's most capable generals, he never again held a command of any importance.

During his hastily organized WAR CRIMES trial after Japan's SURRENDER, Homma claimed to have known nothing of the "Death March" until the end of the war. This appears to have been true. Bent on capturing Corregidor, Homma entrusted the movement and the imprisonment of the surprisingly large enemy host to underlings, particularly Col. Masanobu Tsuji, who was imposed on Homma as his Chief of Staff in Feb. 1942.

Tsuji, a genuinely odious individual, was blamed by most testimony as having instigated the Death March as well as atrocities during the Japanese occupation of the Philippines. None of this was held to extenuate Homma's guilt. A plea by Homma's wife, both in trial testimony and in person to Gen. DOUGLAS MACARTHUR, resulted in a commutation of the sentence from hanging to a more honorable firing squad. Homma was executed on April 3, 1946.

(Tsuji, disguised as a Buddhist monk, slipped into China, where he became an adviser to CHIANG KAI-SHEK. He returned to Japan in 1949.)

Homosexuals

During the war, the U.S. armed services defined homosexuality as an automatic cause for rejection. But that policy produced an unexpected result.

During induction examinations, enlistees and draftees were asked questions about their sexual preferences. If a man or WOMAN did not indicate a preference for the opposite sex, he or she would not be inducted (except in rare cases where the examiner was disinterested in the response). The result was that patriotic homosexuals lied about their preferences, claiming to be heterosexual, while heterosexuals wishing to avoid duty could feign homosexuality and be rejected.

Once a homosexual got into the service, unofficial recognition of his or her life-style led classification officers to find ways to fit them into the military organization. "During World War II," wrote Allan Berube in *Coming Out Under Fire*, "medical officers began to generalize about what special talents they believed gay male soldiers possessed and what job classifications typically included them. . . . Effeminate gay men, butch lesbians, and others assigned to cross-gendered jobs did not represent the majority of gay male and lesbian GIs— they were merely the more visible."

A 1945 study of 183 homosexual servicemen showed they included a gunnery officer aboard a DESTROYER and a specialist in air combat intelligence. Servicewomen, who were supposed to have assignments that released men for combat duty, were expected to remain female in what had traditionally been an all-male profession. Col. OVETA CULP HOBBY, director of the WAC, speaking to a group of Women's Army Corps officers, warned against encouraging mannish behavior. "The last thing we want to accomplish," she said, "is to masculinize a great group of women."

Under the U.S. Articles of War, acts of sodomy were criminal and conviction could mean prison sentences of five years for Army officers or enlisted men, ten years for sailors, and twelve years for Navy officers. Typically, servicemen convicted of sodomy were segregated in "queer stockades" or, as a more lenient punishment, given involuntary discharges. Reforms enacted during the war allowed the discharge of homosexuals as undesirables and the retention and "rehabilitation" of men and women who had engaged in homosexual acts "through intoxication or curiosity."

From 1941 to 1945 the punishment policy changed. According to *Coming Out Under Fire*, More than 4,000 sailors and 5,000 soldiers, most of them men, "were hospitalized, diagnosed as sexual psychopaths, and discharged from the service with the label of homosexuality appearing on their military records."

Honduras

Capital: Tegucigalpa, pop. 1,107,859 (1940). In keeping with its longtime endorsement of U.S. (and United Fruit Company) interests, Honduras was overwhelmingly pro-American. It broke off relations with Germany and Italy in Sept. 1941, declared war on Japan on Dec. 8, 1941, on Germany and Italy on Dec. 13, and, following the U.S. lead, ended relations with VICHY FRANCE on Nov. 13, 1942. Honduras took over AXIS-owned property and joined with U.S. antisubmarine forces in coastal patrols by Honduras air force planes. The United Fruit Company planted an experimental rubber plantation in hopes of establishing a second cash crop. (The export of bananas had drastically fallen off because U.S. shipping had been shifted to the carrying of war cargoes.)

Hong Kong

A British Crown Colony off the southeast coast of China and one of the first targets of the JAPANESE CAMPAIGN IN THE FAR EAST. Nearly 500,000 people lived in Hong Kong on the eve of war; all but about 10,000 of them were Chinese.

The British government evacuated women and children to MANILA on June 30, 1941, in anticipation of a Japanese attack. The Japanese responded by posting troops athwart the Kowloon Peninsula, blockading the colony from land.

A full-scale attack came on Dec. 8, 1941. Six days later the Japanese issued an ultimatum: surrender or heavy bombing and shelling. The governor refused to surrender and the Japanese carried out their threat. The bombing severed water mains, and Japanese held key reservoirs, making siege by thirst a horrifying possibility. On Dec. 25 the exhausted, outnumbered British garrison surrendered.

The Japanese occupation forces allowed Hong Kong's sanitation facility to deteriorate and treated the Chinese cruelly. When the British returned to Hong Kong at the end of the war in Aug. 1945, they declared 16,000 Chinese tenements uninhabitable.

Hood

The largest warship afloat when the war began, the British battle cruiser *Hood* had a brief but vio-

lent career. She served with the Home Fleet and in the Mediterranean in 1939–1941. The *Hood* was part of the British task force searching for the German battleship *BISMARCK* and heavy cruiser *Prinz Eugen* when they escaped into the North Atlantic in May 1941.

The *Hood* and battleship *PRINCE OF WALES* encountered the *Bismarck* in the Denmark Strait on May 24, 1941. Although the German ships were outgunned, and the *Bismarck* was hit and damaged, the *Hood* was apparently struck by a 15-inch (380-mm) shell from the *Bismarck* that penetrated to her magazines. The ensuing explosions blew the *Hood* in half. Within ninety seconds only a pall of smoke remained. She took 1,338 crewmen to their deaths, including Vice Adm. L. E. Holland; there were but three survivors.

The *Hood* was the last battle cruiser to be constructed by any nation (although the Soviet *Kirov*-class nuclear cruisers built in the 1980s are considered battle cruisers by some naval analysts). Begun in 1916 as one of a class of four ships, work on the others ceased in 1917 when the Germans stopped work on a new class of capital ships. The *Hood* was completed in March 1920, too late to participate in World War I.

When World War II began the ship displaced 42,100 tons; she was 860½ feet long and had steam turbines that could drive her at 31 knots. The *Hood*'s main battery was eight 15-inch guns (similar to the *Bismarck*'s main battery) with twelve 5.5-inch (140-mm) guns plus antiaircraft guns. As a battle cruiser, her design sacrificed armor in favor of speed and a heavy gun battery.

Hooligan Navy,

see UNITED STATES, COAST GUARD.

Hoover, J. Edgar (1895–1972)

Director of the U.S. FEDERAL BUREAU OF INVESTIGATION. Hoover, who had built up the reputation of the FBI through shrewd use of publicity in the gangster era, used similar techniques to make "G-men" heroes of the U.S. war effort.

He put his byline over magazine articles portraying the FBI as a relentless hunter of NAZI and Japanese spies. One of his articles claimed FBI discovery of MICRODOTS, although it was British intelligence that told the FBI about the use of the secret-writing technique. The British introduced the FBI to a microdot-equipped double agent, DUSKO POPOV, who had been asked to get information on PEARL HARBOR prior to the Japanese attack. Hoover personally discredited Popov and expelled him from the United States.

Hoover also fostered the frequently recorded tale that he was the first ranking U.S. government official to learn of the Japanese attack because an FBI agent in HAWAII supposedly reached Hoover by telephone and held the receiver out his office window so that Hoover could hear the bombs exploding. Recent research has shown that the FBI Hawaii-to-mainland communication on Dec. 7, 1941, was by an FBI radio operator standing on the roof of a Honolulu building.

Hoover gave FBI cooperation to the makers of the MOVIE *The House on 92nd Street,* which starred William Eythe, Lloyd Nolan, and Signe Hasso and was distributed in 1945. The film, using a documentary technique that suggested the story was true, featured a full-scale FBI operation, complete with scientific and technological aids. In the story the FBI supposedly lets a German-American go to Germany for ESPIONAGE training so that he can act as a double agent for the FBI when he returns to the United States.

The script gives the impression that the FBI had prior knowledge of a real, highly publicized German operation (see SABOTAGE) when, in fact, the arrival of German saboteurs by U-BOAT stunned the FBI. And, in fact, Hoover, given the chance to use Popov as a double agent, rejected the notion.

Hoover's search for wartime spies and saboteurs was sometimes extended to include surveillance of writers suspected of being Communist sympathizers. (See ERNEST HEMINGWAY and JOHN STEINBECK.)

Hope, Bob (1903—)

Comedian and entertainer of servicemen and women. Hope's first tour to entertain troops took him to Alaska and the ALEUTIAN ISLANDS in 1942. With him were singer Frances Langford, comic Jerry Colonna, and guitarist Tony Romano, all of whom would frequently join him again. That first tour was so successful that Army and Navy officials

asked him to go out again and again. He and his troupe would perform for the rest of the war in bases and aboard warships from North Africa and SICILY in Europe to TARAWA and SAIPAN in the Pacific.

He huddled with the troops during air raids, endured a forced landing in an Australian jungle, and often got close enough to hear gunfire above the applause. "We were giving a show on NOEMFOR ISLAND," he wrote during the war. "They shot a Jap 1,200 yards from the stage. I don't know whether he was coming or going to the show."

The UNITED SERVICE ORGANIZATIONS (USO) usually set up his shows, which were staged both in the United States and overseas. "I've just returned from a tour of Army camps," he once told his weekly radio audience. "The USO sent me to Europe to boost the morale of the soldiers in the United States."

Hopkins, Harry L. (1890–1946)

President ROOSEVELT's personal assistant and unofficial secretary of the President's secret "war Cabinet," which included JAMES F. BYRNES, director of the OFFICE OF WAR MOBILIZATION; Adm. WILLIAM D. LEAHY, the President's Chief of Staff; perennial presidential adviser BERNARD BARUCH, and Samuel I. Rosenman, special counsel to the President.

Knowledge of the meetings was not as secret as Roosevelt wished. Leaks showed that actual Cabinet members were not in the President's inner circle. The meetings reflected President Roosevelt's desire to conduct his own foreign policy—a decision that Hopkins encouraged. Hopkins showed his own power in the realm of foreign affairs when he succeeded in getting his protégé, EDWARD R. STETTINIUS, appointed secretary of state in Nov. 1944.

A close confidant of Roosevelt when he was governor of New York, Hopkins followed Roosevelt to WASHINGTON and became federal emergency relief administrator. In 1939 Roosevelt named Hopkins secretary of commerce, a post he held until 1940, when illness forced him to resign. He returned to serve Roosevelt in Dec. 1940 as head of the LEND-LEASE Administration. Roosevelt sent Hopkins as a personal emissary to LONDON and to MOSCOW to work out details of the aid program. He was also instrumental in setting up the National Defense Research Council, out of which evolved the OFFICE OF SCIENTIFIC RESEARCH AND DEVELOPMENT.

In Feb. 1944 Hopkins' son Stephen, an eighteen-year-old soldier, was killed in the fighting on KWAJALEIN. Gen. GEORGE C. MARSHALL, Chief of Staff, wrote to Hopkins suggesting that his son Robert, serving with the Army in Italy, be removed, at least temporarily, from the thick of the fighting. "I hope you will not send for him," Hopkins answered. "The last time I saw him in Tunis he told me he wanted to stay until we get to BERLIN."

Hopkins, who attended the major ALLIED CONFERENCES with Roosevelt, became an adviser to President HARRY S TRUMAN after Roosevelt's death. Hopkins went to Moscow as Truman's personal envoy and solved problems that had arisen at the SAN FRANCISCO CONFERENCE over the use of the veto in the UNITED NATIONS.

His journey to Moscow and his relentless work schedule aggravated his ill health. He was unable to attend the POTSDAM CONFERENCE in July 1945. Still an old-line New Dealer at heart, he became chairman of the Woman's Cloak and Suit Industry in Sept. 1945 and died four months later.

Hornet (CV 8)

The last U.S. AIRCRAFT CARRIER completed before America's entry into the war. Her career was brief and violent, and she was perhaps best known for having launched bombers to strike TOKYO and other Japanese cities under the command of Lt. Col. JAMES DOOLITTLE.

The DOOLITTLE RAID was her first operational assignment. In preparation, on Feb. 2, 1942, while still in the Atlantic, she launched two B-25 MITCHELL bombers to demonstrate the feasibility of launching the land-based, medium bombers from an aircraft carrier. She then sailed south, through the Panama Canal, and on to Oakland, Calif., where she embarked sixteen B-25B bombers. She then put to sea and rendezvoused in the mid-Pacific with a force commanded by Vice Adm. WILLIAM F. HALSEY in the carrier *ENTERPRISE* (CV 6). On April 18 the *Hornet* launched the Doolittle raiders from a position 800 miles east of Tokyo in the first strike against the Japanese homeland.

The *Hornet* then participated in the U.S. carrier

victory at the battle of MIDWAY in June 1944. From late Aug. 1942 she participated in the GUADALCANAL campaign. During late Sept. and early Oct. 1942 she was the only U.S. carrier operational in the South Pacific.

On Oct. 26, 1942, in the bitter and continuing battle for Guadalcanal, U.S. and Japanese warships clashed in the battle of SANTA CRUZ. Japanese carrier planes damaged the U.S. carrier *Enterprise* and the new BATTLESHIP *SOUTH DAKOTA* (BB 57), and succeeded in crippling the *Hornet*. She was soon ablaze and abandoned. U.S. DESTROYERS finally sank the crippled *Hornet* the next morning as Japanese destroyers were arriving on the scene. The stricken carrier went down with 111 of her crew.

The *Hornet* was commissioned on Oct. 20, 1941. She displaced 19,800 tons standard, was 809½ feet long, and carried some eighty aircraft.

She had been in commission for one year and six days before being sunk. During her brief career the *Hornet* earned four battle stars. (Another U.S. carrier, the CV 12, was named *Hornet* during the war.)

Hornpipe

Code designation for a message to alert Allied forces of a twenty-four-hour delay in the NORMANDY assault.

Horsa

The first British troop-carrying GLIDER to become operational, the Horsa was built in large numbers and used by the British in AIRBORNE operations from the invasion of SICILY in 1943 through the RHINE CROSSINGS of March 1945.

The prototype Airspeed-designed Horsa first flew in Sept. 1941 and was quickly followed by production orders that totaled 3,655 aircraft. The first operational use came on Nov. 19, 1942, when two were towed from Scotland to attack a German heavy-water plant in southern Norway. There were twenty-seven available in North Africa in July 1943 for the Sicily operation, followed by more than 250 being used in the NORMANDY INVASION, and over 600 at the ill-fated ARNHEM assault in Sept. 1944. In the March 1945 crossing of the Rhine (Operation Varsity), 440 Horsas were employed. Horsas were also flown by the U.S. Army, acquired under reverse LEND-LEASE; Americans used them at Normandy and in Burma and India.

The Horsa was a high-wing aircraft with a tricycle undercarriage. Upon takeoff the main wheels could be jettisoned for combat landings made on a castoring nosewheel and a central skid. It normally carried twenty to twenty-five troops, depending upon their equipment.

Towing speed was 100 mph. The Horsa had a two-man crew.

Horses,
see CAVALRY.

Hosogaya, Vice Adm. Hoshiro (1888–1964)
Commander of Japanese naval operations in the ALEUTIANS area during the war. Hosogaya served as Commander in Chief of the Japanese Fleet in central China waters from Dec. 1940 to July 1941. He was then made Commander in Chief of the Northern Area Force (Fifth Fleet), which was responsible for the defense of the eastward approaches to the Japanese home islands during the first six months of the war.

Hosogaya was then given an aggressive decoy role in Adm. ISOROKU YAMAMOTO's planned operation against MIDWAY in early June 1942. The diversion was locally successful, but completely failed to distract the U.S. carrier forces near Midway because U.S. MAGIC code-breaking efforts had already revealed the focus of the main effort. Japanese carrier aircraft bombed the U.S. naval base at DUTCH HARBOR in the Aleutians twice, after which Japanese troops were landed on Attu and Kiska in the western portion of the chain.

The dreadful weather prevalent in the northern Pacific and the peripheral nature of the theater dampened aggressive action on both sides. Hosogaya's concern was to resupply the island garrisons and he used his Fifth Fleet's relatively few cruisers and six destroyers to escort his transports. On March 26, 1943, Hosogaya's force confronted a U.S. Navy task group south of the KOMANDORSKIYE ISLANDS. In the subsequent battle, the world's last major naval action fought without the aid of aircraft or radar, the outgunned U.S. force under Rear Adm. Charles H. McMorris drove off the Japanese fleet.

Hosogaya pleaded near-exhaustion of his ammunition and fuel and the imminent arrival of U.S. land-based aircraft as reasons for withdrawing. His excuses were probably valid, but his unremarkable career in the frigid backwaters had attracted no patrons in senior positions at naval headquarters. Hence, his withdrawal before a manifestly inferior U.S. naval force was the immediate cause of Hosogaya's reassignment to the reserves, where he finished out the war.

Höss, Rudolf (1900–1947)
Commandant of AUSCHWITZ, a DEATH CAMP. Höss' devout Catholic parents expected him to be a priest. But he enrolled in the NAZI Party when he was twenty-two, and a year later was involved in the revenge murder of a teacher who had turned in a Nazi criminal. He was sentenced to prison and later released in a general amnesty.

Höss joined the SS and in 1934 became a member of a unit assigned to guarding CONCENTRATION CAMPS. (There were not yet any death camps.) His first assignment was the "model camp," DACHAU. After duty as adjutant of the Sachsenhausen concentration camp, in 1940, with the rank of *SS-Hauptsturmführer,* Höss was put in command of Auschwitz.

At Auschwitz, he installed a death camp and, as he later boasted, ran "the greatest extermination center of all time." By his account, more than 2,500,000 people were killed by mass executions or in gas chambers; 500,000 others were starved to death.

Before setting up his own death camp, Höss visited the one at TREBLINKA and saw how inefficient it was to kill large groups of people with carbon monoxide gas. So he began experimenting with ZYKLON-B, which "took from three to fifteen minutes to kill the people in the death chamber. . . . We knew when the people were dead because their screaming stopped. . . . After the bodies were removed, our special commandos took off the rings and extracted the gold from the teeth of the corpses."

Höss made these statements in a statement at the WAR CRIMES trials at Nuremberg. After giving his testimony, he was turned over to the Polish government. He spent almost a year in prison, writing his autobiography. He was hanged—at Auschwitz—on April 7, 1947.

Houston (CA 30)

U.S. CRUISER that was flagship of the U.S. Asiatic FLEET when the United States entered the war. She had a brief but violent wartime career. One of the so-called "treaty cruisers," having been built under terms of the 1922 WASHINGTON Naval Treaty, the *Houston* was commissioned in 1930.

She served as flagship for U.S. naval forces in the Far East from 1931 to 1933, and again arrived in the Far East in Nov. 1940. The *Houston* carried President ROOSEVELT on a cruise of almost 12,000 miles in 1934, from Annapolis, Md., through the Caribbean and Panama Canal, to Portland, Oreg. The cruiser also served as presidential flagship in 1938 and 1939.

At the time of the PEARL HARBOR attack the *Houston* was at Panay Island in the Philippines. She sailed south, stopping in the DUTCH EAST INDIES, and reached Australia on Dec. 28, 1941. After the loss of the British capital ships *REPULSE* and *PRINCE OF WALES* on Dec. 10, 1941, the *Houston* was the largest Allied warship in the western Pacific. She was then assigned to the ABDA naval force in the east Indies. During an air raid on Feb. 4 the *Houston* was hit by a Japanese BOMB that disabled her after turret, putting out of action three of her nine 8-inch (203-mm) guns.

She then operated between Australia and the East Indies until, late in February, in the Battle of the JAVA SEA she engaged a superior Japanese surface force while in company with British, Dutch, Australian, and other U.S. warships. On the night of Feb. 28–March 1, in the Sunda Strait, she was hit by four Japanese TORPEDOES as well as several shells, one of which killed her captain. As the ship lost way she was swarmed upon by Japanese destroyers. The *Houston*'s gunners were credited with damaging three Japanese destroyers and sinking an accompanying minesweeper. Finally, early on March 1, the *Houston* rolled over and sank.

Of more than 1,000 men aboard the *Houston* when she entered battle, there were but 368 survivors. All were taken on Japanese ships and experienced three years of brutality and starvation in Japanese prisons. Her commanding officer, Capt.

Albert H. Rooks, was posthumously awarded the MEDAL OF HONOR.

The *Houston* was launched on Sept. 7, 1929. She displaced 9,200 tons, was 600 1/4 feet long, and had steam turbines that could propel her at 32.7 knots. Her main armament was nine 8-inch guns, with a secondary battery of eight 5-inch (127-mm) dual-purpose guns plus some light antiaircraft guns.

Hs 126

German reconnaissance and artillery observation aircraft flown by the Luftwaffe on all fronts. A highly versatile aircraft, it was also used as a night bomber, for training, and as a GLIDER tug. In the bomber role it was usually used for harassment of front-line enemy troops.

The aircraft became operational in 1938 and some 600 were built, mostly the definitive Hs 126B variant. Early aircraft were sent to Spain for use in the closing stages of the SPANISH CIVIL WAR. An excellent aircraft for its intended role, the Hs 126 was in action through 1945. When the GERMAN CAMPAIGN IN THE SOVIET UNION began in June 1941 there were more than 400 of the Hs 126s assigned to support the three invading Army groups.

Based on the earlier Henschel-built Hs 122, the later aircraft was a high-wing monoplane, with a radial engine, and fixed landing gear with "spats" coverings on the main landing gear and tail wheel. The pilot and observer-gunner sat in a glazed cockpit, usually open for use of a camera, which could be attached to the port side of the cockpit, or a flexible machine gun.

The Hs 126B had a maximum speed of 221 mph and was credited with a range of up to 450 miles. In addition to the flexible 7.9-mm machine gun aft, there was a fixed forward-firing 7.9-mm gun. Five 22-pound BOMBS or a single 110-pound bomb could be carried under the fuselage.

Hs 129

German specialized in aircraft used against TANKS. Originally developed as a ground-attack aircraft, the Hs 129 was adopted to succeed the increasingly vulnerable JU 87D STUKA in the "tank busting" role on the EASTERN FRONT. Although a few saw limited service in North Africa in late 1942, it was against Soviet tanks from late 1942 that the aircraft was principally used. They also flew in small numbers in the West, with some attacking Allied forces in the NORMANDY INVASION.

Design began in 1937 and the prototype of the Henschel Hs 129 flew in the spring of 1939. The aircraft was underpowered, difficult to control, had poor visibility for the pilot, and was cramped. Still, it was superior to its contemporaries and limited production was ordered, albeit with improved (French) engines. Production through Sept. 1944 totaled more than 800 aircraft, most variants of the Hs 129B model.

The Hs 129 was a low-wing, twin-engine aircraft. The main undercarriage fully retracted into the radial engine nacelles, which were fitted far forward. The pilot sat in a heavily armored cockpit. Maximum speed was 255 mph and range was only 350 miles. Armament varied considerably as a number of antitank weapons were tried. The standard armament was two forward-firing 20-mm cannon and two 7.9-mm machine guns; also fitted in various sub-types were a 75-mm gun pack, a 75-mm gun pack (firing twelve 26.4-pound rounds), a variety of ROCKETS, downward-firing 77-mm MORTARS (a battery of six), and a FLAMETHROWER!

Huff-Duff,

see HIGH-FREQUENCY/DIRECTION FINDING.

Hughes, Howard (1905–1976)

U.S. industrialist, aviator, test pilot, and MOVIE producer. In the 1920s and 1930s he gained worldwide fame as a motion-picture producer and aviator, combining his interest in those two areas to produce *Hells Angels,* a classic film.

His aviation ventures included building Hughes Aircraft Co. and gaining a controlling interest in Trans World Airlines. Hughes insisted on flight-testing aircraft and sought to set flight records. The Hughes-designed Racer H-1 set a Burbank, Calif., to Newark, N.J., speed record in 1937, beating the record Hughes himself had set the year before in a Northrop Gamma. His around-the-world flight in 1938 with a crew of four established another record as he circled the globe in three days, nineteen hours, and fourteen minutes.

Hughes is best remembered in the military con-

text for building a massive, eight-engine flying boat, the "SPRUCE GOOSE," intended to fly hundreds of troops per flight to Europe or the Far East as a means of avoiding attacks by U-BOATS. Hughes piloted the massive aircraft on its first and only flight in 1947. His other major military aircraft venture was the XF-11 high-speed reconnaissance aircraft. This aircraft first flew in 1946, too late to be used in the war. One of the two XF-11 prototypes crashed with Hughes at the controls. After the war he became interested in HELICOPTERS and produced the jet-powered XH-17 heavy-lift helicopter. It was designed to carry a 24,700-pound load a distance of 65 miles.

In his final years he became a recluse who never appeared in public and refused even to have his picture taken.

Hull, Cordell (1871–1955)

U.S. secretary of State. Hull began his long service to the nation as an Army officer in the Spanish-American War. He entered national politics in 1907 when he was elected to Congress and, except for a two-year interval, served continually until 1931. A frustrated supporter of the LEAGUE OF NATIONS, Hull shifted to the Executive Branch in 1931, resigning his Senate seat to become President ROOSEVELT's secretary of state. He initiated the administration's "good neighbor" policy toward Latin America and extended U.S. influence in both the Pacific and Europe. In his internationalist view of the world, the expansionism of Japan in the Pacific merged with the *Lebensraum*—living space—demands of ADOLF HITLER. Hull saw early on the need to contain Japan and to ally the United States with Britain and France against Germany.

Hull's attempts to enforce containment of Japan ended on Dec. 7, 1941, when KICHISABURO NOMURA, Japan's ambassador to the United States, met with Hull while Japanese planes attacked PEARL HARBOR. Responding to the treachery, Hull told Nomura that "in all my conversations with you during the last nine months I have never uttered one word of untruth."

The remark personified Hull, a Southern gentleman who extended his sense of moral principles to foreign affairs, seeing in the rise of totalitarianism a breakdown of international law and morality. Although not comfortable with the Soviet Union as an ally, he managed a working relationship with his Soviet counterpart, VYACHESLAV MOLOTOV and established the procedure for the three- and four-power foreign-minister conferences that paced the war. When, in failing health, he resigned in 1944 he had achieved the longest tenure of a secretary of state. He won the Nobel Peace Prize in 1945.

Human Torpedo,

see KAITEN and MANNED TORPEDOES.

Hump, The

Airlift route over the Himalayas from Assam, India, to Kunming, China. The airlift, a desperate attempt to supply China after the BURMA ROAD was cut off, began on April 8, 1942. The first flight was piloted by Col. William D. Old of the U.S. Army Air Forces. Over The Hump came everything needed by the American forces in China or by the armies of Generalissimo CHIANG KAI-SHEK—from gasoline and shoes to medicine and bulldozers. The planes also brought from China to India more than 13,000 Chinese troops for training as part of a plan drawn up by Gen. JOSEPH W. STILWELL.

Flying to and from crude airfields in treacherous weather, straining their limits at altitudes of 18,000 to 22,000 feet, C-47s delivered 700 tons a month. (Later, C-87s, C-46s, C-54s, and C-109 transports took over and the tonnage increased.) The route was dubbed the Aluminum Trail for the 450 planes that went down, and pilots used the gleaming downed planes as checkpoints.

The first flights were under the aegis of the U.S. Tenth AIR FORCE in India. The China National Aviation Corp. (CNAC) began flying The Hump, but Stilwell objected on the grounds that the CNAC civilian pilots were drawing more pay for the flights than military pilots taking the same risk. Accordingly, he got Chiang Kai-shek to lease all planes to the AAF, and in Sept. 1942 that was done.

Despite many problems, the Tenth Air Force flew The Hump until Dec. 1942, when the mission was taken over by the AAF AIR TRANSPORT COMMAND. While this eased the problems of the Tenth Air Force, because ATC was controlled from WASHINGTON, it further complicated the already complex command relationships in the China-Burma-India theater.

ATC planes took 2,278 tons over the Hump in March 1943; by July 1944 the total was 18,975; the record monthly total was 71,042 tons in July 1945. Toward the end of the war about 650 planes flew every day, and their monthly cargo totals exceeded those carried on the Burma Road. The total delivery from 1942 to the end of the war in Aug. 1945 was 650,000 tons.

Hungary

Capital: BUDAPEST, pop. 11,137,993 (1939). A Hungarian prime minister in 1942 boasted that Hungary had invented fascism back in 1919; NAZI Germany and Fascist Italy had merely picked up the old Hungarian idea.

By 1942 fascism had served Hungary well. She was a staunch ally of Germany, and the alliance had been showing benefits since 1938 when, in the dismemberment of Czechoslovakia by the MUNICH PACT, Hungary got about 4,600 square miles of Czech territory and 1,027,450 new citizens. Another reward for Hungary came in 1940 when, after persistent lobbying by Hungary's foreign minister, Germany handed over Transylvania, which had been part of Hungary but whose inhabitants were predominantly Rumanian.

Hungary followed Germany's every lead, signing the ANTI-COMINTERN PACT to join with Japan, Germany, and Italy in a common front against the Soviet Union in 1939; signing the German-Japanese-Italian TRIPARTITE PACT in 1940; resigning from the LEAGUE OF NATIONS; passing ANTI-SEMITIC laws; and declaring war on the United States.

The anti-Semitic laws passed in 1939 barred JEWS from the civil service, most professions, and employment in the theater, cinema, and journalism; set Jewish quotas of 6 percent to 12 percent of the population for participation in business; and authorized the expropriation of any Jewish farmland in excess of half an acre.

On April 3, 1941, Hungarian Premier Pál Teleki killed himself when Adm. Miklós Horthy, the regent of Hungary, agreed to collaborate with Germany in the invasion of Yugoslavia—a month after signing a friendship treaty with Yugoslavia. (See the BALKANS-GREECE-CRETE CAMPAIGN.)

Teleki was succeeded by Lazlo Bárdossy. On June 29, after the bombing of a Hungarian city, Hungary declared war on the Soviet Union. Bárdossy had secretly ordered the bombing to provide a pretext for joining Germany in the war against the Soviets. Those who opposed the war were told it would bring "much bread and little blood." But much Hungarian blood flowed. In Jan. 1943, at the catastrophic battle of Voronezh, Soviet forces wiped out nearly the entire Hungarian Second Army. (See SOVIET OFFENSIVE CAMPAIGN.)

By the beginning of 1944 Horthy's allegiance to Germany was wavering and Allied PROPAGANDA broadcasts were urging Hungarians to raise GUERRILLA forces against their pro-German government. In March Germany sent occupying troops into Hungary. Later ADOLF EICHMANN arrived and set in motion mass deportations of Hungarian Jews to AUSCHWITZ. Horthy offered to release Jews who had visas to British-ruled Palestine. But Germany, which controlled the Hungarian border, refused to allow them to escape. Neutral nations issued visas and churches provided baptismal certificates. A Swedish diplomat, RAOUL WALLENBERG, used legal devices to save numerous Jews.

As Soviet troops began entering Hungary in Aug. 1944, political pressure mounted for Horthy to make a separate peace. He stalled until October, when a German special force, in an operation called Mickey Mouse led by the daring *Oberst* OTTO SKORZENY kidnapped Horthy and, threatening to kill his son, forced him to resign. His successor, Ferenc Szálasi, led his anti-Semitic Arrow Cross Party on an orgy of murder and terror, killing more than 10,000 Jews and sending 40,000 more on a forced march to Austria.

Soviet troops liberated much of the country by Dec. 1944, when the fifty-two-day siege of Budapest began. A provisional national assembly convened in Debrecen, 120 miles east of Budapest, and on Dec. 26, 1944, declared war on Germany. (The official declaration recognized by the Allies was on Jan. 20, 1945, when Hungary signed an armistice with the Allied powers in MOSCOW.)

Bárdossy, Szálasi, and many other collaborators were tried, convicted of WAR CRIMES, and executed. Horthy, captured by Americans, was not indicted as a war criminal.

Hurley, Maj. Gen. Patrick J. (1883–1963)

U.S. diplomat and Army officer. Secretary of War under President Hoover, Hurley, drawn to power, became acquainted with President ROOSEVELT. Hurley impressed Roosevelt, who was always on the lookout for Republicans potentially sympathetic to the New Deal. In Jan. 1942 Roosevelt promoted Hurley, a colonel in the Army Reserve, to brigadier general and sent him to the Far East to work on ways to break the Japanese blockade of the Philippines.

Hurley was a brash, self-made man who had been born dirt poor on what was still the frontier in the Oklahoma Territory. He became a wealthy lawyer with WASHINGTON connections, a man given delicate international missions despite his disdain for diplomacy.

After the fall of BATAAN, Hurley served as U.S. minister to New Zealand for four months. Later in 1942 Roosevelt sent Hurley to the Soviet Union as his special representative. Hurley met with Soviet leader STALIN and visited battlefields where Soviet troops were fighting Germans. Like all Americans and Englishmen Stalin met, Hurley was urged to get an Anglo-American SECOND FRONT started to take some of the combat pressure off the Soviet Union.

Hurley attended the TEHRAN CONFERENCE of Roosevelt, Stalin, and Prime Minister CHURCHILL in Nov. 1943 and drafted the Declaration on Iran, in which the three nations promised to maintain the independence, sovereignty, and borders of Iran. This document was the basis for a crisis over the Soviet Union's failure to withdraw from Iran immediately after the end of the war.

Hurley made Middle East fact-finding tours for Roosevelt in 1943 and 1944. Then Hurley, who had been promoted to major general in Dec. 1943, set off for China on his most arduous and controversial assignment for Roosevelt. Hurley, as a special envoy, was to mediate between Gen. JOSEPH W. STILWELL and Generalissimo CHIANG KAI-SHEK. In Jan. 1942 Stilwell had been put in command of U.S. Army forces in China and Burma and appointed to serve as Chief of Staff to Chiang. Stilwell despised Chiang for sending so many of his troops to confront Chinese Communists and not Japanese troops. (Stilwell referred to Chiang, not so privately, as "the Peanut.")

Hurley did no discernible good in his talks with Stilwell and Chiang. He next became U.S. ambassador to China and was given the hopeless task of bringing together Chiang's Nationalist regime and the Communists. Hurley was given two objectives: unite the Nationalist and Communist armies against the Japanese and get Chiang to form a coalition government that included the Communists. Both objectives were impossible to attain.

The war ended with civil war erupting in China. Hurley blamed the failure of his mission not on intransigent Chinese politics but on "disloyal" U.S. Foreign Service officers. Speaking before a National Press Club audience, Hurley charged that men in the State Department who were either Communists or under Communist influence had undercut him. He resigned in Nov. 15 and became an ardent anti-Communist and a foe of President TRUMAN's China policy.

Hurricane

The principal British fighter in the BATTLE OF BRITAIN, although in publicity it was overshadowed by the less-numerous albeit higher performance SPITFIRE fighter. The Hurricane entered RAF squadron service in Dec. 1937 and by the outbreak of the EUROPEAN WAR almost 500 were being flown by eighteen fighter squadrons. At the start of the Battle of Britain Hurricanes filled twenty-nine of the fifty-eight squadrons in RAF Fighter Command. (There were nineteen squadrons of Spitfires.)

RAF Hurricanes flew throughout the war in Europe as well as in the Middle East and Far East, with the Royal Navy adopting the Sea Hurricane for carrier use. Some of the latter were converted Hurricane Mk I aircraft further modified to "Hurricats" in 1941 for operation from merchant ships. These planes were catapulted off when a German reconnaissance or antishipping aircraft was sighted; after intercepting the bomber (usually an FW 200 CONDOR), the pilot would attempt to reach a shore base, if within range, or parachute into the sea in the hope that he would be picked up by the CONVOY he had protected.

The prototype Hurricane flew on Nov. 6, 1935, the product of Sydney Camm's design team at the Hawker firm. Production orders were soon placed and, including naval models, Hurricane production in Britain and Canada totaled 14,533 aircraft. A number were provided to the Soviet Union, some modified as two-seat attack aircraft; these included planes for the French "Normandie" squadron that operated with Soviet forces.

The Hurricane was a single-place, low-wing aircraft with a large in-line Rolls-Royce Merlin engine. Top speed of the Mk IIB was 339 mph with a range of 470 miles. Armament consisted of eight .303-cal. machine guns. In the ground-attack role two 500-pound BOMBS or eight large ROCKETS could be carried.

Hurricane (Code Name)

(1) British code name for RAF bombing of Duisburg, Oct. 1944; (2) code name for Allied assault force for Biak, NEW GUINEA.

Hurry

British code name for reinforcement of MALTA, Aug. 1940.

Hürtgen Forest

Dense forest southeast of the German border city of AACHEN. In the fall of 1944 the ALLIES held Aachen, where Charlemagne had been crowned and where HITLER had ordered a last-ditch defense. Then, attacking eastward, U.S. troops ran into strong opposition. The Germans, unable to retake Aachen, were expected to blow up the dams on the Roer River, causing flooding that would cut off a large number of Allied troops. To reach the dams, a U.S. attack was launched through the Hürtgen Forest, which was heavily defended.

From the end of Nov. to mid-Dec., four U.S. DIVISIONS fought in the foggy cold of the forest. Most American soldiers experienced for the first time the terror of "treebursts"—ARTILLERY shells that burst in the treetops and sprayed shell fragments downward. Instead of falling flat as protection against the artillery fire, soldiers had to throw themselves against the tree trunks. U.S. troops suffered some of the highest casualty rates of the war. The 1st Division alone sustained 4,000 casualties. Of some 120,000 Americans who fought in the forest, 33,000 were killed, wounded, or taken prisoner. The battle "stands in history comparable to the Argonne in World War I," according to historian John S. D. Eisenhower.

Husky

Code name for Allied invasion of SICILY, July 1943.

I-16

The bullet-shaped Polikarpov I-16 was probably the best-known Soviet fighter of the war. It was a radical design for its time, and although obsolete by the start of the EUROPEAN WAR, it was effective until retired from frontline service in 1943.

The aircraft was conceived in 1932 while N. N. Polikarpov was interned by the secret police. The prototype flew in Dec. 1933, and appeared lackluster. But fitting an imported American Cyclone engine cleared the aircraft for production. Production through early 1940 totaled just over 7,000 single-seat and 1,639 two-seat aircraft. Many were flown by the Republican side in the SPANISH CIVIL WAR.

A low-wing monoplane, the I-16 had a large radial engine with large spinner, a massive wing set well forward, and an open cockpit. The main under-carriage fully retracted. Several training variants with two cockpits were produced, some with the rear cockpit having a plywood cover for instrument training.

The aircraft had a maximum speed of 326 mph. Standard armament was two 20-mm cannon and two 7.62-mm machine guns; small BOMBS or ROCKETS could be carried under the wings.

I-400

The Japanese submarines of the *I-400* class were the largest undersea craft built by any nation during the war. They were designed specifically to launch floatplane bombers against New York and other U.S. cities. However, as the war moved closer to Japan the mission for the *I-400* class was revised with attacking the Panama Canal becoming the first

The most famous photo of the war was Associated Press photographer Joe Rosenthal's shot of the second flag raising on Iwo Jima on Feb. 23, 1945. *(U.S. Marine Corps)*

The world's largest—and smallest—submarines were Japanese. This is the *I-400,* one of a series of aircraft-carrying submarines intended to send bombers against the Panama Canal. The massive conning tower contains a hangar that can hold three assembled and one broken-down floatplane; there is a catapult for launching the aircraft forward of the tower. *(U.S. Navy)*

priority to slow the transfer of Allied warships from the Atlantic to the Pacific. (The Japanese Navy also operated several smaller aircraft-carrying submarines.)

By May 1945 the first two submarines, the *I-400* and *I-401,* were ready for operations and, with two smaller submarines, formed a division of "submarine carriers" that could launch a total of ten floatplanes—four in each of the larger ships and one in each of the smaller submarines. A strike against the Panama Canal was planned, with models of the canal locks near Nanao Bay on the western coast of Honshu being used for target practice. In these trials the *I-400* and *I-401* were able to surface, ready three planes each, and catapult them into the air in 45 minutes. While the submarines and aircraft were training, the decision was made by the naval general staff to attack U.S. warships at the Ulithi anchorage in the CAROLINE ISLANDS.

The Ulithi plan called for the *I-400* and *I-401* to each launch three bombers and the smaller *I-13* and *I-14* to each launch two high-speed reconnaissance planes that would choose targets for the strike. Submarine-delivered KAITEN suicide submersibles were to make a coordinated attack, if possible.

The *I-400* and *I-401* departed Japan on July 26,

with the six-plane raid on Ulithi scheduled for Aug. 17, the planes to be launched in the predawn darkness. But the war ended before the strike could be launched, and in accordance with the surrender terms, the two large submarines surfaced, launched all TORPEDOES, destroyed their aircraft, and returned to Japan flying the black flag of surrender; they were met at sea and placed under U.S. Navy control on Aug. 27 and Aug. 29, respectively. They had never fired a shot in anger.

The third submarine of this class to be completed, the *I-402,* was ready in July 1945 but did not undertake an operational mission. The *I-400* and *I-401* were sailed to PEARL HARBOR for examination by U.S. submarine experts, after which they were sunk. The *I-402* was taken off the Japanese coast, used for target practice by U.S. ships, and then scuttled in Operation Road's End on April 1, 1946.

The Japanese planned to build eighteen of these underwater giants, but because of material shortages and changes in shipbuilding priorities, only five units were laid down and only three were completed. Four were launched in 1944: the *I-400* was completed in Dec. 1944, the *I-401* in Jan. 1945, and the *I-402* in July 1945. The *I-404* was launched in July 1944 but work on her ceased in March 1945 when 90 percent complete; she was sunk by U.S. Navy carrier planes in July.

The *I-400* submarines had a standard displacement of 3,530 tons and submerged displaced 6,560 tons. Each was 400¼ feet long. The massive superstructure of the *I-400* design could accommodate three fully assembled floatplane bombers (with wings folded) plus parts for a fourth aircraft. The Aichi M6A1 *SEIRAN*—not given an Allied code name—was designed specifically to be catapulted from the decks of these submarines.

These submarines had eight 21-inch (533-mm) bow torpedo tubes and carried 20 torpedoes; for surface action each had one 5.5-inch (140-mm) gun and ten 25-mm antiaircraft weapons. A crew of 144 was carried.

Iceberg

Code name for U.S. invasion of OKINAWA, 1945.

Iceland

Capital: Reykjavík, pop. 117,692 (1938). A republic joined to Denmark through allegiance to the same king, Iceland began planning a break from the union as soon as Germany invaded Denmark in April 1940. The little nation wanted to remain neutral, but the ALLIES needed it because of its strategic location, halfway between the United States and England on the Atlantic CONVOY run. On May 10, 1940, the first of more than 60,000 British troops arrived as a force to keep Iceland out of German hands. The British took into custody both the German consul general and German military personnel.

The British were joined in July 1941 by U.S. Marines and, later, U.S. Army troops, who gradually replaced the British.

Ichigo

Code name for Japanese plan to capture U.S. air bases in eastern China.

Ickes, Harold L. (1874–1952)

Key figure in the ROOSEVELT administration. Named secretary of the Interior in 1933, the former newspaperman and lawyer became the President's principal aide for running the domestic side of the war. While still running the Department of the In-

terior he was appointed solid fuels administrator in Nov. 1941, petroleum administrator for war in Dec. 1942, and coal mines administrator in 1943.

He often clashed with business interests. In Feb. 1944, for instance, he tried to get a pipeline built across Saudi Arabia, despite vigorous—and ultimately successful—lobbying by domestic oil companies. After the Aluminum Company of America opposed Ickes' abortive plan to build a dozen government-operated aluminum plants, he told Congress, "When the story of the war comes to be written, it may have to be written that it was lost because of the recalcitrance of the Aluminum Company of America."

Again and again Ickes was locked in struggles with John L. Lewis, president of the United Mine Workers, whose wartime strikes frequently tested Ickes' populist, prolabor instincts. The powerful, arrogant mutual hatred of the two men made negotiations between them impossible, but they slugged on, year after year, strike after strike.

One of his many enemies in WASHINGTON called him "a HITLER in short pants"—a feeble jab compared to Ickes' litany of abuse about what he called Big Biz: money mobsters, dervishes of Wall Street, worshipers of Moloch, plutocrats of privilege. He said a general who opposed him was suffering from "mental saddle sores." In 1938, after Ickes made some biting remark about German persecution of JEWS, German PROPAGANDA Minister JOSEPH GOEBBELS said Ickes was "the evil spirit present in American policy."

Ickes resigned as secretary of the Interior in Feb. 1946 after publicly opposing President TRUMAN'S nomination of Edwin W. Pauley, an oil executive, to be under secretary of the Navy.

IFF,

see FRENCH RESISTANCE.

I. G. Farben

A cartel of German companies. The name comes from Interessen Gemeinschaft Farbenindustrie Aktiengesellschaft (community of interests of dye industries, incorporated). Far from just an association of dye manufacturers, I. G. Farben was an old-line German cartel. Its directors, who had opposed the anticartel WEIMAR REPUBLIC, were early supporters of HITLER and the NAZI Party. The Nazis, in developing a state-run economy, encouraged cartels like I. G. Farben, which produced more than 85 percent of Germany's high explosives and nearly all its synthetic-rubber tires.

I. G. Farben had many connections with U.S. corporations through patent agreements. The corporations included the Aluminum Company of America, E. I. du Pont, Dow Chemical, and Standard Oil of New Jersey. In 1945, I. G. Farben's indirect holdings of the Winthrop Chemical Co. of Delaware were sold by the U.S. Alien Property Custodian to Sterling Drug, Inc. of Delaware. The terms, according to a U.S. Department official, "virtually prevented its return to German control after the war through 'fronts,' 'cloaks,' or other devices." The same had been said after similar alien-property sales after World War I.

From Germany's abundant coal reserves I. G. Farben scientists developed synthetic gasoline and a synthetic rubber known as Buna. One of the giant I. G. Farben plants that produced both Buna and synthetic gasoline was located at the CONCENTRATION CAMP at AUSCHWITZ. The ZYKLON-B poison gas used at DEATH CAMPS was produced by two German firms that had acquired the patent from I. G. Farben.

After the war I. G. Farben was declared a threat to peace, its breakup was ordered, its major executives were charged with WAR CRIMES, and twenty-four of them were put on trial for enslavement, mass murder of SLAVE LABOR workers, and plundering of conquered countries. The coming of the Cold War, however, convinced U.S. and British policymakers that preservation of German industry was needed to keep the West prepared for conflict with the Soviet Union. The proposed breakup of I. G. Farben was canceled and the executives were released.

I-Go-1A Guided Missile

This was Japan's wartime entry in the development of an antiship GUIDED MISSILES. The I-Go-1A was a short-wingspan flying BOMB (similar to the U.S. BAT and several German projects). The missile was air launched and guided to its target by radio control. Flight tests demonstrated a range of 6 miles. The total missile weight was 1,760 pounds. It was intended for use by the Army Air Force and was to be launched from a Ka-67-I-KAI PEGGY twin-engine bomber.

The first I-Go-1A missiles were completed in 1944, but only ten were built before the war ended. It was never used in combat.

Il-2 *Shturmovik*

One of the most famous Soviet aircraft of the war period, this was a highly effective ground-attack aircraft (*Shturmovik*—armored attacker). Entering service in 1941, the Il-2 became one of the world's most effective close-support, antitank, and "train busting" aircraft. Serving to the end of the war, the IL-4 also had a very low loss rate, especially after being modified to provide a second crewman, who fired a 12.7-mm machine gun to protect the aircraft from a rear attack by German fighters. The Il-2 fought in every region where Soviet troops were engaged.

The prototype (BSh-2) flew on Dec. 30, 1939, and, after several modifications, entered production. The Il-2 was in combat from July 1941 and in a telegram to factory workers, on Dec. 24, 1941, STALIN declared that the Il-2 was "as essential to the Red Army as air and bread." About 35,000 were produced—more than any other aircraft type during the war.

A low-wing aircraft with an in-line engine, the Ilyushin-designed Il-2 was a heavily armored and heavily armed aircraft. It had two wing-mounted 20-mm cannon and two 7.62-mm machine guns; later, the two-seat aircraft had an aft-firing gun. In addition, four 220-pound BOMBS and eight 82-mm ROCKETS could be carried under the wings. Later variants were fitted with high-velocity 20-mm cannon and then two 37-mm guns in place of the 20-mm cannon.

Il-4

Standard medium bomber of the Red Air Force during the war. This highly successful aircraft was the first Soviet bomber to strike BERLIN when, on the night of Aug. 7–8, 1941, five Soviet Navy Il-4 aircraft flying from a base in Estonia made a token strike against the city. The Il-4 was successful as a conventional bomber and as a naval strike aircraft, carrying aerial TORPEDOES and MINES. Late in the war, as newer combat aircraft were available, the Il-4 flew as a trainer and GLIDER-tug aircraft.

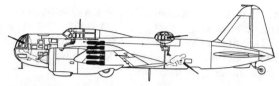

Il-4 (DB-3B) bomber.

The twin-engine aircraft made its maiden flight in 1935. It was the first operational aircraft to bear the initials of designer Sergei Il'yushin, entering squadron service in 1937. In June 1938 an Il-4 prototype flew nonstop from MOSCOW to Dalno, near Vladivostok, a distance of 4,960 miles with a flight time of twenty-four hours and thirty-six minutes. The following April the same prototype took off from Moscow for a polar flight to the United States. Bad weather forced the plane off course and it crash-landed on an island off New Brunswick, having flown 4,970 miles in twenty-two hours and fifty-six minutes. Despite its failure to reach the United States, the flight was widely acclaimed, with President ROOSEVELT personally lauding the effort.

The Il-4 (known by the designation DB-3 until 1940) was a relatively large aircraft, with a streamlined, low-wing configuration and glazed nose. The main landing gear was fully retractable (with a fixed tail wheel). The plane could reach 253 mph in the early models and, with upgraded engines, 265 mph. Maximum BOMB load was 5,500 pounds (as much as a B-17 FLYING FORTRESS); with a 1,100-pound bomb load the plane could reach targets 1,200 miles from base. Alternatively, a torpedo could be carried under the fuselage. Defensive armament consisted of three 7.62-mm machine guns (increased to four plus a 12.7-mm gun in later models). The crew numbered three or four.

Imperator

Code name for proposed Allied raid on French coast, 1942.

Implement

British submarine attacks against ore ships off Spain, May 1944.

Independence

Code name for French offensive toward Belfort, France.

Independence (CVL 22)

Lead ship for a class of small or light AIRCRAFT CARRIERS (CVL) built on the hulls of CRUISERS. These ships formed carrier DIVISIONS with the larger ESSEX (CV 9) class to comprise the core of the U.S. Navy's fast carrier striking forces during the war. These ships spearheaded U.S. striking forces in the Pacific in 1943–1945. The *Essex* was commissioned on the last day of 1942, and sixteen sister ships were in service before the war ended.

Shortly after the United States entered the war the shortage of fast carriers led to the hulls of nine *Cleveland* (CL 55) class cruisers being reordered as light carriers. The lead ship, the *Independence,* was launched on Aug. 22, 1942, and entered service in Jan. 1943. She and her sister ships participated in all major U.S. carrier actions from then until the end of the war.

Eight of these CVLs and seven larger carriers formed the U.S. carrier striking force in the battle of the MARIANAS in June 1944, while eight CVLs along with eight larger carriers fought together at LEYTE GULF in Oct. 1944. The light carrier *Princeton* (CVL 23) was the only U.S. fast carrier lost after the battle of MIDWAY in June 1942. The *Princeton* was struck by two small Japanese BOMBS at Leyte Gulf and, despite heroic efforts to save her, she sank. Shortly after her TORPEDO magazine blew up; 106 men were lost and 1,400 survived. Capt. John M. Hopkins, about to take command of the carrier, was badly injured. The ship's medical officer, himself wounded, amputated Hopkins' injured foot with a sheath knife. (Hopkins survived and after the war, fitted with an artificial foot, went on to command a new carrier named *Princeton,* the CV 37.)

The cruiser *Birmingham* (CL 62), alongside to help fight fires in the *Princeton,* suffered the loss of more than 200 men when the carrier blew up.

After the war the lead ship of the class, the *Independence,* was used as a test ship at the Bikini ATOMIC BOMB TESTS. Heavily damaged, she survived and was used as a radiological test platform at San Francisco until she sank in 1951.

These ships had a distinctive configuration, with their flight decks ending some 40 feet short of their narrow bows and a small island structure fitted with four rectangular funnels angled out from the full aft of the island. About forty-five aircraft were normally embarked—F6F HELLCAT fighters and TBF/TBM AVENGER bombers. The CVLs had a standard displacement of 11,000 tons and were 622½ feet long. Steam turbines could drive them at 31.6 knots. Each ship was armed with BOFORS 40-MM and OERLIKON 20-MM antiaircraft guns.

India

Capital: Delhi, pop. 338,119,154 (1941). When the UNITED KINGDOM declared war on Germany on Sept. 3, 1939, India, as a colonial member of the BRITISH COMMONWEALTH, involuntarily went to war. India, not having yet achieved dominion status, was under British rule. GEORGE VI not only had the title of king of England but also emperor of India. In his name, India was at war. (Dominions, such as Canada and Australia, had legislative autonomy.)

Under the Government of India Act of 1935, however, India had legislatures in all eleven provinces. In eight of them, the powerful anti-British Indian National Congress Party had majorities. When war was declared, the party pulled its representatives out of the legislatures "in order to dissociate India from the war."

From then until the end of the war the Congress Party, under the leadership of MOHANDAS GANDHI and JAWAHARLAL NEHRU, would tie the struggle for Indian independence to the British war effort against Japan. Indian troops fought valiantly for England in North Africa, Iraq, and Syria early in the war. But politically the British made little headway in getting India's politicians to provide the kind of support that was coming from the people of India. Further complicating the political conflict was the endless scheming of Hindu and Moslem nationalists over the question of which religious group would ultimately govern India.

When the attack on PEARL HARBOR launched the JAPANESE CAMPAIGN IN THE FAR EAST in Dec. 1941, India's status changed from theoretical belligerent to potential battlefield. Japan took Malaya, Burma, and, by March 1942 was poised for invasion of India.

Gandhi demanded immediate independence as the price for India's participation in the war and threatened mass civil disobedience. The British viceroy's council, made up of British and Indian representatives, declared the Congress Party an illegal organization and in Aug. 1942 began arresting Ghandi, Nehru, and other party leaders. Rioting broke out in Bombay and other cities. Hindu supporters of Gandhi destroyed railroad stations and cut communications lines with troops on the border in the northeastern province of Assam, the potential gateway for invasion. The turmoil continued for more than a month, disrupting military operations and causing an exasperated British Prime Minister CHURCHILL to reiterate his longtime opposition to Indian independence: "I have not become the King's First Minister in order to preside over the liquidation of the British Empire."

Both Germany and Japan took advantage of the anti-British sentiments to sponsor FIFTH COLUMN movements. British intelligence thwarted most of Germany's subversive activities. But one of Gandhi's political opponents, Jagadis Chandra Bose, operating in Germany, did manage to recruit the nucleus of what he called the Indian National Army. His first volunteers were revolutionary Indian exiles and PRISONERS OF WAR. After Japan entered the war Bose went to Japan and from there began to raise an army of three divisions, recruiting from Indian POWs captured in Malaya and Burma. Many of them later claimed that they had been forced into the Japanese-sponsored army under duress.

About 7,000 men of this Indian National Army joined Japanese troops in the invasion of India in March 1944. The Japanese-Indian force reached Imphal and Kohima, about thirty miles from the Burmese border, in an attempt to seize the Bengal-Assam railroad that carried supplies to China. In fighting that went on until August the Japanese were repelled.

Japan and Germany had underestimated the reaction of the India *not* represented by the Congress Party. Indians were overwhelmingly loyal to England. The Royal Indian Air Force increased in size from two squadrons to ten, and every man was Indian. The Royal Indian Navy, which had 1,200 men at the beginning of the war, ended the war with 30,000. More than 2,000,000 Indians of every class and religion volunteered for the Indian Army in the largest volunteer recruitment in history. At first there were few Indian officers, but by the end of the war they were in the majority and, though still under British command, included officers of brigadier rank. About 700,000 Indian troops served in the Burma phase of the ALLIED CHINA-BURMA-INDIA CAMPAIGN.

The Indian home front mobilized down to the village level. Textile mills turned to the manufacture of CAMOUFLAGE netting and the parachutes used to drop supplies to Allied forces in Burma. Armies of laborers built new roads and railways, 120 field hospitals, and scores of airfields. The British sent Indians to munitions and aircraft plants in England for training. Back in India, the trainees helped build new plants, hastening the coming of industry to a new India.

But the old India of disease and famine still existed. Crop failures, the cutoff of food from Burma, priorities that placed military demands over civilian needs—all these combined to produced widespread starvation in 1943–1944. An estimated 1,500,000 Indians died of starvation and disease.

The disaster inspired new efforts to find a way to bring the modern age to India. The viceroy, now Field Marshal Lord PERCIVAL WAVELL, established India's first department of planning and development. He worked hard to solve the Hindu-Moslem problem but was not able to bring leaders of the two religious groups together. His successor, Adm. Lord LOUIS MOUNTBATTEN, the last viceroy of India, oversaw the granting of independence to India on Aug. 15, 1947.

Indianapolis (CA 35)

Last major U.S. warship sunk in World War II. The CRUISER *Indianapolis* was sunk on July 30, 1945, by the Japanese submarine *I-58* under Lt. Comdr. Mochitsura Hashimoto after having delivered components for the ATOMIC BOMBS to be dropped on Japan to the U.S. base at TINIAN.

A heavy cruiser, the *Indianapolis* was one of eighteen 8-inch (203-mm) gun ships built by the U.S. Navy between the wars. In the 1930s she embarked President ROOSEVELT on several occasions, once for a "good neighbor" cruise to South America. At the time of the PEARL HARBOR attack the *Indianapolis* was exercising near Johnston Island in the Pacific and immediately joined other U.S. warships searching (unsuccessfully) for the Japanese air-

craft carriers that launched the attack.

During 1942–1943 the *Indianapolis* ranged far in the Pacific, escorting convoys to Australia and bombarding Japanese positions in the ALEUTIANS and intercepting Japanese shipping in those northern waters. In Nov. 1943 she became the flagship of Vice Adm. RAYMOND A. SPRUANCE, commander of the Fifth FLEET. In that role the cruiser participated in the assaults on MAKIN and TARAWA in the MARSHALL ISLANDS, often approaching the shore to provide fire support from her 8-inch guns. She next carried Adm. Spruance in the landings in the GILBERT ISLANDS and the MARIANA ISLANDS, including the battle of the PHILIPPINE SEA in June 1944. The cruiser then joined the fast-carrier force (TASK FORCE 58), serving as Spruance's flagship for air strikes on TOKYO in Feb. 1945, followed by participating in the landings at IWO JIMA and OKINAWA as fleet flagship and also providing gunfire support for the landings.

The *Indianapolis* was damaged by a KAMIKAZE that struck the ship off Okinawa on March 31, 1945. The ship returned under her own power to the U.S. West Coast for repairs. On July 16 she departed San Francisco carrying components for the first atomic bombs. She traveled unescorted to Tinian, with a short stopover at Pearl Harbor, traveling 5,000 miles in just ten days. After unloading her cargo, the *Indianapolis* departed GUAM on July 28, again sailing alone, en route to Okinawa.

At 12:15 A.M. on July 30 she was struck by two torpedoes. The cruiser capsized and sank within two minutes. No SOS was sent before she went down. Not until the morning of Aug. 2 were survivors sighted by a plane on a routine patrol. When PBY CATALINA flying boats and ships arrived on the scene they found only 318 of her crew of 1,199 men. Floating among the survivors were the remains of scores of men who had been attacked by sharks.

Capt. Charles B. McVay, III, commanding officer of the *Indianapolis*, was found guilty by court-martial of hazarding his ship's safety by failing to zigzag. However, he was restored to active duty without punishment. McVay was the first U.S. Navy officer to be court-martialed for losing his ship to an enemy in at least a century. (Ironically, a message from the submarine commander that he had sunk a U.S. battleship was intercepted by U.S. naval intelligence, but was dismissed as an exaggeration and received little attention.)

The *Indianapolis* earned ten BATTLE STARS during the war.

The ship was launched on Nov. 7, 1931, and commissioned one year later. She had a standard displacement of 9,800 tons and was 610 feet long. Her maximum speed was 32 knots. In addition to her nine 8-inch guns, she carried 5-inch (127-mm) and lighter antiaircraft guns plus several floatplanes for gunnery spotting.

Indigo

Code name for plan for movement of U.S. troops to Iceland, 1942.

Indochina

Capital: Hanoi, pop. 23,853,861 (1939). When Japan went to war against China in 1937, France controlled Indochina—ancient Vietnam, Cambodia, and Laos—through local puppet rulers. Following the fall of France in June 1940, Japan began making demands that France, with barely 13,000 troops in all of Indochina, had to accept. Japan, ignoring protests from the United States and England, had a strategic need to cut off supplies reaching China via a railroad from the Indochinese port city of Haiphong.

Japanese forces, while using French airfields, railways, and ports at Saigon and Cam Ranh Bay, allowed the French to continue administering Indochina. The United States sought to restrain Japan in Indochina by declaring an embargo on petroleum products to Japan and freezing Japanese assets. Ultimately, Japan retaliated with the attack on PEARL HARBOR.

In March 1945, anticipating an Allied invasion of Indochina, Japan attacked French garrisons in Hanoi and at other sites. The Japanese also convinced the puppet emperor to declare his kingdom's independence from France.

French troops, fighting as GUERRILLA units, were given some support by British air drops. But no such aid came from the United States. After the war, Gen. CLAIRE CHENNAULT, commander of Army Air Force units in China, said he had been ordered "to proceed with 'normal' action against

the Japanese" in Indochina provided he did not help the French "so the problem of postwar separation from their colony would be easier."

Surviving French troops and civilians, weak and ill-equipped, began fighting their way through Japanese lines to China. Thousands were taken prisoner, 2,200 were killed, and about 3,000 reached China.

After Japan's surrender, following Allied procedures decided upon at the POTSDAM CONFERENCE, Indochina was divided at the 16th Parallel, with Chinese forces occupying the north and British to the south. The Communist Viet Minh, under the leadership of Ho Chi Minh, proclaimed a revolutionary government. But the French, determined to retain Indochina, sent in troops and began the decades of fighting that would become the Vietnam War.

Infatuate

Code name for British assault on Walcheren, Oct. 1944.

Influx

Code name for planned 1940 British invasion of SICILY.

Insect

British code name for the reinforcement of MALTA, June 1942.

Interim Committee

Civilian committee established in April 1945 by President TRUMAN to consider the political, military, and scientific issues involved with employment of the ATOMIC BOMB. Members were Secretary of War HENRY STIMSON, presidential representative (and later Secretary of State) JAMES F. BYRNES, Under Secretary of the Navy Ralph A. Bard, Assistant Secretary of State William L. Clayton, and scientists VANNEVAR BUSH, James B. Conant, and Karl T. Compton, with George Harrison as secretary. No military personnel were assigned to the committee, which met several times a month. The Interim Committee was assisted by an advisory panel of scientists who were involved in development of the bomb.

The Interim Committee unanimously recommended on June 1 that: (1) the bomb should be used against Japan as soon as possible; (2) the bomb should be used on a dual target—a military installation or war plant surrounded by housing; and (3) the bomb should be used without explicit prior warning. (Under Secretary Bard subsequently changed his mind and wrote a letter of dissent on June 27.)

Interlude

U.S. code name for Allied rehearsal for the MOROTAI operation, Sept. 1944.

International Military Tribunal,

see WAR CRIMES.

Invader,

see A-26.

Iowa (BB 61) Class

The last U.S. BATTLESHIPS to be constructed. The four *Iowa*-class ships were the largest dreadnoughts to be built by any nation except for the two Japanese *YAMATO*-class ships. In addition to the *Iowa*, the other ships of this class, all completed in 1943–1944, were the *New Jersey* (BB 62), *MISSOURI* (BB 63), and *Wisconsin* (BB 64). Two additional ships of the *Iowa* class were never finished, their construction canceled at the end of the war.

All four completed *Iowa*s served in the Pacific during the war. The *Iowa*, before departing from the Atlantic, carried President ROOSEVELT and U.S. military leaders from Norfolk to Mers el-Kébir (Oran) in Algeria in Nov. 1943 for the CASABLANCA CONFERENCE. During that voyage an escorting U.S. DESTROYER accidently fired an armed TORPEDO at the battleship during an exercise. The weapon exploded in the *Iowa*'s wake without causing any damage, except to the destroyer commander's career.

In the Pacific the battleships were used primarily for antiaircraft defense of AIRCRAFT CARRIER task groups and for bombarding hostile islands in preparation for AMPHIBIOUS LANDINGS. Only once were the *Iowa*-class ships readied to engage a hostile surface force: in the battle for LEYTE GULF, on Oct. 25, 1944. While steaming to attack a Japanese carrier group, Adm. WILLIAM F. HALSEY ordered the formation of a battleship-CRUISER group under Vice Adm. WILLIS (Ching) LEE to engage Japanese surface ships. This force consisted of the *Iowa* and *New Jersey,* four other modern battleships, seven cruisers, and eighteen destroyers; however, the battleships turned back toward Leyte Gulf before making contact with the Japanese ships because of attacks on the U.S. ESCORT CARRIER groups off the Philippines. Thus, the *Iowa*s never fired at other warships.

At the end of the war the *Missouri* was the stage for the Japanese SURRENDER ceremonies in Tokyo Bay.

After World War II all ships were mothballed except for the *Missouri,* which was retained in service as a training ship. All four were reactivated for the Korean War (1950–1953), the *New Jersey* served briefly in the Vietnam War (1968), and all four were again reactivated in the 1980s during the Reagan administration's military buildup.

The main battery of the *Iowa*-class ships was nine 16-inch (406-mm) guns in triple turrets. The guns had a range of 23 miles, firing a 2,700-pound armor-piercing round. The ships carried an antiaircraft battery of twenty 5-inch (127-mm) guns, eighty 40-mm BOFORS guns, and almost sixty 20-mm OERLIKON guns—almost 160 antiaircraft weapons per ship! Each *Iowa* also carried three floatplanes for gunfire spotting. The ships had a standard displacement of 45,000 tons and were 887¼ feet long; geared turbines could drive them at a speed of 33 knots, although speeds of 35 knots were reported. Wartime complement was some 2,500 to 2,900 men per ship.

Iran

Capital: Tehran, pop. 12,500,000 (est. 1942). Although officially neutral during the war, Iran had been a major exporter of grain to Germany, which sent in technicians who helped to tilt the iron ruler of Iran, Reza Shah Pahlavi, toward the AXIS. A large German mission had built up in Tehran by mid-July 1941 when the British and Soviet Union began planning a military move against the country; at the same time, they stepped up pressure for the expulsion of the Germans. The ALLIES saw Iran as a vital resource both for its petroleum and as a supply route for war matériel to the Soviet Union.

Prime Minister CHURCHILL preferred calling the country by its old name, Persia, because "dangerous mistakes may easily occur through the similarity of Iran and Iraq."

On Aug. 25, 1941, the Soviets struck from the north, the British from the southwest and, in four days, took over Iran. On Sept. 16 the Shah abdicated in favor of his twenty-three-year-old son, Mohammed Reza. Under a treaty hammered through the Iranian Parliament, Iran granted the Allies whatever was needed to win the war in exchange for guarantees of wartime protection and withdrawal of all troops within six months after the end of the war.

In the summer of 1942 the first of about 30,000 U.S. troops and advisers arrived in Iran. While the Soviets bought up most of Iran's harvests at bargain prices, the U.S. shipped in grain. Still, a bread shortage touched off rioting, which occupying troops put down. They also uncovered a German SABOTAGE and rebellion underground group, aided by agents who had been parachuted into Iran.

By Nov. 1943, when President ROOSEVELT and Prime Minister Churchill met for their TEHRAN CONFERENCE, the food crisis was over and Iran was more firmly on the Allied side. As a reward for Iran's help, Roosevelt and Churchill promised "maintenance of the independence, sovereignty, and territorial integrity of Iran."

The Soviet Union, mounting a campaign for petroleum concessions, supported an anti-Shah party called the *Tudeh* (masses), backing its attempt to bring down the Shah and give oil concessions to the Soviets. Red Army troops even disarmed and jailed government security forces. In Dec. 1944 armed *Tudeh* units, with obvious Soviet blessing, took over much of the northern area of Iran.

As U.S. and British troops began preparing to leave Iran in 1945, the Soviet Union began proclaiming its intention to stay. By refusing to leave Iran after the war, the Soviets triggered one of the first clashes of the U.S.-Soviet Cold War. After complaints to the UNITED NATIONS and pressure from the other two former occupying powers, the Soviets finally began leaving Iran in April 1946. But Soviet agents had fostered revolution. In Dec. 1946, after bloody battles with Soviet-aided *Tudeh* rebels, the Iranian government declared martial law. Iranian troops drove the Soviets' followers across the border into the Soviet Union.

Iraq

Capital: Baghdad, pop. 3,995,000 (est. 1943). A military revolt in 1936 put the former monarchy of Iraq into an army-backed parliamentary government. Responding in fear to the Italian invasion of weak Ethiopia in 1935, Iraq in 1937 signed a mutual-aid treaty with Afghanistan, Iran, and Turkey. But that same year Kurdish Gen. Bekr Sidqi, who had overthrown the monarchy, became one of the many politicians of the era to be removed from power by ASSASSINATION. Four military officers, banding together as the "Golden Square," took over the country, propped up the royal family, installed a pro-German prime minister, and pushed an anti-British nationalistic policy aimed at repudiating a 1940 treaty that gave the British air bases at Basra and Habbaniya.

In April 1939 King Ghazi's speeding car hit a post, killing him instantly. The regime, aided by behind-the-scene German and Italian advisers, spread the lie that the British had killed the king. Mobs killed the British consul and, in a PROPAGANDA-fanned attack on Zionism, several JEWS were killed.

The anti-British mood was still strong when the EUROPEAN WAR began in Sept. 1939, but Iraqi politicians tried to remain neutral until they could determine which way the war was going. England, meanwhile, became concerned about ominous German diplomatic and subversive moves, masterminded by FRANZ VON PAPEN, German ambassador to Turkey. When the British were about to reinforce their Iraqi bases, Iraqi leaders resisted; the British had just suffered defeats in Libya and Greece, and Germany was in the ascendancy.

Iraqi troops attacked British air bases in May 1941. In the ensuing turmoil, Iraqis killed 350 Jews and the European colony in Baghdad fled to the U.S. and British embassy compounds. Aided by Kurds, Assyrians, and forces from Palestine, the British gained control of the country. The officers of the Golden Square were hanged, a moderate, pro-British government assumed office, and U.S. and British supplies began moving through Iraq to the Soviet Union. On Jan. 17, 1943, Iraq declared war against the AXIS powers.

Ireland

Capital: Dublin, pop. 2,965,854 (1936). Defined as a "republic associated with the BRITISH COMMONWEALTH," Ireland had such a vague association that when the war began on Sept. 1, 1939, Ireland reiterated its neutrality, which it maintained throughout the war.

Ireland's age-old problems with England had theoretically ended in 1922 with a treaty that, among other points, provided independence for Ireland but allowed that defense of its coasts would be "by the imperial forces" of the United Kingdom. This meant that the Royal Navy could use bases at three Irish ports. As war neared in the late 1930s, however, Ireland's prime minister, EAMON DE VALERA, demanded British withdrawal because the presence of the Royal Navy violated Ireland's neutrality. Later, de Valera attempted to get Britain to pay the price of a "united Ireland"—essentially the turning over of Northern Ireland to the Republic of Ireland—in return for the end of neutrality. The British did not pay this price, but, when de Valera denounced conscription in Northern Ireland as "an act of aggression," the British government exempted Northern Ireland from conscription.

When U.S. troops landed in Northern Ireland in Jan. 1942, Ireland protested—astounding President ROOSEVELT, who had assumed that Irish neutrality did not encompass part of the United Kingdom. In March 1944 the United States pressed Ireland to expel diplomats of the AXIS powers. De Valera refused. The British government suspended all travel between the United Kingdom and Ireland. Ireland successfully rode out the crises and enjoyed postwar friendships with all the belligerents.

Iron Cross

The highest German military award in World War II. The Iron Cross was awarded for bravery to men of all services. The eight classes of the Iron Cross are listed below in descending order; take note that two classes were presented only to single individuals.

1. Great Cross of Iron (awarded to HERMANN GÖRING).
2. Knight's Cross to the Iron Cross with Golden Oak Leaves and Swords and Diamonds (awarded to JU 87 *STUKA* pilot HANS ULRICH RUDEL, who flew 2,530 combat missions).
3. Knight's Cross to the Iron Cross with Oak Leaves and Swords and Diamonds (twenty-seven awarded).
4. Knight's Cross to the Iron Cross with Oak Leaves and Swords (154 awarded).
5. Knight's Cross to the Iron Cross with Oak Leaves (860 awarded).
6. Knight's Cross to the Iron Cross (approximately 7,500 awarded).
7. Iron Cross 1st Class (several thousand awarded).
8. Iron Cross 2nd Class (several thousand awarded).

The Iron Cross was established as an award by King Frederick William II on March 17, 1813. The medal's designer was BERLIN architect Karl Friedrich Schinkel. The Iron Cross was awarded continuously by German governments through World War I. The award was reinstated by the THIRD REICH on Sept. 2, 1939; subsequently, HITLER instituted the Knight's Cross and Oak Leaves variations of the award.

Ironbottom Sound

American term for passage between GUADALCANAL and Florida Island in the SOLOMONS, so named because of the large number of U.S. and Japanese warships—as many as forty-eight—sunk in the area from Aug. 1942 to early 1943. "You may search the seven seas in vain for an ocean graveyard with the bones of so many ships and sailors," wrote historian SAMUEL ELIOT MORISON, "as that body of water . . . named Ironbottom Sound."

Ironclad

Later code name for British assault of MADAGASCAR; originally named Bonus.

Irving

The J1N *Gekko* (Moonlight) was an outstanding Japanese night fighter, although originally developed as a reconnaissance aircraft (Allied code name Irving). This role change was similar to those made to the highly successful Ki-46 DINAH and C6N MYRT. A naval aircraft, the Irving reflected a requirement derived during operations in China in the late 1930s. It entered service in late 1942 and was initially identified by the Allies as a twin-engine fighter aircraft (hence the male code name; see AIRCRAFT DESIGNATIONS). It was soon adopted in the field for night-intercept missions with the specialized J1N1-S being fitted with air-intercept RADAR. By the end of the war Irvings were being employed on KAMIKAZE missions.

First flown in May 1941, the Irving probably underwent more modifications while in service than any other Japanese aircraft. Production of Nakajima-designed aircraft totaled 479, with production ending in Dec. 1944.

The twin-engine Irving was a low-wing, twin-engine aircraft with a long glazed cockpit housing the three-man crew. In night-fighter adaptations the crew was two. The J1N1 recce aircraft had a top speed of 329 mph and was credited with a range of 1,675 miles. Standard armament in the recce role was one 13-mm machine gun fired from the rear of the cockpit, with some models instead having a 20-mm cannon in a dorsal turret. Those built as night fighters had four fuselage-mounted 20-mm cannon, two firing upward and two down, or two upward-firing guns and one forward-firing 20-mm gun.

Isabella

German code name for modification of Felix operation.

Ismay, Maj. Gen. Hastings L. (1887–1965)

Chief of Staff to Prime Minister CHURCHILL during the war. A preeminent staff officer, Ismay served as an assistant secretary of the British Committee of Imperial Defence (1925–1930), deputy secretary (1936–1938), and then secretary (1938–1939) of the committee. He next served from 1939 to 1940 as the deputy military secretary of the War Cabinet.

When WINSTON CHURCHILL became prime minister in 1940, Ismay became his Chief of Staff in Churchill's additional role of Minister of Defence. In this role, Ismay was highly successful in establishing a close and effective relationship between Churchill and the CHIEFS OF STAFF, of which he was a full member.

General of the Army DWIGHT D. EISENHOWER

wrote of Ismay in *Crusade in Europe*: "One of the prominent military figures in Great Britain, he was the immediate associate of Mr. Churchill. . . . Ismay's position of the secretarial staff to the War Cabinet and the British Chiefs of Staff was, from the American point of view, a critical one because it was through him that any subject could at any moment be brought to the attention of the Prime Minister and his principal assistants. It was fortunate, therefore, that he was devoted to the principle of Allied unity and that his personality was such as to win the confidence and friendship of his American associates. He was one of those men whose great ability condemned him throughout the war to a staff position. Consequently his name may be forgotten; but the contributions he made to the winning of the war were equal to those of many whose names became household words."

After the war Ismay, achieving the rank of full general, was the first secretary general of NATO from 1952 to 1957.

Isolationism,

see AMERICAN FIRST COMMITTEE and UNITED STATES.

Italian Campaign (1943–1945)

In a May 1943 WASHINGTON CONFERENCE code-named Trident, President ROOSEVELT and British Prime Minister CHURCHILL decided on an Allied strategy to get a restive Italy out of the war and draw Germans into battle there before the NORMANDY INVASION, scheduled for May 1944. Besides the effect on morale of defeating an AXIS partner, the liberation of Italy would threaten German forces in the Balkans and provide the ALLIES with Italian air bases that would widen the air war against German-occupied territory.

The first move was the conquest of SICILY. For the invasion of the island, Gen. DWIGHT D. EISENHOWER, who had commanded the NORTH AFRICA INVASION, was made Supreme Allied Commander. The Sicilian operation, code-named Husky, ended in thirty-eight days with the island secured. As a consequence of the invasion, Italian *Il Duce* BENITO MUSSOLINI was deposed and events were set in motion leading to Italy's withdrawal from the war.

On Sept. 3, while Italian Army officials were se-

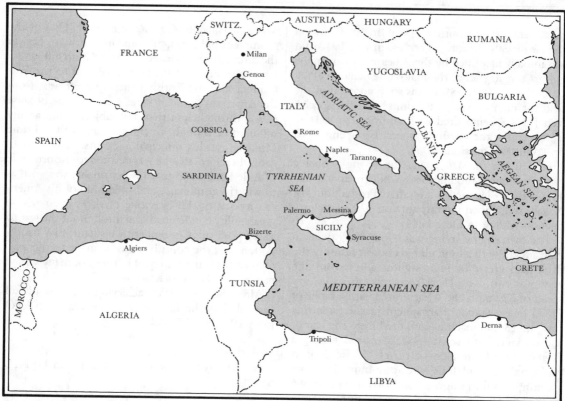

Mediterranean Sea at the start of the European War.

cretly in Sicily to sign a surrender agreement (see SURRENDER, ITALY), the British Eighth Army was crossing the Strait of Messina and landing on the Calabrian coast against token Italian resistance.

Euphoria over the secret surrender inspired Allied leaders to think that Italy would fall into their hands. Plans were under way to fly AIRBORNE troops to ROME. Pro-Allied politicians finally said that they could not guarantee Italian Army seizure of the airfields and German antiaircraft batteries to aid the airborne. The delay kept the 82nd Airborne DIVISION grounded; it was to have guarded the north flank at SALERNO, where Gen. MARK W. CLARK'S Fifth ARMY began landing on Sept. 9. That landing, like the others in the Italian campaign, was affected by how many LSTs (LANDING SHIPS, TANK) were available. The availability of LSTs was also influencing events in the Pacific and was a factor in determining the date of the Normandy landings.

While Clark was landing at Salerno, British forces landed at TARANTO. They advanced northward, and quickly took Bari and Brindisi. The new head of the Italian government, Marshal PIETRO BADOGLIO, fled Rome with King Victor Emmanuel III and established a provisional capital in Brindisi.

Clark's troops faced some desperate hours when German counterattacks threatened to drive the invaders into the sea. But Allied ground, naval, and airborne power secured the beachhead and by Sept. 26 more than 189,000 troops, 100,000 tons of supplies, and 30,000 vehicles had been landed for the drive up the peninsula.

British forces, meanwhile, pressed northward. Although many roads and bridges were blocked or destroyed by the retreating Germans, resistance was relatively light and the troops managed to advance 300 miles in seventeen days. Capri and other islands in the Bay of Naples surrendered, and on Oct. 1, to the cheers of jubilant Neapolitans, the Fifth Army took Naples. The badly damaged harbor was quickly repaired. With the capture of Foggia and its airfields, the Allies seemed to have control of land, sea, and the air.

But the Germans had been working hard to build a series of strong defensive lines across Italy from coast to coast. The advancing Allies ran into the first, the GUSTAV LINE, early in November. Stalled by terrain, winter, and solid German defenses, the Allies tried an indirect move: an AMPHIBIOUS LANDING at ANZIO to disrupt the German rear while Allied forces breached the Gustav Line.

The strategy did not work. Ferocious German assaults and ARTILLERY fire pinned down the troops on the Anzio beachhead and brilliant generalship by *Generalfeldmarschall* ALBERT KESSELRING undercut Allied strategy. The plan was for Clark to break through the Gustav Line by crossing the Garigliano and Rapido Rivers and proceeding up the Liri Valley, the path to Rome. Meanwhile, French and British forces were to feint simultaneously and then hit the center of the line.

Theoretically, Kesselring would be momentarily paralyzed by indecision as to which threat he should first expect, allowing both the Anzio and river-crossing operations to go forward. But Kesselring anticipated the plan and was prepared for it. The Rapido crossing was so disastrous that Clark's conduct of it later became the subject of an inconclusive Congressional investigation, led by Texan members of Congress. (Most of the soldiers killed on the Rapido were Texans of the 36th Infantry Division.)

Another controversy erupted over the bombing of Monte CASSINO, a height crowned by an ancient abbey—but also a Gustav Line strongpoint.

Months of battle at Anzio, in the Liri Valley, and around Monte Cassino ended with a May offensive, code-named Diadem, that cracked the German defense lines. The Anzio invaders broke out. French troops, including Moroccan *GOUMIERS,* surged through supposedly impassable mountains. The Polish CORPS, after taking heavy casualties, planted the Polish flag on Monte Cassino. Valor was commonplace in this motley army that forged common purpose—BRITISH COMMONWEALTH forces from India, New Zealand, and South Africa, along with troops of French, Poles, Brazilians, GHURKAS. JAPANESE-AMERICANS, many of whose relatives were in U.S. internment camps, fought in the all-Nisei

442nd Regimental COMBAT TEAM, which became the most decorated military unit in U.S. history.

When the Anzio breakout finally came in a combined offensive with the Fifth Army and the Eighth British Army, Clark's forces bolted eastward. Had they continued on that course, German forces retreating from the south might have been blocked and eliminated, shortening the war in Italy by several months. Clark chose instead to take Rome.

Clark's decision did not necessarily lengthen the Italian campaign. He was losing men at a steady rate, and the loss was gradually removing the offensive capabilities of the Allies' armies. They were up against what British Field Marshal HAROLD ALEXANDER called "the best soldiers in the world—what men! I doubt if there are any other troops in the world who could have stood up to it [the continued bombing and shelling] and then gone on fighting with the ferocity they have."

But the decision to take and occupy Rome did nothing to shorten the war, and this is the basic reason that Clark's judgment has often been questioned. From the landing at Salerno to the liberation of Rome on June 4, 1944, the campaign took 275 days and cost the Fifth Army 124,917 casualties, including 20,389 dead, of whom 11,292 were American.

The Germans retreating northward from Rome made a stand at Florence, which was entered by advance units of a South African armored division on Aug. 4. The Germans then dug in behind the GOTHIC LINE, strung across northern Italy from just above Leghorn to the Adriatic Sea. U.S. and British armies cracked the line with an offensive that began on Sept. 10. By then, the German Army was already being pressed on two fronts: across northern France following the June Normandy invasion and in southern France, which Allied forces had invaded on Aug. 15. In October would come another liberation: Greece, which the Germans were evacuating.

Although the Gothic Line was the last such extended defensive fortification, the Germans established new defensive positions in northern Italy and held off the Allies through the fall and winter. In April 1945 the Eighth Army pushed through west of Ravenna and the Fifth Army fought its way, sometimes in hand-to-hand combat, up the Po Valley. On April 27 Italian GUERRILLAS, who were roaming the north heeding neither Germans nor Allies, kidnapped Mussolini and killed him the next day. On April 29 all remaining German forces in Italy surrendered.

Italy

Capital: ROME, pop. 44,026,000 (est. 1939). When the EUROPEAN WAR began in Sept. 1939, Italy and Germany were tightly allied. Italy had signed the ANTI-COMINTERN PACT against the Soviet Union in 1937. And, as HITLER was secretly preparing for war in May 1939, Italy and Germany had affirmed the "inner affinity of their ideologies" in the PACT OF STEEL, a military alliance tying Italy's fate to Germany's.

Italy's inner affinity to Germany was rooted in fascism. This totalitarianism in modern form was born in Italy in 1922, when BENITO MUSSOLINI, the founder of the Fascist Party, took over the government after King Victor Emmanuel III asked him to form a cabinet. Mussolini promised Italy a restoration to its imperial glory. To do this, he made Italy a strong, undemocratic state whose two powerful institutions, the Catholic Church and the monarchy, supported him.

To build up his war machine, Mussolini built up the population, using such techniques as a bachelors' tax and rewards for large families. He set up a "corporative state," with all major manufacturers and other corporations put under him and a bloated bureaucracy. Some foreign observers hailed Italy's new efficiency, and one phrase—*the trains run on time*—summed up the corporate state's surface changes in Italy. But many Italians fled totalitarianism, with its infringements on privacy and attempts at thought control. One of Italy's most famous scientists, ENRICO FERMI, left rather than take a loyalty oath. In the United States he would play a key role in the development of the ATOMIC BOMB.

Unchecked by legislature or cabinet and backed by landowners and industrialists, Mussolini began a hasty expansion of Italian armed forces. He announced to the world that Italy and fascism were on the march to war and conquest. Italy's World War II history had three phases, beginning with the prewar conquests of territories that would eventually become battlefields.

1934–1939

Mussolini took power with the promise "to hand over to the King and the Army a renewed Italy," complete with a new Roman empire, built around triumphs in the Balkans and Africa.

Italy had seized Libya from Turkey in 1912 and made it a colony. Under Mussolini, beginning in 1934, the provinces of Libya became extraterritorial parts of Italy and the sites of extensive agricultural development. (For more about Italian relations with LIBYA, ETHIOPIA, ALBANIA, and GREECE, see those entries. See also the NORTH AFRICA CAMPAIGN and the NORTHWEST AFRICA CAMPAIGN.)

Italy had invaded Ethiopia in 1895 and, humiliated in battle, had been forced to withdraw and recognize Ethiopia's independence. Mussolini was determined to cleanse the record. He invaded Ethiopia in 1935, shocking the Western world with his use of bombers and poison gas (see CHEMICAL WARFARE) against spear-wielding tribal warriors. The war ended with a harsh Italian conquest in 1936 and led to Italy's withdrawal from the LEAGUE OF NATIONS.

Mussolini's first target in Europe was Albania. In preparation for conquest, he had heavily subsidized Albania's army, whose officer corps was almost entirely Italian, on loan. In 1939, he invaded the country, meeting little resistance. He had hoped that his invasion would bring Greece and Rumania into Italy's orbit. But those countries turned to England and France for territorial guarantees. Mussolini's dream of an empire also ran into Hitler's doctrine of *Lebensraum*—living space. Hitler was developing his own paths of conquest through the Balkans.

Instead of clashing over their conflicting interests, Mussolini and Hitler found advantages in alliance, though, ultimately, it was Hitler who initially gained more from the association than Mussolini. On Oct. 21, 1936, Germany and Italy signed a secret protocol that promised that they would develop a united foreign policy. The next month Mussolini, in a speech, did not reveal the agreement but did mention an AXIS around which other European powers "may work together." The Axis would symbolize the binding between the two powers. Japan would later become an Axis power, and during World War II that would be the shorthand word for the three enemies of the ALLIES.

In 1937 Italy added its signature to the Anti-Comintern Pact that Germany and Japan had signed the year before, in a move aimed at curbing Soviet aggression. And Mussolini turned his attention to the SPANISH CIVIL WAR, sending some 100,000 troops between Dec. 1936 and April 1937, along with planes and equipment, to the aid of Generalissimo FRANCISCO FRANCO. Other Italians—Communists and other anti-Fascists—managed to slip into Spain and, in international brigades, fought both Franco and Mussolini's Blackshirt legions. Italian submarines—operating as "pirates" without identification—sank several Soviet and other merchant ships attempting to bring weapons to the Republican (Loyalist) side.

When Germany invaded Poland on Sept. 1, 1939, Italy remained on the sidelines. She was not prepared for a full-scale war; her army was full of disgruntled draftees who had been in uniform since 1933, and she had a growing number of citizens who did not understand why so much money was going to guns and so little to butter. Still, Mussolini yearned for war and feared it would end without Italy's participation.

1940–1943

On June 10, 1940, Mussolini, assuming that France was about to be defeated by Germany, declared war on England and France (without consulting Hitler). "This," Mussolini proclaimed, "is the struggle of the peoples who are poor and eager to work against the greedy who hold a ruthless monopoly of all the wealth and gold of the earth." As the self-appointed new commander of Italian armed forces, he ordered an attack into France across the Alps. His forces were rebuffed with heavy casualties by outnumbered French defenders.

"The deed of June 10, which, according to the dictator's PROPAGANDA, was to be a mere prelude to a peace conference, placed Italy in the midst of a war whose end could not be foreseen," wrote postwar Prime Minister Alcide De Gasperi. Disastrous losses at TARANTO (three Italian battleships out of action) and in Libya (130,000 Italian PRISONERS OF WAR taken by the British) in 1940; the abortive invasion of Greece (German troops rescuing reeling Italians) in 1941; and the liberation of Ethiopia by the British—all this strengthened a "feeling of opposition and hostility toward the war," De Gasperi recalled, and "there began to take shape that state of mind which was to give birth to the final catastrophe."

Italy slavishly followed every German lead. Against Italian tradition, Mussolini ratified Hitler's ANTI-SEMITISM, enacting laws that restricted JEWS in some professions and barred them from the armed forces and the civil service. But among the Italian people Nazi racial hatreds did not take hold.

Italy declared war on the Soviet Union after the German invasion in June 1941 and declared war on the United States on Dec. 11, 1941, all without cause other than blind faith in Hitler. Both moves built up the Italian population's resistance against the war. Americans were well liked in a country whose every town and city had citizens with relatives in the United States. And by joining Germany in the war against the Soviet Union, Italy committed still more young men to death in useless distant battle.

Hitler had assured Mussolini that no Italians would be needed on the EASTERN FRONT. But early in 1942 Germany asked for troops. Mussolini offered two divisions; Germany managed to get him to send nine. The Italian troops marched off to still other faraway disasters.

1943–1945

On July 16, 1943, six days after the Allies invaded SICILY, beginning the ITALIAN CAMPAIGN, President ROOSEVELT and Prime Minister CHURCHILL jointly appealed to the Italian people to decide whether they "want to die for Mussolini and Hitler or live for Italy and civilization." That day Italian Fascist leaders began the process that would bring down Mussolini.

While Hitler and Mussolini were meeting at Feltre in northern Italy on July 19, U.S. planes bombed Rome, avoiding the center of the Eternal City but pulverizing areas around a railway junction and the airport, killing about 2,000 people. The bombing accelerated the moves to oust Mussolini.

On July 25 King Victor Emmanuel had *Il Duce* arrested and replaced him with Marshal PIETRO BADOGLIO, Chief of the Italian General Staff. "Italy has found it necessary to rid herself of a political system that she found harmful to the nation," the king said. "Fascism in Italy is over, forever."

Badoglio declared martial law, formed a cabinet,

and said that the war would go on. Secretly, however, he began negotiations with representatives of Gen. DWIGHT D. EISENHOWER through U.S. diplomat ROBERT MURPHY. Badoglio sought to somehow take Italy out of the war without angering Hitler. But Hitler sensed Badoglio's double-dealing. Two days after Mussolini's fall, German troops began passing through the BRENNER PASS and sealing off other Alpine passes as Germany began planning to occupy Italy and continue the fight.

Intensive Allied bombing of northern Italian cities began. Bombs tore through the roof of the convent of Santa Maria delle Grazie in Milan, where sandbags protected Leonardo da Vinci's "The Last Supper." The University of Milan and some 11,700 other buildings were destroyed. Turin and Genoa were also severely damaged. After the second bombing of Rome, the government declared it an OPEN CITY.

Negotiations with Allied officers dragged on until Sept. 3, 1943, when Badoglio secretly approved a conditional surrender and Allied forces landed in southern Italy to begin their long and bloody fight up the peninsula. On Sept. 8 Eisenhower announced the surrender, calling upon the Italians to "help eject the German aggressor from Italian soil." In a radio address Badoglio called the surrender "an armistice."

Italian Army units in Italy and abroad were left on their own. Most of the 1,090,000 Italian soldiers in Italy, demoralized and cut adrift by their high command, were easily disarmed by 400,000 Germans. The Allies hoped that Italian Army units would fight alongside against the Germans. Few did, but the Allies eventually got some help from Italian GUERRILLAS, many of them Communists fighting against both Hitler and the king.

Some 230,000 Italian troops were in France, about 400,000 elsewhere in Europe, and about 260,000 in Greece and the Aegean Islands when Italy surrendered. Nearly 10,000 were killed in Greece when they chose to fight rather than surrender. Records indicate that 500,000 were taken prisoner, but thousands were never heard from again; they are presumed to have died in German POW camps.

About 200 Italian warplanes escaped, but about forty were shot down or otherwise lost to the Allies. Although most of the Italian fleet escaped to MALTA and surrendered to the British there, German bombers sank the battleship *ROMA* with GUIDED MISSILES; 1,254 were lost from a crew of 1,849.

Hope quickly died for a peaceful end of Italy's war. Both Badoglio and the king fled to the Adriatic port of Bari. As Allied armies dug in for long, hard battles, on Oct. 13 Badoglio declared war on Germany, assuring that at war's end Italy would not be treated as an enemy. Mussolini was snatched from Italian custody in a daring rescue by OTTO SKORZENY, a leader of German COMMANDO-like operations. Mussolini established a German-sponsored Fascist Social Republic in northern Italy. Theoretically, Germany had returned him to power. In demonstration of this, Italian Fascists who voted for Mussolini's ouster—including his son-in-law, Count GALEAZZO CIANO—were shot by an Italian firing squad in Verona.

Italians were under double occupation by the advancing Allies and the retreating Germans. The Allies did not want Fascist armies in their ranks. The Germans ordered all able-bodied Italians to join the German Army "to throw back the invader." Most men in German-held areas went underground, risking death for the act but believing that liberation soon would come. Others were rounded up by SS patrols and taken away for forced labor.

U.S. troops fought their way into Rome on June 4, 1945, and the next day King Victor Emmanuel abdicated, as he had promised. Prince Humbert was given the empty title "Lieutenant General of the Realm" and Badoglio stepped down as prime minister. In reality, the government was in the hands of Italians selected by Allied military government officials, who turned control over to Italians in the wake of the advancing Allied armies.

The liberation of Rome was only one event in the Italian Campaign, which continued up the peninsula. Tiny San Marino, a republic with a population of 23,000 surrounded by Italian territory, declared its neutrality when fighting began raging around it. But German troops crossed its borders in Sept. 1944 and it became one of the many battlefields of Italy. The fighting went on until May 1945, when, in the last days of the war, the German armies in northern Italy surrendered.

As the war was ending, Yugoslavian guerrillas seized TRIESTE, an Italian port city on the Adriatic, along with the adjacent Italian territory of Istria, whose population was dominantly Slav. Allied officials, at first fearing a confrontation with the Yugoslavians, finally worked out an arrangement. But not until 1953 did the city itself get returned to Italy.

Italy, Air Force

Italian aviation in the 1920s and 1930s captured the world's imagination—setting speed and other performance records, periodically winning the coveted Schneider aviation trophy, and making mass flying boat flights, including a trans-Atlantic demonstration to the United States. Yet, when war came the *Regia Aeronautica* failed to perform effectively in modern conflict.

Although the Italian Air Force had been in action in the conquest of Ethiopia and the SPANISH CIVIL WAR, it was totally unprepared for combat when BENITO MUSSOLINI declared war on England and France in June 1940. At the time Italy had about 2,500 military aircraft in service. Only 11,000 more were produced during the next three years, far fewer than any of the other major belligerents. Further, Italian aircraft were mostly obsolete, and lacked an effective tactical doctrine. Only the twin-engine S.M. 79 *Sparviero,* a veteran of the Spanish conflict, was considered a realistic threat to the British fleet in the Mediterranean when the war began. But as more advanced fighters joined the British fleet even that threat went down in smoke.

Although air power prophet Giulio Douhet had been Mussolini's first under secretary for Air, the Italian Fascist government had not developed a viable strategic bomber force, as had the United States and Britain.

Like the Italian Army, commitment of the Air Force to a campaign invariably meant defeat.

Under the Mussolini-Douhet doctrine, there could be no dispersal of air power by assigning aircraft to the Army or Navy. The Italian Navy had created its own air arm during World War I, which proved relatively effective. With the creation of the Italian Air Force in 1923 all of the nation's military aircraft were transferred to the *Regia Aeronautica.* The lack of naval reconnaissance aircraft contributed to the humiliating defeat by the British on March 28–29, 1941, in a battle off Cape Matapan, the southernmost point of mainland Greece. As a result of this and other failures of the Air Force to support the Navy, a naval aviation and carrier conversion program were initiated, but did not come to fruition before the Italian SURRENDER in Sept. 1943.

After the Italian capitulation, both the pro-German and pro-Allied factions operated small air forces.

Italy, Army

The Italian Army—like the Air Force and Navy—failed to perform effectively in the war. Indeed, on several occasions the Italian Army's failures forced the German Army to intervene.

The Italian Army had opposed the rise of fascism in Italy led by BENITO MUSSOLINI. However, in 1933 Mussolini permanently took control of the War Ministry and hence the Army. Mussolini's sending the Army into Ethiopia in 1935, to fight spear-wielding natives with planes, tanks, and poison gas, had given many Italians the belief that they had a viable Army.

When Italy declared war against England and France in June 1940 the Army had a paper strength of seventy-three divisions but only forty-two could be mobilized for active service; TANKS and ARTILLERY were in short supply and often obsolete. While the army was predominantly infantry, there were three armored divisions and a few motorized ones, but also several light ones—two parachute and six Alpine. Several of the Army's division were comprised of Fascist militia or Blackshirts.

When the Army moved into southern France in June 1940, it was decisively defeated. When the Italian Army in North Africa moved eastward toward Egypt, it was again defeated, this time by inferior British forces. More than 133,000 Italian soldiers—including six senior generals—had been taken prisoner. ADOLF HITLER had to help his AXIS partner by establishing the AFRIKA KORPS to save the Italians from being completely routed.

In Oct. 1940—without advising Hitler—Mussolini ordered the Italian Army to invade Greece. Soon the Italians were on the defensive, again forcing Hitler to intervene, and causing a delay in the GERMAN CAMPAIGN IN THE SOVIET UNION. After Germany invaded the Soviet Union, Italian troops and aircraft were sent to help in the campaign. Meanwhile, in North Africa the Allied advances from the east and, following the NORTH AFRICA INVASION, from the west, forced the capitulation of the remaining Italian forces in North Africa.

German and Italian forces fought stubbornly in SICILY in mid-1943, but that battle was soon over and in Sept. 1943, when the Anglo-American juggernaut invaded the Italian mainland, there were but twelve divisions available to resist the assault— had the post-Mussolini government chosen to do so. There were just over 1,000,000 Italian troops on the mainland when the government capitulated. They were quickly disarmed by the German forces in Italy, although some continued to fight on the Fascist side. But the Italian Army in reality ceased to exist.

Generalfeldmarschall ALBERT KESSELRING, the CinC of German troops in Italy and North Africa, wrote of the Italians: "Their mobilization machinery was just not adjusted to the requirements of an army of a million men or for a long emergency. As I was able to verify on more than one occasion, peacetime working conditions prevailed even during the most critical periods of the war. And although [Marshal UGO] CAVALLERO accepted the principle of TOTAL WAR, and the initial steps were taken to weld the various organizations of civil life into a co-ordinated war machine, that machine very quickly broke down."

And, he continued in *Kesselring: A Soldier's Record*, "If Mussolini was unable to inspire a wartime spirit into the nation he ought to have abandoned the thought of entering the struggle. Yet it may be inferred from the bitter GUERRILLA warfare of the Partisans against the German *Wehrmacht* that the Italian population were by no means devoid of martial spirit."

Italy, Navy *(Rivesta Maritime)*

During the late 1920s Italy began a naval modernization program that produced some of the most attractive and fastest warships in the world. Like its air force, Italy's Navy was developing what appeared to be an impressive capability. Further, the Navy was completely mobilized in the spring of 1935 during the crisis over the Ethiopian campaign, with the subsequent SPANISH CIVIL WAR and occupation of Albania keeping the Navy on a war footing.

When Italy went to war against Britain and an essentially defeated France on June 10, 1940, the Navy was unprepared for combat. The Italian dictator, BENITO MUSSOLINI, assured the Italian military leaders that the war would last only four months. At the time the Italian fleet consisted of:

    2 battleships (12.6-inch/320-mm guns)
    7 heavy cruisers (8-inch/203-mm guns)
    12 light cruisers (6-inch/152-mm guns)
    2 light cruisers (5.9-inch/150-mm guns)
    73 destroyers
    106 submarines

Another four battleships of the new *Littorio* class were fitting out and two older ships were being modernized. The new battleships, at 35,000 tons standard displacement with nine 15-inch (381-mm) guns and a speed of 32 knots, on paper would be the equal of any British dreadnought. Italy, like Germany, had no aircraft carriers. The Italian Air Force controlled all military aviation, the Italian peninsula being considered a massive aircraft carrier in the center of the Mediterranean.

Thus, when the war began the Italian Navy lacked its own air arm, had no RADAR, and was severely short of fuel oil (which soon had to be provided by Germany).

The French capitulation in June 1940 left the Italian fleet as the dominant naval force in the Mediterranean. Its immediate role was to escort supplies being shipped to the Italian forces fighting the British in North Africa. The Royal Navy, outnumbered and heavily committed elsewhere, began attacking the CONVOYS to North Africa with submarines, surface warships, and aircraft based at Malta. After a brief engagement between British and Italian surface ships, in which an Italian cruiser was sunk, the major Italian warships were held at their bases.

In response, in a daring raid on the night of Nov. 11–12, 1940, twenty-one SWORDFISH bombers from the British carrier *Illustrious* struck the Italian battle fleet at anchor in TARANTO. Three of the Italian battleships were sunk or disabled, at the small cost of two British aircraft.

The Italian Navy suffered another humiliating defeat on March 28–29, 1941, in a battle off Cape Matapan, the southernmost point of mainland Greece. An Italian battle force, led by the new battleship *Vittorio Veneto,* put to sea at German request to intercept British convoys from Alexandria reinforcing Greece. Encountering a superior British force—with two battleships and an aircraft carrier—the Italian warships fled toward Taranto. Swordfish torpedo planes from the carrier *Formidable* scored hits on the Italian battleship and one cruiser. The battleship escaped, but in a night engagement, aided greatly by radar, British warships sank three Italian heavy cruisers and two destroyers. *Not one British ship was even hit in the battle!*

Demoralized, the Italians then employed mostly land-based aircraft, submarines, and (nonsuicide) MANNED TORPEDOES against the British fleet. They were unable to stop the British attacks against the convoys to North Africa, nor did they stop the continued British reinforcements sent to Malta. Indeed, against the wishes of the German naval command, HITLER ordered German U-BOATS to operate in the Mediterranean to supplement Italian forces.

In July 1940 the Italian Navy had asked permission to bring a number of submarines from the Mediterranean to Atlantic ports in German-controlled France to participate in the BATTLE OF THE ATLANTIC. From the port of Bordeaux, twenty-six Italian submarines were sent into the Atlantic to operate in the Azores area and west of Spain, where British antisubmarine forces were limited. The first patrol began in Oct. 1940. The Italian boats failed to accomplish any results, either in attacking British convoys or providing reconnaissance or even weather information to the German naval command. Italian submarine officers were sent to U-boat schools and were taken on war patrols in German submarines. Still, the German U-boat command's war diary noted, "They are not hard or tough enough for this type of warfare. Their thoughts are too slow and orthodox, when they

should be adapting themselves to changing conditions. They are inadequately disciplined and cannot remain calm in the face of the enemy."

By May 1941 the number of Italian submarines assigned to the Atlantic was but ten. Through 1943 Italian submarines sank some 600,000 tons of Allied shipping, a small amount for the number of boats available.

More successful against the British were the Italian "naval assault teams," which operated MIDGET SUBMARINES, two-man human torpedoes (called "pigs" by the Italians), and explosive-laden motor boats. The midget submarines were ineffective in the Mediterranean, but saw some success against the Soviets in the Black Sea.

The human torpedoes—a torpedo with a detachable warhead with two crewmen riding astride the torpedo—were used successfully against British ships at Alexandria, Algiers, and GIBRALTAR. The crewmen wore a Scuba-type breathing apparatus, and torpedoes could be carried into the attack area by submarines. At Alexandria in Dec. 1941 the human torpedoes scored their greatest accomplishment, when three of the craft sank the British battleships *Queen Elizabeth* and *Valiant* as well as a tanker. The battleships were sunk in shallow water, but were not returned to active service for the remainder of the war, a considerable accomplishment for six men. These torpedoes also sank several merchant ships during the war.

The explosive motorboats were small, high-speed craft laden with explosives; a single crewman was to drive it toward an enemy ship in harbor, with the crewman sliding off just before impact. Their principal success was at Suda Bay, Crete, in March 1941 when, in a night attack, they put a British cruiser out of action and sank a tanker and cargo ship.

The naval assault teams also used swimmers carrying small limpet MINES that were placed against ships' hulls with some success, twice at Gibraltar and once at Algiers.

When Italy capitulated to the ALLIES on Sept. 9, 1943, the Italian fleet had in service three battleships, six cruisers, and five destroyers, plus several submarines. Many other ships were undergoing repairs. The surface ships were ordered to Malta, to surrender to the Allied high command. That afternoon, while at sea, German aircraft began attacking the Italian warships. GUIDED MISSLES sank the battleship *Roma* with most of her crew; the battleship *Italia* was also hit but survived.

Interned after surrender, several of the Italian warships were transferred to the Soviet Union after the war, including the battleship *Giulio Cesare*.

The Italian fleet accomplished little for its size and purported capabilities. Italian naval historian Comdr. Marc Antonio Bragadin concluded: "The decisive Allied victories, and thus their final triumph, were essentially the result of the *sea* mentality of CHURCHILL and ROOSEVELT, as opposed to the *land* mentality of Hitler and Mussolini."

Ivan

Code name used for JOSEF STALIN in Allied communications.

Iwo Jima

Pacific island, 660 miles from Japan, that was the site of one of the bloodiest battles of the war. The volcanic island, about five and a half miles long and two and a half miles wide, was well fortified and had two airfields where B-29 SUPERFORTRESS bombers flying to and from the MARIANA ISLANDS could make emergency landings. The island would also serve as an advance base for P-51 MUSTANGS and P-47 THUNDERBOLTS, which had shorter ranges than the bombers. From Iwo Jima, the fighters could escort the B-29s over Japan.

Softening up of Iwo's defenses began in Nov. 1944 with U.S. Navy shelling and U.S. Army Air Forces bombing by B-24 LIBERATOR and B-25 MITCHELL bombers for seventy-four consecutive days. It was the longest pre-invasion bombardment of the war—and for good reason. Reconnaissance photos had shown a massive Japanese defensive network above and under the ground: more than 600 pillboxes and gun positions, a labyrinth of caves, 21,000 Japanese troops.

UNDERWATER DEMOLITION TEAMS surveying and clearing the shore areas were mistaken for an actual landing force and came under heavy fire and suffered 170 casualties. But in firing on the scouting teams the Japanese gave away hidden gun positions, inadvertently helping invasion planners.

With Secretary of the Navy JAMES V. FORRESTAL and journalists watching from an amphibious command ship, on the morning of Feb. 19, 1945, the AMPHIBIOUS LANDINGS of Operation Detachment began. As the landing elements of the 4th and 5th Marine DIVISIONs scrambled onto the volcanic sands, there was only scattered Japanese fire. Then, with seven BATTALIONS on the beach, the Japanese unleashed a rain of fire. Antitank guns picked off Marine tanks and wheeled vehicles churning through the soft, sooty sand. Marines pinned down on the steep beach were sprayed with fire. By nightfall, there were 566 Marines dead and 1,854 wounded on the beachhead.

The invasion plan called for the taking of 550-foot Mount Suribachi, the main bastion at the extreme southern tip of the island, and an airfield directly inland. By the second day the Marines advancing on Mount Suribachi had advanced only 200 yards. For three days the 28th REGIMENT of the 5th Division battled their way up the volcano, attacking strongpoints with FLAME THROWERS, GRENADES, and demolition charges.

By 10 A.M. on Feb. 23 the Marines had reached the top and raised a small American flag. That afternoon, when the slopes were cleared of Japanese defenders, a larger flag was sent ashore and five Marines and a Navy hospital corpsman raised it on a piece of Japanese pipe. Photographer Joe Rosenthal of the Associated Press took the photograph that won him the Pulitzer Prize.

At the sight of the first flag, bells and whistles of the offshore fleet sounded and Forrestal turned to Marine Lt. Gen. HOLLAND M. SMITH. "Holland," Forrestal said, "the raising of that flag on Suribachi means a Marine Corps for the next 500 years." He was right. The photograph and the sculptured version by Felix W. de Weldon symbolized being a Marine.

The battle went on, and three of the flag raisers would die, for not until March 9 were the Marines able to break through the Japanese main defenses. On March 16, Iwo Jima was declared secured. But some fighting continued against Japanese in caves and pillboxes.

Nearly all of Iwo Jima's 21,000 defenders were killed, as were 6,821 Americans, nearly all of the

Marines. Adm. CHESTER W. NIMITZ said that on Iwo Jima "uncommon valor was a common virtue." Twenty-seven MEDALS OF HONOR were awarded to Marine and Navy heroes, the most for any single operation of the war.

Even before the island was declared secure a B-29 made an emergency landing on Iwo Jima. When the war ended in August the number of emergency landings by B-29s totaled 2,400, with crews aggregating more than 24,000 men. The taking of Iwo Jima, which had cost so many American lives, saved the lives of countless others.

J2F Duck

A two-seat amphibious floatplane, the "Duck" as it was invariably known, was a highly useful utility, photographic, and antisubmarine aircraft. In some models a litter could be fitted. Before the war they were flown as utility planes from AIRCRAFT CARRIERS, and during the war they operated from Coast Guard cutters.

The prototype XJF-1 flew on May 4, 1933. After limited production the first flight of the definitive J2F design flew on June 25, 1935. The aircraft was subsequently flown by the U.S. Navy, Marine Corps, and Coast Guard from land bases. The aircraft was evaluated by the U.S. AAF (with the designation OA-12). When production ended in 1945, deliveries had totaled forty-eight JF and 585 J2F Ducks plus eight JFs and four J2Fs for Argentina.

The Grumman-built aircraft was a biplane with equal-span wings and a large, single-step float faired into the fuselage. There were small, fixed stabilizing floats. The aircraft was amphibious with wheels being fitted to the main float. The space between the fuselage and float could be used for cameras or to carry a passenger. The Navy variants had arresting gear and catapult points for operation from carriers. The pilot and observer-gunner sat in an enclosed cockpit.

The J2F-6 (produced in the largest number of any variant) had a maximum speed of 190 mph with a range of 850 miles. Against submarines the Duck could carry two 325-pound BOMBS or DEPTH CHARGES under the wings. A forward-firing .30-cal. machine gun could be fitted, as well as a flexible gun fired from the after cockpit.

A young Japanese-American girl sits amidst her family's belongings as she and thousands of other Americans are moved from the West Coast to internment camps in an ill-conceived, insensitive relocation brought about by fear of collaboration with the Japanese. *(National Archives)*

J4F Widgeon

U.S. flying boat–amphibian that served in a variety of roles, including hunting submarines. Originally designed for commercial use, the Grumman G-44 design first flew in June 1940. Commercial sales were immediately forthcoming as were government orders. In the antisubmarine role the aircraft could carry only one DEPTH CHARGE or BOMB under the starboard wing and had a relatively short range. Still, on Aug. 1, 1942, a Coast Guard J4F-1 piloted by Ens. Henry C. White sank the *U-166* off the approaches to the Mississippi River, the first U-BOAT sinking by the Coast Guard.

The aircraft was used by the U.S. Navy and AAF as utility transports and, by the latter service, for search-and-rescue, with the Coast Guard and, to a lesser extent, the Navy using them to hunt U-boats off the U.S. East Coast.

The first military model was for the U.S. Coast Guard, the three-seat J4F-1 for antisubmarine warfare, with twenty-five aircraft delivered in 1941. Another 131 were built for the Navy as the J4F-2, which were used primarily as five-seat utility transports; fifteen of the Navy's planes went to the Royal Navy under LEND-LEASE, being called Gosling I and (after 1944) Widgeon I and were flown as utility aircraft. The AAF impressed fifteen commercial G-44s, which were designated OA-14. Another twelve aircraft of this type were built for the Portuguese Navy and fourteen of the U.S. Navy's aircraft went to the Brazilian Air Force. Thus, Grumman built 156 J4Fs plus 120 commercial planes; after the war forty-one more Widgeons were built in France, the last delivered in 1952.

The streamlined Widgeon was a high-wing aircraft, with twin wing-mounted, in-line engines, and fixed wing floats. The flying boat hull had retractable main wheels and tail wheel. The maximum seating was five.

The Widgeon had a maximum speed of 153 mph and a maximum range of 920 miles. A single 200-pound depth bomb or rescue gear could be carried.

(U.S. services and RAF also flew the earlier twin-engine Grumman Goose, designated JRF by the U.S. Navy and Coast Guard, and OA-9 by the AAF.)

Jack

The Jack was the first Japanese fighter to develop horsepower comparable with that of advanced Allied fighters. The Japanese Navy's J2M *Raiden* (Thunderbolt)—given the Allied code name Jack—was originally thought to be an Air Force fighter when first seen by American fliers in 1944.

Teething problems and slow production delayed the Jack's entry into combat. Although a few were sent to the Philippines in 1944, their principal use was the effort to defend Japan against U.S. B-29 SUPERFORTRESS bombing raids in 1944–1945. However, the fighters were too few and too late to have an impact on the aerial bombardment of Japan. Although small and light by U.S. standards, the later model aircraft had impressive fuel and pilot protection, and mounted a heavy armament in addition to their performance. However, the J2M lacked the maneuverability of its predecessor, the ZERO.

The work of Jiro Horikoshi, designer of the A6M Zero, the prototype J2M1 flew in March 1942. Although there were major problems, the plane's speed, rate of climb, and stability led the Navy to continue development. While the improved J2M2 overcame many of the problems, there were new difficulties with the engine. Finally, slow production began; by war's end just over 500 aircraft had been produced.

The Jack had a bullet shape, from some viewpoints resembling the U.S. P-47 THUNDERBOLT. A low-wing monoplane, the fuselage was dominated by the large radial engine with a large spinner; turbochargers were fitted for high-altitude intercepts of U.S. bombers. The landing gear, including tail wheel, were fully retractable. Later models had a "blister" canopy. It was not a carrier-capable aircraft.

The J2M2 variant had a maximum speed of 371 mph. It could climb to 20,000 feet in just over fifty-two minutes. While the J2M had two wing-mounted 20-mm cannon and two 7.7-mm machine guns in the fuselage, later variants had four 20-mm guns, with some aircraft modified to provide two oblique-firing 20-mm cannon so the aircraft could attack a bomber while flying under it.

Jackson, Robert H. (1892–1954)

Chief U.S. counsel on the International Military Tribunal for WAR CRIMES. Jackson, appointed a Supreme Court Justice by President ROOSEVELT in 1941, was asked by President HARRY S TRUMAN to set up the procedure by which the ALLIES would put German leaders on trial as war criminals. Jackson plunged into the task, taking the lead in establishing the structure of the four-nation tribunal, which consisted of four judges and four alternates from the United States, England, the Soviet Union, and France.

As Robert E. Conot wrote in *Justice at Nuremberg,* "Jackson raised the sword of justice and made it clear he intended to wield it with or without the participation of the British, Russians, and French." Chief Justice Harlan Stone, who did not like the idea of the war crimes trials, called it "Jackson's high-grade lynching party."

Jackson, functioning as a prosecutor, frequently cross-examined defendants. Off the bench, in a letter to Truman, he objected to the *in*justice of the trials. The Allies, he wrote (but apparently focusing on the Soviet Union), "have done or are doing some of the very things we are prosecuting the Germans for. . . . We are prosecuting plunder and our Allies are practicing it. We say aggressive war is a crime and one of our allies asserts sovereignty over the Baltic States based on no title except conquest."

His closing argument was an eloquent condemnation of each defendant and a ringing justification for the trial: These "defendants now ask this tribunal to say that they are not guilty of planning, executing, or conspiring to commit this long list of crimes and wrongs. They stand before the record of this trial as bloodstained Gloucester stood by the body of his slain king. He begged of the widow, as they beg of you: 'Say I slew them not.' And the queen replied, 'Then say they were not slain. But dead they are. . . .' If you were to say of these men that they are not guilty, it would be as true to say that there had been no war, there are no slain, there has been no crime."

Jael

Code word for the "overall deception policy" of the Allied high commands. Jael was created to en-

courage the Germans to make erroneous strategic decisions, especially in preparing for the NORMANDY INVASION. The code word was later changed to Bodyguard, inspired by Prime Minister CHURCHILL's remark, apparently in reference to Jael, "In wartime, truth is so precious that she should always be attended by a bodyguard of lies." Jael/Bodyguard had two main subplans, COCKADE and ZEPPELIN, which pertained to the masking of Allied strategic intentions. As part of the deception, just before the invasion, James Clifton, a British actor who resembled Gen. BERNARD L. MONTGOMERY, paraded around GIBRALTAR in the hope of convincing German agents there that no cross-Channel operation could be near with Montgomery in Gibraltar.

James, Lt. M. E. Clifton (1897–)

British Army officer who bore considerable resemblance to Gen. BERNARD L. MONTGOMERY, and impersonated him in a visit to GIBRALTAR just before the NORMANDY INVASION of June 1944. James, assigned to the Army Pay Corps, was a former provincial actor.

It was hoped that the deception—part of Operation Copperhead—would lead the Germans to believe that the next Allied assault would be in the Mediterranean area. German records, however, show no indication that any note was taken of the Monty deception. After the war James told of the deception in *I Was Monty's Double.*

Japan

Capital: TOKYO, pop. 72,222,700 (est. 1938). In 1937, on the eve of war against China, Japan was already an empire. Under the surrender terms ending the Russo-Japanese War of 1905 Japan had won the KURIL ISLANDS and China's Liaotung Peninsula with its strategic port of Dairen from Russia. In a conquest Japan called "annexing," she had taken the ancient kingdom of Korea in 1910. By entering the winning side in World War I she had acquired German Pacific possessions that became known as the JAPANESE MANDATED ISLANDS.

The Japanese government was built on the emperor, who had full executive power, with the advice of his Cabinet and Privy Council. He exercised legislative powers with the consent of the Imperial

Diet. It consisted of a House of Peers and a House of Representatives. The 404 peers included princes, counts, barons, and men of great wealth; the representatives were voted into office. Emperor HIROHITO's Cabinet was dominated by military officers whose faith in warrior virtues—Shintoism—and the emperor was translated into a policy of expansionism.

Japan again began expanding her empire on Sept. 18, 1931, when Japanese troops, claiming that Chinese saboteurs were tampering with the roadbed of the Japanese-owned South Manchuria Railway, seized the Chinese city of Mukden (now Shenyang). The bogus "Mukden incident" launched a swift conquest of northeastern China, where the Japanese set up the state of Manchukuo ("the state of Manchu"). The weak LEAGUE OF NATIONS belatedly condemned Japan in 1933, and Japan quit the League.

Japan felt an affinity for the similar policies of NAZI Germany and on Nov. 25, 1936, signed the ANTI-COMINTERN PACT with Germany. The pact, aimed at the international communism sponsored by the Soviet Union, pledged the safeguarding of "common interests" against threats by the Soviet Union.

Japan again moved against China in 1937, when another staged event was used as a pretext for attacking Chinese troops near Peking. The undeclared war, which Japan always called the "China Incident," was envisioned by the Japanese militarists as a way to create another puppet state similar to Manchukuo. In one of the early actions of the war, Japanese warplanes bombed the U.S. Navy gunboat *PANAY* (PR 45), prompting the first of an escalating set of protests from the United States.

Although China was torn by internal strife, armies under CHIANG KAI-SHEK and MAO TSE-TUNG managed to cooperate enough at the beginning to slow down Japan's conquest. The war put a strain on Japan's RESOURCES but at the same time spurred her creation of the GREATER EAST ASIA CO-PROSPERITY SPHERE, a "new order" that would change the balance of power in the Pacific. In 1939 Japan announced a three-year plan for a "major transformation of Japan's economic and defense power" that would make Japan, China, and Manchukuo self-sustaining in terms of iron, steel, coal, key chemicals, automobiles, and railway rolling stock. (For more about the war, see also CHINA.)

Obviously missing from the list of vital resources was petroleum. In early 1939 Japan made a diplomatic effort to obtain oil from Saudi Arabia. The mission failed, however, when the United States outbid the Japanese in getting concessions from the Saudis. Most of Japan's petroleum was then coming from the United States. But this source was threatened as Japan's aggressive moves drew increasingly strong protests from the United States.

After the Germans won the battle of France and installed the VICHY FRANCE regime, Japan, about to sign the TRIPARTITE PACT and become a member of the AXIS, got German approval to occupy French INDOCHINA, from which supplies had been flowing to China. In Indochina, Japan would have bases for further expansion and acquisition of Southeast Asia's oil, rubber, tin, quinine, and timber. Japanese military and political leaders plotted the seizing of the Pacific colonial territories of the Dutch and British, particularly the oil-rich DUTCH EAST INDIES. Japanese occupation forces in China intensified an antiforeigner campaign, focusing particularly on British subjects.

In July 1939 President ROOSEVELT reacted to Japan's militarism by notifying Japan that the United States would terminate the 1911 U.S.-Japanese commercial treaty, cutting Japan off from vital imports. Japan had become extraordinarily dependent upon the United States, which supplied Japan with 66 percent of its oil, virtually all of its aviation fuel, 90 percent of its metal scrap, and 91 percent of its copper.

Japan needed more oil for its growing industry, more room for its growing population, and that meant a need for more military strength to carry out an aggressive foreign policy. The rise of the military came against a background of worsening relations with the United States. The Japanese Cabinet, after a series of shake-ups, hardened its militant, expansionist policies. On April 13, 1941, Japan and the Soviet Union signed a neutrality pact that contained a Soviet pledge to respect the borders of the puppet state of Manchukuo and a Japanese pledge to do the same in Mongolia. The pact gave Japan protection on its Soviet flank. The pieces were now in place for a war against the United States and European colonial powers.

The military-dominated Japanese Cabinet expelled the remaining moderates and in July 1941 ordered a Japanese invasion of the rest of Indochina and the call-up of more conscripts. President Roosevelt responded by freezing all Japanese assets in the United States and cutting off all oil exports to Japan. Prime Minister Fumimaro Konoe tried to work out a diplomatic solution to the crisis, but the military favored a tougher stand and at a conference in October urged that the nation "get ready for war."

Konoe resigned and was replaced by the Minister of War, Gen. HIDEKI TOJO. With the military primed for war, he reiterated Japanese demands: the United States must end aid to China, accept the Japanese seizure of Indochina, resume normal trade, and not reinforce U.S. bases in the Far East. He publicly maintained that the demands were not negotiable and set a deadline for U.S. acceptance. But, unaware of U.S. success in MAGIC code-breaking, he told the Japanese ambassador to the United States, KICHISABURO NOMURA, that negotiations were still possible.

Talks began between U.S. Secretary of State CORDELL HULL and Nomura (aided by special envoy SABURO KURUSU), but the two nations were at an impasse. On Nov. 26 Hull once more stated the U.S. position, which centered on Japanese withdrawal from China and Indochina. Tojo saw Hull's statement as an "ultimatum" and cocked the gun of war. He ordered a Japanese task force, secretly assembled off the Kuril island of Etorofu, to sea. The ships were to carry out the attack on Pearl Harbor on Dec. 8, Japan time, which was Sunday, Dec. 7, Hawaii-WASHINGTON time.

At 2:05 on the afternoon of Dec. 7, Hull learned that Japanese aircraft had bombed Pearl Harbor. Twenty minutes later Hull met for the last time with Nomura and Kurusu and rebuked them for their nation's perfidy.

To Americans, the raid on Pearl Harbor was "a sneak attack," and Japan became a synonym for treachery. In Tokyo, U.S. Ambassador JOSEPH GREW did not receive word of Japan's declaration of war on the United States and England until 11 A.M.

on Dec. 8, seven hours and forty minutes after the attack. Japan's political strategy called for the United States to soon propose talks for a negotiated peace. But the attack infuriated U.S. citizens, who girded for a vengeful war and a decisive defeat of Japan. (For accounts of military actions, see JAPANESE CAMPAIGN IN THE FAR EAST, U.S. SOLOMONS–NEW GUINEA CAMPAIGN, JAPAN'S CHINA-BURMA CAMPAIGN, ALLIED CHINA-BURMA-INDIA CAMPAIGN, and U.S. CENTRAL PACIFIC CAMPAIGN.)

After years of war against China, Japan had still not mobilized her population for TOTAL WAR. Boys of seventeen were made eligible for military service and boys of fourteen got training for the air forces. Most colleges were closed to release students for work in war plants. But Japan never went on a war economy. Her leaders, planning on a short war, convinced themselves that Japan's conquests alone would ensure victory; the raw materials would merely be shifted from peaceful to war use, then back to peaceful use again after victory.

Tojo transformed a political organization, the Imperial Rule Assistance Association, into a virtual government agency for controlling industrial, agricultural, and patriotic groups. The KEMPEITAI—military police who functioned as Japan's internal security force—expanded to control PROPAGANDA, censorship, and antisubversive activities. Hundreds of antimilitarists were arrested. The Greater East Asia Ministry administered a harsh rule over the growing number of occupied areas.

Tojo reorganized his Cabinet in 1943, bringing in industrialists and financial experts. He also became almost a one-man Cabinet, holding down the posts of prime minister, foreign minister, minister of war, minister of education, minister of munitions, and chief of the General Staff. After the fall of SAIPAN in June 1944, B-29 SUPERFORTRESSES were within striking distance of the home islands. Tokyo began to learn about STRATEGIC BOMBING in Nov. 1944.

"Those who continued to hope, after MIDWAY, for a favorable change in fortune knew, after Saipan, that their hopes had lost all meaning," wrote historian Robert J. C. Butow. The remaining optimists, he added, began talking about *Nippon seishin*, Japan's spirit. "Their plea," he wrote, "was simply this: 'Japan may be weak in resources, but she is strong in *spirit*. This will lead the nation to victory!' "

Tojo's Cabinet fell soon after Saipan fell. On July 22, 1944, Gen. Kuniaki Koiso organized a new Cabinet that lasted until April 4, 1945, when some Japanese civilian leaders, though relatively powerless, were desperately sending out peace feelers. On the night of March 9–10, 1945, a B-29 fire raid on Tokyo had killed more than 83,000 people and injured over 100,000. Nearly two-thirds of Japan's merchant fleet had been sunk and resources from the occupied areas of Southeast Asia could no longer pass the gauntlet of U.S. naval and air forces. Rationing had cut the average Japanese's daily diet to 1,200 calories. Japan was under siege.

On April 9, Adm. Kantaro Suzuki, who was close to Hirohito, formed a Cabinet dominated by elder statesmen. With the tacit understanding that he carried out the emperor's will, Suzuki began a delicate, almost invisible effort to end the war, first by "unofficial conversations" with a Soviet diplomat in Tokyo, then through aides of ALLEN DULLES, who was head of OFFICE OF STRATEGIC SERVICES operations in Switzerland. But ultimately Japan balked at the demand of UNCONDITIONAL SURRENDER and the war went on.

Publicly, Japan banned any calls to end the war; about 400 people were arrested on April 15 for being peace sympathizers. The SURRENDER of Germany on May 7 inspired a announcement that Japan would fight on alone.

But on July 26 a proclamation was issued from the POTSDAM CONFERENCE of President HARRY S TRUMAN, STALIN, and Churchill (later replaced by CLEMENT ATTLEE). The proclamation said that the ALLIES "agree that Japan shall be given an opportunity to end this war." The alternative, the proclamation said, was "the utter devastation of the Japanese homeland."

The Cabinet was still debating how to surrender on Aug. 6, when a B-29 dropped an ATOMIC BOMB on HIROSHIMA. On Aug. 8, the Soviet Union, ignoring a neutrality pact, declared war on Japan and sent troops into Japanese-held Manchuria. Despite these shocks, the Army leadership held out. On Aug. 9 a second atomic bomb destroyed NAGASAKI.

Still the Army insisted, in a general's words, "we must fight the war through to the end no matter how great the odds against us!"

On the morning of Aug. 15 Radio Tokyo announced that Emperor Hirohito, who never before had spoken on the radio, would make an announcement at noon. The announcement, secretly recorded the night before, admitted Japan's surrender without actually using the word. After some minor negotiations, the United States announced the end of the war on Aug. 14. The formal Japanese surrender took place on Sept. 3, 1945.

Japan, Air Force

The Imperial Japanese Army's Air Force was intended primarily to support ground operations. It was fully subordinate to the Army high command, in the same manner that naval aviation was a part of the Navy (in contrast to the two other AXIS nations, in which an independent air force controlled everything that flew). Thus the two Japanese air forces had separate training establishments, and developed and flew separate aircraft, even though there was similarity in some missions, such as land-based medium bombers.

The Army Air Force had been established in 1925 with the status equal to that of ARTILLERY, CAVALRY, and infantry corps. (The naval air arm had been created in 1912 and saw combat in 1914.) The Army Air Force flew in action in China in 1928 during the Tsinan incident, and in Manchuria (against the Soviets) and in China during the 1930s.

On the eve of the PEARL HARBOR attack the Japanese Army had 1,375 aircraft, all designated for specific operations when the Pacific War began:

For Malaya campaign	550
For Philippine campaign	175
China	150
Manchuria (reserve)	450
Japan	50

When the war began Army aircraft provided close air support and interdicted Allied troops behind the lines. Once the areas were secure, the aircraft were usually based there for defensive operations.

During the war the Japanese Army, like the Navy,

suffered from production problems and, in general, Army aircraft were inferior to both Japanese naval and Allied aircraft from 1943 on. At the end of the war there were more than 10,000 Army and naval aircraft—most of them trainers—in the home islands that would be sent against the Allied invasion in force in Operation *Ketsu-Go*. Toward the end of the war Japanese Air Force planes also flew suicide missions, but they had far less effect than the Navy's KAMIKAZE operations.

Japan, Army

The Japanese Army was a large, effective fighting force that enjoyed continued success against Chinese troops in Manchuria and China in the 1930s, and in the Far East against Australian, British, Dutch, and U.S. forces in 1941–1942. However, beginning with the U.S. invasion of GUADALCANAL in Aug. 1942, the Japanese were rarely able to take the offensive and were invariably defeated by U.S. commanders, soldiers and Marines, and weapons. (The exception was in the China-Burma areas, where the Japanese continued to enjoy some successes against Allied forces. See ALLIED CHINA-BURMA-INDIA CAMPAIGN and JAPAN'S CHINA-BURMA CAMPAIGN.)

By 1937 the Japanese Army had a strength of some 300,000 troops in seventeen divisions plus CAVALRY, artillery, antiaircraft, and aviation units. A major buildup was undertaken from 1937 to 1941 as preparations were being made for war. By the fall of 1941 the Army had about 1,700,000 men in fifty-one divisions, of which twenty-eight were engaged in operations in China and thirteen were stationed in Manchuria and Korea for defense against the Soviet Union. Only ten divisions remained in the home islands, five newly formed. The Imperial General Headquarters decided to allocate five divisions from China and six from Japan to the Southern Operations—the assault on British, Dutch, and American holdings in the Far East. These troops were grouped as: 14th Army—Philippines, 15th Army—Burma and Thailand, 16th Army—DUTCH EAST INDIES, 23rd Army—HONG KONG, and 25th Army—Malaya and North Borneo.

In addition, the Navy would provide several battalions of Special Naval Landing Force (marines) for assaults. Only limited shipping—cargo ships,

Japanese troops celebrate the capture of an American position during their drive on the Bataan Peninsula in the Philippines. Japanese troops went to war with the United States on Dec. 7, 1941, with extensive combat experience from China and Manchuria. (*Courtesy* Bataan Magazine)

transports, and a few specialized landing ships—were available to move these troops southward. (This lack of shipping was a principal reason for not attempting a landing on Oahu in conjunction with the air attacks on PEARL HARBOR).

The Japanese Army in Dec. 1941 was experienced and hardened by its fighting in China. According to a leading Japanese historian, Professor Saburo Ienaga, "The military went into the Pacific War still clinging to the concept of fighting spirit as decisive in battle. The result was wanton waste of Japanese lives, particularly in combat with Allied forces whose doctrine was based on scientific rationality." In his *The Pacific War 1931–1945* he quoted the Army's 1908 criminal code—still in effect: "A commander who allows his unit to surrender to the enemy without fighting to the last man or who concedes a strategic area to the enemy shall be punishable by death." In 1941 Army Minister HIDEKI TOJO published a field service code that stated: "Do not be taken prisoner alive." Little wonder then the tenacity of the Japanese fighting man. At the same time, this outlook led to Japanese treating PRISON-

ERS OF WAR whom they captured with hatred and savagery.

The Japanese soldier was also individually hardened, most being from peasant stock, and hence combat units were "lean and mean." There were no cooks for troops; the soldier carried his rice and other rations, was responsible for his own cooking, and often was ordered to forage for rations. Few amenities followed the troops into the field—little if any mail, no entertainment except "comfort" units of prostitutes, iron discipline, and hard marches. In the field soldiers appeared unkempt and their march order was ragged. Rather, the emphasis was on fighting skills.

Throughout the war Japanese Army (and Army Air Force) weapons were inferior to Western weapons (unlike the Navy). Light TANKS, for example, that were highly effective in China were outclassed by U.S. tanks, especially the SHERMAN TANK, while being vulnerable to U.S. antitank weapons. Rifles, submachine guns, machine guns, and artillery were also less capable than their Western counterparts.

The result of this inferiority, as well as poor logistics to support troops in the field, led to tremendous losses. Hundreds of thousands of Japanese soldiers died during the war from starvation and malaria on the Asian mainland and especially on isolated islands in the Pacific.

During the war Japan raised more than 100 divisions and numerous separate units with the Army reaching a peak strength of 5,000,000 men. The standard division (triangular when the war began) had a strength of some 16,000–20,000 men; there were no tanks in a division, except in the reconnaissance or cavalry regiment, and artillery was inferior to Western divisions, the largest guns normally assigned to a division being 75-mm weapons. (U.S. DIVISIONS had 105-mm and 155-mm guns; see ARTILLERY.)

There were numerous independent brigades and lesser units, and several airborne regiments (called *Teishin Rentai* or raiding regiment). These were actually battalions of about 600 men comprised of a headquarters unit and three companies, plus a supply section; several were combined with GLIDER units and other forces to form raider brigades of 1,475 men and were further combined with transport aircraft into a raiding group of some 5,600 troops. Airborne forces were intended to parachute behind enemy lines and cause confusion and disruption. The Japanese set up nine parachute training centers in 1940 and used about 100 German instructors to help train over 14,000 parachutists for the Army and Navy (marines).

Japanese Army paratroopers were employed, however, only in small-scale operations, mostly in China. (Also see JAPAN, NAVY.)

As the war neared an end in the Far East the Japanese Army was still largely intact, much of it on bypassed Pacific islands and atolls, in China, Indochina, and the Japanese home islands, plus the massive, 700,000-man Kwantung Army in Manchuria, the last intended to help deter a Soviet attack. (Late in the war some units and equipment of the Kwantung Army had been moved to Leyte and the homeland.) When the Soviet Union attacked Japan in Aug. 1945, Japanese forces in Manchuria and Korea were easily overrun and defeated by the well-trained, well-equipped Soviet Army.

At the end of the war the Japanese Army had fifty-three infantry divisions and twenty-five brigades with a total of 2,350,000 troops in the homeland, ready for a suicidal defense against the expected Allied invasion. (These troops were to be backed up by almost 4,000,000 civilian Army and Navy workers and a civilian militia of 28,000,000, the last armed mostly with sharpened poles, MINES, and GRENADES.)

Japan, Navy

The Imperial Japanese Navy at the beginning of the Pacific War was large and highly innovative, especially with respect to submarines and aircraft carriers. Further, Japanese naval aviators had combat experience from the war in China.

However, the Japanese Navy lagged in the development of RADAR and SONAR, and failed to understand the importance of unrestricted submarine warfare—the value of attacking U.S. merchant ships and transports, and the need to defend Japanese merchant shipping. Also, Japan would be unable to replace the aircraft carriers, aircraft, and trained pilots lost in the first year of the war.

At the start of the war the Japanese Navy had in service ten battleships, six fleet and four light carriers, eighteen heavy and eighteen light cruisers, 113 destroyers, and sixty-three submarines. These warships outnumbered the combined U.S., British Empire, Dutch, and FREE FRENCH forces in the Pacific except for CAPITAL SHIPS, light cruisers, and submarines.

The audacious Japanese carrier attack on PEARL HARBOR sank or severely damaged seven U.S. battleships, while two days later the battleship *PRINCE OF WALES* and battle cruiser *REPULSE* were sunk by Japanese land-based aircraft, changing the balance to ten Japanese capital ships and two U.S. ships. With respect to aircraft carriers, against the ten Japanese ships there were three American.

The bold Japanese naval strokes upon the opening of the war were totally victorious. At the cost of relatively few aircraft (only twenty-seven at Pearl Harbor) and no warship larger than destroyer, the Japanese effectively destroyed U.S. and British naval power in the region (including the eastern Indian Ocean). And, troops were transported for assaults on the Philippines, Malaya, the DUTCH EAST INDIES, and numerous smaller island groups. Adm. ISOROKU YAMAMOTO, during the planning for the war, had told the Japanese government that he could control the seas for six months. After that, he predicted, American naval power could be rebuilt. (See JAPANESE CAMPAIGN IN THE FAR EAST and JAPANESE CAMPAIGN IN THE CENTRAL PACIFIC.)

The Japanese Navy suffered a minor setback after five months, in the Battle of the CORAL SEA. But at MIDWAY one month later, the Japanese suffered a major defeat with the loss of four carriers and, even more important, their planes and most of their trained pilots. Two months later U.S. Marines landed on GUADALCANAL, the first U.S. offensive of the war. The lengthy U.S. SOLOMONS–NEW GUINEA CAMPAIGN further inflicted losses on the Japanese Navy that it could not effectively replace. (The U.S. Navy also suffered losses, including two AIRCRAFT CARRIERS, but their replacements were almost ready for sea.)

As the war progressed many shortfalls of the Japanese Navy came to light. While the Japanese had unequaled night-fighting capability when the war began, by 1943 U.S. radar more than reversed that advantage. Japanese pilot training failed to provide replacements for the casualties at Midway and in the

Solomons. As U.S. SUBMARINES increased in numbers, and their TORPEDO problems were solved, Japanese merchant and naval ships fell easy victim as antisubmarine and CONVOY measures were totally inadequate.

The new ships and aircraft that did join the Japanese fleet were of dubious effectiveness. The super-battleships *YAMATO* and *Musashi*, the largest dreadnoughts ever built, fell easy victim to U.S. air attacks; advanced Japanese aircraft experienced major problems, often from lack of adequate engines, and were too few to have an effect on the war.

As one Japanese later observed, while the United States was developing the ATOMIC BOMB, Japan was launching BALLOON BOMBS against the United States. The most effective Japanese naval weapon of the war was undoubtedly the KAMIKAZE—suicide aircraft attacks on U.S. and British ships. But even that weapon could not deter the Allied advances toward the Japanese home islands. (While Japanese Navy and Army suicide air attacks were a threat, the KAITEN submarines were essentially impotent.)

When the war ended the largest Japanese warship afloat was the battleship *Nagato*. She was towed to Bikini and destroyed in an ATOMIC BOMB TEST in July 1946.

	JAPANESE NAVY	ALLIED NAVIES
Aircraft Carriers	10	3
Battleships	10	10
Battle Cruisers	—	1
Heavy Cruisers	18	14
Light Cruisers	18	22
Destroyers	113	100
Submarines	63	69

Naval Aviation   The Japanese naval air arm was the largest and most capable in the world when the war began. Japanese carrier planes and naval land-based aircraft had seen extensive action in China. The new A6M ZERO fighter and G4M BETTY twin-engine bomber were among the best combat aircraft in service anywhere.

Not only were there six large and four light aircraft carriers in service, but the larger ships were concentrated in the First Air Fleet under Vice Adm. CHUICHI NAGUMO, and that force would strike Pearl Harbor with 350 aircraft. Another fifty aircraft were aboard the six carriers for defensive air patrol and scouting.

The Japanese Navy had 1,250 aircraft on Dec. 7, 1941—more than many of the world's air forces.

Japanese Campaign in the Central Pacific (1942)

Japan's thrust toward PORT MORESBY and then GUADALCANAL in the spring of 1942 was only one phase of a strategic offensive. A more important phase focused on MIDWAY and the ALEUTIANS.

The Midway operation had two objectives: The first was the seizure of Midway Island as an advance base to help provide early detection of U.S. AIRCRAFT CARRIERS seeking to raid Japan, as had occurred in the DOOLITTLE RAID of April 1942. The planned attack on the Aleutians was a diversion, to draw out what was left of the U.S. Pacific FLEET so that it could be engaged and destroyed, the second objective of the Midway operation. With these objectives achieved, the invasion of HAWAII itself would become possible. The plan of Adm. ISOROKU YAMAMOTO, CinC of the Japanese Fleet, depended upon secrecy and good fortune—both of which would be denied in the battle.

Adm. CHESTER NIMITZ, CinC of the U.S. Pacific FLEET, knew of Adm. Yamamoto's plan in advance through American decrypts of Japanese naval codes. Rather, Nimitz's problem was how to obtain sufficient forces to intercept the approaching Japanese fleets. Adm. Yamamoto had assembled four large and two medium carriers, eleven battleships, sixteen cruisers, and fifty-five destroyers plus a large submarine force to engage the U.S. fleet and support the invasion of Midway. Simultaneously, the assault on the Aleutians was to be carried out by two medium carriers, six cruisers, and thirteen destroyers.

In contrast, Nimitz could assemble but three carriers, eight cruisers, and seventeen destroyers plus submarines to stop the Japanese. In his novel about World War II, *War and Remembrance*, Herman Wouk accurately described the feeling of many American commanders as they tallied up the U.S. carrier force going to sea: "The *HORNET* [CV 8], the *ENTERPRISE* [CV 6], with possibly the patched leaky *Yorktown* [CV 5] and their meager train,

against that Japanese armada! . . . As a fleet problem, it was too lopsided for any peacetime umpire to propose" in prewar games at the U.S. Naval War College.

But code-breaking (see MAGIC), luck, and skill were on the American side. Nimitz knew of the Japanese plans; Adm. Yamamoto had dispersed his forces into several separate task forces that were not mutually supportable; one of the Japanese scout planes looking for the American force was delayed; U.S. commanders had better tactics; a U.S. carrier strike was skillfully led to the elusive Japanese carriers by its commanders; ineffective land-based bomber strikes from Midway and then the slaughter of U.S. carrier-launched TORPEDO planes had led to the U.S. dive bombers catching the Japanese carriers at a vulnerable moment.

The tide of battle was turned in a few moments at Midway when U.S. SBD DAUNTLESS dive bombers smashed and left sinking three of the Japanese carriers. A short time later the SBDs destroyed the four large carriers. Sunk on June 4 were the *Kaga*, *Akagi*, *Soryu*, and *Hiryu*—all veterans of the PEARL HARBOR attack—along with hundreds of their veteran pilots and skilled mechanics, and all of their aircraft. The U.S. Navy lost one carrier, the *Yorktown*, in the June 4–5 battle, sunk by a combination of air-submarine attacks.

Although the Japanese failed to seize Midway, they did occupy Attu and Kiska Islands in the Aleutian chain; Japanese troops would occupy those remote islands until the spring of 1943, although they would have minimal effect on the course of the war. But this would be the last successful Japanese offensive of the war. The U.S. Navy had, for the second time, stopped the Japanese advance. (See battle of CORAL SEA and JAPANESE CAMPAIGN IN THE FAR EAST.) It would take three more years of war before Japan capitulated, but the defeat of Japan began with the loss of four carriers and the turning back of the invasion force at Midway.

Japanese Campaign in the Far East (1941–1942)

While Japan's war with China raged on, Japanese troops marched into French Indochina in Sept. 1940 without opposition from the VICHY FRENCH

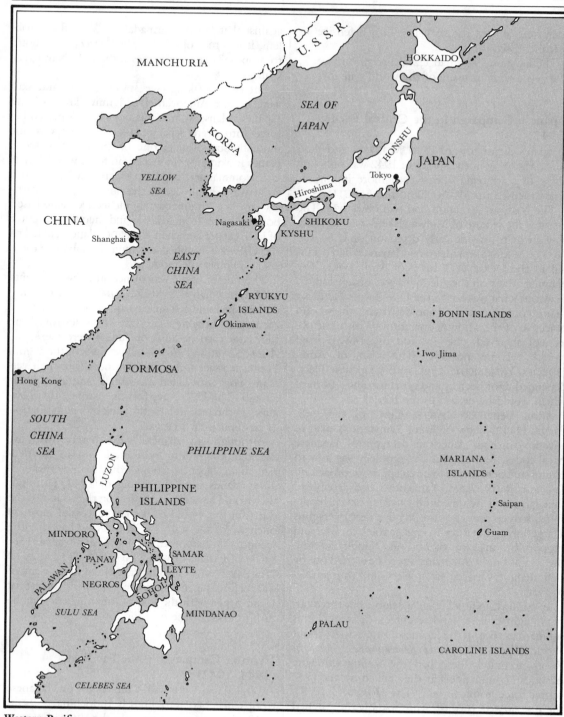

Western Pacific.

government. The Japanese move illuminated part of Japan's plan for a GREATER EAST ASIA CO-PROSPERITY SPHERE, a version of Hitler's European "New Order." The United States responded to Japan's aggression with an oil embargo and stopped the export of iron, steel, and rubber.

By the fall of 1941, diplomatic relations between Japan and the United States had faltered over the issues of U.S. aid to China, the Japanese invasion of Indochina, the U.S. government's freezing Japanese assets in the United States, and other acts of economic pressure on Japan. With only a six-month supply of petroleum available in Japan, and fearful of further U.S. political-economic actions, the Japanese Cabinet, under Premier HIDEKI TOJO, agreed that it had to choose between a war with the United States and dissolution of the empire.

The Japanese Navy, under the direction of Adm. ISOROKU YAMAMOTO, undertook an audacious surprise carrier attack on PEARL HARBOR to prevent the U.S. FLEET from interfering with the Japanese conquest of the Philippines, Malaya, and the DUTCH EAST INDIES. Yamamoto, the CinC of the Japanese Fleet, estimated that the attack on the U.S. fleet—if successful—would give the Japanese six months of freedom from attack to secure its goals in the Far East.

The raid, on the morning of Dec. 7, 1941, was a tactical surprise and success. The raid, however, failed to sink any of the three U.S. AIRCRAFT CARRIERS in the Pacific nor did it prevent Pearl Harbor from being used as an advanced base for U.S. SUBMARINE and carrier operations during the early days of the conflict in the Pacific.

The next day the U.S. Congress voted a declaration of war against Japan. Three days later, on Dec. 11, Germany and Italy declared war against the United States, bringing the United States firmly into the Allied camp against the AXIS powers.

Hours after attacking Pearl Harbor, Japanese bombers struck U.S. bases in the Philippines and on the islands of GUAM and WAKE. They also hit SINGAPORE. Guam would fall to the Japanese in a day, Wake and Singapore in a few weeks. The Japanese invaded the Philippines in massive numbers. The U.S.-Filippino forces, led by Gen. DOUGLAS MACARTHUR, attempted to make a stand on Luzon's BATAAN Peninsula; Bataan fell on April 9.

Thousands of American and Philippine troops became PRISONERS OF WAR. The remnants of the exhausted U.S.-Filipino forces, running low on ammunition and food, burrowed into the tunnels of CORREGIDOR, a rocky fortress in MANILA Bay. MacArthur's successor, Maj. Gen. JONATHAN WAINWRIGHT, surrendered his troops on May 6; die-hard U.S. defenders fled into the hills, initiating a widespread GUERRILLA war there and on Luzon.

When the British fleet in the Far East attempted to stop the landings on the Malaya peninsula in Dec. 1941, land-based Japanese bombers sank the capital ships PRINCE OF WALES and REPULSE. Prime Minister CHURCHILL later wrote of their loss: "In all the war I never received a more direct shock." Japanese forces overran the peninsula, and after long and heavy fighting, the island fortress of Singapore fell on Feb. 15, 1942. Japanese troops also overran NEW BRITAIN, NEW IRELAND, and the ADMIRALTY and SOLOMON ISLANDS.

On Feb. 27 Japanese air and naval forces sank a U.S. and an Australian CRUISER—the largest Allied warships in the Far East—and four DESTROYERS in the battle of the JAVA SEA. The battle had delayed the Japanese invasion of Java by only one day, allowing Japan an open road to the Dutch East Indies.

The Japanese had landed troops on the southern tip of Burma on Dec. 8, 1941; they initially encountered strong resistance from the British. Japanese forces attacked farther up the peninsula and bombed the capital, Rangoon. After heavy fighting to hold Mandalay and the BURMA ROAD, the British defenders began a long retreat to the borders of India. The Burmese end of the Burma Road fell on April 29, and Mandalay fell on May 2.

By the spring of 1942 Japan had gained control of the entire Western Pacific, and had a massive foothold in China, Indochina, Malaya, and Burma, and threatened Australia and British interests in the Indian Ocean. Japanese losses had been minimal—a few dozen planes, a few hundred troops, and several warships, the largest of which were destroyers. The success was beyond the expectations of Japanese military and political leaders, and beyond the greatest fears of Allied leaders.

In May, Adm. Yamamoto had hoped to bring the U.S. carrier force to a decisive battle in the central Pacific, but instead agreed to support an assault on

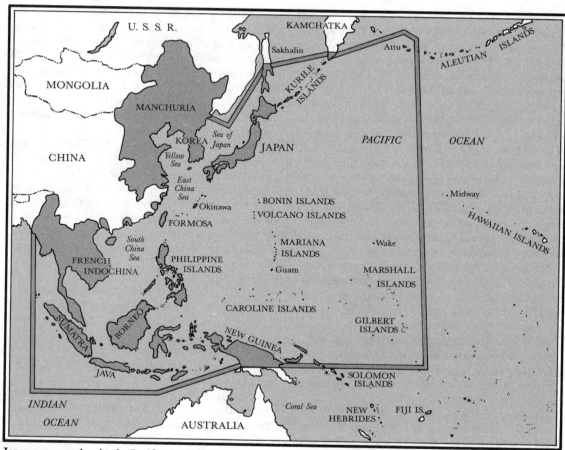

Japanese expansion in the Pacific, June 1942.

PORT MORESBY, New Guinea. The port would be the launch site for Japan's thrust to Australia. The U.S. Navy detected the approaching Japanese carrier and landing forces, and attacked first. The ensuing battle of the CORAL SEA, on May 7–8, 1942, marked the first Japanese defeat of the war. Adm. Yamamoto had been absolutely correct in his estimate that Japan could have six months of freedom of action in the Pacific.

Frustrated in their attempts to take Port Moresby, and suffering the loss of the light carrier *SHOHO* and damage to two larger carriers, the Japanese took a different approach to the capture of Port Moresby. Troops were landed on the island of GUADALCANAL to establish an airfield, and a seaplane base was set up on adjacent Tulagi Island. But

the principal Japanese forces were steaming eastward, for the decisive carrier battle to be fought near MIDWAY.

Japanese Mandated Islands

Pacific islands that were taken from Germany and ceded to Japan under the Versailles Treaty at the end of World War I. They included the MARSHALL ISLANDS, the CAROLINE ISLANDS, and all of the MARIANA ISLANDS except GUAM, which the United States had acquired after the Spanish-American War. The LEAGUE OF NATIONS theoretically kept watch over the mandated lands (which also included NEW GUINEA, ceded from Germany to England and Australia), but in reality the weak League did little to enforce rules against fortification of the mandated islands. Japan quit the League in 1933, and the fortifying of the islands intensified.

Japan kept visitors from the islands and banished Christian missionaries to atolls and other sites deemed nonstrategic. As the world would learn during the war, Japan, in great secrecy, had transformed the mandate into a license to convert many of the islands into air and naval bases that threatened the shipping lanes between Hawaii and Australia.

After the war the UNITED NATIONS placed the formerly mandated islands under U.S. trusteeship and gave the United States the right to fortify them.

Japanese-Americans

U.S. citizens who were interned or singled out for discriminatory treatment during the war. As far back as the 1930s U.S. military officials feared that allegiance to Japan would make traitors of both Japanese aliens in the United States and Japanese-American citizens. The fears were particularly prevalent in the U.S. territory HAWAII, where military intelligence officials had drawn up secret lists of ESPIONAGE suspects in the large Japanese community.

Immediately after the Japanese attack on PEARL HARBOR, many Hawaiians focused their hate and fright on the Japanese and AJA (Americans of Japanese Ancestry) populations. "Caps on Japanese Tomato Plants Point to Air Base" said the headline on one of several hysterical newspaper stories. Every Japanese fraternal or business organization was suspected of subversion; old and poor fishermen were accused of equipping their fishing boats with powerful radios for sending spy reports to Japan.

The panic quickly shifted to the mainland. Military and civilian officials in California began worrying about Japanese-Americans. On Feb. 19, 1942, President ROOSEVELT issued an executive order identifying certain military areas in the United States as places from which German, Italian, and Japanese aliens—*and* Japanese-Americans were to be barred.

California's Attorney General Earl Warren (future Chief Justice of the United States) said the lack of any acts of SABOTAGE proved nothing; the Japanese-Americans were just holding back "until the zero hour arrives." Walter Lippmann, one of the nation's most influential journalists, joined the chorus for quick action against Americans of enemy-alien descent. About 2,000 people of German and Italian ancestry were interned. (See ALIENS.) But the official spotlight was on Japanese-Americans.

On March 18, the War Relocation Authority (WRA) was established as part of the Office of Emergency Management and plans were made for what MILTON EISENHOWER, director of WRA (and brother of Army Maj. Gen. DWIGHT D. EISENHOWER), described in a June report to Roosevelt: the federal government would "take all people of Japanese descent into custody, surround them with troops, prevent them from buying land, and return them to their former homes at the close of the war."

The WRA rounded up nearly 120,000 men, women, and children on the West Coast who were of Japanese descent; about two thirds of them were citizens and more than one fourth of them were children under fifteen. There were three categories: Nisei (persons born in the United States of immigrant Japanese parents and therefore United States citizens); Issei (Japanese immigrants); and Kibei (native U.S. citizens of Japanese immigrant parents but educated largely in Japan). They were taken to ten "relocation centers" scattered from the interior of California to isolated areas in Utah, Arkansas, Arizona, Idaho, Colorado, and Wyoming.

The internees ate in mess halls, used communal washrooms, and lived in tar paper barracks, with a 20-by-25 foot room allowed each family. No one was allowed to have a razor, scissors, or radios. Barbed wire surrounded the camps, which were guarded by armed U.S. soldiers. Children went to WRA-operated schools. One of the assignments: write an essay about why you are proud to be an American.

The only major disturbances were at the Tule Lake Relocation Center, in California near the Oregon border, which in June 1943 was designated a "segregation center" for Japanese-Americans who had proclaimed their loyalty to Japan or who had been designated by the Department of Justice as disloyal to the United States. The Army had to tighten control because of strikes and demonstrations.

A Japanese-American who refused to register for relocation, Gordon Hirabayashi, fought the issue all the way to the U.S. Supreme Court, claiming that the Army had violated his rights as an American citizen. The Supreme Court ruled that the threat of invasion and sabotage gave the military the right to restrict the Constitutional rights of Japanese-Americans.

Not until early in 1943 were Japanese-Americans allowed to enter the service. In Hawaii, 9,500 volunteered, and about 2,700 were accepted. More than 17,000 Japanese-Americans fought for the United States in World War II. The all-Nisei 442nd Regimental COMBAT TEAM, fighting in the ITALIAN CAMPAIGN, became the most decorated military unit in U.S. history. The unit won 4,667 medals, awards, and citations, including one MEDAL OF HONOR, fifty-two Distinguished Service Crosses, and 560 Silver Stars. When many of the soldiers wrote home, the addresses were detention centers. The mother of one medal winner was not allowed to leave the center to receive her son's posthumous award.

In 1990, after years of delay, the United States apologized to the 60,000 survivors of interment and their heirs and began paying to each of them reparation of $20,000.

Japan's China-Burma Campaign (1941–1943)

The Japanese attack on PEARL HARBOR instantly changed the course of the long war between Japan and China. On the day following the attack, China, which had been fighting Japan since 1931, finally declared war on Japan—and on Germany and Italy. Generalissimo CHIANG KAI-SHEK was tying his fate to that of the Western ALLIES.

Chiang had a practical reason for his belated declaration of war on Japan. In April 1941 Japan and the Soviet Union had signed a neutrality pact that recognized Manchuko, the Japanese puppet state in what had been northwest China. The United States, eager to simultaneously chide both the Soviets and Japan, had reacted by declaring China eligible for the kind of LEND-LEASE aid the United States already was giving England and Greece.

To pin down that favored status now that the United States was at war, Chiang made his country an instant Ally: He followed up his declaration of war by sending three reserve armies to the Burma border and offering this force to aid the Allies in Burma, where the Japanese were on the march.

After quickly winning control of the Malayan peninsula, Japan had moved against Burma. The oil of Burma attracted the petroleum-starved Japanese, as did Burma's mountainous barrier with India. Possession of Burma would protect the flank of Japan's GREATER EAST ASIA CO-PROSPERITY SPHERE from British interference.

On Dec. 23 and Dec. 25, 1941, Japanese aircraft bombed Burma's capital of Rangoon and Japanese forces began their drive on Burma by taking the long narrow strip of territory that runs down the eastern edge of Thailand. The Japanese fought British imperial troops in hand-to-hand fighting to seize Moulmein, a Burmese port on the Salween River, on Jan. 31, 1942. In bitter jungle fighting, the Japanese moved relentlessly northward, cutting up the retreating British forces.

Gen. Sir HAROLD ALEXANDER, newly arrived to take command of British forces in Burma, narrowly escaped capture when Rangoon, battered by two months of Japanese air raids, fell on March 6. Now, as the British continued to retreat northward, Chiang's armies entered Burma.

The Chinese were nominally under the command of U.S. Lt. Gen. JOSEPH STILWELL, commanding general of the newly created China-Burma-India (CBI) theater and Chiang's Chief of Staff. Stilwell was no admirer of Chiang. Privately Stilwell called Chiang "the Peanut" and heartily distrusted him. Chiang got Stilwell out of China by putting him in charge of the Chinese Expeditionary Force in Burma.

Both the British forces under Alexander and Stilwell's Chinese troops were doomed to defeat. Burmese refugees by the tens of thousands clogged the scant roads, impeding Allied movement. Japanese troops, superior at jungle fighting, continually outguessed and outmaneuvered their foes. The Chinese fought well, at least at first, but coordination among Allied units was arduous and often hopeless. It would be a problem that would plague the CBI throughout the war.

Alexander assembled virtually all combat-ready Imperial troops in Burma as the I Burma Corps ("Burcorps") and put them under Lt. Gen. WIL-

LIAM J. SLIM, who organized the British retreat and established a SCORCHED EARTH POLICY by destroying trains, river boats, bridges, and the oilfields at Yenangyaung and Chauk.

On April 29 the Japanese cut the BURMA ROAD at Lashio, cutting off Chiang's only route for Lend-Lease and other supplies. The road had run from a railhead at Lashio to Kunming in Yunnan, an industrial center in southwest China. By then both Stilwell and Slim realized that the battle for Burma was lost and the Allies must prepare to defend India.

Slim would later write of men "gaunt and ragged as scarecrows" stumbling into Assam, India, yet still carrying their arms and keeping their ranks. Stilwell, who had made the long walk out of Burma with his men, bitterly said of the humiliating retreat across Burma: The British and the Americans "share one common ancestor. Ethelred the Unready."

Stilwell tried to correct that by a plan to create a modern, well-trained Chinese Army of thirty divisions. With the Burma Road severed, supplies now were flying across THE HUMP of the Himalayas from India to China in U.S. transport planes. On their return journeys they carried out Chinese troops for Stilwell to train and arm in India as a cadre for the army he envisioned.

Chiang resisted the plan, for he saw such a force as a source of rival power. Chiang also resisted Allied advice to throw more of his troops against the Japanese in China. The prevailing Chinese attitude of *wu-wei erh wo pu-wei* ("through not doing all things are done") fit well with the likelihood that Japan's defeat would not come in China, but through Anglo-American action against the homeland. Chiang's philosophical strategy also fit well into military reality. For the loss of Burma and the Burma Road severely limited any campaigning against Japanese troops in China.

Allied strategy focused on the defense of India along the Assam frontier, which was threatened by both Japanese without and anti-British unrest within. In the most publicized Allied action, Brig. Gen. ORDE WINGATE led a harassing force of CHINDITS behind enemy lines to slow the Japanese advance. The raids did little to change the military situation. The far-reaching effect was much more important: Wingate showed that a force moving through jungled, mountainous terrain could be supplied by air.

As the monsoon rains began to cease in Jan. 1944, a daring strategy took shape: Defense would be in the form of offense. Wingate's air-land tactics would be adapted for what would be the ALLIED CHINA-BURMA-INDIA CAMPAIGN.

Java Sea

Shallow Pacific sea north of Java and south of Borneo. Scene of a battle in the JAPANESE CAMPAIGN IN THE FAR EAST. On Feb. 27, 1942, as a Japanese fleet covering an invasion force approached Java, an ABDA (American-British-Dutch-Australian) fleet fired at the Japanese ships from long range. The Allied fleet consisted of a CRUISER from each country and some DESTROYERS—with no air cover. The American cruiser was the *HOUSTON* (CA 30), the largest U.S. warship in the Far East and the flagship of the U.S. Asiatic FLEET.

When the two fleets closed, the Japanese badly damaged the British *Exeter,* which withdrew from the battle. In well-coordinated attacks the Japanese then sank four Allied destroyers and two cruisers. During the night of Feb. 28–29 the *Houston* and the Australian cruiser *Perth* were sunk after sinking a Japanese transport and a minesweeper, and damaging six other ships.

On March 1, as the damaged *Exeter* with her two escorting destroyers slipped out of Surabaya in eastern Java, all three ships were sunk. The invasion had been delayed only for a few hours.

"Of the entire Allied fleet which had operated during those dreadful days throughout the DUTCH EAST INDIES," says a British account of the disaster, "only four American destroyers . . . managed to escape to Australia. . . . The Japanese conquest of the East Indies had been completed in three months; they could be well content, for they had expected it to take six."

Jedburghs

Members of American-British teams who secretly arrived in France to aid the FRENCH RESISTANCE. A Jedburgh team consisted of an American working for the OFFICE OF STRATEGIC SERVICES, a Briton from a British intelligence service, and a Free French officer or enlisted man. All wore uniforms when they were parachuted into France, in hopes that if they were captured the Germans would not execute them as spies.

One of the team members was a radio operator. The teams provided communications, leadership, and advice to local GUERRILLA organizations. The teams also assured Allied officials that arms and other equipment being dropped to guerrillas was being used properly and in keeping with Allied strategy.

Allied aircraft dropped ninety-three Jedburgh teams into France following the NORMANDY INVASION. Some teams also parachuted into Belgium, Holland, and Norway. The teams were recruited and trained in a joint effort of the OSS and a British secret agency, the SPECIAL OPERATIONS EXECUTIVE.

Although there is a Jedburgh in southeast Scotland, it had no apparent connection with the team name, which supposedly was a randomly selected code word. But some hidden British wit may have inspired it, for "Jedburgh justice"—punishing malefactors first and trying them afterward—was a phrase known at least to Scots.

Jeep

A four-wheeled, four-place utility vehicle widely used by U.S. forces and Allies. Gen. DWIGHT D. EISENHOWER cited the jeep as one of the four weapons that helped most to win the war (the others being the C-47 SKYTRAIN/DAKOTA transport, BAZOOKA, and ATOMIC BOMB).

Jeeps were used by millions of American servicemen, from President ROOSEVELT to privates, seamen, and airmen. Several hundred were assigned to each combat DIVISION, and many thousand more were used by headquarters commands and at military bases.

The jeep prototype was completed by the Bantam Car Co. in 1940. Because that firm lacked a major production capability, the vehicle was mass-produced as the M38 utility vehicle by the Willys-Overland Motors Co. and Ford Motor Co.

It could be adapted as a litter carrier or fitted with a pedestal mount for a heavy machine gun, and could tow a 1/4-ton trailer or light gun. It had a four-cylinder engine with four-wheel drive; maximum speed on a good road was in excess of 60 mph.

Jeep. *(By Bill Mauldin)*

Its forte was rough terrain, where four-wheel drive was invaluable. The jeep was an open vehicle, fitted with a canvas cab that afforded minimal protection from rain or cold. The vehicle was approximately 11 feet long and 5 feet 2 inches wide, and empty weighed approximately 2,600 pounds.

The exact origins of the term *jeep* are not known. It may have come from the letters *GP* indicating general-purpose vehicle.

Jericho

Code name for RAF bombing of German prison in Amiens, France, to permit the mass escape by British prisoners; some 250 men escaped in the attack, 1944.

Jerico Trumpet

Name given to sirens on the fixed landing gear of German JU 87 *STUKA* dive bombers.

Jet-Propelled Aircraft

The first operational jet-propelled aircraft flew during the war, following development efforts in several European countries in the 1930s. Jet propulsion offered tremendous power and hence speed, with more efficient aircraft designs possible because there was no requirement for a propeller. However, jet-propelled aircraft consumed large quantities of fuel and had low acceleration rates.

It was an RAF officer, Frank Whittle, who first took out patents for the world's first practical turbojet in 1930 after the Air Ministry rejected his earlier jet engine designs. (His basic patents lapsed in 1935 because he could not afford the renewal fees.) In 1939 the Air Ministry did award his company, Power Jets, Ltd., a contract for an engine to be tested in a special aircraft produced by Gloster Aircraft Co. Designated E.28/39, that experimental aircraft flew on May 15, 1941.

Meanwhile, several other nations initiated jet aircraft development. The world's first jet aircraft to fly was the experimental Heinkel He 178, powered by an engine designed by Hans von Ohain, which made a successful flight on Aug. 27, 1939.

The first jet-propelled fighter to enter combat was the Messerschmitt ME 262 *Sturmvogel* (Stormbird), with preproduction aircraft flying combat missions as early as April 1944. The first kill of a manned aircraft (see below) by a jet-propelled aircraft occurred in the first week of Oct. 1944 by an Me 262 that downed a U.S. B-17 FLYING FORTRESS of the Eighth AIR FORCE.

The Me 262 was an effective fighter, and could have influenced the air war over Germany—especially Allied STRATEGIC BOMBING—if they had been immediately employed as fighters (HITLER wanted to use them as bombers) and if the production bottlenecks could have been overcome. The swept-wing Me 262 was powered by twin Junkers turbojet engines. The first Me 262 had flown (with piston engines) on April 18, 1941, and with turbojet engines on July 18, 1941.

The Germans developed other jet fighter-type aircraft during the war as well as the Ardo AR 234 *BLITZ* (Lightning) high-speed bomber with the Ar 234C being a four-engine fighter variant, while the Heinkel HE 162 *VOLKSJÄGER* (People's Fighter) was a single-jet, low-cost fighter intended to be flown by pilots with minimal training. Several other German jet aircraft flew during the war (as well as the rocket-propelled ME 163 *KOMET*).

The first Allied jet aircraft to enter operational service was the Gloster METEOR, powered by two Rolls-Royce turbojet engines, which entered operational RAF service in July 1944. Meteors immediately began flying sorties against German V-1 BUZZ BOMBS that were flying against England. By the beginning of 1945 Meteors were flying missions over Europe to counter the appearance of the German jet-propelled Me 262. However, there were no jet-versus-jet engagements.

A twin-engine aircraft, the Meteor first flew in March 1943.

The first U.S. jet-propelled aircraft was the Bell XP-59A Airacomet, which flew on Oct. 1, 1942, being powered by two General Electric Type I-A turbojets based on the British-designed Whittle engine. Although P-59B fighters reached Italy by the end of the war, they did not enter combat.

The U.S. Navy shared in jet development with the AAF, but the slow acceleration rate of early jet engines made their feasibility for operation from AIRCRAFT CARRIERS questionable. The British did land a de Havilland Vampire I jet aircraft aboard a carrier in Dec. 1945. Earlier the U.S. Navy had landed a Ryan FR-1 FIREBALL composite piston-jet aircraft aboard a carrier on only its jet when the piston engine suffered a failure.

The Japanese flew the Nakajima *Kikka* (Orange Blossom), a Navy fighter with twin jet engines, for the first time on July 7, 1945. This aircraft was based on the Me 262 with the twin turbojets also based on German designs (copied from photographs). The plane crashed on its second test flight and the nineteen additional aircraft being built were incomplete when the war ended.

An Italian jet-propelled aircraft, the Caproni-Campini CC.2 flew in 1940, but no operational aircraft designs were produced.

(The Soviet Union apparently did not undertake jet aircraft development until after the war, using captured German technology and subsequently purchased British jet engines.)

Jewish Brigade

Jewish unit in the British Army. At the start of the war many JEWS from Palestine joined the British armed forces. (At the time Britain had the LEAGUE OF NATIONS mandate to rule Palestine.) Many served in operations against German and VICHY FRENCH supporters in Syria. Among them was a young officer named Moshe Dayan who lost his left eye during a British military operation in Syria. (Dayan would go on to become a leading Israeli military hero and government minister.)

As German troops of the AFRIKA KORPS approached Egypt in the summer of 1942 and threatened the whole British position in the Middle East, the British command assigned the Jewish defense force or *Haganah* "post-occupation" missions to form the nucleus of GUERRILLA groups behind German lines.

Early in 1943 Jewish leaders offered to send volunteers (some refugees from Germany) from Palestine behind German lines in Eastern Europe to support underground resistance movements. Several members of the *Haganah*—men and WOMEN—were parachuted into Europe by the British. Finally, in 1944 the British Army organized the Jewish BRIGADE under the command of Brig. Ernest Frank Benjamin. Late in 1944 this unit was sent to Italy and joined the Allied army fighting there. After the war the unit served in occupation duties in Austria and Germany.

Including the Jewish Brigade, a total of 28,000 men and 4,000 women of the Jewish community in Palestine served in the British armed forces during the war. Both men and women were among agents parachuted behind German lines for special missions.

The brigade traced its origins to local Jewish defense groups established in Palestine in the late 1870s when there was large-scale immigration from Eastern Europe to Palestine. The Turkish rulers of the area were unable to provide protection for remote settlements. This task was assumed by the Jewish Guardsmen or *Hashomer* in 1907 as immigration increased in the wake of the abortive Russian Revolution of 1905. This self-defense force was reformed as the *Haganah* or "defense" in 1917 after the Balfour Declaration stated that the government of Britain, which was at war with Turkey, would look with favor on the establishment of a Jewish state within Palestine. The *Haganah* concept was not to have a few defenders, but to teach military skills to all Jews in Palestine, in essence a militia. The British government, however, allowed only

limited weapons to this group (initially thirty rifles, twelve light machine guns, plus shotguns). To help train the *Haganah,* in 1937 then-Capt. ORDE C. WINGATE arrived in Palestine, although he was officially there to collect intelligence and curb attacks by Arab marauders. Working with the Jewish leadership, he helped to form an effective fighting force.

Jews

In the late 1920s, the earliest NAZIS scrawled on walls and on the windows of Jewish stores, *Juda Verrecke!*—"Death to Judaism!"—using the word reserved for the killing of cattle, *verrecke.* The message was there on the wall, but in the beginning most of the potential victims paid it little heed. ANTI-SEMITISM had a long history in Germany as well as the rest of Europe. For a short time during his rise to power, HITLER even had the support of the Jewish National Union, which supported his campaign against the immigration of "peddler Jews" from Eastern Europe.

Hitler had repeatedly stated his own anti-Semitic views on "racial purity" in *Mein Kampf,* "My Struggle," his autobiography, whose first volume was published in 1925. But as he evolved from leader of a Bavarian fringe group to leader of a national party, his views seem to temper. "He has stopped breathing fire at the Jews and can make a speech nowadays lasting for four hours without mentioning the word 'Jew'," said the president of the German Federal Republic on the eve of Hitler's elevation to dictatorial chancellor of Germany.

As soon as Hitler became chancellor in 1933, however, there was no doubt that he would embark on a methodical anti-Semitic campaign that would have four phases: economic persecution of German Jews; enactment of laws to remove Jews from the mainstream of German life; roundups and forced migrations of Jews in Germany and conquered territories; eradication of Jews from Europe by mass murder.

Economic Persecution

On April 1, 1933, Hitler launched a boycott of Jewish businesses, saying, "I believe that I act today in unison with the Almighty Creator's intention: by fighting the Jews I do battle for the Lord." SA thugs enforced the boycott by standing in front of the doors to Jewish stores and shops, intimidating anyone who dared to enter. A week later Hitler removed Jews from the civil service. Within the next year "non-Ayrans"—Jews or anyone who had one Jewish parent or Jewish grandparent—were removed from banks, the stock exchange, the law, journalism, and medicine.

Laws Against Jews

In the fall of 1935 the Nazis pushed through the Reichstag the Nuremberg Laws, named after the Bavarian city that was a center of Nazism. A "blood" law stipulated that only persons of "German or related blood" could be citizens; Jews became *Staatsangehörige,* subjects that belong to the state. The "Law for the Protection of German Blood and German Honor" prohibited marriage or sexual relations between Jews and non-Jews; Jews were also forbidden to employ female servants under the age of forty-five.

Regulations stemming from the laws led to the withdrawal of political rights and to outright persecution. On the pretext of Nuremberg law violations, Nazis seized Jewish businesses and authorized the breaking of commercial contracts and the dismissal of Jewish employees. In schools, "racial science" became compulsory, as did membership in HITLER YOUTH (restricted, of course, to Ayrans); Jewish organizations set up more and more Jewish schools. Eventually, Jewish children were barred from public schools.

Between 1933 and 1937 an estimated 129,00 Jews fled Germany and Nazi-annexed Austria (including ALBERT EINSTEIN and Sigmund Freud). The outside world did not welcome the mass of refugees. "Today," the Zionist leader Chaim Weizmann said in 1936, "almost six million Jews are doomed to be pent up in places where they are not wanted, and for whom the world is divided into places where they cannot live, and places into which they cannot enter." In one of the most publicized prewar incidents, the liner *St. Louis* departed from HAMBURG, Germany, on May 13, 1939, carrying 937 Jews bound for Havana, Cuba, where all but twenty-two were refused entry. The United States denied entry to the ship and her passengers. The *St. Louis* returned to Europe, where the passengers

disembarked and scattered. Nearly 600 of them would die in CONCENTRATION CAMPS.

On Nov. 9, 1938, *KRISTALLNACHT,* the "Night of Broken Glass," demonstrated beyond any doubt that German anti-Semitism was becoming murderous; more than 200 Jews were killed in the Nazi-sponsored orgy of violence. More than 20,000 Jews were arrested and 10,000 were sent to the concentration camp at Buchenwald.

Germans got used to seeing neighbors disappear into the camps. As a German described those days in a postwar reminiscence, there was little interest in the fact that the Nazis were rounding up "all these second-rate people, like Jews, and Gypsies, and layabouts, and Bible punchers and homosexuals, and all these lower elements that don't want to work."

This acceptance of concentration camps by ordinary citizens paved the way toward the FINAL SOLUTION, the killing of all European Jews. But first they had to be found and put under control.

Rounding up the Jews

On Sept. 21, 1939, twenty days after the EUROPEAN WAR began with the invasion of Poland, REINHARD HEYDRICH, chief of the REICH CENTRAL SECURITY OFFICE, convened a meeting in Berlin on "the Jewish problem in the occupied zone" of Poland. At the meeting were commanders of SS units that already had seized and murdered groups of Polish Jews. Heydrich vaguely mentioned that he had an "ultimate aim" for the Jews but stressed that immediate needs called for western Poland to be "cleared completely of Jews" and the "concentration of Jews in cities."

The Jews of WARSAW and other cities were herded into ghettos, the two largest being the WARSAW GHETTO and the LODZ GHETTO. Then Jews forcibly removed from other areas were added to the already jammed ghettos. Others were sent to camps and put to work as SLAVE LABOR. Jews had to wear arm bands emblazoned with the Star of David. Jews were allotted half the ration authorized for non-Jewish Poles. A German doctor calculated that this was a sentence to starvation. German occupation forces randomly killed Polish Jews, taunted and tortured them, or made them perform despicable acts. A favorite: forcing Jews at gunpoint to gather up sacred Torah scrolls and burn them while they danced around the fire singing, "We rejoice that this shit is burning."

From the invasion of Poland to the invasion of the Soviet Union on June 22, 1941, perhaps as many as 30,000 Jews were killed either by German guns or by starvation and disease in ghettos and labor camps. With the invasion of the Soviet Union would come the systematic killing of all Jews.

Mass Murders

"I never saw a written order," ADOLF EICH-MANN, the SS officer in charge of the final solution, said at his trial. "All I know is that Heydrich told me, 'The Führer ordered the physical extermination of the Jews.'"

The SS used two methods for the extermination: *Einsatzgruppen,* ACTION GROUPS, who followed the German Army into conquered areas and engineered mass killings; and DEATH CAMPS, set up especially for the purpose of killing as many people (nearly all of them Jews) as quickly and as efficiently as possible. Nazi leaders believed that the Jews had to be wiped out swiftly because, as a guideline to the final solution put it, "our next generation will not be so close to this problem and will not see it clearly enough."

The action groups, according to the Nuremberg International Military Tribunal on WAR CRIMES, killed 2,000,000 men, women, and children in occupied countries. As the chief of one of the groups described the technique: Victims were taken in trucks to the execution site, usually an antitank ditch. "Then they were shot, kneeling or standing, by firing squads in a military manner and the corpses thrown into the ditch."

Death camps, using ZYKLON-B poison gas, carbon monoxide, or gunfire, killed millions more. Others died in concentration camps and from isolated mass murders, such as death marches in Hungary and the Babi Yar massacre in the Soviet Union. The massacre was named after a ravine near Kiev. German troops rounded up nearly 35,000 Jews, killed them in two days, dumped the bodies into the Babi Yar ravine, and covered the bodies with heaps of soil. Soviet poet Yevgeny Yevtushenko, in one of his most famous poems, wrote, "I am each old man slaughtered, each child shot. None of me will forget."

The Nuremberg war crimes trials estimated that the Germans killed at least 5,700,000 Jews. Other estimates put the number closer to 6,000,000. The most authoritative recent estimate was prepared by Yehuda Bauer of Yad Vashem Research Institute, which was created by the Israeli Knesset in 1953 to study what became known as the HOLOCAUST. These estimates are:

Polish-Soviet area	4,565,000
Germany	125,000
Austria	65,000
Czechoslovakia	277,000
Hungary	402,000
France	83,000
Belgium and Luxembourg	24,700
Netherlands	106,000
Italy	7,500
Norway	760
Rumania	40,000
Yugoslavia	60,000
Greece	65,000
Total	5,820,960

(Hungary, France, Italy, and Yugoslavia may be underestimated. Rumania excludes Bessarabia and northern Bukovina, annexed by the Soviet Union in 1940, and northern Transylvania, annexed by Hungary in 1940.)

Surviving Jews

Before the Nazis took control of Germany in 1933, about 500,000 Jews lived in Germany and 185,000 in Austria. An estimated 200,000 German Jews left Germany before the war virtually sealed the border in 1939, and 126,000 left Austria by the end of 1939. In the two countries, some 28,000 Jews survived the war, almost every one as a DISPLACED PERSON; about 10 percent of the Jews were children, but practically none of them younger than six. News about the systematic killing of Jews reached the United States, via Jewish sources, in July 1941, when Yiddish newspapers began publishing accounts of mass deaths following the German invasion of the Soviet Union. On Oct. 26, 1941, *The New York Times* published a short account that said "reliable sources" reported the killing of 10,000 to 15,000 Jews in Poland. Such reports, usually based on good documentation, continued to reach the United States and England through the end of

1942, when prominent magazines and authors publicized the genocide.

Many, however, dismissed the reports as anti-Nazi PROPAGANDA; a Gallup poll published on Jan. 7, 1943, showed that only 47 percent of the respondents believed that 2,000,000 Jews had been murdered in Europe. But, after intensive campaigning by Christian and Jewish relief organizations, in Nov. 1943 the Congress passed a "Rescue Resolution" calling upon President ROOSEVELT to set up a commission to find a way "to save the surviving Jewish people of Europe from extinction at the hands of Nazi Germany."

Roosevelt on Jan. 22, 1944, set up the War Refugee Board (WRB) "to rescue the victims of enemy oppression who are in imminent danger of death." A representative of the board in Turkey, assisted by the International RED CROSS, succeeded in getting Rumania to release 6,400 Jews; German pressure soon blocked that exit. Thousands of others escaped via Sweden and Switzerland.

Jews in Hungary had fared well until 1944; Hungary had even taken in Jews from Poland and Slovakia. But within weeks after Germany occupied Hungary in March 1944, trains began carrying Jews to the AUSCHWITZ death camp.

On June 12, Roosevelt warned Hungary that if it did not stop the deportation of Jews, after the war "Hungary's fate will not be like any other civilized nation's." U.S. bombers punctuated the warning with a raid on BUDAPEST on July 2. The deportations temporarily stopped, and desperate efforts by the WRB, neutral nations, and the Red Cross were made to get the remaining Jews out. A Swedish diplomat, RAOUL WALLENBERG, went to Budapest and, along with papal representatives (including the future Pope John XXIII) and Swiss, Portuguese, and Spanish diplomats, saved thousands. In Hungary and elsewhere, the WRB was credited with saving about 200,000 Jews and 20,000 non-Jews.

As liberation of Hungary neared, the government was overthrown and Hungarian Fascist thugs began shooting Jews and dumping their bodies in the Danube. Soviet troops, fighting a desperate battle for Budapest, liberated the Jewish ghettos in Jan. 1945, but the killing of Jews continued until the surrender of the city on Feb. 12.

After the war a controversy arose about the failure of the ALLIES to bomb any of the Nazi death camps or concentration camps. The most consistent explanation, at the time and in postwar years, was that Allied strategy focussed on the war rather than aid to inmates, however humane that aid might have been. Actually, the concentration camp at Buchenwald was bombed on Aug. 24, 1944. Bombs destroyed two war plants attached to the camp (a frequent arrangement for providing slave labor). An unknown number of prisoners were killed and injured.

Efforts by Quakers and U.S. Jewish organizations to get refugees into the United States resulted in the admission of 982 refugees (89 percent Jewish) in Aug. 1944. Under the supervision of the WAR RELOCATION AUTHORITY, which ran the internment camps for JAPANESE-AMERICANS, the European refugees were sent to a vacant U.S. Army camp in upstate New York. All of them signed documents promising that they would return to their countries after war. In Dec. 1945 President TRUMAN said they could all become immigrants.

The killing of Jews, which Prime Minister CHURCHILL called "probably the greatest and most horrible crime ever committed in the whole history of the world," inspired the Allied decision to treat Nazi leaders as war criminals.

In Allied countries, Jews were citizens who went to war.

England Thousands of British Jews as well as Jews from Palestine (including Eastern European immigrants) served in all of the British armed forces during the war. Some volunteered to parachute into German-occupied areas on clandestine missions. In Palestine, the JEWISH BRIGADE was raised and fought as part of the British Army in Italy in 1944–1945.

United States During the war an estimated 550,000 Jews, including women, fought in the U.S. armed forces. About 8,000 were killed in the war, with many more wounded. They fought in every theater, with scores of them flying bomber missions over Germany before U.S. ground forces first engaged German troops in 1943. Among those killed were Maj. Gen. Maurice Rose, a rabbi's son and commander of the 3rd Armored DIVISION, killed when he surrendered to German troops and was inadvertently shot by a nervous German soldier; and Sgt. Meyer Levine, bombardier in the B-17 FLYING FORTRESS flown by COLIN KELLY against Japanese ships off the Philippines. (He later lost his life while trying to save his crewmates when their bomber crashed in a storm off NEW GUINEA.)

During the war innumerable Jewish scientists—many immigrants from Nazi domination—helped develop the weapons that beat Germany and then Japan. Among them were Philip Abelson and ROBERT OPPENHEIMER, who worked on the ATOMIC BOMB, and Albert Einstein, who helped to sell the bomb program to President Roosevelt.

Soviet Union   Hundreds of thousands of Jews served in Soviet armed forces. Gen. Lev Dovator, a colorful Cossack commander, helped delay the German offensive at Rostov, after which he was killed in a CAVALRY charge. Soviet submarine commander Capt. 3rd rank Israel Fisanovich was highly decorated by the Soviet Navy and received the Navy Cross from the U.S. Navy for his successes against German shipping in the Arctic. (He was killed when a British bomber accidently sank his submarine.)

STALIN was personally anti-Semitic and lashed out at people he saw as his enemies simply because they were Jews. Stalin, however, did use Jews throughout his government and in the military. His commissar of foreign affairs from 1930 to 1939 was a Jew, MAKSIM LITVINOV; subsequently, Litvinov served as ambassador to the United States from 1941 to 1943, and then as deputy commissar for foreign affairs until 1946.

Sycophants and anti-Semites among his associates copied Stalin's own attitude, joining this with the old Czarist loathing of Jews. Occasionally, the government moved openly against Jews. Jewish newspapers were suppressed; the glorification of "Russian nationalism" played on old anti-Jewish feelings among Russians; Jews had harder times getting into influential positions. But as a pragmatist Stalin never unleashed anti-Semitism as a state policy, particularly during the war.

Jill

The principal Japanese Navy TORPEDO bomber during the last year of the war. The B6N *Tenzan* (Heavenly Mountain) aircraft (Allied code name

Jill) did not become operational until mid-1944, after which it was employed in large numbers as a torpedo aircraft and then as a KAMIKAZE. It was first used in combat in the battle of the MARIANAS, when almost all of the ninety-nine torpedo planes on the Japanese carriers were Jills, but they had no effect on the battle. The Jill replaced the aging B5N KATE in the naval torpedo and reconnaissance roles, being generally similar but with a much more powerful engine.

The Jill prototype flew in early 1941. Production was delayed by engineering defects and problems with carrier trails and it was belatedly placed in production. An improved engine was provided in the B6N2 variant. Production totaled 133 of the B6N1 (plus two prototypes) and 1,133 of the B6N2 variants. A B6N3 with a more powerful engine was developed but not produced.

With a conventional carrier aircraft design, the Jill was a low-wing, single-engine aircraft. It had a long, fully glazed cockpit. The lack of armor or leak-proof fuel tanks made the Jill as vulnerable to Allied fighters as was the Kate. Maximum speed was 299 mph for the B6N2 with a range of 1,085 miles in the torpedo role and 1,980 miles in the reconnaissance role.

It could carry an aerial torpedo or 1,764 pounds of BOMBS under the fuselage. Two 7.7-mm machine guns—one on a flexible mount in the rear cockpit and one in the ventral position—were fitted in the three-place aircraft.

Joan Eleanor

Nickname for a small (6½ inches long, 2¼ inches wide, and 1½ inches long) radio transmitter-receiver used by OFFICE OF STRATEGIC SERVICES agents. The 4-pound radio was invented by Navy Lt. Cmdr. Steve Simpson, an RCA engineer in civilian life, and DeWitt R. Goddard, another RCA engineer who was given a Navy commission to work with Simpson. The radio was battery-powered and transmitted to a larger unit, connected to a recorder, in a plane circling overhead. Because of its design and the wavelength on which it broadcast, the transmitter was difficult for German direction finders to detect. Joan Eleanor was the code name for the system, Eleanor being the unit on the ground and Joan (named for WAC Maj. Joan Marshall) the unit in the plane.

Jodl, *Generaloberst* Alfred (1890–1946)

Chief of the operations staff of the High Command of the German Armed Forces. HITLER's senior military adviser, Jodl was chief of the operations staff from 1939 to May 7, 1945, when he signed the German SURRENDER at Reims. Like his longtime army comrade *Generalfeldmarschall* WILHELM KEITEL, Jodl worshiped Hitler. Generals who detested the toadying of Jodl called him a *Nikesel,* a windup toy donkey that continually nodded its head. (Keitel was also called a *Nikesel.*) When Hitler increasingly concentrated on directing the war against the Soviet Union, Jodl became the overseer of warfare on the Western Front.

On the stand at the WAR CRIMES tribunal in Nuremberg, Jodl remained loyal to Hitler. "He came to power," Jodl said, "borne up by the love of the German people. He was almost overwhelmed by this love. . . ." Asked about the SS and CONCENTRATION CAMPS, Jodl replied that he knew "almost nothing." He was convicted of war crimes and hanged. In 1953 a West German de-Nazification court, decreeing that as a soldier Jodl had not broken any international law, posthumously exonerated him.

Johnny Walker

British 500-pound BOMB designed to create a large bubble of gas under a warship to "lift" the ship and "break its back." The bomb had a main charge of only about 100 pounds of Torpex/aluminum in a shaped charge and a hydrogen gas generation device to create the bubble.

It was delivered to RAF Bomber Command in early 1943 but was not used until the Sept. 1944 attack on the battleship *TIRPITZ.* On that raid seven LANCASTER bombers each carried twelve of the Johnny Walker bombs. They inflicted no damage and were never again used. The bombs that were dropped all had self-destruct mechanisms to prevent them from falling into German hands. Forty-three years after the attack Norwegians did find one of the bombs near the Kara Fjord.

The bomb was 72 inches long; little other data are available.

Johnson, Wing Comdr. James E. (1915—)

RAF ACE who led all Western fighter pilots against the Luftwaffe with thirty-eight kills. "Johnnie" Johnson participated in the effort to halt the Germans' advance in France in 1940 as leader of No. 610 Squadron. He rose to wing commander during the war, achieving most of his thirty-eight kills of German fighters in 1943–1944 while his units escorted U.S. bombers on daylight raids over Germany.

He also served in the Korean War and subsequently attained the rank of air vice marshal in the RAF. Johnson became a prolific writer on aviation subjects.

Johnson, Lt. Comdr. Lyndon B. (1908–1973)

A member of Congress since 1937, Johnson was a lieutenant commander in the Naval Reserve. In 1941 he told his constituents if a war started he "would be in the front line, in the trenches, in the mud and blood with your boys, helping to do that fighting." Soon after the Japanese attack on PEARL HARBOR, Johnson requested active duty and, after some delay, was sent to the West Coast on an inspection tour of shipyards and WAR PRODUCTION plants.

After four months on the West Coast, he was assigned to represent the Navy on a three-officer survey team sent by President ROOSEVELT to report on the war in the Southwest Pacific. He and the other two officers left on May 7, 1942, for Australia. On June 6, they flew to Garbutt Field in northern Queensland, headquarters of the 22nd Bomb GROUP, and flew as passengers on three of the B-26 MARAUDER bombers attacking a Japanese air base on the northeastern coast of NEW GUINEA.

During an attack on the bombers by Japanese ZEROS, Johnson was "just as calm as if we were on a sightseeing tour," a crewman later reported. One of the other two inspection officers was on a plane that was shot down. Johnson returned unscathed and received the Silver Star directly from Gen. DOUGLAS MACARTHUR.

On July 9, 1942, President Roosevelt ordered all CONGRESSMEN in the armed services to return to Congress. Eight members of Congress were then on active duty. Four resigned from Congress and remained in the armed services. Four, including Johnson, resigned from the armed forces.

Johst, Hanns (1890—1978)

German novelist and playwright. Johst served as president of the equivalent of a writers' guild in the THIRD REICH. He was a leader in setting the NAZI stamp of approval on German art and culture. The protagonist of his most famous novel, *Schlageter,* proclaimed: "When I hear the word culture, I reach for the safety-catch of my revolver."

Joint Board

Predecessor of the U.S. JOINT CHIEFS OF STAFF (JCS). Established in 1903 in the aftermath of the Spanish-American War, it was reorganized in 1919 and served through 1941 as the principal coordinating agency of the U.S. Army and Navy. The Board considered all matters that required cooperation between the two services.

It had no executive functions or command authority (as did the JCS), and until 1939 reported to the secretary of war and secretary of the Navy. In the 1919 changes a Joint Planning Committee was established to assist the board and develop papers on specific issues. On July 5, 1939, President ROOSEVELT placed the Joint Board under his immediate "supervision and direction."

The Board's membership consisted of six members: the Army Chief of Staff and Chief of Naval Operations, their principal deputies, and the chiefs of their War Plans Divisions.

Joint Chiefs of Staff

The executive body for the direction of U.S. participation in the war. President ROOSEVELT and Prime Minister CHURCHILL decided at their AR-CADIA CONFERENCE in Washington in Dec. 1941– Jan. 1942 to create the Anglo-American COM-BINED CHIEFS OF STAFF. The British component already existed as the CHIEFS OF STAFF, which consisted of the heads of the British services. There was no comparable U.S. body of senior military officers.

Without specific executive action or congressio-

nal legislation, the senior U.S. military officers met as a body for the first time with their British colleagues to form the *Combined Chiefs of Staff* on Jan. 23, 1942. At the time the term *Joint Chiefs of Staff* (JCS) was used for the Americans although several members were not chiefs of their services. The JCS initially consisted of:

Adm. HAROLD R. STARK, Chief of Naval Operations

Gen. GEORGE C. MARSHALL, Chief of Staff, Army

Adm. ERNEST J. KING, Commander in Chief U.S. FLEET

Lt. Gen. HENRY H. ARNOLD, Chief of the Army Air Forces

In March 1942 Lt. Gen. Arnold became commanding general Army Air Forces and Adm. Stark was ordered to London with Adm. King becoming the only Navy representative in the JCS. In July 1942 retired Adm. WILLIAM D. LEAHY was appointed Chief of Staff to the Commander in Chief (Roosevelt) and became de facto chairman of the JCS. Thus, the JCS membership stabilized at four members for the remainder of the war—Leahy, Marshall, King, and Arnold.

(The first official chairman of the JCS was Gen. of the Army OMAR BRADLEY who assumed that position in 1950.)

The JCS served as both the U.S. component of the Combined Chiefs of Staff and as the executive for U.S. military operations.

Joint Psychological Warfare Committee

U.S. intelligence organization. The committee consisted of representatives of the Army, Navy, State Department, Board of Economic Warfare, OFFICE OF WAR INFORMATION, and the OFFICE OF STRATEGIC SERVICES.

Jones, Prof. R. V. (1911—)

British scientist who, WINSTON CHURCHILL said, "did more to save us from disaster than many [scientists] who are glittering with trinkets," commenting on Jones' clear-cut approach to scientific intelligence. Jones was educated at Oxford under FREDERICK LINDEMANN, Churchill's scientific adviser. From 1939 to 1946 Jones was head of scien-

Top U.S. military commanders: from left to right, Gen. Henry H. Arnold, Chief of the Army Air Forces; Gen. Dwight D. Eisenhower, Supreme Allied Commander in Europe (not a member of the Joint Chiefs of Staff); Adm. Ernest J. King, Commander in Chief, U.S. Fleet and Chief of Naval Operations; and Gen. George C. Marshall, Army Chief of Staff. *(Imperial War Museum)*

tific intelligence on the Air Staff and scientific adviser to MI6 Secret Intelligence Service. He was cited especially for his efforts to counter German RADAR, the V-1 BUZZ BOMB, and the V-2 MISSILE.

After the war he was personally decorated by President TRUMAN as well as by the British government.

Joyce, William (1906–1946)

A British subject, known as "Lord Haw-Haw," who broadcast propaganda to England from Germany. Joyce got his nickname from British listeners because he used an assumed aristocratic accent to deliver his pro-Nazi broadsides. A member of Sir Oswald Mosley's British Union of Fascists, he went to Germany in 1939 and became one of Propaganda Minister JOSEPH GOEBBELS's radio stars. Joyce, born in Brooklyn, N.Y., to an English mother and Irish-American father, had moved to Great Britain with his family in 1921. He claimed to be an American citizen when he was put on trial for treason in London's Old Bailey after the war. The court held that as the holder of a British passport he was a subject of the Crown. He was found guilty and executed on Jan. 3, 1946.

JRM Mars

The Mars flying boats were the world's largest operational seaplanes and the largest U.S. Navy aircraft of the war era. They were ordered as patrol bombers but served as long-range transports and aerial ambulances. The prototype XPB2M-1R aircraft was delivered to the Navy in Nov. 1943 and that month, carrying 13,000 pounds of cargo, flew from Patuxent River, Md., to Natal, Brazil, a nonstop flight of 4,375 miles in twenty-eight and a half hours. The designation of production aircraft was changed from XPB2M-1R to JRM-1, reflecting the shift to the utility/cargo role. (The "R" in XPB2M-1R indicated transport; the name was changed to JRM-1 to add the "J," which indicated utility.) Twenty additional JRM-1 aircraft were ordered in Jan. 1945 but only five were built plus a single enlarged JRM-2, with deliveries beginning in 1945. The JRMs were given "Mars" names, such as Caroline Mars (for the CAROLINE ISLANDS).

The prototype XPB2M-1 was ordered in 1938; it was "launched" on Nov. 8, 1941, and made its first flight on July 3, 1942. It was a graceful-looking, high-wing, four-engine aircraft. The flying boat, with large fixed stabilizing floats under the wings, and large twin tail fins with oval vertical surfaces. It was to carry several tons of bombs or four aerial TORPEDOES, and defensive gun turrets were to have been fitted. The subsequent JRM production aircraft had single tail fins with the gun positions faired over. The XPB2M had a gross weight of 140,000 pounds and the JRMs 145,000 pounds. The aircraft could carry 34 tons of cargo or 132 passengers or eighty-four litters plus a medical team.

The XPB2M-1R was credited with a maximum speed of 221 mph and a range of 4,945 miles. It was flown by a crew of eleven.

(In 1942–1943 the Navy acquired three Boeing four-engine "Clipper" flying boats from the Army and two from Pan American Airways; They served the Navy with their commercial designation B-314. Two other "Clippers" acquired by the Navy from Pan Am were the two surviving Martin four-engine flying boats, which were known by the designation M-130 in naval service.)

Ju 52

German tri-motor transport that was surpassed only by the U.S. C-47 SKYTRAIN/DAKOTA (DC-3) in popularity and importance among transport aircraft of the war. Developed as a transport, the aircraft was also employed as a bomber with German and Nationalist forces in the SPANISH CIVIL WAR (1936–1939). The aircraft's historic role in that conflict occurred in late July 1936 when twenty German Ju 52s were used to ferry troops of Gen. FRANCISCO FRANCO from Morocco to Spain, overflying Republican warships that would have intercepted the troops had they gone by sea.

When Germany went to war in Sept. 1939 the Luftwaffe had 552 transport aircraft of which 547 were Ju 52s! The aircraft, which flew on every front, were vital to the German assaults on Norway, Denmark, Holland, and CRETE, and for operations on the EASTERN FRONT as well as in North Africa. During the war the Ju 52 served as a troop and paratroop transport, medical evacuation aircraft, cargo carrier, and glider tug.

The Ju 52 was a tri-motor, low-wing aircraft with a relatively large cargo compartment. The fuselage was made of corrugated duralumin skin. It had a fixed, tail-sitting undercarriage. When employed as

an airliner the Ju 52 could carry fifteen to seventeen passengers; as a troop carrier it could carry twenty soldiers and their equipment.

The first Junkers-produced Ju 52 flew on Oct. 13, 1930, as a single-engine transport. A succession of single- and then tri-motor development aircraft followed, some fitted with skis and floats. The first definitive tri-motor aircraft flew in April 1932 with production following for commercial use by several nations. The first military version was delivered in 1934, intended for use as a bomber with a four-man crew, up to four defensive machine guns, and a BOMB load of 3,307 pounds. During 1934–1935, 450 aircraft were delivered to the German Air Force; production in Germany totaled 4,845 aircraft. After the war production continued in Spain and France, where 170 and some 400 were built, respectively; the aircraft was in commercial operation in several countries after the war and was flown by the French Air Force in the Indochina War.

The aircraft was affectionately referred to by pilots and troops as "Auntie Ju" and "Iron Annie."

The Ju 52 had a maximum speed of 168 mph with a cruise speed of 124 mph. Normal range was 568 miles with a maximum of just over 800 miles.

Ju 87 *Stuka*

The backbone of German air support for the BLITZKRIEG assaults against Poland, France, and the Soviet Union. The Ju 87 *Stuka*, a key factor in German ground victories, was also an effective anti-shipping aircraft. Aviation historian William Green called the *Stuka* "an evil-looking machine, with something of the predatory bird in its ugly contours—its radiator bath and fixed, spatted undercarriage resembling gaping jaws and extended talons. . . ." (*Stuka* was a derivation of *Sturzkampfflugzeug,* a term descriptive of all dive bombers.)

Ju 87 deliveries to Luftwaffe squadrons began in the spring of 1937. Late that year Ju 87s began to arrive in Spain to support the Nationalist forces in the SPANISH CIVIL WAR. Despite relatively poor performance, the Ju 87 was effective against both ground targets and shipping. The Ju 87 saw combat on every front on which the Germans fought during the war. Designed to serve as "long-range artillery" to support the German Army, the Ju 87's bombing accuracy was less than 30 yards. However, the aircraft's effectiveness presupposed control of the air and when that could not be guaranteed by German fighters, the slow, lightly armed Ju 87 was extremely vulnerable to interception.

In the May 1940 assault on Holland and France, the Ju 87 devastated the city of ROTTERDAM. The plane was employed in the BATTLE OF BRITAIN beginning in July 1940, with some 280 Ju 87s available for strikes on Britain. But the *Stuka* was withdrawn on Aug. 19 following heavy losses from RAF fighters. (For example, on Aug. 17 of the eighty-five Ju 87s attacking targets in Britain, twenty-six were shot down and another fourteen were damaged). Subsequently, the aircraft was flown extensively in the Mediterranean and on the EASTERN FRONT, again with great success. Flying in the anti-shipping role, the Ju 87 was able to heavily damage two British aircraft carriers in the Mediterranean, and to sink and damage many other ships. (The only dive bombers to surpass the Ju 87's effectiveness in attacking warships were the U.S. SBD DAUNTLESS and the Japanese VAL.) Late in the European War the Allied control of the air over Germany forced the employment of the Ju 87 as a night bomber.

The Ju 87 was the product of the Junkers firm, pushed into service by *Generaloberst* ERNST UDET, who in 1931 had observed the dive-bombing technique being developed by the U.S. Navy. Encouraged by HERMANN GÖRING, the Reich minister for aviation, Udet demonstrated dive bombing in Germany. By the end of 1935 the Junkers firm had produced the prototype Ju 87, which was flight-tested late that same year. After its combat introduction in Spain, Göring ordered production accelerated and through 1944 more than 5,000 aircraft were produced. Italy, Rumania, Hungary, and Bulgaria also flew the Ju 87 during the war.

The single-engine plane had inverted gull-shaped wings, an in-line, water-cooled engine, and large, fixed landing gear with "spats" covers. BOMBS were carried under the wings and fuselage, and the cockpit held a pilot and radio operator, the latter firing a machine gun to protect the rear of the plane when in a dive. In production aircraft an autopilot was fitted to take control if the pilot blacked out during a dive. The Germans found that when dive bombers pushed over into their dive they had a terrifying effect on troops; Ernst Udet conceived the idea of increasing the natural howling of the dive by attaching sirens to the undercarriage. The plane was considered easy to fly and very popular with its pilots and the troops they supported.

The Ju 87C variant had upward-folding outer wing panels, a tail hook, and other features for use from the never-finished aircraft carrier *GRAF ZEPPELIN*. The Ju 87D-3 was experimentally fitted with twin pods on its wing, each for carrying two agents who were to be dropped behind enemy lines; despite extensive tests, this scheme was not adopted.

Maximum speed of the Ju 87D model was 255 mph; cruising speed was 198 mph. Range with a 3,960-pound bomb load was 620 miles; with maximum fuel and a token bomb load the aircraft could fly almost double that distance. A higher-performance variant, the Ju 187 with a remote-controlled gun turret and retracting undercarriage was under development when the war ended. The two-seat Ju 87 had two fixed, forward-firing 7.9-mm machine guns and a twin 7.9-mm machine gun on a flexible mount in the rear cockpit. For short-range missions the Ju 87 could carry one 3,970-pound bomb or a variety of lesser weapons or two under-wing pods with multiple machine guns or paired 20-mm cannon.

Ju 88

Highly versatile German medium bomber, in many respects similar to the British MOSQUITO. The twin-engine Ju 88, produced in greater numbers than any other German bomber, was flown in the bomber, antitank, TORPEDO, day- and night-fighter, photo-reconnaissance, and training roles. They were also used to carry ME 109 and FW 190 fighters on *Huckepack* (pick-a-back) bombing missions.

Following a rapid development, the first Ju 88s entered Luftwaffe service early in 1939 as high-speed bombers. These planes participated in virtually all German aerial campaigns. They were used extensively in the BATTLE OF BRITAIN but suffered heavy losses in the daylight raids. Bomber and then specialized variants were produced into 1945.

The pick-a-back concept, suggested as early as 1941, provided for a high-performance fighter to be mounted atop an unmanned, BOMB-laden Ju 88.

The planes were to take off in tandem and, upon reaching the target, the Ju 88 would be released and guided to its target by the fighter, which then would return to base. (The United States had a similar program called APHRODITE.) The first pick-a-back or *Mistel* (Mistletoe) mission was flown on June 24, 1944, but the bomber was released prematurely when a Mosquito night fighter appeared on the scene. Subsequent missions were flown against Allied shipping but without significant effect. A variation of the *Mistel* concept was the *Fuhrüngsmaschine,* with a long-range reconnaissance Ju 88H carrying an Fw 190 fighter that would be launched if the recce aircraft were attacked and then, after engaging the enemy plane, return to base independently.

The Junker's bomber was developed in response to a 1935 Air Ministry requirement and the prototype Ju 88V1 flew on Dec. 21, 1936, just eleven months after design work had commenced. Additional prototypes and preproduction models followed, with changes being made in engines and wingspan as well as other features. Variant development continued into 1945. Total production was about 9,000 bomber variants and about 6,000 non-bombers, a total of 14,676 production aircraft plus prototypes being built.

The twin-engine aircraft had low-mounted wings with the radial-engine nacelles almost even with the nose. Variants had in-line and radial engines, with the main landing gear fully retracting into the nacelles. The Ju 88 featured a large glazed cockpit and nose, which afforded the pilot excellent visibility. Some of the fighter variants had a solid nose, with those aircraft retaining a bomb bay that could carry weapons or additional fuel; RADAR was fitted in the night fighters. The recce variants had fuel and cameras in the bomb bay and additional fuel in underwing drop tanks. The Ju 88P antitank variant had tank-busting cannon armament; the Ju 88P-1 variant had a 75-mm gun with a barrel that projected some six feet ahead of the aircraft; other Ju 88P models had two 37-mm cannon.

The early Ju 88A4 bombers had a maximum speed of 273 mph and a range of 1,550 miles. They could carry up to 3,960 pounds of bombs in their internal bay and for short, overload fights another 2,205 pounds of bombs could be carried under the wings. The bombers' defensive armament consisted of several 20-mm cannon and 13-mm and 7.9-mm machine guns; the bomber variants normally had a crew of four—pilot, copilot/bombardier, radio operator/gunner, and flight engineer/gunner.

The first fighter variant to enter production was the Ju 88C. The C-6 model had a top speed of 311 mph and was credited with a range of 2,130 miles. Armament consisted of three 20-mm cannon in the nose and several machine guns. The fighters flew with a crew of three, with a fourth added to night fighters that entered service in 1944.

Ju 188

An improved and "stretched" version of the JU 88 high-speed bomber. Outwardly resembling its predecessor, the later Junkers aircraft was larger and slightly faster (325 mph for the Ju 188A-1), but carried a slightly smaller BOMB load; the high-speed, high-altitude Ju 88S variant had a service ceiling of 38,000 feet and a speed of almost 430 mph, and, like other high-performance aircraft, was unarmed. The Ju 188 was in service from 1942 with just over 1,000 aircraft produced.

Ju 290

German maritime patrol and transport aircraft. The Ju 290 was a progressive development of the prewar Ju 90 civil transport. It was also proposed as a heavy bomber and as successor to the FW 200 CONDOR maritime patrol aircraft. However, the Ju 290 was underpowered for the heavy bomber role and was instead produced in transport and maritime variants.

As a transport the Ju 290 could carry about forty armed troops or cargo. An unusual Ju 290 transport feature was a hydraulically powered loading ramp that could be lowered from the after fuselage to permit troops and small vehicles to be rapidly loaded and unloaded. It could also be used for dropping heavy equipment by parachute. Early transport aircraft as well as Ju 90s were pressed into service to supply the German army at STALINGRAD in Jan. 1943. Subsequently, Ju 290 transports flew throughout the Mediterranean.

The first maritime patrol variant (Ju 290A-2) flew in the summer of 1943, being developed as a replacement for the vulnerable Fw 200C. These planes were heavily armed with two hydraulic dorsal turrets, each mounting a 20-mm cannon plus five other 20-mm guns and one 13-mm machine gun. For attacking Allied shipping they could carry two Hs 293 or two FRITZ-X GUIDED MISSILES. Surface-search FuG 200 RADAR was fitted in these aircraft.

Beginning in Oct. 1943, the maritime patrol variants flew searches over the Atlantic to guide U-BOATS to Allied CONVOYS; they were also operational over the Mediterranean. Following the NORMANDY INVASION, the aircraft based in France were withdrawn from the maritime role in Aug. 1944 and allocated to transport duties, especially dropping agents behind enemy lines.

Three of these aircraft, stripped of armor and guns, were fitted with additional fuel tanks and used to fly high-priority cargo from Odessa and Mielec nonstop to and from Japanese-occupied Manchuria. One of several ultra-long-range recce aircraft of the Ju 290A-9 series was fitted as a fifty-seat transport for use by HITLER, but was never used by the German leader; that plane was flown to Spain on April 26, 1945 (and later used by the Spanish Air Force).

Several further developments of the Ju 290 were started but none was produced. These included the Ju 290D and E model long-range bombers; the latter was to have an internal BOMB bay for a weapons load of 40,572 pounds.

Ju 90 aircraft were lengthened, refitted, and armed as a prototype for the military Ju 290 program. The first of the newly built Ju 290A models flew in Aug. 1942.

The Ju 290 had a conventional bomber configuration with a mid-wing mounting four radial engines and a twin-tail arrangement. The Ju 290A-5 maritime aircraft's top speed was 273 mph carrying two missiles; maximum range was 3,820 miles.

Ju 390

German trans-Atlantic bomber. The Junkers bomber was a scaled-up derivative of the JU 290, a four-engine aircraft whose design dated back to early 1935. The larger aircraft was labeled the "Ural bomber" because it was conceived for strategic bombing missions deep in the Soviet Union. The larger Ju 390 was intended for long-range recon-

naissance or bombing missions *against the United States* from bases in Europe.

The second Ju 390 prototype began a flight-test program in October 1943. The aircraft was delivered to Mont de Marsan, south of Bordeaux, France, in Jan. 1944 for operational evaluation by *Fernaufklärungs-Gruppe* (long-range reconnaissance group) 5. After a few trial flights this aircraft—with fuel for a thirty-two-hour mission—flew across the Atlantic to a point some twelve miles off the U.S. coast, north of New York City, and returned successfully to its base.

Only one other prototype was completed, being first flown in Aug. 1943. These were the largest aircraft ever built in Germany. (Only the Me 323 six-engine powered GLIDER had a greater wingspan than the Ju 390.) A third prototype Ju 390 was not finished, and Japanese efforts to produce a modified Ju 390 under license did not come to fruition. Passenger versions of the four-engine Ju 90/290 began service in 1937. The aircraft was used for cargo and troop carrying during the war by the Luftwaffe; some were fitted with defensive machine guns. An ocean reconnaissance version to succeed the FW 200 CONDOR was flown in prototype form in 1943 and about thirty actually became operational; a large number were unfinished when the war ended.

The six-engine Ju 390 was a large, low-wing aircraft with the leading edges of the outer wing panel swept back. It had a twin-fin tail and a massive landing gear with four twin-wheel main units and a tail wheel. Fitted with a FuG 200 search RADAR, the aircraft had a defensive armament of two hydraulically operated dorsal turrets, each with a single 20-mm cannon; two more cannon mounted in the nose and tail; and three single 13-mm machine guns amidships. Later models were to have quad 13-mm gun turrets in the nose and tail. In the bomber role four antiship missiles or a total of 15,872 pounds of BOMBS were to be carried under the wings.

The production bomber-reconnaissance Ju 390A aircraft was to have had a maximum speed of 314 mph without external weapons, with a cruising speed of 222 mph and a range of 6,000 miles in the reconnaissance role. With 4,255 pounds of bombs the range was to be 5,750 miles—from Europe to New York and return. Fully loaded, these aircraft would weigh 166,450 pounds.

Jubilee

Code name for British-Canadian raid on DIEPPE, France, Aug. 1942; the raid was originally given the code name Rutter.

Judy

The Japanese D4Y *Suisei* (Comet) was intended as a replacement for the highly successful D3A VAL dive bomber. Produced in substantial numbers late in the war, the aircraft—given the Allied code name Judy—was employed largely for KAMIKAZE attacks. The Judy entered naval service in 1942.

At the battle of MIDWAY the carrier *Soryu* had two of the aircraft embarked to serve as long-range scouts; the failure of scouting planes was a major factor in the Japanese defeat at Midway. Not until the June 1944 battle of the MARIANAS were significant numbers of the aircraft available; ninety-nine Judy dive bombers were embarked in the Japanese carriers in that engagement, but their accomplishments were nil. Subsequently the available aircraft were used in suicide attacks.

A product of the Yokosuka Naval Air depot, the Judy first flew in Dec. 1940. A total of 2,038 aircraft were produced during the war at Yokosuka and by the Aichi firm. These included 296 of the D4Y4 "suiciders" (see below).

A low-wing aircraft with fully retractable landing gear (the Val had a fixed undercarriage), the Judy was unusual in being produced with both in-line and radial engines. The first production variant was the D4Y1 Model 11 powered by a license-built German DB 600 in-line engine. But maintenance problems and slow production of that liquid-cooled engine led to the D4Y2 Model 22 being produced with a more-powerful radial engine. The major production model was the D4Y3 Model 33 fitted with a radial engine while the D4Y4 was a specialized single-seat, kamikaze variant. A few earlier aircraft were modified as night fighters, with 20-mm cannon and air-to-air ROCKETS, but lacking RADAR, they had limited success. The Judy had neither armor for the crew nor protected fuel tanks, making it highly vulnerable to Allied fighters—that could catch up with it.

The D4Y3 was a 350-mph aircraft with a range of 945 miles. Armament consisted of two 7.7-mm machine guns and a rear-firing flexible 7.9-mm gun, with up to 1,234 pounds of BOMBS being carried in the bomb bay (1,102 pounds) and externally. A two-man crew flew the aircraft.

July 20 Plot

A conspiracy to assassinate HITLER. On July 20, 1944, at a conference Hitler called at his field headquarters, the WOLF'S LAIR, in Rastenburg, a bomb exploded, killing one person and mortally wounding three others. Because an officer had casually moved the briefcase containing the bomb, the explosion was deflected by the heavy wooden table enough to save Hitler, although his hair was singed and his hearing was temporarily impaired. Hours later, Hitler met Italian leader BENITO MUSSOLINI, who called Hitler's escape "a miracle."

The plotters included several politicians and senior active-duty and retired officers of the Army and the *ABWEHR*. ERWIN ROMMEL, one of three field marshals implicated in the plot, did not take part in the assassination attempt. The man who placed the briefcase bomb was *Oberst* Claus Schenk, Count VON STAUFFENBERG, an officer who had lost his left hand and fingers on his right hand fighting in Tunisia. (He had to use tongs to activate the bomb.)

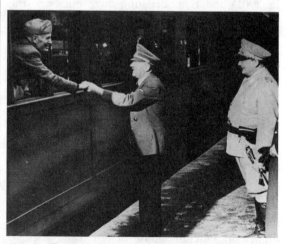

Shortly after the July 20, 1944, attempt on his life, Hitler welcomes Benito Mussolini while a beaming Hermann Göring looks on. Hitler, whose hearing and right arm were affected by the blast, extends his left hand to Mussolini. *(German Army via Imperial War Museum)*

Stauffenberg departed from Hitler's headquarters before the bomb exploded and, assuming that Hitler was dead, flew to BERLIN, which the plotters had hoped to seize with Home (Replacement) Army troops. The nominal leader of the plotters, General Ludwig Beck, former head of the German General Staff, whose opposition to Hitler went back to 1938, was to become the head of the provisional government. But when news of Hitler's survival reached Berlin, loyal Army officers began rounding up the conspirators. By midnight, Stauffenberg had been shot by a firing squad and Beck, after bungling his suicide, was killed by a coup de grace from a sergeant's gun.

In a rampage of vengeance, some 7,000 suspected plotters were rounded up. Many turncoats, seeing the plot fail, tried to betray the cause or plead innocence. Most of them were also arrested and put to death. The conspirators, Hitler decreed, "must be hanged like cattle." The first eight tried were strung up on meat hooks in nooses of piano wire, and a movie, for Hitler's viewing, was made of their final agony. About 200 accused plotters were executed. Thousands of friends and relatives were sent to CONCENTRATION CAMPS.

An earlier attempt on Hitler's life, in March 1943, also failed when a bomb, disguised as a package containing bottles of brandy, failed to explode. This attempt, like another failure shortly afterward, went undetected at the time. The plotters were hampered by Hitler's extremely successful security maneuvers. "The only preventive measure one can take," he once said, "is to live irregularly—to walk, to drive, and to travel at irregular times and unexpectedly. . . ."

The July 1944 attempt was the last of many assassination attempts engineered by the conspirators, some of whom had been plotting for years to overthrow Hitler, achieve a separate peace with the Americans and British, and establish a non-NAZI government in Germany. The July bomb (and those used in at least two previous attempts) were British-made. The *Abwehr* had confiscated many bombs over the years and they found their way to the plotters. Such bombs, dropped by RAF planes, had been intended for use for assassinations by GUERRILLAS—not by German army officers.

Juno

(1) German code name for offensive operations against British forces in Norway in June 1940; (2) Allied code name for Courseulles beach in the NORMANDY INVASION used by Canadian 3rd Division.

Jupiter

Code name for planned British invasion of northern Norway.

Justice, Military

Men and WOMEN entering the service during the war learned that putting on a uniform also meant living under a set of laws that differed considerably from the laws of civilian life. As an old Army saying put it, "There's music and there's *military* music; there's justice and there's *military* justice."

Members of the military charged with violation of regulations were tried under a legal system that used a graduated procedure for meting out justice. The system put the accused "under court-martial jurisdiction," but relatively few were actually court-martialed. Enlisted men and women in the Army or AAF charged with minor offenses went before their own officers for "company punishment"; sailors went before their commanding officer's "captain's mast." More serious charges rated trial by court-martial, a three-stage system with the highest, a general court-martial, having the power to impose life sentences and even the death penalty. More than 90 percent of those who were court-martialed were enlisted men.

Courts-martial at any level were rare. The number of soldiers tried by court-martial in World War II averages 3 out of 1,000, compared to a rate of about 9 out of 1,000 in World War I. General courts-martial were even rarer.

Existing records on World War II military justice are incomplete. Unpublished historical records of the office of the Judge Advocate General (JAG) contain remarkably thorough information on justice in the European theater of operations but little on the Pacific theater of operations. The records give a good picture of wartime military history, however, because the overwhelming majority of courts-martial took place in the European theater, which had far more U.S. troops in 1943–1945 than the Pacific theater. Crimes against civilians and other serious crimes were also more prevalent in the European theater, where contact with civilians was much more likely.

Thus, even though the figures used below are from only one of the two major theaters of war, they reflect wartime military justice. The records also reflect the SEGREGATION that prevailed in the armed services during the war, for statistics were often broken down by race, since blacks and whites were segregated. When there is no numerical breakdown by race, a history notes, "In studying these figures, a rule-of-thumb measurement to be kept in mind is that approximately 10 percent of the troops in the Theater were Negroes."

Between Jan. 26, 1942, and May 31, 1945, a total of 4,182,263 men and three women (in the WAC) in the European theater came under courtmartial jurisdiction; only 22,214 went before a general court-martial. Of them, 2,123 were acquitted. The 16,987 others got sentences that included death, dismissal, or dishonorable discharge. (The statistics at this point do not differentiate between men and women, but the indications are that the WAC enlisted woman and the two WAC officers did not come before general courts-martial.)

For the 16,987 convicted, there was still an appeal. The "convening authority" of a court-martial automatically reviewed all sentences of death and most long-term sentences. The convening authority suspended the discharges of 11,893, sending 1,109 back to duty and the rest to "disciplinary training centers." Of those, 7,249 eventually were restored to duty. The remaining 2,149 went to federal penitentiaries.

Of 443 death sentences, 108 were confirmed by the convening authority and sent to the JAG branch office that had been established in May 1942 at Cheltenham, Gloucestershire, England. In Oct. 1944 the branch office, as it was simply called, moved to Paris. The Branch Office was the last reviewing entity, since the WAR DEPARTMENT did not accept appeals for clemency. The policy was to end the appeals process with the theater commander. Thus, it was Gen. DWIGHT D. EISENHOWER, Supreme Allied Commander, not the secretary of war, who ultimately decided the fate of men in the European theater condemned to death.

The first case involving the death penalty occurred in Dec. 1942 when an American private on guard duty at an ordnance depot in Northamptonshire, England, got into an argument with a second lieutenant and shot him, killing him instantly. The private was sentenced to death, and on March 12, 1943, became the first U.S. soldier to be executed in Shepton Mallet, a British prison, built in 1625–1627. Shepton Mallet, closed after World War I, was reopened for World War II and transferred to American authorities for U.S. military prisoners in mid-1942. (In the movie *The Dirty Dozen* Shepton Mallet was the model for the prison from which hard-core soldier criminals were recruited for hazardous operations.)

The protocol for executing U.S. servicemen in England called for following British practices. The official Home Office executioner, an expert hangman, performed thirteen of the hangings; his uncle performed the other four. (At an American execution, the official hangman recalled, "you could be sure of the best running buffet and unlimited canned beer.") Two soldiers were sentenced to "execution by musketry"—the firing squad—which traditionally may be ordered if the victim was a fellow soldier. According to an exhaustive study by the British publication *After the Battle,* of the nineteen U.S. servicemen executed in England, eleven were executed for murder and eight for rape.

Courts-martial for murders and rapes in England were held, whenever possible, in the community where the crimes were committed. In France, soldiers sentenced to death for capital crimes committed against civilians were hanged in the villages where the crimes were committed.

The official JAG summary of executions in the European theater segregates the executions by crime and race and uses the then-current term "colored." The summary follows:

	TOTAL	MURDERS	RAPE	MURDER/ RAPE	DESERTION
White	15	6	4	4	1
Colored	55	22	25	8	0

The single execution for desertion (see Pvt. EDDIE D. SLOVIK) was the first U.S. military execution for a battlefield offense since the Civil War.

The execution total in the European theater,

then, is 140. The U.S. Army Judiciary Operations Office has drawn together all of the execution cases involving U.S. forces in all theaters in World War II; this total (shown below with a comparison with World War I) puts the total at 142, indicating that there were two executions in the Pacific theater.

	RAPE	RAPE/ MURDER	MURDER	MURDER/ MUTINY	DESERTION
WWII	51	18	72	0	1
WWI	11	3	2	19	0

Although there are discrepancies in the two reports about punishment for rape, rapists rarely were handled in the way Gen. GEORGE S. PATTON promised on the eve of the Allied NORTH AFRICA INVASION. To his forces assigned to the Morocco phase of the landing, Patton said simply: "Any American servicemen molesting a Moroccan woman will be shot." There were 904 recorded courts-martial for rape in the European theater; 461 men were found guilty. As shown above, executions for rape in that theater totaled twenty-nine.

According to wartime JAG dogma, imprisonment was to be kept to a minimum, since the aim was not pure justice but keeping as many men as possible in combat. "Confinement is a contribution to the enemy," a JAG report said, "since it not only immobilizes the confined soldiers as an effective [sic], but also immobilizes other soldiers to guard and feed him."

One "suggested solution," according to JAG records, was to "create disciplinary detachments in combat units so that recalcitrants will perform the most arduous duties while sharing the dangers encountered by their comrades. Only the worst criminals will be confined in military prisons during an active campaign."

Generally, JAG separated from other prisoners those convicted of murder, manslaughter, arson, robbery, rape, sodomy (see HOMOSEXUALS), mayhem, or larceny of property worth $50 or more. The most frequently committed offense was Absence Without Leave—AWOL. Most AWOLs were unmarried draftees who had not graduated from high school and who had earned low marks on the ARMY GENERAL CLASSIFICATION TEST. Volunteers with more than two years of Army service, for exam-

ple, accounted for only 22 percent of the AWOL cases. About 30 percent of the men in the wartime Army were married; they accounted for 43 percent of the AWOLs when the records of married and unmarried men were compared.

The leading offenses in the European Theater:

CRIME	NUMBER ACCUSED	FOUND GUILTY	GUILTY OF LESSER OFFENSE
AWOL	5,984	5,634	0
Desertion	4,072	2,930	990
Murder*	446	206	128
Rape**	904	461	67
Striking officer	197	170	9
Drawing weapon against officer	196	152	5
Plundering and pillage***	34	16	5

*Nationality of victims: 214 Americans, 109 Allied nationals, 107 enemy nationals.
**Nationality of victims: 484 German, 125 French, 101 English.
***Does not include the extraordinary railroad pillaging cases; see below.

Wholesale pillaging of supply trains presented the Army with an uncommon phenomenon in the military—organized crime. The Great Trains Robberies Case strained the Army's traditional justice system and inspired a novel solution: combat for criminals.

Systematic looting of supply trains in France plagued logistics officers. So brazen were the looters that they set up a BLACK MARKET at a railroad yard and made it, in the words of investigators, "a public market place." The black marketeers were stealing and selling cigarettes, shoes, RATIONS, and whatever else they could steal. The trains, according to investigators, were being "ravaged as though they had been in the hands of bandits."

The railroad ring forced the Army to put armed guards on trains and diverted personnel and equipment, adding another burden to the strained logistical system. The robberies led to the placing of undercover agents from the Army Criminal Investigation Division (CID) in the railway operating BATTALIONS that were running Army trains between Dreux and PARIS.

On Nov. 26, 1944—during an ARTILLERY ammunition shortage at the front—the CID agents swooped down on suspects, arresting 400 enlisted men and officers on charges of diverting essential war supplies. The Army sent 115 of the accused to training for transfer to combat units. Of the 190 enlisted men tried, seventeen were convicted. Three officers were convicted and five, including the battalion commander, were acquitted. Army prosecutors hit on the idea of "petitions for clemency" in which an accused man agreed to stoppages of their pay—and volunteered for combat. The petitions sent 149 additional men into combat.

Eisenhower used a similar technique as a way to find more infantrymen to replace those who had been killed or wounded. He promised a pardon and a clean record to anyone under court-martial who would volunteer to fight. Reportedly, every soldier facing fifteen years or more at hard labor volunteered.

K (Operation)

Operation K was the second Japanese air attack on PEARL HARBOR. The raid was flown by H8K1 EMILY flying boats on the night of March 4–5, 1942; it was the operational debut for the four-engine flying boats.

The planes were based at Jaliut atoll in the MARSHALL ISLANDS, some 2,300 miles from Pearl Harbor. The two planes, each carrying a ton of BOMBS, were refueled by Japanese submarines at French Frigate Shoals, 650 miles northwest of Pearl Harbor. One Japanese submarine had served as a radio beacon between Jaliut and the French Frigate Shoals, another was standing off Oahu to rescue the crews if the planes came down at sea after the attack, and a third (which was sunk before the raid) was to provide weather reports from the target area.

They arrived over Oahu at 1 A.M. on March 5 and bombed "blindly" through a low overcast. Their target was the naval base at Pearl Harbor. One plane's bombs fell in the sea and the four bombs from the second plane struck near Punch Bowl crater, causing no damage. U.S. military aircraft were blamed for the bombing.

Both planes returned safely to Jaliut.

A similar bombing raid against MIDWAY by Emily flying boats was planned, but had to be canceled when the submarine that was to refuel those planes arrived at French Frigate Shoals to find a U.S. ship in the area.

K-9

U.S. Army abbreviation for canine—guard dogs used for patrolling facilities in the United States and

Lt. John F. Kennedy, Jr., very much out of uniform, displays the swashbuckling manner of a PT-boat skipper. Kennedy commanded PT 109, which was rammed by a Japanese destroyer in The Slot, near Guadalcanal, in Aug. 1943. Two crewmen were killed. Kennedy and other survivors swam to an atoll and were soon rescued. The saga became part of the Kennedy legend. (*John F. Kennedy Library*)

in rear areas overseas. Usually, but not always German shepherds, these dogs were trained to detect and attack intruders. They were usually used by military police units.

Kaiser, Henry J. (1882–1967)

American industrialist who used assembly line techniques to mass-produce LIBERTY and VICTORY SHIPS and ESCORT CARRIERS during the war. A self-made man who dropped out of school at thirteen, Kaiser became a leader in the construction field.

During the war his shipyards produced Liberty-type merchant ships in record numbers at record building rates. When the U.S. Navy opposed the construction of escort carriers, Kaiser took his proposals to President ROOSEVELT, who authorized the program. The fifty so-called "Kaiser carriers" of the *Casablanca* (CVE 55) class were built at his Vancouver, Wash., yard in record time: the 6,730-ton ships were ordered on June 18, 1942; the first carrier was completed in July 1943 and the fiftieth one year later. They were invaluable in both the Atlantic and Pacific conflicts.

At the Navy's request Kaiser became chairman of the Brewster Aircraft Co. in 1943 but that firm was unsuccessful in producing naval aircraft and he left that position after little more than a year. He also became associated with HOWARD HUGHES in the construction of a massive flying boat transport, but Kaiser withdrew when it appeared that the project would not succeed. (See SPRUCE GOOSE.)

After the war Kaiser entered the automobile business while continuing his interest in many other enterprises.

Kaiten

Japanese suicide submarines. The failure of conventional air, surface, and submarine forces to halt the U.S. offensives in the Pacific led the Japanese to adopt suicide forces—KAMIKAZE aircraft and the kaiten or "human torpedo." (These were different from Japanese MIDGET SUBMARINES, which were not suicide weapons.)

The kaiten was a 24-inch (610-mm)-diameter Type 93 TORPEDO—the "Long Lance" launched from surface ships—that was cut in half with a cockpit section inserted for a pilot and control panel. The kaiten was to be carried to the approximate location of a U.S. ship or naval anchorage by a submerged submarine, released, and propelled at high speed by its oxygen-fueled engine to smash into the enemy ship. With a speed of 40 knots for one hour, the kaiten could outrun any American warship. There was no provision for the kaiten to be recovered by the launching submarine. Although the Japanese Naval General Staff had insisted that a means be provided for the pilot to be ejected from the kaiten about 150 feet from impact, no pilot is known to have attempted to escape from his speeding torpedo as it approached a target.

The first group of kaiten pilots began training in Aug. 1944 and several submarines were modified to carry the submersibles. The kaiten were lashed to the deck, with provision made for the pilots to leave the submarine (with appropriate ceremony) and enter the kaiten while underwater, after which it was launched. The kaiten pilots all were volunteers and unmarried (except for one who was given permission to marry while in training).

The first kaiten mission occurred in Nov. 1944, when three submarines, each carrying four kaiten, departed Japan to attack U.S. fleet anchorages in the CAROLINE ISLANDS. On the morning of Nov. 20 the first kaiten were launched. Three could not be launched because of mechanical difficulties. Five others set off for anchored U.S. warships. Explosions followed, with the Japanese claiming three U.S. AIRCRAFT CARRIERS and two BATTLESHIPS! In reality, one U.S. tanker was blown up and sunk. One submarine, still carrying her four kaiten, was detected by U.S. warships and sunk.

More kaiten missions followed; in all, nine were carried out, most with several submarines carrying the suicide craft. The last kaiten operation saw six submarines going to sea between July 14 and Aug. 8, 1945, each carrying five or six kaiten—a total of thirty-three suiciders. Again, mechanical problems plagued the operation, and three submarines had to return to Japan. The kaiten from the others attacked U.S. ships off OKINAWA in the most successful of the suicide operations. One DESTROYER ESCORT was sunk by kaiten. The kaiten-carrier *I-58* attacked the U.S. CRUISER *INDIANAPOLIS* (CA 35) at sea and sank her with torpedoes rather than suiciders; the ship had just carried ATOMIC BOMB components to TINIAN.

The kaiten effort had failed—only two U.S. ships had been sunk, one each on the first and the last kaiten operation. Eight of the carrying submarines were sunk with almost 900 crewmen and human torpedo pilots. An American admiral later wrote in the U.S. Naval Institute *Proceedings*: ". . . the Imperial Navy did a lot better with its torpedoes *before* the human guidance system was added."

Kaltenbrunner, Ernst (1903–1946)

SS general and director of the REICH CENTRAL SECURITY OFFICE after the assassination of REINHARD HEYDRICH in June 1942. An early functionary of the NAZI Party in his native Austria, Kaltenbrunner, a lawyer, became the leader of the Austrian SS and, after the *ANSCHLUSS,* became the chief for internal security in Austria, with the rank of SS lieutenant general. After he took over Heydrich's post, he concentrated on rounding up JEWS and, through his aide ADOLF EICHMANN, was a major supervisor of the HOLOCAUST. When he knew the war was lost, Kaltenbrunner tried in vain to negotiate peace talks. Evidence at his Nuremberg WAR CRIMES trial included his signature on numerous documents ordering mass killings of Jews and PRISONERS OF WAR. He was sentenced to death and hanged on the night of Oct. 15–16, 1946.

Kamelie

Code name for German occupation of Corsica, 1942.

Kamikaze

Organized Japanese naval suicide air attacks. "The only weapon I feared in the war," was the way Adm. WILLIAM F. HALSEY, U.S. Third FLEET commander, described Japanese suicide aircraft. The Japanese Navy began organized suicide attacks against warships on Oct. 25, 1944, in the battle for LEYTE GULF. Previously, individual Japanese pilots had crashed into American ships when their planes were damaged or they were wounded and had no hope of returning to base. Despite a massive naval and air force suicide effort, there was no change in the U.S. drive toward the Japanese homeland. Capt. Motoharu Okamura, then commander of the 341st Air Group, in June 1944 told Vice Adm. TAKIJIRO ONISHI, "In our present situation I firmly believe that the only way to swing the war in our

favor is to resort to crash-dive attacks with our planes. There is no other way. There will be more than enough volunteers for this chance to save our country, and I would like to command such an operation. Provide me with 300 planes and I will turn the tide of the war."

Subsequently, as Japan's military situation continued to deteriorate, Adm. Onishi formally organized the kamikaze (divine wind) attacks. "Divine wind" referred to winds of terrific strength that in 1274 and again in 1281 reputedly destroyed the fleets of Mongol hordes sailing to invade Japan.

The initial kamikaze attacks of Oct. 1944 were flown by twenty-four volunteer pilots of the Japanese Navy's 201st Air Group on Leyte. Flying A6M ZERO fighters, the pilots attacked a force of U.S. "jeep" or ESCORT CARRIERS that had just been mauled by Japanese surface warships in the Leyte

A Japanese naval officer salutes before starting off on a *kamikaze* attack mission. The *kamikaze* pilots—all volunteers—were the result of the failure of conventional air and naval attacks to stop the U.S. offensives in the Pacific. *(Japanese Navy)*

Gulf battle. The escort carrier *St. Lô* (CVE 63), struck by a bomb-laden Zero believed to have been piloted by Lt. Yukio Seki, erupted in explosions. The "jeep" carrier sank in less than an hour; about 100 men went down with the ship. Two other escort carriers were heavily damaged by kamikazes on Oct. 25 but remained afloat. The Japanese Army Air Force also flew suicide missions, those operations being designated *Taiatari* (suicide).

During the battles for the Philippines, IWO JIMA, and OKINAWA, the Japanese sent an estimated 2,257 aircraft on organized kamikaze attacks against U.S. and British warships from Oct. 1944 until mid-Aug. 1945. (Of these, 936 returned to base for a net expenditure of 1,321 aircraft.) The kamikazes sank twenty-six combat ships (minesweeper and larger) and damaged some 300 others; the largest warships to be sunk were three escort carriers, thirteen DESTROYERS, and one DESTROYER ESCORT. Several U.S. aircraft carriers were knocked out of operation by suiciders, but none was sunk. (British carriers with armored flight decks were rarely put out of action by kamikaze strikes.) Suicide planes killed an estimated 3,000 men on board ships and injured about twice that number.

In addition to employing conventional aircraft in kamikaze attacks, the Japanese produced a specialized suicide aircraft known as the BAKA to U.S. forces. The Japanese officially designated the aircraft *Ohka* or "cherry blossom." Baka translates as "fool." This was a rocket-powered aircraft carried toward its target under a bomber aircraft; the first Baka attack is believed to have occurred on April 1, 1945, against U.S. warships off Okinawa; they scored no successes. These Bakas were assigned to the 721st Air Group, under command of Capt. Okamura, who had urged the kamikaze concept on Adm. Onishi. The D4Y JUDY naval dive bomber was, toward the end of the war, produced in a specialized kamikaze attack variant.

The last suicide flights were flown immediately after the Japanese surrendered, on Aug. 15, 1945. The field commander of the kamikaze forces, Vice Adm. Matome Ugaki, led a flight of eleven D4Y Judy aircraft toward the U.S. ships off Okinawa. Four of the planes returned to base, apparently because of mechanical problems; the seven survivors led by Ugaki disappeared at sea.

After the war, discussing the gaming of war in the Pacific at the Naval War College, Fleet Adm. CHESTER W. NIMITZ, the Commander in Chief in the Pacific, said: "Nothing that happened during the war was a surprise . . . absolutely nothing except the kamikaze tactics toward the end of the war; we had not visualized these."

The Japanese also developed suicide submarines called KAITEN; these were different from the MIDGET SUBMARINES, which were not suicide craft.

Kampfgeschwader 200

German Air Force unit responsible for special operations, including flying captured Allied aircraft. *Kampfgeschwader* (Bomber Wing) 200 was established on Feb. 20, 1944, to "insert" agents into Allied territory, supply them, and evacuate them if necessary. In some instances special troops were flown behind Allied lines to carry out reconnaissance or sabotage tasks.

Among the aircraft flown by KG 200 were the Arado AR 196 and AR 232 reconnaissance and transport aircraft; Blohm and Voss BV 222 flying boat; Focke-Wulf FW 190 fighter-bomber and FW 189 reconnaissance aircraft; Heinkel HE 111 bombers, Junkers Ju 90, JU 188, Ju 252, JU 290, and JU 390 transports and bombers; captured American B-17 FLYING FORTRESS and B-24 LIBERATOR bombers; and a variety of captured French and Italian aircraft plus several types of GLIDERS. The wing also employed various GUIDED MISSILES.

These planes flew a variety of missions throughout Europe.

The first commander of KG 200 was *Oberst* Heigl, followed by *Oberst* Werner Baumbach, who commanded the wing from Oct. 1944 until the end of the war.

Karl Gustav Gun,

see GUSTAV.

Kasserine Pass

A gap in Tunisia's western Dorsal mountains where U.S. troops fought—and lost—their first major battle of World War II. The 2-mile-wide pass, between two 4,000-foot mountains, was a gateway to Tunis and a key objective for both sides during the Allied NORTHWEST AFRICA CAMPAIGN. German *Generalfeldmarschall* ERWIN ROMMEL, boldly striking at Allied lines in Tunisia as he retreated before the British Eighth Army, hurled his AFRIKA KORPS TANKS and men eastward in an offensive that began on Feb. 14, 1943. Allied forces, which had landed in the NORTH AFRICA INVASION of Nov. 1942, reeled back.

Rommel saw the pass as a soft spot in the Allied line and struck on Feb. 19 with a sharp attack that was repulsed. More German armor arrived during the night and on Feb. 20, with Rommel himself at the front, the Germans attacked again and smashed through, inflicting heavy casualties. The Americans pulled out, leaving behind much of their equipment; nearly 1,000 Americans were killed and hundreds were taken prisoner.

The Americans, with British forces and strong air power, rallied, and Rommel ran into strong opposition north of the pass. He retreated back through the pass on Feb. 23. Allied troops reoccupied the pass but failed to pursue the retreating and vulnerable Rommel.

Kate

Principal Japanese TORPEDO plane in the war. The B5N or Type 97 (given the Allied code name Kate) was Japan's primary carrier-based attack plane when the war began, with eighteen- or twenty-seven-plane units on all of the larger carriers; detachments were provided to smaller carriers. In the PEARL HARBOR raid, the six carriers launched ninety-four Kates—a quarter of the attacking planes. They devastated the American "battleship row" with aerial torpedoes and with level bombing employing modified armor-piecing naval shells as BOMBS, sinking four BATTLESHIPS (two a total loss) and heavily damaging three others. Subsequently, Kates delivered death blows to three U.S. AIRCRAFT CARRIERS—the *LEXINGTON* (CV 2), *Yorktown* (CV 5), and *HORNET* (CV 8). Kates served throughout the war, flying from land bases and, until Nov. 1944, from carriers. Their final carrier operation was the battle of LEYTE GULF in Nov. 1944, when four Kate torpedo planes were among the 116 aircraft on the decks of the four Japanese carriers.

Conceived in 1936, the prototype of the Nakajima Kate first flew in Jan. 1937. It was intended for both torpedo and level bombing, in the latter role the bombardier viewing the target through the opening of small folding doors under the fuselage. The early B6N1 aircraft flew bombing missions over China, most of them converted to B5N1-K trainers. The definitive B6N2, which first flew in Dec. 1939, equipped carrier squadrons from 1939–1940; a total of 1,149 of both variants were built.

The low-wing monoplane had a clean configuration with a fully retractable undercarriage. The large wings folded upward for carrier stowage, arranged so that the wing tips overlapped the fuselage. The plane had a long, "greenhouse"-style cockpit. The radial engine had a variable-pitch propeller. The plane lacked armor protection for the crew and self-sealing fuel tanks, hence was highly vulnerable to Allied fighters. Late in the war some were fitted with surface search RADAR or MAGNETIC ANOMALY DETECTORS for (land-based) antisubmarine operations.

The B6N2 had a maximum speed of 235 mph with a maximum range of 600 miles. The aircraft could carry a 1,764-pound torpedo or three 550-pound bombs. A single flexible 7.7-mm machine gun was fitted in the after cockpit. It was flown by a three-man crew.

Katyn Massacre

Mass slaughter of Polish officers by the NKVD, the Soviet secret police. On April 12, 1943, the German radio announced that the bodies of 4,150 Polish officers, all bound and shot in the back of the head, had been found in eight communal graves in the Katyn Forest near Smolensk. The Germans said the officers had been rounded up by Soviets in 1939 and 1940 and later killed. The Soviets denied the charge and, when the Polish government-in-exile in LONDON asked for an International RED CROSS investigation, the Soviet Union broke off diplomatic relations with the Poles.

The officers were among more than 15,000 who had disappeared after surrendering to the Soviets in 1939 during the Polish Army's retreat from advancing Germans. The Soviets claimed that Germans had killed the Poles during the German invasion of the Soviet Union.

Not until 1989 did the Soviets officially begin to admit that the Poles had been murdered by units of the NKVD (the predecessor of the KGB). The mass killings took place in the spring of 1940 when Soviet troops held the area—before the German invasion. The murders were reportedly ordered by Soviet leader STALIN because of his innate hatred of Poles. Another reason, put forth by a Soviet researcher in 1990: the NKVD was evacuating prison camps to make room for deportees from Estonia, Latvia, and Lithuania. The other vanished Polish officers were never accounted for.

Kauffman, Comdr. Draper (1911—)

Much of the U.S. military expertise in BOMB DISPOSAL was acquired through the efforts of Draper Kauffman. A 1933 graduate of the U.S. Naval Academy, Kauffman was forced to immediately resign from the Navy because of poor eyesight. He worked for a steamship line until 1940 when he became an ambulance driver in the French Army. Captured by the Germans in June 1940, he was released two months later and made his way to England where he joined the Royal Naval Volunteer Reserve and became a bomb disposal officer. He was commended several times, on one occasion by King GEORGE VI.

He resigned his British commission to accept an appointment as lieutenant in the U.S. Navy on Nov. 7, 1941. He was rushed to PEARL HARBOR after the Japanese attack to help recover unexploded Japanese bombs (and awarded the Navy Cross for that work). He then set up the U.S. Navy's bomb disposal school and assisted the Army in setting up a comparable activity.

In June 1943 Kauffman was assigned to organize the Navy's first UNDERWATER DEMOLITION TEAM (UDT). He was awarded a gold star in lieu of a second Navy Cross for leading a demolition team during the assaults on SAIPAN and TINIAN in June–July 1944.

He then served in UDT staff positions, with responsibility for planning operations in the IWO JIMA and OKINAWA landings. He also participated—again under fire—in both of those amphibious operations.

After the war he was assigned as an ordnance expert in the Bikini ATOMIC BOMB TESTS. His postwar naval career included the command of a DESTROYER, destroyer DIVISION, AMPHIBIOUS SHIP,

CRUISER, and duty ashore; he was promoted to rear admiral in 1961. Kauffman retired after serving as superintendent of the Naval Academy from 1965 to 1968.

Kaydet,

see PT-13.

KE

Code name for the Japanese withdrawal from GUADALCANAL, Feb. 1943.

Keitel, *Generalfeldmarschall* Wilhelm (1882–1946)

Chief of Staff of the High Command of the Armed Forces of Germany. Wounded in World War I, Keitel remained a professional soldier during the period of the WIEMAR REPUBLIC. In 1935, with HITLER in power and the German Army building for war, Keitel became head of the Armed Forces Office of the Defense Ministry.

Generalfeldmarschall WERNER VON BLOMBERG, minister of defense, dismissed Keitel as lacking competence for the post. Blomberg and *Generaloberst* Baron Werner Freiherr von Fritsch, chief of the High Command of the German Army, were dismissed on trumped-up charges in 1938 in a purge of anti-NAZI Army officers. Hitler assumed supreme command of the armed forces and picked the malleable Keitel as Chief of Staff of the High Command of the Armed Forces.

After the fall of France in June 1940 Hitler assigned Keitel to conduct the armistice negotiations at Compiegne and promoted him to *Generalfeldmarschall*. He became one of Hitler's closest military advisers, but his influence was diluted by his acceptance of whatever strategic decisions Hitler made. Behind his back officers called him *Laikaitel*, after the German word for lackey. Keitel called himself "a loyal shield-bearer" for Hitler.

Keitel did at first oppose the German invasion of the Soviet Union, but he soon was endorsing all that Hitler did there—including the massacre of civilians by ACTION GROUPS. "Any act of mercy is a crime against the German people," Keitel declared. He also accepted the notorious *Nacht und Nebel* (night and fog) decree, which authorized the "disappearance" of anyone charged with "endangering German security."

After the war these acts led to his arrest for WAR CRIMES. Tried before the International Military Tribunal at Nuremberg, Keitel was found guilty of participating in a conspiracy, crimes again humanity, crimes against peace, and war crimes. He was hanged at Nuremberg on Oct. 16, 1946.

Kelly, Capt. Colin P., Jr. (1915–1941)

U.S. Army pilot who supposedly crashed his damaged B-17C FLYING FORTRESS bomber into the Japanese battleship *HARUNA* off the coast of Luzon on Dec. 10, 1941. When the war began Kelly was with the 19th Bomb GROUP in the Philippines. Kelly had taken off from Clark Field on Luzon to attack Japanese shipping. During the bombing by three B-17s, Kelly's plane was attacked by two Japanese A6M ZERO fighters, one of them probably flown by SABURO SAKAI. One crewman was killed instantly and the plane burst into flames. After Kelly ordered the six other crewmen to bail out, the plane exploded and crashed into a sugarcane field near Clark Field. Kelly's body was found nearby.

He became one of America's first heroes of the war when Manila newspapers reported his sinking the *Haruna* by plunging his crippled plane into the battleship. At the time, however, the *Haruna* was at anchor in the Japanese home islands. Kelly was awarded the Army's Distinguished Service Medal (not the MEDAL OF HONOR as in some accounts). He may have attacked a heavy cruiser, but she was neither sunk nor damaged.

The AAF's Kelly Field in Texas was named for Colin Kelly.

Kempeitai (Military Police)

Japanese military police and intelligence service. It served as a domestic as well as military agency and hence was also involved with censorship and counter-ESPIONAGE activities.

The *Kempeitai* was also involved in extra-legal activities, such as helping to smuggle heroin into China (in return for large contributions for the purchase of aircraft for the Army). It was also used to terrorize the populations in occupied areas. Japanese historian Saburo Ienga wrote that in the occu-

pied areas *"Kempeitai* security measures were intended to intimidate the population into submission." He quoted a persistent rumor: "If the *Kempeitai* took you away, that was the end. You would not come back alive. They wanted everyone quaking with fear."

Even in Japan itself the *Kempeitai* was used to control dissidents, to intimidate and even terrorize. Only some members of the Supreme Court and lawyers were able to effectively stand up to the police agencies.

Lt. Gen. Sanji Okido was commander of the *Kempeitai.* After the war the service was abolished.

Kempka, *Sturmbannführer* Erich (1910—)

HITLER's longtime chauffeur and frequent witness to history. Kempka's last order from Hitler came on April 30, 1945, when Kempka was told to fetch gasoline from the Chancellery garage and take the gas containers to the Chancellery garden. After the suicides of Hitler and his bride, EVA BRAUN, Kempka carried Eva's body out of the *FÜHRER-BUNKER* and helped to cremate her body and Hitler's in the garden. Kempka had been ordered to fetch 200 liters of gasoline, but in a battered BERLIN occupied by the Red Army he could find only 180.

Recurrent claims that Hitler remained alive after the war were settled by evidence that included Kempka's detailed account of the last hours, suicides, and cremation of Hitler and Eva Braun.

Kennedy, Lt. John F. (1917–1963)

Naval officer who served on PT-BOATS. Kennedy, son of JOSEPH P. KENNEDY, SR., prewar U.S. ambassador to Great Britain, wrote his senior honors essay on England's appeasement policy. It was published in 1940 as *Why England Slept,* a title riposte to WINSTON CHURCHILL's *While England Slept* (1938).

Kennedy tried to enlist in the U.S. armed services in 1941. The Army rejected him because of his chronic back trouble. Through family connections he was accepted into the Navy three months before the Japanese attack on PEARL HARBOR. He was assigned to PT-boat duty and in the spring of 1943, as a lieutenant (junior grade), he took command of *PT 109* at a base on Tulagi, an island off GUADALCANAL in the SOLOMON ISLANDS.

The PT boats patrolled THE SLOT (Georgia Sound) that ran between two groups of islands. Japanese convoys were using The Slot as a passage for reinforcing their garrisons in the Solomons. On May 30, 1943, Kennedy's *PT 109* and several other boats were ordered about 30 miles north to a base in the RUSSELL ISLANDS, which U.S. forces had taken in February, and then to NEW GEORGIA, a group of islands that would not be declared secure until Aug. 15.

The "TOKYO EXPRESS," the persistent Japanese reinforcement effort in The Slot, continued. The PT-boats were on the sidelines of the CRUISER and DESTROYER battles to impede or derail the Tokyo Express. Operating from a base on the tiny island of Lumbari, off Rendova, the boats searched for Japanese landing barges or small craft flitting between the islands the Japanese still held. On the night of July 19–20, a Japanese float plane bombed the *109,* injuring two members of the ten-man crew.

Kennedy and the other Lumbari PT boats went on frequent patrols, always at night, between then and the night of Aug. 2–3, when, warned by code-breakers, the boats set up a rear guard in Blackett Strait for a destroyer force, under Capt. ARLEIGH BURKE, that would go after the Express. Heading south, the Japanese evaded the PT blockade. After landing 900 troops and supplies on the New Georgia island of Kolombangara, the Express sped north.

One of the Japanese destroyers, barreling up The Slot, rammed the *PT 109.* Two men were killed. Kennedy rescued at least one of the badly injured men. The survivors clung to the hulk of the *PT 109* through the night, then made it to a little atoll they named Bird Island. Through cooperative native islanders, the survivors got word to an Australian COASTWATCHER secretly stationed on Kolombangara. He arranged for their rescue.

The Kennedy saga, well publicized in newspapers and then in a *New Yorker* article by JOHN HERSEY, became part of the Kennedy legend. But, once, when someone remarked on his heroism, Kennedy is reported to have said, "It was involuntary. They sank my boat."

Kennedy remained in the Navy until Jan. 1945, entered politics, was elected to Congress from Massachusetts in 1946 and to the Senate in 1952. When he ran successfully for President in 1960, tieclip replicas of *PT 109* were coveted campaign mementoes.

Kennedy, Joseph P., Jr. (1915–1944)

Project APHRODITE pilot killed in a bomber explosion. Kennedy, son of the former Ambassador to Great Britain, was a U.S. Navy lieutenant. He volunteered for Project Aphrodite, which was experimenting with radio-controlled bombers being flown against German targets. On Aug. 12, 1944, Kennedy and a copilot took off from Fersfield aerodrome in England in a PB4Y-1, a Navy version of the B-24 LIBERATOR. The bomber was loaded with more than 10 tons of explosives. The two airmen were to bail out before the plane reached the English Channel, where a controller aircraft would take over and direct the drone to its target, V-1 BUZZ BOMB launch sites near Calais. But twenty-eight minutes after takeoff the plane exploded over the small town of Newdelight Wood on the east coast of England. His death was veiled in mystery for years because the Aphrodite Project was highly secret; the British did not want their own people to know that bomb-laden planes under radio control were flying over the country.

Kennedy was awarded the Navy Cross posthumously and a DESTROYER named after him was launched in July 1945. His younger brother Robert served on board that ship, the *Joseph P. Kennedy Jr.* (DD 850), as an apprentice seaman.

Kennedy, Joseph P., Sr. (1888–1969)

U.S. Ambassador to Great Britain from Jan. 1938 to Dec. 1940. An isolationist, he testified before Congress in 1941 opposing LEND-LEASE legislation. He was skeptical about Britain's chances of winning the war against Germany. President ROOSEVELT concluded that "Joe has been an appeaser and always will be an appeaser." Kennedy, who had been chairman of the Securities and Exchange Commission, organized and became the chairman of the first U.S. Maritime Commission in 1937. In building up the U.S. merchant fleet, he greatly helped prepare the United States for the war he later wanted to avoid.

Kenney, Lt. Gen. George C. (1889–1977)

Gen. DOUGLAS MACARTHUR's air force commander through most of the war. Kenney had enlisted in the U.S. Army as a flying cadet at the start of World War I. He served in the U.S. 91st Aero SQUADRON in France during the war, shooting down two German planes.

Kenney was a lieutenant colonel in Jan. 1941. He took command of the Fourth AIR FORCE on the U.S. West Coast with the rank of major general in March 1942; in July he went to Australia to take command of the Allied Air Forces in the Southwest Pacific and the Fifth Air Force to command land-based air operations for MacArthur. When he assumed command of the U.S. air units in Australia, there were few combat planes and even fewer of them in flying condition. MacArthur's air forces had third priority for U.S. aircraft production, after U.S. AAF units in Europe and the Navy. With those planes he was able to obtain, Kenney built a highly effective force, especially adept at low-level attacks against Japanese shipping as well as providing support to Allied ground operations, the latter including flying troops over the 14,000-foot Owen Stanley mountains of NEW GUINEA. In Oct. 1942 he was promoted to lieutenant general.

From June 1944 Kenney commanded the AAF Far East Air Forces, which consisted of the Fifth and Thirteenth Air Forces; he held that position until the end of the war.

From 1946 to 1948 Kenney was the first commander of the U.S. Strategic Air Command.

In his *Reminiscences,* Gen. MacArthur wrote: "Through his extraordinary capacity to improvise and improve, he took a substandard force and welded it into a weapon so deadly as to take command of the air whenever it engaged the enemy."

Kent, Tyler G.

Code clerk at the U.S. Embassy in LONDON who was arrested on May 20, 1940, for ESPIONAGE. Kent took some 1,500 pieces of correspondence and cables and passed them on to AXIS agents. Kent, who was ANTI-SEMITIC and anti-ROOSEVELT, was convicted of passing confidential documents to Axis agents. When news of the arrest broke, the U.S. and British governments tried to play down the affair.

Anti-Roosevelt rumors spread that Kent had been imprisoned to keep him quiet, allegedly because he had found evidence in secret CHURCHILL-Roosevelt correspondence that in 1940 they were conspiring to involve the United States in the war. The evidence, finally released in 1972, did not support the conspiracy rumor. The papers that Kent conveyed did indicate Anglo-American naval cooperation. But they also showed that Roosevelt was reluctant to go further without congressional and public approval.

Kesselring, *Generalfeldmarschall* Albert (1885–1960)

Generalfeldmarschall of the Luftwaffe and later Commander in Chief of German forces in Italy. An adjutant and general staff officer during World War I, he remained in the Army after the war, transferring to the Air Force in 1935. He became a friend of *Reichsmarschall* HERMANN GÖRING, who helped Kesselring make his rapid rise in the Luftwaffe leadership.

When the POLISH CAMPAIGN began on Sept. 1, 1939, Kesselring was commander of *Luftflotte* 1, and in the FRANCE AND LOW COUNTRIES CAMPAIGN he commanded *Luftflotte* 2. His Luftwaffe bombers severely damaged ROTTERDAM after it had been declared an OPEN CITY, but Kesselring denied responsibility. Impressed by the Luftwaffe's performance in the two campaigns, HITLER made Kesselring a *Generalfeldmarschall.*

Kesselring commanded *Luftflotte* 2 unit during the GERMAN CAMPAIGN IN THE SOVIET UNION and then, in Feb. 1942, was made Commander in Chief of the German armed services in the South, an area that included Italy and North Africa. He often issued orders to *Generalfeldmarschall* ERWIN ROMMEL that Rommel ignored. But it was Kesselring who supervised the German withdrawal from Tunis in May 1943.

In Sept. 1943 Kesselring was put in command of the central Italian front and given overall command in Italy three months later, when Rommel left to take charge of German defenses against the expected Allied invasion of France. Kesselring had disagreed with Rommel, who, in the face of the Allied invasion and Italy's SURRENDER in Sept.

1943, urged a withdrawal to the north and a defense along the Apennines.

Kesselring, who had a great affection for things Italian, knew the country and showed tactical mastery of the rugged Italian terrain. Again and again he blunted the Allied ITALIAN CAMPAIGN. His opponent, U.S. Gen. MARK W. CLARK, considered Kesselring one of the ablest officers in the German Army.

Even before Italy's surrender Kesselring was treating Italy as an occupied country. Italian GUERRILLAS were hunted down, hostages were taken, reprisal executions were ordered. In March 1944, after a bomb killed thirty-two German police troops in ROME, the Germans rounded up 335 Romans and took them to one of the Fosse Ardeatine caves, where they were shot. Their bodies were covered with lime, then the tunnel leading to the bodies was sealed by a blast of dynamite. The Germans published an announcement about the retaliation in Rome's newspapers.

Kesselring theoretically was so far up the chain of command he had no knowledge of this or other atrocities. In March 1945 Hitler ordered Kesselring to Germany to defend the Reich from the relentless ALLIED CAMPAIGN IN EUROPE. (Rommel had killed himself in Oct. 1944.) Kesselring saw the situation was hopeless, but he soldiered on and did not take part in the flurry of peace-seeking in the last weeks of the war.

He was captured by U.S. troops in May 1945 and held for WAR CRIMES connected with the massacre in Rome. In May 1947 Kesselring was sentenced to death by a British military court in Venice. His sentence was commuted to life imprisonment and he was released in 1952.

Military historian S.L.A. Marshall, in his introduction to the Kesselring memoirs, *Kesselring: A Soldier's Record,* wrote, "Albert Kesselring is a multiple person. No other great German commander had such a variety of major tasks within one war. None other may claim as many curiously conflicting public reputations. Supreme Commander! Convicted war criminal! Hitler henchman! Objective solder! Depending on the point of view, Kesselring is an inspired leader, a military meddler, a felon, an honourable opponent, a genius at military organization, a confused operator,

a horse for work, a weak vessel—all these things and a few more."

Ketsu-Go (Operation Decision)

Japanese code name for the final defense of the home islands against the expected Allied invasion, 1945.

Keyes, Lt. Col. Geoffrey (1917–1941)

British COMMANDO leader killed by friendly fire during an attempt to kill Gen. ERWIN ROMMEL. The son of Adm. of the Fleet ROGER KEYES, at age twenty-four the younger Keyes held the rank of lieutenant colonel and led several commando operations in the Middle East.

The younger Keyes led a raid on AFRIKA KORPS headquarters in Libya on the night of Nov. 17–18, 1941. The raiders encountered difficulty from the start, as rough seas swamped several of their landing boats and only thirty-eight of the fifty-five commandos were able to get ashore. The actual raid on Rommel's quarters was reorganized, the attack being assigned to Keyes and eighteen others. They were to trek some 125 miles from their landing site. When they reached their target the house was dark. Keyes and two others burst in and began firing with automatic weapons. Rommel was not there. He was in Italy at the time for conferences; further, he and his senior officers had ceased using the house some time before, and a supply unit was using it.

In the firefight in the darkened house Keyes was fatally wounded and the captain who had entered with him was also hit. Several Germans were killed.

Keyes was posthumously awarded the VICTORIA CROSS.

Keyes, Adm. of the Fleet Sir Roger (1872–1945)

A leading British practitioner of AMPHIBIOUS LANDINGS and COMMANDO operations. In World War I Keyes had been senior staff officer in the ill-fated Dardanelles amphibious campaign. Subsequently, he planned and led the British assault against German submarine bases at Ostend and Zeebrugge in Flanders. The attackers met with strong defenses. Under heavy fire, blockships were scuttled to stop the egress of submarines and Keyes gave the order to withdraw. Most of the British force was able to reach the open sea, but 1,200 British sailors and troops were killed, wounded, or captured. After only a few hours the Germans were able to dredge a channel around the sunken ships at Zeebrugge, while the blockships at Ostend were unable to block that harbor at all. Thus, the raid was a failure, and had cost heavily. Britain, however, needed a victory and the raid was hailed as a great triumph. WINSTON CHURCHILL would write, "The famous story of the blocking of Zeebrugge on St. George's Day by Admiral Keyes . . . may well rank as the finest feat of arms in the Great War, and certainly as an episode unsurpassed in the history of the Royal Navy." This raid became the basis for his role in World War II.

After the war, having failed to become First Sea Lord—the head of the Royal Navy—Adm. of the Fleet Keyes retired in 1931 and entered Parliament. He retained his interest in naval matters. In 1940 Churchill wanted aggressive commando raids carried out against the German-held French coast. On July 17, 1940, he named Keyes to head COMBINED OPERATIONS.

Keyes rapidly organized a number of raids. He sought to bring Army raiding units, Marines, and AIRBORNE troops as well as ships and RAF aircraft under his command. In all of these efforts he antagonized other British military leaders who were desperately seeking to build up conventional air, ground, and naval forces. Even the Royal Marines were becoming antagonized by Keyes, who wished to employ them for garrison duty in the Azores.

Most of Keyes' operations were failures, hampered by poor intelligence and poor planning. The British CHIEFS OF STAFF attempted to redefine the role of Combined Operations—under their direction. Keyes could not accept a new charter that inhibited his freedom of action. Finally, on Oct. 4, 1941, Churchill sacked Keyes. He wrote: "My dear Roger, I am sorry that you do not feel able to fall in with the proposal which the COS [Chiefs of Staff] have made to you. I have really done my best to meet your wishes. I have to consider my duty to the State which ranks above personal friendship. In all the circumstances I have no choice but to arrange for your relief."

Keyes was oblivious to the situation, responding to Churchill that he be instead appointed First Lord of the Admiralty or First Sea Lord. Churchill did not respond to these suggestions. Keyes was succeeded by Capt. LOUIS MOUNTBATTEN.

Kharkov

Major Soviet industrial city in the eastern Ukraine and an urban battlefield during both the GERMAN CAMPAIGN IN SOVIET UNION in 1941 and the SOVIET OFFENSIVE CAMPAIGN in 1942 and 1943. Kharkov was a high-priority objective because of the iron and coal mines near the city, which was also a railroad and industrial hub. Kharkov changed hands four times during the war and was the focus of JOSEF STALIN's "no retreat" orders, which lead to the killing and capture of hundreds of thousands of Red Army troops, which liberated it for the last time on Aug. 23, 1943. NIKITA KHRUSHCHEV, in his secret denunciation of Stalin before the Twentieth Party Congress in 1956, mentioned disasters centering on Kharkov as proof of Stalin's wartime incompetence.

Khrushchev, Nikita (1894–1971)

Trusted aide of Soviet dictator STALIN and wartime Communist Party official. Khrushchev served on the Southwest and Western Fronts as a member of their Military Councils. (A council served as the military-political command structure for operational units.) In May 1942 he was political adviser to Marshal Semyon K. Timoshenko during the disastrous Soviet defeat at KHARKOV. He would later use what he saw there to denounce Stalin's incompetence as a military strategist.

After Kharkov, Khrushchev was political adviser to Marshal A. I. Yeremenko, who was responsible for the defense of STALINGRAD until Marshal GEORGI ZHUKOV went over to the offensive. In late 1943 he returned to political and reconstruction duties.

When political officers were given military ranks in Dec. 1942, Khrushchev became a lieutenant general. His associations in the field provided him with a cadre of wartime leaders whom he later appointed to high defense positions; during the war Khrushchev developed a lasting animosity toward Zhukov.

His memoirs shed some light on the wartime activities of Stalin. For example, he quoted Stalin as saying, after Germany and the Soviet Union signed their NONAGRESSION PACT, "I know what Hitler's up to. He thinks he's outsmarted me, but actually it's I who have tricked him."

Khrushchev was among the Soviet leaders who grabbed the reins of power after Stalin's death on March 5, 1953. He took the important post of first secretary of the Communist Party in Sept. 1953 and soon became de facto head of the Soviet government, holding that power until forced to resign in Oct. 1964.

Kikusui (Floating Chrysanthemums)

Japanese code name for KAMIKAZE attacks against U.S. naval forces off OKINAWA, April 1945.

Kilroy

A mythical character who materialized in World War II wherever there was a U.S. serviceman, a piece of chalk, and a wall. The GI graffiti, which also showed up on objects and in seemingly inaccessible places, has been traced to Sgt. Francis J. Kilroy of the AAF AIR TRANSPORT COMMAND. According to that story, friends of the real Kilroy posted his name throughout the world as an inside joke that was picked up by others. Another version makes Kilroy a shipyard inspector who signed his work. But a parallel story is told about the origins of the term "Uncle Sam," who was said to have been a meat plant packer during the War of 1812 who put his stamp on his work. Whatever the origin, *Kilroy was here* could be found scrawled from the ALEUTIANS to Zanzibar. The three-word phrase was usually accompanied by the sketch shown here.

Kilroy.

Kimmel, Adm. Husband E. (1882–1968)

Although Adm. Kimmel's World War II service was effectively confined to one day—Dec. 7, 1941—the consequences of that day haunted him for the rest of his life. As Commander in Chief of the U.S. Pacific FLEET, Kimmel and his Army counterpart, Lt. Gen. WALTER C. SHORT, were held responsible for the disaster inflicted by the Japanese attack on PEARL HARBOR. The controversy, over how much Kimmel and Short could and should have known or did, began immediately after the attack and never ended.

Up to Dec. 7, 1941, Kimmel's naval career had been highly successful. He was aide to Assistant Secretary of the Navy FRANKLIN D. ROOSEVELT in 1915 and then served in U.S. BATTLESHIPS in European waters during World War I. He had commanded several ships, including the battleship *New York* (BB 34). Kimmel, at the time a rear admiral commanding the CRUISER force at Pearl Harbor, was appointed to command the Pacific Fleet in mid-January 1941. He relieved Adm. JAMES O. RICHARDSON, whom President Roosevelt fired because of his opposition to basing the fleet at Pearl Harbor.

He was known for his emphasis on "order, routine, and efficiency," according to historian Gordon Prange. But, Prange added, if Kimmel had a great lack, it was that "his solid knowledge of naval history, tactics, and strategy was unfired by the spark of creative imagination."

This lack of imagination seemed to be what hamstrung Kimmel and Short in their response to the worsening political situation between the United States and Japan in late 1941. Kimmel was not derelict in his preparations for war at Pearl Harbor, but he did not expect the war to begin with an attack on Hawaii. Therefore, he did not vary his ships' routines, prepare antitorpedo defenses around his battleships, or, most fatal of all, conduct long-range aerial patrols along the most likely attack routes.

With his fleet devastated, Kimmel took what limited actions he could, including an abortive attempt to relieve WAKE ISLAND. Vice Adm. W. S. Pye temporarily relieved Kimmel as fleet commander on Dec. 17 (pending the arrival of Adm. CHESTER W. NIMITZ from WASHINGTON). Although there were proposals to court-martial Kimmel (and others) in the aftermath of the Japanese attack, Kimmel's request for retirement from the Navy became effective on Feb. 28, 1942. He joined a shipbuilding firm specializing in drydock construction and pressed for a public hearing, which he finally received in 1945–1946 as part of the congressional inquiry into the Pearl Harbor attack. The inquiry did not prove to be the full exoneration he sought for the remainder of his life.

His autobiographical *Admiral Kimmel's Story,* alleging to tell "for the *first* time . . . the story of what really happened at Pearl Harbor," was published in 1955.

King, Fleet Adm. Ernest J. (1878–1956)

Architect of U.S. naval strategy in the war. Adm. King staged two campaigns during his forty-four-year naval career: one to be appointed the Chief of Naval Operations (CNO) and the other to have the Navy's war in the Pacific the dominant campaign of World War II.

King had served in surface ships, SUBMARINES, and aviation, earning his pilot's wings in 1927 (at age forty-eight), commanding the large AIRCRAFT CARRIER *LEXINGTON* (CV 2), and serving as chief of the powerful Bureau of Aeronautics from 1933 to 1936. By the eve of World War II, King's reputation was as an acerbic, intolerant, arrogant lady-killer. His temper was famous for its intemperateness. One of his daughters remarked, "He is the most even-tempered man in the Navy. He's always in a rage." He had often said that he wanted promotion only on merit and would not cater to anyone. His stiff-necked attitude seemed to have cost then-Vice Adm. King his last chance to be CNO in 1939 and he foresaw retirement in 1942. But King's high self-esteem was in large measure justified. He was brilliant and broadly experienced. He had been highly competent in nearly every post he filled.

In Dec. 1940 King was appointed commander of the Atlantic Squadron as a rear admiral. In Feb. 1941, however, the squadron was upgraded and King became Commander in Chief Atlantic FLEET with the rank of full admiral. He was now charged with prosecuting President ROOSEVELT's undeclared war against German U-BOATS. King's fortune in being CinC of the Atlantic Fleet and not CNO at the time of the Dec. 7, 1941, attack on PEARL HARBOR, coupled with Roosevelt's high opinion of his abilities, led to his appointment as Commander in Chief U.S. Fleet in late Dec. 1941. (King abbreviated the title as *Cominch,* not *Cincus*—he didn't like the latter's sound.)

In March 1942, King added CNO to his titles. A close friend, surprised by the appointment, asked him, "Ernie, how in the world did they ever pick you for the top spot?" King's answer was frank and realistic: "When they get in trouble, they send for us sons-of-bitches."

The first few months of 1942 saw King's greatest misjudgment and his greatest contribution to U.S. success in the war. His stubborn refusal to institute CONVOYS along the U.S. East Coast, which he based on a shortage of the escorts he deemed indispensable to defeat the U-boats, meant little effective U.S. response to the massive merchant ship sinkings for several months.

King looked at the gloomy situation in the Pacific and argued that some offensive counterstroke was essential in 1942. He claimed not to be rejecting the overall Germany First strategy of the ALLIES, but that only offensive action would preserve the U.S. ability to begin striking back at Japan. He believed that the U.S. war economy would be able to support both a decisive campaign in Europe (requiring primarily Army resources) and a naval campaign across the Pacific (a Navy–Marine Corps war), a belief that was eventually accepted and proved correct. The July 1942 decision to retake GUADALCANAL and Tulagi was in line with King's desire to strike anywhere, but he soon presented strong opposition to Gen. DOUGLAS MACARTHUR's desire to make a NEW GUINEA campaign the primary effort in the Pacific. King advocated what became the U.S. CENTRAL PACIFIC CAMPAIGN—a thrust through the GILBERT, MARSHALL, and MARIANA island chains. Because appointment of a single commander in the Pacific proved impossible, a two-track campaign developed that strained the Japanese and possibly shortened the Pacific war.

King's relationship with the COMBINED CHIEFS OF STAFF was inevitably turbulent. He strenuously, often tactlessly defended his support of a vigorous naval war in the Pacific, but he also showed the strongest grasp of requirements of overall Allied strategy of any U.S. participant. King proved to be an effective ally of Gen. GEORGE C. MARSHALL in his campaign for a cross-Channel assault on France.

King was promoted to Fleet Admiral in Dec. 1944. When he stepped down as CinC U.S. Fleet and CNO in Dec. 1945 he had built the largest, most lavishly endowed, and possibly most competent naval force ever assembled by a single nation—much of it the product of his strategic concepts.

King was seldom loved, but he was greatly respected.

Kingcobra,

see P-63.

Kingman

Code name for the Wendover (Utah) U.S. Army Air Base, employed as the test and training center for the 509TH COMPOSITE GROUP, which delivered the ATOMIC BOMBS on Japan in Aug. 1945.

Kingpin

Allied code name for Gen. HENRI GIRAUD.

Kinkaid, Adm. Thomas Cassin (1888–1972)

By the end of World War II, Thomas Kinkaid was one of the U.S. Navy's most widely experienced naval fleet commanders, having first served Adm. WILLIAM HALSEY as a carrier commander and later Gen. DOUGLAS MACARTHUR as his Seventh Fleet commander.

Kinkaid had served in surface ships and commanded a CRUISER. From 1938 to 1941, he was U.S. naval attaché in ROME. As a rear admiral, Kinkaid commanded a cruiser DIVISION after the PEARL HARBOR attack and fought in the major naval battles of the first year of the war, including CORAL SEA in May 1942 and MIDWAY a month later. He commanded the *Enterprise* (CV 6) task force for the GUADALCANAL campaign.

Kinkaid was then appointed commander of the naval forces in the North Pacific, where his ships blockaded and bombarded Japanese-held Attu and Kiska in the ALEUTIAN ISLANDS, engaged in the battle of the KOMANDORSKIYE ISLANDS against a Japanese cruiser-destroyer force, and conducted the recapture of Attu in May 1943 and Kiska in August 1943.

In Nov. 1943, Kinkaid, by then a vice admiral,

took command of the Seventh Fleet, assigned to support Gen. MacArthur, which he led until the end of the war. The Seventh Fleet at HOLLANDIA in April 1944 had two heavy cruisers (both Australian), three light CRUISERS, and numerous DESTROYERS and lesser warships; the Fifth Fleet provided most of the carrier-based aircraft and bombardment ships as the Navy's leadership would not "trust" MacArthur with AIRCRAFT CARRIERS and modern BATTLESHIPS.

But by the time the Seventh Fleet supported the AMPHIBIOUS LANDINGS on Leyte in the Philippines in Oct. 1944, Kinkaid had a bombardment force of six battleships (all prewar and five of them PEARL HARBOR survivors), four heavy cruisers, and four light cruisers. Kinkaid also had eighteen ESCORT CARRIERS.

Throughout his association with the theatrical Gen. MacArthur, Kinkaid performed ably and professionally. He was able to avoid confrontations with MacArthur while successfully on occasion cajoling Adm. CHESTER W. NIMITZ for more ships and aircraft. His fleet's final operation was the landing of U.S. forces in Korea.

Kirk, Vice Adm. Alan G. (1888–1963)

Senior U.S. naval fleet commander in European waters. When Capt. Kirk became director of the Office of Naval Intelligence (ONI) in March 1941, he strove to assert ONI's responsibility as the interpreter of enemy intentions as well as a collector of information. This role was opposed by Adm. RICHMOND KELLY TURNER, head of the Navy's War Plans, who carried the day—and, some analysts argue, crippled the U.S. Navy's ability to properly interpret Japanese capabilities and intentions before the Japanese attack on PEARL HARBOR. Kirk was already experienced in a war zone, having served as U.S. naval attaché in LONDON from June 1939 until March 1941.

Kirk was promoted to rear admiral in Nov. 1941 and in March 1942 returned to his former post in London as naval attaché in the U.S. Embassy. He also served as Chief of Staff to Adm. HAROLD R. STARK, Commander U.S. Naval Forces in Europe.

In Feb. 1943 Kirk succeeded Rear Admiral HENRY K. HEWITT as commander of the Atlantic Fleet's amphibious forces. In that assignment he trained the naval forces that would launch U.S. troops on the easternmost beaches of the American zone in SICILY. His task force got its troops ashore in high surf among rock outcroppings that resulted in heavy landing craft losses, but remarkably few casualties.

Kirk's experience with British civilian and military leaders made him a likely choice as commander of the American naval forces in the NORMANDY INVASION under British Adm. Bertram Ramsay. (Kirk suggested that the American beaches be renamed from "X" and "Y" to "Omaha" and "Oregon"; Omaha stuck, Oregon was later changed to "Utah.") The landings at Utah Beach went relatively smoothly, in large part because most troops landed a mile south of the original objective and inadvertently found a weakly defended area. The landings on Omaha Beach were so fiercely contested that it appeared that Omaha might have to be abandoned. Kirk has been criticized for deciding to launch his landing craft from well out at sea (as much as 11 miles). Historian SAMUEL ELIOT MORISON argued that Kirk feared coastal defense guns thought to be in place at Pointe du Hoc; they were later discovered to be dummies.

Once the beachhead had been secured, Kirk oversaw resupply operations through ARTIFICIAL HARBORS until Cherbourg was captured on June 25, 1944, and cleared to permit the first ship to unload on July 16. In October he was named commander of all naval forces in France, which allowed him to oversee all major river-crossing operations, including the RHINE CROSSINGS in March 1945. He was promoted to vice admiral in May 1945 and served on the Navy's General Board until Feb. 1946, when he retired as an admiral and became the U.S. ambassador to Belgium and minister to Luxembourg (1946–1947), ambassador to the Soviet Union (1949–1952), and to Nationalist China (1962–1963).

Kiska,

see ALEUTIAN ISLANDS.

Kitbag

Code name for British naval raid on Frosjoen, Norway, Dec. 1941.

Klabautermann (Hobgoblin)

German code name for operations against Soviet traffic on Lake Ladoga, July 1942.

Knox, W. Franklin (1874–1944)

Secretary of the Navy. A prominent newspaperman and staunch Republican, "Frank" Knox was appointed Secretary of the Navy by President ROOSEVELT in 1940 as he broadened the political complexion of his Cabinet to gain support for his military buildup.

Knox had enlisted as a private in the U.S. Volunteer Cavalry in 1898 and served in Cuba with the "Rough Riders." After the war he began newspaper and political careers, reaching the position of general manager for the Hearst Newspapers in 1931. On the political side, Knox was vice chairman of Teddy Roosevelt's 1912 campaign committee, a candidate for the New Hampshire governorship in 1924, and the Republican candidate for vice president in 1936.

In 1917 he was commissioned as a captain in the Army; mustered out as a lieutenant colonel. After the war, he retained his reserve commission and was generally referred to as Col. Knox.

He presided over the Navy's expansion in the war. Upon his sudden death on April 28, 1944, he was succeeded by Under Secretary JAMES V. FORRESTAL.

Knudsen, William S. (1879–1948)

Automobile executive who became a wartime government official. The Denmark-born industrialist was president of General Motors in Jan. 1941 when President ROOSEVELT named him director of the Office of Production Management (OPM), which handled issues involving industrial production, raw materials, and labor.

At his first meeting, Knudsen, wondering about the setup of the new WAR AGENCY, asked Roosevelt, "Who's boss?" "I am," Roosevelt replied.

When power shifted to the War Production Board in Jan. 1942, Knudsen was commissioned a lieutenant general in the Army and put in charge of production at the WAR DEPARTMENT. From July 1944 to April 1945 he was director of the Allied air forces matériel and service command. He returned to GM in June 1945.

Koch, Karl (1897–1945)

Commandant of the Buchenwald CONCENTRA-TION CAMP. Koch was commandant from the time it opened in 1937 until his arrest in 1944 by his SS superiors.

Koch, a sadist married to a sadist, was tried for the "unauthorized" murder of two prisoners at Buchenwald. At the time, his lawyer later said, there were three kinds of homicides in Germany: the state-authorized and thus "legal" murder of JEWS; "mercy killings" of the aged, infirm, and mentally ill; and the "unauthorized" kind of murders committed by Koch. He was also charged with theft of state property—the personal belongings of inmates—which had made him a millionaire. He was tried and hanged in 1945.

His widow, Ilse, known as the "Bitch of Buchenwald," was acquitted on charges of receiving stolen goods. But after the war she became more notorious than her husband.

At the Nuremberg WAR CRIMES trial, exhibits included a piece of tattooed skin tanned at Buchenwald for her. A former Buchenwald guard said, "After the tattooed prisoners had been kept in the dispensary and killed by injection," the "finished products" were given to Ilse Koch, "who had them fashioned into lampshades and other household articles." These included lampshades, gloves, and book covers.

Witnesses told of how Ilse, a large, red-haired woman, rode around the camp on horseback, striking prisoners with her whip. She also occasionally selected one of the condemned to have sex with her.

She was convicted of crimes against humanity and sentenced to life imprisonment. Gen. LUCIUS D. CLAY, military governor of the American occupation zone, commuted the sentence to four years, touching off a U.S. Senate investigation that criticized Clay's decision.

Ilse Koch was arrested again in 1949, tried in a West German court for crimes against Germans, and once more sentenced to life imprisonment. She hanged herself in her cell with a bed sheet in 1967.

Koenig, Gen. Marie-Pierre (1898–1970)

FREE FRENCH commander in North Africa. After serving in the French Army in World War I, Koenig served in the Foreign Legion in North Africa. In the spring of 1940 he was with the Legion as part of the Anglo-French force sent to Norway, but subsequently evacuated.

Returning to France, he fought in the FRANCE AND LOW COUNTRIES CAMPAIGN and, after the French defeat, he went to England to join Gen. CHARLES DE GAULLE. He was subsequently sent to North Africa and led Free French troops that fought with the British Eighth Army. After the Allied victory in North Africa, Koenig was sent into France to command the French Forces of the Interior (GUERRILLAS) prior to the NORMANDY INVASION. After the liberation of PARIS he was appointed the military governor by de Gaulle.

In the mid-1950s he served briefly as minister of national defense.

Königsberg

German term for battle line established west of MOSCOW, in the winter of 1942.

Koga, Vice Adm. Mineichi (1885–1944)

When the Japanese carrier force attacked PEARL HARBOR, Adm. Koga's China Area Fleet was based at SHANGHAI and subsequently provided naval support during the eighteen-day Japanese campaign to capture HONG KONG. Koga rose to prominence when he took command of the Combined Fleet after Adm. ISOROKU YAMAMOTO was shot down by U.S. fighters on April 18, 1943.

Koga, conservative and cautious, originally had resisted the decision to fight the great industrial power of the United States. By the time of Yamamoto's death his hesitancy seemed sensible. Japan's carrier force had suffered severe losses in ships, aircraft, and pilots in several 1942 battles; the Japanese had abandoned GUADALCANAL; and the war was perceptibly shifting in favor of the United States.

When he became CinC of the Combined Fleet Koga anchored his defense of the SOLOMONS at RABAUL, the large naval base at the eastern end of NEW GUINEA. Several surface engagements in 1943, in which the U.S. Navy began to predominate, were capped by the Battle of Empress Augusta

Bay on Nov. 2, a clear U.S. defeat of a powerful Japanese cruiser squadron. A few days later, U.S. aircraft attacked Rabaul and damaged several warships that had arrived from TRUK as reinforcements. Also in November, when the U.S. forces were unopposed by naval forces or aircraft in the TARAWA invasion, it was obvious how weak the Combined Fleet had become.

Koga, judging correctly that the MARSHALL ISLANDS would be the next U.S. target, sent troop reinforcements to several key eastern islands. His efforts were frustrated by U.S. code-breaking, which allowed the U.S. forces to sidestep these points and capture KWAJALEIN and ENIWETOK with relatively small losses.

These defeats persuaded Adm. Koga that Truk, the "GIBRALTAR of the Pacific," was no longer safe for his fleet. He withdrew his major units in early February, a move that preserved them from the massive two-day U.S. air assault that sank 200,000 tons of shipping and destroyed 250 to 275 aircraft. During this period, Koga met in TOKYO with the Imperial General Staff and informed them that he no longer had a Combined Fleet worthy of the name.

Koga reorganized his forces as the Mobile Fleet, but looked to the "unsinkable" aircraft carriers of Japan's island possessions as the only means to replace his lost floating airdromes. He had hoped to base his fleet at SAIPAN in the Marianas, but supply limitations and growing U.S. submarine depredations forced him to spread his forces. Koga staked his hopes on a major fleet engagement in which he would concentrate his land-based and carrier-based air forces on the U.S. fleets when they invaded the MARIANA ISLANDS, a move he had expected. On March 31 and April 1, 1944, U.S. carriers conducted air raids on the Palaus, home to many of Koga's major units and his headquarters. Aware that the anticipated decisive battle was at hand, he boarded a plane to fly to Davao to survey other elements of his dispersed fleet. The aircraft encountered stormy weather and crashed, killing all on board.

Koltso (Ring)

Soviet code name for the final attack against the German Sixth Army at STALINGRAD, Jan. 1943.

Komandorskiye Islands

Island group in the Bering Sea off the Soviet Union's Kamchatka Peninsula and site of a battle in March 1943 between a U.S. task group and a Japanese fleet attempting to reinforce the Japanese garrison on Attu in the ALEUTIAN ISLANDS.

The U.S. task group—the heavy CRUISER *Salt Lake City* (CA 25), the light cruiser *Richmond* (CL 9) and four DESTROYERS—had been patrolling the waters off the western Aleutians to interdict Japanese ships attempting to resupply or reinforce the Japanese-occupied islands of Attu and Kiska.

Before dawn on March 26, 1943, the U.S. ships' RADAR detected what at first was thought to be merchant ships or transports. As the ships closed, however, the Americans discovered that what they faced were two heavy cruisers, two light cruisers, four destroyers, and three transports.

In what would be a running duel, the U.S. ships commenced firing, scoring hits on one of the Japanese heavy cruisers. As the Americans began a high-speed withdrawal under a smoke screen, the Japanese concentrated fire on the *Salt Lake City*. She was hit six times. "My speed is 22 knots," she radioed . . . then "My speed 14" until the report was "My speed zero."

Three U.S. destroyers, under intense fire, made a TORPEDO run on the Japanese. The destroyers, says a battle report, "appeared to be smothered with splashes. It was incredible that they should survive, but they continued in."

The Japanese broke off, turning away without carrying out their supply mission. The *Salt Lake City* was repaired and began moving again.

Konev, Marshal of the Soviet Union Ivan S. (1897–1973)

Master of Soviet offensive operations. After being conscripted, Konev served as a noncommissioned officer in the czarist Army in World War I. He entered the Red Army and Party in 1918 and was a political commissar during the civil war, taking part in the savage repression of the Kronshtadt naval mutiny of 1921. He then transferred to the regular officer corps in 1924 and served in progressively higher command assignments, rising to commander of the North Caucasus Military District in Jan. 1941.

Konev was recalled to MOSCOW in the fall of 1941 and given command of the Nineteenth Army and Western Army Group in the battle for the Soviet capital in 1941. He subsequently commanded other Army groups, and was commander of the Second Ukrainian and then First Ukrainian Fronts in the great offensive operations into Poland and in the battle for BERLIN in 1943–1945. In this period he was promoted to Marshal of the Soviet Union.

Immediately after the war he became chief of Soviet Ground Forces and deputy minister of war (1946–1950), followed by other senior assignments, including CinC of the WARSAW Pact Forces and first deputy minister of defense (1955–1960) and the CinC of Soviet occupation forces in Germany (1961–1962).

He was twice named a HERO OF THE SOVIET UNION.

Konstantin,

see ACHSE.

Korea

Capital: Seoul, pop. 22,355,485 (1938). Japan, which had long coveted the rich rice fields and farmland of Korea, took it over after the Russo-Japanese War of 1904–1905—despite a pledge that Japan would bestow "complete independence." Japan made a military occupation official through "annexation" of Korea on Aug. 22, 1910. By then Japan had for five years dominated the Korean government and had disbanded the Korean Army. The Japanese ruled harshly, forcing the Koreans to give up their language and religion, take Japanese names, and work as virtual slaves for Japanese masters. Japanese military rulers jailed or executed thousands of Koreans.

In March 1919 Koreans who had managed to get out of their native land set up a Korean provisional government in SHANGHAI. One of the leaders was Syngman Rhee, who had attended Princeton University. Rhee and others tried in vain to get Korea's cause before the LEAGUE OF NATIONS and U.S. officials.

After Japan's invasion of China in 1937, the Korean resistance movement recruited young Korean

men into all-Korean units that in April 1939 joined with Chinese forces in combat against the Japanese in China. Japan countered by sending Korean volunteers into China to fight on the Japanese side.

In Nov. 1943, at the CAIRO CONFERENCE of President ROOSEVELT, Prime Minister CHURCHILL, and Generalissimo CHIANG KAI-SHEK of China, the three leaders agreed that "in due course Korea shall become free and independent." The Soviet Union reiterated this pledge when it entered the war against Japan on Aug. 8, 1945. Soviet troops entered Korea from the north on Aug. 12, two days before the Japanese SURRENDER. U.S. occupation troops arrived in Korea on Sept. 8. The two nations set the 38th Parallel as the demarcation line between the occupation zones.

In Dec. 1945 U.S. Secretary of State JAMES BYRNES and Soviet Foreign Minister VYACHESLAV MOLOTOV worked out an agreement for a provisional government for Korea. But the Cold War already had begun, and, despite prodding by Americans and Koreans, the Soviets refused to carry out the agreement.

The United States ended its occupation on Aug. 15, 1948, by establishing the Republic of Korea (South Korea) under the leadership of Syngman Rhee. On Sept. 9, under Soviet backing, Korean Communists in the north announced the creation of the Democratic People's Republic. Border raids from the north started in 1949 and led to full-scale invasion on June 25, 1950. The United States, responding to pleas for help from South Korea, sent in troops and the three-year Korean War began.

Kozhedub, Maj. Gen. Ivan N. (1920—)

Top-scoring Soviet fighter ACE of the war. He did not enter combat until March 1943, having previously served as a flight instructor. He first saw action at KURSK, shooting down his first German aircraft on July 6, 1943—using up all of the ammunition in his Lavochkin LA-5 fighter to shoot down a single JU 87 *STUKA*.

Following this inauspicious beginning, his score of German planes grew steadily. On Feb. 15, 1945, while on a lone reconnaissance patrol he caught sight of a Messerschmitt ME 262 jet-propelled fighter. Kozhedub opened fire on the low-flying jet and, in what he described as a "lucky shot," he became the only Soviet pilot to destroy a JET-PRO-PELLED AIRCRAFT.

Flying only the La-5, Kozhedub was credited with sixty-two kills of German aircraft. He was three times awarded the HERO OF THE SOVIET UNION.

Kreisau Circle

Anti-HITLER organization made up of professional people, military officers, and intellectuals. It was founded in 1933 by Count Helmuth James Graf von Moltke, who worked in the foreign affairs section of the German High Command. The group took its name from Moltke's estate in Kreisau (now Krzyzowa, Poland). In the orgy of arrests that followed the JULY 20 PLOT on Hitler's life in 1944, many of the circle were arrested and executed. Neither the circle nor Moltke had been involved in that plot or any other plots to kill Hitler. Moltke had been arrested in Jan. 1944 for warning a member of the circle that he was about to be arrested. Tried for treason as one of the July 20 plotters, Moltke was hanged on Jan. 23, 1945.

Kremel (Kremlin)

German deceptive operation in the Soviet Union, May–June 1942.

Kretschmer, *Fregattenkäpitan* Otto (1912—)

Top-scoring German U-BOAT captain in the war—known as the "tonnage king." While in the submarines *U-23* and *U-99,* Kretschmer was the most successful submarine commanding officer of any navy in the war, being credited with sinking 300,000 tons of Allied shipping and three British destroyers.

On March 17, 1941, Kretschmer's *U-99* was on the surface, having expended all his TORPEDOES in an attack on CONVOY HX 112 south of Iceland. The convoy escort was Capt. DONALD MACIN-TYRE'S experienced 5th Escort Group with five destroyers and two corvettes.

Kretschmer had set course to return to base when the *U-99* inadvertently encountered two of Macintyre's destroyers. The officer on the watch dived the boat, but she was immediately detected by the escorts' SONAR. (Kretschmer might have escaped in the darkness on the surface as the escorts had no RADAR.) Macintyre's own ship, the destroyer

Walker, released a single pattern of DEPTH CHARGES that wrecked the *U-99* and forced her to the surface. Another destroyer opened fire on the damaged submarine, which rapidly sank. Kretschmer and all but two of his crew were rescued.

Kretschmer was one of only five German naval officers to win the highest award for bravery and valor—the Knight's Cross with Oak Leaves and Swords to the IRON CROSS; his was the first such award made to the U-boat service. (Kretschmer was in a British PRISONER OF WAR camp at the time of the award.)

After the war Kretschmer and Macintyre met again. Wrote Macintyre, "We warmed to each other eventually and became, I believe, good friends." Kretschmer later reached the rank of rear admiral in the postwar West German Navy.

Kristallnacht

The name given the Nov. 9, 1938, attacks on German JEWS. Crystal Night, the "Night of Broken Glass," was secretly ordered by NAZI officials. The terror followed the fatal shooting of a German diplomat in Paris by a German Jewish refugee. SA and SS units, operating under methodically drafted orders, burned more than 200 synagogues and wrecked some 7,500 Jewish stores and warehouses, killing more than 200 Jews and severely injuring more than 600. Under Nazi pressure, insurance claims were paid—and were then confiscated by the state.

Krueger, Gen. Walter (1881–1967)

Walter Krueger, who was born in Flatow, Germany, and emigrated to the United States at the age of eight, was the only foreign-born officer to command a U.S. ARMY in World War II. He did not graduate from West Point (or any other college) but enlisted to fight in the Spanish-American War out of high school. He subsequently received a commission while serving in the Philippines. In World War I, Krueger was commander of the American Expeditionary Force's TANK Corps.

In 1941 Krueger was promoted to lieutenant general, given command of the Third Army, and was considered one of the most venerable men in the Army, highly revered for his knowledge of training, tactics, and military history. Lt. Col. DWIGHT D. EISENHOWER, who became Krueger's Chief of Staff in June 1941, later wrote that he "had an Army-wide reputation as a hard-bitten soldier. But . . . few officers had a clearer grasp of what another war would demand of the Army; few were physically tougher or more active. Relentlessly driving himself, he had little need of driving others—they were quick to follow his example."

Krueger demonstrated an ability to control large numbers of men during the LOUISIANA MANEUVERS of 1941. In the first year and a half of the war Krueger also earned great credit, second only to Gen. LESLEY J. MCNAIR, for the preparation of most of the Army DIVISIONS that would fight overseas. His chance to command a combat army came in Feb. 1943 when Gen. DOUGLAS MACARTHUR requested him to command the newly forming Sixth Army.

Krueger proved himself once again capable of raising and training a large army. He also showed an ability for managing that army over widely scattered venues during MacArthur's leap-frog landings on NEW GUINEA and surrounding islands in 1944 and later operations in the Philippines.

But Krueger's methodical, even plodding preparations were referred to on occasion as "Molasses in January." And he was seen as unenterprising, timid, overcautious, perhaps too old to run a modern army. His delay in moving off the beaches at Leyte and into the mountains is claimed to have prolonged that campaign by allowing the Japanese defenders to regroup. His forces, however, were always very well prepared and provisioned. Krueger may well have been deliberate, but his Army's casualty rate was relatively low and he never seems to have lost MacArthur's confidence. MacArthur had selected him to lead the U.S. AMPHIBIOUS LANDINGS at Kyushu had the invasion of Japan been carried out as planned.

Krupp

The great German industrial complex that built and supplied the NAZI war machine, making widespread use of SLAVE LABOR, PRISONERS OF WAR, and CONCENTRATION CAMP inmates. The Krupp Works was centered in ESSEN, which was incessantly bombed by the RAF.

After Germany's defeat in World War I, Krupp supposedly was forbidden to make armaments. But Krupp had been clandestinely working on research and design of TANKS and guns; many of the guns used in Germany's rise to power had been designed in the 1920s.

Baron Gustav Krupp von Bohlen und Halbach, Krupp's chairman of the board (and husband of Bertha Krupp, the arm firm's heiress), at first secretly opposed the rising ADOLF HITLER, fearing him a dangerous socialist radical. But when Hitler became chancellor in 1933, Krupp became an ardent supporter. Hitler made Krupp chairman of a fund raised by industrialists for the Nazi Party. Krupp was also a large contributor to the "Circle of Friends of HEINRICH HIMMLER," which underwrote "special tasks of the SS."

In return, Hitler rewarded the Krupp Works with tens of thousands of slave laborers. As a convenience, Krupp factories were set up near the Buchenwald and AUSCHWITZ concentration camps.

A Krupp doctor, in an affidavit used as evidence in the Nuremberg WAR CRIMES trials, told of a visit to the Krupp workers' annex at the Buchenwald concentration camp, where 600 doomed Jewish WOMEN were kept: "I found these females suffering from open festering wounds and other diseases. . . . They had no shoes and went about in their bare feet. The sole clothing of each consisted of a sack with holes for their arms and head. . . . The amount of food in the camp was extremely meager and of very poor quality."

Baron Krupp von Bohlen und Halbach was indicted for war crimes but was not tried because of his "physical and mental condition." His son, Alfred, who had taken over management of Krupp in 1943, was tried at Nuremberg, together with nine Krupp directors. (Trials of other Krupp executives were scheduled but never held.) In 1948 Alfred was sentenced to twelve years in prison and his property was confiscated. He was released in 1951 as part of a general amnesty and the confiscation order was annulled.

Kugelblitz (Ball Lightning)

German code name for German Third PANZER Army operations against Soviet GUERRILLA center near Vitebsk, Feb. 1943.

Kuril Islands

Island chain, north of the Japanese home islands. Japan maintained several bases in the isolated, sparsely populated Kurils. The carrier task force for the attack on PEARL HARBOR assembled in Hitokappu Bay off the Kuril island of Etorufu in late Nov. 1941.

A major base on Paramushir was frequently bombed by U.S. bombers stationed in the ALEUTIAN ISLANDS. The Soviet Union acquired the Kurils, along with southern Sakhalin Island, in the political alignments that followed the end of the war. The Japanese had been given the Russian-occupied Kurils and the southern half of Sakhalin under the surrender terms ending the Russo-Japanese War of 1904–1905.

Kursk

The largest TANK battle of the war. The battle at Kursk, located some 125 miles north of Kharkov, evolved from the German attack, given the code name *Zitadelle* (citadel), that was to attack Soviet forces in the Kursk salient and strike a blow before the Soviet Army could recover from losses suffered in the 1942–1943 winter campaign. For this operation all available German armor was to be concentrated in two great "pincers" to encircle the Soviet forces. The German Ninth Army (with eighteen divisions) and Fourth PANZER Army (with seventeen divisions) were to carry out the attack. They had an aggregate of 2,500 to 3,000 tanks and self-propelled guns and 1,800 tactical aircraft. The German's Mark VI TIGER used at Kursk was the most powerful tank in the world at that time. (Soviet sources put their own tank strength at more than 3,000, including available reserves.)

Delays in the delivery of equipment, conflicting opinions of generals at HITLER's headquarters, and Hitler's vacillations delayed the start of the attack until July 4, 1943. By that time several senior generals were urging Hitler to abandon the offensive since it was obvious that the Soviets were aware of the German preparations. (The Soviets had dependable information on the assault because of the LUCY SPY RING.) But *Zitadelle* began as rescheduled.

The German assault on the northern side (Ninth Army) soon became bogged down after penetrating only a few miles. A Soviet counterattack that began on July 11 precluded further advances. In the south, German troops had more success, gaining a bridgehead across the Psel River on July 10. This led to the tank battle at the village of Prokhorovka. The battle began on July 12 with 600 German tanks and some 850 Soviet tanks engaging. Overhead a furious air battle raged with aircraft of both sides proving adept at "tank busting." Altogether, some 6,000 tanks and 4,000 planes on both sides would take part in the Kursk battle.

As both sides brought up reinforcements Hitler ordered an end to the engagement because of the Allied landing in SICILY on July 10 and his fear that there would soon be a landing on the Italian mainland. The German troops began a withdrawal and on July 17 the Soviets opened an offensive. At the same time, Soviet GUERRILLAS launched attacks in the German rear areas.

When the battle ended in mid-August the estimated losses on the German side were 70,000 troops killed and captured and 2,950 tanks and 1,400 aircraft destroyed—irreplaceable losses only a few months after the disaster at STALINGRAD. Soviet losses were also heavy, but the men and weapons could be quickly replaced. The Kursk battle marked the end of German offensives on the EASTERN FRONT; it was followed immediately by the first Soviet summer offensive of the war.

Kurusu, Saburo (1888–1954)

Japanese diplomat who attempted to negotiate peace with the United States. A career Japanese diplomat, Kurusu married an American while the Japanese counsel in Chicago (1913–1919). Subsequently he held diplomatic posts in the Philippines, Chile, Italy, Germany, and Peru. As the ambassador to Germany in 1939–1940 he helped negotiate the TRIPARTITE PACT.

In Nov. 1941, when critical negotiations were being carried out between the United States and Japan, he was sent to WASHINGTON as special envoy to assist Ambassador KICHISABURO NOMURA. Unknown to the two ambassadors, the decision had already been taken to go to war on Dec. 7.

Following the PEARL HARBOR attack Kurusu was repatriated to Japan. He then toured the country giving speeches to encourage the war effort.

Kuter, Maj. Gen. Laurence S. (1905–1979)

U.S. Army Air Forces planner and commander. A 1927 graduate of the Military Academy, he served briefly in ARTILLERY before he was assigned to the ARMY AIR CORPS in 1929 and then entered flight school.

In 1939 Kuter was assigned to the air section of the operations staff of the Army General Staff as a lieutenant colonel. In Feb. 1942 he was promoted to brigadier general, the youngest general officer of any U.S. service. He was then deputy commander of the Northwest African Tactical Air Force, and subsequently assigned as the assistant chief of the air staff for plans. In that role he was the top AAF planner. Kuter believed that all heavy bombers in the Pacific should be under one command (the Twentieth AIR FORCE) and that postwar AAF planning should not be based on the ATOMIC BOMB.

In July 1945 he was appointed deputy to the Commanding General AAF Pacific Ocean Area.

After the war he was the first commander of the Military Air Transport Service (1948–1951), head of the Air University (1953–1955), and, with the rank of full general, commander of U.S. Far East Air Forces (1955–1959).

Kuznetsov, Adm. N. G. (1904–1974)

Commander in Chief of the Navy during the war and architect of STALIN's naval buildup of the late 1930s and late 1940s. Stalin apparently met Kuznetsov in 1932 when he was commanding officer of a cruiser (at age twenty-eight). Subsequently assigned to the Pacific Fleet, he was one of several officers Stalin summoned to MOSCOW for high-level discussions about an oceanic naval strategy in the mid-1930s. Shortly thereafter, in 1936–1937, Kuznetsov was sent to Spain as Soviet adviser to the Republican naval forces during the SPANISH CIVIL WAR. Upon his return to the Soviet Union in Jan. 1938, Kuznetsov was appointed CinC of the Pacific Fleet. (Many of his comrades who served in Spain were recalled to be executed in the Stalinist purges.)

He was summoned to Moscow for consultation at least twice more, and in 1939 Kuznetsov became the people's commissar for the Navy and CinC of Naval Forces. He served as head of the Navy through the war, although most of the Navy's decision-making power was vested in the Supreme Naval Council and operational forces were generally under Army front or area commanders.

Kuznetsov would later write a vivid description of his relationship with Stalin: "When I was installed in the position of People's Commissar of the Navy in April, 1939, Stalin no longer appreciated objections and did not pay any special attention even to specialists. There had already formed around him a kind of thick cloud of toadying and servility, which made it difficult for people who did not occupy high positions to get through to him, and his opinions evoked no objections, even from his closest advisers. Young people like myself who had been raised to the heights by the waves of the 'turbulent period' of 1937–1938 [i.e., purges], having tried to 'have our own opinions,' were quickly convinced that our lot was more to listen than to speak."

Kuznetsov was relieved as commander in chief of the Navy in 1947 and charged with treason for having approved the transfer of a German acoustic TORPEDO to the British during the war.

Kuznetsov was brought before a military court, but his case was "dismissed" and he was reduced in rank to rear admiral and exiled to the Pacific Fleet. In 1950 he was (for a second time) appointed to command the Pacific Fleet and a year later then-Vice Adm. Kuznetsov was recalled to Moscow by Stalin and appointed minister of the Navy and CinC. Reportedly, after Stalin's death in 1953, Kuznetsov had arguments over naval programs with Stalin's successors. Although Kuznetsov was promoted to the top naval rank of Admiral of the Fleet of the Soviet Union in March 1955, in mid-1955 NIKITA KHRUSHCHEV replaced Kuznetsov with Adm. S. G. GORSHKOV (Kuznetsov being formally retired in Jan. 1956).

Kwajalein

Large atoll—78 miles long with a cluster of about eighteen small islands—in the MARSHALL ISLANDS. Kwajalein, the Japanese administrative and communications center for the Marshalls, was a major objective of the U.S. CENTRAL PACIFIC CAMPAIGN.

U.S. strategists expected the capture of Kwajalein would be as bloody as the taking of TARAWA in the GILBERT ISLANDS in Nov. 1943. But after weeks of bombing by U.S. aircraft from AIRCRAFT CARRIERS and airfields in the Gilberts, the big atoll had been pounded into submission. In the AMPHIBIOUS LANDINGS that began on Jan. 31, 1944, a vanguard of Marines from the 53,000-man U.S. assault force landed on tiny islands near Roi and Namur in the northeast corner of the atoll. The Marines fought their way inland, subdued the defenders, and set up ARTILLERY that bombarded Roi and Namur.

The next morning the Army's 7th DIVISION landed on Kwajalein Island while the 4th Marine Division landed at Roi and Namur. The Marines met little resistance, but the Army troops needed four days to secure the island against savage Japanese resistance. Nearly 8,400 of the 10,000 Japanese died—many of them by suicide—defending Kwajalein. About 500 Americans were killed.

After the war Kwajalein became a U.S. missile test range.

L-5 Sentinel

This U.S. Army and Marine Corps ARTILLERY spotting and liaison aircraft was about twice as heavy as the widely flown L-SERIES GRASSHOPPER aircraft. In 1941 the Army acquired a commercial Stinson 105 Voyager and designated it O-62 for trials. Army procurement began in 1942, initially with the designation O-62 and then L-5. The Army acquired more than 3,000 of these aircraft; the Marines and Navy used another 458 with the designation OY. The Army also acquired a few commercial Voyagers, eight of which were initially designated AT-19 for use as trainers; these later became L-9s.

The planes were used in several combat areas; the Marines launched and recovered OY-1 Sentinels from a LANDING SHIP, TANK off IWO JIMA. Although larger and not produced by the Piper firm,

these aircraft were invariably referred to as Piper Cubs or Grasshoppers by front-line troops.

The L-5 was a development of the L-1 Vigilant built by Stinson. With the designation O-49 and then L-1, the Army from 1940 procured several hundred, a few of which went to the RAF under LEND-LEASE. Several L-1s were configured as ambulances; seven of those were additionally fitted with twin floats.

The L-5 was a high-wing aircraft with a top speed of 130 mph. It carried a pilot and observer, seated in tandem.

La-5

One of the most effective Soviet-made fighters of the war. The aircraft made its combat debut in Oct. 1942 at the battle of STALINGRAD and was flown as

In many respects the most important ship of the war was the landing ship, tank (LST). Although more than 1,100 LSTs were built during the war, there were never enough of them. The *LST 4* is shown here during the invasion of southern France in Aug. 1944. *(U.S. Navy)*

484

a first-line aircraft until the end of the war. The top Soviet fighter ACE, IVAN N. KOZHEDUB, scored all sixty-two of his aerial victories in the La-5, including one jet-propelled Messerschmitt ME 262. The derivative La-9 with a larger engine became operational at the end of the war and the ultimate La-11 version was a mainstay of the Soviet Air Force in the immediate postwar period. Total La-5 production is estimated at 9,920 aircraft.

The La-5 was an improvement on the LaGG-3, with a more powerful engine and other refinements. The aircraft was first flown early in 1942. Performance and handling were excellent and it was quickly placed into production. Only range was a problem. The plane earned designer S. A. Lavochkin the award Hero of Socialist Labor.

The aircraft had a conventional fighter arrangement, being a low-wing aircraft with a large radial engine and distinctive spinner. The main undercarriage was fully retractable. Variants—not built in large numbers—included the two-seat La-7U reconnaissance aircraft and an interceptor variant with a small ROCKET for boost power.

The La-5FN had a top speed of 402 mph with a range listed at 530 miles. Its armament was two 20-mm cannon and it could carry 330 pounds of BOMBS.

La Guardia, Fiorello H. (1882–1947)

New York politician who served briefly in CIVIL DEFENSE. Mayor of New York City from 1934 to 1945, La Guardia ("The Little Flower") was one of the most colorful politicians of his era. President ROOSEVELT in Aug. 1940 named him chairman of the U.S. section of the Canada-U.S. Joint Defense Board and in May 1941 director of the newly created Office of Civilian Defense. In Feb. 1942 La Guardia resigned and Roosevelt sought a high-ranking wartime job for him. The president suggested to Chief of Staff Gen. GEORGE C. MARSHALL that La Guardia be commissioned a general and sent to Gen. DWIGHT D. EISENHOWER as a specialist in military government. Marshall, who disliked putting politicians into uniform, successfully resisted. In March 1946 La Guardia succeeded Herbert Lehman as director general of the UNITED NATIONS RELIEF AND REHABILITATION ADMINISTRATION.

Lachsfang (Salmon Catch)

German code name for proposed German-Finnish drive to Kandalaksha-Belomorsk, mid-1942.

Laconia affair

One of the most controversial events of the BATTLE OF THE ATLANTIC. The 19,659-ton British troop ship *Laconia,* a former Cunard White Star liner, was sunk by the German submarine *U-156* on Sept. 12, 1942, in the South Atlantic, just below the Equator. At the time the ship, bound for England, was carrying 2,228 passengers, including eighty women and children, and 1,800 Italian PRISONERS OF WAR.

After discovering that the survivors included hundreds of Italians, the *U-156*'s commanding officer, *Korvettenkapitän* Werner Hartenstein, began taking survivors on board the submarine and put out an emergency call for assistance. Two other U-BOATS and an Italian submarine were ordered to the scene to assist Hartenstein. The Germans advised Allied forces that the submarines were on the surface for humanitarian reasons, although the call was generally considered to be a trap to lure Allied ships to the area.

On Sept. 16 a U.S. Army B-24 LIBERATOR from Ascension Island attacked the surfaced *U-156,* which had a large RED CROSS flag displayed forward. The U-boat, damaged, cast off the lifeboats she was towing (one was sunk by the BOMBS) and submerged.

Following this attack on the clearly marked submarine, *Kontradmiral* KARL DÖNITZ issued the "*Laconia* order," which expressly forbade submarine commanders from rescuing survivors from torpedoed ships. Donitz's order of Sept. 17 stated: "Rescue runs counter to the primary demands of warfare for the destruction of enemy ships and crews." At the WAR CRIMES trials after the war Dönitz was charged under this order.

Lafayette,

see *NORMANDIE*.

LaGG-3

A widely used Soviet fighter in the early war period although it showed limited performance. In production only from 1941 until mid-1942, the

LaGG-3 saw extensive service although it was quickly replaced on assembly lines by the far superior LA-5 fighter.

The LaGG-3, which was designated for its designers—Lavochkin, Gorbunov, and Gudkov—was in turn a derivative of the LaGG-1, which had first flown in March 1939 and entered only limited production. The LaGG-3 had a larger engine and although of wood construction was considered a rugged aircraft. Total production of the LaGG-1 and LaGG-3 was 6,528 aircraft, mostly the latter design.

The low-wing monoplane had an in-line engine and bore some resemblance to the U.S. P-40 WARHAWK.

Maximum speed of the LaGG-3 was 348 mph with range credited at 400 miles; later aircraft with an improved engine could reach 357 mph. Armament varied considerably. Standard armaments included one 20-mm cannon plus one 12.7-mm and two 7.62-mm machine guns, with up to 484 pounds of BOMBS or ground-attack ROCKETS being carried.

Lancaster

British heavy bomber. Described by aviation historian Owen Thetford as "perhaps the most famous and certainly the most successful heavy bomber used by the RAF in the Second World War," the Lancaster was developed as a result of the failure of its twin-engine predecessor, the Manchester. Employed exclusively against German targets in Europe during the war, the Lancaster was the world's only aircraft capable of carrying the gigantic 22,000-pound GRAND SLAM BOMB. The bomber began wartime service with a minelaying mission in Heligoland Bight on March 3, 1942; its first night bombing mission was flown against Essen on March 10–11.

Subsequently the Lancaster was used primarily in night bombing missions but, on occasion, flew daylight strikes, such as the low-level raid against the

MAN diesel engine factory at Augsburg on April 17, 1942. Lancasters sank the battleship *TIRPITZ* at anchor in a Norwegian fjord on Nov. 12, 1944 (using 12,000-pound TALLBOY BOMBS). Even heavier bombs were delivered by Lancasters against tunnels, dams, viaducts, and other difficult-to-reach targets in Europe. During 1942 the Lancaster became the dominant aircraft of the RAF Bomber Command; by Jan. 1942 there were 256 Lancasters (of 882 bombers) and by Jan. 1943 the command had 652 Lancasters (of 1,093 bombers). In terms of loss rate for bomb load delivered, the Lancaster was the most effective heavy bomber of the war. From 1941 to 1945 Lancasters flew 156,000 sorties over Germany, dropping 608,612 tons of bombs.

A massive-looking aircraft, the Lancaster was a mid-wing, four-engine bomber with characteristic nose, ventral, and tail gun turrets. The twin tail fins were set forward of the tail (the aircraft was originally fitted with triple fins). In most aircraft a RADAR "can" protruded beneath the after fuselage. From the outset the Lancaster could carry a 4,000-pound bomb; this was increased in modified aircraft until it could carry the heaviest payload of any wartime aircraft.

The original Avro Lancaster was a twin-engine Manchester airframe fitted with four Rolls-Royce Merlin engines. This aircraft first flew on Jan. 9, 1941; the first production Lancaster flew in Oct. 1941. The aircraft's combat debut came the following spring. The Lancaster production run totaled 7,377 aircraft (including 430 built in Canada). In planning for the STRATEGIC BOMBING of Japan when the war in Europe was over, the Lancaster Mk IV had more powerful Merlin engines and the Mk V a heavier gun armament and longer fuselage. These aircraft in production were renamed Lincoln. The prototype aircraft flew on June 9, 1944, but the first aircraft for service trials were not delivered until Aug. 1945. Hence no Lancaster or Lincoln saw combat against Japan. (The RAF planned to have thirty-six squadrons of these aircraft assigned to the U.S. Twentieth AIR FORCE by mid-1946 for operations against Japan.)

The Lancaster I bomber had a maximum speed of 287 mph and could fly a 1,660-mile mission with 14,000 pounds of bombs for just over 1,000 miles while delivering a 22,000-pound bomb against a

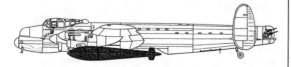

Lancaster Mk 1 with Tallboy bomb.

target. The defensive armament consisted of six .303-cal. machine guns in nose, dorsal, and ventral power turrets (the last eventually deleted) plus four .303-cal. machine guns in the tail turret. The Lancaster was flown by a crew of seven.

(After the war the Lancaster succeeded the B-24 LIBERATOR in the maritime reconnaissance role with RAF Coastal Command until replaced by the Shackleton. The Lancaster served in the RAF until December 1953, the last aircraft being a photo-reconnaissance variant.)

Land, Vice Adm. Emory S. (1879–1971)

Chairman of the U.S. Maritime Commission during the war with responsibility for building thousands of merchant ships, including the LIBERTY and VICTORY programs, as well as LANDING SHIPS, TANK and ESCORT CARRIERS.

A 1902 graduate of the Naval Academy, Land served two years in surface ships before entering the Navy's Construction Corps. He served mostly in the Bureau of Construction and Repair and as a staff specialist to FLEET commanders, including Adm. W. S. Sims when he was head of U.S. naval forces in Europe in 1918. After the war Land qualified as a naval aviator.

In 1932 he became chief of the Bureau of Construction and Repair as a rear admiral. He retired in April 1937 and was immediately appointed to the newly created Maritime Commission. In Feb. 1938 he replaced JOSEPH P. KENNEDY, SR. as chairman. As chairman Land held major responsibilities for American shipbuilding in the war; in 1942 he was given the additional duties of head of the War Shipping Administration. His efforts helped to create the largest merchant fleet in history.

Land was promoted to vice admiral in 1944. He resigned as Maritime Commission chairman in Jan. 1946.

Landcrab

Code name of U.S. recapture of the island of Attu in the ALEUTIAN ISLANDS from the Japanese, May 1943.

Landing Craft

Short-range craft for AMPHIBIOUS LANDINGS employed by most belligerents in World War II. They were needed in short-range operations to carry troops, weapons, and vehicles across rivers and along coasts, and in long-range operations for ship-to-shore movement of troops, vehicles, and supplies.

The U.S. Navy and Marine Corps experimented with a number of landing craft designs in the 1930s, including AMPHIBIOUS TRACTORS. ANDREW J. HIGGINS, a New Orleans boatbuilder, in 1926 had built a shallow-draft boat called the *Eureka* for use on the lower Mississippi River and along the Gulf Coast. In the summer of 1936 the Marines tested Higgins' boat, which immediately proved superior to all previously tested craft. It had a shallow draft and could easily run onto the beach and pull off again. After a 1939 exercise a Marine participant wrote, "The Higgins boat gave the best performance under all conditions. It has more speed, more maneuverability, handles easier, and lands troops higher on the beach" than the other craft evaluated. While the Marines enthusiastically supported Higgins, the Navy's Bureau of Ships opposed the design of an "outsider" and sought to procure for the Marines its own, less-capable craft.

The Higgins design won. In 1942 the U.S. Senate War Investigating Committee, chaired by the indomitable HARRY S TRUMAN, observed: "It is clear that the Bureau of Ships, for reasons known only to itself, stubbornly persisted for over five years in clinging to an unseaworthy TANK lighter design of its own. . . . The Bureau's action has caused not only a waste of time but has caused the needless

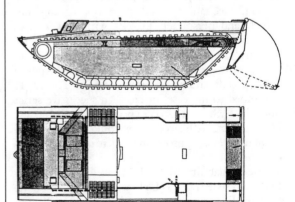

LVT-4 amphibious tractor.

expenditure of over $7,000,000 for a total of 225 Bureau lighters which do not meet the needs of the Armed Forces."

The German conquest of most of Western Europe in 1940 inspired intensive development of Allied landing craft. In those traumatic days of June 1940, Prime Minister CHURCHILL proposed that planning be undertaken for actions against enemy-held coasts and directed that suitable craft be developed for landing tanks on beaches. (In 1917, Churchill had suggested bullet-proof lighters and tank-landing lighters for amphibious operations.) Work was already under way on such craft in Britain as a result of experiments with assault boats in 1938–1939. Now, under Churchill's direction, in July 1940 the Admiralty ordered twenty new, larger craft—the landing craft, tank (LCT).

The initial LCTs displaced 226 tons light, were 152 feet long, and had a maximum speed of 10 knots. Their cargo capacity was three 40-ton tanks or six smaller, 16-ton tanks, or 250 tons of general cargo. Delivered from 1941 onward, large numbers of LCTs were employed for raids on the Continent as well as for coastal operations in Libya. Improved, larger LCTs followed. Even the later LCTs were small enough to be built by engineering firms that were not engaged in shipbuilding. Thus the labor and facilities needed for warships and merchant ships were not interrupted by the large LCT program.

The United States followed with massive landing craft construction programs and, in addition to LCTs, the American firms produced 50-foot landing craft mechanized (LCM), 36-foot landing craft vehicle and personnel (LCVP—with bow ramps) and landing craft personnel (large) (LCP(L)—without bow ramps), and rubber assault craft (LCR) in various sizes—on the order of 70,000 of all types of landing craft and amphibious tractors. The LCTs continued to increase in size with successive series until the U.S.-built LCT(7) became a "ship." These 203 ½-foot, 1,095-ton ships could carry five medium tanks and, appropriately, were called AMPHIBIOUS SHIPS.

The availability of LCTs as well as the larger LANDING SHIP, TANKS (LST) were critical for operations in European waters, and their shortage contributed to the delay in opening a SECOND FRONT by invading the Continent from 1942 to 1943 and again to mid-1944.

Specialized landing craft were also produced in large numbers by the Japanese Navy and the German Navy, the latter primarily for the planned invasion of England, Operation SEA LION, but also for coastal operations in the Aegean and other coastal areas. The Soviet Navy conducted large numbers of short-range amphibious landings using mostly landing craft converted from other types of ships and craft.

Landing Ships,
see AMPHIBIOUS SHIPS.

Landing Ships, Tank
Probably the most important ship in the Allied war effort. The landing ship, TANK or LST was the backbone of amphibious landings in the Mediterranean, European, and Pacific areas. In 1944 Prime Minister CHURCHILL declared: "The whole of this difficult [strategy] question only arises out of the absurd shortage of the L.S.T.s. How it is that the plans of two great empires like Britain and the United States should be so much hamstrung and limited by a hundred or two of the particular vessels will never be understood by history."

The first LSTs were converted by the British from shallow-draft tankers. These and an initial British new construction class of three LST(1) series were not successful.

In Nov. 1941 a delegation from the British Admiralty arrived in the United States to pool ideas with the U.S. Navy's Bureau of Ships. Within a few days the basic design for the definitive LST(2) was ready. It was approved in record time.

The USS *LST 1* was laid down on June 10, 1942, and was completed only six months later—on Dec. 14, 1942. More ships followed—by 1943 there were more than 1,000 LSTs under contract in U.S. shipyards. (Of the 1,052 ships actually completed, 113 were transferred to Britain and four more were turned over to the Greek Navy.) The definitive LST(2) design first saw combat in the SOLOMON ISLANDS and in SICILY in 1943. The pioneer *LST 1* participated in the invasions of Sicily and SALERNO in 1943, and ANZIO and NORMANDY in 1944.

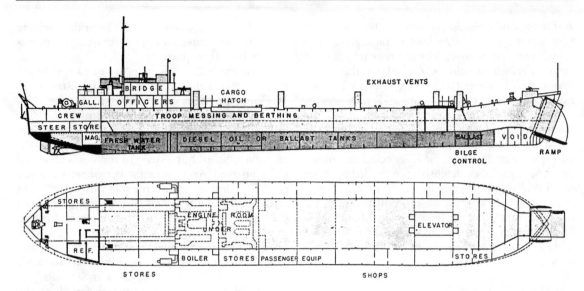

LST (landing ship, tank).

There were many LSTs—but never enough. There were constant demands for the ships. The U.S. Navy—which controlled their construction—wanted them for the Pacific campaigns; the Army wanted them for assaults in Europe; Churchill wanted them for peripheral operations, in the Mediterranean, Aegean, and Norway, to help keep the pressure on Germany until the French coast could be assaulted in mid-1944.

In response to the problems of LST allocation, the British initiated their own, small LST production with the LST(3) design. No diesel engines were available in Britain or from the United States, and there was a shortage of welding facilities in British and Canadian shipyards. As a result, the LST(3) had standard steam reciprocating engines (which were being installed in corvettes and frigates) and were mostly riveted. This provided larger, deeper draft, and slower landing ships without any increase in payload. Only sixty-four LST(3)s were built in British and Canadian yards, completed in 1944–1945.

LSTs demonstrated a remarkable capacity to absorb damage and survive. Despite the sobriquet "Large Slow Target," which was bestowed by irreverent crew members, the LSTs suffered few losses in proportion to their numbers. Their structural arrangement provided unusual strength and buoyancy. Of the 1,052 American-built LSTs, most of which were in combat, only twenty-six were lost to enemy action and another thirteen were victims of weather, groundings, or accidents. None of the British LSTs was lost.

The LSTs also proved to be highly versatile. In the basic configuration they were sometimes used as hospital ships (on D-day at Normandy LSTs brought 41,035 wounded men back across the English Channel), for providing ammunition to BATTLESHIPS, for carrying railroad rolling stock (on rails fitted in the tank deck), and to launch light observation aircraft (fitted with flight decks or the Brodie aircraft launch/recovery system). Other LSTs were fully converted to various types of repair ships, landing craft tenders, wounded-evacuation ships, and (British) command ships. Perhaps the most unusual LST configuration was the fitting of small flight decks for launching Army Piper Cub–type observation planes in the Sicily and Anzio landings. In the Pacific, for the invasion of Iwo Jima, an LST was fitted with a wire/trapeze for the launching *and recovery* of Marine-piloted Piper Cubs used for artillery spotting.

The LST(2) was 328 feet long with a beam of 50 feet; displacement was 4,080 tons fully loaded with

2,100 tons of cargo, although for beaching 500 tons was a more feasible load (typically eighteen 30-ton tanks or an equivalent in other vehicles and cargo). Vehicles could be parked on the upper (main) deck or lower (tank) deck, which were connected by ramp in the early ships and an elevator in the later units. There were two or six davits for landing craft, and a large LCT-type landing craft could be carried on the main deck. In addition to a crew of about 210 men, the LSTs could accommodate 160 troops. Self-defense was provided by up to seven BOFORS 40-MM guns and six OERLIKON 20-MM guns in the U.S. ships, while those that served with the British had a 12-pounder and six 20-mm guns. Diesel engines drove the ships at a maximum speed of 11.6 knots, but their transit speeds were 8 or 9 knots.

Langley (AV 3, ex-CV 1)

The U.S. Navy's first AIRCRAFT CARRIER, generally called the "Covered Wagon" by Navy fliers. After serving from 1922 to 1937 as a trials carrier (CV 1) for the U.S. Navy, she was converted to a seaplane tender (AV 3), losing the forward 40 percent of her flight deck.

Supporting PBY CATALINA flying boats, the *Langley* was assigned to the U.S. Asiatic FLEET and was at Cavite in the Philippines when the Japanese struck on Dec. 8, 1941. She departed immediately, sailing to Balikpapan, Borneo, and Australia, arriving at Darwin on Jan. 1, 1942. She operated along the coast until Feb. 22, 1942, when she departed Freemantle, Australia, in a CONVOY, carrying thirty-two P-40E WARHAWK fighters desperately needed by Allied forces in the DUTCH EAST INDIES. On Feb. 27 she departed the convoy to make a run in to the port of Tjilatjap, Java.

After rendezvousing with two U.S. DESTROYERS, the *Langley* was attacked in a series of strikes by Japanese twin-engine bombers. The ship's commanding officer had requested a fighter escort from Java, but none could be spared from the intensive fighting there. Twice the *Langley* evaded BOMB salvoes from bombers flying too high to be reached by the *Langley*'s antiaircraft guns. On the third run bombers smashed the *Langley* with three hits and two near-misses. The twenty-nine-year-old ship staggered under the blows. Planes on her abbreviated

flight deck erupted into flame. The bridge steering gear and gyro compass were destroyed. There was soon a 10° list to port.

Six Japanese ZERO fighters appeared and began strafing the helpless ship. Comdr. Robert P. McConnell made a gallant effort to save his ship, but had to give up when propulsion was lost. He ordered the *Langley* abandoned at 1:32 P.M. on Feb. 27 while the two destroyers were available to take off survivors. All but sixteen of the ship's crew and the embarked Army aviation personnel were rescued. The destroyers sank the ship with TORPEDOES and gunfire, 74 miles from Java. Fearing a return of the Japanese planes, the destroyers departed before the *Langley* went down, causing a short-lived controversy that the Japanese may have captured her. (The Japanese did capture and put into service a U.S. destroyer found in dry dock at Surabaja.)

The *Langley* survivors were transferred to the U.S. Navy oiler *Pecos* (AO 6); she was sunk by Japanese carrier planes on March 1, and her survivors—many from the *Langley*—were rescued by a U.S. destroyer.

The *Langley,* originally built as the naval collier *Jupiter* (AC 3), was launched in 1912 and commissioned the following year. After World War I she was extensively converted to serve as the Navy's first aircraft carrier and renamed for aviation pioneer Samuel Pierpont Langley.

In her third configuration as a seaplane tender she was fitted to serve as a mobile base for two SQUADRONS of patrol bombers. Her displacement was 11,050 tons standard and she had a length of 542 feet. The Navy's first large electrically propelled ship, she had a top speed of 15 knots. As a seaplane tender she was armed with four 5-inch (127-mm) guns for surface targets and two 3-inch (76-mm) antiaircraft guns, plus several machine guns. Her crew numbered about 300.

Language

The war brought hundreds of new words and phrases into the American language. Some, spawned by the New Deal, were old words given new meanings: *ceiling* and *floor* pertained to prices and wages, which could be *frozen; Good Neighbor* became a policy for dealing with Latin America. Sometimes old words combined for a new meaning:

hot and *money* put together meant cash that was moving quickly out of tottering Europe to be invested in the peaceful and stable United States.

Europe added grim new words to the U.S. vocabulary: BLITZKRIEG, GESTAPO, TOTAL WAR, SCORCHED EARTH, QUISLING. Air raids inspired *air-raid bulb* (a dim blue street light), BLACKOUT, ACK-ACK. One word, *coventryize* (to make rubble of a city), did not last long, but the place that inspired it, COVENTRY, lived on as a symbol of NAZI ruthlessness. The RAF nicknamed its two-ton BOMB the *block-buster* because it could wipe out an entire city block. The word lingered and came to mean a theatrical kind of "hit," a well-received play or movie.

Besides overseeing the British *war effort,* Prime Minister CHURCHILL also kept watch over the English language. He insisted that the NORMANDY INVASION needed a better code name than Roundup, endorsing Overlord as more fitting for such an illustrious endeavor. And when his director of military intelligence used the word *intensive* in plans for the invasion, Churchill shot him a memo: "*Intense* is the right word. You should read Fowler's *Modern English Usage* on the use of the two words."

America's entry into the war brought American words into the war lexicon. H. L. Mencken, in *The American Language,* notes that U.S. WAR CORRESONDENTS "adorned the daily history of the war with multitudinous bright inventions, but the actual soldier, like his predecessors of the past, limited his argot to a series of derisive names for the things he had to do and endure, and the ancient stock of profanity and obscenity." Four-letter words were "put to excessively heavy service. One of them, beginning with *f,* became an almost universal verb, and with *-ing* added, a universal adjective; another, beginning with *s,* ran a close second to it." (Novelist NORMAN MAILER was forced by his publisher to have the soldiers in *The Naked and the Dead* say *fug* in place of the actual word they relentlessly spoke.)

Mencken cites SNAFU, one of the war's many acronyms, as "one of the few really good coinages of the war."

Acronyms flourished. The Navy had manufactured many before the war, including CINCUS for Commander in Chief, U.S. FLEET. After the Japanese sinking of so many ships at PEARL HARBOR,

Adm. ERNEST J. KING took over the post and changed CINCUS to COMINCH. RADAR (for Radio Detecting And Ranging), was a Navy acronym, as was SONAR (Sound Navigation Ranging); both would lose their acronym status and become words. Other acronyms included WAC (WOMENs Army Corps), SHAEF (SUPREME HEADQUARTERS ALLIED EXPEDITIONARY FORCE), and AWOL (absent without leave).

An amateur lexicographer, writing just after the war, noted that the armed services tended to create acronyms of four letters or more that could be pronounced (as in WAVES and WACs while civilian WAR AGENCIES favored three-letter, unpronounceable acronyms: OPA for OFFICE OF PRICE ADMINISTRATION, OWI for OFFICE OF WAR INFORMATION, WRB for War Resources Board, OPM for Office of Production Management, WMC for War Manpower Commission, OWM for the OFFICE OF WAR MOBILIZATION. From these agencies also came such lasting abstractions as *priorities* (as in "setting priorities"); *expediter* (someone who made work or materials move through WAR PRODUCTION processes); and *nonessential* (as in "nonessential civilian items").

SELECTIVE SERVICE, better known as "the draft," gave the wartime language *1-A* for "eligible for induction" and *4-F* (officially written as IV-F) for inductees declared physically or mentally disqualified, and *draft dodger.* Once in the service, an inductee or enlistee could be dismissed via a *Section 8*—the discharge of an inept or "undesirable" SAD SACK.

Some other words of war:

blitzkrieg: A combination of two German words, *Blitz* (lightning) and *Krieg* (war), but not a German word. The British coined it to describe the fast-rolling, PANZER-led German offensive into Poland that started the EUROPEAN WAR. Word detective William Safire traces its first use (as "Blitz-Krieg") to the Oct. 7, 1939, issue of *The War Illustrated.* The British then appropriated the first half of the word for air raids; see "LITTLE BLITZ."

boondocks: Isolated countryside, especially jungles. U.S. Marines and soldiers began using the term while fighting insurgents in the Philippines in the early 1900s. The troops seem to have garbled the word *bundok,* from a native language, Tagalog; *bundok* means "mountain."

bought the farm: Died. One theory holds that farm-state soldiers would say that after the war they wanted to buy a farm. So when they died, their city-bred comrades would remember them by hoping they got the peace they wanted by buying a celestial farm.

brass: High-ranking officers. The term reached U.S. soldiers via the British Army, which used it to allude to the gold braid on officers' hats. The term (also *top brass* or *big brass*) lived on in civilian life as veterans got new jobs and new bosses.

briefing: A military term derived from *brief,* a lawyer's summary of a case's basic points. A briefing session theoretically gave those going into an operation all they needed to know. The idea was later extended to describe the sessions that public relations officers held for WAR CORRESPONDENTS. An after-battle report, usually given by combatants to intelligence officers, became a *debriefing.*

broad: Originally a *bawd* or whore, but given a more wholesome meaning of attractive woman by Oscar Hammerstein in the lyrics of *South Pacific,* which was set in World War II.

combat fatigue: A vague psychological term that replaced the World War I term "shell shock."

door-key children: Youngsters of parents who worked in defense plants and were not home when the children arrived from school. The children were also known as "defense work orphans."

GI or GI Joe: A U.S. soldier (rarely, if ever, used for sailors or Marines). The *GI* is believed to come from *Government Issue,* the general term for matériel distributed to soldiers, and got applied to everything uniquely Army, from *GI haircut* to *GI soap* and *GI chow. GI* was also used to express distaste for military officers making life too military, as in the question a new arrival to a unit invariably asked: "Are they very GI around here?" *Joe* was a general name for any male. In 1942 *GI Joe* was picked up as the name for a COMIC character in *YANK* magazine. The legislation giving schooling and home loans to veterans became known as the GI BILL OF RIGHTS.

gook: A derogatory name for an Asian native. Although in some use during World War II, it gained greater currency in the Vietnam War as the term frequently used by U.S. soldiers and Marines to describe Vietnamese or other natives. It has been traced to usage by U.S. forces fighting insurgents in the Philippines early in the century.

gremlin: A British term, used by RAF pilots. A gremlin was "a mischievous sprite" or "fanciful creature" that caused inexplicable trouble in and around aircraft. The term was picked up by U.S. fliers, especially those stationed in England.

home front: A term resurrected from World War I to describe the civilian efforts supporting the war. A typical usage was in the June 1942 issue of *The American Home* magazine. In it was a red, white, and blue sign to be pasted in the window, proclaiming "On Guard the Home Front. This is a 100% American Home Cooperating for Victory."

milk run: Frequent or regular operation, especially the habitual AAF bombing of a certain target against little opposition. The term stemmed from the quiet, uneventful early morning delivery route of a milkman—a service that ironically began its eventual disappearance during the war.

pinup: A photograph of a beautiful woman, usually a movie star such as Rita Hayworth or Betty Grable, which servicemen hung up in their lockers. In the MOVIE *Guadalcanal Diary* William Bendix has Betty Grable's picture pinned on a tree trunk next to his shaving mirror. The studio got 20,000 requests a week for this bathing suit photo, whose point of view is from the back, with the movie star looking over her shoulder and smiling. The first use of the term *pinup* is believed to have been on April 30, 1943, in *Yank.* Prior to that, *Yank* referred to the photos as "dream girls." Similar glamour photos were the models for NOSE ART used in U.S. warplanes.

roger: Pilot code for "your message received and understood." The response was *roger wilco,* meaning "message received."

Rosie the Riveter: The symbol of women working in defense plants. The mythical Rosie, portrayed in a song as "working overtime on a riveting machine," was the subject of a *Saturday Evening Post* cover by Norman Rockwell; a sexier, scantily clad Rosie appeared in *Esquire* magazine.

short snorter: A piece of U.S. currency, usually of small denomination, on which Allied airmen signed their names. The bills were the membership cards in a global fraternity. It had neither comprehensible rules nor explanation for its existence, and its members usually assembled at a bar in an officers club. When a *short snorter* was filled with names, another bill was attached to the original; the longer the string of bills, the more the holder had been around. Signers of the bills called themselves *short snorters,* a term that came from *short snort,* a quick drink.

short-arm inspection: Examination of male genitals for signs of venereal disease. (See MEDICINE, MILITARY.)

take-home pay: The amount of money left over from a pay check (or pay envelope) after deductions for taxes and WAR BONDS. "Pay-as-you-go income" taxes were a new event in the lives of many Americans, and no longer was a worker's pay what he or she was handed at the end of the work week.

war of nerves: Psychological warfare, using PROPAGANDA to undermine the enemy's morale.

Lanikai

Sailing ship taken over by the U.S. Navy shortly before war began in the Pacific to scout out the destination of Japanese amphibious forces. However, the ship's commanding officer, Lt. Kemp Tolley, surmised that the real intention of the *Lanikai*'s mission was to provoke the Japanese into action against the United States.

On Dec. 2, 1941, President ROOSEVELT had directed the Navy to charter three small vessels "to observe and report by radio Japanese movements in the west China Sea and Gulf of Siam [Thailand]." Tolley's orders were to specifically patrol the entrance to Cam Ranh Bay in French Indochina and report the direction taken by the Japanese fleet when it went to sea.

The *Lanikai* was placed in Navy commission on Dec. 5 at the Cavite navy yard near MANILA in the Philippines. Tolley was ready to depart on his mission on the morning of Dec. 8, 1941. As soon as word was received of the Japanese attack on PEARL HARBOR that morning (Dec. 7 Hawaii time), Tolley returned to Manila. During the following weeks the *Lanikai* was employed as a dispatch vessel and patrol ship in Manila Bay.

On Dec. 26, with several passengers in addition to his crew of six U.S. sailors and twelve Filipinos, Tolley set out for the DUTCH EAST INDIES. The ship evaded the Japanese forces off the Philippines. Safely reaching Java, the ship was bombed there by Japanese planes, but escaped unscathed. (The BOMB concussions killed numerous nearby fish, which the crew collected.) In Feb. 1942 the *Lanikai* escaped from the Japanese forces advancing toward Java and on March 18 reached Freemantle, Australia. She then sailed along the Australian coast keeping a lookout for Japanese activities. On Aug. 22 she was decommissioned and transferred to the Australian Navy, which operated the ship—without masts—as a boom defense vessel for the remainder of the war. The Aussies kept her original name.

The *Lanikai* received one U.S. Navy BATTLE STAR. Tolley, later reaching the rank of rear admiral, became a prolific writer and recounted the ship's odyssey in *Cruise of the Lanikai.*

A two-masted, schooner-rigged yacht with a diesel engine, the *Lanikai* was built in 1914 in the United States. She displaced 150 tons and was 87 1/4 feet long. When taken over by the U.S. Navy she was armed with a 3-pounder cannon of Spanish-American War vintage and two .30-cal. machine guns. She was manned by a crew of about twenty.

Lanphier, Maj. Thomas G. (1915—)

U.S. Army Air Forces pilot generally credited with shooting down the aircraft carrying Adm. ISOROKU YAMAMOTO. Then-Capt. Lanphier of the 70th Fighter SQUADRON was assigned to lead the four-plane attack section for the interception of Yamamoto on April 18, 1943, over Ballale in the SOLOMON ISLANDS. Another sixteen P-38 LIGHTNING fighters would fly cover to protect the attack section, all taking off from GUADALCANAL for the 435-mile flight to the intercept point under the command of Maj. John W. Mitchell.

In the ensuing melee, the G4M BETTY bomber carrying Yamamoto and the accompanying bomber were shot down, and the admiral was killed. Lanphier got one bomber, and Lt. Rex Barber of the 339th Fighter Squadron destroyed the other. Lanphier's kill was credited with being Yamamoto's bomber.

One of the P-38s and its pilot were lost in the operation. Mitchell and the four pilots of the attack section received the Navy Cross for the action.

Latvia

Capital: Riga, pop. 1,994,506 (1938). A republic born in 1918, Latvia was ruled by an authoritarian government that maintained a neutral policy and remained unaffiliated with either its Fascist or Communist neighbors. But with their NONAGRESSION PACT, announced on Aug. 23, 1939, Germany and the Soviet Union erased their neighbor.

Latvia was consigned to the Soviet "sphere of influence," as set forth in a secret protocol of the pact. On Oct. 5, 1939, the foreign minister of Latvia was summoned to MOSCOW and presented with a "mutual assistance" treaty that authorized Soviet forces to garrison military and naval bases in Latvia. Near the end of the year, in a show of German-Soviet cooperation, some 60,000 Latvians of German descent were put on board German ships in Riga and taken to Germany.

Soviet troops invaded Latvia on June 16, 1940. Accompanying Soviet officials staged a mock election that created a puppet legislature whose first official act was passage of a resolution calling for the incorporation of Latvia into the Soviet Union. All members of foreign legations and consulates were ordered out of the country by Aug. 15, and from that date Latvia was effectively sealed off from the world.

Thousands of Latvians were sent to Soviet prison camps and forced-labor brigades. The International RED CROSS reported that 34,250 Latvians were missing and presumed deported. Another 1,450 were executed.

Germany invaded Latvia in 1941 as part of its invasion of the Soviet Union. Latvia was placed under the control of the *Reichskommissariat für dat Ostland,* the ruthless civil administration for occupied Soviet territories in the East. Thousands of Latvian Jews were murdered or sent to German CONCENTRATION CAMPS, and thousands of other Latvians were forced into virtual slavery for their German masters.

When the Germans retreated before the Soviet offensive of 1944, Soviet occupation of Latvia resumed. Bitter fighting against the Germans, continuing into May 1945, made much of Latvia a battleground. As the end of the EUROPEAN WAR neared, the Soviet Union announced the capture of 180,000 German prisoners in Latvia. The end of the war brought new agony for Latvia, as the Soviet occupiers launched a new wave of deportations and executions. (To the United States, Latvia remains an independent state, its status as a republic of the Soviet Union unrecognized.)

Laval, Pierre (1883–1945)

French politician and VICHY FRANCE collaborationist. Laval, who was premier of France and foreign minister in 1931–1932 and premier from June 1935 to Jan. 1936, lost popular support for his appeasement of Italy following its invasion of Ethiopia in 1935. He emerged from the political shadows as France was about to surrender to Germany in June 1940. He helped to make Marshal HENRI PHILIPPE PÉTAIN premier and, in reward, was made deputy head of state and foreign minister in the Vichy France regime.

Pétain fired Laval in Dec. 1940, but, under German pressure, he was reinstalled in April 1942. An avid follower of the NAZI line, Laval became the virtual dictator of France in Nov. 1942 when, following the Allied NORTH AFRICA INVASION, the Germans invaded and occupied Vichy France. Laval shipped French workers to Germany, enforced laws that stripped French JEWS of their rights, and aided the Germans in their hunt for non-French Jews.

"I wish for the victory of Germany," Laval said. After the United States entered the war he said, "An American victory would mean a victory for the Jews and the Communists."

When it became obvious that the Germans were not going to achieve victory, in Aug. 1944 Laval was whisked out of Paris in an SS car and driven to Germany. On May 2, 1945, five days before Germany surrendered, he flew to Spain, then to Austria, where U.S. Army officers arrested him and returned him to France. He testified as a defense witness in the collaboration trial of Pétain, then was himself put on trial for treason and convicted. On the day he was scheduled to be shot by a firing squad he attempted to kill himself. A physician saved him and he was taken out and shot on Oct. 15, 1945.

Layton, Capt. Edwin T. (1903–1984)

Head of U.S. Navy intelligence for the Pacific FLEET during the war and largely responsible for the use of intelligence derived from Japanese code-breaking in the battles of CORAL SEA and MIDWAY, and later engagements.

During the 1920s and 1930s Layton served in surface ships, interspersed with tours ashore—in Japan for language training, in Peking and later TOKYO as assistant naval attaché, and in WASHINGTON. After a little more than a year as commanding officer of a DESTROYER-minesweeper, then-Lt. Comdr. Layton became intelligence officer on the staff of the U.S. FLEET commander at PEARL HARBOR, Adm. JAMES O. RICHARDSON. He continued to serve in that assignment for Richardson's successors, Adms. HUSBAND E. KIMMEL (1941) and CHESTER W. NIMITZ (1942–1945).

Layton's code-breakers at Pearl Harbor made major inroads in reading the Japanese naval codes and analyzing radio transmissions for naval ship movements. However, just before the outbreak of war there was a constant struggle between Layton and the intelligence staff in Washington. Layton later charged that the refusal of those in Washington to share information with his staff contributed to the failure to know the location of Japanese warship movements at the outbreak of the Pacific War. His autobiographic study of naval intelligence in the Pacific War—"*And I Was There*"—was published shortly after his death. The book cited incompetence, bureaucratic feuding, and empire building in Washington, particularly by Capt. RICHMOND KELLY TURNER, then director of Navy war plans.

Layton was a champion of using code-breaking information (MAGIC) in planning operations, and had a strong supporter in Adm. Nimitz. At the end of the war Layton, then a captain, was ordered by Nimitz to join him at the SURRENDER ceremony on the USS *MISSOURI* (BB 63) in Tokyo Bay as a mark of the admiral's regard for his staff's intelligence work.

From Feb. 1946 Layton held several shore assignments, including the task of setting up the U.S. Navy's intelligence school, and, as a rear admiral, assistant director of intelligence for the JOINT CHIEFS OF STAFF and assistant chief of staff to the Commander in Chief Pacific Fleet. He retired in Nov. 1959.

L.B.

British code name for reinforcement of MALTA, May 1942.

League of Nations

A peacekeeping organization formed by the victorious nations after World War I. Each signer of the Treaty of Versailles had a vote in the League, whose Executive Council was to consist of representatives of the United States, the British Empire, Japan, Italy, France, and four nations selected by the Body of Delegates. Although President Woodrow Wilson was the principal architect of the League, the United States did not join, primarily because of opposition by isolationist senators.

The League did settle some minor disputes between small nations, but even its meager influence over international events diminished to utter ineffectiveness. The League failed China after Japan's seizure of Manchuria in 1931 and it would subsequently fail the victims of Italy, and Germany.

When Italy invaded Ethiopia in Oct. 1936, Emperor HAILE SELASSIE personally went before the League to plead for aid to his country. His plea was in vain. Similarly, the League did nothing when Germany militarized the Rhineland in 1936, openly violating the Treaty of Versailles.

Germany and Japan left the League in 1933, Italy in 1937. The Soviet Union was expelled in 1939 for its aggression against Finland. After the MUNICH PACT the League was moribund. It did not formally dissolve until 1946, following the creation of the UNITED NATIONS, whose structure was patterned after the League's.

Leahy, Fleet Adm. William D. (1875–1959)

Leahy, whose naval career dated to the Spanish-American War, served as both civilian and naval officer in World War II. His civilian appointments stemmed from his meeting with FRANKLIN D. ROOSEVELT during his 1913–1920 term as assistant secretary of the Navy. They met again when Roosevelt was President and Leahy was Chief of Naval Operations from 1937 to 1939 (and practically running the NAVY DEPARTMENT because of the illness of the secretary of the Navy).

After Leahy's retirement in 1939 Roosevelt appointed him Governor of Puerto Rico. A year later Leahy became U.S. Ambassador to VICHY FRANCE. As Ambassador, Leahy's role was to keep the lines of communication open while the United States remained neutral. Leahy hoped to encourage the

senescent Marshal HENRI PÉTAIN to resist HIT-
LER's demands, but he had little success. Leahy was
recalled soon after the United States became a belligerent in Dec. 1941.

In June 1942 Leahy became Chief of Staff to
Roosevelt and thus de facto served as Chairman of
the U.S. JOINT CHIEFS OF STAFF. Leahy demonstrated great tact in dealing with inter-service disputes among the service chiefs and in relations with
his British colleagues. Leahy's role was unique. As
the President's Chief of Staff Leahy served as inter-
locutor between Roosevelt and the JCS, which he
served as chairman. It was not important for Leahy
to make decisions; his job was to transmit the decisions back and forth between the strong-minded
Gen. GEORGE C. MARSHALL and Adm. ERNEST J.
KING and the equally self-possessed Roosevelt. Further, Leahy and HARRY HOPKINS were the only
Roosevelt aides who could originate White House
MAP ROOM messages to Prime Minister CHURCH-
ILL. For his service, and because of his position,
Leahy was the first of the seven U.S. senior officers
promoted to FIVE-STAR RANK in Dec. 1944.

Leahy proved as useful to Vice President HARRY
S TRUMAN, when he suddenly succeeded Roosevelt
after FDR's death in April 1945. Leahy's enduring
distrust of Soviet intentions fit in well with Truman's growing determination to take command of
the postwar world. After four more years as Truman's Chief of Staff, Leahy retired in 1949.

Lebanon

Capital: Beirut, pop. 1,126,601 (1944). A French-
Lebanese treaty in 1936 recognized Lebanon as an
independent state, but France retained the right to
maintain its own armed forces in the new country.
Moslem and Christian rivalry so marred the political process that the emergence of a working republic
seemed unlikely. In France, meanwhile, ratification
of the treaty dragged on until, with the outbreak of
the EUROPEAN WAR in Sept. 1939, the French essentially returned to the pretreaty status quo, sending more troops into Lebanon.

After the fall of France in June 1940 the commanding general in Lebanon expelled British and
other German foes and opted for VICHY FRANCE,
the collaborationist regime established in France.
In May 1941 Germany began using Syrian air bases,

and British and FREE FRENCH forces marched on
Lebanon and Syria. (See also SYRIA.) On July 10,
with British forces nearing Beirut, the Vichy troops
surrendered. Most of the Vichy French soldiers returned to France, but many of their officers joined
the ranks of the Free French and reinstalled French
colonial rule over Lebanon, with the British providing defense of the region.

In Nov. 1941 the French proclaimed Lebanon's
independence but not until Aug. 1943 was an election scheduled. When, after much struggle, a new
government was finally installed, it struck down
laws pertaining to French rights in Lebanon. The
French promptly arrested all leading politicians, dissolved the legislative chamber, and set up a puppet
government. The move united Lebanon's squabbling politicians, brought sharp criticism down on
the Free French from their exasperated Allies, and
set up true independence for the nation in Sept.
1944. The last British and French troops left in
1946.

Leclerc, Maj. Gen. Jacques Philippe (1902–1947)

Leading FREE FRENCH Army commander. In the
battle of France in May–June 1940 he was twice
captured by the Germans and twice escaped. He
made his way to England and enlisted in the Free
French forces. Fearing for his family still in France,
he adopted the nom de guerre Leclerc in place of de
Hauteclocque.

Gen. CHARLES DE GAULLE sent him to Africa as
the military governor of Chad and Cameroun,
before being appointed general officer commanding
French Equatorial Africa. His troops captured
Kufra in southern Libya, and distinguished them-
selves in action against Germans and Italians on the
Egyptian border, and in Ethiopia and French
Somaliland. In Dec. 1942 he led a troop column
1,500 miles across the Sahara from Chad to join the
British Eighth Army in Libya in Jan. 1943.

Leclerc was next given command of the French
2nd Armored Division, forming in England. The
division was landed in France shortly after the NOR-
MANDY INVASION. The division subsequently led
the entry of Allied forces into PARIS. Lt. Gen.
OMAR N. BRADLEY described Leclerc as "a magnificent TANK commander."

After the war he was sent to Indochina, but his uncompromising policies led to his recall in 1946. A year later, while serving as inspector general of French troops in North Africa, he was killed in an air crash. He was posthumously promoted to marshal of France.

Ledo Road

A military highway from Ledo, India, to a junction of the BURMA ROAD. U.S. Gen. JOSEPH W. STILWELL based much of the ALLIED CHINA-BURMA-INDIA CAMPAIGN strategy on the building of this new land route—a 300-mile highway through virgin jungle and mountain ranges—to reestablish a road link into China. (The lower portion of the Burma Road had been in Japanese hands since early 1942.)

Stilwell's plan called for a road from Ledo near the India-Burma border, into Burma through the Pangsan Pass in the Patkai Range, down the Hukawng Valley, then south and east down the Mogaung Valley to Myitkyina in the upper Irrawaddy Valley, south to Bhamo, then southeast again to link up with the Burma Road.

The U.S. Corps of Engineers, using many black units (see SEGREGATION), began building the road in the fall of 1942. By Dec. 1943 it was ready to be used to pour troops into Burma. Myitkyina was captured in Aug. 1944 and Wanting in Jan. 1945, making the link and allowing the first convoy to reach Kunming in Jan. 1945 on what Chinese leader CHIANG KAI-SHEK would rename the Stilwell Road.

Lee, Vice Adm. Willis A., Jr. (1888–1945)

The U.S. Navy's premier BATTLESHIP force commander during the war. "Ching" Lee went into battleships immediately after graduating from the Naval Academy in 1908, and although he served in other ships, he remained a battleship sailor first and foremost. He also became an expert rifle marksman, winning five gold medals in the 1920 Olympic Games in Antwerp. Between the wars he also commanded a succession of DESTROYERS as well as a light CRUISER.

In June 1939, as a captain, he became assistant director of fleet training in the NAVY DEPARTMENT. He became head of the division in Jan.

1941, with responsibility for training the sailors to man the large number of new ships being delivered to the Navy. In Feb, 1942, as rear admiral, he became the Chief of Staff to the CinC U.S. Fleet, Adm. ERNEST J. KING. After six months he went to the Pacific where he served as commander of a battleship DIVISION, the Commander Battleships Pacific FLEET, and then Commander Battleship SQUADRON 2. His ships supported the carrier strikes and amphibious assaults of the U.S. CENTRAL PACIFIC CAMPAIGN.

He saw action in the GUADALCANAL area on the night of Nov. 14–15, 1942, when he commanded two U.S. battleships engaging a Japanese battle force. Lee was awarded the Navy Cross. He also was decorated for his role in commanding surface ships in the battle of the MARIANAS in June 1944 as well as other actions against the Japanese. He was promoted to vice admiral in March 1944.

Still commander Battleship Squadron 2, he returned to the United States in 1945 to develop anti-KAMIKAZE tactics. He died of a heart attack on Aug. 25, 1945.

Leigh-Mallory, Air Chief Marshal Sir Trafford (1892–1944)

Leigh-Mallory began the EUROPEAN WAR as Commander of No. 12 GROUP RAF Fighter Command and was known as an ambitious "thruster." He fell out with Keith Park, his counterpart at No. 11 Group, and HUGH DOWDING, head of Fighter Command. Their dispute, which ripened into outright hostility during the BATTLE OF BRITAIN, concerned how best to meet the German air assaults.

History has sided with Park's squadron-by-squadron attacks launched only when the Luftwaffe aircraft destination and strength was clear, but timed to intercept the aircraft before they bombed. Leigh-Mallory's alternative—forming aircraft into five-squadron masses known as "Balbos"—was unwieldy and time-consuming.

Leigh-Mallory intrigued against Park and Dowding and managed to contribute to their replacement after the battle in what was commonly regarded then (and now) as shabby treatment for two outstanding heroes of the air battle. As a result, Leigh-Mallory attracted the active loathing of many of his fellow airmen. His pompous, overbearing manner did not help him win friends among British or American airmen.

During his term as No. 11 Group commander, Leigh-Mallory actively supported large fighter sweeps—Rhubarbs—into France that proved more costly to the RAF than to the Germans. Nevertheless, he was aggressive, experienced, and more willing than many airmen to discuss close-air support of ground forces.

As Commander in Chief Fighter Command from Nov. 1942 to Oct. 1944 he seemed to be the natural choice for Commander in Chief Allied Expeditionary Air Force (AEAF) for Overlord, the NORMANDY INVASION. Under the guidelines set down by Gen. DWIGHT D. EISENHOWER, Leigh-Mallory was to control "only those air forces that were definitely allocated as a permanently integral part of the expeditionary forces."

As AEAF chief, Leigh-Mallory adopted the so-called Transportation Plan proposed by civilian planners, in which a heavy bomber offensive against the marshalling yards in France and Germany disrupted the transportation network in France, isolating the Normandy beachhead from reinforcement. Although resisted mightily by Bomber Command and the U.S. Eighth AIR FORCE, the plan was supported by Deputy Supreme Commander ARTHUR TEDDER, who assumed overall supervision of the effort.

Leigh-Mallory distrusted AIRBORNE assaults and implored Eisenhower to cancel the night drops on Normandy only hours before they were to begin because he feared high casualties. Eisenhower had him record his concerns in a letter, but did not heed them.

Leigh-Mallory's position in the Overlord hierarchy was anomalous, in large part because Tedder was himself an airman, and because many of the major air officers refused to subordinate their strategic planning to Leigh-Mallory's invasion-related needs. Add to that his abrasive personality and his role in the relief of Park and Dowding and it is sadly not surprising that his appointment in Oct. 1944 as commander Allied Air Forces in Southeast Asia was regretted by very few of the Allied commanders in Europe.

He was killed in an air crash en route to take command.

LeMay, Maj. Gen. Curtis E. (1906–1990)

Innovative and aggressive U.S. bomber commander. LeMay began his flying career as a fighter pilot, but in the 1930s he became a strong advocate of STRATEGIC BOMBING and established a reputation as one of the most skillful bomber navigators of the ARMY AIR CORPS.

In 1942, as a colonel, he trained the 305th Bomb GROUP flying the B-17 FLYING FORTRESS, and then led the group against German targets from bases in England. Promoted to brigadier general, in July 1943 he moved up to command the 3rd Air DIVISION of the Eighth AIR FORCE in England. Holding that position for a year, he pioneered the development of advanced bomber tactics.

Maj. Gen. LeMay became commander of the XX Bomber COMMAND in the China-Burma-India theater in Sept. 1944. His B-29 SUPERFORTRESS strikes against targets in Formosa, Manchuria, and Japan had limited effect. Similar problems with the XXI Bomber Command in the MARIANAS led to LeMay's being given that command in Jan. 1945. Deciding that high-level, daylight PRECISION BOMBING raids were ineffective against Japan, LeMay stripped most guns from his B-29s and sent them against Japanese cities at low level, at night, to spread incendiary BOMBS. The first major firebomb raid, against TOKYO on March 9–10, 1945, devastated Tokyo, burning out 16 square miles of the city. More incendiary raids followed until the end of the war.

LeMay briefly commanded the Twentieth Air Force in July–Aug. 1945, before becoming Chief of Staff to Gen. CARL SPAATZ, head of the strategic bombing force in the Pacific. In this period of the incendiary and ATOMIC BOMB raids, LeMay declared: "I'll tell you what war is about. You've got to kill people, and when you've killed enough they stop fighting."

As a full general, LeMay was head of the U.S. Strategic Air Command from 1948 to 1957, and served as Chief of Staff of the U.S. Air Force from 1961 until retiring in Jan. 1965.

In 1968 LeMay was the American Independent Party candidate for vice president of the United States during the unsuccessful bid for the presidency of George C. Wallace.

Lend-Lease

U.S. program begun so that aid could be sent to Great Britain while the United States was still theoretically neutral. The program, recommended by President ROOSEVELT and authorized by Congress, went into effect on March 11, 1941. Originally entitled "An Act to Promote the Defense of the United States," Lend-Lease gave the President the power to "sell, transfer title to, exchange, lease, lend, or otherwise dispose of" defense matériel whose transfer would, in the President's opinion, help U.S. defense. Three hours after signing the act into law, Roosevelt ordered twenty-eight PT-BOATS and PT submarine chasers (PTCs) turned over to the Royal Navy. Prime Minister CHURCHILL called Lend-Lease "Hitler's death warrant."

Two major transactions, arranged to skirt the NEUTRALITY ACT of 1935, preceded Lend-Lease. In June 1940, after the evacuation of DUNKIRK, the United States sent "surplus" munitions—worth about $43,000,000 but technically not sold—to England, which was suffering a shortage of ammunition. And in Sept. 1940 the United States authorized the DESTROYERS-FOR-BASES DEAL that transferred fifty overage destroyers to England in exchange for ninety-nine-year leases to set up air and naval bases in Newfoundland, British Guinea, Bermuda, the Bahamas, Jamaica, St. Lucia, Trinidad, and Antigua. The destroyers were given new names that were common to both countries, such as HMS *Broadway.*

Lend-Lease aid, which totaled more than $50 billion, went to forty-four countries during the war. The BRITISH COMMONWEALTH, which included the United Kingdom, Australia, New Zealand, and South Africa, received the largest amount of aid: $31,392,361,000, and the Soviet Union the second largest: $11,297,883,000. Because of anti-Communist sympathies among voters and members of Congress, Lend-Lease was not extended to the Soviet Union until Nov. 1941, five months after Germany's invasion. The flow of matériel to the Soviet Union, much of it through Iran and Alaska, began on June 1, 1942.

Most Lend-Lease aid consisted of U.S.-manufactured munitions, aircraft, and ships. The law called for reciprocal aid and payment for the U.S. goods.

Several nations did give the United States "reverse lend-lease" in the form of overseas bases, supplies, and services, with England transferring several CORVETTES to the United States. This amounted to $7,387,041,673. Belgium was the only nation to send back more ($191,215,983) than it received ($148,394,457).

After the war, Lend-Lease evolved into foreign aid in the form of loans, anti-Communist military aid, and, in 1947, into the Marshall Plan, which offered U.S. help to European nations that joined in postwar recovery efforts.

Leningrad

The old capital of Russia and the second largest city of the Soviet Union. The GERMAN CAMPAIGN IN THE SOVIET UNION, launched in June 1941, reached the outskirts of Leningrad in September.

In Aug. 1941 the Germans surrounded the city and cut the Leningrad-Moscow railway. An attempt to take the city failed, and the Germans began a siege, releasing PANZER divisions to fight elsewhere. HITLER wanted to level Leningrad and hand the territory over to the Finns, who, fighting on the side of the Germans, had advanced on Leningrad from the north. (But the Finns halted and would go no farther than the border Finland had before the Soviet invasion of 1939.)

A siege pleased HITLER, who on Sept. 29 sent a directive to his generals: *"The Führer has decided to have St. Petersburg* [as Hitler insisted on calling the city] *wiped off the face of the earth.* [The emphasis is his.] The further existence of this large city is of no interest. . . . for *the problem of the survival of the population and of supplying it with food is one which cannot and should not be solved by us."*

German ARTILLERY and aircraft pounded the city, and Leningrad's 3,000,000 people began starving. The only supply open was across Lake Ladoga. Soviet naval units brought in food and fuel and took out refugees. When the lake froze, the Soviets sent supplies in by truck. About 500,000 people got out, but the starving in the city continued. Incredibly, so did war production. The factories, despite bombardments and a malnourished work force, turned out tanks, ammunition, and other war matériel.

Soviet forces vainly tried to break the siege, but not until Jan. 1943 were they able to make a breach wide enough and deep enough to relieve the city. By then, amid reports of cannibalism and desperate thefts of food, hundreds of thousands had died. The complete lifting of the siege came in Jan. 1944 when Soviet forces, fighting along a broad front (see SOVIET OFFENSIVE CAMPAIGN), drove the Germans more than 50 miles from the devastated city. For the first time in 900 days the survivors of Leningrad could walk the rubble-filled streets without fear of a Luftwaffe air raid.

STALIN declared Leningrad a Hero City. Dimitri Shostakovich, an air raid warden, wrote his Seventh Symphony during the siege. He was evacuated to perform it in MOSCOW. The U.S. premiere of what became the Leningrad Symphony raised money for relief. The saga of Leningrad's ordeal was well publicized in the United States and did much to bring the Soviet-German conflict into American consciousness.

Lever

Code name for Allied operation to clear area between Reno and the southwest shore of Lake Comacchio, Italy.

Lexington (CV 2)

One of the two largest U.S. AIRCRAFT CARRIERS of World War II. The *Lexington* was sister ship of *SARATOGA* (CV 3). At the time of the Japanese attack on PEARL HARBOR on Dec. 7, 1941, the *Lexington* was at sea, en route to MIDWAY to deliver a squadron of Marine SB2U VINDICATOR dive bombers to help defend the island. Upon learning of the attack, the carrier turned back toward Pearl Harbor, without having sent off the Marine planes. (Her own aircraft were also on board.) The *Lexington* and other U.S. warships in the area futilely searched for the Japanese carriers. She returned to Pearl Harbor on Dec. 13. She was then involved in the abortive effort to rescue WAKE from Japanese attackers.

The *Lexington* operated in defensive roles until mid-Feb. 1942 when she began offensive patrols in the CORAL SEA area. She returned to the Coral Sea in early May and, in company with the carrier *Yorktown* (CV 5), fought the battle of the Coral Sea on May 7–8. Her planes sank the Japanese light carrier *SHOHO* and helped damage the larger carriers *Shokaku* and *Zuikaku*.

Planes from the two larger Japanese carriers attacked the *Lexington* just before noon on May 8 hitting the carrier with two torpedoes and three bombs. Fires below decks got out of control and she had to be abandoned. Only 216 of her crew were lost as accompanying warships took off the 2,735 survivors. The coup de grace to the *Lexington* was two TORPEDOES from the U.S. DESTROYER *Phelps* (DD 360). The "Lex" was the first U.S. carrier sunk in the war.

The *Lexington* earned two BATTLE STARS in the war.

She had been converted during construction from a battle CRUISER to a carrier. She was launched on Oct. 3, 1925, and was placed in commission on Dec. 14, 1927. She had a standard displacement of almost 36,000 tons and was 888 feet overall in length. As built she had a cruiser's gun armament of eight 8-inch (203-mm) guns (removed in 1942) plus lighter weapons. During the war she carried some eighty aircraft. After her loss the Navy named the new CV 16 the *Lexington*.

The only larger aircraft carrier than the "Lex" and "Sara" completed during the war was the 64,800-ton Japanese *Shinano*, which was sunk by a U.S. SUBMARINE before she became operational. The U.S. Navy built three 45,000-ton carriers of the *Midway* (CVB 41) class during the war, but the first ship was not commissioned until Sept. 10, 1945.

Leyte Gulf

Site of the climactic naval engagement of the war. The Oct. 1944 battles for Leyte Gulf destroyed the major remnants of the Japanese fleet and insured the success of Gen. DOUGLAS MACARTHUR's invasion of Leyte. (See PHILIPPINES.) The U.S. Navy's destruction of the Japanese fleet left the Japanese garrisons in the Philippines without air support or protection of their supply lines to Japan. The battle of Leyte Gulf is sometimes called the second battle of the Philippine Sea.

On Oct. 17, as the main U.S. invasion force headed for the landings on the east coast of the Philippine island of Leyte, the Japanese launched *SHO-GO,* the defense of the Philippines. Four naval forces joined the operation. The First Diversion

Attack Force was the largest concentration of battle-ships and heavy cruisers in a single task force in the entire war: seven battleships, eleven heavy cruisers, two light cruisers, and nineteen destroyers. In the force were the super dreadnoughts *Musashi* and *YAMATO,* the largest battleships ever built. The Japanese Second Diversion Attack Force consisted of two heavy cruisers, one light cruiser, and four destroyers. The third force, known as the Main Body, had one large aircraft carrier, three light carriers, two battleship-carriers, three light cruisers, and eight destroyers. A fourth group, the "C" Force, had two battleships, one heavy cruiser, and four destroyers.

As the First Diversion Attack Force approached the Philippines on Oct. 23, two U.S. SUBMARINES spotted the fleet and fired TORPEDOES at three cruisers, sinking two of them; the damaged cruiser withdrew, taking two destroyers with her. When the submarines alerted U.S. fleets to the approaching Japanese, twelve fast U.S. AIRCRAFT CARRIERS were ordered to close with the Philippines and fly off search planes.

U.S. carrier planes spotted both the First Diversion and C Forces. But before the carriers could fly off strikes, still another Japanese group, the Second Air Fleet, with some 450 planes, attacked the U.S. carriers from bases in Formosa and the Philippines.

During the ensuing air battle, the Japanese lost dozens of planes—Comdr. DAVID MCCAMPBELL of the carrier *ESSEX* (CV 9) shot down at least nine Japanese fighters himself; other Japanese planes were downed by U.S. antiaircraft fire. A Japanese bomber did get through, however, and fatally hit the light carrier *Princeton* (CVL 23) with two 500-pound BOMBS. Explosions of aviation gas in the *Princeton* spewed flying, flaming debris onto the deck of the nearby cruiser *Birmingham* (CL 62), which was aiding the stricken *Princeton.* The explosions killed 229 men and wounded 420 aboard the cruiser. The carrier lost 106 men of her 1,500-man crew when she sank.

Meanwhile, U.S. carrier strikes against the First Diversion Attack Force focused on the battleship *Musashi* as she steamed through the Sibuyan Sea, the island-dotted waters northwest of Leyte. Pounded by bombs and gouged by repeated tor-pedo hits, the *Musashi* struggled for hours before she sank, taking with her nearly half of her 2,399-man crew. The U.S. carrier planes also damaged the *Yamato,* the smaller battleships *Nagato* and *HARUNA,* a heavy cruiser, and a destroyer.

Early on Oct. 25, the ships of C Force, after threading their way through the Mindanao Sea south of Leyte, attempted to enter Leyte Gulf via the Surigao Strait. The force ran into a trap set by Vice Adm. THOMAS C. KINKAID, commander of the U.S. Seventh FLEET, which was providing close protection for MacArthur's invasion forces. Kinkaid had strung the 12-mile-wide channel with a trip wire of thirty-nine PT-BOATS and a screen of destroyers. Behind them were eight cruisers and six old BATTLE-SHIPS.

The PT-boats fired thirty-four torpedoes and hit a light cruiser in the springing of the trap. In a fierce torpedo-gun duel, both of the Force C battleships and two destroyers were sunk and another destroyer badly damaged. The surviving destroyer beat a hasty retreat, passing the Second Diversion Attack Force, which was also headed for the strait. The destroyer did not report the ambush, and the three cruisers and four destroyers of the Second Diversion Attack Force ran into a PT boat attack. In the darkness, as the Second Force began a withdrawal, one of its heavy cruisers collided with a Force C cruiser damaged in the original trap.

Two Japanese forces had been savaged and the First Diversion Attack Force had withdrawn. But there still was a fourth Japanese group to reckon with, the Main Body. Its *Sho-Go* mission had been to draw off U.S. fast carriers so that the other Japanese units could break through U.S. ships protecting the AMPHIBIOUS LANDINGS and tear apart the invasion shipping in Leyte Gulf. When U.S. search planes spotted the carrier-dominated Main Force, Adm. WILLIAM F. HALSEY ordered his Third Fleet north, believing that Kinkaid's Seventh Fleet could stop any remaining Japanese ships coming through either the Surigao Strait or the San Bernardino Strait, a gateway to Leyte.

Halsey's planes, flying through antiaircraft fire from seventeen Japanese ships, sank three carriers and a destroyer and damaged a carrier and a light cruiser. Only when the U.S. planes attacked did they find the Japanese carriers had only a few planes on board and were not a real threat. But to the south there was trouble.

A series of delayed and confusing messages passed between Kinkaid and Halsey. Kinkaid's ESCORT CARRIERS and destroyers were suddenly confronting the remaining ships of the still-powerful First Diversion Force: the giant *Yamato,* three other battleships, six heavy cruisers, two light cruisers, and thirteen destroyers.

The Japanese ships had no scout planes, and thus the First Diversion Force was taken by surprise when lookouts sighted the U.S. escort carriers supporting the Leyte landings. The *Yamato* fired her massive 18.1-inch (460-mm) guns at another warship for the first—and the last—time.

"I knew we were in a tough spot," Rear Adm. Clifton A. F. Sprague, commander of one of the escort carrier groups, later said. "I didn't think anything could save me, since the Japs were reportedly making 30 knots my way. The only thing to do was to think of something to do. I ordered my screen [of destroyers and DESTROYER ESCORTS] to drop back astern of the carriers and make smoke. We made smoke, too, and immediately launched all our planes. Fortunately, the wind was right. My course was 90 degrees and the wind was from 70 degrees, so I could run and launch at the same time."

The destroyers sped into battle, David-size ships against Goliaths. They damaged several Japanese ships and hit a cruiser with TORPEDOES. Japanese guns sank two destroyers and one destroyer escort. The gallant action slowed and distracted the Japanese force, giving the carriers more time to launch planes and strike.

Japanese gunfire battered the escort carriers, one of which sank, taking about 100 of her 850-man crew down with her. But the carrier pilots performed brilliantly, sinking one heavy cruiser and damaging several other Japanese warships. When Japanese destroyers launched a torpedo attack on the escort carriers, a TBM AVENGER from the *St. Lô* (CVE 63) strafed a spread of the torpedoes and caused one to explode. A shot from the *St. Lô*'s five-inch (127-mm) gun deflected another torpedo in that spread.

The escort carriers escaped from the guns of the superbattleship *Yamato* only to encounter an even more deadly menace—KAMIKAZES, Japanese suicide aircraft making their debut in battle. One hit the *St. Lô* as ammunition and gasoline were being readied for returning aircraft. She went down with about 100 of her men. (The *St. Lô,* originally named the *Midway,* had been renamed a month earlier; in the lore of the sea it is unlucky to rename a ship.)

At the same time, the retreating First Division ships—four battleships, three heavy cruisers, two light cruisers, and thirteen destroyers—were under continuing air attack and heading back through San Bernardino Strait. The Japanese lost another destroyer and a light cruiser.

In history's last battleship-versus-battleship engagement, the two U.S. fleets that came to Leyte Gulf stayed; the Japanese fleets were destroyed. Although the Japanese still had six battleships and a few cruisers, they were all the major operational warships that Japan had left. The Leyte Gulf battles marked the end of the Japanese Imperial Fleet. (See JAPAN, NAVY.)

Liberator,
see B-24.

Liberia
Capital: Monrovia, pop. 1,500,000 (est. 1939). Politically close to the United States since its founding in 1822 by freed American slaves, Liberia had both strategic and commercial ties to its mother country. After World War I, Firestone Tire and Rubber Co. bought up Liberian land at low prices and established one of the largest rubber plantations in the world. An American, not a Liberian, controlled customs, and much of its military and financial affairs were in American hands.

On March 31, 1942, Liberia and the United States signed a defense treaty that was fulfilled in June, when thousands of U.S. troops—in black units with white officers, under Army SEGREGATION policy—arrived in Liberia. They protected the rubber plantation and built roads and airfields to serve the planes being ferried from U.S. aircraft plants to bases as far away as China. U.S. funds also paid for the construction of a naval base and the improvement of port facilities.

Liberia did not declare war on Germany and Japan until Jan. 27, 1944; it became a member of the UNITED NATIONS in April.

Liberty Ships

Mass-produced cargo ships built in larger numbers than any other ship design in history. Liberties served in virtually every theater of the war, most carrying cargo for Allied military forces and civilian populations, with almost 200 serving as U.S. Army and Navy auxiliary ships.

The Liberty design was based on a British "tramp" steamer of 1879. The plans were modified prior to the U.S. entry into World War II, with President ROOSEVELT personally reviewing them. Reportedly, he dubbed the ship the "ugly duckling."

Mass production was undertaken at nineteen American shipyards with more than 2,700 ships being completed from 1941 to 1945. The exact number is not known, but the most reliable government data indicate that there were 2,580 standard Liberty ships (designated EC2—for Emergency, "C" for cargo, and "2" for large size), sixty Ocean-class ships for Britain, twenty aircraft transports, twelve colliers, eight tank carriers, and sixty-two tankers.

During the war the Navy converted 133 Liberties to auxiliary configurations—net cargo ships, naval cargo ships, store-issue ships, repair ships, water carriers; the Army took twenty-six, which they converted to hospital ships, repairs ships, and mule carriers; another twenty-two were fitted to carry PRISONERS OF WAR from Europe to the United States; and one was modified to lay pipeline under the English Channel. (See PLUTO.)

A total of 195 of the ships were lost to BOMBS, TORPEDOES, MINES, collisions, accidents, and other causes.

The first ships built were the sixty for Britain. The first U.S. ship was the *Patrick Henry,* launched on Sept. 27, 1941. That same day a total of fourteen Liberties were launched. The shipyards competed to build the ships in record-breaking times. By Dec. 1943, a month in which 113 Liberties were delivered, each ship averaged only twenty-seven days on the building ways with fourteen days for fitting out. The record was claimed to be seven days, fourteen

hours, and twenty-three minutes on the building ways!

The Liberties were 441½ feet long and had simple, "expanding steam" engines that could provide a speed of 11 knots. They had a deadweight tonnage (carrying capacity) of 10,920 and a gross tonnage of 7,500 tons. Their almost 11,000-ton carrying capacity was equal to 300 railroad freight cars. That translated to 2,840 JEEPS, or 440 medium TANKS, or 230,000,000 rounds of rifle ammunition, or 3,440,000 C-RATIONS.

Liberties were usually armed, generally with a single 5-inch (127-mm) gun aft and about ten OERLIKON 20-MM antiaircraft guns. These guns were manned by an ARMED GUARD of ten to twenty sailors, in addition to a ship's crew of about forty-five.

After the war Liberties were used to help rebuild the merchant fleets of several countries. The U.S. Navy converted sixteen to RADAR picket ships to provide early warning in the event of a Soviet bomber attack against the United States.

Libya

Capital: Tripoli, pop. 910,669 (1940). Libya, an Italian colony since 1912, began receiving thousands of Italian colonists in 1938. Italy sent more than 30,000 farm workers, then some 3,000 rural families, to solve the overpopulation problem in Italy. Italians sunk artesian wells, planted trees to reclaim the desert, and planted olive groves and vineyards.

War stopped the vast agricultural experiment in 1940, when Italian troops invaded Egypt, starting a disastrous military adventure that ended in 1942 with the annihilation of Italian troops and the British liberation of Libya.

Libya remained under Allied military administration until the UNITED NATIONS general assembly decided that Libya should become a sovereign state, with Libyans creating their own constitution. In 1951 the United Kingdom of Libya became the first nation to gain independence under the authority of the United Nations.

Liddell Hart, Capt. Basil (1895–1970)

Leading British military thinker and prolific author. A student at Cambridge at the outbreak of

World War I, he served in the British Army and attained the rank of captain before being gassed at the battle of the Somme in 1916. He retired from the Army in 1927 to devote full time to writing and lecturing.

By the start of World War II he had written several books on military matters and was a strong proponent of armored warfare and greatly influenced German thinking in this area. German tank expert Gen. HEINZ GUDERIAN wrote of Liddell Hart and other British soldier-writers of the 1920s and 1930s: "These farsighted soldiers were even then trying to make of the tank something more than just an infantry support weapon. They envisaged it in relation to the growing motorisation of our age, and thus they became the pioneers of a new type of warfare on the largest scale."

During World War II he continued to write and lecture, and had an opportunity to interview senior German officers who were PRISONERS OF WAR in Britain. He continued to be an active thinker, writer, and lecturer until his death.

Lidice

Czech village razed by Germans. The destruction of Lidice (along with Levzacky) was ordered in retaliation for the ASSASSINATION of SS leader REINHARD HEYDRICH. On June 9, 1942, an SS detachment herded all the inhabitants of Lidice into the village square. A boy and a woman who tried to escape were shot to death. All males over sixteen were locked up, and the next day all of them were shot, as were others found elsewhere; a total of 191 males were killed. Seven women were killed and 195 other women were sent to CONCENTRATION CAMPS, where at least forty-five died. Four pregnant WOMEN were taken to hospitals, where they gave birth. Their infants were killed and the mothers sent to a concentration camp. Most of the village's ninety children were put in "educational institutions." The younger ones were taken to Germany where they were raised as Germans.

The village was burned, dynamited, and leveled to the ground. A German newspaper boasted that Lidice had been "erased." But it endured as a symbol of NAZI atrocities; it lived on as towns renamed in its memory: Lidice, Ill., and Lidice, Mexico; and it lived on in Edna St. Vincent Millay's "The Mur-

der of Lidice." After the war, seventeen of Lidice's scattered children were found and sent back to Czechoslovakia by the UNITED NATIONS RELIEF AND REHABILITATION ADMINISTRATION. The SS captain who headed the detachment that razed Lidice was hanged in Prague in 1951.

Lightfoot

British code name for the second battle of EL ALAMEIN, Oct. 1942.

Lightning,

see P-38.

Lila

German code word for occupation of the VICHY FRENCH port of Toulon and capture of the French fleet, Nov. 1942.

Lily

The Japanese Army's Ki-48 was a twin-engine light bomber, a type popular in many air forces in the late 1930s. The 45th *Sentai* (division) was equipped with the Ki-48 in 1940 and that fall deployed to northern China for combat operations.

Against little opposition from the Chinese Air Force, the Ki-48 performed well, with its high speed being cited in crew reports. From Dec. 8, 1941, the Ki-48 was used to attack British, Dutch, and U.S. forces in the Philippines and Southeast Asia. When challenged by Allied fighters, the Ki-48s were vulnerable, despite their speed, having inadequate defensive guns and crew armor, and no self-sealing fuel tanks. Shifting to night attacks increased survivability, but reduced effectiveness.

An improved Ki-48-II with more speed and armor protection flew in Feb. 1942 and was placed in production; despite further improvements in armament, the Ki-48 was simply not able to keep up with the advanced U.S. fighters in the South Pacific. Production of the Ki-48 ended in Oct. 1944, but in 1945 they were still encountered in night operations over OKINAWA. Many were employed (in daylight) as Army suicide planes, some fitted with a long rod protruding from the nose to trigger a 1,764-pound BOMB when it struck an Allied ship. Others were modified for various research roles, including launching the I-GO-1 antiship

GUIDED MISSILE and another as test platform for a jet engine. Production totaled 1,977 aircraft.

The Ki-48 was a twin-engine, mid-wing aircraft, with a glazed nose and almost all glazed crew housing.

The Ki-48-I had a maximum speed of 298 mph, increased to 314 mph in the II variant. Normal range was some 1,200 miles, with a maximum of 1,500 miles. Maximum bomb load was 882 pounds for the Ki-48-I and 1,764 pounds for the Ki-48-II, although normal bomb loads were less. Three flexible 7.7-mm machine guns were fitted, with a 12.7-mm machine gun in the dorsal position in some II variants. A crew of four flew the Ki-48.

Lindbergh, Charles A. (1902–1974)

American aviation hero who campaigned against U.S. involvement in the war. Lindbergh became one of the nation's all-time heroes in 1926 when he made the first solo nonstop flight across the Atlantic. In 1932 Lindbergh's infant son was kidnaped and murdered. Fleeing the publicity surrounding the sensational trial and 1936 execution of the accused kidnaper, Lindbergh and his wife went to Europe. There he inspected German aircraft plants under the guidance of HERMANN GÖRING and was decorated by Göring, in the name of HITLER, with the German Eagle medal. In 1940, back in the United States, he spoke passionately against U.S. involvement in the war while warning of Germany's growing air power.

Lindbergh became the leading advocate of the isolationist, anti-British AMERICAN FIRST COMMITTEE. In Sept. 1941, during a speech in Des Moines, Lindbergh declared that "the three most important groups who have been pressing this country toward war are the British, the Jewish, and the ROOSEVELT Administration." He continued to say of the JEWS: "Their greatest danger to this country lies in their large ownership and influence in our motion pictures, our press, our radio, and our government." His blatant ANTI-SEMITISM lost him much of the support of even staunch isolationists. President Roosevelt publicly denounced Lindbergh, who resigned his Army Air Force reserve commission.

When the United States entered the war, Lindbergh joined the war effort by becoming a technical representative of the United Aircraft Corporation, which built the F4U CORSAIR fighter. During a tour of the Pacific to inspect Corsairs, he also became interested in the range-extension problems of the P-38 LIGHTNING. He flew several combat missions, officially as a civilian observer. In that status, he was credited (though not officially at the time) with shooting down a Japanese plane. In 1954, for his services to the United States, President EISENHOWER appointed him a brigadier general in the Air Force Reserve.

Lindemann, Frederick A. (1886–1957)

Scientific adviser to Prime Minister CHURCHILL. A brilliant, tart-tongued physicist, Lindemann (Lord Cherwell) was a prime thinker and organizer in what Churchill called the WIZARD WAR. Lindemann's greatest value, Churchill wrote, was his ability to "decipher the signals from the experts on the far horizons and explain to me in lucid, homely terms what the issues were."

Churchill credited Lindemann with "bending" German radio directional beams, diverting Luftwaffe bombers from their targets. Lindemann also endorsed research into the PROXIMITY FUZE and RADAR, major products of the Wizard War. He was the only scientist to serve on Churchill's wartime Cabinet. His advocacy of STRATEGIC BOMBING strongly influenced the 1942 decision to strengthen the Bomber Command.

Long before the EUROPEAN WAR began, Lindemann, whom Churchill called "the Prof," suggested the creation of a scientific committee to study air defenses. This became the Committee for the Scientific Survey of Air Defense, better known as the Tizard Committee, after its chairman, Sir HENRY TIZARD. Lindemann, possessive of his longtime relationship with Churchill, worked at keeping Tizard out of inner scientific councils. This typified Lindemann's egocentric character, which often was a barrier to scientific cooperation.

When Churchill again became prime minister in 1951, he made Lindemann chief of British nuclear research.

Link Trainer

An airplane-like training device to simulate flight conditions on the ground. The student was fully enclosed to learn "blind" flying and navigating. The pedestal-mounted Link trainer changed angle as the pilot operated the "stick" and pedals, with his flight path automatically recorded on a chart on the instructor's table.

The device was named for Edwin A. Link, an American inventor who produced his first mechanical aircraft trainer in 1929. The Army began buying Link trainers in 1934 and several thousand were delivered to the AAF and Navy during the war.

Linz,

see HITLERZENTRUM.

Lithuania

Capital: Kaunas, pop. 2,349,423 (1939). Lithuania proclaimed its independence in 1918 but the status of some territory adjacent to Poland was in question. In 1920, while the LEAGUE OF NATIONS was trying to solve the problem, Poland occupied the disputed land, which included the city of Vilnius. The seized territory was recognized by most countries as part of Poland. But Lithuania, after breaking off relations with Poland, denounced the seizure and claimed Vilnius as its historic capital. (By 1931, the city's 128,600 residents included only about 2,000 Lithuanians.)

Lithuania was bargained away in secret protocols attached to the Soviet-German NONAGGRESSION PACT of Aug. 23, 1939, and another, less-known agreement signed the following month. After World War II began, Lithuania, like Finland, Estonia, and Latvia, was placed in the Soviet "sphere of influence." On Oct. 10 the Soviets forced on Lithuania a "mutual assistance" pact that allowed Red Army garrisons into bases in Lithuania.

On Jan. 15, 1940, Soviet troops entered the country, accompanied by Soviet officials who set up a puppet government and mock election for the purpose of voting to incorporate Lithuania into the Soviet Union as a republic. Every foreign legislation and consulate was closed in Aug. 1940 and, with Lithuania thus sealed off from the world, mass arrests and deportations to the Soviet Union began. In one night alone 30,455 politicians and intellectuals were deported to Soviet prison camps.

Part of Lithuania, known as the "Memel triangle," remained German territory. Memel, Lithuania's only port city, and about 1,000 square miles around it, had been under international control from 1919 to 1923, when Lithuanians seized and claimed it. In 1938, campaigning under the slogan "Home to the Reich," the predominantly German population of Memel won control of the legislature and, with the help of Memel STORM TROOPERS essentially made the territory part of Germany. In March 1939 Lithuania bowed to reality and, in a nonaggression pact with Germany, surrendered Memel. On Jan. 10, 1941, Germany sold the Memel territory to the Soviet Union for $7,500,000 in gold.

When Germany invaded the Soviet Union six months later, revolt against the Soviet occupiers swept Lithuania. The Soviets, hastily withdrawing from Lithuania, killed at least 5,000 political prisoners. With the conquering Germans came new persecution. The country was put under the *Reichskommissariat für das Ostland,* the ruthless civil administration for occupied Soviet territories in the East. Thousands of Lithuanians were murdered or sent to German CONCENTRATION CAMPS. The Germans massacred 90 percent of the large Jewish population, swollen by the recent migration of Lithuanian Jews from Polish-occupied territory. Thousands of German families were moved into Lithuania as the first wave of an envisioned colonization of the nation.

In July 1944 Red Army troops entered eastern Lithuania, driving Germans—and tens of thousands of fleeing Lithuanians—to the German border. By the time Soviets occupied all of the country, about 80,000 Lithuanians had fled to Germany. Another 60,000 were sent to Soviet prison camps, and the transforming of Lithuania into a Soviet state began. From the end of the war to 1946 about 145,000 Lithuanians were deported to the Soviet Union; another 60,000 were removed in 1949. (The United States considered Lithuania an independent state under occupation.)

"Little Blitz"

Luftwaffe attempt to relieve the pressure of the Anglo-American STRATEGIC BOMBING on Germany by bomber raids against England in early 1944. The first strike of this so-called "Little BLITZ"—a reference to the massive bombing of England in the fall and winter of 1940–1941—began on the night of

Jan. 21–22, 1944, with an attack of 447 bombers. Most were twin-engine JU 188 and JU 88 medium bombers. Heavy British antiaircraft fire and other problems caused the BOMBS to fall wide of their targets and twenty-five of the attacking planes were shot down.

The bombing continued for almost three months as German bombers made thirty-three night raids and one day raid, mostly on LONDON. Although small in comparison with the 1940–1941 attacks, the Little Blitz delivered 2,400 tons of bombs that killed 1,347 civilians and injured another 2,515. (During the same period RAF Bomber Command alone dropped 48,000 tons of bombs on Germany and 11,000 tons on German-occupied territory.)

While Luftwaffe bombers were able to operate over England at night, RAF Fighter Command still ruled the skies by day and few German reconnaissance aircraft were able to photograph the targets to permit useful damage assessment and planning. By the end of April 1944 the raids ended because of mounting aircraft losses.

The raids marked the end of the German bomber as a long-range weapon. HITLER, however, continued to list bombers among his miracle weapons that would turn the tide of the war. He even insisted that the world's first operational jet-propelled fighter, the ME 262 *Sturmvogel,* be employed as a bomber, preventing it from being used to intercept the Allied bombers destroying Germany.

Rather, the next German weapons to fall on Britain would be V-1 BUZZ BOMBS.

Little Boy,

see ATOMIC BOMB.

Litvinov, Maksim Maksimovich (1876–1951)

Born Meir Walach, he was a longtime Soviet foreign affairs expert and ambassador to the United States during the war. After the Revolution of 1917 he represented the Bolshevik Party in LONDON, where he was imprisoned as a hostage.

Litvinov first achieved international prominence when he led the Soviet delegation to prepare for the LEAGUE OF NATIONS World Disarmament Conference in 1927 and proposed sweeping disarmament programs.

From 1930 he was commissar for Foreign Affairs and, with HITLER gaining power in Germany, urged the League of Nations to make plans for collective resistance against Germany (1934–1938) and negotiated anti-German treaties with France (1935) and Czechoslovakia (1935). Because Litvinov was Jewish and closely identified with anti-German positions, STALIN dismissed him in May 1939 in preparation for concluding the German-Soviet NONAGGRESSION PACT in Aug. 1939.

Litvinov became ambassador to the United States in Nov. 1941, holding that position until July 1943, and he served as deputy commissar for foreign affairs until retiring from the government in Aug. 1946.

Locomotive

British submarine operation to carry Norwegians and stores to Spitsbergen, Sept. 1943.

Lodestar,

see C-56.

Lodz Ghetto

The section of the Polish city of Lodz set aside for JEWS. The industrial city, about 70 miles southwest of WARSAW, was an early target of NAZI persecution during the invasion of Poland in Sept. 1939. The city's 233,000 Jews made up about one third of the population. On Feb. 8, 1940, the Germans chose the most run-down section of the city for a ghetto and loaded more than 160,000 Jews into 31,721 apartments there; 725 apartments had running water. In May the Germans sealed off the ghetto.

As was the practice in other ghettos, the Germans put the administration under a *Judenrat,* a Jewish Council. In Dec. 1941, although some 95 percent of the Jews in the Lodz ghetto were working in war industries, the Germans ordered the Jewish Council to select 20,000 Jews for "resettlement." The Germans wanted the removal of the aged, sick, and children under ten, with quotas set at 1,000 a day; one-way train fares were charged. The Lodz Jews were being sent to DEATH CAMPS, first Chelmno, then, when it was closed, to AUSCHWITZ. Knowledge of this fate sparked some resistance in the ghetto, but it remained essentially under Jewish

Council control until June 1944, when the final death-camp trips began. About 10,000 Lodz victims survived at the end of the war.

Loge (Theater Box)

Luftwaffe code name for LONDON during the BATTLE OF BRITAIN.

London

The capital of the BRITISH COMMONWEALTH, London became the symbol of a staunch people defying HITLER and his bombers as the city stood firm in the BATTLE OF BRITAIN. From the day England went to war on Sept. 3, 1939, to the last V-2 MISSILE fell on March 28, 1945, Londoners endured.

EDWARD R. MURROW and other U.S. journalists gave Americans their first vivid knowledge of war through reports about London, battered each night and abiding each day during the Battle of Britain and the BLITZ. American NEWSREELS showed the thousands of children evacuating the city . . . the silvery BARRAGE BALLOONS floating over the city . . . Prime Minister CHURCHILL emerging from his underground CABINET WAR ROOMS and grimly inspecting the rubble of his city . . . the dome of St. Paul's Cathedral looming through the smoke of an incendiary raid. Londoners were always portrayed as having a stiff upper lip and forever making tea. *Vogue* magazine reported that fashionable London women headed for the air-raid shelter in the basement of the Dorchester Hotel, where "Everyone spends the *alerte* being shampooeed [*sic*] and set, and manicured, and massaged, and foam-bathed."

They also died. As 1940 was ending the toll was 15,000 dead. On Dec. 29, London's sky was reddened by 1,500 fires. Among the historic treasures destroyed or damaged were the Guildhall, eight of the churches that Sir Christopher Wren built after the Great Fire of 1666, and three churches that had survived the Great Fire. Other landmarks would be hit: Westminster Abbey, Buckingham Palace, the Chamber of the House of Commons.

In one raid in April 1941 German bombs killed more than 1,000 people. In May, in the battle of London—the Blitz—375,000 Londoners were left homeless and 1,150,000 houses were damaged.

The bombs stopped, and London began to return to something close to normal.

Then, early in 1942 came the Americans, filling the cinemas, adding more manpower to a city that had long had a shortage. "They were not welcomed by the British men, but to the English girls they were wonderful," said a British woman remembering how the Yanks brought "a wave of glamour, romance, and excitement that has never been experienced before or since."

The air-raid sirens sounded now and then, but for most days and nights London was once again a bustling city. The wreckers tore down the tottering ruins, many shelters were closed, and glass began to appear in windows that had been blasted and boarded. Dotty wildflower collectors enthused over the new species of ragwort and fireweed that were overgrowing the ruins.

In June 1944 it started all over again. V-1 BUZZ BOMBS rained down, killing more than 2,500 Londoners in two weeks. Another 400,000 houses were destroyed. The children and the aged once more were evacuated, this time not in anticipation of raids but sometimes during them. Next came the V-2s, which, unlike the buzz bombs, made no sound before they hit. Londoners, though, practically noted that V-1s and V-2s could not see, and so the BLACKOUT was reduced to a DIMOUT.

The last rocket fell on March 27, the last buzz bomb on March 28. In May, just before V-E DAY, the shelters closed. For London, the war was over.

London (Code Name)

Code name for U.S. Army VIII CORPS front line near Wesel, Germany.

London Cage

Mansion in Kensington Palace Gardens where British intelligence officials conducted interrogations, particularly of high-level German PRISONERS OF WAR.

London Controlling Station

Secret Allied unit that organized deceptive plans to mislead German strategists. Prime Minister CHURCHILL established the unit, which was usually referred to as the LCS. The chief of the LCS was called "the Controller of Deception."

London Gun

The name given to Germany's *Vergeltungswaffe* (reprisal weapon) 3. It was a cannon, with a barrel 416 feet long, designed to fire 55-pound shells at London from a huge underground bunker at Mimoyecques, near Calais. ADOLF HITLER gave high priority to the V-3, and some 5,500 people, including miners, had been assigned to the building of the gun site. Plans called for two batteries, with twenty-five guns each. Heavy bombing so damaged the site that the project was abandoned. (The earlier reprisal weapons were the V-1 BUZZ BOMB and the V-2 MISSILE.)

Lonely Eagles,

see BLACK EAGLES.

Long Lance

The Japanese Type 93 Long Lance was the largest TORPEDO used by any navy in the war. Its explosive charge of 1,080 pounds compared to 879.5 pounds in the U.S. Mk 17 torpedo, the largest American torpedo of the war (although none was used in combat).

The Long Lance torpedoes were carried in several classes of Japanese cruisers and destroyers, which, with their great speed and range, and large warhead, were highly effective against Allied warships in the early surface battles of the Pacific War.

The secret to the Long Lance's high performance was the use of oxygen as the propellant. The French Navy had first considered using oxygen as a torpedo propellant, but abandoned the concept because of the hazard of accidental explosion. The British similarly rejected the concept, but the Japanese persevered and the Type 93 was approved for production in 1933 (year 2,593 of the Japanese calendar). It was believed that oxygen torpedoes would outrange naval guns, creating a revolution in naval tactics.

By Dec. 1941 the Japanese had produced some 1,350 Long Lance torpedoes, about one half the total production. In the latter half of 1942, with the Japanese Navy moving to the defensive, two naval officers conceived of the KAITEN or "human torpedo" based on the Type 93 torpedo. In Feb. 1944 the Naval General Staff gave permission to produce the kaiten and 100 torpedoes were converted in 1944 and 230 in 1945.

The Long Lance torpedo weighed 5,952 pounds, was 29½ feet long, and 24 inches (610 mm) in diameter (the standard Allied and AXIS torpedoes were 21 inches/533 mm in diameter). The range varied with setting—21,900 yards at 48–50 knots, 35,000 yards at 40–42 knots, and 43,700 yards at 36–38 knots. A larger Type 93 Model 3 was put in production in 1945, but was not used in combat; it weighed 6,173 pounds and carried a warhead of 1,720 pounds or twice the size of the largest U.S. torpedo warhead.

Long Range Desert Group

British–New Zealand raiding and reconnaissance force that operated in the North African desert against the AFRIKA KORPS from Aug. 1940 until late 1942. The group—all volunteers—worked behind German and Italian lines, often guiding and supporting British SPECIAL AIR SERVICE and SPECIAL BOAT SECTION operations. The group's patrols sometimes remained behind enemy lines for months at a time to carry out ambushes or garner intelligence.

In early 1943 the group became part of the Raiding Forces Middle East command that coordinated British COMMANDO operations in the Mediterranean and Balkan areas.

The Long Range Desert Group was founded by Maj. R. A. Bagnold.

Look

Code name for Gen. DWIGHT D. EISENHOWER.

LORAN

Acronym for Long-Range Navigation, a U.S. Navy system of radio navigation beacons used by the Allied navies during the war. LORAN produced short-pulse radio signals transmitted from a series of land-based stations. A ship or aircraft fitted with a LORAN receiver could measure the difference in the time of arrival of two signals and, based on where the signals intersected on a chart, determine the ship's or aircraft's position. LORAN was invaluable for ships and aircraft operating at night, in fog, or in other conditions when celestial navigation sights were not possible.

The U.S. Coast Guard, part of the Navy during the war, set up the LORAN stations beginning in

1941. The first LORAN stations outside of the United States were in Nova Scotia and Greenland; subsequently they were set up wherever Allied forces had territory. Immediately after the MARIANA ISLANDS were captured by U.S. Marines, the Coast Guard set up LORAN stations that helped guide the B-29 SUPERFORTRESS bombers attacking Japan; on IWO JIMA and OKINAWA the Coast Guard began surveying sites for LORAN sites under Japanese fire.

The wartime LORAN-A system could measure thousandths of a second and could provide navigational accuracy of no more than two miles of error at a distance of 600 miles from the transmitting stations.

Lord Haw-Haw,
see WILLIAM JOYCE.

Los Alamos

The secret laboratory where the ATOMIC BOMB was developed (also called Site Y). A boys' boarding school occupied Site Y's isolated New Mexico mesa when Brig. Gen. LESLIE R. GROVES, director of the atomic bomb program (MANHATTAN PROJECT), first saw Los Alamos and decided that it would be a good location.

"From the standpoint of security," he wrote in *Now It Can Be Told,* "Los Alamos was quite satisfactory. It was far removed from any large center of population, and was reasonably inaccessible from the outside. . . . Also, the geographically enforced isolation of the people working there lessened the ever-present danger of their inadvertently diffusing secret information among social or professional friends outside."

The people Groves brought there—hundreds of scientists and technicians, plus Army support units—were allowed to use only a Santa Fe post office address, Box 1663. All outgoing mail had to be submitted, in unsealed envelopes, to military censors. If a censor deemed the letter could be sent, he would send it but without the usual censors' mark. All incoming mail also went to the censors. Friends and relatives on the outside, for the most part, did not know exactly where Box 1663 was or what the people who were there did for the war

effort. One of the rumors was that Los Alamos was a home for pregnant WACs.

Under the ESPIONAGE Act, no one could discuss what he or she was doing in the middle of a New Mexico mesa. Journeys out of Los Alamos were granted only by special permission and all social life was to be restricted to fellow employees. As Phyllis K. Fisher described it in *Los Alamos Experience,* "We're not to be friendly with residents of nearby towns. (I hadn't noticed any nearby towns. If we go to Santa Fe [about an hour away over rough roads] . . . we are to keep to ourselves and not talk to outsiders. . . . However, we are allowed a half-smile and a slight nod to persons we already know there."

Groves set up a nursery school for working mothers. Some were scientists; others were starting new careers as secretaries and teachers. There was a grammar school and a high school and a small-scale democracy in the form of a community advisory council. Single men and WOMEN lived in dormitories and paid $13 a month. Families lived in Army-built housing, with rents ($17 to $67 a month) based on salaries. Couples without children lived in three-room apartments; for couples with children there were four- and five-room apartments.

So many babies were born in the small hospital that Groves seriously ordered J. ROBERT OPPEN-HEIMER, the scientific director of Los Alamos, to do something about it. Oppenheimer refused. His wife had their second baby there on Dec. 7, 1944.

Louis, 1st Sgt. Joe (1914–1981)

Heavyweight boxing champion, 1937–1949, who left the ring in 1942 to join the U.S. Army.

On June 22, 1938, Louis defended his title in a fight that had international interest. He was fighting Max Schmeling, the German champion and, to NAZIS, a symbol of the Aryan race. Louis, a black, was facing the only man who had ever knocked him out. (Schmeling had finished Louis off in the twelfth round of a 1936 nontitle match.)

Louis knew that the world was watching more than a boxing match. Only two years before, at the Olympic games in BERLIN, Hitler had snubbed Jesse Owens, the black star of the Olympics.

In Madison Square Garden on June 22 the German ambassador to the United States was at ringside. HITLER had cabled Schmeling, addressing him as "the coming world's champion." Hitler was wrong. Louis battered Schmeling, winning a technical knockout in two minutes and four seconds of the first round. (Schmeling would become a paratrooper in the German Army.)

On the day he was drafted into the Army, Jan. 9, 1942, Louis beat Buddy Baer in the first round and gave his purse to the Navy Relief Fund. Two months later, he knocked out Abe Simon in the sixth round and gave his purse to the Army Relief Fund. A few days before he spoke words that became famous during the war: "We will win because God's on our side."

Louis spent the war fighting exhibition matches and visiting hospitals and bases. He fought 100 fights during his four years in the Army. Because of Army SEGREGATION policies, bases had two canteens, one for black soldiers and one for whites. The black canteen at Fort Riley, Kan., was much smaller than the white one. Louis teamed up with a former UCLA football star, 2nd Lt. JACKIE ROBINSON, and between them they got the Army to improve the black canteen.

Louisiana Maneuvers

The U.S. Army's last and largest prewar maneuvers. Held in Sept. 1941 in Louisiana, the exercises saw the U.S. Second and Third ARMIES in a mock war involving 420,000 troops and several hundred aircraft. Included was the First Armored CORPS with an unprecedented concentration of 300 light TANKS; more tanks were scattered in other units participating in the war games.

During the maneuvers Gen. GEORGE C. MARSHALL, Army Chief of Staff, made key decisions about the future employment of several officers, including Col. DWIGHT D. EISENHOWER, who had planned the successful strategy for the winning side in the maneuvers, and Maj. Gen. GEORGE S. PATTON, an armored DIVISION commander in Louisiana. Patton had successfully moved his division some 380 miles at night, around an opposing army, a remarkable feat and a harbinger of his tactics in the coming war.

Lovett, Robert A. (1895–1986)

U.S. assistant secretary of war for Air. A New York investment banker and railroad executive turned wartime government official, Lovett was appointed in April 1941 to the newly created post. He immediately convinced President ROOSEVELT of the need to rapidly launch a sustained aircraft production program.

As a result of Lovett's efforts, the B-17 FLYING FORTRESS was built through the combined efforts of Boeing, Douglas, and Lockheed, and the B-24 LIBERATOR was built through a similar cooperative arrangement with Vultee, Ford, Douglas, and North American. By the fall of 1941 he had in production the B-17 and B-24, the B-25 MITCHELL, the B-26 MARAUDER, the A-20 HAVOC, the P-39 AIRACOBRA, the P-40 WARHAWK, and the C-47 SKYTRAIN.

Lovett remained in that post until the end of the war. After the war he returned to government service as under secretary of State in 1947–1949, deputy secretary of Defense, 1950–1951, and secretary of Defense, 1951–1953.

Low, David (1891–1963)

British cartoonist famous for his caricatures of political figures on both sides of the war. His "Colonel Blimp," a fat, pompous sputterer of reactionary slogans, became a symbol for wartime feet-dragging and fossilized ideas.

LQ

U.S. Navy code name for Q-SHIP project, 1942.

L-Series Grasshoppers

These light aircraft were produced in large numbers for the U.S. Army for ARTILLERY spotting, observation, and front-line liaison. The ARMY AIR CORPS had neglected this type of aircraft and in 1941 the Army belatedly selected three commercial aircraft for evaluation for these roles. In 1941 the Army acquired four aircraft of three designs: the Taylorcraft Model D, which became the O-57 and then L-2; the Aeronca Model 65TC, which became the O-58 and then L-3; and the Piper Cub J3C-65, which became the O-59 and then L-4. All were changed from observation (O) to liaison (L) designations in 1942 and named Grasshopper by the Army.

The planes entered combat in Nov. 1942 when the U.S. AIRCRAFT CARRIER *Ranger* (CV 4) carried three L-4 aircraft in addition to her naval aircraft for the NORTH AFRICA INVASION. On Nov. 9, as soon as an airfield was available ashore, the three Grasshoppers took off, and were promptly fired on by a U.S. CRUISER. Two landed safely near a French fort; the third, hit by U.S. Army ground fire, made a "controlled crash" and the wounded pilot crawled away before the plane exploded. Subsequently, the Grasshoppers flew on all U.S. fronts, with the Marine Corps and Navy also using them. In the 1944 invasion of southern France Army pilots flew Grasshoppers off LANDING SHIPS, TANK to support the assault.

All of these Grasshoppers were single-engine, two-seat light aircraft with a high-wing configuration that became popularly known as the Piper Cub regardless of the firm that produced them. Not counting the four evaluation aircraft per firm, Taylor built 1,936 O-57/L-2 Grasshoppers and the Army took over forty-one from private users; Aeronca produced 1,435 O-58/L-3 aircraft and the Army took over forty-eight more from private users; and Piper built 5,549 O-59/L-4 Grasshoppers and another 117 were acquired from private users. In addition, the Marines and Navy acquired 350 Pipers, designated AE, HE, and NE, which were used for training and as aerial ambulances. Including the L-1 Vigilant and L-5 SENTINEL aircraft of this type, the U.S. military forces procured more than 12,500 of these aircraft during the war.

While all Grasshoppers were built with small Continental engines, all three firms developed a GLIDER variant by simply removing the engine and wheels, substituting a new nose and simplified cross-axle landing gear.

All of the aircraft had a top speed of about 85 mph. They normally carried a pilot and observer, seated in tandem.

LST,

see LANDING SHIPS, TANK.

Lucas, Maj. Gen. John P. (1890–1949)

Commander of AMPHIBIOUS LANDING at ANZIO during the ITALIAN CAMPAIGN. Lucas' failure to advance from the beachhead after the Jan. 22, 1944, landing was blamed on his timidity. He landed virtually unopposed. While insisting on the buildup of his beachhead, he gave the Germans time to move in major units against him.

U.S. Maj. Gen. Geoffrey Keyes, in an interview after the war, said Lucas had been following instructions that limited his action. He quoted Lucas as saying to him, "If they wanted me to read beyond their instructions, or if they changed their points of view and wanted to do something else, they could have told me. . . . [N]ot one of them said to keep going. . . . Then they said, 'Oh my, Lucas hasn't done a thing!'"

Lucas was replaced during the battle by Maj. Gen. LUCIAN K. TRUSCOTT, JR.

Lucky

Signal code name for U.S. Third ARMY, 1944–1945.

Lucy Spy Ring

Soviet ESPIONAGE operation run during the war. It was named after "Lucy," Karl Sedlacek, a Czech military intelligence officer who worked as a journalist in Switzerland under the cover name Thomas Selzinger.

One of the Soviets running the ring was Sando Rudolfi. An undercover agent for the Comintern, he spied in PARIS in the early 1930s, and in 1936, after changing his name to Alexander Rado, code-named Dora, he became the resident director of the Soviet intelligence network in Switzerland. He was imprisoned by Soviet authorities in 1945 when his network, betrayed from within, collapsed. His arrest reflected STALIN's distrust for spies, even his own.

Rado (sometimes using the anagram Dora) produced amazing information. He was able, for instance, to warn the Soviets about the exact time of a planned German offensive at KURSK, giving the defenders in that battle a great advantage. U.S. spy ALLEN DULLES, who operated for the OFFICE OF STRATEGIC SERVICES out of Switzerland, said that Rado was able to get intelligence from the German High Command "on a continuous basis, often less than twenty-four hours after its daily decisions concerning the Eastern front were made."

Ludendorff Railway Bridge

Bridge at Remagen, Germany, that was the site of the first of the Allied RHINE CROSSINGS. The standing order from Gen. DWIGHT D. EISENHOWER, Supreme Allied Commander, was to take any Rhine bridge that still stood. But the German Army had orders, too—directly from HITLER: Anyone failing to defend vital objectives like Rhine bridges would be put to death.

The advance units of the U.S. 9th Armored DIVISION reached Remagen, a town 20 miles northwest of Koblenz, on March 7, 1945. A PLATOON, the first unit to see the intact Ludendorff Railway Bridge, rushed toward it just as its German defenders set off an explosive charge. Because of a misplacing of the charge, the bridge did not fall, and the Americans rushed across it, against gunfire from the east bank.

"We ran down the middle of the bridge, shouting as we went," Sgt. Alexander Drabik recalled. "My men were in SQUAD column and not one of them was hit."

More Americans poured across the bridge. Combat engineers arrived to shore the bridge and disable the unexploded charges still wired to it. Eisenhower was elated when he heard the report of the crossing. "This was one of my happy moments of the war," he said. He changed his battle plans and ordered all available troops to head for Remagen.

Hitler, by now in his *FÜHRERBUNKER* in BERLIN, raged at the news. He ordered the German officers who were supposed to destroy the bridge executed. (Eight were put to death. The officer who set the faulty charges survived because he had been captured by the Americans.) On March 10, still raging over the crossing, Hitler fired the German commander in the West, *Generalfeldmarschall* GERD VON RUNDSTEDT.

Hitler ordered all available weapons, including heavy ARTILLERY, V-2 MISSILES, and ME 262 *STURMVOGEL* jet aircraft hurled against the bridge. But within twenty-four hours of its capture 8,000 U.S. troops and their equipment and vehicles had crossed the Rhine and engineers were building other bridges nearby.

The battered bridge collapsed without warning on March 17, killing twenty-seven Americans. By then, the last stage in the defeat of Germany had begun, and the importance of the Ludendorff Railway Bridge was well known to both the ALLIES and Germans. "The prompt seizure and exploit of the crossing," said Gen. GEORGE C. MARSHALL, Army Chief of Staff, "demonstrated American initiative and adaptability at its best, from the daring action of the platoon commander to the Army commander who quickly redirected all his moving columns in a demonstration of brilliant staff management." *Reichsmarschall* HERMANN GÖRING said the capture of the bridge "made a long defense scheme impossible and upset our entire defense scheme along the river."

Luftwaffe,

see GERMANY, AIR FORCE.

Luger

German automatic pistol. The Luger was the official sidearm of the German Navy from 1904 and the Army from 1908 until 1938, although it was used by German troops throughout the war. (It was succeeded as the principal sidearm by the Walther P38.) The Luger was also adopted by several other European countries.

The 9-mm Luger had a toggle-locked breech mechanism with a relatively short, 4-inch barrel. A box magazine fit into the hand grip and carried eight rounds.

The pistol was developed by the German engineer George Luger, based on a Borchardt pistol design. The first model was called the Pistol Parabellum Model 1900 and had a 7.65-mm cal. round; the Model 1902 introduced the 9-mm cal. round.

Lumberjack

Code name for simultaneous assaults by the U.S. First and Third ARMIES to destroy German forces in the Eifel, Feb.–March 1945.

Lustre

British code name for aid to Greece.

Lut (Langen Unabhängiger Torpedo)

German submarine TORPEDO intended to permit long-range attacks against Allied CONVOYS. As soon as a U-BOAT succeeded in approaching a convoy, data collected by echo-ranging (SONAR) was automatically set into the *Lut* torpedoes, which were fired in a spread of six at intervals of several seconds. The torpedoes' tracks opened out in a fan pattern until their spread covered the extent of the convoy. At a prescribed distance they began running loops across the convoy's mean course, the size of the loops being preset, in doing so eventually covering the entire convoy track.

In theory these torpedoes were certain of hitting every ship in the convoy; the theoretical possibility of 95 percent to 99 percent hits in an average convoy was achieved in firing trials.

The *Lut* was introduced into U-boats in late 1944. Only the effectiveness of Allied antisubmarine efforts in that period and the limited number of submarines available prevented the *Lut* from having a disastrous impact on the BATTLE OF THE ATLANTIC.

The *Lut* was sometimes referred to as the zigzag torpedo.

Lüth, *Kapitän zur See* Wolfgang (1913–1945)

One of the top-scoring German U-BOAT ACES of the war. He sank some fifty Allied ships during sixteen war patrols, the last setting an endurance record of 220 days at sea. Lüth began the war in one of the small submarines called "canoes," the *U-9*. In his first action he was set upon by four British destroyers that wrecked his craft, which he was still able to bring back to port. He went on to command the larger *U-181*, one of the high-scoring German submarines, in which he made a record-breaking war patrol into the Indian Ocean and to the Far East.

He was the first member of the U-boat service to be awarded Oak Leaves, Diamonds, and Swords to the Knight's Cross of the IRON CROSS for his exploits in command of the *U-181*. (The only other U-boat commander so honored was GÜNTHER PRIEN.) At the end of the war he was commander of the naval school complex in Flensburg where the government of KAREL DÖNITZ was housed; on the night of May 14, 1945, he was shot and killed by a warning shot fired by a nervous sentry.

Lütjens, *Vizeadmiral* Günther (1889–1941)

Admiral embarked in the German battleship BISMARCK during her ill-fated sortie. Shortly after the start of the EUROPEAN WAR, *Kontradmiral* Lüt-

jens, as commander of the Scouting Forces of the German fleet, carried out cruiser-destroyer operations against British shipping in the North Sea. Subsequently promoted to *Vizeadmiral*, in Germany's DENMARK AND NORWAY CAMPAIGN in April 1940 he led the battleships *Gneisenau* and *Scharnhorst* to sea in support of the German landings at Narvik in northern Norway. In that operation the battleships sank the British aircraft carrier *Glorious*. The German Navy suffered heavy losses in the Norwegian invasion; the *Gneisenau* was hit by shells from a British battleship, but survived.

That summer Lütjens was named fleet commander. His two predecessors had been relieved within the past few months because of disagreements with *Grossadmiral* ERICH RAEDER, head of the German Navy. In early Feb. 1941 he again led the *Genisenau* and *Scharnhorst* to sea, this time to raid British CONVOYS in the North Atlantic. Their successful cruise sank 116,000 tons of Allied shipping before the ships put into the German-held port of Brest on the French coast.

Returning to Germany, Lütjens made ready to take the battleship *Bismarck,* Germany's newest and largest warship, into the North Atlantic to raid convoys. Lütjens had wanted to wait until one of the other battleships or the new TIRPITZ would be ready to participate in the operation. But after meeting with HITLER when he visited the *Bismarck* on May 5, Lütjens sailed for Norway. He sortied for the Atlantic on May 21, 1941, accompanied by the heavy cruiser *Prinz Eugen*. The two ships broke into the North Atlantic, but were quickly engaged by British warships. Despite initial success in the dramatic sinking of the battle cruiser *HOOD,* Lütjens was unable to continue the operation. Not realizing he had escaped his pursuers, Lütjens sent a lengthy radio message that the British were able to detect and from it determine the *Bismarck*'s location.

Damaged in the *Hood* engagement, and with her rudder jammed by a TORPEDO hit from an aircraft, on May 27 the *Bismarck* sunk under a tremendous pounding from British warships. Lütjens was not among the 110 survivors.

Luxembourg

Capital: Luxembourg, pop. 301,000 (est. 1938). A grand duchy smaller than Rhode Island and hemmed in by Germany, Belgium, and France, Luxembourg clung to neutrality as a form of survival. Germany formally insured its friendship to the tiny country on Aug. 27, 1939. When the EUROPEAN WAR began in Sept. 1939, the duchy mobilized a voluntary defense corps of 125 men to augment the 300-man army and 250-man police force.

Neutrality and peace ended on May 10, 1940, when German troops crossed the border and began a futile campaign to absorb the tiny nation into the THIRD REICH. More than 45,000 Luxembourgers fled to France, along with the Grand Dutchess Charlotte, who would form a government-in-exile. Some of the young men would later join a small military unit to fight alongside the other ALLIES.

The Germans staged a census on Oct. 10, 1941, to find Luxembourgers of German racial origin. Asked to declare whether they were German, 98 percent said they were not. When the German conquerors declared compulsory military service for young males, the country staged a general strike. In retaliation, the Germans declared martial law and in an eight-day rampage, killed twenty-one people, sent others to CONCENTRATION CAMPS, and deported families to Germany.

The Allies liberated Luxembourg on Sept. 10, 1944. But in Dec. 1945, as the grand duchy began to get used to peace, the battle of the Bulge began, devastating about one third of the little country. Gen. GEORGE S. PATTON, who led the liberation forces, was buried in a U.S. military cemetery in Luxembourg.

M

M1 Garand

Basic rifle of U.S. soldiers and Marines during the war. The M1 Garand semiautomatic rifle was perfected in 1930 and six years later the U.S. Army began to issue it as the standard infantryman's rifle. The Marine Corps began issuing the M1 in 1942. In both services the M1 replaced the M1903 SPRINGFIELD. The U.S. Army infantry DIVISION of July 1943 had 6,518 M1 rifles for the division's 14,253 men; an armored division had 2,063 M1s for 10,937 men; and an AIRBORNE division had 6,169 M1s for 12,979 troops; only the .30-cal. M1 CARBINE was issued as an individual weapon to U.S. soldiers in larger numbers than the M1 rifle. Over 4 million Garands were produced during the war.

The M1 was a .30-cal., gas-operated, semiautomatic weapon, weighing 9.6 pounds, loaded with an 8-round clip. Effective range was 550 yards (maximum was over 3,000 yards) with a rate of fire of 20 rounds per minute. The rifle was noted for its reliability and accuracy.

It was developed by John Cantius Garand (1888–1974), at the time an employee of the U.S. Armory at Springfield, Mass. Garand had first become interested in guns while running a shooting gallery. As a government employee, he received neither a patent for the rifle nor any royalties from its sale.

M3,

see GREASE GUN.

Gen. Douglas MacArthur wades ashore at Leyte as he returns to the Philippines in Oct. 1944. Beyond him, in a helmet, is Philippines President Manuel Quezon; on MacArthur's right is his Chief of Staff, Lt. Gen. Richard K. Sutherland. *(U.S. Army)*

M6A1 *Seiran* (Mountain Haze)

Floatplane developed by the Japanese Navy to be launched from submarines for attacks against U.S. cities. The plane became operational in early 1945 and was immediately assigned to two submarines of the *I-400* class as well as to smaller aircraft-carrying submarines to practice for an attack against the Panama Canal. The planes were finally embarked in the submarines, which departed Japan on July 26, 1945, for a six-plane bombing raid against U.S. warships at Ulithi anchorage in the CAROLINE ISLANDS. The attack, however, was canceled when Japan surrendered; the planes were destroyed and the submarines returned to Japan. Thus, the M6A1 never flew a combat mission.

The prototype Aichi-built floatplane was completed in Nov. 1943. Seven additional prototypes were followed by twenty production aircraft with improved engines, the last two fitted with wheels instead of floats; those two planes were designated M6A1-K *Nanzan* (Southern Mountain).

The M6A1 was a low-wing monoplane with a streamlined fuselage and an in-line engine; the twin, cantilever floats were mounted under the wings. The floats could be jettisoned after launch to improve performance. The wings folded backward against the fuselage, and the horizontal tail surfaces folded downward. With fluorescent paint applied to certain spots on the aircraft to aid assembly in darkness, a trained team of four men could have a plane ready for flight in just six minutes.

Maximum speed of the M6A1 was 294 mph with a range of 740 miles. One 1,874-pound or two 551-pound BOMBS or an aerial TORPEDO could be carried under the fuselage. (In the planned attack against the Panama Canal both bombs and torpedoes were to be used.) The plane had a crew of two, with the second crewman firing a flexible 13-mm machine gun from the rear cockpit.

The plane was not assigned an Allied code name as its existence was unknown until after the war.

MacArthur, Gen. of the Army Douglas A. (1880–1964)

Douglas MacArthur's life and career is a parade of superlatives. He garnered virtually every possible award at West Point and graduated in 1903 with an average exceeded only by one other person, Gen. Robert E. Lee. During World War I combat in France, commanding the 42nd (Rainbow) DIVISION, MacArthur was awarded several decorations for valor and became the youngest general officer in the U.S. Army. He was one of the few men to be twice nominated for the MEDAL OF HONOR (finally awarded in March 1942 after his escape from the Philippines).

In 1930 MacArthur became one of the youngest Army Chiefs of Staff ever appointed. Upon retiring from the U.S. Army in 1934 after his tour as Chief of Staff, he was appointed head of the Philippine Army by President MANUEL QUEZON, averting an anticlimactic retirement. For his new role, MacArthur chose the title of field marshal.

The next six years put the final stamp on MacArthur's Caesarean (to borrow biographer-historian William Manchester's apt characterization) self-image. The negative superlatives in MacArthur's character became entrenched—his ambition, vaingloriousness, amassing of a sycophantic court, and, most important, a view of U.S. strategy that was persistently distorted in favor of his own, Far Eastern priorities.

In July 1941 MacArthur was recalled to active U.S. service and named commanding general of U.S. Army forces in the Far East. By then, with war against Japan becoming likely, MacArthur had become convinced that he could defend against and even defeat a Japanese invasion of the Philippines. MacArthur's conviction, expressed with his usual vigor, overturned a central assumption of the U.S. war plans and led directly to the stubborn, ultimately futile stands on BATAAN and CORREGIDOR in 1942. These battles, although tragic for Americans in the short run, disrupted the schedule of the JAPANESE CAMPAIGN IN THE FAR EAST and probably spelled the difference in turning back the Japanese attempt to occupy the southern coast of NEW GUINEA later in 1942.

MacArthur was not in the Philippines when the final surrender came—in April 1942 for Bataan, in May for Corregidor. On March 23 he received orders from President ROOSEVELT to escape to Australia, leaving recently promoted Lt. Gen. JONATHAN M. WAINWRIGHT in command of the remaining U.S. forces in the Philippines. Mac-

Arthur and his wife, his son Arthur, their Chinese nurse, and several aides embarked in four PT-BOATS (commanded by Lt. JOHN D. BULKELEY), which raced 560 miles to Mindanao in thirty-five hours, eluding Japanese surface and air forces. From that island, taking off shortly after midnight on March 17, his party was flown to Australia, a distance of 1,580 miles, in B-17 FLYING FORTRESSES.

At that low point, when he commanded little more than attention, MacArthur could have been dismissed by history as an aging warrior whose failure to respond to the threat of Japanese air attacks on the day PEARL HARBOR fell cost the Philippines most of their recently reinforced air power. His Medal of Honor might have been merely a morale-boosting retirement present. That such was not his fate is attributable as much to MacArthur's outstanding military abilities as to his talent for self-promotion.

He carved out a Supreme Command in the Southwest Pacific and defied attempts by Adm. ERNEST J. KING and Adm. CHESTER W. NIMITZ and Gen. GEORGE C. MARSHALL, ostensibly his superior, to direct his strategy. His campaign to take New Guinea from the Japanese was characterized by a masterful series of leap-frogging landings that bypassed 135,000 Japanese troops. The dreaded fortress of RABAUL with its 50,000 defenders was never attacked by land, but allowed instead to rot in uselessness until the end of the war. And, he never lost sight of his goal to "Return to the Philippines" at the head of a conquering army, an operation that began in Oct. 1944.

MacArthur's Philippine campaign combined an audacious use of mobility and surprise in the southern part of the archipelago and grinding attrition in Luzon. Opinion is divided on its military merit, with most analysts concluding that the southern liberations unnecessarily diverted men and matériel from the Luzon campaign.

Subsequently, MacArthur was named commander of all U.S. Army troops in the Pacific area and, with the conclusion of the Philippines campaign, was to lead those troops—in collaboration with Nimitz's Navy-Marine forces—in the final assaults on the Japanese homeland. The capitulation of Japan in Aug. 1945 was followed by MacArthur accepting the Japanese SURRENDER on the deck of

the U.S. BATTLESHIP *MISSOURI* (BB 63) on Sept. 2, 1945. Subsequently, he became Supreme Allied Commander in Japan, dictating the founding of a constitutional monarchy, instituting many reforms of Japanese society, even as he assumed the trappings of viceroy, responsible for the disarming and then the rebuilding of the Japanese nation.

He again became a commander at war on July 7, 1950, when he was named Commander in Chief of the United Nations force fighting aggression in Korea. His boldness in demanding a Navy-Marine AMPHIBIOUS LANDING at Inchon in Sept. 1950 was one of most important strategic decisions of his career and turned the tide of the Korean War. However, MacArthur's public disagreement over U.S. strategy with President TRUMAN led to his dismissal in 1951, after which, like the soldier of the old West Point ballad he quoted in his 1951 appearance before a joint session of Congress, he just "faded away." While during and after World War II many Republican leaders sought him as their candidate, when he became available for candidacy after the war he had no political base with which to challenge Truman.

Although his relations with his subordinate commanders were remote, MacArthur recognized talent and directed some brilliant performers who showed imagination, aggressiveness, and flexibility. At all times, however, MacArthur insisted that he was to be seen as the one source of wisdom in the Southwest Pacific. His commanders chafed under a news blackout of their deeds, many of his troops actively loathed his histrionics and (inaccurately) deemed him a coward, calling him "Dugout Doug."

His nominal peers and superiors were alternately blackmailed and fawned upon. A great controversy endures about the casualty rates suffered by MacArthur's forces. Some contend that he lost fewer men in the entire New Guinea campaign than EISENHOWER did on Omaha Beach in the NORMANDY INVASION. Others argue that MacArthur manipulated "body counts," describing extended and bloody battles as "mopping-up" operations.

MacArthur remains one of the most striking—and capable—military figures that the United States has produced.

Macintyre, Capt. Donald (1904–1981)

High-scoring British antisubmarine practitioner. Macintyre commanded two of the most effective escort groups in the BATTLE OF THE ATLANTIC.

Macintyre initially served in surface ships and, after pilot training, in carrier and shipboard aircraft from 1928 to 1934. Returning to surface ships, he commanded the sloop *Kingfisher* in 1935–1936 when she was assigned to the Royal Navy's antisubmarine school. He then commanded a succession of destroyers, and early in the EUROPEAN WAR participated in the Norwegian campaigns as well as antisubmarine operations.

Macintyre took command of the destroyer *Walker* and the 5th Escort Group in March 1941 and in his first CONVOY escort operation, the destroyer *Vanoc* sank the *U-100* commanded by Joachim Schepke and his own ship sank the *U-99* commanded by OTTO KRETSCHMER; these were the top-ranking German submarine ACES. Schepke was killed and Kretschmer captured in these actions.

Promoted to commander in 1942, Macintyre briefly served as the British liaison officer at the U.S. naval base in Argentia, Newfoundland. He returned to sea in the destroyer *Hesperus* in command of the B.2 Escort Group in 1942–1944. The ship fought one of the most dramatic duels of the war on the night of May 11–12, 1942: The *U-223,* forced to surface by the *Hesperus'* DEPTH CHARGES, missed the destroyer with five TORPEDOES. Attacked by additional depth charges set to explode just beneath the surface, fired at by the destroyer, and then rammed, the badly damaged *U-223* was still able to escape.

Under his command the *Walker* and *Hesperus* sank five U-boats; his escort groups sank more.

Macintyre transferred to the frigate *Bickerton,* again in command of the 5th Escort Group, in 1944. On Aug. 22 his flagship was sunk by a U-BOAT's torpedo. Back ashore, he requalified as a pilot. Promoted to captain by the end of 1945, Macintyre served in a number of aviation, antisubmarine training, and fleet assignments prior to his retirement in 1955.

His autobiographical *U-boat Killer* gives a vivid description of hunting submarines: "It was a rare treat for an escort [group] commander to get more than an hour or so off the bridge at one time. Watch would follow watch and day would fade into night, but the escort commander, and usually his Yeoman of Signals, would continue at their post attending to the thousand and one little problems of a convoy getting into its stride."

In another descriptive passage, he writes: "In my sea-cabin under the bridge the endlessly repeated orders to the quartermaster at the wheel and his replies formed, with the ping of the ASDIC [SONAR], a continuous noise background, night and day, day after day, a background which I soon ceased consciously to hear and through which I could sleep soundly only to be instantly awake should the noise pattern vary. An undertone of urgency or anxiety in the voice of the officer of the watch, or an echo to the ping, would sound an alarm in my sleeping brain, and on many occasions I found myself halfway to the bridge before the reason for my waking had penetrated to my conscious thoughts."

Macintyre wrote several other graphic books on naval warfare.

Madagascar

French colonial possession in the western Indian Ocean. On May 5, 1942, in the first Allied invasion of the war, British troops landed on Madagascar to prevent the VICHY FRENCH government on the island from providing support to Japanese naval forces in the Indian Ocean. The operation, given the code names Bonus and Ironclad, required British forces to steam 9,000 miles from England, with a stopover at Freetown, South Africa. The naval force, led by a battleship and two aircraft carriers, included one of the first Allied LANDING SHIP, TANKS, the converted tanker *Bachaquero.*

When the assault components of three brigades went ashore, French troops resisted. But the British, supported by naval gunfire and carrier aircraft, overcame all resistance on May 7. The British lost 105 men and the French some 150. A French submarine attempting to attack the British naval force was sunk by carrier-based SWORDFISH aircraft.

Mae West

Slang for life jacket, generally any type used in aircraft and ships, although originally referring to those that had heavy, kapok padding in front—an analogy to the ample bosom of film star Mae West (1892–1980). Life jackets had kapok fillers to keep them afloat, or were inflatable by carbon dioxide (CO_2) cartridges. U.S. forces late in the war used inflatable life belts, but these were sometimes dangerous for heavily loaded troops, as the weight of helmet, backpack, and even weapons could turn the man upside down when he hit the water from a sinking landing craft.

Some of the Mae Wests had small light bulbs attached. Naval officer-author NICHOLAS MONSARRAT wrote in his *Three Corvettes*: "These lights— they are small naked bulbs clipped to the lifejacket and connected to a battery in the breast-pocket— have been the salvation of countless men, and the lack of them must have been the death of countless more: a man in the water at night is almost impossible to see, and his voice, even in still weather, is lost in engine and water noises."

Magic

U.S. code-breaking effort against the Japanese. From 1935 to 1939 the U.S. Army and Navy were able to read Japanese diplomatic codes generated by machine cipher as a result of intensive work by American mathematicians and cryptologists working under the direction of Russian-born WILLIAM F. FRIEDMAN, the chief cryptanalyst of the U.S. Army Signal Corps. In March 1939 the Japanese began to employ a new code machine and cipher, given the Allied name PURPLE.

That code was broken through herculean efforts by U.S. code-breakers and the clandestine entry into a Japanese consular office by U.S. Naval Intelligence that provided photographs of the machine's switches. In Sept. 1940 the Americans were able to replicate the Purple machine and thereafter read the diplomatic codes.

At the time of the Japanese attack on PEARL HARBOR the Army and Navy were operating Purple machines in Washington, at the Army signal intelligence unit in the Philippines, and at the British code center at BLETCHLEY PARK. (The Purple machine intended for the Navy intelligence team at Pearl Harbor was instead sent to Bletchley Park when the war began in the Pacific.)

The U.S. code-breaking efforts were subsequently successful against Japanese military codes.

They were directly responsible for warning the U.S. Pacific Command (Adm. CHESTER W. NIMITZ) of the Japanese movements in preparation for the carrier battles of CORAL SEA and MIDWAY in 1942, and provided the flight itinerary for Adm. ISOROKU YAMAMOTO, leading to his ASSASSINATION in April 1943. The rapidity with which Purple could be deciphered and transmitted to U.S. forces in the Pacific enabled American submarines to intercept specific Japanese ships at precise locations within hours of Japanese radio transmissions.

Magic Carpet

Code name for the rapid return of U.S. troops from Europe and the Far East by warships and transports immediately after the war.

Maginot Line

Line of forts along the French-German border, hailed in prewar years as the strongest fixed fortification in the world. Begun in 1929 and completed in 1934, the Maginot Line guarded the French border, from Luxembourg to Switzerland. It consisted of old border fortifications and immense new ones, some extending six stories underground and able to garrison about 300,000 troops, complete with heavy guns, hospitals, electrical power generators, and a small-scale railroad. The fortresses were linked by pill boxes, minefields, zigzagging barbed wire, and tank traps. Bombproof guns were aimed permanently at Germany. The line—actually a zone 10 to 50 miles deep—was backed up by strongly fortified towns, including Verdun, Metz, and Nancy.

As British historian A. J. P. Taylor noted, the French "treated the line as purely defensive and had no means of sallying out from it. . . . So confident of this were the Germans that they took few defensive precautions. In this absurd way the Maginot Line benefitted the Germans and weakened the French." The Germans had only nineteen divisions along the line, compared to fifty-nine French divisions.

The German BLITZKREIG of 1940 outflanked the line, leaving it virtually untouched by war. By skirting the line the Germans doomed Belgium, which had resisted French plans to extend the Maginot Line along the Franco-Belgian frontier.

The fortifications were named after André Maginot, French minister of war from 1877 to 1932.

Magnet

Code name for movement of first U.S. troops to Northern Ireland, early 1942.

Magnetic Anomaly Detector

Device for locating U-BOATS through their distortion of the earth's magnetic field. Magnetic Anomaly Detectors (MAD) were developed from magnetometers used in mineral exploration. They had limited range and were most effective in shallow waters. When employed by aircraft, MAD could locate a fully submerged submarine. It was a low-level detection device with the aircraft having to fly at an altitude of 100 feet to detect a submarine at a depth of 300 feet.

A U.S. invention, MAD entered service in 1943 and was initially fitted in Navy PBY CATALINA flying boats. These aircraft were soon dubbed "Madcats." The first Navy squadron to fly Madcats sank three U-boats near the Strait of Gibraltar from Feb. to May 1944. Earlier, the squadron had not been able to make any kills off the U.S. Atlantic Coast because of the lack of U-boat activity. Other U.S. antisubmarine squadrons soon were achieving kills by pinpointing contacts with MAD, although against a dwindling number of German submarines.

Because a MAD-equipped aircraft detected a submarine directly below it, and there would be a few seconds until the BOMBS could be released, a "retrobomb" was developed for use by MAD aircraft. This weapon was a 35-pound, impact-fused bomb with a small, solid-fuel ROCKET in the tail. The rockets propelled the bombs *backwards* off their launch rails, bringing the bombs to a stop in midair; the bombs then fell vertically into the sea. A PBY could carry twelve of these retrobombs on rails under each wing; they were automatically released in salvos of eight bombs at half-second intervals. The bombs were launched at slightly differing angles to increase the probability of a hit on the submarine.

About 400 MAD devices were produced for installation in U.S. aircraft during the war.

Magneto

Code name for the Yalta Conference.

Mailer, Norman (1923—)

Author of the first major American novel of the war, *The Naked and the Dead*, published in 1948.

Mailer enlisted in the Army in 1944, when he was a year out of Harvard, dreaming of writing a war novel. He was assigned to an intelligence and reconnaissance unit in the Philippines where, he later said, he was in "a couple of firefights and skirmishes" during the liberation of the Philippines, which began in Oct. 1944.

Mailer began writing the book while he was in the Philippines by keeping a diary, which he sent back to his wife in the form of letters. When he was discharged in 1946, he began assembling the diary excerpts and produced a novel about action on the fictional island of Anopopei in the Philippines. He struggled in vain with his editor and publisher to keep the rich raw language of combat. He had to make characters say *fug* as in "Fug you." They were allowed some profanity, as in "Fug the sonofabitch mud" and "Fug the goddam gun."

Mailfist

Code name for British capture of SINGAPORE, 1945.

Majestic

Allied code name for the planned invasions of the Japanese home islands. These were to have been the largest AMPHIBIOUS LANDINGS of the war.

In late May 1945 the U.S. JOINT CHIEFS OF STAFF issued a directive on the conduct of the Pacific conflict to force Japan's unconditional surrender. Japan's ability and will to resist would be reduced by blockade, aerial and naval bombardment, and the seizure of portions of the industrial heartland of the main island of Honshu. The invasion would actually be carried out in two steps.

First, Kyushu would be invaded to isolate this southernmost of the main islands, to destroy the Japanese combat forces there, and to provide sites for airfields and other bases for the invasion of Honshu. This assault, code-named Olympic and then changed to Majestic because of a possible security compromise in early Aug. 1945, was scheduled for Nov. 1, 1945. The assault would be carried out by Gen. WALTER KRUEGER's Sixth ARMY.

The second phase, known as Operation Coronet, would be the invasion of Honshu in March 1946. Lt. Gen. ROBERT EICHELBERGER's Eighth Army would be landed on the TOKYO plain.

Gen. of the Army DOUGLAS MACARTHUR would

have overall responsibility for the invasions of Japan with Fleet Adm. CHESTER W. NIMITZ commanding all naval aspects of the campaign. For the invasion of Kyushu the Third and Fifth FLEETS would operate simultaneously for the first time—combining all available U.S. warships in the Pacific. Adm. RAYMOND A. SPRUANCE's Fifth Fleet would provide the amphibious and covering forces, including ten AIRCRAFT CARRIERS and sixteen ESCORT CARRIERS, with eight of the latter carrying Marine aircraft to provide close air support. In all, Spruance would have some 3,000 ships under his command (with many coming from the Atlantic area).

Adm. WILLIAM F. HALSEY's Third Fleet would provide a mobile striking force of carriers and BATTLESHIPS with their escorts. Vice Adm. Bernard Rawlings would command TASK FORCE 37 comprised of Commonwealth ships assigned to the Third Fleet. Halsey would have operational control of seventeen aircraft carriers, eight fast BATTLESHIPS, twenty CRUISERS, and seventy-five DESTROYERS.

These would have been the largest amphibious operations yet undertaken. The overall code name for the assault on Japan was Downfall. In addition, the XXIV CORPS of the Tenth Army was to have landed in southern Korea.

The Japanese were expected to have opposed the landings with massive suicide forces: At the end of the war the Japanese Army had a total of 2,350,000 troops in the homeland, ready for a suicidal defense against the expected Allied invasion. These troops were to be backed up by almost 4,000,000 civilian Army and Navy workers and a civilian militia of 28,000,000, the last armed mostly with sharpened poles, MINES, and GRENADES. In addition, about 10,700 aircraft were in the home islands to be used in suicide attacks against Allied ships, assisted by a large number of HUMAN TORPEDOES.

Major Martin,

see MINCEMEAT.

Makin Island

Japanese-held atoll in the GILBERT ISLANDS where Marine raiders landed from two U.S. SUBMARINEs in Aug. 1942. The raid was intended primarily as a diversion to distract the Japanese from sending reinforcements to GUADALCANAL and Tulagi, where Marines had landed earlier in the month.

The Marines, CARLSON'S RAIDERS under Lt. Col. EVANS F. CARLSON, were taken to the islands on two large submarines, the *Argonaut* (SM 1) and the *Nautilus* (SS 168). The force included thirteen officers (including Carlson and Maj. JAMES ROOSEVELT, son of President ROOSEVELT) and 208 Marine enlisted men. The raiders went to shore in inflated rubber landing craft powered by outboard motors.

The Marines landed without being spotted, but one of them accidentally discharged his rifle, alerting the Japanese. They attacked with machine guns, grenade launchers, and FLAMETHROWERS and called in bombers. The submarines gave some fire support with their deck guns and even sank a small Japanese freighter and a patrol boat.

As the Marines attempted to withdraw that night, some Marines drowned when boats overturned in the surf. About 100 raiders made it back to the submarines that night. Carlson and the rest of the Marines stayed on the island the rest of the day, blew up an aviation gas dump, and seized Japanese documents. That night, most of the remaining Marines made it to the submarines. In all, seven Marines drowned, fourteen were killed, and nine were captured and later executed. (After the war the Japanese officer responsible for the execution order was judged guilty of WAR CRIMES and hanged.)

In Nov. 1943, as part of the assault operation, code-named Galvanic, that took TARAWA, Makin was invaded by 6,470 U.S. Army troops, who easily defeated the small Japanese garrison.

Malaya

Capital: SINGAPORE, *pop. 5,560,444 (1941).* British Malaya (then its official name) consisted of the Straits Settlements, the Federated Malay States, and the Unfederated Malay States. The Settlements, which ranked as a British colony, included Singapore, nearby islands, and portions of the peninsula; the Malay States were also on the peninsula, except for Brunei, which was part of the island of Borneo. Much of the British administration of the territory was through sultans.

One of the richest colonies in the BRITISH COM-

MONWEALTH, Malaya surpassed the Netherlands East Indies in the production of both tin and rubber, vital RESOURCES for England. The fall of France in June 1940 jeopardized these resources, for German-controlled VICHY FRANCE handed French INDOCHINA over to Japanese control, giving Japan a base for operations on the Malaysian peninsula.

On Dec. 8, 1941, Japanese troops, after landing with virtually no opposition on the coast of Thailand, passed through Thailand for the invasion of Malaya. A key objective in the JAPANESE CAMPAIGN IN THE FAR EAST, Malaya fell in Feb. 1942.

The Japanese interned British civilians and other Europeans, who somehow managed to educate their children (even holding standard school-entrance examinations) and maintain a fairly effective medical campaign against malaria and tuberculosis during the war. As the Allies readied a force in mid-1945 to liberate Malaya, Japan surrendered.

Mallory Major

Code name for Allied air offensive against Po River bridges, Italy.

Malmedy

Site of one of the most brutal military atrocities of the war. On Dec. 17, 1944, during the battle of the BULGE, German SS troops herded about 100 captured U.S. soldiers into a field at a road junction near the Belgian town of Malmedy and murdered them with machine gun fire. Many survivors of the machine gun fusillade were killed by pistol shots to the head. A few escaped, but between 71 and 129—the number became a postwar controversy—were killed in what was the bloodiest atrocity committed against U.S. troops during the war.

In 1946 the German officers responsible for what became known as the Malmedy Massacre were tried for WAR CRIMES. A U.S. military tribunal sentenced forty-three of the SS officers to death, twenty-three to life imprisonment, and eight to lesser sentences. But a subsequent, stormy U.S. Senate investigation, led by Sen. JOSEPH MCCARTHY, ended with the claim that U.S. interrogators had mistreated the SS officers in gaining their confessions. In March 1948, the Army commuted all but six of the death sentences, and in Jan. 1951—when McCarthy was

at the height of his power—JOHN J. MCCLOY, the American High Commissioner for Germany, commuted the last of the death sentences to life imprisonment. Shortly thereafter, release of all the convicted officers began.

Malta

British-controlled island 58 miles from SICILY. Naval and air bases on Malta gave the British virtual control of the Mediterranean. Operations out of Malta harassed German supply lines to North Africa from Italy; in Oct. 1941 British attacks sank 65 percent of the AXIS supply ships heading for Axis-held ports in North Africa.

But Malta itself was vulnerable to attack. Soon after Italy's entry into the war in June 1940, Italian air attacks began. All Malta had in the way of air defense were four Sea GLADIATORS. Because there were no spare parts, only three were flown at any one time; any three in the air got the names "Faith," "Hope," and "Charity."

In Dec. 1940 a large German Luftwaffe unit arrived in Sicily and the "toe" of Italy. The mission of the unit, *Fliegerkorps* X, was to neutralize Malta. The formidable *Fliegerkorps* X was an antishipping air corps that had played a major role in the DENMARK AND NORWAY CAMPAIGN. Its assets were fifty HE 111 medium bombers, eighty JU 87 *STUKA* dive bombers, seventy JU 88 fighter-bombers, twenty-six ME 110 fighter-bombers, and forty ME 109 fighters.

On Jan. 10, 1941, the *Stukas* pounced on the British carrier ILLUSTRIOUS, which was about 85 miles off Malta escorting a convoy of merchant ships. The *Stukas* made seven direct bomb hits on the carrier before she reached Malta, afire and steering by her engines.

The attack on the *Illustrious* was the beginning of Malta's long ordeal. Air attacks on the island and on convoys trying to reach it would continue until the end of 1942. In Feb. 1942, when the besieged island was under almost continuous attack, there were as many as thirteen raids in a single night.

As Malta's plight became critical, more and more planes flew in from aircraft carriers. On April 1, 1942, Prime Minister CHURCHILL personally asked President ROOSEVELT for the loan of the U.S. carrier WASP to take planes to Malta. Roosevelt agreed, and forty-seven SPITFIRE fighters flew off

The dockyard at Malta undergoing savage attack by Luftwaffe bombers. Under the crane at the right is the heavily damaged aircraft carrier *Illustrious*. Despite intensive German and Italian bombing, Malta remained a vital British base for attacking Italian convoys attempting to resupply Rommel's Afrika Korps. *(Imperial War Museum)*

from the *Wasp* on April 20. On May 9 the *Wasp* delivered another sixty Spitfires.

In Aug. 1942, the greatest concentration of British carriers ever assembled—four aircraft carriers, along with two battleships, seven cruisers, and twenty-four destroyers—were brought together to escort fourteen merchant ships in Operation Pedestal. As Spitfires were being flown in, a German U-BOAT surfaced and fired a spread of torpedoes. Four slammed into the carrier *Eagle,* which sank in eight minutes. Destroyers rescued about 900 of the ship's 1,160-man crew.

The following day there were four major air attacks on the convoy. Of the fourteen merchantmen that had set out, only five arrived and three of them were damaged. Operation Pedestal cost the Royal Navy one aircraft carrier, two cruisers, and a destroyer. A second carrier and two other cruisers were damaged. But Malta got another lease on life. Thirteen convoys, every one mauled by air attacks, struggled into Malta between Aug. 1940 and Jan. 1943. The relentless air raids killed nearly 1,500 Maltese civilians.

In April 1942, amid rumors of an imminent German invasion, King GEORGE VI, in an unprecedented gesture, bestowed upon all residents the George Cross for valor to honor "her brave people." Operation Hercules, an invasion using both German and Italian paratroops, was being planned. HITLER, unsure of his Italian ally, called off Hercules, despite the appeals of *Generalfeldmarschall*

ERWIN ROMMEL. Rommel later blamed the failure to neutralize Malta for his ultimate defeat in North Africa.

Malyy Saturn (Little Saturn)

Soviet code name for a reduced version of Operation Saturn.

Manchester

British twin-engine medium bomber that was the basis for the highly successful four-engine LANCASTER heavy bomber. The Manchester was called "one of the RAF's great disappointments" by aviation historian Owen Thetford.

The Manchester was designed around two of the new Rolls-Royce Vulture engines that were unreliable and did not achieve their designed power. The aircraft was thus operational only from Nov. 1940 to June 1942. Their first combat mission was a raid on Brest on the night of Feb. 24–25, 1941. Frequent night missions over occupied Europe and Germany followed until more capable aircraft became available.

The first Avro Manchester flew in July 1939 and from mid-1940 until Nov. 1941 a total of 209 production aircraft were delivered (in addition to two prototypes).

The Manchester was a "boxy," mid-wing aircraft with an unusual three-fin tail configuration. The main wheels fully retracted into the engine nacelles. It was noted for its heavy payload and strong defensive armament (eight guns in three power-operated turrets).

Maximum speed was 265 mph; maximum range was 1,630 miles with 8,100 pounds of BOMBS and 1,200 miles with 10,350 pounds. Twin .303-cal. machine guns were fitted in the nose and dorsal turrets, and four guns in the tail turret. The Manchester was flown by a crew of seven.

Mandalay,

see BURMA.

Mandibles

British code word for proposed operations against German forces in the Dodecanese, 1940.

Manhattan Project

The code name for the U.S. program to build the ATOMIC BOMB. The code name was derived from another code name, the Manhattan Engineer District, a nonexistent region invented by the U.S. Army Corps of Engineers to conceal the atomic bomb enterprise. The Manhattan Project controlled hundreds of millions of dollars worth of facilities, materiel, and machinery at Oak Ridge, Tenn.; Hanford, Wash.; and Los Alamos, N.M.; plus smaller activities elsewhere.

The project recruited the leading physicists in the United States. Of some 300 leading U.S. physicists, about 125 worked on the project. In addition, thousands of technicians and military personnel were assigned to the research, development, and building of the first bombs. The man in overall charge of the project was an Army officer, Maj. Gen. LESLIE R. GROVES.

Manhole

Code name for RAF to infiltrate a Soviet adviser team by GLIDER into Yugoslavia, Feb. 1944.

Manila

Capital of the Philippines and a battleground during the liberation of the nation from Japanese occupation. When Japan invaded the Philippines on Dec. 8, 1941 (Dec. 7 Hawaii time), Manila was a major objective. On Dec. 27, as fighting neared the capital, Gen. DOUGLAS MACARTHUR, commander of U.S.-Filipino forces in the Philippines, declared Manila an OPEN CITY and led his men on a retreat into the jungles of the BATAAN Peninsula. But Japanese military leaders disregarded the open city designation and bombed the port and part of *Intramuros*—the Walled City—the original Spanish fortified settlement and a place of numerous churches, which was surrounded by a 25-foot wall about 2½ miles in circumference.

Japanese troops entered the city on Jan. 2, 1942, and soon established a PRISONER OF WAR facility in the old Spanish Bilibid prison in downtown Manila. There they later incarcerated thousands of American prisoners captured on CORREGIDOR and elsewhere in the Philippines.

When U.S. liberation of the Philippines began in Oct. 1944, the city became a major objective, but it was not until early in 1945, as the Americans, joined by Filipino GUERRILLAS, began advancing on the city from the north. Gen. TOMOYUKI YAMASHITA, commander of the Japanese troops, ordered withdrawal from the city, forbidding unnecessary destruction. While Yamashita got his troops out of the city and into the hills of Luzon, about 15,000 sailors and marines and 4,000 soldiers under Vice Adm. Sanji Iwabuchi were encircled in the city by U.S. troops.

Iwabuchi ordered his men to fight to the last and slaughter their enemies, both military and civilian. The Japanese retreated across the Pasig River, which divides the city, and set up a last stand in the concrete buildings of the business district. The Japanese went on a rampage of massacre and burning in the city's residential neighborhoods. U.S. troops and Filipino guerrillas managed to slip behind the Japanese defenses and save thousands of residents. But to drive the Japanese out of the city meant house-to-house fighting and hand-to-hand combat.

When the Japanese in the *Intramuros* refused to surrender, U.S. ARTILLERY demolished it. On March 3, after more than a month of fighting that left most of the Japanese, including Iwabuchi, dead, the city was declared secured. About 70 percent of the city had been destroyed and about 100,000 Filipino civilians had been killed.

Manna

Code name for British occupation of southern Greece.

Manned Torpedoes

Manned torpedoes or "Chariots" were used extensively by Britain, Italy, and Germany to attack enemy ships in harbors. These craft differed from the Japanese KAITEN or "human torpedoes" in that they were not suicide craft.

The manned torpedoes had to be carried to their target area by submarines or other ships, or based close to their target area. The "pilots" would sit astride the torpedo-like vehicle, using individual breathing devices, and place their explosive warhead next to the target ship. The pilots would then attempt to ride their vehicle to safety (i.e., rendezvous with a subarmine).

Britain   The Royal Navy's Chariots were developed by two submarine officers, Comdr. Geoffrey Sladen and Lt. Comdr. W. R. (Tiny) Fell, in early 1942. The Chariots were similar in size to a standard 21-inch (533-mm) torpedo with a 600-pound detachable warhead. An electric battery would propel the craft for four hours at four knots, or six hours at 2.9 knots, providing a nominal range of 18 miles.

The first operational vehicles were delivered in June 1942. After training exercises, in which one pilot died from oxygen poisoning, in Oct. 1942 an attack was mounted against the German battleship *TIRPITZ,* moored in a Norwegian fjord. A Norwegian fishing craft carried the two Chariots, kept under cover, to a secluded fjord near the German warship. But when the Chariots were put into the water they were swamped by rough seas and the mission aborted.

Next, eight Chariots and their pilots were dispatched from MALTA on board three submarines. One submarine was lost to unknown causes en route to the objective (with three Chariots and their crews lost). The two other submarines launched their Chariots against the port of Palermo in northern SICILY on the night of Jan. 2–3, 1943. Five Chariots were sent toward the harbor; three suffered operational problems and were lost. The pilots of the two remaining vehicles penetrated the harbor and dropped their warheads near Italian ships, and attached several limpet MINES. Both crews then scuttled their craft.

The new Italian cruiser *Ulpio Traiano* was sunk and an 8,500-ton liner damaged in the attack. One Chariot and crew was recovered by a British submarine; the eight other pilots were captured and, at the express request of ADOLF HITLER, sent to Germany and PRISONER OF WAR camps. Operation Principal was considered a success.

Subsequently, Chariots were used for beach reconnaissance in preparation for Operation Husky, the invasion of SICILY. After the Italian capitulation, in June 1944 a joint British-Italian effort sent Chariots against the 10,000-ton Italian cruiser *Bolzano* at Muggiano in German-controlled Italy. Two British Chariots sank the *Bolzano.*

Italy   Italian manned torpedoes—called *Maiali* and "pigs"—were the most successful Italian naval force of the war. They were used with success against British ships at Alexandria, Algiers, and GIBRALTAR. At Alexandria in Dec. 1941 the manned torpedoes scored their greatest accomplishment, when three of the craft sank the British battleships *Queen Elizabeth* and *Valiant* as well as a tanker. The battleships were sunk in shallow water, but were not returned to active service for the remainder of the war, a considerable accomplishment for six men.

The Italian craft also sank several merchant ships during the war, some at Gibraltar while operating from a secret base in the hulk of an Italian merchant ship half-sunk at Algeciras, Spain, across the bay from the British naval base.

Germany   The German Navy developed several manned torpedo vehicles late in the war. The *Neger* (Nigger) type, a one-man craft carrying a G7e torpedo, was mass-produced, with about 200 being built, followed by 300 of the similar *Marder* (martens) type. These numbers far exceeded the vehicles built by the British and Italians.

Negers—which ran awash and could not fully submerge—sank two British minesweepers on July 6, 1944, off the NORMANDY beaches, and damaged a Polish destroyer beyond repair. It is possible that a British destroyer was also sunk by one of these craft. Similarly, *Marders* sank a British destroyer on Aug. 3, 1944, and a couple of lesser ships. But casualties among the German craft were very heavy.

See also MIDGET SUBMARINES, X-CRAFT.

Manstein, *Generalfeldmarschall* Erich von (1887–1973)

Head of the Operations Section of the German Army General Staff and Chief of Staff during the

POLAND CAMPAIGN in Sept. 1939. A brilliant strategist, Manstein was the architect of both the war-launching campaign in Poland and the FRANCE AND LOW COUNTRIES CAMPAIGN that surged across Europe in 1940. His infantry force was the first to cross he Seine.

HITLER had decided on Manstein as commander of the ground forces for Operation SEA LION, the invasion of England. When Sea Lion was indefinitely postponed, Manstein was assigned to the German invasion of the Soviet Union in June 1941. He moved from Chief of Staff to *Generalfeldmarschall* GERD VON RUNDSTEDT to the command of a PANZER corps on the EASTERN FRONT. He defeated the Soviets in the Crimea, taking more than 400,000 prisoners, and captured SEVASTOPOL after a siege of 250 days. He succeeded in besieging LENINGRAD but, despite the furious demands of Hitler, was not able to take it. (See GERMAN CAMPAIGN IN THE SOVIET UNION.)

After the fall of Sevastopol in July 1942, Hitler directed Manstein to take Leningrad while simultaneously ordering most of Manstein's troops to *Generaloberst* FRIEDRICH PAULUS' embattled Sixth Army at STALINGRAD. In December Manstein launched Operation Winter Storm, a valiant but vain attempt to save the Sixth Army. His maneuver did, however, save other German forces on the southern wing of the front.

Early in 1942 military conspirators planning to overthrow Hitler had approached Manstein, known to be no supporter of Hitler in his role as military genius. Manstein often argued openly with Hitler and even dared to dismiss some of *Der Führer*'s ideas as nonsense. But Manstein had held off the conspirators, saying he would join the conspiracy after the fall of Sevastopol; then he promised to join after the fall of Stalingrad.

The disastrous defeat of Paulus at Stalingrad changed Manstein's mind again. He felt that he could not now desert Hitler. In Feb. 1943, with a force designated Army Group South, he retook KHARKOV. Manstein's Operation Citadel would be Germany's last offensive in the Soviet Union. Hitler turned down Manstein's suggested strategy of a long withdrawal that would pull Soviet forces, setting up disabling attacks on their flanks.

Hitler's imposed delays enabled the Red Army to reorganize and gather strength for what would be the SOVIET OFFENSIVE CAMPAIGN. Manstein began his skillful retreat. On March 30, 1944, Hitler sent his personal plane to Manstein's headquarters at Lvov in the western UKRAINE. Manstein was flown to Hitler who personally dismissed him from command. He never had another.

After the war he was tried before a British military tribunal for WAR CRIMES. He was charged with killing JEWS and failure to protect civilian lives. An order of the day he had issued on Nov. 20, 1941, said, "The German soldier in the East . . . must have understanding of a severe but just revenge on sub-human Jewry." He was acquitted of killing Jews but convicted on the lesser charge and sentenced to prison for eighteen years. He served four.

Historian B. H. LIDDELL HART called Manstein the "ablest of all the German generals . . . a man who combined modern ideas of mobility with a classical sense of maneuver, a mastery of technical detail, and great driving power."

Mao Tse-tung (1893–1976)

Chinese Communist leader who warred with the Chinese Nationalist Army of CHIANG KAI-SHEK and the Japanese. A member of the Communist Party since its founding in SHANGHAI in 1921, Mao combined his experience as a student with his life as a peasant.

He was an intellectual—a library to him, he said was "like a vegetable garden to an ox"—and he was a military tactician: "The enemy advances, we retreat; the enemy halts, we harass; the enemy tires, we attack; the enemy retreats, we pursue."

From 1934 to 1938 Mao built a peasant army trained in GUERRILLA tactics. This was to be different from Chinese armies of the past. There would be no war lords, no looting, no rape. His soldiers were taught a song whose lyrics gave strict instructions about behavior. One verse said: "Be honest in all transactions with the peasants."

In his civil war with Chiang Mao escaped a trap set in the fall of 1934 and led some 90,000 on the near-legendary Long March, a 6,000-mile withdrawal to fight again. On the march Mao wrote poetry: "And then, the last pass vanquished, the Armies smile." In 1937, when Japan launched an invasion of China, Mao offered his people a simple but powerful rallying cry: "Go north to fight the Japanese!" Going north also meant establishing

Communist control in a sympathetic area near easy contact with comrades in the Soviet Union.

Entrenched in Yenan, Mao instituted intensive training to "correct unorthodox tendencies," using techniques of "criticism and self-criticism." In public meetings errant Communist Party members confessed their guilt and vowed repentance.

He worked to forge a united front with Chiang against the Japanese, using a wily peasant proverb to postpone differences during the war: "Each dreaming his own dreams while sleeping in the same bed."

His Red Army, moving east from Yenan, fought the Japanese much more effectively than Chiang's armies. As the Pacific War neared its end, Mao was a victor against the Japanese and in control of areas of China north of the Yangtze River, a vast region where 90,000,000 Chinese lived.

Prodded by U.S. envoys PATRICK J. HURLEY and Gen. GEORGE C. MARSHALL, Mao and Chiang talked of a coalition, but nothing came of it. In the ensuing civil war, Mao lived up to another proverb: "Political power comes from the barrel of a gun." After three years of fighting, he marched into Peking and on Sept. 21, 1949, proclaimed the People's Republic of China. In Dec. 1949 Chiang moved the remnants of his army from mainland China to the island of Taiwan.

Map Room

Space at the White House where President ROOSEVELT kept track of the war. Shortly after Capt. John McCrea was assigned to the White House as naval aide on Jan. 16, 1942, he realized the need for a specific room for keeping current situation maps of the war and for filing the large volume of classified military messages at the White House. McCrea, who had previously served as a member of the secretariat for the WASHINGTON CONFERENCE in Dec. 1941 and, before that, as an aide to the Chief of Naval Operations, modeled his room on the Admiralty map room in LONDON.

The Map Room was provided with a special case containing a full set of National Geographic Society maps, arranged on rollers so that Roosevelt, while seated in his wheelchair, could pull down the maps to study them. Prime Minister CHURCHILL was attracted to the map collection, and, at Roosevelt's request, the National Geographic Society prepared a duplicate map case inscribed *WSC from FDR, Christmas 1943* and taken with Roosevelt to the CAIRO CONFERENCE.

The White House Map Room kept track of movements and strengths of the Allied and AXIS forces. The room was manned twenty-four hours a day by military personnel. President Roosevelt usually visited the Map Room twice a day when he was in the White House. Access to the room was limited, with the classified files being made available only to the President, his military aides, and his adviser HARRY HOPKINS.

In the fall of 1943 Capt. McCrea was transferred to command of the BATTLESHIP *IOWA* (BB 61), which carried President Roosevelt across the Atlantic on the first leg of his journey to the TEHRAN CONFERENCE.

Maquis,

see FRENCH RESISTANCE.

Marauder,

see B-26.

Mareth Line

A series of fortifications in North Africa. The 22-mile-long line, which ran from the town of Mareth to the Matmata Hills, was built by the French to protect the eastern border of Tunisia. The French called it the "African Maginot," after France's MAGINOT LINE.

Lt. Gen. Sir BERNARD MONTGOMERY was stopped by the line in March 1943 while he was pursuing German-Italian forces after the battle of EL ALAMEIN. After preparing for what he called "a dog-fight battle," he broke through on March 27, 1943, and took 7,000 prisoners. The Mareth fortifications were manned by Italian forces. *Generalfeldmarschall* ERWIN ROMMEL had left for Germany by the time the battle started.

Margarethe

Code name for German occupation of Hungary, 1945.

Mariana Islands

The Mariana Islands, part of Japan's inner ring of defense, were a key objective of the U.S. CENTRAL

PACIFIC CAMPAIGN because of their importance as potential staging sites for U.S. forces in the conquest of Japan. SAIPAN and TINIAN, especially, would make ideal airfields from which Army Air Forces B-29 SUPERFORTRESS bombers could mount attacks against the Japanese home islands. In addition, the island of GUAM, captured by the Japanese in Dec. 1941, had been a U.S. possession. (The other islands in the Marianas group, which had previously been controlled by Germany, were mandated to Japan in 1919 and had been known as the JAPANESE MANDATED ISLANDS.)

The Marianas were 1,500 miles east of the Philippines and an equal distance from the Japanese home islands; they lay across the Japanese lines of communication and supply between Japan and conquered territories in MALAYA and the DUTCH EAST INDIES. Psychologically, the capture of the Marianas would return Guam to the American flag and would signify the growing might and momentum of the impending Allied victory.

The first moves against the Marianas came from carriers of the U.S. Fifth FLEET under Adm. RAYMOND SPRUANCE, who had commanded the Navy's victorious fleet at MIDWAY in 1942. TASK FORCE 58 planes struck the Japanese in the Marianas in Feb. 1944 to destroy enemy installations and take photographs for the subsequent invasion. Set for June 15—one week after the NORMANDY INVASION—the assault would use both Marines and Army troops. It had the code name Forager.

Saipan was selected as the first target, mainly because it offered the closest base to Japan from which to stage the B-29 raids. Its capture would also effectively block the Japanese forces on Guam from direct support from Japan. The U.S. Fifth Fleet steaming toward the Marianas consisted of more than 800 ships, including fifteen fast AIRCRAFT CARRIERS and eleven ESCORT CARRIERS, with twenty-eight SUBMARINES positioned to intercept Japanese warships as they approached the Marianas.

Aware of the importance of the coming battle in the Marianas, the Japanese quickly gathered a large fleet, built around nine carriers, for one massive strike at the American fleet. However, as the Japanese warships proceeded eastward they were harassed by the U.S. American submarines, which extracted a toll in DESTROYERS and carriers.

The two fleets' aircraft met in battle on June 19, in what is considered the last major carrier-versus-carrier battle of the Pacific War. The Japanese lost 400 aircraft on that day in what U.S. pilots called the "Marianas Turkey Shoot." In a running, two-day series of strikes and counterstrikes, the Japanese lost nearly all their aircraft, including 100 land-based aircraft, and three carriers (two by U.S. submarines and one by aircraft). The Americans lost 100 aircraft, many during night landings on June 20–21, when they returned after a long-range final raid against the fleeing Japanese ships.

The battle of the Philippine Sea, as the carrier battle was called, broke the back of Japanese naval air power, although it did not deliver the final crushing blow the Americans had sought. The Japanese fleet was still a dangerous surface opponent and it would take the battle of LEYTE GULF to destroy the Imperial Fleet.

After less than a month of savage fighting, Saipan fell. Even before July 9, when the island was declared secure, AAF P-47 THUNDERBOLT fighters were landing on the newly captured airstrips. The loss of Saipan, coming with the debacle of the carrier battle, brought down the government of Premier HIDEKI TOJO, who resigned on July 18.

The smaller island of Tinian was the next target. It would offer more airfields for B-29 raids against Japan, including the ultimate ATOMIC BOMB raids. Aerial reconnaissance was flown for a month to gain accurate topographical information. Detailed maps were made in foam rubber, a new process developed by a special Navy unit and first used for operations in the ALEUTIANS in mid-1943.

The Japanese organized fierce BANZAI CHARGES, but the Marines stood fast and dug in. By Aug. 12, the last pockets of Japanese had been eliminated, and Tinian secured.

The assault on Guam, originally planned for July 18, was postponed because of the possible intervention of the Japanese carrier force steaming toward the Marianas, and the need to include the Army reserve in the Saipan assault. The decisive U.S. victory in the Battle of the Philippine Sea denied the Japanese Navy any influence on the fighting in the Marianas. But the fierce fighting on Saipan dictated finding another reserve force for the Guam assault.

With coral reefs ringing the island, and steep cliffs

along the northern coast, only a 15-mile stretch of beach on the west coast would permit an AMPHIBIOUS LANDING. Recognizing this fact, the Japanese concentrated their main defense there. The battle on Saipan was three days along when Marines went ashore at Guam on July 21. On Aug. 10 the Marines declared Guam secure.

SEABEES improved Apra Harbor, constructing a new breakwater, dredging the harbor, and building new docks. Guam became a major U.S. naval base in the Western Pacific and headquarters for Adm. CHESTER W. NIMITZ during the final stages of the Pacific War.

The amphibious campaign in the Marianas had proven the worth of UDT reconnaissance prior to the assault, added napalm to the growing arsenal of assault arms, and demonstrated how hopeless the Japanese situation had become. Human waves and banzai charges could not defend against a smoothly coordinated attack, preceded by a deluge of shells and BOMBS.

Marie

British code word for proposed Anglo–FREE FRENCH operation against Jibuti, 1940–1941.

Mariner,

see PBM.

Marita

German code name for the attack on the Balkans, 1941.

Market

Code name for Allied AIRBORNE operation to seize bridgehead at Arnhem in the Netherlands, in conjunction with the land operation, code name Garden. (See MARKET-GARDEN.)

Market-Garden

Allied plan to capture bridges over Dutch waterways by combined AIRBORNE (Market) and ground (Garden) assaults, thus opening a rapid and direct northern route for the Allied advance into Germany during the ALLIED CAMPAIGN IN EUROPE. The third of the airborne landings, at ARNHEM, was a complete disaster and costly military failure.

The ground offensive was carried out by the British XXX Corps (part of the British Second Army and 21st ARMY GROUP). Intending to capture bridges over Dutch rivers and canals in advance of the XXX Corps advance, the U.S. 101st Airborne DIVISION was dropped on canal crossings between Eindhoven and Veghel, the U.S. 82nd Airborne Division on the bridges over the Maas and Waal Rivers. The British 1st Airborne Division and, subsequently, the Polish 1st Airborne Brigade were dropped at Arnhem to capture bridges over the Rhine River—a 60-mile "jump" into German-held territory for the Allies. The massive airborne landings began on the morning of Sept. 17, 1944.

The two U.S. divisions largely accomplished their goals. The British parachute drop and GLIDER landing zones were too far from the Arnhem bridges, permitting an assault on only the northern end of the bridges. The British underestimated the ability of German troops in the area to recover from the surprise of the aerial assault, Allied air support was inadequate, and the British troops lacked effective tactical communications. As a result, the British airborne troops failed to capture an entire bridge, while the XXX Corps failed to advance fast enough to support—and then rescue—the airborne troops. Some British troops held the northern end of the Arnhem bridge for nine days and nights—a week longer than expected.

Combat commander-paratrooper-historian Julian Thompson, a Royal Marine officer, wrote: "Overconfidence, lack of a sense of urgency, and inflexibility plagued this operation from its inception. Practically no lessons learned in previous operations, other than purely procedural ones, were applied to Market. The German [airborne] attack on Crete had been avidly studied by their airborne counterparts in Britain and America. The two factors that swung this battle in favour of the Germans, the use of ground attack aircraft in support and the introduction of reserves by air at a critical part of the battle, were ignored by the Market planners."

Of over 10,000 British troops parachuted and glider-landed at Arnhem, only 2,398 escaped across the river; some 1,400 died and over 6,000 became German PRISONERS OF WAR, half of those wounded. (The Polish brigade had landed south of the river.)

The blame for the Arnhem disaster—graphically portrayed in Cornelius Ryan's book *A Bridge Too*

Operation Market-Garden in Sept. 1944 was the largest Allied airborne operation and the most disastrous. This is a landing zone near the Dutch city of Arnhem. Paratroopers and equipment float down from U.S. C-47 Dakota transports. In the foreground are British Horsa gliders; after landing they were "broken open" to permit rapid unloading. *(Imperial War Museum)*

Far—rested on the shoulders of the "brass": British Lt. Gen. Frederick Browning, commander British I Airborne Corps; U.S. Lt. Gen. LEWIS H. BRERETON, commander of the First Allied AIRBORNE ARMY; Lt. Gen. Brian Horrocks, commander XXX Corps; Gen. Miles Dempsey, Second Army commander; and Field Marshal BERNARD L. MONTGOMERY, the 21st Army Group commander. The problem was not that they sought a bridge too far but, according to one British officer who jumped into Arnhem, they had created "A grand military cock-up."

Mars

(1) Code name for U.S. 5332nd BRIGADE (Provisional) in the China-Burma-India theater; (2) Soviet code name for offensive against the German Ninth Army in the Rzhev salient, fall and winter 1942. See also JRM MARS.

Marshall, Gen. of the Army George C. (1880–1959)

Few other military leaders proved to be as central to their nation's conduct of a major war as did George Marshall. He combined in an incomparable way his ambition for high command with a respect for the American emphasis on the military's obedience to civilian control. Only George Washington rivaled him in his ability to implement military strategy within a civilian democracy.

Marshall's almost unique fitness for high command was seen early by such admirers as Lt. HENRY ARNOLD who in 1914 said to his wife that he had just met a future Army Chief of Staff. Several of his superior officers in the pre–World War I Army commented in fitness reports that they would gladly serve *under* his command. He built on his reputation with brilliant staff work in the Allied Expeditionary Force in World War I.

During the interwar years, Marshall served in near-obscurity in many typical assignments, using them to develop his command of good doctrines and good people. While in command of the Infantry School at Fort Benning he built a file of promising officers, many of whom would later serve in high commands. He developed a field manual that

Gen. of the Army George C. Marshall was the principal U.S. military strategist during the war. As Army Chief of Staff he prepared the Army and AAF forces to fight on all fronts. *(U.S. Army)*

stressed the importance of not relying on the "school solution," which many of his most successful protégés would demonstrate later.

A brigadier general and deputy Chief of Staff in 1938, Marshall attended a meeting at which President ROOSEVELT held forth on favoring bombers over ground forces in the buildup of the Army. "Don't you think so, George?" Roosevelt asked. "Mr. President, I'm sorry but I don't agree with you on that," Marshall replied, shocking others at the meeting. He was told that he had finished his career with that remark; he was a new deputy and outranked by thirty-three other generals.

But when Roosevelt decided on a new Army Chief of Staff in Sept. 1939, he chose Marshall, beginning a partnership that would continue through Roosevelt's lifetime. Marshall, the man who in 1938 was not supposed to know his way around WASHINGTON, persuaded Congress to change the laws regarding the retirement of older officers and to accept SELECTIVE SERVICE. With the promotion and retirement policy changed, Marshall was able to jump dozens of younger officers into responsible positions throughout the Army. In a confrontation in May 1940, the month Germany invaded France, Marshall convinced a reluctant Roosevelt of the need to increase the Army's budget significantly.

Marshall, who strongly backed the Allied "Germany First" strategy, believed that the United States had to strike back soon because a democracy would not long support an indecisive war. Soon after the U.S. entry into the war, he began pushing for a landing in northwest Europe. He opposed the British alternative of landing in North Africa and developing an indirect threat to Germany through Italy and the Balkans. But he and other American strategists were overcome by superior British staff work and a realization that no such invasion could occur much before mid-1943. In each succeeding Allied strategic conference Marshall advocated a landing in northern France, gaining only grudging British consent in late 1943. By that time, Marshall's 1939–1941 program to expand the Army was in high gear, giving the United States a predominance in land power.

To the initial surprise of many, Marshall was not chosen to lead the campaign in France; it would

have been the crowning event of his career. But Roosevelt believed he could not do without Marshall in Washington and by that time no other man could have fulfilled Marshall's unique position as defender of the Army and counselor to the President.

Marshall's view of Pacific strategy was conditioned by his belief that it should not detract from the ability to land in France as soon as possible. Moreover, the Pacific War had strong partisans in Adm. ERNEST J. KING and Adm. CHESTER W. NIMITZ and in Gen. DOUGLAS MACARTHUR, whose prominence and ego frustrated attempts to apply a formally unified strategy. As a result, Marshall supported MacArthur only up to a point in the latter's pursuit of more troops and greater authority against the opposition of King and Nimitz.

By the end of the war Marshall had earned a reputation as the Olympian Father of the Modern American Army, which had increased more than forty times during his tenure. He was also regarded as almost superhuman in his judiciousness, his talent for noticing qualified officers and promoting them into high command, and his ability to support Army goals without wrecking overall Anglo-American accord.

Marshall's postwar career as secretary of State and secretary of Defense would add to the luster of the man CHURCHILL called "the noblest Roman of them all." In his two years as secretary of State he developed still another monument to his genius, the European Recovery Program, a restoration of the Continent that became known as the Marshall Plan. For it he received the Nobel Peace Prize in 1953.

Marshall Islands

A cluster of thirty-one atolls and hundreds of reefs in the Western Pacific, east of the CAROLINE ISLANDS. There are two main chains, Ratak (Sunrise) and Ralik (Sunset). Each atoll consists of a group of small islands encircling a lagoon. The Marshalls, purchased from Spain by Germany in 1899, were occupied by Japan during World War I and after the war made JAPANESE MANDATED ISLANDS by the LEAGUE OF NATIONS. Japan began secretly and illegally fortifying and building airfields on the islands in the 1930s.

From the launching of the JAPANESE CAMPAIGN IN THE FAR EAST in 1941 to the capture of the Marshalls by U.S. troops in Feb. 1944, the fortified islands were used as "aircraft carriers" and submarine bases from which Japan launched attacks on Australian and Philippine sea lanes. After the U.S. conquest of the GILBERT ISLANDS in Nov. 1943, the U.S. CENTRAL PACIFIC CAMPAIGN targeted the Marshalls as the next objective; the invasion operation was called Flintlock.

As a prelude to Flintlock, U.S. planes based in the Gilberts in Jan. 1944 began repeatedly bombing KWAJALEIN, the Japanese administrative and communications center for the Marshalls and a principal target of the Marshalls invasion.

After the war, in July 1946 one of the isolated atolls—Bikini—was chosen as the site for the ATOMIC BOMB TESTS known as Operation Crossroads and for subsequent nuclear-weapons testing. Prior to the 1946 test the 167 natives who lived on Bikini were removed to Rongerik atoll, north of Kwajalein. At another atoll, ENIWETOK (later, Enewetak), the United States exploded the first hydrogen bomb in 1952.

Made a trust territory after the war, the Marshalls in 1986 became a self-governing republic of some 40,000 citizens. The United States provides for its defense and supplies economic aid. (The United States also has promised to settle all legal claims filed in connection with nuclear testing at Bikini and Eniwetok from 1946 to 1958.)

Marston Mat

Steel matting used extensively by the U.S. military during the war to construct runways and other surfaces. Each piece of matting, officially called Pierced Steel Planking (PSP) and resembling a sliver of Swiss cheese, was 10 feet long and 12 inches wide and weighed 66 pounds. The pieces locked together to form firm surfaces. The name was derived from Marston, N.C., 35 miles west of Fort Bragg, N.C., where it was used to form a runway 3,000-feet long and 150-feet wide during the U.S. Army field maneuvers in November 1941. It was used extensively in most theaters of World War II, with a lightweight aluminum version also being developed (32½-pounds per section).

Martlet,

see F4F.

Maruta

Japanese code name for BIOLOGICAL WARFARE experiments.

Master

Signal code name for U.S. First ARMY, 1944–1945.

Matador

Code name for British plan to move into Kra Isthmus, 1942.

Matterhorn

Code name for U.S. STRATEGIC BOMBING of Japan from bases in China, 1944.

Mauldin, Sgt. Bill (1921—)

An Army sergeant who showed the GI view of the war in cartoons. Mauldin drew his cartoons "Up Front with Mauldin" for the Army newspaper STARS AND STRIPES. His principal characters were two footsore, drooping, disheveled infantrymen named Willie and Joe. Their war was from FOXHOLE to foxhole, and it never got any better. It only got worse.

Willie and Joe were composites of the GIs Mauldin met as he wandered the battlefields of Europe. He was at the beachhead at ANZIO and in the hedgerows of France. He temporarily attached himself to fifteen different DIVISIONS and he always went to where the infantry was—*Up Front,* the title of one of his books. In *Up Front* he wrote, "I'm convinced that the infantry is the group in the army which gives more and gets less than anybody else. I draw pictures for and about the dogfaces because I know what their life is like and I understand their gripes. They don't get fancy pay, they know their food is the worst in the army because you can't whip up lemon pies or even hot soup at the front, and they know how much of the burden they bear."

Maunsell Forts

Chain of antiaircraft towers standing on stilt-like supports in the Thames Estuary early in the war to

"Just gimme a coupla aspirin. I already got a Purple Heart."

Bill Mauldin's view of World War II.

"Joe, yestiddy ya saved my life an' I swore I'd pay ya back. Here's my last pair of dry socks."

close the ring of ANTIAIRCRAFT WEAPONS deployed around the city of LONDON.

The first forts were prefabricated concrete gun platforms, sunk into the river bed so that they were above water at high tide. These were Navy manned and fitted with 3.7-inch (94-mm) and BOFORS 40-MM antiaircraft guns.

The Maunsell Forts followed. They were built in groups of six: four forts mounted 3.7-inch guns, one a Bofors 40-mm for defense against low-flyers, and the central fort fitted as command post with fire control RADAR, all six being connected with catwalks. They were manned by the British Army.

Mavis

The only long-range maritime reconnaissance aircraft in Japanese naval service when the war began, the H6K Type 97—given the Allied code name Mavis—served early in the war in bombing strikes against targets in the DUTCH EAST INDIES and at RABAUL. However, it was employed primarily as a reconnaissance aircraft and transport. As a bomber,

the Mavis was vulnerable to Allied fighters because of its lack of armor and self-sealing fuel tanks. In 1943, as the H8K EMILY flying boat entered service, the surviving aircraft were fitted with benches and used as troop transports. (These transports were given the Allied code name Tillie.)

The four-engine Mavis was developed in response to a 1934 specification for a flying boat with exceptional range capabilities. Five prototypes were ordered from Kawanishi, with the first aircraft flying in July 1936. These had minor differences; two were configured as transports. The H6K2-L variant could carry eighteen passengers (or ten in seats and four in sleeping berths), and eighteen aircraft were flown by Japan Air Lines on Western Pacific routes. The first series production military aircraft was the H6K4, an armed aircraft that could carry BOMBS or aerial TORPEDOES. There were sixty-six of these flying boats serving with the Japanese Navy on Dec. 7, 1941. Production continued until 1943 with 215 of all variants being produced.

The Mavis had a superficial resemblance to the

U.S. Navy's PBY CATALINA flying boat, having a parasol wing raised above the long, narrow fuselage on inverted V-struts and braced by parallel struts attached to the hull; four radial engines were mounted in the leading edge of the wing. There were fixed stabilizing floats under the wings. The aircraft had a twin-tail arrangement.

The H6K4 had a maximum speed of 211 mph, increased with upgraded engines to 239 mph in the H6K5. Range was 3,780 miles and 4,210 miles, respectively. As a bomber the plane could carry four 1,100-pound or twelve 132-pound bombs or two 1,764-pound torpedoes on the wing-support struts. Defensive armament consisted of single 7.7-mm machine guns in an open bow position (enclosed turret in the H6K5), an open dorsal position, and two beam blisters; a 20-mm cannon was fitted in a tail turret. The plane had a crew of nine.

McAuliffe, Brig. Gen. Anthony (1898–1975)

Acting commander of the U.S. 101st AIRBORNE DIVISION in the battle of the BULGE (see ARDENNES) in Dec. 1944. During the battle McAuliffe's paratroopers occupied BASTOGNE, a Belgian crossroads town that was a key German objective. McAuliffe's outnumbered troops fought off the Germans and stalled their advance. But on Dec. 20 the Germans surrounded the town and besieged the Americans.

On Dec. 22, the Germans demanded that McAuliffe surrender. He replied with one word: "Nuts!" When the American officer who delivered the reply was asked what it meant, he said, "It means—go to hell!" (A legendary version of the story has McAuliffe use *nuts* in a lewd connotation, which the delivery officer translates as *balls.*)

Gen. GEORGE S. PATTON's Third ARMY troops fought their way to Bastogne and lifted the seige on Dec. 26.

After the war McAuliffe became commanding general of the Seventh Army in Germany and later U.S. Army commander in Europe. He retired as a full general in 1956.

McCain, Vice Adm. John Sidney (1884–1945)

McCain, like WILLIAM F. HALSEY, came to naval aviation late in his Navy career, being qualified in 1936 at age fifty-two after having waited nine years for acceptance to flight school. He and Vice Adm. MARC MITSCHER were strong advocates for naval air power and had remarkably parallel World War II careers, although Mitscher's was the brighter star. Both were commander, Air Forces in the Southwest Pacific, both were deputy chief of naval operations for air, and both commanded the fast carrier forces that were the core of the U.S. CENTRAL PACIFIC CAMPAIGN.

"Slew" McCain before becoming a flier had served in surface ships, being executive officer of a BATTLESHIP and commanding officer of an ammunition ship. He commanded the AIRCRAFT CARRIER *Ranger* (CV 4) in 1937–1939 and at the time of the PEARL HARBOR attack he was commanding naval aircraft on the U.S. West Coast. In May 1942 he was named commander, Air Forces, South Pacific Area under Vice Adm. ROBERT L. GHORMLEY. McCain provided what meager aircraft resources he had during the first months of the GUADALCANAL campaign. He was then selected as chief of the Bureau of Aeronautics in Oct. 1942 and became the first deputy chief of naval operations for air in Aug. 1943, at which point he was promoted to vice admiral. McCain oversaw development and training of the carrier TASK FORCES and land-based naval and Marine Corps aircraft that would fight in all theaters of the war.

In Aug. 1944 McCain was named commander of carrier Task Group 38.1 under Mitscher. After service off Leyte (where his Task Group missed most of the battle of LEYTE GULF because of its detachment for refuelling), McCain relieved Mitscher as commander of the fast carrier force (TASK FORCE 38) of Halsey's Third FLEET. His carriers fended off KAMIKAZES, using tactics McCain had to devise, and raided Hainan and Formosa during a two-week operation in the South China Sea in Jan. 1945.

McCain was then relieved by Mitscher (with the fast carrier force becoming TF 58), returning home for leave until late May when he in turn relieved Mitscher for the final month of the OKINAWA campaign and the massive carrier raids on Japan. In June 1945, with McCain in command, TF 38 was hit by a damaging typhoon. In Dec. 1944 a typhoon caused damage for which Halsey received most of the blame. McCain came in for his share of criticism this time and was nearly relieved of command.

By the end of the war, McCain showed signs of declining health and was relieved in Sept. 1945. He died on Sept. 6 en route to his new post as deputy director of the Veteran's Administration. He was posthumously promoted to admiral.

His bony frame, sunken cheeks (due to false teeth), and prominent nose earned him the nickname of "Popeye" by men under his command; his friends call him "Slew." (His son, John Sidney McCain, Jr., a submariner, rose to four-star rank and was U.S. Commander in Chief Pacific Command during much of the Vietnam War; his grandson, John Sidney McCain III, was a Navy flier, shot down and imprisoned during the Vietnam War, and subsequently a U.S. Senator.)

McCampbell, Comdr. David (1910—)

The U.S. Navy's top-scoring fighter pilot, credited with thirty-four kills of Japanese aircraft.

Not commissioned after graduation from the U.S. Naval Academy in 1933 because of the Depression, McCampbell was called to active duty a year later and served in surface ships for three years. After flight training he became a carrier pilot, and was aboard the USS WASP (CV 7) when she was sunk in Sept. 1942.

He then joined the carrier ESSEX (CV 9), and while commander of Air GROUP 15 in 1944 he shot down thirty-four enemy aircraft in the MARIANAS and LEYTE GULF battles. He was awarded the MEDAL OF HONOR for his prowess as a fighter pilot in the June 1944 Marianas "turkey shoot." In a single sortie on Oct. 24, 1944, at Leyte Gulf he downed nine Japanese aircraft plus two probables—a feat unequaled by any other American pilot in any war. His wingman was credited with at least six enemy planes destroyed in the same sortie.

Raymond F. Toliver and Trevor J. Constable in their *Fighter Aces* reported: "Frequently, a leader and his wingman would both fire at a target, and as in the case of McCampbell in several occasions there was doubt as to who actually knocked down the enemy. McCampbell often gave the victory credit to his wingman, and bore a reputation for generosity in this regard."

All of McCampbell's aerial victories were made while flying the F6F HELLCAT.

After the war he commanded an AIRCRAFT CARRIER and had several shore assignments before retiring in 1964 as a captain.

McCarthy, Capt. Joseph R. (1908–1957)

U.S. Marine who entered politics during the war. When America entered the war, McCarthy, politically ambitious and Wisconsin's youngest circuit judge, was exempt from service because he was a judge. But in June 1942 he joined the Marines and was immediately commissioned as a first lieutenant. He heard one case in uniform instead of robes, and then went off to a training camp.

He served first in HAWAII with the 4th Marine Air Base Defense WING. He was next stationed in the New Hebrides in Aug. 1943 and later served with the 1st Marine Aircraft Wing on GUADALCANAL. Most of the time he was an intelligence officer, although he did go on combat missions, usually taking the place of a gunner in two-man aircraft and operating an aerial camera.

In mid-1944, while still in the Pacific War, McCarthy decided to run for the Republican nomination for the U.S. Senate. His campaign literature called him "Tail-Gunner Joe" and said "he left the bench and enlisted as a buck private in the Marine Corps." On a thirty-day leave, he appeared in uniform at rallies and actively campaigned, despite regulations that prohibited politicking by servicemen and WOMEN. He lost the Republican primary. In Feb. 1945, with the war far from over, he resigned his Marine commission and returned to the bench and to politics.

In 1946 he was elected to the Senate from Wisconsin. One of the first issues he raised in his flamboyant early Senate career involved the massacre of about 100 captured U.S. soldiers by SS troops at MALMEDY, Belgium. After the war, the SS killers were tried for WAR CRIMES; forty-three were sentenced to death. In their appeals, the SS men claimed that U.S. interrogators had tortured them to get confessions.

The controversy about the confessions reached the U.S. Senate and in April 1949 a three-Senator investigating subcommittee was appointed to look into the allegations. McCarthy was not a member of the subcommittee but he dominated the hearing, arguing with Army witnesses and demanding lie-detector tests for the U.S. officers who obtained the confessions.

The Malmedy hearings launched McCarthy into the headlines. On Feb. 9, 1950, shifting his interest from championing SS killers to searching out Communists in government, he told a West Virginia audience, "I have here in my hand a list of 205 . . . a list of names [the number later changed to 57] that were made known to the Secretary of State as being members of the Communist Party and who nevertheless are still working and shaping policy in the State Department."

McCarthy's accusation rocked the government, ushering in the era of "McCarthyism"—government and congressional investigations of persons presumed to be Communists or subversives. When his hunt reached the U.S. Army, his credibility had evaporated. The Senate passed a resolution of censure against him in Dec. 1954 for conduct "contrary to Senate traditions." The censure effectively ended his political career. Not one Communist in government was identified through the extensive McCarthy-dominated investigations.

McCloy, John J. (1895–1989)

Assistant secretary of War and high commissioner in Germany. McCloy, a New York lawyer, served briefly as a special assistant to Secretary of War HENRY L. STIMSON and became assistant secretary of War in April 1941. He remained in this post until Nov. 1945.

Before and after the NORTH AFRICA INVASION McCloy plunged into negotiations to thwart Gen. CHARLES DE GAULLE's plan to purge French colonial officials with whom the United States wished to work. McCloy prided himself in being a "realist" in dealing with the political results of warfare.

In April 1945 McCloy visited Gen. DWIGHT D. EISENHOWER, Supreme Allied Commander, and urged him to keep destruction of the industrial RUHR at a minimum, citing Hannover, Düsseldorf, and ESSEN, site of the KRUPP works. When Eisenhower wrote Gen. GEORGE C. MARSHALL, Army Chief of Staff, about McCloy's remarks, Marshall replied that McCloy represented one of two "schools of thought" about postwar Germany: a "pastoral" defeated nation or one with "some industrial capability to benefit the related economy of other European countries." Marshall did not have to say which school was McCloy's.

McCloy was involved in developing the details of Germany's SURRENDER, worked on details of the WAR CRIMES trials at Nuremberg, and was a key U.S. participant in arranging the administration of occupied Germany. He later became U.S. military governor. "One of my tasks in Germany," he later said, "was to pick up NAZI scientists and send them over to the United States."

McClusky, Comdr. Clarence Wade, Jr. (1902–1976)

U.S. Navy hero of the battle of MIDWAY. At the time of the PEARL HARBOR attack then-Lt. Comdr. "Wade" McClusky was commanding officer of Fighting SQUADRON (VF) 6 on the AIRCRAFT CARRIER ENTERPRISE (CV 6).

McClusky had served briefly in surface ships after graduating from the Naval Academy, and earned his Navy wings in 1929. He flew fighter and bomber aircraft from the carrier SARATOGA (CV 3), and then observation planes from BATTLESHIPS.

At thirty-nine he was considered an "old man" to command a fighter squadron in 1941. His pilots flew their F4F WILDCATS against the Japanese in a series of strikes against the MARSHALL ISLANDS and other Japanese-held islands. In March 1942 McClusky became the air GROUP commander in the Enterprise. The "Big E" accompanied the HORNET (CV 8) on the DOOLITTLE RAID and then raced toward the CORAL SEA, but missed the carrier battle of early May 1942.

But at Midway in early June McClusky led the seventy-nine planes of the Enterprise air group. When the three U.S. carriers launched strikes against the Japanese force on the morning of June 4, for a number of reasons their squadrons became separated. McClusky found himself leading thirty-three SBD DAUNTLESS dive bombers. When the planes arrived at the expected position of the Japanese carriers, the sea was empty. After searching for twenty-five minutes, McClusky sighted a Japanese destroyer speeding north. She was the Arashi, which had been attacking a U.S. SUBMARINE. McClusky followed her heading and a few minutes later he sighted the four Japanese carriers of the striking force.

Adm. RAYMOND SPRUANCE, commander of the U.S. carrier force said after the battle: "McClusky is the outstanding hero of the Midway battle. His decision to go on and find the Jap decided the fate of our carrier TASK FORCE and our forces at Midway and perhaps at Pearl Harbor and the Hawaiian islands."

McClusky's dive bombers—joined by SBDs from the two other U.S. carriers—sank four Japanese carriers that day. As McClusky pulled out from his dive on a Japanese carrier, his SBD was attacked by two Japanese ZERO fighters. McClusky brought his plane to within 20 feet of the water and his radioman-gunner opened fire with his twin .30-cal. machine guns. One Zero was shot down and the other turned away, but not before they riddled the SBD with bullets; McClusky was hit in the left arm and shoulder by five bullets. But he flew on. McClusky received the Navy Cross for his leadership at Midway.

McClusky retired in 1956 as a rear admiral.

McGovern, Capt. George (1922—)

McGovern was the pilot of a B-24 LIBERATOR named "Dakota Queen" in the 15th AIR FORCE in Italy. He came home from the war, became a Methodist minister, a history professor, and then a politician. The Democratic presidential candidate in 1972, he ran on an antiwar platform, condemning the Vietnam War. He spoke little about his own experiences in World War II. His wife, Eleanor McGovern, wrote in *Uphill* how, when he came home, she would be "jolted out of sleep by his half-conscious cries—'The plane's on fire' or 'The flak's getting heavy'."

McGuire, Maj. Thomas B. (1912–1945)

U.S. fighter ACE who was within two aerial kills of the record forty accomplished by Maj. RICHARD I. BONG when he was lost in action. Also flying the P-38 LIGHTNING fighter, McGuire shot down thirty-eight Japanese aircraft in twenty months of combat in the South Pacific before he was lost in action.

He was killed on Jan. 7, 1945, when his P-38 stalled and crashed into the sea during an aerial battle. He was posthumously awarded the MEDAL OF HONOR.

McNair, Lt. Gen. Lesley J. (1883–1944)

Commander of Army Ground Forces and often called the general who trained the U.S. Army. McNair, a veteran of combat in World War I, between the wars specialized in training. He saw active duty in the NORTHWEST AFRICA CAMPAIGN and was wounded by shell fragments while at a forward observation post in Tunisia.

He resumed command of the Army Ground Forces until May 26, 1943, when the WAR DEPARTMENT announced that he had been given "an important overseas assignment." He was made commander of the "First ARMY GROUP," a fictitious organization created on paper (and with special effects; see CAMOUFLAGE) as part of a deception plan prior to the NORMANDY INVASION. The plan, code-named Fortitude, was designed to make the Germans believe that the Allied landings would be in the Pas de Calais.

After the invasion, McNair went to a forward area in France to watch, from a slit trench, a carpet bombing that preceded the breakout from Saint-Lô. (See ALLIED CAMPAIGN IN EUROPE.) Many bombs fell short, killing at least 100 American soldiers, including McNair.

McNutt, Paul V. (1891–1955)

Director of the War Manpower Commission. The former governor of Indiana, McNutt was the U.S. High commissioner to the Philippines from 1937 to 1939. In April 1942 President ROOSEVELT appointed him director of the War Manpower Commission, designed to be one of the most powerful WAR AGENCIES. But Congress watered down its powers. In 1945 McNutt returned to the Philippines as High Commissioner. In 1946, when the Philippines became a republic, McNutt was named U.S. ambassador to the new independent nation.

Me (Bf) 109

The outstanding fighter aircraft at the start of the EUROPEAN WAR and the most famous German aircraft of the war. The German Me 109 was an outstanding performer, having captured several flight records in the late 1930s, attaining a speed record of 379.4 mph on Nov. 11, 1937, a record that stood for two years. (The aircraft was referred to as the Bf 109 for the *Bayerische Flugzeugwerke,* which Professor Willy Messerschmitt joined in 1927; when that firm failed, Messerschmitt formed his own company to take over its interests, hence the application of the initials Bf although the plane was produced under his own imprimatur.)

The Me 109B-1 and 109C models fought in the SPANISH CIVIL WAR. Based on experience in that conflict, the Me 109E entered quantity production and became the standard Luftwaffe fighter for the first three years of the war. The aircraft fought in every theater in which German forces were engaged. However, heavy losses in the BATTLE OF BRITAIN against RAF HURRICANES and SPITFIRES led to adoption of the more streamlined Me 109F and, subsequently, the Me 109G "Gustav," first reported in mid-June 1942 on the Russian and North African fronts. The Me 109G models were flown through the end of the war (that series being produced in larger numbers than all other 109 types combined).

The final major Me 109 operation of the war occurred on April 7, 1945, when *Fliegerdivision* IX with 150 Me 109 fighters, mostly piloted by students, attempted to intercept a massive U.S. daylight bombing raid over Germany. Only fifteen of the fighters returned to their bases.

In addition to flying in the fighter role, both F and G models carrying ROCKETS were used as ground-attack aircraft. The Me 109G-8 was a photo-reconnaissance variant with reduced speed and the Me 109G-12 aircraft was a two-seat trainer. The Me 109T was a modified 109E intended for flying from the aircraft carrier *GRAF ZEPPELIN.* One of several other unusual Me 109 developments was the *Zwilling* (twin), the Me 109Z having two fuselages joined by a short main and tail wing section, which as a fast bomber would have carried one 1,102- and two 551-pound BOMBS. The prototype was completed in 1943—at the same time the U.S. AAF was developing a similar twin P-51 MUSTANG (which became the P-82 Twin Mustang).

The prototype Me 109 flew in Sept. 1935 followed by several improved models that captured several performance records. The Me 109B-1 was the first production model. Because of the poor fighter aircraft available to the Italian Air Force, sufficient Me 109s were transferred to Italy to equip two fighter wings; Spain had acquired Me 109s as

early as 1937. During and after the war several other air forces flew the Me 109. Production totaled more than 33,000 aircraft between 1936 and the final days of the war, which was more than 60 percent of all single-engine fighters built by Germany. Production continued after the war in Czechoslovakia and Spain.

The Me 109 was a low-wing monoplane with a flush-riveted aluminum skin. The fuselage had an oval section with an enclosed cockpit. The narrow-track undercarriage retracted flush into the wings, but there was a fixed tail wheel. The Me 109E-3 had a maximum speed of 354 mph and a range of 410 miles; the Me 109G-6 could attain 387 mph and was credited with a 615-mile range. The Me 109G-10 was rated at 428 mph.

The Me 109E had a standard armament of two 20-mm cannon and two 7.9-mm machine guns—a more powerful punch than contemporary fighters. The Me 109G series had a single 20-mm or 30-mm cannon plus two 7.9-mm or 13-mm machine guns (the cannon firing through the propeller spinner). A pair of underwing 20-mm gun pods could also be fitted.

Me (Bf) 110

German long-range fighter. The Me 110 was a twin-engine fighter intended to escort bomber formations to their targets deep in enemy territory; however, the aircraft was a failure in this role, as were most other efforts at heavy two- and four-engine escorts (the most effective aircraft in this role being the single-engine U.S. AAF P-51 MUSTANG).

Ten Luftwaffe groups had the Me 110C when the EUROPEAN WAR began in Sept. 1939. Because of the limited air opposition over Poland, the fighters were employed mainly in the ground-attack role. In the subsequent BATTLE OF BRITAIN the Me 110s suffered severely in engagements with RAF HURRICANES and SPITFIRES and were withdrawn from combat. But production continued and efforts were made to adopt the Me 110 to the bomber-intercept role with a 30-mm cannon fitted beneath the fuselage and the ground-attack version carrying two 1,100-pound BOMBS (in place of the 551-pound bombs previously carried), later supplemented by wing racks for four 110-pounders.

These bombers and fighter variants were used

mostly on the EASTERN FRONT and in North Africa, where their long range was useful and fighter opposition was limited. Over Germany the Me 110C fighters were adapted for night intercept— the Me 110F-4 without RADAR but with a third crewman, followed by radar-equipped variants. These and other Me 110s continued to attempt daylight intercepts of the streams of RAF and U.S. AAF bombers over Germany until late in the war, but with little effect. There were also photo-reconnaissance configurations of the Me 110.

Designed by the versatile Willy Messerschmitt, the prototype Me 110 flew on May 12, 1936. There were problems in acquiring adequate engines, and delays prevented the planned use of the plane in the SPANISH CIVIL WAR. Squadron deliveries began in 1939 with production continuing into 1945, although it was tapering off in favor of single-engine fighters (only forty-five Me 110Gs were produced in 1945). Total Me 110 production was 5,873 aircraft.

The streamlined, low-wing Me 110 was powered by two in-line engines; the long, narrow fuselage ended in a small twin tail fin arrangement. The main undercarriage retracted into the engine nacelles with a fixed tail wheel. The large cockpit held a crew of two with the radioman-gunner firing a flexible twin machine gun. Maximum speed was 342 mph for the Me 110G-4, which had a range of 1,300 miles with internal fuel.

There was a variety of armament configurations for the aircraft; the Me 110G-4 had two 30-mm and two 20-mm cannon in the solid nose, and the gunner fired a twin 7.9-mm machine gun.

The aircraft was also referred to as the Bf 110 for the *Bayerische Flugzeugwerke*; see ME 109.

Me 163 *Komet* (Comet)

The only rocket-propelled aircraft to enter combat. Few aircraft have legitimately deserved the accolades "unique" and "sensational." The swept-wing, tailless, rocket-propelled Me 163 interceptor was such an aircraft.

Intended to kill Allied bombers over the THIRD REICH, at full power the Me 163 had an endurance of only 230 *seconds!* With a maximum powered flight of twelve minutes through judicious adjustment of throttle, the Me 163 would climb above an Allied bomber formation, reaching 40,000 feet in four minutes, and then weave in and out of the formation both powered and gliding. To further enhance its effectiveness, the Me 163 was directed to intercepts by ground control RADAR.

The first Me 163B encounter with Allied aircraft occurred on July 28, 1944, and within a month twenty-nine aircraft had been delivered to the Luftwaffe. The ALLIES countered the threat by routing bombers around the bases of the short-range Me 163 and using fighters to attack their bases to catch them on the ground. Because of fuel shortages, lack of trained pilots, and Allied bombing of Me 163 bases only one Me 163 wing became operational before the war ended.

The small Messerschmitt-produced aircraft was built around a rocket engine designed by HELMUTH WALTER that burned hydrogen peroxide (known as *T-Stoff*) with a solution of hydrazine hydrate in methanol (*C-Stoff*) as a catalyst. The aircraft had a metal fuselage with a plywood wing covered by fabric. The wing was swept back 23.3°. There were a tall tail fin and a rudder but no horizontal tail surfaces. The Me 163 took off on a two-wheel trolley, which dropped away as the aircraft became airborne. A center skid was lowered for landing (the steerable tail wheel was retained in flight). Although the Me 163 handled beautifully in flight, remains of the highly volatile fuel combined with a skid landing technique caused numerous accidents and pilot fatalities. The Me 163D project, in the flight test stage when the war ended, had a normal retractable undercarriage and a greater endurance.

Development of an aircraft around a rocket engine designed by the ingenious Walter began in the late 1930s. A rocket-propelled aircraft (DFS 194) was completed early in 1940. The airframes of two Me 163 prototypes were finished a year later with preliminary flight tests being flown in a glider mode. Powered flight-testing began in Aug. 1941, and the fourth powered test surpassed the existing world speed record of 469.22 mph; in Oct. 1941, after being towed aloft, a prototype reached 623.85 mph in level flight. The first Me 163B fighter version flew in Aug. 1943; this aircraft had increased fuel and armament. Not until a year later did the Me 163B enter operational service, with several improved Me 163 fighter variants in development when the war ended. A two-seat trainer was tested in a glider mode. When production ceased in Feb. 1945 a total of 279 Me 163s had been delivered; further production was impossible because of the lack of components.

Maximum speed operational was 596 mph at 30,000 feet. The single-seat Me 163 carried two 30-mm cannon.

Me 210/Me 410 *Hornisse* (Hornet)

A twin-engine German fighter-bomber and reconnaissance aircraft, the Me 210 entered combat on the EASTERN FRONT in late 1941. A variety of problems plagued the aircraft and it was withdrawn from production. Redesigned and reengined, it emerged as the Me 410 *Hornisse,* which entered service early in 1943. This plane could carry a 4,400-pound BOMB load with reconnaissance variants having cameras fitted in the bomb bay. Only 325 Me 210s were produced, followed by 1,913 of the improved Me 410 variants. Top speed was 388 mph for the Me 410A-1 with four 20-mm cannon mounted in the nose; both fixed and flexible machine guns were also fitted.

Me 262 *Sturmvogel* (Stormbird)

The world's first operational jet fighter. Leading British test pilot and naval aviator Capt. Eric Brown has described the Me 262 as "the most formidable combat aircraft to evolve in World War II." The failure of the Me 262 to affect the aerial battle over Germany in 1944–1945 was due primarily to the vacillation of the German leadership as well as to production delays caused by Allied bombing. Still, the speed with which German industry and the Luftwaffe developed and placed the Me 262 into combat service is almost unprecedented for an aircraft of its complexity and advanced design.

Preproduction aircraft flew combat missions beginning in April 1944. They were able to intercept and shoot down previously invulnerable P-38 LIGHTNING and MOSQUITO reconnaissance aircraft. Despite some successes against U.S. bombers during raids over the THIRD REICH, the Me 262s were vulnerable to Allied fighter-bombers on the ground and during landing and takeoff, and lacked the numbers to provide an effective aerial defense.

The swept-wing Me 262 was powered by twin turbojet engines mounted under the wings; the aircraft had a conventional tail assembly. Production aircraft were provided with a tricycle undercarriage, ejector seat, and pressurized cockpit. (The first four prototypes had retractable tail wheels.) The aircraft was relatively easy to fly. HITLER demanded that the aircraft be fitted with racks for two 551- or 1,102-pound BOMBS for service as a fighter-bomber. Experiments were also conducted with the aircraft *towing* a 2,205-pound bomb! A two-seat Me 262B trainer and a RADAR-equipped night fighter adaption of that variant were also developed. An Me 262 single-seat aircraft successfully demonstrated night-fighting techniques when assisted by ground searchlights, scoring several kills against Mosquito night intruders.

The Me 262 design stemmed from studies initiated by Willy Messerschmitt in the fall of 1938 for an aircraft to be powered by axial-flow turbojet engines. The first Me 262 flew with tow *piston* engines on April 18, 1941. The first Me 262 flights with turbojet engines occurred on July 18, 1941. Delays were caused by disputes within the national leadership and Luftwaffe over the feasibility and role of the aircraft, technical problems, and Allied bombings. Several prototypes were ordered and in June 1943 the Me 262 was released for series production with a delivery rate of sixty per month planned from May 1944; the twenty-three preproduction aircraft were completed by that time, with production rates of 500 aircraft per month being planned, the production planes being designated Me 262A *Schwalbe* (Swallow). A total of 1,433 aircraft were produced (including prototypes), with between 100 and 200 participating in combat operations before the end of the war. Another 497 aircraft were reportedly destroyed by Allied bombers before delivery to the Luftwaffe.

Maximum speed for the Me 262A was 540 mph at 20,000 feet. Combat range was 300 miles at sea level, 520 miles at 20,000 feet, and 650 miles at 30,000 feet. ROCKET boosters were also considered to further accelerate the Me 262's performance.

The single-seat fighter was heavily armed, with four 30-mm cannon fitted in the nose. In addition, later variants could carry up to twenty-four 55-mm air-to-air rockets or air-to-air missiles. Several armament variations were evaluated, such as a long-barrel 50-mm cannon for attacking bomber formations. A planned Me 262D was to have been fitted with twelve 50-mm rifled MORTAR barrels in the nose of the aircraft, pointing forward and upward; when lined up under a bomber, the mortar rounds would be fired in salvoes. A proposed Me 262E interceptor variant was to carry forty-eight of the 55-mm rockets.

Me 321 *Gigant* (Giant)

One of the largest aircraft of the war, the Me 321 was a cargo GLIDER. Its development was supported by HITLER, who saw the giant glider in the invasion of Britain that would follow the (rapid) conquest of the Soviet Union. First flown in March 1941, the only aircraft capable of towing it into the air was the four-engine Ju 90. Later, groups of *three* ME 110 twin-engine fighters were used to tow the glider, which was further assisted by ROCKET boosters. Eventually the twin HE 111Z was developed as a tow plane.

The gliders were used in the Soviet campaign (albeit not at STALINGRAD). Use of the Me 321 was limited, being succeeded by the power variant, the ME 323. Two hundred of the gliders were produced through 1942. The aircraft's impressive dimensions included a span of 180 1/2 feet, length of 92 1/3 feet, with a normal loaded weight of 75,840 pounds. Loads of 44,090 pounds could be carried although half that cargo or 130 troops was a more normal load. Large, clamshell nose doors opened to facilitate loading troops and vehicles. The crew was six, including two gunners who manned 7.9-mm machine guns, supplemented by guns fired through ports by embarked troops.

Me 323

A six-engine, powered version of the ME 321 *GIGANT* cargo GLIDER. The powered version of this massive German aircraft was initially fitted with four engines, but in production six engines were mounted to provide the lumbering aircraft with a flight range of 685 miles. The powered glider first flew in late 1941 and proved a highly successful transport. The Luftwaffe took delivery of 198 aircraft through early 1944, and it saw extensive service on the EASTERN FRONT and in the Mediterra-

nean. Normal cargo load was some 22,000 pounds or 130 troops. Maximum speed was 136 mph.

Experiments with the giant plane included carrying a 17.7-ton BOMB, but as the weapon was being released the rear fuselage of the aircraft began to break up and the plane crashed. (The plane had been damaged a few days earlier in a strafing attack by U.S. fighters.)

The Me 323 had a maximum loaded weight of 99,210 pounds. With normal fuel but no cargo it could reach 150 mph. Range carrying cargo was 685 miles in the Me 323E-2 variant. Up to seven crewmen flew the plane, which had a defensive armament of two 20-mm cannon in wing turrets, plus several machine guns. The single Me 323E-2/WT aircraft had a battery of no less than eleven cannon and four machine guns.

Medal of Honor

The highest U.S. military decoration. During the war the Medal of Honor was presented to 433 men (the last awards for World War II actions were made in the 1970s). By service the awards were:

SERVICE	TOTAL NUMBER	POSTHUMOUS AWARDS
Army	256	137 (53%)
Army Air Forces	37	23 (62%)
Navy	56	32 (57%)
Marine Corps	83	51 (61%)
Coast Guard	1	1

Almost all of the awards to AAF personnel were for air action; an exception was the award to Col. Dennis T. Craw, killed on the ground during the NORTH AFRICA INVASION. Seven of the Navy winners were enlisted hospital corpsmen who won the award while serving with Marine units; the lone Coast Guard recipient was also working with Marines when he gave his life.

Thus, a total of 433 men won the medal. The highest-ranking Army officer to win the Medal of Honor was then-Gen. DOUGLAS MACARTHUR, for his defense of the Philippines; the next senior Army officer was Lt. Gen. JONATHAN WAINWRIGHT, who succeeded MacArthur as commander of Filipino-American forces in the Philippines, and surrendered them to the Japanese. Three Navy rear admirals won the Medal of Honor: Daniel J. Callaghan, who died in the CRUISER *San Francisco* (CA 38) in the battle of SAVO ISLAND; Isaac C. Kidd, who died in the BATTLESHIP *ARIZONA* (BB 39) AT PEARL HARBOR; and Norman Scott, who went down with the cruiser *Atlanta* (CLAA 51) off GUADALCANAL. The senior Marine to receive the medal was then-Maj. Gen. A. A. VANDEGRIFT, the Marine commander on Guadalcanal, who was later given the medal for services in the SOLOMONS from Aug. 7 to Dec. 9, 1942.

There were several occasions when multiple awards of the Medal of Honor were made in the same action. The largest number of awards were given for the invasion of IWO JIMA and the attack on Pearl Harbor, with fourteen Medals of Honor presented for each of those violent actions.

The Medal of Honor is the oldest U.S. decoration in continuous use, dating from 1862. Given to Army and Navy personnel, it is the only U.S. military decoration hung from a ribbon around the recipient's neck. (The Army and Navy medals differ slightly in design.) Holders of the Medal of Honor who reached age sixty-five may apply to have their names placed on the Medal of Honor Roll, established by an Act of Congress in 1916, which carried a lifetime pension of $10 per month. There is also a provision for an increase of 10 percent of retirement pay to Medal of Honor winners.

Tradition has it that a Medal of Honor wearer is entitled to a salute from another serviceman or -woman regardless of rank, but that is myth and neither custom nor regulation. Also, the decoration is sometimes referred to incorrectly as the *Congressional* Medal of Honor. (The Congressional Medal of Honor is a gold medal awarded by Congress to military and civilian personnel for outstanding achievements; recipients have included CHARLES A. LINDBERGH and Hyman G. Rickover.)

See also AWARDS AND DECORATIONS.

Medals,

see AWARDS AND DECORATIONS.

Medicine, Military

World War II was a turning point for the care of U.S. combat casualties. In World War I about four out of every 100 wounded men could expect to live; in World War II, about fifty out of every 100 lived.

If a critically wounded man was given treatment within an hour, his chance of recovery was 90 percent. After eight hours, his chances dropped to 25 percent.

Offsetting the improvement from war to war were the high casualty rates of a type of combat not known to American forces in World War I—AMPHIBIOUS LANDINGS. Beachhead casualty rates reached as high as 25 percent. In beachhead operations, the average wounding rate of 11.04 per 1,000 men was seven times the average rate for a DIVISION in combat in the war and was more than twice the average for nearly all other combat action. Medical evacuation of the wounded from the beachhead was impeded by the constant flow of successive waves of landing forces.

On the beachhead and elsewhere in combat, U.S. military medicine facilities were designed to get the wounded to surgery during what the surgeons called the "golden period," the first six hours after wounding. In the European theater, out of every 100 wounded soldiers, typically twenty-one did get treatment during the golden period, forty-seven in the next six hours.

The concept of triage—sorting the wounded in terms of probable survival—was practiced during the war. The likely-to-die were given drugs to ease their pain and set aside; the wounded not likely to die were given second priority to those who could be saved by immediate treatment.

This theory was more vividly described by Lt. Gen. GEORGE S. PATTON during a visit to a U.S. Army medical unit in Casablanca following the NORMANDY INVASION. He told the physicians, "If you have two wounded soldiers—one with a gunshot wound of the lung and the other with an arm or a leg blown off, you save the s.o.b. with the lung wound, and let the g.d.s.o.b. with the amputated arm or leg go to hell. He is no g.d. use to us anymore."

The wartime "miracle drugs"—sulfa, streptomycin, and penicillin—saved countless lives. Men in combat carried first-aid packets of sulfanilamide and sulfathiazole to be sprinkled over wounds. Studies showed that this "frosting" of wounds did little to help the wounds heal, but the sulfa did appear to help stave off infection until further treatment was available.

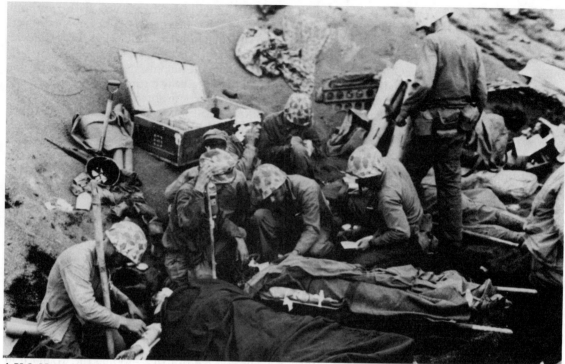

A U.S. Navy chaplain (center) kneels beside a badly burned Marine at an aide station on Iwo Jima. Around him Navy doctors and enlisted hospital corpsmen work to save wounded Marines. *(U.S. Marine Corps)*

During the U.S. Civil War, 80 percent of the wounds were caused by bullets; in World War I the wounds-by-bullet rate dropped to 35 percent. In World War II 80 percent of the wounds were caused by high explosives or fragments from mines, artillery, or mortar shells.

In some Pacific areas, malaria was the most common cause of death or illness. To stop the spread of malaria meant eliminating its carrier, mosquitoes. In permanent installations, ditches were drained and the new chemical DDT (dichloro-diphenyl-tri-chloroethane) liberally applied by heavy sprinklings of powder or, later in the war, by aerosol "bombs." It killed fleas, lice, mosquitoes, and other insects, aiding in the control of malaria, typhus, and other diseases.

Troops in malarial areas had to take daily doses of Atabrine, a newly discovered substitute for quinine, the old standard drug. There was a constant shortage of quinine; most of the tropical countries that

produced the raw product had been conquered by the Japanese. The relatively small amount available was restricted for those who were allergic to atabrine or who had severe infections.

Like quinine, atabrine did not cure; it suppressed symptoms so the infected victim could continue functioning. Attempts to find a better substitute than atabrine involved the testing of it on volunteering conscientious objectors and prison inmates. Likely substitutes did appear, but not in time to be used effectively in Pacific combat zones.

Infectious diseases were drastically cut by inoculations. No troops in the world got more needles than the American GI. Soon after induction servicemen and servicewomen were given smallpox, typhoid, and tetanus shots. Anyone going overseas got, depending upon destination, inoculations against cholera, yellow fever, typhus, and even plague.

Every inductee also saw graphic movies about

venereal disease. (One, stressing the dangers of "fraternization," was narrated by a training-film actor, Ronald Reagan.) In the early years of SELECTIVE SERVICE, inductees were rejected if they had venereal disease. After March 1942, inductees with some types of venereal disease were accepted for limited service, and in Dec. 1942, VD carriers were inducted and given treatment before beginning training. The "venerals," as they were called, were treated and usually cured with sulfa and penicillin. The rate of prevalence of syphilis among white draftees was 17.4 per 1,000; among black draftees the rate was 252.3 per 1,000.

"While chaplains were free and in most commands were urged to stress moral principles and control through continence," an official Army history says, "the Army approached its prevention and control program from a practical medical point of view closely related to manpower economics."

Some soldiers were slow to accept the use of the chemical prophylaxis kit, which many believed reduced virility. One told an officer he had found it difficult to swallow the contents of the entire tube before having sex. Others said they would rely on home remedies, such as drinking lemon juice.

A 1910 federal law, known as the Mann Act or White Slave Act, forbade the transfer of women across state lines for immoral purposes. Using this law, military authorities barred prostitutes from areas around U.S. military camps when local authorities failed to curb prostitution.

Servicemen heading off on leave or liberty were given prophylaxis kits, usually consisting of a condom and anti-VD ointments, or could pick them up at stations near their bases. There were usually separate prophylaxis stations for white or black servicemen, reflecting the SEGREGATION policy in effect during the war.

"Memphis Belle"

First U.S. bomber to complete twenty-five combat missions over Europe and one of the most publicized aircraft of the war. A B-17F FLYING FORTRESS of the 91st Bomb GROUP of the Eighth AIR FORCE based in England, the "Memphis Belle" was the subject of a widely distributed 1944 documentary film of that name and a movie made in 1990. William Wyler directed the first film, based largely on

the plane's twenty-fifth mission against the German naval base of Wilhelmshaven.

The ten-man crew flew the "Memphis Belle" for twenty-five missions without significant injury; the only Purple Heart awarded to the crew was to the tail-gunner, John P. Quinlan, for what he described as a "pin scratch on the leg." The crew was credited with shooting down eight German fighter aircraft.

After completing twenty-five missions in June 1943 the crew was inspected by a number of VIPs, among them King GEORGE VI and Queen Mary. The crew then flew the aircraft back to the United States to participate in a morale-building tour on behalf of WAR BONDS sales. Subsequently the commander of the "Memphis Belle," Capt. Robert K. Morgan, flew the first B-29 SUPERFORTRESS to bomb Japan.

Menace

Code name for failed FREE FRENCH expedition to Dakar, Sept. 1940.

Mengele, Josef (1911–1979)

SS physician who performed heinous experiments on inmates of AUSCHWITZ, a DEATH CAMP in German-occupied Poland. He was known as the Angel of Death.

Mengele, who had doctorates in both medicine and anthropology, was assigned to Auschwitz in May 1943 after he was wounded on the EASTERN FRONT while serving as a medical officer with a *WAFFEN* SS. *SS-Hauptsturmführer* Mengele was infamous for the way he selected those who lived and those who died when the trains carrying JEWS and other condemned arrived at Auschwitz. As the men, women, and children left the cars and passed by, Mengele motioned with his hand or riding crop and called, *"Links!"* ("Left!")—to the gas chambers—or *"Rechts!"* ("Right!")—to the SLAVE LABOR camp and almost certainly nothing more than a short lease on life.

Once, when a mother refused to be separated from her teenage daughter, she rushed to the girl's side, biting and scratching the SS guard who tried to keep them apart. Mengele pulled out his pistol and shot both mother and daughter. Then, in a rage, he sent everyone he had selected for survival to the gas chambers, saying, "Away with this shit!"

He preserved twins for his genetic "studies." He had a pair of boys killed so that he could perform autopsies and settle a diagnostic argument with another SS doctor. He had the eyes plucked out of Gypsy corpses to study iris pigmentation. "More than any other SS doctor," Dr. Robert Jay Lifton wrote in *The Nazi Doctors,* "Mengele realized himself in Auschwitz. There he came into his own— found expression for his talents, so that what had been potential became actual. . . . The all-important Auschwitz dimension was added to his prior psychological traits and ideological convictions to create a uniquely intense version of the Auschwitz self as physician-killer-researcher."

Mengele slipped out of Auschwitz just before it was liberated, lived for several years in West Germany, then escaped to South America, where he became a legendary figure. (He was the model for the NAZI doctor planning to clone HITLER in the movie *The Boys from Brazil.*) Legends placed him in Paraguay, a refuge for ex-Nazis. One legend had him advising Paraguayan authorities on how to wipe out the country's Indian population. Another had him selling manure spreaders for a German firm. Still another had him working in a Mennonite dispensary.

Mengele is believed to have moved from Paraguay to Brazil in 1960. While living under an alias he was reported drowned in 1979. Years later pathologists examined the remains and confirmed his identity.

Menzies, Maj. Gen. Sir Stewart Graham (1890–1968)

Director of MI6, the British Secret Intelligence Service, from 1939 to 1953. Menzies (pronounced *MING-iss*) was responsible for much of Britain's intelligence activities during the war, including operations at BLETCHLEY PARK.

Menzies served as an officer in the Army's Life Guards from 1910 to 1939 and saw action in France during World War I. As a colonel he was deputy to Adm. Sir Hugh Sinclair (head of MI6 from 1923 until his death in 1939), and then succeeded to head MI6. His position was particularly difficult during the war in that he worked for Prime Minister CHURCHILL, who had an insatiable appetite for intelligence and secret projects.

A strong proponent of code-breaking, under Menzies' personal sponsorship Bletchley Park developed the BOMBE machines that began deciphering the German ENIGMA machine cipher in 1940. He was promoted to major general in 1945. He remained head of MI6 until 1953, when he retired in the aftermath of the defection of British intelligence officials Donald McLean and Guy Burgess to the Soviet Union.

Merkur (Mercury)

Code name for German AIRBORNE invasion of CRETE, May 1941.

Merrill's Marauders

U.S. COMMANDO force led by Maj. Gen. Frank Merrill that operated behind Japanese lines in Burma. After serving on the staff of Gen. JOSEPH W. STILWELL, in Jan. 1944, as a brigadier general, Merrill was given command of the recently formed 5307th Composite Unit (Provisional), which quickly became known as "Merrill's Marauders." The unit was formed and trained in India of volunteers from other units.

Copying tactics used by the British CHINDITS, the U.S. group began operations behind Japanese lines in Feb. 1944 in the ALLIED CHINA-BURMA-INDIA CAMPAIGN. American raiders enjoyed several successes. They were usually supplied by air drops of supplies with wounded (including Merrill himself because of illness) being evacuated by air.

The unit was known by the code name Galahad.

Messe, Field Marshal Giovanni (1883–1968)

Commander of the Italian Expeditionary Corps that fought in the GERMAN CAMPAIGN IN THE SOVIET UNION. Messe fought on the EASTERN FRONT in 1941–1942, and in early 1943 became commander of the Italian First Army in Tunisia.

He was taken prisoner by the British when Italian forces surrendered in 1943. BENITO MUSSOLINI immediately promoted Messe to field marshal upon his capture. After the Italian capitulation in Sept. 1943, Messe became Chief of Staff of the Italian Army in the government of PIETRO BADOGLIO. He left the Army in 1945.

Meteor

First operational Allied jet fighter. Design of the Meteor, by a Gloster team led by W. G. Carter, was underway when the Gloster G 40 turbojet test aircraft flew in May 1941. By Sept. 1941 contracts were placed for eight prototypes and a production run of twenty Meteor turbojet fighters. The first entered service in July 1944 with RAF squadron No. 616 and immediately began flying sorties again German V-1 BUZZ BOMBS that were flying against England. The first combat victory for an Allied jet-propelled fighter occurred on Aug. 4, 1944, when Flying Officer T. D. Dean slid his Meteor's wing beneath a V-1, then banked sharply, and sent the V-1 crashing to earth. Dean's guns had jammed; later that same day another Meteor downed a V-1 with gunfire.

By the beginning of 1945 Meteors were flying missions over Europe to counter the appearance of the German jet-propelled ME 262. However, there were no jet-versus-jet engagements (the first being in the Korean War between U.S. F-80C Shooting Stars and Soviet MiG-15s; see P-80 SHOOTING STAR).

The first Meteor flight occurred on March 5, 1943, by which time production was well underway. One of the first production aircraft was sent to the United States in exchange for a P-59A AIRA-COMET turbojet aircraft. Three hundred and nine of the wartime models were built (i.e., through III); production continued after the war with the last Meteor (an F 8 variant) delivered in 1950. Early in its development the aircraft was named Thunderbolt, but was changed to Meteor to avoid confusion with the U.S. P-47 fighter.

The Meteor was a streamlined aircraft with its twin turbojet nacelles faired onto the elliptical wings. The cockpit was forward of the wing. A nosewheel tricycle landing gear was fitted. Initially a single-seat aircraft, later night-fighter marks were two-place aircraft. Top speed was 410 mph for the Mk I (increased in later models). Armament consisted of four 20-mm cannon.

Mexico

Capital: Mexico City, pop. 19,478,791 (1939). The Mexican government worked closely with the United States in preventing Mexico from becoming a haven for German ESPIONAGE agents slipping out of the United States. All citizens of AXIS and pro-Axis countries were removed by Mexican authorities from the area near the U.S. border and none were allowed to become naturalized citizens of Mexico. At the same time, U.S. citizens and British subjects were given virtual unrestricted entry into Mexico.

On May 22, 1942, following the sinking of two Mexican merchant ships in the Gulf of Mexico by U-BOATS, Mexico declared a state of war with Japan, Germany, and Italy. To relieve the manpower shortage on U.S. farms, Mexico sent 75,000 volunteer farm hands, called *braceros,* to the United States in 1942 and 1943, an additional 113,431 in 1944, and 139,688 in 1945.

By a special agreement, both countries could recruit the other's nationals for the armed services (except for U.S. recruitment of *braceros* and Mexicans studying in the United States). More than 15,-000 Mexicans served in the U.S. armed forces. The Mexican Air Unit was a SQUADRON that flew P-47 THUNDERBOLT fighters and saw action in the Pacific.

M.G.1

British code word for CONVOY to MALTA, March 1942. Of the eleven resupply convoys that reached Malta between Aug. 1940 and Jan. 1943, this convoy delivered the least supplies, 5,000 tons. (See also VIGOROUS.)

MI5

British Security Service responsible for counterespionage activities in the United Kingdom. The director general of MI5 when Britain went to war was Maj. Gen. Sir Vernon Kell, who held that post from 1909 until May 25, 1940. He was fired by First Lord of the Admiralty WINSTON CHURCHILL after several alleged acts of SABOTAGE and spying in Britain. (For example, popular myth had it that the battleship *Royal Oak* was sunk by sabotage; see GÜNTHER PRIEN.)

The head of MI5 for most of the war was Sir David Petrie, who served in that post from Nov. 1940 until 1946. Petrie was given a commission in the Army Intelligence Corps—a 2nd lieutenant, acting colonel, local brigadier.

The MI5 organization appears to have been highly successful. Only one man is known to have spied in Britain during the war and evaded capture. At least two others have claimed that they parachuted into Britain during the war and successfully returned to Germany without being detected, but their stories cannot be checked. (See XX COMMITTEE.)

The principal branches of MI5 during the war were: (A) administration, (B) counterespionage, (C) security, (D) military liaison, (E) aliens, and (F) overseas control.

The designation was originally MO5, for Military Operations, and then MI5, for Military Intelligence, with its formal title being Imperial Security Intelligence Service.

MI6

British Secret Intelligence Service. The Chief of SIS when the war began was Adm. Sir Hugh Sinclair, who had held that position since 1923. Sinclair died on Nov. 4, 1939, and in his place was appointed Col. STEWART MENZIES, who held that post until 1953. Menzies, later promoted to major general, was responsible for much of Britain's successful intelligence activities during the war, including the ULTRA efforts. During his tenure Soviet intelligence operatives gained a major foothold in the organization.

MI6 had two major branches: "Y" for headquarters activities and "YP" for overseas stations. The former had the following sections: (I) political, (II) military, (III) naval, (IV) air, (V) counterespionage, (VI) industrial, (VII) financial, (VIII) communications, (IX) cipher, and (X) press.

The designation of the SIS when established in 1909 was MO6, for Military Operations, and then MI6, for Military Intelligence.

Michaelis

Code name for Allied task force for the seizure of Saidor, NEW GUINEA.

Microdots

The photographic reduction of writing or other material by photographic means to facilitate transfer from one location to another. The Germans are often given credit for inventing microdots; how-

ever, Alexander Foote, a Soviet agent in the war, wrote in his book *Handbook for Spies* that the Soviet intelligence service had used microdots before World War II.

Although the Germans did not invent microdots, there is considerable evidence that they made important contributions to the development of microdot technology and used microdots aggressively before and during the war. (The French are credited with using microdots since the siege of Paris in 1870; the size of microdots at that time was 70-mm and contained 300,000 characters; microdots were sent across enemy lines by balloons and pigeons.)

The United States learned of microdots through the German agent DUSKO POPOV, who was under control of British intelligence when he came to the United States in 1941.

Midget Submarines

Midget submarines were employed extensively by Britain, Italy, and Japan in the war. Although Germany produced a large number of midgets, few were employed operationally.

Britain   The Royal navy's midgets were designated as X-CRAFT (see separate entry).

Italy   The Italian Navy built twenty-six midget submarines of the CA and CB classes between 1938 and 1943. Many more were planned. (The first letter of their designation indicated *Costiero* or coastal; the second letter indicated the series.) All had two 17.7-inch (450-mm) TORPEDOES and crews of two (CA) or four (CB).

The Italians planned to modify one 13½-ton CA-type craft to be carried to the U.S. East Coast by a larger submarine and attack a U.S. harbor. That project was never carried out. Six of the 25-ton CB-type craft were sent by rail to Rumania in early 1942 for use in the Black Sea. One was lost and the other five were taken over by German forces when the Italian government surrendered to the Allies in Sept. 1943 and ceded to the Rumanian Navy. These five units came under Soviet control about Aug. 30, 1944, after the surrender of Rumania. Other CBs were captured by the Germans in Italian ports in 1943, with some being later taken over by Yugoslavia.

The Italian midgets sank no enemy ships, except possibly in the Black Sea. German and Italian records indicate the *CB-2* sank a Soviet submarine, but that kill is questionable.

Japan   The Japanese Navy had the most successful experience with midget submarines. These were carried into operational areas by surface ships or larger submarines with about 440 completed from 1934 to 1945. All had two 18-inch (457-mm) torpedo tubes and were operated with crews of two to five men.

In the PEARL HARBOR attack five midgets were dispatched to torpedo U.S. ships in the harbor during the confusion of the air attack. One did penetrate the harbor, but inflicted no damage. All were lost (although they were intended to be recovered); of the ten crewmen, nine died—and were hailed as heroes in Japan—with the survivor becoming the first PRISONER OF WAR held by the United States.

Midgets were also in action off MADAGASCAR on May 31, 1942, with two craft attacking British ships at Diégo-Suarez. They sank a British tanker and damaged the battleship *Ramillies.* Neither midget returned. At the same time, three midgets were launched into Sydney Harbor, Australia. Although several U.S. and Australian warships were in the harbor, the midgets inflicted no damage and none survived the attack.

Midgets also operated off GUADALCANAL, the ALEUTIANS, and Philippines, but without success.

Germany   Germany initiated a major midget submarine program in the fall of 1943 to attack Allied shipping in the coming assault on northwestern Europe. These submarines could operate farther offshore than the MANNED TORPEDOES.

The first type was the 6¼-ton, one-man *Biber* (Beaver), of which 324 were placed in service, each carrying two 21-inch (533-mm) torpedoes. These were quickly followed by the 390 of the *Molche* (Salamander) type, their larger, 10¾-ton displacement providing improved underwater performance. Neither of these midgets accomplished much, but helped to cause the Allied navies to expend considerable time in countermeasures.

The larger units of the Type XXVIIA *Hecht* (Pike) class had U-series numbers; these were 11¾-ton craft, carrying one 21-inch (533-mm) torpedo and manned by a crew of two. The 15-ton Type XXVIIB *Seehund* (Seal) was similar but had a greater range and carried two torpedoes. The first of these

craft went into action in Dec. 1944 and had effective performance—the *Seehund* is capable of a week at sea—while being difficult to detect. Details of their operations are not known, but some 100,000 tons of Allied shipping were probably sunk between Jan. and May 1945. About thirty-five were lost, many to bad weather.

The Germans also produced several prototypes of other small undersea craft. Like many German advanced weapons, the midgets came too late to affect the war.

Midway

A U.S. Navy base on two small islands that form a coral atoll in the central Pacific. Attacked unsuccessfully by the Japanese in Dec. 1941 and Jan. 1942, Midway became the focal point of a decisive battle in June 1942 when the Japanese attacked for the third time.

Japanese strategy called for the capture of Midway and the western ALEUTIAN ISLANDS to create a Japanese defense line from Kiska in the Aleutians to Midway, WAKE, the MARSHALL ISLANDS and the GILBERT ISLANDS, then west to PORT MORESBY and the DUTCH EAST INDIES. The capture of Midway would also be a dramatic response to the April 1942 DOOLITTLE RAID on TOKYO, would deprive the United States of a forward base for SUBMARINES, and would serve as a stepping-stone for the capture of HAWAII.

Japanese Adm. ISOROKU YAMAMOTO, Commander in Chief of the Combined Fleet, realized the potential naval strength of the United States and believed that Japan had to annihilate the U.S. Pacific Fleet in 1942 or lose the war. He correctly assumed that an assault on Midway would force Adm. CHESTER W. NIMITZ to use everything he had to defend Midway, which was vital to the defense of PEARL HARBOR.

Yamamoto committed almost every Japanese warship to Operation *Mi,* the Midway-Aleutians assault. He had four major sea forces built around eight of Japan's ten operational aircraft carriers. *Mi* was to open with carrier air strikes on DUTCH HARBOR in the Aleutians followed by AMPHIBIOUS LANDINGS on the islands of Adak and Kiska on June 12. This phase of the operation was designed to distract U.S. attention from Midway.

The actual attack on Midway would begin on June 5 with carrier aircraft smashing the island's defenses and wiping out its aircraft. The next day the Japanese would occupy tiny Kure Island, 60 miles northwest of Midway, and establish a base for seaplanes to support the Midway invasion. Japanese submarines were fanned out athwart the expected paths of U.S. ships steaming for Midway from Pearl Harbor and toward the Aleutians.

What Yamamoto did not know was that U.S. Navy code-breakers (see MAGIC) had been piecing together a relatively accurate picture of his plan. Nimitz—over the objections of some officers who were skeptical about the code-breakers' analysis—decided to send his only three AIRCRAFT CARRIERS against Yamamoto. The carriers were the ENTERPRISE (CV 6), the HORNET (CV 8), and the *Yorktown* (CV 5), badly damaged in the battle of the CORAL SEA. (She had limped into a Pearl Harbor dry dock for repairs on May 27. Some 1,400 workmen had swarmed over her and on May 30 she was patched up, refueled, and back to sea with an air group formed with planes of three carriers.)

On June 3 a Navy PBY CATALINA spotted the Japanese invasion fleet heading for Midway, but air strikes by Midway-based B-17 FLYING FORTRESS bombers and PBYs did little damage. The next morning aircraft from four Japanese carriers blasted Midway.

On the Japanese aircraft carriers torpedo-armed aircraft were being held in readiness to attack any U.S. warships located by search planes. Word from the attackers on Midway led to changed orders for the waiting aircraft: Swap the torpedoes for bombs and attack Midway again.

While the laborious task was being performed on the two Japanese carriers, a Japanese search plane spotted U.S. warships 200 miles away. But Rear Adm. FRANK FLETCHER, commanding the U.S. carrier striking force, had already been informed that at least two Japanese carriers were within striking distance. Fletcher's advance knowledge would set in train the entire course of battle.

Fletcher then ordered Rear Adm. RAYMOND A. SPRUANCE to take the *Enterprise*—the "Big E"—and *Hornet* and attack the carriers. Fletcher would follow on board the *Yorktown* as soon as his scout bombers returned.

Spruance, heading toward the Japanese at 25 knots, made a crucial decision: He would launch his planes before the Japanese could fly off a second strike at Midway. This meant launching from 200 miles, beyond the 175-mile combat radius of the TBD DEVASTATOR torpedo bombers he would be launching. The Big E launched fourteen TBDs, thirty-three SBD DAUNTLESS dive bombers, and an escort of ten F4F WILDCAT fighters. The *Hornet* flew off thirty-five SBDs, fifteen TBDs, and ten fighters. Ninety-eight minutes later the *Yorktown* launched seventeen SBD dive bombers and twelve TBD torpedo planes escorted by six fighters.

When the *Hornet*'s thirty-five SBDs and F4F fighters reached the reported position of the Japanese carriers, they saw only the empty Pacific. Trying to return, two SBDs and all the fighters came down at sea; thirteen SBDs made it to Midway; only twenty torpedo bombers made it back to the carrier.

The *Hornet*'s fifteen-plane Torpedo Squadron Eight lost contact with the other attack planes but spotted four Japanese carriers. Capt. MARC MITSCHER, commanding officer of the *Hornet,* described what happened next: "Beset on all sides by the deadly 'ZERO' fighters . . . and faced with a seemingly impenetrable screen of cruisers and destroyers, the squadron drove in valiantly at short range. Plane after plane was shot down by fighters, antiaircraft bursts were searing faces and tearing out chunks of fuselage, and still the squadron bored in."

Not one of the fifteen Devastators escaped the inferno of Japanese fire. None of their torpedoes hit. Only one man survived from Torpedo Eight. He was rescued the following day by a PBY.

Next came Torpedo Six from the Big E. Of the fourteen Devastators that attacked, only four survived. Again, none of their torpedoes hit. Then came Torpedo Three from the *Yorktown*. All twelve were shot down. None of their torpedoes hit.

The sacrifice of the torpedo squadrons made the destruction of the Japanese carriers possible. When a torpedo plane makes a run, it speeds toward its target at wave-top level. The Japanese antiaircraft and fighter planes were thus drawn down to that low level. While that attack was going on, U.S. dive bombers from the *Enterprise* appeared overhead. They were virtually unopposed by Japanese fighters.

Throughout the torpedo attack sailors in the four Japanese carriers worked feverishly to prepare planes for a counterattack. Bombers were stacked on the hangar decks of the *Akagi* and *Kaga*. Just as the first Zero was starting down the *Akagi*'s flight deck, a bomb slammed into the carrier. The sixty-odd aircraft on the *Akagi*'s hangar and flight decks, many of them armed and fueled, burst into flame and began exploding into one another.

Four bombs hit the *Kaga*, touching off an inferno among her fueled and armed planes.

Now seventeen dive bombers from the *Yorktown* arrived and selected the *Soryu* as the target. Three bombs hit. Again the explosions and fires caused by the bombs were fed by the fueled and armed aircraft on the carrier's hangar and flight decks.

The fourth Japanese carrier, the *Hiryu*, flew off a strike against the U.S. carriers. The *Yorktown*, hit by three bombs, lost all headway. In a second attack she took two torpedoes in her port side and began to list. "Abandon ship!" was ordered. While DE-STROYERS and CRUISERS rescued her 2,270 survivors, her own dive bombers, which were on board the *Enterprise*, joined with planes from that carrier to kill the *Hiryu*. They hit her with four bombs that started uncontrollable fires. The last of the four Japanese carriers off Midway was doomed.

The *Yorktown* had been abandoned prematurely. When a belated attempt was made to save her, a Japanese submarine torpedoed her and a destroyer alongside.

Besides destroying four Japanese aircraft carriers, U.S. aircraft, in other action during the battle, sank a cruiser and badly damaged another cruiser and two destroyers. All 250 aircraft on the four carriers were lost, as were many of their pilots, air crewmen, and skilled mechanics. Thus ended the first decisive defeat suffered by the Japanese Navy since 1592. The battle also marked the zenith of Japanese expansion in the Pacific.

The northern phase of the battle was relatively successful for the Japanese. Adm. Nimitz had little with which to stop the Japanese move on the Aleutians. Carrier aircraft inflicted heavy damage on the U.S. base at Dutch Harbor and the Japanese made unopposed landings on Kiska and Attu. They would keep their toehold on the North American continent until mid-1943.

Mihajlović, Gen. Draža (1893–1946)

Yugoslav GUERRILLA leader. After the German conquest of Yugoslavia in April 1941, Gen. Draža Mihajlović, a Serbian royalist, organized Yugoslav resistance groups into a force known as the Chetniks. Most of his followers were proroyalist and pro-Serbian. They often clashed with the left-wing partisans, guerrilla forces of JOSEF TITO. Mihajlović, who fought German troops only in Serbian territory, disdained Tito's pan-Yugoslavian policies. Tito's supporters interpreted this as pro-German sentiment and Mihajlović gradually lost support both in the field and from the Yugoslav government-in-exile in LONDON. Tito set up a provisional government, which ran the country after Soviet and Tito forces liberated it. Lacking all support and sought as a war criminal, Mihajlović went into hiding. He was captured in March 1946 and charged with TREASON and collaboration with the enemy. The U.S. government asked that U.S. Army personnel who knew Mihajlović during the war be allowed to testify on his behalf. Tito turned down the request. On July 17, 1946, Mihajlović was executed by a firing squad.

Milch Cow

German submarines used as tankers to refuel other U-BOATS. Beginning in April 1942 the Germans employed milch cows to refuel other U-boats to enable them to operate at greater distances, especially off the U.S. Atlantic Coast, in the Caribbean, and in the Indian Ocean.

The first milch cow was the *U-459*, a Type XIV submarine built specifically for the tanker role. Completed in April 1942, she was relatively large although she had no torpedo-launching tubes, having only antiaircraft guns for self-protection. The *U-459*'s cargo was almost 500 tons of fuel, sufficient to add an extra four weeks on station for twelve Type VII submarines or eight more weeks at sea for five Type IX submarines. Four torpedoes were carried outside of the pressure hull for transfer to other submarines.

The *U-459* carried out her first refueling on April 22, 1942, some 500 miles northeast of Bermuda. Within two weeks she refuelled fourteen submarines before returning to her base in France. Fuel, supplies, and even torpedoes were transferred by block-and-pulley lines as the U-boats moved on parallel courses on the surface.

Subsequent refueling operations became highly vulnerable to Allied naval attack because they concentrated several U-boats in one location. Radio messages to set up their refueling rendezvous were intercepted because the German ENIGMA ciphers had been broken by the Allies. Nine Type XIV submarines were built, all of which were sunk during the war, the last being the *U-490* on June 11, 1944. In addition, several other large submarines were employed in the milch cow role.

The Type XIV submarines had a surface displacement of 1,688 tons and were 220¼ feet long. They were normally fitted with two 37-mm antiaircraft guns and one 20-mm gun. Their crew numbered fifty-three officers and enlisted men.

Millennium

Code name for the RAF Bomber Command's THOUSAND-PLANE RAID against Cologne, May 30, 1942.

Miller, Maj. Glenn (1904–1944)

U.S. dance band leader who joined the Army Air Force. Glenn Miller, one of the nation's most popular band leaders, became Maj. Glenn Miller in 1942, giving up a phenomenally successful career: a thrice-weekly radio show, two MOVIES, the first "golden record" for selling more than 1,000,000 records (the 1941 hit "Chattanooga Choo Choo"). The nation bought his records and hummed his tunes, which became the musical memories of a generation going to war—"Moonlight Serenade," "In the Mood," "Little Brown Jug," "Tuxedo Junction." (See also SONGS.)

The Glenn Miller Orchestra played for the last time on Sept. 27, 1942. Miller, unlikely to be drafted because of his age, volunteered and assembled an Air Force band of servicemen musicians, including members of symphony orchestras. The band played to entertain troops and to recruit enlistees. (A similar band, under Navy auspices, was put together by band leader Artie Shaw, who had enlisted in the Navy.)

The Glenn Miller Air Force band went overseas in June 1944 and spent six months playing for troops in England. The band was scheduled to go next to PARIS. On Dec. 15 Miller flew off to make advance arrangements in bad weather in a small plane. He was never seen again.

Mincemeat

Ingenious British operation to make the German high command believe that instead of SICILY, the ALLIES would invade the Balkans in mid-1943. It was necessary to make the Germans believe that they had, by accident, intercepted highly confidential documents that foretold Allied war plans with the goal of forcing the Germans to disperse troops that would otherwise be defending the beaches of Sicily.

British naval intelligence took the corpse of a man who had recently died in England and preserved his body in dry ice. They quickly developed a *persona* for him—"Major Martin, Royal Marines": William Martin, a captain and acting major, born in Cardiff, Wales, in 1907, and assigned to Headquarters, COMBINED OPERATIONS.

The corpse was outfitted in a Marine officer's uniform, complete with service ribbons, identity disks and papers, theater ticket stubs, pound notes, loose change, even a statement from his club for lodging in LONDON. Most important, chained to him was a locked briefcase with official documents and a personal letter from one senior Allied officer to another. The letter and papers indicated that Major Martin was en route by aircraft from England to Allied headquarters in North Africa.

Major Martin was then placed in a sealed steel canister and taken on board the British submarine *SERAPH,* which sailed to a position off of Huelva on the coast of Spain. There, Lt. N. L. A. (Bill) Jewell, the submarine's commander, and only his officers—all sworn to secrecy—opened the canister on the deck of the surfaced submarine. (The crew was told they were laying a secret weather reporting device.) Major Martin was fitted with a life jacket and, after a final check of the body and its outfit, the 39th Psalm was read and the body gently pushed into the sea where the tide would bring it ashore.

German operatives, who had inundated Spain, quickly learned of the body that had been found by a fisherman on April 30, 1943, while it was being washed toward the shore. While British officials, who also learned of the body, demanded its return, the briefcase was carefully opened by the Germans, its contents photographed and returned, after which the briefcase was given to British diplomats by Spanish officials. The photographs were rushed to BERLIN for analysis by German intelligence. Major Martin's death was mentioned in the next British casualty list and a month later published in *The Times* to further support the ruse. (It had previously been announced that several British officers had died when their aircraft was lost at sea.)

When Major Martin's body and possessions were finally turned over to British officials and the briefcase examined, it was found that the papers had been read and carefully refolded and resealed—obviously by the Germans. The British CHIEFS OF STAFF wired to Prime Minister CHURCHILL, then in the United States: "Mincemeat Swallowed Whole." Churchill's Chief of Staff, Gen. HASTINGS L. ISMAY, later wrote: "The operation succeeded beyond our wildest dreams. To have spread-eagled the German defensive effort right across Europe, even to the extent of sending German vessels away from Sicily itself, was a remarkable achievement."

Major Martin—whose real identity is unknown—was laid to rest in the graveyard at Huelva.

The main instigator of the operation was Ewen Montagu, a lawyer who served in British naval intelligence during the war and afterwards became the judge advocate of the Fleet. He received the Military Order of the British Empire for conceiving Operation Mincemeat. Montagu told the story of Major Martin in his book *The Man Who Never Was,* which was later made into a movie.

Mines

Mines were used on land and at sea, and a few in the air, by all major belligerents in the war. In general, mines were a cheap method of destroying the enemy. Further, mines could be used to "channel" enemy forces into areas—to roads or waterways where they would be more vulnerable to other weapons. Also, just the threat of mines being in an area could sometimes deny it to enemy movements.

Land Mines Many millions of land mines were used in the war. They varied greatly in size and design. The German Army, for example, had more than forty types of antivehicle mines during the war.

Most land mines were intended to be buried and detonated by the pressure of a man or a vehicle coming down on them. While most mines detonated where they were placed, the German BOUNCING BETTY was propelled 3 to 6 feet above the ground where it exploded with its shrapnel having maximum effect against troops.

Mines were very useful in BOOBY TRAPS.

Buried mines could be located by hand-held magnetic detectors or by soldiers on their hands and knees probing with bayonets; tanks could be fitted with a variety of mine-exploding devices, some called "flails." Paths through minefields could also be cleared by a device known as the BANGALORE TORPEDO.

Naval Mines Hundreds of thousands of naval mines were used during the war, sinking about 200 surface warships, many submarines, and thousands of merchant ships. (The largest U.S. warships sunk by mines were DESTROYERS during the NORMANDY INVASION and off OKINAWA.) There were four basic types of naval mines: acoustic mines, exploded by the noises produced by a ship's engines or propellers; contact mines, which detonated when struck by a ship; magnetic mines, exploded by the disturbance caused when a steel-hull ship passed; and pressure mines, which reacted to the pressure changes caused by a ship's passage.

Mines were almost always moored to the bottom with the sensor and explosive canister floating just beneath the surface. There were means of sweeping all of these mines, but such work could be very dangerous. "Degaussing" cables carrying an electrical charge could be placed around or in ships to reduce their magnetic signature and hence their vulnerability to that kind of mine. The three influence-type mines could be fitted with counters that would allow a certain number of ships to pass before becoming active, thus further complicating minesweeping. Similarly, the U.S. Navy fitted some mines with dual capabilities—a pressure sensor combined with either a magnetic or an acoustic mechanism.

Naval mines could be laid by surface ships, submarines, and aircraft. Air-dropped mines were parachuted into coastal waters and even rivers; for example, German aerial minelaying in the Thames estuary in Nov. 1939 threatened to close the port of LONDON. That month, mines sank twenty-seven merchant ships of 120,958 tons and a destroyer, with other ships, including a cruiser, being damaged.

The Germans employed a magnetic mine that was planted on the seafloor, not moored. This was a particularly difficult mine to sweep. The Germans also parachuted mines onto land targets during the BLITZ.

German U-BOATS laid 338 moored mines off the U.S. East Coast during the war, sinking or damaging ten merchant ships.

Probably the largest single mining operation of the war was Operation Starvation, when in early 1945 U.S. AAF B-29 SUPERFORTRESS bombers planted 12,053 mines in Japanese coastal waters in a five-month period, halting most seaborne traffic. Some reports contend that 670 Japanese ships, mostly coastal vessels, were sunk in that operation; sixteen B-29s were lost in the effort's 1,528 sorties (nine to enemy action, the rest operational).

Most navies used small surface craft as minesweepers, but the German and Japanese air forces experimented with using large magnetic loops fitted in aircraft to detonate influence mines.

Aerial Mines   Early in the war the British developed aerial mines that were to be suspended from barrage BALLOONS to explode when the cables were snared by enemy aircraft. However, the device was found to be too dangerous to people on the ground.

Missouri (BB 63)

An *IOWA* (BB 61)–class BATTLESHIP that served as stage for the Japanese SURRENDER at the end of the war. The *Missouri* was the last battleship to be completed by the United States, being constructed at the Brooklyn Navy Yard in New York. She was christened on Jan. 26, 1944, by Miss Margaret Truman, daughter of Senator HARRY S TRUMAN of Missouri.

The warship entered the Pacific in Nov. 1944 and beginning in Jan. 1945 served as a screening ship for AIRCRAFT CARRIERS during air strikes against Japan and provided gunfire support for the landings on IWO JIMA and OKINAWA. On July 15, 1945, her 16-inch (406-mm) guns joined those of other U.S. ships in bombarding the Japanese home island of

Hokkaido in the first U.S. surface attack on Japan. The only damage the *Missouri* sustained in war was from a Japanese KAMIKAZE that struck her on April 11, 1945, but it inflicted superficial damage on the heavily armored ship. For much of her time in combat she was flagship of Adm. WILLIAM F. HALSEY, commander of the U.S. Third FLEET.

The *Missouri* entered Tokyo Bay on Aug. 29, 1945, and was designated to host the formal Japanese surrender ceremonies on Sept. 2. She returned to the United States later that month, and President Truman was on board in New York City as the nation celebrated Navy Day on Oct. 27, 1945.

Mister P

Code name adopted for Prime Minister CHURCHILL at the CASABLANCA CONFERENCE in 1943 after he learned that President ROOSEVELT had chosen the name Admiral Q. "We must," remarked Churchill, "mind our P's and Q's."

Mitchell,

see B-25.

Mitscher, Vice Adm. Marc Andrew (1887–1947)

The preeminent U.S. carrier force commander in the World War II U.S. Navy. After serving in several surface ships, "Pete" Mitscher was certified as Naval Aviator No. 33 in June 1916. He spent the next twenty-five years devising and refining AIRCRAFT CARRIER operations. When PEARL HARBOR was attacked, Capt. Mitscher commanded the carrier *HORNET* (CV 8) in the Atlantic. By that time, he had gained respect and affection for his quiet, modest demeanor and his thorough understanding of naval air.

Mitscher's first mission was to deliver the B-25 MITCHELL bombers of the DOOLITTLE RAID to within striking distance of TOKYO in April 1942. Two months later, aircraft of the *Hornet*, *ENTERPRISE* (CV 6), and *Yorktown* (CV 5) sank four Japanese carriers at MIDWAY. He was promoted to rear admiral in July 1942 and served for six months as commander of a HAWAII-based patrol SQUADRON.

In Jan. 1943, he became commander Fleet Air in the Southwest Pacific under Adm. WILLIAM F. HALSEY, adding commander Air SOLOMON IS-

LANDS in April, supervising Navy and Army air operations. As ComAirSols, Mitscher was executor of the shooting down of Adm. ISOROKU YAMAMOTO by U.S. AAF P-38 LIGHTNING fighters under his command.

With the stream of fast carriers now entering the fleet, Mitscher was chosen to work them up into a TASK FORCE. After several months of training, Mitscher's Fast Carrier Task Force, Pacific Fleet formed the core of Task Force 58, the main naval striking arm in the Pacific. With Adm. RAYMOND SPRUANCE as his commander, Mitscher's carriers supported landings in the MARSHALL ISLANDS, raided TRUK, guarded the HOLLANDIA landings, and awaited the Japanese fleet's response to the June 15 landings in the MARIANAS.

Spruance decided to keep his carriers near SAIPAN, a decision Mitscher strongly, but privately, disagreed with. After the "Turkey Shoot" of June 19, Mitscher did not send out search flights until the next day (a decision historian SAMUEL ELIOT MORISON later criticized, but claimed to sympathize with). His air strike in the afternoon of the next day at the retreating fleet took off knowing that their return would be in the dark; results were meager.

Mitscher, already known for his care for his pilots, cemented his high reputation by ordering that his fleet's lights be turned on to help the aircraft find their way home. This gesture probably saved many lives and maintained morale at an already high peak. (The decision has been criticized on two grounds: It unnecessarily exposed the entire fleet to submarine attack and it was too general, which resulted in pilots being greatly confused by the variety of lights below.)

Mitscher's carriers sank several Japanese ships in the Sibuyan Sea (including the super-battleship *Musashi*) and four aircraft carriers off Cape Engaño during the battle of LEYTE GULF in Oct. 1944, destroying the Japanese Navy's ability to do battle. From Jan. to May 1945, Mitscher's carriers supported the IWO JIMA and OKINAWA landings, raided Japan and Formosa on several occasions, and suffered heavily from KAMIKAZE attacks. In May, Mitscher had to shift his flag twice, from *Bunker Hill* (CV 17) to *Enterprise* to *Randolph* (CV 15) as each carrier was seriously damaged.

Mitscher's health too was damaged and he looked far older than his fifty-eight years; he may have had a heart attack in the spring of 1945, but he carried on. After his relief at the end of May, Mitscher became deputy chief of Naval Operations for Air in July 1945, head of the Eighth FLEET until Sept. 1946, and then CinC of the Atlantic Fleet. He suffered a fatal heart attack in Feb. 1947 while in this last post.

M-minute

Minute in H-HOUR on D-DAY designated as the start of an Allied military operation.

Model, *Generalfeldmarschall* Walther (1891–1945)

A World War I infantry officer, Model was one of the first ranking German Army officers to support HITLER. At a time when old-line Prussian officers were sneering at or plotting against Hitler, Model embraced the NAZI Party.

He was a staff officer in the POLAND CAMPAIGN and FRANCE AND LOW COUNTRIES CAMPAIGN and commanded the Third PANZER Division and the Ninth Army in the GERMAN CAMPAIGN IN THE SOVIET UNION, where his bold actions when sent to trouble spots earned him the nickname *Führer's Feuerwehrmann*—Hitler's fireman.

After the JULY 20 PLOT against Hitler's life in 1944, Model immediately sent a message of allegiance. Following Hitler's dismissal of *Generalfeldmarschall* Hans Günther von Kluge in Aug. 1944 during the ALLIED CAMPAIGN IN EUROPE, Model became Commander in Chief of the Army West until the reinstatement of Kluge's predecessor, *Generalfeldmarschall* GERD VON RUNDSTEDT. (Kluge, suspected of TREASON and guilty of disobeying a Hitler order not to retreat, killed himself.)

Model was in command in the RUHR in April 1945 when Allied troops, after the RHINE CROSSINGS, encircled German forces; some 300,000 German troops surrendered. Model, who had been disgusted by the surrender of *Generalfeldmarschall* FRIEDRICH VON PAULUS at STALINGRAD, believed that field marshals did not surrender. He shot himself and died on April 21.

Mohawk,

see P-36.

Mölders, Gen. Werner (1913–1941)

Luftwaffe's leading fighter ACE. Mölders was credited with 115 kills (fourteen while in the German Condor Legion flying for the Nationalists in the SPANISH CIVIL WAR). He was the most decorated German soldier in World War II. Mölders, who once had to parachute out of his burning ME 109, died in a plane accident. He was a passenger in a HE 111 bomber that crashed while carrying him to the funeral of another Luftwaffe fighter ace, ERNST UDET, who had killed himself.

Molotov Cocktail

Antitank weapon. The shortage of antitank weapons to fight German tanks in 1941–1942 led to improvisation among Soviet defenders, including the widely used Molotov cocktail. This weapon consisted of a bottle of gasoline or other flammable liquid and a rag stuffed into the top of the bottle and lighted moments before being thrown at German troops or vehicles.

The weapon was effective against trucks and lightly armored vehicles. It could destroy a TANK only if it hit the engine air intake or was thrown into an open hatch.

It was named for V. M. MOLOTOV.

Molotov, Vyacheslav M. (1890–1986)

Soviet commissar for Foreign Affairs. An old-line Bolshevik whose pre-Revolution name was Scriabin, Molotov preceded JOSEF STALIN as secretary of the Communist Party central committee. After Stalin took over that post in 1922, Molotov emerged as one of Stalin's principal aides and became one of the nine members of the Politburo. During May Day rites in 1939, Commissar for Foreign Affairs MAKSIM LITVINOV stood proudly with Stalin. Three days later, Litvinov, a well-respected diplomat, was replaced by Molotov, president of the Council of People's Commissars, equivalent to premier.

Soon after his appointment, the British ambassador to the Soviet Union described Molotov as "a man totally ignorant of foreign affairs to whom the idea of negotiation . . . is utterly alien." But Stalin, seeing Germany as a potential ally, decided that

Litvinov, a Jew who had married an English woman, would not appeal to ADOLF HITLER. On Aug. 24, 1939, Molotov signed the NONAGGRESSION PACT between Germany and the Soviet Union.

Molotov resigned as premier in 1941 when Stalin took over that post. Three weeks after the German invasion of the Soviet Union in June 1940, Molotov signed a mutual-aid agreement with the United Kingdom, joining his nation with the ALLIES. He became Stalin's indefatigable advocate for an Allied SECOND FRONT. In May 1942, while Soviet troops were retreating, Molotov flew to LONDON then to WASHINGTON to importune first CHURCHILL and then ROOSEVELT. His argument: If Great Britain and the United States open a Second Front it would pull some forty German divisions away from fighting the Soviets on the Eastern Front. Molotov, dour and an unflinching purveyor of Stalin's policies, participated in major Allied meetings, including the YALTA CONFERENCE and SAN FRANCISCO CONFERENCE in 1945. In 1957, with NIKITA KHRUSHCHEV firmly in power, Molotov was publicly denounced for being a henchman for Stalin, expelled from the Communist Party, and made the ambassador to Outer Mongolia.

Mongolia

Capital: Ulan Bator, pop. 1,000,000 (est. 1939). A republic then recognized only by the Soviet Union, Mongolia played no active role in World War II. In the spring and summer of 1939 the Mongolian border with Japan became the stage for a demonstration of Japanese and Soviet war machines. In the undeclared war, Soviet troops soundly beat the Japanese after initial reverses.

The Soviets had come to the aid of the Mongolians after Japanese troops invaded from the Japanese puppet state of Manchukuo (Manchuria). One Japanese division lost 12,000 of its 15,000 men. The Soviet commander, who used massive tank attacks to achieve victory, was Maj. Gen. GEORGI ZHUKHOV, future defender of MOSCOW and leading Soviet war hero.

Monsarrat, Nicholas (1910—)

Pen name of John Turney, who produced the most exciting and perceptive novels of the tedium, adventure, frustrations, and successes of the BATTLE OF THE ATLANTIC. Monsarrat's first book, *Think of Tomorrow,* was published in 1934, but received little attention. In the 1930s, he produced a number of novels, newspaper articles, some verse, and a play.

A lawyer by education, he entered the Royal Navy in 1940 and served at sea for three years in several antisubmarine ships, and although an "amateur sailor," he rose to command a CORVETTE, an unusual achievement for a lieutenant in the Royal Navy Volunteer Reserve. While at sea he produced three short books about small ships fighting submarines that were combined in *Three Corvettes,* followed by *H.M.S. Marlborough Will Enter Harbor.* In 1945 his *Leave Cancelled* provoked a furor in detailing the twenty-four hour honeymoon of a British officer and his young bride.

He left the Navy in 1946 as a lieutenant commander. He then directed the British information office in Johannesburg, South Africa, where he completed his classic *The Cruel Sea* (published in 1951). He then pursued a prolific writing career.

Monte Cassino,

see CASSINO.

Montgomery, Field Marshal Bernard Law (1887–1976)

Few non-American military leaders—allied or enemy—have aroused the dislike in American hearts as did Montgomery (Viscount Montgomery of Alamein). This haze of resentment has tended to obscure Montgomery's great talents and undeniable success. As a lifelong student and practitioner, Montgomery distrusted amateurs, and few Allied military commanders he encountered could match his training and combat experience.

Montgomery had led an infantry platoon into an attack at Ypres in Oct. 1914, been badly wounded, and served as staff officer for the remaining three years of World War I. During the interwar years, Montgomery rose as a commander and instructor.

He led the British 3rd Division in the battle of France during Germany's FRANCE AND LOW COUNTRIES CAMPAIGN and was evacuated from DUNKIRK. He was later promoted to major general and

Britain's most famous and controversial general during a tea break in North Africa. Field Marshal Montgomery, known to all as "Monty," demanded carefully planned and prepared operations, to the infuriation of his American contemporaries and, on occasion, to the benefit of his German opponents. *(Imperial War Museum)*

became a corps commander, subsequently taking command of the British Eighth Army in Egypt on Aug. 12, 1942.

At the time the Eighth Army was beginning to rebound physically from Gen. ERWIN ROMMEL's drubbings but was still sagging mentally and emotionally. Montgomery's histrionic proclamation was a well-timed bit of backbone-stiffener: "Here we will stand and fight; there can be no further withdrawal. . . . We will stand and fight *here.* If we can't stay here alive, then let us stay here dead."

The subsequent battles of Alam Halfa and EL ALAMEIN raised his reputation above all other British generals. At Alam Halfa in late August he broke Rommel's attack. In late Oct. 1942, after the extended preparations that were to become his hallmark, Montgomery forced Rommel to retreat after a bitter battle. His pursuit of Rommel across Libya to Tunisia has been criticized for its deliberateness, but he arrived in North Africa as Rommel's conqueror. At that moment, "Monty" probably came closest to matching the ideal Montgomery he would later craft in his mind and then in his writings. His flanking of Rommel's MARETH LINE in southern Tunisia contrasted sharply, not least in his own mind, with the American retreat through KASSERINE PASS in Feb. 1943. Although many British Eighth Army veterans at that time held the opinion that they were much the better force, Montgomery abraded American egos by his apparent belief that this was an immutable condition.

Montgomery's performance in the invasion of SICILY and the ITALIAN CAMPAIGN demonstrated both his great strengths and his weaknesses. He showed a willingness to adjust to circumstances, as when the direct route along the southeastern coast of Sicily was found to be nearly impenetrable. He seldom faltered in his drive and was loath to yield ground already taken. But he spent days carefully preparing the cross-strait bombardment in support of his landings on Italy's "toe" in Sept. 1943. Likewise, his push up from TARANTO a few days later was delayed by measured preparation.

Montgomery's was not the braggart's swagger, but rather the demeanor of the insufferable schoolteacher. His penchant for overstating how closely the battle conformed to his earlier plans hurt Montgomery in two ways: It alienated those who might have otherwise heeded the valid points he raised and it obscured his talent for adapting to circumstance.

He arrived in England on Jan. 2, 1944, to take command of 21st ARMY GROUP for Overlord, the NORMANDY INVASION, and immediately began stating the changes he wanted in Overlord plans, most of which had already been prepared. In his preinvasion briefings, Montgomery talked of taking Caen the first day and Falaise within days. (Until a U.S. Army Group was activated in Normandy on Aug. 1944, Montgomery would command all Anglo-American ground troops; on the day that the U.S. ground forces came under their own group commander, Montgomery's promotion to field marshal was announced.)

Montgomery did not fulfill his inflated expectations for a breakout from Normandy. But his constant probing—and several outright assaults—kept most of the German armor facing the Allied left while Gen. OMAR BRADLEY's forces fought through on the right. Montgomery's forces ultimately broke out after the Americans on the right and he almost immediately began calling for a "dagger-like thrust" into north Germany, with him as the guiding light.

Gen. DWIGHT D. EISENHOWER, the Supreme Commander, rejected many of Montgomery's proposals, which would have had more validity had Montgomery not shown himself to be relatively cautious and nonopportunistic. Bradley wrote in his memoirs, *A Soldier's Story,* that after the Normandy breakout, "In the fluid situation that was to obtain until the end of the war Montgomery's luster was dimmed not by timidity as his critics allege, but by his apparent reluctance to squeeze the utmost advantage out of every gain or success. For Monty insisted upon a 'tidy' front even when tidiness forced him to slow down an advance. On the other hand, we Americans preferred to push ahead, unscrambling our troops on the run, in an effort to prevent a fluid front from hardening into a set battle. For each set battle meant that another enemy crust had to be broken and this could only be accomplished with casualties and delay."

Montgomery's attitude toward Eisenhower, a supercilious tolerance, ignited Eisenhower's impressive temper on several occasions as Montgomery intrigued to have himself named overall land forces commander. When Montgomery took over command of the northern shoulder of Allied forces during Germany's Dec. 1944 ARDENNES counteroffensive, Montgomery "tidied up the lines" and then launched what most Americans saw as a belated counterattack. His Jan. 1945 press conference, which made it appear as if he had come in and straightened a real mess all on his own, nearly led to his removal. By the end of the war, he and most of the American commanders, especially Bradley and Gen. GEORGE S. PATTON, were barely civil to each other. On more than one occasion Eisenhower had been prepared to "fire" Montgomery.

After the war Montgomery went on to become chief of the Imperial General Staff and an important early leader of NATO. He was probably the most skillful and successful British commander of World War II, but his personality made it impossible for any American military commander to acknowledge it willingly—and at times to even work with him.

Moorbrand (Swamp Fire)

German code word for operation to destroy the Pogostyle salient on the EASTERN FRONT, mid-1942.

Morgenthau, Henry, Jr. (1891–1967)

Secretary of the Treasury from 1934 until 1945 and close adviser to President ROOSEVELT. Morgenthau, an advocate of a balanced budget even in wartime, had to supervise the financing of a war that was costing $150,000,000 a day while taxes were bringing only $49,000,000 a day into the U.S. treasury. He eased wartime inflation and postwar recovery through a system of financing based on the sale of WAR BONDS, the imposing of heavy taxes on excess profits and high incomes, and the extension of income taxes to a wider population. (Before the war, 11 percent of the population paid income tax; by 1945, 37 percent did.)

The son of a German-born diplomat and philanthropist, Morgenthau took a particular interest in the shaping of an agrarian, thoroughly disarmed postwar Germany, but his MORGENTHAU PLAN was rejected. President TRUMAN so abhorred the plan that he asked for Morgenthau's resignation.

Morgenthau Plan

A proposal for postwar Germany by U.S. Secretary of the Treasury Henry Morgenthau. President ROOSEVELT and Prime Minister CHURCHILL showed some interest in the plan, when Morgenthau presented it at the second QUEBEC CONFERENCE in September 1944. The plan, which called for making postwar Germany an "agricultural and pastoral" nation, was quickly killed off by Roosevelt and Churchill advisers.

Morison, Rear Adm. Samuel Eliot (1887–1976)

Naval historian. Trumbull professor of history at Harvard University, Morison was commissioned by President ROOSEVELT as a lieutenant commander in the Naval Reserve in May 1942 to obtain firsthand experience so he could write an operational history of the Navy at war. Morison sailed in eight surface warships (including a Coast Guard cutter) and saw combat operations firsthand on several occasions. However, as historian Clark G. Reynolds observed, "Curiously, he did not serve aboard an aircraft carrier or submarine, the two major warship types of the conflict."

Morison left active duty in 1946, but the Navy continued to provide him with a staff as he compiled his fifteen-volume, comprehensive *History of U.S. Naval Operations in World War II*. Although a semiofficial work, the series was an extremely useful and popular history of the war at sea. In the work Morison occasionally slipped into flag-waving hyperbole; it also suffered from his not having knowledge of the Allied code-breaking efforts during the war.

Morison retired from the naval reserve with the rank of rear admiral in 1951. The author of numerous other books on naval and maritime subjects, Morison twice won the Pulitzer Prize for literature—for his biography of Columbus, *Admiral of the Ocean* (1942) and *John Paul Jones* (1959).

Morotai

Island in the northern Moluccas (Spice Islands), DUTCH EAST INDIES. Morotai, about 50 miles long by 25 miles wide, was seized during the JAPANESE FAR EAST CAMPAIGN in Jan. 1942. The island was retaken, against little opposition, by U.S. Army troops in an AMPHIBIOUS LANDING on Sept. 15, 1944. The landing was part of Operation Stalemate during the U.S. CENTRAL PACIFIC CAMPAIGN—the taking of Morotai and PELELIU to protect the flank of Gen. DOUGLAS MACARTHUR, who was to invade the Philippines in October. The Peleliu landing was very costly, especially in comparison with the conquest of Moratai, site of an airfield from which strikes could be made on the Philippines.

Mortars

Muzzle-loading, high-trajectory weapons used by all ground combat forces in the war. Mortars were very effective weapons because of their accuracy and their being easy to move. (Navies also had mortar-like antisubmarine weapons in ships; see SQUID, HEDGEHOG, and MOUSETRAP.)

The standard U.S. Army and Marine Corps mortars were the 60-mm M2 and the 81-mm M1. Both were infantry weapons that could be taken apart and carried as backpacks. They could also be carried in and fired from HALF-TRACK vehicles. All were drop-fire weapons (the round being dropped into the muzzle).

The 60-mm weapon fired a 31-pound round to a maximum distance of 1,985 yards. The 81-mm mor-

German soldiers fire an 81-mm mortar during combat on the Kerch Isthmus in April 1942. That body of land, which bridges the Sea of Azov and Crimea, was vital for the German expansion eastward. *(German Army via U.S. Army)*

tar used 6.9-pound and 10.6-pound high-explosive rounds and could lob its projectile 3,290 yards. Both mortars had a sustained rate of fire of 18 rounds per minute. The 60-mm mortar weighed 42 pounds ready to fire; the 81-mm weapon weighed 132 pounds. Mortar rounds were sometimes called "bombs."

An Army rifle COMPANY had three 60-mm mortars in its weapons PLATOON; the weapons company organic to an infantry BATTALION had six 81-mm mortars.

Also used by U.S. combat troops was the 4.2-inch (107-mm) M2 chemical mortar. While intended for firing CHEMICAL WARFARE rounds (smoke and gas), it was employed for general infantry support. The 4.2-inch mortar fired a 24-pound high-explosive round with a maximum range of 4,500 yards. The 4.2-inch mortar weighed 330 pounds ready to fire. These weapons were used by separate chemical mortar battalions.

Two larger mortars entered U.S. service in 1944, the 105-mm T13 and the 155-mm T-25. Only a few of these weapons were produced and only the 155-mm mortar was used in combat, in the Southwest Pacific. They were difficult to handle and saw little service.

Several larger mortars were used by foreign armies, such as the Soviet 160-mm M1943 mortar, which was a 2,380-pound weapon towed by truck.

Moscow

Capital of the Soviet Union and a primary objective of the GERMAN CAMPAIGN IN THE SOVIET UNION. On Dec. 18, 1940, in his directive on Operation Barbarossa, the invasion of the Soviet Union, HITLER said, "The capture of this city means a decisive political and economic victory, beyond the fall of the country's most important railroad junction." Moscow was the hub of Soviet communications and an important war production center, as well as capital of the country.

Germany's Moscow offensive, Operation Typhoon, began on Oct. 2, 1941. At first the Germans moved swiftly, encircling two armies and taking 650,000 PRISONERS OF WAR. By mid-Oct. 1941 the Germans were 60 miles from Moscow and the city was being bombed frequently. Soviet government agencies and foreign embassies were leaving the city and setting up a quasi-capital at Kuibyshev on the Volga River, 550 miles southeast of Moscow. JOSEF STALIN and other Soviet leaders remained, running the war from air raid bunkers deep in the Kremlin.

Children and nonessential workers were evacuated. There was little fuel. Thousands of windows had been blasted out by BOMB explosion, and there was no way to keep apartments warm. A midnight curfew was imposed. People needed a special permit to live in Moscow.

Beyond the city, Operation Typhoon had bogged down in rains and mud. "The infantryman slithers in the mud, while many teams of horses are needed to drag each gun forward," wrote Gen. Günther Blumenritt, Chief of Staff of the Fourth Army. "All wheeled vehicles sink up to their axles in the slime."

Blumenritt's commanders started asking, "When are we going to stop?" They all knew that Napoleon's army had been destroyed by the winter of 1812. Many of them began rereading the grim account of that winter by Marquis de Louis Caulaincourt, aide-de-camp to Napoleon on his Russian campaign. Soviet GUERRILLAS to the rear of the advancing Germans were attacking supply lines. The troops had no winter clothing.

Against the advice of his generals, Hitler ignored the reality of weather and lesson of history. He ordered a final effort to take Moscow. He wanted his troops to blow up the Kremlin to demonstrate to the Soviet people that communism had been destroyed.

The Germans launched a campaign on Dec. 7 when the snow was thick on the ground and darkness was falling as early as 3 P.M. Some infantry troops got as far as the suburbs. They were driven off by Red Army soldiers aided by workers armed with hammers and whatever other weapons they could find.

When Hitler reluctancy allowed a withdrawal to a previously prepared line, temperatures were dropping to 28° below zero. "That was the end of Hitler's bid for Moscow," wrote historian B. H. LIDDELL HART in *The German Generals Talk.* ". . . Never again would any German soldiers catch sight of the Kremlin, except as prisoners."

Moscow's evacuees began coming back, though the year 1942 would be almost as much of an ordeal. There was still little fuel. There were still no restaurants. But the theater companies were back, and Moscow began to live again.

Moscow Conferences

On Aug. 12, 1942, Prime Minister CHURCHILL, Premier STALIN, U.S. envoy AVERELL HARRIMAN, representing President ROOSEVELT, and French delegates representing Gen. CHARLES DE GAULLE met in Moscow to plan the opening of a SECOND FRONT.

The next meeting was held from Oct. 18 to Nov. 1, 1943, when U.S., British, and Soviet officials met to discuss both the war and the postwar world. U.S. Secretary of State CORDELL HULL and British Foreign Minister ANTHONY EDEN met with Soviet Foreign Minister VYACHESLAV MOLOTOV. The three nations agreed that after the war they would continue Anglo-Soviet cooperation and not maintain troops in other countries. They also agreed to recognize China as a major power, to return war criminals to the nation where the WAR CRIMES were committed, and to demand the UNCONDITIONAL SURRENDER of Germany, Japan, and Italy.

Mosquito

In many respects the Mosquito was the most versatile aircraft of the war, serving in the photo-reconnaissance, bomber, antiship, fighter-bomber, nightfighter, and PATHFINDER roles. In most roles the Mosquito was superior to its contemporaries and was the fastest aircraft of any type in the RAF from Sept. 1941 until early 1944. As *Jane's All the World's Aircraft* editor J. W. R. Taylor observed, "The Mosquito was the realization of an ideal: an unarmed bomber that would depend for its defence on sheer performance."

The first Mosquito deliveries to the RAF occurred in mid-1941 and the operational debut occurred on Sept. 20, 1941, when a PR variant photographed occupied France. Chased by three German ME 109 fighters, the Mosquito easily eluded its pursuers at 23,000 feet. The precision strike capabilities of the Mosquito were often demonstrated, as in the Sept. 1942 rooftop attack on GESTAPO headquarters in Oslo, Norway. During the intensive Allied attacks against German V-1 BUZZ BOMB sites in the summer of 1944, Mosquito squadrons averaged one V-site destroyed for each 39.8 tons of BOMBS dropped compared with 219 tons for the B-25 MITCHELL, 182 tons for the B-26 MARAUDER, and 165.4 tons for the B-17 FLYING FORTRESS. During the war Mosquitos bombed BERLIN itself on no fewer than 170 occasions, including the first daylight raid ever on the city, on Jan. 30, 1943. Mosquito strikes on Berlin varied from one or two "nuisance" aircraft to a raid of 122 aircraft in Feb. 1945. In the antishipping role the Mosquito effectively used 6-pounder guns and ROCKETS to destroy AXIS merchant ships and small combat craft.

The Mosquito began as an initiative of de Havilland Aircraft in the summer of 1938. Following the outbreak of war in Sept. 1939, the Air Ministry agreed to limited production. The prototype Mosquito I flew on Nov. 25, 1940, and demonstrated the speed and agility of the design. Next an armed fighter prototype flew on May 15, 1941, and the third—a photo-reconnaissance (PR) prototype—flew on June 10, 1941. Meanwhile, the original order for fifty bombers was changed to twenty bombers and thirty fighters, soon followed by more orders. During the war 6,710 Mosquitos were delivered (with another 1,071 built after the war).

The key to the Mosquito's excellence lay in two Rolls-Royce Merlin engines merged with the smallest practical airframe, and extreme aerodynamic cleanliness. Fabricated of wood, in the bomber and reconnaissance roles the Mosquito was unarmed, relying (effectively) on its speed to escape interception. The engine nacelles reached as far forward as the nose of the fuselage, which ended in a tapered tail with a tall fin and tail wheel. Most variants had two-man crews. A score of Mosquitos modified to carry the HIGHBALL "bouncing bomb" were refitted for carrier operation.

The Mosquito Mk IV bomber variant had a top speed of 380 mph and a range of 1,370 miles with maximum bomb load. It could carry four 500-pound bombs in an internal bay; later bomber marks could carry 4,000 pounds.

The Mosquito Mk VI fighter was also rated at 380 mph while the Mk XXX could reach 407 mph. Normal range was 1,200 miles, which could be extended with drop tanks to over 1,700 miles. Armament was four 20-mm cannon in the nose, and some fighter variants also had four .303-cal. guns. Two 500-pound bombs could be carried in the bomb bay plus another two under wings when the plane was used as a fighter-bomber.

Mountbatten, Adm. Lord Louis (1900–1979)

British naval officer who began the war as the commanding officer of a destroyer and ended it as Supreme Allied Commander in Southeast Asia. Mountbatten's father had been First Sea Lord at the outbreak of World War I and had been forced to resign because of his German heritage. The younger Mountbatten saw considerable combat in destroyers and his destroyer was sunk off CRETE in 1941 by German bombers.

At age forty-one, Mountbatten was given the rank of commodore and made chief of COMBINED OPERATIONS on Oct. 17, 1941. He was soon promoted to acting vice admiral and given equivalent rank in the other services and made a member of the CHIEFS OF STAFF, reflecting the importance that Prime Minister CHURCHILL placed on COMMANDO activities. Mountbatten supervised the DIEPPE raid of Aug. 1942 and other commando strikes.

In Aug. 1943 President ROOSEVELT and Prime Minister Churchill appointed him Supreme Commander of the Southeast Asia Command (as a full admiral). He directed much of the ALLIED CHINA-BURMA-INDIA CAMPAIGN, deftly handling both the complex international politics of the area and the rivalries of Allied officers. (The Allied leadership appointed only three Supreme Commanders during the war: DWIGHT D. EISENHOWER, DOUGLAS MACARTHUR, and Mountbatten; see UNIFIED COMMANDS.)

Mountbatten's biographer Philip Ziegler wrote that the admiral was far from being Churchill's first choice for the Southeast Asia Command. It was only after a half dozen more senior officers had been rejected, Ziegler said, that Churchill "quickly convinced himself that this had been his intention from the start, and that a young and dashing admiral . . . was the obvious choice to breathe life into the tired old military machine and rescue the British armies from a long-drawn-out and painful slog through the Burmese jungle."

In 1947–1948, as the last viceroy of India, he oversaw the granting of independence to India. After the war he served as First Sea Lord and Chief of the Defence Staff. He was killed by a bomb exploded by Irish Republican Army terrorists.

Mousetrap,

see HEDGEHOG

Movies

For American moviegoers, the war began long before PEARL HARBOR. British filmmakers, urged on by their government support of pro-British movies, produced films that had exactly that effect on U.S. audiences. The British established a Film Division in the Ministry of Information and put it under Kenneth Clark (who, as Sir Kenneth Clark, would later become known as the host of the public television series *Civilization*). He enlisted outstanding directors and moviemakers, along with British stars of stage and screen.

From their labors came, for instance, *49th Parallel,* government funded and created with an eye to develop anti-NAZI sentiment in the United States, where it was shown as *The Invaders.* Shot mostly in Canada and released in 1941, the movie had a music score by Ralph Vaughan Williams and starred Laurence Olivier, Raymond Massey, Leslie Howard, and Eric Portman. A hit in U.S. movie houses, it told the story of the six survivors of a German U-BOAT sinking as they wandered through Canada, heading for the neutral United States (across the 49th parallel). Other British films that became U.S. hits were *In Which We Serve* (1942), a Royal Navy epic, and *Target for Tonight* (1941), a documentary of an RAF raid on Germany.

The British government subsidized *Henry V,* starring and directed by Olivier. Although by its release in 1944 the United States was already in the war, the Film Division still saw it as a valuable PROPAGANDA film. In keeping with wartime sentiments, scenes about British traitors were cut from Shakespeare's script.

During the years when the United States was officially neutral, anti-German feelings showed up in unexpected places. In *Babes in Arms* (1939), Mickey Rooney and Judy Garland sing "Chin Up, Cheerio, Carry On," a ditty in which they urge: "turn the Blitz on Fritz." Another 1939 U.S. movie, *Confessions of a Nazi Spy,* so ardently attacked the GERMAN-AMERICAN BUND that the Bund threatened a libel suit. *The Mortal Storm* (1940), with Margaret Sullavan, James Stewart, Robert Young, and Frank Morgan, dramatized the life of a middle-class German family devastated by the rise of Naziism. In the classic film *The Great Dictator* (1940), Charlie Chaplin, as a character named Adenoid Hynkel, savagely ridiculed ADOLF HITLER. In *Sergeant York* (1941) a peace-loving Gary Cooper, playing the title role, becomes a sharpshooter renowned for killing Germans—although in World War I.

Before and during the war, movie audiences saw the war on censored—but often vivid—NEWSREELS and in documentary, fifteen-minute films called *The March of Time,* launched in 1935 and sponsored by *Time, Life,* and *Fortune.* The May 1938 *March of Time* film *Inside Nazi Germany* gave many Americans their first graphic view of Naziism. An early view of modern war came in *Spanish Earth,* whose scenes from the SPANISH CIVIL WAR showed the bombing of Madrid and the intervention of Italian and German forces against the Royalists. ERNEST HEMINGWAY, one of several American writers involved in the film, wrote and spoke the narration.

Numerous "war movies" were ground out for avid moviegoers, many of them defense workers who, like movie houses, worked day and night shifts. A typical array of movies during a week of the war (March 14, 1943) included *Commandos Strike at Dawn,* starring Paul Muni; *The Navy Comes Through* with Pat O'Brien and George Murphy; Tim Holt and Bonita Granville in *Hitler's Children;* *To the Shores of Tripoli* with John Payne, Maureen O'Hara, and Randolph Scott; and a Donald Duck cartoon named after one of the war's popular SONGS, *The Führer's Face.*

Walt Disney produced films telling civilians how to help win the war and soldiers how to avoid venereal disease. Minnie Mouse, about to feed Pluto leftover bacon grease, is told: "Housewives of America! One of the most important things you can do is to save your waste kitchen fats, bacon grease, meat drippings, frying fat. For fats make glycerin and glycerin makes explosives." Popeye fought Japanese spies, Bugs Bunny sold WAR BONDS.

A story about a British couple coping with the war, *Mrs. Miniver,* won the Academy Award in 1942. Greer Garson (who also won an Oscar) and Walter Pidgeon played the stiff-upper-lip couple. The 1943 Academy winner was *Casablanca,* in which Americans learned about VICHY FRANCE through the dialogue of Humphrey Bogart, Ingrid Bergman, Paul Henreid, and Claude Rains. No other so-called war film won an Academy Award during the U.S. war years.

Some films reflected real events: *Bataan* (1943) with Robert Taylor, Thomas Mitchell, George Murphy, Lloyd Nolan, and Desi Arnez; *Guadalcanal Diary* (1943), based on the book by Richard Tregaskis and starring Preston Foster, Lloyd Nolan, William Bendix, Richard Conte, and Anthony Quinn; *Thirty Seconds Over Tokyo* (1944), in which Spencer Tracy, Van Johnson, and Robert Walker very loosely reenact aspects of the DOOLITTLE

RAID; and *They Were Expendable* (1945), in which Robert Montgomery, who actually was a U.S. Navy captain in the war, plays a character based on JOHN BULKELEY, a heroic PT-BOAT skipper, with John Wayne as one of his young officers.

Many well-known moviemakers also went to war. Head of film production for the War Department was Frank Capra, who was commissioned a U.S. Army major. His outstanding work, considered one of the war's most striking examples of U.S. propaganda, was a series of *Why We Fight* films aimed at indoctrinating members of the armed services. Another Hollywood director, John Ford (commissioned a lieutenant commander in the U.S. Navy), made the great documentary *The Battle of MIDWAY* (1942). *Fighting Lady,* shot aboard the carrier *Yorktown* (CV 10) during action in the Pacific, stunned its 1944 audience with combat film in color.

The U.S. film industry produced about 4,000 war-training films for the armed services at cost. About one-third of Hollywood's prewar movie work force, some 7,000 men, went into the service. Many served in related jobs as cameramen and camouflage experts. In a highly publicized dissent from the war, Lew Ayres, who played the sensitive German soldier in *All Quiet on the Western Front* (1930), declared himself to be a conscientious objector.

Among servicemen employed in training film-making was AAF Capt. Ronald Reagan, who also played a shy, lovesick draftee in the film version of the Irving Berlin musical *This Is The Army* (1943). Playing the future President's father was the future senator from California, George Murphy.

Film star Jimmy Stewart flew twenty combat missions in Europe; Clark Gable, Henry Fonda, and Charleton Heston also saw combat in the war. Other stars who went to war included Robert Taylor, Robert Stack, Alan Ladd, Tyrone Power, Glenn Ford. Gable's wife, actress Carole Lombard, was killed on Jan. 16, 1942, in a plane crash in Nevada while on a tour entertaining troops; a LIBERTY SHIP was named after her.

The movie that eloquently marked the end of the war was *The Best Years of Our Lives,* a 1946 Academy Award winner in which Harold Russell, who actually did lose his arms in the war, played a character returning home with two artificial arms. Hollywood, which never found a way to make a good war

movie during the war, would make up for it years later with such films as *Twelve O'Clock High* (1949) with Gregory Peck, Gary Merrill and superb combat footage of the Eighth AIR FORCE; *Run Silent, Run Deep* (1958), an epic about U.S. SUBMARINES in the Pacific, with Clark Gable and Burt Lancaster; *Battle Cry* (1959), with Van Heflin, Aldo Ray, and Tab Hunter; *A Walk in the Sun* (1946), with Richard Conte, John Ireland; *The Young Lions* (1958), with Marlon Brando, Montgomery Clift, and Dean Martin, a breakthrough film that looked at the war from both the Allied and German points of view.

MP-38 Submachine Gun

Standard German submarine gun of the war. HITLER, opposed to the use of submachine guns by German troops (based on his own World War I experience in the Army), ruled that infantry would be better served with rifles. Thus, German troops had to rely on captured foreign submachine guns, especially the Soviet BURP-GUN, until large-scale German production was belatedly undertaken. The MP-38 and the nearly identical MP-40 were widely distributed. By the time of the NORMANDY INVASION in June 1944 the German infantry division had more individual firepower than the larger U.S. divisions because of this weapon.

The 9-mm MP-38 and MP-40 submachine guns were blowback-operated weapons that could fire only in a fully automatic mode. The MP-38 had a corrugated upper receiver and the MP-40 a smooth receiver; otherwise the weapons were identical, although the latter weapon was intended for large-scale production. They both were all-metal weapons with a tubular, extending stock, and were fitted with a 32-round magazine clip that served as a forward grip. Effective range was 200 yards with a firing rate of 500 rounds per minute.

The MP-38 was developed by the Erma firm in Germany in the mid-1930s. It was adopted by the German Army in 1938 and entered small-scale production. It was probably the world's first submachine gun to be made without any wooden components, being fabricated entirely of metal and plastic.

Mulberry

Code name for ARTIFICIAL HARBORS built by the ALLIES during the NORMANDY INVASION to protect shipping from heavy weather; Gooseberry was a part of this system.

Munich Pact

Agreement that began with the demise of Czechoslovakia, although at the time hailed as an important move toward peace. Czechoslovakia was not represented at the meeting in Munich on Sept. 29–30, 1938, at which German Führer ADOLF HITLER, Prime Minister NEVILLE CHAMBERLAIN of Britain, Premier ÉDOUARD DALADIER of France, and *Il Duce* BENITO MUSSOLINI of Italy decided the fate of Czechoslovakia.

Hitler had demanded that Czechoslovakia give up the Sudetenland, the German name for the German-speaking region in northern Czechoslovakia. Chamberlain met first with Hitler in "consultations" at BERCHTESGADEN and Godesberg. Chamberlain then convinced Daladier to join with England in pressing the Czech government to bow to Hitler's demands, thus averting war. France, Czechoslovakia, and Germany had mobilized, and Hitler was threatening a march into Czechoslovakia.

The Munich Pact, signed by England, France, Italy, and Germany, created a new Czechoslovakia, stripped of the Sudetenland, an area where about 3,000,000 ethnic Germans lived, and created a new Czech state highly vulnerable to takeover by Hitler.

Although hailed as a successful move for peace, the Munich Pact became a symbol of appeasement. (Chamberlain, back in England after the Munich meeting, said it had achieved "peace for our time.") The Munich Pact emboldened Hitler and set the European stage for World War II.

Murmansk

Soviet ice-free port on the Kola Gulf of the Barents Sea and a crucial delivery point for Allied supplies. This was the usual destination of the RUSSIAN CONVOYS that ran a gauntlet of German U-BOATS, aircraft, and surface RAIDERS to reach Murmansk. From June 1941, when Germany invaded the Soviet Union, to Sept. 1943, when the SOVIET OFFENSIVE CAMPAIGN was rolling, more than 20 percent of the supplies heading for Murmansk went to the bottom of the sea. (See CONVOY PQ 17.)

Murphy, Lt. Audie (1924–1971)

The most-decorated American soldier of the war. Murphy was awarded the MEDAL OF HONOR for single-handedly turning back a Germany infantry company during the ALLIED CAMPAIGN IN EUROPE in Jan. 1945. He was said to have killed 241 Germans. His thirty-seven medals and decorations included the Distinguished Service Cross, the Silver Star (with oak leaf cluster), the Legion of Merit, and the Croix de Guerre (with palm).

In the action that won him the Medal of Honor, Murphy stayed behind to cover his infantrymen before a German tank attack. He climbed on a burning abandoned U.S. tank destroyer and fired its .50-cal. machine gun, killing fifty Germans and stopping the attack.

After the war he became an actor. He appeared in forty-five films, starring in *The Red Badge of Courage* (1951), *Destry* (1954) and *To Hell and Back* (1955), which was based on his autobiography. He died in a plane crash.

Murphy, Robert D. (1894–1978)

U.S. diplomat. Murphy, first secretary in the U.S. Embassy in PARIS at the fall of the city in 1940, served as the major U.S. envoy to French North Africa, which was under the control of VICHY FRANCE until the Allied NORTH AFRICA INVASION in Nov. 1942. Murphy played a key role in handling the political aspects of the NORTHWEST AFRICA CAMPAIGN. He was a negotiator of the Italian SURRENDER in 1943 and, as political adviser to Gen. DWIGHT D. EISENHOWER, helped to establish the political system for the Allied military government of Germany after the war.

Murrow, Edward R. (1908–1965)

CBS radio broadcaster who vividly reported on the BATTLE OF BRITAIN, from London rooftops during a raid. "This"—a slight pause—"is London," the deep, resonate radio voice said, and millions of American listeners sat by their radios to hear Murrow report on the German air raids on England. From Murrow Americans learned what the war was doing to ordinary people: "three red busses drawn up in a line waiting to take the homeless away ... men with white scarfs around their necks instead of collars and ties, leading dull-eyed, empty-faced women across to the busses. Most of them carried little cheap cardboard suitcases and sometimes bulging paper shopping bags. That was all they had left."

Of Murrow poet Archibald MacLeish wrote, "You burned the city of London in our houses and we felt the flames that burned it. You laid the dead of London at our doors and we knew that the dead were our dead."

Music,

see SONGS.

Musket

Code name for projected Allied AMPHIBIOUS LANDING near TARANTO, Italy, 1943.

Musketoon

Code name for British submarine *Junon* putting COMMANDOS ashore on the Norwegian coast to blow up a power station, Sept. 1942.

Mussolini, Benito (1883–1945)

Fascist leader of Italy. Mussolini's schoolteacher mother and irreligious father named him after the Mexican revolutionary leader Benito Juárez, instilling in him the rebellious mood that would put him on a political path.

As a young teacher he developed an interest in socialism and the *Italia irredenta* ("Italy unredeemed") movement, which advocated the repossession and unification of Italian-speaking territories then under control of other countries. His interest in radical politics resulted in his arrest in 1911 for leading a workers' demonstration in his native province of Forli. He spent five months in prison.

He rose steadily in the ranks of Italian socialism and in 1914 began publishing a newspaper, *Il Popolo d'Italia,* which advocated Italy's entry into World War I. When Italy did join on the side of the Allies, Mussolini entered the army. He was wounded by a hand GRENADE explosion during training.

The war drastically changed his politics. His newspaper, financed now by capitalists who feared postwar communism, turned against socialism.

Also backing him were fellow war veterans who were disillusioned by a war that had cost 600,000 Italian lives but won Italy nothing. Mussolini's final break with the left came in 1919 when he founded *Fasci di Combattimento,* which at first supported worker-controlled factories. (The name came from the emblem of ancient Roman authority: a bundle of rods, with an ax blade protruding.) But, exploiting the fears of landowners and industrialists, he veered to the right and deployed armed gangs to fight Socialists and Communists in the streets.

Mussolini began styling himself as *Il Duce* ("the leader") and organized Fascist groups throughout Italy. His black-shirted thugs ended a general strike and became such a powerful force that the Italian government virtually recognized the Fascists as an arm of the state. When Mussolini convened a Fascist convention in Naples in Oct. 1922 and called for a "March on ROME," the government panicked. King Emmanuel III asked him to form a Cabinet, and Italy's long rule under fascism began.

Mussolini swiftly took over the government, reigning as a dictator, his armed gangs now a personal army. He outlawed other political parties, and declared that "the prestige of nations is determined absolutely by their military glories and armed power." Young boys were recruited into a young Blackshirts movement. Colossal buildings soared in what the Fascists billed as the return of Imperial Rome. The Italian Fascist flag carried the inscription "The Country Is Nothing without Conquest," and Mussolini began carrying out this slogan as soon as he had built up the Italian armed forces.

On Oct. 3, 1935, he sent forces from Italian Eritrea and Italian Somaliland into Ethiopia, which Italy had futilely tried to conquer in 1896. This time Italy hurled the power of a modern army and air force against the spear-wielders of Ethiopia and, despite gallant resistance, took over Ethiopia in 1936.

Mussolini, with a new addition to Italy's African empire, now looked to the Balkans. But his dreams of a Balkans-Mediterranean empire were thwarted by the strategies of HITLER, with whom Mussolini had a complex relationship. During his own rise to power, Hitler had been inspired by Mussolini's use of armed gangs against the state and had imitated the Italian Blackshirts with his own Brown Shirts. But Hitler's designs on Austria and the 1934 murder of Austrian Chancellor Engelbert Dollfuss by Austrian NAZIS had turned Mussolini against Hitler.

Promising to support Austrian independence, Mussolini had told an Austrian official that Hitler was "a horrible sexual degenerate, a dangerous fool." Mussolini said that the rise of Nazism resembled the attacks of "the old Germanic tribes in the primeval forest against the Latin civilization of Rome." Italian fascism, he said, "is a regime that is rooted in the great cultural tradition of the Italian people; Fascism recognizes the right of the individual, it recognizes religion and family. National Socialism . . . is savage barbarism."

Despite this aversion toward Hitler in 1934, Mussolini was enthralled by Hitler and well aware of his power. On Oct. 21, 1936, Germany and Italy signed a secret protocol that promised a coordination of their foreign policy. The next month, without revealing the agreement, Mussolini, in one of his frequent arm-waving, strutting speeches, mentioned an AXIS around which other European powers "may work together," coining the word that would be used to describe the enemies of the ALLIES through World War II.

In Sept. 1937 Mussolini crossed the Alps into Germany, met an affable Hitler, and was given a grand tour of German might, climaxed by a huge rally in BERLIN. Hitler called him a man of destiny, and Mussolini, speaking in German, said, "I have a friend. I go with him through thick and thin to the very end."

An interpreter who saw the two dictators conversing was surprised by the differences between them: Mussolini "more vivacious," had a hearty laugh compared to Hitler's sneering, and had a "Caesarian head . . . with its powerful forehead and broad, square chin thrust forward under a wide mouth." But the two dictators were alike in some ways. They were both very conscious of their health. Both were vegetarians. In 1943, however, a doctor recommended by Hitler put Mussolini on a meat diet.

A few weeks after the 1937 Berlin rally Mussolini signed the ANTI-COMINTERN PACT against the So-

viet Union and, remarking about Hitler's plans to annex Austria, said "Let events take their natural course." Now that Italy and Germany were allied, Mussolini told his people, their country would never be bombed and no enemy would ever step foot on Italian soil.

Mussolini also accepted Germany's ANTI-SEMITISM as doctrine. A policy against Italy's JEWS had been implied in a cultural agreement, signed in Nov. 1938, that urged "training popular mentality along parallel lines in order to make the Italo-German association an instinctive national reaction." The next year brought the grandly named PACT OF STEEL, in which Germany and Italy agreed to "act side by side" to aid each other militarily if either country "became involved in warlike complications."

Even without the pact, Mussolini would have continued to follow Hitler into war. But Italy waited until June 10, 1940, when France had been defeated and England seemed destined to fall, to declare war on the two countries. "This," Mussolini proclaimed, "is the struggle of the peoples who are poor and eager to work against the greedy who hold a ruthless monopoly of all the wealth and GOLD of the earth." He made himself the commander of Italian armed forces and planned to ride a white horse in triumph after Italian victories.

Italy saw not victories but a series of disasters that slaughtered Italian troops and weakened civilian morale. On July 16, 1943, six days after the Allies invaded SICILY, Italian Fascist leaders met with Mussolini and asked for a session of the long-ignored Fascist Grand Council. Mussolini stalled, saying that he had a meeting with Hitler on July 19. At that meeting he had hoped to somehow get Italy out of the Pact of Steel. But, under Hitler's spell, he was unable to do so.

On July 24 the Grand Council met for the first time since Dec. 7, 1939. After listening to Mussolini's windy view of recent events, the Fascist leaders voted, 19 to 8 (with 1 abstention), to depose him. The king summoned him the following day and told him he had been removed. *Il Duce* was then arrested and taken away. The king replaced Mussolini with Marshal PIETRO BADOGLIO, chief of the Italian General Staff.

Badoglio began secret negotiations with Allied officials for an Italian SURRENDER, which he signed on Sept. 3. At that point, Mussolini was still being held by Italian authorities, who may have wanted to use delivery of him to the Allies as a bargaining chip. But Mussolini, who had moved around to various hiding places, was rescued by the daring German operation led by OTTO SKORZENY on Sept. 12. He was flown to Vienna and then to Munich, where he was reunited with his wife. On Sept. 14 he met Hitler at WOLF'S LAIR, in Rastenburg. Mussolini's son Vittorio watched the emotional meeting. "Deeply moved," he later wrote, "the two men clasped each other by the hand for a long time."

Hitler set up Mussolini in northern Italy as the head of a puppet state, the Italian Social Republic.

In return, Hitler forced him to cede TRIESTE, the Istrian Peninsula, and the South Tyrol to Germany.

Mussolini ruled his nonexistent republic from Gargagno on Lake Garda, his long-time mistress, Clara Petacci, then thirty-three, at his side. He had no real power except what the Germans doled out. He used this power once, in an act of murderous vengeance. Mussolini's oldest child, Edda, was married, through her father's arrangement, to Count GALAEZZO CIANO. For a time Ciano was considered to be a potential successor to Mussolini. Edda was Mussolini's favorite. (His son Bruno, an air force officer, died at twenty-one in a 1941 air crash. A child born in 1915 to one of his mistresses died during the war, reportedly in an institution.)

Late in Aug. 1943, the German authorities in Italy had taken Ciano into custody. In Jan. 1944

The end of Italian fascism came in April 1945 with the execution of Benito Mussolini. Captured by Italian partisans on April 27, 1945, he was shot the next day and, with his mistress, Clara Petacci, and several members of his government, publicly displayed in Milan—hanging from a gas station girder. *(Imperial War Museum)*

Mussolini ordered a show trial of Ciano and four other former Fascist Grand Council members who had voted to depose Mussolini. They were sentenced to death and shot by a firing squad on Jan. 11.

In his last days Mussolini, without consulting Hitler, thought that he might be able to bring about an end to the war and sent Vittorio to the Archbishop of Milan to see if peace talks between Germany and the Allies could be started on Italian soil, with Mussolini as a key negotiator. The archbishop forwarded the offer to the Vatican, which relayed it to Allied officials, who rejected it.

In April 1945, with the Allied ITALIAN CAMPAIGN in its decisive stage and sweeping into northern Italy, Mussolini visited his wife in Milan and urged her to flee Italy. He left Milan in a motorcade that included a car in which Clara was a passenger. On April 27, near Dongo on Lake Como, Italian partisan GUERRILLAS stopped the motorcade and pulled Mussolini and Clara from their cars. The next day they were shot, along with twelve other captured Fascist leaders.

The partisans hung the bodies, upside down, from a girder in a gas station being built in Milan. Someone bound Clara's skirt to keep her legs from being exposed. Allied officials ordered that the bodies be cut down. Mussolini was buried next to Bruno in a graveyard in Predappio, Benito Mussolini's birthplace.

Mustang,
  see P-51.

Myrt

A highly successful carrier-based reconnaissance aircraft, given the Japanese designation C6N and named *Saiun* (Painted Cloud); its Allied code name was Myrt. The plane became operational in 1944 in the recce role, but with the demise of the Japanese carrier force it flew from land bases and was also occasionally employed as a high-altitude night fighter against U.S. B-29 SUPERFORTRESS bombers. The Myrt's speed made it almost immune to interception by Allied fighters.

The Myrt first flew on May 15, 1943, with nineteen prototypes being produced to accelerate flight tests and evaluation. The first production aircraft were delivered to the Navy in Aug. 1944 although some prototypes had earlier been flown on operational sorties. Production totaled 463 aircraft. Variants included the C6N1-B TORPEDO bomber and the C6N2 and C6N3 with upgraded engines.

The aircraft was a single-engine, low-wing machine with a long, glazed canopy. It was designed by Nakajima.

Maximum speed of the C6N1 was 379 mph with a range in excess of 3,300 miles with a drop tank. Armament of the three-place aircraft was one 7.9-mm machine gun firing from the rear cockpit, with the night-fighter variant (C6N1-S) being fitted with two 20-mm cannon. It carried two crewmen.

N3N Yellow Peril

The U.S. Navy's principal basic training aircraft during the war. It was invariably known by its nickname, derived from the bright yellow color used for Navy basic trainers.

The prototype XN3N-1 flew in Aug. 1935. It was produced by the Naval Aircraft Factory in Philadelphia, Pa., with 996 being built. A few went to the Coast Guard in 1941. When the last N3Ns were discarded in 1961 (those used at the U.S. Naval Academy to teach midshipmen the rudiments of flying), it marked the end of the biplane in U.S. military service.

The N3N biplane had a large radial engine without cowling cover; the instructor and student sat in separate, open cockpits. The aircraft had a steel-tube fuselage and all-steel wings, making it a relatively rugged aircraft. It could fly as a seaplane with a single large float and small stabilizing floats under the lower of the equal-span wings, or with a conventional wheeled undercarriage for land operation.

Nagasaki

Japanese port city destroyed by the second ATOMIC BOMB used in the war. Nagasaki, a large shipbuilding and ship-repair center, also produced naval ordnance, including the specially modified TORPEDOES for the attack on PEARL HARBOR.

The atomic-bomb mission to Nagasaki on Aug. 9, 1945, was similar to the HIROSHIMA mission three days before. The bomb was to be dropped from a B-29 flying from TINIAN ISLAND. But the

The Normandy invasion was the largest amphibious operation in history, made all the more difficult by the decision to land on open beaches with artificial harbors rather than immediately trying to seize a French port. Here a dozen LSTs unload while others and scores of cargo ships stand offshore, awaiting their turn. *(U.S. Coast Guard)*

bomb, called "Fat Man," was different from "Little Boy," the Hiroshima bomb.

Fat Man was more practical than the uranium-core Little Boy because far less fissionable material (plutonium instead of uranium) was needed. But it was so complicated that its concept was tested at ALAMOGORDO, N.M. The test, on July 16, 1945, was called TRINITY. Fat Man worked on an implosion principle: Explosive charges, designed to focus their force, surrounded a core of plutonium, squeezing it to produce the chain reaction.

Elements of Fat Man were flown to Tinian from LOS ALAMOS, the New Mexico laboratory where the atomic bomb had been developed. The bomb was assembled by scientists and technicians from Los Alamos and loaded aboard a B-29 named "Bockscar" by its commander, Frederick Bock. But the pilot would be Maj. CHARLES W. SWEENEY; the weaponeer in charge of Fat Man was Navy Comdr. F. L. ASHWORTH. Unlike Little Boy, Fat Man had to be completely assembled before being placed aboard Bockscar and would be fully armed at take-off.

Because of a defective fuel pump discovered too late to repair, Bockscar carried some 600 gallons of gasoline that could not be pumped into the engines. Thus, the B-29 had to fly carrying that dead weight, cutting down its effective range.

Bockscar's primary target was Kokura, site of a major arsenal. Bockscar flew there and made three runs over the city but found cloud cover that made visual bombing impossible. The B-29 then flew to the secondary target, Nagasaki.

Bockscar would have enough fuel for one run over Nagasaki and a landing at OKINAWA, the alternative landing field. If Bockscar made more than one Nagasaki run, the crew would have to ditch in the Pacific and hope for rescue by a U.S. SUBMARINE.

Clouds over Nagasaki were so thick that Ashworth had to approve a RADAR run rather than the visual run called for in the mission plan. The run started on radar but, at the last moment, the clouds opened up and Sweeney was able to see the city below. The bombardier lined up on a stadium in the valley, but the bomb, set to detonate at 1,650 feet, exploded over ridges that confined the effects of the blast, which was equivalent to 22,000 tons of TNT.

The bomb destroyed 44 percent of the city, killing about 35,000 people and injuring 60,000, by U.S. estimates. Subsequent investigation put the death toll at 70,000 by the end of 1945 and, in the next five years, a total of 140,000, due to radiation, of which the lethal effects were not well understood at the time the two bombs were dropped. The figures indicate a death rate similar to Hiroshima's 54 percent.

Capt. William C. Bryson, who visited Nagasaki in mid-Sept. 1945, wrote his wife a description of what he saw and smelled: "A smell of death and corruption pervades the place . . . the absolute essence of death in the sense of finality without hope of resurrection."

Nagumo, Vice Adm. Chuichi (1887–1944)

Commander of the Japanese carrier striking force that attacked PEARL HARBOR and roamed throughout the Southwestern Pacific and Indian Oceans in the first few months of 1942. Nagumo had never before had anything to do with naval aviation. His appointment as commander of the First Air Fleet on the eve of the war had come as a reward for his long and active service.

Nagumo was seen as a man of action rather than introspection, happier at sea in command than in a staff job ashore. He was known as generous and outgoing, compassionate, and interested in the welfare of his men. Neither Nagumo nor his very capable Chief of Staff, Rear Adm. Ryonusuke Kusaka, was a gambler, as was Adm. ISOROKU YAMAMOTO, Commander in Chief of the Combined Fleet and advocate of the Pearl Harbor operation.

Nagumo and Kusaka saw the Pearl Harbor raid, which they had opposed, as protecting the flank of the JAPANESE CAMPAIGN IN THE FAR EAST. Even though the attack on Pearl Harbor had exceeded expectations (except for the absence of U.S. aircraft carriers), Nagumo declined to make additional strikes against the base's fuel storage and dockyard, feeling that withdrawal without loss was most important, particularly in view of other tasks awaiting his fleet. After replenishing in Japan, Nagumo's carrier fleet covered the Japanese landings in Indonesia and raided Darwin, Australia, on Feb. 19, 1942. Beginning in late March, Nagumo led a five-carrier task force into the Indian Ocean where it bombed

Colombo and Trincomalee in Ceylon and sank the British carrier *Hermes* and two cruisers, along with almost 100,000 tons of merchant shipping. Japanese aircraft losses were minimal and no ships were even damaged in the rampage. His force returned to Japan in mid-April.

Nagumo returned to changed circumstances. Yamamoto now strongly felt that failure to strike Pearl Harbor again was a mistake that could only be corrected by a major battle on Japanese terms. Once again, Nagumo's First Air Fleet (minus two fleet carriers damaged in the May 1942 battle of the CORAL SEA) would have a major role in a surprise attack: bomb MIDWAY and enemy carriers. Under Yamamoto's plan, his Combined Fleet battleships would sink the U.S. FLEET that came out to rescue the island.

Thanks to code-breaking, the U.S. Navy knew of the plan and the timing. When Japanese radio analysts in TOKYO discovered that a three-carrier U.S. force had put to sea, they notified Yamamoto, but he declined to break radio silence and tell Nagumo.

Nagumo's two objectives—bombing Midway and bombing and torpedoing enemy ships—required conflicting weapons loads on his aircraft. Because successive reports kept changing the tactical picture, Nagumo wavered between rearming his second wave with bombs and fitting them with torpedoes. All the while, U.S. Navy, Marine, and Army Air Forces aircraft were attacking fruitlessly but distractingly. Had he been granted ten more minutes of grace, Nagumo might have gained a draw or even a win in the carrier battle of Midway. Instead, three of his four fleet carriers were fatally bombed by carrier-based dive bombers. The fourth was doomed but it evaded destruction long enough to launch strikes that contributed to the sinking of the U.S. carrier *Yorktown* (CV 7).

Nagumo retained command of the First Air Fleet, consisting now of only the two carriers that had been damaged at Coral Sea, the *Shokaku* and *Zuikaku*. His conduct at the battle of the EASTERN SOLOMONS on Aug. 24, 1942, was irresolute—with some reason: his air groups were shredded during its attacks on enemy carriers. His air arm grew weaker and weaker because of actions like the battle of SANTA CRUZ on Oct. 26, 1942.

He was replaced as head of the rebuilt carrier force by Vice Adm. Jisaburo Ozawa on Nov. 16, 1942, and later given the empty command of the Japanese Central Fleet, an entity with its headquarters on SAIPAN and possessing no major warships. His 6,800 men were among the Japanese forces defeated by the U.S. Marines and soldiers in the June 1944 invasion. He committed suicide on July 6, 1944.

Nagumo's First Air Fleet had accomplished far more than had been expected in its first six months, sinking more ships and helping to occupy more territory in so short a time than any other naval force in history. Had it not been for the disaster at Midway, Nagumo might have been regarded as one of the most successful naval combat leaders of any navy.

Nanking

Capital of China from 1928 to 1937 (now Nanjing). CHIANG KAI-SHEK's Kuomintang government made this port its capital in 1928. Although Japan first invaded China in 1931, not until July 1937 did the undeclared Chinese-Japanese war sweep much of China. On Nov. 20 the Kuomintang government abandoned Nanking and withdrew to Chungking. The Japanese occupation—known in the West as the "rape of Nanking"—shocked the civilized world. More than 50,000 civilians were slaughtered and 20,000 cases of rape were later documented. Japan established a puppet regime, the Reformed Government of the Republic of China, in Nanking. After the SURRENDER of Japan, the Chinese government moved back to Nanking, which remained the capital until it was occupied by Chinese Communist forces in 1949.

Napalm

Powder used to thicken gasoline—called "jellied gasoline"—for use in BOMBS. The substance ignited easily and clung to the ground, foliage, or buildings as it burned. Napalm bombs consisted of aircraft jettisonable fuel (drop) tanks, filled with the substance and fitted with an igniter.

The first combat use of napalm was in the air attacks supporting the invasion of TINIAN in June 1944. It was used in subsequent assaults in the Pacific, being dropped by fighter-bombers and heavy bombers. For example, during sixteen days of "softening-up" attacks against IWO JIMA in Jan. 1945, B-24 LIBERATOR bombers dropped 1,111 drums of napalm.

The term *napalm* was derived from the aluminum salts of *na*phthalenic and *palm*itic acids.

Nate

The Ki-27 Type 97 (Allied code name Nate) was the standard fighter of the Japanese Army Air Force from 1937 to 1942 (when it was replaced by the Ki-43 OSCAR). The Nate saw combat in China and Manchuria before the outbreak of World War II. The aircraft performed poorly over Manchuria against the Soviets. It was then flown by the Army throughout the South Pacific area from Dec. 1941 until late 1942. In the final stages of the war a few Nates flew as KAMIKAZE aircraft, carrying 1,102 pounds of BOMBS.

The first prototype flew on Oct. 15, 1936, and it entered production the following year. There were several modifications during the production run of 3,398 aircraft (by Nakajima and by the Manchurian Aircraft Manufacturing Co.).

A simple design, Nate was Japan's first low-wing monoplane fighter and the first to have an enclosed cockpit. It had a fixed landing gear with "spats."

The Ki-27b model was rated at 286 mph with a maximum range of 390 miles. Armament of the single-place aircraft was two 7.7-mm machine guns, and 220 pounds of bombs could be carried.

National Defense Research Committee,

see OFFICE OF SCIENTIFIC RESEARCH AND DEVELOPMENT.

National Guard

U.S. military force. Because of the worsening situation in Europe, a congressional resolution of Aug. 27, 1940, ordered the National Guard into active military service for twelve consecutive months. The units were inducted in Sept.–Oct. 1941 with a total of 300,034 men being brought into active service. They were organized into eighteen infantry DIVISIONS, twenty-nine aviation observation SQUADRONS, and several nondivisional units.

With the Japanese attack on PEARL HARBOR, the National Guard units were retained on active duty for the duration of the war. These units fought in most theaters—nine divisions in North Africa and Europe and nine in the Pacific, suffering 185,561 battle casualties, and receiving numerous unit and individual AWARDS AND DECORATIONS, including fourteen MEDALS OF HONOR.

At the end of the war all National Guardsmen were separated from federal service and, for a short period, there was no National Guard.

The National Guard developed from the colonial militia concept, with two Massachusetts units tracing their origins to the year 1636. The term *National Guard* was first applied to units of the New York State militia in 1824.

National Redoubt

A mythical last-ditch Alpine stronghold where HITLER was to direct the resurrection of a defeated Germany. Allied intelligence believed in the existence of a "National Redoubt" in the fastness at Hitler's mountain retreat, BERCHTESGADEN. Fear of this redoubt affected Gen. DWIGHT D. EISENHOWER'S strategy in the closing weeks of the war. After linking with Soviet forces at the Elbe River, he ordered the VI CORPS southeast, ready to take on what turned out to be the phantom Germans of the redoubt.

A U.S. intelligence report described the redoubt in lurid terms: "Here, defended by nature and by the most efficient secret weapons yet invented, the powers that have hitherto guided Germany will survive to reorganize her resurrection; here armaments will be manufactured in bombproof factories, food and equipment will be stored in vast underground caverns and a specially selected corps of young men will be trained in guerrilla warfare, so that a whole underground army can be fitted and directed to liberate Germany from the occupying forces." Eisenhower's chief of staff, Gen. WALTER BEDELL SMITH, solemnly accepted this report (which, historian WILLIAM SHIRER said, appeared to have been written by "British and American mystery writers"). In a postwar assessment, Gen. OMAR BRADLEY wrote: "Not until after the campaign ended were we to learn that this Redoubt existed largely in the imaginations of a few fanatic Nazis. It grew into so exaggerated a scheme that I am astonished we could have believed it as innocently as we did. But while it persisted, this legend of the Redoubt was too ominous a threat to ignore and in consequence it shaped our tactical thinking during the closing weeks of the war."

National Socialist German Workers' Party

The political organization, known as the NAZI Party, founded by ADOLF HITLER. He built the Nazi Party to replace the almost defunct German Workers' Party, which he joined in 1919 and took control of in 1921. The party initially was legitimate, one of many in the democratic process of the fledgling WEIMAR REPUBLIC. But it soon became the instrument of Hitler's total power.

In 1923 Hitler's storm troopers (see SA) surrounded a Munich beer hall where political rivals were holding a rally. Hitler, firing a pistol at the ceiling, attempted to take over the rally and declared the start of a revolution. The next day police broke up a Nazi march in Munich, killing sixteen Nazis (three policemen also were killed). Hitler and eight others were tried and convicted of conspiracy to commit treason. The attendant publicity catapulted the Nazi Party to national notoriety and began its ascendancy to power.

The Nazi Party emphasized nationalism, combined with ANTI-SEMITISM, and gave only lip service to socialism while savagely attacking Communists. German industrialists and powerful conservatives, fearful about voters' drift to the left, allied themselves with the Nazi Party, also known by its German initials NSDAP. Frantic over the worldwide economic depression of 1929, Germans turned to the Nazis in increasing numbers. Hitler said of his party in a 1933 speech: "We are the result of the distress for which others are responsible."

In 1933, when the Nazi Party became powerful enough to challenge President PAUL VON HINDENBURG, he made Hitler chancellor and gave the Nazi Party three of the eleven seats in a coalition cabinet. Hitler convinced the cabinet to agree to elections. But the Nazis, using their SA storm troopers to club down the opposition, began the process that doomed the Weimar Republic.

On the night of Feb. 2, 1933, the Reichstag building, which housed the federal Parliament, was gutted by fire. The Nazis blamed the Communists, and history, although lacking solid evidence, blames the Nazis. A week later the Nazis won 44

percent of the vote, increased their seats in the Parliament, and, by allying with the Nationalist Party, were able to pass the Law to Remove the Distress of People and State. The law stripped the Parliament of virtually all of its power and essentially handed it to Hitler.

All other parties were then banned, and the Nazi Party became an organ of the state. As the supreme leader or *Der Führer,* Hitler was the dictator of both the nation and the party. Serving under him was *Reichsleitung,* the Reich leadership, made up of trusted aides who oversaw specific party and thus national interests. Under this scheme, a Nazi-chosen *Gauleiter* or district leader, watched over each *Gau* or district. These leaders, controlling political, economic, and labor affairs in their districts, became petty despots answerable only to the Reich leadership.

Hitler, who traced his party's origins to Frederick the Great, saw the Nazis' ideals reflected in the Nordic "superman" envisioned by his hero, the composer Richard Wagner. The party viewed the *Reich,* the empire, as the rightful heritage of the Germans, whom Hitler called "the highest human species given by the grace of the Almighty to this Earth."

Party members carried a forty-eight-page membership booklet that included a foreword by Hitler, the names of the sixteen Munich *Putsch* "martyrs," a photograph of and personal details about the member, spaces for contribution stamps, and party regulations.

Navajo Code Talkers

Navajo Indians who served in the U.S. Marine Corps as radio operators speaking a code in their language. The Navajos, working in pairs as transmitter and receiver, baffled Japanese electronic eavesdroppers, giving the Marines secure communications in several Pacific battles; at IWO JIMA code talkers handled more than 800 messages in forty-eight hours. In the impenetrable code, many Navajo words were adapted to war: bird names for warplanes, "eggs" for BOMBS, "rabbit trail" for road. The names of places and people were spelled out, with each letter of the alphabet spoken as one, two, or three Navaho words.

About 300 Navajos served as Marine code talkers.

Some, recruited directly at the Navajo reservation on the Arizona–New Mexico border, were barely fifteen years old when they went to war. A few were temporarily taken prisoner—by fellow Marines, who mistook them for Japanese spies.

Naval Air Transport Service

U.S. naval aviation group that provided transport of high-priority men, parts, and supplies to the FLEET. The Naval Air Transport Service (NATS) was established on Dec. 12, 1941, with a single flying boat. The following March the first of thirteen Navy transport squadrons that would serve in NATS during the war was commissioned at Norfolk, Va. The squadrons were soon operating scheduled flights to major naval air bases throughout the world, with additional priority flights being flown as needed.

On Dec. 1, 1943, the Naval Air Ferry command was commissioned as a wing of NATS to ferry naval aircraft from manufacturing plants to embarkation points for ultimate delivery to the fleet.

NATS was reorganized as a fleet command in March 1945 to bring it under the immediate direction of the Commander in Chief U.S. Fleet and subordinate fleet commanders. That same month NATS was assigned responsibility for evacuating wounded naval personnel from forward areas.

In addition to regular Navy transport squadrons, NATS supervised large contract operations by Pan American Airways and American Export Airlines. By the end of the war NATS was flying some 3,600,000 plane miles per month.

Navy Department

Administrative headquarters for the U.S. Navy and Marine Corps, located in temporary buildings on the Mall in WASHINGTON during the war. Although the Coast Guard was a part of the Navy in World War II, some administrative functions were retained by the Treasury Department.

The Secretary of the Navy was head of the Navy Department and a member of the President's Cabinet. The post of secretary was held by W. FRANKLIN KNOX from July 1940 until his death on April 28, 1944; he was succeeded on May 19 by the under secretary of the Navy, JAMES V. FORRESTAL.

His principal military subordinate was the Chief of Naval Operations (CNO). Adm. HAROLD R. STARK served as CNO until March 1942 when Adm. ERNEST J. KING, the CinC U.S. Fleet, additionally took on the position of CNO. (That was the first time the two posts were combined since the position of CNO was established in 1915.)

Nazi

Acronym formed from the first two letters of *National* and the second syllable of *sozialist* in *Nationalsozialistische Deutsche Arbeiterpartei* (NSDAP), the NATIONAL SOCIALIST GERMAN WORKERS' PARTY.

The Nazis' stiff-arm salute was universally used by civilians and Party members. The Nazi salute replaced the traditional military salute in 1944 following the JULY 20 PLOT on HITLER'S life.

Nazi-Soviet Pact,

see NONAGGRESSION PACT.

Nehru, Jawaharlal (1889–1964)

Indian political leader. A nationalist educated in England, Nehru headed the Indian National Congress and was second only to MOHANDAS GANDHI in the long political struggle for Indian independence from England. Going beyond Gandhi's acceptance of dominion status for India, Nehru demanded absolute independence and set an anti-British course that threatened the British war effort in Asia. He, along with Gandhi and other nationalist leaders who resisted British war activities, was arrested in Aug. 1942 and imprisoned until June 1945. In 1947 Nehru became the first prime minister of newly independent India and remained in office until his death.

Nell

The G3M Type 96 medium bomber, given the Allied code name Nell, was the backbone of the Japanese Navy's land-based air arm at the beginning of the war. It flew against targets in China from bases on Formosa beginning in Aug. 1937; subsequently, G3M squadrons were based in China. Although already being phased out of service in favor of the G4M BETTY, the twin-engine Nell was flown extensively at the beginning of the war. Sixty of these planes, flying from bases in INDOCHINA with twenty-six Betty bombers, sank the British CAPITAL SHIPS *PRINCE OF WALES* and *REPULSE* on Dec. 10, 1941. During the last three years of the war the planes flew mostly as transports, GLIDER tugs, and trainers.

The prototype G3M1 flew in July 1935 followed by three additional prototypes and twenty-one service aircraft being built before an engine upgrade led to the designation G3M2. Some of the early aircraft were modified to serve as ten-place transports (redesignated L3Y1). Mitsubishi production reached a total of 1,100 aircraft, including planes with further-improved engines.

The Nell was a twin-engine, mid-wing aircraft with a twin-tail configuration. The undercarriage retracted partially into the radial engine nacelles. Unusual for a bomber, the aircraft had a solid nose with glazed dorsal and, in some models, side blisters for machine guns. Their armament, however, was unable to defend them against Chinese fighters when they struck at targets beyond the range of their own escort fighters.

The early designs for the aircraft provide for three *retractable* gun turrets—two dorsal and one ventral—each housing a single 7.7-mm machine gun. In response to the need for more defensive armament, the dorsal turrets were deleted and the upper blister fitted with a single, flexible 20-mm cannon (the nose 7.7-mm turret was retained); the side blisters were fitted with 7.7-mm guns and a fourth 20-mm cannon could be fired from the cockpit. The plane was designed from the outset to carry an aerial TORPEDO; alternatively, 2,200 pounds of BOMBS could be carried externally, under the fuselage.

Maximum speed was 232 mph for the G3M2 with a maximum range of 2,770 miles. The crew numbered seven in the regunned aircraft.

Nelson, Donald M. (1888–1959)

Industrial executive who became chairman of the U.S. War Production Board. Nelson was executive vice president of Sears, Roebuck and Co. when President ROOSEVELT appointed him to the National Defense Advisory Commission in 1940. In Aug. 1941, after serving as director of purchases for the Office of Production Management, Nelson was appointed director of the Supply Priorities and Allocations Board, which was replaced in Jan. 1942 by the War Production Board (WPB). As WPB chairman, Nelson presided over the greatest WAR PRODUCTION achievement ever known. Cutting off civilian goods, fighting with the military over priorities, he won few friends.

One of his most controversial decisions came in June 1944 when he issued a regulation allowing plants that had fulfilled military contracts to begin reconversion to peacetime production. The war was far from over; that month Allied troops had launched the NORMANDY INVASION and the invasion of the MARIANA ISLANDS. The armed services, fearing a shortage of matériel as a result of the reconversion authorization, fought it in WASHINGTON, with the aid of some contractors. In the political fighting that followed, Nelson lost even more support and in Aug. 1944 was eased out of the WPB when Roosevelt made him his "personal representative" to Chinese leader CHIANG KAI-SHEK, a position he held until May 1945.

Neptune

Code name for naval aspects of Overlord (NORMANDY INVASION), June 1944.

Netherlands

Capital: The Hague, pop. 8,728,560 (1938). As war neared in the late summer of 1939, Queen Wilhelmina of The Netherlands and King Leopold III of Belgium jointly offered to mediate between Germany and England and France. Holland declared its neutrality, while prudently mobilizing. At stake was not only the safety of Holland itself but also a colonial empire that included the DUTCH EAST INDIES, which was coveted by Japan, Germany's AXIS partner.

But the EUROPEAN WAR began on Sept. 1, and within a few weeks German troops were massed on Holland's border. By the spring of 1940, Holland's military leaders knew it was only a matter of time before the Germans would invade. On April 9 all military leaves were canceled and a month later pro-NAZI Dutch politicians were arrested and interned.

On May 10 the German BLITZKRIEG struck, confusing The Hague with two false air raids as German planes appeared above the capital but did not drop bombs. (See FRANCE AND LOW COUNTRIES CAMPAIGN.) The invaders gave the Dutch an ultimatum:

cease resistance or ROTTERDAM, Utrecht, and other cities would be destroyed.

While the Dutch attempted to negotiate, the bombing of Rotterdam began and much of the city was destroyed; 814 persons were killed and 78,000 lost their homes. Queen Wilhelmina and the leading members of her government escaped to LONDON, where a government-in-exile was established. Most of the Dutch Navy also escaped.

German policy sought to make Holland a "Germanic" state. A Dutch engineer, Anton Mussert, had founded a Dutch National Socialist Party with Nazi sympathies. He was appointed Reich Commissioner for the Netherlands and brought Dutch Nazis into the government.

Anti-Jewish laws were imposed soon after the German conquest, with Arthur Seyess-Inquart as Reich Commissioner. He sealed off Amsterdam's old Jewish quarter and seized hundreds of JEWS after a clash between Jews and German troops. About 400 young Jewish men were sent to Mauthausen CONCENTRATION CAMP and executed. Partially in response to the seizure, a general strike was staged on Feb. 25, 1941. The German Army brutally put down the strike and imposed martial law. SS troops rounded up 110,000 Dutch Jews, including many hidden by Christians. More than three years later, in Aug. 1944, ANNE FRANK was found. Her diary immortalized a young girl's courage. Most of the Dutch Jews were sent to AUSCHWITZ and only 5,000 to 6,000 survived.

"The Dutch never accepted the German contention that, for them, the war was over," wrote Foreign Minister Eelco Nicholaas van Kleffens in an account of Dutch life under occupation. "Listening in secret to the forbidden broadcasts from London, they acknowledged only the Netherlands government in London, and their acts of resistance and sabotage grew more audacious as time passed."

The Dutch underground saved countless Allied fliers who parachuted into Holland or survived crash landings. (After the war, Dutch excavators, restoring the dikes of flooded lands, found the wreckage of more than 7,000 downed Allied and German planes.)

As Dutch resistance movements intensified their SABOTAGE and killings of German troops toward the end of the war, Seyess-Inquart ordered more and more retaliation. About 4,000 Dutch men and women were shot. Another 25,000 starved to death after the government-in-exile in Sept. 1944 ordered that railways in the south of Holland be sabotaged to aid the ALLIED CAMPAIGN IN EUROPE. On trial for WAR CRIMES at Nuremberg, Seyess-Inquart insisted that he had been "only harsh." He was found guilty and hanged. Mussert was arrested in May 1945, tried as a collaborator, and hanged on May 7, 1946.

Neutrality Act

Law prohibiting U.S. involvement in other nations' conflicts. In Aug. 1935, reacting to growing fears of war in Europe, Congress passed a Neutrality Act that prohibited the sale of munitions to belligerents. In Jan. 1937, a second Neutrality Act extended the prohibition to both sides in the SPANISH CIVIL WAR. The third Neutrality Act, passed in May 1937, gave some discretionary power to the President but still maintained the neutrality policy.

The act of 1935, made further restrictive by amendment in 1937, prohibited U.S. firms from exporting arms, either directly or by transshipment, to any belligerent. Isolationists considered the legislation the best way to keep the United States from involvement in a war in Europe.

Under the 1937 act (reluctantly signed into law by President ROOSEVELT), when the President proclaimed that a state of war existed between nations, the warring nations could not receive any U.S. arms or loans. The act empowered the President to forbid U.S. citizens to travel on belligerents' ships; to forbid U.S. ships to carry U.S. goods; and to force belligerents to pay for goods before shipment, a policy called "cash and carry."

When the EUROPEAN WAR began in Sept. 1939, President Roosevelt called Congress into special session for the purpose of revising the Neutrality Act yet again. This time, after sometimes stormy debate, Congress passed legislation specifically repealing the embargo on the sale of munitions. The cash-and-carry policy was retained.

On Sept. 5, President Roosevelt issued his first neutrality proclamation, declaring that the use of U.S. territorial waters for hostile operations would be regarded as unfriendly, offensive, and a violation of U.S. neutrality. A day earlier, the U.S. Chief of

Naval Operations, Adm. HAROLD R. STARK, ordered the establishment of aircraft and ship patrols to observe and report the movement of foreign warships within designated areas in the western Atlantic; the reporting areas were soon expanded to the eastern coast of Canada down to the West Indies.

At the time, the predominant U.S. naval strength was in the Pacific under the Commander in Chief Pacific Fleet. In Jan. 1939 an Atlantic Squadron had been formed; on Jan. 1, 1941, the squadron was reorganized as the U.S. Atlantic Fleet under the command of Adm. ERNEST J. KING.

A NEUTRALITY PATROL was carried out in the Atlantic area by Navy and Coast Guard ships and aircraft, which had several encounters with German U-BOATS. In the most serious incident, the U.S. DESTROYER *REUBEN JAMES* (DD 245) was torpedoed and sunk on Oct. 31, 1941. A week later Congress revoked the Neutrality Act. Two amendments were passed: one to permit the arming of American merchant ships to defend themselves (see ARMED GUARD) and the other to abolish the restriction that prevented American-flag merchant ships from entering European waters.

Neutrality Patrol

Operation begun on Sept. 5, 1939, to enforce provisions of the U.S. NEUTRALITY ACT. The patrol was conducted by U.S. Navy ships of the Atlantic Squadron (later the Atlantic Fleet) and aircraft, both land- and carrier-based, the former including P2Y and PBY CATALINA flying boats. The first non-U.S. base used for Neutrality Patrol forces was Bermuda, one of several sites acquired by the United States in the LEND-LEASE exchange of overage destroyers to Britain for bases.

On Nov. 15, 1940, a Navy seaplane tender arrived in Bermuda to support PBY operations from there. Another tender arrived at Argentia, Newfoundland (another Lend-Lease base) on May 15, 1941, to support PBY flights. An airfield was soon under construction at Argentia. PBYs from Patrol Squadron 52 at Argentia helped to search for the German battleship *BISMARCK* in the North Atlantic in late May. (The German warship was located by a British PBY that had a U.S. naval liaison officer on board.)

There were several U.S. warship encounters with German U-BOATS after HITLER proclaimed the seas off Iceland a danger zone for Allied and neutral shipping. On Sept. 4, 1941, the U.S. DESTROYER *GREER* (DD 145) was 175 miles from Reykjavík, Iceland, when she made contact with and trailed a German submarine; the U-boat fired a TORPEDO at the destroyer, which then counterattacked with DEPTH CHARGES. Neither ship was damaged.

On Oct. 17 the destroyer *Kearny* (DD 432) was torpedoed by a U-boat while helping protect a British convoy. With eleven killed and twenty-four wounded, the *Kearny* was able to reach Iceland under her own power. The next U-boat attack against an American destroyer was fatal. On Oct. 31 the twenty-one-year-old *REUBEN JAMES* (DD 245) was some 600 miles west of Ireland when a U-boat torpedo struck her. Only forty-five of some 160 men aboard the destroyer survived. The U-boat escaped unscathed.

While the nation was still technically at peace, the Neutrality Patrol helped to avenge the attacks on American destroyers when, on Nov. 6, off the coast of Brazil a U.S. CRUISER and destroyer intercepted and captured the German blockade runner *Odenwald*, which was en route to Germany from Japan with a cargo of 3,800 tons of vitally needed rubber and other cargo. Because the United States was not at war, there was a formal question about the legality of the capture. Accordingly, the U.S. force commander declared that the ship was captured as a "suspected slaver"!

Cutters and planes of the U.S. Coast Guard also participated in the Neutrality Patrol. (The Coast Guard was transferred to the Navy from the Treasury Department on Nov. 1, 1941.)

New Britain

Largest island in the Bismarck Archipelago, northeast of NEW GUINEA. The island, mandated from Germany to Australia after World War I, was invaded by Japanese forces in Jan. 1942. Japan made a stronghold of RABAUL, the chief town, on the eastern tip of the crescent-shaped island. From Rabaul the Japanese commanded New Guinea and the SOLOMON ISLANDS. The destruction or capture of Rabaul thus became a prime Allied objective.

On Dec. 26, 1943, the 1st Marine DIVISION landed at Cape Gloucester, at the western tip of

New Britain. Secondary landings were made at Tauali and Arawe on the southern coast. Monsoons—16 inches of rain falling in a single day—and violent winds gave the invaders more opposition than enemy troops. Falling trees alone killed twenty-five Marines. Japanese attempts to repulse the landings failed. The Marines' main objective was the airfield at Cape Gloucester, which was secured on Dec. 29.

From here were launched frequent air raids on Rabaul as part of a strategy that called for isolating the highly fortified complex of Japanese bases and airfields rather than launching a costly assault.

New Caledonia

A French island strategically located on the northeast approach to Australia. The onetime penal colony declared itself to be FREE FRENCH territory in July 1940 and it quickly became an Allied base.

The first U.S. forces arrived in March 1942 and formed the Americal DIVISION (*Ameri*can-New *Cal*edonia), the only U.S. division in the war to have a name instead of a number. (In 1954 it was redesignated the 23rd Infantry Division.) The island also served as a landing site for U.S. aircraft being ferried to Australia. Its chief town, Nouméa, for a time was the headquarters for the South Pacific Forces and Area naval command.

New Galahad

Code name for U.S. long-range penetration group operations in Burma.

New Georgia

Group of islands in the SOLOMON ISLANDS. The chief island, about 50 miles long and 10 miles wide, was invaded by the Japanese in Nov. 1942. A Japanese airfield here was used for attacks on U.S. bases in the Solomons, particularly GUADALCANAL. U.S. strategists needed to gain control of the air over the area to press the U.S. SOLOMONS–NEW GUINEA CAMPAIGN.

One aspect of the campaign was the isolating of the major Japanese base at RABAUL in NEW GUINEA. By taking New Georgia and moving up the Solomons toward New Guinea, U.S. air forces would be in position to hammer at Rabaul.

The AMPHIBIOUS LANDINGS on New Georgia consisted of six separate operations. The first landings were made on June 21, 1943, when a Marine force took a 3-inch (76-mm) coastal gun at the southern end of the island. The main landings began on June 30 when Marine and Army forces went ashore on Rendova Island, across the lagoon from the Japanese air base at Munda Point on New Georgia Island. On July 5 the 43rd Infantry DIVISION hit New Georgia.

Meanwhile, in Kula Gulf, between New Georgia and Kolombangara Island, Japanese transports and destroyers were heading for Kolombangara and Vella Lavella Islands to reinforce garrisons. A U.S. force of DESTROYERS and CRUISERS attacked the Japanese, taking out two destroyers, but the cruiser *Helena* (CL 50) was hit by three TORPEDOES and sunk.

Ashore, the Americans met fierce resistance but were aided by close support from Marine air squadrons based on Guadalcanal. The Munda airfield was finally taken on Aug. 5. Bypassing heavily defended Kolombangara, U.S. and New Zealand forces on Aug. 15 took Vella Lavella.

New Guinea

One of the world's largest islands, separated from Australia by the Torres Strait. When the war began, the western half was a Dutch colony and largely unexplored; the eastern half, which included Papua, was under British and Australian administration. New Guinea marked the farthest southern conquest of the Japanese's vast Pacific offensive in late 1941 and early 1942.

At the beginning of the Japanese drive, most of Australia's troops were in North Africa fighting alongside the British Eighth Army. Only a relative handful of soldiers guarded New Guinea on Australia's northern flank. When the Japanese landed on the northern coast of New Guinea in early March 1942, the invasion was unopposed. The Australian garrison had withdrawn. But the Australians knew they had to hold PORT MORESBY, capital of Papua, on the southern coast because if the Japanese were to take it, their bombers could attack Australia.

Although a major Japanese invasion force had been turned back in the battle of the CORAL SEA in

May 1942, the Japanese had strong points at Lae, site of a key air base; Buna, across the Papua peninsula from Port Morseby, and Finschhafen, an old German fort guarding the port at the tip of Huon Bay on the northern coast.

When Gen. DOUGLAS MACARTHUR launched his phase of the U.S. SOLOMONS–NEW GUINEA CAMPAIGN at the end of 1942, he began at Buna, where about 7,000 Japanese stood off a combined U.S.-Australian force. MacArthur ordered Lt. Gen. ROBERT L. EICHELBERGER to take command in the field, relieve the commanding general of a U.S. DIVISION, and "take Buna or don't come back alive."

Eichelberger relieved several Army officers and launched an attack that took Buna in thirty-two days. Next came Lae, where MacArthur launched two assaults, by sea and by air. On Sept. 4, Australian troops landed near Lae and the next day U.S. paratroopers made an AIRBORNE assault on Nadzab, 20 miles northwest of Lae, which was taken on Sept. 16 as the Japanese defenders fled into the jungle, where many died of hunger and disease. Finschhafen fell on Oct. 2 to an Australian force that had landed from U.S. amphibious ships on Sept. 22.

In the second phase of the reconquest of New Guinea, MacArthur swept along the north coast, sidestepping some concentrations of Japanese troops to let them "wither on the vine." Isolated between Allied-held bases and cut off from supplies because of Allied control of the air and sea, thousands of Japanese starved. Some tried to grow their own food while being preyed upon by vengeful natives who had been treated like slaves under Japanese occupation. By early 1944, Allied forces held most of eastern New Guinea. HOLLANDIA, taken in April 1944, became a major military base for the invasion to liberate the Philippines. Although the SURRENDER of Japan was on Aug. 14, 1945, the final surrender of Japan's New Guinea forces did not take place until Sept 11.

New Zealand

Capital: Wellington, pop. 1,624,714 (est. 1939).
A self-governing dominion of the BRITISH COMMONWEALTH, New Zealand declared war against Germany when England did, but in a separate action. New Zealand forces fought in Greece, CRETE, Libya, the NORTH AFRICA CAMPAIGN, and in the battle for CASSINO during the ITALIAN CAMPAIGN. Maori tribesmen, exempt from conscription, formed a volunteer battalion that served in the Middle East. New Zealand imposed rationing of its plentiful meat and dairy products so that as much food as possible could be sent to England.

Newsreels

Short news films usually shown between full-length features when people went to the MOVIES. Most Americans got their first view of modern war through the newsreels before PEARL HARBOR. The war came into darkened movie houses, between Depression-era comedies and gangster films, scenes of death and terror competing with scenes of imagined glamour and fake gunfire. Through newsreels Americans saw the Japanese bombing Chinese cities in the early 1930s; German and Italian planes strafing refugees in the SPANISH CIVIL WAR; and the events leading up to the EUROPEAN WAR: British Prime Minister NEVILLE CHAMBERLAIN with his umbrella outside Number 10 Downing Street after the MUNICH PACT, the massed SWASTIKA flags of NAZI Germany at rallies for HITLER, the PANZER columns rumbling into Prague.

Newsreels covered the war, along with earthquakes and floods, as exciting imagery. The war scenes were mosaics of far-off events, which the moviegoer later put together with information from the other two media for understanding the war: daily newspapers and radio news broadcasts. When the United States entered the war, newsreels became more susceptible to U.S. government CENSORSHIP because it was easier to control the movement of cameras than it was the reporting of WAR CORRESPONDENTS. Tied more to patriotic bond rallies and press agentry gimmicks of Hollywood, newsreels lost their impact, giving way to a new medium: the documentary film, which wedded the real-scene filming of the newsreel to the story-telling tradition of the movies. Outstanding documentaries included *The Fighting Lady*, filmed aboard the AIRCRAFT CARRIER *Yorktown* (CV 10) during action in the Pacific; *The Battle of Midway*; and *With the Marines at Tarawa*.

Nicaragua

Capital: Managua, pop. 983,160 (est. 1940). Anastasio Somoza, named president of Nicaragua in March 1939, was in Washington less than a month later, meeting with President ROOSEVELT, thus beginning his four decades of close dealings with the United States. He got a commitment of U.S. funds for the building of a cross-country military highway, the appointment of a U.S. Army officer to start Nicaragua's first military academy, and the first payment on $4,000,000 in loans. On Dec. 9, 1941, Nicaragua declared war on Japan, Germany, and Italy, and confiscated the properties of their nationals in Nicaragua.

Nick

Highly successful Japanese night fighter. The Kawasaki Ki-45 *Toryu* (Dragon Slayer) was a twin-engine Army Air Force aircraft, employed as a night fighter in the Southwest Pacific from 1942 and extensively in the Philippines in 1944, and later for the defense of the Japanese home islands. It could also carry small BOMBS—as well as cannon—for ground attack and antishipping roles; at the end of the war it was also used for KAMIKAZE attacks.

The Nick prototypes, the first of which flew in early 1939, were plagued with engine problems. When an appropriate power plant was available, the aircraft was ordered into production in Oct. 1941, officially rated as a "heavy fighter." A total of 1,698 aircraft were built, the Army's only operational night fighter.

The Nick variants carried a heavy gun armament—one 37-mm cannon and two 20-mm cannon firing forward, and a single 7.9-mm flexible machine gun in the rear cockpit. One aircraft was tested with a 75-mm antitank gun, but it was too heavy for the aircraft's light frame. Two 551-pound bombs or drop tanks could be carried under the wings.

The plane had a conventional configuration with an elliptical wing, a solid, pointed nose, and a large cockpit with a rear position for the radioman-gunner. Some models fitted with RADAR in the nose had no nose guns but two upward-firing 20-mm guns plus the 37-mm cannon in a ventral housing. The main undercarriage retracted into the radial engine nacelles.

Maximum speed for the Ki-45 KAIa variant was 340 mph with a range of 1,400 miles. It was flown by a two-man crew.

Niemöller, Pastor Martin (1892–1984)

Protestant churchman who rallied Christians against the NAZIS. He was famous for his statement on how the Nazis were able to take over Germany:

First they came for the socialists, and I did not
  speak out—
because I was not a socialist.
Then they came for the trade unionists, and I did
  not speak out—
because I was not a trade unionist.
Then they came for the Jews, and I did not speak
  out—
because I was not a Jew.
Then they came for me—
and there was no one left to speak for me.

Niemöller was the leader of the Confessional Church, which claimed adherence to fundamental Lutheran beliefs and opposed the pro-Nazi German Christian Church. He was the vicar of the Church of Jesus Christ at Dahlem, a Berlin suburb. A German submarine commander in World War I, he was a strong German nationalist. He morally opposed HITLER and preached against ANTI-SEMITISM, CONCENTRATION CAMPS, and Nazi philosophy.

In his Sunday sermon on June 27, 1937, he told a jammed church, "No more are we ready to keep silence at man's behest when God commands us to speak." Three days later he was arrested and shortly thereafter placed in a concentration camp. He was one of about 800 Confessional Church leaders arrested in 1937. He was a prisoner at DACHAU when U.S. forces liberated the camp in April 1945.

Night of the Long Knives,

see SA.

Nightshirt

Code name for British projects to increase the effectiveness of a ship's ASDIC (SONAR) by injecting oil and then bubbles underwater to reduce propeller noises.

Nimitz, Fleet Adm. Chester W. (1885–1966)

Nimitz commanded the immense U.S. Navy effort in the Pacific with little self-promotion but great confidence, based on a career that had already shown a flexibility of mind and a firmness of character. His interests before World War II ranged from SUBMARINES—he was the Navy's expert on diesel engines—to naval aviation—in 1923–1924 he devised the circular screen formation that was later adopted for carrier TASK FORCES in the war. His commands included submarine units, a heavy CRUISER, cruiser DIVISION, and BATTLESHIP division.

When PEARL HARBOR was attacked, Nimitz was a rear admiral serving as chief of the Bureau of Navigation, which oversaw personnel matters. With the need for a new Pacific Fleet commander to replace Adm. HUSBAND E. KIMMEL at Pearl Harbor, someone with Nimitz's intelligence and flexibility was the obvious choice. He took command amidst the wreckage of the Hawaiian naval base on Dec. 31, 1941. Faced with the shock and despair that pervaded the fleet, Nimitz chose to replace only one of Kimmel's aides with his own, retaining virtually all other members of Kimmel's staff. The act preserved the experience and restored the morale in a very capable group of officers.

Early in his career, Nimitz was known for his "serene self-control," a strong grounding in military and naval art, "dedication to duty, decisiveness, utter fearlessness, and unswerving loyalty to seniors and subordinates." He also prized the intelligence that his code-breaking units were deriving from interception of Japanese communications, and he used the information often and well. Nimitz showed himself to be a keen judge of his subordinates, promoting personalities as diverse as WILLIAM F. HALSEY, RAYMOND A. SPRUANCE, and THOMAS C. KINKAID. Nimitz gave second chances to many of his commanders, most of whom can be said to have redeemed themselves.

Nimitz was Commander in Chief Pacific Fleet and of the Pacific Ocean Area (CinCPOA) UNIFIED COMMAND for most of the war. As CinCPOA he directed all U.S. military forces in the Central Pacific, and provided support to the Southwest Pacific forces of Gen. DOUGLAS MACARTHUR. Nimitz thus had to work with two strong personalities: Adm. ERNEST J. KING, Commander in Chief U.S. Fleet and Chief of Naval Operations, and MacArthur.

In strategic terms, Nimitz and King believed that a drive to take the Japanese island groups in the Central Pacific offered the best chance to draw the Japanese fleet into battle. MacArthur advocated a drive along the NEW GUINEA coast to the Philippines. Eventually they compromised by pursuing both lines of attack—a highly successful strategy. The major problem of strategy arose over the issue of whether to invade Formosa or the Philippines in 1944; the JOINT CHIEFS OF STAFF and President ROOSEVELT had difficulty coming to a decision and in a unique session, Roosevelt met with MacArthur and Nimitz at Pearl Harbor (without the JCS). MacArthur's Philippine strategy won.

After an initial period in which he had to more or less patiently carry out only an "offensive defensive" strategy, beginning in 1943 Nimitz commanded immense resources, centered on fast-carrier task forces, large amphibious assault forces, and extensive afloat support resources. His main striking force for the U.S. CENTRAL PACIFIC CAMPAIGN from June 1944 on had two commanders—Spruance and Halsey—who alternated planning the next offensive and carrying out the one at hand. Thus, Nimitz exploited his burgeoning resources at a high intensity.

Perhaps Nimitz's greatest accomplishment was his ability to sustain a consistent strategic effort while adapting to circumstances at the campaign level. He sped up the timetable for the capture of the MARSHALLS in 1944, backed Halsey in his recommendation for the acceleration of the schedule to land on Leyte, and eventually conceded the need to forgo recapture of Formosa for a full effort in support of MacArthur's Philippine campaign. Considering the military and political implications of the Central Pacific command, Nimitz was the perfect choice. He left the Pacific post in Nov. 1945 and then served two years as Chief of Naval Operations.

(His son, Rear Adm. Chester W. Nimitz, Jr., was a submarine commander during the war, with his submarine, the *Haddo* [SS 225], sinking five Japanese ships of 14,500 tons.)

Nishizawa, Chief Warrant Officer Hiroyoshi (1920–1944)

Leading Japanese fighter ACE of the war. Called the "Devil" by his fellow pilots, he scored 104 aerial victories during the war, at least ninety of them against U.S. aircraft. (Various accounts credit him with seventy-four to 200 kills; 104 appears the best estimate.)

He enlisted in the Navy flight-training program in 1936 and completed his training in March 1939. His combat career began in early 1942 at RABAUL. Flying the A6M ZERO, he scored his first aerial kill on Feb. 3. In April he was transferred to eastern NEW GUINEA. He fought in the U.S. SOLOMONS–NEW GUINEA CAMPAIGN until Nov. 1942, raising his score to thirty U.S. aircraft destroyed.

He continued flying in the Southwest Pacific until Nov. 1943, when he was promoted to warrant officer and assigned to air defense duties in Japan. Nishizawa flew to the Philippines in Oct. 1944 and on Oct. 25 he flew a fighter escort for the first KAMIKAZE attacks against U.S. warships, shooting down his final two aircraft on that mission. He was killed on Oct. 26, 1944, over Clark Field on Luzon in the Philippines when the twin-engine transport he was piloting to bring pilots back from the island of Cebu was shot down by U.S. Navy F6F HELLCATS.

Upon his death he was honored by being mentioned in a dispatch to all naval units and was awarded a posthumous double promotion, to lieutenant (j.g.).

Nissen Hut

Similar in appearance to a QUONSET HUT, the Nissen Hut was a half-cylinder structure fabricated of corrugated iron. It was easily erected and flexible in use. It was named after Lt. Col. P. N. Nissen, its British designer.

Nissenthal, Jack (1919—)

RAF RADAR specialist. An early radar technician, he was one of the first proponents of ground control intercept: having radar operators on the ground in direct communication with fighter pilots during intercepts, a scheme subsequently adopted by the RAF and U.S. air services. As an RAF flight sergeant, he participated in the DIEPPE raid on Aug.

19, 1942, in an effort to obtain information on a German Freya 28 radar installation. During the raid he had an "escort" of Canadian soldiers charged with making certain that, because of his knowledge of British radar, he was not captured alive by the Germans.

Nixon, Richard M. (1913—)

Navy lieutenant assigned to the NAVAL AIR TRANSPORT SERVICE. Nixon, a California lawyer who went to WASHINGTON to work for the OFFICE OF PRICE ADMINISTRATION, shifted to the Navy. As a lawyer he received a direct commission as a lieutenant (junior grade). After training, he was sent to NEW CALEDONIA, a South Pacific island that served as a landing site for U.S. aircraft being ferried to Australia. In Oct. 1945 he became a lieutenant commander and entered the Naval Reserve. He was a commander in the reserve in 1953 when he took office as vice president to fellow war veteran DWIGHT D. EISENHOWER.

NKVD *(Narodnyy Komisariat Vnutrennikh Del)*

The People's Commissariat for Internal Affairs and the Soviet state security apparatus during World War II. The NKVD combined internal police and foreign intelligence activities that were previously assigned to separate agencies. (In 1943 the functions were somewhat separated, but NKVD remained the principal agency for internal security, while the KGB became responsible for state security.)

Like other organs of the Soviet state, the NKVD entered the war with many of its leaders and agents executed or imprisoned in STALIN's purges of the 1930s. The notorious head of the NKVD (since 1938) was LAVRENTI BERIA, who supervised such diverse NKVD activities as ESPIONAGE against Britain and the United States as well as Germany; developing the Soviet ATOMIC BOMB; providing security for Stalin and, during conferences in Soviet territory, for Allied leaders; operating prison camps; insuring that Soviet troops stood up well in battle (see SMERSH); and following in the wake of Soviet troops to seize political prisoners, enemy technology, and industrial and military equipment.

The NKVD was also responsible for several major

executions, including the KAYTN MASSACRE of Polish military prisoners.

The NKVD and its predecessor agencies trace their origins to the Cheka, established by the Bolsheviks. The name was derived from the initials of *Chrezvychaynaya Komisiya* (Extraordinary Commission), that term a shortened version of All-Russian Extraordinary Commission for the Struggle Against Counterrevolution and Sabotage. The Cheka's purpose was to combat counterrevolutionaries and to punish "spies, traitors, plotters, bandits, speculators, profiteers, counterfeiters, arsonists, hooligans, agitators, saboteurs, class enemies, and other parasites." (See also IVAN SEROV.)

Noah's Ark

Code name for British plan for the occupation of Greece upon German troop withdrawal, 1944.

Noemfor

A coastal island on the western side of Geelvink Bay, NEW GUINEA. U.S. forces captured the island in July 1944. It was an objective of Gen. DOUGLAS MACARTHUR'S "leap-frogging" campaign against Japanese forces in western New Guinea to establish air bases for his Philippines campaign. He used the leap-frogging technique to isolate units of the Japanese forces without staging major assaults.

The AMPHIBIOUS LANDING on July 2 at Noemfor was relatively without opposition. A simultaneous landing at another coastal island, BIAK, ran into ferocious resistance. (See also HOLLANDIA.)

Nomura, Kichisaburo (1887–1964)

Japanese ambassador to the United States when the Japanese attacked PEARL HARBOR. A naval officer and veteran of the Russo-Japanese war, Nomura, although blinded in his right eye by a terrorist's bomb in 1932, remained an admiral in the Imperial Japanese Navy until he resigned in 1937 to serve on the Supreme War Council and later as foreign minister.

His selection in Feb. 1941 as ambassador to the United States signaled a possible thaw in U.S.-Japanese relations, for the six-foot-tall Nomura had made many friends among U.S. naval officers and diplomats while he was a naval attaché in Washington and later a member of the Japanese delegation

to the Washington Naval Conference of 1921–1922. President ROOSEVELT was assistant secretary of the Navy when he first met Nomura, and when the President met him again in 1941 he said he would address him as "admiral" rather than "ambassador" because of the naval tie between them.

Month after month, as relations between the two countries worsened, Nomura met frequently with U.S. Secretary of State CORDELL HULL, usually in Hull's apartment to avoid press notice. In Aug. 1941 Nomura asked the Foreign Ministry to send a special envoy "well informed on the state of things at home and abroad." The foreign ministry sent SABURO KURUSU, who, as Japanese ambassador to Germany, had signed the TRIPARTITE PACT in 1940. The former Japanese consul in Chicago, he was the husband of an American woman. He prided himself on his knowledge of idiomatic English.

Nomura and Kurusu met with Hull for the last time at 2:20 P.M. on Dec. 7, 1941, fifteen minutes after Roosevelt informed Hull that Japanese aircraft had attacked PEARL HARBOR. Although the two diplomats became immediate symbols of Japanese treachery, historical evidence shows that neither one was aware of the plans for the attack. Nomura was interned until Aug. 1942. When he was repatriated, he was not given any military duty to perform during the war.

Nonaggression Pact

Agreement between Germany and the Soviet Union that set the stage for World War II. On Aug. 23, 1939, the Soviet Union and Germany stunned the world by announcing a Nonaggression Pact. The two nations, ideological enemies in public, had been negotiating in secret for some time, but the breakthrough came swiftly when the two leaders, ADOLF HITLER and JOSEF STALIN, directly intervened.

During the spring and summer of 1939, newly named Soviet Foreign Minister VYACHESLAV MOLOTOV had conducted fruitless negotiations with the British and French seeking a three-nation nonaggression pact. (Discussions also had been going on among military representatives of the three nations.) The Germans believed that the Soviets were playing the Germans off against the British and French. The Germans sweetened their negotiation offers by hinting that a slice of Poland could be included. This intrigued Stalin. Then, on Aug. 20 Hitler sent a personal message to Stalin: War was imminent between Germany and Poland. He asked Stalin if he would meet with German Foreign Minister JOACHIM VON RIBBENTROP. Stalin replied that he would welcome Ribbentrop to MOSCOW on Aug. 23.

Less than an hour after getting Stalin's message, Hitler had the German radio network announce agreement on the pact. That same day, the Soviets issued a similar communiqué. The signing of the agreement in Moscow by Molotov and von Ribbentrop was an anticlimax. Nine days later, on Sept. 1, 1939, Germany invaded Poland. Later that month Soviet and German negotiators sliced up Poland. The Soviet government explained that it was sending troops into Poland to aid Russian "blood brothers," Ukrainians and Byelorussians living in Poland.

The pact shocked the world, especially Communists and Communist sympathizers, who had zealously condemned Nazism. British author Evelyn Waugh saw it as "the Modern Age in arms"—two evils allied, "huge and hateful, all disguise cast off." Stalin, toasting von Ribbentrop on the night of the signing, said, "Just think how we used to curse each other!" Not quite two years later, reacting to Germany's invasion of the Soviet Union, Stalin, in a rambling radio address, did not admit that he had been betrayed. He defended the pact as one that "not a single peace-loving state could decline."

Not until 1945 did secret protocols of the pact become known, and not until 1990 were full texts of the protocols made public. Secretly, the pact established the borders of German and Soviet "spheres of influence" in Eastern Europe, dooming Estonia, Latvia, and Lithuania to Soviet takeover.

Norden Bombsight

U.S. aiming device used for high-altitude bombing. Faith in U.S. PRECISION BOMBING rested essentially on the Norden bombsight, which, spokesmen for the Army Air Forces boasted, could "drop a BOMB into a pickle barrel from 25,000 feet." When visibility was good, the bombsight did give the bomber a high degree of accuracy. But in cloudy weather, or when the target was otherwise obscured, the optically aimed bombsight was not ef-

fective. Reportedly, on clear days, one in five bombs released by a Norden bombsight would strike within 1,000 feet of the target.

Development of the bombsight was begun in 1928 by Carl L. Norden, a Dutch-American inventor, who worked with Theodore H. Barth, an engineer. The bombsight first saw widespread use in U.S. heavy bomber raids over Europe in 1942.

The bombsight was linked to the plane's autopilot. The bombardier entered data on air speed, wind, and bomb weight into the bombsight, which calculated the trajectory of the bombs. Near the target the bombardier took control of the plane. As he aligned the bombsight's telescope on the target, his movements were transmitted to the plane's controls. The bombsight automatically released the bombs at what it determined the proper release point, following directions for bomb-drop intervals given it by the bombardier.

Details of the bombsight were kept classified until 1947. The bombsight was not used in the B-25 MITCHELL bombers of the DOOLITTLE RAID on Japan to keep it from falling into enemy hands.

Nordhausen,

see CONCENTRATION CAMPS.

Nordlicht (Northern Light)

Code name for German offensive against LENINGRAD, fall 1942.

Nordmark (Northern Border)

German code name for operation by the battleships *Gneisenau* and *Scharnhorst* and lesser warships to raid British CONVOYS between Norway and the Shetlands, but no convoys were sighted; Feb. 1940.

Nordpol (North Pole)

German code name for projected assault into the Toropets bulge in the Soviet Union, March 1942.

Nordwind (North Wind)

Code name for German attack north of Alsace, Dec. 1944 (see *WACHT AM RHEIN*).

Norm

Highly advanced Japanese floatplane reconnaissance aircraft. The E15K *Shiun* (Violet Cloud) was one of several Japanese naval aircraft developed for use in the Southwest Pacific, where support ships could provide base facilities in sheltered bays for floatplane aircraft. Given the Allied code name Norm, this was a highly advanced recce aircraft intended to be able to evade Allied fighters. However, its complex scheme for retractable wing floats and lack of armor and fuel tank protection doomed it to failure.

The design was far in advance of contemporary Western single-engine recce aircraft with the prototype E15K1 making its maiden flight on Dec. 5, 1941. Several technical problems came to light; after modifications, the plane was placed in limited production. Only fifteen were completed through 1944—six prototypes and trial aircraft and nine production units. The six planes were sent to Palau for combat evaluation, but were quickly shot down by U.S. naval fighters.

The Kawanishi E15K was a low-wing, streamlined aircraft with a large radial engine mounting contra-rotating propellers. The aircraft had a massive centerline float and retracting wing floats.

Maximum speed of the E15K was 291 mph, with a range of 2,100 miles. A single 7.7-mm machine gun was fired from the rear cockpit. Two 132-pound BOMBS could be carried to provide a limited attack capability.

The aircraft had a two-man crew.

Normandie

French luxury liner taken over by U.S. Navy. Seized by the U.S. government at New York City on Dec. 12, 1941, the *Normandie* was transferred to the Navy on Dec. 24, promptly renamed *Lafayette,* and designated as a troop transport (AP 53).

Her conversion began almost immediately at a Manhattan pier, but on Feb. 9, 1942, she caught fire. The tons of water poured into her by firefighters caused the ship to capsize early the next morning. Sabotage was suspected but not proved; the most likely cause was a welder's torch. After a massive salvage operation that began in May 1942, the ship was righted on Aug. 7, 1943. The salvage had cost an estimated $3,750,000.

Although redesignated as an aircraft transport (APV 4) and placed in dry dock in Oct. 1943 for conversion, work was abandoned because of the extent of the fire damage and the condition of her machinery. She was stricken from the Navy List in late 1945 and scrapped the following year.

The *Normandie* was laid down at Saint-NAZAIRE, France, in 1931 and was launched on Oct. 29, 1932. She made her first trans-Atlantic crossing in 1935 and served in Atlantic passenger service until 1940. As a liner she was 1,027 feet long—the world's first ship to exceed 1,000 feet—with a gross tonnage of 82,800, and had a maximum speed of 30 knots. The ship could carry 2,000 passengers in luxury and splendor.

Normandie Squadron,

see FRANCE, AIR FORCE.

Normandy Invasion

History's largest AMPHIBIOUS LANDING. On June 6, 1944, after four months of heavy bombing of rail and road targets in France (see STRATEGIC BOMBING) and numerous exercises off the British coast (see SLAPTON SANDS), the ALLIES launched the invasion that would liberate Western Europe.

The U.S. buildup in England for the invasion consisted of 1,527,000 troops, including 620,504 men of the ground forces in twenty-one DIVISIONS plus support troops. The massive invasion fleet, the mightiest armada ever assembled, included more than 4,400 ships and LANDING CRAFT to carry the 154,000 troops—50,000 of them the assault troops of D-DAY—and 1,500 tanks. With the invasion fleet was an aerial armada of 11,000 fighters, bombers, transports, and GLIDERS to provide protection, support, and supplies.

Of the forty-seven Allied divisions used in the invasion, twenty-one were American; the rest were British, Canadian, and Polish. There were also French, Italian, Belgian, Czech, and Dutch troops. Opposing them were about sixty German divisions in France and the Low Countries. In what would be the area of the invasion there were nine German infantry divisions and one PANZER division arrayed along fortifications called the ATLANTIC WALL.

Allied planners had chosen the Normandy coast over the more obvious Pas de Calais area, but an elaborate deception plan increased German suspicion that Calais was the invasion coast. The Germans kept their Fifteenth Army in the Calais area.

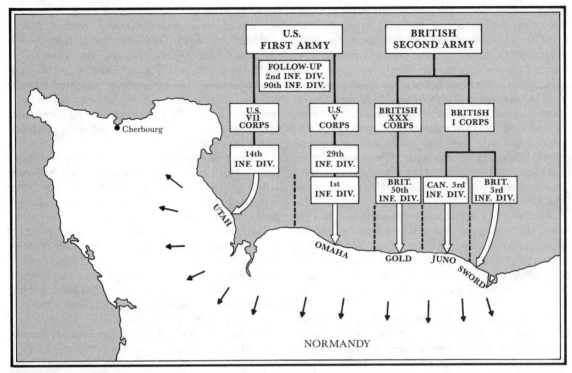

Normandy Invasion: Operation Overlord, June 6, 1944.

The tactical aspect of the deception plan was code-named Fortitude; on the strategic level it was called BODYGUARD. The First United States ARMY GROUP (FUASG) had been created on paper. A fleet of landing craft, deemed unseaworthy, bobbed in British ports across from Calais. The commanding officer of FUASG was Gen. GEORGE S. PATTON. Instructions for acts of SABOTAGE were radioed to the FRENCH RESISTANCE. (See also CAMOUFLAGE.)

The date of the invasion was based on considerations of tide (lowest at H-HOUR), weather (low winds to hold down Channel chop), and light (moonlight on the eve of D-Day; good light at H-hour). These considerations bracketed the period from early May to early June. The date June 5 was finally set. But bad weather forced a lonely decision by Gen. DWIGHT D. EISENHOWER as commander of the ALLIED EXPEDITIONARY FORCE. He postponed the date by twenty-four hours. With the possibility of bad weather still hovering, he nevertheless gave the order to launch the invasion.

Hours before the troops landed at 6:30 A.M. on June 6, one British and two U.S. AIRBORNE DIVISIONS were dropped into the dark French countryside in a massive parachute-GLIDER assault behind German lines. This vanguard force fought to secure and hold bridges, roads, rail lines, and airfields needed for the Allied advance inland.

American forces landed on two western beaches, Utah and Omaha. British and Canadian troops landed farther east on beaches designated Gold, Juno, and Sword. While Gen. BERNARD MONTGOMERY served as overall commander of the ground forces, Lt. Gen. OMAR BRADLEY commanded the American First ARMY in the landings, and Gen. Sir. MILES DEMPSEY led the British Second Army.

Allied air forces controlled the skies over the 50-mile front. But bombing and strafing, and, from warships, gunfire and rocket barrages could not silence the well-entrenched German guns, especially on Omaha Beach, where casualties numbered 2,000 in contrast to only 210 on Utah. Beginning the series of disasters at "Bloody Omaha" was the sinking of two beach-control craft that struck MINES.

"They came ashore on Omaha Beach, the slogging, unglamorous men that no one envied," Cornelius Ryan wrote in his superb account of the invasion, *The Longest Day.* Some of the men "hadn't a chance. German gunners on the cliffs looked almost directly down on the waterlogged assault craft that heaved and pitched toward these sectors of the beach. Awkward and slow, the assault boats were nearly stationary in the water. They were sitting ducks. . . . [M]en plunged over the sides into deep water, where they were immediately picked off by machine gun fire."

To the east, British and Canadian troops met with less resistance and suffered fewer casualties than the Americans did. The British 3rd Division defeated a counterattack by a panzer tank battalion northwest of Caen, throwing *Generalfeldmarschall* ERWIN ROMMEL'S forces completely on the defensive.

By day's end, close to 150,000 Allied troops and their accompanying vehicles, equipment, munitions, and provisions were unloaded. In a week the troop buildup numbered a half-million men. By late July 2,000,000 troops and 250,000 vehicles had landed in France, using prefabricated harbors and floating piers. (See ARTIFICIAL HARBORS.) Allied D-Day losses approximately equalled those of German Forces: some 15,000 killed and wounded. But, according to a report by Rommel, his casualties for the entire month of June would total "28 generals, 354 commanders and approximately 250,000 men."

North Africa–Middle East Campaign (1940–1943)

The long and complex campaign for North Africa began with England fighting one AXIS partner, Italy, and then, in battles that would track the sands from Egypt to Morocco, with Germany's Desert Fox, ERWIN ROMMEL.

The Italian phase of the campaign began shortly after Italy declared war on England on June 10, 1940. Gen. ARCHIBALD PERCIVAL WAVELL, Commander in Chief of British forces in the Middle East, decided to remind Italy that Europe was not the only place where there was war. Wavell sent a few armored cars across the border between British-administered Egypt and the Italian colony of Cyrenaica, Libya. The British tore down the barbed-wire fence the Italians had put up, showed the flag around two Italian forts, captured a truck and its stunned Italian Army passengers, and returned to Egypt. This was the opening scene in a campaign that would seem as endless as the sands on which it was fought.

Wavell's move was bold enough to appear foolhardy. He had fewer than 40,000 men between Italian forces numbering some 200,000 to the west in Libya and about 250,000 to the south in Italy's Ethiopian and Somaliland colonies.

Italian dictator BENITO MUSSOLINI, dreaming of a new Roman Empire, saw the EUROPEAN WAR as his chance to expand his colonies in North Africa. With France conquered by Italy's AXIS partner Germany, he had no fear of reaction from French colonies. As for the British in Egypt, there were not enough of them to be a threat.

On Aug. 4, 1940, Italian forces invaded British Somaliland, southeast of Egypt, on the Horn of Africa. The British withdrew and on Aug. 17 the Italians captured the port town of Berbera, the colony's capital. Wavell realized that the Italian invasion of this obscure corner of the world could have far-reaching consequences, for the neutral United States could declare the Red Sea unsafe and cut off a vital British supply line.

While Wavell pondered his problems to the south, more trouble came from the west. On Aug. 19 Mussolini, who had been told by HITLER that a German invasion of England was imminent (see SEA LION), sent a message to Marshal d'Armata Rodolfo Graziani, Commander in Chief of Italian forces in North Africa: "Now, on the day on which the first platoon of German soldiers lands on British soil, you too will attack."

When no invasion of England came, Mussolini nudged the reluctant Graziani to still make a move. On Sept. 13 Graziani did, sending five divisions across the Egyptian border. Advancing slowly against a British force fighting withdrawal, heavy ARTILLERY fire, and RAF bombing, the Italians reached Sidi Barrani, a coastal town about 65 miles within Egypt. The Italians stopped and began constructing an elaborate defense system for miles around the town.

On Dec. 9 about 30,000 British troops of Wavell's Western Desert Force, in a "five-day raid" code-named Compass, attacked Sidi Barrani. The raiders caught the Italians by surprise and took more than 20,000 PRISONERS OF WAR. "Something is wrong with our Army," Count GALEAZZO CIANO, the Italian Foreign Minister, wrote in his diary, "if five divisions allow themselves to be pulverized in two days."

But the raid was far from over. The British force's commander, Lt. Gen. Richard O'Connor, decided to transform the raid into an assault into Libya. He captured Bardia, just over the Libyan border, rounded up more prisoners, and pushed on toward TOBRUK, then to Benghazi and beyond. In ten weeks O'Connor's overwhelmingly outnumbered force covered 500 miles, captured the province of Cyrenaica, and, incredibly, took 130,000 prisoners.

O'Connor wanted to roll on to Tripoli. But Wavell, under pressure to provide troops to Greece, cut back the Libyan forces and hoped that an even smaller force could hold on to Cyrenaica. Tripoli could wait. Wavell had not counted on what would happen after the arrival of *Generalleutnant* Rommel in Tripoli on Feb. 12. Rommel, just appointed commander of Germany's AFRIKA KORPS, had been sent by Hitler to help Mussolini get back his lost territory.

Although Rommel was theoretically under an Italian general, he led the offensive, adding Italian forces to his fast-moving tank columns. In March he headed east to regain Cyrenaica. By mid-April he had gotten back all that the British had taken except Tobruk, to which the British had withdrawn, and he had captured O'Connor, along with another British general. (O'Connor, who had just been knighted by King GEORGE VI, was taken as a prisoner of war to Italy; he escaped in Dec. 1943.)

Rommel's first desert offensive ended with the Germans over the Egyptian border and in possession of Halfaya Pass. He had bypassed Tobruk. The port, temporarily safe within an arc of strong points and reinforced from the sea, settled in for a siege. The British mounted two futile attempts—operations Brevity and Battleaxe—to dislodge Rommel. Battleaxe was a disaster, with the British losing half of their armor to Rommel's 88-MM FLAK guns and other superior weapons.

Prime Minister CHURCHILL had a personal stake in the desert battles because he had rejected the counsel of his military advisers, who had wanted to keep in England the tanks and fighter aircraft that Churchill sent to Wavell. Now, with much of that precious matériel gone, Wavell had to go, too. He was replaced by Gen. Sir Claude Auchinleck, who in Nov. 1941 launched Crusader, a thrust across the border with the double objective of reclaiming land from Rommel and covering a breakout from besieged Tobruk.

In a confusing, seesawing battle that lasted until mid-December, Auchinleck's Eighth Army (evolved out of the Western Desert Force) lifted the 242-day siege of Tobruk and drove Rommel back to El Agheila, where he had started a year before. Official estimates of losses gave the percentage points to the Eighth Army, which lost about 15 percent of its effectiveness compared to Rommel's 23 percent and the Italian forces' 44 percent.

The Afrika Korps, battered but undaunted, had, in retreat, a great advantage over the British Eighth Army: shorter supply lines. The Germans still held Tripoli. Rommel called the arrival of equipment and gasoline to the ports "as good as a victory in battle." German supply ships were escaping the punishment that might had been inflicted if the Royal Navy and RAF had not been hard pressed in the campaign to sustain besieged MALTA.

On Jan. 21, 1942, only sixteen days after he had driven back to El Agheila, the Desert Fox roared out of his den, recaptured Benghazi, looted the British supplies piled up there, and smashed forward to within 35 miles of Tobruk. The British had withdrawn to the Gazala Line, a string of strong point "boxes" linked by minefields, running from Gazala on the coast to Bir Hacheim, a FREE FRENCH outpost about 40 miles southwest of Tobruk.

Both sides regrouped and resupplied, the British strengthening the center of the Gazala Line, Rommel awaiting more men, supplies, and fuel. The long pause ended on May 26 when Rommel swept around the southern end of the line, hoping to take Bir Hacheim and then pick off the boxes, one by one.

But in a fierce battle dubbed "the Cauldron" by the British, Rommel was pinned between British strongpoints. He eluded what looked to be potential annihilation, overcame the gallant defenders of Bir Hacheim, crushed a series of boxes, and dashed for the huge British supply dump east of Tobruk on June 17 and four days later took Tobruk and its 30,000 defenders. "The booty was gigantic," Rommel's Chief of Staff later recounted. "It consisted of supplies for 30,000 men for three months." The gasoline stocks, however, were burned before the town fell.

The capture of Tobruk won Rommel the baton of a field marshal. When he got the telegram from Hitler announcing the promotion, Rommel is said to have remarked, "It would be better if he had sent me another division."

The desert war by then had become personalized. In British dispatches the combined German-Italian forces were referred to as *Rommel*. Churchill himself, in rare words of praise for a German, told the House of Commons in Jan. 1942, "We have a very daring and skillful opponent against us, and, may I say across the havoc of war, a great general."

After the fall of Tobruk the British drew another line in the sand, this time at Mersa Matruh, well into Egypt, and prepared to defend from there. Beyond, at EL ALAMEIN, was the last-ditch defense of Alexandria and Egypt itself.

Rommel's forces took Mersa Matruh at the end of June, replenished from its stores, and rolled on to the El Alamein Line, a 35-mile-wide defensive complex whose flanks were guarded by natural obstacles. To the north was the sea and to the south was the 700-foot dip of the vast Qattara Depression, 7,000 square miles of impassable terrain.

Despite Rommel's acquisition of British supplies along the way, he was still stretching his resources and his men. Honed but wizened by weeks on the desert, they were exhausted. RAF attacks on Rommel's columns slowed his advance. When he reached the El Alamein Line on July 1 he did not have the strength to break it.

The fall of Tobruk had struck Churchill hard. He went to Cairo, checked the scene himself with a foray to El Alamein, and replaced Auchinleck with another general, William Gott. When Gott was killed while flying to take command, Lt. Gen. BER-NARD L. MONTGOMERY was sent from England to replace him.

Montgomery immediately began reorganizing the Eighth Army, sacking officers, stepping up training, arranging for closer air support. "Here we will stand and fight; there can be no further withdrawal," he told the men of the Eighth Army, predicting that Rommel would make an attack in August on the south end of the line, that he would be beaten, and that the Eighth Army would expel him from North Africa. Montgomery was right in all his prophecies.

Rommel attacked on Aug. 31—at the Alam Halfa ridge where Montgomery had expected to be hit—and ran into a wall of heavy defensive fire. He withdrew, well aware that there was another general in the desert making a legend of himself.

Meanwhile, off Tobruk, the RAF destroyed the tanker convoy that was bringing Rommel the gasoline he needed for resupply. As Rommel was losing supplies, Montgomery was gaining them. From the United States were coming SHERMAN TANKS and self-propelled artillery supplied at Churchill's specific request to President ROOSEVELT.

In late October, after methodical preparations, Montgomery forced the German-Italian forces to retreat in what would go into British military history as the second battle of El Alamein. The Eighth Army had savaged four German divisions and eight Italian divisions, taking 30,000 prisoners.

Pursuit of Rommel began. On Nov. 20, 1942, Benghazi fell and by Nov. 23 Rommel once more was in El Agheila, but in headlong retreat. The Eighth Army pressed on, taking Tripoli on Jan. 13, 1943, and, although Montgomery had to fight through the MARETH LINE, he ultimately drove 1,750 miles to join the Allied troops who had landed in French North Africa in Nov. 1942. The linkup came on the Tunisian frontier in April 1943. (See NORTH AFRICA INVASION and NORTHWEST AFRICA CAMPAIGN.)

North Africa Invasion

Initial move in the NORTHWEST AFRICA CAMPAIGN—given the code name Operation Torch. The invasion began on Nov. 8, 1942, when U.S. and British troops, under the command of Gen. DWIGHT D. EISENHOWER, landed in Casablanca,

Morocco, and Algiers and Oran in Algeria. Algiers quickly surrendered, but French troops at Oran and in Morocco surprised the invaders by holding out. The ALLIES were invading what was a part of the technically neutral country of VICHY FRANCE, with which the United States still had diplomatic relations.

The invaders went ashore in three landings, with all ground forces under U.S. Army generals: 34,300 troops landed on a front centered at Casablanca, under the flamboyant but highly capable Maj. Gen. GEORGE S. PATTON; 39,000 U.S. troops at Oran, under Maj. Gen. Lloyd Fredendall; and 10,000 troops under Maj. Gen. Charles Ryder, with 23,000 British troops at Algiers. Casablanca was an all-American landing. Anglo-American troops went ashore at Oran and Algiers—with Americans in the first waves in an attempt to reduce French opposition. (President ROOSEVELT had insisted that the initial landings should be by U.S. forces alone to dampen the resistance of the French, who had more reasons to oppose the British than the Americans.)

Adm. JEAN FRANÇOIS DARLAN, commander of the Vichy France defending forces, at first agreed to order a cease-fire, but only with the approval of the Vichy government. Vichy refused, fearing that approval would trigger a German retaliatory invasion of unoccupied France (which did in fact begin on Nov. 11).

Darlan on Nov. 13 signed a cease-fire agreement with Eisenhower, who acknowledged that the invaded territory belonged to France. German troops from SICILY had already been flown in, against no opposition, to an airport near Tunis. By then the Allied invasion was successful. But heavy fighting lay ahead.

Operation Torch saw the largest concentration of Allied naval forces yet assembled in the war. The Allies mustered twelve AIRCRAFT CARRIERS, several of them small, American-built ESCORT CARRIERS, generally referred to as "jeep" or "Woolworth" carriers. One of the "jeeps" carried seventy-eight U.S. Army P-40F WARHAWK fighters and three spotter planes to be flown to airfields that ground troops were to capture. Some 350 naval fighters and bombers provided air support, along with longer-range aircraft flying from GIBRALTAR, Eisenhower's headquarters for the invasion.

The invasion fleet was not intercepted by German reconnaissance aircraft or U-BOATS, and the German high command, believing that the shipping was en route to besieged MALTA, was taken by surprise.

U.S. troops suffered 556 killed, 837 wounded, forty-one missing. British casualties totaled 330. About 700 French defenders were killed and about 1,400 wounded.

Local irregulars, all anti-Vichy, formed the Corps Franc d'Afrique; they, along with Free French troops, joined the Americans and British in the next phase of the campaign: to drive AXIS forces out of North Africa.

Northwest Africa Campaign (1942–1943)

For both military and political reasons, an operation in North Africa had long attracted Allied strategists. The fall of France in June 1940 left the French territories in North Africa as a potential arena for war. The British wanted to keep the Germans from controlling French North Africa and its military installations, including a sizable fleet. The Germans and their Italian allies were already in northeast Africa and could bring down reinforcements through Italy.

French North Africa was essentially under French control, with the administrators there politically tied to the pro-German VICHY FRANCE government. The few Germans were mostly functionaries—the kind fictionalized by SS Maj. Heinrich Strasser in the movie *Casablanca*.

President ROOSEVELT and Prime Minister CHURCHILL had been discussing a joint U.S.-British campaign in French North Africa since their ATLANTIC CONFERENCE in Aug. 1941, when both knew that U.S. entry into the war was inevitable. The proposal returned as a definite strategic proposal at one of their WASHINGTON CONFERENCES (also known as the Arcadia Conference or the United Nations Conference) of Dec. 1941–Jan. 1942, when Churchill suggested to Roosevelt a "North-west Africa Project" for "closing and tightening the ring around Germany."

The "project" would put U.S. forces in action, boost American morale, and give some response to STALIN's demands for a SECOND FRONT. Militarily, an invasion would provide a staging area for action against Italy and would put pressure on the advancing German forces of Gen. ERWIN ROMMEL to the east. But no other major campaign of the war was fraught with more political problems. Although the United States had diplomatic relations with the Vichy regime, the British viewed it, rightly, as a German puppet state. Royal Navy attacks on French warships in 1940 to prevent their falling under German control had incensed the FREE FRENCH of Gen. CHARLES DE GAULLE as well as Vichy France. So a solo British operation against French North Africa was diplomatically impossible.

But the reasons against an operation were offset in June 1942 when unexpected German gains in Libya left the British Eighth Army in battered disarray. Churchill flew to Washington on June 17 to meet again with Roosevelt, and the two leaders agreed on an imminent landing in North Africa. The operation was initially given the code name Super Gymnast, but was later changed, at Churchill's insistence, to Torch—a more dynamic title.

Roosevelt overruled resistance by the U.S. JOINT CHIEFS OF STAFF, who favored a larger and later landing operation in Europe. As planning for Torch went on through the summer of 1942, the Soviets continued putting on pressure for a Second Front. Foreign Minister VLACHESLAV MOLOTOV, during a visit to Washington in May, had been assured by Roosevelt that a Second Front was possible in 1942. In Moscow in August, Soviet leader Stalin, in his first meeting with Churchill, asked,

"Are you going to let us do all the work while you look on? Are you never going to start fighting?" Churchill, throttling his fury, placated Stalin by telling him about Torch.

This first Anglo-American assault of the war would be under the overall command of Lt. Gen. DWIGHT D. EISENHOWER, a relatively unknown plans officer for Gen. GEORGE C. MARSHALL. Torch was an Anglo-American operation with Eisenhower having overall military command. All naval forces would be under Royal Navy Adm. Sir ANDREW BROWNE CUNNINGHAM, while RAF Air Chief Marshal ARTHUR W. TEDDER would direct all air operations.

In planning Torch, Eisenhower had more problems with the U.S. Navy than with the British. Although he glossed over this in his public history, *Crusade in Europe,* in his diary he wrote, "One thing that might help win this war is to get someone to shoot King [Chief of Naval Operations ERNEST J. KING]. . . . He's the antithesis of cooperation, a deliberately rude person, which means he's a mental bully." For King—the most senior U.S. naval officer—the principal theater of war was the Pacific, and every warship or escort or landing craft diverted to North Africa afflicted war in the Pacific.

On Oct. 21, 1942, one of Eisenhower's deputies, Maj. Gen. MARK CLARK, sailed from Gibraltar in the British submarine *SERAPH* for a secret meeting with the U.S. consul-general in North Africa, ROB-

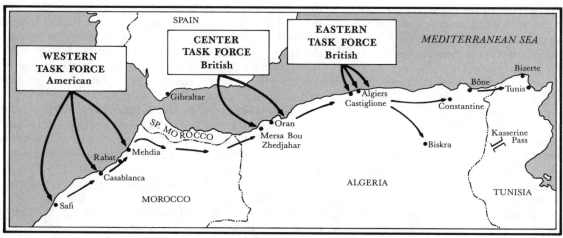

North African invasion.

ERT MURPHY, and Vichy representatives in North Africa. The purpose of the meeting was to secure from the French pledges to help—or at least not to resist—Allied landings.

During a clandestine meeting in a beach house, 60 miles west of Algiers, from the morning of Oct. 21 into late the following night, Clark got an agreement for tacit cooperation. Unknown to the French, who were promised a month's warning prior to any landing, invasion ships were about to leave the United States and were due to arrive two weeks later off the North African coast. Clark nearly drowned in heavy surf while returning to the submarine in a canvas boat.

The strategic purpose of the NORTH AFRICA INVASION was the clearing of AXIS forces out of North Africa through a linking of the invasion forces with Gen. BERNARD MONTGOMERY's British Eighth Army, which in October had broken through *Generalfeldmarschall* Erwin Rommel's lines at EL ALAMEIN. The German forces were retreating westward across Libya. But the Allied drive eastward faltered, due primarily to rains that turned the poor roads into quagmires, and the loss of air superiority. The Germans, reacting quickly, began pouring troops and supplies into Tunisia from SICILY by sea and by air, seizing airfields at Tunis and Bizerte.

By Nov. 12 British AIRBORNE troops had taken the airfield at Bône, but Allied forces, especially green American troops, moved slowly and failed to take advantage of Axis reverses in Egypt. Allied operations, Eisenhower later wrote, "have violated every recognized principle of war, are in conflict with all operational and logistic methods laid down in textbooks, and will be condemned in their entirety" in future war college classes.

Slogging through mud and hampered by meager supplies, Allied troops aiming for Tunis were stopped by outnumbered Germans. The buildup continued, with the German and Italian forces in Tunisia numbering nearly 100,000 as the new year began.

In a dramatic demonstration of the success of the invasion, Roosevelt and Churchill, accompanied by the combined CHIEFS OF STAFF, began their CASABLANCA CONFERENCE at a seaside villa on Jan. 14. As they were ending their conference, Montgomery's Eighth Army was driving westward. He took

Tripoli on Jan. 23, 1943, and paused for what was expected to be the final push to drive the Axis out of North Africa.

The retreating Rommel, however, audaciously linked his AFRIKA KORPS with a German PANZER division on the Tunisian front and launched an offensive against the Allied forces to the east. The German attack introduced the Mark VI TIGER TANK, which mounted the 88-mm antitank gun. He envisioned a breakthrough that would cut the Allied line in half and give the Germans another supply port, Bône. His frequent target was American troops—because they "had no practical battle experience." Initially, U.S. losses were heavy, including forty tanks in a single battle.

At dawn on Feb. 14, the Germans broke out of the Faïd area, attacking in a double thrust that drove a wedge through the Allied lines and forced U.S. troops back to what would be a crucible that tested the Americans, the KASSERINE PASS. The Germans' attack on the pass began on Feb. 19. They smashed through the next day, inflicting heavy casualties, advanced on the road toward Thala, 20 miles north of the pass, and thrust toward Tebessa, near the Algerian border.

American units beat the Germans back at Tebessa. Then Allied forces surged into the area, driving back the Germans over the ground they had taken and pounding them from the air. Rommel retreated through the pass, but, as the official Army history puts it, "ground operations against the retreating enemy became extraordinarily hesitant at just the time the enemy was most vulnerable."

The Germans and Italians faced the Eighth Army at the MARETH LINE, a 22-mile series of fortifications, running from the sea to the Matmata Hills, built by the French against a possible Italian invasion of Tunisia. Under a command reorganization, Gen. Sir HAROLD ALEXANDER, Commander in Chief Middle East, became deputy commander for ground forces, which included the British Eighth Army, U.S. Army forces, along with the Free French—some 500,000 troops in all. This set the stage for the linkup of Allies advancing from east and west.

From Feb. 26 to March 20, a series of battles weakened Axis forces and gave the Allies time for the final blow: a breach of the Mareth Line. On

April 8 patrols from U.S. forces in the east and British Eighth Army coming from the west greeted each other near Gafsa, and the linkup began. Rommel, ailing, had already flown to Germany, never to return to Africa.

Weakened by the long retreat from El Alamein, low on fuel, ammunition, and food, the enemy pulled back to a bridgehead encompassing Bizerte, Tunis, and the Cape Bon peninsula. Hundreds, then thousands of Axis prisoners were rounded up. Tunis fell to the British, Bizerte to U.S. and French forces. All resistance ended on May 13. German and Italian generals arranged massive surrenders. An estimated 240,000 prisoners were taken.

The Allies, in the words of Alexander, now were "masters of the North African shores."

Norway

Capital: Oslo, pop. 2,907,000 (est. 1939). Britain, violating international law, on April 8, 1940, began laying mines in Norwegian waters to thwart neutral Norway's iron-ore trade with Germany. The next day, Germany invaded Norway, using paratroops, air-landed troops, and troops carried into Norwegian ports in merchant ships and warships. This dazzling display of BLITZKRIEG appeared to be an incredibly rapid counter to the British mining. Actually the Germans carried out an operation, Exercise Weser, that had been developed two months before.

The British and French managed to land troops to aid reeling Norwegian defenders, but much of Norway fell to the Germans within a month. The rest of the country was lost when the British and French forces were forced to evacuate. King Haakon VII, the royal family, and Norway's gold reached London, where a government-in-exile was established.

Norway was put under the rule of a Reich commissioner who declared that the only legal party was the pro-Nazi National Unity Party headed by VIDKUN QUISLING, the former minister of war and the leader of Norwegian collaboration. He had met with HITLER and encouraged him to invade Norway. Quisling's name became synonymous with treason.

The German conquerors made Quisling *"Führer"* of Norway, dethroned King Haakon, and empowered Quisling to "reconstruct" the country into a Fascist state. Loathed by the overwhelming majority of his fellow citizens, Quisling ruled as a dictator, sending thousands to German CONCENTRATION CAMPS and killing hostages rounded up in retaliation for acts by Norway's vigorous resistance movement. He became prime minister of a puppet government on Feb. 2, 1942.

Defiance came from every side. Teachers resigned. Bishops and clergymen resigned. The state church, to which 97 percent of the population belonged, separated from the state. When the Germans seized Norway's food reserves and sent them to Germany, both Sweden and Denmark got food into Norway, Swedish organizations feeding some 100,000 Norwegian children.

Aided by resistance groups, British COMMANDOS made frequent raids into Norway, and Allied bombers targeted German occupation facilities. As the Germans stepped up retaliation against such actions, the tide of war was turning. In Oct. 1944 German troops, retreating before a Soviet offensive in Finland, crossed into Norway. The Germans declared a SCORCHED EARTH policy in northern Norway, evacuating the population, razing villages, killing cattle and reindeer. Free Norwegian forces from England along the coast fought side by side with the Red Army.

Between 10,000 and 15,000 Norwegians who had crossed the border to Sweden were given police training and when liberation came on May 8, 1945, they were sent into Norway to help resistance groups maintain order.

Quisling was arrested, tried, and shot by a firing squad. Also executed were about fifty collaborators, including members of Quisling's cabinet and police officials. Some 46,000 were tried for collaboration after the war, but only a few were severely punished. Gen. Nikolaus von Falkenhorst, the commander of German troops in Norway, was sentenced to death by a British military tribunal for killing commandos taken prisoner. The sentence was reduced to life imprisonment and Falkenhorst was released in 1953.

Nose Art

Paintings, usually of scantily clad women, placed on the noses of U.S. aircraft. Besides women, the nose art included characters from the COMICS and Walt Disney cartoons, various animals, and good-luck symbols.

A nose art artist, Ted Simonaitis, described his range as "the sentimental, the comical, semi-nudes in good taste, and the downright raunchy." Artists often copied the images of popular "pinup girls," such as Betty Grable and Rita Hayworth. Ironically, as servicemen nose artists were copying long-legged "Varga girls" from *Esquire* magazine, the U.S. Post Office was trying to pull *Esquire* out of the mails. (See CENSORSHIP.)

Melissa Keiser, described by the Smithsonian's *Air & Space* magazine as the National Air and Space Museum nose art specialist, said the farther aircrews got from headquarters, the naughtier was their art. "The girls on the planes in England were pretty much covered up, presumably because they were so close to Command," she said. "But when you got way out in the South Pacific they tended to shed more clothing."

This produced problems, especially when heroic planes flew back to the United States for WAR BOND rallies. Some officers ordered nose art cleaned up before appearing in public.

Bombers carried most of the nose art because there was more room for it, although a fighter might get a name. Lt. (j.g.) GEORGE BUSH named his "Barbara." A tradition quickly grew: Nose art kept a plane lucky and so it was never removed. Another crew might add a name or some words, but the original art stayed.

Novikov, Chief Marshal of Aviation A. A. (1900–1976)

Commander of the Soviet Army Air Force during most of the war. Novikov graduated from the prestigious Frunze Military Academy in 1930. After serving briefly on the staff of a rifle corps, he was transferred to the Air Force, passed the examination for observer-pilot in 1935, and became a squadron commander.

When Germany invaded the Soviet Union in June 1941, Novikov was commander of the Soviet Air Force units in the LENINGRAD military district with the rank of major general of aviation. Immediately after the war began, Soviet ground and air forces were reorganized into fronts, and Novikov became commander of the Northern Front's air forces. In that role, Novikov planned and directed one of the first offensive operations of the Air Force when, early on June 25, 460 of his planes made the first massed strike against German airfields. Catching the Germans by surprise at nineteen airfields, the Soviet fliers destroyed forty-one aircraft on the ground without suffering any losses themselves.

In Feb. 1942 Novikov was appointed the first deputy head of the Soviet Air Force and worked mainly in developing mass air attacks in support of Soviet ground forces. On April 11 he became commander of the Soviet Air Force and the deputy people's commissar of Defense for Aviation with the rank of colonel general of aviation. He held that post until the end of the war, being promoted to chief marshal of aviation in Feb. 1944. In 1945 he was twice decorated as HERO OF THE SOVIET UNION.

Under his direction the Soviet Air Force rapidly integrated into effective formations the mass of aircraft arriving from Britain and the United States, and from the relocated Soviet aircraft industry.

In March 1946 STALIN dismissed Novikov. Allegedly libeled by Stalin's son, Vasili, Novikov was arrested and imprisoned. He was released after Stalin's death in March 1953. Later that year he became head of the Soviet strategic bomber force, a position he held for two years.

Nuremberg,

see WAR CRIMES.

Oak Ridge

Site, near Clinton, Tenn., of secret production work on the ATOMIC BOMB. Oak Ridge uranium separation plants extracted the easily fissionable U-235 from the abundant but less fissionable U-238.

The secret facility, which covered 93 square miles, was known as the Clinton Engineer Works. Its lasting name came from a permanent housing area built on a series of ridges overlooking what the Army called the reservation. Not until 1947 was the name Oak Ridge made official and the fictional Clinton Engineer Works dropped.

The reservation was established by a confidential presidential proclamation, which was shown to the governor of Tennessee by an Army officer after the land had been acquired. Owners were paid the ap-praised value of their land; if they did not accept the offer, a Federal judge initiated condemnation proceedings.

Construction on the first plant, code-named Y-12, began in Feb. 1943 and by November it was in operation. The work force for this plant and subsequent ones grew to 82,000 by May 1945. To accommodate the workers in what had been empty land the government built houses, dormitories, apartment houses and set up trailer parks for nearly 4,000 government-purchased trailers. A government-hired management firm ran the laundry and cafeterias, the utilities, a school system for more than 7,000 students, and set up a fire department, police force, and hospital. The government, striving to found a "typical American community," built movie theaters, soda foun-

U.S. Marine Corps "Buffalo" armored amphibious tractors move past a battleship bombarding the island of Okinawa. (U.S. Navy)

tains, snack bars, athletic fields, and started a weekly newspaper.

The creation of Oak Ridge was incredibly demanding. Maj. Gen. LESLIE R. GROVES, director of the MANHATTAN PROJECT for building the bomb, had to, in his words, "design, build, and operate an extremely large plant with equipment of incredible complexity, without the benefit of any pilot plant or intermediate development. . . . Always we were driven by the need to make haste. Consequently, research, development, construction, and operation all had to be started and carried on simultaneously and without appreciable prior knowledge."

Copper would have been sufficient for some of the conductor material needed at Y-12, but, due to other WAR PRODUCTION demands, there was a copper shortage. So Groves decided to substitute silver for copper. He sent an officer to the U.S. Treasury to ask for somewhere between 5,000 and 10,000 tons of silver. A shocked Treasury official said, "Colonel, in the Treasury we do not speak of tons of silver; our unit is the Troy ounce."

Out of Oak Ridge on July 24, 1945, came enough uranium for the first atomic bomb, which would be dropped on HIROSHIMA on Aug. 6.

Oak Ridge continued to be a nuclear production and research facility after the war.

Oask,
see EICHE.

Octagon
Code name for U.S.-British QUEBEC CONFERENCE, Sept. 1944.

Odessa
Secret organization of former SS officers, founded after World War II. Odessa's main function was believed to be arranging for the escape of SS officers wanted for WAR CRIMES. The name is a German acronym from *Organisation der Entlassene SS Angehörige* (Organization for the Release of Former SS Members). The Odessa had agents throughout Germany who, through an underground known as *Die Spinne* (The Spider), arranged for ex-SS to escape or elude Allied hunters.

U.S. and Israeli intelligence officials believe that Odessa engineered the escape to South America of ADOLF EICHMANN, the SS "expert" on JEWS; JOSEF MENGELE, the SS physician who performed heinous experiments on inmates of AUSCHWITZ; and other, lesser-known SS officers. Existence of the organization became known to Allied occupation officers immediately after the war. One of the founders was believed to be OTTO SKORZENY, the daring special operations leader who in the West was called HITLER'S COMMANDO.

SS officers reportedly smuggled huge sums out of Germany to finance the escapes. Fleeing SS men were provided with false identities and passage was arranged out of Germany at the end of the war. One major terminal of the Odessa escape route, according to Israeli intelligence, was Buenos Aires, Argentina. Israeli hunters found Eichmann there and brought him to Israel for trial.

Oerlikon 20-mm Gun
Swiss-design rapid-fire, antiaircraft gun extensively used by Allied and Axis navies during the war. The gun had established a favorable reputation in the SPANISH CIVIL WAR and it was adopted by the Japanese Navy, which made several improvements (although few guns were procured). Subsequently, the British adopted it for merchant ships, which influenced the U.S. Navy's late 1941 decision to begin installing Oerlikons in warships. The original guns were of Swiss manufacture, but soon they were being produced indigenously. Several thousand were produced for the U.S. Navy and about 5,500 for the British Commonwealth fleets.

The gun was particularly used on small craft and SUBMARINES. However, the relative short range of the 20-mm gun, about 4,000 yards, gave it a limited effectiveness against aircraft, while the small size of its rounds also limited its effectiveness against KAMIKAZES.

The Oerlikon operated on the blow-back principle, with the explosive force of the propellant moving the breach to accept the next round. The gun's high rate of fire (450 to 480 rounds per minute), its light weight, and the ability to bolt it to the deck without electrical connections made it suitable for ships and small craft of virtually any size. Single, twin, triple, and even quad mounts were provided in ships from PT-BOAT size (one or two mounts) to

BATTLESHIPS and AIRCRAFT CARRIERS, which could mount scores of 20-mm guns.

The 20-mm/70-cal Oerlikon was fired by a gunner, one or two ammunition loaders, and either a radio talker or pointer to point out approaching aircraft to the gunner. The 20-mm guns had either a simple open sight, or a gyroscopic sight that took into account the ship's pitch, roll, yaw, and speed changes.

Weights of the gun mounts varied, being about 950 pounds for the single-barrel and up to 1,400 pounds for the twin, plus 240 pounds for the optional flat shield. The standard drum-type magazine held 60 rounds of semi-armor-piercing, high-explosive, and tracer ammunition. The rounds weighed about 8.5 ounces and were 7.18 inches long.

Office of Price Administration

U.S. government agency that controlled prices and rents. The OPA, as it was usually called, traced its origin to the Office of Price Administration and Civilian Supply within the Office for Emergency Management, which was established in April 1941. The Office of Price Administration was established in Aug. 1941 and became an independent agency in Jan. 1942, after considerable congressional debate.

OPA stabilized prices of goods, services, and residential rents. A later presidential directive gave the OPA RATIONING powers. One of the OPA's first acts was to bring a new phrase into the LANGUAGE: price freeze. Effective May 1942, the OPS froze prices for nearly all everyday goods and about 60 percent of all foods at March 1942 levels. But the cost of living, fueled primarily by uncontrolled prices on subsidized commodities, rose steadily, as did wages. Stabilization was threatened.

In Oct. 1942, an amendment extended OPA price control over more services (but not theater tickets) and to nearly all food prices. Rents were frozen, in most cases as of March 1942 in 459 "defense rental areas" with about 20,000,000 dwelling units. Between Aug. 1939 and Sept. 1946 rents rose less than 5 percent.

Amendments controlling the OPA came annually because the OPA lived from year to year by reluctant congressional authorization. In 1943, for example, Congress directed that anyone in the OPA who handled price policies had to have business or industrial experience. (Wags called the mandate the "anti-college-professor amendment.") Farm-state members of Congress constantly pressured the OPA to raise price ceilings on agricultural products.

The first administrator of the OPA was LEON HENDERSON, an economist. The OPA was a vast bureaucracy, run, said its many critics, by "Washington warlords." More than 63,000 paid workers were supplemented by some 235,000 volunteers, most of them serving on 5,0661 local price and rationing boards. These grass-roots units of the OPA handled such local matters as whether a veterinarian's request for more rationed tires weighed more heavily than a dentist's request.

When the war ended, rationing immediately stopped, except on sugar. Price lids also remained. OPA's annual authorization expired on June 30, 1946—and prices skyrocketed almost 25 percent. But Congress, concerned about this surge, brought OPA back to life in July; prices and rents in effect on June 30 were restored. Controls were gradually removed through 1946. From 1946 to 1947 wholesale prices increased more than they had during the entire war.

Office of Scientific Research and Development

U.S. agency that directed much of the research into such wartime projects as the ATOMIC BOMB, the PROXIMITY FUZE, and penicillin. The director of the OSRD was VANNEVAR BUSH. The office, established in June 1941, grew out of the National Defense Research Council (NDRC), which was the original agency for the handling of atomic bomb research through the URANIUM Committee.

At the end of 1941 the atomic work passed to the OSRD under Bush. Within the OSRD the atomic bomb project was known as the S-1 program, signifying that it was no longer a research project but was under development in Section One of the OSRD. When research showed that the atomic bomb was potentially a practical weapon, its further development was taken over by the MANHATTAN PROJECT, under the direction of Maj. Gen. LESLIE R. GROVES.

The OSRD worked on a wide spectrum of projects, including psychological studies aimed at classification and selection of personnel; techniques for secretly examining the mail of suspected spies; and providing scientists for the ALSOS MISSION, which, following Allied forces as they liberated occupied Europe, sought out evidence of German and Italian nuclear weapon work.

Office of Strategic Services

U.S. wartime intelligence agency. President ROOSEVELT created the Office of Strategic Services (OSS) on June 13, 1942. The OSS, which was placed under the jurisdiction of the JOINT CHIEFS OF STAFF, replaced the Office of Coordinator of Information, a quasi-intelligence organization. Roosevelt named WILLIAM J. DONOVAN, who had been Coordinator of Information, director of the new agency.

Donovan, a New York lawyer and a retired U.S. Army officer, roughly modeled the OSS on the SPECIAL OPERATIONS EXECUTIVE, a British secret agency that ran resistance groups and GUERRILLA activities in German-occupied countries. The OSS was organized into five branches: Secret Intelligence (SI) for intelligence gathering and ESPIONAGE; Secret Operations (SO) for such missions as parachuting agents into enemy territory; Research and Analysis (R and A—also known as the "Chairborne Division") for such work as determining the effect of Allied bombing on German-occupied Europe; Morale Operations (MO) for "black" PROPAGANDA efforts, such as broadcasting from England fake German radio stations ostensibly operated by nonexistent anti-NAZI groups; and counterintelligence (X-2) for protecting U.S. intelligence.

The OSS recruited a great variety of Americans: university professors like Arthur M. Schlesinger, Jr.; lawyers, including future Supreme Court Justice Arthur Goldberg; advertising men, journalists, and writers (including Gene Fodor, originator of the Fodor Guides); and economists (for such matters as analysis of German war production in terms of good air-raid targets). Cookbook author Julia Child served in the OSS in WASHINGTON and later in China. She recalls that the outfit was called "Oh! So Secret!" Others, because of the notables in the OSS ranks, said it meant "Oh, So Social."

Under a formal agreement with British intelligence officials, the OSS did not launch independent missions from England. At the beginning, OSS strength lay in North Africa, where it had gathered intelligence in advance of the Nov. 1942 invasion. The first of many OSS forays into Europe originated from North Africa, where OSS officials had recruited two agents who set up an intelligence network in southern France.

Later, as relations improved between U.S. and British intelligence officials, the OSS generated joint missions with the British. To aid FRENCH RESISTANCE units, three-person teams—an American, a Briton, a Free French soldier—were dropped into France. They were known as JEDBURGHS.

The Jedburghs were dropped after the NORMANDY INVASION, as were OSS Operational Groups (OGs), known as Donovan's "private army." These units of four officers and about thirty men, all of whom spoke at least passable French, worked behind the lines and often fought in small fire fights. (The BRITISH SPECIAL AIR SERVICE had similar units.)

As the Allied armies advanced across Europe, OSS agents were parachuted into Germany, equipped with small transmitter-receiver radios (see JOAN ELEANOR). By the end of the war the OSS had placed nearly 200 agents in Germany; many were German PRISONERS OF WAR who were given fake identification papers and specific assignments, such as, locate V-1 BUZZ BOMB sites and find out the effects of air raids on BERLIN.

The OSS developed independent operations in neutral countries, with operatives in Lisbon, Stockholm, Madrid, Istanbul, and Bern. ALLEN W. DULLES, head of OSS operations in Switzerland, established contacts with anti-HITLER Germans and worked on SURRENDER overtures.

OSS agents operated in the China-Burma-India area, often in collaboration with British forces. But Gen. DOUGLAS MACARTHUR refused to allow the OSS to operate within his Southwest Pacific Command.

The OSS was officially abolished by President TRUMAN'S executive order on Sept, 20, 1945, with its functions temporarily transferred to the State Department and the War Department. But from the OSS would emerge the Central Intelligence Agency. In Jan. 1946 Truman established the Central Intelligence Group; the name was changed to

Central Intelligence Agency under the National Security Act of July 1947. Among the Directors of Central Intelligence have been veterans of OSS: Allen Dulles, William Colby, Richard Helms, and WILLIAM CASEY, who was chief of the LONDON OSS headquarters under Donovan.

Office of War Information

U.S. war agency. President ROOSEVELT established the Office of War Information on June 16, 1942, and named journalist–radio broadcaster Elmer Davis the director. His deputies would include MILTON EISENHOWER, Robert E. Sherwood (who often worked as a presidential speech writer), and author Leo Rosten.

The OWI, absorbing the Office of Facts and Figures, the Office of Government Reports, the Division of Information, and the Foreign Information Service, mushroomed into a major agency, with regional offices, hundreds of writers, and a peak payroll of 5,693. In 1943 Congress ordered a cutback, but this did not stop the OWI from sending no less than 440 employees to Europe to cover the NORMANDY INVASION.

Under OWI auspices, *Newsweek, The New Yorker, Life,* and several other magazines published free miniature editions, without advertising, for distribution to service men and women overseas. Book publishers were also recruited to provide paperback, small-format (but unabridged) books for free distribution to service men and women.

The OWI also ran eighteen radio stations beaming "Voice of America" broadcasts overseas in forty languages. Latin America was off-limits to such broadcasts; PROPAGANDA for that region was under the control of Nelson A. Rockefeller, coordinator of the Office of Inter-American Affairs.

OWI officials mobilized the advertising industry, directing propaganda and war-effort ads in print and on radio; during 1942 alone the major radio networks devoted more than 4,000 hours to OWI-endorsed war programs and announcements. The OWI also ventured into MOVIES, releasing 77,387 prints on 177 subjects.

The Surveys Division of OWI made studies of public opinion and morale, including a survey of drinking in and around military bases. ("No American army in all history," the survey said, "has been

so orderly.") OWI propaganda specialists, operating through the Psychological Warfare Branch of the Army, supervised the distribution of leaflets urging German soldiers to surrender, and ran such operations as the dropping of packets of salt to villages in Burma in 1945 to alleviate a salt shortage and, through the accompanying message, gain support for the ALLIES.

President TRUMAN abolished the OWI on Aug. 31, 1945, but continued its functions, which were taken over by the State Department and, eventually, by the U.S. Information Agency.

Office of War Mobilization

U.S. war agency that coordinated the actions of other agencies involved in production, distribution of goods, and the use of resources. President ROOSEVELT created the OWM in May 1943 in the wake of criticism by Senator HARRY S TRUMAN's investigation committee. Truman's powerful committee, saying that the war effort lacked central authority, had called for a super-agency. Roosevelt put the OWM under the control of JAMES F. BYRNES, who operated out of a White House office. Power shifted from the War Production Board to the OWM, which acted as a referee in interagency disputes. It also ruffled the military by reviewing contracts awarded by the armed services. In Oct. 1944 the OWM was succeeded by the Office of War Mobilization and Reconversion, which established policies for demobilization and the transition to a peacetime economy.

O'Hare, Lt. Comdr. Edward H. (1914–1943)

The U.S. Navy's first fighter ACE. A pilot in Fighting SQUADRON (VF) 3 on the carrier *LEXINGTON* (CV 2) at the time of the PEARL HARBOR attack, Lt. O'Hare first saw combat on Feb. 20, 1942, as the *Lexington* force attempted to attack the Japanese base at RABAUL on NEW BRITAIN. While steaming off BOUGAINVILLE, shipboard RADAR detected approaching Japanese bombers and O'Hare piloted one of several F4F WILDCAT fighters sent to intercept the attackers. Within four minutes, he shot down five twin-engine G4M1 BETTY bombers, becoming the first Navy pilot to become an ace.

(Although all but one or two of the eighteen attacking planes were shot down by fighters and shipboard gunners, the element of surprise was lost and the planned raid against Rabaul was aborted; no damage was inflicted on the U.S. ships.)

O'Hare was awarded the MEDAL OF HONOR for this action.

After briefly serving as executive officer of VF-3, O'Hare was detached from the *Lexington* in April 1942 (shortly before she was sunk at the Battle of CORAL SEA). After a brief reunion with his family, on April 21 he went to the White House for presentation of his medal by President ROOSEVELT. That day he was also promoted to lieutenant commander.

In Nov. 1943 O'Hare commanded the air GROUP that went aboard the carrier *ENTERPRISE* (CV 6). On the night of Nov. 26, in the Navy's first night air operations, undertaken in support of the AMPHIBIOUS LANDINGS in the GILBERT ISLANDS, Lt. Comdr. O'Hare took off in an F6F HELLCAT with another fighter, to be guided to intruding Japanese planes by radar fitted in a TBF AVENGER. The Avenger shot down two enemy bombers, and was vectoring the fighters to others when, apparently, the Avenger's gunner mistakenly shot down his plane.

O'Kane, Lt. Comdr. Richard H. (1911—)

U.S. Navy SUBMARINE ACE. O'Kane commanded the submarine *Tang* (SS 306) for five war patrols in 1944 during which she is credited with sinking twenty-four Japanese ships of 93,824 tons.

A 1934 graduate of the Naval Academy, he served in surface ships until 1938 when he then entered submarine service. O'Kane was on board the submarine *Argonaut* (SM 1) patrolling near MIDWAY on Dec. 7, 1941. He subsequently served as executive officer in the submarine *Wahoo* (238), one of the top-scoring submarines in the Pacific.

As a lieutenant commander he took command of the submarine *Tang* (SS 306) when she was commissioned in Oct. 1943. After fitting out and training, the *Tang* departed PEARL HARBOR on her first war patrol on Jan. 22, 1944. Heading for the CAROLINE-MARIANA areas, the *Tang* claimed her first victim on Feb. 17, sinking a large Japanese cargo ship. In five war patrols under O'Kane's command,

the *Tang* achieved a U.S. submarine record exceeded in number of enemy ships sunk only by the *TAUTOG* (SS 199) and in tonnage sunk only by the *FLASHER* (SS 249).

The *Tang* met her demise in a striking way when, on the night of Oct. 24–25, 1944, O'Kane sighted a Japanese convoy steaming near Formosa. The *Tang* was able to sink two tankers and an escort ship. With two TORPEDOES remaining, O'Kane attacked a transport. He fired those two "fish": the first ran "hot and straight"; the second torpedo left the tube but O'Kane, on the bridge during the night attack, saw this last torpedo broach the surface and then circle back toward the submarine.

O'Kane rang up full speed and threw the rudder hard over in an effort to evade the torpedo. The *Tang* was hit in the stern. There was a massive explosion and the submarine sank rapidly, stern first. Of nine men on the bridge, only three, including O'Kane, escaped from the conning tower and were alive on the surface when dawn came. On the bottom at 180 feet, inside the *Tang* the surviving crewmen destroyed secret documents and equipment. Thirteen men then escaped from the forward torpedo room using Momsen breathing devices. Only five of them survived the escape attempt.

The eight *Tang* survivors were picked up by a Japanese destroyer. They endured ten months in a Japanese PRISONER OF WAR camp, all being beaten and abused by their captors. Liberated at the end of the war, O'Kane was presented with the MEDAL OF HONOR by President TRUMAN in 1946 for his successful fifth war patrol. He retired from the Navy in 1957 with the rank of rear admiral.

Okha,

see BAKA.

Okinawa

Pacific island group in the center of the Ryukyu Islands, the islands nearest the Japanese home islands. Allied strategists saw Okinawa as the near-culmination of the U.S. CENTRAL PACIFIC CAMPAIGN: the capture of an invaluable advanced staging base for the expected invasion of Japan. (See MAJESTIC.) The Japanese saw the defense of Okinawa as their last chance to hold off an invasion of Japan itself.

The AMPHIBIOUS LANDING to take Okinawa, code-named Iceberg, was massive and bloody. The 100,000 Japanese troops on the island planned to sell themselves dearly, using the last units of the Imperial Fleet, KAMIKAZE raids, and suicidal BANZAI charges. The creed of the 32nd Japanese Army on Okinawa was: "One plane for one warship. One boat for one ship. One man for ten enemy. One man for one tank."

The invasion fleet consisted of the largest number of ships involved in a single operation during the entire Pacific War: nearly 1,500 combatant and auxiliary vessels. In addition, the British sent a fast carrier task force of twenty-two ships, with 244 aircraft in four carriers to supplement the Americans' nearly 1,000 carrier aircraft. About 500,000 men—U.S. Army, Navy, Marines, and Royal Navy—would participate in the operation.

The invasion was originally scheduled for March 1, 1945, but because of delays in the Philippines campaign and at IWO JIMA, Iceberg was set back to April 1, Easter Sunday. Pre-invasion bombardment of Okinawa began a week before the landings, and on March 26 U.S. forces seized five small islands of the Kerama Retto group, just west of Okinawa, to cut off a force of enemy suicide boats and establish a preliminary fleet anchorage.

The landing began at 4:06 Easter morning, starting with a feint toward the southeastern shore of the island. The real landing would be along a 5-mile stretch of beach on the southwestern coast, near two important airfields. The Marines and Army troops came ashore and within four days had attained most of their objectives, with limited opposition.

The Japanese initial response was aimed at the landings in the form of intense kamikaze attacks on the naval task force. More than 1,900 kamikaze sorties would be flown between now and July, sinking or damaging 263 ships of all types. By verified count 2,336 Japanese aircraft were destroyed by U.S. AIRCRAFT CARRIER planes and guns.

Ashore, the Japanese made their stand behind what became known as the Shuri line, from an ancient nearby castle. Allowing the U.S. invaders to take the airfields, the Japanese bided their time.

On April 4, Army troops ran up against the Shuri line for the first time. They fought for eight days to take a ridge and clear the Japanese out of numerous caves. A major offensive against the line failed on May 11. Finally, the 1st Marine DIVISION took Shuri Castle on May 29. By that time Japanese strength was failing. More than 62,500 Japanese and Okinawans had been killed around Shuri, and 5,000 more had been killed on Ie Shima, a small island off Okinawa's west coast. There ERNIE PYLE, one of America's best known WAR CORRESPONDENTS, was killed by a Japanese sniper.

The Japanese evacuated Shuri, moving south to establish another defensive line at Yaeju Dake and Yazu Dake. The two commanders of the forces died within five days of each other. Lt. Gen. SIMON B. BUCKNER died of shrapnel wounds on June 18; Lt. Gen. Mituru Ushijima committed suicide on June 23.

On April 13, word was passed about the death of President ROOSEVELT and memorial services were held wherever possible. Fighting on Okinawa continued until the last week of June and the campaign was officially ended on July 2. Both sides suffered horrendous casualties. More than 107,000 Japanese and Okinawian military and civilian personnel died. U.S. losses were 31,807 Marines wounded, 7,163 killed or missing in action; the Navy sustained 9,731 casualties in ships.

There were also more than 25,000 "nonbattle" casualties due to combat fatigue. An official report on the battle said, "The rate of psychiatric cases was probably higher on Okinawa than in any other previous operation in the Pacific." The cases were attributed to the intensity of the fighting and the persistent artillery and mortar fire.

Olive

Code name for Allied attacks on the Gothic Line, Italy.

Olympic

Code name for U.S. plans for the AMPHIBIOUS LANDING in Kyushu, Japan in Nov. 1945. (See MAJESTIC.)

Omaha

Code name for U.S. invasion beach at Normandy on the Calvados coast.

Onishi, Vice Adm. Takijiro (1891–1945)

Planner of the PEARL HARBOR attack and founder of the Japanese KAMIKAZE force. In early 1941 Adm. ISOROKU YAMAMOTO, Commander in Chief of the Japanese Navy, directed then-Rear Adm. Onishi, one of Japan's leading naval aviators, to prepare the preliminary study and plan for an attack on Pearl Harbor. Comdr. MINORU GENDA collaborated in the planning.

Yamamoto told Onishi, "If we have a war with the United States we will have no hope of winning unless the United States Fleet in Hawaiian waters can be destroyed." His study of a carrier-based air attack in Pearl Harbor, submitted in April 1941, stated that the attacking force would have a 50-50 chance of success.

At the beginning of the war he commanded the highly successful air assault on the Philippines. Subsequently, his abrasive and arrogant manner led to his being assigned to minor positions. However, on Oct. 17, 1944, he took command of the 1st Air Fleet in the Philippines and directed land-based aviation in the battle of LEYTE GULF. On Oct. 25 he initiated organized suicide air attacks against U.S. ships, a tactic that would continue until the end of the war.

In May 1945 he was appointed vice chief of the Naval General Staff. Onishi strongly opposed the Japanese surrender and on Aug. 16 he committed ceremonial suicide *(seppuku)*, taking eighteen agonizing hours to die.

OPA,

see OFFICE OF PRICE ADMINISTRATION.

Open City

City declared undefended and free of military activity. For this guarantee, an open city is given immunity from attack or bombardment. Cities given this status during the war had widely varying experiences.

ROTTERDAM: When the German BLITZKRIEG struck the Netherlands in May 1940, the Germans said they would spare the city if the Dutch surrendered. While the Dutch attempted to negotiate, the bombing of Rotterdam began and much of the city was destroyed; 814 persons were killed and 78,000 lost their homes.

PARIS: Declared an open city on June 13, 1940, the day before it fell to the Germans, it was not damaged until fighting erupted during its liberation in Aug. 1944.

Belgrade: After German troops invaded Yugoslavia on April 6, 1941, it was declared an open city, but German planes bombed it.

MANILA: As Gen. DOUGLAS MACARTHUR began evacuating the city in Dec. 1941 he declared it an open city; two days later Japanese planes began a heavy bombing campaign, a prelude to their occupation. (In month-long fighting by U.S. troops liberating the city in 1945, much of Manila was destroyed.)

ROME: The Eternal City escaped much damage during the war and was declared an open city by the Germans in the fall of 1943 as Allied troops advanced in Italy. Although the ALLIES hoped to honor that declaration, they did bomb military targets on the outskirts of the city. In a letter to EAMON DE VALERA, president of Ireland, on April 19, 1944, President ROOSEVELT said, "If the German forces were not entrenched in Rome, no question would arise concerning the city's preservation." A Gallup poll taken in the United States around that time showed that 74 percent of the respondents approved the bombing of "historic and religious shrines" for military necessity.

Operations Research

The application of organized and systematized analysis to specific situations, such as military operations. The term "operational research" traces back to 1937 when some workers at the Air Ministry Research Station were given the task of figuring out how to put to use a promising new radio-echo detection system that later would be called RADAR. The word *operational* was inserted into the group's research title to set off what they were doing from traditional research and development activities. Thus was born operational research, usually just called OR.

Among the advocates of operational research was Professor SOLLY ZUCKERMAN, a zoologist (monkeys were his special interest). Applying scientific analysis to war, he called a military operation "an experiment of a very crude kind."

Operational researchers discovered, for example, that the mathematical concept of "constant effectiveness ratio" could be applied to warfare; results obtained in one theater of war or in a series of battles could be considered "constant" elsewhere. One constant effectiveness ratio study showed that whether British aircraft laid mines in German sea lanes or German planes dropped MINES in British ports, the effectiveness ratio remained constant: for every sixty mines laid, one ship was sunk.

OR analysts poured over reports of the bombing of railways in Italy and then translated that data into plans for the massive bombing of German railroads. Knocking out a railroad system was merely an exercise in network mathematics. OR analyzed the convoy system and found that the percentage of losses in large convoys was much smaller than losses in small ones. A mathematical analysis showed that seven escorts could protect sixty ships as well as six escorts could protect forty.

OR looked into how antisubmarine warfare aircraft fought their war and saw what they did as an operational system. When one of the planes spotted a U-BOAT on the surface charging its batteries, the pilot made a DEPTH CHARGE run. The U-boat had about two minutes to try to escape before the attack. The depth charges were set to explode when they were 100 feet below the surface.

OR figured out that the U-boats were escaping because they were nowhere near 100 feet down by the time the depth charge exploded. OR suggested that the depth charges be set to explode at 25 feet. So devastating was the effect of the change that the Germans believed the British had developed a powerful new explosive.

U.S. military officers discovered operational research (which became *operations* research when it crossed the Atlantic) soon after they began joint warfare with the British. One of the first U.S. organizations devoted to OR was the Naval Research Laboratory's Operations Research Group (ORG). The ORG studied several naval problems, including what to do about Japanese KAMIKAZE attacks.

A special ORG research section found that the kamikazes were far more effective than dive bombers or torpedo planes: of the kamikazes that managed to aim themselves at ships, 5 percent were getting through intense antiaircraft fire and making hits that sank ships.

The ORG looked at antiaircraft guns' angles of aiming and rates of fire, at the dive angles of the kamikazes, and at the varying ability of large and small ships to take evasive action. The conclusion: a ship under attack should base its evasive tactics not on eluding the kamikaze but on bringing its best concentration of antiaircraft fire to bear on the attacker; a ship should turn beam toward a kamikaze coming in high and turn beam away from a plane coming in low.

The WASHINGTON-based Operations Research Group was also asked to find out why there were so few successes in what had seemed to be a sensible Navy plan for hunting U-boats. The plan took advantage of the U-boat's need to surface frequently to recharge the batteries that powered it underwater. If patrol planes could cover a large enough area in sea lanes where U-boats were known to patrol, at some time in, say, forty-eight hours, a submarine would surface and would be detected. But the plan was not producing very many sightings or kills.

The researchers came up with a new tactic: A plane flew outside the area where a U-boat was believed to be, inducing the U-boat to surface and head along the safest course—that of the disappearing plane. But, in a countermove, the plane returned, and, with the aid of surface ships, attacked. The OR gambit was tested in Atlantic patrols, and it worked.

"By the time the war ended," Andrew Wilson, defense correspondent of the London *Observer*, wrote, "there was scarcely a field of military activity, on the Allied side, that had not been profoundly affected by operational research. Its impact ranged from improvements in tank gunnery and field engineering to the complete recasting of aid and naval procurement programmes."

Oppenheimer, J. Robert (1904–1967)

Director of the LOS ALAMOS laboratory where the first ATOMIC BOMBS were built. Educated at Harvard, Cambridge, and Göttingen, he became a full professor at the age of thirty-two, and taught at both the California Institute of Technology and the University of California.

VANNEVAR BUSH, director of the OFFICE OF SCIENTIFIC RESEARCH AND DEVELOPMENT, which initiated the U.S. efforts to build the atomic bomb, and Gen. LESLIE R. GROVES, head of the MANHATTAN PROJECT that produced the bomb, selected Oppenheimer to run the scientific aspect of the project. Groves made Oppenheimer director of the central laboratory for designing and developing the bomb, Los Alamos, in New Mexico.

Oppenheimer's left-wing associations, vaguely connected with the Communist Party, initially snagged his appointment. Knowing "we were not going to find a better man," Groves, in his book *Now It Can Be Told,* says, "I felt that his potential value outweighed any security risk," and so he signed a memo taking full responsibility for hiring Oppenheimer.

"He accomplished his assigned mission and he did it well," Groves said, summing up in a few words Oppenheimer's long labor. Much of his task involved keeping thousands of people productively working under circumstances that battered sensitive egos and continually bruised delicate scientific protocol.

After the first atomic bombs had been dropped at HIROSHIMA and NAGASAKI, he left Los Alamos and resumed teaching. But he was so often called upon to consult on government atomic projects that he could not maintain a teaching career. In 1947 he became director of the Institute for Advanced Study at Princeton, N.J., whose nonteaching faculty included ALBERT EINSTEIN.

In 1947 the Atomic Energy Commission (AEC) replaced the Army as controller of atomic-weapon production and policy. Oppenheimer was chairman of the AEC's General Advisory Committee of the U.S. Atomic Energy Commission. In Oct. 1949, following the first Soviet atomic-bomb test, Oppenheimer's committee declined to endorse proposals to build a thermonuclear weapon, the hydrogen bomb. In the atmosphere created by the anti-Communism crusade of Sen. JOSEPH MCCARTHY and the cracking of a Communist ESPIONAGE ring (see JULIUS ROSENBERG), Oppenheimer's old left-wing connections were resurrected and reassessed.

In June 1954, after an extraordinary, highly publicized security hearing, the AEC announced that Oppenheimer was being denied further access to classified information because of "concern for the defense and security of the United States."

The AEC (predecessor of the Nuclear Regulatory Commission) concluded that, although there was no doubt about Oppenheimer's loyalty, his left-wing associations made it doubtful that he should be trusted with atomic secrets. In Dec. 1963 he received the ENRICO FERMI Award for his outstanding contributions to atomic energy.

Orange

Code name for U.S. prewar plans for war with Japan.

Oration

Code name for RAF to parachute advisory team into Yugoslavia to assist GUERRILLA operations.

Orkan (Tornado)

German code name for proposed operation to eliminate the Sukhinichi salient in the Soviet Union, mid-1942.

Orphan,

see APHRODITE.

OS2U Kingfisher

U.S. Navy floatplane used during much of the war, employed for spotting gunfire from BATTLESHIPS and CRUISERS and, especially, rescuing downed airmen. Considered a two-place aircraft, in one rescue operation in TRUK lagoon on April 30, 1944, an OS2U piloted by Lt. (j.g.) John Burns picked up nine Navy fliers; unable to fly back to the TASK FORCE because of the load, Burns simply taxied out to sea and rendezvoused with a U.S. SUBMARINE that took the fliers on board. On another occasion, the OS2U that located Capt. EDDIE RICKENBACKER and his companions lost in the South Pacific taxied across 40 miles of rough seas to reach safety. The OS2U was far more popular and more widely used than the later SO3C SEAMEW and SC SEAHAWK.

The prototype of the Vought-Sikorsky OS2U made its first flight on July 20, 1938. Production began almost immediately and the first units reached the fleet in Aug. 1940. Battleships and the larger heavy and light cruisers were normally assigned three or four of the aircraft. During the war several inshore patrol squadrons flew the identical OS2N Kingfisher, produced by the Naval Aircraft Factory in Philadelphia as well as the Vought-Sikorsky OS2U. Total production through Nov. 1942 was 1,218 OS2U aircraft and 300 OS2Ns. Of these, 154 Vought aircraft went to other countries, including 100 to the Royal Navy. The aircraft served in the U.S. Navy into 1946.

A graceful-looking aircraft, the low-wing monoplane had a radial engine and a large cockpit fully faired into the after fuselage. A large single float was provided plus small, fixed stabilizing floats under the wing. The floats could be replaced by a fixed undercarriage for operation from land bases.

The aircraft had a maximum speed of 164 mph and a range of 800 miles. A fixed forward-firing .30-cal. machine gun and a flexible .30-cal. gun in the rear cockpit were provided. Small bombs totaling 240 pounds could be carried under the wings (although more were sometimes carried in an overload condition).

There were provisions for one or two passengers in addition to the two-man crew.

Oscar

The Ki-43 Type 1 *Hayabusa* (Peregrine Falcon) was the most widely flown fighter of the Japanese Army Air Force during the war (Allied code name Oscar). Entering squadron service shortly before the PEARL HARBOR attack, the Oscar was highly maneuverable with a good rate of climb, but somewhat underpowered and, despite updates, unable to compete effectively with U.S. fighters in the latter stages of the war. An official U.S. AAF analysis, however, described later models as "an increasingly dangerous opponent." The Oscar saw combat in all Pacific areas where the Japanese Army conducted air operations, and most Japanese Army ACES scored most of their kills in this aircraft. At the end of the war the Oscar was employed with the Army's *Taiatari* (suicide) units.

First flown in Jan. 1939, the Oscar was designed by Nakajima engineer Hideo Itokawa. Army pilots initially disliked the fighter, which they found less maneuverable than its predecessor,

the Ki-27 NATE. The Oscar was modified, primarily with a "butterfly flap" that was extended in combat to provide additional lift, increase turn rate, and improve control response. The Oscar remained in production throughout the war. Only forty Oscars were in Army service at the time of Pearl Harbor. A more-powerful engine and other features characterized the Ki-43-II, put in production in 1943, and the Ki-43-III, produced from Dec. 1944. Oscar production totaled 5,919 units—more than any other Japanese aircraft of the war. The Oscar was also flown by the Thai Air Force. (After the war they were also flown by Indonesians against the Dutch, and briefly, by the French in the INDOCHINA conflict.)

The Oscar was a simple, streamlined aircraft; the radial-engine, low-wing aircraft resembled the A6M ZERO and to some extent Western fighters. It had a bubble canopy and was one of the first Japanese fighters to have armor; later models were also fitted with protected fuel tanks.

The major production variant, the Ki-43-II, had a maximum speed of 329 mph, which was increased in the IIIa to 358 mph. Normal range for the II was 1,095 miles, extended to 1,990 miles with a drop tank, reflecting the Japanese interest in long-range fighter operations.

Most aircraft had two 12.7-mm machine guns, making them highly undergunned by Western standards. The IIIb variant, of which only two prototypes were produced, instead had two 20-mm cannon. The II and III variants could carry two 551-pound BOMBS.

OSS,

see OFFICE OF STRATEGIC SERVICES.

Overcast

Code name for operation to relocate German scientists and engineers in the United States after the war. The operation began in July 1945; the most prominent scientist brought to the United States was WERNHER VON BRAUN.

Overlord

Code name for Allied invasion of Western Europe (NORMANDY INVASION), 1944.

OWI,
  see OFFICE OF WAR INFORMATION.

Oxford

The Airspeed firm's Oxford—known as the "Ox-Box" to British fliers—was a twin-engine bombing and gunnery trainer in service from 1937. Almost 400 were in RAF service by the time the EUROPEAN WAR began; production was stepped up with several firms producing a total of 8,751 of the planes for Commonwealth as well as British use as trainers, flying ambulances, and utility aircraft.

Oyster

British code name for daylight air attack on the Philipps factory in Eindhoven, the Netherlands, 1942.

P

P-36

The first U.S. fighter aircraft in combat in the war. The P-36 was flown primarily by foreign air forces, although a few were flown by the U.S. Army at the start of the war in HAWAII and in the Philippines. Those P-36s (as well as a few older P-35 and P-26 fighters) were unable to halt the onslaught of attacking Japanese. And, when U.S. troops invaded North Africa in Nov. 1942 they fought against these fighters flown by VICHY FRENCH pilots.

The first commercial Hawk 75 variant of the P-36 was flown in 1937 by CLAIRE L. CHENNAULT, head of the Chinese Air Force. A year later 112 Hawk 75s were sent to China; they suffered more losses from inexperienced pilots than from Japanese fighters. More Hawk 75s were built for Argentina (where 200 were built under license), Thailand (Siam), and France. France had bought 200 before the EUROPEAN WAR started. After a French pilot shot down a German aircraft in Sept. 1939, France ordered another 430 Hawk 75 aircraft. These were followed by orders from Iran, Norway, and the DUTCH EAST INDIES.

After the fall of France, forty-four captured Hawk 75s were sold by the Germans to Finland; 227 others were taken over by the British. Called Mohawk in RAF service, about 100 of these planes were sent to North Africa beginning in Dec. 1940; when newer fighters became available to the British in North Africa, their Hawk 75s were sent on to South Africa as trainers. Another 100 of these Mohawks were sent to India in Dec.

The U.S. destroyer *Shaw* (DD 373) blows up after being struck by a Japanese bomb during the Pearl Harbor attack. At right can be seen the stern of the battleship *Nevada* (BB 36), the only dreadnought to get under way during the raid. *(U.S. Navy)*

1941; they saw action against the Japanese, flying on the Burma front until Jan. 1944. (British Mohawks saw no combat in Europe.) When Norway was lost to the Germans, thirty Norwegian Hawk 75s in production were used in Canada for flight training, then sold to the U.S. Army (as P-36G), and later transferred to Peru. Dutch pilots in Java flew Hawks against Japanese planes, again with little effect.

The Curtiss P-36 lost a U.S. Army fighter competition to what would become the P-35 designed by ALEXANDER P. DE SEVERSKY. Still, in July 1936 the Army ordered three YP-36 prototypes and flight tests began in Feb. 1937. In July the Army ordered 210 production aircraft, of which 177 were the P-36A and thirty-one were P-36C aircraft. The first Army deliveries were in April 1938; one plane of this order became the prototype P-40 WARHAWK and another the XP-42. Over 500 Hawk 75s were produced for other air forces (plus the 200 built in Argentina).

The P-36 was a low-wing monoplane, with a large radial engine, a configuration that became common for many war-era fighters. The tail-sitting aircraft had a fully retractable landing gear (including tail wheel).

Top speed of the P-36A was 300 mph with a range given at 825 miles. That airplane had two .30-cal. machine guns in the engine cowling; this was increased in the P-36C by two more .30s in the wings. There were several attempts to increase the P-36 firepower, among them the XP-36E with one .50-cal. machine gun in the cowling and eight .30-cal. wing guns (an attempt to match the new European eight-gun fighters) and the XP-36F with a .23-mm cannon fitted beneath each wing in addition to one .30-cal. and one .50-cal. guns in the cowling. The single P-36B had an improved engine providing a speed of 313 mph. The P-36 was a single-seat aircraft.

P-38 Lightning

The U.S. Army's highest-performance and longest-range fighter when the United States entered the war. Although produced in smaller numbers than other major AAF fighters, the P-38 served in virtually every theater of the war. In Europe P-38s were used in the early efforts to provide a long-range

escort for B-17 FLYING FORTRESS and B-24 LIBERATOR bombers. In the Pacific P-38s were used for the attack on Japanese fleet commander Adm. ISOROKU YAMAMOTO on April 14, 1943, over BOUGAINVILLE (sixteen P-38s shot down the BETTY bomber carrying Yamamoto as well as a second Betty and three ZERO fighters for the loss of one U.S. plane; those P-38s flew 550 miles from their base on GUADALCANAL). The top U.S. AAF ACES of the war, RICHARD BONG and Thomas B. McGuire, scored their kills against Japanese aircraft in P-38s. Thus, it was appropriate that a P-38 was apparently the first U.S. aircraft to land in Japan after the Japanese capitulation.

This aircraft was the first venture into military aircraft of the Lockheed Corp. Flight testing of the XP-38 began on Jan. 27, 1939, and production was initiated before service-test models ordered in April 1939 had been completed. Production lagged and only sixty-nine aircraft were in service on Dec. 7, 1941, but a total of 9,923 aircraft were delivered through Aug. 1945. These included a few two-seat reconnaissance (RP-38) and RADAR-equipped night-fighter (P-38M) variants, and two-seat "J" and "L" models that had a bomb-aimer position in a lengthened, glazed nose; the F-4 and F-5 were single-seat photo variants of the P-38. Those with bombardiers (and a NORDEN BOMBSIGHT) were used in Europe to lead formations of P-38s that would release their BOMBS on signal from the lead ship. Later bomb leaders had radar (in place of the Norden) to permit bombing through clouds. A few P-38F models had a second seat (but no controls) jammed in to teach pilots P-38 tactics.

The twin-engine aircraft had twin tail booms, with the small, bullet-like fuselage mounted on the wing between the fuselages. This arrangement alleviated the need to synchronize guns firing through propellers. The usual armament was four .50-cal. machine guns and one 20-mm or 23-mm cannon, with up to 3,200 pounds of bombs being carried externally in some models.

The plane's high speed (up to 414 mph in later models), long range, and fast rate of climb made it a worthy opponent. As a fighter-bomber with 2,000 pounds of bombs it had a combat range of almost 700 miles. In a fighter-escort role the range of the later models approached 2,000 miles.

P-39 Airacobra

Along with the P-40 WARHAWK, the P-39 was the principal "pursuit" aircraft of the U.S. Army when America entered the war. At the time the P-39 was already approaching obsolescence in comparison with contemporary European fighters. The official U.S. AAF history states: "Especially disappointing was the P-39, whose low ceiling, slow rate of climb, and relative lack of maneuverability puts its pilot at a decided disadvantage wherever they fought."

The P-39 saw relatively little action with U.S. forces and never achieved the popularity of the P-40. It was used with some success as a ground-attack aircraft. The peak AAF inventory was 2,150 in early 1944. The P-39 was the only U.S.-built fighter to serve in large numbers with a former AXIS air force *during* the war: Italian fighter squadrons were provided with 149 P-39N and P-39Q variants in 1944—after Italy surrendered to the Allies—to provide fighter-bomber support for Yugoslav GUERRILLAS. About one half of the total P-39 production—some 5,000 aircraft—were also supplied to the Soviet Union under LEND-LEASE.

The Bell XP-39 prototype flew in April 1938 followed by a U.S. order for thirteen YP-39s for evaluation. However, the French Air Force did place an order, which was taken over by the British in 1940; the first of these Airacobras reached the RAF in July 1941 and were employed only briefly in the ground-attack role in North Africa. Some of the French-British order was taken over by the AAF as training aircraft. The P-39C was the first combat version ordered for U.S. service and the P-39D was the first to enter quantity production. Total P-39 deliveries between 1940 and 1944 was 9,558 aircraft; variants reached the designation P-39Q (there were no I, H, or P). A single P-39C acquired by the U.S. Navy for evaluation as a carrier fighter was designated XFL-1 and named Airabonita; no others followed.

The P-39 was a sleek-looking, low-wing fighter with the unusual arrangement of the engine being *behind* the cockpit, with a 37-mm cannon firing through the propeller spinner. In addition, four .30-cal. and then .50-cal. machine guns were fitted in the wings; a 500-pound BOMB could be carried. The P-39D had a top speed of 368 mph; engine limitations prevented effective combat above about 13,000 feet.

P-40 Warhawk

U.S. fighter aircraft. The P-40 and the P-39 AIRACOBRA were the principal U.S. Army "pursuit" aircraft or fighters when the United States entered the war. At the time Army officials considered the P-40 little more than an advanced training plane. In 1941–1943 P-40s were in action at PEARL HARBOR during the Japanese carrier attack, in the PHILIPPINES, the DUTCH EAST INDIES, and North Africa. It was flown by the FLYING TIGERS in China against Japanese aircraft in 1941–1942. The P-40 was generally outclassed by contemporary Allied and AXIS fighters, but acquitted itself well in combat because of its rugged construction and the skill of its pilots.

The Curtiss P-40 was a development of the firm's earlier P-36. The later plane, a single-engine, monoplane fighter, had a liquid-cooled engine with a top speed of about 350 mph. The aircraft's altitude was limited to about 12,000 feet. The plane's success was due, according to the official U.S. AAF history, "to the fact of its employment chiefly against the Japanese rather than the German Air Force. . . ."

The P-40 was the first American mass-produced fighter plane; 13,738 P-40s were built by Curtiss between 1940 and 1944. Some 2,000 were sent to Britain, France, China, Canada, New Zealand, and the Soviet Union. (The British called them Tomahawks and Kittyhawks.)

Armament in the early P-40s consisted of two .30-cal. machine guns, increased to six .50-cal. guns in later models. Small BOMBS could be carried; however, in India the 51st Fighter GROUP (AAF), after a series of experiments, modified P-40s to carry a 1,000-pound bomb. These planes were informally referred to as "B-40" and were highly effective as dive bombers. The P-40 had a single pilot.

P-47 Thunderbolt

One of the most widely flown U.S. Army fighters. In 1944–1945 the P-47 or "jug" was flown by more than 40 percent of all AAF fighter GROUPS serving overseas. The only AAF fighter that surpassed the all-around performance of the P-47 was the P-51 MUSTANG. The P-47 saw extensive combat in both the European and Pacific theaters as an interceptor, bomber escort, and ground-attack aircraft.

The P-47 was designed by Republic Aviation Corp. in 1940 when the U.S. AAF belatedly recognized the need for a high-performance fighter that could compare with European fighters. The original aircraft had a liquid-cooled engine, but concern over production rates led to adoption of the new Pratt & Whitney R-2800 air-cooled engine.

The XP-47B—with an air-cooled engine—first flew on May 6, 1941. A large number of "teething" problems delayed the plane's production. The first AAF P-47 group reached England in January 1943 but did not enter combat in Europe until April 1943. Acceptance progressed rapidly and at the end of the Pacific War there were thirty-one AAF fighter groups with P-47s. The total P-47 production was 15,683 aircraft, several hundred of which went to FREE FRENCH, British, and Soviet fighter units.

The low-wing aircraft's appearance was dominated by the large radial engine that demanded a large fuselage. An elliptical wing plan form and telescopic landing gear were required to provide ground clearance for the large, four-blade propeller. The P-47 was the heaviest piston-engine fighter ever produced for the AAF. During production of the P-47D model the bubble-type cockpit was adopted, providing all-around visibility for the pilot.

Combat range as a fighter-bomber was initially about 500 miles and as an escort fighter 1,000 miles; in later models these ranges were extended to some 800 and 2,000 miles! Top speed was increased from some 425 mph in early models to 460 mph, although the rate of climb declined in the later, heavier models. An XP-47J fitted with a supercharger reached 504 mph. The production aircraft had a powerful gun armament, consisting of six or eight .50-cal. machine guns plus the capacity for six 5-inch air-to-ground ROCKETS and 2,000 pounds of BOMBS. This weapons payload made the P-47 an effective fighter-bomber. It was flown by a single pilot.

P-51 Mustang

The P-51 was the most capable U.S. land-based fighter of the war. But in the words of the official U.S. Army Air Forces history, because of AAF reluctance to adopt the plane, the Mustang "came close to representing the costliest mistake made by the AAF in World War II."

By 1943 the U.S. STRATEGIC BOMBING effort against Germany had failed because of the high loss rate; only the availability of the P-51 from Dec. 1943 permitted a resumption of daylight bombing. Its first long-range escort mission on Dec. 13 was 490 miles from bases in England to Kiel and back, a fighter escort record at that time. The following March the P-51s accompanied the heavy bombers all the way to BERLIN and back, a round trip of 1,100 miles.

Aviation historian William Green has called the P-51 "probably the best all-around single-seat piston-engined fighter to be employed by any of the combatants" in the war. The Mustang was designed by North American for the British in 1940 as a substitute for the U.S. P-40 WARHAWK, which was considered unsuitable for European operations. It was a single-engine, low-wing fighter, much lighter than either the P-47 THUNDERBOLT or P-38 LIGHTNING. It had a very clean airframe, differing from nearly all contemporary fighters in having square-cut wing tips and tail surfaces. The P-51 could be easily distinguished by the large under-fuselage air intake for the radiator.

The first aircraft, with the North American desig-

P-51 Mustang fighters, fitted with long-range drop tanks, high over Europe. Only this escort aircraft—which had earlier been rejected by the Army Air Forces—permitted U.S. heavy bombers to operate over Europe in daylight. *(Imperial War Museum)*

nation NA-73, flew for the first time in Oct. 1940 with an Allison in-line, liquid-cooled engine. Production began in the second half of 1941 with orders for the RAF; deliveries were delayed by the decision to provide the plane with the Rolls-Royce Merlin 61 engine. After trials with a pair of XP-51s the U.S. AAF belatedly began ordering the aircraft, initially called the Apache. The first AAF P-51 fighter group was deployed to Britain in Nov. 1943.

Production totaled 14,819, of which 7,956 were the definitive P-51D variant. A single-seat photo version was designated F-6 and 500 aircraft carried the attack designation A-36, being fitted with dive brakes and wing racks for BOMBS. Ten TP-51D two-seat trainers were built (with a single "bubble" canopy), one of which was modified for use by Gen. DWIGHT D. EISENHOWER to inspect the Normandy beachheads in June 1944.

By the end of the war in Europe all but one fighter group in the U.S. Eighth Air Force had been converted to P-51s. Following the capture of IWO JIMA in Feb. 1945 the AAF based P-51s there to escort B-29 SUPERFORTRESS raids against Japan. The U.S. Navy flight-tested a P-51 with an arresting hook aboard an AIRCRAFT CARRIER in 1944, but no naval use followed.

The early aircraft, built to meet the short-range needs of the RAF, had a combat range of less than 400 miles; this was steadily increased, reaching 1,800 miles with the P-51H model, which had a top speed of 487 mph. Its ceiling was over 40,000 feet, making it a truly high-altitude aircraft. The P-51 normally was armed with six .50-cal. machine guns and could carry 5-inch ROCKETS or up to 2,000 pounds of BOMBS. Early British Mustangs had four 20-mm cannon in place of the machine guns. The P-51 had a single pilot (the P-82 Twin Mustang was a side-by-side two-fuselage, two-seat version).

P-59A Airacomet

First U.S. JET-PROPELLED AIRCRAFT. The P-59A was a response by Bell to a Sept. 1941 U.S. AAF requirement for an aircraft built around two Whittle-type turbojet engines. The aircraft was designated XP-59*A* as a deceptive move, as the original XP-59 was a different Bell aircraft design, with a piston-pusher engine. The P-59As were employed for trials and training; none saw combat.

The first XP-59A flew on Oct. 1, 1942, being powered by two General Electric Type I-A turbojets based on the British-designed Whittle engine. Three XP-59A prototypes were followed by thirteen YP-59A evaluation aircraft, two of which went to the U.S. Navy with the designation XF2L-1. The first of twenty production P-59A fighters were delivered in the fall of 1944, followed by thirty lengthened P-59B models—for a total of sixty-six P-59s. Plans to procure another 300 of the P-59B variant were halted in favor of the Lockheed P-80 SHOOTING STAR.

The P-59A was a single-seat, mid-wing aircraft with a slender fuselage with the twin turbojet nacelles fitted on each side of the fuselage, under the wings. The aircraft had a fully retractable, nose-wheel undercarriage. Different modifications of GE turbojet engines were fitted in successive batches. A few aircraft were fitted as drone aircraft directors with a second, *open* cockpit ahead of the pilot, the first such modified XP-59A flying on Oct. 30, 1942.

The XP-59B had a maximum speed of 413 mph—less than contemporary piston-engine fighters—with a range of 525 miles. The standard P-59 armament was one 37-mm cannon and three .50-cal. machine guns in the nose; small BOMBS could be carried under the outer wing sections.

P-61 Black Widow

The first American plane developed specifically for service as a night fighter. The Northrop-built P-61 saw combat in the European and Southwest Pacific theaters in 1944–1945. It was a twin-engine, twin-fuselage, and twin-tail aircraft, somewhat resembling the P-38 Lightning, but much larger, comparable to medium bombers rather than fighters. The long nose housed an air-intercept RADAR. It was one of the most maneuverable aircraft of its size. Toward the end of the war a modification of the P-61 for use as a long-range day fighter was begun, but the war ended before the project was completed.

The first XP-61 was flown on May 26, 1942, but both flight testing and production were delayed. The first production aircraft was delivered late in 1943.

Only 682 aircraft were delivered by Aug. 1945, with just another twenty-four delivered after the war. (The P-61 remained in service until 1952, with the Marine Corps flying a pair of the planes with the designation F2T; thirty-six photo-reconnaissance variants were produced as the F-15 Reporter.) Painted with a glossy black finish, the night fighters began serving in Europe in Aug. 1944 and subsequently in the Philippines.

Maximum speed was about 360 mph. The standard armament was four nose-mounted 20-mm cannon and four .50-cal. machine guns in a top turret; up to 6,400 pounds of BOMBS could be carried externally in some models. Combat range with external tanks was more than 1,000 miles.

The P-61 was flown by a pilot, radar operator, and gunner.

P-63 Kingcobra

U.S. fighter aircraft developed from the P-39 AIRACOBRA. The P-63 Kingcobra was one of three U.S. fighters to make its first flight after U.S. entry into the war and then to enter service before the end of the war. Although manufactured in large numbers, the P-63 Kingcobra was never used as a first-line combat plane by the U.S. AAF; most aircraft were provided to the Soviet Union under LEND-LEASE.

Like its predecessor, the P-63 had the cockpit fitted *ahead* of the in-line engine; in most appearance features the low-wing aircraft resembled the P-39.

The XP-63 flew for the first time on Dec. 7, 1942, but production by the Bell Corp. had already been ordered in Sept. 1942. Few were flown by the U.S. AAF, with its peak inventory, in Aug. 1944, being only 339 aircraft. Total P-63 fighter production was 2,970 aircraft with 2,456 transferred to the Soviet Union; another 300 went to FREE FRENCH forces and the British tested two aircraft. Variants reached P-63E with another 332 RP-63 aircraft being built with "thick skins" as manned targets for student gunners firing dummy bullets.

The P-63A had a maximum speed of 408 mph with a combat range of 450 miles. Armament consisted of one 37-mm cannon and four .50-cal. machine guns; three 500-pound BOMBS could be carried externally. The P-63 was a single-seat aircraft.

One P-63 was modified to test a V-tail configuration; two were modified for swept-back wing tests by the Navy; and several were fitted with a second cockpit for research and test work.

P-80 Shooting Star

First U.S. jet-propelled combat aircraft. Developed late in World War II, the aircraft did not see action in that conflict, but was the first U.S. jet aircraft to see combat in the Korean War. (On Nov. 8, 1950, a U.S. F-80 destroyed a MiG-15 in what is believed to have been the first "conclusive" air combat between two JET-PROPELLED AIRCRAFT.) The P-80—redesignated F-80 in 1948—and the later, two-seat T-33 trainer variant ushered the U.S. AAF into the jet age. Two YP-80A aircraft reached a U.S. base in Italy shortly before V-E DAY but did not see action.

Development of the P-80 began in May 1943 as the AAF invited the Lockheed Corp. to submit a proposal for a fighter built around the de Havilland H-1 turbojet engine developed in Britain. Designed in record time, the XP-80 flew for the first time on Jan. 8, 1944. (The first U.S. jet-propelled aircraft, the XP-59A AIRACOMET, had flown on Oct. 1, 1942.) Two additional XP-80A prototypes and thirteen YP-80A service test aircraft were rapidly delivered (only the first aircraft had the H-1 engine, produced as the Allis-Chalmers J36; subsequent P-80s had the General Electric I-40/J33 engine). Series production followed; 5,000 were ordered or planned, but after postwar cancellations only 917 P-80A models were delivered, starting in 1945, followed by 798 P-80C models from 1948. An improved J33 engine fitted in 240 P-80A models became P-80B; one modified P-80A became the XP-80R, which reached a speed of 623.8 mph. Several aircraft were modified for photo-reconnaissance, being labeled FP-80 or F-14 (and RF-80 in 1948). The two-seat T-33 model, delivered from 1948, was flown by the Air Force, Navy (TO-2/TV-2), and several foreign countries with 5,819 produced in the United States plus license production in Canada and Japan, reflecting the excellence of the basic P-80 design.

The U.S. Navy and Marine Corps took fifty of the P-80C models, designating them TO-1 and later TV-1; one, flown by Marine pilot Marion Carl, was fitted with arresting gear and flew carrier trials late in 1946. The two-seat TO-2/TV-2 could operate from AIRCRAFT CARRIERS.

The Lockheed-built P-80 was a streamlined, low-wing aircraft with the twin turbojet engines faired into the fuselage and with the air intakes in the sides of the fuselage forward of the wing leading edges. It had a nosewheel undercarriage. A bubble canopy provided the pilot with excellent visibility.

The P-80A was rated at a top speed of 558 mph and had a range of 540 miles. The standard armament was six .50-cal. machine guns in the nose; later P-80s were additionally fitted to carry two 1,000-pound BOMBS or ten 5-inch ROCKETS.

P.108B

Italy's only four-engine heavy bomber of the war. Although Italy began the war with a large force of twin-engine medium bombers, she had no four-engine aircraft. The P.108B entered service in 1942 and was active in the Mediterranean area, flying several bombing missions against GIBRALTAR. In one of those strikes Bruno Mussolini, son of Italian dictator BENITO MUSSOLINI, was killed. The aircraft also flew on the EASTERN FRONT.

Design of the P.108 began in 1937 at the Piaggio firm. The prototype flew in 1939. The single P.108A (solid nose) was refitted with a 102-mm cannon for the antishipping role. The 163 production aircraft were designated P.108B.

The P.108 was the largest Italian aircraft of the war. It resembled the early B-17 FLYING FORTRESS, being a four-engine, low-wing aircraft with a tall tail fin. An unusual feature was the placement of remote-controlled gun turrets on the outboard engine nacelles; the guns were operated by a crew member within the fuselage. The P.108B production aircraft had a glazed nose. The large internal BOMB bay could accommodate 7,716 pounds of bombs or three aerial TORPEDOES.

Top speed was 270 mph with a range of 1,550 miles. The aircraft had twin 12.7-mm guns in the engine turrets, and four additional machine guns—nose, tail, and waist positions—for defensive armament. The aircraft was flown by a crew of seven.

Civil and military transport variants of the P.108 were planned, but never built except for a prototype German-requested P.108C cargo aircraft. Several P.108B aircraft were converted into transports for

use by the Luftwaffe. When Italy capitulated in Sept. 1943 the Germans also took possession of the single P.108A.

Pact of Steel

A treaty in which Germany and Italy agreed to "act side by side and with united forces to secure their living space." They also promised that each would "immediately" aid the other militarily if either country "became involved in warlike complications." The treaty, signed in BERLIN on May 22, 1939, also stipulated that neither country would negotiate a separate peace or armistice.

High-ranking German officers had seen little worth to the pact, for they had a low opinion of Italian military forces. But HITLER and Italian leader BENITO MUSSOLINI both wanted it, as did their foreign ministers—but for different reasons. Italy, ill prepared, was hoping to stave off war; Germany, about to go to war, wanted Italy tied to a mutual fate.

On July 19, 1943, facing a crisis brought on by the Allied invasion of SICILY, Mussolini met with Hitler and planned to say that Italy was going to withdraw from the pact. Mussolini, characteristically overcome by Hitler's personality, did not raise the issue. Six days later he was deposed.

Palestine

A place of frequent clashes before, during, and after World War II. Formerly part of the Ottoman Empire, at the beginning of the war Palestine was a LEAGUE OF NATIONS mandate under British administration. The territory was bounded by Lebanon, Syria, Egypt, and Transjordan, another British mandate. The administrative center was Jerusalem. The other cities were Tel Aviv, Haifa, Jaffa, Gaza, Nablus, and Hebron.

NAZI persecution of JEWS drove thousands of them out of Europe and into what they hoped would be a homeland. The flood of Jewish immigrants drastically changed the social fabric of Palestine. In 1919 there were 65,300 Jews in the territory; by 1936 the number had risen to 400,000, representing 28.5 percent of the population.

The British straddled the issue of Jewish immigration, trying to cut it back while simultaneously using Jewish units to maintain order. A young British officer, CAPT. ORDE C. WINGATE, trained Jews for the *Hagannah,* the approved Jewish defense force. Some Jews went into Wingate's Special Night Squads to fight Arab bands attacking kibbutzim with what would become COMMANDO tactics. (In Burma in 1942 he formed similar hit-and-raid units called the CHINDITS.)

After the fall of France in June 1940 the Jewish units served with British forces in Iraq, Syria, and Egypt. Jews from Palestine served individuals in all of the British armed forces. Others formed the JEWISH BRIGADE, which saw action in Italy in 1944–1945.

European Jews illegally arrived on dangerously run-down ships. One capsized, drowning 252 refugees; another sank, with the loss of 700 lives. At the same time, Zionist leaders organized an underground army, stole LEND-LEASE arms designated for the British, and worked to get help from Jews in the United States. About 3,500 Jews deserted from a Free Poland army training in Palestine. Many of them became the cadre of Jewish terror organizations.

When the war ended, President TRUMAN urged the British to allow 100,000 European Jewish refugees to immigrate to Palestine. As the 100,000 issue remained unanswered in 1946, terrorism against the British increased. On May 14, 1948, the British mandate expired and the nation of Israel was proclaimed.

Panama

Capital: Panama City, pop. 631,637 (1940). The takeover of the government by Arnulfo Arias in 1940 put an anti-American dictator in control of the country that encompassed the vital Panama Canal. Arias was so pro-AXIS that he refused to allow Panama-flag merchantmen to arm for defense against German U-BOATS. Overthrown in Oct. 1941, he was replaced by a pro-Allied government that began arming the ships. Panama became so aligned with the United States that, following the PEARL HARBOR attack, Panama declared war on Japan before the U.S. Congress did. Declarations of war against Germany and Italy soon followed.

Many Latin American countries suffered economically during the war because of a cutback in trade with the United States. But Panama prospered

because of a surge in canal construction and the deployment of U.S. forces to protect the canal. In 1939 the U.S. Congress had approved, primarily as a defense measure, the construction of a third set of canal locks. Excavation began in July 1940 but was stopped in May 1942 because other wartime projects had higher priority.

Panay (PR 5)

The first U.S. warship sunk by enemy action in the twentieth century. One of several shallow-draft craft built in the 1920s to protect American interests in China, the *Panay* was sunk by Japanese bombers in 1937.

Completed in 1928, the *Panay* was a shallow-draft river gunboat intended to patrol the Yangtze River against pirates and warlords interfering with commercial shipping. Often the *Panay* would provide armed guards for Western craft travelling the river. After the Japanese invaded China, in Nov. 1937 the U.S. river gunboats evacuated most of the American Embassy staff from the capital of NANKING (now Nanjing). The *Panay* remained to take off the last Americans when the situation in Nanking became untenable.

On Dec. 11 the last Americans from the embassy came on board the *Panay,* as did several newsmen and a few foreigners, and she moved upriver to avoid becoming involved in the fighting around the capital. Three American merchant tankers moved upstream with her. The senior Japanese naval commander in Shanghai was informed of this movement, a precaution taken to avoid accidental attacks by Japanese forces.

On Dec. 12 Japanese naval aircraft were ordered by the Army commander in the area to attack "any and all ships" in the Yangtze above Nanking. Knowing of the presence of the *Panay* and the merchant ships, the Navy command questioned the order. Still, at 1:27 that afternoon nine Japanese naval bombers began attacking the *Panay*. The aerial bombardment continued until the ship sank in shallow water at 3:54 P.M. Three U.S. sailors and an Italian on the ship were killed, and forty-three other Navy men and five civilians were wounded. A formal protest was immediately sent to the Japanese government. The Japanese accepted responsibility, although they claimed that the attack was unintentional. (The weather was good, visibility was clear, and the ship had two large American flags spread out on her awnings to aid aircraft recognition.) The Japanese government paid an indemnity of $2,200,-000 in April 1938, officially ending the incident.

(On the same day as the *Panay* was sunk, two American merchant ships were attacked, and a Japanese Army artillery regiment shelled the British gunboat *Ladybird* and took her into custody.)

The *Panay* was one of six river gunboats built in China for the U.S. Navy. She was launched on Nov. 10, 1927. With a standard displacement of 474 tons and 191-feet long, the *Panay* was armed with two 3-inch (76-mm) guns and several machine guns. Her crew numbered sixty officers and enlisted men.

Pantelleria

A rocky island, well fortified by Italy, about 70 miles southwest of SICILY. Reputed to be a miniature GIBRALTAR, the 32-square-mile island was targeted as an obstacle that had to be overcome before the Sicilian invasion. On June 11, 1943, after five days of intense air and naval bombardment, the island surrendered before a scheduled landing took place.

Panther

Code name for British X Corps drive across the Garigliano, Italy.

Panther tank

One of the best tanks of the war, the Panther PzKw *(Panzerkampfwagen)* V was more than a match for any Allied tank when introduced in 1943. At the time of the NORMANDY INVASION the typical German PANZER division in France had one battalion of PzKw IV tanks and one of Panthers. Comparing the Panther with the standard U.S. tank, the SHERMAN, noted U.S. Army historian Russell F. Weigley wrote: ". . . the usual [U.S.] dependence of the Sherman in combat against the Panther had to be upon greater numbers of tanks, unless the Sherman's crew were exceptionally skilled tank tacticians. With numbers, Sherman could surround a Panther and hit its vulnerable flanks and rear."

The Panther's principal armament was a long-barrel 75-mm cannon—decisively superior to the short-barrel 75-mm gun in the Sherman in terms of muzzle velocity and range. One 7.92-mm machine gun was also fitted. Maximum road speed was rated at 46 mph and cross-country speed was 24 mph. The tank had a crew of four.

Development efforts that would lead to the Panther began as early as 1935. Although originally intended as a replacement for the PzKw IV, the Panther increased in weight from its original 35 tons to almost 43 tons in some models. The Panther introduced several engineering advances such as syncromesh gears, hydraulically operated brake steering, and improved suspension. However, mechanical difficulties made every one of the first batch of Panthers unfit for battlefield use.

Almost 6,000 Panthers were built. After the war the French Army continued to operate them.

There were several Panther variants. One, however, was a deception: For the ARDENNES offensive of Dec. 1944 a number of Panthers were disguised using metal sheets to resemble the U.S. M36 TANK DESTROYERS. Together with some captured U.S. vehicles, the modified Panthers were given American markings and sent forward to create confusion among Allied units, and had some success.

Panzer

German term for both armor and TANK. It was also used to refer to armored formations, as panzer division or battalion. The largest panzer formation was the army.

Panzer Army Africa was organized as Gen. ERWIN ROMMEL's headquarters in North Africa in Aug. 1941. It was renamed the German-Italian Panzer Army in Oct. 1942, and abolished in Feb. 1943.

The First and Second Panzer Armies were the former I and II Panzer Groups, renamed for the EASTERN FRONT campaign in Oct. 1941; the Third and Fourth Panzer Armies were similarly renamed from the III and IV Panzer Corps in Jan. 1942.

The Fifth Panzer Army was formerly the XC Corps, renamed in Tunisia in Dec. 1942; that command surrendered on May 9, 1943. The Fifth Panzer Army was reestablished in France in Aug. 1944, formerly being designated Panzer Group West. It fought in NORMANDY and in the ARDENNES, being disbanded in April 1945.

The Sixth Panzer Army was established in Sept. 1944 to command armored units being withdrawn in the face of Allied advances in northwestern

Europe. It took part in the ARDENNES operation, and then transferred to the EASTERN FRONT, fighting until the end of the war.

Panzerfaust

Highly effective, simple-to-use German antitank weapon. The weapon was used extensively by German troops and captured weapons were often used by U.S. and Soviet troops, the latter also provided with the Russian-made copy designated RPG-1.

The *Panzerfaust* 30 and successive models consisted of a steel launch tube containing a percussion-fired propellant charge that launched a hollow-charge antitank GRENADE with a short, tube-like body and fins. It was a single-shot, disposable weapon with a range of about 30 yards. The weapon weighed only 11 pounds and was 41 inches long, making it easy to carry and use. It had a simple sight, facilitating its use by untrained soldiers.

The later *Panzerfaust* 60, with an improved sight, had a longer range and weighed 13½ pounds, with the subsequent *Panzerfaust* 100 being larger with a greater range, but still retaining simplicity.

Panzerschiff,

see POCKET BATTLESHIPS.

Papen, Franz von (1879–1969)

NAZI politician and diplomat. Von Papen was instrumental in convincing German industrialists and President PAUL VON HINDENBURG to make ADOLF HITLER chancellor in 1933.

Born to wealth and power, von Papen entered the German Army and in 1914 became military attaché in the German Embassy in WASHINGTON. He was expelled for his ESPIONAGE activity.

As Hitler began his rise to power, von Papen became an envoy to wealthy reactionary Germans who worried that the Nazis were radical socialists. As a reward for being the middle man in getting Hitler made chancellor, von Papen was named vice chancellor.

He and Hitler broke over Hitler's failure to pay enough attention to German conservatives. Von Papen had no stomach for Nazi street-gang violence, and in June 1934 publicly condemned Nazi suppression of religion and the press. Hitler arrested von Papen and killed two of his associates.

Hitler released von Papen in July 1934 and made

him a special envoy to Austria, where he helped to set up Hitler's takeover in the *Anschluss* of 1938. From 1939 to 1944 von Papen was ambassador to Turkey, a center for espionage; his embassy ran the spy known as CICERO.

Tried for WAR CRIMES at Nuremberg, von Papen was acquitted. Later, a German de-Nazification court found him guilty of wartime criminal conduct. He appealed his eight-year prison sentence and served less than two years.

Paraguay

Capital: Asunción, pop. 954,848 (est. 1938). With large and influential German and Italian communities and bordered by pro-AXIS Argentina and Brazil, Paraguay moved cautiously to ally herself with the United States and other Western Hemisphere nations. But in June 1942 she finally expelled Axis diplomats who had been sponsoring an anti-ALLIES PROPAGANDA campaign, along with a government official who had been spreading VICHY FRANCE sentiments in the armed forces. Paraguay finally became an Ally herself, and thus a member of the UNITED NATIONS, by declaring war on Germany and Japan on Feb. 7, 1945.

Paris

Capital of France and a city that endured conquest, occupation, and ADOLF HITLER's threat to burn it at its most glorious wartime moment: Liberation.

As German troops neared Paris in June 1940, the city was proclaimed an OPEN CITY and surrendered without a show of resistance. Under the terms of the armistice signed with Germany on June 22, Paris was one of the six zones of the occupied territory and no longer was capital of France. The collaborationist government of VICHY FRANCE established the seat of government in Vichy.

HITLER paid a conqueror's visit to the city early on the morning of June 23, accompanied by his chief architect, ALBERT SPEER. He went sightseeing at the Opéra, the Eiffel Tower, and Napoleon's Tomb, and declared: "I thank Fate to have seen this city whose magic atmosphere has always fascinated me."

Hitler expressly ordered that German soldiers in Paris be on their best behavior. Looters, he warned, would be shot. Around the city Hitler's PROPA-

GANDA operatives had pasted posters showing a German holding a child; the headline said: "Frenchmen! Trust the German soldier!" But the conquerors had their privileges. Bottles of champagne were labeled for reserve for German armed forces. Seats on public transport were also reserved.

Americans pined over the occupation of Paris. "The Last Time I Saw Paris" became a hit-parade SONG. What most Americans did not know was that in July 1942 Germans, with aid of the Vichy government and local police, rounded up 13,000 refugee JEWS in Paris and sent them to CONCENTRATION CAMPS. Another 50,000 Jews in the occupied territory met the same fate.

At first, many Parisians merely shrugged at the inconvenience of war. Worldly impresarios knew the show must go on, especially when there were so many soldiers to entertain. In the summer of 1941 a German soldier could choose between 175 movie houses, sixty-six dance halls and night clubs, and sixty theaters.

Parisians tried to live as normally as possible, but there were problems, such as a power shortage. Clothes, shoes, and even sewing thread became hard to find. Women had trouble finding a place to dry their hair. One enterprising hairdresser hooked his dryer to stove pipes that passed through a furnace; the hot air was then pumped by teams of boys on stationary bicycles. To dry 160 heads a day the boys pedaled 320 kilometers.

To hold down unemployment, Germans who had bought control of French establishments offered jobs to French men and women. Industries thrived in the suburbs. Enough manufacturing was going on in the industrial suburbs of Paris to draw U.S. and British air raids; the city itself was spared bombing.

The FRENCH RESISTANCE was active in Paris, and many patriots or hostages were shot for attacks on Germans. After Germany's invasion of the Soviet Union in June 1941, the French Communist Party, centered in Paris, rose against Germany, with many leaders of the Resistance coming from the ranks of the Communist Party.

By 1944, the poorer districts of Paris were suffering. Only the well-off could afford BLACK MARKET prices on scarce goods. People yearned for liberation, particularly after the NORMANDY INVASION in June 1944. On Aug. 19, as Allied Forces neared Paris, the Communist wing of the Resistance called for a rising and a seizure of the city from the German occupiers.

Generalleutnant DIETRICH CHOLTITZ, German commander in Paris, was under orders from Hitler to defend the city at any cost—including its destruction. When the Resistance insurrection erupted, Choltitz at first attempted to negotiate. Through the Swedish consul general, Choltitz worked out a shaky truce with FREE FRENCH Resistance supporters of Gen. CHARLES DE GAULLE. But the truce broke down, and Choltitz called out tanks.

Learning of the street fighting and the imminent Allied liberation, Hitler asked his military staff during a meeting in Rastenburg, "Is Paris burning?" Choltitz refused to carry out the order, and, as serious confrontations loomed between Germans and patriots, Allied troops were reported nearing Paris.

Gen. De Gaulle had convinced Gen. DWIGHT D. EISENHOWER, Supreme Allied Commander, that Allied forces would meet no opposition entering the city, which Eisenhower had planned to bypass because of logistics problems. On Aug. 25, U.S. forces entered against little opposition. Resistance fighters and jubilant citizens aided U.S. and French forces in silencing a few remaining strongpoints.

Most U.S. troops who marched down the Champs-Elysées kept on marching and went on to continue the war. Some, however, bivouacked in the city, setting up tents in parks. Visiting the troops became a popular occupation for the liberated Parisians. "We felt like we were in a zoo," one soldier remembered. French women even took over the meal preparation duties that GIs called KP, for kitchen police. Sergeants quickly handed the KP chores back to the soldiers. Barbed wire finally had to be strung around the U.S. bivouacs to keep Parisians from swarming over the soldiers.

De Gaulle entered the city triumphant on Aug. 26, though collaborationist snipers in the Place de l'Hôtel opened fire during his arrival. "There are moments that go beyond each of our poor little lives," he said. "Paris! Paris outraged! Paris broken! Paris martyrized! But Paris liberated! . . ."

Paris

Code name for U.S. Army XVIII CORPS line west of Erle, Germany.

Parsons, Commo. William S. (1901–1953)

"Deak" Parsons was the U.S. naval officer who armed the ATOMIC BOMB dropped on HIROSHIMA. Parsons worked on a number of high-technology developments in the 1930s and early in the war, among them RADAR and the PROXIMITY FUZE. In June 1943 he was assigned to the MANHATTAN PROJECT in charge of the ballistic aspects of the atomic bomb. According to Fletcher Knebel in his atomic bomb history *No High Ground,* the head of the Manhattan Project, Maj. Gen. LESLIE GROVES "considered him indispensable, and long before had picked him to arm the first A-bomb in the war." Thus, Parsons flew as weapons officer on the Aug. 6, 1945, flight of the B-29 SUPERFORTRESS "Enola Gay" from TINIAN, arming the bomb by hand after the plane had taken off.

Promoted to commodore on Aug. 10, 1945, Parsons returned to WASHINGTON to head atomic bomb programs in Navy headquarters and serve on the military liaison committee of the new Atomic Energy Commission. He was promoted to rear admiral in 1948. At the time of his death on Dec. 5, 1953, he was deputy chief of the Navy's Bureau of Ordnance.

Partisans,

see GUERRILLAS.

Pastorius

Code name for German plan to land SABOTAGE agents in the United States.

Patch, Lt. Gen. Alexander McCarrell (1889–1945)

In March 1942, Patch took a U.S. Army expeditionary force to NEW CALEDONIA in the Southwest Pacific and there formed the Americal DIVISION, (*Ameri*can New *Cal*edonia), the only U.S. division in the war to have a name instead of a number. After training in New Caledonia, the Americal arrived in GUADALCANAL to relieve the 1st Marine Division in Dec. 1942 in the continuing fight against the Japanese for control of that important island.

Patch was then named commander of the Army's XIV CORPS, which included the Americal Division, the 2nd Marine Division, and the 25th Infantry Division. He began the final offensive against the Japanese on Guadalcanal on Jan. 10. The Japanese

elected to pull their troops out and on Feb. 9, Patch informed Vice Adm. WILLIAM F. HALSEY: "TOKYO EXPRESS no longer has terminus on Guadalcanal."

Patch took command of the Seventh ARMY in March 1944. This Army, based first in SICILY and then in Italy, was the American spearhead for the Allied landings in southern France on August 15, 1944 (Operation Anvil/Dragoon). The Seventh moved swiftly up the Rhône Valley as part of Gen. JACOB DEVERS's 6th ARMY GROUP.

Patch's link-up with Gen. OMAR BRADLEY's 12th Army Group near the German border occurred twenty-seven days after the landings. During that time, Patch had lost his son in battle; Bradley felt that the loss was "so devastating as to impair his effectiveness as an Army commander." This is not a commonly held view, however.

Although possessed of a temper "like the devil before dawn," Patch apparently lived up to his leadership ideals, which he once described as based on character and represented by courage of purpose, honesty, and an unselfish attitude. He was often seen in easy conversation with the men in his army.

Patch thought aggressively, but did not act foolhardily. When asked about a plan of Gen. GEORGE PATTON that would encroach on Seventh Army territory, he merely replied "We're all in the same army," thus bearing out Patton's comment that "Patch was always extremely easy to work with." Patch was credited with a deadpan sense of humor, as when he congratulated Patton, a longtime friend, on being the *last* man to reach the Rhine in 1945. Patton, not unarmed with wit either, replied, "Let me congratulate you on being the first man to leave it," a reference to Patch's pullback from the Rhine in Dec. 1944 in response to a counterattack by German forces. Patch's Seventh crossed the Rhine in early March, took Munich and Nuremberg, and met the 15th Army Group's forces coming through the BRENNER PASS on May 4.

In June 1945 Patch was given command of the Fourth Army in the United States and in October was named to a group studying the Army's postwar posture. Within days after completion of the study in Nov. 1945, Patch died of pneumonia.

Pathfinders, Aircraft

Specialized aircraft, mostly MOSQUITO variants, used by the RAF to make targets (with special

BOMBS and flares) for follow-on attacks by bombers not fitted with sophisticated navigation aids; in some instances larger aircraft were used, including four-engine STIRLING bombers. This scheme was highly efficient for night area bombing operations by the RAF Bomber Command.

The Bomber Command's pathfinder force was eventually organized as No. 8 Group.

The U.S. AAF used modified P-38 LIGHTNING fighters as pathfinders for fighter-bomber strikes in both Europe and the Pacific. Those aircraft carried a bombardier in a lengthened nose section and were fitted with a NORDEN BOMBSIGHT. On signal from the bombardier in the lead plane the formation would salvo its bombs.

Pathfinders, Paratroopers

Paratroopers dropped ahead of the main force to mark the drop zone (with flares or electronic beacons) for AIRBORNE assaults.

Patria

German passenger ship that served as the last capital of the THIRD REICH. When *Grossadmiral* KARL DÖNITZ became head of the German state in succession to ADOLF HITLER, he had his offices in the ship, which was moored at Flensburg on the German-Danish border. His government was dissolved by the ALLIES on May 23, 1945, when Dönitz was arrested.

Built in Germany in 1938, the Hamburg-American Lines ship was 562 feet long and 16,595 deadweight tons. After Dönitz was arrested the *Patria* was taken over by the British and then transferred in 1946 to the Soviet Union and renamed *Rossiya*. She served in the Soviet merchant fleet into the 1980s.

Patterson, Robert P. (1891–1952)

U.S. assistant secretary of War Patterson served in France in World War I and won the Distinguished Service Cross for "extraordinary heroism." In the summer of 1940, when President ROOSEVELT appointed seventy-two-year-old HENRY L. STIMSON secretary of War, the President also named Patterson, a federal appeals judge, assistant secretary of War. Five months later he became under secretary of War.

Patterson stepped up U.S. WAR PRODUCTION by scrapping unwieldy contract procedures and slashing through bureaucratic red tape. He often went to the front himself to see weapons in action. He also took a personal interest in MILITARY JUSTICE and took steps to reform the Army penal system.

When Stimson resigned in Sept. 1945, President TRUMAN offered Patterson either a seat on the U.S. Supreme Court or appointment as secretary of War. Patterson said he would serve where he was most needed, and Truman made him secretary of War. The following month Patterson proposed a unified defense structure, the future Department of Defense.

Patton, Gen. George Smith, Jr. (1885–1945)

Speaking to a group of officers of the U.S. 2nd Armored DIVISION at Fort Benning, Ga., in 1940, Patton said, "War will be won by Blood and Guts alone." From then on his nickname was Old Blood and Guts. It was during this interwar period that Patton often advanced another theory: The best way to defeat an enemy was to go around him and force him to defend against you out of his prepared positions.

Patton was an American pioneer in the use of armored formations, beginning with his service in World War I and continuing through the LOUISIANA MANEUVERS in 1941. In 1927, Maj. Gen. W.R. Smith, in a comment on the efficiency report of then-Capt. Patton, wrote, "This man would be invaluable in time of war, but is a disturbing element in time of peace." His work with armor led to his being given command of the Western Task Force that landed in Morocco as part of Operation Torch, the NORTH AFRICA INVASION in Nov. 1942.

"Now if you have any doubts as to what you're to do," he told his junior officers, "I can put it very simply. The idea is to move ahead. You usually will know where the front is by the sound of gunfire, and that's the direction you should proceed. Now, suppose you lose a hand or an ear is shot off, or perhaps a piece of your nose, and you think you should walk back to get first aid. If I see you, it will be the last goddamned walk you'll ever take."

After the short campaign against French forces in

Morocco, Patton served a short and controversial term as the senior U.S. military administrator in Morocco, where his relative naiveté about politics led him to accept what appeared to many to be a fascistic French government. Patton was rescued from this ill-fitting role because of the U.S. II CORPS' failure to withstand a German counterattack in Feb. 1943. Patton is given credit for reviving the morale and improving the fighting ability of II Corps in a very short time; he drove the troops hard, sacking commanders who, in his opinion, did not act aggressively enough. Although he registered no striking victories, he proved that American forces could fight well against the Germans under the right circumstances.

His performance had been successful enough to

One of the most knowledgeable and aggressive American commanders was Gen. George C. Patton. Also outspoken and impulsive, he was an embarrassment to the U.S. military leadership on several occasions. Here he watches his forces maneuver against German troops in North Africa. *(U.S. Army)*

gain him promotion to lieutenant general and command of the U.S. Seventh ARMY in the invasion of SICILY in July 1943. In this campaign, Patton conducted headline-making warfare, becoming, on the home front, a celebrity general and on the war front, an increasingly difficult general to manage.

He gloried in the publicity he got for his capture of Palermo with a "reconnaissance in force" that transgressed his basic instructions. But he was stunned when the publicity machinery turned against him, reporting how he chewed out and even slapped soldiers he accused of malingering in field hospitals. He was nearly cashiered for the slapping incident, but Gen. GEORGE C. MARSHALL and Gen. DWIGHT D. EISENHOWER, both longtime backers of Patton, decided that the Army needed him for his genuine and rare talent for quick exploitation of enemy weaknesses.

Nevertheless, Patton languished in disuse for several months before being called to England to "command" a dummy First U.S. ARMY GROUP (FUSAG) before and during the NORMANDY INVASION, a successful deception that played on the great German respect for Patton's military abilities. Patton's reward for his good behavior was command of the Third Army, which was activated in Normandy six days after the start of the American breakout.

Under his direction the Third Army first cut across the Brittany peninsula to isolate Atlantic ports (including Brest, which was an essential port to sustain the Allied drive across France). The effect was electric, particularly when Patton turned the main thrust east and drove for the Seine river. This rapid flanking move, combined with a failed German counteroffensive at Mortain, unhinged German defenses and led to the nearly complete encirclement of German forces west of the Seine in the Falaise Gap.

By early Sept. 1944 Patton was confident that given enough fuel and ammunition he could jump the Rhine River on the run if the Allies gave German defenders no time to regroup. But Patton's nemesis, British Field Marshal BERNARD L. MONTGOMERY, felt the same way and had his own plans (including Operation MARKET-GARDEN), which envisaged stopping Patton's supplies to increase his own. To Patton's great anger, his supplies were reduced and his offensive stalled in favor of Montgomery's effort.

Patton enjoyed no more success than any other general in the autumn's positional warfare. However, when the ARDENNES counteroffensive hit in December, launching the battle of the Bulge, much of Third Army was able to wheel 90° to the left and enter besieged BASTOGNE on Dec. 26. This counterthrust is widely regarded as the most remarkable of Patton's many feats because of its complexity and the speed with which he was able to accomplish the reorientation. Patton kept up his pressure on the Germans and crossed the Rhine in late March, a day before the main crossing farther north by Montgomery. (See RHINE CROSSINGS.) His forces advanced through southern Germany and into Czechoslovakia before the surrender. He fumed before Prague, which he had been ordered not to take because it was a Soviet political objective.

Patton at war was nearly peerless; Patton in peace was less skillful, and his political naiveté about the use of former NAZIS in occupation government posts led to his transfer to command of the 15th ARMY GROUP. On Dec. 9, 1945, he suffered a broken neck in an automobile accident near Mannheim and died twelve days later.

He was renowned—and disliked by some—for his in-depth knowledge of military history, flamboyant personality, style of dress (he designed a distinctive uniform for tankers and carried an ivory-handled pistol), and for his rigid enforcement of military dress and discipline.

Paukenschlag (Drumbeat)

German code name for U-BOAT attacks against U.S. merchant shipping off North American coast and in the Caribbean, early 1942.

Paul

This twin-float reconnaissance aircraft, like many other Japanese floatplanes, was intended to operate from island bases in the South Pacific area. The E16A named *Zuiun* (Auspicious Cloud) was given the Allied code name Paul. The aircraft had a secondary dive-bombing role and carried a relatively heavy defensive armament.

The plane revealed major problems in flight tests; the first of three prototypes flew in May 1942 and the design was not approved for production until Aug. 1943. The aircraft saw relatively little service in the war and most of those surviving in 1945 were employed in KAMIKAZE attacks.

The Aichi-built E16A had a streamlined appearance with a long, glazed cockpit for the two-man crew. It had a radial engine and a low-wing configuration with two large floats fitted under the inboard wing sections on vertical N-struts. The wings folded upward for stowage on seaplane carriers.

Including the prototypes, a total of 256 aircraft were built through Aug. 1945.

The aircraft had a maximum speed of 273 mph and, in the search role, a range of 1,500 miles. As a dive bomber 551 pounds of BOMBS could be carried. The plane had two wing-mounted 20-mm cannon and a flexible 13-mm machine gun in the after cockpit.

Paulus, *Generalfeldmarschall* Friedrich von (1890–1957)

Commander in Chief of the German Sixth Army encircled and defeated by the Red Army at STALINGRAD. A career staff officer since World War I, Paulus served in the POLAND CAMPAIGN in Sept. 1939 and the FRANCE AND THE LOW COUNTRIES CAMPAIGN in 1940. As deputy chief of staff he was the key planner for Operation Barbarossa, the German invasion of the Soviet Union in June 1941.

He took command of the Sixth Army in Jan. 1942. In Oct. 1942 Paulus reached Stalingrad and occupied most of the city the next month. But the Red Army encircled the Germans and began relentlessly wiping them out.

HITLER refused to admit that the Sixth Army was doomed. He ordered that it hold Stalingrad. He promoted Paulus to *Generalfeldmarschall,* probably believing that no German officer of that rank would surrender. But on Jan. 31, 1943, unable to feed his exhausted army, Paulus surrendered, in defiance of Hitler's fight-to-the-death orders.

Of his 284,000 men, more than half were dead or were dying by the time of the surrender. About 35,000 had been evacuated. The remaining 91,000 were marched off to hellish Soviet prison camps. Only about 6,000 lived to return to Germany many years later.

Paulus himself survived. He collaborated with the

Soviets by joining the National Committee for Free Germany, which urged German troops to surrender. He testified as a Soviet prosecution witness at the Nuremberg WAR CRIMES trial. Finally released in 1953, he settled in East Germany.

Pay, Military

U.S. military personnel were paid during the war on the basis of rank (grade) and years of service; there was additional pay for special types of service (e.g., flight and submarine duty), awards (e.g., combat infantryman and medical badges), and overseas service. Military pay, unlike civilian pay, was not subjected to regular income tax deductions until the laws were changed, after the war.

Privates and seamen recruits received $50 per month, while a four-star general or admiral made $666.67 per month. The table shown here provides a "slice" of the June 1942 pay table—enlisted men and officers through the rank of captain (Navy lieutenant) are shown for five years' service; for higher officers the pay shown is that for officers passing the ten-year mark.

ARMY/AAF/ MARINE CORPS	NAVY/ COAST GUARD	MONTHLY PAY
private	seaman 3rd class*	$ 52.50
private 1st class	seaman 2nd class*	$ 56.70
corporal-tech. 5th grade	seaman 1st class*	$ 69.30
sergeant-tech. 4th grade	PO 3rd class	$ 81.90
staff sgt.-tech. 3rd grade	PO 2nd class	$100.80
technical sergeant	PO 1st class	$119.70
master sgt.-1st sgt.	chief PO	$144.90
2nd lieutenant	ensign	$157.50
1st lieutenant	lieutenant (j.g.)	$175.00
captain	lieutenant (j.g.)	$210.00
major	lieutenant commander	$287.50
lieutenant colonel	commander	$335.42
colonel	captain	$383.33
brigadier general	commodore	$500.00
major general	rear admiral	$666.67
lieutenant general	vice admiral	$666.67
general	admiral	$666.67

*Also fireman and airman.
  tech. = technician; PO = petty officer.

Flight pay for aviators and submarine pay added 50 percent to the base pay; overseas duty added another 10 percent of base pay for officers and 20 percent for enlisted men; and parachute pay added $100 per month for officers and $50 per month for enlisted men. Certain qualifications also earned additional pay: $2 per month for distinguished service awards, $5 for the combat infantry badge, and $10 for the medical badge.

In addition, officers received a subsistence allowance, which was payable monthly in cash. An officer without dependents was entitled to $21 for a thirty-day month (i.e., 70¢ per day); an officer with two dependents would receive $42 for a thirty-day month and with three dependents $63. Subsistence was not used in computing additional pay for flight, submarine, or overseas duty.

Also, officer aides to generals received additional pay—$150 to $200 per month—because of certain personal expenses they would incur when they accompanied the general.

PB2Y Coronado

The only four-engine patrol bomber flying boat to enter squadron service with the U.S. Navy. It entered service on the last day of 1940. The Navy had seven of the aircraft on Dec. 7, 1941, including the XPB2Y-1 and XPB2Y-3, the others being PB2Y-2 variants. The aircraft were employed in ocean patrol but during 1944–1945 the operational aircraft were withdrawn from combat service and assigned to search-and-rescue units or to the NAVAL AIR TRANSPORT SERVICE. As transports they could carry thirty-four to forty-four passengers or 16,000 pounds of cargo. Several served as "flagships" for senior admirals, having a VIP configuration for eighteen passengers. The PB2Y-5H "hospital" variant carried twenty-five litters plus a medical team.

The Consolidated PB2Y was the winner of the 1935 Navy design competition for a four-engine flying boat patrol bomber. The XPB2Y-1 made its maiden flight on Dec. 17, 1937. A total of 217 aircraft were built, with ten PB2Y-3B models going to the RAF Transport Command in 1944 for trans-Atlantic routes.

A graceful, high-wing flying boat with large stabilizing floats, the production aircraft had a twin-tail configuration following extensive modification to the single-fin prototype because of early problems with lateral stability. In flight the stabilizing floats folded up to form the wing tips. In combat, the aircraft could carry eight 1,000-pound BOMBS or DEPTH CHARGES in internal wing bays or (rarely) two aerial TORPEDOES under the wings. Some aircraft were fitted with RADAR.

The major production variant, the PB2Y-3 (210 aircraft), had a maximum speed of 223 mph and a range of 2,370 miles or 1,370 miles with 8,000 pounds of bombs. The production aircraft had twin .50-cal. machine guns mounted in nose, dorsal, and tail power turrets (which were removed in the 1944–1945 transport reassignment). The crew normally numbered nine or ten.

PB4Y-2 Privateer

U.S. Navy maritime patrol version of the B-24 LIBERATOR heavy bomber. This aircraft was extensively modified for the maritime patrol and antisubmarine roles. The aircraft was also employed to carry the BAT antiship missile. Few of the production aircraft were completed before V-J DAY and those were employed exclusively in the Western Pacific area.

In May 1943 the Convair firm was directed to convert three B-24D bombers into PB4Y-2 configurations. The first of these prototypes flew on Sept. 20, 1943, and the following month production aircraft were ordered. Deliveries to the fleet began in March 1944 and continued through Oct. 1945. When production ended a total of 736 newly built Privateers were delivered to the Navy and (a few of those) to the Marine Corps. A transport version was also produced for the Navy as the RY-3 with forty-six going to the U.S. Navy and twenty-seven to the RAF as the Liberator IX. (After the war the Coast Guard flew the Privateer as the P4Y-2G.)

The Privateer was distinguished by its tall tail fin, replacing the twin-tail configuration of the B-24; the PB4Y-2 also had a seven-foot fuselage extension forward of the wing. It was a four-engine, high-wing aircraft with gun turret blisters on the after fuselage, a nose turret, two dorsal turrets, and tail turret, each mounting a pair of .50-cal. machine guns—a total of twelve defensive guns. (No ventral turret was provided.) The internal weapons bay could hold 8,000 pounds of BOMBS.

The Privateer had a maximum speed of 237 mph and a maximum range of 2,800 miles. The aircraft's crew numbered eleven, including two electronics operators for the aircraft's surface search RADAR.

After the war the French Navy flew the Privateer in the war in INDOCHINA.

PBM Mariner

This graceful flying boat succeeded the PBY CATALINA as the U.S. Navy's principal seaplane patrol bomber and was flown by most Navy patrol squadrons at the end of the war. The PBM—the world's largest twin-engine flying boat—was noted for its range, bomb load, ruggedness, and sea-worthiness.

Squadron deliveries of the PBM began in Sept. 1940; at the time of the PEARL HARBOR attack the Navy had twenty-two PBMs, including test aircraft. The PBMs flew in a variety of roles during the war (see below).

The PBM was designed by the Glenn L. Martin Co. in competition with the Consolidated PBY, with the Martin effort being a later design. The first aircraft flew on Feb. 18, 1939. Production had been ordered even before the prototype flew, in part because of Martin's considerable flying boat experience. A total of 1,366 aircraft were produced through 1947, including fifty-four for the RAF (some of which were returned to the U.S. Navy). The PBM was produced in larger numbers than any other military flying boat of any nation, except for the U.S. Catalina. (The U.S. Navy retired its last PBM in mid-1956.) During the war a few Mariners were flown by the RAF Coastal Command and in the search-and-rescue role by the U.S. Coast Guard.

The PBM was a twin-engine, gull-wing flying boat with a deep fuselage and twin-fin tail assembly with dihedral on the horizontal tail surfaces. The wing floats were rigid. The aircraft was some 60 percent heavier than the PBY with a greater speed and twice the payload. It was capable of single-engine flight; a PBM once flew for two hours with the starboard engine out. The PBM-3R was a transport variant for the NAVAL AIR TRANSPORT SERVICE with strengthened floors for 9,000 pounds of cargo or seats for twenty passengers, and cargo loading doors; the PBM-3D introduced a large surface RADAR housing immediately aft of the flight deck; the PBM-3S was an antisubmarine version with increased range, the weight of additional fuel being offset by deletion of power turrets and less armor protection for the crew; and the PBM-5A, a post-war development, was an amphibious aircraft with retractable landing gear. (In 1948 the final PBM-5 became the prototype P5M Marlin; the U.S. Navy's last flying boat aircraft to see service, it flew in the Vietnam War.)

The PBM-3D had a maximum speed of 211 mph and was credited with a range of 2,240 miles in a combat configuration. The PBM-3S with four 325-pound DEPTH CHARGES was rated at 3,130 miles.

The PBM had bomb bays within each engine nacelle that could hold BOMBS, MINES, or aerial TORPEDOES—a maximum weapons load of 8,000 pounds. The defensive armament consisted of twin .50-cal. machine guns fitted in power-operated nose, dorsal, and tail turrets; single .50-cal. guns were fitted in the beam positions, an extremely heavy armament for a flying boat. The long-range PBM-3S had only four hand-held .50-cal. guns. The aircraft had a crew of seven to nine.

PBY Catalina

Long-range flying boat. The most successful flying boat ever developed by any nation, the PBY "Cat" was employed during the war in the patrol, bomber, antisubmarine, torpedo, search-and-rescue, and transport roles. RADAR-equipped PBYs—painted black and known as "Black Cats"—carried out nighttime reconnaissance and attacks against Japanese shipping. More Catalinas were produced than any other flying boat in history.

PBYs first flew on wartime patrols with the RAF Coastal Command in Sept. 1940. A Catalina from No. 209 Squadron spotted the fleeing BISMARCK some 700 miles west of Brest, France, on May 26, 1941, after the German battleship had successfully evaded searching British surface ships.

There were thirty-nine PBYs based on Oahu at the time of the Japanese attack on PEARL HARBOR on Dec. 7, 1941. Three of these Catalinas were out on patrol that morning; one detected and attacked a Japanese MIDGET SUBMARINE near the harbor entrance just before the air attack. Of the remaining PBYs, Japanese bombing and strafing destroyed twenty-seven planes and damaged another six.

The U.S. Navy had twenty-eight PBYs in the Philippines when the war erupted. From the start of conflict they scouted out Japanese naval forces and made bombing and torpedo attacks against Japanese shipping. As U.S. forces withdrew from the Philippines, the surviving PBYs flew from the DUTCH EAST INDIES, where the Dutch had thirty-six PBYs when the war began.

PBYs had an important role in the U.S. carrier victory at the battle of MIDWAY, making the initial sighting of the approaching Japanese naval forces. They subsequently were assigned patrol and bombing missions in the Southwest Pacific, and served in all war areas as antisubmarine aircraft. Although "Cats" were active through the end of the war, during the winter of 1944–1945 the last PBYs left front-line patrol bomber service in the Pacific (having been replaced by PBM MARINERS).

The PBY design originated with the Consolidated P3Y, which had been ordered by the U.S. Navy in Oct. 1933. An exceptionally clean, all-metal monoplane, the XP3Y-1 first flew on March 28, 1935. The aircraft was sufficiently impressive for the Navy to broaden its specification to bombing as well as patrol (hence the PB designation). The re-built prototype, designated XPBY-1, flew nonstop from Norfolk, Va., to San Diego, Calif., via the Panama Canal, a record-setting distance of 3,443 miles. Production PBY-1s first entered Navy squadron service in Oct. 1936.

By the end of 1941 the PBY was flown by twenty-three of the Navy's twenty-five patrol squadrons (the others flew the PBO Hudson and PBM Mariner). While not all PBY squadrons were at full twelve-aircraft strength, numerous PBYs were also flown by shore commands and a few by the U.S. Coast Guard. PBYs also went to the Dutch and various British Commonwealth air forces and navies with the first PBY flying across the Atlantic to Britain in July 1939. The Soviets purchased three PBYs and their plans, borrowed eighteen Consolidated technicians, and produced several hundred planes at Taganrog (designated GST). Another 138 American-built PBNs and forty-eight PBYs went to the Soviet Union under LEND-LEASE. Several other Allied countries flew PBYs during the war.

More Catalinas were produced than any other flying boat in history: U.S. Catalina production totaled 1,836 aircraft, including the PBN Nomad variants built by the Naval Aircraft Factory and

The **PBY Catalina** was one of the most versatile flying boats ever built. It was produced in larger numbers than any other military seaplane. The photo shows a variant that had a twin-gun power turret in the nose and a radar dome (radome) fitted atop the cockpit, forward of the twin engines. *(U.S. Navy)*

PB2B Catalinas built by Boeing; Vickers built an additional 562 more in Canada—149 for Canadian service, 183 for the U.S. Navy-designated PBV, and 230 rescue versions for the U.S. AAF as the OA-10. Rescue versions were referred to as "Dumbo," for Walt Disney's flying elephant cartoon character.

A graceful aircraft, the PBY had a high wing mounted on a pylon with large, distinctive supporting struts atop the stepped boat fuselage. It had twin wing-mounted engines. A high tail was fitted with horizontal control surfaces level with the main wing. Beginning with the PBY-4 of 1938, the Catalina had distinctive glazed blisters on the after fuselage, and the PBY-5A and later A-suffix aircraft were amphibious with retracting wheels for beaching or land operation.

The PBY-5A had a maximum speed of 179 mph and a cruising speed of 117 mph with a maximum range of 2,545 miles. In the bombing role a PBY could carry four 1,000-pound or smaller BOMBS, or eight DEPTH CHARGES, or two aerial TORPEDOES under its wings.

Defensive armament consisted of one .30-cal. machine gun in the nose, another in the ventral or tunnel position, and two .50-cal. guns in waist hatches or side blisters. In later models a twin .30-caliber mount was fitted in the nose. The PBY normally flew with a crew of eight: three pilots, one of whom also served as the bombardier and nose gunner, two radiomen, and three machinists, who would fire the aircraft's waist guns and tunnel gun.

Catalina was the Consolidated firm's name for the aircraft; it was officially adopted by the Navy on Oct. 1, 1941.

Pe-2

Probably the most versatile bomber-type aircraft in the Soviet Air Force and produced in greater numbers than any other Soviet bomber. It served on all fronts of the 1941–1945 conflict.

The twin-engine plane was originally intended as

a high-altitude, long-range fighter. A high-altitude fighter variant was developed (the Pe-3) but only twenty-three of these fighters were built before all production reverted to the Pe-2 bomber variants. Subsequently, a modified fighter-bomber was produced, the Pe-3*bis* with provisions for eight 82-mm ROCKETS under the wings in addition to a 20-mm cannon and machine guns. These planes could still carry BOMBS and were highly effective as tank killers. However, they were relatively vulnerable to ground fire, and most of the aircraft were shifted to the antishipping role in the Black Sea, with others becoming photo-reconnaissance aircraft. Other Pe-2 variants included a specialized *Shturmovik* (armored attacker) version, two-seat dive bomber, heavily gunned versions with a power turret and additional gunner, high-altitude fighter, and armed trainer. The Pe-2 and its many variants served the Soviet Union well during the war.

The first prototype flight was on May 7, 1939. The aircraft was designed by V. M. Petlyakov while he was "interned," having been arrested in 1938 on STALIN's orders; the Pe-2 nickname *Sotka* or "little hundred" was derived from KB No. 100, the prison design bureau where Petlyakov and his colleagues were interned. The excellence of the Pe-2 design earned Petlyakov a State Prize from Stalin in early 1941. Still, Petlyakov and his associates interned at KB No. 100 remained under NKVD jurisdiction until the German invasion of the Soviet Union in late June of that year.

The plane was in production until 1946 and remained in Soviet service until the early 1950s, with 11,427 aircraft of all variants being built.

The aircraft was a low-wing, twin-engine aircraft with streamlined in-line engine nacelles that housed the fully retractable undercarriage. The streamlined fuselage—with a fully glazed cockpit—tapered into a twin tail-fin arrangement. It had turbo-superchargers for the twin, liquid-cooled engines, and a pressurized cockpit. The aircraft had all-electric systems for flaps, fuel pump, superchargers, trim tab, and undercarriage, requiring some fifty servomotors. The ruggedness of the plane was demonstrated when the dive brakes failed in a flight test and the plane reached 497 mph before the pilot pulled out of a dive.

The basic Pe-2 was rated at 335 mph and a range

of 1,200 miles. Up to 441 pounds of bombs could be carried in the internal bomb bay and 220 pounds of bombs in the rear of each engine nacelle; four 220-pound bombs could also be carried on wing racks for a total of 2,205 pounds of bombs. Alternatively four 551-pound or two 1,102-pound bombs could be carried under the wings. A 12.7-mm gun was fitted in the dorsal turret and there were four forward-firing 7.62-mm guns. Some aircraft also had a ventral machine gun, aimed through a periscope. The aircraft had a crew of two (three in the version with a gun turret).

Pe-8

The principal four-engine heavy bomber of the Red Air Force during the war. The Soviets conducted only limited STRATEGIC BOMBING operations, and those mostly employed twin-engine aircraft. Entering service in 1940, eleven of the aircraft bombed BERLIN on the night of Aug. 7–8, 1941. The Pe-8 was employed primarily to strike German targets in the Balkans. They were also used as transports, one being used to fly Soviet Foreign Minister VYACHESLAV MOLOTOV to England and the United States in May–June 1942.

The Tupolev design bureau began work on the aircraft in 1934 under the direction of V. M. Petlyakov. The aircraft was originally designated ANT-42 (for A. N. Tupolev) and TB-7 (Air Force heavy bomber) but is best known by its Petlyakov designation (assigned in late 1940). The aircraft first flew on Dec. 27, 1936, and entered service in 1941. Production terminated in Oct. 1941 after seventy-nine aircraft were delivered.

The Pe-8 had a massive appearance, being a low-wing aircraft with four large engine nacelles. The prototypes had four in-line engines, replaced in the production aircraft with radial engines. Early aircraft were re-engined with in-line diesel engines (these aircraft bombed Berlin). Another unusual feature was the fitting of flexible gun positions under the inner engine nacelles.

The standard variants (radial engines) had a top speed of 274 mph and a range of 2,320 miles; the diesel variant was credited with 4,860 miles with 4,400 pounds of BOMBS. The bomb bay could accommodate up to 8,800 pounds of bombs. The Pe-8 defensive armament consisted of two 7.62-mm machine guns in the nose turret, two 12.7-mm machine guns in the inboard engine nacelles, and 20-mm cannon in a dorsal and (electrically operated) tail turrets; the engine nacelle guns were deleted from later production aircraft. The plane was flown by a crew of eleven.

After the war some thirty surviving aircraft were used extensively for research purposes.

Peace Treaties

The formal end of World War II came with the signing of peace treaties between the ALLIES and the AXIS powers and their allies. The process began with treaties covering the minor belligerents. Germany and Japan would be handled separately and with much more complexity.

In July 1946 at a meeting of twenty-one of the UNITED NATIONS in PARIS, drafts on treaties covering the minor European belligerents were discussed. These drafts had been prepared by the BIG FOUR: the United States, Britain, France, and the Union of Soviet Socialist Republics. The Big Four foreign ministers completed their work in Dec. 1946 and formal signing took place in Paris on Feb. 10, 1947. The provisions of the treaties, for each of the defeated nations:

Italy Her Adriatic port of TRIESTE was taken from her and made into a Free Territory under UN administration; later, much of the Trieste area went to Yugoslavia. The Dodecanese Islands were awarded to Greece, two thirds of the Province of Venezia Giulia went to Yugoslavia, and some alpine territory went to France. Her African colonies were taken away. She agreed to pay $125,000,000 in reparations to Yugoslavia, $105,000,000 to Greece, $100,000,000 to the Soviet Union, $25,000,000 to Ethiopia, and $5,000,000 to Albania.

Hungary Prewar boundaries reestablished. Northern Translyvania was returned to Rumania and some territory went to Czechoslovakia. Reparations: $300,000,000 went to the Soviet Union, $50,000,000 to Yugoslavia, $50,000,000 to Czechoslovakia.

Rumania Northern Bukovina and Bessarabia ceded to the Soviet Union, Southern Drobudja to Bulgaria. Reparations: $300,000,000 to the Soviet Union.

Bulgaria Reparations: $45,000,000 to Greece, $25,000,000 to Yugoslavia.

Finland Reaffirmed her cession of Petsamo to the Soviet Union under the 1944 armistice. Reparations: $300,000,000 to the Soviet Union.

Germany The peace treaty with Germany, divided by the Big Four into four occupation zones, was much more complicated. The governing organizations, the ALLIED CONTROL COUNCIL, broke down soon after the war because of disputes, primarily over reparations, between the Soviet Union and the other three nations. The disputes were taken to a higher level, but repeated attempts at settlement by Big Four foreign ministers failed. In Dec. 1946, England and the United States merged their zones under the name Bizonia. In 1948, France joined, making it Trizonia. This set up the emergences of *two* Germanys, the East and the West.

Meanwhile, the cold war was making Soviet-encircled BERLIN a stage for confrontation. In May 1949 the Western powers reacted to a string of Berlin crises by authorizing the creation of the Federal Republic of Germany; in October the Soviets made their zone into the German Democratic Republic.

No peace treaty between the Big Four and defeated Germany was ever signed, as a result of the Cold War. But the Big Four did reach agreement as the sudden and dramatic reunification of Germany neared after the Berlin Wall came down in late 1989. In what amounted to a peace treaty ending the war, in July 1990 the Big Four and the two Germanies guaranteed Poland's border with a united Germany. Technical impediments to the reunion were removed through Big Four cooperation, and reunification became a reality at midnight on Oct. 1–2, 1990.

Japan On Sept. 8, 1951, in the midst of the Korean War, the United Nations and forty-eight other nations signed a peace treaty with Japan, which had been under Allied occupation since its SURRENDER in Aug. 1945. (Burma and India did not attend, but India signed a similar treaty in 1952 and Burma did the same in 1954.)

Under the 1951 peace treaty, Japan recognized the independence of Korea and renounced rights to lands it had occupied. The treaty left the question of reparations to individual countries. Japan signed reparation treaties with Burma in 1954, the Philippines in 1956, and Indonesia in 1958.

In 1947 a U.S.-framed Constitution, modeled on the United States constitution and stripping the emperor of monarchial power, was ratified by Japan. The constitution prohibited Japan from having any "land, sea, and air forces, as well as other war potential." But the occupation powers modified this in 1950, allowing the creation of what became Japan's Self-Defense Force. This gave Japan the last bit of sovereignty that had been retained by the victors of World War II.

Peacemaker,

see B-36.

Pearl Harbor

Major U.S. naval and air base on the Hawaiian island of Oahu, attacked by Japanese aircraft on Dec. 7, 1941. The surprise attack killed 2,403 people, most of them American servicemen, and wounded 1,104 others. The attackers crippled the U.S. Pacific Fleet and destroyed 75 percent of the aircraft on the airfields around Pearl Harbor. In two swift air strikes the Japanese destroyed or damaged 188 planes, eight BATTLESHIPS, three light CRUISERS, three DESTROYERS, and four smaller vessels.

The idea of a surprise attack originated with Adm. ISOROKU YAMAMOTO, Commander in Chief of the Japanese Combined Fleet, who began planning the attack in Nov. 1940, two months after Japan signed the TRIPARTITE PACT that aligned Japan with the AXIS powers, Germany and Italy.

In Jan. 1941 Yamamoto directed Rear Adm. TAKIJIRO ONISHI, a leading naval aviator, to prepare a preliminary study. Onishi secured the assistance of Comdr. MINORU GENDA, air operations officer of the First Carrier Squadron. The plan, completed in April, called for Japan to make a surprise air and submarine attack on Pearl Harbor.

Comdr. MITSUO FUCHIDA, who would direct the air attack, spent months developing the tactics and equipment needed to fly to Hawaii and torpedo the U.S. BATTLESHIPS lined up in "Battleship Row" at FORD ISLAND in the middle of Pearl Harbor.

There is evidence that Yamamoto's idea to attack Pearl Harbor had been inspired by two events: His

reading of a prophetic book and his knowledge of an historic air attack. The book was *The Great Pacific War,* written in 1925 by Hector Bywater, a British naval authority. Bywater's realistic account of a war between the United States and Japan begins with the destruction of the U.S. fleet and the subsequent invasion of the Philippines and capture of GUAM. The historic air attack was the RAF strike, on Nov. 11, 1940, against the Italian fleet at TARANTO; two battleships were torpedoed and extensively damaged. It was the first practical attack of aircraft on battleships.

In mid-November, after the "Hawaiian Operation" was approved by the government, the striking force began to assemble in Hitokappu Bay in the bleak KURIL ISLANDS. Commander of the force, on board the flagship *Akagi,* was Vice Adm. CHUICHI NAGUMO. The striking force was built around Japan's six carriers. The carriers—screened by two battleships, three cruisers, and nine destroyers—departed Hitokappu Bay on Nov. 26 under strict radio silence.

Eight oilers would refuel the striking force. To supplement their normal fuel capacities, the warships were loaded with drums of fuel oil and fuel was carried in the double bottoms of the carriers, a practice usually forbidden. The northern route the force would take, roughly along latitude 43° north, took the ships into stormy seas. But the route kept the striking force out of normal shipping lines and beyond the range of U.S. search planes from WAKE or MIDWAY. Fierce gales, high seas, and dense fog hid the fleet.

Three large fleet submarines scouted ahead of the main force. Twenty-seven other fleet submarines were to deploy around Oahu to attack any U.S. warships that escaped the attack. Five of the submarines carried MIDGET SUBMARINES to penetrate the harbor just before the air attack.

(Only one of the five two-man undersea craft was able to enter the harbor; it fired two TORPEDOES, but hit no ships. All five midgets were lost; one was attacked by a U.S. flying boat and DESTROYER shortly before the air raid. The one surviving crewman of the midgets became the first U.S. PRISONER OF WAR.)

On Dec. 1 the Japanese Cabinet set Dec. 8 (Japanese dates; Hawaii time is a day earlier) as the day

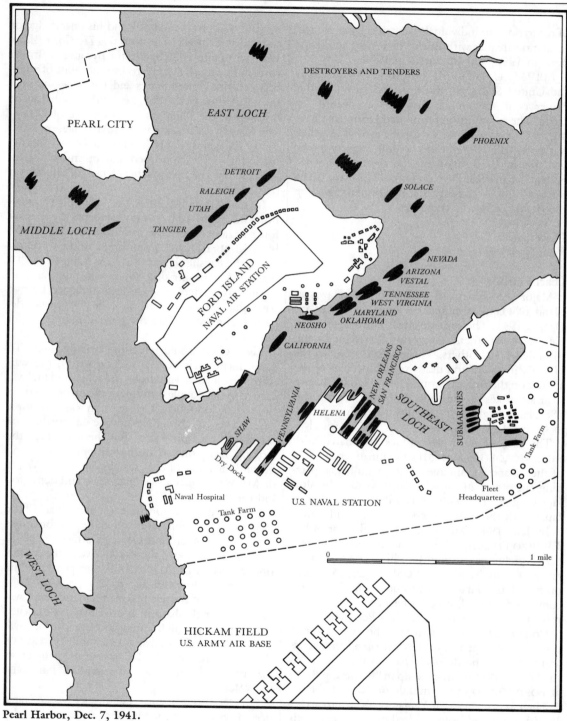

Pearl Harbor, Dec. 7, 1941.

Japanese bombers devastate the U.S. Pacific Fleet at Pearl Harbor. In the center of this photo is Ford Island and, along its eastern side, "Battleship Row." Moments after this photo was taken the battleship *Arizona* (BB 39), the second large ship from the left, blew up and sank. *(Japanese Navy)*

war would begin between Japan and the United States. On Dec. 2 in Japan, Yamamoto's flagship in the Inland Sea sent out a pre-arranged code signal to attack Pearl Harbor on Sunday, Dec. 7, Hawaii time: *Niitaka Yama Nobore* ("Climb Mount Niitaka"—a mountain on Formosa, then part of Japan).

The next day the striking force refueled at sea and turned southeast, then south. At 6 A.M. on Dec. 7, when the striking force was 230 miles north of Oahu, the first wave of 183 planes, led by Fuchida, began their runs down the pitching decks of the Japanese carriers. The forty-three ZERO fighters would gain control of the air over Oahu and strafe airfields. The fifty-one VAL dive bombers, each carrying a 551-pound bomb, would strike the Army's

Wheeler Field and the naval air station at Ford Island. Forty KATE bombers armed with torpedoes and another forty-nine Kates carrying 1,760-pound bombs would attack the U.S. Pacific Fleet.

An hour and fifteen minutes later, while the first wave was still on its way to Oahu, the second wave of 167 planes was launched: thirty-five Zero fighters for cover and for strafing if there was no airborne opposition; fifty-four Kate bombers, each carrying a 551-pound bomb and six 132-pounders to hit the airfields; seventy-eight Val dive bombers with 551-pound bombs, their targets the warships.

Over Oahu, Fuchida gave the attack signal, two telegraph-key dot-dash clusters that meant *to* and *ra;* said together, they happened to mean "tiger." The signal was heard on the *Akagi* and, because of an atmospheric phenomenon, on the flagship of Yamamoto in Japan.

The first wave of 183 Japanese planes struck at 7:55 A.M. Most of the U.S. Pacific Fleet was at anchor, including eight of the fleet's nine battleships. Airfields around the island of Oahu, some 250 Navy, Marine, and Army Air Corps planes were mostly parked wingtip-to-wingtip in neat lines, to make it easier to guard them against SABOTAGE. Nearly all the planes were hit.

There had been warnings—one, wrongly interpreted, resulted in the disastrous sabotage defense. And there would be others, up to minutes before the attack. All were ignored. (See PEARL HARBOR INVESTIGATIONS.)

The airfields and battleships were the principal targets of the first wave, with the second wave striking other ships and shipyard facilities. A direct hit on a mess hall at Hickam Field killed thirty-five men having breakfast. Of the 231 aircraft at Hickam, sixty-four were destroyed and of those that were damaged, only seventy-two were later judged repairable.

At Pearl Harbor, one of the 1,760-pound bombs (actually they were 16-inch armor-piercing projectiles fitted with fins) hit the *ARIZONA* (BB 39) near

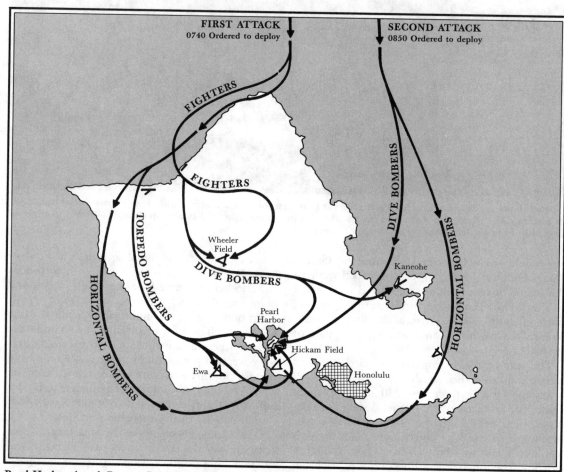

Pearl Harbor Attack Routes, Dec. 7, 1941.

her No. 2 turret and penetrated into the forward magazine, where it exploded, killing 1,104 Navy and Marine officers and enlisted men, including Rear Adm. Isaac C. Kidd, Commander Battleship DIVISION 1, and the ship's commanding officer, Capt. F. Van Valkenburgh (both of whom were posthumously awarded the MEDAL OF HONOR, as was the senior surviving officer of the ship, Lt. Comdr. S. G. Fuqua). The ship may also have been struck by one or two torpedoes and several other bombs.

The *Utah,* a target ship that attackers had been told to ignore, was hit by two torpedoes and capsized, killing at least fifty-eight men. Two torpedoes and a bomb hit the *California* (BB 44), which settled on the bottom. As many as seven torpedoes slammed into the *West Virginia* (BB 48). In fifteen minutes five to seven torpedoes struck the *Oklahoma* (BB 37) and she capsized.

The *Pennsylvania* (BB 38), in drydock, was slightly damaged when a 551-pound bomb went through two decks and exploded. Two duds hit the *Tennessee* (BB 43). One bomb hit the *Maryland* (BB 46). The *Nevada* (BB 36), hit by a torpedo and five 551-pound bombs, somehow managed to get under way and was hit by more bombs when the second wave of Japanese aircraft roared over Pearl Harbor. All but the *Arizona,* the *Utah,* and the *Oklahoma* were salvaged and returned to the fleet.

The three U.S. AIRCRAFT CARRIERS in the Pacific, the prime target of the original Operation Hawaii plan, escaped the air attack. The *LEXINGTON* (CV 2) and *ENTERPRISE* (CV 6) were delivering Marine aircraft to outlying islands, and the *SARATOGA* (CV 3) was in California waters.

The Japanese lost only twenty-seven aircraft in the raid plus the five midget submarines. The carrier planes, however, did not strike the fuel tanks at Pearl Harbor. If they had been destroyed, the Pacific Fleet would have had to shift its base to the West Coast, delaying U.S. offensive actions in the Pacific.

The Japanese had briefly considered an AMPHIBIOUS LANDING to follow the air raid, but the distances involved and the need for available transports for landings in the Philippines, DUTCH EAST INDIES, and other areas deterred that plan.

Pearl Harbor Investigations

The Japanese surprise attack on Pearl Harbor—most Americans called it a "sneak attack"—inspired the rallying cry "Remember Pearl Harbor!" It also inspired the question "How did Pearl Harbor happen?" From that question came eight major investigations and a welter of rumors, accusations, and dark tales of conspiracies.

The first of the investigations, a board of inquiry appointed by President ROOSEVELT eleven days after the attack, convened at the site of Pearl Harbor—Oahu, HAWAII—behind closed doors. The Roberts Commission, named for its chairman, Supreme Court Justice Owen J. Roberts, concluded its investigation on Jan. 23, 1942, by declaring that both Adm. HUSBAND E. KIMMEL, Commander in Chief of the U.S. Pacific FLEET, and Lt. Gen. WALTER C. SHORT, commanding officer of the U.S. Army's Hawaiian Department, had failed to exhibit the qualities expected of high command. Kimmel and Short had already been relieved of their duties, were given no assignments, and soon retired.

The next six investigations, under Army or Navy auspices, were also secretly conducted. Not until the war ended could concern about military security give way to a resolve to publicly air the facts about the Pearl Harbor disaster. A joint congressional investigation began on Nov. 15, 1945, and continued through six months of hearings that produced 15,000 pages of testimony.

Both the majority and minority reports issued in July 1946 again put the basic blame on Kimmel and Short. This time the reasons for the conclusion were specific: The admiral and general had failed to heed the warnings sent to them from WASHINGTON; they had failed to alert their forces properly; they had not coordinated what defenses they did mount; they had not employed their personnel and equipment as well as they should have in anticipating the attack or in defending against it. The committee concluded that Kimmel and Short had made "errors of judgment" but were not guilty of "dereliction of duty."

The Congressional investigation did not end the questions about Pearl Harbor. Many lingered, for several reasons: In 1945 U.S. code-breaking prowess was still not fully known; many MAGIC intercepts would not be declassified for decades; in 1945, with many careers not yet ended, the bickering between military intelligence bureaucracies continued to obscure what was known by whom—and when it was known. Finally, there was a general misunderstanding of just what "warnings" had gone to the military commanders at Pearl Harbor.

Roberta Wohlstetter, in her lucid and exhaustively researched 1962 book, *Pearl Harbor: Warning and Decision,* pointed out, "There is a difference . . . between having a signal available somewhere in the heap of irrelevancies, and perceiving it as a warning; and there is also a difference between perceiving it as a warning, and acting or getting action on it. The distinctions, simple as they are, illuminate the obscurity shrouding this moment in history."

Questions that arise from this moment in history usually begin with this one: *Why did President Roosevelt reject the advice of a military expert and move the Pacific Fleet from the West Coast to Pearl Harbor?*

The question goes to the heart of the "conspiracy theory" that has the President cunningly moving the fleet to use it as bait to lure the Japanese to attack the United States—and thus start the war that Roosevelt wants. The theory starts with the erroneous belief that Adm. JAMES O. RICHARDSON, Commander in Chief of the U.S. Fleet, in Oct. 1940 warned the President that moving the fleet to Pearl Harbor would put it in danger, that is, at hazard to Japanese attack.

In fact, Richardson strongly protested the order to move the fleet because of what he perceived to be substandard facilities at Pearl Harbor. He simply did not like Pearl Harbor as a permanent base for his fleet. But he was not worried about its security. In a letter written on Nov. 28, 1940, to Adm. HAROLD R. STARK, Chief of Naval Operations, Richardson said, "The feature of the [fleet security] problem does not give me a great deal of concern, and, I think, can be easily provided for."

Roosevelt was moving the fleet at the urging of the State Department, which believed that the movement would help to deter Japanese aggression. Richardson's insubordinate objections—raised to *warnings* in retrospective interpretations—led to his removal and replacement by Kimmel, who never

raised the issue of danger for the fleet (redesignated the U.S. Pacific Fleet). "Sailing into harm's way" is what fleets are ultimately supposed to do.

Why weren't the "war warnings" heeded? They were, but not in ways that did any good when the attack came on Dec. 7.

On Nov. 27, 1941, the NAVY DEPARTMENT sent Kimmel a dispatch described as "a war warning." The dispatch said that "an aggressive move by Japan is expected within the next few days." The WAR DEPARTMENT, also on Nov. 27, sent Short a dispatch warning "hostile action possible at any moment. If hostility cannot, repeat cannot, be avoided the United States desires that Japan commit the first overt act."

Each commander reacted in his own way. Kimmel, not wishing to arouse Hawaii's civilian population, did not raise the alert status in the Navy he commanded at Pearl Harbor. But he did send the carriers ENTERPRISE (CV 6) and LEXINGTON (CV 2), with escorts, to deliver planes to WAKE ISLAND and MIDWAY ISLAND because he was thinking offensively rather than defensively. Inadvertently, his decision saved the carriers from being Dec. 7 targets.

Short, in charge of Pearl Harbor defenses, reacted to his warning dispatch by taking precautions against SABOTAGE. This response stemmed from the belief that Hawaii's Japanese and JAPANESE-AMERICANS could not be trusted and in war would turn against America. The Army particularly subscribed to the fear of sabotage by people with Japanese blood. In the mid-1930s then-Lt. Col. GEORGE S. PATTON, chief of Army intelligence in Hawaii, drew up a plan to seize 128 leaders of Hawaii's Japanese community and hold them as hostages in the event of a U.S.-Japanese war.

Short followed Army doctrine in responding to what he saw as a threat of sabotage. One antisabotage move was the massing of aircraft in wingtip-to-wingtip aggregations to make them easier to guard. Unfortunately, Short's move also hastened the planes' destruction when Japanese planes struck at airfields around Pearl Harbor.

The Nov. 27 warnings to Kimmel and Short had been preceded by other warnings going back to at least April. But, warnings about *war* are not warnings about an *attack* on Pearl Harbor. Neither in

Washington nor in Pearl Harbor was there unqualified expectation of an attack at Pearl Harbor.

Kimmel and Short were denied access to the intelligence community's highly secret decryptions of intercepted Japanese diplomatic messages. The intelligence bureaucracies wanted to tightly hold the secrets their code-breaking unveiled. MAGIC was guarded so zealously that few people ever saw an original message. The war warnings might have been better understood by Kimmel and Short if they had seen the diplomatic messages. But it does not seem likely that higher-grade intelligence would have changed their perceptions of how to respond.

One intercepted TOKYO-Washington coded message said that if Japan-U.S. relations were "in danger," Tokyo would broadcast on feigned weather broadcasts the words "east wind rain." Conspiracy theorists contend that the words were broadcast on Dec. 5, but, mysteriously, the "warning" was not given to Kimmel and Short. In fact, according to the Congressional report (and Wohlstetter's research) there is no evidence that the message was ever transmitted.

Why didn't RADAR give warning of the approach of the Japanese planes? It did, but no action was taken.

At 7:02 A.M. on Dec. 7, two Army radar operators on Oahu's northern shore were about to shut down (radars were turned on only from 4 A.M. to 7 A.M.). But they saw on their radar screen what appeared to be a large formation of planes. The operators notified a lieutenant at an information center at Fort Shafter on Oahu. He said, "Well, don't worry about it." He explained later that he assumed the operators had picked up a flight of B-17 FLYING FORTRESS bombers (unarmed, incidentally) coming in from the U.S. West Coast. The congressional majority report said the lieutenant's response "tends to demonstrate how thoroughly unprepared" the Army was on Dec. 7.

Why weren't there any antitorpedo defenses around the battleships? In Feb. 1941 the Chief of Naval Operations said in a letter to Kimmel, "a minimum depth of water of 75' may be assumed necessary to successfully drop torpedoes from planes." The waters of Pearl Harbor were about 40 feet deep. Kimmel believed that the shallowness of the waters was protection enough. What he had not expected was that the Japanese would fit their aerial TORPEDOES

with vanes that would reduce the angle of the torpedoes when they hit the water.

Why didn't Kimmel and Short cooperate? The admiral and general were friends. "The rumor that Short and I did not get along bothered me more perhaps than anything else," Kimmel said. But, as the Army Board noted, they did not extend their friendship to coordinated planning. "Apparently Short was afraid that if he went much beyond social contacts and really got down to business with the Navy to get what he had a right to know in order to do his job," the board said, "he would give offense to the Navy. . . ."

Pedestal

Code name for British CONVOY to MALTA, Aug. 1942.

Peenemünde

Site of German rocket research and construction. The village of Peenemünde, on an island off Germany's Baltic coast, was the center of German development of the V-1 BUZZ BOMB and V-2 MISSILE. Although heavily bombed, Peenemünde continued to be a key research facility throughout the war. It was captured by Soviet troops in April 1945. (See also CONSTANCE BABINGTON-SMITH.)

Peggy

Although in operational service for less than a year, the Ki-67 Type 4 heavy bomber (Allied code name Peggy) proved to be one of the Japanese Army Air Force's most effective and versatile aircraft. In Japanese service it was known as the *Hiryu* (Flying Dragon). This was the first Army bomber to carry an aerial TORPEDO, and was employed by the Army and Navy in the antishipping role as well as a conventional bomber, ground-attack plane, reconnaissance aircraft, interceptor, BAKA carrier, and, in desperation, as a *Taiatari* (suicide) aircraft. Several were also employed as research aircraft. A 75-mm cannon was provided in the Ki-104 variant to provide a "heavy fighter" to intercept high-flying U.S. B-29 SUPERFORTRESS bombers; forty-four aircraft were completed, but the concept was not successful. The Peggy was also selected as carrier for the I-Go-1A GUIDED MISSILE, but that weapon did not become operational before the war ended.

The Peggy was flown by the Japanese Navy in small numbers as a torpedo bomber; the aircraft first saw action in this role in attacks against the U.S. Third FLEET off Formosa in Oct. 1944. Both services continued to employ the Peggy in torpedo attacks.

Design of the Mitsubishi Ki-67 began in 1941 and the prototype flew on Dec. 27, 1942. Although flight tests were successful, modifications delayed production and by early 1944 only twenty-one aircraft had been completed. Production was hampered by U.S. bombing attacks and the earthquake of Dec. 1944; a total of 698 aircraft were built.

The twin-engine, mid-wing aircraft bore a superficial resemblance to the Navy's G4M BETTY bomber, with a prominent glazed nose and tail, and a large tail fin; however, the twin-engine Peggy had a dorsal hump housing the cockpit and ending in most models with a dorsal gun turret. The undercarriage retracted fully into the radial engine nacelles. An internal bay could hold up to 1,746 pounds of BOMBS or an aerial torpedo could be carried externally, under the fuselage. Defensive armament consisted of a 20-mm cannon in the dorsal turret plus three flexible 12.7-mm machine guns and paired 12.7-mm guns mounted in the tail turret.

The Ki-67-Ib had an impressive top speed of 334 mph with a maximum range of 2,360 miles. The crew was six to eight—reduced to three for suicide attacks.

Peleliu

One of the Palau Islands and one of the Pacific territories that made up the JAPANESE MANDATED ISLANDS. Peleliu, about 5 miles long and 2 miles wide, was at the southern end of the chain, about halfway between NEW GUINEA and the Philippines. Here, as part of the U.S. CENTRAL PACIFIC CAMPAIGN, U.S. forces staged a costly AMPHIBIOUS LANDING in Sept. 1944.

To protect the flank for Gen. DOUGLAS MACARTHUR, who was to invade the Philippines in October, on Sept. 15, the 1st Marine DIVISION struck Peleliu while the Army hit MOROTAI in the DUTCH EAST INDIES. Adm. WILLIAM F. HALSEY had argued against the landing because of indications that the Philippines were not well defended. But Mac-

Arthur went on with the Morotai and Peleliu invasions, code-named Stalemate.

U.S. invasion planners had little knowledge of the Palau Islands. The last detailed information had come from Marine Maj. EARL H. ELLIS, who had died under mysterious circumstances while in the Palaus in 1923. Planners were ignorant of the fact that Peleliu, surrounded by coral reefs and mangrove swamps, was heavily fortified in protective jungle, with hundreds of caves serving as natural bunkers. The ignorance would cost many lives.

Intensive pre-invasion bombardment of the beach was ineffective for three reasons: targeting information was faulty, the Japanese defenders were deeply burrowed in, and the Japanese strategy called for a defensive line well behind the beach. In a lesson learned from other U.S. landings, the Japanese realized that by holding back from a beachhead defense they ran less risk from bombardment.

As part of the Japanese plan, the Marines met little resistance when they began landing on the morning of Sept. 15. Then the concealed mortars and machine guns opened up, knocking out twenty-six LANDING CRAFT. In the afternoon, the Japanese sent tanks and troops against the 1st and 5th Marine REGIMENTS. Night brought BANZAI charges as the Japanese poured from caves.

In the first week of fierce combat the Marines suffered 4,000 casualties; the 1st Marine Regiment was nearly wiped out. Marine survivors joined with the Army's 81st Infantry Division in fighting along a central coral ridge. One handful of Marines, out of ammunition, fought off an assault with bayonets, chunks of coral, and their fists.

Marine-piloted F4U CORSAIR fighters, newly arrived on the captured airstrip at the southern end of the island, dropped BOMBS and NAPALM, and strafed the Japanese. The fighting was so close that the Corsair pilots did not bother to raise their landing gear when they took off for a bombing run. They simply dumped their bombs and then banked to come around to land and rearm.

The carnage on Peleliu finally ended amid bombs and FLAME THROWERS in the caves and charred jungles. The 1st Division suffered 6,786 casualties—1,300 killed in action. The 1st Marines casualties amounted to 53.7 percent of their strength, the 5th's loss was 42.7 percent, and the 7th's was 46.2

percent. About 12,000 Japanese had been killed when Peleliu's organized resistance ended on Nov. 27. But many Japanese in the island's caves continued fighting until after the war was over.

Of the nineteen MEDALS OF HONOR awarded to Marines of the 1st Division in the Pacific, eight were won on Peleliu. The courage displayed in taking the island is undiminished by a bitter truth: The invasion was not necessary. MacArthur, already headed for the Philippines, needed no protection. Peleliu could have been bypassed and allowed to "wither on the vine"—the stated strategy in the skirting of other Japanese strongholds.

Penitent

Code name for Allied operations on the Dalmatian coast (Yugoslavia) proposed for the latter years of the war.

Pentagon

Headquarters for the WAR DEPARTMENT and Army staff during the war. Built under the direct supervision of an Army engineer, Col. LESLIE R. GROVES, the massive structure was begun in the summer of 1941 in Arlington, Va., directly across the Potomac River from WASHINGTON at the site of a former airport. The Pentagon was to bring together some 24,000 clerks and staff officers scattered in offices throughout Washington. The Navy high command was invited to move into the Pentagon, but declined and remained in wooden, temporary buildings on Washington's Mall.

The building was occupied beginning in Nov. 1942 and, formally completed in Jan. 1943, would eventually house almost 40,000 workers. Then the world's largest office building, its five-sided, five-story structure covers twenty-nine acres and has about 3.7 million square feet of floor space. It has almost seventeen miles of corridors, arranged to minimize the distances between offices. A central (five-sided) court provides space for workers to relax at noontime. Scores of restaurants, cafeterias, a dispensary, massive telephone complex, bank, and other facilities are provided. The Great Pyramid of Egypt could be placed within the Pentagon with 200 feet to spare on all sides. The reinforced-concrete building was intended as a permanent structure, with massive internal ramps to both handle

the hordes of workers and facilitate its conversion to a veteran's hospital after the war.

Numerous stories about the Pentagon quickly emerged as thousands of workers got lost in its maze of corridors and ramps: The Western Union boy who entered the maze and emerged three days later as a lieutenant colonel, and the woman who was a virgin when she entered and by the time she found her way out had become a mother.

Perpetual

British code name for reinforcement of MALTA, Nov. 1941.

Persecution

Code name for Allied assault force for Aitape, NEW GUINEA.

Peru

Capital: Lima, pop. 7,023,111 (1940). Because of the number and influence of resident nationals from Japan, Germany, and Italy, Peru at the beginning of the EUROPEAN WAR was a hotbed of AXIS PROPAGANDA efforts. But questions about Peru's solidarity with the United States were answered in May 1941 when the crews of five German ships scuttled them because Peru was about to seize them. Peru next denied diplomatic immunity to the mail pouches of Axis diplomats and confiscated the planes of the German Lufthansa airline.

After the Japanese attack on PEARL HARBOR on Dec. 7, 1941, Peru froze Japanese credits and later restricted the movements of resident Japanese. The United States became Peru's only customer for strategic materials, including antimony, copper, molybdenum, tungsten, zinc, and lead.

Peru in Jan. 1944 announced the discovery of a Japanese-German plot to disrupt the country by inspiring ANTI-SEMITIC disorders. In retaliation, Peru liquidated German financial holdings and expropriated Japanese and German property. On Feb. 12, 1945, Peru announced that it had considered itself in a state of belligerency with Japan and Germany and two days later became a member of the UNITED NATIONS.

Pétain, Henri Philippe (1856–1951)

Puppet leader of VICHY FRANCE after France's surrender to Germany. A Marshal of France and hero of Verdun in World War I, Pétain succeeded PAUL REYNAUD as French Premier on May 17, 1940, and signed an armistice with Germany on June 22. The collaborationist National Assembly gave him emergency powers and, as head of state, he moved the government to Vichy, in unoccupied France.

When the war ended, he entered Switzerland from Germany, but returned to France on April 26, 1945, and was arrested by the provisional government of Gen. CHARLES DE GAULLE. "I sacrificed my prestige for the French people," he testified. Convicted of aiding the enemy—not of committing TREASON—the eighty-nine-year-old Pétain was sentenced to death; de Gaulle commuted the sentence to life imprisonment. When Pétain died, he was still hailed by some in France as a misguided patriot.

Pete

Despite its biplane configuration and age, the F1M observation floatplane was a highly successful aircraft flown throughout the war. Given the Allied code name Pete, the F1M was used in the *fighter* as well as observation, gunnery spotting, antisubmarine, and convoy escort roles. It flew in Japanese operations in the Philippines, NEW GUINEA, the SOLOMONS, from Attu in the ALEUTIANS, and in numerous other areas. Toward the end of the war the surviving units were flown as trainers.

The prototype F1M first flew in June 1936. There were major stability problems and some redesign was done before production began. The F1M2 model entered naval service in 1941 and proved extremely agile with a high rate of climb, leading to its use as a fighter. When production terminated in March 1944 a total of 1,118 had been built.

The F1M was an extremely clean design, with a radial engine, two open cockpits, and the upper wing slightly ahead of the lower; a large centerline float was fitted as were stabilizing floats under the outer wing sections.

Maximum speed was 230 mph, and range was credited up to 360 miles. Two 132-pound BOMBS could be carried. Gun armament consisted of two cowling-mounted 7.7-mm machine guns and a third gun in the after cockpit. The crew numbered two.

Philippine Sea,

see LEYTE GULF.

Philippines

Capital: MANILA pop. 16,000,303 (1939). The site of two of America's most disheartening defeats—BATAAN and CORREGIDOR—at the beginning of the Pacific war and then the stage for Gen. DOUGLAS MACARTHUR's dramatic "I shall return" liberation in 1944. The Philippines, a commonwealth under U.S. authority when the Japanese invaded in Dec. 1941, had a long and sometimes bitter relationship with the United States. But during the war the Philippines proved to be a staunch ally.

An archipelago of some 7,000 islands, the Philippines were ceded to the United States (along with Puerto Rico and GUAM) by Spain in the treaty ending the Spanish-American War. The U.S. venture into colonialism got off to a rough start, for Philippine rebels immediately turned from fighting the Spanish to fighting the Americans. The .45-CALIBER PISTOL gained fame in the hands of U.S. troops who intermittently fought the Filipino rebels. The words of a soldier's song told the story:

The rebels up at old Tarlac, four men to every gun.
I think the trouble is at an end. They think it's just
   begun.

(Tarlac, in the mountains of the main northern island of Luzon, would become a battleground again in World War II, but this time Filipino rebels—the Communist-led *Hukbalahap,* dubbed the Huks—fought as GUERRILLAS on the U.S. side, against the Japanese.)

The United States conceded the strength of Filipino nationalism in 1916 when an Act of Congress promised withdrawal of American authority "as soon as a stable government can be established therein." By then, Filipinos were voting for their own legislators and provincial governors. U.S. authority was represented by a governor general appointed by the president. (One of them, HENRY L. STIMSON, would serve as U.S. secretary of War during World War II.)

As a commonwealth, the Philippines remained dependent upon the United States for defense. Retired U.S. Gen. Douglas MacArthur, former

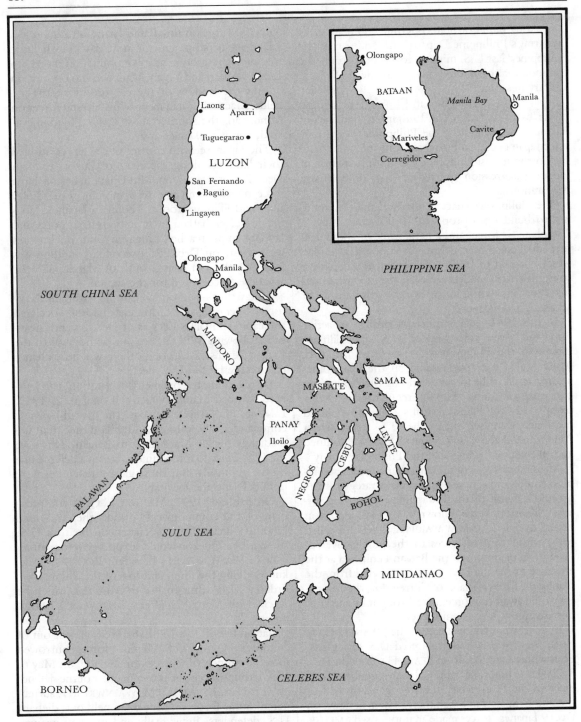

Philippines.

U.S. Army Chief of Staff, onetime commander of the Army's Philippine Department, and son of the Philippines' last U.S. military governor, became the commonwealth's military adviser and head of a U.S. military mission.

Japan's invasion of China in 1937 and the signing of the TRIPARTITE PACT in 1940 intensified fears of Japanese moves against the Philippines, especially since Japan occupied Formosa—only 65 miles from the northernmost Philippine island. Anticipation of Japanese aggression spurred a surge of defensive preparations.

The Philippines enacted universal military training to build up a proposed 10,000-man army, a 250-plane air force, and a naval force of about 100 torpedo boats. MacArthur developed a war plan which, he said in 1939, "will represent a defensive strength that would cause even the strongest and most ruthless nation in the world to hesitate about attacking the Islands."

In July 1941, MacArthur was recalled to active duty and given command of U.S. and Filipino troops in the Philippines; he stuck to his plan, which called for a defense of all the Philippines against attack. The forces defending the Philippines consisted of about 10,000 regular U.S. Army troops, 12,000 Filipino scouts (Filipino enlisted men who were serving in the U.S. Army under American officers), and about 100,000 ill-trained and ill-equipped soldiers of the Philippine Army.

MacArthur's plan put much reliance on these Filipino troops and ignored the official strategy for the ground defense of the Philippines: War Plan Orange, Revision Three, known as WPO-3, a portion of the overall RAINBOW WAR PLAN. WPO-3 called for a withdrawal of forces to the jungle-covered, mountainous terrain of the Bataan Peninsula at the entrance to Manila Bay. There, protected from the rear by the fortress island of Corregidor, the defenders would await reinforcements brought by the U.S. fleet steaming into Manila Bay.

But the speed and violence of the JAPANESE CAMPAIGN IN THE FAR EAST shattered U.S. war plans. Following its air assault on PEARL HARBOR on Dec. 8, 1941 (Philippine time), Japan bombed U.S. bases in the Philippines, destroying nearly half of the 200 U.S. aircraft based there. Then, at dawn on Dec. 9 Japanese forces made an unopposed AMPHIB-IOUS LANDING on tiny Batan Island off Luzon and seized its air strip. On the next day's dawn more troops went ashore at two points on northern Luzon, Aparri and Vigan, again with no opposition during the landing or the capture of nearby airfields. MacArthur had most of his ground forces on Mindanao, the southernmost major Philippine island, about 800 miles away.

The Japanese, with control of the air, continued their landings along the coast of Luzon and, on Dec. 20, at Davao on Mindanao, where a large force quickly overcame resistance by some 3,500 U.S. and Filipino troops. The main Japanese landing force, embarked in seventy-six transports and landing ships, reached Lingayen Gulf, on Luzon's west coast, on Dec. 22; a secondary landing was made on the east coast, south of Manila, and the Japanese forces raced for the capital.

MacArthur—without consulting with U.S. Navy forces operating out of Manila's harbor—declared the capital an OPEN CITY as of Dec. 26 and, ironically following WPO-3, began a withdrawal to the Bataan Peninsula, although there was little chance of a rescue by the U.S. fleet.

Disregarding the open city declaration, the Japanese bombed Manila, which fell on Jan. 2, 1942. Lt. Gen. MASAHARU HOMMA, the overall Japanese commander, chose to take Manila rather than immediately pursue MacArthur to Bataan. This gave the U.S.-Filipino forces time to set up a defense line on the peninsula. But those gallant defenders were only delaying the inevitable.

On Feb. 20, 1942, MANUEL L. QUEZON, president of the commonwealth, and other U.S. and Filipino officials were evacuated on board a U.S. submarine. (Quezon would set up a government-in-exile in WASHINGTON.) President ROOSEVELT, acknowledging the imminent loss of the Philippines, ordered MacArthur to flee to Australia, which he reached on March 17 after a harrowing PT-BOAT voyage.

Bataan fell on April 9. Exhausted, almost out of ammunition, the U.S.-Filipino forces burrowed into the tunnels of Corregidor. Finally, on May 6, MacArthur's successor as commander of the defenders, Lt. Gen. JONATHAN M. WAINWRIGHT, surrendered. Some forces on Mindanao held out; diehard U.S. defenders, individually and in small groups, took to the hills, and a widespread guerrilla war began there and on Luzon.

Japan hoped for a peaceful occupation of the Philippines, which the Japanese saw as a potential partner in the GREATER EAST ASIA CO-PROSPERITY SPHERE. But Filipino resistance grew with each day of occupation. The conquerors then tried to transform the people. Japanese PROPAGANDA pictured the Filipinos as brothers in the war between the nonwhite and white races; the teaching of the Japanese language was made compulsory; radios were altered to prevent listeners from hearing U.S. or British broadcasts. All political parties were abolished and a new Japanese party was introduced to select members of what was a puppet government.

In the mountains and jungles, guerrilla groups grew. Aided in part through the landings of supplies from U.S. SUBMARINES, the mixed units of Filipinos and U.S. holdouts evolved into significant military forces, some of whom were led by U.S. officers dispatched by MacArthur. By mid-1944, guerrillas had their own currency, communications system, recruiting program, and political organization. They controlled 60 percent of Philippine territory, all of it rural or jungled.

MacArthur had vowed, "I shall return," and, after his successes in NEW GUINEA, he pressed for the reconquest of the Philippines. His plan clashed with the Navy island-hopping strategy that saw the taking of Formosa as the next step in the advance of the war directly to Japan. But MacArthur prevailed, convincing President Roosevelt of America's responsibility to the Philippines.

On Oct. 20, 1944, using two assault forces and some 500 ships, MacArthur landed 202,500 troops on Leyte, the central main island and a strategic link to Mindanao, Mindoro, and Luzon. In a display of bravado highly publicized by still and NEWSREEL cameras, MacArthur waded ashore from a LANDING CRAFT to personally lead the invasion.

At his side, also wading through the surf at Leyte, was Sergio Osmeña, the former vice president of the Philippines who had become president upon the death of Quezon on Aug. 1, 1944. Osmeña carried a Philippine flag on a pole that he jammed into the shore, proclaiming the return of democracy to his homeland. U.S. forces captured the harbor and airfield of Tacloban, provincial capital of Leyte, on Oct. 21, 1944, and Osmeña proclaimed it the temporary capital of the commonwealth.

MacArthur, no fan of the U.S. Navy, had made the "I-shall-return" operation an Army show. But it was the Navy, in the fateful battle of LEYTE GULF, that saved his forces from what might have been a disastrous assault by Japanese carrier-based aircraft. The Navy's destruction of the Japanese fleet bearing down on Leyte left the Japanese garrisons in the Philippines without air support or protection of their supply lines to Japan.

The U.S. invasion force met relatively light resistance to the landings near Tacloban. But in another landing at Ormoc on Dec. 7, Japanese troops in pillboxes and caves fought hard, and KAMIKAZE attacks mauled U.S. ships supporting the landings. On Dec. 15, some 16,000 U.S. combat troops and 15,000 construction and Army Air Forces personnel went ashore at Mindoro, where the 500-man Japanese garrison showed little fight. By Christmas 1944 Leyte was declared secured and MacArthur was ready for the next phase of the invasion: the taking of Luzon, held by 250,000 Japanese troops.

But when the first of 200,000 U.S. troops stormed ashore at Lingayen Gulf in western Luzon, the enemy did not appear in any strength, and U.S. commanders uneasily wondered why. The answer: A new Japanese tactic allowed an amphibious landing to take place uncontested, thereby sparing the defenders a punishing bombardment. Inland, the Americans found an intricate defense system of caves, tunnels, and pillboxes. The U.S. troops fought determined defenders who saw resistance here as a way to deflect an American invasion of the home islands.

On Jan. 31, 1945, after another landing south of Manila Bay, U.S. troops fought their way into Manila. Filipino guerrillas and U.S. RANGERS freed U.S. PRISONERS OF WAR, many of them victims of the BATAAN DEATH MARCH. In fierce house-to-house fighting and hand-to-hand combat, the liberation forces won back Manila, which MacArthur declared secure on March 3. He returned civil control of the Philippines to Osmeña, who reinstalled the government in the Malacañan Palace in a demolished Manila.

MacArthur announced on June 30 that most of the country was liberated, but the fighting went on.

Gen. TOMOYUKI YAMASHITA led about 65,000 Japanese troops into Luzon's hills and held out until the end of the war.

The destruction of the country was appalling. Manuel Acuna Roxas, who would become president of the Philippines in 1946, was shocked when he saw the evidence of "unbelievable and vengeful sacking" by the Japanese occupation force.

"In every large city, in hundreds of smaller municipalities and even in barrios," he wrote, "most of the habitable dwellings were destroyed; schools had been sacked and gutted; bridges over the principal rivers and waterways blown up; telephone and telegraph lines disrupted, radio stations dismantled and all the government buildings, with but isolated exceptions, in ruins. . . . All the inter-island vessels were sunk or taken away by the Japanese. No commercial aircraft remained. Street cars and busses were destroyed or stolen. Railroads were bombed into uselessness and most of the rolling stock gone. Most of the precious work animals, the carabaos, were eaten or killed. Farm lands were left fallow and untended."

Reconstruction of the devastated country had to be postponed because the Philippines became a staging area for the planned invasion of Japan. Hundreds of thousands of Allied troops poured into the islands. Inflation drove up prices. Communist insurgents who had been fighting the Japanese, began preparing to fight to take power. Adding to the chaos were purges of collaborationists who had held government posts under the Japanese.

Under the Philippines' last U.S. high commissioner, PAUL V. McNUTT, the United States rewarded the Filipino allies: Congress authorized eight years of free trade, guaranteed generous quotas on sugar, coconut oil, and hemp cordage; pegged the peso to the U.S. dollar; and set up a $400,000,000 fund for payment of war-damage claims, with a priority to Filipino individuals with small claims of $500 or less (many claims involved the death in battle of carabaos). The United States also funded a $120,000,000 public works program and turned over $100,000,000 in surplus properties to the Philippine government. Independence came on schedule on July 4, 1946, when the commonwealth of the Philippines became an independent republic.

Picador

British code name for capture of DAKAR; later Barrister.

Piccadilly

Allied code name for drop site for CHINDITS in Burma.

Picket

British code name for reinforcement of MALTA, March 1942.

Pigstick

Code name for planned AMPHIBIOUS LANDING on Mayu peninsula.

Pilgrim

Code name for projected Allied capture of the Canary Islands, 1942.

Pinpoint

British code name for the reinforcement of MALTA, July 1942.

Pius XII (1876–1958)

Pope during the war. Prior to becoming Pope Pius XII, Eugenio Pacelli spent much of his ecclesiastical career working for the Vatican Secretariat of State. He was papal nuncio to Bavaria during World War I and became papal nuncio to Germany in 1920. In 1930 he became Vatican secretary of state, and he ascended to the papal throne in March 1939.

His reign was marked by controversy over his relationship with NAZI Germany and Fascist Italy and his failure to publicly condemn the HOLOCAUST. The Pope shared with HITLER and Italian *Il Duce* BENITO MUSSOLINI a fear and hatred of Communism. It was anti-communism, rather than an espousal of Fascism, that underlay Pope Pius' foreign policy.

He saw as his first mission the protection of Catholicism against Communism, whether it be by siding with the Fascists in the SPANISH CIVIL WAR or by accommodating the Fascist states of Germany and Italy. He realized that the papacy was supposed to be a moral beacon, but he never let it shine so brightly that its glare put VATICAN CITY in danger. He rationalized his failure to speak out against the NAZI massacre of JEWS by assuming that a denunciation from him would make matters worse for Jews.

The Pope, for example, made no known move to curb Father Josef Tiso, a Roman Catholic priest and a Czech Nazi, who ran the German puppet state of Slovakia. About 70,000 Jews died either in Slovakia or in CONCENTRATION CAMPS in Poland and Germany. Elsewhere in Europe, however, as historian John Toland wrote in *Adolf Hitler,* the Catholic Church "saved the lives of more Jews than all other churches, religious institutions and rescue organizations combined. . . . The record of the ALLIES was far more shameful."

In 1933, soon after Hitler became chancellor, Cardinal Pacelli, as papal secretary of state, had negotiated a concordat with Germany in which Hitler promised the Catholic Church the right "to regulate her own affairs." In 1939, when Cardinal Pacelli became Pope Pius XII, he knew that Hitler had been violating the concordat, but the Pope refrained from criticizing Germany. Told once that the Pope had always been a good friend of Germany, Hitler said, "That's possible, but he's no friend of mine."

Only one high-ranking Catholic prelate openly opposed Hitler. He was Cardinal-Archbishop Clemens August von Galen of Münster. In 1941 he gave a courageous series of anti-Nazi sermons, denouncing as "plain murder" Hitler's so-called euthanasia policy. The Cardinal, dubbed the Lion of Münster for his unrelenting stand against Hitler, was finally arrested in the widespread roundup of suspects following the JULY 20 PLOT against Hitler in 1944. Von Galen was put in the Sachsenhausen concentration camp. He survived the war and died in 1946.

In Aug. 1939, on the eve of the EUROPEAN WAR, the Pope appealed for peace. His next plea, following the fall of France in June 1940, played into Hitler's hand. Hitler believed that England would sue for peace. The Pope, in confidential messages to both Hitler and Mussolini, offered to mediate a peace that obviously would mean ratification of Hitler's conquest of Europe.

President ROOSEVELT, concerned about the Pope's ambiguous neutrality, appointed Myron Taylor, former president of U.S. Steel, as a special representative to the Vatican. (Unlike many other countries, the United States did not have formal diplomatic relations with Vatican City.) Taylor, an Episcopalian, periodically visited the Pope to convey personal messages from Roosevelt. Taylor's most important meeting was in Sept. 1942 when Taylor informed the Pope that there would be no negotiated peace; the Allies would keep fighting until Hitler and Nazism were destroyed.

As the tide of war turned against Germany, so did Vatican policy. After Italy's SURRENDER in Sept. 1943, Vatican City's neutrality was respected by Germany during a brutal occupation of ROME. Undoubtedly with the Pope's tacit approval, many Jews, downed Allied airmen, and escaped PRISONERS OF WAR were hidden in Vatican City, risking its neutral status. In Turkey, Vatican diplomat Angelo Roncalli—who in 1958 would succeed Pope Pius XII as Pope John XXIII—distributed baptismal certificates to help the rescue of some Hungarian Jews.

Only after the defeat of Germany did the Pope speak out. On June 2, 1945, he denounced the Nazis' "arrogant apostasy from Jesus Christ, the denial of His doctrine and of His work of redemption, the cult of violence, the idolatry of race and blood, the overthrow of human liberty and dignity."

Plaster

Code name for "creeping attack" tactic against submarines developed by Capt. F. J. WALKER, Royal Navy.

Platoon

Military unit, the smallest led by an officer in the U.S. Army and Marine Corps. Platoons are found in most types of military organizations and are normally a component of COMPANIES, and in combat units (infantry, TANK) and some support organizations (military police, reconnaissance) they consist of three or four SQUADS. Infantry platoons had some forty to forty-five men, while tank platoons had only twenty men (five tank crews).

Other types of platoons varied from a score of men to military police platoons, which had an authorized strength of 106 by the end of the war. Platoons were normally commanded by lieutenants.

Ploesti

Rumanian city 35 miles north of Bucharest and the center of the nation's oil industry. Germany was heavily dependent upon Rumanian oil during the war, and Ploesti, at the center of a complex of oil fields, refineries, and petrochemical plants, came under intensive U.S. air attack during the war as the AAF prosecuted its so-called "oil campaign" to deprive the German armed forces of petroleum.

The first AAF raid against Ploesti came on June 12, 1942, when thirteen B-24D LIBERATOR four-engine bombers flew from the British airfield at Fayid, Egypt, on a round-trip raid of 2,400 miles. The results were minimal, with four of the valuable planes coming down in Turkey and one crash-landing elsewhere in the Middle East.

Although by 1943 the Ploesti area was providing more than one half of Germany's petroleum, the refineries there were not bombed again until Aug. 1, 1943. With bases available in Libya, the U.S. Eighth and Ninth AIR FORCES launched 177 B-24D bombers, each carrying two tons of BOMBS on a 1,900-mile strike against seven installations in the Ploesti area. The raid—Operation Tidal Wave—was meticulously planned, with the bomber crews rehearsing two full-scale practice missions against a simulation of Ploesti laid out in a remote desert area.

After overflying the Mediterranean, Albania, Yugoslavia, and Bulgaria, the B-24s approached their targets from a height of only 500 feet in a move to deceive German defenders. But some of the groups became disoriented and approached from the wrong directions. The alerted German FLAK batteries and the general confusion over the target took a heavy toll of the B-24s. Fifty-four planes (30 percent) failed to return (with almost 500 crewmen killed, captured, or interned in neutral Turkey). Damage to the Ploesti complex was significant, but within a month the facilities were operating at pre-raid capacity. Five of the fliers on the Aug. 1 mission received the MEDAL OF HONOR—three posthumously—the most ever awarded for a single air action.

The AAF bombers returned again and again to Ploesti, from bases in North Africa and in 1944 from bases in Italy. But Ploesti's petroleum production was not stopped for three reasons: failure to adhere to the oil campaign (such as bombing Ploesti's railroad yards twice in April 1944 with the expectation that the bombings would produce "incidental" damage to the refineries); extensive German defenses; and the priority Germany gave to rebuilding damaged facilities.

With some forty minutes' warning available as the Italian-based bombers passed over Yugoslavia en route to Ploesti, the Germans could get their guns and fighters ready for action, and could light hundreds of smoke pots that would obscure the area, making PRECISION BOMBING impossible.

There was also confusion in the AAF leadership about the oil campaign. The attacks were generally considered part of the effort to destroy German oil supplies, but Lt. Gen. CARL SPAATZ, head of the U.S. STRATEGIC BOMBING effort in Europe, believed that the "cardinal issue" of the oil campaign was to kill German fighters. According to the official AAF history, "He contended that it [the German Air Force] would expend itself against heavy bomber fleets engaged in attacking oil installations but would conserve its strength while targets . . . as rail centers were being bombed."

In May 1944 the Fifteenth Air Force began regular bomber strikes against Ploesti from bases in Italy. Almost 500 U.S. bombers struck the Ploesti area on May 5, almost 700 struck on May 17, some 460 planes on May 31, and 300 on June 6. On June 10 the Fifteenth Air Force also flew P-38 LIGHTNING fighters against Ploesti targets. Thirty-six of the twin-engine fighters carried two 1,000-pound bombs while another thirty-nine P-38s fended off the pugnacious German fighters that sought to protect their source of gasoline; this strike was only partially successful and twenty-three P-38s were lost. (By then Ploesti was the third best-defended target on the continent, the first being BERLIN and the second Vienna, also an oil-production center.)

More strikes followed—761 bombers on June 23, another 377 on June 24; these heavy strikes continued, and soon even blind bombing through dense smoke from so many four-engine bombers was inflicting heavy damage. In addition to AAF daylight raids, RAF twin-engine WELLINGTON bombers struck Ploesti in four night raids. The attacks went on until Aug. 24, 1944, when operations at Ploesti finally ceased—the day after Rumania surrendered. A few days later Soviet troops entered the ruins of Ploesti.

In the AAF effort a total of 13,469 tons of bombs were dropped on Ploesti and 350 heavy bombers plus numerous fighters were lost with most of their crews killed, although many were captured or interned.

Plot E

Cemetery for U.S. troops executed in Europe during World War II. There are five plots to the Oise-Aisne American CEMETERY at Fère-en-Tardenois, France. Four plots—A,B,C,D—contain the 6,012 graves of Americans who fell in France. The honored dead lie under crosses and Stars of David. Plot E, hidden in a wooded area, contains ninety-six graves, each marked by a marble block. These are the graves of the ninety-six soldiers executed in the European Theater during World War II, ninety-five for murder and rape, and one, EDDIE D. SLOVIK, for desertion. (See also JUSTICE, MILITARY.)

Plunder

Code name for crossing of the Rhine by the British 21st ARMY GROUP, March 1945.

Pluto

Anglo-American pipeline across the English Channel to carry petroleum following the NORMANDY INVASION. PLUTO was an acronym for Pipe Line Under The Ocean.

The PLUTO scheme provided for the laying of ten three-inch-diameter flexible pipelines from Sandown on the Isle of Wight to the port of Querqueville near Cherbourg. The first pipeline was to be in place by D+20 (twenty days after D-DAY) and the last by D+75. At the 60-mile distance the theoretical delivery capacity of each of the ten lines was 300 tons of gasoline per day. Once ashore, the pipelines were to be linked by aboveground pipelines to truck terminal points.

After the Allied landings on June 6, 1944, the pipelines were unwound across the bottom of the channel from large drums, 50 feet in diameter. The drums, awkward to handle and tow, were called "Conundrums."

The first PLUTO pipeline was ready on D+19 (June 25). The original PLUTO plan was not fully successful. Damage from ship anchors and other difficulties led to several pipeline failures. In Oct. 1944 a new series of PLUTO-type pipelines was laid across the channel from Dungeness in southeast England to Boulogne. By the end of the year eight pipelines of this series were in use; the total eventually reached seventeen. Still, by early 1945 only 700 tons of gasoline per day were being provided to the U.S. and British armies in France by pipeline, far short of the expected quantity.

In addition to the PLUTO project, flexible steel pipes were run from the beaches at Normandy to offshore mooring buoys, where tankers could tie up to unload gasoline at the rate of 600 tons per hour per ship.

Pocket Battleships

Term given by journalists to German armored ships or *Panzerschiff*. According to WINSTON CHURCHILL, "Their six eleven-inch guns, their twenty-six knot speed, and the armour they carried had been compressed with masterly skill into the limits of a ten-thousand-ton displacement."

Under the terms of the Versailles Treaty of 1919 Germany could build six ships of this type, but only three were constructed before Germany began building battle cruisers and battleships. The most notorious of the three pocket battleships was the short-lived *ADMIRAL GRAF SPEE,* which was scuttled off Montevideo after being defeated by three smaller British cruisers in a battle off the Plate estuary between Argentina and Uruguay. The other ships in the class were the *Admiral Scheer* and *Deutschland;* the latter was renamed *Lützow* on Nov. 15, 1939, because HITLER feared the psychological impact on the German people of the loss of a ship with that name.

At the start of the EUROPEAN WAR the *Deutschland* and *Graf Spee* were on standby stations in the North and South Atlantic, respectively. The *Graf Spee* sank nine merchant ships (50,089 gross tons) before she was destroyed in Dec. 1939; the *Deutschland* sank only two merchant ships and captured a third (11,925 gross tons) before returning to Germany. She subsequently participated in the April 1940 invasion of Norway, where she was damaged by shore guns and then by a British submarine's torpedo. In 1942 she was shifted to a base in Norway for attacks against the RUSSIAN CONVOYS. She was brought back to the Baltic in 1944–1945 and was used to support withdrawing German troops in the eastern Baltic; she foundered off Swinemünde on April 16, 1945, and was scuttled to prevent the ship falling into Soviet hands.

The *Admiral Scheer,* plagued by engine problems, made a raiding cruise into the Atlantic and Indian Oceans from Oct. 1940 to April 1941, steaming 46,419 miles in five months without touching port (she was refueled at sea by German merchant ships). The *Scheer* sank fifteen ships and captured two others (113,233 gross tons). She too operated against Russian Convoys from Norwegian bases, from 1942 until she returned to the Baltic in 1944. There the ship was used mainly for gunfire support against Soviet troops. On April 9–10, 1945, she was sunk in Kiel harbor by British bombers.

Although ostensibly rated at 10,000 tons standard displacement, the *Deutschland* was 11,700 tons; the two other ships displaced 12,100 tons. They were armed with a main battery of six 11-inch (280-mm) guns plus eight 5.9-inch (150-mm) guns and lighter weapons and torpedo tubes. Their maximum speed was 28 knots and each had a crew of some 1,125 men.

Pointblank

Code name for Anglo-American STRATEGIC BOMBING offensive against Germany in preparation for the NORMANDY INVASION.

Poland

Capital: WARSAW, pop. 34,775,698 (1939). From medieval times to World War II, Poland was a land of shifting borders. Conquerors crisscrossed Poland so often that Poland itself was obliterated for more than 100 years until the victorious treaty writers of World War I put her back on the map of Europe. That postwar Poland was formed of land that had belonged to Germany, Russia, and Austria-Hungary. The "Polish Corridor" cut off Germany from East Prussia and gave Poland access to the Baltic via the Prussian port of Danzig (called Gdansk by Poles). The port was declared a "free city" under LEAGUE OF NATIONS administration.

When German armies withdrew from Poland and western Russia in 1918, Bolshevik armies, hoping to link Russia with revolutionaries in Germany, marched on Poland, touching off warfare and protracted boundary talks that were not settled until 1921. At the same time, border troubles erupted between Poland and Germany.

The creators of the new Poland had decreed that people in some areas were later to vote on whether to be part of Germany or remain as part of Poland. The voting, often indecisive, touched off frequent disputes and a military clash in 1921 between Polish and German troops. Poland seized the Lithuanian city of Vilna in 1920 and demanded the Czech territory of Teschen, which it later occupied.

Poland became a republic under a 1921 constitution but a military junta seized power in 1926. Although thinly legitimized by a new constitution in 1935, the government remained under military control, fending off Soviet and German threats to Polish independence.

The rise of ADOLF HITLER and the appeasement policy of France and England narrowed Poland's horizons. On Jan. 26, 1934, Poland and Germany signed a nonaggression pact, but both countries knew that Germany had targeted Poland for takeover. Germany focussed on Danzig, building up a local NAZI PARTY and demanding the city's annexation. After Germany's seizure of Czechoslovakia, encircled Poland seemed next. On March 31, 1939, British Prime Minister NEVILLE CHAMBERLAIN declared that if Poland's independence were threatened, the British "would feel themselves bound at once to lend the Polish government all support in their power."

Poland believed that if Germany did attack, a military response would come from the Soviet Union, which had been denouncing Nazi Germany ever since it supported the anti-Communist side in the SPANISH CIVIL WAR. But the hope of Soviet support was killed on Aug. 23, 1939, when Germany and the Soviet Union astounded the world by announcing their NONAGGRESSION PACT.

On Sept. 1, 1939, Germany invaded Poland and sixteen days later the Soviet Union poured troops into eastern Poland to aid Russian "blood brothers," Ukrainians and Byelorussians who lived in Poland. On Sept. 28, the day after a heavily bombed

Warsaw finally fell to German troops, Germany and the Soviet Union signed another agreement. This one gave eastern Poland to the Soviets and western Poland to the Germans.

Remnants of the Polish Army retreated into France, where Polish emigrants added to their ranks. After the fall of France in June 1940, part of the army and the government fled to England, where refugees and escapees from Poland continued the buildup of the army and provided vitally needed pilots to the RAF.

Germany incorporated about half of Poland into the *Reich* and administered the rest as an occupied country under a former storm trooper, HANS FRANK. Germany did not invoke such direct rule in any other conquered country. Frank decreed that Poles would be made "the slaves of the Greater German Empire." During his savage regime, more than 6,000,000 people, about half of them JEWS, were killed in mass murders, in the WARSAW GHETTO, and in CONCENTRATION CAMPS and DEATH CAMPS. (About 10 percent of Poland's prewar population had been Jewish.) An underground Polish army, controlled by the government-in-exile in LONDON, continually harassed the occupation forces, provoking numerous retaliation murders by the Germans.

Mass deportations and persecution were the fate of many Poles in the area controlled by the Soviets until Germany invaded the Soviet Union in June 1941. In an agreement signed by the Polish government-in-exile and the Soviet Union, the Soviets dropped claims to Polish territory and liberated all Polish citizens. The Soviets also allowed Poles taken as PRISONERS OF WAR in 1939 to enter the Polish Army.

Polish divisions under Soviet command fought the Germans in the Soviet Union and entered BERLIN with Soviet troops. Polish Army divisions fought side by side with other Allied forces in Western Europe and Italy in 1944–1945. Polish pilots fighting in the BATTLE OF BRITAIN shot down 15 percent of all the German planes destroyed; Polish bomber squadrons flew thousands of raids and lost 1,968 men; Polish Navy warships, sailing with the Royal Navy, took part in several battles and escorted convoys in the BATTLE OF THE ATLANTIC.

The cordial relations between the Poles and the Soviets evaporated when the Soviet Union refused to answer questions about thousands of missing Polish officers. After discovery of the KATYN MASSACRE—mass graves of thousands of murdered Polish officers—in a Soviet forest in 1943, diplomatic relations were broken off.

As Soviet forces swept eastward toward Germany, Stanislaw Mikolajczyk, head of the Polish government-in-exile in London, foresaw a crisis. He feared Soviet forces liberating German-controlled Poland would occupy the territory, again raising issues about Poland's boundaries and sovereignty. Mikolajczyk urged U.S. and British officials to guarantee a free postwar Poland. But at the TEHRAN CONFERENCE in Nov. 1943, the Allies gave no such assurance. On Jan. 3, 1944, Soviet troops crossed the prewar Polish border; two days later Mikolajczyk met in Washington with President ROOSEVELT and said the Poles would resume diplomatic relations with the Soviet Union.

On Aug. 1, 1944, the underground Polish Home Army, anticipating a Soviet march on Warsaw, led a rising in the capital. Through leaflets and radio broadcasts, the Soviets had urged the rising against the German occupiers. The Poles were also inspired by a political reality: If Poles, rather than Soviets, liberated the capital, the anti-Communist government-in-exile would be in a strong postwar bargaining position.

Soviet forces were across the Vistula River, in a Warsaw suburb, when the rising began. But they did not aid the Home Army or the thousands of men, women, and children who fought alongside the ill-armed resistance units. In the fierce fighting, the Germans leveled more than 85 percent of the city and killed more than 250,000 Poles. The leader of the rising surrendered on Oct. 2. The Germans sent 600,000 Poles, virtually the entire surviving population, to concentration camps.

Poland's postwar future was ultimately decided in Feb. 1945 at the YALTA CONFERENCE, which pledged free elections but decided not to hinder Soviet plans to make Poland a satellite state. The U.S.-British-Soviet declaration made at Yalta said that an interim government would be formed of the non-Communist Polish government-in-exile and "democratic leaders from within Poland"—actually a Soviet-created government already in place. The

German-Polish border was pushed westward to the Oder-Neisse rivers. Mikolajczyk resigned in 1944, but did go to Poland after the war to become a deputy premier in the Communist-dominated government. Differences with the regime sent him into exile. Poland remained a Soviet satellite until 1989.

Poland, Air Force

At the start of the EUROPEAN WAR the Polish Air Force had 900 first-line aircraft—fighters, bombers, reconnaissance aircraft, of which about one half were relatively modern. Indeed, the only aircraft that could be called "advanced" were the thirty-six PZL P.37B Loś B twin-engine bombers, which had a maximum speed of 273 mph. Most Polish planes were fighters and ground-attack aircraft, with the top fighter being the PZL 11c, a single-seat, high-wing aircraft with an open cockpit and top speed of 242 mph.

On Sept. 1, 1939, these aircraft—every one outclassed by their German counterparts—were pitted against the 1,300 aircraft that the Luftwaffe committed to the BLITZKRIEG against Poland. In addition, another 400 German aircraft were kept ready as a reserve should they be needed.

Despite reports that the Polish Air Force was wiped out on its airfields on the first day of the war (as did happen in June 1941 in the German assault on the Soviet Union), most of the Polish planes survived a day or two by operating from small, auxiliary airfields. But like Poland itself, it was only a matter of time, and within a few days the Polish Air Force ceased to exist.

Many Polish fliers escaped, to Rumania and France, and then on to England. On Dec. 1939 the British government decided that certain Polish squadrons would be reformed in the RAF. Under the Polish government-in-exile, Polish pilots were taken into the RAF, mostly into Fighter Command's No. 302 (City of Poznan) and No. 303 (Kościuszko) squadrons. Some of these pilots had already fought against the Germans with l'Armée de l'Air in France before reaching England. The RAF No. 3 Polish Wing was also established to "process" Polish fliers before being sent to RAF squadrons.

The Poles were aggressive and undaunted—one Polish HURRICANE pilot pushed his attack on a blazing Donier DO 17 so relentlessly that he collided with one of the crew who bailed out. The Hurricane made a forced landing with its propeller smashed and blood on the engine cowling. A total of 154 such pilots fought with the RAF in the BATTLE OF BRITAIN—with at least thirty being killed. Subsequently, these squadrons flew fighter sweeps over occupied France, with the Polish fighter units flying through the end of the war.

Poles also flew with RAF Bomber Command.

Other Poles flew with the Soviet Air Force after the decision was reached in late 1940 to establish a Polish Army on Soviet territory.

Poland, Army

The Polish Army was the first victim of the German BLITZKRIEG.

The Polish Army on the eve of the EUROPEAN WAR had a nominal strength, with some reserves activated, of 1,700,000 under Marshal Rydz-Smigly. But morale in the Polish Army was poor, and the Army was poorly equipped and inadequately deployed to defend the country.

Although the rapid buildup of the German Army in the 1930s, and its emphasis on armored warfare, were obvious to Polish military leaders, there was no interest in developing a proper armored force or fortifications to stop German tanks. The Polish Army on Sept. 1, 1939, had but a single armored brigade with two battalions of 6-ton tanks. The two Polish motorized brigades each had one company of 6-ton tanks and two of small "tankettes" or mini-tanks. Including the thirteen tankettes and eight armored cars in the reconnaissance squadron of each of twelve CAVALRY brigades, the Polish Army could muster some 600 tanks. (This force was opposed in Sept. 1939 by six German PANZER divisions with about 2,000 tanks, although most were PzKw I and II vehicles armed only with machine guns; still there were far more and better tanks in the German force.)

The twelve brigades of Polish horse cavalry bravely charged against the German tanks and armored cars to become the specter of military anachronism.

The dispositions forced on the Polish Army were poor. The Polish government had decided to defend all of the country's 1,750-mile border with Germany. Most of the thirty front-line Polish divisions were deployed on that border and two divisions faced East Prussia. This reduced the central reserve, while the Luftwaffe's attacks prevented those reserves from reaching the front-line positions before they collapsed.

The Polish Army existed as an organized military force for eighteen days in combat—until Sept. 18 when the government and military high command escaped to Rumania. On Sept. 17 the Soviet Union had attacked across the almost undefended eastern border. Warsaw held out until Sept. 27 and remnants of the Polish Army continued to fight against the two aggressors until Oct. 5.

Many Poles were able to flee the country. Those soldiers who reached France and then went on to England continued to fight under the banner of the Polish government-in-exile. A Polish division was among the NORMANDY INVASION forces, and a Polish parachute brigade was dropped into ARNHEM during the ill-fated portion of Operation MARKET-GARDEN, while Polish fighter pilots flying from bases in England gained an unequalled reputation for aggressiveness. (See POLAND, AIR FORCE.)

The British government also sponsored a Polish force built up from the Poles in the Soviet Union. In Sept. 1939 the Soviets captured 230,670 Polish soldiers—from generals to privates; to these were added reserve officers who were arrested, and Poles who had fled to the Baltic States subsequently taken over by the Soviets—a total of some 250,000 Poles. About 15,000—of whom 8,000 were officers—"disappeared" while in Soviet captivity—executed on STALIN's orders by the secret police (see NKVD) in the KATYN MASSACRE.

Subsequently, in late 1940—a year after the Katyn forest killings—the Soviet government raised a Polish force with officers who had been vetted by the NKVD and at least were not opposed to the existing Communist doctrine. Under a Col. Berling (later promoted to general), the Soviets organized, trained, and equipped a Polish command on Soviet territory with headquarters located in the town of Buzuluk, 90 miles east of Kuibyshev. The initial size of the Polish formation was set at 30,000 men, but quickly was raised to 96,000 men in six rifle divisions. These units fought in the SOVIET OFFENSIVE CAMPAIGN and were in combat all the way to the assault on BERLIN.

Meanwhile, after negotiations with the British government and Polish government-in-exile in LONDON, in 1942 the Soviets allowed Lt. Gen. Wladyslaw Anders to recruit an army, which was shipped to the Middle East for training and assignment to the British Eighth Army. While training in Palestine, an estimated 3,500 of their numbers deserted and remained in Palestine, many becoming terrorists in the postwar battle to establish an independent Jewish state. Anders' troops eventually formed a corps and fought with distinction in the ITALIAN CAMPAIGN. The corps' 12th Polish Armored Lancers' Regiment led the attack that captured Monte CASSINO. (The regiment had been famous for "doing the impossible" since Napoleonic campaigns.)

Poland, Navy

When the EUROPEAN WAR began the Polish Navy consisted of four modern British-built destroyers, two modern Dutch-built submarines, and three older French-built undersea craft, and several gunboats, TORPEDO boats, and minelayers.

When the Germans attacked Poland on Sept. 1, 1939, several Polish ships were ordered to flee to Britain, including three destroyers. Luftwaffe bombers sank the fourth destroyer in the opening days of the war. Similarly, the submarines were soon ordered to flee Polish waters, two going to Britain and two being interned in Sweden.

In an attempt to justify their attack on Poland, the Soviet tanker *Metallist* was sunk in Narva Bay on Sept. 26, 1939, according to Soviet spokesmen, by the Polish submarine *Orzel*. In reality, the Soviet submarine *Shch-303* had unsuccessfully tried to torpedo the *Metallist,* after which the tanker was sunk by a Soviet torpedo boat.

With the fall of Poland, many Polish officers and sailors found their way to France and then England. The Polish government-in-exile in LONDON sponsored a Navy and, over the next few years, the new Polish Navy was loaned six ex-British destroyers, and several CORVETTES and the ex-U.S. SUBMARINE *S-25.* The Polish warships fought hard and suffered heavy losses in the BATTLE OF THE ATLANTIC. (The former *S-25* was mistakenly sunk by Allied escort ships off Norway in May 1942.)

Five of the destroyers participated in the NOR-

MANDY INVASION on June 6, 1944. One of these, the *Dragon,* was heavily damaged by a torpedo fired by a German MIDGET SUBMARINE; the ship was beached and declared a total loss. The *Dragon*'s entire crew was transferred to the British light cruiser *Danae,* which was then commissioned in the Polish Navy.

Polish Campaign (1939)

ADOLF HITLER succinctly declared his strategy for *Fall Weiss* (Case White), the code name for the plan to invade Poland: Isolate the country and take it in a lightning thrust, the tactic that would become known as the BLITZKRIEG. "The isolation of Poland," he said in a secret directive, on April 3, 1939, "will be all the more easily maintained, even after the outbreak of hostilities, if we succeed in starting the war with sudden heavy blows and in gaining rapid successes."

When Hitler wrote his April directive, there was little doubt in European capitals that Germany was on a march of conquest. Hitler had taken over Austria and, through the British-French appeasement policy reflected in the MUNICH PACT, had seized Czechoslovakia. He had used threats and hard-line diplomacy to get his way. The next step would have to be war. On March 31, England and France had pledged immediate military assistance to Poland in the event of attack.

Hitler's military planners translated his April directive into an invasion plan, which he received on June 15 from *Generalfeldmarschall* WALTHER VON BRAUCHITSCH, Commander in Chief of the German Army. The "sudden heavy blows" phase was now ready. There remained completion of the "isolation of Poland." This was accomplished in a diplomatic version of the blitzkrieg: On Aug. 21 the Soviet Union and Germany stunned the world by announcing a ten-year NONAGGRESSION PACT. Secretly, the two countries agreed that the Soviets could seize eastern Poland after Germany conquered western Poland.

On the night of Aug. 31, 1939, German SS troops brought twelve CONCENTRATION CAMP prisoners to the German city of Gleiwitz (now Gliwice, Poland) on the Polish border. The prisoners were dressed in Polish Army uniforms and injected with poison. Their bodies were shot and laid out in a nearby wooded area. Another prisoner in a Polish uniform was taken to the Gleiwitz radio station. One of the SS men yelled, in Polish, into a microphone that he and other Poles were launching an invasion of Germany. The SS men fired several shots, killed the last prisoner, and ran off into the night.

The hoax attack, code-named Canned Goods, was used by HITLER to declare the next day, Sept. 1, in a speech before the Reichstag, "Polish regular soldiers fired on our own territory. Since 5:45 A.M. we have been returning the fire. . . ." The EUROPEAN WAR had begun.

German divisions roared across the border in the north and south. Luftwaffe fighters and bombers quickly won control of the air, wiping out the Polish Air Force, destroying rail centers, attacking command centers, and shattering Polish troop concentrations.

England and France declared war on Germany on Sept. 3, but the declaration did nothing to save Poland. By the next day German troops had driven 50 miles into Poland and were on the verge of capturing Lodz. Kraków fell on Sept. 6.

German forces sweeping in from the north took Danzig (Gdansk) and the Polish Corridor—territory taken from Germany in World War I—and headed for WARSAW. The Polish garrison at the Westerplatte fortress in Danzig harbor surrendered on Sept. 7. By the next day German troops were on the outskirts of Warsaw. In the south, a seemingly entrapped Polish force surprised the Germans, wheeling at them, inflicting heavy casualties, and triggering a battle not on the German schedule. When the battle ended, the Germans took some 100,000 Poles as PRISONERS OF WAR.

On Sept. 16 the German high command gave Warsaw an ultimatum: surrender or suffer merciless ARTILLERY bombardment. The Poles rejected the ultimatum, and the shells and bombs began raining down on the capital, whose motto was "Defying the Tempest." Tens of thousands of people were killed and hundreds of fires flamed across the besieged city. On Sept. 27, lacking ammunition, water, food, and electricity, the Warsaw garrison surrendered. Hitler and his triumphant troops entered the devastated city on Oct. 1.

On Sept. 17 Soviet troops marched into eastern

Poland. The Soviet invasion ended at a secretly established line of demarcation. Soviet and German forces met at Brest Litovsk, an historically significant town. There in 1917 Germans and Bolsheviks negotiated Russia's withdrawal from World War I. Among the territories the Bolsheviks handed over to Germany at the time was Poland; the treaty was nullified by Germany's subsequent defeat. Now Germans and Communists were again meeting to carve up Eastern Europe. The Soviets got Brest Litovsk and the eastern half of Poland, which was populated by Ukrainians and White Russians as well as Poles.

On the fighting front, all organized resistance ended by Oct. 6. About 100,000 Poles—thousands of them soldiers—escaped into Rumania, Hungary, and Lithuania. Many made their way to France and then to England, where escaped Polish officials had established a government-in-exile. Thousands of Poles would fight on, joining the Allied forces that had been mobilized against Hitler when he unleashed his blitzkreig against Poland.

Pom-Pom

Slang for highly effective British close-in antiaircraft gun mounting. Officially rated as a 2-pounder, the pom-pom came in single and quad mounts for smaller ships and 8-barrel mounts for battleships, large cruisers, and aircraft carriers. Single and twin mounts were also used ashore.

Developed in World War I and first evaluated at sea in the early 1920s, the pom-pom by the 1930s was fitted in numerous British warships. By the end of World War II there were up to eight 8-barrel pom-pom mountings in the *King George V* battleships and six 8-barrel guns in the *Illustrious* carriers. Destroyers, frigates, and CORVETTES generally had a single 4-barrel mounting. A few destroyers and other ships, including large LANDING CRAFT, had single-barrel pom-poms.

The pom-pom was a recoil-operated, belt-fed weapon. During the war remote power was added (hydraulic) and a cooling-water circulation system. Each barrel had a rate of fire of approximately 100 rounds per minute. The belted ammunition was fed from 114- or 140-round loading trays. Each round weighed just under 2 pounds.

The 2-pounder/40-mm gun had a maximum range of 6,800 yards and a ceiling of 13,000 feet (falling between the BOFORS 40-MM and OERLIKON 20-MM guns).

Early mountings had hand-cranked operating gear, but this was later replaced by powered drive to permit faster training, elevating, and firing. (The gun layer and trainer still turned hand cranks to aim the guns, but the effort to do so was minimal.) These improvements led to a continual increase in weight until the quad pom-pom installation weighed 11 tons; a splinter shield to protect the gun crew could also be provided.

A single-barrel, powered pom-pom was also available for destroyers and smaller ships, but was seen far less than the multibarrel mounts. A twin was also used ashore, but it is unlikely that it was ever used in ships.

The gun was fired with a simple open sight. A few mounts in larger ships had gyro sights.

Popov, Dusko (1912–1982)

Yugoslav business promoter recruited by the *ABWEHR*. He told the British of the recruitment, and when his *Abwehr* controllers sent him to England in Dec. 1940 the XX COMMITTEE, which handled doubled agents, gave him the British code name Tricycle; the Germans had given him the code name Ivan. Among the false information given to the Germans was the size of the British armed forces.

In June 1941 the *Abwehr* ordered him to go to the United States and set up an ESPIONAGE ring. At the request of the Japanese, he was to obtain specific information about PEARL HARBOR and go to HAWAII to make sketches of military facilities there. The instructions were concealed in MICRODOTS on a fake telegram Popov carried. (Microdots were the product of a process that reduced a page of writing to the size of the dot of an i.)

The British informed the FEDERAL BUREAU OF INVESTIGATION of Tricycle's double status before Popov arrived in the United States by Pan American Clipper from Lisbon on Aug. 12, 1941. But the director of the FBI, J. EDGAR HOOVER, denounced him as a Balkan playboy and refused to allow him to go to Hawaii.

Hoover ignored the implications of the microdot message regarding Pearl Harbor, even though by Aug. 1941 the United States and Japan were on a collision course and war was considered likely by many U.S. officials. Hoover, incredibly, ignored the message. Not until Sept. 30 was some of the Popov message passed on to Naval and Army intelligence offices. And even then the significance of the Pearl Harbor inquiries was disregarded.

On Jan. 13, 1942, more than a month after the Japanese attack on Pearl Harbor, Hoover wrote a memo to Maj. Gen. Edwin M. Watson, President ROOSEVELT's appointments secretary. In it Hoover mentions neither Popov nor the Pearl Harbor queries. All he says is that he thought the President might want to see "one of the methods used by the German espionage system in transmitting messages to its agents."

Hoover enclosed a 400x enlargement of a portion of the microdot message and an FBI translation. The portion that Hoover chose to show the President did *not* refer to Pearl Harbor. The translation refers to that part of the message that seeks information about American aircraft production.

Popov had arrived in the United States with a Yugoslav passport and $70,000. He rented a Park Avenue penthouse and began making the rounds of New York City nightclubs, while FBI agents kept him under surveillance and waited in vain to see Popov set up a spy ring. Popov insisted that to convince his German handlers that his mission to the United States was not in vain, he needed information that would look like the authentic gleanings of a German spy.

The British XX Committee showed great cunning in producing that kind of information. But Hoover, inexperienced and anti-British, dredged up little for Popov. Among the 1,421 pages of heavily sanitized pages in the Popov's FBI dossier are secret FBI memos showing that the material given Popov included back copies of the *Infantry Journal* and Army press releases. The Office of Naval Intelligence was "unable to furnish any specific information which would be suitable for counter-espionage data," an FBI memo said.

The FBI file shows that the Popov case was closed on July 20, 1943, when he began working for the British again and did valuable double-dealing against the Germans until the invasion of Normandy in June 1944.

In a bylined article in the April 1946 *Reader's*

Digest, Hoover, without mentioning Popov's name, gave this account of meeting him:

"One day in August 1941 we met a youngish traveler from the Balkans on his arrival in the United States. We knew he was the playboy son of a millionaire. There was reason to believe he was a German agent. With meticulous care we examined his possessions, from toothbrush to shoes. . . ." Hoover goes on to dramatically describe the "discovery" of the microdots and adds: "Seeing that we knew about the dots, he began to talk freely." Hoover, implying that the "Balkan playboy" was a spy, does not reveal that he had been introduced to the FBI by British intelligence as a double agent.

Port Chicago Explosion

Ammunition explosion at Port Chicago, Calif., that killed 202 black sailors who were loading ammunition and injured 233 other men, some of them white. When ordered to resume loading ammunition without leave or counseling, some of the surviving black sailors mutinied. (See SEGREGATION).

The disaster occurred on July 17, 1944, when a detonation of ammunition vaporized one merchant ship being loaded, smashed a second, and destroyed several buildings. Only the remains of fifty-one of the victims could be positively identified. With 202 dead and 233 sailors injured, the unhurt survivors were taken to the nearby Mare Island Navy yard and ordered to begin loading ammunition on other ships.

The formation of black sailors—led by white officers—refused to march to the ferry that was to take them to the ammunition depot. The Navy tried 258 of the black sailors by court-martial. All were found guilty; the fifty convicted of mutiny were given dishonorable discharges and sentenced to prison terms up to fifteen years; another 208 sailors were found guilty of refusing to obey a lawful order and given dishonorable discharges.

The Navy's leadership soon realized what events led to the mutiny by the black sailors at Port Chicago. Those men given the longer prison sentences were released in less than two years. And soon after the explosion many black sailors were assigned to serve in ships, while blacks were also accepted for officer training as the efforts to integrate the Navy were accelerated. (In 1990 the Navy told the survivors that the case was too old for an appeal under military law, but that the President could give a pardon.)

Port Moresby

Port on the south coast of New Guinea. Port Moresby, the administrative center of Australia's Territory of Papua, was a key objective in Japan's plan to capture New Guinea and put northern Australia within range of land-based Japanese bombers.

The undermanned Port Moresby garrison of Australian troops was reinforced in April 1942 by U.S. troops. The following month, the Japanese planned Operation *Mo,* an AMPHIBIOUS LANDING. But this was thwarted by the battle of the CORAL SEA in which the Japanese amphibious force was turned back by a U.S. task force.

In July Japanese troops landed at Buna and Gona on the northern coast of New Guinea as part of a new plan to take Port Moresby by striking across the Owen Stanley Range, which rose as high as 8,500 feet. The Japanese advanced along the Kokoda Trail to within 25 miles of Port Moresby but were thrown back. The Japanese withdrew toward Buna and Gona. But their beachheads had been retaken by Australian forces in Dec. 1942–Jan. 1943, and the Japanese were driven along the northeast coast.

Postage Stamps

Wartime PROPAGANDA efforts extended to postage stamps in many countries. The United States launched its campaign on July 4, 1942, with the 3¢ "Win the War" stamp that portrayed an American eagle with wings in the form of a V-FOR-VICTORY. Three days later, the 5¢ China Commemorative stamp with portraits of Abraham Lincoln and Sun Yat-sen, the first president of the Chinese Republic, was issued; the stamp, which also had the Chinese characters meaning "Fight the War and Build the Country," commemorated the fifth anniversary of Chinese resistance against Japan. (Japan had seized Chinese territory in 1931 but the large-scale invasion came in 1937.)

Next came the 1¢ FOUR FREEDOMS and the "Overrun Countries Series," 5¢ stamps issued in tribute to thirteen countries occupied by the AXIS in Europe and Asia. While conventional commemorative subjects (the transcontinental railroad, the

telegraph, Florida statehood) continued through the war years, patriotic stamps were ever present. They marked the defense of CORREGIDOR, the death of President ROOSEVELT, the founding of the UNITED NATIONS, and, in a series of stamps issued immediately before and after the end of the war, the armed forces: U.S. Marines raising the flag on Mount Suribachi on IWO JIMA; U.S. soldiers marching by the Arc de Triomphe in Paris with a flight of bombers overhead; U.S. sailors in their summer whites; two U.S. Coast Guard LANDING CRAFT. The U.S. MERCHANT MARINE was also honored in the same series with a LIBERTY SHIP stamp. War veterans were commemorated with a 3¢ 1946 stamp showing the honorable discharge emblem affectionately known as the Ruptured Duck.

"War stamps" continued to be issued in the postwar years to honor U.S. military heroes: a 3¢ to honor Gen. GEORGE S. PATTON, JR., a 6¢ for Gen. DOUGLAS MACARTHUR. The 25¢ stamp issued in 1990 to commemorate the centennial of DWIGHT D. EISENHOWER's birth showed the two-term President as a general talking to U.S. paratroopers on the eve of D-DAY and was emblazoned with his five-star insignia.

The ALLIED MILITARY GOVERNMENT issued special U.S.-made stamps for newly liberated areas. The AMG stamps were used until the governments resumed regular postal services.

Germany issued a heavy-handed propaganda "Liquidation of Empire" series, smuggled into Sweden in June 1944. The stamps were copies of British stamps, but with a Star of David replacing the cross on the British crown and the Communist hammer and sickle symbol replacing the pence symbol; a portrait of STALIN replaced the king's.

Italy issued a 1941 stamp showing HITLER and BENITO MUSSOLINI with the slogan *Due Popoli; Una Guerra* (two peoples, one war); British counterfeiters transformed it to a stamp showing Mussolini cowering before Hitler with the legend *Due Popoli; Un Führer (Two Peoples: One Leader!)* Copies of the stamp were sent into Italy shortly before the Italian SURRENDER in Sept. 1943. Other British stamp forgeries were for purposes of ESPIONAGE rather than propaganda. Counterfeits of German stamps were issued to agents so they could mail propaganda material without having to take the risk of going to a post office.

German occupation officials in Poland and Norway issued stamps hailing the THIRD REICH and the NAZI stamps were answered with "retaliatory" stamps issued from LONDON by the governments-in-exile. The latter stamps were declared legitimate by the Universal Postal Union, which gave the exiled leaders recognition as the nations' legal governments.

Potsdam Conference

Allied meeting (July 17 to Aug. 2, 1945) that made the key decisions about postwar Germany. The Potsdam Conference, in a suburb of devastated BERLIN, had been expected to ratify decisions made at the YALTA CONFERENCE of Feb. 1945. But it did not follow the plans of the Yalta BIG THREE: President ROOSEVELT, Prime Minister CHURCHILL, and Soviet leader JOSEF STALIN. At Yalta, they had agreed on broad principles about the postwar world and had planned to meet again after the UNCONDITIONAL SURRENDER of Germany. But Roosevelt died on April 12, 1945, three and a half weeks

before the surrender, and Churchill, defeated in the July British elections, was replaced during the Potsdam Conference on July 28 by England's new Prime Minister, CLEMENT ATTLEE, leader of the Labor Party.

On July 16, President HARRY TRUMAN, awaiting the late-arriving Stalin, was touring Berlin with his new secretary of state, JAMES BYRNES, while in New Mexico scientists were celebrating the successful testing of the ATOMIC BOMB. After being informed, Truman wrote in his diary, "Believe Japs will fold up before Russian comes in." On July 24, after the day's conference, Truman "casually mentioned to Stalin that we had a new weapon of unusual destructive force," but Stalin, who already knew about the bomb through ESPIONAGE, did not seem impressed.

The conference reiterated Yalta decisions regarding the new boundaries of Germany, decided that ethnic Germans in Poland, Czechoslovakia, and Hungary would be returned to Germany, and essentially accepted the reality of Soviet occupation of Eastern Europe.

In a public declaration, the three nations agreed on the abolishing of all traces of "German militarism and Nazism"; the arrest and trial of Germans suspected of WAR CRIMES; the decentralization of the German economy with emphasis on "agriculture and peaceful domestic industries"; and payment of reparations to the Soviet Union and other countries that had suffered under Germany during the war. To coordinate policies over the four separate occupation zones in Germany (U.S., British, French, and Soviet), the conference also created the ALLIED CONTROL COUNCIL. By secret agreement, Soviet reparations would include German industrial equipment taken from the other three zones.

Pound, Sir Alfred Dudley (1877–1943)

Dudley Pound, who became First Sea Lord in 1939, was the Royal Navy's highest ranking strategist and administrator for the first four years of World War II. The man most directly answerable to Prime Minister CHURCHILL on naval matters, Pound was frequently thrust into the role of stifling the Prime Minister's more exotic plans.

Pound was not always able to withstand or shrug off Churchill's barrage of commands, suggestions, and "Action This Day" memoranda. He had little staff and was not inclined to leave the details to the few he had.

His second in command, Adm. ANDREW B. CUNNINGHAM, commented privately after the war: "Churchill wore Pound down. He was so tired of fighting the Prime Minister that he made up his mind only to fight for the essential factors. But apparently he did not regard support of his Flag-Officers at sea as always an essential factor, and I think he always favored getting a scapegoat."

Pound could not forbear from commanding his fleets directly from LONDON, imposing decisions on distant commanders who would have benefitted from greater freedom of action. One of the most tragic single instances came in mid-1942, when Pound ordered CONVOY PQ 17, en route to MURMANSK, to scatter in the face of what he believed to be the imminent threat of the German battleship *TIRPITZ*. Most of the dispersed ships were set upon by German aircraft and U-BOATS and sunk. Despite the PQ 17 disaster, Pound is given great credit for his tenacious, and largely accurate, focus on the BATTLE OF THE ATLANTIC against German submarines, the longest-running and most trying campaign of the war.

Pound suffered from osteoarthritis of the hip, a painful condition that interrupted sleep and contributed to a short temper. His physical ills increased in 1941 when he first began showing symptoms of a slow-growing brain tumor. When Pound suffered a stroke in Aug. 1943 he resigned as First Sea Lord and was replaced by A. B. Cunningham. Pound died on Trafalgar Day, Oct. 21, 1943.

Pound, Ezra (1885–1972)

American poet who made anti-American broadcasts from Rome during the war. Pound went to Europe in 1907 and never returned until he was brought back after the war for trial on charges of TREASON. From about 1924 on, while living in Rapallo on the Italian Riviera, he had a great admiration for the Fascist philosophy of Italian leader BENITO MUSSOLINI. Italian PROPAGANDA officials commissioned Pound to make radio broadcasts in support of Mussolini. He also wrote pro-Fascist articles for the weekly newspaper *Meridiano Di Roma*.

Although Pound was charged with treason, he was never tried. He was held until 1958 in St. Eliza-beth's Hospital, a government-operated mental institution in WASHINGTON, D.C. A psychiatrist familiar with Pound's symptoms later wrote that they seemed to have been exaggerated to make it appear that the poet could not be put on trial for treason for reasons of insanity.

Precision Bombing

The doctrine of precision bombing was extensively promoted by the U.S. Army Air Forces, which stated that it was the "heart" of air power, "the key to our operations," and "fundamental to AAF strategy." The doctrine was first put to test in combat with the arrival of the U.S. Eighth AIR FORCE in England in 1942. The AAF supported the RAF's belief in STRATEGIC BOMBING, the destruction of German war industry. But AAF doctrine diametrically opposed the RAF's preference for nighttime "area bombing."

Much of the claim for high-altitude "pinpoint" bombing rested on the performance of the NORDEN BOMBSIGHT. Bombing was often precise on practice ranges in the United States. But European weather, German defenses, and smoke hampered bombardiers, who depended upon the bombsight's optical view of the target. Using crude radar imagery, bombardiers soon found themselves doing more area bombing than precision bombing. The "distinction between area bombing and precision attack," wrote Air Force historian Bernard C. Nalty, "had become blurred as the fight wore on."

Priceless

Code name for Allied invasion of Italy, Sept. 1943.

Prien, *Korvettenkäpitan* Günther (1908–1941)

German U-BOAT commander who carried out a daring attack in the British fleet anchorage of SCAPA FLOW in the Orkney Islands off the northern tip of Scotland.

Prien joined the German merchant marines at age fifteen and served as an officer in the Hamburg-Amerika Line; he resigned in 1931 during the Great Depression. In 1933 he was called to active duty in the Navy and when the EUROPEAN WAR began he was commanding officer of the *U-47*. *Kommodore* KARL DÖNITZ, head of the submarine force, on Sept. 26, 1939, received aerial photos of Scapa Flow taken by the Luftwaffe. He immediately planned an attack on the heavily defended British base, assigning the task to Prien—in many respects his favorite U-boat commander.

During the night of Oct. 13–14 the U-boat stole through the dangerous channels leading to the main anchorage. Carefully firing a total of seven TORPEDOES (which required reloading while in the harbor), the U-boat sank the 29,150-ton battleship *Royal Oak*. The dreadnought sank in thirteen minutes, with 786 officers and ratings killed. British naval historian John Terraine wrote in *Business in Great Waters*, "It is difficult to think of any U-boat exploit during the war equal to this. . . ."

The *U-47* escaped the frantic British ships and craft seeking the intruder. The British had to abandon their main fleet base; Prien became a national hero and was awarded the IRON CROSS, first class, and had a personal audience with ADOLF HITLER; and Dönitz was promoted to *Kontradmiral*.

Prien next took the *U-47* into Norwegian waters to attack British shipping during the April 1940 battle and then into the BATTLE OF THE ATLANTIC. He had considerable success against British merchant shipping, both in his own attacks and on several occasions sighting CONVOYS and calling in other U-boats. On March 7, 1941, the *U-47* radioed U-boat headquarters that he was in pursuit of Convoy OB 293 in the North Atlantic. Just after midnight two British destroyers with the convoy attacked the *U-47*. The hunt went on for five hours; about 5:20 A.M. a pattern of DEPTH CHARGES rained down on the *U-47:* "A red glow lasting ten seconds was seen in the depths amid the explosions [of the charges], and soon the debris of a shattered submarine came to the surface." The *U-47* was gone. There were no survivors.

German records contend that Prien sank twenty-eight merchant ships totaling 160,930 tons in addition to the *Royal Oak*; although those estimates were high, Prien certainly ranked as a leading submarine ACE.

His previously written memoirs—first published in 1942—sold more than 750,000 copies in Germany. After the war, they were published in English as *I Sank the Royal Oak*.

Prince of Wales

British battleship that helped stop the German battleship *BISMARCK* but eight months later fell victim to Japanese aircraft. When the German dreadnought *Bismarck* and heavy cruiser *Prinz Eugen* broke out into the North Atlantic in late May 1941, the *Prince of Wales,* not fully operational and with workmen still on board, was dispatched with other British warships to intercept the German ships. The *Prince of Wales* and the battle cruiser *HOOD,* accompanied by six destroyers, sought to intercept the German ships in the Denmark Strait.

The opposing warships sighted each other at 5:35 A.M. on May 24. The action began eighteen minutes later. After the first salvo one of the *Prince of Wales'* forward gun turrets jammed.

In the brief but furious engagement, the *Hood* was hit by gunfire from both German ships. A magazine blew up, and she sank with but three survivors from a crew of 1,350. With her consort gone and her gun battery reduced, the *Prince of Wales* turned away. Within a few minutes she had suffered four hits from the 15-inch (381-mm) guns of the *Bismarck* and three from the 8-inch (203-mm) guns of the *Prinz Eugen*. A heavy shell striking her compass platform killed or injured most of the officers and ratings in that control position except for her captain.

She had fired six salvoes before hitting the *Bismarck*. The *Prince of Wales* scored two 14-inch (355-mm) hits. One of these hits caused a fuel oil leak and contaminated other fuel tanks in the *Bismarck*. Her trail of lost oil and the loss of fuel eventually led to her destruction.

After repairs, in Aug. 1941 the *Prince of Wales* carried Prime Minister CHURCHILL to Placentia Bay, Newfoundland, for the ATLANTIC CONFERENCE with President ROOSEVELT. The ATLANTIC CHARTER was signed on board. After returning Churchill to England, the battleship escorted CONVOYS in the Mediterranean.

With the deteriorating situation in the Far East, in late Oct. 1941 the *Prince of Wales* was dispatched to the fleet base at SINGAPORE. She and the battle cruiser *REPULSE* were the only Allied CAPITAL SHIPS between the Mediterranean and the Hawaiian islands on Dec. 7, 1941. That afternoon (Dec. 8 in the Far East), the two British capital ships and four destroyers sortied to attack a Japanese troop landing reported on the coast of Malaya. When Allied aircraft could not be provided to support them, Rear Adm. Sir Tom Phillips in the *Prince of Wales* turned his ships back toward Singapore.

Late that morning the British ships were attacked by eighty-six twin-engine Japanese naval bombers, G3M NELL and G4M BETTY aircraft carrying BOMBS and aerial TORPEDOES. In the ensuing attack both ships were sunk, the *Prince of Wales* shattered by one or two 1,100-pound bombs and six torpedoes. She rolled over and sank. Of 1,612 officers and ratings on board, 1,285 were rescued by the accompanying destroyers. Adm. Phillips was not among the survivors.

The *Prince of Wales* and *Repulse* were the first capital ships of any nation to be sunk by air attack while at sea. Three Japanese bombers were lost in the attack.

The *Prince of Wales* was one of five battleships of the *King George V* class; she was launched on May 3, 1939, and placed in service in March 1941 although all work had not been completed. The ship displaced 36,750 tons standard and was 745 feet long. Her main battery consisted of ten 14-inch guns in one twin and two quad turrets, plus lighter guns. Steam turbines could drive the ship at 27.5 knots.

Principal

Code name for British attack with Chariots against Italian ships in Palermo Harbor, SICILY, Jan. 1943; see MANNED TORPEDOES.

Prisoners of War

Prisoners captured in World War II were the first to be kept under a 1929 agreement that came to be called the Geneva Convention, after the place where representatives of forty-eight governments met to discuss the convention. This was the first such international agreement devoted to the treatment of prisoners of war (POWs).

Some of the practices agreed upon: Food would be equal to that served to troops of the detaining country. Prisoners were not to be individually confined. Officers received pay, usually on the level of comparable officers of the detaining country. Prisoners might be required to work but the work could not be connected with the war effort.

A POW was "required to declare, if he is interrogated on the subject, his true name and rank or his regimental number. . . . No pressure shall be exerted on prisoners to obtain information regarding the situation in their armed forces or their country. Prisoners who refuse to reply may not be threatened, insulted, or exposed to unpleasantness or disadvantages of any kind whatsoever."

Of the belligerents who would participate in World War II, China, France, Germany, England, and the United States were among the thirty-six nations that ratified the convention. Japanese representatives signed, but their government did not ratify it. The Soviet Union, which did not attend the Geneva meeting in 1929, said after war began with Germany in 1941 that it would abide by the 1907 Hague Convention. It did not provide for neutral observation of POW camps.

In Jan. 1942 Japan said it would abide by the convention, but Japan persistently maltreated POWs. On the BATAAN DEATH MARCH an estimated 5,200 Americans died. (Among the U.S. prisoners taken by the Japanese in the Philippines were 104 U.S. Army and Navy nurses.)

There is evidence to support charges that the Japanese performed BIOLOGICAL WARFARE experiments on prisoners. Of the U.S. Army and AAF prisoners held by Japan, 40.4 percent died in captivity, compared to the 1.2 percent of the Army and AAF prisoners who died while in German and Italian custody.

The Japanese compelled about 250,000 Asians and 61,000 Allied prisoners of war—most of them Australian and British—to build, by hand, a 265-mile military railway along the River Kwae Noi (Kwai) into Burma from Thailand. The merciless treatment of the prisoners building the "Railway of Death" was dramatized in Pierre Boulle's novel *The Bridge over the River Kwai* and in the movie *The Bridge on the River Kwai*. Beatings, malnutrition, and lack of medical care killed 12,568 of the prisoners and about 87,500 Asians.

The Japanese transferred prisoners without international supervision. As a result, U.S. SUBMARINES were unaware that some of the ships they sunk carried prisoners. In one six-week period U.S. submarines are believed to have sunk Japanese ships that were carrying a total of 4,000 prisoners. An attempt to get relief supplies to Japanese POWs ended with one "mercy ship" sunk by a U.S. submarine. (See *AWA MARU.*)

Germany in general followed the Geneva Convention in the treatment of U.S. and British servicemen in POW camps. But outside the POW camp system there were atrocities. In the MALMEDY MASSACRE about 100 American prisoners were shot to death; some fifty British airmen who had escaped from a POW camp in 1944 were executed, in violation of the convention.

At a German CONCENTRATION CAMP in Mauthausen, Austria, at least forty-seven American, British, and Dutch officers, all airmen, were beaten and kicked to death in a massacre similar to others in which Soviet prisoners were the victims.

At least fifteen other Americans and British prisoners, including an Associated Press correspondent, were executed at Mauthausen. They had been captured after parachuting into German-occupied Czechoslovakia. They, along with another fifteen American soldiers captured behind the lines in Italy in 1944, were killed in compliance with a take-no-prisoners policy against COMMANDOS, an order that HITLER had personally issued.

During the disastrous commando raid on DIEPPE on Aug. 19, 1942, German-held prisoners were handcuffed in "death slings" that strangled them if they stretched their legs. The Germans for a time shackled 1,000 Canadian prisoners, and the British retaliated by doing the same. On Oct. 18 Hitler issued his Commando Order: surrendering raiders who "do not act like soldiers but like bandits" would be shot, not taken prisoner.

Under the secret Commando Order, hundreds of Allied soldiers and sailors who should have been taken prisoner were summarily executed. Some incidents disclosed at the Nuremberg WAR CRIMES tribunal: 107 Allied soldiers executed by one SS PANZER division in June 1944; ten Norwegian sailors, captured on a torpedo-boat raid, killed and their bodies dumped into the sea; the execution of fifteen American soldiers captured while trying to blow up a railroad tunnel in Italy.

Escapes were legal under international law, and prisoners, particularly downed fliers, often treated escape planning as a normal recreational event. "Escape committees" were formed in camps. (See COLDITZ.) Escapes from German POW camps increased as the war wore on, and many of these escapees were executed when they were recaptured. On March 24, 1944, at the Sagan camp in Silesia, eighty RAF officers, including Greeks, Poles, Norwegians, Frenchmen, and Czechs escaped via a tunnel—the first successful one of some 100 such tunnels. At least fifty were quickly captured and executed. Their names were posted at Sagan as a warning to others.

Other escapees were transferred to Mauthausen and killed under the *Kugel Erlass* (bullet decree), another Hitler order. Extending this order, German officials declared Allied airmen "terror fliers," who, if found on the ground, could be killed on the spot. An unknown number of airmen were killed, some in lynchings carried out by Nazi functionaries.

More than 400,000 AXIS POWs were held in camps in the United States. Thousands of them were "allocated" by the War Manpower Commission for work on farms.

Prisoner information by nationality:

American At the end of the war, Germany held 95,000 U.S. military personnel and Japan held more than 15,000.

British (United Kingdom and BRITISH COMMONWEALTH) Of 308,000 British prisoners held at the end of the war, 200,000 were held in Germany, 200,000 in Japanese custody.

German At the end of the war U.S. forces in Europe held about 2,000,000 German prisoners, who were turned over to the British and French as postwar laborers. The Soviet Union, which did not publicly report its POW figures, held an estimated 2,000,000 German POWs. Many of the Soviet-held POWs were placed in German concentration camps after the civilian inmates had been freed. Some 130,000 prisoners were taken into eleven known POW camps in the Soviet occupation zone of Germany; about 50,000 are believed to have died.

A total of 371,683 German prisoners were held in POW camps in the United States. Included among them were a number of generals, who were given private quarters and enlisted POWs as orderlies. According to FBI records, 1,607 POWs were reported to have escaped from U.S. camps; how many of them permanently escaped is not recorded.

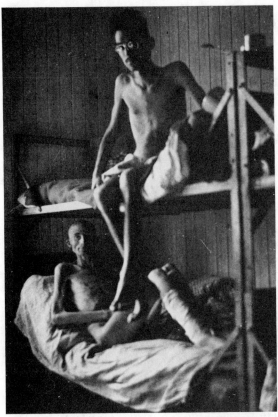

These emaciated men are U.S. Army soldiers liberated from Stalag 11B, a German prisoner-of-war camp. Suffering from malnutrition, they reflected the brutal treatment sometimes accorded to military POWs by the Germans. *(Imperial War Museum)*

Italian A total of 50,273 Italian POWs were kept in camps in the United States; about 1,000 of them were sent to Hawaii in June 1944 as a labor force. The Soviets took about 85,000 Italian troops who fought with German forces on the EASTERN FRONT; the fate of most of them was never known. In 1945 the Germans held 550,000 Italian POWs and U.S. and British forces in Italy held another 428,000.

Japanese At the end of the war the United States held about 20,000 Japanese prisoners; of these, 3,915 were held in camps in the United States.

Following the short Soviet war against Japan in Aug. 1945, the Soviets took tens of thousands of prisoners and, characteristically, did not disclose information about them. In 1990, the president of the Mongolian Red Cross Society said in Tokyo that more than 1,600 Japanese soldiers had died in Mongolian POW camps. They had been brought there in 1945. Another 3,800 Japanese prisoners are known to have died in Siberian prison camps.

Polish Among the first prisoners taken in World War II were 694,000 Polish soldiers captured during Germany's first BLITZKRIEG, the POLISH CAMPAIGN in Sept. 1939. The Soviets, who also marched on Poland at that time, took an estimated 217,000 Polish soldiers prisoners. The fate of tens of thousands is unknown; they vanished from record.

Soviet An estimated 5,250,000 to 5,750,000 Soviets were taken prisoner during the German invasion of the Soviet Union. According to German records, 1,981,000 Soviet POWs died in camps and 1,308,000 were listed as "Death and Disappearances in Transit," "Not Accounted For," and "Exterminations." SS chief HEINRICH HIMMLER said that in 1941 alone "prisoners died in the tens and hundreds of thousands of exhaustion and hunger." Fewer than 1,000,000 were found alive in camps when the war ended. About 1,000,000 were released to render aid to the Germans, including service in German military organizations. (See ANDREI VLASOV.)

The Germans used Soviet POWs as SLAVE LABOR in munitions factories and even as auxiliary troops. About 40 percent of Germany's prisoners of war were employed in 1944 in various kinds of munitions plants. At least 30,000 Soviet POWs were impressed into crews manning antiaircraft guns.

Privateer,
see PB4Y-2

Propaganda
The word, new to most Americans who began hearing it when the EUROPEAN WAR began, stemmed from an old idea: the papal *Congregatio de propaganda fide,* an organization for spreading the faith. *Propaganda* took on a new meaning in World War II: The spread of ideas or falsehoods for the

purpose of helping or hindering an ideology or institution. JOSEPH GOEBBELS, chief of NAZI Party propaganda, introduced the modern version, setting up a vast apparatus to spread and preserve the doctrines of Nazism in Germany, control German public opinion, and make words into weapons.

Goebbels' master, ADOLF HITLER, in *Mein Kampf* (My Struggle) explained the philosophy: "All propaganda has to be popular and has to adapt its spiritual level to the perception of the least intelligent of those towards whom it intends to direct itself."

The "great masses of the people," Hitler also said, "will more easily fall victims to a big lie than to a small one."

The Nazi propaganda machine spewed the big lie beyond Germany's borders. In France prior to the war, German propaganda agents supported separatist movements. The Breton newspaper, *Breiz Atao,* printed not only Breton separatist propaganda but also pro-Nazi propaganda. French newspapermen were arrested in 1939 for accepting bribes to publish German propaganda and to engage in ESPIONAGE.

Wherever there were Germans, Goebbels-fostered German-language newspapers sprang up, especially in South America, where there were many large German communities. Propaganda attachés were installed at leading German embassies. German English-language shortwave radio shows were aimed at many countries. An Englishman, WILLIAM JOYCE, otherwise known as Lord Haw-Haw, was the principal major commentator for Nazi broadcasts beamed to England. He was hanged for TREASON after the war.

The leading commentator for the German-sponsored "Radio Free India" was Subhas Chandra Bose, the violently anti-British president of the Indian Congress. In 1943 Bose slipped out of Germany by U-BOAT and appeared in India as the leader of the India National Army. (See India.) He died in a plane crash in Aug. 1945.

BBC countered Radio Free India with regular commentaries by Eric Blair, who worked for the British propaganda agency, the Ministry of Information. After the war, under the pseudonym George Orwell, he would write searingly about the propaganda world of Big Brother in *1984.*

The Germans also broadcast shortwave shows for specific American audiences: "The College Hour" for intellectuals, the "Folks Back Home in Iowa" for midwesterners, the "Jew in American History" for supporters of ANTI-SEMITISM. Nearly everyone who chose this over Jack Benny or Charlie McCarthy, a U.S. study showed, were members of the GERMAN-AMERICAN BUND.

American propaganda was spread by the OFFICE OF WAR INFORMATION, which looked upon itself as a public relations organization spreading America's story to the world. Its "Voice of America" broadcast in forty languages.

Although not strictly a propaganda effort, the U.S. government during the war did get involved in an immense book-publishing program for "building morale." In cooperation with publishers, librarians, and booksellers, the U.S. government financed the production of Armed Services Editions of books selected by an officer in the Army Special Services Division and the librarian of the Navy. Books included *Oliver Twist, Babbitt,* and collections of short stories by both ERNEST HEMINGWAY and O'Henry.

The books were distributed free to service men and women. From each book the original publishers received a 1¢ royalty, which was sometimes waived. Some 50,000 copies each of fifty different titles were published each month when the program began in Sept. 1943. When the program ended in 1947, 126,000,000 books had been published.

Propaganda in theaters of war was handled by the Psychological Warfare Branch of the U.S. Army, which prepared leaflets, set up radio transmitters for broadcasting to enemy forces, and engaged in activities to "cause the enemy to think and act in a manner detrimental to his war effort."

Providence

Code name for planned U.S. occupation of Buna, NEW GUINEA, 1942; canceled because of Japanese operations.

Proximity Fuze

Fuze that detonated an antiaircraft shell at the closest point to an enemy aircraft. Also called an influence fuze or Variable-Time (VT) fuze, the proximity fuze greatly increased the probability that a shell would destroy an enemy aircraft. Previous "smart" fuzes that detonated at a preset altitude had to be set before the gun was fired and could not allow for the target aircraft's changes in speed and course.

In mid-1940 the U.S. Navy decided that an electronic proximity fuze was practical. This belief was based in part on major British orders with a U.S. firm for magnetrons (small valves) for use in RADAR sets. Beginning with the TIZARD MISSION to the United States in Sept. 1940 there was total pooling of Anglo-American knowledge of radar technology. The proximity fuze in the shell would work on the same concept as radar: transmitting a radio signal that would bounce off an aircraft and reflect back to a receiver in the shell.

The technical challenges were considerable, for a proximity fuze would have to fit into the head of a 5-inch (127-mm) shell, withstand shipboard handling and the forces of being fired from a gun barrel, and be affordable in large numbers. The fuze itself had to contain sending and receiving antennas and a dry-cell storage battery.

In Aug. 1942 the U.S. CRUISER *Cleveland* (CL 55) shot down three target drones with four rounds of 5-inch VT ammunition. Following this dramatic demonstration, the proximity fuze was put into mass production. The decision was made to put the fuze on board ships and not provide it to ground forces because of the fear that unexploded shells might fall into enemy hands.

By early 1943 some 5,000 rounds of proximity-fuze ammunition had been rushed to the South Pacific. The first combat use came on Jan. 5, 1943, when the U.S. cruiser *Helena* (CL 50) brought down a Japanese VAL dive bomber near NEW GEORGIA with a few rounds of VT ammunition. Subsequently, proximity-fuze ammunition was provided to warships in the Atlantic and Mediterranean. These rounds proved three times as effective as time-fuzed ammunition with 9,100 rounds of 5-inch VT ammunition being fired (compared to 27,200 conventional rounds).

On June 12, 1944, the first V-1 BUZZ BOMB fell on LONDON and a short time later the COMBINED CHIEFS OF STAFF agreed on the necessity of using proximity-fuze ammunition in the defense of London. This was followed by deployment of antiaircraft guns firing proximity-fuze ammunition to the continent to defend the port of Antwerp from V-1 missiles and, during the battle of the Bulge, by antiaircraft guns firing fuzed ammunition against entrenched German troops. But it was against the V-1 buzz bomb over England and the KAMIKAZE attacks against U.S. ships in the Pacific in 1944–1945 that proximity-fuzed ammunition made its greatest contribution to the Allied victories.

Before the war Britain had been developing a photo-electric fuze for antiaircraft ROCKETS, which was abandoned, and as an offshoot of its radar program began looking at a proximity fuze, but that research was taken over by the U.S. Navy. In Germany there was extensive research into proximity fuzes for BOMBS and GUIDED MISSILES as well as antiaircraft shells. The most promising antiaircraft effort was given the designation *Kranich* (Crane) and consisted of an ingenious device to detonate the round when within range of an aircraft engine. The amplitude of the vibration caused an electric current to detonate the warhead. It was ready for production when the war ended but, like so many German technical developments, was too late to influence the war.

PT-Boats

Small, fast, TORPEDO craft used by the U.S. Navy in several combat areas. The U.S. Navy called these craft PT- (Patrol Torpedo) boats, although most navies referred to them as MTBs (Motor Torpedo Boats).

The U.S. Navy had little interest in PT-boats until the eve of World War II because of the isolated position of the United States. In 1937 Gen. DOUGLAS MACARTHUR, in planning for the defense of the Philippines, believed that 100 torpedo boats could fend off a potential Japanese invasion. A year later the U.S. Congress voted $5,000,000 for an experimental PT-boat program.

Following a design competition, the Navy ordered from the Elco Boatyard series production of a 77-foot, 46-ton, wood-hull boat with three Packard gasoline engines that could drive the craft at 41 knots. Armament would consist of four TORPEDOES plus two pairs of .50-cal. BROWNING MACHINE GUNS. Each had a crew of two officers and nine enlisted men.

On the morning of Dec. 7, 1941, there were six operational Elco boats in the water at PEARL HARBOR. Another six were lashed on cradles, being loaded on a Navy oiler for transportation to the Philippines. When Japanese bombers attacked Pearl Harbor, the PT-boat sailors—on the boats in the water and in the cradles—blazed away at the attackers with their machine guns, firing more than 4,000 rounds.

Another eleven PT-boats were at the New York Navy Yard that day; they were soon dispatched by cargo ship to the Panama Canal. And the Navy's final six PT-boats—the *PT 31* through *PT 35,* and *PT 41* were in MANILA Bay when the war began. Those boats, forming MTB SQUADRON 3 under Comdr. JOHN D. BULKELEY, fought a heroic delaying action in the Philippines against Japanese aircraft and ships. Normally they were used for patrol duties and to follow up reports of Japanese ship movements. They were under almost constant air attack in daylight, but at night were effective against Japanese small craft in the area.

PT 33 ran aground and was lost; *PT 31* drifted aground with engine problems and when taken under fire by Japanese shore guns was destroyed by her crew. All suffered engine problems. Finally, in March 1942 the four remaining boats carried Gen. MacArthur and a small party away from besieged CORREGIDOR to the southern Philippines, from where they were flown to Australia. During subsequent operations in the Philippines the *PT 34* was sunk in a Japanese strafing attack and the three other boats eventually were scuttled.

Subsequently, PT-boats were in action in the U.S. SOLOMONS–NEW GUINEA CAMPAIGN beginning in Oct. 1942. In that lengthy campaign, PT-boats, operating mostly at night, proved themselves highly effective in attacking Japanese barge traffic attempting to reinforce garrisons under Allied attack, often while fighting off large Japanese warships. In one action a PT-boat launched a torpedo that went completely through the destroyer *Hatsukaze,* but the Japanese ship was still able to get away at 18 knots. (Later a Japanese bomber put a

The *PT 141* at high speed during a training exercise. The "141 boat" has two 21-inch torpedo tubes, with the two after tubes replaced by depth charges. Rapid-fire cannon and machine guns complete her armament. (*U.S. Navy*)

torpedo—which did not explode—completely through the hull of the *PT 167.*) Another Japanese destroyer, maneuvering wildly to avoid PT-boat torpedoes, struck a MINE, and sank. In one night operation the *PT 109* was sliced in half by a Japanese destroyer; the PT-boat skipper, Lt. JOHN F. KENNEDY, and most of his crew survived. In discussing PT-boat operations in this campaign, an official U.S. Navy history notes: "with relatively little damage to themselves [the PT-boats] took terrible toll of the Japanese. Along the coastline [of New Guinea] was the wreckage of hundreds of blasted barges; in former enemy encampments were bodies of thousands of soldiers who died for lack of supplies."

U.S. PT-boats also saw action in the Mediterranean beginning in April 1943, in the NORMANDY INVASION, and, finally in the 1944–1945 recapture of the Philippines. PT-boat sailors referred to their craft as "boats," their force as the "mosquito fleet," and for a motto they usually quoted American naval hero John Paul Jones: "Give me a fast ship for I intend to go in harm's way."

Going in harm's way earned the MEDAL OF HONOR for John D. Bulkeley for his four months of war in the Philippines, and for Lt. Comdr. A. Murray Preston, commander of MTB Squadron 33, for leading two PT boats through mined waters and under heavy shore fire for two and a half hours to rescue a downed U.S. pilot.

Sixty-nine PT-boats were lost during the war, including twenty-six or twenty-seven by enemy action (two by KAMIKAZES) and seven by U.S. and other Allied forces through misidentification.

In addition to several experimental PT-boats, U.S. shipyards built 499 PT-boats during the war, with another four boats being built in Canada for the U.S. Navy. American yards also delivered ninety-one PT-boats to Britain and 166 more to the Soviet Union. PTC "chasers" with additional DEPTH CHARGES in place of torpedoes were also built, mostly for foreign transfer under LEND-LEASE.

Later U.S. PT-boats had lightweight torpedo launchers instead of tubes; some boats carried a few depth charges, and progressively more guns were added—OERLIKON 20-MM and BOFORS 40-MM GUNS, more machine guns, occasionally ROCKET launchers, Army 37-mm guns, and even MORTARS. Other features of later PT-boats included RADAR for night operations, and smoke generators to provide smoke screens in daytime.

PT-19

Although the U.S. Army favored biplanes for primary training during the war, the low-wing PT-19 monoplane and its derivatives were flown in almost as large numbers as the PT-SERIES KAYDET biplanes. Developed by Fairchild, the first PT-19s were ordered in 1940. Large orders with several firms followed; the plane also was used by the Royal Canadian Air Force. However, unlike the PT-series biplanes, this aircraft was not used by the U.S. Navy.

A total of 6,014 of the PT-19 and its derivative PT-23 were built for the U.S. Army (including ninety-three by Fleet in Canada); another 1,727 were built for Canada with the designation PT-26 (including 250 PT-26B aircraft built by Fleet in Canada). The principal differences in the PT-19 and PT-23 were their engines, with the PT-23 having a cowling over the engine. The PT-19B and PT-23A had a blind-flying provision with a hood over the forward cockpit to enable a student to fly "blind" while the instructor was in the open, ever ready to take over the controls. The PT-26 had a single canopy over the two cockpits.

The PT-19 series was a low-wing aircraft with a fixed landing gear. The top speed of the PT-19A was 132 mph, and the PT-23A 128 mph. The instructor and student sat in tandem, open cockpits.

PT-Series Kaydet

The PT-series biplane was the basic training aircraft of the U.S. AAF and Navy. The Army began ordering the PT-13, which was developed as a private venture, in 1936 and it soon became the nation's principal primary military trainer. It was also flown by several other nations.

The Kaydet flew for the Army with the designations PT-13, PT-17, PT-18, and PT-27, and the Navy used NS and N2S. (PT indicated primary trainer; the Navy letters were "N" for training and "S" for Stearman.) Eventually the Army and Navy models were standardized and fully interchangeable. Total PT-series production exceeded 10,000 aircraft.

Designed by Stearman, the Kaydet was produced mainly by Boeing. The two-place, open-cockpit aircraft had a fixed landing gear; it did not have a cowling over the radial engine. Some 300 PT-27 winterized versions were produced for the Royal Canadian Air Force with a single canopy over the two cockpits; the U.S. Navy got a few aircraft with canopies.

The PT-13 had a top speed of 125 mph; later variants could reach 135 mph. The student and instructor sat in separate, tandem cockpits.

Pugilist

Code name for Allied attack on the MARETH LINE, Tunisia, 1943.

Puma

Code name for projected Allied landings in the Canary Islands, 1942.

Pumpkin Bombs

Name given to "stand-in" bombs for the ATOMIC BOMB. Because the B-29 SUPERFORTRESS bombers assigned to deliver the atomic bomb were modified and thus unable to carry conventional bombs, Pumpkins were fashioned by the MANHATTAN PROJECT. Shaped like the FAT MAN atomic bomb and painted orange for visibility, Pumpkins were used for training the bomb deliverers, the 509TH COMPOSITE GROUP based on TINIAN. A Pumpkin contained 5,500 pounds of explosives and had a PROXIMITY FUZE that allowed an air burst, a feature of the atomic bomb. On realistic rehearsal runs for the actual atomic-bomb mission, Pumpkins were dropped on Japanese cities near potential atomic-bomb targets to familiarize air crews with navigation problems and to give them lessons in target recognition.

Punishment

Operation Punishment was HITLER's term for the destruction of Belgrade in the German invasion of Yugoslavia, April 1941.

Purple

U.S. code machine that was used to decipher Japanese diplomatic codes. The American machine was to function as the *97-shiki O-bun Injiki* or Alphabetical Typewriter 97 (the number derived from the Japanese year 2597, when it was invented—1937). The Japanese machine represented a radical departure from the German ENIGMA and other electrical encoding machines because it used a battery of 6-level, 25-point switches with a plugboard to establish the key; Enigma and other encoding machines were based on the use of multiple rotors. The machine was invented by Capt. Risaburo Ito of the Japanese Navy.

The American Purple was largely the result of efforts by America's leading code-breaker, WILLIAM F. FRIEDMAN. The first U.S. device was built in 1940 at the WASHINGTON Navy Yard and the first complete message text was deciphered the following year. Rear Adm. EDWIN T. LAYTON, senior U.S. intelligence officer of the Pacific FLEET, wrote in *And I Was There*, "By the second week in September [1940] the current keys to the Purple cipher had been recovered and the rat's nest of wiring and chattering relays housed in a makeshift black wooden box finally rewarded the months of ingenious labor by producing the first decrypts of TOKYO's most secret diplomatic messages."

Apparently four Purple machines were produced in the United States. One was used at the WAR DEPARTMENT and one at the NAVY DEPARTMENT in Washington by the service intelligence departments, one was sent to Gen. DOUGLAS MACARTHUR's headquarters in the Philippines, and in the spring of 1941 one was carried to England and presented to the British code-breakers at BLETCHLEY PARK. Significantly, the one that went to England had been intended for the intelligence staff at U.S. naval headquarters at PEARL HARBOR.

As tension grew over possible war with Japan, in Washington the Army and Navy alternated on a daily basis the decoding of Japanese message traffic in the Purple code. The decrypts were then hand-carried to a very limited distribution list of senior officials in the Army, Navy, and Department of State.

Purple Heart,

see AWARDS AND DECORATIONS.

PV-1 Ventura,
    see A-28/A-29/B-34 HUDSON.

PV-3 Harpoon,
    see A-28/A-29/B-34 HUDSON.

Pyle, Ernie (1900–1945)

America's best known WAR CORRESPONDENT. Pyle, a columnist for United Feature Syndicate, was writing chatty, offbeat stories about U.S. people and places when the war began. His first war dispatches reported on the BATTLE OF BRITAIN. After America entered the war, he returned to England, wrote about the U.S. troops arriving there, and accompanied some who were sent as replacements following the NORTH AFRICA INVASION.

He always focused on ordinary soldiers—"brave men," he called them—and left the big picture to other writers. His columns were published six times a week in about 300 newspapers. More than 13,000,000 people read his dispatches from the war, and many slipped clippings of the columns into letters they wrote to loved ones serving overseas. He thus had both home front and frontline fans. In 1943 he won the Pulitzer Prize for "distinguished war correspondence."

Pyle slogged along with infantrymen through North Africa, during the invasion of SICILY, the battles to liberate Italy, and the NORMANDY INVASION. "I was at the foot of the mule train the night they brought Capt. Waskow's body down," he wrote in what would be his most memorable column, an unflinching portrait of war in the mountains of Italy in the winter of 1944. "Dead men had been coming down the mountain all evening, lashed onto the backs of mules. They came lying belly-down across the wooden pack-saddles, their heads hanging down on the left side of the mule, their stiffened legs sticking out awkwardly from the other side, bobbing up and down as the mules walked. . . . You feel small in the presence of dead men, and ashamed at being alive. . . ."

As Pyle headed for war in the Pacific, he said, "I feel that I've used up all my chances." Alongside Marines of the 1st Marine DIVISION, he went ashore on D-DAY at OKINAWA, April 4, 1945. Fourteen days later he was with U.S. Army infantrymen on tiny Ie Island, west of Okinawa. Japanese snipers fired on a jeep in which he was traveling. He dived into a ditch. When he raised his head, he was shot in the left temple. He was buried on the island.

On his body soldiers found the draft of a column obsessed with battle deaths "in such monstrous infinity that you come almost to hate them." A MOVIE, *The Story of G.I. Joe,* with Burgess Meredith playing Pyle, was released shortly after his death.

Q

Q-Ships

Heavily armed decoy ships intended to lure enemy submarines into surfacing to attack them with gunfire instead of using their more expensive and limited number of TORPEDOES. Q-ships were successful in World War I, although numerous postwar novels and MOVIES accorded them more successes than they actually scored.

Early in 1942—in response to heavy shipping losses to U-BOATS—President ROOSEVELT proposed to Adm. ERNEST J. KING, the Commander in Chief U.S. FLEET, that a Q-ship program be undertaken. Under the code name Project LQ, the Navy acquired a large trawler and two cargo ships and converted them to Q-ships: 4-inch (102-mm) guns and .50-cal. machine guns were fitted, as were DEPTH CHARGES, SONAR detection gear, and internal communications.

Disguised as innocent, unarmed merchantmen, the trio sailed from New England ports in late March 1942. On March 27, four days after going to sea, when some 300 miles east of Norfolk, the Q-ship *Atik* encountered the *U-123.* After being hit by a single torpedo from the surfaced submarine, the Q-ship's "panic party" took to the ship's lifeboats while a radio SOS was hastily transmitted.

The U-boat took the bait and closed on the surface. As she approached, the *Atik* shed her disguise and opened fire, hitting the U-boat several times and killing one man. The U-boat managed to pull out of gun range and that night she torpedoed and sank the *Atik.* No survivors from her crew of 141

The liner *Queen Elizabeth,* pressed into service as a troop ship, still shows her royal lines. The two British "queens" were sailed independently, using their speed to evade U-boats. *(U.S. Navy)*

or wreckage was found by the Q-ship *Asterion,* which answered the ill-fated *Atik*'s distress call.

The two other ships continued to operate as Q-ships, even though German radio announced the earlier sinking of a Q-ship. A modified tanker and a three-masted sailing schooner were also sent out on Q-ship patrols. Some sonar contacts were made but there were no U-boat attacks against them and the Q-ship project was abandoned in 1944. The score of Project LQ: U-boats—1, Q-ships—0.

The Royal Navy fitted out eight Q-ships in 1939–1940, giving them the code name Freighters. None ever sighted a U-boat and two were sunk in June 1940.

British naval historian S. W. Roskill observed: "The enemy was far too wary to be caught by a ruse which had been so well advertised between the wars and, moreover, secrecy had been so great that the ships were often in considerable danger of being sunk by our own forces. . . . [A] thorough enquiry was ordered. Once all the facts were known, their operations were immediately stopped." The score of Project Freighters: U-boats—2, Q-ships—0.

Quadrant

Code name for U.S.-British QUEBEC CONFERENCE, Aug. 1943.

Quebec Conferences

Two meetings in Canada between President ROOSEVELT and Prime Minister CHURCHILL. For the first conference, code-named Quadrant, Churchill arrived in Quebec on Aug. 10, 1943, and first met with Canadian Prime Minister W. L. Mackenzie King. Roosevelt arrived on Aug. 17 and remained until Aug. 24. The leaders and their advisers agreed on a tentative date (May 1, 1944) for the Allied invasion of France. Also agreed upon was the island-hopping strategy in the Pacific, the establishment of B-29 SUPERFORTRESS bases for the bombing of Japan, and the creation of a Southeast Asia Command under Adm. LOUIS MOUNTBATTEN.

The second conference, code-named Octagon, began on Sept. 12, 1944, when Churchill and Roosevelt, meeting again in Quebec, laid out plans for the occupation of Germany and the defeat of Japan. They set Oct. 20, 1944, for the invasion of the Philippines by U.S. forces under Gen. DOUG-

LAS MACARTHUR. They also indicated their interest in what became known as the MORGENTHAU PLAN, a rollback of Germany to pastoral status. U.S. Secretary of the Treasury Henry Morgenthau presented the plan, which Roosevelt and Churchill soon killed on the recommendation of Roosevelt's startled advisers.

Queen

Code name for U.S. 12th ARMY GROUP operation on the Roer Plain between the Wurm and Roer rivers in Germany.

Queen Elizabeth

British liner employed as a troop transport during the war. The ship entered service with the Cunard Lines in 1940, the largest ship to be built at that time.

She immediately began sailing under government orders, departing the Clyde on her maiden voyage to New York on Feb. 27, 1940. During the war the *Queen Elizabeth* and her running mate *QUEEN MARY* sailed unescorted as troop ships across the Atlantic, able to evade German U-BOATS because of their high sustained speeds. The "queens" averaged three trans-Atlantic crossings a month, each ship carrying some 15,000 troops to England—the equivalent of an army DIVISION—on each trip. By June 1, 1944, they had transported an aggregate of 425,000 American servicemen or 24 percent of the entire U.S. buildup in Britain prior to the NORMANDY INVASION.

She completed her troopship service in March 1946 and was outfitted as a luxury liner, to carry 850 first-class, 720 cabin, and 744 tourist passengers. She commenced regular Southampton–New York service on Oct. 16, 1946. She made that first crossing in four days, sixteen hours, eighteen minutes; it did not break the record of the *Queen Mary*.

The "QE" was laid down on Dec. 4, 1936, and launched on Sept. 27, 1938. Steam turbines could propel the 83,673-ton ship at 31 knots.

Queen Mary

British liner employed as a troop transport during the war. The *Queen Mary* entered passenger service with the Cunard Lines in 1936. During the war she and her running mate *QUEEN ELIZABETH* (see above) carried a large number of the American troops employed in the European theater, and often returned to the United States with German PRISONERS OF WAR.

Twice during the war the *Queen Mary* carried Prime Minister CHURCHILL from England to the United States, for the WASHINGTON CONFERENCE (Trident) in early May of 1943, and again for the second QUEBEC CONFERENCE (Octagon) in Sept. 1944. On the former voyage about 5,000 German POWs also sailed to the United States. (Churchill returned to Britain from the Trident conference by flying boat and from the Octagon conference in the *Queen Mary.*)

The ship returned to trans-Atlantic passenger service in Aug. 1947 after a thorough outfitting.

The *Queen Mary* was laid down in Aug. 1930 and after a suspension of work because of the worldwide depression, she was launched on Sept. 26, 1934. Her first voyage was from Southampton to New York, commencing on May 27, 1936; she made this run (from Bishop Rock to Ambrose Lightship) in four days, twenty-seven minutes (an average speed of 30.14 knots). In 1938 she set a new eastbound crossing record of three days, twenty hours, forty-two minutes. The 80,774-ton ship was rated at 30 knots and, in postwar passenger service carried 700 first, 680 cabin, and 500 tourist passengers. The ship is now preserved as a hotel-restaurant complex in Long Beach, Calif.

Quezon, Manuel L. (1878–1944)

President of the commonwealth of the Philippines. Quezon, an anti-American insurgent in his youth, made peace with the U.S. territorial authorities and entered politics, becoming a member of the Philippine legislature and a resident commissioner to the U.S. Congress from 1909 to 1916. He was elected president of the Philippine Senate in 1916 and still held that post in 1935 when the United States made the Philippines a commonwealth and promised that it would become an independent republic on July 4, 1946.

Following an American-style election campaign, Quezon was elected president of the commonwealth and was sworn in on Nov. 15, 1935. He worked closely with Field Marshal DOUGLAS MACARTHUR, the commonwealth's military adviser and head of a U.S. military mission, to build up

Philippine defenses against Japan and was in his second term as president when the Japanese invaded the Philippines on Dec. 8, 1941.

On Feb. 20, 1942, Quezon, Vice President Sergio Osmeña, and other Filipino officials were evacuated from CORREGIDOR by a U.S. SUBMARINE. (The Japanese radio, in a PROPAGANDA ploy to demoralize Filipinos, announced that Quezon had died under American torture.)

Quezon, Osmeña, and the rest of the Philippine delegation arrived in San Francisco on May 8 and were put onto a special train that took them to WASHINGTON, where President ROOSEVELT personally welcomed them. Quezon set up a government-in-exile in Washington and became somewhat of a celebrity. He kept the American press mindful of his country as an ally. He also joined U.S. military and political officials who pressed for a higher priority to the U.S. war effort in the Pacific. A British Embassy political report in April 1943 noted that the lobbying of Quezon and others in the "Pacific bloc" was making the "Pacific front permanently a more burning issue than the European front is ever likely to be."

Under the Philippine constitution, Quezon was to end his presidential career at the end of his second term. But a friendly U.S. Congress in 1943 voted to have him continue as president until liberation. But Quezon died on Aug. 1, 1944. He was succeeded by Osmeña, who in October accompanied MacArthur when the general led an invasion to liberate the Philippines.

Quicksilver

Code name for the complex operation to convince the Germans that the main landing in the assault on Western Europe would be directed at the Pas de Calais.

Quisling, Vidkun (1887–1945)

Norwegian traitor whose name became a synonym for betrayal. A former army officer, diplomat, and cabinet member, Quisling founded a Norwegian NAZI party soon after HITLER became chancellor of Germany in 1933. In 1939, while Norway was neutral, Quisling conferred with Hitler and Nazi officials and urged them to seize Norway before England did. Quisling aided the Germans when they invaded the neutral nation on April 9, 1940. The German conquerors made him "Führer" of Norway on Sept. 25 and empowered him to "reconstruct" the country into a Fascist state.

Loathed by the overwhelming majority of his fellow citizens, Quisling ruled as a dictator, sending thousands to German CONCENTRATION CAMPS and killing hostages rounded up in retaliation for acts by Norway's vigorous resistance movement, which operated along the border with Sweden. He became prime minister of a puppet government on Feb. 2, 1942.

Norway's liberators arrested him after the German SURRENDER on May 7, 1945. The legitimate Norwegian government, which had been in exile in LONDON, returned and put him on trial for TREASON, murder, and theft. He was convicted and was executed on Oct. 24, 1945. Quisling, CHURCHILL predicted, "will carry the scorn of mankind down the centuries."

Quonset Hut

Widely used structure, produced in the tens of thousands for U.S. and Allied forces during the war. A half-cylindrical design made of corrugated metal, the Quonset hut was used for offices, hospitals, barracks, and warehouses.

The first huts were built for the U.S. Navy in 1941 at Quonset Point, R.I. The design was a modification of the British-produced NISSEN HUT.

R4

British plan in April 1940 to occupy Norwegian ports in the event of a German invasion.

Rabaul

Japanese stronghold on NEW BRITAIN, largest island in the Bismarck Archipelago in the Bismarck Sea. New Britain, an Australian mandated island, was invaded by Japanese forces in Jan. 1942. Japan made a stronghold of Rabaul, the chief town, on the eastern tip of the crescent-shaped island. The buildup included five airfields and a major harbor complex. From Rabaul Japan could control the sea and air approaches to NEW GUINEA and the SOLOMON ISLANDS.

Allied strategy made Rabaul a key objective for capture or neutralization. Eventually ruling out capture, military planners decided to hammer Rabaul with both carrier- and land-based aircraft.

BOUGAINVILLE, largest of the Solomon Islands, was seized with a U.S. AMPHIBIOUS LANDING in Nov. 1943. In Dec. 1943 U.S. Marines landed at the western end of New Britain, but, in keeping with the neutralization strategy, no attempt was made to seize Rabaul at the eastern end.

More than 29,000 Allied sorties were flown against Rabaul. As Allied strength grew in the Pacific, naval and air forces isolated Rabaul, and the 91,000-man Japanese garrison there was allowed to "wither on the vine." The troops there capitulated on Sept. 6, 1945, three weeks after the SURRENDER of Japan.

Radar was a vital component of Allied combat operations in all theaters of the war. This view of the radar antennas of an _Essex_-class carrier indicates the impact of this device on carrier operations—for air and surface search, gunfire control, identification of aircraft, and navigation. (_U.S. Navy_)

Race Riots

Civil disorders, often involving servicemen, touched off by tensions between groups of whites and blacks or whites and Hispanics. So many riots erupted in so many places during the war that in Oct. 1943 a committee of the American Civil Liberties Union published a pamphlet "How to Prevent a Race Riot in Your Home Town." Major racial clashes broke out between servicemen at several U.S. military posts and among black and whites, mostly civilians, in several cities, including New York; Mobile, Ala.; Beaumont, Texas; and Los Angeles, where servicemen attacked Mexican and black ZOOT SUITERS. During a night of racial rioting in New York City on Aug. 1, 1943, five men died and more than 450 were injured.

The worst of the wartime race riots flared in June 1943 in Detroit, where twenty-five blacks and nine whites were killed and nearly 700 people were injured. Property damage amounted to $2,000,000. Detroit, the nation's fourth largest city during the war, was overcrowded and tense, with a population of nearly 3,000,000, including tens of thousands of blacks who had migrated from the South to find jobs in war plants. Until the summer of 1943, clashes between whites and blacks were quickly quelled. Then, on June 20, a steaming hot Sunday, scuffles broke out in Belle Isle, a park jammed with about 100,000 persons, most of them black.

Toward night, the scuffling grew into mob violence and spread from Belle Isle to downtown Detroit. By noon on Monday, four people were dead and 186 injured. Later in the day, Army troops, using tear gas and rifle butts, began driving the rioters off the streets. Eventually, after White House consultations, the Army sent some 5,000 soldiers—all white—to Detroit, and some remained in the city until July.

Fighting among white and black servicemen in segragated U.S. Army posts frequently escalated into rioting. At one post, the commanding officer banned black newspapers, which he blamed for agitating his black troops. Black newspapers were sometimes removed from post libraries and reading rooms. (See SEGREGATION)

In Aug. 1941 a white military policeman and a black soldier were killed and two white MPs and three black soldiers were wounded in a gun battle at Fayetteville, N.C. In April 1942 a white MP and two black soldiers died in a gun battle at Fort Dix, N.J. There were serious disturbances in 1943 at many camps, particularly in the South. A gun battle involving 100 men of a black regiment in Arizona ended with the deaths of an officer, an enlisted man, and a civilian. Sixteen members of the regiment were court-martialed and each was sentenced to fifty years in prison. The infantry regiment was later sent to the ALEUTIAN ISLANDS for the rest of the war.

Radar

Radio Detection And Ranging (radar) provided the means of "seeing" objects at night, in bad weather, and smoke; in clear weather it extended the range of sight. It could detect aircraft and ships by the reflection of radio waves from solid objects and was undoubtedly one of the most important technical devices of the war, having a decisive influence on the BATTLE OF BRITAIN and the BATTLE OF THE ATLANTIC, and making a major contribution to U.S. naval successes in the U.S. CENTRAL PACIFIC CAMPAIGN. (The term *radar* was coined by U.S. naval officers.)

Radar was developed simultaneously in the 1930s by the Americans, British, French, and Germans. Experiments at the U.S. Naval Aircraft Radio Laboratory in WASHINGTON in the fall of 1922 indicated the phenomena of radio-wave reflection, but proposals for follow-up work were not undertaken. Then, in 1930 the U.S. Naval Research Laboratory in Washington found that aircraft flying overhead disturbed the calibration of a high-frequency radio direction finder. This time the lab was directed to investigate the use of radio waves to detect aircraft and surface ships. Research continued and was soon shared with the U.S. Army.

In 1937 the U.S. Navy installed an experimental radar set in the DESTROYER *Leary* (DD 158). Early the following year that set, attached to a gun mount, detected an aircraft at a distance of 100 miles. The more capable XAF radar was installed in the BATTLESHIP *New York* (BB 34) in Dec. 1938. That radar—with a 17-foot rotating "bed spring" antenna—and the competitive CXZ set fitted in the battleship *Texas* (BB 35) were an outstanding success in exercises, detecting aircraft and surface ships, providing excellent navigation aids, and spotting the fall of shots. As a result, the U.S. Navy was firmly committed to radar. Search and (from Dec. 1941) gunfire control radars were rapidly fitted to all surface warships of DESTROYER ESCORT size and larger; small combat craft and submarines received search radars.

Radar development began in both Germany and Britain in 1935, although along different lines. Germany began using wavelengths in the half-meter band, but when even shorter waves in the centimeter range were tried, the German scientists gained the impression that no progress would be made in that direction. Consequently, German developments were confined to the decimeter range, and the standard mass-produced radar of the German armed forces used wave bands between 80 and 150 centimeters.

In Britain the first radar sets used wavelengths of 11 to 12 meters, but as this equipment was cumbersome, experiments were made with progressively shorter waves until 9-centimeter and even shorter wavelengths proved satisfactory. Also, while the Germans looked at radar for range measurement, the British and Americans considered the value of radar in broader terms. German research was halted in 1940–1941 on HITLER's orders. Thus, when the Germans found a 9-centimeter radar in a shot-down British bomber they realized for the first time how far behind they were. The shorter wavelengths used by the ALLIES permitted greater detection ranges and more accuracy.

Ground Radar   The first major use of radar in the war was in the Battle of Britain (with the British referring to radar as R.D.F.—Radio Direction Finding). The initial British interest in radar (1935) was for air defense, both land-based and shipboard. By 1937 the Air Ministry had begun the development of a "chain" of radar stations along the British coast that would give warning of high-flying aircraft at a distance of 100 miles. At the time Britain's greatest fear was attacks by high-speed German bombers.

In July 1940, when the battle began, the British air defense system included twenty-one Chain Home (CH) and thirty Chain Home Low-flying (CHL) radar stations, the former's antennas mounted on 240-foot towers. The CH operated on a wavelength of 5.8 to 13.5 meters, and CHL 1.5

meters. The CHL radars could detect both low-flying aircraft and coastal shipping. The only gaps in the chain were in the northwest of Scotland, the Bristol Channel, and a portion of the Welsh coast. In addition, to help the RAF detect aircraft taking off from airfields near Calais, two gunfire control radars were installed on the Dover cliffs.

The chain radar stations were tied by telephone to operations rooms that directed RAF Fighter Command fighters onto approaching German bombers. Without radar direction it would have been impossible for the RAF Fighter Command to make successful interceptions. Those stations were operational twenty-four hours a day, for six years, until the German SURRENDER. Luftwaffe fighter leader ADOLF GALLAND observed: As Luftwaffe planes assembled over France, their "formations were already picked up and never allowed to escape from the radar eye." He added, "We had nothing like it."

In Germany the Navy, not the Luftwaffe, was the prime proponent of radar development in the mid-1930s. However, in 1936 the FLAK arm of the Luftwaffe became interested in air defense radars and that year saw a demonstration of the *Freya,* which worked on a wavelength of 2.4 meters, considerably shorter than the British CH radars. In 1939 the *Würzburg* radar was demonstrated—with Hitler and HERMANN GÖRING in attendance. Based on these demonstrations, both sets were ordered in quantity for air defense, although production was hampered by the usual lack of urgency and interagency bickering that characterized German military programs.

These and later radar sets were procured in large numbers for the air defense of German-controlled Europe. However, German technology (and production) was unable to keep pace with Allied radar countermeasures that permitted STRATEGIC BOMBING to continue. The U.S. Army's first radar set was the SCR (Signal Corps Radio) 268, developed to control antiaircraft guns. It was demonstrated in May 1937 before top Army and congressional officials. This demonstration led to acceleration of the development of a long-range radar set that could detect early warning of air attack. By 1939 the prototype SCR-270, a mobile set with a detection range of over 120 miles, and the similar fixed SCR-

271 were ready for tests. Subsequent radar sets made use of British-provided technology.

In 1940 the first operational Army radar was installed at the Panama Canal. By the time of the Japanese air attack on PEARL HARBOR the Army had six SCR-270 mobile (truck-mounted) radar sets in operation, and installations were being completed for three SCR-271 fixed sets. The mobile radars were in operation from 4 A.M. to 7 A.M. every day—"the most dangerous hours" for an attack by Japanese carriers, according to Lt. Gen. WALTER SHORT, the U.S. Army commander in Hawaii. The mobile sets were operated by motor generators, which frequently broke down. They were linked to the plotting center by commercial telephones. There was no liaison between the Army and Navy, and personnel were poorly trained.

On the morning of Dec. 7, 1941, instead of closing down the SCR-270 at Kahuku Point at the northern end of Oahu at 7 A.M. as scheduled, Pvt. Joseph L. Lockard and Pvt. George E. Elliott continued to operate the radar because Elliott wanted further instruction. At 7:02 "something completely out of the ordinary" appeared on his radar screen. The privates had detected a flight of planes 137 miles north of Oahu, heading due south.

When they called the plotting center a young officer (in training) made some inquiries and decided that the operators were seeing a flight of B-17 FLYING FORTRESS bombers arriving from the mainland. In fact, those B-17s arrived in the middle of the Japanese attack, which began at 7:55 A.M. Intelligence historian Roberta Wohlstetter believes that if the Oahu radar system was operating properly, under the most favorable conditions radar would have provided a forty-five-minute warning to the Army and perhaps a thirty-minute warning to the Navy. (The Kahuku Point radar reopened at 9 A.M. and tracked the Japanese planes retiring northward, toward their waiting carriers. But the Army failed to inform the fleet headquarters and Navy search efforts looked elsewhere for the withdrawing Japanese carriers.)

Several hours later, in the PHILIPPINES the single operating Army radar did provide warning of a Japanese air strike approaching Luzon from Formosa. This warning, as at Pearl Harbor, went astray and a short time later Japanese bombs smashed U.S. aircraft on the ground at Clark and Iba airfields. (A second radar set in the Philippines was apparently not operational at the time.)

After Pearl Harbor the Army sought to establish a radar warning fence on both the East and West Coasts to give warning of enemy bomber attacks. The full plan—thirty sites along the Atlantic coast and sixty-five on the Pacific coast—was never fulfilled; the maximum number of radars in use at any one time was about seventy-five.

Radars were also deployed with antiaircraft gun batteries in the United States and in the war zones.

Shipboard Radar   At the start of the EUROPEAN WAR the British and German Navies were installing search and gunfire control radars in their ships. The British tried a 1½-meter radar at sea in the minesweeper *Saltburn* in 1937, but it failed because it was impossible to obtain sufficient power on such a short wavelength. Therefore the Royal Navy concentrated on a wavelength of 7 meters and a prototype Type 79 radar was tested at sea in March 1937. This set was installed in the battleship *Rodney* in Aug. 1938 and the cruiser *Sheffield* in Nov. 1938. This set could detect an aircraft at ranges of over 50 miles. Additional and improved sets were fitted in British warships by the start of the war.

The German Navy was the first to take radar to sea, with the *Seetakt* radar rangefinder installed in the POCKET BATTLESHIP *ADMIRAL GRAF SPEE* in 1936. The set could detect large ships at a distance of ten miles and cruisers at six miles. However, German surface-ship radar development lagged behind British and U.S. efforts, in part because of the excellence of German optical equipment. Indeed, on the battleship *BISMARCK* the *Seetakt* had only some 75 percent of the range of the ship's optical rangefinders. However, when the *Bismarck* was in her death throes, her radar-directed guns were able to open fire at British destroyers at a range of about 12,000 yards, preventing them from making a TORPEDO attack and requiring the British to reduce the *Bismarck* to a hulk with long-range gunfire before the ship could be sunk by torpedoes.

In many respects the most important use of radar at sea was the Allied antisubmarine effort. Early in the war the primary U-BOAT tactic was to track CONVOYS and attack on the surface, at night, making use of their higher surface speed and cover of darkness.

The initial radars installed in British escort ships had minimal capabilities against submarines—they were used primarily for convoy station keeping. U-boats were still safer on the surface, where they were safe from SONAR (Asdic) detection.

By mid-1942 most convoy escorts were being fitted with the new 10-centimeter Type 271M radar. This set—first installed in a CORVETTE in March 1941—could detect a surfaced U-boat—a very small, difficult target—at a range of four miles or more. Within a year enough escorts had the 271M that the U-boats were robbed of their concealment at night or in fog. Vice Adm. FRIEDRICH RUGE, a leading postwar German naval historian, wrote that because of radar, "Much time had to be wasted keeping submerged, and, if in the vicinity of a convoy, it would be almost impossible to attain a position ahead for attacking it. The conditions for delivering an attack had in any case become more difficult. Usually the maneuvering could only be done at extreme visibility range, since nearly all the enemy convoy escorts were now equipped with radar." The situation became worse for U-boats with the employment of airborne radar (see below).

The forcing of U-boats to remain submerged led to development of the advanced TYPE XXI submarine, which was intended to carry out its entire patrol submerged and thus, except for its SNORKEL head, be immune to Allied radar detection. And, even the snorkel head could be covered with radar-absorbing (anechoic) material.

Following its prewar efforts, the U.S. Navy soon fitted all surface warships—down to PT-BOATS and minesweepers—and all submarines with radar. Radar was highly effective in naval actions in the Pacific as well as in the Atlantic areas. Radar in U.S. warships totally compensated for the Japanese emphasis on night combat—without radar.

Following the Japanese initiation of KAMIKAZE attacks in the fall of 1944, the U.S. Navy hastily developed radar-picket destroyers, which were available in time for the April 1, 1945, invasion of OKINAWA. These ships manned radar picket "stations" off the island to provide carrier and amphibious forces with early warning of kamikaze attacks, in part to permit interception by defending fighters. These ships themselves suffered heavily from Japanese suicide attacks when the enemy realized their function.

Japanese and Italian radar development lagged far behind that of the United States, Britain, and Germany. The Soviet Union had a radar program under way in the late 1930s, but it was largely suspended during the war with some U.S. radars becoming available during the war through LEND-LEASE.

Airborne Radar Airborne radar also played a crucial role in the Battle of the Atlantic. As early as 1937 the British were experimenting with ASV (Air-to-Surface Vessel) radar; as the U-boat menace became clearer, aircraft radar was emphasized, and in Jan. 1940 the RAF Coastal Command received twelve A-28 HUDSON bombers fitted with the ASV I radar. The more capable ASV II was ordered into production but had to face competition for resources because of the need for night fighters equipped with Air-Intercept (AI) radars to defeat German night bombers during the Blitz.

Radar-equipped antisubmarine aircraft were forthcoming, with U.S. B-24 LIBERATORS, the most capable of the long-range maritime aircraft, SUNDERLAND flying boats, carrier-based SWORDFISH, and other radar-equipped aircraft being key factors in defeating the U-boats.

Simultaneous with the development of ASV-type radars was AI radar for fighter aircraft to intercept night bombers. The RAF BLENHEIM two-engine bomber was fitted with early air-intercept radar to pioneer the night-fighter role. On the night of July 23–24 a Blenheim used AI radar to close on a German DO 17 bomber over the channel and, making the attack by visual sighting, achieved the first radar kill of the war. The size of AI radars initially required that it be fitted in twin-engine aircraft, such as the long series of MOSQUITO night fighters. But Allied efforts soon provided small, pod-mounted radars, used primarily in naval aircraft, such as the F6F HELLCAT, F4U CORSAIR, TBF/TBM AVENGER, ALBACORE, and Swordfish. In the United States, the twin-engine P-61 BLACK WIDOW was the first U.S. aircraft designed specifically as a night fighter; the twin-engine A-20 HAVOC was adopted for that role (becoming the P-70).

The Luftwaffe originally employed standard fighters for night interceptions, relying on searchlights in the target area for illumination of targets.

When the RAF opened its bombing offensive against Germany in May 1940, the Germans quickly adapted their large force of twin-engine fighters—ME 110, JU 88, and DO 17—to the night intercept role.

The RAF led the development of bomber radars for navigation and target acquisition because of the RAF Bomber Command shifting to night bombing. The U.S. AAF—tenaciously holding to daylight bombing—saw little need for radar in its bomber force. However, the long-range, high-flying B-29 SUPERFORTRESS had the AN/APQ-13 bombing radar. (Ironically, when high-altitude operations with the bombsight failed, the B-29s were employed in low-level, nighttime incendiary attacks against Japanese cities.) The AAF also fitted a wing of B-24s with the AN/APQ-5 low-altitude radar bombsight for operations against Japanese shipping in the SOLOMON ISLANDS area in 1943–1944.

Toward the end of the war, in response to Japanese kamikaze attacks, the U.S. Navy sought to provide fleets with more advance warning of air attacks. Avengers were fitted with AN/APS-20 air search radars (designated TBM-3W) to provide detection of Japanese aircraft at ranges beyond those possible with ship-mounted radars. Also, several B-17G aircraft were similarly fitted with the APS-20 (designated PB-1W) in an effort to provide still longer-range aircraft to protect the fleet. These projects—called Project Cadillac—were the beginnings of today's airborne early warning/AWACS aircraft.

The Allies and AXIS developed radar countermeasures to defeat the effectiveness of enemy radars.

Radio Direction Finding,

see HIGH-FREQUENCY/DIRECTION FINDING.

Raeder, *Grossadmiral* Erich (1876–1960)

Architect of the buildup of the German Navy under ADOLF HITLER and Commander in Chief of the Navy for the first three years of the war. Raeder served in the German Navy from 1894, serving in surface ships and in staff positions in World War I, seeing action in several battles.

After working in naval history (and writing a book on cruiser warfare), in 1925 he was appointed a *Vizeadmiral* in the new German Navy and in 1928 was appointed admiral and Chief of the Naval Staff.

During this period he planned the rebirth of the Navy, in violation of the Versailles Treaty. In 1935 Raeder was named CinC and given the new rank of General Admiral (changed to *Grossadmiral* in 1939).

The war came earlier than Raeder had been led to expect by Hitler (see Z PLAN). Raeder planned and directed naval operations in the 1939 assault on Poland, the 1940 invasions of the DENMARK AND NORWAY CAMPAIGN (with the Navy having a key role in the latter), and preparations for the abortive invasion of England (see SEA LION). In the GERMAN CAMPAIGN IN THE SOVIET UNION the naval forces had a secondary but significant role in the Arctic, Baltic, and Black Sea areas.

Following the loss of several major surface ships, Raeder resigned on Jan. 30, 1943, when Hitler demanded that the remaining surface warships be retired in favor of concentration of U-BOAT operations.

After the war Raeder and his wife were arrested by the Soviets and, in July 1945 flown to MOSCOW. For three months he was interrogated, albeit with great care and courtesy. He was then returned to Germany and tried for WAR CRIMES at Nuremberg. (His wife was held in a Soviet prison camp until 1950.)

Raeder's defense against the charge of waging illegal submarine war at sea included testimony from Adm. CHESTER W. NIMITZ, the U.S. CinC in the Pacific during the war; against charges of ANTI-SEMITISM his defense included testimony from several German JEWS who told of his efforts to protect Jewish naval officers and their families. Found guilty, he was sentenced to life imprisonment but released from Spandau prison in 1955.

After his release Raeder published two volumes of autobiography. In the second, *Mein Leben—Von 1935 bis Spandau 1955,* Raeder described Hitler as "an extraordinary man worthy of becoming Germany's leader."

Raiders

German merchant-type ships heavily armed with concealed weaponry and employed to attack Allied merchant ships. These ships generally operated in remote areas, not the major shipping lanes where escorted CONVOYS might be encountered.

The first raiders went to sea in 1940, the *Atlantis* departing Germany on March 11 and the *Orion* on April 7. In mid-April, during the DENMARK AND NORWAY CAMPAIGN, the raiders were ordered to reveal their presence in an effort to lure British warships away from the coast of Norway. The *Orion* scored the first merchant ship kill on April 24 in the North Atlantic.

In May and June three more raiders went to sea—the *Widder, Pinguin,* and *Thor.* These five raiders sank several hundred thousand tons of merchant shipping between June and Sept. 1940. Additional ships followed; those that operated in the Indian ocean sometimes continued eastward to replenish in Japanese-held ports in southeast Asia and even Japan. At least one raider used a Soviet port in the arctic prior to hostilities between the two countries. In all, ten raiders went to sea. The highest-scoring ship was the *Atlantis,* which operated mainly in the Indian Ocean, sinking or capturing a total of thirty-two ships of 201,500 tons in two cruises. One of her captures, a 5,000-ton motorship, was commissioned as an auxiliary in the German Navy.

The *Pinguin* captured three large Norwegian whale-factory ships and eleven small whale catchers; the large ships were sent back to France with 22,000 tons of whale oil; they and most of the smaller whale catchers reached France safely, with one retained in German service to support the *Pinguin.* On a cruise of almost eleven months the *Pinguin* sunk or captured twenty-eight allied ships totaling 136,000 tons and laid mines that sank five others of 29,000 tons.

From June 1941 armed merchant raiders were the only German surface ships to continue operations on the high seas except in the Arctic Ocean. The raider operations continued until 1943. Several of the ships were sunk by Allied warships, but on Nov. 17, 1941, some 200 miles west of the Australian coast, the German raider *Kormoran* encountered the 7,000-ton Australian light cruiser *Sydney,* armed with eight 6-inch (152-mm) guns and eight TORPEDO tubes. The audacious captain of the *Kormoran* was able to keep the ruse until the ships were only 1,000 yards apart. Then the *Kormoran* opened fire; her first salvo from her concealed guns hit the cruiser's bridge and one torpedo also struck the hapless warship. The raider was hit by the warship's gunfire, fires broke out, and eventually she had to be abandoned. But the *Sydney,* hit again by the German guns, also erupted in fire and staggered away. She sank without survivors.

The raiders cost the Allied merchant fleets about 900,000 tons of shipping, including those ships sunk by mines. In addition, their operations pulled many ships away from the critical BATTLE OF THE ATLANTIC.

The raiders were disguised to look like innocent merchant ships. They carried lumber and other materials to quickly alter their appearance if necessary. Behind canvas and false deck houses, the ships were armed with several guns and torpedo tubes. The standard raider gun armament was six 5.9-inch (150-mm) guns plus light antiaircraft guns and several torpedo tubes and, in some ships, mines. Nine of the raiders also carried a floatplane that could be hoisted over the side to take off and search out victims. One raider also carried a small motor torpedo boat.

Railway

British code name for reinforcement of MALTA, June 1941.

Rainbow

German code word for scuttling of U-BOATS rather than surrendering them to the ALLIES at the end of the EUROPEAN WAR. Although the order was not officially given by naval headquarters, 138 German submarines were scuttled by their crews in the first week of May 1945.

Rainbow War Plan

The U.S. strategic plan for war in the Pacific against Japan. War planners used colors to designate enemies; Japan was Orange. The Rainbow plan, developed in the late 1930s, combined several earlier color-coded plans.

By mid-1941 the Rainbow war plan had become the Rainbow 5 contingency war plan, which encompassed a global strategy for fighting Germany and Japan. The U.S. Navy's Plan D was the source of the Atlantic phase of Rainbow 5 and gave the plan a "Europe first" foundation.

This aspect of the plan figured prominently in investigations growing out of the Japanese attack on PEARL HARBOR on Dec. 7, 1941. Adm. HUSBAND KIMMEL, Commander in Chief of the Pacific Fleet, complained to his superiors that he did not have the forces to carry out the plan, which called on his fleet to "capture . . . positions" in the MARSHALL ISLANDS, "destroy AXIS sea communications, and protect the territory of the associated powers [British and Dutch possessions]." In July 1941 Kimmel revised his war plan for the Pacific Fleet while still fulfilling the Rainbow 5 requirements. He planned to use his fleet to "check any Japanese moves toward the eventual capture of Malaysia (including the Philippines) and HONG KONG" or "the capture of GUAM and other outlying positions."

Adherence to the plan would be part of the potential court-martial defense put forward by Kimmel and Lt. Gen. WALTER SHORT, commanding general of the U.S. Army's Hawaiian Department, when their military competence was questioned. Kimmel in particular felt that he could not use up his aviation gasoline stores and patrol aircraft to search for possible attackers because the resources were needed for carrying out the war plan. This was his response to investigators who cited the lack of reconnaissance patrols that could have theoretically located the Japanese fleet bearing down on Pearl Harbor in Dec. 1941.

Raincoat

Code name for Allied assault on Camino Hill, Italy, Dec. 1943.

Ramage, Comdr. Lawson P. (1909—)

A leading U.S. SUBMARINE ACE and MEDAL OF HONOR winner. After serving in surface ships from his graduation from the Naval Academy in 1931 until 1935, "Red" Ramage served in submarine activities for the next decade except for one assignment in a DESTROYER on the U.S. NEUTRALITY PATROL in 1939–1941.

On Dec. 7, 1941, he was on the staff of the submarine force commander at PEARL HARBOR. In 1942 he went back to sea in a submarine that made one war patrol. Lt. Comdr. Ramage took command of the submarine *Trout* (SS 202) in June 1942 and commanded her on several patrols until early 1943, when he was ordered to the new submarine *Parche* (SS 384). Ramage commanded the *Parche* on four

war patrols; on the second, in July 1944, in concert with another submarine he ripped into a Japanese CONVOY. The *Parche* sank two ships and assisted in sinking a third, earning Ramage the Medal of Honor.

In Dec. 1944 Ramage became personnel officer for the Pacific Fleet submarine commander at Pearl Harbor, an assignment he held into 1946.

After the war Ramage held a succession of submarine and surface ship commands, as well as several important staff positions in WASHINGTON. He retired in 1970 as a vice admiral.

Randy

The Japanese Army Ki-102 assault plane—known by the Allied code name Randy—was a modification of the Ki-96 heavy fighter, which did not enter service. The plane's heavy gun armament, with BOMBS in some variants, provided a potent ground-attack capability, while toward the end of the war a night fighter variant was developed to intercept U.S. bombers. Most Ki-102s were retained in Japan to fend off the expected Allied invasions of 1945–1946, but a few saw combat in the OKINAWA campaign. The Ki-102b was used in development of the I-Go-1 antiship GUIDED MISSILE.

The first of three Ki-102 prototypes flew in March 1944, followed by twenty preproduction aircraft. Production of the Ki-102b model followed, with some modified to the Ki-102a high-altitude fighter, needed to counter U.S. B-29 SUPERFORTRESS bombers. The Ki-102c was a night-fighter variant, but the two prototype conversions from Ki-102b aircraft were still in flight trials when the war ended. Production of all models (including prototypes) totaled 238 aircraft through July 1945. (A lightweight variant of the Ki-102 was also proposed.)

The Ki-102 was an attractive, twin-engine aircraft, with separate, glazed cockpits for the pilot and radio- or radar-operator/gunner. Two large radial engines, with large spinners, were fitted on the mid-fuselage mounted wings. The main landing gear retracted fully into the engine nacelles. The heavily modified Ki-102c was fitted with an air-intercept RADAR.

The aircraft's top speed (Ki-102b) was 360 mph and range was computed at 1,250 miles. The aircraft was heavily armed, with a 57-mm cannon in the nose, two 20-mm cannon in the lower fuselage, and a flexible 12.7-mm machine gun in the after cockpit. The night-fighter Ki-102c was to have two 30-mm guns in the lower fuselage and two 20-mm cannon fired upward from the after fuselage. All variants could carry two 551-pound BOMBS. The crew numbered two.

Rangers

U.S. Army unit patterned after the British COMMANDOS. The Rangers originated in the spring of 1942 when American Army volunteers trained with British commandos at the Commando Depot in Archnacarry, Scotland. The training was so realistic that one American drowned, two were wounded by bullets and one by a GRENADE.

In June, Col. LUCIAN K. TRUSCOTT, JR., in charge of the U.S. training operation, suggested that his troops not be given the British designation of commando. The name he suggested was accepted: "Rangers," a name dating to the French and Indian War. A Ranger BATTALION was organized under Capt. William O. Darby, who, to have the rank necessary for commanding a battalion, was promoted to major and then lieutenant colonel within ten weeks.

On Aug. 19, 1942, six officers and forty-five enlisted men from the Ranger battalion joined British commandos and Canadian troops in a raid on the French Channel port of DIEPPE. Among the more than 3,000 men killed or captured were two Ranger officers and four enlisted men killed; four enlisted men were captured.

In their first action as a new U.S. Army unit, the 1st Ranger Battalion made a surprise night landing in Arzew, Algeria, to neutralize coastal defenses for the NORTH AFRICA INVASION. The raid was an exception to the concept of the Rangers, which called for them to be used in small-unit, hit-and-run special operations. Instead, they usually were sent into combat as conventional infantry.

Six Ranger battalions were formed during the war. Five battalions fought in the European theater, the sixth in the Pacific. The Army prejudice against elite forces persisted in both theaters.

The Army lost confidence in the Rangers after a tragically botched Ranger assault at Cisterna near the ANZIO beachhead in Jan. 1944. In that action Rangers shot other Rangers to prevent a piecemeal surrender to German troops. Of 767 men who had begun the operation, only six made it back to friendly lines. Everyone else had been killed or captured.

The Rangers' reputation was later salvaged by a perfectly executed action in Jan. 1945. Rangers, reinforced by Filipino GUERRILLAS, rescued 511 American Allied PRISONERS OF WAR from a camp near Cabanatuan in the Philippines. The Ranger force of eight officers and 120 enlisted men, advancing well ahead of U.S. lines, hit the camp in a night raid. All guard forces were neutralized in thirty seconds and all but two prisoners were saved. (One died of a heart attack during the raid and the other hid at the sound of gunfire and was later rescued.)

Darby, the founding commander in England, became assistant division commander of the 10th Light (Mountain) DIVISION, which fought in northern Italy. He was killed on April 30, 1945, just before the SURRENDER of German forces in Italy. He had been recommended for promotion to brigadier general, and the promotion was made. He was the only Army officer posthumously promoted to star rank during the war.

Rankin

Code name for Allied contingency plan to enter Europe in the event of a sudden German collapse.

Rashness

Code name for revised Carbonado plan.

Rastenburg,

see WOLF'S LAIR.

Rationing

The wartime allotment of scarce goods. Rationing (from *ratio*) originally was a military term for allotting an even share of supplies to each individual. The practice was adapted for U.S. civilians during World War I in a largely volunteer system based on self-denial. But the U.S. rationing system in World War II was complex and backed by laws aimed at guaranteeing not only supplies to the war effort but also fair distribution on the home front.

Although there were shortages, U.S. rationing

was mostly inspired by the government's desire to distribute scarce products equitably among consumers. For industries engaged in WAR PRODUCTION, rationing meant allocations and priorities over raw materials. For most Americans, however, rationing meant getting less of what you wanted.

Rationing at first was voluntary. With nearly 90 percent of U.S. crude rubber imports cut off by Japan's capture of the DUTCH EAST INDIES and Malaya, the United States faced the first of several crises involving RESOURCES. President ROOSEVELT, reluctant to initiate rationing, launched a scrap drive. He asked Americans to round up "old tires, old rubber raincoats, old garden hose, rubber shoes, bathing caps, gloves—whatever you have that is made of rubber." The rubber for recycling was turned in at gas stations, which paid a cent a pound for it and were later compensated by the government.

The scrap-rubber drive, while inspiring patriotism, did not stave off rationing. The effects of U-BOAT attacks on tankers in the Atlantic were being felt by early 1942. On May 14, 1942, in seventeen Eastern states, motorists using their cars for "nonessential" purposes were restricted to about three gallons of gasoline a week. On Dec. 2 gas rationing was extended to the rest of the United States. Car owners pasted ration stamps on windshields: *A* as a car whose trips were nonessential; *B* for cars that belonged to people who needed them for work, such as traveling salesmen; *C* for the cars of such essential drivers as doctors. For a while, *X* stamps were issued to Very Important People, including Members of Congress. But public criticism ended that practice. Regulations encouraged the setting up of "driving clubs," which became known by the lasting name "car pools."

Although the OFFICE OF PRICE ADMINISTRATION (OPA) had set price ceilings early in 1942 on many items, workers in war plants usually had enough income to bid for scarcities by buying them on the BLACK MARKET. Butter was in short supply beginning in Feb. 1943 because the government reserved about 30 percent of production, mostly for the toast and pancakes consumed by the armed services. Rationing began late in 1943 and continued until Dec. 1945. About one third of U.S. cheese production went to military and Allied countries. The scarcity resulted in cheese rationing.

Latin American coffee producers exported record shipments in the war years, but demands of shipping—and increased consumption by civilians and members of the armed services—led to the rationing of coffee from Nov. 1942 to July 1943. Patriots learned to drink their coffee black—or with only one teaspoon of sugar, which was also rationed.

About one third of civilian food items were rationed during most of the war. The OPA issued rationing stamps, which were administered through local, volunteer-staffed rationing boards. Registration began in April 1942. One member of a family handled the registering (which included stating supplies on hand) and got a book for each member of the family. Coffee stamps were removed from books of children under fifteen and rationing books of departing servicemen were turned in.

Grocery shoppers spent red stamps for meat (except for poultry, which was not rationed), butter, fats, cheese, canned milk, and canned fish; green, brown, or blue stamps were used for canned vegetables, juices, baby food, and dried fruits. A shopper could earn two extra red points for every pound of meat drippings and other fats turned in as part of the save-fats campaign. Fats were used in several manufacturing processes, including the production of paints and munitions and the tanning of leather.

Shoppers scanned price tags showing both cents and points: A pound of ham, for example, cost 51 cents and 8 points. Canned and bottled goods carried points: a can of baked beans 10 points, a can of tomato juice 16 points, a 14-ounce bottle of catsup 8 points.

Other rationed goods included fuel oil, AUTOMOBILES, tires, bicycles, shoes, and typewriters. All rationing except sugar and rubber tires ended within two months of the Japanese SURRENDER. Rationing of tires stopped on Dec. 31, 1945. But sugar was still so scarce that rationing continued until June 1947.

Rations

The U.S. armed forces were undoubtedly the best-fed troops of any nation in the war. This was true in the field as well as for troops in garrison, with five basic types of field rations being issued.

The "C" and "K" rations were the most widely distributed, with the "K" ration originally designed for AIRBORNE units, but quickly adopted for all soldiers and Marines in forward areas.

The "C" and "K" rations could be eaten hot or cold, with small (pocket-size) paraffin heaters usually available as well as small gasoline stoves. The rations were well packaged, some able to resist humidity and immersion. The cans were opened by small, folding miniature can openers packaged with each ration, but invariably carried by troops on their DOG TAG chain. Some rations also contained mini-packs of cigarettes.

A Ration   Similar to the garrison ration, with about 70 percent fresh foods.

B Ration   Similar to "A" except that canned meats, fruits, and vegetables, and dehydrated eggs and potatoes were substituted for the fresh foods. Each package was enough for ten men for three meals (one day), hence it was sometimes called a 10-in-1. Two of the daily meals were hot and one cold.

C Ration   This popular meal contained ten cans with selections from the following: chicken and vegetables; frankfurters and beans; ham, eggs, and potatoes; ham and lima beans; meat and beans; meat and noodles; pork and beans; meat and rice; meat and vegetable stew; and meat and spaghetti. Also provided were cereals, crackers, jam, powdered drinks, and sugar.

D Ration   Sometimes called the "iron ration," this was a 600-calorie meal for emergency use (as in the Arctic) consisting of a chocolate bar made from cocoa, oat flour, and powdered skim milk.

K Ration   These were individual meal rations for breakfast. dinner, or supper. Breakfast contained a fruit bar, Nescafe drink powder, crackers, and a can of ham and eggs; lunch and dinner contained a can of potted meat or cheese, crackers, orange or lemon drink powder, sugar, chocolate or other dessert, and chewing gum.

All U.S. troops carried a two-piece aluminum "mess kit," which had a folding handle for ease of handling and washing. Both pieces as well as a three-piece utensil set could be hooked to the handle and immersed in water. The standard U.S. canteen, also aluminum, had a form-fitting cup, also with a folding handle for heating liquids. (The mess kit was carried in a backpack; the canteen had a canvas cover that hooked onto the soldier's or Marine's web belt.)

Rattle

Code name for meeting at Combined Operations headquarters in 1943 to discuss beach selection and deception plans for the NORMANDY INVASION.

Ratweek

Code name for British plan to attack German forces during their withdrawal from Yugoslavia, 1944.

Raubtier (Beast of Prey)

German code name for operation against the Volkhov pocket in the Soviet Union, March 1942.

Ravenous

Code name for British IV Corps plan for the recapture of northern Burma, 1944.

Razon Guided Bomb,

see GUIDED MISSILES.

Razzle

Code name for small British incendiary BOMB used early in the war.

Reckless

Code name for Allied assault force for HOLLANDIA, NEW GUINEA, April 1944.

Recoilless Rifles

Light artillery that sought to eliminate recoil by control of the escape of the propellant (burning) gas to the rear when a round was fired. The most feasible method was to have a perforated base in the shell casing and openings in the breech to vent and defuse the escaping gas. Recoilless rifles, used in World War I on the ground and in aircraft, were guns that could be more easily fired from confined spaces (e.g., buildings, jungle). They were lighter than conventional guns because of the absence of a recoil system, making them useful for AIRBORNE troops.

The British, German, Italian, and U.S. armies all developed recoilless guns during the war. The most audacious effort was a Luftwaffe project to attack shipping. This weapon—to be mounted in a DO 217 bomber—was a 350-mm (13.77-inch) recoilless gun that fired a 1,400-pound armor-piercing shell! The firing was compensated by the rearward ejection of a 1,400-pound cartridge case. The concept was perfected before World War II, but was never deployed; instead, the Luftwaffe did employ, at later stages of the war, smaller recoilless guns from aircraft.

Most recoilless gun developments were for ground forces. The British had several models available by the end of the war. Similar weapons were entering U.S. service, but their impact was minimal. The first U.S. recoilless rifle to see widespread service was the 57-mm M18, which weighed 40 pounds. It could be fired from a man's shoulder, or mounted on a tripod mounted on the ground or on a vehicle.

Red Ball Express

(1) A "special delivery" shipping service across the English Channel to the NORMANDY INVASION beachhead begun by the ALLIES on June 9, 1944, three days after the invasion. It provided 100 tons of shipping space per day for emergency requests from field commanders for special munitions and equipment.

(2) Truck-delivery service on the Continent, providing supplies for the ALLIED CAMPAIGN IN EUROPE. On Aug. 29, five days after the express began, 12,342 tons of supplies were delivered to forward units by nearly 6,000 trucks. By Sept. 5, the day on which the Red Ball's first mission was considered complete, 89,000 tons of supplies had been delivered to the supply dumps serving forward areas.

The Red Ball Express used two parallel highways between Saint-Lô, where the Normandy breakout had begun, and successive terminal points in France as the route was extended to keep up with advancing Allied troops. The route was marked with red ball signs for drivers; others, including hapless pedestrians, were told by signs in French and English that the route was closed to all unauthorized vehicles. To safely avoid a convoy, British soldiers said, you had to "not only get off the road but climb a tree." The Red Ball Express operated twenty-four hours a day and kept rolling until Dec. 1944.

Red Ball drivers were supposed to maintain a steady top speed of 25 mph, with ten-minute breaks before each even hour. Military policemen handled traffic and arrested violators, most of whom were speeders; 50 mph was a more typical speed. The drivers wore out tires and trucks at an unprecedented rate, causing some commanders to doubt the overall effectiveness of the effort. Another criticism: Some drivers simply dumped their cargoes wherever they could, and not at the designated depots, where they were needed.

Red Cross

A national and international humanitarian agency that aided both service personnel and civilians during the war. The American Red Cross, at government request, in Jan. 1941 set up a blood donor program. The blood (segregated into blood from blacks and whites) was processed into plasma and, later, into serum albumin, both of which were used for transfusions. Red Cross chapters collected 13,326,242 blood donations (usually a pint each) during the war.

Red Cross volunteers, freeing surgical-supply manufacturers for more urgent tasks, set up bandage-making assembly lines in churches, synagogues, and town community halls throughout the country. Volunteers, many of them mothers of servicemen, made as many as 3,000,000 wound dressings daily for a wartime total of more than 2.4 billion dressings. At military hospitals, other volunteers read and wrote letters for patients and taught crafts.

More than 27,000,000 food parcels, packed in the United States and shipped to Geneva, were distributed by the International Red Cross to American and Allied PRISONERS OF WAR in Europe. Prisoners held by Japan received about one tenth of the food, medicine, and other supplies sent by the Red Cross, primarily because Japan refused to allow neutral vessels to carry relief supplies in Japanese-controlled waters. (Two ships were allowed to carry Red Cross supplies to prisoners in April 1945. In a tragic incident, one of them, the *AWA MARU,* was torpedoed by the U.S. SUBMARINE *Queenfish.*) Red Cross workers followed liberating Allied forces in Europe, providing food and clothing to people in war-ravaged areas. The International Red Cross, which had managed to get some food parcels to

CONCENTRATION CAMPS, after the war aided relatives trying to find survivors.

Nearly 20,000 professional American Red Cross workers served with the armed services during the war. They operated clubs, rest homes, recreation centers, and canteens at military installations in the United States and overseas. Under an agreement with the UNITED SERVICE ORGANIZATIONS (USO), the Red Cross maintained its role as the prime provider of humanitarian aid at military facilities.

American Red Cross "clubmobiles" in European and North African combat areas (but not in the Pacific) typically provided coffee and doughnuts to soldiers near the front lines. Stories circulated throughout the war about servicemen having to pay for these snacks. But, under War Department regulations, the only fees the Red Cross could charge was for meals and lodgings at clubs. One of the most famous clubs was the Rainbow Corner in London, which remained open every day, twenty-four hours a day, for three and a half years.

Red Orchestra

The term *(Röte Kapelle)* given by German intelligence to an anti-NAZI, Soviet-directed network of ESPIONAGE and subversion rings operating in Germany during the war. Members of the ring included an officer attached to the Luftwaffe Chief of Staff and sources in the cipher section of the German Army Chiefs of Staff.

Among the secrets sent to the Soviets was information on Luftwaffe strength and troop movements on the EASTERN FRONT. The Soviets put the orchestra-delivered information to good use; by some German estimates, the orchestra espionage cost Germany 200,000 men.

In 1941 an *ABWEHR* direction-finding receiver in BERLIN discovered a secret radio transmitter operating in contact with MOSCOW, possibly from Belgium. Three members of the ring were arrested, but a high-ranking member, Leopold Trepper, was released because his credentials as a businessman from France were accepted by the Germans. Trepper ("the Grand Chef," *Abwehr* called him) was able to warn several others.

Other arrests followed in July 1942. About eighty-five suspects were rounded up in HAMBURG alone, along with another 118 in Berlin. Of the first wave of agents arrested, two killed themselves in custody, eight were hanged, and forty-one were beheaded. Among those arrested was a native American, Mildred E. Harnack, who met her German husband at the University of Wisconsin in the 1920s. She was executed on Feb. 16, 1943. (In 1967 the East German government issued commemorative postage stamps honoring Mildred Harnack and others for their work.)

From Aug. 1942 to Oct. 1942 the Germans "played back"—used as double agents—captured Red Orchestra agents who had, under torture, agreed to work against their Orchestra comrades. A special GESTAPO task force, *Sonderkommando Röte Kapelle,* was assigned to investigate the spy ring. The name of the force has caused some misunderstanding about the term.

A Central Intelligence Agency study of the Red Orchestra says that its information would have been even better used by the Soviets if it were not for the Stalin-inspired distrust of anything of German origin. The Red Orchestra, for example, had warned the Soviet Union of the planned German invasion in 1941, but Stalin dismissed the warning.

The CIA study traced the Red Orchestra to Soviet networks in Europe as early as 1930. During the war the network extended beyond Germany to Belgium, Holland, France, Switzerland, and Italy. "Several connections," the CIA study says, ". . . were found in England, Scandinavia, Eastern Europe, the United States, and elsewhere."

According to the CIA account, when Trepper was captured he became a triple agent—a double agent working for his original service. He managed to escape to Poland, then to Vienna. He returned to the Soviet Union, where he was arrested as a failed spy. He was sent to a Siberian labor camp, where he remained until after the death of Marshal STALIN in 1953. Trepper died in 1982.

Redoubt,

see NATIONAL REDOUBT.

Regenbogen (Rainbow)

Code name for attack by German pocket battleship *Lützow* and heavy cruiser *Hipper* on Allied convoys in Arctic, Dec. 1942–Jan. 1943.

Regiment

Major army formation and the principal component of U.S. infantry and AIRBORNE divisions. Regiments were the largest U.S. Army units with infantry, artillery, and armored components. DIVISIONS were usually commanded by a major general. The types of divisions in various armies included infantry/rifle, armored/TANK, ARTILLERY, airborne/parachute, mountain, CAVALRY, defense/fortress, and marine.

The regiment or BRIGADE was the principal troop component of a division; in World War II divisions were generally rectangular (with four regiments) or triangular (with three regiments). U.S. infantry divisions during the war had three infantry regiments; however, U.S. armored divisions had combat commands (designated A, B, and Reserve) that consisted of tank and infantry battalions. In some armies, the division's artillery was organized as a brigade or an additional regiment (the latter in the U.S. Marine Corps), while the U.S. Army grouped artillery units within the division as simply the "division artillery" (with the slang term "divarty" being used).

Reich Central Security Office

Main NAZI secret-police organization. The RSHA, as it was known by its German initials, was established in 1939 to unite all German police security organizations, including the GESTAPO. The chief of the RSHA was REINHARD HEYDRICH. When he was assassinated in June 1942, he was succeeded by ERNST KALTENBRUNNER.

Office III supervised the ACTION GROUPS (Einsatzgruppen) task forces, whose innocuous label hid their sinister purpose. They were extermination units that killed 2,000,000 men, women, and children in occupied countries, usually by shooting them and throwing them into pits.

Office VI of the RSHA supervised activities against JEWS and was headed by ADOLF EICHMANN.

Reinhard

Code name for the SS operation that systematically slaughtered the JEWS of Poland. Under SS *Brigadeführer* Odilo Globocnik, four CONCENTRATION CAMPS were set up in Poland and secretly designated as DEATH CAMPS. Nearly 3,000,000 Polish Jews were killed in them by Nov. 1943. Operation Reinhard, named after Nazi leader REINHARD HEYDRICH, had for its goals not only the extermination of Polish Jews but also the accumulation of their wealth. Globocnik reported that between April 1 and Dec. 13, 1943, alone he had obtained Jewish property, including eyeglasses and gold teeth, worth 180 million Reichsmarks. Globocnik, hunted down by Allied troops—and possibly by armed Jewish bands—reportedly killed himself in May 1945.

Reitsch, Hanna (1912–1979)

German aviatrix and fervent supporter of ADOLF HITLER. A onetime medical student, she left her university to take up gliding and flying. Her aviation feats included the world gliding record for WOMEN—initially five and a half hours, later extended to eleven and a half hours—and the world's altitude record for women in 1934 (9,184 feet). She flew a Focke-Achgelis Fa 61 HELICOPTER inside the Deutschlandhalle in BERLIN in Feb. 1938 to demonstrate the aircraft's agility to German leaders, marking the first indoor flight of a helicopter. In 1942 she became the only woman to be awarded the IRON CROSS (1st and 2nd Class), presented by Hitler for her flying feats.

During the war she flight-tested many aircraft, including JET-PROPELLED AIRCRAFT and the ROCKET-propelled ME 163 *KOMET*. Reportedly she wanted to pilot a V-1 BUZZ BOMB against England, but was denied this request by Hitler.

At the end of the war, with Soviet troops laying siege to Berlin, on April 26, 1945, she flew into the German capital with Gen. Ritter von Greim to bid her farewells to Hitler. The plane was hit by Soviet antiaircraft fire and Greim was wounded. After meeting with Hitler, who appointed Greim to head the Luftwaffe in place of the disgraced HERMANN GÖRING, Reitsch flew Greim out of Berlin.

After the war she resumed her flying career, continuing to set records for both gliding and powered flight. During her lifetime she set more than forty aviation records.

Remagen Bridge,

see LUDENDORFF RAILWAY BRIDGE.

Reno

Code name for Allied plans for operations in the Bismarck Archipelago.

Repulse

British battle cruiser sunk by Japanese bombers at the start of the war in the Pacific. In World War I the *Repulse* served with the Grand Fleet. Between the wars the ship was extensively modernized and in 1923–1924 made an around-the-world cruise. When the EUROPEAN WAR began she was with the British Home Fleet and from Oct. 1939 until Oct. 1941 saw action off Norway, in the North Atlantic, and in the Mediterranean. In May 1941 the *Repulse* participated in the hunt for the German battleship *BISMARCK* but, in part because of a fuel shortage, did not see action against the German ship.

In Oct. 1941 the *Repulse* was sent to the Indian Ocean. On Nov. 28 she rendezvoused with the new battleship *PRINCE OF WALES* at Colombo and they sailed to the fleet base at SINGAPORE. She and the *Prince of Wales* were the only Allied capital ships between the Mediterranean and the Hawaiian islands on Dec. 7, 1941. That afternoon (Dec. 8 in the Far East), the two British capital ships and four destroyers sortied to attack a Japanese troop landing reported on the coast of Malaya. When Allied aircraft could not be provided to support them, the ships turned back toward Singapore.

Late that morning the British ships were attacked by eighty-six twin-engine Japanese naval bombers, G3M NELL and G4M BETTY aircraft carrying BOMBS and aerial TORPEDOES. In the ensuing attack both ships were sunk. The *Repulse* was hit by one 550-pound bomb and five torpedoes. She heeled over and sank, taking with her 327 of her crew of some 960 officers and ratings (the survivors were rescued by accompanying destroyers). Her commanding officer, Capt. William Tennant, survived.

The *Prince of Wales* and *Repulse* were the first capital ships of any nation to be sunk by air attack while at sea. Three Japanese bombers were lost in the attack.

The *Repulse* was launched on Jan. 8, 1916, and completed on Aug. 16 the same year, she and her sister ship, *Renown*, being built in record time. The *Repulse* displaced 26,500 tons and was 794 feet long. Her main battery consisted of six 15-inch (381-mm) guns and lighter weapons. Steam turbines could drive her at 30 knots.

Rescue Ships

U.S. and British ships used to accompany CONVOYS to pick up survivors of sunken ships. Rescue ships were developed because using convoy escorts to pick up survivors would distract them from hunting attacking U-BOATS, while merchant ships stopping to pick up survivors became highly vulnerable to attack.

The first British convoy rescue ship was the small Dutch merchant ship *Hontestroom* of 1,875 gross tons, capable of 12½ knots. She sailed on her first voyage on Jan. 11, 1941. When the BATTLE OF THE ATLANTIC reached its climax in May 1943 the British had ten rescue ships at sea. The number grew to twenty-nine by the end of the EUROPEAN WAR, the last five being converted CORVETTES. The ships were manned by merchant crews with Navy gunners and other specialists on board.

The U.S. Navy adopted ships in production for the rescue role. Thirteen 180-foot, 795-ton submarine chaser escorts were converted to a PCE(R) configuration. In addition, the Navy built ninety wood-hull rescue tugs designated ATR, of which fifteen went to Britain. These were 1,652-foot, 852-ton tugs with special features provided. The large force of U.S. Coast Guard cutters regularly performed rescue functions, especially when they were assigned to convoys. All of these ships were manned by Navy or Coast Guard crews.

Rescue ships, whether ex-merchant or naval, were armed with antiaircraft guns. They carried additional lifeboats and floats, cargo nets that could be rigged over the sides for climbing aboard, and clothing and bedding for survivors. They also carried books and decks of playing cards for use by survivors during the voyage. The ships were staffed with extra cooks and medical personnel.

British records indicate that their ships rescued 4,190 survivors of Allied merchant ships and warships, plus four crewmen from U-boats.

Resources

The natural assets of warring nations. Decisions about the preservation or coveting of resources often underlay decisions about military strategy.

Japan, poor in resources, launched its Far East campaign (see JAPANESE CAMPAIGN IN THE FAR EAST) to get needed oil, tin, and other raw materials possessed by the DUTCH EAST INDIES, Malaya, Indonesia, and the Philippines. Japan was particularly in need of the resources that the United States cut off on the eve of war: petroleum and scrap metal. Germany, lacking rubber, developed synthetic rubber known as buna. Germany's need for natural resources of the East was so critical that U-BOATS were used to transport rubber and other scarce goods from Japan.

When France was about to fall and President ROOSEVELT realized that England would need U.S. help, he promised that the "material resources" of the United States would aid "the opponents of force."

To translate the abstract word *resources* into specific war aims, the U.S. government had begun stockpiling critical materials in 1939 with the importing and storage of about 250 commodities, including rubber, tin, mica, manila fiber for rope, and quinine for the prevention of malaria. To prevent a bidding war, the United States joined with the other major stockpiler, the UNITED KINGDOM, in the formation of the Combined Raw Materials Board in 1942. The board controlled the import and private-industry use of materials deemed necessary for defense.

The United States established three categories:

Strategic materials were essential to the national defense but entirely or principally available only from overseas sources. They included aluminum, antimony, chromium, manganese, manila fiber, mica, nickel, quinine, rubber, silk, tin, tungsten, and wool.

Critical materials were essential. They were attainable because they were available either domestically or through friendly trade but needed to be conserved and controlled. These included asbestos, cadmium, coffee, cork, cryolite, flaxseed, fluorspar, graphite, hides, iodine, kapok, nux vomica [the botanical source of strychnine], opium, phenol and picric acid [used in explosives], platinum, and chemicals used for tanning materials.

Essential materials were needed, presented no procurement problems, but could become critical. They included arsenic, abrasives, ethyl alcohol, he-lium, iron and steel, lead, molybdenum, paper and pulp, wheat, uranium, and zinc. Two other essential materials, sugar and petroleum (in the form of gasoline), were controlled through RATIONING.

When the United States entered the war after the attack on PEARL HARBOR, nearly 90 percent of U.S. crude rubber imports had already been cut off by Japan's capture of the Dutch East Indies and Malaya. The United States sent money and aid to Haiti for the growing of cryptostegia, a rubber-producing vine. This attempt to solve the American rubber shortage ended when U.S. scientists found ways to produce synthetic rubber. In 1944 the production of synthetic rubber reached nearly 800,000 tons.

The production of petroleum was one of the most important U.S. contributions to the war. U.S. forces overseas needed two tons of oil for every ton of munitions, vehicles, food, clothing, and medical supplies. In terms of demand and volume, petroleum was the most important of all munitions.

The oil that fueled the Allied victory came from twenty nations, including some neutral ones. But the bulk of Allied petroleum was produced, refined, and shipped by the United States. The Office of Petroleum Coordinator, under Secretary of the Interior HAROLD L. ICKES, handled U.S. oil policy.

Aviation fuel was a vital U.S. product. In May 1941, there were sixteen plants producing 100-octane fuel in the United States. By the end of 1941 there were seventy-three 100-octane plants. The U.S. refineries began producing 100-octane aviation gasoline in 1938 and were supplying it to England when the war started. (Octane numbers are used to measure the "antiknock" qualities of gasoline.)

During the BATTLE OF BRITAIN, RAF pilots flew planes powered by the 100-octane fuel against Luftwaffe planes flying on 87-octane fuel. On planes otherwise equal, those with greater octane had an edge in speed and rate of climb. An expert calculated that of two bombers flying to a target 1,000 miles away, the one using 100-octane fuel would carry a bomb load 5,000 pounds heavier than the bomber using 87-octane.

Other U.S. petroleum products that aided the war effort were toluene, used in making explosives, and butadiene, used in the manufacture of synthetic rubber.

Retribution

Allied code name for the highly successful operation that kept German and Italian forces from escaping from TUNISIA to Italy after being defeated in North Africa. The purpose of Retribution was summed up in a signal to the fleet from Sir ANDREW CUNNINGHAM: "Sink, burn, and destroy."

Reuben James (DD 245)

First U.S. warship sunk in the EUROPEAN WAR. Early on Oct. 31, 1941, while escorting a CONVOY bound for England, the twenty-one-year-old U.S. DESTROYER was sunk about 600 miles off Ireland. She was torpedoed by the German submarine *U-562*. The single TORPEDO blew up the *Reuben James*'s magazine and she broke in half, her bow section sinking immediately, her stern remaining afloat for five minutes. Exploding DEPTH CHARGES killed some of the survivors. Of her 160-man crew, only forty-five were saved. The *U-562* escaped despite depth-charge attacks by other destroyers in the convoy.

In his memoirs, *Kontradmiral* KARL DÖNITZ wrote, "If Germany were not to abandon altogether her Atlantic operation, in the middle of the war and to the great benefit of Britain, and if the United States persisted in its active intervention in the BATTLE OF THE ATLANTIC contrary to international law, such incidents as the torpedoing of the *Kearney* (DD 432) and the *Reuben James,* were bound to recur repeatedly."

The *Reuben James,* completed in 1920, was one of the 267 flush-deck, four-stack destroyers built for the U.S. Navy during World War I, none of which entered service before the 1918 armistice. The *Reuben James* displaced 1,190 tons standard, was 314⅓ feet long, and was armed with four 4-inch (102-mm) guns and twelve 21-inch (533-mm) torpedo tubes plus depth charges. In World War II these ships served in the U.S., British, and Soviet navies (with seven of the British ships being manned by Canadians).

Reunion

Code name for use of B-17 FLYING FORTRESS bombers to evacuate over 1,000 U.S. fliers from Rumania and nearly 300 from Bulgaria after Rumania quit the AXIS in Aug. 1944.

Rex

Japanese floatplane fighter. An excellent Kawanishi design, the N1K1 *Kyofu* (Mighty Wind), was given the Allied code name Rex. It was so successful in flight trials as a seaplane fighter that the land-based N1K1-J *Shiden* (code name GEORGE) was developed from the floatplane variant. Although only ninety-seven production floatplane variants were produced, they saw extensive combat service, mostly in the DUTCH EAST INDIES. Toward the end of the war they flew in homeland defense against Allied air attacks.

The prototype N1K1 flew on May 6, 1942, the first of four preproduction aircraft. The powerful engine of the prototype required contrarotating propellers to offset the expected airscrew torque. However, complexity of that arrangement led to a single propeller being fitted for the remaining aircraft. It was a mid-wing fighter with a large engine cowling and propeller spinner. It had a massive main float; the originally planned retractable wing floats were also discarded in favor of fixed stabilizing floats because of complexity.

The Rex had a top speed of 302 mph and a range of 655 miles, which could be extended in the search role to 1,035 miles. Armament consisted of two 7.7-mm machine guns and two 20-mm cannon.

It was a single-seat aircraft.

Reynaud, Paul (1878–1966)

French statesman who on March 21, 1940, succeeded ÉDOUARD DALADIER as premier and minister of foreign affairs. An opponent of the MUNICH PACT signed by his predecessor, Reynaud believed he could rally his nation against the Germans. Seven days after taking office he forged an agreement with England that neither country would make a separate peace with Germany. But soon after Germany launched the FRANCE AND LOW COUNTRIES CAMPAIGN in May 1940, the French government began to weaken. Reynaud shuffled his cabinet, bringing in Marshal HENRI PHILIPPE PÉTAIN, and making Gen. CHARLES DE GAULLE his military adviser. But the German juggernaut rolled across France, and on June 10 the government evacuated Paris, moving first to Tours and then, on June 14, to Bordeaux. On June 16 he resigned, knowing that his successor, Pétain, would surrender the nation to the Germans.

In Sept. 1940 Reynaud was jailed by the collaborationist VICHY FRANCE regime and later sent to a German prison. Testifying at the postwar trial of Pétain, Reynaud said he had hoped to carry on the war from French North Africa but was opposed by Pétain. Reynaud was elected to the new constituent assembly in 1946 and resumed his political career.

Rheingold (Rhine gold)

German program to create six new divisions by calling up previously deferred men, Jan. 1942.

Rheinübung (Rhine Exercise)

German code name for the breakout of the battleship *BISMARCK* and the heavy cruiser *Prinz Eugen* into the Atlantic CONVOY lanes, May 1941.

Rhine Crossings

As the ALLIES pushed across Europe and neared the Rhine River early in 1945, HITLER fumed at the widespread desertions and surrenders of his troops. The Rhine had not been crossed by an enemy since Napoleon did it in 1805. Hitler saw the Rhine as a "they-shall-not-pass" symbol of the steadfastness of the THIRD REICH. He approved orders that any commander who gave up a town or communications post was to be put to death. The order especially included bridges across the Rhine.

The campaign for the Rhine bridges began with the March 5, 1945, Allied capture of COLOGNE. The capture did not give the Allies an avenue across the river because most of the city lies on the western bank of the Rhine and German troops destroyed the bridges in their retreat from the city.

Gen. GEORGE S. PATTON's Third Army, reaching the Rhine near Koblenz, was similarly frustrated. But on March 7, as Patton planned an assault crossing *without* a bridge, American troops found a bridge not yet blown up—the LUDENDORFF RAILWAY BRIDGE at Remagen. The passage of U.S. troops across this bridge began the Rhine crossings.

Within days Patton's Third Army crossed the Rhine at Oppenheim, south of Mainz. Allied ground and AIRBORNE forces continued to capture bridges with the help of air support. By March 23 the Allies had a bridgehead 35 miles wide and 12 miles deep. By the beginning of April there were seven Allied armies across the Rhine.

U.S. Army combat engineers (many of them black soldiers consigned to labor units under the Army's SEGREGATION policy) built more than sixty bridges—railroad bridges, highway bridges, and floating bridges of pontoons and rafts—across the Rhine. The 2,800-foot railroad bridge at Mainz (called the Franklin D. Roosevelt Memorial Bridge) was built in nine days and twenty-two hours, beating the ten-day record set by Julius Caesar's engineers in bridging the Rhine.

Rhubarb

British code name for RAF fighter-bomber attacks flown from bases in England against the German-held coast of France in mid-1941.

Ribbentrop, Joachim von (1893–1946)

German minister of foreign affairs. A well-traveled salesman and businessman, Ribbentrop dabbled in military and diplomatic activities after World War I. He went to work as a salesman for the German champagne company Henckel-Trocken and in 1920 married Anneliese Henckel, daughter of one of the owners. He wangled an adoption from an aunt with a noble title and thus was able to add *von* to his name.

He did not join the NAZI Party until 1932, on the eve of ADOLF HITLER's triumphant arrival at the chancellorship. But Ribbentrop's social connections aided Hitler so much that the snobbish, pompous Ribbentrop rapidly became an important counselor. Hitler held secret conferences and formed his 1933 Cabinet in Rippentrop's palatial BERLIN home.

For political purposes, Hitler at first had to appear to rely on the traditional German Foreign Ministry. In reality, he fostered what became known as *Dienststelle Ribbentrop* (Ribbentrop Bureau), a competitive foreign office operated by the ambitious ex-champagne salesman. The bureau, which had more than 300 employees, was abolished when Hitler appointed Ribbentrop foreign minister in 1938.

Two years before, he had been appointed German ambassador to England. An outraged and powerful enemy, HERMANN GÖRING, protested. But, he said later, Hitler "pointed out to me that Ribbentrop knew 'Lord So and So' and 'Minister So and So.' To which I replied, 'Yes, but the difficulty is that they know Ribbentrop.'"

Göring was right. Hitler had made a disastrous appointment. Ribbentrop dismayed his fellow diplomats or, on occasion, amused them. His two years in England can be envisioned by one incident: Presented to King GEORGE VI, Ribbentrop shot out his right arm in the Nazi salute and shouted "Heil Hitler!"—twice.

Ribbentrop had known King George's predecessor, his brother, who reigned briefly as Edward VIII until his abdication "for the woman I love." Ribbentrop, thinking that the ex-king could be restored to the throne after Germany's conquest of England, worked with his friend, FRANZ VON PAPEN, to kidnap the Duke of Windsor. (See WILLI.)

Probably no high-ranking Nazi official was as detested and ridiculed. Historian WILLIAM L. SHIRER, who, as a correspondent in BERLIN in the 1930s saw Rippentrop frequently, described him as "incompetent and lazy, vain as a peacock, arrogant and without humor." Count GALEAZZO CIANO, the Italian Foreign Minister, called Rippentrop "vain, frivolous, and loquacious" and said in his famous diary, "The Duce [BENITO MUSSOLINI] says you only have to look at his head to see that he has a small brain." JOSEPH GOEBBELS said of him: "Von Ribbentrop bought his name, he married his money, and he swindled his way into office."

After the JULY 20 PLOT against Hitler's life in 1944, Ribbentrop fell into disfavor because people in his foreign ministry were implicated. But when he was put on trial at Nuremberg for WAR CRIMES, he said, "Even with all I know, if in this cell Hitler should come to me and say, 'Do this!' I would still do it."

Ribbentrop was found guilty of all four types of major war crimes and sentenced to death. He was the first of the condemned Nazis to be hanged.

Richardson, Adm. James O. (1878–1974)

U.S. admiral fired by President ROOSEVELT for his opposition to basing the U.S. FLEET at PEARL HARBOR.

Richardson served in and commanded several surface ships. Ashore he held the important posts of Navy budget officer and Chief of the Bureau of Navigation, which handled personnel matters. In June 1939 Richardson took command of the U.S. Fleet's Battle Force as a full admiral, in command of the main strike force of the fleet.

The following January he became Commander in Chief U.S. Fleet, second only to the Chief of Naval Operations in the Navy seniority. Based on the U.S. West Coast, the Fleet periodically conducted maneuvers near HAWAII. The spring 1940 maneuver—Fleet Problem XXI—was held during April and early May between the West Coast and Hawaii. On April 29 Richardson received a message from the Chief of Naval Operations, Adm. HAROLD R. STARK, advising him that because of events in Europe, the Fleet might be ordered to remain in Hawaiian waters. On May 7 Richardson was further directed by Stark to announce that the fleet was remaining in Hawaii "to accomplish some things [Richardson] wanted to do while here."

Keeping the Fleet at Pearl Harbor caused personnel problems, there was not enough fuel available, there were insufficient docking and repair facilities, and Richardson felt that the fleet was more exposed to Japanese attack. Richardson protested to Stark, but to no avail.

Richardson then made two trips to Washington to protest the basing policy, in July and again in Oct. 1940. On the latter trip he met with President Roosevelt and voiced his opposition to keeping the fleet in Hawaii. Richardson told a PEARL HARBOR INVESTIGATION by Congress of the conversation. The President, Richardson called, said: "Despite what you believe, I know that the presence of the fleet in the Hawaiian area, has had, and is now having, a restraining influence of the actions of Japan."

Richardson: "Mr. President, I still do not believe it, and I know that our fleet is disadvantageously disposed for preparing for or initiating war operations."

Later Secretary of the Navy FRANK KNOX told Richardson, "You hurt the President's feelings by what you said to him."

Meanwhile, ships and aircraft were being detached from the Fleet and sent into the Atlantic for NEUTRALITY PATROL, again over protests from Richardson. In Feb. 1941 Richardson was relieved as Fleet commander by Adm. HUSBAND E. KIMMEL.

Richardson returned to his permanent rank of rear admiral; he served briefly on the Navy's General Board, and then served as executive vice president of the Navy Relief Society, where he remained until May 1945. He was formally retired from the Navy in Oct. 1942 and given the rank of full admiral on the retired list; he was retained on active duty as a retired officer until March 1946.

Rickenbacker, Edward (1890–1973)

A World War I ACE (twenty-six German planes downed), Rickenbacker served as a civilian in World War II. Offered a commission as a major general, the World War I Army captain refused, saying he would serve the war better as blunt-talking captain of industry, paying his own expenses. (He was president of Eastern Air Lines.)

At the request of Lt. Gen. H. H. ARNOLD, commanding general of Army Air Forces, Rickenbacker studied U.S. aviation training methods and went to England to compare aircraft production there with U.S. production. Oct. 21, 1942, while he was flying to PORT MORESBY on a Pacific inspection mission, the B-17 FLYING FORTRESS in which he was a passenger became lost and ran out of fuel. The plane crash-landed, and Rickenbacker and the others on the plane were given up for dead. But they survived on rafts for twenty-seven days and were rescued. The news startled the nation and became a well-publicized saga of the war.

Ridgway, Lt. Gen. Matthew B. (1895—)

Leading U.S. AIRBORNE commander. On Dec. 7, 1941, Ridgway was in the Army's War Plans Division (with DWIGHT D. EISENHOWER). He had already acquired a reputation as intense, "charismatic and able," in the words of Gen. OMAR BRADLEY.

Bradley, recently placed in command of the unsatisfactory 82nd Infantry DIVISION, requested Ridgway as his Assistant Division Commander. Their efforts completely renovated the division, at which point Bradley was appointed to the 28th Infantry Division (National Guard) to work similar wonders, and Ridgway took command of the 82nd. Soon after Ridgway assumed command, the 82nd was redesignated an airborne division and Ridgway,

who had never had parachute training, remained as its commander. Ridgway learned as he went—making parachute jumps, GLIDER assaults, and, to reassure the troops, riding as passenger in a glider being put through stunts. In March 1943 he took the 82nd to North Africa to prepare for an air drop on SICILY as part of Operation Husky.

Ridgway did not jump with his troops at Sicily, feeling that he could better direct operations from a command ship than from a forward position ashore. Once ashore, Ridgway proved himself a *"great* combat commander," according to his deputy commander, Brig. Gen. JAMES GAVIN. "Lots of courage. He was right up front every minute. Hard as flint and full of intensity. . . ."

Ridgway's paratroopers were used during the first stages of AMPHIBIOUS LANDING at SALERNO in Sept. 1943 when German counterattacks threatened the beachhead and the ITALIAN CAMPAIGN. The 82nd fought on the ground for almost two months until they were withdrawn to prepare for the NORMANDY INVASION.

By then Ridgway was seen as the leading American expert on airborne operations. Bradley's confidence in Ridgway's experience and leadership led him to insist, in the face of considerable opposition by other planners, that the 82nd and 101st Airborne Divisions be dropped behind the German defenses in Normandy.

Although these forces did not achieve their objectives, they disoriented the defenses and contributed to the landings' success. Ridgway dropped with the 82nd, but was unable to direct the battle, which was conducted at the small-unit scale until the airborne forces linked up with sea-landed forces.

After Normandy, Ridgway was given command of the XVIII Airborne CORPS (82nd, 101st, and 17th Airborne Divisions) as part of the AIRBORNE ARMY. Several airborne operations designed to "outflank" German defenders during August and early September in 1944 were canceled because of the rapid Allied progress on the ground. The one that was not canceled—Operation MARKET-GARDEN—achieved only limited success and suffered heavy casualties. Ridgway had little to do with the planning or conduct of that operation, which many historians have sharply criticized.

During the winter fighting, including the AR-

DENNES offensive, Ridgway's 82nd and 101st were heavily engaged. He additionally commanded the 30th Infantry and 7th Armored Divisions during their successful efforts to shore up the northern shoulder of the breach. He then led the XVIII Airborne Corps on its drop across the Rhine, which was counted a success but which, as always, resulted in heavy equipment losses. After helping to seal the Ruhr pocket, Ridgway's four-division Corps (two airborne, one infantry, one armored) led the race across the Elbe River to the Danish border ahead of the Red Army.

At war's end, Ridgway was one of the most highly regarded field commanders in the U.S. Army. He later commanded the UNITED NATIONS forces in Korea and had a highly influential tour as Army Chief of Staff from 1953 to 1955. During that time, he successfully dissuaded President Eisenhower from taking over the French role in INDOCHINA (Vietnam).

Rita

This was the Japanese Navy's first four-engine bomber, being designated G8N *Renzan* (Mountain range) with the Allied code name Rita. It was too late for the war. Although Japanese twin-engine bombers achieved the range and payload of many Western four-engine aircraft, by the end of 1942 the Japanese Navy concluded that a four-engine aircraft was required to perform long-range strikes against enemy bases in support of the fleet. In Feb. 1943 the Nakajima firm was directed to design a four-engine attack bomber, the G8N1 *Renzan*. (The Japanese Navy was already operating four-engine aircraft, the H6K MAVIS and H8K EMILY flying boats.)

Four prototypes were built, the first flown on Oct. 23, 1944. Flight tests went well, but were disrupted by U.S. air attacks, with the third prototype destroyed on the ground in a U.S. Navy strike. The shortage of resources forced cancellation of the planned construction of forty-eight aircraft, including sixteen prototypes and trials aircraft, to have been operational by Sept. 1945. When the war ended, the Navy was still considering the possible production of an all-steel variant (G8N3). The canceled G8N2 variant was to have carried the BAKA man-guided BOMB.

The Rita was a mid-wing, four-engine aircraft, with a large conventional tail fin. The plane's tricycle undercarriage was fully retractable, with the main wheels being housed in large inboard engine nacelles.

Maximum speed was 368 mph with a range estimated at 2,450 miles, being extended in an overload condition to 4,640 miles. A large internal bomb bay was to hold a maximum of two 4,409-pound bombs. Alternatively, the G8N2 was to carry a Baka. Defensive armament was heavy: twin 20-mm cannon in power-operated dorsal, ventral, and tail turrets; two 13-mm machine guns in a power-operated nose turret; and single flexible 13-mm guns in the waist positions.

Ro

Code name for Japanese air operations to augment forces at RABAUL and delay Allied offensive action.

Road's End

U.S. code name for scuttling of twenty-four surviving Japanese submarines at sea on April 1, 1946. (See also DEAD DUCK.)

Roast

Code name for Allied operation to clear Comacchio Spit, Italy.

Robinson, 2nd Lt. Jackie (1919–1972)

Black athlete and Army lieutenant. Robinson, a football, baseball, basketball, and track star at the University of California at Los Angeles, was inducted into the Army in 1942. He applied for officers training school and was turned down. At Fort Riley, Kan., he happened to meet a fellow black athlete, Master Sgt. JOE LOUIS, the heavyweight champion of the world.

Louis called Truman Gibson, a black civic leader who was an adviser on racial issues to Secretary of War HENRY L. STIMSON. As a result of Louis and Gibson's intervention, Robinson did go to officer training and was commissioned a second lieutenant.

Back at Fort Riley he became the morale officer for black troops. (A SEGREGATION policy kept troops racially separate.) Robinson and Louis teamed up to improve recreational facilities for black troops on the base. Robinson was transferred to Fort Hood, Texas. When a bus driver told him to move to the back of a bus, Robinson refused and allegedly threatened the driver. Robinson was acquitted in a court-martial. But he knew that he was a marked man because of his refusal to quietly accept racial discrimination in the Army.

He applied for a medical discharge because of an ankle injured in football. He became a professional baseball player and in 1947 joined the Brooklyn Dodgers, becoming the first black player to break the baseball color barrier.

Rochefort, Capt. Joseph J. (1899–1976)

Head of code-breaking at the U.S. Navy's Pacific FLEET headquarters at PEARL HARBOR.

A graduate of the University of California, Rochefort enlisted in the Navy during World War I. After attaining officer rank he became a Japanese language specialist, studying for three years in Japan, and alternated duty at sea with intelligence work ashore. When assistant operations and intelligence officer on the staff of the Pacific Fleet commander in the 1930s, the admiral noted that Rochefort was "one of the most outstanding officers of his rank" whose "judgment and ability are truly remarkable," . . . especially for a non–Naval Academy graduate, he added.

In 1941 Rochefort established a team of code-breakers at Pearl Harbor. His team's efforts made a direct contribution to the U.S. successes at CORAL SEA, MIDWAY, and later battles.

In Oct. 1942 Rochefort was reassigned to WASHINGTON without any foreknowledge, but was soon given a command, the prerequisite for later promotion to flag officer. The dispute between the Navy's code-breaking staffs at Pearl Harbor and in Washington had led to shabby and even malicious treatment of Rochefort by the Navy's leadership, including blocking a recommendation by the Pacific Fleet commander, CHESTER W. NIMITZ, that Rochefort be given the Distinguished Service Medal for his role in the code-breaking effort that led to the victory at Midway. That was the highest award given to men who were not in combat. For a command Rochefort was given a non-self-propelled floating dry dock. He retired shortly after the war.

After the war, when Nimitz learned of why the medal had not been given to Rochefort he wrote to the Navy Department on Rochefort's behalf. But not until 1986, through the efforts of then-Secretary of the Navy John Lehman, was the Distinguished Service Medal awarded posthumously to Rochefort, with President Reagan personally presenting it to his family at the White House.

See also EDWIN T. LAYTON.

Rocket

British code name for reinforcement of MALTA, June 1941.

Rockets

Unguided missiles used as weapons and signals. Rockets were relatively effective, lightweight, and inexpensive weapons, used by air, ground, and naval forces.

Ground and naval forces used rockets to bombard enemy-held areas. While the rockets lacked the guns' accuracy and ability to penetrate fortified structures, rockets would saturate an area, inflicting heavy casualties on exposed troops. In amphibious landings rocket-firing ships forced defending troops to keep under cover until the assaulting troops were ashore.

United States The U.S. Army employed two principal rocket launchers during the war. The "calliope," a 60-tube launcher fitted atop a SHERMAN TANK, fired 4.5-inch (114-mm) rockets independently or in a salvo; the tank retained its full combat capability. Sets of multiple 4.5-inch rocket tubes were also mounted on standard 6×6 TRUCKS. These launchers, fixed on the trucks, could not traverse, but could be elevated from +45° to −5°.

U.S. and British fire-support ships were generally converted landing ships and craft. The "ultimate" support ship was the U.S. Navy's LSMR series, which had twenty automatic-loading, rapid-fire 5-inch (127-mm) rocket launchers, plus a single 5-inch gun.

Aircraft employed rockets primarily to attack ground troops and submarines on or near the surface. U.S. fighter-type aircraft employed 5-inch rockets against ground targets; Allied antisubmarine aircraft in the Atlantic area used them against surfaced submarines. The American 5-inch aircraft rocket had a 50-pound explosive warhead, highly effective against ground targets. Later versions were designated HVAR (High-Velocity Aircraft Rocket) but were popularly called "Holy Moses." In 1944 the Navy introduced an 11.75-inch (298.5-mm) diameter aircraft rocket called Tiny Tim; it carried a potent, 150-pound warhead for use against ground targets.

Britain   In the antisubmarine role various British carrier- and land-based fighter and attack aircraft carried eight 3-inch, rail-launched rockets with 25-pound solid warheads that could punch a hole in the pressure hull of a U-BOAT. The first such U-boat kill was by a naval SWORDFISH from the British ESCORT CARRIER *Archer;* the plane's rockets damaged the *U-752,* forcing her to surface and then scuttle in May 1943. As British military historian John Terraine has noted: "The moral effect of this weapon, especially against young and inexperienced U-boat crews, was as great as its destructive effect."

The British also developed ship-launched rockets that carried aloft trailing wires, intended to foul the propellers of attacking German aircraft. This device was of marginal value.

Germany   During the war the Germans developed rockets as ground artillery, air-to-ground, and air-to-air weapons. Several fighter aircraft flown by the Luftwaffe had various rockets for use against Allied bombers. One device—not ready for combat when the war ended—fired 400 antiaircraft rockets within a minute. (This concept lead to the postwar U.S. Mighty Mouse rocket system.)

The most-used German rocket weapon was the six-tube *der Nebelwerfer* (smoke thrower). Originally developed to launch smoke shells, it was an antipersonnel weapon although its shrapnel could damage tanks and other vehicles. It was both towed and mounted on vehicles. It was first used on the EASTERN FRONT in 1941. Later used in North Africa and Western Europe, the rockets were called "Screaming Meemies" by their American victims.

In addition, the Germans developed two rocket-propelled interceptor aircraft, the BA 349 and ME 163, the latter becoming operational at the end of the war. They were the only rocket-propelled fighters ever built.

The German Navy also experimented with bombardment rockets, including launching them from underwater. The submarine *U-511,* on trials, launched several from a depth of almost 200 feet.

USSR   The Soviets pioneered rocket weapon development in the 1920s and 1930s; the Soviet Army made extensive use of rocket bombardment, their weapons generally referred to as "STALIN's organ" or *Katyusha,* the latter for a popular song. As early as 1939, in aerial combat with Japanese aircraft over Manchuria, Soviet fighters used air-to-air rockets. During the war against Germany the Soviets used these and air-to-ground rockets against tanks with great effect.

The fighter-interceptor variant of the Soviet La-7 was fitted with a small rocket motor to boost combat speed. Disposable rockets were also used to accelerate aircraft takeoffs, and were fitted to a number of Soviet as well as British, German, and U.S. aircraft. These rockets usually were attached immediately before takeoff and provided additional thrust for a few seconds before burning out.

Roger

Code name for Allied capture of Pkuhet Island off Kra Isthmus, Burma.

Röhm, Ernst (1887–1934)

Early supporter of HITLER and organizer of the SA storm troopers. Röhm, erratic and power hungry, saw himself as the leader of a massive military force serving Hitler. "Since I am an immature and wicked man," he once said, "war and unrest appeal to me more than good bourgeois order."

After the NAZI election victories of 1930, Röhm organized a force of some 170,000 thugs and brawlers who took Hitler's anti-Communist battles into the streets. Röhm built the force to more than 2,000,000 men and campaigned to make a "people's army" consisting of his storm troopers and the regular German Army. Hitler's generals were appalled at the idea and actively fought against it.

Nazi leaders HERMANN GÖRING and HEINRICH HIMMLER, conspiring against Röhm, accused him of two crimes they knew Hitler would not tolerate: Röhm's disloyalty and his homosexual liaisons with a coterie of SA officers. On the night of June 30, 1934—the Night of the Long Knives, as it came to be called by the Nazis—Hitler launched the Blood Purge in which Röhm was assassinated, along with the leadership of the SA. Between seventy and 100 SA members were murdered.

Rokossovsky, Marshal Konstantin (1896–1968)

Leading Soviet field commander. Rokossovsky had key roles in the battle of STALINGRAD and subsequent operations in the SOVIET OFFENSIVE CAMPAIGN.

After being drafted into the czarist Army in 1914 he rose to the rank of sergeant in the CAVALRY. He joined the Bolshevik forces during the Civil War. He held a number of commands in the 1930s, rising to a corps commander in Manchuria. But in Aug. 1937 he was arrested during the STALIN purges and charged with spying for Japan and Poland. He was imprisoned until March 1940 when he was reinstated in the Army.

His adroit command of the IX Mechanized Corps in the UKRAINE during the German invasion of the Soviet Union in 1941 led to his being called to the attention of Gen. GEORGI ZHUKOV. In July 1941 he was given command of the Sixteenth Army, which participated in the defense of MOSCOW. In late 1942 he directed the Don Front armies that made the final assault on the German Sixth Army at Stalingrad. After the decisive battle he was promoted to colonel-general in Jan. 1943 and was promoted again in April. Under Zhukov's sponsorship he held major commands at the battle of KURSK and the subsequent Soviet drive into Poland.

For the final thrust into Germany he was assigned to the Second Belorussian Front, which in the final days of the war pushed his command north toward the Baltic and then covered the northern flank of the Soviet assault on BERLIN.

After the war Rokossovsky was CinC of Soviet forces in Poland from 1945 to 1949, and then minister of defense of Poland in 1949–1956, after which he served as chief inspector and deputy minister of defense of the USSR.

He was decorated twice with the HERO OF THE SOVIET UNION.

Roma

Italian battleship; the first major warship ever sunk by a GUIDED MISSILE.

The *Roma* was one of four battleships of the *Vittorio Veneto* class, three of which were completed in 1940–1942 (the last never finished because of steel shortages). While the first two ships of the class engaged in extensive action during the war, the *Roma*, completed in June 1942, saw no active service. She was hit by Allied bombs while at La Spezia in June 1943. Then, on Sept. 9, 1943, in accord with the Italian SURRENDER terms, she sailed with other units of the Italian Fleet for MALTA. En route, the Italian ships were heavily attacked by German DO 217 aircraft launching FRITZ-X guided bombs. Two struck the *Roma*.

This class of warships incorporated an advanced protective scheme to defeat plunging shells and BOMBS. However, the Fritz-X with a 3,454-pound semi-armor-piercing bomb as warhead penetrated the *Roma*'s armor and exploded. Inrushing sea water and the rupture of electric cables caused fires. As the *Roma* fell out of formation, a second Fritz-X struck her, causing more fires and flooding. Moments after the second hit, the magazine of a 381-mm (15-inch) gun turret detonated, and the ship rapidly capsized, broke in two, and sank. There were 595 survivors from her crew of 1,849.

The same day her sister ship *Italia* (ex-*Littorio*) was also struck by a Fritz-X, but survived.

The *Roma* was built by Cantieri Riunniti dell' Anriatico at Trieste. She was launched on Sept. 6, 1940. With a standard displacement of 35,000 tons, the ship was 789½ feet long, and had steam turbines providing a speed of 31 knots. Her main armament was nine 381-mm guns, with a secondary battery of twelve 152-mm (6-inch) guns and a heavy antiaircraft battery.

Rome

Capital of Italy and a key objective of the long and frustrating ITALIAN CAMPAIGN. The Eternal City lived through three phases during the war: imperial showplace of BENITO MUSSOLINI's Italy; the German occupation that threatened its existence; and the military campaign that made it an objective and a potential target of Allied destruction.

Mussolini's Rome Under the absolute rule of Mussolini, who commissioned an ambitious city plan, Rome in the 1920s and 1930s became what he envisioned as the capital of a new Roman Empire. Massive buildings and triumphant avenues advertised Mussolini's grandiose vision. Mussolini's black-shirted troops paraded frequently along Roman avenues. Roman wits said that Italy had gotten the *passo romano* (goose step) from Germany and Germany had gotten the *passo Brennero* (BRENNER PASS) from Italy. In a typical show of homage to his fellow dictator, Mussolini bedecked the city with Fascist and NAZI banners for a visit of ADOLF HITLER in May 1938.

German Occupation　By late 1941, as Germans poured troops into Italy, they began an unacknowledged occupation, and Rome saw a growing German presence. In 1942, with the Italian people wearying of both Mussolini and war, he turned increasingly to the Germans for support and inspiration.

Mussolini openly accepted Nazi ANTI-SEMITISM and ordered that JEWS be rounded up and handed over to the Germans. Christians, especially in Rome, resisted the order and saved many Jews. (After the war the chief rabbi of Rome converted to Catholicism in gratitude, he said, for the help that Christians gave Jews under the German occupation.)

The Allied invasion of SICILY in July 1943 toppled Mussolini, launched the series of events leading to Italy's SURRENDER on Sept. 3, and, with Germany now considering Italy an enemy, put Rome, a military stronghold, in peril of attack by the ALLIES. Mussolini's successor, Marshal PIETRO BADOGLIO, fled to the south.

On Jan. 22, 1944, while U.S. troops were landing at ANZIO, about 30 miles southeast of Rome, Allied radio messages beamed at the city said, "The hour has arrived for Rome and all Italians to fight in every possible way and with all forces. Sabotage the enemy . . . block his roads of retreat, destroy his communications to the last wire, strike against him everywhere . . . until our troops have arrived." The Roman underground, leery of Allied promises, did not immediately react. But the Rome Committee of National Liberation began secretly preparing a government that would replace Badoglio.

The Allied landing at Anzio produced exultation in Rome, but that began to fade when days and weeks passed and the German grip on the city tightened. Rations dwindled. Meat practically disappeared. Electricity was "zoned" so that each night a different area of Rome went without power.

The Germans decreed the death penalty for a variety of offenses, ranging from aiding escaped prisoners to failing to show up for work. Hundreds of Romans were hauled off to the five-story GESTAPO headquarters on the Via Tasso, questioned under torture, and shot. Many were never heard from again, for they were killed, and then "turned into mist" under the *Nacht und Nebel Erlass,* Night and Fog Decree.

On March 23, 1944, a group of GUERRILLAS planted a bomb that killed thirty-two German police troops. Retaliation was swift by *Generalleutnant* Kurt Maelzer, the commander of German troops, who styled himself the "King of Rome." He ordered the killing of every person living on the street where the explosion occurred. Talked out of this by a German diplomat, Maelzer ordered that ten Romans be killed for every German who died.

There were not enough Gestapo prisoners at the moment, so the Germans rounded up Jews and suspected anti-Fascists. A total of 335 Romans (fifteen over the quota) were taken to one of the Fosse Ardeatine caves. They were shot, their bodies were covered with lime, and then the tunnel leading to the bodies was sealed by a blast of dynamite. The Germans published an announcement about the retaliation in Rome's newspapers.

Military Objective　U.S. Gen. MARK W. CLARK and British Field Marshal Viscount HAROLD ALEXANDER were in what Alexander perceived to be a race for Rome. "I can only assume," Alexander said later, "that the immediate lure of Rome for its publicity value persuaded him to switch the direction of his advance."

More than 500 U.S. planes had bombed railroad marshaling yards and airfields in Rome on July 19, 1943, after President ROOSEVELT had said that the Allies would respect only the neutrality of VATICAN CITY. Nearly a year later, as Allied troops neared the city, Pope PIUS XII met with German generals and diplomats urging that the city not be defended.

Some Allied officers feared that the Germans were planning a STALINGRAD-style street-by-street defense that would devastate the city. *Generalfeldmarschall* ALBERT KESSELRING, commander of German forces in Italy, tried to contact Allied leaders through the Vatican to work out a way to guarantee preservation of Church properties, but his offer was ignored. He then declared Rome to be an OPEN CITY.

The Allies knew the city was a military base, a vital link in the German supply line. The Allies said they would treat Rome as an open city when the Germans withdrew their military apparatus and headquarters. The Germans began withdrawing at the last moment, leaving behind a rear guard that slowly pulled out of the city. The feared battle for Rome never occurred.

Clark's Fifth ARMY troops took the city on June 4, 1944, against little opposition. Clark staged a victorious liberation celebration and then quickly pushed on to continue the war in northern Italy. On the Fourth of July a U.S. color guard raised in the center of Rome the same U.S. flag that had flown over the Capitol in Washington on Dec. 8, 1941, when war was declared on Japan, and on Dec. 11, when war was declared on Germany and Italy.

Romeo

Code name for French COMMANDO force that landed at Cap Negré in the Mediterranean.

Rommel, *Generalfeldmarschall* Erwin (1891–1944)

One of the best known and most capable German generals of the war, Erwin Rommel, was saluted by foes as well as by Germans. After the war WINSTON CHURCHILL wrote: "His ardour and daring inflicted grievous disasters upon us, but he deserves the salute which I made to him—and not without some reproaches from the public—in the House of Commons in January, 1942, when I said of him, 'We have a very daring and skillful opponent against us, and, may I say across the havoc of war, a great general.' "

A delicate child and initially educated at home because of his health, he became an officer cadet in 1910. In World War I he saw action in France, Rumania, and Italy, was wounded twice, and highly decorated. When the EUROPEAN WAR began he was commandant of HITLER's field headquarters in Poland. He was soon given command of the 7th PANZER Division with which, as a brigadier general, he participated in Germany's FRANCE AND LOW COUNTRIES CAMPAIGN in May–June 1940. His tanks spearheaded the German breakthrough near the Meuse. He narrowly escaped capture when the British counterattacked on May 21, but again taking the offensive he almost cut off a large part of the British Army, including the 3rd Division under BERNARD MONTGOMERY. Near Arras on May 21 Rommel turned back the British by attacking with 88-MM FLAK antiaircraft guns that were improvising as antitank guns. He would elaborate on this makeshift ingenuity during the NORTH AFRICA CAMPAIGN and the NORTHWEST AFRICA CAMPAIGN with deadly effect.

Rommel's rise to world fame began when he arrived in Tunisia on Feb. 12, 1941, to aid the Italian forces that had been chased back from the Egyptian border by British forces. Over the next two and a half years Rommel's AFRIKA KORPS would launch three eastward attacks that he would press furiously until his goals of Cairo and the Suez Canal were almost within sight. After the fall of TOBRUK to the Germans on June 21, 1942, HITLER promoted Rommel to Field Marshal. When he got the telegram from the Führer announcing the promotion, Rommel is said to have remarked, "It would be better if he had sent me another division." Rommel never received the weapons and supplies he was promised (for example, to the end of Oct. 1941 of 60,000 tons of supplies promised to Rommel by the Italians, only 8,093 tons reached his forces at Benghazi).

Rommel's attacks never quite succeeded in their aims. Each time, stiffening British resistance and the failure of his supply line brought the offensive to a halt. His strength—persistence in driving forward—proved also to be his weakness as he ran down his mechanized forces. His final check came at the first battle of EL ALAMEIN in Aug. 1942; illness forced his return to Germany in September. Rommel returned when his army was thrown back in retreat by Gen. Bernard Montgomery's meticulously prepared second battle of Alamein in Oct. 1942. Rommel's retreat ended behind the MARETH LINE in Tunisia, where he regrouped. In Feb. 1943 he launched a spoiling attack against British and American forces to his west, but it fell short and his army was soon forced to retreat again when Montgomery staged a

disorganized. This required mobile reserves located near the suspected invasion points and latitude to use them quickly. But Hitler reserved that decision for himself.

When the NORMANDY INVASION began, Hitler was asleep and Rommel was heading for a vacation in Germany. Whether he could have persuaded Hitler that this was the actual landing is debatable. Rommel continued to plead fruitlessly with Hitler for flexibility in his tactics until he was wounded in an air attack on July 17, 1944.

An attempted ASSASSINATION of Hitler three days later (see JULY 20 PLOT) raised suspicions that Rommel had known of it beforehand, which he had. But he had opposed assassination, arguing for the arrest of Hitler by the Army and a trial in a civilian court. On Oct. 14, 1944, SS troops surrounded his house and a German general confronted Rommel with a choice of suicide or a trial. He accepted proferred poison, told his wife and fifteen-year-old son (an antiaircraft gunner) that Hitler was charging him with TREASON, and said he would be dead in fifteen minutes. His death publicly was attributed to his war wounds and he was given a state funeral. (Had he not taken poison and demanded a public trial, Hitler had promised retribution against his wife and son after his sentencing and execution.)

Generalfeldmarschall Erwin Rommel demonstrated his military genius commanding the 7th Panzer Division in the invasion of France in May 1940, then the Afrika Korps in 1941–1943. *(German Army via Imperial War Museum)*

flanking attack around the Mareth Line. Rommel was flown out of Africa in March 1943.

He was then given command of German forces in northern Italy (Army Group B). When U.S. and British forces landed at SALERNO in Sept. 1943, Rommel recommended that all German forces withdraw to a line north of ROME. *Generalfeldmarschall* ALBERT KESSELRING, commander of forces in Rome and southern Italy, proposed a forward defense that significantly slowed the Allied forces.

Rommel, formerly a relatively ardent supporter of Hitler, began to despair of German victory. When appointed to command of forces along France's Atlantic coast, he immediately began upgrading defenses along the beaches. Rommel believed that Germany's only hope of defeating an Allied landing was to confront it in the first few hours, while the troops were still on the beach and

Rommel's Asparagus

Devices planted in open fields to deter AIRBORNE attack. Named for *Generalfeldmarschall* ERWIN ROMMEL, the "asparagus" consisted of sharp posts connected to mines emplaced by German troops in potential areas of Allied parachute or GLIDER landings along the Atlantic Coast of France.

When Maj. Gen. MATTHEW B. RIDGWAY, commander of the U.S. 82nd Airborne DIVISION, parachuted behind the Normandy beachhead on the night of June 5–6, 1944, he immediately encountered a cow, which he almost kissed. The presence of the bovine, he later explained, meant that the fields where his division was landing were not staked with Rommel's antiparachute devices.

Romulus

Allied code name for the Arakan part of Operation Capital.

Roosevelt, (Anna) Eleanor (1884–1962)

Eleanor Roosevelt, wife of President ROOSE-VELT, traveled extensively throughout the world during the war, serving as an observer for her husband and a morale raiser for troops. She occasionally floated trial balloons for her husband in her widely circulated newspaper column, "My Day."

Wearing her RED CROSS uniform, she frequently visited the wounded in U.S. and overseas hospitals. On one trip she traveled 25,000 miles in five weeks, then, back home, made hundreds of surprise phone calls to the mothers and girlfriends of servicemen she had seen.

When the President died on April 12, 1945, it was Eleanor Roosevelt who broke the news to Vice President HARRY S TRUMAN. She served from 1945 to 1952 as a member of the U.S. delegation to the UNITED NATIONS.

Roosevelt, Elliott (1910–1990)

Second oldest son of President ROOSEVELT, Elliott Roosevelt was called to active duty in the Army Air Corps Reserve in 1940. He served as an Army Air Forces photo-reconnaissance officer in Northwest Africa, becoming a colonel and the commanding officer of a photo-reconnaissance wing. He later served as a reconnaissance officer in Europe and was promoted to brigadier general in Feb. 1945.

Roosevelt, Franklin Delano (1882–1945)

On Sept. 1, 1939, when Germany invaded Poland, Franklin D. Roosevelt had been President for almost seven years and was expected to leave office in Jan. 1941. But just as that September changed the world so did it change the plans of Roosevelt.

On Sept. 13 he called Congress into special session to revise the NEUTRALITY ACT so that belligerents could purchase arms on a "cash-and-carry" basis, but U.S. ships were still barred from war zones. He hoped that this would give enough help to England and France to defeat Germany. But his hope was slight. The United States, he knew, could not long remain on the sidelines of the war.

Two days before calling Congress, Roosevelt began a long private correspondence with WINSTON CHURCHILL, the British First Lord of the Admiralty. Their warm and trusting relationship was the heart of the Western alliance against what would become known as the AXIS.

Throughout Roosevelt's presidency, which began slightly more than a month after ADOLF HITLER became chancellor of Germany, Roosevelt had seen and feared the growth of militant Germany and Japan. Now the war had come.

During his first administration, from March 1933 to Jan. 1937, Roosevelt could do little to resist the prevailing neutralism in the United States other than open diplomatic relations with the Soviet Union and advocate a "Good Neighbor" policy in Latin America. The first half of his second term saw him speak more harshly about Germany and Japan, but a rise in military spending did not follow.

When Churchill began his confidential correspondence with Roosevelt in Sept. 1939, Roosevelt started getting a private education about the war. Churchill, far more than any domestic adviser, gave Roosevelt the information and justifications for greatly expanding aid to Britain as part of an overall military buildup.

On June 10, 1940, as France was about to fall, *Il Duce* BENITO MUSSOLINI, declaring war on England and France, attacked France, and Roosevelt threw off the thin veil of neutrality. In one of his "fireside broadcasts" to the nation, he said, "The hand that held the dagger has struck it into the back of its neighbor." Now U.S. policy was this: The United States would "extend to the opponents of force the material RESOURCES of this nation."

A month later the Democratic National Convention, on the first ballot, nominated Roosevelt for an unprecedented third term. Isolationists, rallying around the AMERICAN FIRST COMMITTEE and its major supporter, the "Lone Eagle" CHARLES A. LINDBERGH, opposed Roosevelt's pro-British policies and warned that the United States was not prepared for war. The isolationists were realistic about U.S. preparedness, but Roosevelt was changing that reality.

Simultaneously running for President and fashioning ways to aid England, Roosevelt sponsored further revisions to the neutrality laws, began the building of the "Arsenal of Democracy" with a characteristically expansive call for "50,000 planes a year," won Congressional approval for the drafting of soldiers in the summer of 1940, and offered the

DESTROYERS-FOR-BASES DEAL with Great Britain in Sept. 1940, after shrewdly getting it endorsed by the Republican candidate for President, WENDELL L. WILLKIE.

Roosevelt also undercut Republican criticism of his anti-isolationist policy by appointing Republican HENRY L. STIMSON secretary of War and FRANK KNOX, the 1936 Republican vice presidential candidate, secretary of the Navy. Roosevelt won his third election easily and never lost the momentum of aid to England. Laws prohibited lending money to England. But he gave America and Congress a parable about how a man *lends* his garden hose to his neighbor to keep the neighbor's fire from spreading to the hose-owner's home. This produced the LEND-LEASE Act in March 1941.

Roosevelt proclaimed a "neutrality zone" in which the U.S. Navy would patrol for German U-BOATS and, to guarantee that Germany would not garrison Iceland or Greenland, sent troops to both places. At the same time, Roosevelt formulated Wilsonian war aims, describing the FOUR FREEDOMS (of speech, of religion, from want, and from fear) and drafting with Winston Churchill the ATLANTIC CHARTER, a document that echoed Wilson's Fourteen Points and eventually led to the creation of the UNITED NATIONS.

After the damaging and sinking of U.S. ships by U-boats, Roosevelt ordered the Navy to "shoot on sight" and got Congress to authorize the arming of merchantmen. Some military advisers, including Adm. HAROLD R. STARK, the Chief of Naval Operations, wondered whether Hitler would declare war on the United States.

By Nov. 1941, however, Secretary of State CORDELL HULL had no doubt where war would come from. He and Roosevelt had been negotiating in vain with Japanese envoys over Japan's expansionism in the Pacific. On Nov. 27 Hull said to Simpson, "I have washed my hands of the Japanese situation, and it is now in the hands of you and Knox, the Army and Navy."

On Dec. 7, 1941—"a date which will live in infamy," Roosevelt called it—Japan attacked PEARL HARBOR and Roosevelt suddenly became a wartime Commander in Chief. Roosevelt's performance in that role has been subjected to varying interpretations. Some historians have argued that Roosevelt did not concern himself with military decisions, choosing instead to accede to the consensus of his military advisers. In this view, Roosevelt remained the skillful domestic President, playing RATIONING off against patriotism, looking upon WAR PRODUCTION as a matter of union-management issues, making his running of the home front the principal political issue, especially when he ran for an astonishing fourth term in 1944.

But no less an authority than Adm. WILLIAM D. LEAHY, Chief of Staff to Roosevelt and the Chairman of the JOINT CHIEFS OF STAFF, wrote after the war, "Planning of major campaigns was always done in close co-operation with the President. Frequently we [the Joint Chiefs] had sessions in his study. . . . Churchill and Roosevelt really ran the war . . . we were just artisans, building patterns of strategy from the rough blueprints handed us by our respective Commanders-in-Chief."

Historians Eric Larabee and Kent Roberts Greenfield, general editor of *The U.S. Army in World War II,* among other authorities, argue persuasively that Roosevelt was directly and beneficially involved in the war's direction in several ways. Some examples: He often personally selected his military leaders, including Leahy, Gen. GEORGE C. MARSHALL, and Adm. ERNEST J. KING; he broke a tie among his military advisers, or even bucked their consensus, on more than twenty separate major decisions including the decision to invade North Africa, for MacArthur to retake the Philippines, and to sustain Lend-Lease shipments to the Soviet Union. These moments demonstrate Roosevelt's ability to balance military and political considerations more deftly than all but a few national leaders in history.

The outcome wasn't always triumphant. His insistence on maintaining a fleet at Pearl Harbor left it vulnerable to a surprise attack. His attempts to shape the war in China and Anglo-American policy toward France were unsuccessful. His belief that a personal relationship with Soviet leader JOSEF STALIN could mask incompatible aims in Eastern Europe overlooked his own failing health and the possibility that Stalin saw international relations in a different light. Churchill, who had a sharper perception of Stalin's aims, wrote to Roosevelt in March 1945: "It will be a torn, ragged, and hungry world to help to its feet; and what will Uncle Joe

[Stalin] or his successor say to the way we would like to do it?"

When Churchill, Stalin, and Roosevelt met for the YALTA CONFERENCE in Feb. 1945, Roosevelt was visibly frail and in ill health. Early in April he went to his cottage in Warm Springs, Ga., hoping that a rest would restore his health. On April 12, he complained of a headache and moments later died of a massive cerebral hemorrhage.

Roosevelt's influence on the conduct of this coalition war was pervasive and masterly. He brought to the Anglo-American alliance a personal, even manipulative relationship with Churchill. Roosevelt's insistence on the "Germany First" strategy and on Anglo-American unity became guiding principles that even the prickly Admiral King was forced to adhere to. Few other civilian leaders have displayed to the same degree Roosevelt's ability to trust his advisers in most decisions and overrule them when it mattered most to him.

Roosevelt's unmatched experience as President, his ebullience, his ability to speak easily to a microphone and have his listeners treat his words as personal conversation, his consistency of overall purpose—all were elements in his overwhelming influence on the U.S. conduct of World War II.

Roosevelt, James (1907—)

The oldest son of President ROOSEVELT. A U.S. Marine Corps captain when PEARL HARBOR was bombed, James was in WASHINGTON on Dec. 7, 1941, and was one of the first people the President called when he learned about the raid. As a Marine major, he became the executive officer of CARLSON'S RAIDERS and took part in the assault on MAKIN ISLAND. He often served as his father's aide, physically helping Franklin Roosevelt, a polio victim, get around. The President asked James to stand with him at his fourth Inaugural in 1945. James, a Marine major, wrote him back, "You're the commander in chief—if you want me, you can order me back." And he did.

"It was a cold, blustery day," James recalled. "He took the oath on the White House balcony. He didn't want to wear an overcoat. I sent for one for him, but he wouldn't put it on. The family here thought he looked fine, but he looked tired and gray to me."

Three months later, on April 12, Franklin Roosevelt died.

Roosevelt, Brig. Gen. Theodore, Jr. (1887–1944)

The son of the twenty-sixth President, Brig. Gen. Theodore Roosevelt Jr. saw action in the NORTH AFRICA INVASION and in SICILY. On June 6, D-Day of the NORMANDY INVASION, he was, as the assistant commander of the 4th DIVISION, the only general to land in the first wave. He went with the first wave at his request.

Cool and cheerful under heavy fire, he checked a map and discovered that he was about 2,000 yards from his wave's designated landing area. He decided to head inland—a decision that undoubtedly saved countless lives and helped to establish the beachhead. He won the MEDAL OF HONOR for his valor on Utah Beach. On July 12, at a divisional command post, he died of a heart attack. "There's not a soldier or an officer in this division who won't feel a personal loss," his commanding officer said.

Rooster

Code name for U.S. air transport of the Chinese 22nd Division to Chihchiang.

Rose

Allied code name for Ruhr pocket, April 1945.

Rosenberg, Julius (1918–1953)

A key member of a Soviet spy ring that produced one of the most effective ESPIONAGE coups of the war: information on the tightly guarded ATOMIC BOMB. He and his wife, Ethel Greenglass Rosenberg (1915–1953), were children of Jewish immigrants born and raised in New York City. Julius graduated from City College of New York as an electrical engineer; Ethel finished high school.

The COMMUNIST PARTY OF THE UNITED STATES, following Soviet directives, preached neutrality for the United States before and at the beginning of the EUROPEAN WAR. The Rosenbergs accepted the party line, although in 1940 Julius had gone to work as a civilian for the U.S. Signal Corps. After the German invasion of the Soviet Union the Communist line quickly changed, and the Rosenbergs responded. The couple persuaded DAVID

GREENGLASS, Ethel's brother, to spy for the Soviet Union when he was assigned to the atomic bomb laboratory in LOS ALAMOS in 1944.

In 1945 Julius was dismissed from his Signal Corps job because of his pro-Soviet views and on July 17, 1950, he was arrested for espionage. Ethel was arrested on August 11. The evidence against her was not strong. At her trial she testified that she was a loyal U.S. citizen and had never committed espionage. The key witness against the couple was Greenglass, who received a fifteen-year sentence.

Federal Judge Irving R. Kaufman told them, "I consider your crime worse than murder," when he sentenced them both to death on April 9, 1951. They proclaimed their innocence, winning sympathy and kindling an unending controversy over their guilt and sentencing. They were executed in the electric chair at Sing Sing Prison at Ossining, N.Y., on June 19, 1953. They were the only Americans to be executed for espionage during peacetime in U.S. history. Ethel Rosenberg was the first woman executed for a federal offense since Mary Surratt was hanged in 1865 for her involvement in the assassination of President Lincoln.

New testimony attesting to their guilt came in 1990, with the publication of a memoir of NIKITA KHRUSHCHEV. The Rosenbergs, he said, "provided very significant help in accelerating the production of our atomic bomb." Although he said they were not spies for the Soviet Union, Khrushchev said they "did what they could to help the Soviet Union acquire the atomic bomb so that it could stand up to the United States of America. That was the issue of the times."

Rosie

Allied code name for French naval force landing at southwest Cannes, 1944.

Rosselsprung (Knight's Move)

(1) Code name for German attack on Allied CONVOY PQ 17 in the Arctic, July 1942; (2) code name for German plan for kidnapping Yugoslavian leader TITO, 1944.

Rostov

Soviet city on the Don River, often called the gateway to the Caucasus. The city was fiercely fought over during the war, changing hands four times.

In the Dnieper-to-the-Don phase of the GERMAN CAMPAIGN IN THE SOVIET UNION German troops took Rostov on Nov. 21, 1941. The Red Army, attacking across the frozen Don, forced the Germans out of the city a week later. As a result of this first victory for the Soviets, German forces were shifted from the north, drawing on the strength of the German drive on MOSCOW.

When HITLER ordered *Generalfeldmarschall* GERD VON RUNDSTEDT to halt his retreat from Rostov, von Rundstedt refused and was relieved of his command.

In July 1942 the Germans again took Rostov, this time putting the Red Army to flight. Soviet Marshal STALIN reacted by ordering the execution of a number of high-ranking Red Army officers. In the wake of the Red Army victory at STALINGRAD, the SOVIET OFFENSIVE CAMPAIGN began rolling and liberated Rostov in Feb. 1943.

Rot (Red)

German code name for the second half of the battle of France, June 1940.

Rotterdam

Dutch city that was heavily bombed by the Luftwaffe during the FRANCE AND LOW COUNTRIES CAMPAIGN. The German BLITZKRIEG roared across the Netherlands on May 10, 1940, and surrender was inevitable in days. Rotterdam was declared an OPEN CITY, giving it theoretical protection from assault. But on May 13, while Dutch officials were negotiating a surrender, the city was bombed.

The bombing enflamed the British and may have been indirectly responsible for giving the RAF political and popular support for later bombing of German cities. In the United States, anti-NAZI sentiments were fanned by what was seen as an atrocity. First reports had as many as 30,000 civilians killed.

The bombing, however, seems to have been a result of German bungling rather than a deliberate violation of Rotterdam's open city status. By the German timetable, Rotterdam was to be bombed during warfare, not during negotiations. Whatever the timing and the confusion of communications, 100 HE 111 bombers appeared over the city on the afternoon of May 13. About half of them, responding to frantic flare signals on the ground, pulled away. The rest of the bombers dropped 97 tons of bombs; 814 persons were killed and 78,000 lost their homes.

Rouen

Target of the first U.S. bomber raid in Europe. Twelve B-17 FLYING FORTRESS bombers took off from an Eighth Air Force base in Grafton, England, on the afternoon of Aug. 17, 1942, to bomb the railroad yards at Rouen. In one plane was Maj. Gen. IRA C. EAKER, who had set up the U.S. Bomber Command. One of the pilots was PAUL W. TIBBETS, JR., who in 1945 would pilot the plane that dropped the first ATOMIC BOMB on HIROSHIMA. The B-17s, which dropped more than 18 tons of bombs, were escorted by RAF SPITFIRES and ran into little opposition and returned to base intact. At the same time, six other B-17s flew a diversion mission along the French coast and also returned unscathed, except for bird damage to one bomber.

Roundhammer

Code name for modified Round-Up invasion proposed for late 1943.

Round-Up

Code name for proposed Allied invasion of Western Europe in 1943; predecessor to Overlord.

Royal Air Force,

see UNITED KINGDOM, AIR FORCE.

Royal Flush

One of three phases of U.S. Eighth and Ninth AIR FORCES' strikes against German trains, supply dumps, airfields, and targets of opportunity past the immediate NORMANDY INVASION areas, June 1944.

Royal Marines,

see UNITED KINGDOM, MARINES.

Royal Navy,

see UNITED KINGDOM, NAVY.

Rudel, Hans Ulrich (1916—)

German dive bomber and fighter pilot who flew more combat missions than any other pilot in World War II. In flight school he was considered a slow learner. Rudel's combat career began flying JU 87 STUKA strikes in the Polish campaign of 1939, followed by combat in the Balkans, against CRETE, and on the EASTERN FRONT. German records credited him with destroying more than 500 Soviet tanks in a Stuka carrying 37-mm cannon in addition to bombs. His dive-bombing attack scored a decisive hit on the Soviet battleship *Marat*, sunk at anchor at LENINGRAD. Rudel was shot down more than a dozen times, and seriously injured on several occasions. On Feb. 9, 1945, while attacking Soviet forces crossing the Oder River, his Stuka was struck by antiaircraft fire. He crashed-landed and was seriously injured; one leg had to be amputated (the other had been in a cast for several months). Although forbidden by HITLER to further risk his life, when the war ended he was flying a modified FW 190 fighter with an artificial limb and his remaining leg still in a plaster cast.

With the war ended he and several squadron mates flew to a U.S. air base to surrender.

Rudel was credited with having flown over 2,530 combat missions. Hitler himself designed the unique and penultimate IRON CROSS award for him—the Knight's Cross to the Iron Cross with Golden Oak Leaves and Swords and Diamonds.

Rufe

This was the floatplane version of the high-performance A6M ZERO carrier-based fighter. The Japanese developed a number of floatplane fighters and bombers to operate from tenders among the islands of Southeast Asia. Despite the weight and drag of the large centerline float and fixed stabilizing floats on the wings, the A6M2-N Type 2 floatplane fighter (Allied code name Rufe) was a fast, maneuverable aircraft.

These aircraft were first deployed to TULAGI in the SOLOMON ISLANDS in mid-1942. They were destroyed by AAF B-17 FLYING FORTRESS bombers that struck the area in advance of the U.S. landings on GUADALCANAL in Aug. 1942. The floatplanes also took part in the 1942–1943 campaign in the ALEUTIAN ISLANDS and, in the final months of the war, were used for the air defense of Japan.

The Japanese had initiated floatplane fighter development in 1940, but to provide an interim aircraft the Mitsubishi A6M was adapted for the role. The prototype—using the airframe of an A6M2 Model 11—flew for the first time on Dec. 7, 1941. The aircraft had the main float attached by a forward, angled pylon and aft V-strut. It retained the clean lines of the A6M; however, because no centerline auxiliary fuel tank could be carried, fuel was carried in the float. A total of 327 aircraft were built to this configuration through Sept. 1943. (The Rufe's successor was the REX—the Kawanishi-design N1K1 *Kyofu.*)

The aircraft had a maximum speed of 271 mph and a maximum range of 1,100 miles. Armament consisted of two 7.7-mm machine guns above the engine cowling and two 20-mm cannon in the wings. Two 132-pound BOMBS could be carried.

Rugby

Code name for Allied AIRBORNE force dropped in invasion area of southern France, 1944.

Ruge, *Vizeadmiral* Friedrich O. (1894–1961)

German naval planner and adviser to senior Army commanders. Ruge served in surface ships during World War I and in the postwar period, specializing in MINE warfare.

He was a *Kapitän zur See* and senior officer of minesweepers when the EUROPEAN WAR began and participated in naval operations in the North Sea and English Channel. He remained a staff officer in France until 1943, when he was promoted to *Vizeadmiral* and assigned as senior naval officer in Italy and the commander of German naval forces in the area. That November he was appointed naval adviser to *Generalfeldmarschall* ERWIN ROMMEL, who was charged with building Atlantic coastal defenses against the expected Allied invasion. From Aug. 1944 until the end of the war he served in BERLIN as the Navy's director of ship construction.

After the war he was a PRISONER OF WAR for several months. Released in 1946, he served as an official German historian for the U.S. Navy. With the establishment of the postwar German Navy, Ruge was recalled to active duty and was appointed to head that force, retiring for a second time in 1961. Subsequently, he became a prolific writer and lecturer on naval matters.

Ruhr

Germany's major industrial area and the target of almost continual air raids. The center of Germany's iron and steel industry was in the valley of the Ruhr River, a tributary of the Rhine.

On the night of March 5–6, 1943, the RAF Bomber Command launched the "Battle of the Ruhr," a sustained attack on the heartland of German industry by attacking ESSEN, hub of the KRUPP munitions empire, with 442 planes. In bombings that continued until July 13, the RAF flew 2,070 sorties, heavily bombing several Ruhr cities, including Essen, Düsseldorf, and Dortmund, while simultaneously hitting BERLIN, Nuremberg, Munich, Frankfurt am Main, and other cities.

One of the Ruhr raids concentrated on the Möhne and Eder dams, whose hydroelectric facilities supplied much of the Ruhr's electricity. In a May 19 attack code-named Chastise, specially trained LANCASTER bomber crews dropped UPKEEP "bouncing bombs" that skipped along reservoirs and exploded against the dams.

A ground battle for the Ruhr was waged in March–April 1945 when Allied armies encircled some 300,000 troops trapped in the ruins of the Ruhr. The troops surrendered, but their commander, *Generalfeldmarschall* WALTHER MODEL, killed himself rather than surrender.

U.S. interest in maintaining the industrial Ruhr was emphasized by JOHN J. MCCLOY, assistant secretary of war (and future high commissioner in Germany). He visited Gen. DWIGHT D. EISENHOWER, Supreme Allied Commander, in April 1945 and urged that the conquest of the Ruhr not be too destructive lest it imperil the economic future of Europe.

Rumania

Capital: Bucharest, pop. 19,900,000 (est. 1940). By 1937, when a Fascist government was elected into office, the constitutional monarchy of Rumania was an ideological ally of NAZI Germany. ANTI-SEMITIC laws, modeled on those of the Nazis, were enacted, primarily against JEWS who were doctors, innkeepers, and journalists. King Carol II, concerned about the government's economic policies, dismissed it in 1938 and provisionally appointed the Patriarch of

Rumania, the religious leader of the country, prime minister. His death and peasant unrest intensified the king's search for a totalitarian regime that would keep Rumania independent yet allied with Germany.

On March 24, 1939, Rumania signed an agreement with Germany for the development of Rumanian oil, timber, and mineral industries. To keep her relations balanced, Rumania quickly signed trade agreements with England and France. But clearly Rumania was in Germany's orbit.

The Fascist Iron Guard, which had been suppressed, reemerged, plotting the ASSASSINATION of the king and succeeding in the killing of Prime Minister Armand Călinescu on a Bucharest street on Sept. 21, 1939. Out of the political turmoil came absolute allegiance to Germany, with mixed results for Rumania.

In June 1940, the Soviet Union occupied two Rumanian provinces, apparently with the connivance of Germany, which had at that moment had a NONAGGRESSION PACT with the Soviets. In August a German-Italian commission arbitrating Rumania's territorial disputes with Hungary awarded Transylvania, which had been acquired by Rumania after World War I, to Hungary, which Hitler considered more of an ally than Rumania. Finally, in September Bulgaria acquired a southern part of Rumania occupied primarily by Bulgarians.

Rumania, which had an area of 113,919 square miles and a population of 19,900,000 on Jan. 1, 1940, had in a year shrunk to a nation of 74,000 square miles with a population of 16,000,000. Germany was so concerned about Rumania's plight that it sent in troops to guard its borders and the Luftwaffe to protect Rumanian oil fields and refineries.

King Carol abdicated on Sept. 6, 1940, and the governing of Rumania was left to Prime Minister Ion Antonescu and the Iron Guard, with Carol's teenaged son Mihai as regent. On Nov. 23 Rumania signed the TRIPARTITE PACT, joining itself to the destiny of Germany, Japan, and Italy. Four days later, in a macabre ceremony foreshadowing the terror to come, the Iron Guard executed sixty-four prominent Rumanians over the graves of fourteen Iron Guardsmen who had been executed in 1938, then exhumed their comrades' bodies and reburied them with Iron Guard pageantry.

Germany took over Rumania's economy, harvesting the nation's food crops for Germans and creating a food shortage in Rumania. When Germany invaded the Soviet Union on June 22, 1941, Rumania joined forces, retaking its erstwhile territory and surging forward in the UKRAINE, ultimately to lose more than 400,000 men at STALINGRAD and elsewhere in the fateful GERMAN CAMPAIGN IN THE SOVIET UNION.

In a backlash on the home front, Antonescu (now with the rank of marshal) launched new pogroms against Rumanian Jews. In Dec. 1941 Rumania, along with Hungary and Bulgaria, declared war on the United States. The declaration was "not in response to the wishes of their own people, but as instruments of Hitler," President ROOSEVELT said in a message to Congress asking recognition of a state of war against the countries. Rumania's Dec. 1941 declaration of war on England brought a response on June 12, 1942, when B-24 LIBERATOR bombers from Africa bombed the PLOESTI oil fields, beginning a two-year Allied bombing campaign.

As the SOVIET OFFENSIVE CAMPAIGN rolled across Eastern Europe in the spring of 1944, the Rumanian government frantically tried to find U.S. or British officials in Turkey and Egypt with whom to begin surrender talks. King Mihai materialized, won support from loyal generals, arrested Antonescu, and asked his nation to change sides, taking up arms with the advancing Soviets. The Germans responded by bombing Bucharest, which had already been heavily bombed by the ALLIES. During the collapse of the Rumanian regime more than 1,000 American PRISONERS OF WAR, many of them shot down on Ploesti raids, escaped to Italy.

Rumania's last moves of the war were well timed to get her on the winning side. She declared war on Germany on Aug. 25, 1944, as PARIS fell, and as a belligerent against Germany, became eligible for membership in the UNITED NATIONS. She declared war on Japan on March 7, 1945, as U.S. troops crossed the RHINE.

Rumania signed an armistice with the Soviet Union, which began instituting a Moscow-controlled government. In the years to come the Communist regime would force the abdication of Mihai, install a totalitarian regime, and hold democracy at bay until the tumultuous 1990 uprising that overthrew the Rumanian dictatorship.

Rundstedt, *Generalfeldmarschall* Gerd von (1875–1953)

Commander of German defenses against the NORMANDY INVASION. Son of a Prussian Army general, von Rundstedt was born to be a soldier. He made the Army his life, retiring in 1938. He was recalled on the eve of the EUROPEAN WAR to lead army groups in the POLISH CAMPAIGN and the FRANCE AND LOW COUNTRIES CAMPAIGN.

He was appointed to the command of German forces assigned to Operation SEA LION, the invasion of England. When that did not happen, he went to the EASTERN FRONT as commander of the Southern Army Group in the UKRAINE during the GERMAN CAMPAIGN IN THE SOVIET UNION.

Von Rundstedt showed a Prussian officer's undisguised distaste for HITLER, particularly when *Der Führer* acted as a grand strategist. Von Rundstedt openly referred to Hitler as "that Bohemian corporal."

When von Rundstedt was in retreat from ROSTOV in Dec. 1941 Hitler told him to stand and fight. Von Rundstedt wired Hitler: "It is madness to attempt to hold. First the troops cannot do it and second if they do not retreat they will be destroyed. I repeat that this order must be rescinded or that you find someone else." Hitler shot back: "I am acceding to your request. Please give up your command."

But Hitler could not do without the talents of von Rundstedt. Early in 1942, in anticipation of an eventual Allied invasion of Europe, Hitler made von Rundstedt Commander in Chief West. When the invasion came in June 1944, von Rundstedt could not stop it and, hearing reports that von Rundstedt wished to sue for peace, Hitler again removed him. In the following month the failure of the JULY 20 PLOT on Hitler's life devastated the Army's officer corps, but von Rundstedt was not touched. Although aware of the plot, he had not joined it.

Recalled once more in Sept. 1944, von Rundstedt could do little to stop the ALLIED CAMPAIGN IN EUROPE. The last German offensive of the war was the ARDENNES thrust that triggered the Battle of the Bulge. This is sometimes called the Rundstedt offensive, but historian B. H. LIDDELL HART, who interviewed von Rundstedt after the war, wrote in *The German Generals Talk:* "That title [Rundstedt offensive] acts on Rundstedt like the proverbial red rag, for his feelings about the plan were, and remain, very bitter. In reality he had nothing to do with it except in the most nominal way. . . . The decision was entirely Hitler's own."

The British held von Rundstedt for a WAR CRIMES trial, charging that he had turned British COMMANDOS over to the GESTAPO in June 1942. The trial was canceled because of von Rundstedt's ill health.

Rupert

Code name for British expedition to Narvik, April 1940.

Russell Islands

Island group in the SOLOMON ISLANDS about 30 miles northwest of GUADALCANAL. In Operation Cleanslate, U.S. forces met no opposition when they took the two large islands, Banika and Pavuvu, on Feb. 21, 1943. Bases built here served the subsequent PELELIU and OKINAWA invasions.

Russian Army of Liberators,

see ANDREI VLASOV.

Russian Convoys

Anglo-American merchant convoys that sailed mostly from Iceland to Soviet ports in the Arctic, carrying weapons and munitions to help keep the Soviet Union in the war. Although Britain was hard pressed by German forces in the BATTLE OF THE ATLANTIC and in the Mediterranean when Germany invaded the Soviet Union in June 1941, Prime Minister CHURCHILL immediately offered the Soviet Union major military assistance, most of which initially would be carried by the Russian Convoys.

The convoy route from Iceland—some 1,500 to 2,000 miles, depending upon the ice conditions—ran the gauntlet of German surface warships based in Norway, U-BOATS, and land-based bombers. The weather and sea conditions were arduous. One British ESCORT CARRIER rolled up to 45° and had to heave to; for survivors of ship sinkings, immersion brought death in a couple of minutes; on a raft or in a boat, survival was sometimes measured in hours.

From Aug. 22, 1941, until the end of the year eight lightly escorted convoys were dispatched to the Soviet Union. Most were escorted by only a cruiser and two destroyers. The Germans were slow to react, with several convoys reaching the ports of Archangel or Murmansk without loss. By the end of 1941 a total of fifty-three heavily laden ships safely reached port and thirty-four returned, without loss.

The British Home Fleet was charged with providing escorts for the Russian Convoys but was unable to provide major warships for escort because the Home Fleet's primary responsibility was to be ready in British waters to respond to a German breakout into the North Atlantic. The ships would only sail eastward upon positive intelligence that major German warships would attack the convoys. The actual escorting destroyers, frigates, and CORVETTES were mostly British with a sprinkling of U.S. ships after Dec. 1941. (Soviet air and naval support near the end of the convoy run was rarely effective.)

The year 1942 began ominously when the first convoy, in January, suffered two merchant ships and one destroyer sunk by U-boats. Only two men from the destroyer *Matabele*'s crew of 200 were rescued—testimony to the extreme cold and sea conditions. The U-boats were joined in Jan. 1942 by the massive battleship TIRPITZ, sister ship to the ill-fated *BISMARCK,* which was sent to Norway. HITLER intended the battleship to help defend Norway against a British invasion; the naval high command wanted the ship there to threaten Arctic convoys.

On March 6, 1942, the *Tirpitz* and destroyers sailed from Trondheim, Norway, in the first surface attack against the Russian Convoys. Passing close to convoys PQ 12 (eastbound) and QP 8 (westbound), the *Tirpitz* did not intercept them because of bad weather; similarly, the *Tirpitz* escaped a British battleship-carrier force searching for her although she was attacked (without effect) by carrier-based torpedo planes.

CONVOY PQ 17 in July 1942 proved to be the most disastrous of the Russian Convoys. On July 5, believing that the *Tirpitz* was about to attack, the British Admiralty ordered the convoy to scatter to reduce the number of merchant ships that the German dreadnought could attack. But without the close escort the thirty-three merchant ships were vulnerable to German bombers and U-boats. Only nine reached port as twenty-four ships of 143,977 gross tons were sunk. (The *Tirpitz* did not attack PQ 17.)

The convoy situation changed radically in Sept. 1942 when the British escort carrier *Avenger* was dispatched with convoy PQ 18, carrying twelve HURRICANE fighters and three SWORDFISH bombers to be employed against U-boats. By that time the Luftwaffe had some ninety torpedo planes and 130 level bombers based in northern Norway.

The British, however, had not yet perfected tactics for the escort or "jeep" carrier and, despite heavy antiaircraft gun batteries in the escorting ships, large-scale raids by German bombers succeeded in sinking nine ships, almost a quarter of the convoy's forty merchant ships (plus two tankers to refuel the escorts), at the cost of only five bombers shot down. The Swordfish, however, did keep the U-boats at bay; at least five U-boats attacking the convoy were able to sink only one tanker. Two U-boats were sunk in retribution. The *Avenger*'s fighter aircraft soon got into stride and thirty-four German bombers were destroyed by a combination of shipboard guns and fighters. (In all, convoy PQ 18 lost thirteen ships.)

Each convoy battle had its own drama, pathos, and—increasingly—success. By the end of 1942—as the crucial battle for STALINGRAD was being fought—the Russian convoys had brought the Red Army 7,652 aircraft, 9,848 tanks, 111,301 trucks, and several million tons of food. These supplies certainly contributed to the Soviet successes in the winter of 1942–1943.

While U-boats and bombers continued to sink merchant ships on the Arctic convoy route, the threat from German surface warships persisted. In March 1943 the *Tirpitz,* the battleship *Scharnhorst,* and the heavy cruiser *Lützow* anchored in Altenfjord near North Cape, from which they could quickly close with convoys. The surface ships, however, did not sail against the convoys and, in Sept. 1943, several British X-CRAFT MIDGET SUBMARINES inflicted damage on the *Tirpitz*. She never again went to sea as carrier-based planes damaged her and then RAF bombers, using 12,000-pound TALLBOY BOMBS, sank the ship.

But the *Scharnhorst* did sortie against convoy JW 55B in late Dec. 1943 as the German naval Commander in Chief, *Grossadmiral* KARL DÖNITZ, exhorted his men to give their last ounce of energy to help their embattled comrades on the EASTERN FRONT. Screened by destroyers, the *Scharnhorst* encountered heavy weather and, unable to reach the convoy, was soon trapped by superior British naval forces, including the battleship *Duke of York* and several destroyers. Snared, the *Scharnhorst* inflicted few casualties on the British warships that sank her in the last effort of the German surface fleet to challenge British naval power.

There were seventeen more months of Russian convoy runs, but without the threat of surface ships and the availability of more escort carriers, with improved fighters and antisubmarine aircraft and escort carriers, convoy losses were greatly reduced. At the same time, however, increasing numbers of U-boats were deployed to Norway, especially after the NORMANDY INVASION of June 1944 began to deprive the Germans of bases on the French coast. By the end of 1944 there were thirty-two U-boats available at Norwegian bases to prey on Arctic convoys.

The last convoys were run immediately after the end of the war in Europe, the last, a westbound convoy, arriving in England on May 31, 1945. Although only 22.7 percent of the vast amount of war matériel sent to the Soviet Union went via the Russian convoy route, that route was immediately available in the critical days of 1941–1942, and was the faster route compared to the one via the Persian Gulf.

Of the 811 merchant ships that sailed for Soviet ports in the Arctic in the Russian convoys, 750 arrived safely (92 percent); thirty-five turned back for various reasons, and ninety-eight were sunk—forty-one by U-boats, thirty-seven by aircraft, and three by surface gunfire. Of 715 merchant ships that attempted the return (westbound) voyage, twenty-nine were lost. Remarkably, only 829 merchant seamen were lost although hundreds of others suffered from exposure and frostbite.

The Royal Navy lost two cruisers and several destroyers, frigates, and corvettes—a total of seventeen naval ships (including one submarine). The Navy lost almost 2,000 officers and ratings in those ships sunk in the frigid Arctic waters.

Russian Front,
see EASTERN FRONT.

Rutter
Early British code word for the DIEPPE raid; later Jubilee.

S

6×6 Truck

Standard U.S. Army truck and a major contributor to the mobility of U.S. combat forces. The 6×6 (six wheels, all six drive wheels on three axles) was mass-produced and used by all of the U.S. military services and some Allied forces. It could carry 2½ tons of cargo or twenty troops while towing a 1½-ton-capacity trailer or an ARTILLERY piece; on a first-class highway the cargo load could be almost doubled.

By the end of the war each U.S. Army DIVISION had several hundred trucks, with separate truck transportation COMPANIES and BATTALIONS assigned to higher-level field commands. By late Aug. 1944 there were more than 130 truck companies with almost 6,000 trucks—mostly 6×6 trucks—

operating in France to supply U.S. ground forces (see RED BALL EXPRESS). This was in addition to the trucks assigned to combat units. At times the requirement for 6×6 trucks was so critical that U.S. divisions being prepared in England to move to France were stripped of their trucks, which were rushed to the continent to help supply divisions already fighting.

Developed by General Motors Corp. (GMC), the 6×6 truck had an open cab and cargo bed, which could be covered by canvas, and a tail gate. A machine gun for air defense could be fitted on a ring mount above the cab.

The typical 6×6 had a 104-horsepower, 6-cylinder engine with five forward and one reverse gears. There were several variants, including a look-alike

Troops of the U.S. Third Armored Division follow a Sherman tank through a snow-covered woods during the battle of the Bulge in Dec. 1944. The Sherman, armed with a "short" 75-mm gun, was the principal American tank during the war. *(U.S. Army via Imperial War Museum)*

707

6×4 and a dump truck. Others were fitted with vans for maintenance and communications purposes while the long-bodied 2½-ton truck (with the cab over the engine) could haul light but bulky engineering equipment, such as BAILEY BRIDGE sections. More than 800,000 2½-ton trucks were produced in the United States, most of them by GMC and Studebaker.

SA

NAZI storm troopers, street fighters who helped enforce HITLER'S rise to power. The SA—initials for *Sturmabteilung,* "storm detachment"—began in the 1920 as a legion of thugs at the service of the NATIONAL SOCIALIST GERMAN WORKERS' PARTY. Storm troopers guarded party meetings and fought savagely in street brawls against Communists and other political enemies of the Nazis. In 1931 ERNST RÖHM, an early supporter of HITLER, organized the SA into a private army, complete with a general staff, and put them in uniforms that gave them another name: Brown Shirts. By 1932 the ranks of the storm troopers had grown to some 400,000 and was a force that threatened the weakening WEIMAR REPUBLIC. President PAUL VON HINDENBURG banned the SA, which was succeeded by the SS.

Restored when Hitler became chancellor in 1933, the SA became, along with the SS, a private Nazi police force. Hitler allowed Röhm to build the SA to more than 2,000,000 men. The SA members, brutal enforcers of Nazi policies, carried out missions given unofficial sanction, such as the Nov. 9, 1938, *KRISTALLNACHT* attacks against German JEWS. But when Röhm pressed his plan to make a "people's army" consisting of his storm troopers merged with the regular German Army, Hitler saw Röhm as a rival and his SA as a threat to the army.

Hitler, prodded by JOSEPH GOEBBELS and HEINRICH HIMMLER, believed that Röhm had organized an SA coup. On the night of June 30, 1934—the Night of the Long Knives, as the Nazi called it—the SS swept down on SA officers and men, shooting many on the spot and jailing others for later execution by relays of firing squads. The Blood Purge, another name for that murderous night, ended with the slaying of Röhm, more than seventy left-wing Nazi SA leaders, and 100 or more followers. SS killers, under the cover of the SA purge, also slew an unknown number of political enemies not affiliated with the SA. Hitler's puppet legislature later declared that the SS's actions were legal.

The SA was reorganized, stripped of its power, and became so ineffectual that the WAR CRIMES military tribunal at Nuremberg decreed that, while all members of the SS were war criminals, the SA was an association of "unimportant Nazi hangers-on" and not, like the SS, "a criminal organization."

Sabotage

The damaging or destruction of an enemy's facilities. No nation inflicted any serious harm on an enemy through sabotage during the war. The British SPECIAL OPERATIONS EXECUTIVE was established to foster sabotage in German-occupied countries. But the consensus of military historians is that the fortunes of war were little affected by acts of sabotage performed by valiant GUERRILLAS and FRENCH RESISTANCE agents. A railroad train derailed here, a telegraph office blown up there—the deeds amounted to little more than patriotically inspired vandalism.

Historian John Keegan in *The Second World War,* looking at Allied-sponsored guerrilla, sabotage, and ESPIONAGE activities in German-occupied countries, wrote, "All failed at the price of very great suffering to the brave patriots involved but at trifling cost to the German forces that put them down."

The ALLIES also suffered little from sabotage. In the United States, the FEDERAL BUREAU OF INVESTIGATION (FBI) reported 3,081 "suspected acts of sabotage," but none was serious. JAPANESE-AMERICANS, thousands of whom were interned as potential saboteurs and spies, committed no acts of sabotage. But some were planned by German-Americans. Potentially, the worst damage would have come from eight trained German saboteurs who were landed by U-BOATS on the Atlantic Coast. They were quickly caught.

One saga began shortly after midnight on June 13, 1942, when a U.S. Coast Guardsman, patrolling a beach near Amagansett, N.Y., encountered some men. When he challenged them, one of the men said that he and his companions were fishermen whose boat had run aground. Suspicious, the young Coast Guardsman persisted. One of the men threatened him with a gun then offered him a $260 bribe to forget that he saw them.

The Coast Guardsman ran to a nearby Coast Guard station to report the incident and get reinforcements. Back at the scene, the beach patrol discovered four boxes of explosives, incendiaries, and a German seaman's duffle bag containing German uniforms. The men had disappeared.

The next day a man who identified himself as Frank Pastorius called the FBI in New York; the FBI believed his message was a crank call. He then went to WASHINGTON, where he called FBI headquarters and repeated his story: He was a German saboteur just landed in Long Island. Another group, he said, was to be landed in Florida. "Pastorius" (who used the password for the operation as his telephone alias) was George Dasch, one of eight German-born saboteurs who spent part of their lives in the United States. They had been recruited and trained at a sabotage school in Germany.

Dasch arrived in the United States as a stowaway in 1922 and worked as a waiter in New York, San Francisco, Miami, and Los Angeles. He returned to Germany in March 1941 and went to work for German intelligence monitoring U.S. broadcasts.

Dasch was the leader of his group. The others were Ernest Burger, Heinrich Heinch, and Richard Quirin. Burger was already a NAZI sympathizer when he immigrated to the United States in 1927. Like most of the others, during his time in the United States he joined the GERMAN-AMERICAN BUND. He worked in Milwaukee and Detroit, became an American citizen, and joined the Michigan National Guard. He returned to Germany in 1933. Heinch had been an illegal immigrant.

A four-man group from a U-boat landed near Jacksonville, Fla., on June 17. Their leader was Edward Kerling, who had joined the Nazi Party in 1928 and immigrated to Brooklyn the next year. He had several jobs, including chauffeur for Ely Culbertson, a famous bridge player. His men were Herman Neubauer, who had worked in Hartford and Chicago; Herbert Haupt, who had returned to Germany from Chicago via Mexico and Japan; and Werner Theil, who had immigrated to the United States in 1927, worked in Detroit, Los Angeles, and Philadelphia, joined the Bund, and returned to Germany in 1939.

Dasch was arrested at the Mayflower Hotel in Washington. He directed the FBI to his comrades, who by then were in New York and Chicago. Within a few days the FBI had all eight Germans, along with incendiary devices concealed in pens and pencils; bombs that looked like pieces of coal; fuzes, detonators, primers, timing devices, draft cards, Social Security cards, and $174,588.62 in U.S. coins and currency. They also had plans for the sabotaging of aluminum plants and railroad facilities.

On July 2, 1942, President ROOSEVELT proclaimed that anyone planning to commit sabotage or espionage would be "subject to the law of war" and handed over to military jurisdiction. Dasch and Burger, as American citizens, could be charged with TREASON; the others, for espionage. The military tribunal appointed by the President charged them all with espionage.

The saboteurs' defense attorneys, both Army colonels, challenged the tribunal's jurisdiction and sought writs of habeas corpus, the constitutionally protected right against illegal detention. After two days of hearings, the Court held that the President had acted lawfully. But its published opinion noted that no presidential proclamation could limit the Court's power.

The secret trial was conducted in the Department of Justice Building from July 8 to Aug. 4, with Attorney General Francis Biddle and Maj. Gen. Myron C. Cramer, Judge Advocate General of the WAR DEPARTMENT handling the prosecution before seven general officers appointed by the President. On Aug. 8 the President announced that all eight men had been convicted and six had been executed. The transcript of the trial would remain secret until long after the war.

Although the court sentenced all eight to death, Biddle and J. EDGAR HOOVER, director of the FBI, appealed to the President to commute the sentences of Dasch and Burger for their help in locating and convicting the others. Dasch's sentence was commuted to thirty years and Burger's to life imprisonment. The others were executed in the District of Columbia's electric chair and buried in the District's Potters Field.

In 1948 President TRUMAN pardoned Dasch and Burger on condition that they be deported. They were released from prison and taken to the American Zone of still-occupied Germany, where they were generally shunned.

Several Americans who aided the saboteurs were arrested, and their legal defenses led to several treason decisions by the U.S. Supreme Court.

Sad Sack

The epitome of incompetence in uniform, the Sad Sack cartoon character was created by Sgt. George Baker, a former Walt Disney artist on the staff of the magazine *Yank*. Sad Sack lived on after the war as a comic strip and entered the LANGUAGE as a noun describing "an inept person, especially an inept serviceman."

Saint-Nazaire

Site of the largest dry dock on France's Atlantic coast. The dock was destroyed by British COMMANDOS in March 1942 to prevent its use by German battleships.

Saint-Nazaire, some 125 miles southeast of Brest, was the only dry dock available to the Germans on the Atlantic coast that could accommodate the large battleships *BISMARCK* and *TIRPITZ*. The former battleship was steaming toward the dock when she was sunk by British naval forces in May 1941. After the battleship *Tirpitz* became operational in Jan. 1942, the British naval high command made the decision to destroy the dock to prevent the ship from using Saint-Nazaire as a base from which to raid Allied CONVOYS.

Early on March 28, 1942, while a diversionary air strike was flown against the town, a British destroyer escorted by eighteen motor torpedo boats approached the dock. They were detected and engaged by German shore guns, but the destroyer *Campbeltown,* formerly the USS *Buchanan* (DD 131), rammed into the dock gates and was scuttled by her crew. Those commandos and sailors who were not killed in the fighting were mostly captured.

Late that morning some forty senior German officers were on board the *Campbeltown* to plan her removal; several hundred German soldiers were nearby looking at the ship. Without warning, almost five tons of explosives in the ship blew up. The dock was disabled for the remainder of the war.

The commanding officer of the *Campbeltown,* one of five participants in the raid to receive the VICTORIA CROSS, had his citation read to him while in a PRISONER OF WAR camp.

During the remainder of the war the Saint-Nazaire shipyard supported German U-BOATS with a SUBMARINE PEN located at the port. Saint-Nazire was also site of the French SNCA aircraft factory.

Saipan

A JAPANESE MANDATED ISLAND, about 14 miles long and 2 to 5 miles wide, that was the first objective in the battle of the MARIANA Islands. On June 15, 1944, a landing force of 71,000 Marines under Lt. Gen. HOLLAND M. SMITH, went ashore on the southern coast near Aslito airfield. Clandestine preliminary scouting by UNDERWATER DEMOLITION TEAMS had brought back important information on water depth, channels, tides, and currents.

The 30,000 defenders fought viciously. Before the end of the day, 2,000 Marines were killed or wounded. But 20,000 were on the island. For reinforcements, Holland Smith ordered the Army's 27th Infantry REGIMENT ashore. The soldiers, on the 4th Marine DIVISION's right flank, helped take the airfield.

As Marine and Army troops fought side by side, their respective generals fought their own struggle. Holland Smith, whose nickname was "Howling Mad," was dissatisfied with the Army's performance and its general's apparent inability to press the attack. The Marine Smith relieved his subordinate, Maj. Gen. Ralph Smith, and assumed direct command of the Army operation. (The Army later upheld Ralph Smith's actions.)

By June 20 the southern end of the island was cleared, except for a warren of concealed caves and bunkers. From them emerged at dawn on July 7 about 3,000 of the remaining Japanese, screaming in a BANZAI CHARGE. Staggered by the vicious attack, the Americans fell back, then quickly recovered.

Japanese death-defying fanaticism stunned Americans. *Time* magazine correspondent Robert Sherrod told of seeing a Japanese soldier blasted out of a pile of logs by a concussion grenade, then wounded by another. "He struggled up, pointed his bayonet into his stomach and tried to cut himself open in approved hara-kiri fashion. The disemboweling never came off. Someone shot the Jap with a CARBINE. But, like all Japs, he took a lot of killing. Even after four bullets had thudded into his body he rose to one knee. Then the American shot him through the head and the Jap was dead."

On June 22 Holland Smith declared Saipan secured. By then, all but about 1,000 of the 30,000 Japanese defenders were dead. Some killed themselves in the final moments by jumping from cliffs onto jagged seaside rocks. They were joined by an estimated 22,000 civilians, including whole families. Some were pushed or pulled to their deaths by Japanese soldiers as they themselves jumped; others voluntarily leaped rather than endure the American barbarism they had been warned to expect. American casualties numbered 16,525 killed and wounded.

Sakai, Ens. Saburo (1916–)

One of Japan's leading fighter ACES. An enlisted naval aviator, Sakai was in combat over China in 1938–1941. Then, flying the advanced A6M ZERO fighter, Sakai flew in the Japanese attack on the Philippines, and on Dec. 10, 1941, was the first Japanese pilot to shoot down an AAF B-17 FLYING FORTRESS. (See COLIN P. KELLY.)

Flying from land bases, Sakai also saw combat over JAVA and in the SOLOMON ISLANDS area. On Aug. 7, 1942, moments after his 58th aerial kill over GUADALCANAL, he was severely wounded while engaging several U.S. F4F WILDCAT fighters. Despite being paralyzed on his left side, wounded in the skull, and losing his right eye, Sakai flew his damaged Zero back to RABAUL and landed safely. He had been airborne for eight and a half hours!

Sakai then served as a flight instructor in Japan until mid-1944 when he flew combat missions over IWO JIMA, increasing his score of aerial victories to sixty-four. He volunteered for KAMIKAZE missions and actually took off on a suicide flight, but returned to his base—with honor—having found no suitable targets.

Promoted to ensign late in 1944, Sakai was the highest-scoring Japanese fighter ace to survive the war.

Sakhalin Island,

see KURIL ISLANDS.

Salamander,

see HE 162.

Salerno

Italian port city on the Gulf of Salerno on the Tyrrhenian Sea about 25 miles south of Naples and site of an Allied AMPHIBIOUS LANDING on Sept. 9, 1943. Salerno was chosen for the invasion, code-named Avalanche, primarily because it was at the northern limit for aircraft based on Allied-held SICILY.

While the U.S. Fifth ARMY under Lt. Gen. MARK W. CLARK landed along the coast, U.S. RANGERS and British COMMANDOS landed on the Salerno peninsula, the Rangers to take a pass leading to the Naples plains and the Commandos to capture Salerno itself.

The invaders met little initial opposition. ROCKETS, launched from LANDING CRAFT modified for test-firing, were experimentally added to the naval gunfire for the landings. Some rockets exploded a minefield. They proved their worth and would be used in future Allied assaults.

On land and in the air the Germans, with some Italian troops reluctantly pressed into service, mounted a stiff counterattack under strong air support. The Allied forces, short on shipping, did not get heavy armor until a British armored division started unloading five days after the initial landing.

Pinned down and threatened with being driven into the sea, Clark called on the 82nd Airborne DIVISION, which dropped a total of 4,000 men in night and day jumps on Sept. 13–14. Fighting continued, with British battleships aiding the men on the beachhead. On Sept. 15 the British Eighth Army, driving north from its landing site at Reggio, made contact, and two days later the Salerno beachhead was declared secure.

Salient

British code name for reinforcement of MALTA, June 1942.

Sally

Already obsolete at the time of the PEARL HARBOR attack, the Ki-21 Type 97 heavy bomber (Allied code name Sally) remained the backbone of the

Japanese Army Air Force's bomber squadrons throughout the war. The Sally entered service in 1937 and was used against Soviet forces in Manchuria in 1939 and against the Chinese in the lengthy Japanese warfare in China. The Sally flew against U.S. forces in the South Pacific, but by the end of the war the plane was employed primarily as a transport.

On May 24, 1945, seven Sallys flew from Japan to land at an American-held airfield on OKINAWA; five were shot down, but the two survivors crashlanded at Yontan airfield, and the twelve COMMANDOS from the planes destroyed seven U.S. aircraft, fuel drums, and an ammunition dump before being killed by defending U.S. Marines. At the war's end the Sally joined other Japanese aircraft that were painted white with green crosses to carry VIPs negotiating the Japanese SURRENDER. The Sally thus had the distinction of being in Japanese Army service longer than any other other combat aircraft.

A Mitsubishi design, the Sally was developed as a heavy bomber to strike targets in the Soviet Far East. The prototype flew in 1937. The design was accepted, but it was reengined and was continually refined (by Nakajima as well as Mitsubishi) to increase the BOMB load and defensive armament. The improved Ki-21-II was the definitive variant, with the IIb subseries introducing a dorsal gun turret (in place of the "greenhouse"; see below). A further improvement (Ki-21-III) was rejected in favor of the Ki-67 PEGGY. Production of the Sally continued until Sept. 1944 with 2,064 aircraft being produced.

The Sally was a twin-engine, mid-wing aircraft distinguished by an elongated dorsal "greenhouse" aft of the cockpit, a glazed nose, and tall tail fin. The undercarriage fully retracted into the radial engine nacelles. Up to 2,200 pounds of bombs could be carried in the internal bomb bay. The IIb variant had a defensive armament of one 12.7-mm machine gun in the dorsal turret, four 7.7-mm hand-held machine guns in the nose and other positions, and a remote-controlled 7.7-mm gun in the tail "stinger" position.

Maximum speed for the IIb was 297 mph, while its range was 1,350 miles on combat missions. The aircraft was flown by a crew of seven.

Salzburg Conferences

Austrian site of two German-Italian conferences. On Aug. 11, 1939, Count GALEAZZO CIANO, the Italian Foreign Minister, met with his German opposite number, JOACHIM VON RIBBENTROP, at an estate near Salzburg, about 10 miles from BERCHTESGADEN, the Alpine retreat of HITLER. Ciano was hoping for negotiations to stave off the war, but Ribbentrop told him, "We want war."

On April 28–29, 1942, Hitler met at Salzburg with BENITO MUSSOLINI and other Italian Fascist leaders who committed more Italian troops to the EASTERN FRONT, where German forces were bogging down.

San Antonio

Code name for first U.S. B-29 SUPERFORTRESS bombing missions against Japan flown from the MARIANA ISLANDS, Nov. 1944.

San Francisco Conference

Meeting that established the UNITED NATIONS. When the conference convened on April 25, 1945, the structure of the United Nations had been decided by President ROOSEVELT, Prime Minister CHURCHILL, and Soviet leader JOSEF STALIN. Even though Roosevelt had died on April 12, the conference went on fairly smoothly. Some 10,000 people attended, including an army of stenographers and interpreters, who translated hundreds of documents into the five official languages: English, French, Spanish, Russian, and Chinese.

The basic concept of the UN had been discussed at the DUNBARTON OAKS CONFERENCE of 1944, when U.S., British, and Soviet officials (with some Chinese representation) agreed on the structure for a postwar world organization: a General Assembly of all member nations, which controlled the activities of UN operations; and a Security Council, an executive body whose permanent members would be the United States, England, China, and the Soviet Union plus six nations regularly chosen by the Assembly. The real power of maintaining international peace and security would be vested in the council.

Left unresolved at Dunbarton Oaks was the question of veto rights for major powers. At the YALTA CONFERENCE of 1945, Roosevelt, Churchill, and Stalin had agreed that major powers in the Security

Council would have the right to veto General Assembly sanctions. But Stalin was not satisfied with the one-nation-one-vote formula in the General Assembly. He at first wanted sixteen votes, but settled for three, which would come from the Soviet Union plus two Soviet republics, the Ukraine and Byelorussia.

The San Francisco Conference began with representation from the forty-six nations that had been represented at the UNITED NATIONS CONFERENCE in 1942. During the San Francisco Conference, the two Soviet republics were added, along with Denmark and Argentina. By the time the members signed the charter on June 26, Germany had surrendered and the postwar era had begun. France was added as a permanent member. Poland, whose government was still not organized, was not officially represented but was allowed to become a member. (For a listing of original members, see UNITED NATIONS.)

San Marino,
see ITALY.

Santa Cruz

Island group in the Southwest Pacific. During the bitter and continuing battle for GUADALCANAL, U.S. and Japanese warships clashed in what became known as the battle of Santa Cruz (Oct. 25–26, 1942). Japanese carrier planes damaged the U.S. carrier ENTERPRISE (CV 6) and the new BATTLESHIP *South Dakota* (BB 57), and fatally crippled the carrier *HORNET* (CV 8), which was attacked simultaneously by dive and TORPEDO bombers.

Saratoga (CV 3)

One of the two largest U.S. AIRCRAFT CARRIERS of the war. The *Saratoga,* sister ship of the ill-fated *LEXINGTON* (CV 2), was on the U.S. West Coast at the time of the PEARL HARBOR attack on Dec. 7, 1941. She immediately sailed westward to reinforce the two U.S. carriers then operating in the Pacific and took part in the abortive effort to relieve WAKE ISLAND, under Japanese attack.

She then operated mainly in Hawaiian waters until, on Jan. 11, 1942, she was torpedoed by a Japanese submarine. Six crewmen were killed and the ship suffered damage to her engineering spaces.

She returned to the West Coast for five months of repairs and overhaul.

Subsequently, the "Sara" departed the United States for the battle of MIDWAY on June 1, 1942, but arrived too late for that carrier battle. The *Saratoga* then participated in the U.S. landings at GUADALCANAL in Aug. 1942 and saw combat in several engagements with Japanese ships and aircraft in the area. She was again struck by a TORPEDO from a Japanese submarine on Aug. 31 and had to be towed out of the area by a U.S. CRUISER. After repairs she returned to the SOLOMON ISLANDS in Dec. 1942 and was in combat almost continually from that time.

The *Saratoga* participated in the U.S. assaults on TARAWA and MAKIN in 1943, the MARSHALL ISLANDS landings and attacks on Sumatra in 1944, and IWO JIMA landings in Feb. 1945. In the last operation the "Sara" operated as a night carrier. On the evening of Feb. 21 she was devastated by KAMIKAZE and BOMB hits; the ship erupted in flames and lost 123 crewmen. She was able to steam out of the area and again underwent repairs.

At the end of the war she was pressed into service carrying troops from the Pacific to the United States in Operation MAGIC CARPET. At the time she ceased operating as a carrier she had the greatest number of aircraft landings ever recorded by a carrier—98,549 in seventeen years. The "Sara" had earned seven BATTLE STARS during the war.

On July 25, 1946, she was sunk in the ATOMIC BOMB TESTS at Bikini atoll. The carrier was moored some 300 to 500 yards from the aim point for the bomb; the underwater atomic detonation lifted the massive "Sara" 43 feet out of the water and moved her horizontally several hundred yards. She settled slowly to the 180-foot bottom of the lagoon, disappearing some seven-and-a-half hours after the blast.

The *Saratoga* had been converted during construction from a battle cruiser to a carrier. She was launched on Apr. 7, 1925, and placed in commission on Nov. 16, 1927. She had a standard displacement of almost 36,000 tons and was 888 feet long. As built she had a cruiser's gun armament of eight 8-inch (203-mm) guns (removed in 1941) plus lighter weapons. During the war she carried some ninety aircraft. She set a record big-ship speed of 34.99 knots.

The U.S. carrier *Saratoga* (CV 3) after being attacked by Japanese kamikaze or naval suicide planes off Iwo Jima in Feb. 1945. Within a few minutes the "Sara" was hit by three bombs and two kamikazes. Two hours later she was hit by another bomb and struck by a kamikaze that bounced over the side. The *Saratoga* survived, suffering 123 men dead or missing and 192 injured. She was able to land aircraft again an hour after the second attack, but had to withdraw from battle to a U.S. shipyard for repairs. (*U.S. Navy*)

The only larger aircraft carrier than the "Lex" and "Sara" completed during the war was the 64,800-ton Japanese *Shinano*, which was sunk by a U.S. SUBMARINE before she became operational. The U.S. Navy built three 45,000-ton carriers of the *Midway* (CVB 41) class during the war, but the lead ship was not commissioned until Sept. 10, 1945.

Satin

Code name for planned U.S. II CORPS operation against Sfax, Tunisia.

Saturn

Soviet code name for projected offensive west of STALINGRAD aimed at recapturing Rostov from the Germans, Nov. 1942.

Sauckel, Fritz (1894–1946)

Director of Germany's SLAVE LABOR program. Sauckel, a NAZI functionary since 1927, was *Gauleiter* (district leader) and later *Reichsstatthalter* (governor) of the German state of Thuringia. On March 21, 1942, HITLER made him Germany's slave labor master with the title Plenipotentiary-General for Labor Mobilization. He was also an "honorary" SS general officer.

A member of the prosecution staff at the WAR CRIMES tribunal believed that Sauckel, though a pawn of higher officials, used "complete ruthlessness and unfeeling efficiency in application of a program which took five million into slave labor and countless numbers to their death." Found guilty of war crimes and crimes against humanity, he was hanged at Nuremberg.

Saucy

Code name for Allied limited offensive to reopen land route from Burma to China.

Saudi Arabia

Capitals: Mecca, Riyadh; pop. 5,500,000 (est. 1945). Saudi Arabia was the largest of the four major political entities occupying the vast Arabian Peninsula during the war. The others—Yemen, Kuwait, and Oman—played hardly any role in the war. But the kingdom of Saudi Arabia was the kingdom of oil, and its continual affiliation with the ALLIES became an important diplomatic issue.

On the eve of the EUROPEAN WAR nations that would be belligerents had competed fiercely for rights to Saudi oil. In 1939 the kingdom of Saudi Arabia granted a concession to Standard Oil Company of California, which had first struck oil in potentially commercial quantity in Saudi's El Hasa province in 1938. Standard Oil gave King Ibn Saud of Saudi Arabia $1,500,000 in gold and promised $750,000 a year while exploring for oil. The United States had won out over the bids of Germany and Japan.

Although Saudi Arabia professed neutrality at the onset of the war, the desert kingdom was in fact on the Allied side. The Saudis accepted Allied-directed oil production restrictions. In return, Saudi Arabia got LEND-LEASE aid and Arizona experts on scarce-water farming, along with U.S. crews that dug deep water wells. Thousands of previously barren desert acres bloomed with grains and vegetables.

President ROOSEVELT and Prime Minister CHURCHILL each separately took pains to court King Ibn Saud when the Big Two were traveling to and from the YALTA CONFERENCE in Feb. 1945. The king met with Roosevelt on the U.S. CRUISER *Quincy* (CA 71) in Great Bitter Lake near Cairo. The monarch's voyage to Egypt on board a U.S. DESTROYER was his first trip outside of his kingdom.

Later he met with Churchill at a hotel in an oasis. "A number of social problems arose," Churchill recalled in his history of the war. "I had been told that neither smoking nor alcoholic beverages were allowed in the Royal Presence. As I was host of the luncheon I raised the matter at once, and said to the interpreter that if it was the religion of His Majesty to deprive himself of smoking and alcohol I must point out that my rule of life prescribed as an absolutely sacred rite smoking cigars and also the drinking of alcohol before, after, and if need be during all meals and in the intervals between them. The King graciously accepted the position."

The king also accepted the urging of Roosevelt and Churchill that Saudi Arabia declare war on the AXIS so as to qualify for membership in the UNITED NATIONS. He agreed, and on March 1 the monarchy—except for the "zone of holy shrines"—declared war against Japan and Germany.

Savo Island

Site of a major U.S. naval disaster. Savo Island is just north of GUADALCANAL in the SOLOMON ISLANDS, where U.S. Marine landings on the morning of Aug. 7, 1942, marked the first U.S. offensive operation in the Pacific.

The Japanese reacted immediately against the U.S. invasion force with major air strikes flown from their base at RABAUL. That night a Japanese attack force of five heavy cruisers, two light cruisers, and a single destroyer departed Rabaul to attack the U.S. invasion force.

A U.S. SUBMARINE and several Allied aircraft sighted the Japanese ships, but warning did not reach the U.S. commanders off Guadalcanal. On the night of Aug. 8–9, 1942, the Japanese warships encountered an American-Australian force of CRUISERS and DESTROYERS steaming between the islands of Tulagi and Guadalcanal. The Japanese ships—none equipped with RADAR, as were the Allied ships—opened fire with guns and TORPEDOES, making use of their superior night-fighting tactics. In less than an hour three U.S. heavy cruisers, one Australian heavy cruiser, and one U.S. destroyer were sunk; another U.S. cruiser and two destroyers were damaged.

The Australian cruiser *Canberra* lost only eighty-four men, but the three U.S. cruisers—the *Astoria* (CA 34), *Quincy* (CA 39), and *Vincennes* (CA 44)—suffered the combined loss of 1,203 crewmen. The destroyer *Jarvis* (DD 393) suffered the loss of all 247 men on board when she was damaged by Japanese gunfire and a torpedo in the night attack, and succumbed early on the afternoon of Aug. 9 to Japanese air attack.

The Japanese ships suffered one minor shell hit in the battle, but with daylight the old U.S. submarine *S-44* (SS 155) torpedoed and sank one of the withdrawing Japanese cruisers off New Ireland Island.

The waters between Tulagi and Guadalcanal were soon labeled IRONBOTTOM SOUND because of the number of warships lying on the seafloor.

SB-2

Soviet medium bomber that fought in late 1930s conflicts as well as World War II. The SB-2 was flown on the Republican side in the SPANISH CIVIL WAR and in conflicts with the Japanese in Manchuria in the late 1930s, and in the war with Finland in 1939, by which time it was the most numerous twin-engine bomber in the world. The SB-2 was used throughout the 1941–1945 war, although from 1943 it was succeeded in frontline service by newer bombers.

The Tupolev-developed aircraft was initially designated ANT-40 (for A. N. Tupolev). It apparently first flew on April 25, 1934, and production aircraft were being delivered by the end of 1935. Improvements were incorporated throughout the aircraft's production run, with approximately 6,650 being completed by Jan. 1941. These included several hundred SB-3 trainers (with an open cockpit in the nose for the student), many of which were employed as tugs for military GLIDERS and sailplanes. In addition, over 200 early SB-2s were sold to China in 1937 and licensed production was begun in Czechoslovakia, but all 111 planes went into Luftwaffe service.

A modified SB-2 was produced as the SB-RK dive bomber. The prototype flew in 1940 but only 200 were produced before the factory had to be evacuated in the fall of 1941 to escape the German advance. Some of these aircraft had a twin tail with small, oval fins, and a fully retractable main undercarriage. There was also a PS-41 transport variant with a solid nose.

The twin-engine aircraft had a mid-fuselage elliptical wing, a shortened, rounded nose with a glazed bombardier's position, and a large, rounded tail fin. Most combat machines had in-line engines, with the main undercarriage partially retracting into the nacelles. Some early aircraft had radial engines.

The SB-2*bis* had a maximum speed of 280 mph

and a range of 1,430 miles. An internal BOMB bay could hold up to 1,320 pounds of bombs. A variety of armament combinations were fitted, but the standard SB-2 arrangement was a twin 7.62-mm machine gun in the nose, and single guns in the dorsal and ventral positions. SB-3 trainers, however, had a power turret in the dorsal position.

SB2A Buccaneer

The Brewster Aircraft attempt to develop a replacement for the SBD DAUNTLESS. The XSB2A-1 scout–dive bomber first flew on June 17, 1941, and large-scale production was ordered for British, Dutch, and U.S. Navy service (the British variants being named Bermuda). Although 771 of these aircraft were delivered, they were used for training and as target tugs, and there is no record that any were used in combat. The U.S. AAF gave the aircraft the designation A-34, but none was procured. The effort was terminated in 1943 in favor of the SB2C HELLDIVER.

SB2C Helldiver

U.S. Navy carrier-based scout–dive bomber. Successor to the highly successful SBD DAUNTLESS, the Helldiver never achieved the popularity nor successes of the earlier dive bomber. After several technical problems were overcome, the SB2C saw its first action in a carrier strike on RABAUL on Nov. 11, 1943, and by the battle of the Philippine Sea in June 1944—the last combat sorties by the SBD—there were 165 Helldivers on five of the fleet carriers compared to fifty-seven Dauntlesses on two fleet carriers.

The SB2C went on board all AIRCRAFT CARRIERS of the *ESSEX* (CV 9) class as well as some older ships, but because of the KAMIKAZE threat that developed in late 1944, only some fifteen dive bombers (plus fifteen torpedo bombers) were embarked in U.S. fleet carriers, with the remaining seventy-odd aircraft being fighters. The U.S. Marine Corps also flew large numbers of SB2C dive bombers from land bases. A few were flown by the British.

Following a long line of Curtiss-built dive bombers (most with the company name Helldiver), the SB2C was the firm's first monoplane. The prototype XSB2C-1 first flew on Dec. 18, 1940, but crashed a few days later. Large-scale production had been ordered the previous month for the Navy and Army (as A-25). Through 1945 Curtiss produced just over 5,516 SB2Cs while the Canadian Car & Foundry in Ontario built 860 SBW models and Fairchild-Montreal built 300 similar SBF variants. The AAF ordered 900 planes from Curtiss, but most were transferred to the Marine Corps, reflecting Army aviation's disdain for dive bombing. The British took twenty-six of the Canadian-built Navy aircraft under LEND-LEASE. One XSB2C-2 was fitted as a floatplane, the twin-float conversion being completed in Sept. 1942.

The SB2C had a large fuselage with a large fin and rudder. An internal BOMB bay could carry 1,000 pounds of bombs; an aerial TORPEDO could be carried under the fuselage, but the SB2C was never used in the torpedo role. Bombs and rockets could be carried under the wings. Early aircraft had four .50-cal machine guns in the wings, which were soon replaced by twin 20-mm cannon with a flexible .50-cal. twin mount in the after cockpit. The wings folded for carrier stowage, another advantage over the SBD.

The SB2C-1 had a maximum speed of 281 mph and a range of 1,165 miles when delivering a 1,000-pound bomb load to just over half that distance.

After the war SB2Cs were flown by the French Navy—which used them in combat in Indochina into the 1950s—as well as Italy and Thailand. (Italy designated them S2C-5 vice *SB2C-5* because Italy was not allowed to have "bombers" after the war.)

SB2U Vindicator

U.S. Navy scout–dive bomber that saw limited action in the war. When the Japanese attacked PEARL HARBOR on Dec. 7, 1941, only two of seven U.S. AIRCRAFT CARRIERS had SB2Us embarked, the *Ranger* (CV 4) with twenty-five planes and the *WASP* (CV 7) with thirty-six planes. However, the *LEXINGTON* (CV 2) was en route to MIDWAY Island with eighteen Marine SB2Us when the Japanese struck. After searching for the Japanese carriers, she returned to Pearl Harbor with her Marine aircraft. The Marine fliers then made a nine-hour, forty-five-minute flight from Oahu to Midway, the 1,137-mile route being the longest yet made over water by a single-engine combat aircraft. At the time of Pearl Harbor two Marine squadrons flew the SB2U. The

carriers soon gave up their Vindicators and the only aircraft to see combat were those flown by Marines, including the Midway-based planes in the June 1942 battle of Midway.

The first flight of the XSB2U-1 occurred on Jan. 4, 1936, and the plane entered naval service in 1938. Production of the Vought-designed SB2U totaled only 170 aircraft as the Navy was not fully convinced of the viability of monoplanes as dive bombers. *After* the SB2U was ordered, the Navy gave a contract to Vought for the SB3U biplane scout bomber. An XSB2U-3 was fitted with twin floats to evaluate the possible role of a floatplane bomber, but the concept was not pursued by the United States (an SB2C HELLDIVER was similarly evaluated).

The low-wing SB2U had folding wings and carried its BOMBS externally. Top speed was 250 mph and a single 500- or 1,000-pound bomb could be carried. Flown by a pilot and radioman/gunner, the SB2U had one forward-firing .50-cal. machine gun and a second, flexible gun in the after cockpit.

SBD Dauntless

The most effective dive bomber of World War II in terms of warship tonnage sunk. U.S. Navy SBD scout–dive bombers destroyed four Japanese aircraft carriers in a single day at the battle of MIDWAY on June 4, 1942. At the beginning of the war four of the U.S. Navy's seven AIRCRAFT CARRIERS each embarked two SBD squadrons of eighteen or more planes, and two Marine land-based squadrons flew SBDs. Subsequently, all U.S. large carriers operated SBDs until mid-1944. Their baptism of fire began during the PEARL HARBOR attack on Dec. 7, 1941, when SBDs from the carrier *ENTERPRISE* (CV 6) attempted to land on Ford Island in the center of Pearl Harbor during the raid. Several were shot down by overanxious antiaircraft gunners at Pearl Harbor.

SBDs were used in the early air strikes on Japanese islands in the Pacific, the first flown from the *Enterprise* with thirty-six SBDs against KWAJALEIN on Feb. 1, 1942. At the battle of CORAL SEA in May 1942 the SBDs and torpedo planes sank the Japanese light carrier *SHOHO,* while the dive bombers also damaged a large carrier; at Midway the following month the SBDs sank four large carriers—the

Akagi, Kaga, Horyu, and *Soryu*—and a heavy cruiser. In the ensuing U.S. SOLOMONS–NEW GUINEA CAMPAIGN, carrier- and land-based Navy and Marine SBDs sank considerable Japanese shipping.

In the Atlantic, SBDs flew from U.S. carriers to support the NORTH AFRICAN INVASION in Nov. 1942, and were used in both oceans from aircraft carriers and ESCORT CARRIERS in the antisubmarine role.

The SBD served as the Navy's principal bomber aircraft until mid-1944. The replacement SB2C HELLDIVER was delayed in fleet introduction because of teething problems, and it never achieved the popularity of the SBD. While Helldivers did replace SBDs on the larger carriers in 1944–1945, the older aircraft flew from escort carriers through the end of the war. The Marine air arm reached a peak of twenty land-based squadrons flying the SBD.

The SBD was a low-wing monoplane with a canopy housing the pilot and radioman-gunner. It had large dive brakes and was considered a reliable, rugged, and effective aircraft. Beneath the fuselage was a swinging BOMB cradle (so the bomb would clear the propeller) and bomb racks were mounted beneath the wings. Unlike most contemporary carrier planes, the SBD's wings did not fold for shipboard storage.

The prototype SBD was a production Northrop BT-1 dive bomber, redesignated XBT-2 for development purposes. The BT-series was the product of the genius of aircraft designers Jack Northrop and Ed Heinemann. The XBT-1 flew for the first time on Aug. 19, 1935. Production was initiated for the Navy. Numerous changes were made to produce the XBT-2 and the designation scout–dive bomber was assigned; in highly successful flight tests the aircraft reached a speed of 265.5 mph. SBD production was ordered at the Douglas Aircraft Co. in April 1939 with deliveries of the SBD-1 to Marine units beginning in late 1940; the improved SBD-2 began entering Navy carrier service the following year.

Through 1944 the Navy and Marine Corps took delivery of 4,923 SBDs, some of which were additionally fitted with cameras and had a "P" (photographic) suffix after their model number. The U.S.

AAF received 1,013 similar aircraft with the designation A-24 and, although they were used in combat in NEW GUINEA by the AAF, dive bombing never gained popularity with the Army.

Nine SBD-5s were transferred to Britain for flight tests, but no procurement followed; New Zealand did operate a number of SBDs during the war. The FREE FRENCH Air Force began flying the A-24B in 1943 and the French naval air arm received SBDs for carrier use in late 1944. They survived to be used against Communist troops in the French INDOCHINA war.

The SBD-5, the principal production variant, had a maximum speed of 255 mph and a cruising speed of 185 mph. Normal range was 1,115 miles in a strike role and 1,565 miles when used as a scout. Bomb load (all external) was a 1,600-pound bomb under the fuselage and two 325-pound bombs under the wings. One or two .50-cal. machine guns were fixed in the engine cowling and the gunner had an aft-firing .30-cal. twin gun mount.

SC Seahawk

The U.S. Navy's ultimate catapult floatplane for use from BATTLESHIPS and CRUISERS. The Seahawk was unusual for U.S. floatplanes, being a single-place aircraft; by the time the aircraft entered service, the Navy had sufficient flying boats to perform the search-and-rescue missions previously flown by floatplanes. The first Seahawks to go to sea were assigned to the large cruiser *Guam* (CB 2) in Oct. 1944. Few were in service when the war ended, and their shipboard career was brief, ending in late 1949 as HELICOPTERS took their place on U.S. warships.

The design was initiated in 1942 as a successor to the OS2U KINGFISHER and SO3C SEAMEW floatplanes. The prototype XSC-1 flew on Feb. 16, 1944, and 577 aircraft were delivered through Oct. 1946, including ten two-seat SC-2 variants.

The Curtiss-built Seahawk had a fighter-like, low-wing configuration with a large radial engine, a large centerline float, and wing-mounted stabilizing floats. It could be flown from shore bases with wheels replacing the float. The pilot sat under a bubble canopy. A second person could be crammed into the fuselage, if necessary. The large central float had an internal bay that could carry two 100-pound BOMBS; another two 250-pound bombs could be carried under the wings or a RADAR pod could be substituted for one bomb.

The SC-1 had a top speed of 313 mph and a range of 625 miles. Two fixed, forward-firing .50-cal. machine guns were fitted.

Scapa Flow

British naval base in the Orkney Islands off the northern coast of Scotland. It was the principal British naval base in World War I and scene of the scuttling of the German High Seas Fleet in June 1919 following its surrender to the British.

A British survey of Scapa Flow in 1937 had revealed a gap in the defenses. It was though this gap—a passage many officials felt too shallow and too swept by too strong a current for passage of a U-BOAT—that the *U-47* commanded by *Korvetten-kapitän* GÜNTHER PRIEN entered the base on the night of Oct. 13–14, 1939, and sank the battleship *Royal Oak* with heavy loss of life.

Following the U-boat success, the British fleet was withdrawn to other bases until a new survey of Scapa Flow could be undertaken and the shortcoming in the defenses corrected. (A blockship to plug the gap through which Prien had transited arrived a day after the attack.)

Schild und Schwert (Shield and Sword)

German code name for projected Army Group North offensive in the UKRAINE, 1944.

Schlingpflanze (Vine)

German code name for operation to widen the corridor to the Demyansk pocket in the Soviet Union, Oct. 1942.

Schnorchel,

see SNORKEL.

Schwarz (Black)

German code name for the military takeover of Italy after the fall of the Fascist government, 1943.

Schweinfurt

Center of German ball-bearing production and target of costly U.S. Eighth AIR FORCE raids. The first Schweinfurt raid on Aug. 17, 1943, was a complex mission: Taking off in a coordinated attack,

146 B-17 FLYING FORTRESS bombers would bomb the Messerschmitt factory at Regensburg, near the Austrian border, and would continue on to land at Allied air bases in North Africa; meanwhile, 230 B-17s would bomb the ball-bearing plants at Schweinfurt and return to their bases in England.

The Regensburg strike flight, under the command of Brig. Gen. CURTIS E. LeMAY, took off on time, but bad weather delayed the Schweinfurt-bound B-17s. Instead of taking off ten minutes after the Regensburg flight, the Schweinfurt raiders left their bases more than three hours late. The delay gave German fighters the chance to attack the first flight, land to refuel and rearm, then take off again to attack the second B-17 flight.

The Germans shot down twenty-four of the bombers attacking Regensburg and thirty-six of those bound for Schweinfurt. Others crashed in accidents. Damage was heavy to the Messerschmitt factory; little was inflicted at Schweinfurt.

A 420-plane raid on Schweinfurt was planned for Oct. 14, but by the time the day arrived B-17 losses had been so high only 291 B-17s could be assembled for the attack. They flew with fighter escort as far as AACHEN, the limit of fighter cover.

The bombers came under heavy attack. German fighters shot down sixty B-17s. Five B-17s crashed in England; 138 were badly damaged. The airmen named the day Black Thursday.

The raids caused a 50 percent drop in ball-bearing production. But at the rate the U.S. Eighth Air Force was losing B-17s such big daylight raids could not continue.

As a direct result of the Schweinfurt raids, U.S. tactics changed. Faith in daylight PRECISION BOMBING continued to be strong, but U.S. strategists realized that bombers could not bomb effectively without command of the air. New long-range fighters were needed. Production of the P-51 MUSTANG was speeded up, with dramatic results.

In a raid on Feb. 24, 1944, P-51s escorted the 228 B-17s that set out. Only eleven bombers were lost.

Scorched Earth Policy

The ancient practice of denying anything of value to an enemy, especially when the defender is in retreat. The term was used in the late 1930s when

Chinese, withdrawing from territory invaded by Japan, burned crops and even cities before advancing Japanese troops reached them.

Soviet armies similarly scorched the earth behind them as they retreated during the early stages of the GERMAN CAMPAIGN IN THE SOVIET UNION. The Germans, in turn, after exploiting the nations they conquered in the BALKANS-GREECE-CRETE CAMPAIGN, destroyed whatever they could as they retreated before Allied armies in the closing phase of the EUROPEAN WAR.

HITLER, wishing to punish defeatist Germans in a *Gotterdämmerung* finale of the war, ordered what would have been the most disastrous of all the war's scorched-earth decrees: the total destruction of what remained of Germany. The order came on March 19, 1945, when he directed the military, aided by Nazi civilian functionaries, to destroy what was later listed at the Nuremberg WAR CRIMES trial as "all industrial plants, all important electrical facilities, water works, gas works, food stores and clothing stores; all bridges, all railway and communications installations, all waterways, all ships, all freight cars and all locomotives."

On April 23, 1945, German armaments chief ALBERT SPEER went to besieged BERLIN and, expecting to be arrested for TREASON, confessed that, in "conflict between personal loyalty and public duty," he and other high NAZI officials and army officers had refused to follow Hitler's order. Hitler, by then planning to end his own life, showed little interest in Speer's disobedience.

SD

Sicherheitsdienst, security service, the intelligence-gathering and espionage section of the SS. The SD's first chief was REINHARD HEYDRICH, who later became the head of the REICH CENTRAL SECURITY OFFICE. As described by SS chief HEINRICH HIMMLER, the SD's task was to "discover the enemies of the National Socialist concept." Through a vast network of informers and agents throughout Germany and conquered Europe, the SD worked closely with the GESTAPO. SD killers also carried out the *Nacht und Nebel Erlass*—the Night and Fog Decree—which HITLER had ordered in Dec. 1941 as a way of preventing the creating of "martyrs" by public execution. Under *NN,* as the SD called it,

citizens of occupied countries were taken to Germany in secrecy to "vanish without leaving a trace." Under the decree, "no information may be given as to their whereabouts or their fate." The Germans had a word for what happened to the tens of thousands of victims: They were *vernebelt,* transformed into mist.

In indicting the SD and Gestapo as organizations responsible for WAR CRIMES, the International Military Tribunal at Nuremberg accused them both of "the persecution and extermination of the JEWS, brutalities and killings in concentration camps, excesses in the administration of occupied countries, the administration of the SLAVE LABOR program and the mistreatment and murder of prisoners-of-war."

Sea Lion

German plan for AMPHIBIOUS LANDINGS in England in 1940. After the defeat of Belgium and France in June 1940, the victorious German armies faced an isolated, poorly armed Britain across a channel some 20 miles wide. When the British government scorned German peace feelers, HITLER, on July 16, 1940, issued a directive for the future course of the war: "As England, in spite of the hopelessness of her military situation, has so far shown herself unwilling to come to any compromise, I have therefore decided to begin to prepare for, and if necessary to carry out, an invasion of England. This operation is dictated by the necessity of eliminating Great Britain as a basis from which the war against Germany can be fought, and, if necessary, the island will be occupied."

The operation was given the code name *Seelöwe* or Sea Lion. The German Army immediately began organizing and preparing for an assault. The real burden, however, would fall to the German Navy and the Luftwaffe. The Navy was charged with transporting and protecting the invasion force, including minesweeping and planting defensive minefields; the Luftwaffe was to prevent British air attacks, engage naval vessels approaching the invasion force, destroy coastal defenses, and annihilate British reserves behind the beachheads. To accomplish its missions the Luftwaffe would have to destroy the RAF Fighter Command. Neither the German Navy nor the Luftwaffe was capable of such assignments in view of their weaknesses and the strengths of the RAF and Royal Navy.

Staff studies for an invasion of England had been undertaken by the German armed forces as early as Nov. 1939. The German Army looked at the invasion as a "gigantic river crossing." Early proposals called for up to forty divisions to be landed in several waves over several days. This was soon reduced to a more realistic assault wave that would consist of eleven infantry divisions, possibly two motorized divisions, supported by paratroopers from two Luftwaffe AIRBORNE divisions. The Army units would number 90,000 combat troops with 650 tanks and several thousand horses. They were to land and establish beachheads at Yarmouth and Lowestoft. These first-wave troops would require eleven days to land, after which additional divisions would come ashore at the rate of two divisions every four days.

These plans anticipated virtually no losses in landing craft. Also, other than the relatively few tanks and light artillery, no gunfire support would be available to the troops for several days. The largest ships the German Navy would risk in the Channel area would be destroyers. Rather, the Luftwaffe would provide close air support, as had occurred in previous BLITZKRIEG campaigns, *assuming* that the Luftwaffe had fully defeated the RAF.

By early July 1940 an invasion date of mid-August had been established. Both the Luftwaffe and Navy considered the Army's plan too ambitious. The troops and their equipment would be ferried across the English Channel in specialized landing craft, barges towed by tugs and trawlers, and by coastal steamers; it was highly questionable if sufficient craft were available and could be modified in time to transport the invasion force. A Navy memorandum declared: "The task allotted to the Navy in operation 'Sea Lion' is out of all proportion to the Navy's strength and bears no relation to the tasks that are set [for] the Army and Air Force."

Hitler put off the assault date to Sept. 15 and the size of the invasion was further scaled down as the military staffs began to understand the complexity of an amphibious landing. The assault force was revised to a first wave of nine divisions, a second wave of eight divisions (only four of them PANZER), a third wave of six divisions, plus a reserve force of two divisions. Airborne troops would also participate—three regiments of paratroopers and one of GLIDER troops. By the end of August there were 168 coastal steamers, 1,900 prahms, 221 tugs, the same number of steam-powered fishing trawlers that could be used as tugs, and over 1,000 motor launches available for Sea Lion—a remarkable achievement by the German Navy.

The key factor was control of the air over the English Channel and southern England. Without that control there could be no invasion. For the revised, mid-September invasion date the Luftwaffe was to begin the destruction of the RAF on Aug. 5, but was delayed by bad weather until Aug. 13. This was the beginning of the BATTLE OF BRITAIN.

The Luftwaffe was unable to defeat the RAF Fighter Command and thus achieve control of the skies. It soon became evident that the invasion could not be carried out before late September, when the Channel weather was expected to become too rough for an invasion. At a meeting on Sept. 17 Hitler postponed Sea Lion indefinitely. Preparations were to outwardly continue until Oct. 12 in an attempt to maintain political and military pressure on Britain.

With the suspension of Sea Lion, Hitler's attention turned to the Soviet Union, and never again was there a threat of German landings in England. Still, he harbored the thought that after the rapid, successful conquest of the Soviet Union (by the end of 1941), he could again turn his armies to the invasion of England—or possibly even Ireland. In fact, not until Feb. 13, 1942, were the German forces designated for the invasion officially released from that role. The British continued to maintain some invasion defenses until after the NORMANDY INVASION of June 1944.

Could Sea Lion have been a success? British soldier, historian, and author Peter Fleming, who did the most detailed analysis of the planned landing, wrote: "Operation Sea Lion, as planned and mounted, was doomed to failure and, had it been launched, could only have ended in disaster." Fleming did believe that immediately after the DUNKIRK withdrawal in early June 1940, a landing by three or four German divisions, and the rapid capture of airfields in southeast England, could have opened the country to German conquest.

Grossadmiral ERICH RAEDER, the Commander in

Chief of the German Navy from 1928 to 1943, later observed: "Hitler was never wholeheartedly in favor of Operation Sea Lion. By contrast with the driving force he put behind other operations, he was very sluggish in regard to the planning of the English invasion. It may be that he regarded the preparation as principally the means for bringing heavy moral and psychological pressure on the enemy. This, combined with the air Blitzkrieg on the British capital, he counted on to bring England to negotiate for peace."

SeaBees

U.S. Navy construction troops. Their name was derived from their official designation—Construction BATTALIONS.

The first SeaBee battalions were authorized on Jan. 5, 1942, and were initially composed of men who had worked in construction trades before the war. SeaBees were additionally trained as infantrymen, and often constructed airfields, port facilities, housing, and roads while under enemy fire.

SeaBee units were active in the Caribbean, Azores, North Africa, in the NORMANDY INVASION, the Mediterranean area, and throughout the Pacific. In some respects their most ambitious project was the rapid construction of several huge airfields and support facilities for B-29 SUPERFORTRESS bombers on the islands of GUAM, SAIPAN, and TINIAN, and the ports to bring in the fuel, BOMBS, construction materials, and provisions needed for the bombing of Japan. Naval construction BRIGADES were established to coordinate large projects, as on Guam where Army and Navy construction troops were assigned to the 5th Naval Construction Brigade.

The SeaBees' motto was "Can do."

Seagull

British code name for the operation to destroy German-laid mines off Sulitjelma, Norway, Sept. 1942. See also SOC SEAGULL.

Seahawk,

see SC Seahawk.

Seamew,

see SO3C Seamew.

Second Front

Term used for the often-delayed effort to open a front against Germany in Western Europe. The opening of a second front was continually demanded by Soviet leader JOSEF STALIN, who believed that a second front would draw off German forces from what he considered the "first front" (EASTERN FRONT)—the German-Soviet war. Pressure particularly built up in the summer of 1942, when Soviet reverses prompted the COMMUNIST PARTY OF THE U.S. to sponsor, both openly and covertly, public support for the immediate launching of a second front to aid "fellow workers" in the Soviet Union. The second front opened with the D-DAY NORMANDY INVASION on June 6, 1944.

Section

Small group of soldiers or Marines, either a combat, support, or administrative subunit. For example, a U.S. machine gun PLATOON had two sections, each with two SQUADS with one machine gun. Also found in the U.S. Army were such sections as headquarters, maintenance, administration, liaison, ammunition, message center, wire, litter bearer, and ambulance.

Seelöwe,

see SEA LION.

Segregation

The official policy that kept black and white servicemen and servicewomen in separate military units. In 1940 the U.S. Army had twelve black officers and 5,000 black soldiers. Negroes or "colored," as they were referred to, were not allowed in the ARMY AIR CORPS or Marine Corps. Until June 1942, the Navy admitted blacks only as messboys, and even when blacks were later given other ratings, 90 percent of the Navy's blacks were messboys. Black paratroopers fought forest fires in the United States.

Under pressure from black leaders, President ROOSEVELT established the Fair Employment Practices Committee, which would cancel government contracts of defense-industry employers who practiced discrimination. But this partial breakdown in segregation practices in civilian life did not carry over to military service.

The draft was segregated, SELECTIVE SERVICE regulations calling for separate call-ups of blacks and whites. Using as a yardstick the percentage of young black males in the U.S. population, the Army set 10.6 percent as the proper proportion. But an overwhelming percentage of black inductees got low marks in the ARMY GENERAL CLASSIFICATION TEST and so were given little specialized training and were assigned to labor in service units, such as dockside cargo handling.

As the war continued, the Army Air Forces established several black fighter and bomber GROUPS, including the highly publicized BLACK EAGLES; the Navy commissioned a handful of black officers; and the Marines finally began accepting blacks. But the black Marines were put into a segregated infantry BATTALION that did not go into combat. RED CROSS blood banks at first refused blood from blacks, then accepted it—but kept the blood segregated. White servicemen frequently clashed with blacks and Mexican-Americans, as did civilians. (See RACE RIOTS, ZOOT SUITERS.)

"By the war's end," Army historian Ulysses Lee

Black troops unload equipment at the Normandy beachhead from DUKW amphibious trucks. The Army used "Negro" soldiers largely as stevedores and construction troops until the high infantry attrition rates after the Normandy landings. *(U.S. Army via Imperial War Museum)*

wrote, "the services had learned that segregation hurt the war effort because it wasted black manpower, lowered unit effectiveness, and created unnecessary racial tension. It also subjected the services' civilian leadership to pressure from civil-rights groups. In the end, the war prompted the first small steps toward integrated units and laid the foundation for the armed forces' postwar desegregation."

Even before the U.S. entry into the war, the National Association for the Advancement of Colored People had campaigned vigorously for the integration of the armed services. The NAACP finally won a commitment from President Roosevelt: blacks would be enlisted in numbers that approximated the percentage of their numbers in local populations. But blacks usually were assigned to noncombat duties. In 1941, blacks, who made up about 8 percent of the U.S. population, were represented by the following in the Army: 5 percent of the infantry, 15 percent of the Quartermaster Corps, 25 percent of the Corps of Engineers. Few black women joined the Woman's Army Corps (WAC), which segregated units at the company level. "What these foolish leaders of the colored race are seeking," Secretary of War HENRY L. STIMSON wrote in his diary in Jan. 1942, "is at the bottom social equality."

Early in 1942 then-Brig. Gen. DWIGHT D. EISENHOWER, of the General Staff's War Plans Division, was the liaison between the Army and State Department on the issue of sending black troops overseas. He told a War Department inquiry that he had not found any country where black troops would be welcomed. The War Plans Division (soon to become the Operations Division), he said, had decided to send white and black troops simply as American troops. Official bans on black troops were made by Greenland, Iceland, Labrador, Panama—and even Alaska, where black engineer units would help to build the ALCAN HIGHWAY. Most of the men in the Engineers' force that built the 271-mile LEDO ROAD were black; Chinese officials requested that black units not be used near Kunming because western Chinese had never seen blacks.

Black leaders lobbied to get more blacks into combat, but Army Chief of Staff Gen. GEORGE C. MARSHALL, in an April 1943 memo, flatly stated Army policy: "Quit catering to the negroes' desire for a proportionate share of combat units. Put them where they will best serve the war effort." The WAR DEPARTMENT, however, did decide that black battalions could be attached to white units; a white-led, all-black task force was sent to Liberia. Overseas, nearly all black soldiers worked behind the front lines. Black Transportation Corps drivers, as well as white drivers, drove the RED BALL EXPRESS, which carried supplies to the U.S. First and Third ARMIES in Europe. Black smoke-generator companies laid smokescreens at ANZIO and SALERNO.

To maintain segregated forces, the Army and Army Air Forces usually placed blacks in small, scattered service units or in what a Nov. 1942 Army Ground Forces memo recommended: "combat units not larger than a battalion, organized so as to be self-administered." By the end of 1942, the percentage of black soldiers overseas was far below the percentage of blacks in the Army; in Hawaii, the percentage was 4.63, in Alaska, 1.34. By the spring of 1943 of the 504,000 U.S. soldiers overseas, 79,000 were black, mostly as service troops.

Under pressure to send more blacks into combat, the Army set up two black DIVISIONS, the 92nd and 93rd, both of which had some black junior officers. According to historian Ulysses Lee, the 93rd Division spent a year and a half "moving from one Pacific island to another, relieving elements of other divisions going forward to engage the enemy, taking over positions which were now rear areas, loading and unloading ships, cleaning out Japanese stragglers hiding out in 'secure' islands, and mounting invasions for other troops."

Elements of the 92nd Division fought in Italy in July 1944. One platoon and several other groups were disarmed and arrested for refusing to obey orders to advance toward German positions. An officer investigating a breakdown of morale in the 92nd Division wrote, "Most of the EM [enlisted men] have no confidence in their officers. . . . The men don't feel these officers [both white and black] are fit to lead them into combat."

The Navy usually assigned blacks who were not messboys to tugs and dockside work, but a SUBMARINE chaser had an all-black crew and black officers and the DESTROYER ESCORT *Mason* (DE 529) had an all-black crew. The captain was white, as were all the officers at first. Just before the war ended two black junior officers went on board the *Mason*.

Charges of segregation triggered a black mutiny after the explosion of two cargo ships in the northern California town of PORT CHICAGO on July 17, 1944, where only black sailors were assigned the risky job of loading munitions. (See JUSTICE, MILITARY.)

Black soldiers occasionally clashed with Australian soldiers and civilians; no such incidents occurred in the United Kingdom. Lt. Gen. GEORGE S. PATTON welcomed the all-black 761st Tank Battalion to France in Oct. 1944 with these words: "Men, you're the first Negro tankers to ever fight in the American Army. I would never have asked for you if you weren't good. I have nothing but the best in my army. I don't care what color you are, so long as you go up there and kill those Kraut sonsabitches." The 761th spent 183 days in combat and was credited with capturing thirty major towns in France, Belgium, and Germany. Its record was largely ignored until 1978 when President Jimmy Carter awarded the 761st a Presidential Unit Citation.

By Dec. 1944, heavy casualties in European combat units created a sudden demand for more men, forcing the Army into involuntary integration. Within two months, 4,562 blacks had volunteered for combat. Many of them were noncommissioned officers who took demotion to transfer from supply-handling tasks to infantry units. They went into combat in platoons or companies, and sometimes as individuals. An Army study showed that about two-thirds of the men in an average white company disliked the idea of mixed-race companies before a black platoon entered the company. But, after the test of combat, the percentage fell to 7 percent.

Selective Service

Popularly known as the draft. The nation's first peacetime draft was enacted by Congress as the Burke-Wadsworth Act in Sept. 1940 by surprisingly wide margins in both Houses. Registration of all males twenty-one to thirty-six years of age began on October 16, 1940. On Oct. 29, a blindfolded Secretary of War HENRY L. STIMSON drew a number from the same ten-gallon glass bowl used in the 1917 draft. He handed the number to President

ROOSEVELT, who read it into a microphone: 158 . . . (numbers ranged from 1 to 7,836).

The number 158 was held by 6,175 young men, the vanguard of the 20,000,000 men eligible for the draft between Oct. 1940 and Nov. 30, 1946. Of those called in the first year, 50 percent were rejected for failing to meet minimum standards. These standards included: height—at least 5 feet tall; weight—at least 105 pounds; correctable vision; at least half of thirty-two natural teeth; and no flat feet, hernias, or venereal disease. In addition to the generally poor health of the registrants (a legacy of the 1930s Great Depression), one out of every five was functionally illiterate.

The most frequently cited selective service designations were I-A, for selected inductees, and 4-F (officially written as IV-F) for inductees declared physically or mentally disqualified. In mid-1943, many 4-Fs were shifted to classes eligible for induction. Many had been rejected under higher physical standards; others had been rejected administratively in excess of permitted quotas of limited-service men, men with venereal disease, or illiterates.

Problems of inefficiency and incompetence in processing the registrants through the 6,443 local, volunteer-staffed draft boards led to the resignation of the civilian head (Clarence Dykstra) after six months. He was succeeded by Brig. Gen. LEWIS B. HERSHEY, who remained head of the Selective Service until 1970.

Hershey enforced a system under which local boards had to call up men via their lottery numbers. The sequence in which a draftee's number was called determined the order in which the man was to be considered for military service by his local draft board.

The Selective Service Act originally called for the drafting of men between the ages of twenty-one and thirty-six. Congress later limited induction to men twenty-one through twenty-seven. When the United States declared war, the draft law was changed so that the President had the power to defer men by age group. In Nov. 1942 the drafting of eighteen- and nineteen-year-old men began, and the upper age limit was extended to thirty-seven; this was the age span for the rest of the war.

In letters home from basic training camps many of the first men drafted hopefully scribbled "OHIO"—for Over the Hill In October—in recognition that the Selective Service Act had a one-year term. Resistance to renewing the draft grew in Congress, and the House agreed to a second one-year draft by a single vote (203 to 202) on Aug. 18, 1941. Limitations on the size of the call-up and length of service were later removed. By the end of the war 34,000,000 men had registered. A total of 10,000,000 men were ordered to report for induction, mostly into the Army.

Until 1943, eligible black men were passed over for the draft because of doubts about their capacity to serve and racist apprehensions about the mingling of blacks and whites. (See SEGREGATION.) Using as a yardstick the percentage of young black males in the U.S. population, the Army set 10.6 percent as the proper proportion. But at first this percentage of black inductees was not achieved.

The incongruity of drafting whites while rejecting healthy black candidates when uniformed manpower was in short supply eventually overcame compunctions about drafting blacks, and they were drafted in proportionate numbers. They served almost exclusively in labor units until very late in the war, when losses forced the Army to use black soldiers in combat in both segregated and integrated units.

"Occupational deferment," which local draft boards were entitled to bestow, became a persistent controversy. The deferments were supposed to be based on a list of "essential occupations" drawn up by Hershey in conjunction with the War Manpower Commission (WMC). The WMC saw itself as the arbitrator of needs put forward by the armed services and war industries. But in fact it had little power, for Congress guarded its hold on selective service. One amendment pushed by farm-state members of Congress, for example, specified that farmers would get consideration as essential war workers. Another amendment established that appeals involving occupational deferments would go to area appeals boards, which were controlled by state governors.

The official number of Conscientious Objectors (CO) was 42,793, although most historians believe this number significantly understates the actual count. Standards for conscientious objection were tightened as the war progressed. Before March

1942, the CO was required to show "sincerity of belief in religious teachings combined with a profound moral aversion to war." That definition was changed to "belief in a transcendent creator-deity." So-called "peace" churches, such as the Quakers, accounted for most of the conscientious objectors. But about 75 percent of the drafted Quakers chose to enter the armed forces unreservedly.

The government offered COs noncombatant assignments in the armed forces or unpaid service in work camps set up by churches. The Civilian Public Service Camps (CPSC), home to approximately 12,000 COs, featured long hours, no pay, and sometimes hazardous work. Some CPSC men were not released until 1948.

Between 5,000 and 6,000 men were imprisoned for failing to register or for refusal to serve in any way; most of these were Jehovah's Witnesses. Those convicted in 1942 usually received five-year terms; by 1945, the typical sentence was less than four years.

Seraph

British submarine that carried out a number of unusual missions, one under a U.S. commanding officer.

The *Seraph,* completed in June 1942, went on her first operational mission in support of the planned NORTH AFRICA INVASION. During the last two weeks of Sept. 1942 the submarine carried out a periscope reconnaissance of the Algerian coast. This was the *Seraph*'s first combat mission, under the command of Lt. N. L. A. (Bill) Jewell.

After this mission the *Seraph* returned to GIBRALTAR where, instead of being given orders to operate against the German and Italian forces in the Mediterranean, the submarine was assigned to Operation Flagpole: carrying Gen. DWIGHT D. EISENHOWER's deputy, Lt. Gen. MARK CLARK, to North Africa for secret negotiations with Vichy French officers. Loaded with folding canoes, submachine guns, WALKIE-TALKIE radios, and other supplies, the submarine embarked Clark, two other Army generals, U.S. Navy Capt. Jerauld Wright, a couple of colonels, and three British COMMANDOS.

With this party embarked, the *Seraph* sailed to the Algerian coast. There the collapsible canoes were launched to carry Clark and his party ashore on the night of Oct. 20. His meeting helped to reduce French opposition to the landings (although the French were not told that the troop ships were already at sea and that the landings would commence in a few days).

There were delays and some problems, but the *Seraph* finally came to within 300 yards of the beach on the morning of Oct. 23 to embark her passengers. Because of the importance of returning them to Eisenhower's headquarters at Gibraltar as soon as possible, the Americans were transferred at sea to a PBY CATALINA flying boat.

A few days later Lt. Jewell received orders to sail to the coast of southern France to secretly take aboard Gen. HENRI-HONORÉ GIRAUD. The general was to be asked to follow the Anglo-American troops into North Africa to gain support for the ALLIES from the French colonies. But Giraud would not travel in a British submarine, so strong were the anti-British feelings among Frenchmen at the time. Capt. Wright embarked in the *Seraph* as nominal commanding officer of the submarine, which was temporarily transferred to the U.S. Navy. Lt. Jewell remained on board to actually direct operations (Wright not being a submariner). The Giraud party was picked up from the town of Le Lavendou by the *Seraph* on the night of Nov. 5–6 and transferred at sea to a PBY for the flight to Gibraltar.

The *Seraph* finally sailed on her first war patrol in the Mediterranean—her fourth mission since completion—on Nov. 24. The *Seraph,* however, was soon called upon to join sister submarines in carrying U.S. and British commandos for reconnaissance operations in the Mediterranean. The *Seraph* torpedoed and damaged an Italian merchant ship in Dec. 1942 (that was sunk later the same day by British surface forces). That same month she rammed and damaged an Italian submarine, which she apparently fired a TORPEDO at a night later, but without effect.

In early 1943 the *Seraph* sailed for England and a needed refit. In April she set out again for the Mediterranean, still under command of Lt. Jewell. In addition to her normal crew, packed in dry ice was the unidentified body of a dead man dressed as a Royal Marine officer, with a briefcase that contained several secret documents handcuffed to his wrist.

On the night of April 19–20 the *Seraph* surfaced off the coast of Spain, a life jacket was placed on the body, and it was lowered over the side in Operation MINCEMEAT.

In late June 1943 the *Seraph* loaded radio beacon equipment and, with two other British submarines, moved to within a few hundred yards of the SICILY invasion beaches. On the night of July 9–10 the submarines planted buoys offshore to guide in the first waves of assault craft.

Operating against German and Italian ships through the end of 1943, the *Seraph* attacked several convoys but her only kills were a few barges and other small craft destroyed by gunfire. For the remainder of the war the *Seraph* operated in the western Atlantic and Norwegian Sea, but her remaining patrols were uneventful. She was in active service into the early 1960s; when scrapped in 1965 her conning tower was preserved as a memorial at The Citadel campus in Charleston, S.C. (Clark was a graduate of The Citadel and its president from March 1954 to June 1965.)

While her score of enemy sinkings was virtually nil, the *Seraph* did perform important—and highly unusual—missions during the war. She was launched on Oct. 25, 1941, as one of the sixty-two submarines of the "S" class. She displaced 814 tons surfaced and 990 tons submerged, and had an overall length of 217 feet. She mounted a 3-inch (76-mm) deck gun and an OERLIKON 20-MM rapid-fire cannon, with her main armament being seven 21-inch (533-mm) torpedo tubes (six bow and one stern).

Serov, Gen. Ivan Alexandrovich (1905–1962)

Soviet secret police officer, responsible for intelligence and police activities in Estonia, Latvia, and Lithuania in the wake of the Soviet takeover of those countries in 1940.

Previously an Army intelligence officer, Serov survived the 1930s purges of the GRU and in 1939 transferred to the NKVD. He was deputy chief of SMERSH in 1941, a deputy to LAVRENTI BERIA in 1943–1945, and the deputy chief of SMERSH in Soviet-occupied Germany in 1945.

Serov distinguished himself in the pursuit and liquidation of the anti-Soviet inhabitants of Estonia, Latvia, and Lithuania in 1940 and again in 1944–1947, and he was personally involved in the murder of the Polish officers in the KATYN MASSACRE. In Aug. 1946 he personally took part in the execution of the commanders of the Russian Liberation Army under Lt. Gen. ANDREI VLASOV.

He was deputy chief of the GRU when STALIN died in March 1953 and became one of the conspirators against Beria. He later became chairman of the ministry of state security (KGB). Together with Ambassador Yuri Andropov, he seized the leaders of the Hungarian revolution of 1956 by deceit and took part in their torture and execution, earning the nickname the "hangman of Hungary." In Dec. 1958, Serov became chief of the GRU. Under his leadership, corruption in the GRU attained unbelievable proportions. Serov was demoted and stripped of his decorations in 1962 because of the defection of Col. Oleg Penkovsky to the West.

Sevastopol

Soviet fortress city on the Black Sea and the site of an epic siege during the GERMAN CAMPAIGN IN THE SOVIET UNION. When Soviet defenses collapsed in the Crimea in the fall of 1941, about 106,000 Red Army troops, sailors, and marines remained in Sevastopol, holding the city behind three lines of defense: trenches and MINE fields; a series of forts protected by reinforced concrete walls and bristling with 305-mm guns; and a ring of trenches, gun positions, and machine gun emplacements.

The defenders had forty-two modern guns and numerous mortars. Arrayed against them were more than 200,000 Germans and 670 guns, including giants akin to Big Bertha of World War I. They fired 2,000- or 4,850-pound projectiles designed to penetrate reinforced concrete. The monster GUSTAV, mounted on a railway train, fired 7-ton projectiles that demolished the concrete walls. The giant guns smashed the outlying forts.

For three weeks the Germans bombarded the city from the ground and the air, shaking the earth with their barrages. The Soviets held. "Don't believe Ivan is dead because his legs have been blown off, his scalp is half torn away by shrapnel, and somebody has stuck a bayonet through his guts," a German noncom told his men. "If he has an arm left and a rifle within reach, he'll roll over and shoot you in the back as soon as you're past him."

Soviet ships and submarines, running a gauntlet of bombs and shells, brought men, ammunition, and supplies into the city, but so many ships were sunk that reinforcement troops were warned that they would have to swim to shore, carrying only as much equipment as they could manage.

Soviet attacks on the besieging German and Rumanian forces took the pressure off Sevastopol. But the German-Rumanian Eleventh Army, under *Generaloberst* ERICH VON MANSTEIN, rid the Kerch Peninsula of the Red Army, taking some 170,000 Soviets prisoner. Now Manstein could renew his attack on Sevastopol. On June 7, he drove on the city, whose airfields had been taken. Cut off from air, the Soviets began an evacuation by sea. On July 3, after a siege of 250 days, the city fell. A few of the 30,000 defenders, scattered around the city, offered some resistance. Most, however, were taken prisoner, adding to the ranks of some 60,000 others captured in the final assault. HITLER promoted Manstein to *Generalfeldmarschall.*

In April 1944, during the SOVIET OFFENSIVE CAMPAIGN, the Red Army retook the Crimea and on May 7 began the liberation of Sevastopol. In a savage two-day assault the Red Army wiped out twelve Rumanian and German divisions and reoccupied the devastated city.

Sextant

Code name for U.S.-British CAIRO CONFERENCE, Nov.–Dec. 1943.

Seydlitz

German code name for operation west of Sychevka in the Soviet Union, July 1942.

SHAEF,

see SUPREME HEADQUARTERS ALLIED EXPEDITIONARY FORCE.

Shanghai

China's commercial and industrial capital. When the EUROPEAN WAR began in 1939, Shanghai was China's largest city, but was not under Chinese rule. Japan, which had invaded China in 1931, prized Shanghai and occupied the city in 1937. At least fifty-five Japanese were killed in anti-Japanese terrorism in the city in 1938–1939.

Under a treaty forced on China in 1842, sections of the city had been ceded to foreign powers. It had three distinct parts: the Chinese section of nearly 2,000,000 Chinese; the International Settlement of about 1,000,000 people, administered by the British-U.S.-Japanese Shanghai Municipal Council, and the French Concession of nearly 500,000 people, administered by the French consul general. The Japanese installed a Chinese puppet government during the occupation, which continued until the end of the war.

On Dec. 8, 1941, as part of the JAPANESE CAMPAIGN IN THE FAR EAST, Japan seized the International Settlement and sank or captured several ships in the harbor. The Japanese took over the British-run Hong Kong and Shanghai Bank and closed down all English-language newspapers except one with a pro-Japanese policy.

Allied nationals were essentially interned for the duration of the war. They had to wear distinguishing armbands: *A* for Americans, *B* for British, *H* for Dutch. Some leaders of the English-speaking community were arrested and tortured. Other Westerners turned collaborationist and broadcast pro-Japanese PROPAGANDA on Japanese-run radio stations.

Shangri-La

The name a laughing President ROOSEVELT gave on May 10, 1942, when reporters asked him where the planes of the DOOLITTLE RAID came from. The raid on TOKYO was on April 18. Announcement of the raid was held off until the survivors reached safety; several of the planes had crashed. Ironically, Shangri-La is a place discovered by victims of a Himalayan plane crash. The survivors stumble upon a hauntingly beautiful Tibetan land described in James Hilton's novel *Lost Horizon:* in Shangri-La "forsaken courts and pale pavilions shimmered in repose from which all the fret of existence had ebbed away."

Hilton's novel, published in 1933, was not as widely known as the movie of the same name, which came out in 1937; it was directed by Frank Capra and starred Ronald Colman and Jane Wyatt.

Roosevelt's jocular identification inspired the U.S. Navy to name an aircraft carrier under construction the *Shangri-La* (CV 38).

Shark,

see *Haifisch*.

Shellburst

Signal code name for advanced headquarters of SHAEF in Normandy, June 1944.

Sherman Tank

The most successful Allied TANK of the war. The M4 General Sherman—called just the Sherman by the men who fought with it—was generally outgunned by German tanks, especially the PANTHER and TIGER tanks. The Sherman was a robust tank, with a reliable engine and rubber-block tracks (which had about five times the life expectancy of German steel tracks).

Like the M3 GRANT that it replaced, the Sherman was hastily developed in response to events in the EUROPEAN WAR, which demonstrated that the light-gunned American tanks would be useless in modern combat. The T6 prototype was completed by the U.S. Army's Ordnance Department in Sept. 1941 and large-scale production began in July 1942. During 1943 alone American industry produced 21,000 Shermans with the total WAR PRODUCTION in excess of 49,000 tanks.

The Sherman became the standard U.S. Army and Marine Corps medium tank from 1943 onward and was used extensively in the North African, Pacific, and European theaters. British as well as FREE FRENCH forces used the Sherman in Europe. British tanks fitted with flail MINE exploders were known as the "Crab" while some British and U.S. Army tanks were fitted with the 76.2-mm (17-pounder) gun, which had more penetrating power against German armor than the short-barrel 75-mm weapon. In Europe the Sherman could generally outfight its more heavily gunned German adversaries because of its superior maneuverability and the numbers of Shermans available.

The U.S. Marine Corps first used the Sherman in the Pacific in the 1943 landings in the GILBERT ISLANDS. The tank rapidly proved its worth against Japanese defenses, easily pushing aside the enemy's light tanks. In the 1945 assault on OKINAWA the Marines landed three tank BATTALIONS with just under 150 Shermans; according to Marine historians Jeter A. Isely and Philip A. Crowl, although the Shermans had limitations in the direct-support role, "Without the Shermans, however, the assault would have failed." The Marines found Shermans fitted with FLAME THROWERS particularly effective in attacking Japanese fortifications.

Weights of the Sherman varied with the model; the widely used Mark V weighed 33 tons. Its eight-cylinder, 425-horsepower gasoline engine gave it a road speed of 26 mph; cruising range was 100 miles. In addition to the 75-mm, low-velocity gun, the tank normally had two .30-cal. and one .50-cal. machine guns. The Sherman had armor up to 81-mm thickness. The tank's crew numbered five—commander, gunner, driver, and two loaders.

Shinano,

see *YAMATO*

Shingle

Code name for Allied AMPHIBIOUS LANDING at ANZIO, Italy.

Ship Designations

In 1920, the U.S. Navy instituted a ship-designation scheme to help classify naval ships for identification, correspondence, and marking spare parts. There were initially thirty-three letter symbols for different types of ships, with individual ships indicated by a hull number following the designation. During World War II, hundreds of additional symbols were added, mostly for AMPHIBIOUS SHIPS, LANDING CRAFT, and specialized auxiliary ships.

The symbols used in this book to identify specific ships are listed below; the first letter "A" indicated an auxiliary ship and the "L" a landing ship or craft, with LCI indicating landing craft, infantry.

AC	collier
ACV	auxiliary AIRCRAFT CARRIER
AG	miscellaneous auxiliary ship
AGC	amphibious force flagship
AKA	attack cargo ship
AO	oiler
AP	transport
APA	attack transport
APD	high-speed transport
AV	seaplane tender
AVG	aircraft escort ship
BB	BATTLESHIP
CA	heavy CRUISER
CB	large cruiser
CL	light cruiser
CLAA	antiaircraft cruiser
CV	aircraft carrier
CVB	large aircraft carrier
CVE	ESCORT AIRCRAFT CARRIER
CVL	small aircraft carrier
DD	DESTROYER
DE	DESTROYER ESCORT
IX	miscellaneous unclassified ship
LCI(G)	LCI (gunboat)
LCI(L)	LCI (large)
LCI(M)	LCI (MORTAR)
LCI(R)	LCI (ROCKET)
LCM	landing craft mechanized
LCP	landing craft personnel
LCR	rubber assault craft
LCS(L)	landing craft support (large)
LCT	landing craft tank
LCVP	landing craft vehicle and personnel
LSD	landing ship, dock
LSM	landing ship, medium
LSM(R)	landing ship, medium (rocket)
LST	LANDING SHIP, TANK
LSV	landing ship, vehicle
PR	river gunboat
PT	patrol-TORPEDO (PT) boat
PTC	patrol chaser
SM	submarine minelayer
SS	submarine

Shirer, William L. (1904—)

American foreign correspondent and historian. Millions of Americans heard his voice from BERLIN during the years of HITLER's rise to power. Shirer was in Vienna when the NAZIS seized power. His *Berlin Diary* (1941) covered his years in Germany and elsewhere in Europe from 1934 to Dec. 1940, when he left Germany. He returned at the end of the war. He combined his own witness and formidable research to write *The Rise and Fall of the Third Reich* (1960) and *The Collapse of the Third Republic: An Inquiry into the Fall of France in 1940* (1969). He began publishing his memoirs, *20th Century Journey,* in 1976.

Sho-Go

Code name for Japanese plan to counterattack U.S. forces in the battle for LEYTE GULF, Oct. 1944.

Shoho

First Japanese aircraft carrier sunk in the war. In the first five months of the Pacific War the Japanese lost no warships larger than destroyers (while sinking five British and American BATTLESHIPS, one British battle cruiser, one small British aircraft carrier, and seven Allied CRUISERS).

The carrier *Shoho* was part of the covering group for the Japanese assault force approaching PORT MORESBY on NEW GUINEA to capture that base as a stepping-stone for Japanese operations against Australia. Supporting the assault force was a striking force that included two larger carriers. U.S. decryptions of Japanese communications alerted the U.S. commanders in the Pacific and a carrier TASK FORCE was sent into the CORAL SEA to intercept the enemy forces.

On the morning of May 7, 1942, in the opening blows of the battle of the Coral Sea, U.S. planes from the AIRCRAFT CARRIERS *LEXINGTON* (CV 2) and *Yorktown* (CV 5) fell on the *Shoho*. Ninety-three carrier aircraft attacked: the *Shoho* was smothered with twelve BOMB hits and up to seven TORPEDO hits. She sank in ten minutes, taking to their death some 600 of her 800-man crew. Lt. Comdr. ROBERT DIXON of the *Lexington* radioed to the American force, "Scratch one flattop!"

(The carrier battle continued the following day, when the *Lexington* was sunk and two Japanese carriers damaged.)

The *Shoho* was built as a submarine tender, and completed in 1939. She was converted to a light carrier in 1941–1942. She had been in commission only five months when she was sunk. As a carrier she had a standard displacement of 11,262 tons, was 712 feet long, and had steam turbines providing a speed of 28 knots. She carried thirty aircraft.

Shooting Star,

see P-80.

Short, Lt. Gen. Walter C. (1880–1949)

Walter Short—like Adm. HUSBAND KIMMEL—is remembered solely for what he failed to do: prevent a Japanese attack on PEARL HARBOR from inflicting major damage on U.S. air and naval forces. Short's career ended on Dec. 7, 1941, almost forty years after it began.

From the end of World War I, in which he served

as assistant chief of staff to the Third ARMY, to his appointment as head of the Army's Hawaiian Department in Feb. 1941, Short held a series of posts, including several training commands. Gordon Prange, leading historian of the Pearl Harbor attack, described Short as "a capable and conscientious officer, neither brilliant nor overly aggressive, but polished, competent, honest, and willing to do a good job."

Prange also noted, however, that Short's true personality is the least accessible of all Pearl Harbor participants: "He stands before the inquisitive historian in taut watchfulness, courteous, painstaking, and inscrutable, forever holding the citadel of his own personality."

As with Kimmel, Short's principal error was fundamental: he did not expect the Japanese to attack Pearl Harbor. He seems to have regarded his major mission as training and dealt with other concerns in that light. Hence, his limited encouragement of the use of RADAR surveillance stemmed from his belief that he was using radar more "for training than any idea that it would be real." His clustering of aircraft together to frustrate SABOTAGE made them highly vulnerable to air attack.

The most damning charge against Short (and Kimmel) was that they failed to appreciate the import of the Nov. 27 "war warning" message from WASHINGTON. Other parts of the chain of command, including Army Chief of Staff GEORGE C. MARSHALL, War Plans heads Brig. Gen. LEONARD T. GEROW and Rear Adm. RICHMOND K. TURNER, and many others may be assigned a share of the blame, but Short and Kimmel must be seen to have failed in their duty as the on-scene commanders.

After the attack, little time was lost in relieving Short (and Kimmel) of command, Lt. Gen. Delos Emmons replacing Short on Dec. 17, 1941. Short's requested retirement from the Army was granted and he went to work for Ford Motor Company. Through four years of investigations and hearings, Short maintained his essential innocence of the charge of "dereliction of duty," but remained convicted of a tragic lack of imagination. After his public testimony in front of Congress in 1945–1946, he entered quiet retirement that ended in 1949 with his death.

Shrapnel

British code name for 1940–1941 plans to occupy the Cape Verde Islands.

Shturmovik,

see IL-2 *SHTURMOVIK.*

Shuttle Bombing

Technique employed by the U.S. Army Air Forces in an effort to reach targets in eastern Germany with U.S. heavy bombers—B-17 FLYING FORTRESSES and B-24 LIBERATORS. The plan was that bombers based in England would strike targets in Germany, then fly onward to bases in North Africa and, after resting their crews, refueling, and rearming, attack Germany en route back to England. The North African airfields, however, lacked the facilities to accommodate large numbers of bombers.

In 1942 AAF planners had approached the Soviet government, but it was reluctant to have large numbers of Americans in the Soviet Union. Also, in 1942 the Germans controlled much of the western area of the country. Discussions continued, and in early 1944 permission was given for U.S. planes to use three Soviet bases—Mirgorod, Piryatin, and Poltava. The operation was given the code name Frantic.

The airfields were readied, stocked with fuel and BOMBS, and 1,200 AAF ground crewmen were brought in through Iran. In addition to inflicting damage on German installations, the first Frantic raid was intended to distract German attention from the forthcoming NORMANDY INVASION. On June 2, 1944, Lt. Gen. IRA C. EAKER led a Fifteenth AIR FORCE strike of 130 B-17s and seventy P-51 MUSTANG fighter escorts from bases in Italy against the Debrecen railroad yards in Hungary. The bombers landed at Poltava (only one was lost in the attack) and the fighters at Piryatin. On June 6 these planes bombed Galatz, Rumania, returning to Soviet bases. On June 11 they struck the Foscani airfield in Rumania and continued on to their bases in Italy.

The second shuttle mission was flown from England when Eighth Air Force planes—114 B-17s escorted by seventy P-51s—bombed a synthetic oil plant near BERLIN on June 21 and landed in the

Soviet Union. Within a few hours of their arrival, on the night of June 21–22, German planes struck Poltava, destroying forty-three B-17s and damaging twenty-six others; fifteen of the Mustangs and a few Soviet aircraft were also destroyed. The ammunition dumps and 450,000 gallons of gasoline were ignited by German bombs. Remarkably, only one American was killed, while the Soviets suffered twenty-five fatalities. Not a single German aircraft was shot down.

The surviving U.S. planes flew to bases farther east. The following night the Germans struck the base at Mirgorod. On June 26 the seventy-one surviving B-17s, escorted by fifty-five fighters, left the Soviet bases and struck the oil refinery at Drohobycz, Poland, and continued on to bases in Italy. On June 5 they bombed the rail yard at Béziers, France, and continued back to their home fields in England.

After the Poltava disaster the AAF attempted to establish a night-fighter GROUP to protect the bases, but the Soviets refused. The Soviets also rejected AAF proposals to permanently base heavy bombers in the country (although their fuel and BOMB requirements would have been difficult if not impossible to fulfill).

The bombers' tremendous appetite for fuel and bombs led to employing P-38 LIGHTNING fighter-bombers on the next two shuttle missions. These were flown by Italian-based SQUADRONS in July and August. The first group—seventy-eight P-38s and fifty-eight P-51s—operated from Soviet airfields for nine days in July with the second group (only P-38s) operating from there from July 31 through Aug. 6.

The fighter-bomber raids were proving too costly for the tonnage of bombs dropped, and in early August 1944 the B-17s with P-51 escorts resumed shuttle raids: seventy-six bombers and sixty-four fighters from England bombed a Focke-Wulf aircraft plant near Gdynia, Poland, then flew a strike against a Polish oil refinery from the Soviet Union, and, after refueling and rearming, attacked airfields in the Balkans en route to Italy.

The final Frantic air strike was again by Eighth Air Force bombers based in England. On Sept. 11 a force of seventy-five B-17s and sixty-four P-51s attacked a weapons plant at Chemnitz, Germany,

en route to the Soviet Union. On Sept. 13 the planes bombed a steel works at Diosgyör, Hungary, and landed in Italy.

The Allied advance into France and the Soviet advances in the east alleviated the need for additional shuttle bombing operations. A final Frantic plan was to use Soviet bases in the fall of 1944 to drop supplies to besieged Polish forces in WARSAW being attacked by German forces. The Soviets initially refused and the bombers lacked the range to drop supplies on Poland and return to bases in England. Finally yielding to Allied pressure, on Sept. 18 the Eighth Air Force sent 117 B-17s over the battle area and dropped 1,284 containers with guns, ammunition, GRENADES, medical supplies, and food. Only 130 containers—at most—fell into Polish hands. The Germans gathered in the others.

The AAF also attempted to establish shuttle bombing between Soviet bases in Siberia and U.S. bases in Alaska and the Far East; however, the Soviets—at peace with Japan—refused to participate in such an operation.

The consensus on Operation Frantic is that the raids were worthwhile. However, as the official AAF history notes, "all of the [targets] could have been reached without utilizing Russian bases and with a smaller expenditure of effort. Some of the attacks would probably not have been regarded as worth making but for the desire to use those bases. [Air Force] intelligence, however, estimated that perhaps a few airplanes and men had been saved because of the shuttle method. The much-vaunted purpose of frightening and distracting the Germans did not materialize at all. The German high command was not fooled; it did not even redeploy its fighters. . . . a captured [Luftwaffe] general indicated that Frantic was evaluated by his organization as a mere propaganda stunt."

Siam,

see THAILAND.

Sicily

The largest island in the Mediterranean Sea, separated from the rest of Italy by the Strait of Messina. Allied troops launched the ITALIAN CAMPAIGN here, beginning with AMPHIBIOUS LANDINGS on July 10. By the time the invasion was completed thirty-eight days later it had brought down Italian *Il Duce* BENITO MUSSOLINI and set in motion the events leading to Italy's withdrawal from the war. (See SURRENDER, ITALY.)

AXIS troops in Sicily numbered some 405,000 men—315,000 Italians and 90,000 Germans. But little opposition was met by the first landings—Lt. Gen. GEORGE S. PATTON's Seventh ARMY in the Gulf of Gela and the British Eighth Army under Gen. BERNARD L. MONTGOMERY south of Syracuse.

Close air and naval gunfire support aided the invasion, code-named Husky. When German TIGER tanks attacked a unit near the beachhead, the U.S. DESTROYER *Cowie* (DD 632) brought her 5-inch (127-mm) guns to bear, winning history's first destroyer-vs.-tank battle. In the AIRBORNE phase, GLIDER and parachute troops were flown in on the eve of the invasion. Many were killed or wounded, but not by the enemy. The American paratroopers suffered 27 percent casualties, the British 23 percent as they ran afoul of winds, "friendly" antiaircraft fire, and inexperienced troop transport pilots. Two nights after the invasion, U.S. naval gunfire downed several U.S. planes.

On land, the operation progressed well. Patton pushed on toward Palermo on the northern Sicilian coast while Montgomery, after securing Syracuse, bogged down at Catania. Montgomery's objective was Messina, guardian of the 2-mile-wide strait that separates Sicily from Italy and the jumping-off place for the mainland. Rugged terrain and stubborn German resistance impeded him. Patton reached Palermo on July 22; the British did not reach Messina until Aug. 17.

The delay of the British in reaching Messina, along with skillful moves by Axis commanders, gave the Germans and Italians a chance to make a successful withdrawal across the Messina Strait. Despite intensive U.S. and British air attacks—the Allied air forces had been trying to bomb out the Messina train ferries for months—the Germans were able to evacuate 39,569 troops (including 4,444 wounded), forty-seven tanks, ninety-four heavy guns, 9,605 vehicles, more than 2,000 tons of ammunition, and much more gear, all in six days and seven nights. The Italians evacuated 62,000 troops, forty-one artillery pieces, and twelve mules.

The conquest of Sicily, accomplished in thirty-eight days, paved the way for the invasion of the mainland and gave the ALLIES control of the Mediterranean.

Siegfried

Code name for advance by German Army Group South from Kharkov to STALINGRAD, July 1942. Also called Blau and Maus.

Siegfried Line

The name, used mostly by Allied forces, for Germany's fortified western frontier. The Siegfried Line traced back to 1917, but the government-run TODT ORGANIZATION did not begin building the modern "West Wall," as Germany called it, until 1938.

The Wall, extending 35 miles deep in some areas, consisted of MINE fields, TANK traps, pillboxes, and fortresses. It ran from a complex of fortifications east of Basel, Switzerland, to Karlsruhe, Germany, then followed the Luxembourg and Netherlands borders, with a branch paralleling a stretch of the Rhine River. The southern end of the line faced France's MAGINOT LINE.

U.S. troops breached the Siegfried Line north of AACHEN on Oct. 2, 1944, during the ALLIED CAMPAIGN IN EUROPE.

Silberfuchs (Silver Fox)

Code name for buildup of German troops in Finland for the invasion of the Soviet Union, May–June 1941.

Silberstreif (Silver Streak)

German code name for PROPAGANDA campaign intended to increase Soviet desertions, May–July 1943.

Silverplate

U.S. Army Air Corps code word for the training program for delivery of the ATOMIC BOMB.

Simpson, Lt. Gen. William H. (1888–1980)

The least known of the senior U.S. Army commanders in Europe, William Simpson may have attained a unique position among that group: It is difficult to find an unkind or disparaging word said about him. Gen. DWIGHT D. EISENHOWER said simply, "If he ever made a mistake as ARMY Commander, it never came to my attention. . . . Alert, intelligent, and professionally capable, he was the type of leader that American soldiers deserve."

Commander of two National Guard DIVISIONS (the 30th and 35th), commander of the XII CORPS, and Fourth Army commander in the United States, he finally brought the Ninth Army into battle on Sept. 5, 1944, in the last few weeks of the siege of Brest, France.

A "quiet but strong-willed Texan," tall, rawboned, "and bald as a billiard ball," he was "steady, prepossessing, well organized, earthy, a great infantryman and leader of men," according to 12th ARMY GROUP commander Gen. OMAR BRADLEY. Soon after the Ninth Army entered the line on the left of the 12th Army Group, Simpson and his staff began reflecting his qualities, demonstrating a quiet competence in planning and executing assaults. During the German Army's ARDENNES counteroffensive, Eisenhower allowed Field Marshal BERNARD MONTGOMERY to take control of the Ninth Army. Most unusually for an American general, Simpson replied, "You can depend on me to respond cheerfully, promptly, and as efficiently as I possibly can to every instruction he gives." As the "swing" Army between the U.S. and British army groups, the Ninth proved a valuable asset to both. Bradley describes Simpson's Feb. 1945 attack across the Roer River as "one of the most perfectly executed of the war."

After diplomatically thwarting Montgomery's apparent intention to exclude it from the March 1945 assault across the Rhine River, the Ninth Army (by now 330,000 men in three corps with thirteen divisions) sped eastward and closed the ring around the Ruhr and the remaining German divisions west of the Elbe River.

In April Simpson was 65 miles from BERLIN when he received the order to stop. He argued then, and for twenty years later, that he could have been in Berlin the next day. While that contention is part of heated postwar debate, it reflected his drive and his confidence.

After V-E DAY, Simpson was told to prepare the Ninth Army to move to China, but V-J DAY mooted the plans. Simpson was forced to retire as a lieutenant general soon thereafter with ulcers and a hernia. He was promoted to general on the retired list in 1954—a general who appears to have had no detractors and many admirers.

Singapore

British colonial possession called "The Gibraltar of the East." Site of the last-ditch British defense of MALAYA, the island city was devastated by Japanese bombardment and bombing. Encircled and its water supply cut off, Singapore fell on Feb. 15, 1942. The Japanese invaders had numbered about 35,000 troops; the defenders, 80,000. Nearly all of the defenders were captured.

Sitka

Code name for Allied force for the assault on the islands of Levant and Port Cross in the Mediterranean.

Skorzeny, *Generalmajor* Otto (1908–1976)

WAFFEN SS officer who led several daring COMMANDO-style operations. Skorzeny began his spectacular career as a member of HITLER's *Leibstandarte-SS Adolf Hitler,* Hitler's SS bodyguard regiment. He also fought as a *Waffen* SS officer in the FRANCE AND LOW COUNTRIES CAMPAIGN and the GERMAN CAMPAIGN IN THE SOVIET UNION.

Skorzeny studied British commando tactics and training, hoping to establish a similar special operations unit in the *Waffen* SS. He received little support until he successfully completed his first major mission: the rescue of BENITO MUSSOLINI after the Italian dictator was deposed and arrested in July 1943.

Hitler personally selected Skorzeny for the mission, which was complicated by the fact that Italian authorities kept moving Mussolini. Skorzeny, who organized an intensive intelligence effort to find Mussolini, remained a step behind him in the hide-and-seek with the dictator's Italian captors. Once, reconnoitering a hideout on an island off Sardinia, Skorzeny flew in a plane that was shot down by Allied aircraft.

Skorzeny finally learned that Mussolini was in a heavily guarded resort hotel in the Gran Sassos mountains north of Abruzzi. On Sept. 12, 1943, Skorzeny flew to the high plateau in a GLIDER, one of twelve that landed on a 3,000-foot meadow next to the hotel. Intimidating Mussolini's guards, Skorzeny entered the hotel, found the dazed dictator, told him that Hitler had sent him, and said, "You are free!" Skorzeny shoved Mussolini into a FI 156 STORCH that could barely take off from the rock-strewn meadow. Skorzeny delivered Mussolini to Vienna that night, completing what Skorzeny called an "impossible mission."

Following the JULY 20 PLOT against Hitler's life in 1944, Skorzeny sped to the Ministry of War in BERLIN and for a short while during the confusion virtually ran the German Army. He organized an SS battalion to help guard the ministry, found evidence of the plot, and rounded up many of the conspirators.

Skorzeny's next mission, code-named Mickey Mouse, was inspired by Hitler's desire to keep Hungary in the AXIS. In Sept. 1944 Adm. Miklós Horthy, the dictator of Hungary, had begun trying to negotiate a separate peace with the Soviet Union, whose troops were nearing BUDAPEST. Skorzeny took a special force into Hungary and kidnapped Horthy's son Mikio, threatening to kill him if Horthy did not resign. Skorzeny also seized Horthy's citadel and ruled Hungary for a short time until a Fascist puppet regime was installed.

When Germany launched the ARDENNES offensive that triggered the battle of the Bulge in Dec. 1944, Skorzeny once again showed his genius for special operations. In an operation code-named *Greif* (snatch), he trained a force of English-speaking German soldiers, dressed them in American uniforms, and, with captured U.S. vehicles, sent them behind American lines to raise havoc.

Skorzeny's ersatz GIs cut communications wires, changed road signs, and gave confusing, GI-to-GI information to U.S. troops stunned by the sudden German attack. At the headquarters of the SUPREME HEADQUARTERS ALLIED EXPEDITIONARY FORCE at Versailles, just outside PARIS, extra security was thrown around Gen. DWIGHT D. EISENHOWER because of planted rumors that a Skorzeny-led ASSASSINATION team had targeted Eisenhower. American forces captured many of the disguised GIs and summarily executed them as spies.

Skorzeny was captured by U.S. forces in Austria in May 1945. An American WAR CRIMES tribunal accused him of illegal warfare in the battle of the Bulge. He was acquitted after a British officer testified that British and U.S. special forces had used similar irregular tactics.

German authorities arrested him and placed him in an internment camp in Darmstadt. He escaped in July 1948, assumed a new identity, and helped to found the ODESSA, a secret organization of former SS officers. According to Skorzeny-inspired accounts, Odessa and its escape network, *Die Spinne* (the spider), helped get hundreds of SS officers out of Germany. Odessa-aided escapees reportedly included the infamous ADOLF EICHMANN and MARTIN BORMANN.

Skorzeny settled in Spain, started an import-export business as a cover for *Die Spinne* activities, and helped to maintain the escape network that got SS officers to safety in sympathetic countries in the Middle East and South America. Skorzeny, who had access to caches of SS loot, in 1959 bought a country estate in Ireland and raised horses. He died in Madrid.

Skua

The first aircraft to sink a German warship and the first naval aircraft to shoot down a German aircraft. This British fighter and dive bomber entered service in Nov. 1938. By the time the EUROPEAN WAR began in Sept. 1939 the Royal Navy had thirty Skuas (the only other naval fighter at the time was the naval version of the GLADIATOR). Of the Skuas, eighteen were assigned to the carrier ARK ROYAL; the remainder were based ashore.

When Britain and Germany fought over Norway in April–May 1940, the German Navy suffered heavy losses, including the light cruiser *Königsberg*, attacked by sixteen Skuas attached to the carrier *Ark Royal*, which took off from the air base at SCAPA FLOW in the Orkney Islands. Flying a 660-mile round-trip to strike the ship in Bergen Fjord, Norway, the Skuas scored sixteen hits or near-misses with 500-pound BOMBS. The *Königsberg* erupted in flames, her magazines exploded, she rolled over, and broke in half. Also off Norway, an *Ark Royal* Skua shot down a Dornier DO 18 flying boat, the first German plane to fall to the Fleet Air Arm.

Skuas were also flown from the *Ark Royal* to attack the French battleship *Richelieu* at DAKAR. However, the Skua was outclassed by German fighters and as newer carrier planes became available to the British, the Skuas were withdrawn from frontline service in 1941. They continued to serve as trainers and GLIDER tugs.

The Blackburn-built Skua was the Navy's first operational monoplane. The prototype flew in 1937. A total of 192 aircraft were built.

The plane had a radial engine and was distinguished by the long, squared-off "greenhouse" cockpit; the vertical tail fin, with a large rudder, was forward of the horizontal surfaces. The main landing gear was fully retractable and the wings folded back along the fuselage for carrier stowage.

Maximum speed of the Skua was 225 mph and the aircraft was credited with a range of 760 miles and endurance of four and a half hours. A single 500-pound bomb could be carried under the fuselage; four .303-cal. machine guns were fitted in the wings and the second crewman had a flexible Lewis gun in the after cockpit.

Skymaster,
see C-54.

Skyrocket,
see F5F.

Skytrain/Dakota,
see C-47.

Slapstick
Code name for unopposed British landings at TARANTO, Italy, Sept. 9, 1943.

Slapton Sands
The problem of finding space for training with live ammunition was most difficult for U.S. troops in Britain preparing for the NORMANDY INVASION. In south Devon, on the shore and in the country behind Slapton Sands, about 25 square miles were vacated for live-fire training by U.S. forces.

All 3,000 residents of the 167 farms and seven villages moved out with their household goods, sheep, cattle, pigs, and poultry. Then began the battle of Slapton Sands. Almost every U.S. soldier who landed at Normandy on D-DAY had first won the beachhead at Slapton Sands under live gunfire. Many houses and farm buildings were hit, although

special care was taken not to hit the churches in the area.

The U.S. Army subsequently erected a monument on the beach to commemorate the sacrifices of the Devon people, which saved untold numbers of American lives on D-Day.

Slave Labor
Germany's use of prisoners for work, particularly in war industries. Even before the EUROPEAN WAR began in Sept. 1939 NAZI officials turned to foreigners as a source of labor in the booming German armaments industry. French and Polish workers were imported after the conquest of those nations. The Poles in particular were treated as slaves, establishing what the WAR CRIMES tribunal at Nuremberg would call "a policy of mass deportation and mass enslavement . . . of underfeeding and overworking foreign laborers, of subjecting them to every form of degradation, brutality, and inhumanity."

In the wake of the 1941 winter campaign against the Soviets on the EASTERN FRONT, 370,000 skilled German workers were conscripted into the army and Germany suddenly needed a massive new labor supply. On March 21, 1942, HITLER ordered an even greater exploitation of foreign workers, called for the movement of 300,000 people a month from the East, and named FRITZ SAUCKEL Plenipotentiary-General for Labor Mobilization.

SS officials and labor agents prowled the conquered countries for workers and seized them, a German official said, "like dog catchers used to catch dogs." The workers, by Sauckel's orders, were "treated in such a way as to exploit them to the highest possible extent at the lowest conceivable degree of expenditure." He was hanged for his war crimes.

ALBERT SPEER, minister of Armaments and War Production, made use of CONCENTRATION CAMP inmates by putting them to work in nearby factories. The SS, with Speer's endorsement, built slave-labor factories at AUSCHWITZ, DACHAU, Buchenwald, Mauthausen, and Dora concentration camps. The policy of working inmates to death was called *Vernichtung durch Arbeit,* "destruction through death."

Germany moved hundreds of thousands of "Nordic" young women from the Ukraine to work as maids and, Sauckel said, "as presents for friends." Tens of thousands of young boys were seized in Poland and sent to Germany for what a German document called "the alleviation of the shortage of apprentices." Untold numbers of them died.

The vast industrial empires of I. G. FARBEN and KRUPP used slave labor extensively. "Sanitary conditions are atrocious," a Krupp doctor reported to the directors of the company. Workers, he said, were ill-clothed, often shoeless, fed starvation rations, and were kept in barns, warehouses, even dog kennels. Germany ultimately used about 7,500,000 foreign civilians and 2,000,000 military PRISONERS OF WAR—mostly Soviet—as slave workers.

Sledgehammer

Code name for planning for possible invasion of Western Europe in the fall of 1942.

Slim, Field Marshal William J. (1891–1970)

Leading British desert and jungle warrior. Joining the British Army as a private in 1914, Slim fought at Gallipoli and in Mesopotamia in World War I. Between the wars he was rapidly promoted and by 1941 was commanding the 10th Indian Division in action against VICHY FRENCH forces in Syria. He also saw service in Iraq and Iran before being sent to Burma in 1942. Slim had wanted to stay in the Middle East—"the desert suits the British, and so does fighting in it. You can see your man," he observed.

In Burma, under Gen. Sir ACHIBALD WAVELL, Slim was given command of the I Burma Corps ("Burcorps") formed from virtually all combat-ready Imperial troops in Burma. He attempted to hold the army together as it retreated toward India, his troops being exhausted, short of supplies, and subjected to Japanese air attacks. With reorganization of forces in India he was given command of the XV Indian Corps and in Oct. 1943 was made commanding general of the Fourteenth Army, the major fighting force in Southeast Asia.

Hampered by conflicting American and British objectives, and an aggressive enemy, Slim's command went on the offensive and in early 1944 threw back the Japanese and broke the siege at Imphal. After this success Slim's forces went on a full-scale

offensive (Operation Capital), crossing the Chindwin River to eject the Japanese army from upper Burma. He increased the scope of his offensive (Extended Capital) and drove into lower Burma, where, on May 6, 1945, his Fourteenth Army linked up with British troops landing near Rangoon.

Slim was then told that the Fourteenth Army was to lead the assault against Japanese forces in Malaya and that he would command the new Twelfth Army, which would do the "mopping up." Slim refused the assignment and asked to be relieved. The British high command in LONDON reversed the plan. Slim was then given command of all Allied land forces in Southeast Asia.

After the war Slim was made a viscount and became chief of the Imperial General Staff (i.e., head of the British Army) and then governor-general of Australia.

Slot, The

Nickname given by the ALLIES to the body of water between NEW GEORGIA, BOUGAINVILLE, Choiseul, and Vella Lavella in the SOLOMONS, transited by Japanese warships and freighters attempting to reinforce garrisons in the area. The scene of several naval engagements in 1942–1943.

Slovik, Pvt. Eddie D. (1920–1945)

The only U.S. soldier in World War II executed for desertion. Slovik, a draftee, was a reluctant rifleman assigned to G COMPANY, 109th Infantry REGIMENT, 28th Infantry DIVISION.

The 28th fought hard across France and Germany, took heavy casualties in the HÜRTGEN FOREST, and in the ARDENNES—the battle of the Bulge. Slovik missed those battles because while the 28th was fighting and losing men he was awaiting death for desertion.

He had deserted first in Aug. 1944, the day after he arrived in France with a group of replacements. Combat veterans disliked replacements because they were unreliable. The sergeants had a saying: "Don't send us any more replacements; we haven't got time to bury them." But a company that had lost men certainly needed them.

On Aug. 25, heading toward his assigned unit, Slovik and a buddy disappeared into the confusion of a combat zone. They were taken in by a Canadian unit as soldiers who had lost their units. On Oct. 5, as Slovik later told it, the Canadians turned him and his buddy over to American military policemen and they reported to the 28th Division at Elsenborn, Belgium.

No charges were made against the missing men; it was not unusual for replacements to get lost. They were ordered to the 109th regimental headquarters and assigned to G Company. When Slovik reached the company, he told the company commander that he was "too scared and nervous" to be in a rifle company and, if sent into combat, would run away. The officer shrugged, and the unit went forward. His buddy went to the front and was later wounded in action. Slovik ran away.

The next day he gave himself up and, against the advice of the officer who arrested him, confessed. The Army believed that he had staged this second desertion "with the intent . . . that he would be tried by court-martial and incarcerated and thus avoid the hazardous duty . . . of action against the enemy."

Late in October the 28th Division was going through troubled times. Many men were shooting themselves to avoid duty or were taking the desertion-to-jail route: deserting, letting themselves get caught, and then looking to a prison sentence as a way to serve out the rest of the war. (It was a good gamble. In 1945 special clemency boards were set up to review 27,500 wartime convictions for determining whether any were too harsh. Jailed deserters rarely served sentences extending substantially beyond the war years.) Two military policemen took Slovik out of the stockade for an interview with the division's ranking legal officer.

The legal officer offered Slovik a common deal (see JUSTICE, MILITARY): go directly from stockade to combat and he would not be court-martialed. Slovik refused the deal. On Nov. 11 he was tried and convicted in a trial that lasted one hour and forty minutes. The sentencing vote of the nine-officer court-martial was unanimous: "to be shot to death with musketry." The presiding officer ordered two more ballots. Both were also unanimous.

"I think every member of the court thought that Slovik deserved to be shot," the presiding officer said years later in an interview with William Brad-

ford Huie, author of *The Execution of Private Slovik.* ". . . But in honesty . . . I don't think a single member of that court actually believed that Slovik would ever be shot."

The Army's appeals mechanism upheld the conviction and the sentence, saying that Slovik had "directly challenged the authority of" the United States and that "future discipline depends upon a resolute reply to this challenge. If the death penalty is ever to be imposed for desertion it should be imposed in this case, not as a punitive measure nor as retribution, but to maintain that discipline upon which alone an army can succeed against the enemy."

The final appeal was to Gen. DWIGHT D. EISENHOWER, Supreme Allied Commander. Accompanying the legal papers was a plea from Slovik. He had been a petty criminal back in Michigan, he said, but after getting out of jail he married "a swell wife . . . and had a good record. . . . I'd like to continue to be a good soldier."

The papers on Slovik came across Eisenhower's desk during the battle of the Bulge. As Eisenhower pondered the Slovik case, the first of nearly 20,000 Americans were dying in that battle; some 7,500 men in one unit had just laid down their arms in the largest U.S. Army surrender on record.

On Dec. 23, 1944, with the outcome of the battle of the Bulge still in doubt, Eisenhower endorsed the finding of the court-martial and appeals court, authorizing the first execution of a U.S. Army deserter since the Civil War. Until then, the Army's policy had been to commute all death penalties. Thousands of potential desertion cases never reached the general court-martial stage because of combat-or-else deals like the one offered Slovik.

During the war, a total of 4,072 soldiers would face general court-martial in the European Theater; 2,930 would be found guilty. Although the penalty for desertion before the enemy was execution, Slovik was the only one of them to receive that sentence. (Almost simultaneously with his endorsement dooming Slovik, Eisenhower ordered the execution of three German infiltrators captured in American uniforms.)

The Army's highest legal authorities again reviewed the case from a procedural viewpoint and upheld the verdict and sentencing.

The execution site was St. Marie aux Mines in eastern France, where the 28th Division had its headquarters established. The regimental chaplain, a Catholic priest, heard Slovik's confession and said Mass for him.

Slovik, hands bound, bareheaded, with all Army insignia stripped from his uniform, was marched through the snowswept cold out to a house's courtyard, commandeered for the execution. While the court-martial order was read to him, a sergeant wrapped an Army blanket around him. He was strapped to a post set before a wooden barrier erected to stop rifle bullets that passed through Slovik's body. A black hood made by a local seamstress was placed over Slovik's head.

A twelve-man firing squad under a sergeant marched out, following a path earlier tramped in the snow. They took their positions 20 yards from Slovik. One of the men was from G Company. All were from the 109th and all were skilled marksmen. Following age-old Army regulations, the officer in charge of the execution had loaded the rifles in secrecy, placing a blank round in one of them. Theoretically, each man in the firing squad could assume that he had—or did not have—the blank round. In reality, blanks do not produce as great a recoil as a live round. The man with the blank would know it.

A medical officer had shown the firing squad where to aim: for the heart. At the command *Fire!* they shot Slovik. None of the eleven bullets struck his heart, but, with wounds from his neck and left arm to his abdomen, he died in about three minutes.

The execution had been witnessed by a selected group of enlisted men and officers. One of them was Slovik's regimental commander. In a message to his regiment he summed up the Army's belief in why at least one man had to die for desertion: "The person that is not willing to fight and die, if need be, for his country has no right to life."

S.M. 79 *Sparviero* (Sparrow Hawk)

The most effective Italian bomber of the war, the S.M.79 was an ugly three-engine aircraft presenting a ponderous "hunchback" appearance. Like many other Fascist aircraft, the S.M.79 underwent its combat debut in the SPANISH CIVIL WAR, flying bomber strikes for the Nationalists. Italy entered the EUROPEAN WAR in June 1940 with 594 S.M.79s—almost two-thirds of the Italian Air Force's bomber strength. They were widely flown in the Mediterranean and North Africa in bombing, TORPEDO attack, and reconnaissance roles. When they began bombing MALTA on June 11, 1940, they were faster than the defending British GLADIATOR fighters! In the Mediterranean S.M.79s sank several British destroyers and merchant ships. After Italy's capitulation in Sept. 1943 the aircraft continued to fly for both the Allied and the NAZI-controlled Italian forces. Italy's most famous wartime pilots gained their reputations in the *Sparviero*.

Developed by Savoia-Marchetti, the S.M.79 first entered service in 1934 as an eight-place commercial transport. A year later an S.M.79P established a number of international flight records, while in 1937 modified bomber aircraft garnered a new series of records for Italian aviation. Subsequently, militarized S.M.79-I aircraft were produced for the Air Force as medium bombers. As early as 1937 the Air Force sponsored trials of the S.M.79 in the torpedo attack role, and the aircraft demonstrated considerable merit in this role. The S.M.79-II was produced as a specialized torpedo bomber. The S.M.79-III was a "cleaned-up" aircraft converted from older models or newly built, most by the Fascist air arm after Sept. 1943. A total of some 1,200 aircraft were built for Italian use. The S.M.79B (for *Bi-motore*) was a modified, twin-engine aircraft with glazed nose built for export and sold to Balkan countries, Brazil, and Iraq with a variety of Italian and German engines.

The three-engine S.M.79 was a low-wing aircraft with a fuselage "hump" above of the cockpit to house a machine gun. The after fuselage had minimal taper and ended with a small tail fin. The capacious fuselage was a welded steel-tube structure with aluminum skin over the forward section, plywood covering most of the upper fuselage, and fabric covering the sides and bottom. The fully retractable main undercarriage provided little clearance for the internal BOMB bay and a bomb-aiming/gun gondola under the after fuselage. The aircraft was noted for its ability to sustain damage and still fly.

The S.M.79-I had a maximum speed of 267 mph and with 2,755 pounds of bombs the aircraft had a range of 1,180 miles; as a recce aircraft it could fly 2,050 miles. The S.M.79-II was credited with a top speed of 270 mph and a range of 1,245 miles. The II variant could carry two aerial torpedoes externally. The defensive armament consisted of three 12.7-mm and one 7.7-mm machine guns. A four-man crew flew the aircraft.

S.M.81 *Pipistrello* (Bat)

This trimotor medium bomber and transport saw combat in the Italian invasion of Ethiopia (Abyssinia) beginning in Oct. 1935 and, subsequently, in the SPANISH CIVIL WAR. There were about 100 still in service when Italy entered the EUROPEAN WAR in June 1940. Most of those were employed against the British in North Africa, increasingly as a transport and paratroop carrier. Some were used in the Oct. 1940 Italian assault on Greece and—in July 1941—a small number were dispatched with the Italian contingent to the EASTERN FRONT. They served on both the Allied and Fascist sides after the Italian SURRENDER in Sept. 1943, with a few surviving in the postwar Italian Air Force.

The Savoia-Marchetti *Pipistrello* was a derivative of the S.M.73 commercial transport of the 1930s. It bore a superficial resemblance to the German JU 52/3m and was the forerunner of the S.M. 79 *Sparviero*. The S.M.81 was distinguished from its medium bomber successor by a fixed landing gear with large "spats," a small gun turret instead of the "hump" above the cockpit, and a larger tail fin. The S.M.81B was a twin-engine variant built for Rumania.

The S.M.81 had a maximum speed of 196 mph with a range of 1,240 miles. It could carry 2,205 pounds of bombs internally and had a defensive armament of four or five 12.7-mm machine guns, including two in the dorsal turret. It was flown by a crew of six.

SMERSH *(Smert Shpionam)*

Soviet agency with broad activities in the field of counterespionage—especially tracking down traitors and deserters behind the front lines, shooting retreating soldiers, and arresting men who escaped from German captivity. SMERSH also supervised a network of informers in the armed forces. Among

its millions of victims was artillery officer-writer ALEKSANDR SOLZHENITSYN.

SMERSH was established in 1941 by LAVRENTI BERIA as an agency of the of NKVD; in 1943 all armed forces counterintelligence and security were transferred to SMERSH. During the war the agency was under the command of Beria's deputy and protégé Viktor Abakumov.

Smert Shpionam was an abbreviation of Russian words meaning "death to spies." After the war onetime British intelligence officer IAN FLEMING used SMERSH as the "bad guys" in some of his James Bond novels.

Smith, Lt. Gen. Holland M. (1882–1967)

"Howling Mad" Smith was a pioneer in developing U.S. AMPHIBIOUS LANDING concepts and the senior U.S. Marine field commander. Marine historians Jeter A. Isley and Philip A. Crowl described him as "tough, egocentric, cantankerous, exacting."

After troop commands and duty at Headquarters Marine Corps, including service as assistant to the commandant, in 1939 Maj. Gen. Smith took command of the 1st Marine BRIGADE, the largest Marine unit at the time. In Feb. 1 the brigade was redesignated the 1st Marine DIVISION, the first division formation in Marine history.

In June 1941 Smith began amphibious planning for the Atlantic FLEET and for Army divisions. A year later he went to the West Coast to take command of the Pacific Fleet's amphibious force to organize and train Marines for the Pacific War. After observing the Army landings in the ALEUTIAN ISLANDS, Smith in Sept. 1943 went to PEARL HARBOR and, with the title Commander V Amphibious CORPS, in 1943–1944 he directed the Marine-Army landings in the MARSHALL ISLANDS and then the assaults on SAIPAN and TINIAN in the MARIANAS. During the Saipan operation he relieved Army Maj. Gen. Ralph Smith as commander of the 27th Infantry Division for the "all-round poor performance" of the division. His action led to a major interservice controversy (with the Army's high command supporting their Smith).

In Aug. 1944 Smith became commanding general Fleet Marine Force Pacific (FMFPac), a newly formed command to direct all Marine operations in the Pacific; its principal subordinate commands were the III and V Amphibious Corps. As FMFPac, Smith was also the Marine commander for Adm. CHESTER W. NIMITZ.

In July 1945 he was transferred to Camp Pendleton, Calif. (near San Diego) to direct Marine training, a position he held until retiring in 1946.

Smith, Lt. Gen. Julian C. (1885–1975)

A leading U.S. amphibious commander in the Pacific War. After extensive service in the Caribbean and Central America beginning shortly after he was commissioned in 1909, Smith was a naval observer in LONDON in 1941. After the United States entered the war he commanded the Marine training center at Camp Lejeune, N.C., in 1942–1943. Early in 1943 he took command the 2nd Marine DIVISION and led it in the invasion of TARAWA.

After that bloody landing he became deputy commander of the Fleet Marine Force Pacific (see HOLLAND M. SMITH), and in 1944 commanded the assault troops in the Palau operation. From Dec. 1944 he held administrative assignments in the United States as a lieutenant general. He retired in 1946.

Smith, Lt. Gen. Walter Bedell (1895–1961)

Chief of Staff to Gen. DWIGHT D. EISENHOWER in the European theater. Smith enlisted in the Indiana NATIONAL GUARD in 1910 and fought as an infantryman in France during World War I. He was commissioned as a second lieutenant in 1917 and served mainly as a staff officer between the wars. He was not a college graduate.

When the United States entered the war Smith was assistant to the secretary of the U.S. Army's General Staff. As a brigadier general, Smith became Chief of Staff to Gen. Eisenhower in Sept. 1942. In that role, Smith was a key adviser to Eisenhower and negotiated the Italian SURRENDER in 1943 and the German surrender in 1945. Eisenhower called Smith "the general manager of the war."

Smith was American ambassador to the Soviet Union from 1946 to 1949 while retaining his military rank. He was commanding general of the U.S. First ARMY in 1949–1950 and was director of Central Intelligence from 1950 to 1953; he was pro-

moted to full general in 1951. Smith was under secretary of State in 1953–1954.

SNAFU

Slang phrase. To the homefront, this acronym was defined as Situation Normal All *Fouled* Up, but to servicemen it meant Situation Normal All *Fucked* Up. Variants included FUBAR (Fucked Up Beyond All Recognition) and FUMTU (Fucked Up More Than Usual).

Snorkel

Tube-like device to permit SUBMARINES to take in air for operating their diesel engines while submerged. Submarines had diesel engines to propel them on the surface and to charge their electric storage batteries, which provided energy to electric motors for underwater propulsion. By 1943 Allied antisubmarine forces—mostly using RADAR—could easily detect U-BOATS when they were on the surface charging their batteries or transiting to a patrol area at high speed. (Submerged, submarines could travel at about 10 knots and while on the surface up to 20 knots.)

Several navies had earlier experimented with devices for bringing air into a submerged submarine, with the Simon Lake submersible *Argonaut I* having a breathing tube as early as 1897. The Dutch Navy revived the idea in the early 1930s to provide fresh air for their submarine crews and to bring in air for the diesel engines while submerged. *Kapitein Luitenant ter Zee* J. J. Wichers developed an efficient snorkel with valves to prevent water from coming into the submarine when water washed over the snorkel head, which was raised a few feet above the surface. The Germans captured several Dutch submarines with this device when Holland fell in 1940.

But not until the BATTLE OF THE ATLANTIC turned against the U-boats in 1943 was the snorkel adopted for German submarines. It was tested in the submarine *U-58* in the Baltic that summer, and was fitted in existing submarines as well as those under construction.

The snorkel reduced submerged speeds to 6 knots when in use (otherwise the tube would break off). Snorkeling was also uncomfortable and even dangerous. When a wave closed the valve of the intake the diesel engines would suck the air out of the submarine, the changing pressure damaging crewmen's eardrums and causing intense pain. Also, when snorkeling in daylight the tube (and periscope) left a wake that was highly visible if the water was calm. Still another problem was garbage—a crew of fifty or sixty men eating three meals a day created a lot of debris, which in the past was simply thrown over the side when the submarine was on the surface. Now it had to be "saved" for those rare occasions when the boat did surface, or fired out of a TORPEDO tube with great care not to foul the delicate mechanisms of the tube.

But the snorkel gave U-boats a new lease on life as they were less vulnerable to radar detection when charging their batteries (albeit with a loss of speed compared to surface running). Also, a rubber-like anechoic coating on the snorkel head would absorb radar energy, reducing the effectiveness of the radar. A snorkeling period of about three hours could fully charge batteries, permitting the U-boat to cruise at slow speed for a day or more, with reserve to speed up (submerged) to attack a CONVOY.

In a dramatic demonstration of snorkeling, after the German SURRENDER the *U-977* escaped from Norway to Argentina, traveling sixty-six consecutive days submerged during that voyage.

After the war, the U.S., British, French, and Soviet navies all adopted snorkels for their submarines.

(Called *schnorchel* by the Germans, the British referred to the device as a "snort," and submarines using them as "snorting.")

SO3C Seamew

This U.S. Navy aircraft was designed as a high-speed floatplane scout. Despite its advanced design, it served only briefly in frontline service as a catapult aircraft from U.S. CRUISERS, displaying poor flight characteristics. Intended to replace the SOC SEAGULL, the older plane carried on in the FLEET after the SO3C was discarded.

The prototype XSO3C-1 flew on Oct. 6, 1939, and the first production aircraft reached the fleet in July 1942, first being assigned to the cruiser *Cleveland* (CL 55). Deliveries totaled 794 aircraft with 150 going to the Royal Navy under the name Queen Seamew. Most U.S. and all British aircraft were soon relegated to training duties. And thirty

of the U.S. planes were converted to radio-controlled drones (SO3C-1K). The last U.S. fleet SQUADRON to fly the Seamew discarded the planes at the end of March 1944. Plans to build an improved model and to produce the SOR-1 model by Ryan were dropped.

The SO3C was a streamlined, mid-wing aircraft with an in-line engine. As a floatplane it had a large center float and twin stabilizing floats. When flown with a wheeled undercarriage it had "spats" housings over the wheels. The wheeled versions could be fitted with arresting hooks and catapult attachment points for use from AIRCRAFT CARRIERS. The aircraft could carry two 250-pound BOMBS or DEPTH CHARGES under its wings. As a land plane, it could also carry a 500-pound bomb under the fuselage *if* the pilot armor, .30-cal. flexible machine gun, and self-sealing fuel tanks were removed.

SOC Seagull

This float-equipped biplane was the principal gunfire-spotting and scout plane carried by U.S. BATTLESHIPS and CRUISERS until the end of the war. It was in combat in virtually every engagement involving major surface ships, and also scouted in the South Pacific for PT-BOAT SQUADRONS. During the Japanese carrier attack on PEARL HARBOR on Dec. 7, 1941, a pair of SOCs from the U.S. cruiser *Northampton* (CA 26) encountered an A6M ZERO fighter, apparently damaged during the attack. The pair of SOCs engaged the Zero for some twenty minutes, finally shooting it down.

The SOC outlasted the two floatplanes procured to succeed it, the OS2U KINGFISHER and SO3C SEAMEW. The SOC was also the last biplane to fly from U.S. warships.

The SOC design originated with the Curtiss O3C of 1932. First flown in April 1934, the XO3C-1 prototype was followed by the production SOC, the June 1935 designation change reflecting the combination of scouting ("S") and observation ("O") roles in the same aircraft (with "C" indicating Curtiss). The first operational aircraft were assigned to the cruiser *Marblehead* (CL 12) in Nov. 1935. Production totaled 259 SOCs plus forty-four identical SONs built by the Naval Aircraft Factory. A few served in the Coast Guard.

With SOC/SON production ending in early

1938, the Navy began replacement in the fleet with the monoplane SO3C. But when that aircraft encountered operational problems, the surviving SOCs were returned to first-line service. The aircraft was launched from shipboard catapults and recovered by coming down at sea alongside the warship and being hoisted back aboard by crane. The aircraft could also be fitted with a wheeled undercarriage.

The Curtiss-built SOC was a graceful aircraft with a large central float and small stabilizing floats fitted under the lower wing. The fuselage had a steel-tube structure with fabric covering. The pilot and observer-gunner were housed under a single glazed canopy. The wings folded back for shipboard stowage.

The SOC-1 had a maximum speed of 165 mph with a range of 675 miles. An armament of one fixed, forward-firing .30-cal. machine gun was fitted and the observer had a flexible .30-cal. gun. Two 250-pound BOMBS could be carried under the wings.

SOE,

see SPECIAL OPERATIONS EXECUTIVE.

Solomon Islands

A 900-mile-long string of islands in the southwest Pacific east of NEW GUINEA and the major objective of the U.S. SOLOMONS–NEW GUINEA CAMPAIGN. Taken from Germany after World War I, they were made a British-Australian mandate, with BOUGAINVILLE and two islands north of it becoming part of Australia's Territory of New Guinea. In March-April 1942 Japanese troops occupied the Solomons, landing several thousand Japanese troops at several islands, including Bougainville and GUADAL-CANAL, which became sites of World War II battles. (See also EASTERN SOLOMONS.)

The Japanese, who developed harbors and airfields on key islands, saw the Solomons as strategic bases in the drive to isolate and ultimately invade Australia. When the Japanese landed, some British remained behind as COASTWATCHERS, men who lived in the islands clandestinely, sheltered by natives, who hated the Japanese occupation forces and frequently ambushed Japanese units in the dense jungles.

Solzhenitsyn, Aleksandr I. (1918—)

Soviet Army officer and Nobel Prize winner. With a university degree in mathematics and physics, Solzhenitsyn served for four years as an ARTILLERY officer in the Red Army during the war. In 1945, while a twice-decorated captain serving with an artillery unit in East Prussia, he was arrested and sentenced to eight years of forced labor for derogatory remarks about STALIN that he made in a letter to a friend. He was imprisoned in the Marfino Special Prison No. 16, on the outskirts of MOSCOW, which he described in *The First Circle*. From Aug. 1950 to Feb. 1953 he was at Ekibastuz, part of the complex of labor camps in the steppes of Kazakhstan in Soviet Central Asia. He was then sent to "internal exile" in Kazakhstan, finally being allowed to return to his home in Ryazan in 1957.

His prolific post-prison writings were based on his military and prison experiences. He became internationally known in 1962 with publication of his novel *One Day in the Life of Ivan Denisovich*. His subsequent *The First Circle* and three-volume *Gulag Archipelago* delineated the Soviet penal system of Stalin's era.

Sonar

Sonar—called ASDIC by the British—was the principal means of detecting submerged submarines during the war. *Passive* sonar or hydrophones listened for the sounds of submarines—their machinery noises and cavitation caused by their propellers. Its effectiveness was limited because of the noise generated by the antisubmarine ship, and the low noise levels of submarines while underwater, moving slowly, on electric motors. *Active* sonar produced an acoustic pulse ("ping") that was sent out by the antisubmarine ship that would be reflected back to the sonar set if it struck a submarine (or other solid object, such as a large fish or bottom wreckage).

Hydrophones were used by major navies in World War I and there was considerable sonar development between the wars. The most significant advances were made by the German Navy, which developed groups of hydrophones that could detect incoming TORPEDOES as well as submarines, giving excellent directional data. These sets were fitted in submarines as well as surface ships.

By the beginning of the EUROPEAN WAR in Sept. 1939 all U.S. Navy DESTROYERS had sonar while the Royal Navy had fitted Asdic in more than 100 modern destroyers, about forty-five older destroyers and sloops, and some forty antisubmarine trawlers. Unfortunately, the Navy believed that Asdic could easily defeat the U-boat and in the late 1930s there was little attention given antisubmarine training and tactics by the British.

In the war at sea sonar was limited, especially in the early phases of the BATTLE OF THE ATLANTIC, because German U-BOATS preferred to attack and withdraw on the surface, masked by fog or darkness. (They were faster and more maneuverable on the surface.) Also, the detonation of DEPTH CHARGES when attacking a U-boat would make the attacking ship's sonar unusable for several minutes. However, the widespread use of radar in Allied antisubmarine ships and then aircraft from 1942 onward began to deprive German submarines of their ability to operate on the surface. Also, tactics were developed to overcome the loss of contact during depth charging, especially Operation Plaster used by Capt. F. J. WALKER. The development of the HEDGEHOG permitted the use of sonar throughout an attack as the projectiles detonated only upon contact with a submarine's hull.

There were also efforts to reduce ship-generated noises that interfered with sonar, such as injecting oil and then (more successfully) air bubbles around a ship's propellers (Project Nightshirt) and then through the propellers (Project Agouti). The Germans also developed sonar countermeasures, including the release of bubbles and decoys from submarines, and coating U-boats with anechoic materials. (See ELECTRONIC COUNTERMEASURES.)

The United States, Britain, and Soviet Union also employed fixed hydrophone arrays on the seafloor for detecting submarines entering a harbor or anchorage. (These were the precursors of the U.S. Sound Surveillance System [SOSUS] and Soviet seafloor devices of the postwar period.)

Sonar was used for guidance in several Allied and German torpedoes. (See FIDO and GNAT.)

See also SONOBUOYS.

Songs

Before America's entrance into the war, two events that touched the nation's heart—the fall of France and the bombing of LONDON—were commemorated in song: "The Last Time I Saw Paris" (music by Jerome Kern, lyrics by Oscar Hammerstein II) poignantly marked the fall of France, and "Bless 'Em All" (British songwriters Jimmie Hughes and Frank Lane) captured the undefeatable spirit of the Londoners enduring the bombs and flames of the BATTLE OF BRITAIN.

The passage of the SELECTIVE SERVICE Act in 1940 inspired "Dear Mom" (words and music by Maury Coleman Harris), which Kate Smith introduced:

> Dear Mom . . . your package arrived but was missing
>   a stamp . . .
> your cake made a hit with all the boys in the camp.

After PEARL HARBOR, the music business, like every other U.S. industry, was quick to convert to turning out products for war. The first notable U.S. war song was "Remember Pearl Harbor" (words by Don Reid, music by Don Reid and Sammy Kaye), copyrighted within days of the attack:

> Let's Remember Pearl Harbor as we go to meet the
>   foe.
> Let's Remember Pearl Harbor as we did the Alamo.

The song title became an enduring rallying cry that echoed in politicians' speeches and in exhortations to war workers.

A legend of Pearl Harbor—that a chaplain had helped gunners who were firing at Japanese planes—was made into "Praise the Lord and Pass the Ammunition" (words and music by Frank Loesser):

> Down went the gunner, a bullet was his fate.
> Down went the gunner, and then the gunner's
>   mate.
> Up jumped the sky pilot, gave the boys a look
> And manned the gun himself as he laid aside the
>   Book,
> shouting: "Praise the Lord and pass the ammunition!"
> . . . Yes the sky pilot said it.
> You've got to give him credit,
> for a son of a gun of a gunner was he. . . .

Soon after the U.S. Eighth AIR FORCE began flying missions from British bases, WAR CORRESPONDENTS wrote stories about bullet-riddled U.S. bombers limping home. The stories were set to music in "Comin' in on a Wing and a Prayer" (lyrics by Harold Adamson, music by Jimmy McHugh):

> One of our planes was missing, two hours overdue.
> One of our planes was missing, with all its gallant crew.
> The radio sets were humming, they waited for a word;
> Then a voice broke thru the humming and this is what they heard:
> "Comin' in on a wing and a Pray'r
> Comin' in on a wing and a Pray'r
> Tho' there's one motor gone, we can still carry on . . .
> Comin' in on a wing and a pray'r. . . ."

At WAR BOND rallies, USO dances, and practically any other gathering with the need for a patriotic moment, the band played a medley of songs honoring the Army ("The Caissons Go Rolling Along"), the Navy ("Anchors Aweigh"), the Marines ("The Marine Hymn"), and what at the beginning of the war was called the ARMY AIR CORPS, whose song (words and music by Robert Crawford) was as new as the service:

> Off we go into the wild blue yonder,
> Climbing high into the sun.
> Here they come, zooming to meet our thunder.
> At 'em boys, Give 'er the gun!
> Down we dive, spouting our flame from under,
> Off with one helluva* roar!
> We live in fame or go down in flame.
> Nothing'll stop the Army Air Corps! . . .

The asterisk was to a footnote in the official sheet music edition, which warned: "For radio use substitute 'ter-ri-ble.' "

War in the air added new phrases to the "Marine Hymn," whose "on the land as on the sea" was changed to "in the air, on land and sea"; and to the "Navy Hymn," to which was added, "Oh God, protect men who fly / Through lonely ways beneath the sky."

One of the most famous members of the Army Air Forces was bandleader GLENN MILLER. In February 1942, soon after getting the first "golden record" (for the million-plus sale of "Chattanooga Choo Choo"), Miller disbanded his band, joined the AAF, and organized a swing band of airmen who played for troops. The plane carrying him from England to France in 1944 disappeared over the English Channel and his body was never found.

Songs were considered so necessary for morale that the Army Hit Kit of Popular Songs was regularly sent to bases throughout the world. The one issued in March 1943, for example, had the sheet music for a song made popular by Australian troops, "I've Got Sixpence," and Irving Berlin's "This Is the Army, Mister Jones," from the all-soldier "This Is the Army" musical, which played on Broadway and elsewhere for the Army Emergency Relief Fund. Berlin's all-time hit, "God Bless America" was sung in "This Is the Army." Berlin had removed the song from his World War I soldier show "Yip! Yip! Yaphank."

Some songs touched directly on the war, sentimentally in "I Left My Heart at the STAGE-DOOR CANTEEN," comically in Spike Jones' jeers at "Der Führer's Face." Many songs were more about love than about war. Lyrics talked of loneliness and vows—"Don't Get Around Much Any More," "I'll Walk Alone"—and the fear that "Somebody Else Is Taking My Place."

Glenn Miller's vocalist Marion Hutton relayed a soldier's plea: "Don't Sit Under the Apple Tree with Anyone Else But Me." Songs promised a bright tomorrow: "When the Lights Go on Again All Over the World," "There'll Be Bluebirds Over the White Cliffs of Dover."

The best songs lingered in the American heart long after the war: "As Time Goes By," "It's Been a Long, Long Time," "I'll Be Seeing You," "Sentimental Journey."

In European combat zones, soldiers on both sides sang the haunting "Lily Marlene," which had been written by German composer Norbert Schultze as he went off to battle in World War I:

> *Vor der Kaserne, vor dem gross Tor*
> *Steht eine Laterne und steht sie noch davor*
> *Und wenn wir da einst uns wiedersehn,*

Vor der Laterne werd ich stehn
Wie einst Lilly Marlen. . . .

"Standing by the barracks, standing by the gate," the song begins, telling the story of a woman who waited for a soldier, who hopes that he will live through the war and will someday "stand by the lantern as Lilly Marlen once did."

More than two decades later, British troops told of hearing the song drifting through the desert night during the African campaign of World War II. The German words (and Lilly's name) were translated into English and the song was sung on both sides through the rest of the war.

Sonnenblume (Sunflower)

Code name for deployment of German troops to North Africa, Jan.–Feb. 1941.

Sonnenwende (Solstice)

German code name for counteroffensive at Stargard on the EASTERN FRONT, Feb. 1945.

Sonobuoy

Aircraft-laid hydrophones for detecting U-BOATS. The sonobouy was an American-invented device that was dropped into the water by parachute; upon entry a hydrophone was suspended beneath the buoy to detect submarine propeller sounds that would be transmitted by radio to the circling aircraft. The standard procedure was to lay a pattern of five buoys—one at each corner of a three-mile square and one in the center; the operator in the aircraft would then listen to each buoy in turn to determine the location of a U-boat within the pattern.

The first kill credited to the sonobuoys' use (as well as to aircraft RADAR) occurred on Mar. 20, 1945, off the Orkney Islands when a British-flown B-24 LIBERATOR used a FIDO homing TORPEDO to sink the submarine *U-905.* Two days later another Coastal Command Liberator used the sonobuoys and a Fido to sink the *U-296.*

Each sonobuoy was 3¾ feet long and 4 inches in diameter, and weighed 14 pounds. They could be released from aircraft flying up to about 120 mph. Upon hitting the water the parachute broke away, the buoy's batteries were activated, and the hydrophone was lowered into the water on a 24-foot

cable. The separation was necessary so that the sound of waves lapping against the buoy would not hide faint propeller noises from the U-boat. Effective range of the sonobuoys varied greatly with sea conditions and the target's speed and depth. The range could be as great as 3.5 miles in ideal conditions. The buoy's batteries lasted about four hours, after which a dissolving plug in the buoy would sink the device to prevent its capture by the enemy.

Sorge, Richard (1895–1944)

Soviet master spy. Sorge, half-German, half-Russian, used the cover of a German journalist in Japan while working as an agent for Soviet intelligence. Sorge painstakingly developed a cover by joining the NAZI Party, getting a job on the *Frankfurter Zeitung,* Germany's most respected newspaper, and convincing the editors to send him to TOKYO as the paper's correspondent. By 1936 Sorge had a spy ring whose members included an adviser to the Japanese Cabinet and an American Communist sent to Japan by the Soviets to act as Sorge's interpreter.

Sorge so ingratiated himself with the German diplomatic community in Tokyo that he set up an office in the embassy itself and had access to embassy files. He also curried favor with influential Japanese officials and sought to persuade Japan to avoid war with the Soviet Union. He learned of HITLER's plans for invading the Soviet Union two months before the invasion. But STALIN dismissed the warning.

Sorge was able to inform the Soviets that in Dec. 1941–Jan. 1942 the Japanese planned to move south (toward the DUTCH EAST INDIES and French INDOCHINA). Thus, the Soviets were able to shift their military forces in the Far East to the European front with assurance that the Japanese would not launch an attack to support the German invasion of European Russia.

Japanese counterintelligence cracked his ring in 1944 and Sorge was hanged on Nov. 7, 1944.

South Africa,

see UNION OF SOUTH AFRICA.

South Dakota (BB 57)

U.S. BATTLESHIP that won fame in the South Pacific during the battle of SANTA CRUZ in Oct.

1942 when her antiaircraft guns shot down an estimated twenty-six Japanese aircraft during the day-long engagement. This was the most effective score against aircraft in a single battle of any warship in the war. The *South Dakota*'s gunnery achievement was due to her newly installed BOFORS 40-MM guns, 5-inch (127-mm) dual-purpose guns firing PROXIMITY-FUZE ammunition, and RADAR gunfire control.

In press reports after the battle the *South Dakota* was usually referred to as "Battleship X" for security reasons.

She was commissioned in March 1942 and, after trials and training, reached the Southwest Pacific in early Sept. 1942. Her entry into the war zone was inauspicious with the dreadnought striking a submerged rock and having to return to PEARL HARBOR for repairs.

She was back in the Southwest Pacific in late Oct. 1942 as part of a TASK FORCE including the CARRIERS *ENTERPRISE* (CV 6) and *HORNET* (CV 8). The force, blocking possible Japanese advances toward GUADALCANAL, came under intense air attack early on Oct. 26. Operating near the *Enterprise,* the *South Dakota* and the "Big E" were attacked by waves of Japanese carrier-based dive bombers and TORPEDO planes beginning about 11:45 A.M. The battleship was struck by a 500-pound BOMB atop her heavily armored No. 1 gun turret; damage was minimal but fifty men, including the commanding officer, were injured (one man later died).

The *South Dakota* and the U.S. battleship *Washington* (BB 56), under Rear Adm. W. A. (CHING) LEE engaged a Japanese dreadnought and two heavy cruisers off SAVO ISLAND early on Nov. 15. The *South Dakota* took several Japanese ships under fire, but suffered power failures and was herself struck by twenty-seven shells of varying caliber and was heavily damaged; fortunately, a number of 8-inch (203-mm) shells did not explode when they hit the ship. The *South Dakota* had thirty-eight men killed and sixty injured. (The Japanese battleship was severely damaged and, with a stricken destroyer, were abandoned and scuttled; the two Japanese cruisers were also damaged.)

Following repairs in the United States, the *South Dakota* operated with the British Home Fleet until Aug. 1943. Returning to the Pacific, the battleship saw heavy action in the U.S. CENTRAL PACIFIC CAMPAIGN, operating with fast carriers, bombarding shore positions, and beginning in late July was one of several U.S. warships that shelled the Japanese coast. Her gunners were credited with shooting down a total of sixty-four planes during the war. On June 19, 1944, a Japanese bomb killed twenty-four crewmen and injured another twenty-seven; on May 6, 1945, while taking on ammunition from a supply ship, a powder canister exploded, causing the death of eleven men and injuring another twenty-four.

The *South Dakota* was anchored in TOKYO Bay at the time of the SURRENDER ceremonies on Sept. 2, 1945. She was decommissioned on Jan. 31, 1947, and placed in "mothballs." She was later broken up for scrap. During the war the ship was awarded thirteen BATTLE STARS for her war service.

The *South Dakota,* launched on June 7, 1941, was the first of four similar ships. Her standard displacement was 35,000 tons and she was 680 feet long. Steam turbines could drive her at 27.5 knots. The *South Dakota*'s main battery was nine 16-inch (406-mm) guns and she had a secondary battery of sixteen 5-inch guns plus numerous BOFORS 40-MM and OERLIKON 20-MM antiaircraft guns. (Her three sister ships had two additional 5-inch twin gun mounts for a total of twenty of those weapons.) The *South Dakota* was manned by a crew of 2,350.

Soviet Offensive Campaign (1943–1945)

The Battle of STALINGRAD during the winter of 1942–1943 marked the end of the German offensive in the East and the turning point in the EUROPEAN WAR. That defeat demonstrated three phenomena that would prevail on the EASTERN FRONT for the next two and a half years: (1) ADOLF HITLER's blind refusal to permit breakouts of surrounded troops or strategic retreats—the more than 231,000 troops of *Generalfeldmarschall* FRIEDRICH PAULUS' Sixth Army killed or captured at Stalingrad were among the first to learn this (another 30,000 wounded had been flown out); (2) the failure of the Luftwaffe to provide the promised aerial support or deliver sufficient supplies to sustain the garrison; and (3) the strategic and tactical genius of Soviet commanders, especially Gen. V. I. CHUIKOV and Gen. GEORGI ZHUKOV, who came to Stalingrad after Zhukov's defense had helped to save MOSCOW.

The German armed forces were now being called upon to occupy all of VICHY FRANCE and to reinforce North Africa in response to the Allied NORTH AFRICA INVASION of Nov. 1942, and Anglo-American STRATEGIC BOMBING was demanding the allocation of more defensive forces in Germany; at the same time, ALBERT SPEER was belatedly mobilizing the German industry for war. Stalingrad had also been costly for the Soviets in terms of troops and matériel, but American LEND-LEASE and British weapons were reaching the frontline troops, the Soviet factories relocated away from the battle zone were again producing weapons, and a steady stream of fresh troops were arriving from Asia. Thus, while both sides were suffering heavy losses, the Soviets but not the Germans could replace them.

Hitler and the German high command, contemptuous of the Soviets, failed to comprehend what was occurring on the Eastern Front. Rather, the Germans believed that their failure had been due to the Russian weather. Hitler postponed launching his 1943 offensive several times, oblivious of the increasing concern of his commanders that the Soviets had learned of their plans. Moscow would be the eventual objective of the campaign; the immediate goal was to "straighten the front," to destroy a Soviet bulge in the German lines around a town called KURSK. Given the code name *Zitadelle* (Citadel) by the Germans, the ensuing battle in July 1943 was the largest tank battle in history. After a week's fighting the Red Army held—at a cost to the Germans of over 70,000 men dead and captured and 2,950 TANKS and 1,400 aircraft destroyed—irreplaceable losses only a few months after the disaster at Stalingrad.

Even while the Kursk battle was being fought, the Red Army went on the offensive. Farther north, near Orel, there was a German salient protruding into the Soviet lines. The attack was launched on July 12, and on Aug. 6 the Soviets captured Orel, the defeated Germans losing another 1,500 tanks. Another offensive began on Aug. 3 (this operation under Zhukov, now a marshal), against another German salient, at KHARKOV, south of Kursk. Kharkov fell on Aug. 23; more than 1,500 German tanks were lost in that battle. Smolensk was recaptured by Soviet forces on Sept. 25 and Kiev on Nov. 6.

The year 1944 was worse for the Germans. In Jan. 1944 the Red Army broke through to LENINGRAD; it was not the lifting of the siege, which had gone on since the fall of 1941, but there was now a rail line into the city, and food and munitions would now be more available to fend off the Germans. Farther south Soviet troops continued the drive to eject the Germans from the Ukraine, with a new offensive beginning in Feb. 1944. A third offensive, along the Black Sea coast, isolated the Crimea, defeated the Germans at Odessa and, finally, recaptured SEVASTOPOL on May 9.

One month later, to the north of Leningrad, another Soviet thrust smashed the German-Finnish defensive line and proceeded to push the AXIS forces back toward the Finnish border. More offensive operations followed—striking westward to clear German forces from Estonia and Latvia, and toward Poland, and southwest into Hungary and Rumania (Bucharest fell to the Red Army on Aug. 31, 1944). The drive toward Poland led to an uprising in WARSAW. But the Soviet troops halted short of the city, to rest and resupply—and to let the 60,000 Polish freedom fighters be defeated by German troops, to facilitate setting up a Communist government in Poland when the war was over.

Virtually everywhere the Soviets were on the offensive and, with the British and Americans fighting on the Italian mainland and, from June 1944, in France, and in the skies over the *Reich,* the Germans were hard pressed to allocate forces to meet the onslaughts. Throughout Eastern Europe the Soviets were recapturing the territory held by the Germans and then moving into Eastern Europe. Soviet troops reached the Gulf of Danzig in late Jan. 1945, cutting off a large German army in East Prussia—Hitler refused to allow either an evacuation by sea or a breakout by land.

While the Red Army came into Soviet territory and even Eastern Europe as liberators, they came into East Prussia as victors. As the Soviets approached those Germans living in the region—who learned in time of the German advance—fled to the West. Soon roads were clogged with millions of refugees.

When Soviet troops entered East Prussia all men were immediately rounded up—from age ten to seventy. Those immediately identified as NAZI officials were shot. The remainder were marched off, first to remove mines and tank traps, and bury the dead, and then to be taken to the Soviet Union as forced labor. German historian Jürgen Thornwald quoted a survivor of the Soviet assault in his *Flight in the Winter:* "There was a striking contrast between this well-planned action, carried through under clear directives, and the seemingly disorganized, wild dealings of Red Army officers and men with the life and property of the Germans. . . . It seemed as though the devil himself had come to Silesia. The 'Mongol barbarism of the Asiatic plains' had come not in a PROPAGANDA phrase but in the flesh."

The frontline Soviet troops raped, pillaged, and killed. "Thus," continued the survivor's account, "the German population was delivered into the hands of an uncouth army of millions who had marched over dead bodies and through ruined towns from Stalingrad to Poland, across half of Europe. But what is more, a systematic, relentless propaganda had implanted in these millions a pitiless hate of the Germans." The savagery, however, still paled in comparison with the German SS and even Army activities in the Soviet Union.

Further, as German territory was conquered, the Soviet troops stripped everything that could be carried away—even doors, windows, plumbing, and electrical wiring from houses. Telephones were especially prized, as was any machinery. Livestock that was not commandeered by the combat troops as they went through an area, was herded off across Poland to the Soviet Union.

Throughout this period, Hitler continued to refuse to allow troops to withdraw to more favorable defense lines. City after city was declared a "fortress" that would withstand the Soviet advance, regardless of the refugees in the city, whether the garrison was regular army or People's Army (home guard), or even if they had ARTILLERY or ammunition. Millions of refugees died on the road or under Soviet artillery and air attacks because Hitler would not give them warning or allow them to move westward.

Before dawn on April 16, 22,000 Soviet guns aligned along the Oder River opened fire on the hapless German troops entrenched on the western bank. This was the last river before BERLIN. That day Hitler drafted an order of the day that declared, "We have been waiting for this assault. Since January [1945] every step has been taken to raise a strong eastern front. Colossal artillery forces are welcoming the enemy. Countless new units are replacing our losses. . . . Once again, Bolshevism will suffer Asia's old fate—it will founder on the capital of the German Reich."

For the final assault on the Berlin area the Soviets assembled three front (army group) commands: to the north was the 2nd Belorussian Front of Marshal K. K. ROKOSSOVSKI, in the center Zhukov's 1st Belorussian Front, and to the south Marshal I. S. KONEV's 1st Ukrainian Front. However, in April the 1st Belorussian Front was given to Gen. V. D. Sokolovsky to permit Zhukov to take command of the overall assault on Berlin, with the Eighth Guards Army to have the honor of assaulting the German capital. The three fronts totaled 193 divisions, 2,500,000 men and WOMEN, 6,250 tanks, more than 41,000 artillery and MORTAR tubes, over 3,200 multiple ROCKET launchers, and 7,500 aircraft.

To confront this mass the Germans could assemble but eighty-five emaciated divisions; perhaps 1,000,000 tired, demoralized troops of varying quality; 10,000 guns and mortars; 1,500 tanks; and a few hundred effective aircraft.

The Soviets crossed the Oder. On April 18 Red Army units broke through German defenses less than 20 miles east of Berlin. Two days later Hitler, celebrating his 56th birthday in the *FÜHRERBUNKER* beneath the Chancellery in Berlin, decided to remain in Berlin, convinced that his presence in "fortress Berlin" could make the front hold. But he did authorize the removal of various ministries from Berlin.

Soon artillery shells as well as BOMBS were falling continuously on the center of Berlin. In his bunker, Hitler pondered his maps, moved imaginary armies and relief columns, and struck out at members of his entourage whom he perceived were disloyal, especially those reported to be attempting negotiations with the enemy. By April 24, Soviet artillery was established in nearly every suburb as Berlin was completely encircled and Soviet troops, especially prepared for street-to-street fighting, entered the city. The next day Soviet troops completed the encircle-

Russian and American troops drink beer and champagne as the leading units of U.S. and Soviet armies meet at Torgau on the Elbe River on April 25, 1945. *(U.S. Army)*

ment of Berlin; on the same day, to the west, troops of the U.S. First ARMY and the Soviet Fifth Guards Tank Army met at Torgau on the Elbe River.

On April 30 Hitler committed suicide. The next day the surviving generals in the *Führerbunker* sought out the Soviet commanders to begin negotiations for the surrender of Berlin, which took place on May 2. The European War continued for six more days. The Red Army had decisively defeated the German Army in the largest ground campaign of the war.

Soviet Union,

see UNION OF SOVIET SOCIALIST REPUBLICS.

Soviet-German Nonagression Pact,

see NONAGRESSION PACT.

Spaatz, Gen. Carl (1891–1974)

The leading U.S. AAF intellect and senior AAF field commander of the war. After brief infantry service, "Tooey" Spaatz became an Army fighter pilot and flew in Europe in World War I. He remained in fighter aviation after the war, commanding the Army's only pursuit squadron. But like most of his contemporaries, he soon became a bomber advocate and a leading champion of daylight PRECISION BOMBING.

When the EUROPEAN WAR began he went to England as an observer. He returned to the United States and was the chief of the Army's air staff (under Lt. Gen. H. H. ARNOLD) when the Japanese attacked PEARL HARBOR. He returned to England and in May 1942 took command of the U.S. Eighth AIR FORCE, the first major U.S. air command in

Europe. After haltingly launching the U.S. air campaign against Germany, shortly after the NORTH AFRICA INVASION, on Nov. 30, 1942, he arrived in North Africa as Gen. DWIGHT D. EISENHOWER's air adviser, and in Feb. 1943 he organized and commanded the North West African Air Force. A month later, he was promoted to lieutenant general and became commander of the Twelfth Air Force and deputy commander of the Mediterranean Allied Air Forces, which directed Allied air operations for the landings in SICILY and Italy.

In Jan. 1944 Spaatz became commanding general U.S. Strategic Air Forces in Europe, responsible for Eighth and Fifteenth Air Force operations against Germany. He employed his bombers primarily to make the Luftwaffe send its fighters into battle, where they were vulnerable to his P-51 MUSTANG escorts—a strategy forced on the AAF after disastrous bomber losses in daylight operations over Germany. Spaatz's biographer, David R. Mets, judged Spaatz a pragmatist with "an unerring sense of what would work."

Spaatz was made a full (four-star) general in March 1945 and, after returning briefly to the United States, he became commander of U.S. Strategic Air Forces in the Pacific (Eighth and Twentieth Air Forces) for the planned 1945–1946 air campaign against Japan.

He succeeded Gen. Arnold as commanding general AAF in Feb. 1946. In Sept. 1947 Spaatz became the first Chief of Staff of the U.S. Air Force, a position he held until retiring in April 1948.

Spain

Capital: Madrid, pop. 25,365,000 (est. 1939).
Spain had two political lives during World War II: the SPANISH CIVIL WAR, which ravaged the country from 1936 to 1939, and the dictatorship of FRANCISCO FRANCO, who emerged from the war as *Caudillo,* chief of state. Although Spain proclaimed neutrality during the war, she supported the fellow Fascist states of Germany and Italy.

Both Germany and Italy gave immense aid to Franco's Nationalists in the civil war against the left-wing Republicans, who were supported by the Soviet Union. At first the United States tried to stay aloof. In Jan. 1937, applying the NEUTRALITY ACT to Spain, the United States cut off all war matériel

to both sides—just at the time when the Republicans were going to buy U.S. munitions.

Spain's neutrality began to waver in 1940 when Germany's victories and Italy's entry seemed to tilt the balance in the EUROPEAN WAR. Spanish mobs, in government-sponsored demonstrations, demanded that England turn over GIBRALTAR and France give up Morocco to Spain. In conversations with both HITLER and Italian dictator BENITO MUSSOLINI, Franco said he would enter the war. But when Hitler specifically discussed a plan to send German troops through Spain to seize Gibraltar, Franco insisted he did not yet have the resources to go to war.

Spain permitted German tankers in Spanish bays to refuel U-BOATS and did little to halt widespread German ESPIONAGE, including spying on the British naval base and airfield at Gibraltar. When Germany invaded the Soviet Union, Franco sent the BLUE DIVISION to the EASTERN FRONT to fight with Germany and help with "the extermination of Russia."

As the tide of war began to turn against the AXIS in late 1943, so too did Spain turn, showing a new fervor for the ALLIES. Spanish officials, for example, began allowing men to traverse Spain from VICHY FRANCE on the way to FREE FRENCH Army units in North Africa. The United States authorized sales of 60 percent of Spain's usual petroleum imports; Spain in turn sold to the Allies 77 percent of its production of wolfram, from which tungsten is extracted.

In Jan. 1944, when Spain refused to ban wolfram exports to Germany, the United States cut off all petroleum, creating an instant transportation crisis in Spain. Oil exports were resumed in May after Spain agreed to expel specified German spies operating in Spain and Spanish Morocco; withdraw the Blue Division from the Eastern Front; and release to the Allies three Italian merchant ships in Spanish ports.

Near the end of the war Spain tried desperately to get on the winning side. She severed relations with Japan on April 11, 1945, ten days after U.S. forces landed on OKINAWA, and broke off relations with Germany the day of Germany's SURRENDER. But at the POTSDAM CONFERENCE the United States, Britain, and the Soviet Union declared that

Spain could not be a member of the UNITED NATIONS. Spain was not admitted to the U.N. until 1955.

Spanish Civil War

A military uprising that became a prelude to World War II. What at first seemed like an ideological struggle between two factions in Spain brought onto the international stage three rehearsing belligerents of World War II: Germany and Italy on the side of the Spanish Nationalists, the Soviet Union on the side of the Spanish Republicans. More than 1,000,000 Spaniards died in the war.

The civil war erupted in July 1936 when, after years of political turmoil and months of riotous strikes, the right-wing Nationalists, led by the Spanish Army, revolted against the left-wing Republican government, whose supporters also were known as the Loyalists. Gen. FRANCISCO FRANCO, who had gone to Spanish Morocco to rally army support, was given air cover by German and Italian warplanes when he flew back to Spain. Such aid by the sympathetic Fascist states continued throughout the three-year war.

Italy sent some 100,000 troops between Dec. 1936 and April 1937, along with planes, weapons, and advisers. Germany used the war as a "laboratory." The Luftwaffe tested in combat such planes as the ME 109 fighter, HE 111 and DO 17 bombers and, flying JU 87s and Hs 123s, developed the Luftwaffe's dive-bombing techniques.

In late July 1936, German JU 52 transports ferried Franco's troops from Morocco to Spain, overflying Republican warships that would have intercepted the troops had they gone by sea. In just over a month the twenty Ju 52s flew 461 flights, carrying 7,350 troops, along with their field guns, machine guns, and other equipment. Another 5,455 troops were ferried in September and October, by which time Franco's forces had control of the sea, ending the need for an airlift.

Germany formed the Condor Legion to fight in Spain. Among the 17,000 to 18,000 Germans in the Legion was fighter pilot ADOLF GALLAND, who would become a leading ACE in World War II. On March 31, 1937, German bombers of the Legion struck the Republican-controlled town of Durango, some six miles from the front lines. This was the first defenseless town in Europe to feel the wrath of modern air power. Several churches were hit by German BOMBS, and one bomb killed fourteen nuns in a chapel. German bombing and strafing that day killed a total of 258 persons.

In Europe's first saturation bombing, German planes bombed Barcelona eighteen times in two days. But the bombing that horrified much of the world was the German raid on the old Basque capital of Guernica on April 26, 1937. A town of about 5,000 people with no military targets, Guernica was totally destroyed by incendiary, high-explosive, and shrapnel bombs, some weighing up to 1,000 pounds. The bombing killed 1,654 people and injured 889. The eradication of Guernica became a symbol of the price the innocent paid in modern TOTAL WAR.

Artist Pablo Picasso, commissioned by the Republicans to paint a mural, used the bombing of Guernica as his subject. "Guernica," a jagged panorama of torn bodies and terror from the skies, became one of the most famous paintings of the century. To a United States only beginning to comprehend the reality of total war, the painting, like the NEWSREELS of the time, was one of many emotional images of future Fascist enemies.

ERNEST HEMINGWAY's *For Whom the Bell Tolls,* a best-seller published in 1940, also brought the war to the American public. His hero, Robert Jordan, personified the idealistic young Americans who joined the ABRAHAM LINCOLN BRIGADE, an ill-equipped, ill-trained force of volunteers fighting on the Loyalist side. Hemingway, a WAR CORRESPONDENT in Spain, gave circulation to a new term: the FIFTH COLUMN, subversive elements aiding the enemy.

Through the Comintern, the Moscow-directed coordinator of international communism, the Soviet Union organized international brigades, including the Abraham Lincoln Brigade. Soviet aid, purchased with Spanish government gold, was substantially less than the help sent by Germany and Italy. Soviet advisers came first, then ARTILLERY and fighters and bombers. The total number of Soviet pilots who fought in Spain is not publicly known; estimates run from 150 to 750. At least 2,000 Soviet advisers, fliers, and technicians are believed to have served in Spain. At the peak of the fighting, international volunteers numbered about 18,000.

SPARs

The U.S. Coast Guard organized the all-female SPARs on Nov. 23, 1942, their name being derived from the Coast Guard motto—*Semper Paratus*—Always Ready. By the end of the war there were some 10,000 SPARs on active duty, fulfilling a variety of shore jobs throughout the United States and in Alaska and Hawaii. Their commanding officer was Dorothy C. Stratton, who held the rank of captain at the end of the war.

The Coast Guard had also recruited WOMEN in World War I.

Special Air Service

British COMMANDO organization formed in the Middle East in July 1941 by Lt. David Stirling, then serving with the Army's No. 3 Commando. Initially called a "BRIGADE" to confuse the Germans, the unit began as a detachment of seven officers and some sixty men. Small parties were parachuted into the desert behind German and Italian lines, often in collaboration with the famed British LONG-RANGE DESERT GROUP, to attack bases and supply lines of the AFRICA KORPS.

The success of the commandos, coupled with the addition of a contingent of FREE FRENCH paratroopers, led to formation of the 1st SAS REGIMENT in Aug. 1942. With the advance of Gen. BERNARD L. MONTGOMERY's Eighth Army across North Africa, SAS forces continued to operate behind German lines. Stirling was captured in early 1943 near Gabes, Tunisia, and taken to Italy. He escaped from confinement four times and, ultimately, was placed in the COLDITZ POW camp in Germany for the remainder of the war. (While imprisoned, Stirling drafted a proposal for the use of bases in China for joint Anglo-American commando raids against Japan.)

The 2nd SAS Regiment was established—under command of Lt. Col. W. S. (Bill) Stirling, David's brother—and carried out raids against German targets in SICILY, CRETE, Sardinia, and on the Italian mainland (along with raids by the 1st SAS Regiment).

In March 1944 the two SAS regiments were brought to England. In January 1944 they formed the 1st SAS Brigade, which included other SAS units, two French parachute BATTALIONS, and a Belgian parachute COMPANY along with a sprinkling of individuals of a variety of nationalities. (One Danish officer won the VICTORIA CROSS while leading an SAS operation.) The SAS then concentrated on supporting and training FRENCH RESISTANCE groups to aid the NORMANDY INVASION. At the time of the Normandy landings the SAS brigade had a strength of some 2,500 officers and men.

Highly effective, the SAS fought in German-occupied areas of Europe until the end of the war. At that time it was learned that on several occasions SAS personnel captured by the Germans had been tortured and executed.

During the war the SPECIAL BOAT SECTION (SBS), later renamed Special Boat Service, was formed, initially under the aegis of the SAS.

After the Allied victory, in Oct. 1945 the SAS was disbanded. Subsequently, in 1947 a reserve SAS regiment was formed (mostly of wartime veterans), which was reactivated in 1950 to carry out special operations, from fighting guerrillas in Malaya beginning that year to conducting operations against Irish terrorists in Northern Ireland, combating rebels in the Falklands and South Georgia in 1982, and numerous publicized and clandestine activities during the past forty years.

Special Boat Section

Term used for small boat units within the British COMMANDO structure. These units used canoes, folbots, and kayaks to carry raiders, reconnaissance troops, and demolition specialists into enemy territory. They were carried to paddling distance of their objectives by British submarines, motor torpedo boats, and disguised fishing craft.

The origins of the Special Boat Section (SBS) were in 1941 commando raids in the Mediterranean, with the SBS initially using folbots (collapsible canoes) for preattack reconnaissance of the island of Rhodes off the Turkish coast. More operations in the Mediterranean area followed, SBS "paddlers" often working behind German lines in North Africa and sometimes supporting operations of the LONG-RANGE DESERT GROUP. Subsequently, SBS units carried out raids and reconnaissance missions in European waters.

From 1946 the SBS was an all-Royal Marine unit; it was formally designated as the Special Boat Service in 1975.

Special Liaison Units

An MI6 system set up for the distribution of the use of ULTRA intercepts. Assigned to British and American headquarters, the SLU personnel handled the intercepts so that their use would not alert the Germans to the penetration of their cryptography.

Special Operations Executive

British agency that ran resistance groups and GUERRILLA activities in German-occupied countries and directed SABOTAGE operations both in Europe and Asia. The SOE, formed in July 1940, drew personnel from MI6 and other existing intelligence organizations. It was the model for the U.S. OFFICE OF STRATEGIC SERVICES.

The SOE parachuted advisers and supplies to JOSEF TITO's guerrillas in Yugoslavia and directed the dropping of tons of weapons into German-occupied France. Its agents also set up extremely effective resistance forces in Denmark and Norway. SOE ASSASSINATION specialists trained and equipped the Czechs who were parachuted into Czechoslovakia to kill *Reichsprotektor* REINHARD HEYDRICH.

SOE agents also worked, on a smaller scale, in Malaysia, Burma, and Indochina. At its peak the SOE employed about 13,000 men and WOMEN.

Speedy

Signal code name for U.S. Army II CORPS in TUNISIA and SICILY, 1943.

Speer, Albert (1905–1981)

Architect whom ADOLF HITLER made minister of armament in the THIRD REICH. Germany was not fully mobilized when the EUROPEAN WAR began in 1939; Speer led that mobilization in 1943, and weapons production thereafter increased rapidly, despite British and American STRATEGIC BOMBING, declining only when Allied ground troops overran industrial areas.

Speer heard Hitler give a speech in 1931 and joined the NAZI party. He spoke with Hitler for the first time in 1933 and from then until 1942 he mainly designed government buildings and monuments for Hitler's "Thousand-year Reich." In 1942 Hitler appointed Speer as the minister of armaments and munitions. Despite strong opposition from government leaders, especially HERMANN GÖRING, head of the Luftwaffe, and HEINRICH HIMMLER, head of the SS, Speer was able to rejuvenate German arms production. His use of SLAVE LABOR—for which, for practical reasons, he demanded medical treatment and adequate food—in arms production was the major factor in his being sentenced for WAR CRIMES after the war.

Although Speer was not a member of the JULY 20 PLOT against Hitler, the assassins had listed his name in documents as a prospective member of the post-Hitler government. He survived the massacre of military and government leaders that followed the ASSASSINATION attempt. And, as the Allied armies were closing the ring around BERLIN in the closing days of the European War, he contravened Hitler's SCORCHED EARTH POLICY. In the final days of the conflict, as Hitler threatened more retaliation against the German people, who were unworthy of his leadership, Speer planned to use poison gas to kill Hitler in the *FÜHRERBUNKER* in Berlin. That scheme failed, and after an emotional farewell, he left Hitler for the last time on April 23.

In his autobiographical *Inside the Third Reich*, Speer recalled the scene: "By now it was about three o'clock in the morning. . . . The day had worn me out, and I was afraid that I would not be able to control myself at our parting. Trembling, the prematurely aged man stood before me for the last time; the man to whom I had dedicated my life twelve years before. I was both moved and confused. For his part, he showed no emotion when we confronted one another. His words were as cold as his hand: 'So, you're leaving? Good. *Auf Wiedersehen.*' No regards to my family. No wishes, no thanks, no farewell. For a moment I lost my composure, said something about coming back. But he could easily see that it was a white lie, and turned his attention to something else. I was dismissed."

Speer then walked to the Brandenburg Gate, climbed into a FI 156 *STORCH,* and took off from a

Berlin boulevard, already under Soviet ARTILLERY fire. Hitler committed suicide on April 30. Speer reached the headquarters of Hitler's successor, KARL DÖNITZ, and offered his services to the new führer. Along with other members of Dönitz's government, Speer was arrested. Placed on trial with other war criminals at Nuremberg, he was the only one of the twenty defendants to admit responsibility. He was sentenced to twenty years in prison, and became the longest-serving inmate of Spandau prison except for RUDOLF HESS. Speer was released on Sept. 30, 1966.

In prison Speer clandestinely wrote books that revealed the innermost workings of the Nazi government *(Inside the Third Reich)* and described his incarceration at Nuremberg *(Spandau—the Secret Diaries)*.

Writing about his relationship with Hitler, Speer observed, "One seldom recognizes the devil when he is putting his hand on your shoulder."

Spitfire

The outstanding British fighter aircraft of the war. Although not the predominant RAF fighter during the BATTLE OF BRITAIN, the Spitfire or "Spit" attracted the most attention of any of the antagonists in that battle. It was an effective, superb flying machine that was also highly photogenic. "Spits" were flown by nineteen of the fifty-eight squadrons of the RAF Fighter Command at the start of the Battle of Britain in July 1940. (The most prominent aircraft was the HURRICANE, flown by twenty-nine squadrons.)

The aircraft's combat debut occurred on Oct. 16, 1939, when Spitfires shot down two HE 111s over the Firth of Forth, the first German aircraft to be shot down over Britain since 1918. The fighter gained battle laurels in defeating the German Air Force over Britain in 1940, and then in most theaters where British forces fought.

In 1942–1943 two U.S. AAF fighter GROUPS flew Spitfires pending the availability of American-built fighters. During the NORMANDY INVASION on June 6, 1944, U.S. Navy pilots flew land-based Spitfires to direct gunfire from warships.

The Spitfire was a particularly clean design, with a Rolls-Royce in-line engine and a small air intake under the fuselage. The elliptical wing tips and pointed tail fin were particularly distinctive. The aircraft went through a large number of improvements and modifications during the war, reaching series 24 in postwar variants (plus Seafire models). While less rugged and more vulnerable to enemy fire than the Hurricane fighter, the Spitfire more than compensated for these limitations by its excellent acceleration and maneuverability. The Spitfire's speed made it a fine unarmed photo-reconnaissance aircraft. Beginning in 1941 Spitfires were produced with an arresting hook, folding wings, and other features for naval use, these being dubbed Seafires. Several Spitfires were experimentally fitted with floats.

The immediate predecessor of the Spitfire was the Supermarine firm's Type 224 aircraft, designed to meet an Air Ministry specification of 1930. It was an open-cockpit, gull-winged aircraft with a fixed landing gear. Dissatisfied with that plane—which did meet the Ministry's requirements—Supermarine began the Spitfire as a private venture. The new design was accepted by the Air Ministry in Jan. 1935 and the prototype "eight-gun fighter" flew on March 5, 1936. Production was approved in June 1936 and deliveries to RAF Fighter Command began in June 1938; more than 2,000 Spitfires were on order when Britain went to war in Sept. 1939. By that time nine squadrons had received the aircraft.

A total of 20,351 Spitfires were built through Oct. 1947. It was the only Allied fighter that was in production throughout the EUROPEAN WAR (the U.S. F4U CORSAIR was in production from 1941 into the 1950s); in addition, 2,408 naval Seafires were built. (They served into the Korean War of 1950–1953 and also flew from French aircraft carriers.)

The single-seat Spitfire was originally armed with eight .303-cal. machine guns. Some models carried 20-mm cannon in place of some machine guns. Maximum speed for the Spitfire I was 362 mph at its regular altitude; combat range with fifteen minutes in combat was 395 miles; maximum range was 575 miles.

Splice

British code name for reinforcement of MALTA, May 1941.

Sports

War had a varying impact on major U.S. sports. After the United States entered the war, many colleges cancelled varsity sports, and professional sports limped along with rosters made up of players too young, old, or infirm for war. Only one professional U.S. sport, however, was cancelled: automobile racing, including the Indianapolis 500. Horse racing came close to being totally suspended, but suspension of race meetings was spotty. The Kentucky Derby was run every year during the war.

Baseball, curtailed in World War I, went on as best as it could during World War II, though many stars volunteered for service or were drafted. President ROOSEVELT, in a letter to Judge Kenesaw Mountain Landis, commissioner of baseball, said "it would be best for the country to keep baseball going." Roosevelt also encouraged increasing the number of night games "because it gives an opportunity to the day shift [in war plants] to see a game occasionally."

Professional football, like baseball, relied on over-the-hill players or those who failed their draft physicals. The service academies at West Point and Annapolis, maintaining that sports helped to develop officers, kept full football schedules. Some colleges with Navy trainees on campus had stellar wartime seasons because Navy and Marine Corps trainees, who made up three-quarters of the squads, were allowed to play varsity sports. Because the Army did not let trainees play, colleges with only Army men either cancelled football or fielded substandard teams.

Boxing suffered more than any other sport because every champion or major contender went to war. About 300 boxers entered the service, including heavyweight champion JOE LOUIS, contender Billy Conn, world welterweight champion Barney Ross, and former heavyweight champion Gene Tunney. (During the war in Germany, heavyweight Max Schmeling, defeated by Louis in one round in 1938, served as a German paratrooper and landed at CRETE.)

The Olympics were held, with great NAZI fanfare in BERLIN in 1936. Signs saying *Juden unerwünscht* (JEWS Not Welcome) were taken down from restaurants and hotels, and sidewalk assaults and persecutions of Jews temporarily stopped. In a colossal new stadium adorned with SWASTIKAS, HITLER personally congratulated German winners, but when three Americans (two of them black) won the three medals for the high jump, Hitler left the stadium. Jesse Owens, another black American, won four gold medals for track and was a member of the winning relay team. The international crowd cheered him wildly, but Hitler snubbed Owens, whose prowess, grace, and intelligence dramatically repudiated Hitler's racial quackery.

Japan's conquest of Korea aided Japan's Olympian record, for the winner of the marathon was a Korean, running as a Japanese. The next Olympics were to have been held in TOKYO in 1940. But Japan, at war with China, dropped out and the torch passed to Finland, which was host instead to a Soviet invasion in 1939. The games that were played there were not recognized by the International Olympic Committee.

Spotter

British code name for effort to reinforce MALTA, May 1942.

Springboard

Code name for projected Allied assault on Madeira, 1942.

Springfield

Rifle used by U.S. Army and Marine Corps when the United States entered the war. The M1903 Springfield was rapidly replaced by the new M1 GARAND. The Springfield fitted with a Weaver telescopic sight was retained in large numbers as a sniper rifle.

The Springfield, a .30-cal. bolt-action weapon, weighed 8.75 pounds loaded with a 5-round internal clip. Effective range was approximately 550 yards with a rate of fire of 10 to 15 rounds per minute.

Spruance, Adm. Raymond A. (1886–1969)

Unlike many other commanders who are known for their remoteness and apparent lack of passion, Raymond Spruance was not hiding uncertainty or incompetence. His was a private personality, one of detachment and economy of phrase or expression.

Yet, at the time of the PEARL HARBOR attack, Spruance was already regarded as one of the finest intellects in the U.S. Navy. Spruance was a member of the "gun club" (those favoring BATTLESHIPS in the great fleet battles that were sure to come).

In the first few months of 1942 he served, as a rear admiral, as commander of a CRUISER DIVISION in support of Adm. WILLIAM F. HALSEY's CARRIER striking force. When Halsey was stricken with severe dermatitis in May 1942, Spruance, although not an aviator, was Halsey's first choice to replace him, and Adm. CHESTER W. NIMITZ, Commander in Chief Pacific Fleet, readily concurred.

Spruance had a reputation for careful planning and an unwillingness to make reckless moves. When the appropriate moment in the battle of MIDWAY came, however, Spruance did not hesitate to launch full deck-loads of torpedo and dive bombers at the enemy carriers. The resulting battle sank four of Japan's best carriers and shredded their aircraft. He then pulled his carriers back temporarily, avoiding a night surface battle with the intact, overwhelming Japanese surface fleet.

After Midway, Spruance was appointed, as previously planned, to be Nimitz's Chief of Staff, serving in that assignment from July 1942 to Aug. 1943. As a vice admiral he then assumed command of the Fifth FLEET, the Navy's main striking force. Spruance's first operations as commander were the Nov. 1943 landings in the GILBERT ISLANDS, followed by the seizure of KWAJALEIN and ENIWETOK in the MARSHALL ISLANDS in Feb. 1944. It was then decided that Spruance—promoted to full admiral—and Halsey (Third Fleet) and their staffs would alternate in command of the fleet in order to let one staff plan the next set of operations in the U.S. CENTRAL PACIFIC CAMPAIGN while the other was in action.

Spruance's decisions during the June 1944 invasion of the MARIANA ISLANDS and the battle of the Philippine Sea that resulted have aroused as much controversy as Halsey's later dash to the north during the battle of LEYTE GULF. Spruance was criticized for tying his carrier forces too closely to a defense of the landing forces and for withdrawing to the east overnight, making it impossible for his carriers' aircraft to inflict more than a single strike at their extreme range. This caution is lamented by his critics, who argue that a more aggressive strategy might have sunk the entire Mobile Fleet. (Halsey, who never publicly criticized Spruance, later commented that it might have been better if command of the FLEETS had been reversed in the two great sea battles.)

Spruance's defenders point to the previous Japanese preference for dividing its forces, making a focal point for a strike harder to identify and his battleship commander's unwillingness to risk a night battle. Above all, there are results: Spruance's air GROUPS in one day shot down over 400 Japanese planes, leaving the Japanese with but thirty-five operational aircraft. Moreover, the Japanese lost three carriers, albeit two of them sunk by U.S. SUBMARINES. Although cautious, Spruance's interpretation of his orders was defensible, and his forces were able to take the Marianas while stripping the Japanese of much of their mobile striking power.

After the Marianas were taken, Spruance turned over command of the fleet to Halsey. In Jan. 1945, as planned, Spruance regained command to oversee the IWO JIMA and OKINAWA operations. He is criticized for not providing strong naval support of the Marines ashore at Iwo Jima and for grumbling at the slow progress at Okinawa. The Fifth Fleet's exposure to costly KAMIKAZE air attacks may have prompted his impatience.

Spruance turned over command to Halsey for the last time at the end of May 1945, heading back to Pearl Harbor to begin planning for the invasion of Japan. The Japanese capitulation in Aug. 1945 canceled those plans and Spruance's part in World War II was over. Relieved of command of the Fifth Fleet in Nov. 1945, he became Commander in Chief Pacific (replacing Nimitz). He retired in 1948 but went on to serve as ambassador to the Philippines (1952–1953).

Spruance and Halsey were both considered for FIVE-STAR RANK in late 1944. Halsey, the more senior, received the fifth star in Dec. 1945. However, Congress did vote Spruance special compensation and benefits.

Spruance is remembered as a meticulous planner whose operations often turned out almost precisely the way he had planned. If not dashing or willing to strike impulsively, he nevertheless has to be seen as skillful, coolly competent, and highly successful.

While in some respects the opposite of Halsey, they nonetheless made a highly effective command team.

(His son, Capt. Edward D., commanded the submarine *Lionfish* [SS 298] in the Pacific during the later stages of the war.)

"Spruce Goose"

Largest aircraft built in World War II—although it did not fly until Nov. 2, 1947, and then for only *one minute!* The aircraft was developed by aviation industrialist HOWARD HUGHES. The aircraft was the product of a brief collaboration of Hughes and shipbuilder HENRY J. KAISER that sought to produce a "flying cargo ship" that could move troops and weapons overseas without the risk of loss to enemy submarines. Hughes was to design, build, and test the prototype aircraft; Kaiser would mass-produce them as he had merchant ships. In addition, Kaiser's friendship with President ROOSEVELT was needed to get the project going in the face of apprehension by military leaders. A contract with the government was signed on Nov. 16, 1942.

The aircraft—designated both HK-1 for Hughes-Kaiser and H-4 Hercules—was intended to transport 120,000 pounds of cargo or 750 troops or 350 litter patients plus a medical crew. Under the contract three prototype flying boats were to be built. Only the first was completed—the largest flying machine ever built in terms of wingspan and length until the modern wide-body jets. Called the "Spruce Goose," although it was built mainly of birch, the aircraft had a wingspan of 320 feet and length of 218½ feet with an estimated gross weight of 300,000 pounds. The Hughes flying boat was to have had a maximum speed of 218 mph and range of 3,500 miles. It was a streamlined, high-wing aircraft with eight radial engines. Fixed stabilizing floats were fitted to the wings.

A factory was built at Culver City, Calif., specifically to construct the aircraft. Built entirely of wood, it was 750 feet long, 250 feet wide, and 100 feet high—the largest wooden building in the world at the time. The sections of the flying boat were fabricated in the shed and then transported over two days the 28 miles to Terminal Island on Long Beach Harbor for assembly. That was in June 1946. The assembled aircraft was not launched until Nov. 1, 1947.

With Hughes as pilot and thirty-one others on board, including six from the news media, the aircraft began taxi runs the next day. On the third run, at 1:30 P.M. on Nov. 2, the "Spruce Goose" became airborne for sixty seconds. She flew for just over one mile and reached an altitude of about 85 feet.

The aircraft was a failure. It never flew again. (She is now on display in Long Beach, Calif.)

Squad

The smallest infantry unit. In the U.S. Army and Marine Corps squads were nominally commanded by junior sergeants or corporals. Three rifle squad generally composed a rifle PLATOON.

During the war U.S. Army squads generally consisted of twelve men—ten of whom, including the squad leader, were armed with M1 GARAND semiautomatic rifles, one with a BROWNING AUTOMATIC RIFLE (BAR), and one with an M1903 SPRINGFIELD rifle fitted with a sniper scope. The squad generally operated as a two-man scout SECTION, a four-man fire section (including the BAR), and a five-man maneuver and assault section; the squad leader customarily advanced with the scout section.

From 1943 on, the U.S. Marine Corps had thirteen-man squads with a squad leader and three fire teams, each with three riflemen plus one man armed with a BAR. The Marines used the M1903 Springfield into 1942, after which riflemen carried the M1 Garand. Thus, a Marine squad had ten M1s and three BARs. Accordingly, when ARTILLERY or machine guns and MORTARS could not be used to provide direct support, a Marine squad would tend to be more capable of maneuver and providing fire than an Army squad by virtue of superiority in automatic rifles. (Earlier Marine squads had nine men.)

Squadron

A U.S. AAF, Army, and Navy organizational structure.

Army Air Forces Within the AAF the squadron—a component of a GROUP or, sometimes, a WING—was the smallest unit having both tactical and administrative components, comparable with an Army COMPANY or BATTERY. Squadrons were generally commanded by a captain or major, and had numerical designations, e.g., 71st Fighter

Squadron, 342nd Bombardment Squadron. Three or four squadrons composed a group.

The numbers of aircraft assigned to a squadron varied with type. The normal allocations of aircraft and personnel to AAF squadrons in 1943 were:

TYPE OF SQUADRON	AIRCRAFT TYPES	AIRCRAFT	PERSONNEL
Heavy bomber	B-17 B-24	12	427
Medium bomber	B-25 B-26	16	377
Twin-engine fighter	P-38	25	313
Single-engine fighter	P-47 P-51	25	284

The Navy and Marine Corps also operated aircraft squadrons as their basic aircraft unit.

Army The reconnaissance units—of BATTALION size—in armored and CAVALRY DIVISIONS were designated as cavalry reconnaissance squadrons.

Navy Ship squadrons were administrative commands, primarily for DESTROYERS and SUBMARINES, each composed of two or, on occasion, three DIVISIONS of the same kind of ship—a usual total of eight or twelve units, commanded by a captain.

Squid

Antisubmarine MORTAR that fired DEPTH CHARGES. The Squid was a British development, based on the principle of the ahead-firing HEDGEHOG weapon, but firing 350-pound depth charges that contained some 200 pounds of an advanced explosive, Minol II. The three-barrel Squid hurled the depth charges a distance of some 300 yards. (Smaller escort ships were fitted with a single-barrel or double-barrel version of the Squid.) The three-barrel weapon produced a triangular pattern with about 120 feet per side. The Squid, able to reach depths of 1,500 feet in later models, had the deepest capability of any Allied antisubmarine weapon.

The first Squid sinking of a U-BOAT took place on July 31, 1944; the victim was the *U-333* near the Scilly Isles off the coast of England. (The attacking ships were from an escort group previously commanded by Capt. F.J. WALKER, who had died a few days earlier.)

The Squid was developed from the earlier Fairlie Mortar, a smaller weapon that threw depth charges ahead of the ship. Sea trials of the Squid took place in May 1943. The weapon was first mounted in the frigate *Hadleigh Castle;* subsequently, both U.S. and British escort ships were fitted with Squid.

The Squid was the most effective ship-launched antisubmarine weapon used by the Royal Navy between 1943 and 1945. A single Squid pattern had a roughly 50 percent chance of sinking a U-boat.

U-boat commander Peter Cremer said that "if the Hedgehog was a hand probing for the U-boat with five fingers, the Squid was a paw which struck and crushed everything."

SS

HITLER's elite personal guard, which became a political police force that symbolized NAZI terrorism and slaughter. The *Schützstaffel*—"protection detachment," abbreviated as SS—was created in the early 1920s as a small unit to serve as a bodyguard for Nazi leaders. The SS began to grow in 1929 when Hitler appointed HENRICH HIMMLER *Reichsführer* SS. The SS, with only 280 members, was a tiny, but well-disciplined unit under the 60,000-strong SA, the thuggish Nazi paramilitary organization. Himmler, an ambitious and fanatic disciple of Hitler, saw a major role for the SS as a mystic brotherhood to enforce and perpetuate Nazi ideology. The Black Shirts recruited a more elite-minded German than the street-fighting SA. The black shirts were adopted to distinguish the SS—the initials were emblazoned as lightning bolts—from the brown-shirted SA storm troopers.

By 1930 Himmler had recruited more than 3,000 members of the SS, each a paragon of Nazi standards for racial purity, for SS men were expected to show an Aryan ancestry going back to the eighteenth century. Candidates' pedigrees were examined by the *Rasseund Siedlungshauptamt,* the Race and Settlement Office, headed by Richard-Walther Darré, a pig breeder who was the author of the "blood and soil" theory that claimed European civilization was the work of racially pure Germans. The office also investigated the prospective brides of SS men.

The SS motto was "Believe! Obey! Fight!" But the SS men, who fancied themselves modern Teutonic knights, usually fought by slaughtering unarmed foes. Soon after the invasion of Poland, SS units launched their first reign of terror in a conquered land—what the SS called the "housekeeping of Jews, intelligentsia, clergy, and the nobility."

When Germany invaded the Soviet Union, the SS was given the task of wiping out Soviet JEWS and "Bolshevik agitators." To do this, the SS set up ACTION GROUPS (*Einsatzgruppen*) of 800 to 3,000 men, who followed the German Army's initial advance into the Soviet Union. *Einsatzkommando* detachments rounded up civilians, nearly all of them Jews, and shot them down in massive slaughters. More than 2,000,000 Jews were killed by these SS units, according to WAR CRIMES testimony.

Members of SS Death-Head detachments, who wore skull-and-crossbones insignia on their black tunics, guarded CONCENTRATION CAMPS. When the war started, many Death-Head troops were assigned to a Panzer division in what became an SS branch known as *WAFFEN* SS, the military arm of the SS.

The International Military Tribunal at Nuremberg, which declared the SS, SD, and GESTAPO organizations guilty of war crimes, exempted some clerical and low-level members of the SD and Gestapo from guilt. But the tribunal declared that every individual member of the SS was a war criminal guilty of planning and carrying out crimes against humanity.

Stage-Door Canteen

A New York club for servicemen and -WOMEN, operated by show business personalities. Stage stars passed out coffee and doughnuts, renowned musicians gave impromptu concerts, and after their Broadway performances actresses went from their stages to the canteen dance floor to jitterbug with GIs and sailors.

The original canteen, sponsored by the American Theater Wing War Service, inspired a song, "I Left My Heart at the Stage-Door Canteen," which was sung in the all-Army show "This Is the Army." Another inspiration was a LIBERTY SHIP, the *Stage-Door Canteen,* christened by actress Ilka Chase, a founder of the original canteen, in Oct. 1943.

The club was open only to the guests in uniform, the volunteers, and wealthy "angels," who backed the canteens as they would back a Broadway show. They were allowed to sit in at reserved tables.

Similar canteens opened in WASHINGTON, Phila-

delphia, Cleveland, San Francisco, and Hollywood. The Hollywood Stage-Door Canteen, where movie actors and actresses entertained, was second in fame only to the original. Celebrities basked in the publicity and the patriotism on display. Most of the work was done by noncelebrity volunteers. Perky junior hostesses usually were the dance partners and coffee dispensers. The rules, enforced by chaperones called senior hostesses, forbade hostesses to make dates with servicemen.

At the Washington Stage-Door Canteen Vice President Henry Wallace challenged visitors to Indian wrestling, PAUL MCNUTT, chairman of the War Manpower Commission, and DONALD NELSON, chairman of the War Production Board, washed dishes.

Stalemate

Code name for U.S. invasion of the Palaus.

Stalin, Josef (1879–1953)

Wartime Soviet leader. Born Josef Dzhugashvili in the Soviet republic of Georgia, he called himself Stalin ("man of steel") as a revolutionary name. He was elected general secretary of the Communist Party in 1922 and he rose rapidly and ruthlessly under the tutelage of Lenin.

Through selective murders and widespread purges in the 1930s, Stalin became the absolute ruler of the Soviet Union. His purge of the Red Army on the eve of World War II wiped out one third of the officer corps. He ruled by what Russians would later call the "Great Terror," words that could have meant death for anyone who uttered them in his time.

Between 1928 and his death in 1953 he sent 17,000,000 to 25,000,000 of his people to the *gulag,* the system of *lags* (camps) in Siberia described in ALEKSANDR SOLZHENITSYN'S *Gulag Archipelago.* How many he actually sent and how many died in those camps will never be known.

Following the czarist tradition, Stalin exiled enemies and suspected enemies until, as Soviet historian Ray Medvedev said, he was condemning "anyone he didn't like." Estimates in the 1980s, when secret ledgers began to open and people began to talk, put Stalin's "Great Terror" executions at 1,000,000 and deaths in the camps at 7,000,000.

Medvedev and Robert Conquest of the Hoover Institution estimate that 7,000,000 to 10,000,000 people died in the *gulag*.

A typical "crime" that warranted sentencing to the camps: capture by the Germans in World War II. The United States and England had agreed that any Soviet citizens in their occupation zones of Germany would be returned to the Soviet Union—whether they wanted to or not. Some 2,000,000 were turned over, and most of them were sentenced to the camps, most of which were in Siberia.

Stalin lived and ruled behind a veil of secrecy, using the tools of terror and treachery, the latter being best shown by his cynical agreement with NAZI Germany, the NONAGGRESSION PACT, signed in Aug. 1939. On Dec. 21, Stalin received sixtieth-birthday greetings from HITLER and his foreign minister, JOACHIM VON RIBBENTROP. Stalin replied: "The friendship of the peoples of Germany and of the Soviet Union, cemented in blood, has every reason to be lasting and firm."

The treaty with the Soviet Union's ideological enemy gave Stalin a piece of Poland at no apparent cost. But this cheap acquisition led to his own country's betrayal on June 22, 1941, when Hitler invaded the Soviet Union.

Stalin's military strategy was often driven by ideology. For example, there could be no defensive fortifications because any war would be fought only on enemy land. Because he believed in the invincibility of the Red Army—despite its abysmal performance in Finland—he simply did not accept intelligence reports that the Germans were massing for an invasion. When the GERMAN CAMPAIGN IN THE SOVIET UNION began, Stalin acted dazed for about two weeks. After finally rallying, he took the first of his military titles: Commander in Chief; later he became Marshal and then Generalissimo.

When he broadcast to the Soviet people on July 2, they were startled to hear his Georgian accent. He had never spoken on the radio before. He did not speak again until Nov. 6, when he told his people that while 350,000 Soviet troops had been killed, German losses amounted to 4,500,000. The figures were pure fiction. In reality, LENINGRAD was surrounded, MOSCOW was threatened, about 40 percent of the nation's population was under

Soviet dictator Josef Stalin and his commissar for foreign affairs, V. M. Molotov, huddle during a conference with their western Allies. Stalin took on the rank of *generalissimo* after his armies had defeated Germany. However, he refused to meet with his ally and fellow *generalissimo*, Chiang Kai-shek. *(U.S. Army)*

German control—and Stalin was afraid that the peoples of the conquered territory would rise up against him.

Stalin directed the war from an air-raid shelter in the Kremlin and did not go to the front, but paintings later portrayed him there, rallying the troops, planning the next offensive. He did indeed act as Generalissimo. Dominating his generals, he laid out Red Army strategy, ordered a SCORCHED EARTH POLICY in the wake of retreats, moved more than 11,000 whole factories to the east, and made the war a crusade against "criminal German perverts" who were raping Mother Russia. His own faith in his people and his army, though not sincere, was nevertheless contagious. He did inspire his people, who forgot or ignored the Great Terror crimes that so many had known. Like Prime Minister CHURCH-

ILL and President ROOSEVELT, Stalin symbolized a nation's struggle against Hitler.

The leaders became known in the press as the Big Three, but the depictions of Allied unity masked Stalin's instinctive isolation and his distrust of capitalistic nations. After America's entrance into the war, he pressed continually for a SECOND FRONT, arguing that a U.S.-British invasion of German-occupied Europe would take the pressure off the Soviet Union. Meanwhile, England and the United States should send all the supplies they could. When Churchill told Stalin of the tragic losses suffered by RUSSIAN CONVOYS, Stalin gave Churchill a "rough and surly" answer and hinted that the Soviet Union might have to sue for a separate peace. He won large amounts of LEND-LEASE, which he never revealed to his people. As far as most of them knew, the Soviets had won the GREAT PATRIOTIC WAR on their own.

Churchill and Stalin met for the first time on Aug. 12, 1942. "The first two hours were bleak and somber," Churchill reported, and the one the next day was "a most unpleasant discussion." Roosevelt also wanted a face-to-face meeting with Stalin, even suggesting "a few days together near our common border off Alaska."

Stalin finally suggested that he meet Roosevelt and Churchill in Tehran, Iran, because it had a direct telegraph line to Moscow. Roosevelt demurred and offered communications aid so that the meeting could be in a more convenient place. Stalin held out, and the result was the first Big Three meeting, the TEHRAN CONFERENCE of Nov. 1943. By the time of the conference, the tide of battle had turned and the SOVIET OFFENSIVE CAMPAIGN had begun. Stalin was already looking beyond the war.

Stalin moved Roosevelt into the spacious Soviet Embassy and, subtly playing the President off against Churchill, convinced Roosevelt that he was getting on the right side of Stalin. Roosevelt called him "Uncle Joe," a flippant remark that would haunt Roosevelt as a sign of his naiveté in dealing with Communists.

Churchill glowered at the joshing that went on between the other two leaders. As he saw it, Stalin was trying to split the Anglo-American alliance in preparation for postwar deals. Stalin secretly promised that he would go to war against Japan after the EUROPEAN WAR ended. But not much of substance came of the conference, primarily because of Stalin's clever manipulation of Roosevelt and Churchill.

Stalin again set the site for the next Big Three meeting, choosing his own soil in the Crimea. When the YALTA CONFERENCE convened on Feb. 11, 1945, Stalin had rolled the German Army past his own borders; the Red Army had conquered most of Poland and Hungary. The Great Patriotic War was nearly over. The war for the peace had begun. Only Stalin clearly saw that reality.

Stalin wanted his Red Army to stay in Europe, and his wishes overshadowed all others. Uncle Joe extracted concessions about Poland and the rest of Eastern Europe in exchange for his participation in the war against Japan.

Stalin dealt with new faces from the West at the POTSDAM CONFERENCE of July-Aug. 1945—President TRUMAN for the United States, Prime Minister CLEMENT ATLEE replacing defeated Churchill in mid-conference. But the conference did little more than ratify the Yalta decisions. Uncle Joe got what he wanted: token entry in the war against Japan, five days of Red Army fighting. In exchange he would be allowed to extend his power into northern Korea, Manchuria, and the KURIL ISLANDS.

Stalin later showed Secretary of State JAMES BYRNES a film that portrayed the Red Army winning the war in the Pacific and Japanese officers signing a surrender document on the deck of a Soviet warship. It looked like a mockery of the Allied ceremony on the deck of the *MISSOURI* (BB 63).

Even as the war was ending, the Cold War, was beginning under Stalin's generalship (see the Epilogue to War). What he had tried to contrive in Tehran—Uncle Joe and Uncle Sam against an isolated John Bull—never happened. The United States and England would perpetuate their wartime alliance. But, while the two democracies celebrated the end of World War II, Stalin never let his people emerge from the shadow of war. Their sacrifices went on as he built a superpower from the rubble of his nation and the treasures he would wrest from the nations he made into satellites.

Stalin, Lt. Gen. Vasili

Son of the Soviet leader JOSEF STALIN and a general in the Red Air Force. The younger Stalin trained as a pilot. At the start of the war in June

1941 he was a captain; when the war ended he held the rank of lieutenant general. After the war he became commander of the prestigious MOSCOW Military District. At about the same time he libeled the CinC of the Soviet Air Force, A. A. NOVIKOV, causing his dismissal and arrest. The younger Stalin also denounced other Soviet leaders to his father.

In his autobiography, NIKITA KHRUSHCHEV wrote: "Vasya [Vasili] was a good boy, clever but headstrong. In his early youth he started to drink heavily. He was an undisciplined student and brought Stalin much grief. I think Stalin used to whip him regularly and assigned Chekists [secret police] to keep Vasya under surveillance." Historian Roy Medvedev described him as "coarse, semiliterate, alcoholic."

Stalingrad

Major Soviet industrial center and rail junction on the Volga River—1,500 miles east of BERLIN. Named Tsaritsyn before 1925 (and Volgograd after 1961), during the winter of 1942–1943 it was the scene of the decisive battle of the EASTERN FRONT in which the German advance into the Soviet Union was checked.

The German Sixth Army under *General der Panzertruppen* FRIEDRICH PAULUS was moving eastward. ADOLF HITLER had ordered the taking of Stalingrad to help secure the German drive to the oilfields of the CAUCASUS. The German forces began their attack on Aug. 21 from positions about 40 miles from the city; two days later German TANKS had reached the Volga River, north of Stalingrad, and then fought their way into the city. Advance elements of the LI Corps of the Sixth Army and Fourth PANZER Army entered the city's suburbs on Sept. 12 and for sixty-six days German troops laid siege to the remainder of the city, which ARTILLERY shelling and BOMBS soon turned into rubble. But Soviet troops of the Sixty-second Army under Gen. VASILY I. CHUIKOV held tenaciously to the rubble, forcing the Germans to fight house-to-house. In Oct.–Nov. the Soviet perimeter on the western bank of the Volga was reduced at times to a depth of no more than 1,500 yards in some places.

Meanwhile, a counterattack was planned by Gen. GEORGI ZHUKOV. A Soviet attack within the city began on Nov. 19 (Operation Uranus) while other Soviet forces completely surrounded the German

force on Nov. 22–23, closing the pincers at Kalach. The Sixth Army and part of the Fourth Panzer Army were thus trapped. Gen. Paulus might have broken out at that stage but Hitler, assured by HERMANN GÖRING, head of the Luftwaffe, that aircraft could deliver 500 tons of supplies per day to the encircled troops, ordered Paulus to defend "Fortress Stalingrad."

Within the "fortress" Paulus had five corps headquarters, twenty German divisions, and two Rumanian divisions with a strength believed at the time to be as high as 284,000 men. Aircraft could fly in supplies to six airstrips, one of which could be used at night. British military historian Albert Seaton has calculated that by standards of that time about 7 pounds per man per day were required to maintain the force—about 850 tons. (This figure did not take into account a buildup for breakout or offensive.) More than 400 Junkers JU 52 sorties per day would have been required to provide that supply lift—assuming 100 percent availability and no losses; the entire Luftwaffe transport force at the time contained some 750 Ju 52s scattered throughout Europe and North Africa, while maintenance problems and weather conditions in the area reduced aircraft availability to about 35 percent.

The Luftwaffe's assigned task was impossible. In the next two months the Luftwaffe's best air supply effort could provide the troops in the Stalingrad pocket with an average of only about 80 tons per day.

As the circle drew tighter, aircraft could no longer land to deliver supplies and carry out the wounded, and parachute drops and GLIDER landings were substituted. (While airstrips were available the Luftwaffe had flown out 25,000 wounded.) Meanwhile from the south, Army Group Don under *General der Infanterie* FRITZ VON MANSTEIN attacked Yeremenko and advanced to within 30 miles of Paulus's positions, but was forced to retreat under Soviet pressure.

Paulus still refused to surrender despite his troops being exhausted, starving, sick, and suffering severely from frostbite. On Jan. 8, 1943, the armies of the Soviet Don Front under Lt. Gen. KONSTANTIN ROKOSSOVSKI launched their final attack (Operation *Koltso* or "ring"). Rokossovski commanded seven armies with 281,000 troops and heavy air support. The German troops fought bravely, but late on Jan. 22 Paulus radioed Hitler: "Rations exhausted. Over 12,000 unattended wounded in pocket. What orders should I give to troops who have no more ammunition and are subjected to mass attacks supported by heavy artillery?"

Hitler answered: "Surrender is out of the question. The troops will defend themselves to the last."

The Soviets continued to advance, closing the circle. Paulus ceased issuing rations to the wounded on Jan. 28 to preserve the strength of the fighting troops. (On Jan. 10 Paulus had stopped feeding Russian prisoners and ordered them released, but most had remained within the German pocket.) Soviet thrusts continued to split the surviving German forces into several smaller pockets. On Jan. 30 Hitler promoted Paulus to *Generalfeldmarschall.*

At 6:15 A.M. on Jan. 31 the chief radio operator at Sixth Army headquarters, in the basement of the *Univermag* (department store) on Red Square in Stalingrad, sent the following message: "Russians are at the door. We are preparing to destroy [the radios]." An hour later came the simple message: "We are destroying." Paulus surrendered his headquarters that day. He became the first German field marshal to be captured. Some German units continued to fight until Feb. 2.

The Germans lost some 140,000 troops at Stalingrad, with another 91,000 taken prisoner (many sick and wounded), including Paulus and twenty-three generals. The "survivors" began a long trek by march and train to prison camps throughout the Soviet Union. Only about 6,000 survived Soviet captivity. The Germans also suffered heavy casualties outside of the Stalingrad pockets as units attempted to fight through to them—possibly as many as 100,000 killed and wounded. The Soviets have never released official data on their own losses; many tens of thousands were killed and wounded.

Hitler subsequently stated that the Sixth Army had performed a valuable service at a critical time by tying down several hundred thousand Soviet troops.

Stalingrad marked the extremity of the German drive into the Soviet Union. The loss of an entire army, plus the Luftwaffe casualties in attempting to support the "fortress," could not be quickly replaced, and with the Soviets on the offensive the southern portion of the German front would collapse, opening the way for the SOVIET OFFENSIVE CAMPAIGN. Marshal Chuikov's memoir of the battle was appropriately entitled *Nachalo puti*—The Beginning of the Road.

Stamina

Code name for Allied air supply of Imphal-Kohima garrisons, 1944.

Stark, Adm. Harold R. (1880–1972)

The U.S. Chief of Naval Operations (CNO) at the time of the PEARL HARBOR attack. Stark served as CNO between the tenures of Admirals WILLIAM D. LEAHY and E. J. KING, taking office in Aug. 1939. He brought to the post a reputation as a highly respected and well-liked commanding officer as well as the demeanor of a kindly bishop (to paraphrase historian SAMUEL ELIOT MORISON).

His tenure contributed to U.S. success in World War II in two ways. First, after a survey of U.S. naval ships, aircraft, and personnel, Stark recommended a dramatic expansion of the Navy and presided over the two-ocean Navy buildup that began in early 1940. Second, he soon determined that efforts to save Britain from defeat should be paramount in U.S. strategy.

After President ROOSEVELT was reelected in Nov. 1940, Stark drafted a memorandum that considered four alternative courses of grand strategy. After analyzing each, Stark recommended Plan D—hold the line in the Pacific, put most of the effort into defeating Germany. This "Plan Dog Memorandum" is considered one of the most important single documents drafted during the U.S. prewar period because the strategy it outlined was within U.S. capabilities and was acceptable to both the Army and the British Chiefs of Staff. Throughout 1941 Stark and Gen. GEORGE C. MARSHALL, the U.S. Army Chief of Staff, worked with their British counterparts to refine the Plan Dog.

Stark was less successful in forestalling war in the Pacific. He advocated less confrontation, being reluctant, for example, to impose an embargo on oil shipments to Japan. Like the others in the U.S. high command, Stark was surprised by the attack on Pearl Harbor. His extensive correspondence with Adm. HUSBAND E. KIMMEL contained prudent warnings about the worsening situation in the

Pacific, but Stark was no more prescient than Kimmel about the timing or the weight of the blow.

In March 1942 Stark was succeeded as CNO by the Commander in Chief U.S. Fleet, Adm. King, and Stark was appointed commander of the U.S. Naval Forces, Europe. For the rest of the war he was the senior U.S. naval representative in England, but was not part of Gen. DWIGHT D. EISENHOWER's campaign-planning staff.

Although he was easily overshadowed by the acerbic and brilliant King, Stark is credited with tact and diplomacy in supporting U.S. naval operations in Europe and in dealing with such prickly allies as Gen. CHARLES DE GAULLE. Stark was appointed commander of the Twelfth FLEET in Oct. 1943 and served in both positions until Aug. 1945. After a brief stint in the Office of the CNO, Stark retired in 1946.

(Stark was known to his friends as "Betty," a name bestowed on him at the Naval Academy for reasons having to do with history rather than personality.)

Starkey

Code name for Allied deception operations against Pas-de-Calais, France, 1943.

Stars and Stripes

Newspaper published by and for U.S. soldiers. The paper, named after a soldiers' newspaper of World War I, began publishing in April 1942, first as a weekly publication carrying news from home. The paper began publishing daily a few months later, reportedly under orders from President ROOSEVELT, who wanted to preempt a soldiers' edition of *The Chicago Tribune*.

The *Stars and Stripes* aimed at the GI in the FOXHOLE and rarely missed. It criticized Army policies, carried the officer-deflating cartoons of BILL MAULDIN, and covered the war with its own kind of WAR CORRESPONDENTS—privates, corporals, and sergeants who shared the mud, bad food, and dangers of the men up front.

A typical day's content from a European edition: many short combat stories, usually carrying the by-lines of writers who were there; tips on how to speak German or French; a column announcing the birth of babies back home; a "Foxhole Who's Who" for

announcing battlefield commissions and AWARDS AND DECORATIONS; SPORTS pages, COMICS, and a Mauldin cartoon. The "B Bag" column ("blow it out here") was reserved for GI gripes, such as this one: "I hate to criticize a person I like as much as Bing Crosby, but when he tells the people back home that 'the nearer you go to the front, the cleaner-shaven the men are and the snappier are the salutes,' well, any GI Joe knows he can't have seen much of the front lines. . . ."

Editions of *Stars and Stripes* were published throughout the world, wherever it could find a press. It began publishing in ROME on the day the city was liberated, June 4, 1944; in LONDON the brash tabloid was printed in the plant of the staid *London Times*. When the war ended, *Stars and Stripes* continued to be a newspaper for U.S. forces overseas.

Starvation

U.S. code name for the sowing of some 11,000 MINES in Japanese home waters by U.S. SUBMARINES and B-29 SUPERFORTRESS aircraft; March–Aug. 1945.

Status

British code word for reinforcing of MALTA, Sept. 1941.

Stauffenberg, *Oberstleutnant* Klause Phillip Schenk, Graf von (1907–1944)

A key figure in the JULY 20 PLOT to kill HITLER. Von Stauffenberg, a member of one of Bavaria's oldest aristocratic families, served as a staff officer in the POLAND CAMPAIGN and the FRANCE AND LOW COUNTRIES CAMPAIGN. During the GERMAN CAMPAIGN IN THE SOVIET UNION, as an officer attached to the Army High Command, he saw firsthand the ruthlessness of SS killer squads (see ACTION GROUPS), sights that appalled him as a soldier and as a devout Roman Catholic. In the Soviet Union he met two German officers who were plotting to get rid of Hitler. He joined the plot.

While the plot was taking shape von Stauffenberg joined a PANZER division in the NORTH AFRICAN CAMPAIGN. In April 1943 he was grievously wounded when his car hit a mine, apparently while trying to evade a strafing Allied plane. He lost his left eye, his right hand, and two fingers on his left hand. As he recovered in a Munich hospital, he vowed that he would kill Hitler and establish a military government that would abolish the SS.

The plot was code-named Valkyrie (the militant maidens in *Der Ring des Nibelungen* by Richard Wagner, Hitler's favorite musician). The same code name was used for a plan to marshal the Home (Replacement) Army to protect BERLIN and other cities in the event of a revolt. So the plotters could openly work on the legitimate Valkyrie plan while secretly using some of its elements for their own Valkyrie conspiracy.

Twice von Stauffenberg had carried bombs in AS-SASSINATION attempts that failed. The third time he carried a bomb was on July 20, 1944. Hitler was having a military conference at the WOLF'S LAIR, his tightly guarded headquarters at Rastenburg. Von Stauffenberg had been asked to bring some information to the conference. He carried a briefcase containing a bomb.

The bomb was a British product dropped to GUERRILLAS in German-occupied Europe and seized by the *ABWEHR,* the military intelligence service; its chief, Adm. WILHELM CANARIS, was also an anti-Hitler plotter. The bomb was detonated by breaking a glass capsule containing acid that ate away a wire holding a firing pin. The acid took 10 to 15 minutes to eat through the wire; when the wire parted, it released a firing pin against a percussion cap.

Before entering the large conference room, von Stauffenberg slipped into another room, and, grasping tongs with his three fingers, pushed an arming mechanism that broke the capsule. He asked to be placed as close to Hitler as possible. The request did not arouse suspicion because it was well known that von Stauffenberg had been partially deafened in the incident that had so badly wounded him. The briefcase leaned against a thick oak socle, a block supporting the table, about six feet from Hitler. Von Stauffenberg left the room, got into his car, and was in it, headed for an airport, when he heard the explosion.

Minutes after von Stauffenberg left, one of the conferees, trying to lean closer to the maps spread on the table, moved the bulky briefcase to the other side of the socle. It exploded at 12:42 P.M.

Hitler was stunned and slightly injured. Von Stauffenberg, flying to Berlin, thought *Der Führer* was dead and the first move in the plot a success. Even after he reached Military Headquarters in Berlin and learned that Hitler still lived, von Stauffenberg tried to carry out the rest of the conspiracy. But it was too late. *Generalmajor* OTTO SKORZENY, a *WAFFEN* SS officer famed for his COMMANDO-style exploits, had rushed to Military Headquarters and was uncovering the plot; he even found proof of it in von Stauffenberg's safe. Von Stauffenberg was arrested and within hours summarily executed by a firing squad in a courtyard of Military Headquarters lighted by a truck's headlights. His last words were, "Long live our sacred Germany!"

Stein, Gertrude (1874–1946)

American poet and novelist who was long an expatriate in PARIS. When Paris was liberated, Gertrude Stein and her companion Alice B. Toklas welcomed U.S. WAR CORRESPONDENTS with a celebratory lunch and presented one of them with a manuscript, which he took to New York. It was published as *Wars I Have Seen.* One night she was on a Paris boulevard with Pablo Picasso when a camouflaged truck passed. "[W]e had heard of camouflage but we had not yet seen it," she later wrote, "and Picasso, amazed, looked at it and cried out, yes, it is we who made it, that is cubism."

Steinbeck, John (1902–1968)

Pulitzer Prize–winning novelist (for *Grapes of Wrath* in 1940) who wrote a controversial war book, *The Moon Is Down.* The book recounted the takeover of a small, unnamed Scandinavian country by an unnamed invader. It was obviously based on the German conquest of Denmark and Norway in 1940.

Steinbeck wrote *The Moon Is Down* as a contribution to the war effort. But when the novel appeared in March 1942, many critics perceived Steinbeck's treatment of the occupiers of the unnamed country as too "sympathetic."

In later perspective, the book was seen in better light: Steinbeck had been using his literary skill to show that NAZIS were no melodramatic villains but real human beings. The tragedy was that they were *not* monsters of evil, but ordinary. The Danish underground appreciated the book enough to circulate a mimeographed version of the manuscript among members of the resistance.

Steinbeck once suggested setting up a U.S. PROPAGANDA office to counteract the Nazi propaganda he had seen during travels in Central America. In 1941, when WILLIAM DONOVAN was still "coordinator of information" (his title prior to becoming head of the OFFICE OF STRATEGIC SERVICES), he set up a Foreign Information Service under Robert E. Sherwood, playwright and occasional speechwriter for President ROOSEVELT. Sherwood offered Steinbeck a job with the service, which was later incorporated into the OFFICE OF WAR INFORMATION.

Steinbeck preferred independence. But he worked as a WAR CORRESPONDENT and wrote, with Army Air Forces cooperation, a documentary account of training, *Bombs Away: The Story of a Bomber Team.*

Sten Submachine Gun

A rugged, reliable weapon for close-in combat. One of the first submachine guns designed for mass production, the Sten had a minimum of machined parts. Introduced in 1941, the Sten was provided in large numbers by the British to GUERRILLA groups throughout occupied Europe and was used extensively by British troops, especially paratroopers who called it the "tin tommy gun."

It was distinguished by a tubular receiver with, in most models, a simple metal tubular stock; the Mark 5 had a wooden stock and rear pistol grip, an optional pistol grip on the barrel, and a large front-sight guard.

A 9-mm weapon that operated on a blowback mechanism, the Sten weighed 8.5 pounds and was fed by a detachable 32-round magazine. Effective range was some 200 yards. On fully automatic the Sten could fire at the rate of 550 to 600 rounds per minute. It fired the 9-mm Parabellum cartridge.

Approximately 3.5 million Sten guns were produced during the war. The designation Sten came from the gun's two designers, R. V. Sheppard and H. J. Turpin, plus the first two letters of Enfield, England where the gun was developed.

Stephenson, William S. (1896–1989)

Director of British Security Co-operation in the United States during the war. Canadian born, Stephenson initially served in the Royal Canadian Engineers in World War I, and was gassed at the front. Following his recovery he transferred to the British Royal Flying Corps and as a fighter pilot was credited with shooting down German aircraft before he was himself shot down and taken prisoner. He escaped and returned to British lines.

After the war he became a boxer, earning the title of world amateur lightweight champion. He subsequently became involved in commercial radio development and aviation. While visiting German industrial concerns in the 1930s he began to provide intelligence information to MI6 and WINSTON CHURCHILL.

Churchill, as prime minister, in 1940, appointed Stephenson as his personal representative to President ROOSEVELT and to establish British Security Coordination in the United States. Stephenson became the representative of British intelligence activities in the United States, and British liaison to the FBI and OFFICE OF STRATEGIC SERVICES (OSS). His nominal title was British Passport Control Officer.

Stephenson was knighted in 1945. His code name was Intrepid.

Stettinius, Edward R., Jr. (1900–1949)

Industrialist turned wartime government administrator. Shortly before the German invasion of Poland on Sept. 1, 1939, President ROOSEVELT established the War Resources Board, which consisted mostly of businessmen like Stettinius, chairman of the board of U.S. Steel. In Aug. 1941 Stettinius became administrator of LEND-LEASE and the following month special assistant to the president. Stettinius remained in charge of Lend-Lease until Sept. 1943, when he succeeded SUMNER WELLES as undersecretary of State. He became secretary of State in Nov. 1944 and attended the Feb. 1945 YALTA CONFERENCE. He resigned in June 1945 and President TRUMAN appointed him chairman of the U.S. delegation to the UNITED NATIONS.

Stilwell, Gen. Joseph W. (1883–1946)

When World War II began Stilwell was a major general commanding the U.S. Army's III CORPS in California. Earlier, at the Infantry School at Fort Benning, Ga., he had come to the attention of Gen. GEORGE C. MARSHALL, who pronounced him "farsighted," "highly intelligent," "one of the exceptionally brilliant and cultured men of the army" who was "qualified for any command in peace or war." It was also at Benning that his acerbic intolerance for failure and duplicity earned him his nickname, "Vinegar Joe."

During several prewar stints in China, Stilwell had come to admire the Chinese peasant greatly and to distrust Chinese leadership. In Jan. 1942 Stilwell was put in command of U.S. Army forces in China and Burma and appointed to serve as Chief of Staff to Generalissimo CHIANG KAI-SHEK, a position Stilwell accepted reluctantly. He also was given supervision of LEND-LEASE shipments to China, supplies that Chiang coveted and wished to control.

Stilwell's first objectives were to hold open the BURMA ROAD between India and China and to frustrate the Japanese conquest of Burma. He was unable to achieve either. (See ALLIED CHINA-BURMA-INDIA CAMPAIGN.)

After a two-month campaign in Burma, in which Japanese forces maneuvered skillfully, Chinese commanders refused to accept his orders, and as his shoestring supply route further sapped his army, he was forced to escape to India with just 8,000 troops. Stilwell's press conference in Delhi consisted of few words: "I claim we got a hell of a beating. We got run out of Burma and it is humiliating as hell. I think we ought to find out what caused it, go back, and retake it."

In 1943 he became deputy supreme commander of the China-Burma-India theater to Lord LOUIS MOUNTBATTEN. Stilwell's plan to train thirty divisions American-style and lead them into battle in Burma and China directly challenged Chiang's desire to retain control of all of his army units. Chiang also considered MAO TSE-TUNG'S Communist forces perhaps a greater threat than those of the Japanese; he would not accede to actions that he felt tipped the balance in Mao's favor.

Stilwell particularly disliked Chiang (referring to him not so privately as "the Peanut") and his coterie, whom he saw as representatives of corrupt, unfeeling wealth. He also battled U.S. AAF Maj. Gen. CLAIRE CHENNAULT, founder of the American Volunteer Group (AVG) or FLYING TIGERS, whose vision of the help China needed veered markedly from Stilwell's and who believed that Lend-Lease shipments should favor air power rather than the ground troops Stilwell wanted to build up.

Opinions vary on whether China in fact needed to fight so strenuously. The Chinese people were unlikely to give in to Japan, and an increase in Chinese activity often led to grievous defeat in ensuing Japanese counteroffensives. If this argument is accepted, Stilwell's mission, which he saw as preparing the Chinese Army to fight, was doomed from the start.

In the beginning of 1944, Stilwell led his two Chinese divisions south from China to retake Myitkyina and its vital airfield and to build the LEDO ROAD (later Stilwell Road). The offensive consumed most of seven months, the airfield falling on May 17, but the adjacent town holding out until Aug. 7. The Stilwell Road was not completed until March 1945. The irresolvable conflicts between Stilwell and Chiang festered until Chiang forced Stilwell's recall in Oct. 1944.

Stilwell then served as chief of U.S. Army Ground Forces before assuming command of the Tenth ARMY on OKINAWA in June 1945 and served as military governor of the Ryukyu Islands until after the war. Stilwell and Gen. COURTNEY HODGES (commander of the U.S. First Army) would have led the U.S. ground forces in the planned invasion of Japan.

Stimson, Henry (1867–1950)

U.S. secretary of War. Stimson was a Cabinet officer for four Presidents. He was secretary of War under President Taft, secretary of State under President Hoover, and secretary of War during World War II under President ROOSEVELT and President TRUMAN. He also served President Coolidge as the U.S. negotiator in the ending of the U.S. Marine occupation of Nicaragua in 1927 and as governor general of the Philippines in 1928.

Stimson at the age of fifty volunteered for duty in World War I and went to France with the American Expeditionary Force as a colonel in the field artillery. Thereafter he preferred the title "Colonel" above all others.

As Hoover's secretary of State he once summarized his dislike for intelligence agencies with the remark that "gentlemen don't read other people's mail." The quotation, often cited in discussions about the morality of code-breaking, implies that Stimson was a nice old gentleman who did not live in the world of realpolitik and strutting dictators.

Stimson's public career belies that assessment. As far back as his time as secretary of State he displayed a firm opposition to aggression. In that year, Japanese military leaders, operating on their own initiative, launched a military operation in Manchuria. On Jan. 7, 1932, Stimson, in identical notes to Japan and China, said the United States would not recognize any territorial changes that Japan produced by force in China. This pronouncement, which became known as the Stimson Doctrine, was the first step in the U.S. diplomatic effort to curb Japanese aggression in the Pacific.

Stimson was an elder statesman by June 1940, when President Roosevelt, wanting a respected Republican in his Cabinet, appointed Stimson secretary of War. Stimson, while maintaining his own integrity, vigorously supported Roosevelt's attempts to move the United States out of isolation and build up U.S. defenses. Before U.S. entry into the war Stimson endorsed LEND-LEASE, the arming of U.S. convoys, and extension of SELECTIVE SERVICE. After the Japanese attack on PEARL HARBOR, he skillfully administered the rapid buildup the Army and Army Air Forces.

He was an early advocate of a unified Army-Navy command under a single secretary. He had good reason. There was not even a pretense of unification of the armed services. The secretary of War had to constantly juggle the demands of the Army against those of the Navy, settle petty and major turf battles, and simultaneously help the President determine war policies.

In Stimson's memoirs, *On Active Service in Peace and War*, McGeorge Bundy summed up one of Stimson's most persistent problems: "the peculiar psychology of the NAVY DEPARTMENT, which frequently seemed to retire from the realm of logic into a dim religious world in which Neptune was God, [Alfred Thayer] Mahan his prophet, and the United States Navy the only true Church."

Stimson was particularly interested in developing policy for the use of the ATOMIC BOMB. He kept watch over the development of the bomb for President Roosevelt and, after Roosevelt's death, for President Truman. Stimson recommended to Truman that the bomb be dropped on Japan.

The question of what city to bomb was given to a Target Committee of scientists and military officers. One of the cities selected by the committee was Kyoto, the ancient capital of Japan. Stimson instructed Maj. Gen. LESLIE R. GROVES, director of the atom bomb project, on the historic and religious significance of Kyoto and struck it from the list. When Groves questioned the decision, Stimson said, "This is one time I'm going to be the final deciding authority. Nobody's going to tell me what to do on this. On this matter I am the kingpin."

Stimson resigned as secretary of War on Sept. 18, 1945. He was succeeded by ROBERT P. PATTERSON, assistant secretary of War.

Under Stimson's tutelage, several subordinates became future advocates of a militarily strong America and the projection of U.S. power to advance national interests. They included men who would be key operatives of the Cold War—DEAN ACHESON, a future secretary of State; JOHN MCCLOY, who would become U.S. high commissioner for Germany and head of the World Bank; and ROBERT LOVETT, wartime U.S. assistant secretary of War for air and postwar secretary of Defense.

Godfrey Hodgson, author of *The Colonel,* a biography of Stimson, noted that during the Cuban missile crisis, when McGeorge Bundy, President JOHN F. KENNEDY's national security adviser, himself asked for advice, he got this from Lovett: "I think the best service we can perform for the president is to approach this as Colonel Stimson would."

There was a link between Stimson and still another President. In 1940, when Stimson spoke at his old school, Andover, GEORGE BUSH, a sixteen-year-old in the audience, heard Stimson condemn isolationism and was inspired to enlist as soon as possible. He became the youngest pilot in the U.S. Navy. Hodgson also noted that Stimson was one of the Yale men who initiated Bush into Skull and Bones, the secret society that has been an incubator for the elite of American government and finance.

Stirling

The first Allied four-engine bomber to see service in the war. It entered service with RAF Bomber Command in Aug. 1940, but the production rate was slow and the first major raid did not occur until the night of Feb. 10–11, 1941, when three Stirlings dropped fifty-six 500-pound BOMBS on oil-storage tanks at ROTTERDAM. After that the Stirlings bombed by day as well as night, having a good defensive armament. Stirlings bombed BERLIN for the first time on April 17, 1941, and after that, targets in Czechoslovakia and northern Italy. They flew in all of the THOUSAND-PLANE RAIDS of 1942–1943. By early 1944, however, Stirlings were withdrawn from service as bombers and assigned as GLIDER tugs and transports with the RAF Transport Command. Indeed, Stirling production was shifted to specialized Mk IV and V for those roles. During the last year of the war they were employed extensively to carry aviation fuel to the 2nd Tactical AIR FORCE in Europe, each Stirling IV being able to transport over 600 gallons of fuel in cans to forward airfields.

The Stirling was designed from the outset as a four-engine aircraft, preceded in 1938 by a half-scale trial model. The first Stirling prototype flew on May 14, 1939, but was destroyed in a landing accident. The first production Stirling flew in May 1940 and bomber production (Mk I and III) totaled 1,631 aircraft. (Mk II was applied to three early aircraft that evaluated U.S. engines.) Two Mk III bombers were converted to Mk IV prototypes in 1943 and were followed by the production of 737 glider-tug and transport variants—total production being 2,375 aircraft, including prototypes.

The Short Brothers, which built the Stirling, had previously constructed large flying boats for the RAF. Thus, the firm was well versed in large, four-engine aircraft. The plane had a shoulder-wing configuration with a massive (retractable) undercarriage that gave it a steep ground angle. Most of the fuselage had a constant diameter, with nose and tail gun turrets, and a tall tail fin (with tail wheel). The Mk IV had the nose and dorsal gun turrets deleted and glider-tow gear installed. The Mk V carried no armament, and had a streamlined nose and fuselage.

The Stirling III was credited with a top speed of 270 mph and a range of 2,010 miles with 3,500 pounds of bombs or 590 miles with 14,000 pounds, all carried in an internal bay. The aircraft had two .303-cal. guns in the nose and dorsal turrets, and four in the tail turret. The crew numbered seven or eight.

Stonehinge

British code name for CONVOY to MALTA, Nov. 1942.

Störfang (Sturgeon Catch)

German plan for capturing the Soviet port city of SEVASTOPOL, 1942.

Storm Troopers,

see SA.

Stösser (Sparrowhawk)

German AIRBORNE operation in the battle of the BULGE, with some 1,200 troops participating, Dec. 1944.

Strangle

Code name for Allied air operations to interdict movement of enemy supplies in central Italy; begun in March 1944.

Strategic Bombing

The use of bombers to destroy enemy warmaking capabilities. Between the world wars, both the U.S. Army and the RAF developed the idea of using bombers as a modern version of blockade. By bombing industrial, transportation, and communications targets, bombers could deny the enemy war supplies and would thus play a role similar to that of blockading navies.

When World War II began, both air forces had faith in PRECISION BOMBING as a way to carry out this strategy. But theory soon gave way to reality, and "area bombing"—heavy, sustained air raids on cities—became Allied strategy both in Europe and in the subsequent bombing of Japan. Prime Minister CHURCHILL defined the strategy as an "absolutely devastating, exterminating attack by very heavy bombers . . . upon the NAZI homeland."

The concept of area bombing was applied tactically to the battlefield as "carpet bombing"—a massive bombardment from the air prior to an attack. The most dramatic carpet bombing of the war came in July 1944. The ALLIED CAMPAIGN IN EUROPE was stalled because Allied troops were unable to break out from the NORMANDY INVASION beachhead. Some 3,700 tons of bombs were dropped in the Saint-Lô area. Because some bombs fell into a "safety zone," more than 100 soldiers of the 30th Infantry DIVISION were killed, as was Lt. Gen. LESLEY J. McNAIR, chief of Army Ground Forces, who was observing the bombing.

Air Chief Marshal Sir ARTHUR HARRIS, an early advocate of strategic bombing, took over the RAF Bomber Command in Feb. 1942 and within a month began his nighttime bombing assault on the German war machine. "Bomber" Harris wrote to Churchill in Nov. 1943: "We can wreck Berlin from end to end if the USAAF will come in on it. It will cost us between 400–500 aircraft. It will cost Germany the war." When Harris' promises were drastically unfulfilled, Churchill still listened to him, for Harris always seemed to offer so much for so little.

The U.S. planes—mainly B-17 FLYING FORTRESS bombers—did come in, bringing with them the concept of daylight precision bombing without fighter protection and the sharpshooting that was supposed to be guaranteed by the NORDEN BOMBSIGHT. Bomber Command and the U.S. Eighth AIR FORCE developed a RAF-at-night-U.S.-by-day policy.

American tactics depended upon the massed, mutually covering firepower of bombers flying in formation. The Luftwaffe rapidly developed countertactics. More and more American planes began going down in flames.

After disastrous losses in several raids, especially those on the ball-bearing plants at SCHWEINFURT in Aug. and Oct. 1943, the United States had to change its tactics or accept catastrophic losses. The RAF counseled emulating the night bombing of Bomber Command. But U.S. crews had little if any training in night flying.

What was needed were long-range fighters that could accompany the planes. ROBERT A. LOVETT, U.S. assistant secretary of War for air, in June 1943, after a visit to the Eighth Air Force, saw the need. He stepped up the production of the P-51 MUSTANG. On their first long-range mission in Dec. 1943 P-51s accompanied bombers to Kiel and back,

setting a fighter escort record. U.S. bomber losses dropped from 9.1 percent per raid in Oct. 1943 to 3.5 percent in March 1944. The Allied strategic bombing offensive surged.

By March 1944 Germany had lost command of the air in daylight, and after the Allied breakout from Normandy in July 1944, Germany lost more air-power assets: night-fighter bases and RADAR sites in France. By the fall of 1944 U.S. Army Chief of Staff Gen. GEORGE C. MARSHALL believed that strategic bombing would be a major element in a quick ending of the war. In Oct. 1944, Allied intelligence reported an intercepted message in which ALBERT SPEER, the German minister of armaments and war production, said that Allied bombing had shut down 30 percent to 35 percent of the nation's arms plants. (Later, Speer had another assessment. See STRATEGIC BOMBING SURVEY.)

Air power had been decisive—but certainly would not win the EUROPEAN WAR. That still would take Allied armies to overrun most of Germany.

Lavish claims about the effects of strategic bombing masked what the bombing did achieve and touched off a controversy that still goes on. Attempts to settle the controversy through the Strategic Bombing Survey produced statistics but not definitive answers.

One British historian, Noble Frankland, a veteran of Bomber Command strikes, gave this assessment: "The strategic air offensive against Germany was one of the great campaigns in history. It was great in the sense of the issues involved for, during much of the war, it was the principal and, at times, the only means by which direct offensive pressure could be exerted against Germany. . . . It was great too in the sense of the results achieved, for the strategic air offensive was a decisive factor in the defeat of Germany."

British historian A. J. P. Taylor's assessment: "During 1941 the RAF lost a bomber for every ten BOMBS dropped. . . ." Regarding the RAF's refusal to be diverted from bombing German factories, Taylor noted, "When finally compelled to cooperate, it dropped 20,000 tons of bombs on U-BOAT bases without putting a single U-boat out of action." But he conceded that when American bombers were escorted by P-51 Mustang fighters, the bombing had an immediate impact: Attacks on German synthetic-oil plants severely cut fuel supplies to German warplanes and U-boats.

Part of the controversy over the value of strategic bombing stems from confusion over strategic purposes for the bombing. Franklin, in a series of 1963 lectures later published as *The Bombing Offensive Against Germany,* cites three "great strategic aims" that were "operationally feasible": destruction of oil facilities, destruction of transport facilities, and general dislocation.

Each of the strategic aims had its own RAF advocates (for Harris it was "a burning faith in the idea of general dislocation"), and each got its share of attention. But none except "dislocation" received sustained, concentrated assaults. In the last three months of 1944, for example, Bomber Command dropped 53 percent of its bombs on cities, 15 percent on railways and canals, and 14 percent on oil targets.

Against the RUHR, Germany's major industrial area, Bomber Command flew 2,070 sorties between March and July 1943. HAMBURG was bombed more than 180 times. In July 1943 during the Battle of Hamburg, code-named Operation Gomorrah, massive fires created the war's first FIRESTORM. The longest and most sustained air offensive against a European target was Bomber Command's "Battle of BERLIN." Between Aug. 1943 and March 1944 the RAF flew 10,000 sorties against the city—and lost more than 600 aircraft. The RAF official history concludes, "The Battle of Berlin was more than a failure. It was a defeat."

The major American proponents of strategic bombing included U.S. AAF Generals CURTIS LEMAY, CARL SPAATZ, and HENRY ARNOLD. LeMay took his concepts to the Pacific theater in March 1945.

Before LeMay took command of U.S. strategic bombing against Japan in Jan. 1945, B-29 SUPERFORTRESS bombers flying from China and the MARIANA ISLANDS had been bombing Japanese cities from high altitude. The raids were phenomenally ineffective.

The first B-29 strike against Japan was a raid on the Yawata iron works on June 15, 1944. Of seventy-five bombers in the raid, forty-eight actually bombed Yawata, inflicting little damage. The planes

were based in China, making it an operation that was logistically impossible to support.

The capture of the Marianas provided ideal bases for the B-29 raids against Japan because U.S. control of the Pacific could insure a steady and economical flow of aviation gas, bombs, ammunition, spare parts, and other matériel. The first target chosen for the Marianas-based B-29s was the Nakajima Musashino aircraft engine plant in suburban TOKYO. During 350 sorties there were thirty-four bomb hits within the plant area. Typically, 1.8 percent of the B-29 bombs hit within 1,000 feet of their target.

LeMay abandoned the traditional daylight, high-level, precision-bombing doctrine. He decided to send his entire available force of 334 B-29s into the air at once, stripped of armor and guns, carrying only incendiary bombs, and with orders to make a night attack at "chimney" level. The first target was Tokyo.

On the night of March 9–10, 1945, the B-29s—flying at 5,000 to 7,500 feet instead of 25,000 to 30,000—burned out almost sixteen square miles of industrial and commercial areas of Tokyo. Japanese records show that 83,783 people were killed and over 100,000 injured in that raid. These were higher than the immediate casualties suffered in either of the ATOMIC BOMB raids against Japan.

In the Pacific, as in the European theater, debate continues about the importance of strategic bombing in winning the war. Statistics show that Japanese aircraft production was decreasing before the B-29 attacks. Many of the plants that were bombed were not producing anything. U.S. SUBMARINES and AIRCRAFT CARRIERS had cut the shipping routes to the raw materials the plants needed.

Strategic Bombing Survey

Analysis of the effects of bombing, particularly on German and Japanese cities. In Nov. 1944, under orders from President ROOSEVELT, a survey of the results of STRATEGIC BOMBING was begun by a group of U.S. military officers and civilians. The survey was to examine the air war on Germany to guide planning for a similar campaign against Japan. When the war ended, President TRUMAN ordered the Strategic Bombing Survey to make a Pacific study.

Roosevelt, who wanted the Survey to be dominated by a civilian viewpoint, selected as chairman Franklin D'Olier, president of the Prudential Insurance Company. About 1,000 people, a third of them civilians, worked on the Survey.

By the time Germany surrendered, the RAF had dropped 1,104,320 tons of BOMBS and the U.S. AAF had dropped 997,920 tons. RAF Bomber Command lost 55,573 lives; bomber crews suffered a 20 percent casualty rate, second only to U-BOAT crews among fighting forces. The ultimate goal of the survey was the finding of a correlation between the effectiveness and cost of destroying war-making capabilities and the ending of the war. But the definitive answer was never found. The real consequence of the Survey was the creation of an enormous data base for debates about air power.

Some members of the Survey—Robert S. Mac-Namara, Paul Nitze, George Ball, and John Kenneth Galbraith—went on to political careers and brought with them what they had learned about strategic bombing. The headquarters of the Survey was LONDON, but Survey workers went into combat areas to get information. Five were killed in the line of duty.

Survey members interrogated ALBERT SPEER, Germany's minister of armaments and war production, and *Reichsmarschall* HERMANN GÖRING, chief of the Luftwaffe, and executives of KRUPP. The Survey unearthed (sometimes literally) German records on such matters as production and worker-absentee rates. In Japan the Survey members found similar records and conducted similar interviews.

Late in the spring of 1947 they had completed the Survey, which was released in the form of 321 reports, totaling 3,361 pages. The Survey held that Allied air power "was decisive in the war in Western Europe. . . . Its power and superiority made the success of the [NORMANDY] INVASION. It brought the economy which sustained the enemy's armed forces to virtual collapse. . . ." As to the Pacific: "certainly prior to 31 December 1945, and in all probability prior to 1 November 1945, Japan would have surrendered even if the ATOMIC BOMBS had not been dropped, even if Russia had not entered the war, and even if no invasion had been planned or contemplated. . . ."

Both proponents and opponents of strategic bombing found nuggets to support their positions.

Galbraith: "At best, the bombing was a badly flawed performance."

Speer: "The real importance of the air war consisted in the fact that it opened a SECOND FRONT long before the invasion of Europe. That front was over the skies of Germany. The fleets of bombers might appear at any time over any large German city or important factory. . . . Defense against air attacks required the production of thousands of antiaircraft guns, the stockpiling of tremendous quantities of ammunition all over the country, and holding in readiness hundreds of thousands of soldiers. . . ."

David Halberstam, in *The Best and the Brightest,* applying it to Vietnam: The Survey "proved conclusively that the strategic bombing had not worked; on the contrary, it had intensified the will of the German population to resist. . . ." (The Survey says, "Bombing seriously depressed the morale of German civilians. . . .")

Streicher, Julius (1885–1946)

A leading NAZI JEW-baiter, Streicher published *Der Stürmer,* a virulent anti-Semite journal. (The paper, which had a circulation of 500,000, blamed a Jewish plot for the destruction of the German zeppelin *Hindenburg* at Lakehurst, N.J., in 1937.) He vigorously supported the KRISTALLNACHT orgy of violence against Jews in 1938. A small-time Nazi as *Gauleiter* (district leader) of Nuremberg, he was nevertheless nationally known and, among party leaders, loathed. His obscene outbursts and sadistic behavior finally so outraged Nazi officials that he was drummed out of his party posts in 1940. He was allowed to continue publication of *Der Stürmer,* which Hitler enjoyed reading. Convicted of crimes against humanity for "incitement to murder and extermination" by the WAR CRIMES tribunal at Nuremberg, he was hanged on Oct. 16, 1946. On the steps to the scaffold, he shouted, *"Purimfest!,"* a reference to Judaism's festival celebrating victory over Haman, an oppressor of Jews, who was hanged.

Strong, Maj. Gen. Kenneth W.D. (1900—1982)

Head of intelligence for the Supreme Allied Commander, Gen. DWIGHT D. EISENHOWER. Before the EUROPEAN WAR, Strong had served as assistant British military attaché in BERLIN, and for the first year and a half of the war was head of the German section in the War Office. In 1942–1943 he was head of intelligence for the British Home Forces.

After the debacle at KASSERINE PASS in Feb. 1943, Gen. Eisenhower asked the British to replace his head of intelligence, Brig. Eric Mockler-Ferryman, with another British officer, "who has a broader insight into German mentality and method." Ike added, "In his successor, I now look for a little more inquisitiveness and greater attention to checking and cross-checking reports from various sources." The British proposed Strong, then a brigadier.

He and Ike got on well. In his autobiography, *Intelligence at the Top,* Strong wrote that Eisenhower "had an immense talent for listening to oral explanations and distilling their essence. I was also to discover that the best way to deal with him was to be completely frank, no matter what national considerations or other controversial factors were involved in any issue. . . . Most people in high places have too much to read. . . . Only on a few occasions, when it was essential that something should appear on the record, did I produce a written Intelligence appreciation for Eisenhower."

Eisenhower sent Strong with his Chief of Staff, Brig. Gen. WALTER BEDELL SMITH, to Lisbon in Aug. 1943 to secretly arrange with Italian representatives for the unconditional SURRENDER of Italy.

At the height of the ALLIED CAMPAIGN IN EUROPE, Strong had more than a thousand men and women on his staff. He finished the war as a major general.

He became the first director general of intelligence in the Ministry of Defence in 1964; under his direction the military intelligence staffs of the three British armed services were combined into a defense intelligence staff. Strong retired in 1966.

Stud

One of three phases of U.S. Eighth and Ninth AIR FORCES' strikes against German trains, supply dumps, airfields, and targets of opportunity past the immediate NORMANDY INVASION areas, June 1944.

Student, *Generaloberst* Kurt (1890–1978)

Commander of German AIRBORNE forces during the war. Student was "a tireless officer with great organizational ability whose ideas on the employment of airborne troops in a strategic capacity were revolutionary at that time," wrote British author James Lucas in *Storming Eagles,* his history of German parachute forces.

Student began his military career as a cadet in the Prussian Army and was commissioned in 1911. He transferred to the new German Air Force in 1913 and served as a pilot in the war, becoming commander of a fighter squadron in 1916. After the war he remained in the Army and from 1919 to 1928 was the sole member of the aviation section of the *Reichswehr,* as Germany was forbidden by treaty from having an air force. Secretly he helped to train pilots in the Soviet Union and organize the Luftwaffe. In 1929 he took command of an infantry regiment, but by 1933—when ADOLF HITLER came to power—Student had transferred to the new Air Ministry.

On July 1, 1938, when the Luftwaffe high command decided to combine its parachute, GLIDER, and air transport units into the 7th *Flieger* (airborne) Division, *Generalmajor* Student was named division commander. (This was unlike U.S. or British airborne forces, where the troops were Army and the aircraft were under the Air Force.) Student's 9,000-man division—plus aircraft crews—was larger than any other nation's airborne force except for the Soviet Union.

Under Student's direction, in April 1940 the 7th Airborne Division successfully captured a number of objectives in the airborne assault on Norway during the DENMARK AND NORWAY CAMPAIGN. This was followed by the highly successful air assaults by the 7th Airborne Division to seize Wallhaven, the ROTTERDAM bridges, and the Moerdijk bridges at the start of the FRANCE AND LOW COUNTRIES CAMPAIGN in May 1940. Student was wounded in the Rotterdam operation.

A year later he commanded *Fliegerkorps* (Air Group) IX for the assault on CRETE (Operation *Merkur*), which, despite heavy German casualties, marked the first time in history that an airborne force had captured a major objective without ground or naval support. However, German losses were so high that never again were Student's main forces used in an airborne assault; instead, the increasing German airborne arm was employed as light infantry (as were U.S. and British airborne divisions for extended periods).

By late 1941 the main parachute force, rested and replenished, was sent into action as infantry in the siege of LENINGRAD. However, in 1942 the airborne troops were withdrawn from the Soviet Union, to the Mediterranean area, for a planned airborne assault on MALTA, which was never carried out; the division then planned for an assault on GIBRALTAR, which was also canceled. Some of Student's troops were sent back to fight in the Soviet Union. An airborne brigade was formed from the division and sent to North Africa for a planned, but never executed assault on Cairo, to support the AFRIKA KORPS advance into Egypt; it, too, was canceled. There were some smaller airborne landings in the Mediterranean areas.

When the ALLIES landed in North Africa in Nov. 1942, all available airborne troops were flown into Tunis and Bizerta to confront the Anglo-American forces as infantry.

Meanwhile, in the German military infighting, the head of the Luftwaffe, HERMANN GÖRING, formed more infantry divisions along with the *Fallschirmkorps* (Parachute Corps) I and II, established to control them. Student was now promoted to Commander in Chief Parachute High Command and commander of the First Parachute Army, establishing his headquarters in Nancy, France. Hitler gave Student a defensive mission: training German armies in the West to defend against expected Allied airborne landings. By the time of the NORMANDY INVASION there were some 160,000 troops in the parachute army.

Student's forces fought as infantry in the 1944 battles in France and Belgium. He was promoted to *Generaloberst* in July 1944. When the Allies carried out the massive airborne drops of Operation Market-Garden in Sept. 1944, the ill-fated British parachute and glider assault on the city of ARNHEM was undertaken without knowledge that it was the headquarters area for Student's army command. Student helped to organize an effective German defense.

Student was made commander of Army Group H in Nov. 1944 as the German Army was reorganized in an effort to stem the Allied advances in the West. His appointment, apparently by Hitler, was opposed by the army high command, which felt that Student lacked true command experience. He was soon dismissed as the Army Group commander, but then ordered back as deputy commander. In Dec. 1944 he directed the formation of parachute assault units that participated in the ARDENNES offensive (Operation *Stösser*).

The poor performance of his troops in battle led to his losing favor with Hitler and he was dismissed at the end of Jan. 1945. Göring had tried to defend Student from Hitler, but the German leader is reported to have refuted: "He reminds me of Fehrs, my new servant. When I tell him to do something it takes minutes for him to get it. He's dumb as an ox, but he certainly works hard. It's just that he's so slow."

In April 1945, with Soviet troops assaulting BERLIN, Göring took Student to see Hitler in the *FÜHRERBUNKER*. Hitler told him to take command of certain reserves—Army Group Vistula—which existed only in Hitler's mind. Finally, he set off to reach the headquarters of *Grossadmiral* KARL DÖNITZ, then commander of German forces in the northern part of the country. He arrived at Dönitz's headquarters at Flensburg where, on May 9, he was taken into captivity by British troops.

He was imprisoned for three years while being investigated, but he never was accused of WAR CRIMES. Student was released from Allied custody in 1948.

Student, Operation

German code name for takeover of certain Italian facilities in the event of an Italian capitulation to the ALLIES, 1943; named after *Generaloberst* KURT STUDENT.

Studie England

Code word for German plan for the invasion of England produced in May 1940 by the Naval War Staff under *Kontradmiral* Kurt Ficke. (See SEA LION.)

Stuka,

see JU 87.

The Ju 87 Stuka (seen here over North Africa in Nov. 1941) was one of the most effective aircraft of the war, being highly effective against ground troops, tanks, and ships; however, Stuka formations in the Battle of Britain were devastated by high-performance fighters. *(Luftwaffe via Imperial War Museum)*

Style

British code name for effort to reinforce MALTA, June 1942.

Submarine Pens

Massive sheltered piers for the protection of submarines. After the conquest of France in May 1940, the German Navy established five U-BOAT bases along the French Atlantic coast: Bordeaux, Brest, La Pallice, Lorient, and SAINT-NAZAIRE. The availability of French bases alleviated a 450-mile transit for U-boats from the Atlantic to German bases, saving about a week's time on each patrol.

At those bases the Germans constructed shelters or "submarine pens." By 1942 Lorient was the largest submarine base in the world. In addi-

tion, Lorient was used briefly as headquarters for the admiral commanding U-boats (*Kontradmiral* KARL DÖNITZ) from Sept. 1940 to March 1942, with the U-boat command post located in the nearby chateau at Kernevel, at the mouth of the River Blavet.

The *U-30* was the first submarine to enter a French port from the Atlantic to refuel and rearm for another war patrol, arriving at Lorient on July 7, 1940. Dönitz said that the base's repair facilities "proved to be superior to those of the overburdened dockyards of Germany." In addition to U-boats, Italian submarines were based at Bordeaux from 1940 to 1943.

The TODT ORGANIZATION provided each base with submarine "pens" in which the U-boats could be repaired and replenished; the pens also contained repair facilities and barracks for the submarine crews. The pens had reinforced concrete roofs 15 feet or more thick. Heavy concentrations of antiaircraft guns surrounded the bases. Once the pens were completed in mid-1942 they were immune to even the heaviest bombs then carried by U.S. and British aircraft. (The U.S. and British bomber commands refused to bomb the submarine pens while they were being built.)

Because the pens themselves were essentially invulnerable to STRATEGIC BOMBING, the U.S. Eighth AIR FORCE proposed attacking the adjacent floating docks, storage depots, power houses, railway yards, and barracks to reduce the effectiveness of the bases. From Oct. 21, 1942, until June 1943, "Submarines became the primary concern of the Eighth Air Force," according to the official U.S. AAF history. The AAF estimated that the five bases would each require 250 sorties per week for eight weeks or 10,000 heavy bomber flights to destroy the targets adjacent to the submarine pens. But neither the RAF Bomber Command nor the Eighth Air Force was able to significantly reduce the effectiveness of the submarine bases. Numerous French civilians (as well as Germans) were killed in the bombings.

The French submarine pens were in use until after the Allied landings in June 1944. The last boats departed from them in August 1944. (Lorient and Saint-Nazaire remained in German hands until the end of the war, although they were not usable as submarine bases because of Allied control of the air and surface of the Bay of Biscay.)

The Germans also built sheltered submarine facilities at Bergen and Trondheim in Norway and in Germany (the first, for six U-boats, was completed at Heligoland in 1940). Projects Valentin in Wilhelmshaven, Hornisse in Bremen, and Konrad in Kiel were begun as massive shelters for the construction of TYPE XXI submarines, but were never completed. The one at Kiel, partially completed, was used to construct *Seehund* MIDGET SUBMARINES at the end of the war.

The RAF had some success in damaging these hardened submarine facilities with 22,000-pound GRAND SLAM BOMBS carried by British LANCASTER bombers in 1944–1945.

Submarines

U.S. submarines had a major impact on the Pacific War. They sank large numbers of Japanese warships and, by sinking merchant ships, prevented the Japanese from bringing the RESOURCES of conquered areas to the home islands.

When the war began the Navy had 114 submarines in commission. In the Pacific, there were twenty-two so-called "fleet boats" operating out of PEARL HARBOR with twenty-three fleet boats and six older S-boats based at MANILA Bay in the Philip-

A U.S. submarine ties up at Pearl Harbor after a patrol in Japanese waters. It took more than a year to fix the problems with U.S. submarine torpedoes; with the improved torpedoes, these long-range fleet-type submarines were highly effective against Japanese shipping. *(U.S. Navy)*

pines. On the U.S. West Coast and East Coast were sixty-three additional submarines, including nineteen S-boats, eighteen obsolete R-class submarines, and seven of the O class.

The fleet boats were relatively large, long-range submarines, built in the 1930s to operate with the surface fleet. The newer fleet boats had a surface displacement of some 1,500 tons, were over 300 feet long, and were armed with ten 21-inch (533-mm) TORPEDO tubes, with up to twenty-four torpedoes carried. For attacking small merchant and fishing craft, they had a 3-inch (76-mm) deck gun plus several machine guns. Most S-boats, built in the early 1920s, displaced some 800 tons and were 219 feet long. They could not dive as deep, had less range, and were more cramped than the fleet boats, and had only four torpedo tubes. S-boats, as well as smaller O-class and R-class submarines built in World War I, were in service as training craft, although the latter made a few "war patrols" in the Atlantic (see below). Shortly before U.S. entry into the war one S-boat was transferred to Polish forces in England, and in 1942 five others went to the Royal Navy, as did three R-boats.

Several U.S. submarines were at sea in the Pacific when the war began. They were immediately ordered to commence operations against Japanese merchant ships, throwing aside the mission of providing direct support to the U.S. surface fleet that had been practiced in the 1930s. In their new role, caused by the devastation of the BATTLESHIPS at Pearl Harbor, the submarines were severely hampered by faulty torpedoes. That problem was not fully solved until mid-1943.

The first successful U.S. submarine attack of the war came on Dec. 15 when the *Swordfish* (SS 193) sank the Japanese merchant ship *Atsutasan Maru* off the coast of Indochina. On Jan. 27 the *Gudgeon* (SS 211) became the first U.S. submarine to sink a Japanese warship, the submarine *I-173*. That attack was based on information derived from the MAGIC code-breaking effort. The ability to read Japanese naval codes during the war was a key factor in vectoring U.S. submarines to their targets.

Still, it was not until 1943—when the Japanese antisubmarine forces had suffered major losses from U.S. AIRCRAFT CARRIER strikes, and the torpedo problems were solved—that U.S. submarines

achieved major successes in the Pacific. And, in the closing days of the war, submarine MINE-planting in Japanese home waters, undertaken with AAF B-29 SUPERFORTRESS bombers (Operation Starvation) finally sealed off Japanese ports to merchant shipping. Submarines were also used to land agents and supplies to support GUERRILLA operations in the Philippines, carry out reconnaissance of various Pacific islands, and land troops on MAKIN ISLAND in the GILBERTS and Attu Island in the ALEUTIANS. (See CARLSON'S RAIDERS and TRANSPORT SUBMARINES.) American submarines operated from Australia and DUTCH HARBOR, Alaska, as well as from Pearl Harbor, and near the end of the war, from GUAM.

During forty-four months of war in the Pacific U.S. submarines sank almost 1,300 merchant Japanese ships for a total of 5,300,000 tons. This represented 55 percent of the Japanese merchant tonnage sunk by all causes during the war. U.S. submarines also sank four fleet and four escort carriers, one battleship, twelve cruisers, forty-two destroyers, and a couple of Soviet merchant ships mistaken for Japanese. U.S. submarines also sank twenty-two Japanese undersea craft.

The top-scoring U.S. submarines were the *Tautog* (SS 199), with twenty-five enemy ships sunk, and the *Flasher* (SS 249), with 100,231 tons of shipping to her credit. The *Archerfish* (SS 311) sank the Japanese carrier *Shinano* of some 59,000 tons, the largest ship ever sunk by a submarine's torpedoes (see *YAMATO*). The submarine *Harder* (SS 257) sank three Japanese destroyers in four days, while the *BATFISH* (SS 310) sank three Japanese submarines in four days.

While such numbers paled in comparison with German U-BOAT accomplishments in the Atlantic, they nonetheless had a severe impact on the Japanese war effort, especially in proportion to assets: The U.S. submarine force had about 50,000 men ashore and in submarines—only 1.6 percent of the Navy's personnel. Fifty two U.S. submarines were lost during the war, probably thirty-six to Japanese guns, BOMBS, MINES, and DEPTH CHARGES and one to a torpedo from a Japanese submarine; ten were believed to be operational losses, with at least two of those being sunk by their own torpedoes that made circular runs and four that stranded in shallow water; one was accidentally sunk by U.S. forces; and four were lost in accidents outside the war area, two of those in the Atlantic. In those submarines that were lost, 3,505 men died of some 16,000 who actually made war patrols in the submarines.

(British and Dutch submarines also operated in the Far East, especially in the early months of the Pacific War.)

Although U.S. submarines operated primarily in the Pacific, early in the war U.S. submarines carried out eighty-six patrols along the U.S. East Coast and near the Panama Canal, most by outdated R- and S-boats. The *R-1* (SS 78) reported contact with a U-boat and fired four torpedoes while some 300 miles northeast of Bermuda on April 18, 1942. The Navy gave the submarine credit for a sinking and the skipper received the Navy Cross; postwar records show no U-boat sunk at the time. It was the only U.S. submarine attack in the Atlantic in that period.

Then, in response to an appeal by Prime Minister CHURCHILL during the summer of 1942, President ROOSEVELT ordered that a squadron of six fleet-type submarines be sent into the Atlantic. The Navy had a shortage of submarines in the Pacific at the time. The submarines, to be based in Roseneath, Scotland, participated in the NORTH AFRICA INVASION (Operation Torch), where they had a "nightmarish time. . . . The weather was bad, and recognition signals were mixed up. *Gunnel* [SS 253] was bombed by an Army aircraft. *Shad* [SS 235] was heavily DEPTH-CHARGED by a friendly DESTROYER. None of the boats made a noteworthy contribution to the landing," wrote historian Clay Blair, Jr., in *Silent Victory*.

These submarines carried out twenty-seven war patrols in European and North African waters, most in the Bay of Biscay. Although one or two of the submarines encountered German U-boats and several fired torpedoes at AXIS merchant ships, no sinkings were confirmed. In mid-1943 the submarines were belatedly withdrawn and sent to the Pacific.

When the Japanese attacked Pearl Harbor there were seventy-three fleet boats under construction in U.S. shipyards. Between Dec. 1941 and Aug. 1945, American shipyards delivered a total of 202 new submarines. At the time of the Japanese capitula-

tion the U.S. Navy had 214 large submarines in commission, plus forty-six older O-, R-, and S-craft employed for training.

Substance

British code name for reinforcement of MALTA, July 1941.

Sudetenland,

see CZECHOSLOVAKIA.

Sullivan Brothers

Brothers who were lost with the USS *Juneau* (CLAA 52) when the CRUISER was sunk in 1942. The five Sullivan brothers were all born in Waterloo, Iowa, between 1914 and 1920. The two oldest, George and Francis, enlisted in the Navy in 1937 and served in the DESTROYER *Hovey* (DD 208). On Jan. 3, 1942, they reenlisted, and their three younger brothers, Joseph, Madison, and Albert enlisted with them to avenge a friend who had been killed in the sinking of the *ARIZONA* (BB 39) at PEARL HARBOR.

The five Sullivans went on board the cruiser *Juneau* at the Brooklyn Navy Yard on Feb. 3, 1942. On Nov. 12–13, during fierce night action off GUADALCANAL, the *Juneau* was severely damaged by a Japanese TORPEDO. The next day she was torpedoed by the Japanese submarine *I-26*. One or possibly two torpedoes hit the cruiser and detonated her magazines. The ship blew apart and went down in forty-two seconds. Of the brothers, only George, badly wounded, was able to get off the ship and onto a raft. But, with most of the survivors, he was lost at sea.

A destroyer being built at the Bethlehem Steel shipyard in San Francisco was named *The Sullivans* and launched on April 4, 1943. The sponsor was Mrs. Thomas F. Sullivan, mother of the Sullivans. The ship saw extensive combat in the war and earned nine BATTLE STARS. After the deaths of the Sullivans, Navy regulations were changed so that close relatives were not allowed to serve on board the same ship.

Summersby, Capt. Kay (1908–1975)

Chauffeur for, secretary to, and companion of Gen. DWIGHT D. EISENHOWER. Irish-born Kay

Summersby was in the British Transport Service when she was assigned as the driver for Eisenhower soon after he arrived in LONDON in June 1942 as the commander of the European theater of operations. She later became his secretary at SUPREME HEADQUARTERS ALLIED EXPEDITIONARY FORCE (SHAEF) and was given a direct commission in the WAC.

She became Eisenhower's companion and confidante, and rumors circulated about the extent of their relationship, which continued through the EUROPEAN WAR. She wrote a chatty account of working in SHAEF in a book, *Eisenhower Was My Boss,* published in 1948. A few references from the book appear in *Eisenhower at War 1943–1945,* written by Eisenhower's grandson David Eisenhower and published in 1986. Mentioned in it, for example, is how Eisenhower opened a meeting with President ROOSEVELT in Jan. 1944 by asking Roosevelt for an autographed photograph for Kay, who had driven the President on a tour of the battlefield at Carthage during the CASABLANCA CONFERENCE.

President TRUMAN, according to his daughter Margaret, learned that Eisenhower had written to Gen. GEORGE C. MARSHALL, Army Chief of Staff, asking to be returned to the United States so that he could divorce Mamie Eisenhower and marry Kay Summersby. "Marshall responded with fury," Margaret Truman wrote in *The New York Times,* "telling Eisenhower that his conduct was disgraceful and that if he went through with his plans, Marshall would kick him out of the Army and harass him in other ways for the rest of his life. Eisenhower dropped Kay Summersby. When my father left the Oval Office, he threw out the correspondence between Marshall and Eisenhower, as a courtesy to Eisenhower. In 1975, Kay Summersby told the story in her book *Past Forgetting: My Love Affair with Dwight D. Eisenhower.*"

Sunderland

Highly successful, long-range flying boat operated in the maritime reconnaissance and antisubmarine roles by the RAF Coastal Command. In service at the outbreak of the war, Sunderlands operated in the Far East, and over the Atlantic and Indian Oceans during the war. They were used in the evacuations of British troops from Norway, Greece,

and CRETE. Sunderlands were highly effective because of their long rang, large weapons load, and potent defensive armament—which led to their being labeled *Stachelschwein* (Porcupine) by German fighter pilots. By the end of the war twenty-eight squadrons of Coastal Command flew Sunderlands.

The Sunderland was based on the commercial Short "C" Class Empire flying boats, which first flew in 1936. Production of the Sunderland was ordered in March 1936 with the first military flying boat not taking off until eighteen months later, in Oct. 1937. The aircraft entered RAF service the following summer. Production continued throughout the war; the 749th and last Sunderland was produced in June 1946. It was also flown by the Royal Australian Air Force.

(Two of the original "C" Class flying boats were pressed into military service by the RAF in 1939; they were destroyed off Norway in May 1940 while being used as transports. Two more were then taken over by the RAF, one of which was lost. The latter were used as patrol aircraft by Coastal Command, being fitted with BOMB racks and gun turrets.)

The Short Brothers–built Sunderland was a massive flying boat, with large shoulder wings carrying four radial engines and fixed stabilizing floats. The stepped hull terminated with a tall tail fin and tail-gun turret. (A nose turret was also fitted, as were two flexible waist guns; the latter were replaced in some aircraft with a dorsal turret.) When German U-BOATS were refitted with heavy antiaircraft gun batteries in 1943, Sunderlands were additionally fitted with four .303-cal. machine guns in the nose, which were used to clear gunners from the submarine's deck as the aircraft approached to attack. The aircraft had two decks, with large numbers of bombs, DEPTH CHARGES, and MINES carried internally; they could be shifted in flight to the release positions in the wings.

The aircraft could fly at 210 mph with a range of 1,780 miles; at overload weights the aircraft's range was 2,900 miles. A payload of 4,960 pounds of ordnance could be carried. Early aircraft had two .303-cal. machine guns installed in the nose turret, four .303-cal. guns in the tail turret, and two flexible .303-cal. guns in the waist. Later variants had a dorsal turret with two .303-cal. guns, but in the final production units this was deleted in favor of two flexible .50-cal. waist guns. (When attacked by enemy fighters the Sunderlands would fly down to water level to protect the underside of their hull while fending off attackers with fire from their eight guns.)

Sunderlands were flown extensively after the war, being used by the RAF during the Korean War; the last were retired in 1959.

Sunrise

Allied code name for negotiations for German SURRENDER in Italy, April–May 1945; Prime Minister CHURCHILL had used the code name Crossword for the negotiations.

Super Guns

German cannon used to bombard England from positions in France. The two so-called super guns were 210-mm (8.27-inch) weapons mounted on railway carriages. They were deployed to the French coast and were used to fire into southeastern England from late 1940 until late 1941. The firings produced no known damage, although fragments of the guns' shells were recovered at Rainham, near Chatham, some 55 miles from the nearest point in England to the French coast.

The super guns had eight-groove barrels 109¼ feet long that fired ribbed shells. With a 530-pound powder charge, the guns fired a 236-pound shell with a muzzle velocity of 4,920 feet per second to reach a maximum range of 71.4 miles. Each gun weighed 297 tons.

The guns, ordered in 1935, were completed in 1939 and 1940. They were designated as 21-centimeter *Kanone* 12 (E); the *12* in the designation was the estimated range (12 × 10 kilometers) and the *E* indicated *Eisenbahnlafette* or railway mounting. The guns each had an estimated firing life of 120 rounds.

Although there were larger guns in use during the war, including the massive GUSTAV, the biggest gun in the world, none had a greater range than the super guns. The aborted LONDON GUN or V-3 was to have had a range sufficient to strike London from the French Coast.

Super Gymnast,

see TORCH.

Supercharge

(1) Code name for British XXX Corps follow-up near EL ALAMEIN to Lightfoot operation, Nov. 1942; (2) code name for revised Allied plan for the assault on the MARETH LINE, Italy, March 1943.

Superfortress,

see B-29 SUPERFORTRESS.

Supreme Headquarters Allied Expeditionary Force

Headquarters for Gen. DWIGHT D. EISENHOWER, the Supreme Commander Allied Expeditionary Force, established in June 1942 in Bushey Park, 15 miles west of the center of LONDON. "Ike" did not actually take command at Bushey Park until Jan. 1944. Immediately known by the acronym SHAEF, Eisenhower's headquarters also served as the command structure for Allied ground forces in Europe. (There were separate naval and air commands under Eisenhower; the British 21st ARMY GROUP under Gen. BERNARD MONTGOMERY served as headquarters for all Allied ground forces during the landing phase of the European campaign.)

Just before the NORMANDY INVASION in June 1944, the operational portions of SHAEF and the 21st Army Group headquarters were set up at Portsmouth on England's southwest coast. Portsmouth was the Allied assault force's principal embarkation port, and the Navy had set up a communications system to keep Eisenhower in contact with the assault forces during the early hours of the landings.

SHAEF was moved to Granville, France, after the Normandy landings. In the late summer of 1944 SHAEF moved to its permanent continental location at Versailles, near PARIS. Eisenhower then established a forward command post just outside of Reims, from which point he could reach the front, by road if necessary, because weather prevented his flying.

SHAEF passed out of existence on July 14, 1945, when Eisenhower ceased to be the Allied commander and became commander of only the U.S. forces in Europe.

Surrender, Germany

The ALLIES followed long and twisting roads to Germany's surrender and the celebration of V-E DAY, Victory in Europe Day—May 8, 1945. Of the four major Allies in the EUROPEAN WAR, only two would be shoulder-to-shoulder victors at the end.

The war began with the British and French standing together in Sept. 1939. But the French soon became a conquered people in need of liberation. In Dec. 1941 the United States entered the alliance, replaying its role in World War I: go to Europe and fight Germany. As for the fourth ally, the Soviet Union, it had begun the war as an ally of Germany through the NONAGGRESSION PACT and joined Germany in the conquest of Poland. Then, invaded by Germany, the Soviet Union fought what it saw as its own conflict, the GREAT PATRIOTIC WAR against Germany.

As the war against Germany neared its end, these differences affected the events leading to Germany's surrender. The United States and Britain, as liberators, and France, as a liberated Ally, managed to suppress individual national interests and find the same road. They came from the west, via the long and relentless STRATEGIC BOMBING of Germany and the NORMANDY INVASION. The Soviet Union came from the east, across its ravaged lands, driving back the invaders and then pushing onward, into Eastern Europe.

ADOLF HITLER saw the fall of BENITO MUSSOLINI in July 1943, and Italy's withdrawal from the war the following September (see SURRENDER, ITALY) as problems that could be settled by sending more troops into Italy and treating it as another occupied country. The Allied forces slogging up the Italian peninsula at first saw no effect from Italy's surrender.

By the time of the YALTA CONFERENCE in Feb. 1945, the BIG THREE—President ROOSEVELT, British Prime Minister CHURCHILL, and Soviet Marshal STALIN—could look at a map of Europe and no longer see a NAZI Germany. There was still fighting—hard fighting—to come. But the Big Three (with France's Gen. CHARLES DE GAULLE sulking in the wings) could begin to sketch the results of Germany's UNCONDITIONAL SURRENDER. That was the phrase, first used by Roosevelt at the CASA-BLANCA CONFERENCE in Jan. 1943, that would hover over the rest of the war.

At Yalta, the Big Three had defined the cost of Germany's aggression: "It is our inflexible purpose to destroy German militarism and nazism and to ensure that Germany will never again be able to disturb the peace of the world. . . . It is not our purpose to destroy the people of Germany, but only when nazism and militarism have been extirpated will there be hope for a decent life for the Germans and a place for them in the comity of nations."

April 1945 brought three milestones on the road to surrender: the linkup of U.S. and Soviet troops at Torgau on the Elbe in the heart of Germany; the collapse and capitulation of German forces in Italy; and the suicide on April 30 of Hitler in his *FÜHRER-BUNKER* in a BERLIN about to surrender to the Red Army.

Hitler, just before his death, had made *Grossadmiral* KARL DÖNITZ his successor, with orders to continue fighting. The end of German fighting, however, had already begun. In Feb. 1945 HEINRICH HIMMLER, leader of the SS and overseer of CONCENTRATION CAMPS, had begun discussions with International RED CROSS representative Count FOLKE BERNADOTTE about selectively freeing Scandinavians among camp inmates. These talks evolved into surrender talks.

Coincidentally, around the end of Feb. 1945 peace feelers were sent out by *SS-Obergruppenführer* Karl Wolff, Himmler's former adjutant who was German military governor of northern Italy. Wolff made contact in Zürich with agents of ALLEN DULLES, representative in Switzerland of the OFFICE OF STRATEGIC SERVICES. Wolff's contact was given the code name Crossword and the negotiations themselves the code name Sunrise. By March 8 negotiations had reached the point where Wolff himself met with Dulles and was bluntly told that the surrender of German troops in northern Italy had to be unconditional. On March 15 a British general and a U.S. general went in disguise from Allied headquarters at Caserta to Switzerland to arrange the details.

The Soviet government was informed of these talks, but ever-suspicious Soviet leader Stalin complained bitterly that the secret deal was jeopardizing the Red Army because Germany would be able to move troops from Italy to the EASTERN FRONT. President Roosevelt angrily responded on April 5: "Frankly I cannot avoid the feeling of bitter resentment toward your informers, whoever they are, for such vile misrepresentations of my actions or those of my trusted subordinates."

On April 29, the day before Hitler killed himself, the German Southwest Command, without his knowledge, surrendered all forces in Italy. The local surrender was arranged by U.S. and British officers. But, to allay Soviet suspicions that the other Allies were plotting a separate peace, a Soviet general attended the signing ceremonies, which took place in Caserta.

The next local surrender came on May 4 at the headquarters of British Field Marshal Sir BERNARD L. MONTGOMERY on Lüneberg Heath in the German state of lower Saxony. The surrender, signed by Montgomery as the representative of Gen. of the Army DWIGHT D. EISENHOWER, Supreme Commander, ALLIED EXPEDITIONARY FORCE, covered German forces in Holland, Denmark, and northwest Germany. Montgomery added a handwritten note: "This [surrender] to include all naval ships in these areas."

On May 6, Dönitz, as head of the THIRD REICH, authorized *Generaloberst* ALFRED JODL, Chief of the Operations Staff in the High Command of the Armed Forces, "to conclude an armistice agreement" with Eisenhower's SUPREME HEADQUARTERS ALLIED EXPEDITIONARY FORCE (SHAEF). The Germans hoped to negotiate a separate peace with Eisenhower without surrendering forces in the east to the Red Army, which the Germans feared as a brutal instrument of Soviet vengeance. Eisenhower coldly turned down the attempt to split the Allies and ordered that a surrender reflecting the Big Three demands be signed the following day.

At 2:41 A.M. on May 7, in the war room of SHAEF in the Professional and Technical School at Reims in northeastern France, Jodl and two other German officers representing Dönitz sat across a long table from Lt. Gen. WALTER BEDELL SMITH, SHAEF Chief of Staff, and other representatives of the armed forces of the United States, England, France, and the Soviet Union. The Germans and the Allied representatives (except for the Soviets) signed a surrender document. Eisenhower was not

at the table because he refused to meet with German officers until they had formally surrendered.

The *official* instrument of surrender still had to be signed. This document had been in preparation, under direction of the Big Three, since July 1944. The work on the document had been done by the European Advisory Commission (EAC), set up in 1943 to carry out the details of unconditional surrender and lay out possible solutions to postwar economic and political problems.

SHAEF had not been able to put the EAC document on the surrender table because of two snags: France had not been included in the 1944 draft and the word "dismemberment," added at the Yalta Conference to emphasize the division of Germany, was missing. Harried EAC document writers produced a new draft, but Eisenhower and his officers decided that a military surrender, ending the fighting and stopping the bloodshed, was all that was needed. The political problems could be solved later.

The military surrender provided for the cease-fire to take place at 11:01 P.M. on May 8. SHAEF agreed to this forty-four hour delay between the signing and the cease-fire so that more German troops could hurry westward and surrender to U.S. and British forces rather than the Red Army.

The Soviets insisted that a second ceremonial signing take place on May 9 in Soviet-occupied Berlin, ostensibly because the Soviet officer at the Reims signing, who attended as an observer, did not have a rank high enough to sign. Actually, the Soviets wanted to demonstrate that the other Allies had not signed a separate peace. Dönitz authorized three officers to sign the Berlin surrender documents, which, unlike the all-English Reims texts, were in English, Russian, and German.

A separate document contained detailed instructions for the surrender of all German naval forces, including charts showing the location of minefields in European waters and the surrender of all U-BOATS.

The Allies allowed the Dönitz government to remain in power for sixteen more days. Dönitz, Jodl, and most of the other German officers involved in the surrender were arrested for their WAR CRIMES. Tried and convicted at Nuremburg, Dönitz was given a ten-year prison sentence and

Jodl was hanged. Of two other officers who took part in the surrender, one was hanged and one killed himself before trial.

Surrender, Italy

"The Italian government has surrendered its forces unconditionally," Gen. DWIGHT D. EISEN-HOWER, Supreme Allied Commander, announced on Sept. 8, 1943, on the eve of an Allied AMPHIBI-OUS LANDING at SALERNO on the Italian mainland. A similar announcement was made on Italian radio by Marshal PIETRO BADOGLIO, chief of the Italian General Staff and Italian head of state since the overthrow of BENITO MUSSOLINI on July 25, 1943. But the word *unconditional* was premature.

Negotiations for a surrender began in August, when Eisenhower sent his Chief of Staff, Brig. Gen. WALTER BEDELL SMITH, and head of intelligence, British Maj. Gen. KENNETH STRONG, to Lisbon, in neutral Portugal, for secret talks with Italian representatives. Smith and Strong, with British passports and posing as commercial travelers, carried with them a "Short Terms" surrender document, as it was called by Eisenhower aides who had prepared it. Meanwhile, at higher political levels, both the U.S. State Department and the British Foreign Office had prepared their versions of what became known as the "Long Terms" document that spelled out the Allied "unconditional surrender" war aim.

The chief Italian negotiator in Lisbon was Italian Brig. Gen. Giuseppe Castellano of the Italian Armed Forces Staff. He carried with him a letter from the British Minister in VATICAN CITY attesting that Castellano was an authentic spokesman for Badoglio's government. Castellano was accompanied by a Harvard-educated representative of the Italian Foreign Office, who served as interpreter.

After the Short Terms agreement was tentatively reached, to get Castellano back to Italy safely, he was instructed to take a certain route that was guaranteed to be free of Allied attack for a specified period. The next problem—how he would communicate with the Allied negotiators once he returned to Italy—was solved in a remarkable way, as recounted by Strong in his book *Intelligence at the Top:*

"We contacted LONDON and an officer was dispatched at once with the necessary equipment. . . . We gave a radio set to the Italians and reminded Castellano that Dick Mallaby, a member of SPECIAL OPERATIONS EXECUTIVE recently captured by the Italians, was in Milan. We suggested that they should free him and make use of his expert signal knowledge. Mallaby was released and later became responsible for communications between ROME and Allied Force Headquarters."

Through the radio, Castellano arranged a rendezvous in his native Sicily, which was already in Allied hands. After some fruitless discussion, he flew back to Rome without the Allied negotiators knowing whether they had succeeded in their primary military mission: getting Italy out of the war before the invasion.

Talks in Sicily almost broke down over Castellano's insistence on knowing Allied invasion plans. Badoglio wanted that knowledge because he was playing a desperate game. He believed that the Allied armies had to make a show of strength in Italy so that Badoglio would have a plausible reason to surrender. He feared the Germans would punish Italy for a surrender that was willful rather than one forced by Allied arms. Badoglio simultaneously was trying to convince *Generalfeldmarschall* ALBERT KESSELRING that Italians would fight side-by-side with the Germans against the expected invasion.

But in the end Badoglio was forced to throw in his fate with the ALLIES. He decided to accept the Short Terms document as an "armistice." Castellano returned to Sicily and, on Sept. 3 received, by clandestine radio, authority from Badoglio to sign the Short Terms; the Long Terms would be handled later as a political, rather than military, matter. In a tent in an olive grove at Cassibile, Sicily, Castellano signed for Italy and Smith signed for the Allies, although Eisenhower was present. Meanwhile, the first Allied force to invade Italy, the British Eighth Army, crossed the Strait of Messina and landed on the Calabrian coast against token Italian resistance.

Badoglio had hinted that Italian troops would support an Allied AIRBORNE assault on Rome. The commander of the 82nd Airborne DIVISION, Brig. Gen. MAXWELL TAYLOR, was taken by an Italian frigate to a port in Italy and spirited into Rome in a RED CROSS ambulance. Taylor did not believe such an attack would work, primarily because Badoglio backed off from making any assurances of Italian aid.

As soon as Badoglio announced the surrender on Sept. 8 he fled from Rome, with King Emmanuel and the Italian Cabinet, to Brindisi in southern Italy and proclaimed it the capital of the new Italy. Three days later British forces occupied the city. Meanwhile, Italian Army units in Italy and abroad were left on their own. Most of the 1,090,000 Italian soldiers in Italy, demoralized and cut adrift by their high command, were easily disarmed by the 400,000 Germans under Kesselring. The Allies hoped that Italian Army units would fight against the Germans. Few did, but the Allies eventually got some help from Italian GUERRILLAS, many of them Communists fighting against both Hitler and the king.

Under the Short Terms, the Italian fleet was to surrender to the British at MALTA. As Italian ships headed for Malta, German bombers sank the battleship *ROMA* with a GUIDED MISSILE.

On Sept. 29 the Long Terms version of the surrender was signed on board the British battleship *Nelson* at Malta. On Oct. 13 Badoglio declared war on Germany, assuring that at war's end Italy would not be treated as an enemy.

U.S. diplomat ROBERT D. MURPHY and, for the British, Harold Macmillan (a future prime minister) helped draw up the Long Terms. One of the Allied requirements was the installation of a democratic government. "A republican form of government is not suited to the Italian people," the king, tears in his eyes, told Murphy. But in June 1944, following the Allied liberation of Rome, the king abdicated, Badoglio stepped down, and, the Long Terms satisfied, Italy was on the road to democracy.

Surrender, Japan

The Japanese decision to surrender took the Cabinet and Emperor HIROHITO down a long and twisting road. Ever since the CAIRO CONFERENCE of President ROOSEVELT, Prime Minister CHURCHILL, and *Generalissimo* CHIANG KAI-SHEK of China in Nov. 1943, Japan had known that UNCONDITIONAL SURRENDER was the only kind of surrender that the ALLIES would accept.

Japan paid little heed to the Cairo statement. But the fall of SAIPAN in June 1944 and the pounding of Japanese cities by B-29 SUPERFORTRESSES stimulated some thoughts about peace among Japanese statesmen. By the spring of 1945, after months of heavy firebombing of Japanese cities, the peace efforts intensified. In a delicate, almost invisible effort to end the war, Japanese officials sent out feelers to Sweden, to the Soviet Union, and then to aides of ALLEN DULLES, who was running OFFICE OF STRATEGIC SERVICES operations in Switzerland. They also tried to get help from the Soviets in the hope that Japan could end the war before the Soviet Union came in. Because of U.S. code-breaking, U.S. officials were aware of these overtures.

On July 26, 1945, the small peace bloc in the Japanese government began studying the Potsdam Proclamation (later called the Potsdam Declaration) issued after the POTSDAM CONFERENCE of President HARRY S TRUMAN, STALIN, and Churchill, later replaced by CLEMENT ATTLEE. The document, issued in the names of the heads of government of the United States, China, and England, said that the United States, England, and China "agree that Japan shall be given an opportunity to end this war." The Potsdam document offered a slight change in the unconditional surrender policy: It seemed to apply only to the armed services, not to the nation itself.

The majority of the Japanese Cabinet was in favor of surrender. But two generals held out. Hoping for time to persuade the generals and prepare the Japanese people, the government announced that an offer of peace had been made but that the Cabinet had decided momentarily to withhold comment. The statement used the word *mokusatsu,* which can also mean "ignore." That was the translation used in an English-language radio broadcast. On July 28 American newspapers published stories saying that Japan had "ignored" the peace offer. On Aug. 6, Truman announced that Japan had "rejected" the peace offer and in response a B-29 dropped an ATOMIC BOMB on HIROSHIMA.

While a divided Japanese Cabinet frantically debated how to end the war, the Soviet Union declared war on Japan, and a second atomic bomb destroyed NAGASAKI. Amid fear that the Japanese military would attempt a coup, the Emperor ordered that a rescript, or official answer, be sent accepting surrender. On Aug. 10, through Swiss diplomatic channels, Japan notified the United States that it accepted the Potsdam statement, providing the prerogatives of the emperor as a sovereign ruler would be preserved.

The U.S. replied that the authority of the emperor and the Japanese government "would be subject to the Supreme Commander of the Allied powers." While the Cabinet debated, the military tried desperately to thwart the peace moves. The emperor secretly recorded an announcement of surrender, and gun-toting imperial guardsmen roamed government offices hoping to seize the record.

On the morning of Aug. 15, Radio Tokyo announced that Emperor Hirohito, who never before had spoken on the radio, would make an announcement at noon. "We have ordered Our Government," said the recorded announcement, "to communicate to the Governments of the United States, Great Britain, China, and the Soviet Union that Our Empire accepts the provisions of their Joint Declaration." Nowhere in the long statement did the word *defeat* or *surrender* appear.

President Truman announced the "unconditional surrender" of Japan on Aug. 14. Allied occupation troops began arriving in Japan on Aug. 28. Unlike occupied Germany, Japan would not be divided into occupation zones. Allied authority was vested in the FAR EASTERN COMMISSION.

On Sept. 2, in Tokyo Bay, before an array of Allied representatives—including Lt. Gen. JONATHAN M. WAINWRIGHT, a PRISONER OF WAR since the fall of BATAAN—the Supreme Commander of the Allied Powers, Gen. of the Army DOUGLAS MACARTHUR, oversaw the signing of the surrender on the deck of the battleship *MISSOURI.* The eight-paragraph Instrument of Surrender had been prepared by the War Department. It began with "We, acting by command of and in behalf of the Emperor of Japan. . . ."

Several local surrenders followed. On Sept. 3, at Camp John Hay on Luzon in the Philippines, Wainwright accepted the surrender of Japanese forces in the Philippines. On Sept. 9, the surrender of about 1,000,000 Japanese troops in China took place in the restored capital of NANKING; the same day, U.S. officers accepted the surrender of Japanese forces south of the 38th parallel in Korea; the Soviets accepted the surrender north of the parallel. On Oct. 10 (China's anniversary day), the Japanese garrison at Peking formally surrendered to the Chi-

nese Army, which had been fighting the Japanese since 1937. Other surrenders took place in the MARIANA ISLANDS, the Ryukyu Islands, on WAKE, at TRUK, and at SINGAPORE.

Suzuki, Adm. Kantaro (1867–1948)

Last Japanese wartime prime minister. Suzuki commanded a TORPEDO boat in the Sino-Soviet War (1894–1895) and a destroyer SQUADRON in the Russo-Japanese War (1904–1905). Following a distinguished naval career Suzuki became the grand chamberlain to the emperor in 1929.

Known for his moderate views, in April 1945 he became prime minister although he was opposed by Gen. HIDEKI TOJO. But Suzuki was unable to bring about a peace agreement until after the United States carried out the ATOMIC BOMB attacks on Japan.

Swamp

British code name for intensive RAF Coastal Command attack on German U-BOATS in defense of Operation Overload (NORMANDY INVASION), June 1944.

Swastika

NAZI symbol. The hooked cross—*Hakenkreuz*—was adopted by ADOLF HITLER as the emblem and central flag motif for the National Socialists and, after he became the nation's leader, for Germany itself. He claimed to have invented it in 1920 for the party as the symbol "for the victory of the Aryan man." The swastika, a cross with limbs extending at right angles, was an ancient symbol used by American Indians, and other cultures from Japan to Tibet. Ancient Greeks formed it from four *gammas* of their alphabet. In Sanskrit it symbolized good luck. Emblazoned everywhere—on armbands, flags, uniforms, buildings—the swastika became so powerful an emblem that a postwar Germany law banned its appearance.

Sweden

Capital: Stockholm, pop. 6,284,722 (1938). The constitutional monarchy of Sweden maintained a policy of armed neutrality during the war but leaned always toward the ALLIES. In 1933–1934 Sweden's defense appropriations were $30,000,000; in 1939, she was spending $200,000,000 and supporting an army, navy, and air force numbering 600,000 men. Air raid shelters were built in Stockholm and in other potential targets.

In 1939 Sweden declined HITLER's offer for a nonaggression pact and refused to acknowledge a NAZI "Aryanization" campaign in which commercial businesses were asked to state the race of employees doing business with Germans. Against threats of trade cutoffs, Swedish businessmen filled in the racial questionnaires on the German forms with the same word: *Swedish*. In 1943 all commercial exchange of goods between Germany and Sweden ended.

When the Soviet Union invaded Finland in Nov. 1939, Sweden sent volunteer armed forces, food, weapons, munitions, aircraft, and medical aid to Finland. But Sweden, fearing it too would be attacked, declined to become an active ally of Finland.

Swedish intelligence agents had advance warning of Germany's April 1940 DENMARK AND NORWAY CAMPAIGN and passed the information to the two fellow Scandinavian nations. To defend her borders during the attacks on her neighbors, Sweden shot down German reconnaissance planes, refused to allow German military units to transit Sweden, and braced for an expected invasion. Swedish diplomats learned that the Soviet Union had put pressure on Germany to keep out of Sweden.

When Germany invaded the Soviet Union, Sweden allowed a German division to transit the country en route to Finland. German troops and munitions en route to German-occupied Norway were also allowed to cross through Sweden.

Sweden, which lost much of her foreign trade after the Denmark and Norway invasions, increased trade with Germany, exchanging iron ore for German coal, ball bearings, chemicals, and rubber. An OFFICE OF STRATEGIC SERVICES agent passed information about secret Swedish-German dealing to U.S. diplomats, who worked successfully to get the trade stopped. After the war Sweden said that besides its trade with Germany it also had been secretly supplying England with ball bearings.

Sweden allowed numerous Danish and Norwegian underground agents to slip into the country and then out of the country to join resistance forces in England. Danish physicist NIELS BOHR, one of the thousands of refugees who escaped to Sweden, appealed to Sweden's King Gustav for asylum for Denmark's JEWS. Within two months 7,220 Danish Jews reached safety in Sweden.

Count FOLKE BERNADOTTE, a Swedish RED CROSS official and the king's nephew, acted as a contact between German and Allied officials during the war. Through his efforts nearly 20,000 CONCENTRATION CAMP inmates, most of them Scandinavian, were released to Sweden. Sweden sheltered as many as 200,000 refugees, including thousands of Finnish orphans. RAOUL WALLENBERG, a Swedish diplomat in BUDAPEST, saved thousands of Jews by sheer courage and ingenious use of the diplomatic powers Sweden authorized him to use.

Sweeney, Maj. Charles W. (1919—)

Pilot of ATOMIC BOMB aircraft raid against NAGASAKI. Sweeney was commander of the AAF 393rd Bombardment SQUADRON, the lone squadron of the 509TH COMPOSITE GROUP, established on Dec. 17, 1944, in the United States to deliver the atomic bomb against Japanese targets. The squadron flew specially modified B-29 SUPERFORTRESS bombers.

Sweeney led the squadron from the United States to TINIAN in June 1945. Based at the island's North Field, the squadron flew several practice bombing runs with PUMPKIN BOMBS.

In the atomic bomb attack on HIROSHIMA on Aug. 6, 1945, Sweeney flew the B-29 "The Great Artiste" carrying scientific equipment to measure the effects of the bomb. On the NAGASAKI raid on Aug. 9 Sweeney piloted the B-29 "Bockscar," which dropped the atomic bomb. (On that raid "The Great Artiste," still loaded with scientific gear, was flown by Capt. Frederick C. Bock, the regular pilot of "Bockscar.")

Switzerland

Capital: Berne, pop. 4,260,179 (est. 1941). Surrounded by belligerents of the EUROPEAN WAR, Switzerland maintained its neutrality while simultaneously serving as a go-between nation for the countries at war. Even though she was a member of the LEAGUE OF NATIONS—whose headquarters was in Geneva—Switzerland would not participate in any kind of sanctions.

With the fall of France in June 1940, Switzerland was surrounded by AXIS forces and responded by keeping her troops on constant border alert. Ultimately, her troops could consist of every male between the ages of eight and sixty because of her compulsory militia service law. Another law authorized the callup to national service of all civilians.

A small NAZI party was banned in 1938; when new versions appeared under other names, the leaders were arrested. HITLER in his most rash dreams of conquest never included Switzerland. It was not BLITZKRIEG country, and Swiss proclamations of preparedness were taken seriously. The heart of Swiss defense was a national redoubt in the mountains. Switzerland defensive strategy called for abandonment of lowlands and towns and a final stand in the natural fortress of the Alps.

Switzerland could not ignore the war. The government imposed censorship on all newspapers and news agencies. With trade and tourism casualties of war, the government kept a tight hold on the economy, fixing prices and rents, regulating the sale of coal, and rationing basic foodstuffs.

Switzerland became a center for both public and private negotiations between belligerents. Publicly, Switzerland was the official distribution point for handling parcels and messages for PRISONERS OF WAR of all nations. This was done through the International Committee of the RED CROSS, whose headquarters was in Geneva. Privately, spymaster ALLEN DULLES of the OFFICE OF STRATEGIC SERVICES, used Switzerland as a contact point with German ESPIONAGE agents and Germans putting out peace feelers.

The only major incident to disturb Swiss neutrality occurred on April 1, 1944, when U.S. aircraft accidentally bombed Schaffhausen near the Swiss-German border. At least fifty people were killed and 150 injured; several small factories were extensively damaged.

Sword

Code name for Dourves beach at the NORMANDY INVASION used by British 3rd Division.

Swordfish

The principal British carrier-based bomber of World War II and one of the most famous British warplanes of all times. The Swordfish was affectionately called the "Stringbag" after a wag, commenting on the variety of weapons the plane could carry, remarked that "No housewife on a shopping spree could cram a wider variety of articles into her stringbag." The open-cockpit, biplane Swordfish was obsolete when the war began; it was far inferior in performance to the Japanese KATE and the U.S. Navy's TBD DEVASTATOR TORPEDO planes. Still, flying from British carriers, Swordfish sank the Italian battle fleet at anchor at TARANTO, stopped the German battleship *BISMARCK,* and were responsible for sinking and damaging many other AXIS ships and submarines.

In Sept. 1939 there were nine to thirty-six Swordfish assigned to six of the Royal Navy's seven aircraft carriers (no planes were assigned to the *Argus*); Swordfish were the only planes assigned to four of the carriers.

Their first major action was off Narvik, Norway, in April 1940. Spotting for British warship guns, Swordfish helped sink seven German destroyers, and bombed and sank a U-BOAT and another destroyer. The most famous Swordfish action of the war came on the night of Nov. 11–12, 1940, when twenty-one bombers from the carrier *Illustrious* sank two Italian battleships and damaged a third, plus other ships in Taranto Harbor. Two Swordfish were lost in the raid.

In May 1941 Swordfish from the carriers *Victorious* and *ARK ROYAL* helped to track down the German battleship *Bismarck* as she attempted to evade British pursuers. A torpedo hit by a Swordfish from the *Ark Royal* crippled the *Bismarck*'s steering and permitted British warships to intercept and sink her with gunfire.

Swordfish served on British carriers throughout the war, toward the end flying mainly from ESCORT CARRIERS to hunt U-boats. These planes were particularly valuable on the RUSSIAN CONVOYS and in the BATTLE OF THE ATLANTIC. Flying from an airfield in Belgium, a Swordfish attacked an offshore MIDGET SUBMARINE only three and a half hours before Germany's surrender.

The Swordfish was a biplane of great simplicity, having neither flaps nor variable-pitch propeller; it had a fixed landing gear, and a stall speed of about 60 mph. The aircraft was highly maneuverable. A twin-float version flew from catapults on British cruisers and battleships. Swordfish wings folded backward for shipboard stowage.

The prototype Swordfish first flew on April 17, 1934, the first production contract was awarded in April 1935, and the aircraft entered squadron service in 1936. The Fairey firm produced 692 aircraft; all Swordfish delivered from Dec. 1940 were produced at the Blackburn factory. A grand total of 2,391 aircraft were produced through Dec. 1944.

Maximum speed without torpedo was 139 mph; carrying a torpedo or BOMB load it could reach only 110 mph. Range was 545 miles with a torpedo and 1,030 miles in the reconnaissance role. The Swordfish could carry (externally) an 18-inch, 1,610-pound torpedo or three 500-pound bombs; the Mark II aircraft delivered in 1943–1944 had special provisions for eight ROCKETS to attack surfaced U-boats, while the Mark III, also put into service in 1943, had RADAR for detecting surfaced submarines and their periscopes. There was a single fixed .303-cal. Vickers machine gun firing forward and a second, flexible Vickers gun in the after cockpit. For bombing missions two crewmen were carried; for reconnaissance, three.

Officially the Swordfish was designated TSR for Torpedo-Spotter-Reconnaissance aircraft.

Symbol

Code name for the CASABLANCA CONFERENCE, Jan. 1942.

Syria

Capital: Damascus. pop. 2,800,000 (est. 1942). Ending a seventeen-year struggle for independence, the Syrian parliament in Dec. 1936 approved a French-Syrian treaty ending French rule. But the French legislature stalled, French-Turkey negotiations clouded Syria's future, and, with the outbreak of the EUROPEAN WAR in Sept. 1939, Syria was back where it had started. After the fall of France in June 1940 VICHY FRANCE, the collaborationist regime established by the victorious Germans, took over Syria.

As the British feared, Germany saw Syria as a potential Middle Eastern base. In May 1941 German warplanes flew from Syria on missions against the British in Iraq. A German-sponsored PROPAGANDA campaign stirred up Syrians against the British. On June 8, 1941, the British countered with a propaganda move of their own: Over Damascus and Syrian towns planes dropped tens of thousands of leaflets carrying a promise from FREE FRENCH Gen. Georges Catroux, a close associate of Gen. CHARLES DE GAULLE: "I come to . . . proclaim you free and independent—your state of independence and sovereignty will be guaranteed by treaty."

Simultaneously with the leaflet drop, from Palestine and from Iraq, which the British had recently occupied, came a British force of Australians, Indians, and about 6,000 FREE FRENCH troops. After some stiff resistance, the Vichy officers surrendered on July 12. When the British learned that some of their PRISONERS OF WAR had been shipped to Vichy France, for certain handing over to Germany, the British held the highest-ranking Vichy officers in Syria as hostages until the POWs were returned.

Most Vichy troops chose to return to France, but many of their officers stayed as a Free French government was set up in Syria. To answer Syrian objections, the Free French proclaimed Syrian independence, but not until July 1943 was an election held. The United States, the Soviet Union, and several Middle Eastern countries recognized Syria's independence in 1944.

A few days after the end of the war in Europe in May 1945 several hundred French troops disembarked at Beirut, Lebanon, ostensibly en route to the Far East. Rioting broke out in Syria and, to quell it, the French shelled the Syrian parliament and other buildings, killing about 350 people. (At the SAN FRANCISCO CONFERENCE that would found the UNITED NATIONS, Arab delegates shouted, "French war criminals!" At the first meeting of the UN Security Council Syria and Lebanon would complain that foreigners were in their countries without permission.)

De Gaulle charged that the British had fomented the rioting to get France out of its old colony. Finally, in April 1946 troops of both nations left Syria.

The chief architect of Japanese military aggression in the war was Hideki Tojo, prime minister from Oct. 1941 to July 1944. However, he was always subject to the supreme command, which forced his resignation after the U.S. invasion of the Mariana Islands. Here he reads a document during his trial for war crimes. *(U.S. Army)*

30th Assault Unit

British multiservice combat unit that collected intelligence on German forces during amphibious landings. The 30th Assault Unit (also known as No. 30 COMMANDO), organized in part by IAN FLEMING, came ashore with the first wave of Allied landing forces to seize German documents and equipment before they could be destroyed or lost. (The British had learned that in 1941 the Germans had a similar "intelligence commando" that had entered Athens with the first German troops and seized important documents from the abandoned British headquarters there; other, similar German units were known to exist.)

The 30th Assault Unit entered service at the time of the Anglo-American NORTH AFRICA INVASION in Nov. 1942. The unit subsequently participated in operations in Tunisia, SICILY, Italy, and elsewhere in the Mediterranean, capturing valuable documents as well as cipher, radio, and RADAR equipment and weapons. In Sicily the unit captured a complete set of Italian Air Force ciphers for homing beacons that enabled Allied planes to fly to targets in northern Italy guided by Italian navigation beacons.

The 30th Assault Unit returned to Britain in late 1943 to prepare for the NORMANDY landings in 1944. However, the British 15th ARMY GROUP requested the return of the army component of the unit to Italy for operations there. Thus, only the naval component participated in the Overlord landings. At Normandy the 30th Assault Unit landed with the 47th Royal Marine Commando on the morning of D-DAY to help capture and collect technical intelligence at a German coastal radar station.

T-34 Tank

One of the world's most advanced TANKS when it entered Soviet service in 1941. *Generalmajor* F. W. von Mellenthin, a German staff officer who served on all major fronts during World War II, including duty on the personal staff of *Generalfeldmarchall* ERWIN ROMMEL, wrote that the Soviets began the war "with the great advantage of possessing in the T-34 a model far superior to any tank on the German side . . . they then produced an improved model of the T-34. . . . The Russian tank designers understand their job thoroughly; they cut out refinements and concentrate on essentials—gun power, armor, and cross-country performance. During the war their system of [tank] suspension was well in advance of Germany and the West."

Soon after its introduction the T-34 became the principal Soviet tank on the EASTERN FRONT and over 53,000 were built in 1941–1945. The tank's 76-mm gun could pierce the armor of virtually all German tanks within the gun's effective range. Most of the German Army's antitank guns were unable to penetrate the T-34's armor. In the second half of 1943 the Soviet Army began to receive an upgraded T-34 armed with an 85-mm gun. Although with the larger gun the T-34's mass increased from 26½ to 32½ tons, the tank's mobility remained practically unchanged.

The tank was produced in the Soviet Union until 1948. Production continued in Eastern European countries until 1956. (Although the tank is no longer in Soviet service, several Eastern European, African, and Asian countries still use it.)

The T-34 had a combat weight of 26 to 30 tons (depending upon variant) and carried two 7.62-mm machine guns in addition to the 76-mm gun. The tank was manned by a crew of four.

Ta 152

The Focke-Wulf Ta 152 was the most advanced piston-engine fighter to see service with the Luftwaffe during the war. A development of the "longnose" FW 190D, the Ta 152 had a maximum speed of 463 mph with a service ceiling of over 40,000 feet. (The Ta 152H reached 472 mph at that altitude.) Armament of the sleek-looking aircraft was one 30-mm and four 20-mm cannon. Only sixty-seven of these planes were produced when the war ended.

Ta indicated the designer, Kurt Tank.

Taifun (Typhoon)

German code name for offensive against MOSCOW that began on Oct. 2, 1941.

Tables of Organization

Tables of Organization—documents invariably known as TOs—listed in detail the number of officers and enlisted men in a U.S. Army or Marine unit, their ranks, and their jobs. Tables of Organization and Equipment—called TO&Es—additionally listed the equipment in an Army or Marine unit: the guns, vehicles, radios, flashlights, desks, bunks, mess kits, canteens, and everything else issued to the unit.

The TO&Es addressed all units, from a field ARMY down to a SECTION or SQUAD. During the war, the documents were revised frequently to reflect the experience of battle, the availability of new weapons, and the formation of new types of units. Developed by the WAR DEPARTMENT and Headquarters Marine Corps, the TO&Es could be modified by field commanders to reflect local conditions and troop availability.

Takagi, Vice Adm. Takeo (1892–1944)

Commander of the Japanese carrier force in the May 1942 battle of the CORAL SEA. After the battle Takagi took his carriers *Shokaku* and *Zuikaku* back to Japan for repairs and to rehabilitate their devastated air groups. He thus was unable to participate with those ships in the battle of MIDWAY in early June. Earlier he had commanded a cruiser-destroyer force in the Philippines operation and the battle of the JAVA SEA in Feb. 1942.

Talisman

Code name for planned Allied AIRBORNE assault on BERLIN; changed to Eclipse.

Tallboy Bomb

Large conventional BOMB. This 12,000-pound bomb was second only to the 22,000-pound GRAND SLAM in the size of conventional bombs used in the war. Both were so-called "earthquake bombs," designed by Barnes Wallis of Vickers-Armstrong (Aircraft) to destroy subterranean targets such as bridge and viaduct foundations, with the bombs creating shock waves.

The Tallboy bombs were manufactured in both the United States and Britain, although they could be carried only by British LANCASTER four-engine bombers.

From June 1944 to April 1945 the Lancasters of RAF No. 9 and 617 SQUADRONS dropped 854 of the Tallboy bombs; their principal targets were SUBMARINE PENS and other protected naval structures (199 bombs), viaducts and bridges (160), and V-1 BUZZ BOMB and V-2 MISSILE sites (107). On Sept. 15, 1944, a raid by twenty-eight Lancasters (with fifteen Tallboys) against the German battleship *TIRPITZ* scored a damaging near-miss as the ship lay at anchor in a Norwegian fjord; she required major repairs before returning to sea. (The JOHNNY WALKER bombs dropped by seven of the Lancasters inflicted no damage on the ship.) On Nov. 12, 1944, another RAF strike was flown against the ship as she lay at anchor near Tromso, Norway. This time thirty-two Lancasters scored three direct hits and two near-misses with Tallboys, causing the ship to roll over and sink.

The Tallboy held 5,200 pounds of the explosive Torpex. The casing was 21 feet long with a maximum diameter of 38 inches.

Talon

Code name for British operations against Akyab, Burma, Dec. 1944.

Tank Destroyer

Lightly armored tank-type vehicle for fighting TANKS. The U.S. Army extensively used tank destroyers in the war, although most commanders preferred more versatile tanks. The tank destroyers—with open turret tops and thin side armor—were developed in response to German BLITZKRIEG tactics. U.S. Army supporters of the concept envi-sioned masses of these vehicles with high-velocity guns stopping German armor. Tank destroyer or "TD" BATTALIONS were organized and by late 1942 the U.S. Army had thirty-six such units, each with thirty-six guns, plus command, reconnaissance, and antiaircraft components.

About one half of the TD battalions had towed antitank guns while the other half had self-propelled TD vehicles: the M10 Wolverine with a 3-inch (76-mm) gun, the M18 Hellcat with a 76-mm gun, and the M36 with a 90-mm gun. The widely used M10 had an M4 SHERMAN tank chassis. It was a 29½-ton vehicle with a road speed of 26 mph. A single .50-cal. antiaircraft machine gun was fitted in addition to the 76-mm gun. The M10 had a crew of five.

Tanks

U.S. Army tanks, which lagged in development during the war, were almost always outgunned by their German counterparts. Tanks had their greatest success when used in large formations to break through front lines and overrun the enemy's rear forces. This capability led Gen. GEORGE S. PATTON to contend that a tank's principal weapon was its treads. The tank's mobility enabled attacking forces to exploit breakthroughs before an enemy could solidify secondary defensive lines. Tanks usually operated with infantry; on their own they were vulnerable to a variety of antitank weapons.

The United States was slow to deploy large numbers of tanks. On May 1, 1940—a few days before tanks spearheaded the German assault on France—the U.S. Army had 464 tanks, mainly light tanks of 9 to 11 tons armed with only .50-cal. machine guns; a few U.S. M2 medium tanks had a 37-mm cannon. At the time, the German Pzkw IV tank in wide use had a 75-mm gun.

The success of German armored formations led the U.S. WAR DEPARTMENT to order on July 10, 1940, the creation of an armored force consisting of the 1st and 2nd Armored DIVISIONS, which were activated on July 15, and the nondivisional 70th Tank BATTALION. An Armored Force School was established in Oct. 1940.

In further response to the events in Europe the U.S. Army's Ordnance Department rushed a 75-mm gun tank into production by adapting the T5 prototype medium tank to carry a 75-mm gun in a sponson on the right side; the tank's turret still had only a 37-mm gun. Produced as the M3 GRANT, this tank had limited capability but was invaluable to the British when it began to arrive in North Africa in large numbers in late 1941.

The Grant was a stopgap measure until the U.S. Army could develop and produce a tank with a 75-mm gun. Based on the T6 prototype, this was the M4 SHERMAN, which entered production in July 1942. It became the standard U.S. Army and Marine Corps tank and was used extensively in the North African, Pacific, and European theaters as well as by British and FREE FRENCH. It was, however, still outgunned by modern German tanks, especially the PANTHER and TIGER. (The British did put a larger, 76.2-mm long-barrel gun on some of their Shermans.)

Efforts by the Ordnance Department to develop a heavy tank were continuously retarded by the infantry and evenly armored forces, whose leaders perceived that the Army needed light or at best medium tanks that were fast and could easily accompany the infantry. Finally, in Feb. 1944 the Army Ground Forces recognized the shortcomings of the Sherman and insisted that the Ordnance Department mount a 76-mm long-barrel gun on a Sherman chassis; this compromise vehicle entered service in small numbers. The more capable M26 Pershing eventually entered service with a 90-mm gun. It was the first U.S. mass-produced heavy tank.

When the war ended the U.S. Army had sixteen armored divisions. Infantry divisions each had attached tank battalions as well as TANK DESTROYER battalions when required for specific operations. There were a maximum of sixty-five separate tank battalions at the end of 1944 (plus the fifty-four in the armored divisions) in addition to the tank destroyer battalions. Tank battalions generally had just over 700 men and fifty-three Sherman tanks and seventeen light tanks; toward the end of the war, several additional Shermans with 105-mm howitzers were assigned to each battalion. Thus, a 1943–1944 armored division (with three tank battalions) had 186 medium and fifty-four light tanks. This increased in 1945 to 195 medium plus the light tanks.

Marine divisions normally had one tank battalion assigned.

The Army's I Armored CORPS, established on July 15, 1940, was followed in 1942 by the II, III, and IV Armored Corps, each to consist of two armored divisions and one motorized infantry division. But by 1943 Army planners decided that armored forces had to be fully integrated with infantry, and by early 1944 the armored corps had been redesignated as standard corps.

In addition to tanks, U.S. armored units also had tank destroyers, which were tank-like vehicles with lighter armor and open-top gun turrets. These vehicles were a limited success, for a full-fledged tank was more capable of fighting other tanks and undertaking more roles than could a "TD."

The U.S. Marine Corps operated amphibious tanks, a type of "amtrac," during the war, designated LVT(A) for landing vehicle, tracked (armored). These were fully amphibious vehicles that could "swim" in from AMPHIBIOUS SHIPS with troop-carrying LVTs and crawl up onto the beach. The LVT(A)1 had a 37-mm gun in a turret and a single .30-cal. machine gun; the definitive LVT(A)4 had a short-barrel 75-mm howitzer mounted in an open-top turret, plus machine guns. (See AMPHIBIOUS TRACTORS.)

Only Britain, Germany, the Soviet Union, and the United States produced large numbers of medium and heavy tanks during the war. Of these, the German Panthers and Tigers, the Soviet T-34, and the U.S. Sherman were the most notable. The Japanese employed only light tanks.

The largest U.S. tank operations were in Europe. The German-Soviet tank battles near KURSK in 1943 were the largest tank engagements of the war.

Tanne Ost (Fir East)

German code word for landing on Suursaari Island in the Gulf of Finland, Oct. 1944.

Tanne West (Fir West)

German code name for a projected occupation of the Aland Islands in the Gulf of Bothnia, between Sweden and Finland.

Taranto

Port that was the main base of the Italian fleet and the site of the first major aircraft carrier strike in history. The British scheduled a raid on the fleet on Trafalgar Day, Oct. 21, 1940, but a fire on the new aircraft carrier *ILLUSTRIOUS* forced a postponement until Armistice Day, Nov. 11. Two carriers were to have taken part; damage to the *Eagle* withdrew her from the action.

On the night of Nov. 11, the attack was launched from a point 170 miles southeast of Taranto when twelve SWORDFISH from the *Illustrious* took off. Six Swordfish, carrying flares and bombs, illuminated the harbor and made a diversionary attack on cruisers, destroyers, and harbor facilities. The other Swordfish, carrying torpedoes, headed for six battleships. A single torpedo sank one battleship; two torpedoes holed another battleship and she went down, resting on the sea floor.

The second wave of Swordfish arrived forty minutes later, five of them carrying torpedoes. One of the previously hit battleships was torpedoed again and a third battleship was badly damaged.

The attack had been ordered by Adm. Sir AN-DREW B. CUNNINGHAM, Commander in Chief Mediterranean, who wanted to neutralize the Italian fleet, which could challenge Allied control of the Mediterranean. Italy had entered the European War on June 10, 1940. The fleet had mainly been screening ships carrying supplies to Italian forces in North Africa.

The attack on Taranto helped assure the British control of the Mediterranean by forcing the Italian fleet to withdraw to the west coast of Italy. One of the battleships would never see service again; the other two would be out of action until the spring of 1941.

The success of the British at Taranto inspired Adm. ISOROKU YAMAMOTO, Commander in Chief of the Japanese Combined Fleet, to conceive of an attack by aircraft carriers on PEARL HARBOR. According to DUSKO POPOV, a double agent (recruited as a spy by Germany but working for the British), the German air attaché in TOKYO had escorted Japanese naval officers to Taranto to get a firsthand understanding of the attack. The visit would have happened during the time the Japanese were planning to go to war with the United States.

Tarawa

Atoll in the GILBERT ISLANDS, about 12 miles wide and 18 miles long, taken during the U.S. CEN-TRAL PACIFIC CAMPAIGN. The battle for Tarawa was one of the bloodiest in the history of the U.S. Marine Corps.

Operation Galvanic began on Nov. 20, 1943, with the Army's 27th Infantry DIVISION making an AMPHIBIOUS LANDING on MAKIN Atoll, where CARLSON'S RAIDERS had staged a hit-and-run reconnaissance in Aug. 1942. The Army troops easily dealt with the small Japanese garrison on Makin, but the Marines would call the other atoll, 100 miles to the south, Bloody Tarawa.

The triangularly shaped Tarawa atoll of islands and reefs had a fortress on Betio Island, three miles long and 600 miles wide, in the southwest corner. Betio, site of an airfield, was the target of the main landing on Nov. 20 by Marines of the 2nd Division. Many headed for shore in "amtracs," AMPHIBIOUS TRACTORS, tracked vehicles with little armor.

Across 3½ miles of choppy seas the landing craft bobbed, shielded by a covey of minesweepers and under fire from shore guns. Smoke and coral dust raised by the heavy preinvasion bombardment obscured the command ship's view of the landing craft fleet. Fire was halted for thirty minutes to allow the smoke to clear. This allowed the Japanese to regroup and brace for the assault.

The landing craft came in at extremely low tide, and some of the craft had to stop and unload the Marines half a mile from shore. They began wading ashore in red-stained surf, where many died. Others, trapped in barbed wire strung in shallow water, were cut down by murderous fire. The director of the assault, Col. David M. Shoup, stood in waist-deep water, wounded in the leg, directing the attack. When he made it to the beach, he tried to establish a command post at an apparently unoccupied bunker. It was occupied, and had to be subdued. For his gallantry at Tarawa Shoup would get the MEDAL OF HONOR and would survive to become Marine Commandant. The other three Medals of Honor for gallantry at Tarawa would be awarded posthumously.

The survivors of the landing huddled on the beach, hemmed in by surf and a coconut-log seawall about four feet high. They expected a nighttime BANZAI charge that luckily did not come.

At 6:15 the next morning more Marines came ashore, wading into the same merciless fire that had cut down their comrades. The Marines managed to get tanks and howitzers ashore and, using FLAME THROWERS, TNT charges, and GRENADES, breach the shore defenses and fight their way inland, where defenses were thin. By the end of the second day, Shoup declared, "We are winning."

By the fourth day Tarawa was in American hands, at a great cost. The Marines suffered nearly 3,000 casualties, including 984 dead; total American casualties in the assault were 1,027 dead and some 3,300 wounded. Almost the entire 4,836-man garrison of defenders was wiped out. Only seventeen wounded Japanese and 129 Korean laborers survived.

Tarzan

Code name for projected Allied advance in Indaw-Katha area of Burma, 1944.

Task Force

Tactical organization used by U.S. Army and Navy. Army task forces were organized on a temporary basis, usually combining different types of forces. Some were designated "provisional" and were often designated by the name of their commanding officer.

Navy task forces, organized for specific types of operations, were semipermanent. Their designations were based on fleet assignment; thus, TF 38, for example, was the carrier striking force of the Third FLEET (with subordinate task groups designated as 38.1, 38.2, etc., and task units 38.1.1, 38.1.2, etc.).

Taubenschlag (Dovecote)

German code name for projected attacks against Toropets in the Soviet Union, Oct. 1942.

Tautog (SS 199)

U.S. SUBMARINE that sunk the most enemy ships during the war—twenty-five. (The U.S. submarine credited with sinking the most *tonnage* was the *FLASHER* [SS 249].)

The *Tautog* began her first war patrol out of PEARL HARBOR on Oct. 21, 1941, operating in the area off MIDWAY for forty-five days as a picket against possible Japanese operations in the area. She returned to Pearl Harbor on Dec. 5, and two days later her gunners were among the first to go into action when Japanese planes attacked the U.S. naval base.

The day after the attack the *Tautog* left for a war patrol in the MARSHALL ISLANDS, gathering intelligence. No enemy ships were encountered. On May 17, 1942, on her third war patrol, she sank her first enemy ship, the Japanese submarine *I-28*. Encountering the surfaced I-boat near RABAUL, the *Tautog* fired two TORPEDOES, one of which hit. A third "fish" was fired to finish off the large submarine.

Operating from Fremantle, Australia, as well as Pearl Harbor, the *Tautog* carried out twelve wartime patrols, completing the last in Feb. 1945. Her total score of Japanese ships sunk was two destroyers, one submarine, one landing ship, one small submarine chaser, one tender, and nineteen merchant ships for a total of 71,641 tons; she also carried out a minelaying mission off Borneo and landed agents on Kabaena Island. Her record earned the submarine fourteen BATTLE STARS and a Navy Unit Commendation. (The *Tautog* was also credited with having sunk the medium-size Japanese submarine *RO-30* in April 1942, but that craft is known to have survived the war.)

The *Tautog* then operated for several months off the U.S. West Coast testing new submarine equipment. After being decommissioned in Dec. 1945, she was employed briefly in 1947 as a training submarine and then as a stationary training ship at Milwaukee, Wisc., until stricken in 1959 and sold for scrap.

The *Tautog* was built by the Electric Boat Co., in Groton, Conn. She was a "T"-class submarine, launched on Jan. 27, 1940, and placed in commission that July. With a surface displacement of 1,475 tons and submerged displacement of 2,370 tons, the *Tautog* was 307 1/6 feet long. The submarine was armed with ten 21-inch (533-mm) torpedo tubes—six bow and four stern, and had a single 3-inch (76-mm) deck gun plus machine guns. She was manned by a crew of sixty-five.

Taylor, Maj. Gen. Maxwell D. (1901–1987)

Leading U.S. AIRBORNE commander who undertook a secret mission into ROME for Gen. DWIGHT D. EISENHOWER. After graduating from the Military Academy in 1922 he briefly served as an engineer before entering the ARTILLERY branch. In the

1930s he was sent to TOKYO to study Japanese and then was assigned as assistant military attaché in Peking to observe the Sino-Japanese conflict.

At the time of United States entry into World War II he was on duty in WASHINGTON. In 1942 he was ordered to help form the 82nd Airborne DIVISION and then commanded the division's artillery REGIMENT in the SICILY and Italian mainland operations.

In Sept. 1943, having taken command of the 82nd Airborne Division, Brig. Gen. Taylor was sent on a secret mission into Rome to contact the Italian resistance leaders to determine the feasibility of Allied troops parachuting onto the airfields around the city. He and an AAF officer landed in Italy by a war ship and met with Marshal PIETRO BADOGLIO and other Italian leaders. The American officers found that German presence in the city was greater than expected and the proposed airborne assault was not carried out.

Gen. Eisenhower would write in *Crusade in Europe* that the risks run by Taylor "were greater than I asked any other agent or emissary to undertake during the war—he carried weighty responsibilities and discharged them with unerring judgment and every minute was in imminent danger of discovery and death."

Taylor was then ordered to England to take command of the 101st Airborne Division, which he led in the NORMANDY INVASION, parachuting into France on the morning of June 6, 1944. He also led the division in Operation MARKET-GARDEN into northern Holland in Sept. 1944.

A month later the 101st was caught by the German attack in the ARDENNES, and was surrounded in the battle of the Bulge. Taylor was in the United States at the time. He returned to France in time to participate in the battle.

After the war he served as superintendent of West Point, was U.S. military governor of BERLIN, commanded the Eighth ARMY in Korea, and later all U.S. forces in the Far East. He retired after serving as Chief of Staff of the Army from 1955 to 1959. After Taylor wrote the controversial *Uncertain Trumpet*, President Kennedy appointed him Chairman of the JOINT CHIEFS OF STAFF (1962–1964) and then U.S. ambassador to South Vietnam (1964–1965).

Taylor, Brig. Gen. Telford (1908—)

U.S. chief prosecutor on the international military tribunal that tried NAZIS at Nuremberg for WAR CRIMES. Trained as a lawyer, during the war Taylor worked, as an Army colonel, at BLETCHLEY PARK, the ULTRA code-breaking establishment. After the war, at the request of Justice ROBERT H. JACKSON, first chief U.S. counsel at the trials, Taylor was assigned to the prosecution.

Taylor succeeded Jackson, who returned to his Supreme Court bench after serving as prosecutor at the first of the thirteen Nuremberg trials. The first trial was quadripartite, with judges and prosecutors from the United States, France, England, and the Soviet Union.

Taylor was chief prosecutor at twelve trials before American judges and prosecutors. The other countries had trials in their own occupation zones. Taylor's trials included the DOCTORS TRIAL of physicians accused of barbarous experiments.

TB-3,

see ANT-6.

TBD Devastator

The U.S. Navy's carrier-based TORPEDO bomber when America entered the war. In Dec. 1941 four of the Navy's seven large AIRCRAFT CARRIERS embarked eighteen TBDs in their seventy-two-plane air groups and one carrier had eight planes (later increased).

After limited success against Japanese ships in the early Pacific raids and in the battle of CORAL SEA, the TBDs proved ineffective against Japanese carriers at MIDWAY in June 1942 and were promptly retired in favor of the new TBF AVENGER.

In the Coral Sea battle on May 7, 1942, the U.S. carriers *LEXINGTON* (CV 2) and *Yorktown* (CV 5) sent twenty-two TBDs as well as a large number of dive bombers and fighters to attack a Japanese task force. The planes fell on the hapless Japanese light carrier *SHOHO*, smothering her with thirteen bombs from the dive bombers and seven torpedoes from the TBDs. This was the first Japanese carrier to be sunk in the war. However, later that day another U.S. carrier strike force—which included twenty-one TBDs—attacked two larger Japanese carriers.

Although the SBD DAUNTLESS dive bombers inflicted some damage on the two ships, no torpedoes from the TBDs scored hits.

The following month, at the battle of Midway, the aircraft carriers *Yorktown*, ENTERPRISE (CV 6), and *HORNET* (CV 8) launched their forty-one TBDs against the Japanese carrier force on the morning of June 4. The torpedo planes attacked the Japanese forces before the U.S. dive bombers and fighters arrived on the scene, permitting the defending Japanese fighters and shipboard gunners to concentrate their fire on the hapless torpedo planes; thirty-nine were shot down. Not one torpedo from the forty-one planes struck the Japanese carriers. (Four Japanese carriers were sunk by Navy dive bombers.)

The Douglas-built TBD first flew on April 15, 1935, and reached Navy squadrons in late 1937. A total of 130 aircraft were produced through 1939. One was test-flown with twin floats (as were several other carrier planes of the period). The last TBD was withdrawn from service in Aug. 1942.

The TBD was a single-engine, monoplane aircraft with a large "greenhouse" canopy. The wings folded upward for carrier stowage. The aircraft had a top speed of 206 mph, and a range of 715 miles with a 1,000-pound BOMB. An aerial torpedo could be carried under the fuselage. There was a single .30-cal. fixed gun firing forward and a flexible .30-cal. gun in the dorsal position. The plane was flown by a pilot, navigator/bombardier, and gunner.

TBF/TBM Avenger

The principal U.S. Navy TORPEDO plane of the war. The TBF/TBM Avenger arrived in the fleet too late for the carrier battles of CORAL SEA and MIDWAY, and in the subsequent carrier actions in the SOLOMON ISLANDS, MARIANAS, and LEYTE GULF the major damage was inflicted on Japanese ships by carrier-based dive bombers. Still, the Avenger—the U.S. Navy's only carrier-based torpedo bomber from late 1942—proved highly effective against Japanese merchant shipping in the Pacific and against German U-BOATS in the Atlantic. The U.S. Marine Corps also flew the Avenger from escort carriers for close air support during AMPHIBIOUS LANDINGS.

The TBF-1 first saw action at Midway when, on June 4, 1942, six planes took off from the island to attack Japanese carriers; only one returned, heavily damaged. The avengers scored no hits on the Japanese carriers.

The TBF/TBM was a chunky, single-engine, mid-wing aircraft with a tall-tail configuration. The aircraft had a long cockpit ending in a power turret with a single .50-cal. machine gun. Aft of the bomb bay was a tunnel gun and camera position with a .30-cal. gun manned by the radio operator-photographer. The Avenger was unusual among the torpedo planes with an internal bomb bay for carrying its torpedo. When flying antisubmarine patrols, the Avengers generally carried four DEPTH CHARGES or a 500-pound BOMB (for attacking surfaced submarines) and a FIDO homing torpedo (for submerged targets). Later aircraft could also carry ROCKETS under their wings for attacking U-boats on the surface.

Grumman Aircraft Co. received a contract to produce two prototype XTBF-1 torpedo planes in April 1940; the first flight was on Aug. 1, 1941, with the first production aircraft delivered to the Navy in Jan. 1942. To meet the growing requirements for torpedo aircraft aboard the large number of carriers being built, in March 1942 the Eastern Aircraft Division of General Motors received a contract to produce the Avenger with the designation TBM. Various improvements were made during the war in engines and a wing-mounted RADAR pod was provided to some variants. Near the end of the war a few TBM-3W variants were fitted with the large AN/APS-20 air search radar, while the TBM-3S was a specialized antisubmarine aircraft.

In all, Grumman produced 2,293 TBF variants and Eastern 7,546 TBM aircraft. Britain received 921 planes (initially called Tarpon) and New Zealand another sixty-three. After the war Avengers were flown by several other nations. They remained in U.S. naval service in various roles until 1954. Postwar variants included the TBM-3R cargo version, which could deliver mail and spare parts, as well as nuclear components for ATOMIC BOMBS to aircraft carriers.

All Avengers had a three-man crew. The TBF-1C had a maximum speed of 257 mph and a cruise speed of 153 mph. Range with a torpedo was 1,100 miles and as a scout with additional fuel tanks 2,335 miles. Maximum bomb load was 2,000 pounds. In addition to the .50-cal. gun in the turret and the .30-cal. tunnel gun, the aircraft had one or two cowling-mounted .50-cal. guns.

Ted

Code name for Allied task force in the Aitape area, NEW GUINEA.

Tedder, Air Chief Marshal Arthur (1890–1967)

From Dec. 1943 to the end of the EUROPEAN WAR, Air Chief Marshal Arthur Tedder served as deputy supreme commander under Gen. DWIGHT D. EISENHOWER. Tedder was highly regarded for his intelligence, devotion to a joint Anglo-American strategy, and receptiveness to new ideas and tools.

Tedder was second in command to Air Marshal Arthur Longmore during Greek and CRETE operations in April and May 1941, replacing Longmore as commander of the RAF's Middle Eastern Air Force in mid-1941. He improved the flexibility and effectiveness of RAF close-air support of ground troops during the NORTHWEST AFRICA CAMPAIGN by insisting that operational control of air units remain with the air commander. This arrangement avoided tying any air element too closely to a particular ground unit. He also devised a "pattern bombing" tactic that is credited with helping Gen. BERNARD MONTGOMERY win the second battle of EL ALAMEIN.

In late Feb. 1943 Tedder became commander of all Allied Air Forces in the Mediterranean and immediately established a reputation for air-ground "team play" during the invasion of SICILY in July 1943 and the invasion of Italy in Sept. 1943. His tactical air support innovations were soon doctrine throughout the Allied Air Forces.

As deputy supreme commander and chief air leader of the NORMANDY INVASION, Tedder won approval to direct strategic bombing forces against the French transportation network on March 25, 1944, as a prelude to the Normandy invasion. The transportation-bombing campaign is credited with isolating Normandy from the rest of France and frustrating German reinforcement efforts.

Throughout the ALLIED CAMPAIGN IN EUROPE Tedder maintained his intimate working relationship with Eisenhower, winning him high praise from most British and American military leaders.

Tedder, representing Eisenhower, signed the May 9, 1945, formal ratification of Germany's SURRENDER in BERLIN. Tedder later served as chief of air staff in the postwar RAF and was knighted, becoming 1st Baron Tedder.

Tehran Conference

Meeting of President ROOSEVELT, Prime Minister CHURCHILL, and Soviet leader STALIN. Roosevelt and Churchill went to Tehran, Iran, from the CAIRO CONFERENCE to meet, for the first time, with Stalin and plan the invasion of Europe. The four-day conference began on Nov. 28, 1943. Publicly, the BIG THREE (as the leaders were called in newspapers) recognized "the assistance which Iran has given in the prosecution of the war" and promised the reward of economic aid during and after the war. They also agreed to give military aid to TITO in Yugoslavia.

"We leave here friends in fact, in spirit, and in purpose," the leaders said after the conference, although Roosevelt and Churchill were already well aware that Stalin would not be a postwar friend. Secretly, the three leaders signed an agreement to go to war against Bulgaria if that country attacked Turkey. Stalin also secretly promised to go to war against Japan after the defeat of Germany.

Telegraph

Code name for Gen. WALTER BEDELL SMITH.

Teller, Edward (1908—)

U.S. physicist and one of the builders of the ATOMIC BOMB. Teller was at Göttingen University in the company of a band of distinguished physicists in April 1933 when HITLER proclaimed the first of the NAZI racial laws. Like many of the physicists in Germany, Teller was a JEW. And, besides being targeted by ANTI-SEMITISM advocates, Teller, Hungarian-born, was not even a German citizen. He left for England and eventually the United States.

Teller was part of the team assembled by J. ROBERT OPPENHEIMER at LOS ALAMOS, the laboratory in New Mexico where the bomb was developed and built. Teller focused on the plutonium-core version, Fat Man, dropped on NAGASAKI. Even while the atomic bomb was being developed, Teller championed a new weapon: the hydrogen (thermonuclear) bomb, a much more powerful weapon.

The hydrogen bomb's energy is measured in megatons, equivalents of millions of tons of TNT, compared to the kiloton, thousands of tons of TNT used to calculate atomic bomb blasts. Teller called it the Super.

Teller, angered at Oppenheimer's wartime disinterest in the Super, kept lobbying for it, evolving from a relatively unknown physicist to a zealous advocate for a weapon that could help the United States in the Cold War. When President TRUMAN on Sept. 23, 1949, announced that the Soviets had exploded the first hydrogen bomb, Teller led the campaign to build the Super.

Largely because of his efforts, the hydrogen bomb was built. The first one was exploded in 1952. Teller became popularly known as the "father of the H-bomb."

Tempest

A development of the TYPHOON high-performance fighter, the Tempest was the most advanced British piston-engine fighter to see combat in the war. The name Tempest was adopted by the Hawker firm to avoid confusion with other advanced fighter projects. The first production model was the Mk V, which entered RAF service in Jan. 1944. The aircraft was employed primarily in "train busting" operations over German-controlled Europe and in intercepting V-1 BUZZ BOMBS over England. From June to Sept. 1944 Tempests destroyed 638 V-1s. Subsequently, in aerial combat over Europe, Tempests destroyed twenty ME 262 turbojet fighters.

A series of Tempest prototypes fitted with different engines flew during 1942–1943, with the Mk V fitted with the Napier Sabre IIB in-line engine selected for service. The first of 805 of these aircraft were delivered before the end of the war, with production of more advanced models continuing after the conflict.

The Tempest generally resembled the low-wing Typhoon, but had a "bubble" cockpit providing the pilot with increased visibility. Top speed was 435 mph with a range of 1,530 miles. Four 20-mm cannon were fitted and for ground attack the aircraft could carry two 1,000-pound BOMBS or eight large ROCKETS.

Tennant, Vice Adm. William (1890–1963)

Naval officer who directed the evacuation of British troops from DUNKIRK and commanded the battle cruiser *REPULSE* when she was sunk by Japanese bombers.

A lieutenant in a cruiser at the Battle of Jutland in 1916, Tennant was a captain and was appointed senior naval officer Dunkirk in May 1940. He was expected to facilitate the evacuation of some 45,000 troops from the French port. Instead, under Tennant's direction, naval and civilian ships and craft brought out 338,226 British and French troops.

Official British military dispatches noted that on the night of June 2–3, Tennant "toured the beaches and the harbors in a motorboat, and, being satisfied that no British troops were left ashore . . . ," returned to England.

After Dunkirk, he was given command of the *Repulse.* He told his crew, "We are off to look for trouble. I expect we shall find it." The *Repulse* and the battleship *PRINCE OF WALES* were sent to SINGAPORE. On Dec. 10, 1941, the two warships were sunk off Malaya by Japanese planes. Tennant refused to leave the ship but was pushed into the sea by some of his officers.

After Tennant gave a firsthand account of the disaster to King GEORGE VI, he was promoted to rear admiral. He subsequently commanded a cruiser squadron and was commander of the 1943 invasion of MADAGASCAR. He then directed the construction of the ARTIFICIAL HARBORS for the NORMANDY INVASION.

After the Normandy landings, Tennant was made British naval commander for the Levant and eastern Mediterranean. After the war he commanded the British West Indies squadron. He was knighted in 1948 and promoted to admiral; he retired in 1949.

Terminal

Code name for Allied conference at Potsdam, Germany, July–Aug. 1945.

Texan,
> see AT-6.

Thach, Capt. John S. (1905—)

"Jimmy" Thach was an innovative U.S. Navy fighter pilot. After brief service in BATTLESHIPS in 1929–1930, he became a carrier fighter pilot. During the 1930s he served in a variety of aviation units and in the summer of 1939, while assigned to the AIRCRAFT CARRIER *SARATOGA* (CV 3), he developed the fighter maneuver known as the "Thach weave," a two-plane defensive tactic that became the standard for U.S. Navy and Army fighter pilots in the Pacific War.

After the *Saratoga* was damaged by a Japanese TORPEDO in early 1942 Thach, in command of Fighting Squadron (VF) 3, went aboard the carrier *LEXINGTON* (CV 2). One of VF-3's pilots, Lt. EDWARD O'HARE, became the first U.S. fighter ACE of the war during operations in the western Pacific.

After the "Lex" was sunk in May 1942, VF-3 was shifted to the carrier *Yorktown* (CV 5), from which Thach flew in the Battle of MIDWAY. Thach himself shot down six Japanese A6M ZERO fighters in the battle to qualify as an ace. After the *Yorktown* was sunk at Midway he spent the next two years training fighter pilots in the United States.

Thach went back to sea in mid-1944 as the air operations officer and principal tactical adviser to Vice Adm. JOHN S. MCCAIN, the fast carrier commander in the Philippines and LEYTE GULF operations. Promoted to captain in March 1945, immediately after the war Thach returned to a training assignment. He subsequently commanded aircraft carriers, served as the navy's senior aviator in 1963–1965, and as a full admiral, served as CinC U.S. Naval Forces in Europe before retiring in 1967.

Thailand (Siam)

Capital: Bangkok, pop. 14,976,000 (1938). In 1936, responding to a surge of nationalism, the constitutional monarchy of Siam abrogated its treaties with the United States and other nations and proclaimed independence from any foreign interference in its affairs; new treaties establishing this principle were signed in 1937. Two years later, the government announced that Siam was to be known as Thailand ("Land of the Free"), but most of the world continued to call the nation Siam.

When the EUROPEAN WAR began in Sept. 1939, Thailand declared its neutrality. France and England, whose colonial territories surrounded Thailand, hoped that it would remain a buffer state against Japan. But other countries had reason to worry about Thailand's growing friendship with Japan. China especially wondered after examining new Thai schoolbooks that showed "Greater Thailand" encompassing several Chinese provinces.

After the fall of France in June 1940, the Thai pressed the German collaborationist government of VICHY FRANCE for border changes with French INDOCHINA. When Vichy refused, Thai troops crossed the border and skirmished with French forces. Japan mediated the dispute, which ended with Vichy France ceding about 21,000 square miles to Thailand. (Later, German pressure on Vichy resulted in a Japanese takeover of Indochina.)

On Dec. 8, 1941, Japan followed its declaration of war on the United States and England by an AMPHIBIOUS LANDING on the coast of Thailand, with the connivance of Prime Minister Lang Pipul. The troops then passed through Thailand for the invasion of British Malaya. Pipul, a former field marshal, embraced Japanese policy, declaring war on the United States and England on Jan. 25, 1942, and recognizing the Japanese puppet government in China. In Oct. 1942 Pipul suspended the Parliament and became a dictator controlled by the Japanese occupation authorities.

The Japanese used about 250,000 Asians and 61,000 Allied PRISONERS OF WAR—most of them Australian and British—to build, by hand, a 265-mile military railway along the River Kwae Noi (Kwai) into Burma from Thailand. The merciless treatment of the prisoners building the "Railway of Death" was dramatized in Pierre Boulle's novel *The Bridge over the River Kwai* and in the movie *The Bridge on the River Kwai*. Beatings, malnutrition, and lack of medical care killed 12,568 of the prisoners and about 87,500 Asians.

As a reward for cooperation, Japan ceded to Thailand four northern Malayan states and territory from Burma, a total of about 30,000 square miles. But Japan, beset by a widespread GUERRILLA movement, inflicted a harsh occupation. The puppet government did whatever the Japanese ordered—from trying to outlaw the old Thai habit of betel-chewing to changing the constitution to accommodate totalitarianism.

After Japan's surrender in Aug. 1945 Thailand swiftly nullified its 1942 declaration of war against the ALLIES. But peace-treaty negotiations with England and France continued until 1946, when Thailand gave back all territory acquired during the war and was rewarded with membership in the UNITED NATIONS.

Theaters,
see UNIFIED COMMANDS.

Third Front
Term used by Prime Minister CHURCHILL in Nov. 1943 for the ITALIAN CAMPAIGN, as it tied down some twenty German divisions and prevented their use against the Soviet Union.

Third Reich
HITLER's name for what he saw as a new German empire. *Reich,* the German word for kingdom, was used by Hitler to symbolize his new Germany. When he became chancellor in 1933, Hitler proclaimed the birth of the Third Reich and said it would last for 1,000 years. He saw his Reich following two others in a German historical theory that held Germany's unity evolved from two Reichs. The First Reich was the Holy Roman Empire of the German Nations—European tribes united with the Franks by Charlemagne in the ninth century. For the next ten centuries Germanic peoples lived in kingdoms and duchies under an emperor.

The rise of Prussia and the defeat of France in the war of 1870–1871 led to the unification of German states under Otto von Bismarck, "iron chancellor" of the Second Reich, which lasted until Germany's defeat in World War I. The term Reich went into eclipse under the WEIMAR REPUBLIC. Revived by Hitler, Reich symbolized the NAZI vision of Germany as an empire that would conquer Europe.

Thompson Submachine Gun
Submachine gun popularly known as the "Tommy Gun." The Thompson was used by Ameri-

can gangsters and FBI G-men in the 1920s and 1930s, and by U.S. soldiers, sailors, and Marines in World War II. It first proved its lethality at short range when used by U.S. Marines in Nicaragua in 1926. The Thompson was the world's only widely used submachine gun until 1941 when Britain began producing the STEN gun. However, that weapon, of welded-steel construction, lacked the "tough guy" image, aesthetic lines, and punch of the Thompson. (The U.S. services also used the M3 GREASE GUN during the war.)

Originally designated the M1928 and later the M1 submachine gun, the Thompson was a .45-cal., delayed-blowback weapon capable of selective fire. It weighed 12.1 pounds with a 20-round magazine, and could be used with 20-, 30-, and 50-round magazines; the smaller magazines were in clip form and the 50-round magazine was a drum. Effective range was about 600 yards with a rate of fire up to 100 rounds per minute on full automatic.

Despite its weight, the Thompson was popular throughout the war, being used especially by AIRBORNE troops and COMMANDOS. In July 1943 a U.S. airborne division was authorized 383 Thompsons.

Its inventor was Col. John Taliaferro Thompson (1860–1940). A West Point graduate, Thompson served in the U.S. Army's Ordnance Department from 1890 to 1914, when he retired. World War I brought him out of retirement and in 1920 he invented the "Tommy gun."

Thousand-Plane Raids
Attacks by more than a thousand Allied bombers in a single raid. The first thousand-plane raid of World War II, on May 30–31, 1942, was carried out by the RAF Bomber Command against the German city of COLOGNE. During the three-hour night raid, 1,455 tons of bombs were dropped by 1,158 bombers, destroying more than 600 acres of the city including an estimated 13,000 houses. The Germans reported 469 dead in the raid with more than 4,000 injured. The British lost forty bombers during this first major attack in a campaign to destroy German industry with "area bombing" rather than PRECISION BOMBING.

Other thousand-plane raids were launched in May and June 1942 against ESSEN and BREMEN.

These were the first unqualified successes of heavy bombers in World War II. Although massive Allied bombing raids would continue over Germany, thousand-plane missions would not be resumed for nearly three years.

Thruster

Code name for proposed Allied expedition against the Azores, 1942.

Thunderbolt,

see P-47.

Thunderbolt (Operation)

Code name for Allied offensive near Metz France.

Thunderclap

Code name for RAF attack plan to destroy German morale; executed in a modified form against DRESDEN; Feb. 13–14, 1945.

Thursday

Code name for second CHINDIT operation in Burma, 1944.

Thwart

Code name for British submarine *Seawolf* landing agents on the Norwegian coast, July 1940.

Tibbets, Col. Paul W., Jr. (1915—)

Pilot of the first aircraft to drop an ATOMIC BOMB on Japan. After flying antisubmarine patrols along the East Coast of the United States, Tibbets was assigned to the Eighth AIR FORCE in England flying B-17 FLYING FORTRESS bombers. He flew on the first U.S. air strike against German-occupied Europe (see ROUEN) and subsequently saw combat in North Africa before returning to the United States in 1943 to make the transition to the B-29 SUPERFORTRESS bomber.

Late that year he was chosen to command the 509TH COMPOSITE GROUP that would deliver atomic bombs against Japan. After training at remote Wendover Field in Utah, the group deployed from the United States to TINIAN in May–June 1945. The 509th flew training flights from Tinian and during July the unit flew twelve strikes with special high-explosive bombs against Japan. (See PUMPKIN BOMBS.) On Aug. 6, 1945, Tibbets piloted the B-29 "Enola Gay" in the attack on HIROSHIMA.

A postwar movie reenactment of the Hiroshima bombing had Tibbets saying: "My God, what have we done?" Tibbets, in his book *Mission: Hiroshima,* said, "I'm sure those dramatic words were not spoken. . . . [W]e were certainly aware that thousands of people were dying at that moment on the ground below. It is not easy for a soldier to be detached from the misery he has created. . . . Let it be understood that I feel a sense of shame for the whole human race. . . ."

Tidal Wave

Code name for U.S. AAF bombing raid against the German petroleum center of PLOESTI, Rumania, on Aug. 1, 1943.

Tiger

(1) Anglo-American AMPHIBIOUS LANDING exercise off SLAPTON SANDS, England, in preparation for the NORMANDY INVASION, April 1944; (2) British code name for sailing five fast merchant ships from GIBRALTAR to Alexandria in May 1941 to deliver TANKS and HURRICANE fighters to the Middle East; the CONVOY was attacked by German aircraft, but the only loss was to a MINE.

Tiger Moth

Basic trainer for the RAF and Commonwealth air forces. Entering service with the RAF in 1932, the Tiger Moth was flown in large numbers through the war. More than 1,000 were in RAF service when the EUROPEAN WAR began in Sept. 1939. The plane was also flown by the Royal Navy, several Commonwealth nations, and the U.S. Army (as the PT-24).

The de Havilland–designed Tiger Moth first flew in Oct. 1931 and soon went into production. Production in Britain totaled 4,200 with almost 3,000 more built in Australia, Canada, and New Zealand. In addition, another 420 were built as "Queen Bee" radio-controlled targets. It remained in service as an RAF trainer until 1947 and flew for several more years in other countries.

The biplane Tiger Moth had a fixed landing gear and in-line engine; the instructor and student sat in open cockpits.

Top speed was 109 mph for the Tiger Moth II (improved engine) with a range of 300 miles and a three-hour flight endurance.

Tiger Tank

The most advanced tank used during the war by the German Army. Officially designated PzKw *(Panzerkampfwagen)* VI, the 55-ton tank was rushed into service in 1943 as a response to the Soviet T-34 tank as well as the heavier Soviet JS and KV tanks. Only limited numbers of Tigers were available during the war, but in 1944–1945 American soldiers tended to refer to almost any German tank as a Tiger.

The Tiger was armed with the highly effective German 88-mm cannon making it deadly as an antitank weapon. The Tiger had heavy frontal armor, which could defeat most Allied antitank guns, but was relatively vulnerable from other aspects. In one documented engagement, a Tiger survived fourteen hits from the "short" (low-velocity) 75-mm gun of a U.S. SHERMAN TANK. However, Tigers suffered major engine problems.

The Tiger had a maximum speed of only 23½ mph with a highway range of about 60 miles. It was operated by a five-man crew. In production through Aug. 1944, a total of 1,350 of these Tiger Is were delivered to the German Army.

An improved Tiger II or "King Tiger," weighing 70 tons, was introduced in 1944. This was the heaviest operational tank produced by any nation during the war. Although heavily armored—still mounting the 88-mm gun—the Tiger II had limited mobility and was mechanically unreliable. Its speed was similar to the Tiger, with a slightly greater range. Production totaled 485 tanks.

A Tiger-Maus or "Lion" tank was designed as a 70-ton successor to the Tiger II. However, it did not proceed beyond the design stage. This tank was to have had a 150-mm gun.

Tigercat,
see F7F.

Tindal

Allied code name for deception operations against German forces in Norway, 1943.

Tinian

One of the JAPANESE MANDATED ISLANDS and a target in the battle of the MARIANAS. After the conquest of SAIPAN in early July 1944, on July 24 U.S. Marines attacked the smaller island of Tinian, another prospective site for airfields from which B-29 SUPERFORTRESS bombers could fly to attack Japan.

In the face of intense Japanese fire and fierce BANZAI charges, the Marines continued the assault, killing more than 1,000 Japanese defenders. At dawn the next day, more than 40,000 additional Marines came ashore. By Aug. 12 the last pockets of Japanese had been wiped out and Tinian was secured. Marines counted 317 dead, 1,550 wounded, twenty-seven missing. The Japanese lost nearly 5,000 men.

Tinian, about 1,450 air miles from Tokyo, was chosen over GUAM (100 miles farther away) as the airfield from which the ATOMIC BOMB missions would be flown. The 509TH COMPOSITE GROUP, the B-29 force that would deliver the bombs, began arriving on Tinian in June 1945. Navy SEABEES built six runways, each nearly 2 miles long and the width of a 10-lane highway, giving little Tinian the largest airport in the world.

Tirpitz

One of the two largest warships built by Germany, being a near sister ship of the battleship *BISMARCK*. Unlike her sister ship, however, the *Tirpitz* never fired her heavy guns in anger against an enemy ship.

Commissioned in Feb. 1941, the *Tirpitz* spent almost a year working up to battle efficiency in the Baltic Sea. On Jan. 12, 1942, HITLER gave the naval staff his permission to base the *Tirpitz* in Norway to attack the RUSSIAN CONVOYS traveling from Iceland to Soviet ports in the Arctic. Hitler also perceived (incorrectly) that the British would eventually invade Norway and he saw the stationing of capital ships there as a deterrent.

The impact of the *Tirpitz* was considerable:

Prime Minister CHURCHILL wrote to the Chiefs of Staff Committee on Jan. 25, "The destruction or even crippling of this ship is the greatest event at sea at the present time. No other target is comparable to it. If she were even only crippled it would be difficult to take her back to Germany. . . . The entire naval situation throughout the world would be altered, and the naval command in the Pacific would be regained. . . . The whole strategy of the war turns at this period on this ship, which is holding four times the number of British capital ships paralysed, to say nothing of the two new American BATTLE-SHIPS retained in the Atlantic."

Beginning on the night of Jan. 29–30, 1942, with a raid by sixteen HALIFAX and STIRLING bombers, which could not locate the target, the British continually sought to destroy the *Tirpitz*. This was the first of several RAF Bomber Command strikes and Navy carrier-based strikes flown against the German warship.

On March 5, 1942, the *Tirpitz* and an escort of destroyers sailed from Trondheim in the first surface attack against the Russian Convoys. Passing close to convoys PQ 12 (eastbound) and QP 8 (westbound), the *Tirpitz* did not intercept them because of bad weather; similarly, the *Tirpitz* escaped a British battleship-carrier force searching for her although she was attacked, without success, by carrier-based torpedo planes. (The battleship's anti-aircraft guns shot down two of the attacking planes.) By midday on March 9, the *Tirpitz* was safely in Vest Fjord.

The German surface forces in the Trondheim area were now the *Tirpitz*, the POCKET BATTLESHIP *Admiral Scheer*, two heavy cruisers, and several destroyers; coupled with U-BOATS and a large force of Luftwaffe bombers, this was a considerable threat to the Russian Convoys.

On the night of March 27–28, 1942, the RAF sent forty-three bombers against the *Tirpitz*, thirty-four on the following night, and thirty-four more bombers on the night of March 30–31—all without scoring a hit on the battleship.

More ineffective raids were flown in April. The following month the pocket battleship *Lützow* joined the German force in northern Norwegian waters (at which time one of the heavy cruisers returned to Germany for repairs). But as M. J. Whit-

ley wrote in his *German Capital Ships of World War Two*, "The usefulness of this large force in Norway was more illusionary than real, for the fuel position was critical and all operations had to be carefully weighed to see if the fuel expenditure was worthwhile. Sea training under way had to be slashed drastically, with the resultant decline in efficiency."

An attempt to attack CONVOY PQ 17 in July 1942 was judged by the German naval high command to be worth a major expenditure of fuel. It proved to be the most disastrous of the Russian Convoys. Late on the afternoon of July 2 the *Tirpitz*, a heavy cruiser, destroyers, and torpedo boats went to sea. Although ULTRA intercepts indicated no movement of the battleship, on July 5, believing that the *Tirpitz* was about to attack, the British First Sea Lord, Adm. A. D. POUND, ordered the convoy to scatter to reduce the number of merchant ships that the German dreadnought could attack. But without close escort, the thirty-three merchant ships were vulnerable to German bombers and U-boats. Only nine reached port as twenty-four ships of 143,977 gross tons were sunk. The *Tirpitz* did sail—but did not attack PQ 17—and was back safe in harbor on the morning of July 6.

Frustrated, the naval high command ordered the *Tirpitz* to remain at anchor. (Other German surface ships did engage merchant ships during this period, but submarines and bombers were the principal threat to the convoys.) In Oct. 1942, while the warship was at anchor in the Trondheim area, a disguised fishing vessel carried two British human torpedoes or "chariots" to a position off the coast. The two-man craft then traveled up the fjord to lay their explosive charges under the ship. The effort—Operation Title—failed because of water conditions and German defenses.

Early in 1943 the battleship *Scharnhorst* joined the *Tirpitz*. So great was the threat that the Allies suspended convoys to the Soviet Union for several months. Finally, in Sept. 1943 the *Tirpitz* and *Scharnhorst* and their escorts went to sea. On Sept. 8 the warships' guns bombarded the Allied coaling station on the island of Spitsbergen while the destroyers landed troops. It was the only time the *Tirpitz* would fire her guns in anger.

The warships returned safely to port. There, on Sept. 22 three British X-CRAFT MIDGET SUBMA-

RINES, towed into the area by submarines, attacked the *Tirpitz* at Alten Fjord. (A total of six of the X-craft were sent on the mission, dubbed Operation Source.) Two submarines, the *X-6* and *X-7,* each laid two charges of two tons of explosives under the battleship. Although the *Tirpitz* spotted the submarines, and captured two crewmen, when the charges detonated they inflicted major damage. Repairs were begun and in mid-March 1944 the *Tirpitz* began sea trials.

In early April British aircraft carriers began flying strikes against the *Tirpitz.* The battleship sustained major damage. More carrier strikes were made, but without effect. The RAF returned in Sept. 1944, flying from a base in northern Russia, the distance being too great for a strike from British bases. On Sept. 15, 1944, a raid by twenty-eight LANCASTERS with fifteen carrying TALLBOY BOMBS and twelve JOHNNY WALKER explosives struck the battleship. More damage was inflicted by a single near-miss by a Tallboy—the other bombs having no effect. On Nov. 12, 1944, another RAF strike was flown against the ship as she lay at anchor near Tromso, Norway, this time with thirty-two Lancasters. The planes scored three direct hits and two near-misses with Tallboys, causing the ship to roll over and sink. The loss of life was heavy.

The *Tirpitz* had a standard displacement of 42,343 tons and at full load was 52,700 tons. She was 813 1/2 feet long. Steam turbines could drive the ship at 30 knots. The principal armament was eight 15-inch (381-mm) guns with a heavy secondary gun battery and antiaircraft battery. Her complement totaled some 2,530.

Tito, Josef (1892–1980)

Wartime resistance leader in Yugoslavia. Born Josef Brozovich (or Broz), he took the name Tito when he became a Communist leader. Soon after Germany invaded Yugoslavia in April 1941, GESTAPO agents, joining with Belgrade police, rounded up Communists, killed them, and hanged them from lampposts. Tito slipped out of Belgrade and formed a GUERRILLA resistance group he called the partisans. They cooperated at first with a competing resistance group, the Chetniks, led by Gen. DRAŽA MIHAJLOVIĆ, a veteran of the Serbian Army in World War I. But Tito broke with the Chetniks,

won British support, and was warmly endorsed by Prime Minister CHURCHILL.

Tito was an inspiring leader who fought alongside his troops and shared their hardships. "His alert, light-blue eyes missed nothing," a British observer wrote. "He gave an impression of great strength held in reserve, the impression of a tiger ready to spring."

In March 1945 Marshal Tito, as he called himself, agreed to the formation of a coalition cabinet. But he held all the power, including control of the secret police (OZNA), and when elections were held Nov. 1945 the only candidates were his. His regime executed Mihajlović in 1946.

Tito resisted the efforts of STALIN to control postwar Yugoslavia and broke with the Soviet bloc in 1948. Tito then became a leading spokesman for nations that refused to take sides in the Cold War. Making himself president for life in 1963, he ruled Yugoslavia until his death.

Tizard, Sir Henry Thomas (1885–1959)

British scientist chiefly responsible for the British RADAR warning system. Tizard was employed as a test pilot for the Royal Flying Corps (although he had a sight defect). He worked in industry and the government between the wars, calling himself a scientist in and out of civil service. As ADOLF HITLER rebuilt the Luftwaffe in the 1930s, Tizard advocated construction of the "chain" series radar installations along the coast of Britain. He had considerable influence in this regard, in part by being chairman of the Air Ministry's committee on air defense.

In Aug. 1940 he led a delegation to the United States to exchange scientific and military information, a historic exchange. (See TIZARD MISSION.) Subsequently, conflicts with FREDERICK LINDEMANN, scientific adviser to Prime Minister CHURCHILL, led to Tizard's being relegated to minor activities.

Tizard became the chief scientific adviser to the Ministry of Defence in 1948.

Tizard Mission

British transfer of advanced weapons technology to the United States. The famed mission had its origins in Lord Lothian, the British ambassador to the United States. He and his scientific attaché became convinced by May 1940 that a scientific exchange between the two countries would be mutually beneficial. (At the time the United States was not in the war.)

In July 1940, after discussions with LONDON, Lord Lothian proposed such an exchange to President ROOSEVELT and received immediate approval. In late Aug. 1940 a mission of British and Canadian scientific and military personnel, led by Sir HENRY TIZARD, arrived in WASHINGTON. The British mission was authorized to exchange secret data on CHEMICAL WARFARE, communications, explosives, fire-control equipment, RADAR, aircraft superchargers, and underwater detection systems. At that time, according to the official U.S. AAF history, "the British unquestionably had more to offer than did the Americans."

The Tizard mission led to a continuing exchange of scientific and military information throughout the war period.

Tobruk

Port in northeastern Cyrenaica, Libya. Tobruk, a pawn of desert war, changed hands three times during the three years of the British NORTH AFRICA CAMPAIGN.

Tobruk was made into a fortress by Italy in the 1930s as the Italians strengthened their North African colonies. One large project was the building of a 1,100-mile coastal road linking Tripoli, Bengasi, and the little town of Tobruk, which had a large natural harbor. The Italians built a naval base there, tunneling into the rocky headland to carve bomb-proof shelters and storage depots.

The British Western Desert Force, responding to an ill-fated Italian thrust into Egypt, attacked Tobruk on Jan. 21, 1941, and it fell the following day. The British continued on, conquering all of Cyrenaica. But in March *Generalleutnant* ERWIN ROMMEL, commander of Germany's AFRIKA KORPS, arrived in Libya and launched an attack that won back the occupied land—except for Tobruk.

Tobruk, a pocket of British resistance for Rommel, twice repelled attacks in April. On May 15, the British mounted the first of two futile attempts to dislodge Rommel. By early spring it had been obvi-

ous that Tobruk, cut off by land from Egypt, was besieged. The beleaguered British could be supplied only by sea.

When Tobruk was taken by the British in January, the Royal Navy had formed an Inshore Squadron, a motley collection of captured Italian ships, merchant ships, patrol craft, gunboats, and whatever destroyers could be found. Usually denied air cover because of RAF commitments elsewhere, the Inshore Squadron was continually under fire. The Luftwaffe pounded the ships and the harbor, which was also targeted by German and Italian artillery.

Bombs and artillery reduced much of Tobruk to rubble, but the British held on, faithfully expecting relief would come from Egypt. It came on Dec. 10, when operation Crusader, a thrust across the border, drove Rommel back and covered a breakout by Tobruk's garrison of Polish, British, Indian, Australian, and Czech troops.

But battle was to come to Tobruk again when Rommel, capping a fierce offensive, took the town on June 21, 1942, capturing some 30,000 BRITISH COMMONWEALTH troops. Then, in the desert duels between Rommel and Gen. BERNARD L. MONTGOMERY, after the crucial second battle of EL ALAMEIN the British Eighth Army stormed after Rommel and in the pursuit recaptured Tobruk on Nov. 13, 1942.

Todt Organization

A quasi-military German agency created for major construction projects. These included the SIEGFRIED LINE, SUBMARINE PENS, and the *Autobahnen*, Germany's system of high-speed highways. The agency, which extensively used SLAVE LABOR, was named after Fritz Todt, the Reich minister for Armaments and Munitions from 1940 to 1942, when he died in an airplane accident. He was succeeded by ALBERT SPEER.

Toenails

Code name for landing of U.S. Army 43rd Infantry DIVISION on NEW GEORGIA Island in the SOLOMONS, July 1943.

Togo

Code name for second phase of Japanese Ichigo operation.

Tojo, Hideki (1884–1948)

Wartime leader of Japan. An Army career officer, Tojo gained prominence as commander of the Japanese military police in Manchuria. He later became Chief of Staff of the army there. An advocate of military control of the state, he became vice minister for war in 1938 and war minister in 1940. When Japan's moderate government fell in October 1941, Tojo took over as prime minister and eventually also became both war minister and Army Chief of Staff.

For the American people he personified the Japanese enemy and, although linked in cartoons and in wartime folklore with HITLER and MUSSOLINI, he was not their equal. He shared power with a "supreme command" and, unlike the dictators of Germany and Italy, did not build a fanatic following among his countrymen. After the fall of SAIPAN in 1944, Tojo was forced to resign. He shot himself in Aug. 1945 when U.S. troops came to seize him, but he recovered and stood trial for WAR CRIMES. Sentenced to death by an International Military Tribunal, he was hanged on Dec. 22, 1948.

Token

Code name for rehearsal for the Allied AIRBORNE landing across the Rhine River in March 1945.

Tokyo

The capital of Japan, home of the emperor, and a port-industrial complex on the northeast coast of Tokyo Bay. Tokyo's population in 1940 was about 7,350,000; by the end of the war it had dropped to some 3,500,000.

From at least 1937 there was concern about the possibility of air raids against Japan by Soviet bombers during the Sino-Russian war. But the Japanese attitude toward air attack was naive at best; the principal counter to fires ignited by BOMBS were bucket brigades manned by neighborhood associations.

The first air attack against Tokyo came on April 18, 1942, when U.S. AAF Lt. Col. JAMES DOOLITTLE led sixteen B-25B MITCHELL bombers launched from the U.S. AIRCRAFT CARRIER *HORNET* (CV 8). (See DOOLITTLE RAID.)

The second raid against Tokyo took place on Nov. 24, 1944, when eighty-eight B-29 SUPERFORTRESS bombers flying from China attacked Tokyo, although few of the aircraft were able to hit the objective, the Nakajima aircraft engine works. Cloud cover and high winds deterred effective high-level daylight bombing of Tokyo as well as other Japanese targets. Relatively small, high-altitude STRATEGIC BOMBING raids by B-29s continued, but with little success. Bomber crews were briefed not to hit the emperor's palace.

On the night of March 9–10, 1945, 279 B-29 Superfortress heavy bombers flying from bases in the MARIANA ISLANDS dropped 1,665 tons of petroleum-based incendiaries on Tokyo. Fierce fires took hold and, fanned by 20 mph winds, precipitated a FIRESTORM. About 16 square miles were almost completely burned out and over a million people—one seventh of the capital's population—lost their homes. Japanese records show that 83,783 people were killed and over 100,000 injured in that raid. These were higher casualties than immediate losses in either of the ATOMIC BOMB raids against Japan. According to aviation historian Roger Freeman, "This staggering raid, bringing destruction on an unprecedented scale, rocked the Japanese nation; public morale never recovered."

Tokyo at the time had just over 110 square miles of built-up area, the largest city in Japan. The B-29 raids destroyed about one half of that area.

Beginning on Feb. 16, 1945, U.S. Navy carrier-based aircraft periodically attacked targets in the Tokyo area. Sixteen carriers launched several hundred fighters and bombers in the first series of strikes. There were no Japanese counterattacks against the U.S. carriers.

Japan surrendered on Aug. 15, 1945, and the first U.S. troops arrived in Japan by transport aircraft on Aug. 28, followed by Marine and Navy landings. The Japanese surrender took place on Sept. 2, 1945, on board the U.S. BATTLESHIP *MISSOURI* (BB 63) moored in Tokyo Bay with other units of the U.S. Pacific Fleet. Gen. of the Army DOUGLAS MACARTHUR, who accepted the Japanese surrender, established his postwar headquarters in Tokyo.

Tokyo Express

American name for Japanese effort to resupply GUADALCANAL by destroyers and transports, from Aug. 1942 to early 1943.

Tokyo Rose

GI name for what legend made a single person: a traitorous American citizen who broadcast PROPAGANDA aimed at U.S. forces. Actually, several English-speaking women played records of dance bands and light classical music and offered servicemen a variety of news: bogus CASUALTY figures on U.S. military units; tales of infidelity by wives and sweethearts back home, prophetic reports of upcoming operations. The voices merged into a mythical character called "Tokyo Rose," and the daily broadcasts became popular among U.S. servicemen throughout the Pacific.

After the war, the U.S. government identified "Tokyo Rose" as Iva Ikuko Toguri d'Aquino, a Japanese-American born in Los Angeles. When Japan attacked PEARL HARBOR on Dec. 7, 1941, she was a young woman visiting a relative in Japan. She married a Portuguese national in 1945.

Returned to the United States, she was tried in 1949 for treason and undermining U.S. troops' morale. At her trial she insisted she had been forced to make the broadcasts. She said she was one of at least twenty "Tokyo Roses" who worked for the Japanese Broadcasting Company. Acquitted of treason but convicted of the lesser charge, she was sentenced to ten years. President GERALD FORD pardoned her in 1977.

Tomahawk,

see P-40.

Tony

The first operational Japanese fighter with an in-line engine, the Ka-61 *Hien* (Swallow) was one of the most widely flown fighters of the Army Air Force. It was initially mistaken for the Messerschmitt ME (Bf) 109 when first seen by Allied airmen in the late summer of 1942. The Tony did employ a Japanese adaptation of the German DB 601 engine, and the early models had the German Muser 20-mm cannon, but that was soon replaced by a Japanese model. It saw action over NEW GUINEA, Formosa, and OKINAWA, and was used in the defense of the Japanese homeland.

The Tony first flew in Dec. 1941 and entered production shortly afterwards, with 2,646 of the series I being built. Armament was steadily increased and improved models remained in production until Jan. 1945. The Ka-61-II had a more powerful engine, larger wing, and redesigned cockpit. Production difficulties, however, limited that design to eight aircraft, followed by a more extensive redesign—the Ki-61-II KAI—of which only ninety-nine were completed because U.S. air attacks destroyed the engine plant. When its engine functioned properly, the Ki-61-II KAI was the only Army fighter that could fight at the operating altitudes of B-29 SUPERFORTRESS bombers.

Resembling Western high-performance fighters, the Tony was a long-wing aircraft with an in-line engine. It was the first Japanese fighter with factory-installed armor and self-sealing fuel tanks, marking a move away from lightweight fighters. Armament consisted of two 20-mm cannon and two 12.7-mm machine guns. Two 551-pound BOMBS could be carried.

The Ki-61-Ib could reach 368 mph and was credited with a range of 685 miles; the Ki-61-II KAI was rated at 379 mph with a 995-mile range.

Top Policy Group

A secret committee formed by President ROOSEVELT to advise him on the development of the ATOMIC BOMB. The group consisted of the President, Vice President Henry Wallace, Secretary of War HENRY L. STIMSON, Gen. GEORGE C. MARSHALL, Army Chief of Staff, Dr. VANNEVAR BUSH, director of the OFFICE OF SCIENTIFIC RESEARCH AND DEVELOPMENT, and Dr. James B. Conant, chairman of the National Defense Research Committee. The committee's major decision was the recommendation that the U.S. Army Corp of Engineers be assigned the task of handling the construction work that would be needed and that the engineers select a competent Army officer to head the program. The program became the MANHATTAN PROJECT and the engineer selected was Col. LESLIE R. GROVES, who would direct the mammoth project and direct the army of scientists that built the atomic bomb.

Torch

Code name for Allied invasion of French North Africa, Nov. 1944.

Toreador

Code name for Allied AIRBORNE assault on Mandalay.

Tornado

Code name for Allied force for the assault on Wakde-Sarmi area, NEW GUINEA.

Torpedoes

Weapons used during the war by aircraft, surface warships, and submarines to attack surface ships and submarines. Torpedoes were highly effective, with a single hit usually being sufficient to sink or inflict severe damage on merchant ships and on warships up to destroyer size, although larger ships were on occasion sunk by a single torpedo hit, as the British aircraft carrier *ARK ROYAL*.

Torpedoes can best be addressed by the types of platform that used them.

Aircraft   Aircraft-launched torpedoes were used against surface ships. The U.S. Navy had the 22.5-inch (571.5-mm)-diameter Mark 13 antiship torpedo available for aircraft when the war began. The Mark 13 had a 600-pound high-explosive (TPX) warhead.

The standard Navy torpedo aircraft at the outbreak of the war was the TBD DEVASTATOR, a graceful but slow and vulnerable aircraft. TBDs sank the light aircraft carrier *SHOHO* at the battle of CORAL SEA in May 1942, but at the battle of MIDWAY the following June all three U.S. TBD torpedo squadrons were decimated by Japanese defenses without any U.S. planes scoring a hit on any of the four Japanese fleet carriers—all of which were then sunk by SBD DAUNTLESS dive bombers. Although the subsequent TBF/TBM AVENGER was a more capable torpedo aircraft, dive bombers continued as the major U.S. naval striking force. Large numbers of aerial torpedoes, however, did sink the Japanese super-battleships *YAMATO* and *Musashi*.

From May 1943 U.S. and British aircraft also used the FIDO acoustic homing torpedo against *submerged* submarines. (The German Navy used acoustic homing torpedoes against surface escort ships; see GNAT.)

Surface Ships   U.S. DESTROYERS and PT-BOATS employed torpedoes to attack Japanese surface ships. Destroyers carried the 21-inch Mark 8 and Mark 15 torpedoes. In the battle of the JAVA SEA in Feb. 1942 the four U.S. destroyers present fired twenty-two torpedoes at Japanese warships without effect. But in the 1943 naval battles in the SOLOMON ISLANDS torpedo attacks by U.S. destroyers and PT-boats were successful. The Mark 8 had a 466-pound TNT warhead while the Mark 15 had a warhead of 825 pounds of HBX Torpex explosives. About 500 Mark 8 torpedoes were given to Britain in 1940 for use with the fifty U.S. LEND-LEASE destroyers.

Motor torpedo boats—called PT-boats in the U.S. Navy—carried the Mark 8 and Mark 15 torpedoes at the beginning of the war. They were first used by PT-boats in the 1941–1942 struggle in the Philippines. Afterwards PT-boats were used with great effectiveness in the Solomons and Philippines (1943–1944) and in the Mediterranean area (1943–1944). From 1943 the PT-boats carried the Mark 13 aircraft torpedo, which was launched from lightweight racks rather than torpedo tubes. These 22.5-inch (571.5-mm)-diameter weapons were only 13 feet long compared to 21 feet for the Mark 8.

Submarines   When the war began older U.S. S-class submarines carried the 18-inch (457-mm) Mark 10 and fleet submarines the 21-inch (533-mm) Mark 14 torpedoes. They could also be used against *surfaced* submarines. (During the war there was only one sinking of a submerged submarine by another undersea craft: in Feb. 1945 when the British *Venturer* sank the German *U-864*. The lack of homing guidance prevented standard torpedoes from being able to attack submerged submarines because the target submarine's depth could vary.)

Both U.S. torpedoes encountered major problems with failures of contact and magnetic proximity fuzes when the war began. The problems were not fully corrected until 1943. Still, the Mark 14, which was the only torpedo in fleet submarines until 1944, is credited with sinking some 4 million tons of Japanese shipping (compared to 1 million tons for the later Mark 18). The Mark 10 had a 497-pound TNT warhead and the Mark 14 one of 643 pounds of Torpex.

The electric, wakeless Mark 18 torpedo became available to U.S. submarines in 1944. Design of the Mark 18 was based in part on captured German torpedo technology. (All other U.S. torpedoes except the Fido had steam propulsion using alcohol as fuel.) Also in service late in the war was the short-range, high-speed Mark 23, but this weapon was unpopular with submarine commanders. These torpedoes all had a diameter of 21 inches.

U.S. submarines fired approximately 14,750 torpedoes at 3,184 ships. Of those, 1,314 were sunk for a total of 5.3 million tons; in addition, U.S. submarines received "probable credit" for another seventy-eight ships of 203,306 tons.

American surface ship and submarine torpedoes were inferior to Japanese torpedoes in terms of speed, range, and warhead. The Japanese Type 93 "long-lance" torpedo, with a 24-inch (610-mm) diameter, was the world's largest used in the war. U.S. torpedo production during the war totaled 64,000.

Total Germany

Royal Navy code signal, sent at 11:15 A.M. on Sept. 3, 1939, indicating to naval forces that a state of war existed between Britain and Germany.

Total War

War that demands a nation's total RESOURCES and hardly distinguishes civilian from soldier. The concept of total war was rooted in NAZI mobilization for World War II: There could be no limit on commitment of labor or materials. All major belligerents, with the exception of Italy, followed a policy of total war, although the United States and the other ALLIES never acknowledged the term; it smacked too much of "totalitarianism."

After the war, however, scholars both in the United States and England used the term *total war* to explain such actions as the massive bombing of DRESDEN and other German cities; the development and dropping of the ATOMIC BOMB; and the mobilization of WOMEN in the armed service and war plants. Phenomenal U.S. WAR PRODUCTION also showed how what Americans called the "war effort" was at the same time total war, American style.

In a typical use of the term, JOSEPH GOEBBELS, German PROPAGANDA minister, in a memorandum to HITLER written on July 18, 1944, advocated a radical intensification of the German war effort for a "total war." Goebbels pleaded that the bureau-

cratic apparatus of the regime and army be abolished and total mobilization of production and manpower be put in the hands of one commissar. He argued that Germans were ready for such ultimate sacrifice for the defense of their nation, just as the British and Soviet peoples had responded to CHURCHILL's and STALIN's appeals.

Japan set up an Institute of Total War, in which civilians and military representatives planned not the war effort but the administration of conquered territory. Italy, on the other hand, at the outbreak of the EUROPEAN WAR had little capacity to produce heavy armaments and did little to change the situation. Italian industrialists did not look forward to the prospect of war, given the disastrous state of the economy. Italy also lacked strategic raw materials and fuel. But the real reason for Italy's lack of preparedness was the failure of the regime to understand the nature of total war fully and to organize wartime production properly. Significantly, Italy was the first AXIS nation to surrender.

Totalize

Code name for Canadian attack toward Falaise, Normandy, Aug. 1944.

Tovey, Adm. of the Fleet John C. (1885–1971)

Commander in Chief of the British Home Fleet from 1940 to 1943, Tovey became particularly famous for leading the British pursuit of the German battleship *BISMARCK*.

Tovey, who first attracted notice as an aggressive destroyer commander during the battle of Jutland in World War I, was known as a man possessed of "tenacity of purpose" (or as another admiral half-kiddingly phrased it "sheer bloody obstinacy"). He had strong opinions, great optimism, and a deep religious faith.

Soon after the EUROPEAN WAR began he was elevated to second-in-command of the Mediterranean Fleet under Adm. ANDREW BROWNE CUNNINGHAM. When France surrendered in June 1940, Tovey commented to Cunningham, "Now I know we shall win the war, sir. We have no more allies."

In Dec. 1940 he replaced Admiral Sir Charles Forbes as CinC of the Home Fleet. He was to prevent German surface raiders from attacking Atlantic

CONVOYS, maintain the British naval blockade of Germany, oversee the defense of Soviet-bound convoys, and organize British troop convoys to the Mediterranean. His percipient and dogged chase of the *Bismarck* in May 1941, which was hampered by the raw unreliability of his newest battleships (*PRINCE OF WALES* and *King George V*) and the low fuel states of most of his ships, culminated in his cornering and sinking the *Bismarck* before she could take refuge in Brest.

Tovey was frequently angered by orders issued from First Sea Lord Admiral DUDLEY POUND, many of them at Prime Minister CHURCHILL's impatient behest. When Pound signaled to keep pummelling the *Bismarck* until she sank—even if it meant *towing* the *King George V* home—Tovey called it "the stupidest and most ill-considered signal ever made." He probably rated as only slightly less ill-advised Pound's decision to scatter the MURMANSK-bound convoy PQ 17 in July 1942 when it appeared likely that the *Bismarck*'s sister ship, the *TIRPITZ*, was about to descend on it.

In May 1943, Tovey was promoted to Admiral of the Fleet and was appointed Commander in Chief of the Nore (Eastern England), a post he held until the end of the war. It seemed a quiet demotion for so active and aggressive a commander (although the command did have an important role in the buildup for the NORMANDY INVASION).

Naval historian Stephen Roskill recalled in his *Churchill and the Admirals,* "when difficulties with Admiral E. J. KING, USN, were becoming acute, Churchill put forward a proposal to send Tovey to WASHINGTON in place of Sir Percy Nobel, who had been head of the British naval mission for two strenuous years and was pressing to return home. Churchill, obviously recalling his brushes with Tovey over the Atlantic Battle and the Arctic convoys in 1942, evidently considered he would prove a worthy opponent to the redoubtable 'Ernie King.' 'Admiral Tovey' . . . 'would put up a splendid fight there,'" Churchill was reported to have said.

Adm. Tovey was made 1st Baron Tovey of Langton Maltravers.

Tracer

British code name for reinforcement of MALTA, June 1941.

Tractable

Code name for the second Allied attack toward Falaise, Normandy, Aug. 1944.

Tradewind

Code name for Allied assault force for Morotai, NEW GUINEA.

Transfigure

Code name for plan to drop Allied AIRBORNE troops west of the Seine River to block German escape routes.

Transport Submarines

The U.S. Navy conducted experimental exercises in the late 1930s with SUBMARINES landing raiders by rubber craft. Submarines could clandestinely approach an enemy's shore and send raiders or COMMANDOS ashore for raids or to garner intelligence. With the outbreak of World War II such plans were put aside as available submarines of all nations were sent to seek out and destroy enemy warships and merchant shipping. But as the war progressed, U.S. and British submarines were employed in several AMPHIBIOUS LANDINGS.

The two largest submarine landings of the war were conducted by the U.S. Navy. The first was a Marine raider operation against the Japanese-held MAKIN ISLAND in the GILBERTS. The raiders were to be carried to the island in two large submarines, the *Argonaut* (SM 1) and the *Nautilus* (SS 168). The former, 381 feet long, was the U.S. Navy's largest undersea craft; originally built as a submarine minelayer, she was converted to a transport submarine during the first half of 1942. The *Nautilus* was slightly smaller, 371 feet long. Both ships had two 6-inch (152-mm) deck guns. Reload TORPEDOES and some other gear were removed to accommodate the raiders—two companies of the 2nd Marine Raider BATTALION under Lt. Col. EVANS F. CARLSON totaling thirteen officers and 208 enlisted men. The raid was carried out in early Aug. 1942, the raiders going ashore in seventeen rubber boats. (See also CARLSON'S RAIDERS.)

The next major U.S. submarine landing was also a two-submarine operation, in May 1943, involving the *Nautilus* and her sister submarine *Narwhal* (SS 167). The target was Attu, one of two of the ALEUTIAN ISLANDS that the Japanese had occupied in June 1942 as part of the diversion for the attack on MIDWAY. The two submarines unloaded their spare torpedoes and other equipment to make space for the Army's 7th Scouts. They conducted a rehearsal at DUTCH HARBOR on April 30, and then took aboard 200 scouts, who successfully landed by rubber boats five hours before the main assault on May 11. (The submarines also served as navigation beacons for the main landing force.) The submarine landings were a useful complement to the main landings, but were not a critical factor in the recapture of Attu, Operation Landcrab.

During the U.S. landing on TARAWA atoll in Nov. 1943 the *Nautilus* obtained last-minute information on surf and weather conditions and landed seventy-seven scouts from the 5th Marine Reconnaissance COMPANY and an Australian by rubber boat on Kenna Island. All landed safely, and the next day the *Nautilus* used her 6-inch guns to pound the twenty-five-man Japanese garrison on the island. The small garrison was either killed by the gunfire or committed suicide, and the island soon became the site of an American airfield.

Both the *Nautilus* and *Narwhal,* joined by several other submarines, also kept up a steady flow of supplies to the American-Filipino GUERRILLAS in the Philippines. These two large submarines could each carry some 90 tons of munitions plus special personnel on each voyage to the Philippines; the smaller, fleet-type submarines carried about 35 tons of arms and supplies on each mission to the Philippines. (Early in 1942 U.S. submarines had carried out the GOLD reserves of the Philippines as well as military nurses, code experts, and other high-priority passengers.) The major use of submarines in transport and landing operations was in the Mediterranean region. Clandestine operations from submarines were undertaken throughout the Mediterranean during the war on an almost-regular basis. Using folbots and rubber rafts, commandos would go ashore from submarines off Sardinia, Italy, Greece, and various Aegean islands as well as along the German-held coast of Libya. These commandos blew up train tracks, bridges, airfields, and other installations; conducted coastal and shore reconnaissance; and carried munitions and other supplies to guerrillas.

Submarines also made a few supply trips to the besieged British island base of MALTA, but this was a much smaller effort than the transport of supplies to the Philippines by U.S. submarines.

British and Dutch submarines carried commandos on several raids against Japanese-held islands in Southeast Asia. They were also used in attempts to infiltrate agents and supplies into Malaya. But unfavorable coastal conditions made it more effective to use long-range aircraft based in India to parachute people and supplies.

The Japanese Navy also employed submarines extensively in the resupply role, but apparently not in direct support of amphibious landings. Interestingly, the Japanese developed submarines that could carry LANDING CRAFT and AMPHIBIOUS TRACTORS. The main use of these efforts was in the resupply of garrisons on Pacific islands isolated and bypassed in the U.S. SOLOMONS–NEW GUINEA CAMPAIGN and U.S. CENTRAL PACIFIC CAMPAIGN.

See also *SERAPH.*

Trappenjagd (Bustard Hunt)

German code name for operation on the Kerch Peninsula, May 1942.

Treason

The only crime mentioned in the U.S. Constitution, defined as levying war against the United States or providing aid and comfort to its enemies. The most publicized U.S. treason cases involved PROPAGANDA broadcasters (see AXIS SALLY, TOKYO ROSE), as did the major British case (see WILLIAM JOYCE).

On Aug. 6, 1942, in the first such prosecution of treason since the Whiskey Rebellion of 1794, German-born Max Stephan, a naturalized U.S. citizen, was found guilty of treason and sentenced to hang. The sentence later was commuted to life imprisonment. Stephen, a Detroit restaurant owner, aided German PRISONERS OF WAR who escaped from imprisonment in Canada.

Two important U.S. Supreme Court decisions regarding treason grew out of the convictions of eight German-born agents for SABOTAGE convictions. The eight were landed by two U-BOATS and quickly caught before they committed any acts of sabotage. Six were executed after trial before a special military tribunal. The United States charged that two Americans, including the father of one of the saboteurs, were guilty of treason for aiding the German agents.

Anthony Cramer, a naturalized citizen, met two of the saboteurs, Edward Kerling and Werner Thiel, at two eating places in New York City. Before the war Cramer and Thiel had run a delicatessen. When Cramer was arrested for giving aid and comfort to the two saboteurs, he said they were just talking about old times. The United States was not able to prove that Cramer had done anything specific to help Kerling and Thiel. But a jury convicted him.

The Supreme Court overturned the conviction, ruling that the Constitution put strict rules on convictions for treason: A person must confess openly or two witnesses must testify to the same overt act.

The man convicted of treason in the second case was Hans Max Haupt, a naturalized American citizen, whose son Herbert had already been executed when Hans Haupt went on trial. Hans had sheltered Herbert for six days, helped him buy a car, and helped him try to get a job making parts for the secret NORDEN BOMBSIGHT.

The Supreme Court upheld this treason conviction. The majority opinion held that Hans Haupt's trial judge had correctly framed the case for the jury: It must decide whether what Haupt did was motivated by a desire to help his son or a desire to help Germany against the United States. As a commentary on the case put it, "The jury had found him a traitor, and in law they had sufficient evidence."

Treason can be relative. The pro-NAZI government of VICHY FRANCE condemned Gen. CHARLES DE GAULLE for treason. But after the war it was the prime minister of that Vichy government, PHILIPPE PÉTAIN, who was put on trial for treason. And it was de Gaulle, as president of France, who commuted Pétain's death sentence.

Treblinka

DEATH CAMP where about 300,000 JEWS from the WARSAW GHETTO were killed. It was the only death camp that had a major revolt by prisoners.

The camp, which got its name from a nearby village about 50 miles northeast of Warsaw, was designed to be a death camp, not a CONCENTRATION CAMP. Prisoners built the barracks, set up the gas chambers disguised as showers, erected barbed-wire fences, and dug large burial pits.

To keep secret what Treblinka was to become, the prisoners who built it were executed. They were replaced by Jews rounded up to serve as a permanent cadre, *Hofjuden,* or Court Jews, who maintained the camp and served the SS supervisors and the Ukrainian guards.

As in most camps, there was a special spur line for the trains carrying victims from collection points. Later, a building at trackside was made to look like a provincial railroad station. And signs like *Tailors* or *Carpenters* led incoming inmates to believe that they were sent to a work center.

When the first shipment of prisoners reached Treblinka in June 1942, men were held in place; women and children were taken off to what they were told were "showers." The men went to the same destination, except for about 200 men selected to survive, at least for a while. Some became what the Germans called *Totenjuden,* Jews of Death. They would remove the bodies from the gas chambers. Specialists among the Jews of Death, "the dentists," pulled gold teeth and removed jewels concealed in the victims' mouths. Then squads of *Totenjuden* dumped the bodies into the ditches.

The victims had removed their clothes before entering the gas chambers. The clothes and personal belongings were piled in a square. *Platzjuden,* Jews of the Square, separated the victims' property into categories for subsequent disposal by SS enterprises. Other groups chopped wood, did camp chores, and gathered branches to weave into the barbed wire in an attempt to conceal the camp from the air. There were also *kapos* who acted similar to trustees in a prison.

The Germans wanted the camp to be run by inmates not only because this relieved the captors of work but also because it was a particularly sadistic form of torture for those who lived while others died. These Jews knew that, ultimately, they would someday walk down what the Germans called "the road to heaven" and that they would die in the gas chambers or at the side of a ditch, a bullet in the back of the head. But they served in the hope that they would survive.

Although scorned by the doomed, the Jews of Death also endured their own form of torture for they knew they held the testimony of Treblinka. That testimony could be given only if some prisoners escaped. The Jews of Death began a revolt on Aug. 3, 1943. About twenty guards were killed with weapons taken from an armory opened with keys crudely fashioned by an inmate locksmith.

"All the members of the committee and most of those who played a role in the uprising of the camp died in the revolt," according to Jean-François Steiner, author of *Treblinka,* an account of the revolt. "Of the thousand prisoners who were in the camp at the time, about six hundred managed to get out and to reach the nearby forests without being recaptured." But when Soviet liberation forces arrived a year later, they found only forty former prisoners still alive. Steiner's book, based on interviews with some of those survivors, said the others were killed, some by Poles, others by the GESTAPO or other German hunters.

After the revolt, the Germans demolished the camp; the land was plowed, and many documents destroyed. But the Soviets who liberated the camp found enough evidence to show that 840,000 people, nearly all of them Jews, died at Treblinka.

Tricycle,
see DUSKO POPOV.

Trident
Code name for U.S.-British WASHINGTON CONFERENCE, May 1943.

Trieste
Disputed territory that almost touched off a battle between Allied troops and Yugoslavia. As the war was ending in Europe, JOSEF TITO and his Yugoslav GUERRILLA army seized Trieste, an Italian port city on the Adriatic. Spurred by Prime Minister CHURCHILL's threat of expulsion "by force of arms," the Yugoslavs withdrew but the threat lingered, since they held adjacent Italian territory.

Anglo-U.S. administrators who were aiding in the postwar rehabilitation of Italy worked out a temporary compromise on the Trieste issue. This evolved into the "Free Territory of Trieste," administered by the UNITED NATIONS. The territory's Zone A, which included the city, was put under Anglo-U.S. control, and Zone B was put under Yugoslav control. Zone B gradually became part of Yugoslavia. Zone A was finally turned over to Italy in 1953.

Trinity
Code name for the test site and the testing of the first ATOMIC BOMB, near ALAMOGORDO, New Mexico, on the morning of July 16, 1945.

After six months of road building, barracks building, cable laying, and other preparation at the site, July 4, 1945, was set as the target date for the test. Maj. Gen. LESLIE R. GROVES, in charge of the project, was under pressure to get the bomb successfully tested before the end of President TRUMAN's meeting with Soviet leader STALIN and British Prime Minister CHURCHILL (later to be replaced by CLEMENT ATLEE) at the POTSDAM CONFERENCE. But J. ROBERT OPPENHEIMER, director of the LOS ALAMOS laboratory, had a host of technical problems to solve. He kept pressing Groves to postpone the test date. Reluctantly, Groves advanced the test to July 16.

Oppenheimer, somewhat of a mystic, selected the code name for the test, Trinity. As Richard Rhodes recounts in *The Making of the Atomic Bomb,* Groves assumed that Oppenheimer had chosen *Trinity,* so often used to name rivers and mountains in the West, because the name would be inconspicuous. But that was not what Oppenheimer said when Groves asked about the source of Trinity.

"Why I chose the name is not clear," Oppenheimer replied, "but I do know what thoughts were in my mind." He mentioned two poems by John Donne. One, a sonnet, begins:

Batter my heart, three-person'd God, for, you
As yet but knock, breathe, shine, and seek to mend.

The bomb was to be detonated on a platform atop a steel tower 100 feet high at a spot in the sand and sagebrush designated as Ground Zero. Earth-and-concrete bunkers for observers, cameras, and instruments were built 10,000 yards to the north, west, and south of Ground Zero.

As the test day neared, scientists calculated—or

guessed—the probable explosive power of the bomb. Most calculations put it at the equivalent of 20,000 tons (20 kilotons) of TNT. But many scientists doubted that figure. They started a pool, with an entry fee of $1. EDWARD TELLER picked 45,000 tons, Oppenheimer a mere 300. Another physicist picked zero; he was one of the scientists who doubted that the "gadget," as they called it, would work.

ENRICO FERMI, an eminent physicist, irritated Groves "when he suddenly offered to take wagers from his fellow scientists on whether or not the bomb would ignite the atmosphere, and if so, whether it would merely destroy New Mexico or destroy the world." Groves himself was concerned enough about the unknown effects of the bomb to telephone the governor of New Mexico early on the morning of the test and cryptically warn him that he might shortly have to declare martial law because of an emergency Groves was not at liberty to describe.

Before dawn on the day of the test, 30-mile-per-hour gusts of wind whipped the sands and thunderstorms were rolling across the sky. At 2 A.M. July 16, with the bomb partially armed and sitting on a platform at the top of the tower, "It was raining cats and dogs, lightning and thunder," a physicist recalled. He and others wondered what would happen if lightning struck the bomb—which was to be electrically detonated.

At a 2 A.M. weather conference the meteorologist predicted that the weather would be clear enough to conduct the test at 5:30 A.M. "You'd better be right on this," Groves said. "Or I will hang you."

Distinguished visitors and workers not needed during the test assembled on Compania Hill, about 20 miles northwest of Ground Zero. "We were told," physicist Edward Teller recalled, "to lie down on the sand, turn our faces away from the blast, and bury our heads in our arms. No one complied. We were determined to look the beast in the eye." He did smear suntan lotion on his face, put on sunglasses, and hold a piece of welder's glass to his eyes.

The firing circuit closed at 05:29:45. "For a brief period," Groves officially reported, "there was a lighting effect within a radius of 20 miles equal to several suns in midday; a huge ball of fire was formed which lasted for several seconds. This ball mushroomed and rose to a height of over 10,000

feet before it dimmed." Groves estimated the energy generated by the bomb to be more than that of 15,000 to 20,000 tons of TNT.

The light from the explosion was seen clearly at about 180 miles away, the sound was heard about 100 miles away, windows broke in Gallup, New Mex., 235 miles away. "A massive cloud was formed which surged and billowed upward with tremendous power, reaching the substratosphere at an elevation of 41,000 feet, 36,000 feet above the ground, in about 5 minutes," Groves' report continued. ". . . A crater from which all vegetation had vanished, with a diameter of 1,200 feet and a slight slope toward the center, was formed. In the center was a shallow bowl 130 feet in diameter and 6 feet in depth. . . . The material within the outer circle is greenish and can be distinctly seen from as much as 5 miles away. The steel from the tower was evaporated."

Another tower, a half mile from Ground Zero, was anchored in concrete and built to resemble the structure needed to support a building 15 to 20 stories tall. "The blast tore the tower from its foundations, twisted it, ripped it apart and left it flat on the ground." Groves wrote. "The effects on the tower indicate that, at that distance, unshielded permanent steel and masonry buildings would have been destroyed. . . . I can no longer consider the PENTAGON [which Groves had built] a safe shelter from such a bomb."

Kenneth T. Bainbridge, the scientist in charge of the test, interrupted jubilant congratulations by saying to Oppenheimer, "Now we are all sons of bitches." Later, Bainbridge remembered, Oppenheimer said "It was the best thing anyone said after the test."

Oppenheimer watched the test in silence, remembering a line from the Hindu scripture, the *Bhagavad-Gita:* "Now I am become Death, the destroyer of worlds."

The $102 in the bomb-power pool was won by physicist Isidor I. Rabi, who watched the ball of flame light the sky and thought of his wooden house back in Cambridge, Mass.

Tripartite Pact

The treaty, signed by Germany, Italy, and Japan on Sept. 27, 1940. The treaty called for each to provide military assistance in case of attack by any nation not yet in the war. The pact was aimed at giving America pause about intervention against what was now a three-nation AXIS.

The pact, signed in BERLIN, asserted Japan's recognition of "the leadership of Germany and Italy in the establishment of a new order in Europe" while recognizing Japan's dominance over "Greater East Asia." Hungary, drawn into the Axis by Germany, signed the pact on Nov. 20.

Japanese diplomat SABURO KURUSU, who would later take part in Japan's pre–PEARL HARBOR negotiations with the United States, helped shape the Tripartite Pact. Japan judged the pact to be valuable for it showed that Germany and Italy recognized Japan's policy for a "new order" in East Asia, the GREATER EAST ASIA CO-PROSPERITY SPHERE.

Trojanisches Pferd (Trojan Horse)

Code name for German occupation of Budapest; part of Operation Margarethe.

Troop

The reconnaissance units—of COMPANY size—in armored and CAVALRY units. Within the cavalry reconnaissance SQUADRON (BATTALION) of a U.S. armored DIVISION there were a headquarters and service troop, three reconnaissance troops, an assault gun troop, plus a light TANK company.

Truk

An island group in the CAROLINE ISLANDS where the Japanese, in violation of laws governing the JAPANESE MANDATED ISLANDS, built a major naval base. It was the headquarters of the Japanese Combined Fleet. Consistently bombed and shelled by U.S. air and naval forces in 1944–1945, it was not invaded. Instead, like the Japanese stronghold of RABAUL, it was allowed to "wither on the vine."

Truman, Harry S (1884–1972)

Vice President who succeeded President ROOSEVELT upon his death on April 12, 1945. Truman, who had been a field artillery captain in France in World War I, retained his reserve commission. Soon after the United States entered the war, Truman, then a Democratic Senator from Missouri,

requested a call to active duty from Gen. GEORGE C. MARSHALL, Army Chief of Staff.

Truman later said that Marshall had told the Senator he was "too damned old." When Truman pointed out that Marshall was older, the general diplomatically replied that Truman was of greater value as chairman of the Special Committee to Investigate the National Defense Program.

The committee, created in Feb. 1941, soon became known as the Truman Committee, after its feisty chairman, who uncovered widespread waste and corruption in the U.S. defense effort. After the Japanese attack on PEARL HARBOR the committee—and Truman—gained even more publicity because the revelations now were affecting American lives.

The committee's work so changed government procurement and contract practices that by some estimates it saved taxpayers more than $15 billion. A poll of newspaper correspondents in 1944 rated Truman as second only to President Roosevelt in contributions to the war effort.

Roosevelt, seeking his fourth term, had to dump his vice president, Henry Wallace, because of pressure from conservatives in the Democratic Party. To avoid a floor fight at the Democratic Convention, Roosevelt chose a compromise candidate to replace Wallace—Truman. When Truman, who was supporting JAMES BYRNES, balked, Roosevelt called the party's national chairman, Robert Hannegan, who held the telephone receiver so others in the room, including Truman, could hear Roosevelt's voice.

"Bob," the President asked, "have you got that fellow lined up yet?" Hannegan said he hadn't. "Well," Roosevelt replied, "tell him that if he wants to break up the Democratic Party in the middle of a war, that's his responsibility."

Truman accepted.

He was little prepared for the presidency when it came. He had to be informed about the ATOMIC BOMB, knew little about the SAN FRANCISCO CONFERENCE that was to start thirteen days into his presidency, and had no agenda for the looming close of the EUROPEAN WAR. His rescuer was HARRY HOPKINS, Roosevelt's closest adviser.

Truman sent him to STALIN with instructions on what to say to the Soviet leader about the forthcoming POTSDAM CONFERENCE: "that I was anxious to have a fair understanding with the Russian Government—that we never made commitments which we did not expect to carry out to the letter—[that] we expected him to carry his agreement out to the letter and we intended to see that he did." Truman also told Hopkins that he "could use diplomatic language or he could use a baseball bat."

Germany was defeated by the time of the conference in July 1945, and Truman waited anxiously for information about the TRINITY test of the atomic bomb. Informed that the test had been successful, he tried as casually as possible to tell Stalin about it. He later wrote that he had mistakenly "liked the little son-of-a-bitch."

To help him on decisions about the bomb Truman appointed the INTERIM COMMITTEE, which suggested that the bomb be used on a city without warning. Truman accepted the advice, authorizing the dropping of the bombs. Truman was en route home from Potsdam on board the CRUISER *Augusta* (CA 31) on Aug. 6 when he received word that the atomic bomb had been dropped on HIRO-

SHIMA. By the time the ship reached port on Aug. 9 the second bomb had been dropped on NAGASAKI and events began rapidly moving toward the SURRENDER of Japan. Truman never regretted making the decision to drop the bombs because, as he saw it, the decision hastened the end of the war and saved countless American lives.

Truman, who was a wartime President for so few months, inherited a postwar world dominated by issues involving U.S.-Soviet relations. The war that he did preside over, both as the unexpected President and the elected President in 1948, was the Cold War. In a letter he wrote to a friend in 1958 he summed up, in his unmistakable words, what he thought he had done:

"I reduced the national debt by 27 billion dollars, balanced the budget for six of my eight years, met TITO, Stalin, et al. in Yugoslavia, Persia and the Near East, kept Stalin out of Greece and Turkey and BERLIN and put the UNITED NATIONS into Korea and saved that Republic. Also kept crooked old CHIANG KAI-SHEK from being

The Big Three at the Potsdam conference, meeting near Berlin after the end of the war in Europe. From left are Winston Churchill, who would soon be voted out of office; Harry S Truman, who had recently become President; and Josef Stalin, who dictated Soviet policy for three decades. *(U.S. Navy)*

mopped up by placing the Seventh FLEET between him and danger."

Truscott, Lt. Gen. Lucian K., Jr. (1895–1965)

In the spring of 1942 Army Chief of Staff GEORGE C. MARSHALL sent Col. Lucian Truscott to England with orders to find a way for U.S. troops to take part in British COMMANDO raids. From Truscott's experience came his suggestion that the U.S. Army organize units similar to the commandos. This was the origin of what Truscott would call the RANGERS.

To gather firsthand experience, Truscott, newly promoted to brigadier general, participated in the Aug. 1942 reinforced raid at DIEPPE. The heavy casualties convinced many American officers that they must wait at least until 1943 to launch an invasion of France.

Truscott returned to the United States after Dieppe to command Goalpost, one of three NORTH AFRICA INVASION task groups formed under Maj. Gen. GEORGE PATTON's Western Task Force that landed south of Casablanca in Nov. 1942. Cited for brilliant battle leadership, Truscott later said he was lucky to have been opposed by troops who did not have their hearts in the fight.

After serving as Gen. DWIGHT D. EISENHOWER's field deputy in TUNISIA, Truscott, by now a major general, took command of the 3rd Infantry DIVISION for the campaign in SICILY. Again he proved himself aggressive and imaginative, as well as fully cooperative with Patton's larger schemes. He would become the only general to have successively commanded a REGIMENT, a division, a CORPS, and a field ARMY in combat during World War II.

The ITALIAN CAMPAIGN, which began for Truscott's 3rd Division with an AMPHIBIOUS LANDING at SALERNO in Sept. 1943, was gruelling and frustrating. In Jan. 1944, as part of VI Corps, the 3rd landed at ANZIO in an attempt to threaten the German line from the rear. Maj. Gen. JOHN LUCAS's command of VI Corps was deemed too cautious and Truscott succeeded him in March 1944, leading VI Corps out of encirclement to link up with forces from the South.

VI Corps was then pulled out of Italy for the invasion of southern France (code-named Anvil-Dragoon) in Aug. 1944. Truscott's subsequent drive up the Rhône Valley has been called a "shining example of boldness and initiative" capped by the five-day battle of Montélimar, which stripped the German Nineteenth Army of most of its equipment and many of its troops. Truscott regarded the fourteen-day campaign as his finest tactical achievement.

Truscott was promoted to lieutenant general and became commander of the Fifth Army in Italy in early 1945, leading its last offensive up to the BRENNER PASS. Knowledge of Truscott's abilities and achievements was often limited to those best placed to judge him. And among such judges he was ranked very high in all phases of command from training and planning to vigorous execution.

Tu-2

Highly effective Soviet light bomber and ground attack aircraft. The Tu-2 design was begun by Andrei N. Tupolev in 1938, while he was imprisoned. This aircraft originated as a low-level and dive bomber to support ground forces. Tu-2 entered combat in 1944 and proved an outstanding aircraft.

First flight of Tupolev's ANT-58 prototype took place in Jan. 1941 with others following; the definitive ANT-60 prototype flew in Dec. 1941 with production being delayed because of a shift in factories and redesign. Output through 1948 was only about 3,000 aircraft, low by Soviet standards, especially for a successful aircraft. (Tupolev and his design team were released from prison in April 1943, in part so he could devote more attention to manufacturing the Tu-2; that summer he received the STALIN Prize for his design efforts.)

The Tu-2 was an attractive mid-wing aircraft with twin radial engines, comparatively large wing area, and twin tail. All wheels fully retracted. There were two separate glazed crew positions in the fuselage, while the underside of the nose was also glazed. (Early prototypes had in-line, liquid-cooled engines.) A large number of specialized variants appeared, although few were produced in numbers—long-range aircraft (Tu-2D), camera version (Tu-2R), *Shturmovik* (Tu-2Sh), and TORPEDO bomber (Tu-2T). After the war the basic Tu-2 evolved into the Tu-6, -8, and -10 aircraft. After the war the Tu-2 was given the NATO code name Bat.

Maximum speed of the early aircraft was 340 mph, increased in later models with improved engines; the Tu-2M was rated at 376 mph. Range was 1,300 miles, later increased to 2,200 miles. The plane could carry up to 5,000 pounds of BOMBS in an internal bomb bay for short distances, with 2,200 pounds being normal. Gun armament for the Tu-2 generally consisted of two 20-mm cannon in the wing roots plus some combination of 12.7-mm single or paired 7.62-mm dorsal and ventral machine guns.

Tube Alloys

Code name for British participation in the ATOMIC BOMB project.

Tulagi,

see GUADALCANAL.

Tulsa

Code name for Gen. DOUGLAS MACARTHUR's preliminary plan for the capture of RABAUL.

Tungsten

British code word for carrier-based air attacks against the battleship *TIRPITZ* in Norwegian waters, April 1944.

Tunisia

Capital: Tunis, pop. 2,608,313 (1936). Part of France's North African colonial empire at the beginning of the war, Tunisia was a target of Italian interest early in 1939, a few months before the EUROPEAN WAR began. The Italian problem died down as Tunisians rallied in favor of the French, who administered Tunisia as a protectorate with a sultan as nominal ruler. When France fell in June 1940, Tunisia, like the other French North African colonies, was placed under the control of the pro-German VICHY FRANCE regime.

On Nov. 9, 1942, the day after the Allied NORTH AFRICA INVASION, Germany occupied Tunisia, making much of the country a battlefield for the NORTHWEST AFRICA CAMPAIGN until the surrender of AXIS forces in May 1943. As the war neared its end, Tunisian nationalists stepped up demands for independence, which did not come until 1956.

Turkey

Capital: Ankara, pop. 17,820,950 (1940). Politically aligned with the UNITED KINGDOM and France at the beginning of the war, Turkey signed treaties with them after the EUROPEAN WAR began in Sept. 1939, irritating Germany and Italy. Attempts to produce a treaty with the Soviet Union broke off, primarily over Soviet efforts to get concessions about the passage of warships through the Turkish Straits, the only outlet from the Black Sea for major Soviet warships.

Under the internationally sanctioned Montreux Convention, a 1936 supplement to earlier treaties, Turkey was allowed to fortify the straits while allowing free passage to merchant ships and warships under certain carefully spelled out conditions. If Turkey were neutral, she could bar the passage of belligerents. Turkey's complex rights to the historically strategic straits complicated her foreign relations before and during the war.

After the fall of France in June 1940, Turkey's frontiers were threatened by two events on her borders: the collaborationist regime of VICHY FRANCE took control of Syria; at the same time, a rebellion broke out in Iraq. By June 1941 British troops were fighting in both places.

Further danger to Turkey came when Germany launched the BALKANS-GREECE-CRETE CAMPAIGN, invading Greece and Yugoslavia in the spring of 1941. Turkey continued the balancing act: She mobilized her troops against the Germans. Then she signed a friendship agreement with Germany. But when Germany's ally, Italy, wanted to send warships from the Mediterranean into the Black Sea, Turkey stood by the Montreux Convention and would not let them pass.

A grandiose Japanese plan, played in a war game in May 1942, called for a sweeping AXIS worldwide victory, with Germany, triumphant in the Soviet Union, taking Iran and then, triumphant in Egypt, forging a solid NAZI Middle East with a conquest of Turkey while Japan, the new master of India, linked up in Iran.

A German march through Turkey was not that farfetched; rumors of a German ultimatum haunted Turkish strategists. Then, in three fateful events, Turkey's dangers were gone: the German retreat from EL ALAMEIN in Oct. 1942, the Allied NORTH AFRICA INVASION in Nov. 1942, and the German retreat from STALINGRAD in Jan. 1943. No longer was Germany a threat to Turkey or the Middle East.

It was British Prime Minister CHURCHILL, not HITLER, who arrived in Turkey in Jan. 1943. Churchill stopped off at the Turkish port of Adana on the way home from his CASABLANCA CONFERENCE with President ROOSEVELT. He promised Turkey arms and whatever military aid that was needed as a reward for the way it had skewed its neutrality toward the ALLIES.

At the TEHRAN CONFERENCE in Nov. 1943, Roosevelt and Churchill secretly agreed, with Soviet leader JOSEF STALIN dissenting, that the United States and England would go to war against Bulgaria if that country attacked Turkey. Still Turkey wavered when pressed by the Allies to join them. Not until Aug. 1944 did Turkey break off diplomatic relations with Germany. In Feb. 1945 Turkey declared war against Germany and was rewarded with membership in the UNITED NATIONS.

Turner, Adm. Richmond Kelly (1885–1961)

The premier U.S. amphibious commander in the Pacific War. A Naval Academy graduate, Turner served in a variety of surface ships before taking command of a DESTROYER in 1924. Three years later, at age forty-two, he took flight training, after which he served in several aviation assignments.

In 1935, the year Turner was promoted to captain, he went to the Naval War College as a student, after which he remained at the school to head strategic studies. He returned to sea in 1938 to command a CRUISER. With war in Europe and the Far East, in Oct. 1940 Turner became director of war plans in the NAVY DEPARTMENT and a few months later was promoted to rear admiral. He sought to influence naval intelligence in evaluations of Japanese intentions, coming in particular conflict with the fleet intelligence staff at PEARL HARBOR. (See EDWIN T. LAYTON.) When the United States entered the war, Turner was assigned to the staff of Adm. ERNEST J. KING, the U.S. FLEET commander, thus having a major role in planning strategy for the Pacific campaigns.

Turner was assigned as commander Amphibious Force in the Pacific in July 1942 and directed the AMPHIBIOUS LANDINGS at GUADALCANAL in Aug. 1942. He continued to command landings in the SOLOMON ISLANDS until mid-1943, when he took command of the V Amphibious Force in the Central Pacific (part of the Fifth Fleet); in March 1944 he was promoted to vice admiral and given the additional title of commander Amphibious Forces Pacific. In those positions Turner directed the landings in the GILBERT, MARSHALL, and MARIANA island groups and at IWO JIMA and OKINAWA.

The Fifth Fleet commander, Adm. RAYMOND A. SPRUANCE, asked for Turner, having worked with him at the Naval War College. Spruance said, "Our ideas on professional matters were thoroughly worked out together, and we usually thought alike. I was greatly impressed with RKT's brilliant mind, his great capacity for hard work and his fine military and personal character."

In May 1945, Turner was assigned to Pacific Fleet headquarters on GUAM to plan the invasion of Japan. (See MAJESTIC.) He was promoted to full admiral at the time.

After the war Turner served as the U.S. naval representative on the military staff committee of the UNITED NATIONS until he retired from the Navy in July 1947.

Twilight

Code name for U.S. plan to base B-29 SUPERFORTRESS bombers in the China-Burma-India theater.

Twining, Lt. Gen. Nathan F. (1897–1985)

Leading U.S. AAF tactician. Twining held major aviation commands in the Pacific and Mediterranean areas. After enlisted service with the Army NATIONAL GUARD on the Mexican border in 1916, Twining went to West Point and then almost immediately into flight training. After various aviation jobs, from Aug. 1940 to July 1942 he held staff positions at ARMY AIR CORPS and then AAF headquarters, including being executive assistant to Lt. Gen. HENRY ARNOLD.

In July 1942, as a brigadier general, he became Chief of Staff to the U.S. South Pacific air command, and in Jan. 1943, as a major general, commander of the Thirteenth AIR FORCE in the South Pacific. (On Feb. 1 the B-17 FLYING FORTRESS in which Twining and fourteen other men were flying came down at sea near the New Hebrides. The men spent six days on a raft before being rescued.)

In late 1943 Twining traveled to the Mediterranean, taking command of the Fifteenth Air Force in Italy in Nov. 1943. He held that assignment until July 1945, directing bomber raids against PLOESTI and the SHUTTLE BOMBING raids to the Soviet Union. In early 1944 he was given the additional position of Commander Mediterranean Strategic Air Forces to coordinate AAF and RAF bomber strikes against Germany.

In Aug. 1945 he took command of the Twentieth Air Force on GUAM to direct B-29 SUPERFORTRESS bomber operations against Japan. He did not know about the ATOMIC BOMB and refused to let the attack on HIROSHIMA be launched until he did know; Twining later recalled, "I was led inside the fence and they told me what it [the bomb] would do. Of course, I did not believe them. It was an awful looking thing . . . warts all over it . . . terrible."

After the war Twining went on to hold a number of aviation commands, served as Chief of Staff of the Air Force from 1953 to 1957, and became the first Air Force officer to serve as Chairman of the JOINT CHIEFS OF STAFF, from 1957 to 1960.

Type XXI

The most advanced submarine to become operational in World War II. The German Type XXI U-BOAT was superior to all submarines of wartime construction in performance—speed, depth, underwater endurance, and probably in running quietly.

When the EUROPEAN WAR ended in early May 1945 there were 140 Type XXIs ready for service. Only one undertook an operational cruise, the *U-2511*. She had departed for a war patrol in the Caribbean when she received orders to return to Norway because of the pending German SURRENDER.

Another 139 Type XXI submarines were at forward bases in Norway, preparing to go to sea, and scores more were in German waters being fitted out, training, or being readied to transit to Norway. Had the war been prolonged a few weeks or months

many of those submarines would have been at sea. But it was already too late for them to have had an impact on the war as Soviet armies were then encircling Berlin and the Anglo-American armies were poised on the Elbe River. If the Type XXI submarines had become operational a few months earlier the war could well have continued for several months but not years.

The Type XXI U-boats displaced 1,621 tons on the surface and 1,819 tons submerged; they were 251¾ feet long, and diesel-electric propulsion could propel them underwater at 16 knots for an hour (compared to perhaps 10 knots for one-half hour in other modern submarines). The Type XXI had six 21-inch (533-mm) TORPEDO tubes and carried twenty-three torpedoes.

Type XXIII

Coastal counterpart of the advanced TYPE XXI U-BOAT. U-boat historian *Fregattenkäpitan* Günther Hessler wrote that the six Type XXIII submarines that went to sea "provided limited, though convincing proof, of the fighting qualities of these boats." The first unit to go to sea on a war patrol—the *U-2324*—sailed from Kristiansand, Norway, on Jan. 31, 1945. Royal Navy reports indicate that the six boats undertook a total of eight patrols in British home waters, sinking a total of six small merchant ships (19,277 tons). All escaped detection after their attacks.

Sixty-one of these submarines were completed, with scores of additional units on the building ways when the war ended.

Although the Type XXIII submarines were relatively quiet and fast (12½ knots submerged), their short endurance and armament of only two TORPEDOES severely limited their effectiveness.

Like the larger Type XXI, these submarines were mass-produced; the smaller boats consisted of four, all-welded prefabricated sections. The submarines were 112 feet long and had a surface displacement of 232 tons. No deck guns were fitted. They were manned by a crew of fourteen.

Typhoon

High-performance British fighter and ground attack aircraft. While not successful in the interceptor role for which it was designed, the Typhoon was an excellent ground-attack aircraft. The aircraft entered RAF service in July 1941 and despite initial successes against German fighter aircraft, was soon shifted primarily to antishipping, antitank, and "train busting" missions. By D-DAY the RAF had twenty-six Typhoon squadrons providing support to the Allied invasion of France. On a single day—Aug. 5, 1944—these aircraft destroyed 135 enemy tanks.

The prototype Typhoon flew on Feb. 24, 1940, and large-scale production was ordered before the end of the year. Although a Hawker design, most of the 3,330 aircraft (almost all Mk IB) were produced by Gloster Aircraft.

A relatively large, single-seat fighter, the low-wing Typhoon IB had a top speed of 417 mph with a range of 980 miles. The early Typhoons (Mk IA) were armed with twelve .303-cal. machine guns, but the dominant production aircraft (Mk IB) had four 20-mm cannon. For the ground attack role the aircraft could carry two 1,000-pound BOMBS or eight large ROCKETS.

Typhoon, Task Force

Code name for Allied task force for the Sansapor-Mar operation, NEW GUINEA.

U-505

U-505

The first enemy ship to be boarded on the high seas by the U.S. Navy since the War of 1812. The Type IXc U-BOAT was operating submerged some 150 miles west of the coast of French West Africa on the morning of June 4, 1944, when she was attacked by the U.S. DESTROYER ESCORT *Pillsbury* (DE 133).

The U.S. warship was part of an ESCORT CARRIER group commanded by Capt. DANIEL V. GALLERY in the carrier *Guadalcanal* (CVE 60). Gallery had drilled his ships' crews to be prepared to board a damaged U-boat forced to the surface to either remove code machines and documents or possibly to salvage the entire submarine.

The *Pillsbury* had been guided to the *U-505* by HIGH-FREQUENCY/DIRECTION FINDING (Huff Duff). The escort attacked with DEPTH CHARGES, and the U-boat's captain, taken by surprise, thought his submarine had been mortally stricken. He brought her to the surface and ordered his men to abandon ship.

The *Pillsbury*'s crew, well trained under Gallery's guidance, immediately launched a whale boat, which drew alongside the abandoned submarine. While two sailors raced to the U-boat's radio room to remove cryptographic equipment, other American sailors led by Lt. (j.g.) Albert L. David disconnected the demolition charges the Germans had set and shut off an open 8-inch waterline. The U-boat was taken in tow and brought to Bermuda. All sailors of the escort group were sworn to secrecy in the

U.S. soldiers smiling with the imperturbable attitude of youth, crowd the deck of an LCU as the craft heads toward the beaches at Normandy. American troops were well trained, generally well led, and very well equipped. (*U.S. Navy*)

hope of keeping the U-boat's capture a secret. The *U-505* booty contributed greatly to the Allies' reading of ENIGMA communications.

The *U-505* was the fourth Axis submarine captured at sea by Allied navies during the war. Previously, the British had captured the Italian *Galilei* (1940), and the German *U-110* (1941) and *U-570* (1941). The *U-110* was lost while in tow (but her cryptographic material was saved) and the *U-570* was placed in commission as the British submarine *Graph* (her crew had jettisoned her cryptographic material before surrendering).

After the war the *U-505* was taken on tour of U.S. ports and then emplaced as part of the Chicago Museum of Science.

U-boats

German submarines or *Unterseeboot* almost defeated Britain in 1917 and again came close in the spring of 1943 (see BATTLE OF THE ATLANTIC). Although forbidden by the Versailles Treaty to have submarines, in the 1920s Germany initiated a clandestine submarine program by setting up a design office in Holland that developed and helped build submarines for Finland, Spain, and Turkey. In all, prototypes for five designs were tested.

The first German-built U-boats were launched in 1935, part of what WINSTON CHURCHILL would describe as a "brazen and fraudulent" treaty violation. In an effort to arrest German naval rebuilding, the British Admiralty decided to propose a new, bilateral treaty. Signed in 1935, it allowed the German Navy to build up to 60 percent of British strength in submarines, although if *Germany* decided that circumstances were exceptional, it could build up to parity with the Royal Navy.

Still, despite the impact of submarines in World War I, the German Navy, under *Grossadmiral* ERICH RAEDER, stressed surface warships, planning for a conflict with the Soviet Union and Poland, not for war with Britain. Indeed, the ambitious Z PLAN shipbuilding program emphasized surface ships and did not provide anything like the 300 U-boats that head of the submarine force *Kommodore* KARL DÖNITZ believed were necessary for waging a successful war in the Atlantic.

When the EUROPEAN WAR began in Sept. 1939 the German Navy had only fifty-seven U-boats in commission, of which only twenty-six were large enough to operate in the Atlantic. The average number of submarines at sea, in the Atlantic and North Sea, during Sept. 1939 was twenty-three. The U-boats suffered from faulty TORPEDOES and lacked the assistance of naval reconnaissance aircraft to locate merchant convoys. There were too few U-boats for Dönitz to employ the WOLF PACK tactics he had developed just prior to the war.

The U-boats enjoyed several early successes, including sinking a battleship inside of the primary British base (see GÜNTHER PRIEN) and an aircraft

The scourge of the Atlantic and peripheral seas in the European War was the German U-boat. But by May 1945 the U-boats were being attacked in their home waters, when they ran trials or training operations, or were in transit to open seas. This is the Type XXI submarine *U-2534* being attacked by RAF Mosquitos while trying to reach Norway on May 6, 1945. *(Imperial War Museum)*

carrier. Further, with the conquest of Norway and then France in 1940, the U-boats had access directly onto the Atlantic Ocean, alleviating the need to transit around the British Isles to reach the open seas from German ports. (See SUBMARINE PENS.) Finally, with new construction providing more submarines by the end of 1941 there were an average of more than thirty submarines at sea and by the end of 1942 more than 100. But the number peaked in May 1943—when there were an average of 118 U-boats at sea. In that month the Battle of the Atlantic was decided. Forced out of the main shipping areas by Allied antisubmarine ships and aircraft, Dönitz moved his submarines to more remote operating areas while he sought to develop submarines and tactics that could cope with enhanced Allied forces. Unknown to Dönitz, beyond the capabilities and numbers of Allied forces, his submarines were being destroyed because of Allied code-breaking efforts (ULTRA).

A number of countermeasures were tried. Submarines were heavily armed with antiaircraft guns, called "flak traps," and they would sail from French ports through the Bay of Biscay on the surface as they headed for the Atlantic. It was hoped this would reduce their nighttime vulnerability to Allied RADAR-equipped aircraft; but the Allied aircraft simply outgunned (and ROCKETED) the U-boats. The SNORKEL permitted U-boats to recharge their batteries while only exposing a relatively small breathing device, but this, too, was countered.

Rather, the best hope for the U-boat appeared to be advanced submarines that would have (1) no need to surface (but would use a snorkel) while (2) being able to move rapidly while underwater if necessary (without using a SNORKEL). First came the TYPE XXI, the most advanced U-boat of the war. However, Allied bombing of canals, factories, and shipyards, and the laying of MINES in their work-up areas in the Baltic slowed this mass-production program. Although more than 140 Type XXI submarines were completed when the war ended, only one had begun a war patrol. The TYPE XXIII was a much smaller, mass-produced craft with the first unit going to sea for operations in the North Sea in Jan. 1945. A total of six of these U-boats put to sea and they sank six Allied ships. Dönitz had told HITLER that with these

new submarines "the mighty sea power of the Anglo-Saxons is essentially powerless."

(Beyond these submarines, work was under way on the still-more-advanced, closed-cycle submarines designed by Dr. HELMUTH WALTER, which would be air-independent for sustained periods of time.)

But like so many other German "wonder weapons," these advanced U-boats were too few, too late. A short time later Dönitz succeeded Hitler as führer and on May 4, 1945, he was forced to accept the Allied SURRENDER dictates. Under the terms of the surrender all U-boats at sea were ordered to surface immediately and, in plain language, report on a specific wavelength their positions to the nearest Allied forces. They were to jettison all ammunition, disarm torpedoes and mines, and fly a large black or blue flag by day, and show navigation lights by night as they followed directions for proceeding to Allied ports.

Germany continued building U-boats up to the end of the war; a total of 1,153 U-boats of all types, plus many MIDGET SUBMARINES, were completed through April 1945. Of the boats commissioned, 830 took part in some 3,000 war patrols in all theaters and sank over 3,500 ships totalling 18.3 million tons (British records cite 2,603 ships aggregating 13.5 million tons), of which 2,452 ships of 12.8 million tons were sunk in the Atlantic. In addition, U-boats sank 175 naval warships and auxiliaries.

The German Navy lost 784 submarines to all causes during the war:

636 to direct enemy action

63 by air attack on U-boats bases and yards

85 through collision, internal explosions, mines in Baltic waters, etc.

Another 154 surrendered (two after fleeing to South America at the end of the war) and—against Allied orders—218 were scuttled by their crews.

Of the 40,000 men who served in U-boats, about 28,000 were killed; another 5,000 survivors of sunken U-boats were taken prisoner by Britain and the United States. But there was never a shortage of volunteers to man the undersea craft. As the author of *Das Boot,* Lothar-Günther Buchheim, observed: "Hardly any units of the German armed forces can have had more blind faith in their commander than the submarine units had in Dönitz."

Udet, *Generaloberst* Ernst (1896–1941)

The highest-scoring German pilot to survive World War I and a leader in the development of the Luftwaffe. During the 1914–1918 conflict he shot down sixty-two Allied planes. After the war he achieved international fame as a sports and test pilot. In 1931 Udet observed the dive-bombing technique being developed by the U.S. Navy. Encouraged by HERMANN GÖRING, the Reich Minister for Aviation, Udet demonstrated dive bombing in Germany. Udet entered the Luftwaffe in 1935 and the following year was made inspector of fighters and dive bombers. In 1939 he was appointed the director general of equipment with the rank of *Generalleutnant* and the following July was given the rank of *Generaloberst*.

As British historian Alfred Harris observed, Udet's "brilliance as a pilot in no way fitted him for the vitally important task of organising the production of aircraft for the Luftwaffe; one by one his successive and sometimes conflicting programmes ran into difficulties." As a result, few replacement aircraft were forthcoming after the heavy Luftwaffe losses in the BATTLE OF BRITAIN and the subsequent Operation Barbarossa against the Soviet Union.

Udet suffered severe depression and on Nov. 17, 1941, shot himself.

U-Go

Japanese code name for operations across the border from Burma into India, March 1944.

Ukraine

A Soviet region of steppes and rich soil, savagely fought over during the GERMAN CAMPAIGN IN THE SOVIET UNION and the SOVIET OFFENSIVE CAMPAIGN. The Czars called the Ukraine the granary of the empire, its Donets mines the empire's coal pit. HITLER made the Ukraine a major objective in his projected conquest of the Soviet Union. He coveted the Ukraine's soils and riches but hated its people, who were special targets for annihilation. More than 5,000,000 Russians died during the fighting and the three-year German occupation.

Ultra

The generic term for ENIGMA-based communications intelligence used by the United States and Britain during the war. Before 1941 the decryptions of German radio traffic was circulated under the code name BONIFACE, the implication being that the information was supplied by a secret agent. Subsequently, the classification Ultra Secret was employed.

The precise use of the term, however, was only as a security grading for outgoing signals and documents; the actual information itself was always referred to as "Special Intelligence."

Unconditional Surrender

Allied policy for ending the war. President ROOSEVELT used the phrase at a press conference at the CASABLANCA CONFERENCE in Jan. 1943. Observers later claimed that a seemingly offhand remark had ruled out the kind of armistice and negotiations that had ended World War I. But Prime Minister CHURCHILL had long before stated that there could be no negotiating with Germany.

The policy, repeated at the MOSCOW CONFERENCE in Oct. 1943, was seized by HITLER in an attempt to persuade his people to fight to the finish. But Germany did accept unconditional surrender, as did Japan (except that Emperor HIROHITO was allowed to stay on his throne). Italy's surrender, although total, was somewhat conditional because Allied negotiators worked to get some Italian Army units to go over to the Allied side. (For details, see SURRENDER entries.)

Undertone

Code name for U.S. Third and Seventh Army operations to break through the West Wall and establish a bridgehead over the Rhine in the vicinity of Worms-Mainz, Germany, March–April 1945.

Underwater Demolition Teams

U.S. Navy term for "frogmen," who surveyed and cleared obstructions and MINES from assault beaches and offshore waters.

The Navy's first Underwater Demolition Teams (UDT) were organized in early 1943, with the first class of frogmen graduated from the Navy's UDT school at Fort Pierce, Fla., in July 1943. The head of the school was Lt. Comdr. DRAPER KAUFFMAN, a Navy BOMB disposal expert who had learned his trade in Britain during the BLITZ.

The frogmen—mostly Navy but with several Marines assigned—had to be able to swim at least two miles, and were trained to measure depth and bottom contours, and to clear mines and other underwater obstacles, and, if necessary, blast passages through coral reefs. They were brought into the landing area, often at night, by small LANDING CRAFT and rubber boats.

The UDTs were first used in an AMPHIBIOUS LANDING at Roi-Namur Islands at KWAJALEIN in Feb. 1944. All subsequent Navy-Marine and many Army landings had UDTs clearing the beaches ahead of the assault troops. By the end of the war there were about a dozen teams, each with an authorized strength of sixteen officers and eighty enlisted men, all swimmers. A team was divided into four operating PLATOONS of three officers and fifteen men, plus a headquarters platoon of four officers and twenty men.

Unexploded Bomb (UXB),

see BOMB DISPOSAL.

Unified Commands

U.S. unified and Allied commands consisted of forces from more than one military service and from more than one nation, respectively. World War II saw the unification of forces in the field—ground, air, and naval—on an unprecedented basis. And, on a practical basis, the U.S. and Allied components were often indistinguishable within Allied commands.

U.S. Commands In the official history of the U.S. JOINT CHIEFS OF STAFF (JCS), Grace Person Hayes observed, "the surprise attack [on PEARL HARBOR] indicated dramatically the difficulties inherent in coordinating responsibility for defense of the whole Hawaiian area. It likewise made President ROOSEVELT and his advisors determined that there be no uncertainty as to responsibility for protection of the Panama Canal."

Consequently, on Dec. 12, 1941, meeting with the President, U.S. military leaders decided to establish the first unified commands: On Dec. 17,

1941, the command of all U.S. military forces in the HAWAII area were placed under the Commander in Chief Pacific FLEET (Adm. CHESTER W. NIMITZ) and those in the Panama area under the CinC Panama and then Caribbean area under Lt. Gen. FRANK ANDREWS.

In the Pacific, with U.S. forces fighting an "offensive defensive," two unified commands were established in the Pacific. Prime Minister CHURCHILL had urged President Roosevelt to appoint a single Allied commander for the Pacific, and the JCS agreed with that position. Hayes wrote: "The obvious choice for the position, obvious because of his popularity, was General [DOUGLAS] MACARTHUR, to whose direction the Navy would never have given a fleet. Apparently there was no naval commander acceptable as senior to General MacArthur, and so the solution was to establish two commands under the Joint Chiefs of Staff."

On March 18, 1942, Gen. MacArthur was appointed commander of the Southwest Pacific area and on March 24 Adm. Nimitz was named commander of the Pacific Ocean area. The JCS formally established their commands on March 30 and both men controlled all U.S. *and Allied* forces within their respective areas.

The line between the two theaters was the 160th degree of east longitude; almost immediately, however, it would be changed to the 159th degree to put GUADALCANAL under Adm. Nimitz's command because Navy and Marine units were to be used in that operation.

In general, the dual command scheme worked well. Gen. MacArthur was certainly "his own man"; Nimitz, although a unified commander, worked for Adm. ERNEST J. KING, the CinC U.S. Fleet and Chief of Naval Operations, and through King for the Joint Chiefs of Staff. There was continued debate between the Navy and MacArthur, and between the JCS and MacArthur. The situation reached a near crisis on several occasions. In mid-1944, when the JCS could not decide whether to assault Luzon or Formosa, Roosevelt met personally with MacArthur and Nimitz at Pearl Harbor. No members of the JCS were present, except Adm. WILLIAM D. LEAHY, Roosevelt's own Chief of Staff. MacArthur wanted to liberate the Philippines; King, Gen. H. H. ARNOLD, the head of the Army

Air Forces, and others wanted to first capture Formosa. Nimitz saw the advantages of both strategies. Roosevelt backed MacArthur and the liberation of the Philippines was undertaken.

Australian ground forces were fully integrated into MacArthur's command; when the British Pacific Fleet was established it became a part of Nimitz's command.

On Jan. 3, 1945, the U.S. Southwest Pacific Area and Pacific Ocean Area were abolished; MacArthur was placed in command of all U.S. ground forces in the Pacific and Nimitz all naval forces in preparation for the final assaults on IWO JIMA, OKINAWA, and the Japanese home islands.

The complexity of STRATEGIC BOMBING operations against Germany (including coordination with the RAF Bomber Command) and to a lesser degree against Japan, led to the JCS establishing the U.S. Strategic Air Forces in Europe and U.S. Strategic Air Forces in the Pacific that were operationally outside the control of the respective U.S. area commanders (Nimitz and Gen. DWIGHT D. EISENHOWER). In Europe Lt. Gen. CARL SPAATZ headed this organization from Jan. 1944 until June 1945 (when he became commander of Army Strategic Air Forces in the Pacific). Similarly, the Twentieth AIR FORCE was established in the western Pacific in April 1944 directly under the JCS with Gen. Arnold, head of the AAF, as nominal Twentieth Air Force commander. Arnold's staff in WASHINGTON assumed dual assignments, but in fact this was unsuccessful because of the burden on the AAF staff. Arnold exercised his command chiefly through a special Chief of Staff, who was at the Twentieth Air Force base complex in the MARIANA ISLANDS. As a result of difficulties in this arrangement, the responsibilities for the B-29 SUPERFORTRESS bomber operations were shifted to the U.S. Army Strategic Air Forces in the Pacific.

Allied Commands The first Allied command was the ABDA—American, British, Dutch, Australian—naval forces. British Gen. Sir ARCHIBALD WAVELL became CinC of ABDA forces on Jan. 15, 1942. But a month and ten days later—on Feb. 25—the command was dissolved and the defense of Java left to Dutch forces.

There were six Supreme Allied Commanders during World War II. In July 1942 Eisenhower was named to command the Anglo-American NORTH AFRICA INVASION (Operation Torch) and went on to command all Allied forces in North Africa, and became Supreme Allied Commander Mediterranean. Churchill and Roosevelt, in Aug. 1943, were faced with selection of an Allied commander for the NORMANDY INVASION (Operation Overlord). Churchill had earlier offered Gen. ALAN BROOKE the supreme command of the cross-Channel forces, but Roosevelt wanted to select Gen. GEORGE C. MARSHALL on the principle, Churchill later recounted, "that the Commands should go to whichever country has substantially the largest number of troops employed." Churchill accepted this but, in the event, Roosevelt named Eisenhower as the Supreme Commander of the ALLIED EXPEDITIONARY FORCE.

In Jan. 1944 British Gen. Maitland Wilson succeeded Eisenhower as Supreme Allied Commander in the Mediterranean, being himself succeeded in Nov. 1944 by Gen. HAROLD ALEXANDER.

On the same basis of national contribution dictating the area commander, in Oct. 1943 Adm. LOUIS MOUNTBATTEN was made the Supreme Commander in Southeast Asia. This was an Allied command that succeeded the British command in the area.

In China, Generalissimo CHIANG KAI-SHEK was the nominal Supreme Commander. But in that area there were mainly Chinese ground troops; the U.S. Fourteenth Air Force was the principal non-Chinese, non-ground force in the area. (In the interests of Chinese-U.S. collaboration, U.S. Army Lt. Gen. JOSEPH W. STILWELL served as Chief of Staff to Chiang Kai-shek.)

The final Supreme Allied Command of the period went to Gen. MacArthur. On Aug. 14, 1945, with the Japanese SURRENDER, MacArthur was appointed Supreme Allied Commander Allied Powers for the occupation of Japan.

One other major Allied command was contemplated in World War II: In early 1943—with the outcome of the BATTLE OF THE ATLANTIC in doubt, there were proposals for a "Super" CinC with strategic responsibilities for all forces engaged against the U-BOATS. However, as British cabinet historian S. W. Roskill observed in portraying the British Naval Staff's viewpoint, "while unified strategic control was undoubtedly a need 'devoutly to be wished' and one that might be achieved by gradual stages, a new authority could not possibly be suddenly super-imposed on the whole complicated structure of British-American-Canadian operational practice."

Another issue was the nationality of the commander: to the U.S. Navy and Army Air Forces the Atlantic was a secondary theater; to the British it was a matter of life and death. The U.S. Navy, in the person of Adm. King, refused to even establish an overall U.S. antisubmarine command in the Atlantic until mid-1943. (See FLEET.) The AAF and RAF commanders, as well as others in the U.S. government, strongly supported the appointment of a "Super-Air Officer" CinC to achieve "unified air control of the Atlantic," but even this move proved to be too controversial to be accomplished.

Union of South Africa

Capital: Pretoria, pop. 9,979,900 (est. 1938). A dominion within the BRITISH COMMONWEALTH, South Africa on the eve of the EUROPEAN WAR was a nation teetering toward neutrality—with a tilt toward NAZI Germany. Local Nazis, members of an organization known as the Greyshirts, got aid from the large and active German legation in Pretoria. Nazi PROPAGANDA stoked anti-British feelings and sustained the ANTI-SEMITISM and anti-black movements in South Africa.

In 1938 newspapers and members of Parliament revealed that Nazis were urging Germans and citizens of German-descent colonies that their allegiance lay with the Fatherland, not England. The Nazis were especially active in the mandate territory of South-West Africa, a former German colony that South African troops wrested away from Germany in World War I. But, as a new war with Germany seemed about to start, the Afrikaans-speaking (Boer) population was so anti-British that many seemed willing to support the Nazis over the British.

German–South African trade had been growing, despite worldwide economic problems. The pro-German United Party of Prime Minister J.B.M. Hertzog pointed out that a barter agreement— South African wool for German railway equipment and other manufactured products—was due for renewal. After his party won a resounding victory in 1938 elections, Hertzog, a former Boer general hostile to the British, said there was no need for his nation to get involved in a war in Europe.

When the UNITED KINGDOM declared war on Germany on Sept. 3, 1939, South Africa, as a Dominion, had the right to decide on its own declaration. Hertzog called for a continuance of neutrality. Hertzog's deputy prime minister, Gen. Jan Christian Smuts, Boer hero of the Boer War but a World War I fighter for England, was outraged. Parliament rebuffed Hertzog's neutrality policy by a vote of 80 to 67. On Sept. 5 Hertzog resigned and the next day South Africa declared war on Germany. Smuts became prime minister and minister of defense.

German propaganda intensified, with Afrikaans-speaking broadcasters drumming on anti-British sentiment. Smuts bought all rifles in the hands of quasi-military organizations, interned thousands of pro-German citizens, especially in South-West Africa, and forbade the wearing of uniforms or the staging of parades by private organizations.

Smuts ruled out conscription, but one out of every three white men between twenty and sixty years of age answered the call for volunteers. The 102,000 "non-European" men (as nonwhites were called) who volunteered were not allowed to serve under arms; they were trained in such noncombatant duties as drivers and medical orderlies.

In the winter of 1940–1941 South African troops fought Italian forces in what was then Italian-held territory in Somalia and continued on to join with British troops in the liberation of Ethiopia. South African troops and air forces also fought in North Africa and in the invasion of MADAGASCAR.

The battles reflected the "only in Africa" political restrictions on South African troops. When the Smuts government was reelected in 1943, Parliament changed the law, allowing servicemen to choose whether they would go overseas. Few chose to stay. South African soldiers, airmen, and sailors joined other Commonwealth forces fighting in Italy.

British West Africa. The British believed that, since the Gold Coast was administering part of the former German colony of Togoland, Germany might attempt to invade the Gold Coast. In response, the British launched propaganda and recruitment campaigns there. More than 70,000 Gold Coast men served in the armed forces (about half of them in Asia). Unlike the South African "non-Europeans," they were armed soldiers.

After the war, the rise of revolutionaries in the Gold Coast and Kenya led some British to believe that African soldiers developed anticolonial attitudes while serving in British armies. But few postwar African revolutionary leaders served in the military. The veterans, however, became educated, learned skills, and, having seen some of the world, eagerly supported anticolonial movements.

Union of Soviet Socialist Republics

Capital: MOSCOW, pop. 170,467,186 (est. 1939). Born in revolution in Oct. 1917, the Soviet Union inherited much of the Russian czarist empire. Five lands of the czars, however, declared their independence; by the end of World War II those lands would be wholly or partially in a new empire: the nations of Estonia, Latvia, and Lithuania would become new republics in the Union of Soviet Socialist Republics; Finland would give up about 16,000 square miles, and Poland would yield 60,000 square miles to the Soviets, an annexation that moved the Polish-German border 100 miles westward.

The worldwide depression of the late 1920s and 1930s had affected the Communist state less than it had capitalist countries, but the Soviet system was faltering. JOSEF STALIN, the secretary of the Communist Party, had tightened his grip on the country through endless purges of party members, intellectuals, military officers, and other "enemies of the people." Farm and factory production was down.

When the EUROPEAN WAR began in Sept. 1939, the Soviet Union was so financially strapped that it had just given Poland the former crown jewels of Russia, valued at $14,000,000, in lieu of an overdue indemnity payment.

Laziness and drunkenness were cutting production to such an extent that in 1939 tardiness and absenteeism became grounds for firing, and executives who failed to enforce the rules were jailed. Peasants who disobeyed a growing list of farming regulations were deported to Siberia and other sparsely populated areas that the Soviet Union was trying to develop. Between 1926 and 1939 more than 3,000,000 people were shipped from Russian parts of the country to the Urals, Siberia, and the Far East, vastly increasing the proportion of Russian citizens in largely Asiatic areas.

In the east, the occasional clashes between small Soviet and Japanese military units along the disputed Russo-Manchurian border rekindled the enmity between the two nations. In Jan. 1939 the tensions flared into large-scale warfare. Soviet troops, under the command of Gen. GEORGI ZHUKOV, were sent to Mongolia to aid Mongolian forces fighting some 60,000 Japanese troops. Both sides used tanks and airplanes in several months of heavy fighting. The Soviets were superior to the Japanese in both tank and air warfare. In a final offensive that began on Aug. 20, Zhukov encircled the Japanese Sixth Army and inflicted heavy casualties. Japanese dead and wounded totaled 18,000; the Soviets said their losses numbered 293 killed and 653 wounded. A truce on Sept. 15 laid the foundation for a joint border commission and a nonaggression treaty signed on April 13, 1941.

The Japanese request for a truce may have been inspired not only by defeats in the field but also by a sudden and startling elevation of the Soviet Union to alliance with Germany, the "Fascist enemy" that the Soviet Union had opposed in the SPANISH CIVIL WAR. But Stalin would pay any cost to have the Soviet Union play a major role in Europe. He had foreseen political realignments foreshadowed by the 1938 MUNICH PACT, which had handed Czechoslovakia over to Germany. The next nation German Führer ADOLF HITLER planned to take, Stalin assumed, was Poland, which had spurned offers of heavy-handed protection from the Soviet Union.

The two dictators settled Poland's fate on Aug. 23, 1939, when they announced their agreement on a NONAGGRESSION PACT. Nine days later, Germany invaded Poland, beginning World War II in Europe. Later in September Soviet and German negotiators sliced up Poland and, in a secret protocol, established the borders of German and Soviet "spheres of influence" in Eastern Europe, dooming Finland, Estonia, Latvia, and Lithuania to Soviet takeover.

The Soviet Union got about three fifths of Poland and about 13,000,000 people; the Soviets said that more than 10,000,000 of the new citizens were Ukrainians and Russians who lived on land that the Poles had illegally annexed. Germany and the Soviet Union traded inhabitants of their new territories, with about 140,000 people of German descent going from Soviet territory to Germany and about 1,000,000 Ukrainians, Belorussians, Russian Jews, and Polish Communists migrating from Germany to Soviet territory.

The Soviets acquired the three Baltic states later in 1939 merely by menacing them. Finland needed convincing. After claiming that Finland had shown "profound hostility" toward the Soviet Union, Red Army troops invaded. Finland astonished the world by turning back the superior forces. (See FINLAND.) When President ROOSEVELT condemned the invasion, the Soviets responded by withdrawing from the New York World's Fair. The nearly dormant LEAGUE OF NATIONS came to life and, condemning the flagrant aggression, expelled the Soviet Union.

The Soviet Union's alliance with Germany ended on June 22, 1941, when Germany launched Operation Barbarossa—the invasion of the Soviet Union with a front that reached from the Black Sea to the Baltic. Within five months after the invasion, some 500,000 square miles of Soviet territory was under harsh conquest, LENINGRAD was encircled, and German troops came within 25 miles of Moscow. In the first three months of what the Soviets call the Great Patriotic War, more than 3,000,000 Soviets died or were taken prisoner. Only about three out of every 100 Soviet PRISONERS OF WAR survived. The Soviet Union, a devastated battlefield, lost a total of 20,000,000 to 25,000,000 people, the largest losses of any nation in the war. (See GERMAN CAMPAIGN IN THE SOVIET UNION and SCORCHED EARTH POLICY.)

Soon after the U.S. entry into the war Stalin campaigned for a SECOND FRONT that would take German troops away from the battles in the Soviet Union. But until the NORMANDY INVASION in June 1944, Stalin had to be satisfied mainly with LEND-LEASE aid, which amounted to more than $11 billion. In addition, hundreds of millions of dollars in funds and supplies reached the Soviet Union private relief through Russian War Relief, the RED CROSS, and other Anglo-American sources. The Soviets gave little publicity to U.S. aid, consistently dimin-

ished U.S. combat victories, and even attributed the liberation of PARIS to the Red Army and French Communist partisans. (In a report issued in 1990, the Soviet government admitted still owing the United States $674,000,000 in Lend-Lease debts.)

Stalin, now allied with two capitalist states, rationalized the odd alliance as adroitly as he had rationalized a pact with Hitler. He abolished the Comintern, a Soviet apparatus for aiding Communist movements in capitalistic nations; he eased restrictions on worship (cracking down again after the war); and he pledged adherence to principles of the UNITED NATIONS, including self-government for Eastern Europe nations. (They did not see free elections until the freedom surge of 1989–1990.)

During and immediately after the war Stalin, obsessed by fears of disloyalty, drastically changed the political map of the Soviet Union. Several formerly autonomous regions were absorbed into a reorganized federation of sixteen republics. The people of the former German Volga autonomous region were sent to Siberia. The fate of most of the Tartars and other indigenous peoples of the other regions, which had been occupied by the Germans, is not known. The local names of all towns were replaced with Russian names, and Russian-speaking Soviets were sent into the areas.

Relations between the United States and the Soviet Union, though officially close, began to cool as the war neared its end. Red Army troops fighting their way across Eastern Europe waged their own war, while the allied U.S.-British forces under Gen. DWIGHT EISENHOWER waged theirs. Although joint military strategy was practically nonexistent, joint political parleys were frequent. The most significant was the YALTA CONFERENCE in Feb. 1945, where Stalin traded his promise to join the war against Japan for a Soviet sphere of influence in Eastern Europe.

The Soviet Union declared war on Japan on Aug. 8, 1945, two days after the ATOMIC BOMB was dropped on HIROSHIMA, and sent more than 1,000,000 troops swarming into Japanese-occupied Manchuria and Korea from many border points. By the time of the SURRENDER of Japan on Aug. 14, Soviet forces occupied the major cities of Manchuria and were moving toward the 38th Parallel, the line set at the POTSDAM CONFERENCE as the boundary between Soviet and U.S. occupation. Soviet engineers began dismantling Manchurian factories and shipping them to the Soviet Union.

The war bestowed upon the USSR vast tracts of land taken from Germany, Rumania, Czechoslovakia, and Japan. No other major power that fought in World War II gained new territory. Before the war, the Soviet Union was the largest country in the world, covering one-seventh of the Earth's land surface. After the war, its territory covered one-sixth of the planet's land.

For its short-lived participation in the Pacific war the Soviet Union was given the KURIL ISLANDS, north of the Japanese home islands, and the southern end of nearby Sakhalin Island; the former independent republic of Tannu-Tuva in Outer Mongolia (64,000 square miles); joint ownership with China of Manchuria's two main railroads; and rights to reestablish a naval base at what had been imperial Russia's Port Arthur on the Yellow Sea.

In Europe, the Soviet postwar occupation zone encompassed eastern Germany and Poland and through Czechoslovakia and eastern Austria to Hungary, Rumania, and Bulgaria. The Soviet Union transformed all but Austria into satellites and, with the addition of Albania, welded them into what in Cold War terms were called the Warsaw Pact countries, arrayed against the North Atlantic Treaty Organization. The confrontation continued until the surge of democracy rolled across Eastern Europe in 1989, toppling Communist governments, reuniting a democratic Germany in Oct. 1990, and threatening a breakup of the Soviet Union from the Baltic to the Central Asian republics.

Union of Soviet Socialist Republics, Air Force

The Soviet Air Force, officially the Air Force of the Workers-Peasants Red Army, was employed primarily to support ground forces during the war.

The Air Force had undergone a period of innovative development in the late 1920s and early 1930s. In the prewar period Soviet dictator JOSEF STALIN had strongly endorsed aviation development. In 1933 he had established Aug. 18 as Aviation Day, an annual holiday. There was a deluge of books, articles, films, posters, and even postage stamps

commemorating Soviet aviation, and a squadron of airplanes was established to carry propaganda films, speakers, and presses across the broad Soviet state while also demonstrating Soviet aviation achievements. Stalin met regularly with Air Force officials and designers, as well as with the leading pilots, and witnessed several test flights of aircraft. And, the first presentations of the HERO OF THE SOVIET UNION award went to seven fliers who rescued survivors of a research ship that sank in icy Arctic waters. The Air Force was helped more directly by the government sponsoring a massive paramilitary training program, with civilian glider, sports flying, parachute, and even aviation mechanic clubs.

Soviet fliers gained combat experience in the SPANISH CIVIL WAR from 1936 to 1938, with a reported 722 pilots flying for the Republican side; during the fighting with the Japanese on the border between Outer Mongolia and Manchuria in 1938; and particularly in the three-and-a-half-month conflict with Finland that began in Nov. 1939. However, those operations demonstrated major shortcomings in Soviet military aviation. Much of the Red Air Force leadership was purged in the late 1930s. The service lost not only its most experienced officers—including successive heads of the Air Force—but many senior aircraft designers were arrested (some continued to work while imprisoned).

On the eve of the war with Germany the Red Air Force had over 400,000 officers and men; but there were shortages of air crews with some units having only 70 percent of the needed fliers for their assigned aircraft. A long-range air force, directly under the Soviet high command, controlled long-range bombers and transports, with each front (army group) or military district being assigned fighter and light bomber divisions. There was a central training command, although with the expansion of the Air Force, including the calling up of reserves, its training capabilities were badly overtaxed. There was a separate naval air arm, directly subordinated to the fleet commands. (See UNION OF SOVIET SOCIALIST REPUBLICS, NAVY.)

When the Great Patriotic War—the name given by the Soviets to the war against Germany—began on June 22, 1941, the Red Air Force employed 1,540 new combat aircraft in the border area plus at least 6,000 obsolete aircraft (probably in addition to some 1,400 naval aircraft assigned to the three Soviet European fleets).

The Air Force, like the Red Army, suffered massive casualties in the initial German attack. About 400 Soviet aircraft were shot down by noon on that first day plus another 800 destroyed on the ground as German aircraft struck a reported sixty-six Soviet airfields. German sources list only thirty-five of their planes lost on that first day of the four-year conflict (although official Soviet statements contend that Red pilots flew about 6,000 sorties on June 22 and destroyed more than 200 German planes). A German intelligence analysis written after five months of war against the Soviets observed, "the Red Air Force is materially and with regards to its training clearly inferior to the German." Nearly 3,000 Soviet aircraft were probably destroyed in the first ten days of fighting.

In the wake of the Soviet rout, several Air Force commanders in the combat areas were removed from office, a few arrested, and several just disappeared, undoubtedly the victims of secret police (NKVD) firing squads. The commander of the Red Army Air Force when the war began, Lt. Gen. of Aviation Pavel F. Zhigarev, who was promoted to that position in the spring of 1941, survived in the top post until April 1942, when he was relieved by Col. Gen. of Aviation (later Marshal) A. A. NOVIKOV, who served until the end of the war. Zhigarev appears to have survived on the Air Force staff until May 1945, when he was named commander of the 10th Air Army in the Far East. (A couple of Zhigarev's predecessors were executed, undoubtedly on Stalin's orders.)

During the conflict the Red Air Force operated primarily in the direct support role, attempting to gain control of the air over the battlefield and attacking German troops and, especially, tank formations. One of the major components of the Red Air Force was the SHTURMOVIK (armored attacker)—aircraft armed with cannon and sometimes ROCKETS, and heavily armored against ground fire, used to attack German tanks; these included the twin-engine TU-2SH and the single-engine IL-2, which destroyed thousands of enemy tanks.

Another major mission of the Air Force was supporting GUERRILLA operations in the large area oc-cupied by German forces. Soviet records indicate that 109,000 sorties were flown behind enemy lines, some planes landing on airfields temporarily held by partisans. These flights carried in agents and 17,000 tons of guns, radios, medicine, and food to support attacks against the German rear areas. Flying back to Soviet bases, these flights carried more than 83,000 men and women—many wounded—into Soviet-held areas.

Long-range or strategic operations were limited, although the four-engine ANT-6 (TB-3) bomber did fly bombing missions against the Japanese in Manchuria, targets in Finland, and made night attacks against BERLIN. There were ten bombing raids against Berlin flown by the Air Force and Navy until early Sept. 1941, when the loss of bases in the Baltic States prevented further strikes. These raids inflicted only token damage, but were important for the morale of Soviet fliers.

The larger Soviet bombers were found to be highly vulnerable to German fighters, and were used primarily at night and mostly to deliver supplies to guerrillas and, on occasion, to drop paratroops. Shturmoviks, twin-engine bombers, and fighters were the principal aircraft flown by the Red Air Force during the war. Although Soviet aircraft were usually outclassed by their German opponents early in the war, advanced types were produced that included several outstanding models. But more often than not, after the Soviet victory at STALINGRAD in Jan. 1943 the Soviets generally outnumbered the Luftwaffe in the battle area. A reported 1,400 Soviet aircraft fought at Stalingrad and 5,300 participated in the Soviet counteroffensive at KURSK in July 1943, while more than 6,000 took part in the final assault on Berlin. Also, German aircraft were often immobilized during the Soviet winters while the Soviet operations were rarely limited by the cold.

Soviet data indicate that in Jan. 1945 there were 15,500 first-line aircraft in the Soviet Air Force, plus substantial reserves, training, and administrative aircraft. German estimates put the total as high as 39,700 aircraft.

During the war Soviet industry delivered about 125,000 aircraft to the Air Force, a remarkable achievement in view of the dislocation of the aviation industry from Western Europe to the Ural

Mountain area in advance of the German invasion. In addition, over 14,000 aircraft were provided directly by the United States and some 7,400 from Britain, of which over 3,100 were produced by the United States. Although Anglo-American aircraft were limited in their numbers, they were very important to Soviet defensive operations in early 1942, before the relocated Soviet factories could resume full production. Aluminum and aviation fuel provided by the United States under LEND-LEASE were also crucially important.

Women There had been Russian women military pilots since 1911, when Princess Eugenie Mikhailovna Shakhovskaya became a reconnaissance pilot with the 1st Field Air Squadron (she later served in the *Cheka,* the secret police). In the subsequent Communist state women were given professional equality, and many women qualified as pilots between the world wars.

In Oct. 1941, short of pilots, the Soviet Air Force formed a woman's flying corps. Early in 1942, after a strenuous training program, three regiments of women pilots were formed—fighter, light bomber, and night bomber regiments (the last flying Po-2 biplanes). Subsequently, male pilots were assigned to two of the regiments, but the 46th Night Bomber Air Regiment remained all women, including air crew members and mechanics as well as pilots; at that time all fliers were twenty-three years of age or younger.

The regiment (about thirty first-line aircraft) saw considerable action in their canvas-and-wood biplanes, flying low and slow over enemy areas at night to attack specific targets and to keep the enemy on edge. The unit entered combat in mid-1942 and in Feb. 1943 was awarded the honorary title Guards for its combat achievements.

The intensity of the regiment's operations was demonstrated in Dec. 1944 when the unit was based on an airfield only four miles from the front lines. Each available plane flew fourteen to eighteen sorties on one night, the flights to attack German frontal positions taking five to seven minutes; the average in this period was thirteen or fourteen sorties during winter nights, and six to ten during the shorter summer nights. The all-woman 46th Guards Tamansky Night Bomber Air Regiment ended the war fighting in Germany, its last combat mission being flown on May 5, 1945.

Women served in many other Soviet Air Force units, a few as pilots and air crewmen; many more served in training and administrative assignments.

See also GERMAN CAMPAIGN IN THE SOVIET UNION and SOVIET OFFENSIVE CAMPAIGN.

Union of Soviet Socialist Republics, Army

The Soviet Army, officially the Workers-Peasants Red Army, was the largest ground force in the war.

In the 1920s and 1930s the Soviet Union had developed a highly innovative army, especially in aviation, TANK, and AIRBORNE fields. This period of innovation was short-lived, however. In Jan. 1935 the Soviet dictator, JOSEF STALIN, initiated a purge of his political opponents, and from 1937 the purge extended into the ranks of the military: Three of the five Soviet marshals were arrested, tried, and executed as were all eleven vice commissars of defense. (They were charged either with helping "enemies" or other counterrevolutionary activities.) Scores of senior Army officers followed, being arrested and executed. Of an estimated 75,000 senior and middle-grade officers, about 30,000 were executed or imprisoned (many in what would become known as the Gulag Archipelago). Not even the Army's political officers were immune—all seventeen army commissars were executed as were twenty-five of the twenty-eight corps commissars, and all but two of the thirty-six brigade commissars, and numerous others. In many instances wives and sisters were arrested and deported to "internal exile"; few were intentionally killed. (Some of the imprisoned Army leaders were released in 1941 after Germany invaded the Soviet Union.)

During this period, in 1936–1939 Stalin sent several hundred Soviet officers to Spain as advisers to the Republican side during the SPANISH CIVIL WAR, giving them valuable experience (although many were purged when they returned to the Soviet Union).

In the Far East, beginning in July 1938 Soviet and Japanese troops engaged in a series of border battles, near Vladivostok and then on the border of Outer Mongolia and Manchuria. While both armies engaged in the fighting were roughly the same size, the Soviets had more tanks and vehicles—and the leadership of Gen. GEORGI ZHUKOV who, at the battle of Khalkin-Col, demonstrated brilliant tactics in handling large tank formations. Some of the new T-34 TANKS participated in this battle.

On Sept. 17, 1939, shortly after the EUROPEAN WAR erupted, Soviet troops crossed the eastern border of Poland, seizing territory as the Polish Army was fully engaged on the western front against the German Army. Opposition was negligible (there were a few brief clashes with German units during the invasion). Thousands of Polish troops surrendered to the Soviets, many of whom would become victims of the KATYN MASSACRE.

The Soviet Union went to war with Finland in Nov. 1939 to push the border farther away from LENINGRAD. Here the effect of the purges and the lack of initiative by the surviving generals was shown when the initial Soviet assaults were thrown back with heavy losses—some estimates are as high as 273,000 dead on the Soviet side in the brief conflict. Only overwhelming numbers gave the Soviets victory, permitting them to adjust the boundaries to provide more protection for Leningrad. The three-and-a-half-month conflict—popularly known as the "winter war"—highlighted many faults in the Red Army, some of which would be corrected before the Red Army was given its supreme test.

The Great Patriotic War—the name given by the Soviets to the war against Germany—began on June 22, 1941, when German troops invaded the Soviet Union along a front of more than 1,500 miles (from the fall of 1941 the front was never less than 2,400 miles and in late 1942 reached 3,060 miles). The Red Army, forbidden by Stalin from occupying forward defensive positions or carrying out effective reconnaissance (because he did not want to antagonize HITLER), had about 5,000,000 men. In the western Soviet Union were some 2,680,000 troops comprising 170 divisions—103 rifle, forty tank, twenty motorized, and seven CAVALRY (of about brigade size).

The German invasion was successful in all areas, throwing back the defenders and advancing all along the entire front. By Dec. 1941 the Red Army had lost an estimated 1,500,000 men killed and 2,500,000 taken prisoner, with most of the Soviet tanks and aircraft destroyed. (Only three in 100 of the Russian prisoners survived German captivity.) The Soviet call-up of available reserves by the end of

1941 gave the Red Army a strength of just over 4,200,000 troops.

German units in the GERMAN CAMPAIGN IN THE SOVIET UNION in 1941–1942 came within sight of their goals: Leningrad was encircled and besieged, MOSCOW's skyline was viewed by the advanced German patrols, and German troops entered STALINGRAD (now Volgograd) in their thrust to the Caucasus mountains and the Russian oil fields. The tenacity of the Soviet soldiers halted the German advances, with the assistance of a harsh winter, for which the German troops were unprepared. The Soviets were partially armed with U.S. and British weapons, mostly shipped in the RUSSIAN CONVOYS. With Japan engaged in war with the United States in the Pacific, troops from the Far East could be brought to the German front and by the end of 1942 the Red Army fighting in the West numbered at least 9,000,000 (including aviation units).

The turning point for the Red Army came at Stalingrad, when, by Jan. 1943, the Soviets were able to entirely destroy the German Sixth Army and go on the offensive. Soon Soviet tactics as well as numbers were demonstrated to be superior to the Germans'. At KURSK in July 1943 the war's largest tank battle took place and an overwhelming Soviet victory resulted.

The Soviet "steamroller" gathered momentum and rolled westward. By the spring of 1944 most of the pre-1939 Soviet territory that had been occupied by the Germans was again under Soviet control. By April 1945 Soviet troops were fighting in the streets of BERLIN. According to WINSTON CHURCHILL, "It is the Russian Army that tore the guts out of the German military machine."

Throughout the European War the Soviets maintained about thirty (under strength) infantry divisions and several armored brigades in the Far East. The victory in Europe was followed by a massive shift of forces to the Far East when, in accord with Allied agreements nine months before, the Soviets entered the war against Japan in Aug. 1945. When the offensive began the Soviet ground forces in the Far East totaled 1,578,000 troops in eighty divisions—seventy rifle, two tank, two motorized, six cavalry—plus four tank and mechanized corps (about the size of Western divisions) and forty-six independent brigades. Over 3,700 aircraft were ready to support these troops. Manchuria and the upper half of the Korean peninsula as well as the island of Sakhalin fell to the Soviet ground and airborne assaults during the eleven-day conflict in the Far East.

Stalin personally directed operations of the Red Army from Moscow's Kremlin. In addition to direct communications with field commanders, Stalin had personal representatives at various command headquarters, as well as senior political officers who also reported to him (including NIKITA KHRUSHCHEV). Stalin's control included making all major decisions for the procurement of important weapons, the assignments of senior officers, and even the designation of military units.

During the war the role of political officers ("commissars") was reduced, and by Dec. 1942—when Stalin apparently felt he could trust his Army—the political officers became assistants to the military commanders. While Soviet officers were not up to the professional level of German officers, they learned quickly and, as large numbers of troops and weapons became available, won battlefield superiority. Further, the T-34 and some other weapons (especially ground-attack aircraft) were qualitatively superior to German weapons.

As Russian-born journalist Alexander Werth wrote in *Russia at War, 1941–1945,* by the end of the war, "The Army was enormously popular—too popular, indeed, for Stalin's and the Party's taste, though, for a short time after V-E DAY, Stalin was determined to cash in on the Army's popularity and, in June [1945], went so far as to assume the title of Generalissimo." (The only other Generalissimo of the war was China's Chiang Kai-shek.)

At its wartime peak in mid-1945 the Red Army was reported to number 11,365,000 men and women (there were another 2,000,000 Soviets serving in the Air Force and Navy). Reportedly, the Soviet order of battle included 510 rifle divisions and brigades, thirty-four cavalry divisions, forty artillery divisions, twenty-five tank corps, thirteen mechanized corps, and almost 400 separate brigades and regiments (although most units were smaller than their U.S. counterparts).

The war had cost the Red Army, Navy, and Air Force some 12,000,000 men and women killed—almost one half of all soldiers killed in the war—and probably several times that number wounded.

After the war there was a rapid demobilization as the Soviet economy could not support a large Army while technicians and workers were desperately needed in the civilian economy. (In the reorganization of 1946 the name Workers-Peasants Red Army was abolished, with the term Ground Forces being generally substituted.)

See also SOVIET OFFENSIVE CAMPAIGN.

Union of Soviet Socialist Republics, Navy

The Soviet Navy had a minor oceanic role in the war but provided invaluable support to the Red Army on rivers and on coastal and enclosed seas.

After World War I the fleet reached a nadir with only a few obsolescent warships available. However, by the late 1920s, dictator JOSEF STALIN embarked on a major industrial rebuilding program that included the production of large naval ships. By the 1930s keels were being laid down for large cruisers and battleships, with aircraft carriers being planned for construction. This ambitious naval program was aborted by the German invasion of the Soviet Union in June of 1941.

Like the Red Army and Air Force, the Navy's leadership had also been devastated by purges. When the Soviet Union went to war the Commander in Chief of the Navy was NIKOLAI G. KUZNETSOV, who was thirty-five years old when named head of the Navy. He served as People's Commissar of the Navy from April 1939 until Jan. 1947, when STALIN "fired" him (demoting him to vice admiral and exiling him to the Far East; in July 1951 Stalin return Kuznetsov to the top Navy position, which he held until he was again fired in Jan. 1956 by NIKITA KHRUSHCHEV).

At the time of the German assault there were three European fleets, a separation forced by geography; there was also a small Pacific Ocean Fleet based in the Far East:

	NORTHERN	BALTIC	BLACK	PACIFIC
Battleships	——	2	1	——
Heavy Cruisers	——	2	3	——
Light Cruisers	——	1	3	——
Destroyers	5	12	8	10
Old Destroyers	3	7	5	2
Submarines	15	65	47	91
Aircraft	116	656	625	500

When the war began the Baltic was the main naval area as the northern wing of the German assault sought to envelop the Baltic States and capture LENINGRAD. As ports along the Baltic fell to the Germans, the Baltic fleet became bottled up in Leningrad and the nearby island port of Kronstadt in the Gulf of Finland. There, during the 900-day siege of Leningrad, the heavy guns of Soviet warships assisted in the defense efforts. Submarines trying to break out to operate in the Baltic had to evade net and MINE barriers placed across the entrance to the Gulf of Riga, and Finnish and German antisubmarine ships and aircraft. Still, the few submarines that did get out caused the Germans significant losses in merchant ships on the ore routes between Sweden and Germany.

In the Black Sea the Soviet fleet immediately attacked Rumanian coastal targets. But the German drive into the Ukraine soon put the Luftwaffe within striking range of the western area of the Black Sea and the surface ships were forced to withdraw. In their place, Soviet submarines preyed upon enemy shipping and, more important, supplied coastal garrisons cut off by the rapid German advances and, on occasion, helped in their evacuation.

Following the turn of the tide at STALINGRAD in early 1943, the Black Sea Fleet supported Soviet land operations along the coast as Soviet armies pushed westward. The Luftwaffe was still a threat, as were small German and Italian submarines transported overland to operate in the Black Sea.

In the Northern (Arctic) Fleet area Soviet submarines had some successes against German shipping. The Arctic ports of MURMANSK and Archangel (Arkhangel'sk) were vital for the RUSSIAN CONVOYS carrying arms and other supplies from the United States and Britain to the Soviet Union. The Soviets were able to give only minimal air and naval support to the convoys, for Murmansk and other area ports were under periodic German air attack as the German armies attacked eastward along the Arctic coast.

In the Far East the fleet was inactive for most of the war. In Aug. 1945, in accord with the ALLIED agreements at the YALTA CONFERENCE, the fleet supported the Red Army's drive into North Korea and the seizure of Sakhalin Island.

Also important were the Soviet river and inland sea operations, especially on the Sea of Azov. There a flotilla under the command of Rear Adm. S. G. GORSHKOV proved invaluable in supporting Army operations. The flotilla was abolished in Nov. 1942 when the coastline fell under German control. The flotilla was reestablished in 1943 as the Red Army advanced and Gorshkov again took command; in 1944 he became head of the Danube flotilla, supporting the Red Army's thrust into Eastern Europe.

When the war ended the Soviet Navy had made good most of its battle losses, through new construction (mostly in the Far East as the shipyards at Leningrad were mostly idle and those along the western Black Sea coast devastated during the war). Also, after the SURRENDER of Italy in Sept. 1943 the United States and Britain delivered several major warships and submarines to the Soviet Union as a substitute for the Soviet share of the surrendered Italian fleet, which could not reach Soviet ports because of the U-BOAT threat. Separately, the United States provided the Soviet Union with large numbers of minesweepers and submarine chasers as well as PBY CATALINA patrol aircraft.

Naval Aviation   The Soviet Navy had its own air arm of land-based fighters and medium bombers subordinated to the four fleets. (The Navy had no aircraft carriers, although Stalin had planned to construct them in the early 1940s and again in the early 1950s; the Navy attempted to obtain the German carrier *GRAF ZEPPELIN* after the war.)

Naval aircraft fought the Germans in all coastal areas, often operating under Air Force operational control. The first Soviet air attack on BERLIN was flown by five Navy IL-4 twin-engine bombers, flying from a base in Estonia on the night of Aug. 7–8, 1941.

Naval Infantry   Although Naval Infantry or "marine" units had been part of the Russian Navy since 1705 when Peter the Great first established a naval infantry regiment for his Baltic Fleet, there does not appear to have been units of this type in the fleet between the World Wars. In 1939 a brigade was established in the Baltic Fleet and used in the war with Finland (1939–1940). By mid-1941, when the Soviet Union was invaded by Nazi Germany, there were twenty-five individual naval rifle brigades and twelve artillery brigades.

When the war ended in 1945 there were almost 500,000 sailors fighting ashore, some in what were called Naval Rifle units and some in Red Army units, while the troops with the fleet were still called Naval Infantry. Many of these men were from the crews of ships immobilized at Leningrad or sunk, with 147,000 from ships in the Far East that were idle for most of the war.

There were significant AMPHIBIOUS LANDINGS during the conflict with approximately 100,000 naval infantrymen remaining under fleet and flotilla control; they were used to defend naval bases and islands as well as to carry out amphibious landings with army troops. The Soviet Navy conducted 114 amphibious landings during the war, some quite small—essentially raids of platoon size. But four of the landings, two at Kerch-Feodosiya and one at Novorossiysk on the Black Sea, and one at Moon Sound in the Baltic, each involved several thousand troops.

United Kingdom

Capital: LONDON, pop. 46,212,599 (est. 1939). When "England" declared war on Germany in 1939, the declaration was actually in the name of the United Kingdom: The British Isles, which encompassed the island of Great Britain, comprising England, Scotland, and Wales, together with Northern Island, which lies on the northeastern area of the island of Ireland. All were united under the monarchy, with GEORGE VI as their king. Other UK possessions included the islands off the English and Scottish and Northern Island coasts, including the CHANNEL ISLANDS.

England, with London as its hub, was the focal point of the war. But the rest of the British Isles contributed substantially to the war: coal and food from Wales and Scotland, and from Scotland's shipyards around Glasgow, ships. Hundreds of thousands of British and U.S. troops trained in Northern Ireland, "the GIBRALTAR of the North." The first U.S. troops to enter the European theater landed at Belfast in Jan. 1942. (A government leaflet issued to tell the British about U.S. soldiers advised: "Don't talk about Chicago gangsters as if they represented 90 percent of the population of America.")

As HITLER led Germany down the road to war and conquest, the UK took the road of appeasement but at the same time prepared for the possibility of war, financed by a tax called the national defense contribution. In 1937 the Parliament debated air-raid precaution expenditures and by Aug.

1938 was considering the evacuation of women and children from major cities. The MUNICH PACT of Sept. 1938, engineered by Prime Minister NEVILLE CHAMBERLAIN, was denounced as a surrender to Hitler by prominent politicians, including WINSTON CHURCHILL, ANTHONY EDEN, and Alfred Duff Cooper, First Lord of the Admiralty. Hitler, in a well-publicized speech in Oct. 1938 predicted war if Churchill, Eden, or Cooper entered the Cabinet.

After war was declared on Sept. 3, 1939, Churchill and Eden did become members of Chamberlain's Cabinet (Churchill becoming First Lord of the Admiralty). Evacuation of cities was already under way when the war started. Gas masks were distributed to every man, woman, and child. Rationing began. BLACKOUTS became part of the UK's way of life. Men and women were conscripted into defense work.

Following the fall of France in June 1940, newly named Prime Minister Churchill declared that the BATTLE OF BRITAIN had begun and the UK's "finest hour" had come. The British people, particularly Londoners, endured night after night of bombing from Sept. 1940 to May 1941, when German resources shifted for the invasion of the Soviet Union in June.

Throughout the war, wrote Oxford historian Robert Buchanan McCallum, "The day-to-day life of the people of Britain was absorbed by two main concerns, security and production." By the summer of 1942 two thirds of the population between fourteen and sixty-five were working full-time in civil defense, industry, or the armed services. All farming came under government control, and arable acreage was increased by 50 percent. Coal miners and other workers deemed essential were not allowed to leave their jobs. Labor shortages were so severe that men called up for military service were sent instead to the mines.

After intensive but unsuccessful attacks on British airfields and RADAR stations, Germany shifted its major target to London, and, to Americans, the most remembered story of the EUROPEAN WAR was what England called "the Blitz." (See BATTLE OF BRITAIN.) But bombs also rained on southern ports and the industrial north. COVENTRY became a symbol of merciless bombing. Southhampton, with 2 percent of the population of Greater London, was bombed by as many as 251 planes in a single night. Plymouth, with a population similar to Southhampton, was erratically bombed by hundreds of planes, the largest raid one by 354 planes.

In the industrial north, Liverpool, Manchester, and Birmingham were heavily bombed. In Scotland, a March 1941 survey showed people believing that Germans did not plan to bomb Scotland because their war was much more with the British. But Glasgow and its Clydeside shipyards were pounded in 1942, as was Belfast, where more than 900 persons were killed in raids in April and May 1941. A diarist, writing an imaginary message to Hitler, wrote of the feelings of many in the UK during the war's finest hours: "We are a little frightened, we who have been happy. We are not frightened enough to become what you want. . . . If you kill us, we only die."

United Kingdom, Air Force

The Royal Air Force was ill-prepared for the EURO-PEAN WAR. From the end of World War I, the RAF—established on April 1, 1918—had concentrated its resources on the development of an independent bomber force. This obsession with bombers was based on the preaching of the apostles of independent air power, Hugh Trenchard in Britain, Guilio Douhet in Italy, and William (Billy) Mitchell in the United States. As a result, in the 1930s the belief grew up, in the words of Prime Minister Stanley Baldwin, "The bomber will always get through."

Thus, in the austerity of the 1920s and 1930s, the RAF had emphasized bombers. Fighters, naval aircraft, and even transports fell by the wayside. When Britain entered the European War on Sept. 3, 1939, the RAF had 1,900 first-line aircraft, about one half the Luftwaffe strength, with 174,000 personnel. The major commands were: Bomber, Fighter, Transport, and Coastal, the last being land-based patrol and antisubmarine aircraft, under naval operational control. (The Royal Navy regained control of ship-based aircraft in 1939.)

Many British aircraft were obsolete. However, in part because of private ventures, new fighters were becoming available, especially the eight-gun HURRI-CANE and SPITFIRE fighters. These aircraft proved valuable in the attempt to halt and to slow the German invasion of France, and then were means by which the RAF triumphed in the BATTLE OF BRITAIN. Meanwhile, RAF bombers began attacking Germany—at first with propaganda leaflets. Losses to Luftwaffe FLAK and fighters were heavy, and soon Bomber Command was forced to switch to night bombing.

The RAF played an invaluable role in every theater where the British fought. Too often, however, the RAF was outnumbered and outgunned by the Luftwaffe during the 1940–1942 period. Only when Germany was heavily committed in the Soviet Union and British aircraft production was reaching its stride did the RAF begin to have an impact. Night bombing of German industrial cities did reduce the effectiveness of German industry, and force the heavy deployment of antiaircraft guns and defensive fighters. When the U.S. heavy bombing effort began to be felt in 1943, the Allied air forces had the ability to BOMB Germany around the clock.

Similarly, over the sea Coastal Command had been starved in peacetime with priorities going to Bomber Command rather than to antisubmarine aircraft. This lack of long-range land-based maritime aircraft was sorely felt in the BATTLE OF THE ATLANTIC. A key factor in the turn of the tide in that campaign in the spring of 1943 was the availability of such aircraft, especially the American-built B-24 LIBERATOR, which was highly coveted by Coastal Command.

In addition to the Hurricane and the Spitfire, and the LANCASTER four-engine bomber, several other RAF aircraft had a notable affect on the European War, especially the twin-engine MOSQUITO. That aircraft, made of wood, was successful in a number of roles. And, the METEOR was the only Allied JET-PROPELLED AIRCRAFT to see combat during the war. But the RAF failed to produce an effective land-based maritime patrol aircraft or a transport on par with the U.S. C-47 SKYTRAIN /DAKOTA or the German JU 52.

United Kingdom, Army

When the war began the British Army numbered 897,000 troops—deployed around the world. Major British Army units were to be found in India, Malaya, Egypt, and France as well as in Britain itself. In 1940 an Anglo-French expedition to Norway was planned, but that was preempted by the German DENMARK AND NORWAY CAMPAIGN. Although British troops were landed in Norway to counter the German invasion, they were soon forced to withdraw in the face of aggressive German ground and air forces.

The next attempt by the British government to influence events on the continent came with the German FRANCE AND LOW COUNTRIES campaign. By the time of the German invasion the British Expeditionary Force had deployed five regular and five territorial (reserve) divisions in France as well as RAF squadrons. Additional troops and planes were moved across the English Channel in the unsuccessful attempt to stem the German advance. But almost everywhere the Germans were successful, cornering most of the British Expeditionary Force at the French port of DUNKIRK. In an evacuation of epic proportions, the British Army was saved, but forced to abandon its guns, vehicles, and other matériel in France.

The British Army now numbered 1,650,000 through the calling up of reserves and recruiting efforts. The Army in Britain was poorly equipped and would have been hard pressed to halt a German AMPHIBIOUS LANDING of the proper proportion. However, the invasion could not come until the RAF was defeated, and the BATTLE OF BRITAIN proved that was not to be. (See also SEA LION.)

The only other place on the continent of Europe that the British Army would fight in 1940–1942 was Greece. The Italians invaded Greece in Oct. 1940, the Greeks pushed back the Italians, and ADOLF HITLER was forced to send German troops to their assistance. The British pledged to support Greece and 58,000 troops from the Middle East, mostly Australian and New Zealand, with a significant number of British, were transported to Greece. But they were too few and, with strong Luftwaffe support, the German Army overran Greece.

The British Army in 1940 was also fighting in North Africa. The Italian Army, attempting to march from Libya into Egypt, was soundly defeated by the British Eighth Army, forcing Hitler to dispatch the AFRIKA KORPS to North Africa. Although the German force was small, its commander, *Generaloberst* ERWIN ROMMEL, would prove to be

the most difficult opponent that the British Army would face.

This was the only area in Europe–North Africa–Middle East where British troops were directly engaged with the Germans until Nov. 1942 and the Allied NORTH AFRICA INVASION (Operation Torch). British and American troops landed at three points along the northwest African coast, and pushed eastward, while the Eighth Army, under Gen. BERNARD L. MONTGOMERY, attacked Rommel from the east. In early 1943, on the eve of the final Anglo-American assault on the remnants of the Afrika Korps and the Italian forces in North Africa, Prime Minister CHURCHILL declared, "After the war when a man is asked what he did it will be quite sufficient for him to say, 'I marched and fought with the Desert Army'." And, continued Churchill, "When history is written your feats will gleam and glow and will be a source of song and story long after we who are gathered here have passed away."

From North Africa, the British Army—shoulder-to-shoulder with the U.S. Army—went on to assault SICILY then the Italian mainland. In Nov. 1944 the Anglo-American Normandy invasion was the largest amphibious assault of the war. The British 21st ARMY GROUP under Gen. Montgomery controlled all ground forces during the actual invasion, with the U.S. forces then being shifted to the U.S. 12th Army Group under Lt. Gen. OMAR N. BRADLEY. However, during the ensuing Allied Campaign in Europe, U.S. troops were regularly assigned to the 21st Army Group to help it maintain momentum against the Germans (often with complaints from the U.S. field commanders). Montgomery attempted to make a rapid breakthrough to the Rhine River through Holland, with airborne troops capturing key bridges in advance of British ground troops. This assault—code name MARKET-GARDEN—was successful at the first two river crossings, but at the third a series of mistakes led to the tragic debacle at Arnhem and a halt to the Montgomery plan.

British troops continued to move forward until they reached the lines agreed to by national leaders, with the British to the left of the Allied line.

In the Far East the Japanese air-ground-naval assaults on HONG KONG, Malaya, and various British islands easily won the day. The Japanese assault into

Burma, pointed at India, was initially successful, but also one of the most difficult campaigns of the war. British Army participation in Burma was considerable, but elsewhere in the Pacific area it was minimal, although an invasion of Malaya was being planned at the time of the Japanese SURRENDER. (See JAPAN'S CHINA-BURMA CAMPAIGN and THE ALLIED CHINA-BURMA-INDIA CAMPAIGN.)

When the war ended in the Far East, the British Army stood at some 2,920,000 officers and men.

United Kingdom, Marines

The Royal Marines had a rich tradition of AM-PHIBIOUS LANDINGS. However, after World War I this aspect of naval operations was completely neglected, and on the eve of the EUROPEAN WAR the 12,390 Marines in active service were primarily manning guns in British warships and providing security guards ashore.

In 1937 the Navy's CinC at Plymouth, Adm. Sir Reginald Plunkett-Ernle-Erle-Drax, proposed that "one or two brigades of Royal Marines should be entered [into service] and specifically trained as an amphibious striking force. It would be of great value if even one division of the British Army could be given special training in combined operations." No specialized landing forces were raised before the German invasion of Poland in Sept. 1939. Although an all-service amphibious training center had been established, it was left mainly to specially organized COMMANDO units to conduct most British amphibious raids until the larger landings of 1942–1944, when British Army units were employed.

The Royal Marines were employed in "small packets" of tens, twenties, and fifties. In May 1940 they were sent to Iceland and the Faroe Islands to protect them from German incursions. Marines then carried out several operations along the Dutch and French coasts in May 1941 to help in the evacuations from Europe, and in subsequent raiding operations along the European and Mediterranean coasts. Usually coming ashore from destroyers or cruisers, on occasion submarines were also used. In 1942 some 100 Marines were sent to Burma to provide riverine support for Army operations; in May 1942 the battleship *Ramillies* sent fifty Marines ashore to help in taking the island of Madagascar

from its VICHY FRENCH defenders. Separate Marine raiding companies as well as battalion-size "commandos" were formed, with Marines also participating in actions of the SPECIAL BOAT SECTION.

In the NORMANDY INVASION of June 1944 two Marine commandos—No. 47 and No. 48—went ashore on D-DAY and suffered heavy casualties. After Normandy these Marines and other units forming the Royal Marine Special Service Brigade were employed as infantry. Some of those Marines were used to assault Walcheren Island near Antwerp. Again, casualties were heavy.

Thus, the Royal Marines belatedly returned to the amphibious assault role, although on a much smaller scale than the U.S. Marine Corps or even the Japanese Special Naval Landing Force.

United Kingdom, Navy

The Royal Navy began the EUROPEAN WAR in a most favorable position. It far outnumbered the German Navy, which it could bottle up in the North Sea, while the U-BOAT threat—which had almost won the war for Germany in 1917—was considered controllable because of recent ASDIC (SONAR) developments. And, the Fleet Air Arm had been transferred from RAF control to the Navy, although it still suffered from twenty years of neglect.

Although the Italian Navy in the Mediterranean posed a potential threat, the British warships in the Mediterranean working with the French Navy could counter that force. Indeed, for several years the French and British Navies had fully cooperated in planning, working out communications, and exchanging liaison officers.

When Britain declared war on Germany the Royal Navy had in service, including from the Dominions:

12 battleships	49 light cruisers
3 battle cruisers	184 destroyers
6 aircraft carriers (1 modern)	58 submarines
15 heavy cruisers	

Additional ships were under construction, with a new class of aircraft carriers of the *Illustrious* class being particularly significant.

The war in Europe that began in Sept. 1939 saw

the British and French navies and air forces at the ready—but not engaged with the enemy. But while things were quiet ashore and in the air, they were not at sea. On the day Britain declared war on Germany, Sept. 3, a German U-boat sank the liner *Athenia,* the beginning of the BATTLE OF THE ATLANTIC. Before 1939 was over, the British had lost a battleship and an aircraft carrier to U-boat TORPEDOES as well as lesser naval ships and merchant ships.

The first major success of the war at sea was the defeat of the German POCKET BATTLESHIP *ADMIRAL GRAF SPEE,* which was forced to seek haven at Montevideo in Dec. 1939. Believing that a superior force had assembled over the horizon, the commanding officer scuttled his ship (and then committed suicide). But if 1939 ended on a high note for the Royal Navy, it disappeared rapidly in the new year. The British and French governments decided that it was necessary to land troops in neutral Norway, and to MINE Norwegian coastal waters to prevent their use by German ships and to halt the iron ore shipping from Sweden to Germany. However, the Allied effort was delayed, and in April the Germans struck, invading Denmark and Norway. Furious naval engagements off the Norwegian coast followed. The Royal Navy inflicted major damage on the German fleet, but in turn suffered losses, including the outdated carrier *Glorious,* sunk by German surface ships while carrying RAF fighters evacuated from Norway.

Within a month of the German assault on Norway, the German BLITZKRIEG smashed into France. The French Army collapsed and the Royal Navy was soon evacuating, under heavy Luftwaffe attack, troops from DUNKIRK and other French ports. The loss of France was ominous for the Royal Navy, for it would permit the basing of German submarines on the French coast, greatly enhancing the effectiveness of the U-boat fleet. (See SUBMARINE PENS.)

Then, with the fall of France, the country was divided into the German-occupied territory and VICHY FRANCE. The French fleet would be a welcome prize for the German Navy; some ships were interned at TOULON in metropolitan France, and various African ports, especially at Oran (Mers el-Kébir) and the British port of Alexandria, Egypt.

The shock of the defeat of France and, on June 10, Italy declaring war on Britain and France, gave Britain's new prime minister, WINSTON CHURCHILL, grave concern over the fate of the French ships. He had his admiral commanding FORCE H at GIBRALTAR and the admiral at Alexandria demand that the French ships (1) join the British against the Germans and Italians, (2) sail to British ports to be interned for the duration of the war, or (3) sail to a French port in the West Indies or to the United States to be demilitarized.

The French admiral at Oran refused all options and, while his ships were at anchor, the British force—using naval bombardment and aircraft from the carrier *ARK ROYAL*—attacked the ships, sinking several and inflicting heavy casualties. At Alexandria the two admirals were able to come to an amicable and face-saving agreement (there the situation was quite different as the French ships were at anchor under the guns of British warships). Several French ships in British ports were boarded by deception and captured (with the killing of one British officer).

Now Britain stood alone. Churchill, desperate for antisubmarine ships to fight U-boats, made an agreement with President ROOSEVELT to swap rights to British bases in the Western Hemisphere for U.S. DESTROYERS, and fifty World War I–built ships—still useful—were soon flying the White Ensign and Canadian colors. (see DESTROYERS-FOR-BASES DEAL.) But the Battle of the Atlantic was a long, cold, deadly conflict, and not until May of 1943 was the issue firmly decided—in favor of the Allied navies.

In the Mediterranean, Force H from "Gib" and the Mediterranean Fleet from "Alex" fought the Italians with tenacity. A surprise air attack on the fleet base at TARANTO in Nov. 1940 and the battle off Cape Matapan in March 1941 firmly established the British as victors over the Italian Fleet. However, the Luftwaffe turned that situation around. Specialized antishipping aircraft (see HANS GEISLER) and U-boats took a heavy toll of British ships in the Mediterranean, and the spring 1941 evacuation of Greece and then CRETE further exposed British warships to intensive German air attacks. In 1941–1942 the carriers *Ark Royal* and *Eagle* were sunk by U-boat torpedoes, while the carriers *Illustrious* and *Indomitable* were smashed by

JU 87 *STUKA* dive bombers and limped out of the area (to be repaired in the United States). Throughout the period the Royal Navy kept MALTA—the thorn in the side of the AFRIKA KORPS— supplied with food, ammunition, and aircraft, enabling that island fortress to survive.

In the midst of these losses, in late 1941 the battleship *PRINCE OF WALES* and the battle cruiser *REPULSE* were hurriedly dispatched to the Far East, in a futile attempt to counter the pending Japanese aggression. On Dec. 10, 1941, Japanese naval bombers easily sunk the two warships, the first capital ships to be sunk by aircraft while at sea. A few months later the Japanese carrier striking force that had attacked PEARL HARBOR, after giving support to Japanese operations in Southwest Pacific, entered the Indian Ocean to strike British ports and bases, and while doing so sank the carrier *Hermes* and two cruisers.

The war at sea was stretching the Royal Navy to the utmost. But the admirals, officers, and ratings never wavered. The situation began to change with the highly successful Anglo-American invasion of North Africa in Nov. 1942, followed by the two navies teaming for aggressive operations in the Mediterranean, culminating with the surrender of the surviving Italian warships at Malta in Sept. 1943.

The Royal Navy continued to be heavily engaged in the Battle of the Atlantic, while also escorting the RUSSIAN CONVOYS, needed to help keep the Soviet Union in the war during the German offensives of 1941–1942. Similarly, British (and at times U.S.) naval forces were engaged in operations against German surface ships in Norwegian waters, including the battleship *TIRPITZ,* which was disabled by naval aircraft bombs and X-CRAFT, and finally sunk by RAF heavy bombers using special bombs.

The Royal Navy again joined with its American cousins in June 1944 for the NORMANDY INVASION, the largest amphibious operation in history. While the U.S. Navy, Marine Corps, and Army carried out the amphibious operations in the Pacific, beginning in April 1944 British carriers began strikes against Japanese targets in the DUTCH EAST INDIES; on Nov. 22, 1944, the British Pacific Fleet was established and from then until the end of the war a British carrier force (four carriers, two battleships,

five cruisers, eleven destroyers) operated as a part of the U.S. Third and Fifth FLEETS.

The SURRENDER of Japan on Sept. 2, 1945, found warships of the British Pacific Fleet at anchor in TOKYO Bay alongside the U.S. Pacific Fleet. The fleet had suffered the loss of four battleships, two battle cruisers, five aircraft carriers, three ESCORT AIRCRAFT CARRIERS, thirty-three cruisers, 154 destroyers, and ninety submarines, plus numerous lesser ships. It had been a costly as well as well-earned victory for the Royal Navy.

United Nations

World organization formed during the war. The term *United Nations,* attributed to President ROOSEVELT, was the official collective name of the ALLIES fighting the AXIS. Widespread use of the term began after the UNITED NATIONS CONFERENCE in Washington in January 1942. Although the historic founding of the United Nations was at the SAN FRANCISCO CONFERENCE in 1945, the beginnings of the organization trace to the DUMBARTON OAKS CONFERENCE of 1944 and the YALTA CONFERENCE of 1945.

At these conferences, the major powers worked out the basic structure: a General Assembly of all member nations, which controlled the activities of UN operations; and a Security Council, an executive body whose permanent members would be the United States, England, China, and the Soviet Union plus six nations regularly chosen by the Assembly. France was later made a permanent member of the Security Council.

The original UN charter also provided for the creation of a Secretariat for administrative work, an International Court of Justice, a Trustee Council for administering territories that were not self-governing, and an Economic and Social Council, which coordinated the UN's economic, social, cultural, and humanitarian activities.

At its founding the United Nations totaled forty-six—those nations that had signed the UN declaration at the UN conference in 1942. At the beginning of the war the Allies numbered twenty-six. When the four sponsoring nations—the United States, England (the United Kingdom), the Soviet Union, and China—invited forty-two other nations and added Argentina and Denmark, the Soviet

Union insisted that two of its republics (Belorussia and the Ukraine) be treated as individual members. The original members of the United Nations were:

Argentina, Australia, Belgium, Bolivia, Brazil, Belorussia (Soviet republic), Canada, Chile, China, Colombia, Costa Rica, Cuba, Czechoslovakia, Denmark, Dominican Republic, Ecuador, Egypt, El Salvador, Ethiopia, France, Greece, Guatemala, Haiti, Honduras, India, Iran, Iraq, Lebanon, Liberia, Luxembourg, Mexico, Netherlands, New Zealand, Nicaragua, Norway, Panama, Paraguay, Peru, Philippines, Poland, Saudi Arabia, South Africa, Soviet Union, Syria, Turkey, Ukraine (Soviet republic), United States, United Kingdom, Uruguay, Venezuela, and Yugoslavia.

United Nations Conference

Meeting of Allied nations on the war. On Jan. 1, 1942, Prime Minister CHURCHILL arrived in Washington from Canada to discuss mutual war matters with President ROOSEVELT. Churchill suggested the conference (also known as the Arcadia Conference) to establish Allied plans in the wake of the PEARL HARBOR attack.

The next day, the two leaders joined with representatives of twenty-six nations to sign an agreement on the peace aims of the ALLIES, based on the ATLANTIC CHARTER, which Roosevelt and Churchill had drafted in August 1941. The two leaders then continued conferring until Jan. 14.

Roosevelt first used the term *United Nations* at this conference. In the United Nations Joint Declaration each nation agreed to use its full RESOURCES against the enemy, and not to sue for a separate peace. The signatories were:

Australia, Belgium, Canada, China, Costa Rica, India, Cuba, Czechoslovakia, Dominican Republic, El Salvador, Greece, Guatemala, Haiti, Honduras, Luxembourg, Netherlands, New Zealand, Nicaragua, Norway, Panama, Poland, South Africa, Soviet Union, United Kingdom, United States, and Yugoslavia.

United Nations Relief and Rehabilitation Administration

Organization that provided food, shelter, fuel, clothing, and medical aid to people in countries liberated by the ALLIES. Established in Nov. 1943 by forty-four Allied nations, UNRRA (known universally as *un-rah*) was the first service organization of the UNITED NATIONS. Each nation agreed to contribute 1 percent of its 1943 gross national income to set up UNRRA, but the United States initially paid more than half of UNRRA's budget. After the war UNRRA cared for millions of DISPLACED PERSONS in Europe and set up extensive relief activities in the Soviet Union and China. The first director general was Herbert H. Lehman, former Democratic governor of New York. Former New York City Mayor FIORELLO LA GUARDIA succeeded Lehman in March 1946.

United Service Organizations

Provided "home away from home" aid and entertainment for members of the U.S. armed forces. The USO, as it has always been called, was founded in Feb. 1941, its name reflecting its origin. Six service agencies combined their efforts to establish the USO: the Young Men's Christian Associations, National Catholic Community Service, National Jewish Welfare Board, the Young Women's Christian Associations, the Salvation Army, and the National Travelers Aid Associations.

USO clubs, staffed primarily by volunteers, helped servicemen and women who found themselves away from home. Other clubs, set up in overstrained boom towns, provided entertainment for war workers. The USO was restricted to the United States and safe places overseas. But USO camp shows, with troupes of Hollywood stars and starlets or Broadway casts, went behind the lines in combat areas.

Funding for the USO came through local "War Chests," wartime versions of Community Chests. (War Chests were overseen by the President's War Relief Control Board, which also included the United Seamen's Service, War Prisoners Aid, and organizations sponsoring war relief to foreign countries.)

United States

Capital: WASHINGTON, pop. 131,669,275 (est. 1940). For most Americans of the forty-eight United States, the war that began in Sept. 1939 was a European affair. For the AMERICAN FIRST COMMITTEE and other American isolationists, events were all too reminiscent of World War I, when Americans were drawn into a conflict that did not concern them. President ROOSEVELT himself sounded like an isolationist when he said in Aug. 1936, just before the start of the SPANISH CIVIL WAR, "We shun political commitments which might entangle us in foreign wars. . . ."

Through a frequently amended NEUTRALITY ACT, Congress again and again showed its reluctance to allow U.S. resources to be used by belligerents. But Congress modified its stand when Roosevelt summoned it into special session after the outbreak of the EUROPEAN WAR in Sept. 1939. From then on, the United States was entangled in what was no longer a foreign war.

The National Defense Act of 1939 more than doubled the size of the Army Air Corps and appropriated funds for pilot training of civilians who would be called up in time of war. In June 1940 Congress passed the so-called "11% Fleet Expansion Bill," which provided for construction of two BATTLESHIPS, three large AIRCRAFT CARRIERS, fourteen CRUISERS, and thirty-eight DESTROYERS. The next month the "two-Ocean Navy" bill led to orders for seven battleships, six battle cruisers, eight large aircraft carriers, twenty-seven cruisers, and 162 destroyers. Congress also specifically provided funds for building bases on obscure Pacific islands, including MIDWAY and WAKE, and in the territories of Hawaii and Alaska, where potential statehood was not an important issue.

SELECTIVE SERVICE, popularly known as the draft, was heatedly debated in Congress but it became law in Sept. 1949, and the first draftees had their numbers called in Oct. 1940. Seven months later, Congress passed LEND-LEASE legislation, enabling the United States to go to the aid of England in its darkest hours. No matter how hard isolationists campaigned, the march of the United States toward the European War seemed inevitable.

Then, on Dec. 7, 1941, war came to the United States not from Europe but from the Pacific, when the Japanese attacked PEARL HARBOR in the territory of Hawaii and the Philippines, a U.S. possession since the Spanish-American War. (Under a 1934 act of Congress, the Philippines would become an independent republic on July 4, 1946.)

Disbelief, despair, and some panic seized the nation. Nearly every community had a CIVIL DEFENSE organization whose wardens ran air-raid drills and enforced BLACKOUTS. The government took more than 125,000 JAPANESE-AMERICANS from their West Coast homes and put them in "relocation camps."

Although war bloodied both the territories of Hawaii and Alaska, the war barely touched the United States. On Feb. 24, 1942, the Japanese submarine *I-17* shelled the oil refinery at Ellwood near Santa Barbara, Calif., with her 5.5-inch (140-mm) gun. It was the first enemy attack on the continental United States since the War of 1812. In Aug. 1942 the Japanese submarine *I-25* launched a float plane piloted by Warrant Flying Officer Nobuo Fujita from a position off the coast of Oregon to drop incendiary bombs on U.S. forests. A second fire-bombing mission was flown by the E14Y Glenn floatplane.

In the windows of mansions, farm houses, tenements, and apartments, parents hung little red-bordered flags. A blue star on a white field symbolized a member of the family in the armed services. A gold star gave remembrance to someone who would not be coming back.

Income taxes, a concern of few Americans during the Depression, rose sharply during the war. In 1942 the ordinary income tax rate went up from 4 percent to 6 percent, and a special "defense tax" of 10 percent, imposed in 1940, became a "victory tax." People with incomes over $2,000 paid a 13 percent tax; the levy rose to 82 percent on incomes of $200,000. In 1940 the Internal Revenue Service handled only 7,437,307 returns; in 1942, an estimated 27,000,000 people paid income tax and 43,000,000 paid the victory tax. In 1940 only 11 percent of the people were paying income tax; by 1945, 37 percent of them were paying. In addition, Americans were buying billions of dollars worth of WAR BONDS.

Even before the U.S. entry into the war the government was the nation's biggest employer, and its ranks tripled between Sept. 1939 and July 1943. Many of the new employees worked for equally new WAR AGENCIES. New acronyms—OPA, WAVES, SHAEF—entered the LANGUAGE, along with new words, from ALCAN HIGHWAY to ZERO.

About 3,000,000 babies were born in 1942 and 1943, compared to about 2,000,000 babies a year before the war. But the big baby boom would not come until the war ended. The greatest population effect was the movement of people. Never before had there been such migratory changes. More than 27,300,000 people moved during the war. The armed services drew more than 11,000,000 men and WOMEN from their homes. Defense jobs drew millions more, and "Rosie the Riveter" became a symbol of a new army of women in the work force. The three Pacific Coast states, centers of shipbuilding and aircraft industries, increased their population by over 34 percent between 1940 and 1945. During those same years some 1,602,000 people left farms, mostly for work in war plants.

But farm production soared under a government "Food for Freedom" program that publicized farms as part of the war effort. The manufacture of farm machinery and spare parts was given high priority (another war word). The government provided special wartime subsidies and price supports to farmers and declared bees and wool "war-essential." (Honey was a substitute for rationed sugar and beeswax was used to waterproof equipment. Most wool went into military uniforms.)

American farmers had 10 percent fewer workers and 5 percent more acreage than farmers had in World War I. But the World War II farmers produced 50 percent more food than had been produced in the previous war.

Ranking with desertions from farms as a significant migration was the movement of black Americans moving out of the rural South to jobs in the North or into the SEGREGATION of the armed services. Shortly before the U.S. entry into the war, A. Philip Randolph, president of the Brotherhood of Sleeping Car Porters, organized a "March on Washington" against segregation. Roosevelt got the march postponed by promising federal action. He established the Fair Employment Practices Committee, which threatened to cancel government contracts of defense-industry employers who practiced discrimination. Some 2,000,000 black men and women worked in war plants, but segregated housing and transportation made life difficult in their new places. RACE RIOTS broke out in several cities.

Americans, emerging from the trials of the Depression, expected that the harsh demands of war would bring new hardships. But for most Americans life during the war was far better than life during the Depression. There were, of course, inconveniences. Silk and rayon stockings disappeared—as did a brand-new "miracle fiber," nylon. So women substituted liquid leg makeup and some even painted on seams. And there was a butter shortage. But at least it forced changes in laws that had long favored dairy farmers: wartime margarine became a permanent butter substitute.

Food RATIONING inconvenienced shoppers and gasoline rationing cut back on pleasure driving in the family car. But no one really suffered from rationing. People who complained were chided with a question that became a cliché of the times: "Don't you know there's a war on?"

When compared to 1939, the wartime economic picture was extraordinarily bright. The gross national product doubled and unemployment plummeted from 9,000,000 to 1,000,000. Consumers were spending more and, thanks to price controls, getting more for their money. Although WAR PRODUCTION kept home appliances and many other consumer goods off store shelves, shoppers still bought more shoes and clothes than they had in 1939. Their wartime diet contained more calories than their Depression diet, and consumption of meat and home-heating fuels, despite rationing, was well above 1939 rates.

Paul Gallico, in *While You Were Gone,* a 1946 book aimed at returning servicemen, told them about "hardships" on the home front: "women took to wearing slacks in the streets, old toothpaste tubes had to be turned in for new ones. . . . Ice cream was reduced to ten flavors, and civilian suffering really hit its stride when the War Production Board banned the use of metals for asparagus tongs, beer mugs, spittoons, bird cages, cocktail shakers, hair curlers, corn poppers, and lobster forks."

Radio commercials nearly doubled between 1941 and 1945. One reason was a newsprint shortage that curtailed newspaper advertising; another was the rise of radio as a source of news. Americans lived through the BATTLE OF BRITAIN with EDWARD R. MURROW, whose eyewitness broadcasts in 1940 became the model for on-the-spot coverage of war news. Sponsored television programs went on the air in New York City on July 1, 1941, but commercial television became an early casualty of war.

Advertising tied products to the war effort and kept scarce items in buyers' memories by promising that peacetime wonders would flow from lessons learned during wartime. In a magazine ad combining a torpedo and a washing machine, for example, a sheet-metal company said, "When we've *won* this hard war, the steel in your *new* automobile will be battle-proved, the sheet metal in your gleaming washing machine, hot-water tank, bathtub and sink will have profited from wartime experiences and research." An insecticide ad had a termite boasting, "Boy! Am I helping the Japs!" Ads flying a *Help Win the War* banner included one from Kleenex: "Don't be a Public Enemy. Be patriotic and smother sneezes with Kleenex to help keep colds from spreading to war workers." A cigarette company, explaining that it was in a white package because the dye was needed for Army CAMOUFLAGE, advertised, "Lucky Strike green has gone to war."

A Massachusetts woman reminiscing about the way the war ended, remembered the Main Street parade, the church bells ringing, the end of rationing, the return of cinnamon and her favorite ice cream. But, she added, "The men didn't come home right away." For some, the wait would not be long. For others, the wait would never end.

United States, Air Force

The United States entered the war with a rapidly growing Army Air Forces (AAF). That designation had come into being on June 20, 1941, as one of three Army operational forces, the others being the Army Ground Forces and the Services of Supply (later Army Service Forces).

During the 1930s the Army's aviation leaders had stressed the need for heavy bombers—to protect the American coast from hostile invasion. Arguments between the Army and the Navy forced President ROOSEVELT himself to dictate the ranges out to which Army planes could fly from the coast. This emphasis led to the Army developing the effective B-17 FLYING FORTRESS and B-24 LIBERATOR bombers, and paved the way for "the ultimate" wartime bomber, the B-29 SUPERFORTRESS. However, fighters were ignored and when the United States

entered the war most of the AAF fighters available were either obsolete or little more than advanced trainers. (The Army did have good transports because of American civil aviation developments.)

With Europe about to go to war, in early 1939 the Army was authorized a strength of 6,000 airplanes—more than double its previous authorization. A massive training program was initiated to provide pilots and air crews for those planes, but even this effort was insufficient and, with France having fallen to German aggression, in June 1940 a program of 12,835 aircraft was approved with a goal of April 1942.

The Dec. 7–8, 1941, attacks by Japanese aircraft on PEARL HARBOR and the Philippines destroyed much of the available AAF strength in the war zone. Subsequently, more losses were suffered in the DUTCH EAST INDIES. But more aircraft—and pilots—were authorized; at the end of the war the AAF had taken delivery of almost 230,000 aircraft in a five-year period. At its peak, the AAF had a total strength of 2,411,294 men and WOMEN. (See WAC, WASP.)

Because the AAF was a part of the Army, when the U.S. and British service chiefs met in late 1941 to recommend Allied strategy, thus forming the COMBINED CHIEFS OF STAFF, Gen. GEORGE C. MARSHALL, U.S. Army Chief of Staff, permitted Lt. Gen. H. H. ARNOLD, head of the AAF to sit as a full member—the opposite to British Marshal of the RAF Lord Portal, Chief of Air Staff. Indeed, Marshall gave the AAF commanders and planners considerable latitude during the war. As they fought the war, in the words of Maj. Perry McCoy Smith (later major general, U.S. Air Force), the AAF commanders ". . . were convinced that American airpower was winning World War II. The enormous role that the Russians, the British, and the Chinese, as well as the United States Navy, Marines, and Army were playing in the victory was not recognized by the Air Force planners. Conflict and war, they felt, would always occur, but wars would be brought quickly to an end through American airpower. . . ."

U.S. air power—including STRATEGIC BOMBING—made a vital contribution to the war. But it could not have been won in any theater without the U.S. Army and Navy, and in Europe without the

British (from 1939 to 1943) and Soviet armed forces.

United States, Army

When Europe went to war on Sept. 1, 1939, the U.S. Army had approximately 174,000 men on active duty, most assigned to more than 130 camps, posts, and stations throughout the continental United States; approximately one quarter were overseas, most of those in Hawaii. This strength included the Army AIR CORPS. (See UNITED STATES, AIR FORCE.) The Regular Army was supported by the 200,000-man NATIONAL GUARD organization.

In 1939 three infantry DIVISIONS (1st, 2nd, and 3rd) were organized as were two CAVALRY divisions (1st and 2nd). Several other divisions were at BRIGADE strength and there was one mechanized brigade (7th Cavalry). Few of the Army's units were at full strength or had their full allowance of equipment.

During 1940 the Army, under the direction of Gen. GEORGE C. MARSHALL, who became Chief of Staff in Sept. 1939, underwent major reorganization. Four field ARMIES were established with responsibility for the command and training of ground forces; a separate Armored Force was established (as was a TANK DESTROYER Command the following year) to foster the development of TANK tactics, which had served the Germans so well in BLITZKRIEG campaigns of May–June 1940. (Although the Army had a Tank Corps in World War I, it was abolished in 1920 as the tank was thought of as an infantry support weapon; and, because the tanks were to work with the infantry, the Army concentrated on light tanks that could easily cross bridges and move forward with troops.)

By a joint resolution of Congress, from Sept. 16, 1940, to Oct. 6, 1941, the entire National Guard was brought into federal service: by then a total of 300,000 men organized into sixteen infantry divisions and twenty-nine air observation squadrons plus nondivisional units. These units were integrated into the regular Army for a period of one year. As a result of this call-up and subsequent mobilization, on Dec. 7, 1941, the U.S. Army had 1,686,000 men in thirty-six active divisions—twenty-nine infantry, five armored, and two cav-

alry—plus supporting units. Most formations lacked training and were short of equipment.

When war began, the Army was mostly at continental bases with three divisions overseas—the 24th and 25th Infantry Divisions in Hawaii and the Philippine Division (12th) in the Philippines. (The Philippine Division fought with great heroism until the fall of CORREGIDOR on May 9, 1942, when the division ceased to exist as an entity.)

On Dec. 6, 1941, Brig. Gen. LESLEY J. McNAIR, Jr., who the previous year had taken charge of training the Army, estimated that the United States would require 200 divisions to win a war against Germany and Japan. Early in 1942 the newly established JOINT CHIEFS OF STAFF projected a U.S. Army of 334 divisions would be needed to carry out Allied strategy.

During 1942 the Army was able to add thirty-seven more divisions, bringing the total to seventy-two (the Philippine Division had been lost) with a total Army ground manpower of 3,730,000 (plus 1,270,000 in the Army Air Forces). But the Army was unprepared and ill trained and the nation lacked the AMPHIBIOUS SHIPS for a cross-Channel invasion of Europe in 1942 or 1943. Indeed, the Allied decision makers—ROOSEVELT and CHURCHILL—had few options for employing Army ground forces in the Germany First strategy. The only place where the British were fighting Germans on the ground was in Northeast Africa. The decision was made to use the Army to invade Northwest Africa—held by neutral VICHY FRANCE—as a means of (1) putting the Army into the field, (2) showing the Soviets, who were calling for a SECOND FRONT, that America was moving, and (3) eventually relieving pressure on the British Eighth Army by coming at the German AFRIKA KORPS from a second direction.

By the time of the North African invasion the Army had already sent thousands of troops to the Southwest Pacific area to strengthen defenses of Australia and those islands still held by U.S. forces. The landing of U.S. Marines on GUADALCANAL in Aug. 1942 led to the commitment of Army ground troops (the AAF being already heavily engaged in that theater). Indeed, by the time of the North Africa invasion in Nov. 1942 the Army had more troops committed to the Pacific than to North Africa. (Small Army garrisons had also been sent to

Iceland and Northern Ireland, while staffs to support future operations were being set up in China and England.)

Thus, a direct confrontation with German troops was delayed until Feb. 1943 when they met in battle in south central Tunisia (with U.S. troops being put to flight at KASSERINE PASS). But North Africa was a secondary theater to the Germans, and the astute leadership of generals such as DWIGHT D. EISENHOWER, OMAR BRADLEY, and GEORGE S. PATTON, ably tutored by Gen. Sir HAROLD ALEXANDER and other British leaders, coupled with increased amounts of war matériel, permitted the American forces to take the measure of Germany's best. The North African campaign was followed by the assaults on SICILY, then the Italian mainland. Finally, in June 1944 the U.S. Army was ready for the NORMANDY INVASION of France (to be followed by a smaller landing in Southern France). However, the Army was still short of men and divisions.

The last new U.S. Army division was formed in Aug. 1943, bringing the total to ninety, but one was inactivated in May 1944, providing the eighty-nine divisions that would be available through the end of the war. (The Marine Corps would grow to six divisions.) The Army would have to commit against superior Axis forces, but the shortfalls would be compensated by ARTILLERY and, especially, aircraft, both tactical and strategic.

When Gen. Eisenhower gave the "go" command for the cross-Channel invasion in June 1944 the assault force consisted of only seven American divisions (five infantry and two AIRBORNE) with three British and one Canadian divisions also hitting the beach on D-DAY.

While the Army proved itself in combat against the best of the German legions and triumphed, the Army was continually plagued by shortages of ground combat troops (especially infantry), lags in the production of artillery shells, and the shortage of trucks to keep the forward-moving armies supplied. When the war in Europe ended Gen. Eisenhower had under his command sixty-one of the U.S. Army divisions (68 percent of the total) plus thirty Allied divisions.

From the time that the decision was made to invade North Africa, Gen. Eisenhower, a protégé of

Gen. Marshall, was chosen to command all U.S. Army and AAF forces in Europe (except that AAF strategic bombers were joined with the RAF Bomber Command under the direction of the COMBINED CHIEFS OF STAFF). Ike, as he was invariably called, remained in command of the American Army in Europe until the end of the war.

In the Pacific, Gen. DOUGLAS MACARTHUR (Commander in Chief Southwest Pacific Area from March 1942) made do with relatively few troops. But his "leap-frog" tactics and the naval and air support available enabled him to move effectively up the ladder of islands in the SOLOMONS and beyond. At the same time the Central Pacific commander, Adm. CHESTER W. NIMITZ (Commander in Chief Pacific Ocean Area) was moving westward through Pacific island groups, employing both Marines and soldiers, ably supported by his massive Third and Fifth FLEETS and their overwhelming air power.

Only in the China-Burma-India theater were U.S. ground forces unequal to the job; the Japanese were too strong, the terrain too difficult, the command structure too complex, and the logistic lines too long for the small number of troops committed to have a decisive impact on the war. (This is not to detract from those advances that were made, especially by irregular groups, such as MERRILL'S MARAUDERS.)

At the end of the European War, in May 1945, the U.S. Army had 8,300,000 men and women, including 2,500,000 million in the Ground Forces comprising the eighty-nine divisions and numerous separate combat units. (The total U.S. armed forces at that time was 12,350,000.) The woman's component—the Woman's Army Corps or WAC—reached a peak strength of 99,288 in April 1945. (On July 1, 1943, the WAC had become a full-fledged branch of the Army.)

When the European War was over the Army began shifting more forces to the Pacific, in preparation for the planned invasion of Japan and the subsequent campaign that was expected to continue into at least 1946 and possibly 1947. Estimates of 1,000,000 casualties (dead and wounded) led to the urging of the Soviet Union to enter the Pacific war. Under an agreement made at the YALTA CONFERENCE Soviet troops would join the war against the Japanese within nine months—by Sept. 1945.

In preparation for the invasion of the Japanese homeland, in Jan. 1945 the old UNIFIED COMMANDS—Southwest Pacific Area and Pacific Ocean Area—were abolished. In their place, Gen. MacArthur was placed in command of all ground forces in the Pacific and Adm. Nimitz in charge of all naval forces. The Army Air Force command structure was more complicated, in part because of the AAF insistence that the STRATEGIC BOMBING effort remain under direct and centralized control of the airmen. Thus, MacArthur would command the U.S. massive Army-Marine ground assault against the Japanese home islands, carried to Japan and supported by the Third and Fifth Fleets.

But—because of naval and air blockade and the use of ATOMIC BOMBS—the invasion of Japan was unnecessary. Instead, the Army that remained in the Far East after Japan's capitulation became an occupation force (as it had in Germany).

Prof. Russell F. Weigley, leading historian of the U.S. Army at war in Europe, concluded in his *Eisenhower's Lieutenants*: "Pitted against the German army, the United States Army suffered long from a relative absence of the finely honed professional skill of the Germans, officers and men, in every respect of tactics and operations. In part because of American inexperience, in part because of unresolved inconsistencies in the American conception of war reverberating downward from the strategic to the tactical sphere—as in the lack of firepower in the assaults of the infantry PLATOONS—the German army remained qualitatively superior to the American army, formation for formation, throughout far too many months of the American army's greatest campaign. In the end, it was its preponderance of material RESOURCES that carried its army through to victory in World War II."

See also WAC.

United States, Coast Guard

A U.S. military service, the Coast Guard was a part of the Treasury Department until a presidential order of Nov. 1, 1941, made it a part of the Navy. During the war Coast Guardsmen served at sea, operating a variety of ships and LANDING CRAFT; and ashore, providing port security, and in the air.

During 1940 and 1941 the Coast Guard's cutters—the term for all vessels over 100 feet—received their wartime armament: additional guns, DEPTH CHARGES, and SONAR gear. Some of the cutters were provided with belts of degaussing cables in their hulls to protect them against MINES. Additional men were recruited to man the cutters and patrol boats. (Ten 250-foot cutters were transferred to Great Britain in 1941 under LEND-LEASE.) As war approached, in June 1941 President ROOSEVELT signed an executive order that permitted Coast Guardsmen to serve in Navy ships and to operate four large transports that were taken over from commercial service.

Also in 1941, the Coast Guard adopted the full U.S. Navy uniform, with the only Coast Guard distinguishing marks being the insignia for specialized corps (e.g., engineer officers), buttons, officer cap devices, and Coast Guard shield worn on the lower right sleeve of enlisted jumpers. Thus, the Coast Guard was well integrated into naval operations when, a month before the PEARL HARBOR attack, it became part of the Navy. The subsequent changes that followed the integration were small: cutters were painted dark gray and the national colors were flown from ships twenty-four hours a day, not just in daylight, as had been the Coast Guard custom.

When the United States entered the war the Coast Guard had 25,000 officers and enlisted men. The service reached a peak wartime strength of 241,000 men and WOMEN (see SPAR). In addition to vital port security, beach patrol, lifesaving, and merchant ship-inspection roles, during the war Coast Guard personnel operated 802 cutters of various sizes and hundreds of small craft, plus 351 Navy ships (including thirty DESTROYER ESCORTS, seventy-five frigates, and a host of amphibious, landing, and auxiliary ships), and 288 Army ships. They were often under fire, aboard cutters escorting Allied CONVOYS in the Atlantic and manning LANDING CRAFT and LANDING SHIPS, TANK participating in Pacific invasions; indeed, Coast Guardsmen participated in every major AMPHIBIOUS LANDING carried out by U.S. forces. One Coast Guardsman participating in the GUADALCANAL operation, Signalman 1st Class Douglas A. Munro, was fatally wounded while helping evacuate Marines under Japanese gunfire. He became the only Coast Guardsman to be awarded the MEDAL OF HONOR during the war.

In the BATTLE OF THE ATLANTIC the 327-foot Coast Guard cutter *Alexander Hamilton* (WPG 34) was sunk by a German U-BOAT off Iceland on Jan. 29, 1942, while towing a disabled storeship. Twenty-six of her crew died. Several smaller Coast Guard ships were also sunk in action, but Coast Guard cutters or Coast Guard–manned Navy ships were credited with sinking eleven U-boats (another submarine was sunk by a Coast Guard aircraft; see below).

The Coast Guard was called upon during the war for a number of unusual and special missions, among them destroying German weather stations on Greenland and sinking or capturing German supply ships. In the NORMANDY INVASION of June 1944, in addition to manning and escorting landing ships, Coast Guard 83-foot patrol craft also rescued 1,438 men from sinking or burning ships. And Coast Guardsmen established and maintained the LORAN navigation stations that provide accurate navigation data for Allied ships and aircraft.

Aviation In the air the Coast Guard fliers flew several hundred of their own and Navy aircraft, mostly on search-and-rescue missions. Ens. Henry C. White, a Coast Guard pilot flying a J4F WIDGEON, sank the *U-166* in the Gulf of Mexico on Aug. 1, 1942. Also, the Coast Guard was charged by the Navy with responsibility for HELICOPTER development during the war, including flight trials from ships.

United States, Marines

The U.S. Marine Corps—a separate service within the U.S. NAVY DEPARTMENT—that carried out the major assaults of the Pacific War. During the 1920s and 1930s the Marine Corps concentrated on the development of tactics and equipment for AMPHIBIOUS LANDINGS. Also, the U.S. Marine Corps was the only force of its type with an integral air arm, and close coordination between ground and air units became a hallmark of the Marines. (Marine pilots were trained to fly from AIRCRAFT CARRIERS, and most Marine combat aircraft were similar to those flown by the Navy, providing considerable tactical flexibility.)

In addition, Marines were used for "police actions" in Central America in that period, and detachments of Marines served in larger U.S. warships,

guarded U.S. embassies, and provided detachments at most U.S. naval bases in the United States and overseas. From 1927 until Nov. 1941, there was also a Marine detachment in China to help protect U.S. interests in that strife-torn country.

When the EUROPEAN WAR began the Marine Corps' strength was 18,000 men—about the same size as the New York City police force. An increase in strength was authorized, through both recruitment and calling up reserves until, when the Japanese attacked PEARL HARBOR on Dec. 7, 1941, the Marine strength was 70,425; a few months earlier two DIVISIONS had been formed, the first units of that size in Marine history.

When the United States went to war there was a Marine BRIGADE in Iceland, a REGIMENT in the Philippines (recently arrived from China), and defense BATTALIONS on WAKE and MIDWAY ISLANDS, plus a smaller DETACHMENT on GUAM. A dozen Marine F4F WILDCAT fighters were also on Wake, and provided a heroic defense before the island fell to the Japanese. There were insufficient Marines on Guam to effectively resist the Japanese assault, while the Marines in the Philippines fought a lengthy defensive battle, with most of the survivors becoming Japanese PRISONERS OF WAR.

The first American offensive of the war was the Marine landing on GUADALCANAL in Aug. 1942. This was also the first of a long series of landings as Marines demonstrated their amphibious prowess at MAKIN, TARAWA, NEW GEORGIA, BOUGAINVILLE, ENIWETOK, the MARIANA ISLANDS, PELELIU, OKINAWA, and IWO JIMA as well as lesser-known assaults. Although the U.S. Army conducted more and larger amphibious assaults, none came close to the ferocity of some of the Marine assaults. The Marines also flew combat missions in support of their own troops; when the Japanese Navy introduced KAMIKAZE attacks in late 1944, Marine F4U CORSAIR fighters went aboard carriers to help fend off the suiciders. (Marine aircraft regularly flew from ESCORT CARRIERS for close air support of ground operations.)

When the war ended Marine Corps strength—men and WOMEN MARINES—totaled 484,631, with six Marine divisions and five aircraft WINGS, their operations coordinated by two amphibious CORPS. Marines were fighters—medical, chaplain, and certain other specialized personnel in Marine units were Navy; they were fully integrated, wearing Marine "utilities" when serving in combat units.

The size of the Marine Corps also led to the first three- and four-star commandants being appointed during the war: Thomas Holcomb, commandant from 1936 to 1943 became the Corps' first lieutenant general, and ALEXANDER A. VANDEGRIFT (1944–1947), became the first full general in Marine history.

United States, Navy

The large, modern fleet available to the United States for the war had its beginnings in 1933 when FRANKLIN D. ROOSEVELT became President, bringing to that office a deep understanding and love of the Navy (Roosevelt having been assistant secretary of the Navy in World War I). Roosevelt also looked at naval construction as a means of helping economic recovery. His rebuilding plans were enthusiastically endorsed in Congress.

Further, Roosevelt's strong support of the British cause led to U.S. warships becoming involved in aiding British antisubmarine operations beginning in 1940 (see NEUTRALITY PATROL). Combat with German U-BOATS followed, with the *REUBEN JAMES* (DD 245) being sunk by a submarine in Oct. 1941 and several other U.S. destroyers being attacked. This undeclared war in the Atlantic led to a weakening of the Pacific FLEET, which had been based at PEARL HARBOR in early 1941 as a "deterrent" to Japanese aggression in the Pacific. The Pacific Fleet was forced to send numerous warships to the Atlantic. At the same time, new Navy patrol planes were also sent to the Atlantic, reducing the Pacific Fleet's scouting capabilities.

When the war began the United States had three fleets:

	ATLANTIC	PACIFIC	ASIATIC
AIRCRAFT CARRIERS	4	3	——
ESCORT CARRIERS	1	——	——
BATTLESHIPS	8	9	——
CRUISERS			
Heavy	5	12	1
Light	8	9	2
DESTROYERS	87	71	13
SUBMARINES	60	22	29

In addition, large numbers of warships were under construction or on order—fifteen fast battleships, eleven large aircraft carriers, and scores of cruisers, destroyers, and submarines. All were the most effective of their respective types being built by any nation. In addition, U.S. yards would produce thousands of antisubmarine craft, minesweepers, motor torpedo boats, AMPHIBIOUS SHIPS, and LANDING CRAFT during the war.

Massive recruiting efforts were undertaken to man these ships and the Navy grew from just over 160,000 officers and enlisted men on Dec. 7, 1941, to 3,380,000 when the war ended. (This included the large naval air arm; see below.)

The Japanese attack on Pearl Harbor on Dec. 7, 1941, led to a rapid recasting of U.S. war strategy. The only significant losses at Pearl Harbor were battleships and patrol aircraft; thus, the early Navy operations in the Pacific were carried out mainly by carrier task groups and submarines. Adm. ERNEST J. KING, who had become Commander in Chief U.S. Fleet in Dec. 1941 and, additionally, Chief of Naval Operations in March 1942, favored an emphasis on naval operations in the Pacific. President Roosevelt and Prime Minister CHURCHILL, however, had earlier decided on a "beat Germany first" strategy; still, King sought to keep the majority of U.S. naval forces in the Pacific. The U.S. Navy's victories at CORAL SEA and MIDWAY permitted King to advocate the invasion of GUADALCANAL by a Navy-Marine force in Aug. 1942, thus initiating the naval offensive in the Pacific.

Large naval forces, however, were needed in the BATTLE OF THE ATLANTIC, and then for the Allied AMPHIBIOUS LANDINGS in North Africa, SICILY, and at Normandy. U.S. shipyards were able to produce the massive numbers of ships required for a multiocean war (with several hundred ships also transferred to Britain and other Allies).

Beyond ship numbers, the Navy was able to develop a large air arm and continue innovative developments in antiair and antisubmarine weapons, RADAR, and SONAR. The major Navy technical failure was in TORPEDOES. Immediatley after the war began, U.S. submarines entered Japanese waters to attack merchant shipping and warships. They were largely ineffective because of faulty torpedoes (a problem that also plagued British and German submarines). Not until early 1943 were the torpedo problems fully solved and submarines able to demonstrate their effectiveness. (By that time Japanese warship losses had drastically curtailed Japan's antisubmarine capability.)

The major shortfall in U.S. naval operations appears to have been the reluctance to establish CONVOYS off the U.S. Atlantic Coast and in the Caribbean when German U-boats began attacks in the western Atlantic in early 1942. Indeed, not until May 1, 1942, did Adm. King establish the U.S. Tenth Fleet (under his direct command) to coordinate U.S. antisubmarine activities in the Atlantic.

When the war ended the U.S. fleet was larger than the combined strength of the rest of the major navies at the start of the war except in battleships. Although the U.S. Navy had suffered major losses, all were replaced many times over. In some respects the most important aspect of the war was the ascendancy of the aircraft carrier over the battleship. This direction was understood by the U.S. naval leadership even before the war, as evidenced by the extensive carrier-building program (Adm. King was himself an experienced aviator and aviation planner).

In the EUROPEAN WAR the U.S. Navy had a major role (albeit at times subordinate to the Royal Navy) in the antisubmarine campaign in the Atlantic and the various Mediterranean and European landings. But in the Pacific the Navy had the principal role, carrying and supporting Army and Marine units in their assaults on various Pacific atolls and islands, and in destroying the Japanese Fleet.

Naval Aviation   The U.S. naval air arm, which predated World War I, was fully integrated into the fleet. Although by law only naval aviators could command aircraft carriers and seaplane tenders, all had served in surface warships, as did all graduates of the Naval Academy at Annapolis, Md., before they could enter specialized aviation (or submarine) training.

The naval air arm expanded more than tenfold during the war, from just under 4,000 aircraft at America's entry into the war to over 40,000 when Japan surrendered, including Marine aircraft (see UNITED STATES, MARINES). High-performance fighter, dive bombing, and torpedo aircraft were provided to all carriers; from 1943 radar-equipped night aircraft were available for U.S. carriers, with a couple of carriers operating all-night-flying air groups.

Although prewar agreements with the Army had provided for that service to fly land-based patrol and antisubmarine aircraft and the Navy to be limited to flying boats, soon after the war began it was obvious that the Army Air Forces was ill suited for overwater operations. Accordingly, the Navy built up a large force of land-based patrol/antisubmarine aircraft (including the B-24 LIBERATOR, which was an outstanding antisubmarine aircraft) as well as seaplanes, mostly PBY CATALINA and then PBM MARINER flying boats.

Naval pilots (including Marine and Coast Guard) were trained by a large naval air training establishment. Also, the NAVAL AIR TRANSPORT SERVICE provided long-range delivery of mail, spare parts, and personnel to the fleet throughout the world.

See also WAVES.

Unknown Soldier

After World War II, the Unknown Soldier was selected from the remains of the unidentified dead in military cemeteries. The ceremonies were patterned after those used for the first Unknown Soldier in World War I. But this time it was not a matter of selecting an Unknown from one theater of war. The Korean War had been fought, and an Unknown from that war was also chosen.

The ceremonies began on May 10, 1958, when the caskets of six Unknowns of the Pacific theater were brought to Hickam Air Force Base in HAWAII. One of the six anonymous caskets, chosen by a veteran of both World War II and the Korean War, was transferred to Guantánamo Bay, Cuba, where it was put aboard the CRUISER Boston (CAG 1). An Unknown from the Korean War, chosen in similar ceremonies, was also placed on board the Boston.

At the same time, the remains of thirteen Unknowns from the European and North Africa theaters were rearranged by mortuary technicians at the Army mortuary in Frankfurt, Germany, to assure the anonymity of the thirteen dead. They were sent to an American cemetery in France, where one casket was chosen, flown to Naples, and placed on board the U.S. DESTROYER Blandy (DD 943), which rendezvoused at sea with the *Boston* and transferred the casket.

Then, off the Virginia Capes, the *Boston* met the cruiser *Canberra* (CAG 2), named for the Australian cruiser sunk with three U.S. cruisers in the battle of SAVO ISLAND in Aug. 1942. All three caskets were transferred to the *Canberra*. A MEDAL OF HONOR winner chose one of the World War II caskets, not knowing whether the Unknown was originally from the Pacific or Europe. The *Canberra* headed for deeper water for the burial at sea of the unselected Unknown.

The two caskets of the World War II Unknown and the Korean Unknown were transferred to the *Blandy,* which took the unknowns to the United States. On Memorial Day 1958 the two Unknowns were buried at Arlington National Cemetery in WASHINGTON.

Upkeep Bomb

"Bouncing" BOMB intended to destroy dams in the Ruhr Valley of Germany. Barnes Wallis, designer of the "earthquake bombs," conceived the Upkeep to overcome the problems of attacking dams, whose destruction would deprive the Germans of hydroelectric power and flood industrial areas.

The Upkeep bombs were cylindrical (resembling DEPTH CHARGES), and were carried in an open bomb bay of modified LANCASTER bombers. Before being released, the bombs were started spinning backwards at 500 revolutions per minute to extend their range and momentum. Released from a height of only 60 feet while the four-engine bomber sped over the water at 210 to 220 mph, the spinning bomb would skip across the water and "crawl" down the face of the dam to detonate some 30 feet below the surface.

The Upkeep bombs were used only once, in Operation Chastise on the night of May 16–17, 1943, when nineteen Lancasters of RAF squadron No. 619 attacked four Ruhr Valley dams. Eleven planes dropped their single Upkeep bombs on their targets, destroying the Möhne and Eder Dams, and damaging the Bever Dam. Eight Lancasters were lost with fifty-three of their crewmen killed and three captured. Wing Comdr. G. P. (Guy) Gibson, commanding officer of No. 617 squadron—quickly dubbed the "Dambusters"—was awarded the VICTORIA CROSS for the operation. (The squadron was established on March 21, 1943, especially to carry the Upkeep and other Barnes Wallis bombs.)

The dams were repaired by the fall of 1943, but their destruction in May 1943 inflicted extensive damage on Ruhr Valley industry and forced the Germans to devote considerable RESOURCES to defending those and other dams.

The Upkeep bombs weighed 9,200 pounds with a warhead of 5,720 pounds of Torpex explosive. The bomb was developed in parallel with the antiship HIGHBALL BOMB.

Upsilon

Code name for British submarine *Junon* that landed supplies on the Norwegian coast for British COASTWATCHERS, Nov. 1942.

Uranus

Soviet code name for the STALINGRAD counteroffensive, Nov. 1942.

Uruguay

Capital: Montevideo, pop. 2,093,331 (est. 1938). Three months after the EUROPEAN WAR began, Uruguay suddenly found itself the stage for a wartime drama: the death of the German POCKET BATTLESHIP *ADMIRAL GRAF SPEE,* which had sailed into Montevideo harbor after being damaged in a running battle with the Royal Navy. Uruguay rejected Germany's request for extended time to repair the ship and threatened to intern her. The ship's captain scuttled her just outside the harbor. Two weeks later, Uruguay interned the *Tacoma,* an auxiliary ship to the *Graf Spee,* when the *Tacoma* refused to leave port. The German sailors from the two ships were interned.

In June 1940 the Uruguay government announced that a pro-German FIFTH COLUMN was plotting a coup so that Uruguay could become an agricultural colony for Germany. Two U.S. CRUISERS soon appeared in a well-orchestrated demonstration of U.S. support of the government. Uruguay ended relations with Germany, Italy, and Japan on Jan. 25, 1942, ended relations with VICHY FRANCE on May 12, 1943, and declared war against Germany and Japan on Feb. 15, 1945.

U.S. Central Pacific Campaign (1943–1945)

Hard-won victories at GUADALCANAL and NEW GUINEA gave the ALLIES launching sites for attacks on the islands that years before Japan had secretly transformed into fortresses. The decision for an aggressive Pacific strategy had come from the QUEBEC CONFERENCE of Aug. 1943 when Prime Minister CHURCHILL agreed on an Allied island-hopping strategy in the Pacific and the establishment of B-29 SUPERFORTRESS bases for the bombing of Japan.

Even before the conference, code-named Quadrant, a U.S. thrust from New Guinea in June 1943 won Kiriwina and Woodlark, two small islands to the east. Aircraft from airfields built here could strike wherever air power was needed in the Solomons or New Guinea.

When the decision to go on the offensive was made, the United States had about 461,000 ground and air forces arrayed against Japan, compared to some 411,000 in Europe. U.S. might would be used offensively now for the rest of the war. After the battle of MIDWAY and the U.S. SOLOMONS-NEW GUINEA CAMPAIGN, Japan would never again gain the initiative. She would adopt a defensive strategy, using her fortress islands as a shield to protect Japan itself, the home islands.

Beneath the Pacific, American SUBMARINES were being directed to targets by code-breakers who had cracked enciphered Japanese radio messages to merchant convoys. By the end of the war, about two thirds of Japan's merchant fleet would be sunk by U.S. submarines, which would also send 201 Japanese warships to the bottom.

While the Navy, under Adm. CHESTER W. NIMITZ, advanced across the Central Pacific, Gen. DOUGLAS MACARTHUR's Allied forces thrust northward from Australia, cleared or bypassed Japanese strongholds in New Guinea, and readied an invasion of the Philippines to fulfill MacArthur's vow: "I shall return."

Two vital bulwarks of Japan's defenses were the GILBERT ISLANDS and MARSHALL ISLANDS. They were actually groups of atolls, each with some twenty to fifty islets, islands, and reefs of sharp, hard coral surrounding a lagoon—an incredible challenge to planners of AMPHIBIOUS LANDINGS. With the volcanic CAROLINE ISLANDS and the jungled

The strategists of the U.S. Central Pacific Campaign under the guns of the heavy cruiser *Augusta* (CA 31) off Saipan in July 1944: from left, Adm. Chester W. Nimitz, CinC Pacific Ocean Area; Adm. Ernest J. King, CinC U.S. Fleet and Chief of Naval Operations; and Adm. Raymond A. Spruance, Commander Fifth Fleet. *(U.S. Navy)*

MARIANA ISLANDS, the Gilberts and Marshalls formed the Japanese bastion across the Pacific. Except for GUAM in the Marianas, these were JAPANESE MANDATED ISLANDS, taken from Germany and ceded to Japan under the Versailles Treaty that ended World War I. In great secrecy, using the mandate as a license of conquest, Japan had fortified the islands, converting many of them into air and naval bases that threatened to cut off the United States and HAWAII from the Philippines and Southeast Asia.

The United States opened its island-hopping offensive with Operation Galvanic, the invasion of the Gilbert Islands atolls of MAKIN and TARAWA. Army troops easily dealt with the small Japanese garrison on Makin, but the Marines would call the other atoll Bloody Tarawa, where men had to leave grounded LANDING CRAFT and wade or die in reddening, waist-high surf. Of 4,700 Japanese defenders, only seventeen, all wounded, were taken alive.

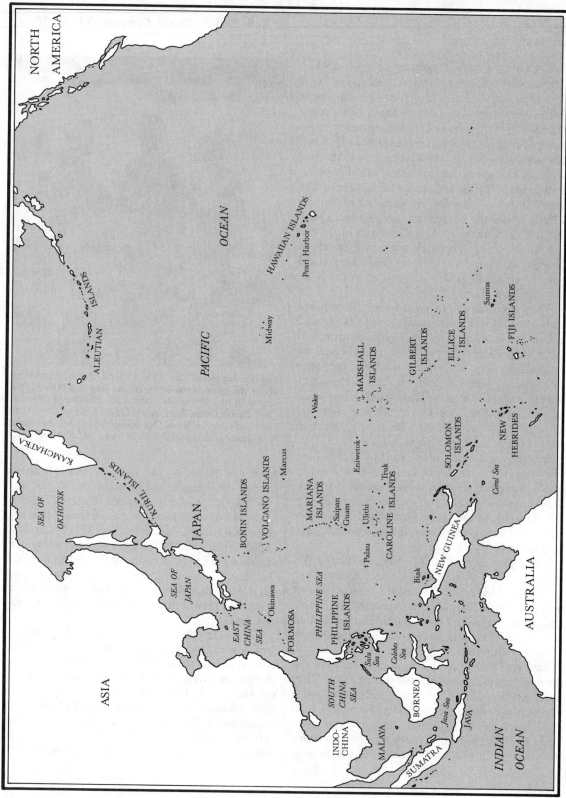

Pacific Ocean area.

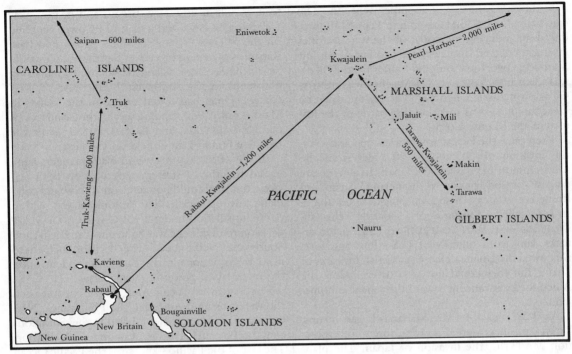

Central Pacific.

The next targets were KWAJALEIN, the Japanese administrative and communications center for the Marshalls, and ENIWETOK, an atoll in the northwestern segment of the Marshalls. While covering the invasion of Eniwetok, U.S. carriers devastated the huge Japanese air and naval base of TRUK in the Carolines.

Now came the Marianas, 1,500 miles from Japan. Strategically, the large islands of SAIPAN, TINIAN, and GUAM offered attractive staging sites for U.S. forces. Saipan and Tinian, especially, would make ideal airfields for Army Air Forces B-29s from which to mount attacks against the Japanese home islands. The Marianas also lay across the lines of supply between Japan and conquered territories in Malaya and the DUTCH EAST INDIES. To cut these strategic shipping lines would badly hurt the Japanese economy and military capability.

On June 15, 1944, two Marine divisions hit the bunker-lined beaches of Saipan. Thousands of Saipan civilians, believing Japanese propaganda about

bloodthirsty Americans, committed suicide by leaping off seaside cliffs.

Other amphibious assaults took Guam, where a handful of Japanese soldiers would hold out into postwar years, and Tinian, the island from which the ATOMIC BOMB would be carried. Psychologically, the capture of the Marianas and the liberation of Guam, conquered by the Japanese in the dark days after Pearl Harbor, signified the growing might and momentum of the impending Allied victory.

The Philippine invasion, scheduled for Dec. 1944, was moved up to October. Four U.S. Army DIVISIONS landed at Leyte while Japanese attempts to stop the invasion triggered a climactic naval engagement—the battle for LEYTE GULF. The U.S. Navy destroyed the Japanese fleet and left the Japanese garrisons in the Philippines without air support or protection of their supply lines to Japan, thus assuring the ultimate success of MacArthur's invasion.

Meanwhile, the island-hopping went on. The epic battle for IWO JIMA, begun in Feb. 1945, produced an enduring memorial of the war: Marines raising the American flag at the summit of Mount Suribachi. Iwo Jima, only 660 miles from TOKYO, was taken at the cost of 6,821 Marine lives in thirty-six days of ceaseless fighting. The seizure of those 10 square miles was the bloodiest battle in the history of the Marine Corps.

Then came the largest amphibious operation yet, the invasion of OKINAWA, 350 miles from the southernmost main islands of Japan. In a desperate defense of soil viewed as homeland, Japan unleashed a strategy based on suicide: KAMIKAZE strikes called *Kikusui,* or "floating chrysanthemums"—HUMAN TORPEDOES. The suicide attacks damaged a number of U.S. ships and foreshadowed the fanatic defense against an invasion of Japan. But they could not stop or even slow the Allied forces advancing toward the Japanese homeland.

As B-29 raids from the Marianas began hitting Tokyo, planners started arraying forces for Operation MAJESTIC, the invasion of Japan. The planners, gazing on a far horizon, saw a Japanese death struggle that would not end until the spring of 1946.

At that time, most of the invasion planners did not know the greatest secret of the war: On one of the Pacific's hard-won islands a new weapon was being readied. The island was Tinian. The weapon was the ATOMIC BOMB. It would end the war in Aug. 1945.

U.S. Solomons–New Guinea Campaign

The battle of MIDWAY in June 1942 convinced the U.S. Navy that it had gained, at least temporarily, the initiative in the Pacific. To exploit this advantage, Allied strategists considered two potential moves for the naval forces that had not only defeated the Japanese at Midway, but had also thwarted the Japanese in the battle of the CORAL SEA in May 1942. Both potential Allied moves centered on RABAUL, the NEW BRITAIN port and air base that the Japanese had captured in Jan. 1942, gaining control of the sea and sky around NEW GUINEA and threatening Australia.

Gen. DOUGLAS MACARTHUR was urging a full-scale assault against New Britain and nearby New Ireland. The Navy had a plan of its own, centered on the SOLOMON ISLANDS. This too would have Rabaul as the major objective. But the assault would be on the Solomon Islands, a 900-mile-long string of islands in the southwest Pacific east of New Guinea. Japan had seized several of the islands in March–April 1942, landing several thousand troops on BOUGAINVILLE and GUADALCANAL, with the Japanese building an airfield on the latter.

In WASHINGTON Army and Navy planners hammered together a strategy agreeable to both services. But they could not agree on who would command the operation. The Solomons was within Army jurisdiction under a JOINT CHIEFS OF STAFF decision to divide the war zone into the Pacific and Southwest Pacific areas. The decision helped to make many actions in the Pacific dependent upon the interplay of powerful personalities.

The Southwest Pacific Area, which encompassed the waters around Australia, the Philippines, New Guinea, the DUTCH EAST INDIES, the Solomons and the Bismarck Islands, was under MacArthur. The rest of the Pacific—known as the Pacific Ocean Area (POA) command—was under Adm. CHESTER W. NIMITZ. The POA consisted of three subareas: South Pacific (Vice Adm. ROBERT L. GHORMLEY, replaced by Adm. WILLIAM F. HALSEY); Central Pacific (including HAWAII, the GILBERT ISLANDS, MARSHALL ISLANDS, CAROLINE ISLANDS, and MARIANA ISLANDS); and North Pacific Area (including the ALEUTIAN ISLANDS). The area commanders reported to Nimitz.

A compromise, reached in early July 1942, gave the Navy initial control of the assault on the Solomons—in large part because only the Navy had the resources to assault the island, the 1st Marine DIVISION. But the decision reserved for a later time when and where command would shift to the Army. The compromise anticipated that at the time of the shift there would be Army divisions available and air bases in Allied hands, eliminating the need for direct aircraft carrier support of land operations.

The battle of Guadalcanal was fought while naval battles raged in the seas around the island: CAPE ESPERANCE, SAVO ISLAND, EASTERN SOLOMONS, SANTA CRUZ—each was a test of U.S. naval strength and tactics, and proof that the island-hopping strat-

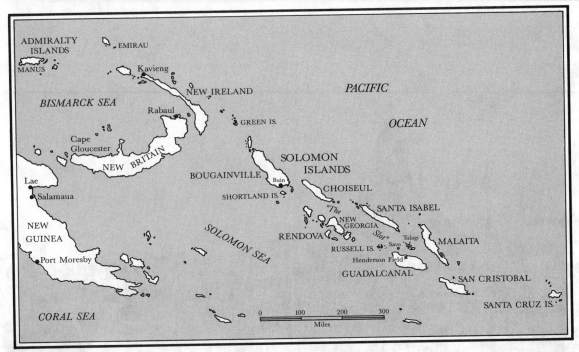

Solomon Islands.

egy would work. After Guadalcanal, U.S. forces moved up the Solomon archipelago, making AM-PHIBIOUS LANDING successively at NEW GEORGIA, Vella Lavella, and Bougainville.

MacArthur launched his part of the campaign at the end of 1942; he began at Buna, which took thirty-two days to capture, then pressed on to Lae, where he launched two assaults, by sea and by air. In the second phase of the reconquest of New Guinea, MacArthur swept along the north coast, sidestepping some concentrations of Japanese troops to let them "wither on the vine," which they did. Thousands of Japanese starved. Some tried to grow their own food while being preyed upon by vengeful natives who had been treated like slaves under Japanese occupation.

By early 1944 Allied forces held most of eastern New Guinea.

USO,

see UNITED SERVICE ORGANIZATIONS.

Utah

Code name for beach in NORMANDY INVASION used by U.S. Army VII CORPS.

UXB,

see BOMB DISPOSAL.

V-1 Buzz Bomb

The first GUIDED MISSILE in history to be launched in large numbers against an enemy. The German Air Force began launching the V-1 (for *Vergeltungswaffe* or reprisal weapon) against LONDON on June 13, 1944, exactly one week after the D-DAY landings at Normandy. Of four missiles that crossed the English Channel on that date, three inflicted no casualties; one reached the Bethnal Green section of London where it exploded, killing six persons and injuring nine more.

Soon V-1s were falling like lethal hailstones. In the first two weeks of the V-1 campaign they fell at an average of nearly 100 every twenty-four hours. On Sunday, June 18 a V-1 fell on the Guards Church at Wellington Barracks in London; the structure was destroyed and almost 200 persons were killed and injured.

Britains referred to them as "doodlebugs" or "buzz bombs" because of the strident sound of the missile's pulse-jet engine. Also called a "flying bomb," the missile resembled a small aircraft. It was launched from a short-length catapult and climbed to a height of some 3,000 feet and reached a cruising speed of almost 400 mph as it streaked toward its target. When the missile had traveled a preset distance, the engine cut off and the missile tipped over and dived toward the earth. The 1,870-pound warhead detonated just above the ground, inflicting considerable damage. WINSTON CHURCHILL wrote:

A V-1 buzz bomb falls on the Picadilly section of London. The onslaught of the V-1s—and then the V-2 missiles—was more difficult than the early Blitz and Little Blitz bombing raids because the missiles fell around the clock and were less discriminate in the selection of their targets. *(U.S. Army)*

"This new form of attack imposed upon the people of London was a burden perhaps even heavier than the air-raids of 1940 and 1941. Suspense and strain were more prolonged. Dawn brought no relief, and cloud no comfort [in the 1940–1941 BLITZ the Luftwaffe bombers attacked London mainly on cloudless nights]." London was the worst hit, but the damage was widespread, with parts of Kent and Sussex becoming known as "bomb alley" because many V-1s fell along a route short of London. "One landed near my home at Westerham, killing, by cruel mischance, twenty-two homeless children and five grownupas collected in a refuge made for them in the woods," lamented Churchill.

During an eighty-day period the V-1s wrecked or damaged more than 1,000,000 buildings in England, killed 6,184 persons, and seriously injured 17,981 others. The port of Antwerp, important for the supply of Allied armies in Western Europe, was also a target for the V-1s.

German records indicate that 8,564 of the missiles were launched against England and Antwerp; about 43 percent failed, or were diverted or destroyed by fighters, antiaircraft fire, or BARRAGE BALLOONS. Fighters—especially the jet-propelled METEOR—could intercept the missiles; over a thousand antiaircraft guns were set in belts beneath the missiles' path. In addition, under Operation Crossbow, Allied bombers sought out V-1 production facilities and launch sites. (Churchill recorded that almost 2,000 U.S. AAF and RAF Bomber Command airmen died in those attacks.) Still, 2,419 missiles fell on England and 2,448 on Antwerp.

The first V-1 was launched from the missile development center at PEENEMÜNDE on Dec. 24, 1942. The designation of the Fiesler-developed missile was Fi 103; to disguise its real purpose it was also referred to as the FZG 76 (*Flakzielgerät* or long-range aiming device). A Luftwaffe weapon, its development was accelerated in an effort to beat the German Army's V-2 MISSILE into action. More than 29,000 V-1 missiles were built, mainly by SLAVE LABOR at a gigantic underground factory called Mittelwerke near Nordhausen (where the V-2 was also built). The Luftwaffe's 155th (W) FLAK Regiment was responsible for launching the V-1. On its best day, Aug. 2, 1944, units of the regiment sent off 316 buzz bombs from thirty-eight catapults.

From July 1944 some 1,200 of the missiles were air-launched from HE 111H twin-engine bombers. Also, a scheme was developed for the Ar 234B *BLITZ* jet-propelled bomber to tow a V-1 for air launching. A proposed *piloted* version of the V-1 was flight-tested but never used operationally. Those tests were flown by HANNA REITSCH and OTTO SKORZENY, among others.

The V-1 was $25^{11}/_{12}$ feet long, with a wingspan of $17^{5}/_{12}$ feet, and weighed 4,806 pounds at launch. The standard range was 150 miles with a speed of 400 mph.

After the war the United States and Soviet Union took large numbers of V-1s for evaluation. Subsequently, they were produced in the United States with the Navy planning to launch them in large numbers from ships against Japan in the intended invasion of the Japanese home islands. The Navy also experimented in launching these missiles from surfaced SUBMARINES, tests that led to development of submarine-launched cruise missiles.

V-2 Missile

German ROCKET weapon and precursor to the postwar Intercontinental Ballistic Missiles (ICBM). Germany developed the V-2 (for *Vergeltungswaffe* or reprisal weapon) from rocket experiments going back to the 1930s. The fourth in the experimental series, known to German scientists as the A-4, was first successfully fired on Oct. 3, 1942, from the PEENEMÜNDE research facility on the Baltic Sea. The first operational launches were on Sept. 6, 1944, when two missiles were fired at PARIS. Two days later, two V-2s struck England, followed by 1,188 more missiles striking England during the next six months.

Whereas the V-1 BUZZ BOMB that had preceded the V-2 could be shot down by antiaircraft guns or fighters, once launched the V-2 was invulnerable to interception. Upon launching the rocket-propelled missile rose vertically to an altitude of about six miles, then arced upward to about 50 miles. Preset controls cut off the fuel—liquid oxygen and alcohol—to provide desired range. Then the missile tipped over and hurtled down toward its target, reaching a speed of nearly 4,000 mph—a mile per second. The entire flight—200 miles from launch

German technicians fuel and ready a V-2 missile, which appeared too late to influence the war. Once launched, there was no means of intercepting the ballistic missile. *(German Army via Imperial War Museum)*

point to target—took only three or four minutes.

The missile smashed into the ground without warning. The explosive force of its 2,145-pound high-explosive warhead was absorbed by the ground as the missile penetrated several feet before exploding. Still, it was a terrifying and deadly weapon.

The V-2 campaign against England killed 2,754 persons and seriously injured 6,523 others. The second target for the V-2 campaign was Antwerp, a port important to the Allied armies in Western Europe. A total of 1,610 missiles fell on Antwerp; total casualties to the V-1 and V-2 attacks on Antwerp were 3,470 Belgian citizens and 682 Allied servicemen. A further 151 V-2s were sent against Brussels and a few against Paris as well as eleven fired

against the LUDENDORFF RAILROAD BRIDGE at Remagen, the last being the only "tactical" use of the weapon.

Detection of V-2 launch sites was almost impossible, since the rockets needed no permanent launch pads. They were taken to a site by a vehicle, set on a platform, and fired. The platform and vehicle then quickly left the area. Not until March 27, 1945, when the last V-2 launch site was overrun by Allied troops did the missiles stop coming.

Developed for the German Army by a team of scientists led by Dr. WERNHER VON BRAUN, the V-2 flew its first successful test flight—a distance of 118 miles—on Oct. 3, 1942. It landed within 2½ miles of its aim point. Several earlier test vehicles had failed and despite several misfires, on Dec. 22, 1942, HITLER ordered the V-2 into production. Meanwhile, British intelligence had learned about the work at Peenemünde and on the night of Aug. 17–18, 1943, a raid of 571 four-engine bombers wrecked much of the test center and killed 735 military personnel and civilians.

Late in 1943 the missile entered limited production at a plant south of Peenemünde. Mass production was subsequently undertaken at the massive Mittelwerke near Nordhausen, where in underground facilities SLAVE LABOR produced more than 10,000 V-2s (including over 1,000 in the month of Oct. 1944). The Army's 836th *Artillerie Abteilung* was given responsibility for launching the missiles. In all, some 4,320 missiles were fired operationally, many of them failures. Another 600 missiles were fired in trials and training.

The V-2 was 46 feet long and 5 feet in diameter. It was a wingless missile weighing 28,373 pounds at launch. Several variants were developed. The A-4b was a winged missile—called a "glider"—with a range of 465 miles; two were test-fired. The A-9 and A-10 were further improvements, the latter a two-stage version intended for striking the United States from launch sites in Europe. When Soviet troops reached bomb-wrecked Peenemünde, they found that work had started on V-2s to be launched at sea. These sea missiles, towed by U-BOATS to points 100 to 200 miles off the East Coast, could have hit U.S. cities; they were considered an interim weapon until the A-10 would be available.

U.S. and Soviet forces captured V-2s and their

scientists. Sixty-nine captured V-2s were test-fired in the United States; on Sept. 6, 1947, one was fired from the flight deck of the AIRCRAFT CARRIER *Midway* (CVB 41). In both the United States and Soviet Union, the V-2s and their makers served as the basis for ballistic missile and space programs.

V-3,

see LONDON GUN.

Val

Principal Japanese dive bomber of the war. The carrier-based D3A Val had a major role in the PEARL HARBOR attack on Dec. 7, 1941, and in the subsequent Japanese carrier actions in the Pacific and Indian Ocean.

At Pearl Harbor the 129 Vals launched from six carriers (37 percent of the planes in the two attack waves) struck at Army and Navy airfields as well as the U.S. warships. In the subsequent Japanese carrier sweep of the Pacific the Vals were highly effective; in the Indian Ocean on April 5, 1942, an attack of fifty-three Vals sank two British heavy cruisers in just nineteen minutes—every BOMB released at the radically maneuvering warships was a hit or near miss (one plane's bomb failed to release). By mid-1944 the Vals were largely replaced in the dive bomber role by the D4Y JUDY bomber and A6M ZERO fighter-bombers; at the start of the June 1944 battle of the MARIANAS the nine Japanese carriers had only twenty-seven Vals compared to ninety-nine Judy dive bombers. Further, the Val's effectiveness deteriorated as naval pilot quality declined after mid-1942.

The Val was the latest in a long line of Aichi dive bombers based extensively on the German Heinkel designs. The D3A1 version entered production in 1937; it was replaced on the production lines in 1942 by the improved D3A2, with a total of 1,294 of the two models being produced when the lines closed in 1944.

The dive bomber was a low-wing aircraft with a fixed undercarriage fitted with distinctive "spats." Top speed was 266 mph and the aircraft was highly maneuverable. Up to 882 pounds of bombs were carried externally and two forward-firing 7.7-mm machine guns were fitted, plus a flexible gun aft. The Val had a crew of two.

Valkyrie

Both the code name for a plan, known to HITLER, to mobilize the Home (Replacement) Army to protect BERLIN and other cities in the event of a revolt and, with this as a cover, the code name for the unsuccessful JULY 20 PLOT to assassinate Hitler.

Vandaman, Brig. Gen. Arthur (1882–1987)

U.S. AAF officer who, with access to ULTRA, flew on a bomber mission over Europe and was shot down over Germany. So far as is known, he was the only U.S. officer with knowledge of Ultra that was captured by the Germans.

Vandaman had enlisted as an Army pilot in 1917 and was commissioned in 1920. He held mostly air engineering assignments and, from July 1937 to June 1941, was assistant U.S. air attaché in BERLIN. Vandaman then held senior positions in AAF matériel agencies, being promoted to brigadier general in March 1942. In May 1944, he was ordered to the Eighth AIR FORCE in England as assistant chief of staff for intelligence. He flew a mission over Germany and was shot down on June 27, 1944. He was a PRISONER OF WAR until April 23, 1945, when he was liberated and returned to the United States.

After the war he reverted to his permanent rank of colonel, but was promoted to major general in 1948.

Vandegrift, Gen. Alexander A. (1887–1973)

Vandegrift is best known for his leadership of the 1st Marine DIVISION on GUADALCANAL from Aug. to Dec. 1942. He was "a professional, a soft-spoken, tough-minded commander in the mold of Stonewall Jackson," wrote Robert Leckie, author of *Strong Men Armed*.

In April 1942 Vandegrift assumed command of the 1st Marine Division as a major general. He was confident that six months of hard training would produce an effective weapon by late 1942. On July 1, however, he was ordered to land his Marines on Guadalcanal a month later—the date was later changed to Aug. 7.

Despite the sudden acceleration of his timetable, Vandegrift managed to pull together a landing force, combat-load his transports, and deliver his 19,000 Marines to the beach on Aug. 7. The great fortune of landing unopposed on Guadalcanal (the smaller island of Tulagi was taken after a severe fight) and securing the airfield was nearly eclipsed two days later by the night battle of SAVO ISLAND in which four Allied CRUISERS were sunk. Vandegrift was again forced to improvise as the transports were hurriedly and incompletely unloaded and pulled out.

Vandegrift led from makeshift quarters on Guadalcanal during his division's four months of action, "at the constant risk of his life," as his citation for the MEDAL OF HONOR reads. He initially concentrated on holding the perimeter around the airfield (renamed Henderson Field) and defeating Japanese attacks. His forces gradually built up to 23,000 including elements of the Army's 164th REGIMENT and the "Cactus Air Force," which usually included pilots from sunk or damaged U.S. AIRCRAFT CARRIERS.

After withstanding three months of Japanese attacks and having his Marine pilots frustrate Japanese reinforcement efforts in mid-November, Vandegrift was at last able to begin to expand the U.S. hold on Guadalcanal. By Dec. 9, when he and his division were relieved by Maj. Gen. ALEXANDER PATCH, defeat of the Japanese on Guadalcanal was no longer in doubt.

Vandegrift was promoted to lieutenant general in July 1943 and took command of the I Marine Amphibious CORPS, which assaulted BOUGAINVILLE in Nov. 1943. Aided by a deceptive raid on Choiseul Island as well as the surprising (to the Japanese) choice of Empress Augusta Bay as the landing site, Vandegrift's forces succeeded in establishing and expanding a beachhead. On Nov. 8, 1943, Vandegrift turned over command on Bougainville to Gen. ROY S. GEIGER and returned to the United States. In Jan. 1944 he became commandant of the Marine Corps and in March 1945 became the first commandant to be promoted to four-star rank. He served as commandant until Dec. 1947 and retired in 1949.

Vandenberg, Arthur H. (1884–1951)

U.S. senator. A prewar isolationist, Vandenberg became a strong supporter of President ROOSEVELT. As a Michigan newspaper editor he opposed the policies of President Woodrow Wilson but did support Wilson's war policies. Vandenberg also endorsed Wilson's doomed campaign to get the Senate to approve U.S. membership in the LEAGUE OF NATIONS.

Vandenberg, appointed to the Senate to fill a vacancy prior to the election in 1928, chose to run and easily won a six-year term. He became a member of the Senate Foreign Relations Committee and veered from a mild internationalist to an isolationist determined to limit presidential power in foreign affairs.

But, with the United States at war, Vandenberg became an architect of bipartisan foreign policy based on consultations with President Roosevelt and congressional leaders. He urged THOMAS E. DEWEY, the 1944 Republican presidential candidate, to keep foreign policy out of the campaign. Unlike the Senate that opposed internationalism after World War I, the post–World War II Senate, thanks largely to Vandenberg, endorsed U.S. membership in the UNITED NATIONS. Roosevelt made Vandenberg a delegate to the SAN FRANCISCO CONFERENCE that drafted the UN charter.

Vandenberg, Lt. Gen. Hoyt S. (1899–1954)

Leading planner of the U.S. Army Air Forces. A Military Academy graduate, Vandenberg was commissioned in 1923. He served in various aviation and staff positions and from 1939 until March 1942 was the operations and training officer of the AAF air staff. Then sent to England, Vandenberg helped plan the NORTH AFRICA INVASION (Operation Torch) and was subsequently made the Chief of Staff Twelfth AIR FORCE when it was established in North Africa. He returned to WASHINGTON in Aug. 1943 to become deputy chief of the air staff. That fall he was part of a U.S. delegation sent to MOSCOW to coordinate SHUTTLE BOMBING operations with the Soviet government.

He remained in that post only a few months, being assigned in March 1944 as deputy air commander of the Allied Expeditionary Force (under Chief Air Marshal ARTHUR TEDDER) as well as commander of the U.S. air components in May 1944. In this role he was instrumental in providing the air support for the NORMANDY INVASION. In Aug. 1944, as a major general, Vandenberg took command of the Ninth Air Force, providing tactical air support for the Allied Forces coming ashore in France. He held that position at the end of the war.

In April 1948 he became the second Chief of Staff of the U.S. Air Force, serving until June 1953, when he retired.

Vanguard

Code name for Allied plan for AMPHIBIOUS LANDING on Rangoon, 1944.

Varsity

Code name for Allied AIRBORNE operation in the RHINE CROSSING, March 1944.

Vasilevsky, Marshal Alexander M. (1895–1977)

Soviet chief of the General Staff and, late in the war, a senior field commander. Vasilevsky was a Russian Army officer in World War I and joined the Bolshevik forces in 1919 and fought in the Civil War. He then held command and staff positions, and attended the Academy of the General Staff.

Shortly after the German invasion of the Soviet Union in June 1941, he became deputy chief of the General Staff and head of the important operations section of the staff, positions that brought him in daily contact with STALIN. His role in helping stem the German advances led to his being made chief of the General Staff in June 1942. With the subsequent success of Soviet armies his role declined and, in Feb. 1945 he asked Stalin for a field command.

He was directed to coordinate the First Belorussian and First Baltic Fronts, both engaged in heavy combat with the Germans. Following the death of Gen. Ivan Chernyakhovsky in Feb. 1945, he additionally took command of the Third Belorussian Front for the assault on Eastern Prussia.

After the defeat of Germany, Vasilevsky was sent to the Far East to command Soviet troops in the invasion and occupation of Manchuria and northern Korea.

From 1949 until Stalin's death in March 1953 he was minister of the Armed Forces (renamed ministry of Defense in 1950); he was then first deputy minister from 1953 until his retirement in Dec. 1957. He was twice awarded the HERO OF THE SOVIET UNION.

Vatican City

The square-mile enclave of the Pope in the heart of ROME, Vatican City was a vestige of the once vast and powerful Papal States. Italy recognized Vatican City as an independent state in 1929 under the terms of the Lateran Treaty. Scores of Allied soldiers and downed Allied airmen made their way to Rome, eluded German occupying forces, and slipped into the Vatican, which, although officially neutral, gave them secret sanctuary.

V-E Day

Victory in Europe Day. On May 7, 1945, the Associated Press flashed word of the German SURRENDER at Reims a day ahead of the scheduled official announcement. (WAR CORRESPONDENT Edward Kennedy, the AP reporter responsible for the premature announcement, was suspended by Allied supreme headquarters.)

The actual surrender had been on May 7, at 2:41 A.M., when German *Generaloberst* ALFRED JODL, chief of the operations staff of the High Command of the German Armed Forces, signed the UNCONDITIONAL SURRENDER at Allied headquarters in Reims. Ratification in BERLIN by Soviet authorities came just before midnight on May 8. President TRUMAN announced the surrender on May 8.

Venereal Disease,

see MEDICINE, MILITARY.

Venezuela

Capital: Caracas, pop. 3,951,371 (est. 1941, including est. 100,600 "indigenous forest population" of Indians). Ruled by strongmen through the twentieth century, Venezuela was a relatively stable and prosperous nation. When the war began, Venezuela declared its neutrality. But after the U.S. entry into the war, Venezuela joined other Latin American nations in opposing the AXIS. She broke off diplomatic relations with the Axis powers, restricted radio communication to the Americas, and signed an agreement to sell rubber to the U.S. In 1945, after declaring "belligerency" against Germany and Japan, the government arrested ten Germans charged with planning to SABOTAGE Venezuelan oil fields and tankers carrying oil to Europe.

Ventura,

see A-28.

Venus

Code name for British submarine *Ula* landing stores on Norwegian coast, Sept. 1943.

Vergeltung (Revenge)

German code name for Luftwaffe attacks on LONDON on Sept. 7–8, 1940, during the BATTLE OF BRITAIN. See also V-1 BUZZ BOMB and V-2 MISSILE.

Veritable

Code name for Canadian First Army offensive to clear the area between the Maas and Rhine Rivers, Feb. 1945.

V-for-Victory

Popularized by British Prime Minister CHURCHILL. He launched the V-for-Victory campaign on July 20, 1941, in a message broadcast to the people of German-conquered European nations, saying, "The V sign is the symbol of the unconquerable will of the occupied territories, and a portent of the fate awaiting the NAZI tyranny."

The opening notes of Beethoven's Fifth Symphony were played frequently on BBC broadcasts aimed at German-occupied countries. The notes—*da da da daaah*—were a musical version of dot-dot-dot-dash, the Morse code for V.

Vichy France

The French regime that Germany authorized for unoccupied France. The government was established on July 2, 1940, with its capital at Vichy, 200 miles southeast of PARIS, a famous spa whose name previously had been associated with water from its thermal springs. Under the secret terms with Germany, signed by Marshal HENRI PHILIPPE PÉTAIN, the regime stated, "The AXIS Powers and France have an identical interest in seeing the defeat of England accomplished as soon as possible. Consequently, the French Government [as Vichy saw itself] will support, within the limits of its ability, the measures which the Axis Powers may take to this end."

As postwar French legal scholars ruled, Vichy was not the French government, for on July 11 Pétain abrogated the French Constitution. But Vichy won recognition from many countries, including the United States. The U.S. Ambassador, WILLIAM D. LEAHY, tried in vain to steer Vichy away from Germany. Leahy publicly admitted admiration for Pétain—an admiration that the British never forgot nor entirely forgave.

PIERRE LAVAL, a former premier, became vice premier of Pétain's Vichy regime. "A new order," Pétain declared, "is about to begin." As proof, the French slogan of "Liberty, Equality, Fraternity" was replaced by "Work, Family, Fatherland." Laval was vice premier until Dec. 1940 and again from April 1942 to April 1945. (In the interval, while Laval had temporarily fallen from power, Adm. JEAN DARLAN was vice president.) On his return to power, under German pressure Laval had the title "chief of government." He totally collaborated, ordering compulsory labor on German projects, enacting laws that stripped French JEWS of their rights, and aiding the Germans in their hunt for non-French Jews who had sought refuge in Vichy France from death or forced labor in Germany.

Vichy also had control over French colonial possessions, including those in North Africa. Prior to the Allied NORTH AFRICA INVASION on Nov. 8, 1942, U.S. diplomat ROBERT D. MURPHY and Gen. MARK W. CLARK dealt with French colonial officials, some of whom were anti-Vichy, to stop French resistance to the invasion. Vichy responded to the invasion by breaking off relations with the United States; Germany responded by violating the 1940 armistice and invading unoccupied France. From then through the beginning of the liberation of France with the NORMANDY INVASION of June 1944, the Vichy regime was ignored by Germany. As Allied forces rolled across France, Resistance leaders replaced Vichy officials and DE GAULLE'S FREE FRENCH made plans for dealing with the traitors: death for Laval and others, dishonor for lesser people who aided the Vichy rulers.

Victor

Code name for series of U.S. Eighth ARMY operations in the Philippines.

Victoria Cross

The highest British military award. Given for conspicuous bravery in action, the decoration was established in 1856, to be conferred by the sovereign alone. An important clause in the Royal Warrant for the decoration was that "neither rank, nor long service, nor wounds, nor any other circumstance or condition whatsoever, save the merit of conspicuous bravery" should be the rationale in its award.

In 1902 the sovereign approved the posthumous award of the Victoria Cross as well as to women serving under orders or direction of military authorities.

During World War II a total of 182 awards were made. In addition, the Victoria Cross was presented to the U.S. UNKNOWN SOLDIER at the Arlington National Cemetery.

Queen Victoria herself chose the design for the decoration, based on the Maltese Cross, Royal Crest, and the words "For Valour." It is made of bronze, cast from metal melted down from cannon captured at the Russian port of SEVASTOPOL during the Crimean War. Although the Victoria Cross was established in 1856, the first award was to a twenty-year-old Irishman on board a British ship in the Baltic for picking up a live shell and throwing it over the side. That event occurred nineteen months before the Royal Warrant for the award.

Victory Gardens

Backyard and community gardens tended by American nonfarm families to help the war effort. Some 20,000,000 Victory Gardens sprouted in backyards, vacant lots, and parks throughout the United States. Local governments changed zoning laws to allow rabbits and chickens to be kept within urban boundaries. The OFFICE OF WAR INFORMATION and the Office of CIVIL DEFENSE both mounted intensive publicity campaigns for Victory Gardens to, as one ad said, "beet the enemy."

Gardening was hailed as a way to fight juvenile delinquency (a new term), to get people's minds off the horrors of war, and to exercise productively. By some estimates, the gardens produced 40 percent of U.S. vegetables at the height of the effort. Ironically, some of the vegetable shortage was caused by the internment of JAPANESE-AMERICANS, who had made up much of the California agriculture labor force.

Victory Ships

Mass-produced fast merchant ships, a large number of which were completed as AMPHIBIOUS SHIPS. Built from 1943 onward in six shipyards, these ships were similar in size to the earlier LIBERTY series, but were of a more advanced design and significantly faster.

A total of 531 Victory ships were built—414 as Navy, Army, and merchant cargo ships, and 117 as attack transports (designated APA). The cargo ships had a deadweight tonnage (cargo capacity) of 15,580 tons; the APAs were slightly smaller, and carried about twenty LANDING CRAFT of the LCM and LCVP types, and had bunks for almost 1,600 troops.

The merchant ships were 455 feet long and the APA design 436½ feet. Both types had steam turbine propulsion providing a speed of 17 knots (compared to 11 knots for the Liberty ships). Most of the class were armed, the standard being a 5-inch (127-mm) gun aft and varying numbers of BOFORS 40-MM and OERLIKON 20-MM antiaircraft guns.

All Victory ships carried the Maritime Administration designation VC2—"V" for Victory, "C" for cargo, and "2" for large size.

Vigorous

Code name for British CONVOY to MALTA and Alexandria, June 1942.

Vindicator,

see SB2U.

Vinson, Carl (1883–1981)

Long-serving member of the U.S. House of Representatives and chief congressional architect of the U.S. Navy's large construction programs of 1940–1941. After attending military college and law school, Vinson served as a lawyer, member of the Georgia legislature, and as a judge before being elected to Congress as a Democrat, taking his seat in Nov. 1914. He served until Jan. 1965—a longevity record for the House.

A strong supporter of the Navy, Vinson had a key

role in passage of the so-called "11% Fleet Expansion Bill" of June 1940 and Two-Ocean Navy bill of July 1940 as well as subsequent naval increases.

V-J Day

Victory over Japan Day. Although Emperor HIROHITO decided upon the SURRENDER of Japan on Aug. 14, TOKYO time, his announcement the following day was Aug. 14, U.S. time. The official announcement came from President TRUMAN at 7 P.M. on Aug. 14. Millions of wildly happy Americans took to the streets to celebrate. Offensive action against Japan ended on Aug. 15. A second, much more somber V-J Day came on Sept. 2, when representatives of Japan and the Allied nations signed the instrument of SURRENDER on board the BATTLESHIP *MISSOURI* (BB 63) at anchor in Tokyo Bay.

Vlasov, Lt. Gen. Andrei A. (1900–1946)

Soviet general who led Soviet troops fighting on the German side. A Soviet adviser to CHIANG KAI-SHEK in China in 1938–1939, Vlasov took command of the 4th Armored Corps in the Soviet Union in 1941, and, after the German invasion, seemed on his way to becoming one of the most illustrious senior Soviet generals. He won the Order of Lenin during the battle of MOSCOW in 1941. While commanding general of the 20th Army, he led his troops brilliantly, winning the Order of the Red Banner and a promotion to lieutenant general.

After the battle of Moscow, he was sent to Volkhov and given command of the 2nd Shock Army. On July 12, 1942, while trying to break out of a German encirclement near Volkov, he was captured, along with most of his men. At first the Germans used Vlasov as a PROPAGANDA broadcaster and stoked his anti-STALIN feelings. Later he formed a "liberation committee" that attracted other Soviet PRISONERS OF WAR. From this evolved the Russian Army of Liberation, which, until late in the war, saw little military service.

In Jan. 1945 Vlasov took command of a 50,000-man army formed by the Committee for the Libera-

tion of Russia, a NAZI-sponsored organization consisting of Russians, Ukrainians, Cossacks, and other anti-Stalinists. On May 1–2, when Czechs in Prague staged an uprising against German occupation troops, Vlasov's force, together with a Russian Liberation division, went to the rescue of the Czechs.

Thus, on May 8—the day of the war's end in Western Europe—tens of thousands of Russian turncoats turned again and fought Germans. The anti-Stalinist army swept the Germans out of the city, pulled out of Prague, and tried to surrender themselves to U.S. troops rather than the advancing Soviet forces. But the Americans refused. Under a secret agreement, made at the YALTA CONFERENCE, Soviet citizens who fell into American custody had to be repatriated, even against their will. The Americans turned Vlasov and six other Soviet generals over to the Red Army. The generals, including Vlasov, were hanged.

V-mail

Condensed letters sent to and from U.S. servicemen and servicewomen overseas. After being written and posted, the letters were photographed on microfilm. Then the rolls were transported to distribution centers where they were enlarged to four-by-five-inch prints and put into conventional postal delivery systems. "Write plainly," the correspondents were warned on the V-mail form. "Very small writing is not suitable." About 150 words fit on the form. The logo for this mail, encompassing the Morse code for V, was $V \ldots \_ \, Mail$.

Vogelsang (Bird Song)

German code name for anti-GUERRILLA operation in the Bryansk Forest of the Soviet Union, June 1942.

Vulcan

Code name for final Allied offensive to clear German forces from Tunisia, May 1943.

V-weapons,

see V-1 BUZZ BOMB and V-2 MISSILE.

WAC

The U.S. Women's Army Corps (WAC) began as the Women's Army Auxiliary Corps (WAAC), authorized on May 14, 1942. The WAAC grew rapidly, reflecting an early statement by Gen. GEORGE C. MARSHALL, Army Chief of Staff: "I want a women's corps right away and I don't want any excuses." By July 1942 there was one officer and 727 enlisted WOMEN; the corps increased to a peak strength of 5,746 officers and 93,542 enlisted women in April 1945 (the total force declining by almost 9,000 by the end of the war). They served throughout the United States and some 10,000 were overseas—in England, Italy, North Africa, Australia, NEW GUINEA, India, HAWAII, and Alaska. About 40,000 were assigned to the AAF.

By mid-1943 the average age of WACs was twenty-eight years, although 41 percent of the corps were under twenty. Records indicate that 42 percent were high school graduates and 8.8 percent were college graduates. While recruiting standards were high, their public image was questionable. In June 1943 newspaper columnist John O'Donnell wrote: "That old devil sex is certainly rearing its ugly head along the Potomac these days." He then repeated rumors of sexual promiscuity among the women in uniform, and of pregnant WACs being shipped home from overseas. President ROOSEVELT and Secretary of War HENRY STIMSON angrily denounced such stories and, like Gen. Marshall, gave unqualified support to women in uniform. Members of Congress had mixed feelings about women

The U.S. submarine *Pogy* (SS 266) is "side-launched" into the Mississippi River at Manitowoc, Wisc. The U.S. industry mass-produced tanks, planes, guns, surface ships, and submarines in greater numbers than any other nation during the war—in some categories more than all other belligerents combined. *(U.S. Navy)*

in the armed forces, and refused to give the director a general's star, although she commanded more people than in an Army field CORPS.

The first director of the WAAC and then the WAC was OVETA CULP HOBBY, who resigned on July 12, 1945, as a colonel. She was succeeded by Lt. Col. Westray Battle Boyce, who served until 1947.

As originally established as the WAAC, the service had its own rank structure, different from the Army. It was made a regular contingent of the Army on July 1, 1943, renamed Women's Army Corps, and accorded the status of other Army service corps, such as chemical, engineers, military police, ordnance, quartermaster, and signal.

Wacht am Rhein (Watch on the Rhine)

Code name for German offensive in the Ardennes, Dec. 1944.

Waco,

see CG-4 and CG-13.

Wadham

Code name for Allied invasion proposal against the Cotentin Peninsula, 1943.

Waesche, Adm. Russell R. (1886–1946)

Commandant of the U.S. Coast Guard during the war. He directed the massive wartime expansion of the Coast Guard, which, under Navy operational control, contributed effectively to combat operations in several theaters.

Following graduation from the Coast Guard Academy in 1906, Waesche served mostly at sea until 1932, commanding several cutters. He then served as Coast Guard liaison to the War Plans Division of the Office of the Chief of Naval Operations. After assignment at Coast Guard headquarters, in 1936 he was appointed commandant of the Coast Guard with the rank of rear admiral. He was appointed to successive four-year terms until retiring in 1946, being promoted to vice admiral in 1942 and full admiral two years later, the first Coast Guard officer to hold those ranks.

Waffen SS

Military arm of the SS (*Schutzstaffel*—"protection detachment"). What had started out as HITLER'S personal military force, separate from both the German Army and any police organization, in June 1940 became officially known as the *Waffen* (armed) SS. Before the EUROPEAN WAR began, the SS in these units were called "asphalt soldiers" because they spent so much time parading. They goose-stepped amid masses of SS banners and staged theatrical formations. Before the war they also had a horse show jumping team and sponsored fox hunts.

There were 15,000 men in these units when the war started. The *Waffen* SS members wore distinctive black dress uniforms for parades and guard duty and gray uniforms for field training and combat. Handpicked by *Reichsführer* HEINRICH HIMMLER, a *Waffen* SS man was expected to be the embodiment of NAZI ideology.

The *Waffen* SS grew into the largest SS branch. At its height, the armed SS numbered nearly 1,000,000 men organized in SS rifle corps and SS PANZER corps. They fought in Poland, in the FRANCE AND LOW COUNTRIES CAMPAIGN, in Italy, the Balkans, and the Soviet Union. They quickly developed a reputation for being ruthless, ideologically driven soldiers. Himmler set the tone with a speech on the enemy they were fighting in the Soviet Union: "a mixture of races, whose very names are unpronounceable, and whose physique is such that one can shoot them down without pity or compassion."

The first documented *Waffen* SS atrocity in the West was the murder of about 100 survivors of the 2nd Battalion, Royal Norfolk Regiment. The soldiers had surrendered at LeParadis in northwestern France after inflicting heavy casualties on the attacking SS troops. (After the war, the SS company commander, Fritz Knöchlein, was tried by the British and hanged in Jan. 1949.)

About half of the *Waffen* SS divisions were made up of foreign volunteers in keeping with Himmler's desire for an international organization of all peoples of "Nordic blood." There were divisions for 310,000 ethnic Germans from other countries, including the Netherlands, France, Norway, Belgium, and Hungary. The Germanic countries were identified by special color insignia while others had national insignias. Near the end of the war, SS recruits were young conscripts, many without Nazi leanings or any understanding of the SS mystique.

Wainwright, Lt. Gen. Jonathan M. (1883–1953)

Left in command when President ROOSEVELT directed Gen. DOUGLAS MACARTHUR to leave the Philippines, Wainwright soon became the senior U.S. PRISONER OF WAR held by the AXIS during the war.

In Sept. 1940 "Skinny" Wainwright had been promoted to temporary major general and took command of the Philippines DIVISION under Gen. Douglas MacArthur. During 1941 MacArthur and Wainwright struggled to use the mingling of U.S. soldiers and Philippine scouts to mold an effective army, but there was little time. The success of the Japanese attack on PEARL HARBOR converted a plan for defeating a Japanese invasion of the Philippines to a sacrificial holding action in which Wainwright would figure to the last day.

Wainwright commanded the North Luzon CORPS, which took the brunt of the Japanese landings in December. His numerical advantage in forces, which neither he nor MacArthur suspected, was outweighed by a wide variation in training among his men, shortages of equipment, and lack

Lt. Gen. Douglas MacArthur, recalled to active duty in the U.S. Army in July 1941, and Maj. Gen. Jonathan Wainwright, commander of the Philippine Division, discuss the defense of the Philippines in late 1941. *(U.S. Army)*

of supporting aircraft; many of his Filipino troops broke under Japanese pressure. MacArthur soon realized that victory was out of the question and that defense of MANILA would only expose the city to carnage. He had to withdraw into the BATAAN Peninsula. Wainwright's North Luzon Corps delayed the Japanese advance long enough to permit the South Luzon Corps to pull back into the peninsula. Delaying tactics, including the blowing up of bridges, bought enough time to allow the withdrawal of 80,000 troops (and at least 20,000 civilians) into Bataan.

Wainwright's exhausted, malaria-ridden forces, already down to half rations (later cut to 3/8), were reformed as I Corps on the left of the line, which was pushed slowly south by Gen. MASAHARU HOMMA's equally fatigued army. On March 11, MacArthur left by PT-BOAT for Australia on President ROOSEVELT's direct order. Wainwright was promoted to temporary lieutenant general and given command of all Philippine forces. He moved to the fortress island of CORREGIDOR.

In early April, Japanese forces finally overwhelmed the Bataan garrison and forced its surrender. Wainwright and 13,000 other troops held out for another month on Corregidor, surrendering on May 6. A bitter outcome of his temporary promotion was its use as a lever to force the surrender of all forces in the islands, although several detachments might have held out far longer.

Wainwright spent the next three and a half years in captivity on Luzon, on Formosa, and finally in Manchuria. When finally liberated in Aug. 1945 he went to TOKYO and joined MacArthur in the final SURRENDER ceremony. He was skeletal and depressed, convinced that he had been blamed for "losing" the Philippines. Upon his return to the United States he was hailed as hero, rode in several victory parades, was promoted to full general, and was awarded the MEDAL OF HONOR. He retired from the Army in 1947.

Wake Island

A coral atoll about 2,000 miles west of HAWAII and the site of the first sustained battle between U.S. and Japanese forces in the war. The United States took possession of Wake in 1898, but not until 1935 did it gain attention as a refueling stop for Pan American Airways Clippers, which that year began flying between San Francisco and MANILA. Wake was promoted by Pam Am as the place "Where America's Day Begins." At the same time, U.S. strategists had included Wake in the RAINBOW WAR PLAN, making it a forward base for any thrust toward the JAPANESE MANDATED ISLANDS.

As a result of the war plan, funds were allocated in 1938 to build air and SUBMARINE support facilities on Wake, but construction was delayed until early 1941, when about 1,200 civilian workers arrived. A small Navy-Marine contingent also landed on Wake, along with a six-man Army communications unit.

By Nov. 1941 Marine Maj. JAMES P. S. DEVEREAUX commanded a 388-man Marine defense detachment on Wake. The Marine's major weapons were eight 5-inch (127-mm) guns taken from World War I BATTLESHIPS, sixteen 3-inch (76-mm) antiaircraft guns, and twenty-four 50.-cal. machine guns. On Dec. 4, from the AIRCRAFT CARRIER *ENTERPRISE* (CV 6) came twelve F4F WILDCAT fighters flown by pilots of Marine Fighter Squadron (VMF) 311.

On the morning of Monday, Dec. 8, Wake heard by radio of the Japanese attack on PEARL HARBOR. (Wake is west of the International Dateline, so Sunday, Dec. 7 at Pearl Harbor was Monday, Dec. 8 at Wake.) At noon, with four F4Fs on patrol, Japanese bombers from KWAJALEIN attacked Wake. Their BOMBS destroyed seven F4Fs on the ground and inflicted major damage on Wake's facilities. A Pan American Clipper was caught at Wake during the raid. The Clipper was loaded with 200 tires for the P-40 WARHAWKS of the FLYING TIGERS in China. When the Japanese planes departed, the tires were burned to keep them out of Japanese hands and the Clipper took off.

The defenders, under attack by Japanese planes and ships, damaged three cruisers, two destroyers, and other ships of an invasion force on Dec. 11. The Japanese then battered the island for twelve days before landing on Dec. 23. The island commander, Navy Comdr. Winfield S. Cunningham, sent the last message from Wake: "Enemy on island—issue in doubt." A short time later, he surrendered. In the battle for Wake the Japanese lost an estimated 820 men in the air and on the ground.

American casualties totaled 120 killed, forty-nine wounded, and two missing.

Wake's gallant defense inspired *Wake Island,* one of the earliest war MOVIES and gave Americans reeling from the Pearl Harbor attack a feeling of pride. What they did not know was that the long ordeal for Wake's PRISONERS OF WAR had just begun.

About 1,200 U.S. civilians and military prisoners were loaded aboard a converted passenger ship on Jan. 12, 1942, and transported to camps in China. During the twelve-day voyage five were beheaded for no apparent reason. Of those remaining on Wake, all but ninety-eight American civilians were soon removed. The ninety-eight were put to work with the heavy construction equipment.

On Oct. 7, 1943, Rear Adm. Shigematsu Sakaibara, commander of the Japanese garrison on Wake, claiming that the prisoners had been in radio contact with U.S. forces, executed the prisoners.

The Japanese intended to make Wake an important air base and eventually stationed about 4,400 troops there. But the island proved useless to Japan. U.S. planes bombed it repeatedly during the Japanese occupation and U.S. ships frequently shelled it as the island became a training range for fliers and gunners.

The besieged garrison had few supplies and suffered from malnutrition; there were only about 1,200 Japanese left when Sakaibara surrendered on Sept. 4, 1945, two days after Japan's formal SURRENDER in TOKYO Bay. Sakaibara was arrested and later tried and convicted of WAR CRIMES. He was executed on GUAM on June 18, 1947.

Waldheim, Kurt (1918—)

German officer wounded on the EASTERN FRONT in Dec. 1941 and, after convalescence, sent as an intelligence officer to Belgrade, Yugoslavia, and later to Greece. Austrian-born, he led a relatively unpublicized life until he became the fourth secretary-general of the UNITED NATIONS in Jan. 1972. He was elected to a second term in Dec. 1976. After failing to get a third term, he returned to his native Austria, where he successfully ran for president in 1986. In his autobiography, Waldheim obscured part of his war record, apparently because in places where he was stationed Germans committed atrocities against GUERRILLAS and other civilians. Although no direct connection was made between Waldheim and the atrocities, revelations about his suppressed war record badly damaged his reputation.

Walker, Capt. F. J., (1896–1944)

The Royal Navy's most successful antisubmarine group leader. During the war Walker commanded first the high-scoring 36th Escort Group and then the 2nd Escort Group. The former accounted for fourteen U-BOATS sunk during Walker's tenure, including six destroyed in a twenty-seven-day operation in the eastern Atlantic early in 1944. (One of Walker's escorts was sunk by a submarine's GNAT acoustic TORPEDO in that operation.)

Capt. Walker developed the scheme of "double teaming" a U-boat opponent in his brilliant "creeping" attack tactic: one escort ship slowly kept pace with the submerged submarine by using her echo-ranging ASDIC (SONAR). When sufficient data were available for an attack, Walker would have a second escort race in to attack with DEPTH CHARGES (including SQUID-launched charges). This tactic eliminated the loss of acoustic contact when the attacking escort passed over the U-boat to release depth charges. Walker called this tactic Operation Plaster.

"There were no reports on this tactic to U-boat Command, because once held in the vice of the 2nd [Escort Group]'s Asdic, no U-boat survived. Walker hunted to the death," wrote British historian John Terraine.

Capt. Walker died in July 1944 of a stroke caused by exhaustion.

Walkie-talkie

Back-carried voice radio weighing a few pounds that was widely used by U.S. forces. It was a battery-operated FM set that was manually tuned over the 40 to 48 megacycle range; it was generally carried by one man with the PLATOON leader or COMPANY commander using a handset on a cord plugged into the radio. Its designation was SCR (Signal Corps Radio) 300. Range was about two miles.

A still-smaller set, the SCR-536 "handie-talkie," was an AM radio.

Wallenberg, Raoul (1910–1947[?])

Swedish diplomat credited with saving 20,000 Hungarian JEWS by his bold and courageous work. In July 1944 Wallenberg, a member of a prominent Swedish family, went to BUDAPEST under the auspices of the International RED CROSS on a mission to save the Jews being sent off to the DEATH CAMP at AUSCHWITZ. Wallenberg, made an attaché in the Swedish legation in Budapest, rented buildings, gave them Swedish diplomatic status, and housed hundreds of Jews there. He also issued dubious—but effective—passports that gave Swedish protection to thousands of Jews. He was supported by advice and funds from the U.S. War Refugees Board.

When Germans tried to seize Jews from Wallenberg's protected area, he rushed outside and shouted, "This is Swedish territory. . . . If you want to take them, you will have to shoot me first." He plucked Jews out of death marches, removed them from ghettoes, and is credited with having saved about 20,000 in his Swedish territory and aiding in the protection of 70,000 confined Jews who survived until liberation.

On Jan. 16, 1945, during fierce fighting for Budapest, Soviet troops liberated Wallenberg's facilities and the area around them. But Soviet officials, apparently believing Wallenberg was an American spy, would not aid him in getting the Jews to freedom. On Jan. 17, he went with a Soviet officer and his driver to Soviet military headquarters at Debrecen, about 120 miles east of Budapest. He was not seen again and was assumed to have been arrested. Postwar efforts to trace him led to reports that he was seen in various Soviet prisons.

The Soviets, in response to international interest in Wallenberg, had said in 1957 that he had died in Lubyanka Prison in Moscow on July 17, 1947, of "a heart attack." The Soviets said his arrest and imprisonment was a "tragic mistake."

Walrus

Widely flown British reconnaissance and air/sea rescue flying boat. A lumbering biplane based on a private venture of the Supermarine Aviation Works, the Walrus flew with the Royal Navy from 1936 until the end of the war. An amphibian, the Walrus was regularly carried by British battleships and cruisers; it was launched by catapult and after a mission came down on the water alongside the ship and was hoisted back aboard by crane. The Walrus flew in every part of the world that the Royal Navy operated.

The single-engine aircraft with a top speed of 135 mph and a range of 600 miles. The four-man crew had minimal self-defense with two .30-cal. machine guns, and could carry 1,000 pounds of BOMBS.

Walter, Helmuth (1900–)

German engineer and scientist who developed a closed-cycle propulsion plant for submarines. In June 1943, after the devastating U-BOAT losses of May in the BATTLE OF THE ATLANTIC, Prof. Walter proposed to *Grossadmiral* KARL DÖNITZ, the CinC of the Navy, the mass production of high-speed submarines that could remain fully submerged for long periods.

These submarines, with a streamlined hull, would be propelled by a Walter closed-cycle turbine plant with an engine that used the thermal energy produced by the decomposition of a high concentration of hydrogen peroxide. It was a complex system, but produced steam and oxygen at a high temperature (1,765° F) that passed to a combustion chamber where they met to ignite fuel oil. Thus, the turbine could be operated in a closed (submerged) atmosphere to provide sustained high underwater speeds.

At the urging of Walter, an experimental submarine, the *V-80,* was built in 1940 with a Walter turbine plant. That submarine reached over 26 knots submerged for short periods of time. (Submarines of the war period had a maximum underwater speed of ten knots.) In 1942 several Type XVIIa Walter experimental boats were ordered and plans were made for building twenty-four operational Type XVIIb submarines. Red tape in the German war machine slowed the program while skepticism among many naval engineers and others led to further delays.

In Dec. 1943 the first two Walter boats, the *U-792* and *U-794,* were ready for sea trials. They attained 25-knot underwater speeds for short periods; their longest fully submerged run was five and a half hours at 20 knots. In March 1944, after riding the *U-794,* Dönitz ordered the design into mass production. Plans were also drawn up for a larger, two-turbine design, the Type XVIII, which would be a large, long-range undersea craft. Again, bureaucratic squabbling and then a shortage of high-test peroxide caused the adoption of a smaller Walter-propelled submarine, the Type XXVI. Two hundred of these 850-ton submarines were ordered in May 1944. They were to have a submerged range of 158 miles at 25 knots, or 273 miles at 15 knots. These submarines were to have a surface displacement of 842 tons and a length of 184½ feet. Armament was to be ten 21-inch (533-mm) TORPEDO tubes (no reloads provided); they would need crews of about thirty-five men.

The plan was for 100 of these Walter boats to be operational by the end of 1945. However, Allied bombings wrecked this timetable and none was completed when the war ended in early May 1945. Seven of the Type XVII Walter submarines were completed by the end of the war, but had not yet finished trials and training when hostilities ceased.

After the war the Soviets and British carried out research with Walter propulsion plants, while the United States experimented with a shore-based turbine plant.

Wannsee Conference

Meeting to plan the "FINAL SOLUTION of the Jewish Question." Early in 1942 a "Führer order" calling for a plan to exterminate JEWS was sent by HERMANN GÖRING to several leading NAZI officials, including REINHARD HEYDRICH, Chief of the REICH CENTRAL SECURITY OFFICE (known by its German initials, RSHA); ADOLF EICHMANN, chief of the RSHA's Central Office of Jewish Emigration and the Nazi's official expert on Jews; representatives from the Occupied Eastern Territories, ministries of Justice and the Interior and the Foreign Office, and Nazi organizations.

The group met at an RSHA office in the BERLIN suburb of Wannsee on Jan. 20, 1942. Eichmann acted as recording secretary as Heydrich outlined his program for what the minutes of the conference call "the final solution of the Jewish question."

The problem involved about 11,000,000 Jews, he said. As he sketched his plan, the Jews "capable of work" would be moved in "big labor gangs, with separation of sexes," from Europe to the conquered territory of the East. Survivors of this SLAVE LABOR, representing "the strongest resistance" and "the germ cell of a new Jewish development," would be killed. The word *killed* does not appear in the minutes of the meeting; Heydrich said that the strong survivors, "representing a natural selection," must be "treated accordingly." This was code for treating an extreme threat with extreme measure: death.

War Agencies

U.S. government organizations set up primarily to handle economic, production, and other home-front problems produced by the war. The creation of the agencies began two years before the U.S. entry into the war. In 1939 President ROOSEVELT established a War Resources Board, headed by EDWARD R. STETTINIUS, JR., chairman of the board of U.S. Steel. The WRB, as it was called, ushered a host of new defense and war acronyms into the LANGUAGE. The appointment also established the practice of appointing prominent industrialists to war agencies. They were called "dollar-a-year men" because that was their official salary; they had to be paid something to be government employees.

In May 1940 Roosevelt set up the Office of Emergency Management and the Advisory Commission to the Council of National Defense. The council consisted of the secretaries of War, Navy, Interior, Agriculture, Commerce, and Labor. The commission had little power and was resented by military leaders, but its demise pointed up what would be the administration's policy for running the war: much of the work would be done by newly created agencies rather than by old-line Cabinet departments.

Roosevelt's next agency, established in Jan. 1941, was the Office of Production Management (OPM), which handled issues involving industrial production, raw materials, and labor. It was directed by WILLIAM S. KNUDSEN, president of General Motors, with Sidney Hillman as associate director. Hillman was a powerful labor leader of the nation's major union entity, the Congress of Industrial Organizations (CIO). During the 1944 Democratic Convention, when Roosevelt was asked about a running mate, he was quoted as saying, "Clear it with Sidney." The phrase became a Republican rallying cry during the campaign.

The OPM and the Supply Priorities and Allocations Board were replaced in Jan. 1942 by the War Production Board with DONALD M. NELSON, a former Sears Roebuck executive, as chairman. The WPB appeared to be powerful and reigned over the nation's prodigious WAR PRODUCTION. But the armed services retained the power of awarding and scheduling production contracts. And several other seemingly lesser agencies, such as the Petroleum Administration for War and the Office of Rubber Director, dispensed raw materials.

The War Manpower Commission (WMC), headed by PAUL V. MCNUTT, theoretically controlled labor for the war effort. But the WMC was relatively weak, for it could never get the armed services to refrain from taking skilled labor from the factory and shipyard workforce. The OFFICE OF WAR MOBILIZATION appeared in May 1943 as a superagency that coordinated the policies of various wartime agencies.

Concern over the economic impact of the war inspired the establishment of other agencies. In Jan. 1942 Congress passed the Emergency Price Control Act, which had been under debate since the middle of 1941. The act led to the creation of the OFFICE OF PRICE ADMINISTRATION, which controlled prices and rents and, later, RATIONING. The Office of Economic Stabilization, set up within the Office for Emergency Management under JAMES F. BYRNES in Oct. 1942, worked with the National War Labor Board to "hold the line" on wages and fight inflation. Other wartime organizations, usually designated as "office of" or "board of," handled special problems, ranging from overseeing LEND-LEASE and CIVIL DEFENSE to keeping track of alien properties and watching over the operations of petroleum pipelines.

War Bonds

Low-interest loans made to the U.S. government by private citizens and organizations to help finance the war. More than $190 billion worth of war bonds was subscribed to during the war. Most of the financing was through eight "war loan" drives between Dec. 1942 and Dec. 1945, when $156.9 billion was raised—with the aid of war heroes,

MOVIE stars, and such stars of the COMICS as Batman, Superman, and Dick Tracy. Two out of every three Americans, many of them using payroll deduction plans, subscribed to Series E bonds, first issued in Sept. 1943. Millions of school children got war-bond stamp books. They bought 25-cent war-bond stamps and kept pasting them into the book until until it was filled and could be turned in for a $25 bond.

The rate of interest was 1.8 percent compared to 4.25 percent on similar bonds issued in World War I. The bonds, besides psychologically uniting civilians in the war effort, curtailed civilian spending. Small investors bought about $40 billion worth of bonds; the rest were purchased by commercial banks, insurance companies, brokers, savings and loans associations, states, and local governments.

War Brides

The term used to describe WOMEN who married American servicemen overseas. "Operation War Bride" brought 600 British war brides to the United States on a passenger ship in 1946. That year, according to U.S. immigration figures, 60,000 British women had filed for emigration to the United States as brides or prospective brides. Another 8,000 applications came from French, Italian, and Dutch women and 4,000 from Australian and New Zealand women.

War Cards

Garish cardboard illustrations of scenes of war, enclosed with bubble gum. In the 1930s American children who collected baseball cards discovered a new product: war cards. The scenes showed Japanese soldiers bayoneting Chinese babies, bodies being blown apart in SPANISH CIVIL WAR air raids, and similarly gruesome moments of war. The cards began fading away after the U.S. entry into the war.

War Correspondents

Reporters, photographers, and broadcasters who covered the war. Some 800 correspondents, including twenty-four WOMEN, were accredited by the U.S. military. Thirty-eight were killed and thirty-six were wounded and given the Purple Heart. The casualty rate for correspondents was 22 percent (compared to 5 percent for servicemen in combat).

Among those killed were ERNIE PYLE, one of the best-known correspondents of the war, and Raymond Clapper, who worked for Scripps-Howard newspapers and was syndicated in 180 newspapers. Clapper was killed in Feb. 1944 when the Navy plane he was in, returning to its carrier, collided with another.

Although subject to front-line CENSORSHIP, correspondents generally gave military censors little concern. The correspondents had quasi-officer status and most of them (Pyle was an exception) tended to see the war from the viewpoint of an officer and a strategist. Correspondent Fletcher Pratt wrote, "The official censors pretty well succeeded in putting over the legend that the war was won without a single mistake by a command consisting exclusively of geniuses."

U.S. war correspondents in World War II were writing for their side of the war. There was no objectivity about who were the heroes and who were the villains. JOHN HERSEY, a correspondent for *Time-Life,* referred to "Japs" as "a swarm of intelligent little animals" in his account of a Marine skirmish, *Into the Valley.* In a foreword to a 1989 edition he said that the words bothered him when he read them as a postwar writer.

Novelist JOHN STEINBECK, a correspondent for the *New York Herald Tribune* during the war, wrote in *Once There Was a War* (1959): "We were all part of the war effort. We went along with it, and not only that, we abetted it. . . . Yes. we wrote only a part of the war but at that time we believed, fervently believed, that it was the best thing to do."

War Crimes

Acts committed by AXIS military and civilian leaders who were tried by international tribunals in Nuremberg and TOKYO and by an estimated 2,000 other individual trials in defeated and formerly enemy-occupied countries. Although a UNITED NATIONS War Crimes Commission was formed in 1943, the Soviet Union refused to participate, and another system had to be found to bring to justice those who committed what President ROOSEVELT called "acts of savagery." The focus was on Germany and what Prime Minister CHURCHILL, referring to

German guards hang civilians at an internment camp in Europe. This photograph was found on a captured German soldier. *(Imperial War Museum)*

the HOLOCAUST, called "probably the greatest and most horrible crime ever committed in the whole history of the world."

An International Military Tribunal for the Far East, with headquarters in Tokyo, tried twenty-five Japanese military officers and civilians charged with crimes against peace, crimes against humanity, murder, and atrocities. The trials, unlike the German proceedings in Nuremberg, were largely ignored by the U.S. public. The only celebrated defendant was HIDEKI TOJO, Japan's Prime Minister who, for Americans, personified the Japanese enemy. In a trial that dragged on until Nov. 1948, Tojo and six others were sentenced to death; sixteen other Japanese were sentenced to life imprisonment. Gen. MASAHARU HOMMA, blamed for the BATAAN DEATH MARCH, was among those executed. In war crimes trials in SINGAPORE and other Far East cities, about 900 people were condemned to death.

The Nuremberg trial of NAZI leaders, conducted by a joint U.S.-British-French-Soviet military tribunal, began on Nov. 20, 1945, with U.S. Supreme Court Justice ROBERT H. JACKSON as chief prosecutor and TELFORD TAYLOR as chief prosecution counsel. Each of the four nations supplied two judges, one of whom was an alternate. The principal U.S. judge was Attorney General Francis Biddle.

The United States and Great Britain had not wanted the trial held in the Soviet occupation zone; the Soviets preferred BERLIN. Nuremberg, though heavily damaged, was chosen; it had a relatively intact Palace of Justice with an adjacent prison.

Evoking unprecedented legal procedures, the tribunal indicted twenty-four Germans; twenty-two went on trial. Robert Ley, leader of the German Labor Front and the "Strength through Joy" recreational organization, who had called for the "extermination" of JEWS, committed suicide in his cell before the trial began. Gustav KRUPP von Bohlen und Halbach, whose vast armaments empire relied on SLAVE LABOR, was judged unable to stand trial because of his "physical and mental condition."

The four separate charges drawn up for the trial were *Count 1*, conspiracy to commit the crimes cited in the other three counts; *Count 2*, crimes against the peace (planning, preparing, starting, or waging aggressive war); *Count 3*, war crimes (violations of the laws or customs of war); *Count 4*, crimes against humanity (murder, extermination, enslavement, persecution on political or racial grounds, and involuntary deportation and inhumane acts against civilian populations).

The defendants, arrayed in two rows of seats under heavy military police guard, listened to simultaneous translations as prosecutors proved charges with the use of the Nazis' own meticulous documentation of systematic mass murder and other crimes. In defense, the accused essentially claimed they were mere ignorant pawns of their master, ADOLF HITLER.

Among the exhibits displayed as evidence were the shrunken head of a CONCENTRATION CAMP inmate, used as a paperweight, and a piece of tattooed human skin, accompanied by an affidavit from a concentration camp guard: prisoners at Buchenwald "with the best and most artistic specimens were kept in the dispensary and killed by injection." The prisoners' tattooed skins were then turned over to Ilse Koch, the wife of KARL KOCH, the commander of the camp. The guard said she "had them fashioned into lampshades and other household articles."

The verdict and sentences were handed down on Sept. 30–Oct. 1, 1946. The sweeping verdict, going beyond the twenty-two defendants, acquitted members of the General Staff and High Command, despite "clear and convincing" proof of criminal acts. As groups, the SA (Brown Shirts) and Hitler's Cabinet were also acquitted. But the dreaded Nazi secret police apparatus—the SS, SD, and GESTAPO—all were declared criminal groups.

The defendants, the verdicts, and sentences were:

MARTIN BORMANN, confidential aide to Hitler. Tried, found guilty, and sentenced to death *in absentia*. In 1973 a West German court declared him officially dead.

KARL DÖNITZ, *Grossadmiral* and Hitler's successor. Guilty of Counts 2 and 3. Sentenced to ten years in prison. He served his complete sentence.

HANS FRANK, governor general of Poland. Guilty on Counts 3 and 4. Hanged.

Wilhelm Frick, Reich Minister of the Interior from 1933 to 1943, protector of Bohemia and Morovia, and author of the Nuremberg Laws that legalized the persecution of Jews. Guilty on Counts 2, 3, and 4. Hanged.

Hans Fritzsche, deputy minister of PROPAGANDA. Acquitted.

Walther Funk, economics minister and *Reichsbank* president, who conspired with HEINRICH HIMMLER to put the gold fillings, jewels, and other loot from victims of DEATH CAMPS in a false bank account. Guilty on Counts 2, 3, and 4. Life imprisonment. He was released in 1957.

HERMANN GÖRING, commander of the Luftwaffe and *Reichsmarschall*. Guilty on all four counts. Sentenced to be hanged. An hour and a half before his execution was scheduled he killed himself with poison.

RUDOLF HESS, deputy führer before he flew to Scotland in 1941. Guilty on Counts 1 and 2. Life imprisonment. He died in prison in 1987.

ALFRED JODL, chief of the operations staff of the High Command of the Armed Forces. Guilty on all four counts. Sentenced to be hanged, he requested a soldier's death by firing squad, but this was refused—he was hanged.

ERNST KALTENBRUNNER, director of the REICH CENTRAL SECURITY OFFICE after the ASSASSINATION of REINHARD HEYDRICH in June 1942. Guilty on Counts 3 and 4. Hanged.

WILHELM KEITEL, chief of the High Command of the Armed Forces. Guilty on all four counts. He, too, asked for a firing squad—he was hanged.

Baron Constantin Freiherr von Neurath, foreign minister from 1932 to 1938 and Reich protector of Bohemia and Moravia from 1939 to 1943. An aristocrat who claimed allegiance to Germany but not Hitler, Neurath nevertheless acted like a Nazi, abolishing political parties, muzzling the press, closing universities, and enforcing racial laws. Guilty on all four counts. Sentenced to 15 years in prison, he was released in 1954 and died, at age eighty-three, two years later.

FRANZ VON PAPEN, Nazi politician and diplomat. Acquitted (but later found guilty of wartime criminal conduct by a German "de-Nazification" court; see below).

ERICH RAEDER, *Grossadmiral* and Commander in Chief of the German Navy. Guilty on Counts 1, 2, and 3. Life imprisonment. He was released in 1955 and died in 1960.

JAOCHIM VON RIBBENTROP, minister of Foreign Affairs from 1938 to 1945. Guilty on all four counts. Hanged.

Alfred Rosenberg, ANTI-SEMITIC, and anti-Catholic ideologue and minister for the Occupied Eastern Territories. His institute for "scientific and cultural research" was a front for the looting of Jewish art collections and libraries. Guilty on all four counts. Hanged.

FRITZ SAUCKEL, director of slave labor. Guilty on Counts 3 and 4. Hanged.

Hjalmar Schacht, former *Reichsbank* president and minister of Economics. Arrested after the JULY 20 PLOT against Hitler, Schacht was placed in a concentration camp. He was acquitted at Nuremberg. Later a de-Nazification court declared him a "major offender" (see below). Cleared by an appeals court, he founded a foreign trade bank and prospered as an adviser to Iran, Syria, Libya, and other countries.

Baldur von Schirach, leader of HITLER YOUTH, 1931 to 1940; *Gauleiter* of Vienna, 1940. Grandson of a Union officer in the U.S. Civil War, Schirach, at thirty-eight, was the youngest defendant at Nuremberg. As leader of the 9,000,000 members of Hitler Youth, at twenty-four he had the SA rank of *Gruppenführer,* equivalent to a major general. He wrote lavish poetry about Hitler ("a genius grazing the stars") and endorsed the expulsion of Jews from Austria as "contributing to European culture." Guilty on Count 4. He was sentenced to, and served, twenty years imprisonment.

Arthur Seyss-Inquart, Nazi chancellor of Austria and administrator of occupied Holland. Under his reign, some 110,000 Dutch Jews had been sent to concentration camps; no more than 6,000 survived. As Dutch resistance movements intensified their SABOTAGE and killings of German troops toward the end of the war, he ordered more and more retaliation. About 4,000 Dutch men and WOMEN were shot. Guilty on Counts 2, 3, and 4. Hanged.

ALBERT SPEER, Hitler's chief architect and subsequently minister of armaments and WAR PRODUCTION, who had slave labor factories built next to concentration camps. He admitted his guilt but was found guilty on Counts 3 and 4. He was sentenced to, and served, twenty years imprisonment.

JULIUS STREICHER, publisher of an anti-Semite journal. Guilty on Count 4. Hanged.

The hangings, carried out by U.S. Army Master Sgt. JOHN WOODS, an experienced hangman, took place after midnight on Oct. 16, 1946. The bodies of Göring and the ten others were taken by trucks to DACHAU, where the bodies were cremated in the concentration camp's crematorium. The ashes were dumped into a brook in Munich.

From the loathsome evidence and horrifying testimony at the Nuremberg trials came much of what the world would learn about the Holocaust, concentration camps, death camps, and slave labor. For many years, numerous other de-Nazification trials would be held. Defendants were classified in five categories: (1) major offenders subject to life imprisonment or death; (2) "activists," military criminals, or profiteers, liable for up to ten years in prison; (3) lesser offenders, especially people who entered the Nazi Party at a young age, two to three years; (4) "followers," a fine; (5) Nazis who had resisted Hitler and had suffered for it, exoneration.

A U.S. military tribunal at Nuremberg in Dec. 1946 tried twenty-three SS physicians and scientists who performed usually lethal experiments on Jews and other prisoners. The trial ended in Aug. 1947 with sixteen defendants found guilty. Seven were sentenced to death by hanging; five to life imprisonment. The others received long prison sentences. (See DOCTORS TRIAL.)

From Dec. 1963 to Aug. 1965, a West German court at Frankfurt am Main tried twenty-one former SS officers at the death camp at AUSCHWITZ. Charged with complicity in thousands of murders, nineteen were convicted and sentenced to prison terms ranging from three years to life.

Some war criminals, such as JOSEF MENGELE escaped; others, such as ADOLF EICHMANN, were tried elsewhere. Unknown numbers of Nazis were tried in secret by Soviet tribunals, which meted out unpublicized justice.

War Department

Administrative headquarters for the U.S. Army. At the start of the war the War Department's offices were located in a number of government and leased buildings in WASHINGTON. Beginning in Nov. 1942 the principal offices of the War Department moved into the new PENTAGON building, located in Arlington, Va., just across the Potomac River from Washington.

The secretary of War, HENRY L. STIMSON, was head of the War Department and a member of the President's Cabinet. His principal military subordinate was the Army's Chief of Staff, Gen. GEORGE C. MARSHALL.

War Powers Act

The powers Congress granted the President during the war. The powers themselves were essentially bureaucratic. But from them stemmed a welter of controls.

Congress passed the first War Powers Act on Dec. 18, 1941, ten days after President ROOSEVELT asked Congress for a declaration of war. The act primarily gave the President power over the awarding, settlement, and termination of defense contracts; to redistribute the functions of government agencies except for the General Accounting Office; and to enforce regulations freezing foreign credits. The act also allowed the President to impose CENSORSHIP.

The second War Powers Act of March 27, 1942, gave the Interstate Commerce Commission the right to control motor carriers and water carriers; authorized the requisition of property by the WAR DEPARTMENT and NAVY DEPARTMENT; provided free postage to service men and WOMEN. The act also gave the President the right to set priorities for WAR PRODUCTION and allocate RESOURCES. The President delegated this power to the War Production Board, and this was the pattern: In the *name* of the War Powers Act a wide spectrum of powers was assumed by government agencies.

Through supplementary laws and executive orders, government controls were imposed over manpower, production, distribution of goods, foreign commerce, communications, transportation, the handling of finances; prices were set on profits, housing, food, fuel, and medical services.

From this same broad interpretation of the War Powers Acts came government actions ranging from powerful and unprecedented to tiny and ludicrous: the "relocation" of JAPANESE-AMERICANS to internment camps; orders to bakers to conserve production facilities by refraining from the use of double wrappers on bread; orders to the U.S. Mint to make ZINC COINS and discontinue nickel-copper five-cent pieces.

The two War Powers Acts enacted during a shooting war would loom years later when Congress tried again to decide whether presidential powers included the right to dispatch troops and make moves leading to or threatening war. The Vietnam-era War Powers Act, passed in 1972, required the President to give an accounting of his actions within thirty days of committing troops.

War Production

The unprecedented U.S. effort to produce the weapons and other matériel needed to win the war. At the TEHRAN CONFERENCE in 1943, Soviet leader JOSEF STALIN, in a rare acknowledgment of U.S. war efforts, offered a toast: "To American production, without which this war would have been lost."

Stalin was not exaggerating. From 1941 to mid-1945, U.S. plants produced more than 300,000 airplanes, 100,000 TANKS and armored vehicles, such as HALF-TRACKS; 5,600 merchant ships, 79,-125 LANDING CRAFT, 2.4 million military trucks (many 6×6s), 3.3 million rifles and CARBINES, 2.6 million machine guns, 20.8 million helmets, 41 billion rounds of ammunition, and innumerable other tools of war.

The U.S. production effort was threatened early in the war by Japan's swift conquests in the Pacific, giving the enemy control of the oil of the DUTCH EAST INDIES, virtually all of the world's natural rubber, and 70 percent of the world's tin. As the RESOURCES from conquered areas were cut off, England was forced to rely more and more upon U.S. resources, especially oil. England, Canada, and the United States formed boards that helped to coordinate the three nations' production and resources allocations.

The mobilization of U.S. industry had been well under way before PEARL HARBOR. "We must be the great arsenal of democracy," President ROOSEVELT said on Dec. 29, 1940, in one of his radio "fireside chats" to the nation. By the time of the Japanese attack, military spending was at a level of nearly $2 billion a month.

In Jan. 1942 President Roosevelt stepped up production by setting objectives and establishing the first of a series of new WAR AGENCIES, the War Production Board (WPB), with DONALD M. NELSON as chairman. The watchword was conversion: A kitchen sink factory began making cartridge cases and a factory that made shirts switched to making mosquito netting. The WPB, while having little power over contract negotiations, gained power from Congress to set priorities and stop production of "nonessential" civilian goods, such as AUTOMOBILES, home appliances, lawn mowers, home oil burners, bird cages, cocktail shakers, and more than 400 other civilian products.

The armed services, not the WPB, controlled specifications on manufactured goods, awarded contracts, and set production schedules. The military suspended competitive bidding and gave out cost-plus-fixed-fee contracts that guaranteed profits. The services paid manufacturers up to 30 percent in advance and promised to cover postwar retooling costs. Competitors that colluded to set prices were granted immunity from antitrust prosecution if they could show that their actions aided the war efforts.

Many factories did compete—for raw materials and manpower—while civilians and military procurement officers wrangled over what manufacturers should get what scarce products. Aircraft manufacturing and shipbuilding set records.

Aircraft The most remarkable U.S. production records were for aircraft delivered—in one month, March 1944, amounting to 9,113 planes. The following table compares U.S. aircraft production with that of Japan, Germany, and the UNITED KINGDOM. (No such figures are available from the Soviet Union, although Stalin reported that Soviet aircraft production reached a rate of 40,000 planes per year in 1944.)

YEAR	JAPAN	GERMANY	UK	USA
1939	4,467	8,295	7,940	2,141
1940	4,768	10,826	15,049	6,086
1941	5,088	11,776	20,094	19,433
1942	8,861	15,556	23,672	47,836
1943	16,693	25,527	26,263	85,898
1944	28,180	39,807	26,461	96,318
1945	8,263*	—	12,070**	46,001†

*Seven and one-half months for Japan
**Nine months only for U.K.
†Eight months only for U.S.A.

The United States produced more airframes, as measured in weight, than all other countries combined—1,101,116,000 pounds, including spares. During the war, Britain produced 208,520,000; Germany 174,939,000; Japan estimated about 100,000,000, and the Soviet Union (based on Stalin's numbers) a maximum of 200,000,000. During this period the United States produced over 800,-000 aircraft engines.

Of the U.S. planes, some 77 percent were for the U.S. Army Air Forces and 23 percent went to the U.S. Navy. About 45,000 U.S.-produced aircraft went to ALLIES—mostly the United Kingdom and the Soviet Union.

Warships Two major U.S. warship shipbuilding programs got under way on the eve of the war. In June 1940 Congress passed legislation increasing the strength of the Navy. This so-called "11% Fleet Expansion Bill" provided for the construction of two BATTLESHIPS, three AIRCRAFT CARRIERS, fourteen CRUISERS, and thirty-eight DESTROYERS. (SUBMARINES were not included in the bill.) In July 1940 Congress passed "the Two-Ocean Navy Bill" that let orders for an additional seven battleships, six battle cruisers, eight large aircraft carriers, twenty-seven cruisers, and 162 destroyers.

In the fall of 1941, U.S. shipyards got orders for fifty DESTROYER ESCORTS for LEND-LEASE transfer to Britain. Then came PEARL HARBOR and the beginning of a record-setting era for U.S. shipbuilding. In 1939 American shipbuilders had 156 building ways large enough for seagoing merchant ships and combat ships. By the end of the war there were eighty-four shipyards with 578 such building ways. In addition, about 5,000 war plants produced components and supplies needed by the shipyards. Employment increased from about 100,000 in 1939 (one third of the workers in government-operated naval shipyards) to a peak of 1,722,500 at the end of 1943.

COMBAT SHIPS* AND CRAFTS PRODUCED, 1941–1945

Private yards: 1,027 of 2,538,065 displacement tons
Government yards: 325 of 3,501,040 displacement tons

*battleships, aircraft carriers, cruisers, destroyers, destroyer escorts, high-speed transports (destroyer-escort type), frigates, minelayers (destroyer type), gunboats, submarines.

NAVAL AUXILIARY SHIPS PRODUCED, 1941–1945

Private yards: 166 of 1,061,959 displacement tons
Government yards: 13 of 69,310 displacement tons

In addition, hundreds of merchant ships were converted to naval auxiliaries.

Merchant Ships Merchant ship production also had a prewar congressional mandate. The Merchant Marine Act of 1936 led to government contracts for fifty ships per year beginning in 1938. When the EUROPEAN WAR began in 1939, this quota was doubled, then doubled again in 1940, with an added British order for sixty more ships. At the beginning of 1941 the U.S. Government ordered the first 200 LIBERTY SHIPS and 227 Lend-Lease cargo ships.

MERCHANT SHIPS BUILT OF 2,000 GROSS TONS AND OVER

	Cargo Ships	Tankers	Passenger/Cargo
1941	61	28	6
1942	652	61	11
1943	1,410	231	20
1944	1,175	240	48
1945	833	188	46

The automotive industry was the principal armory in the arsenal of democracy. About 35 percent of the nation's ordnance production was in and around Detroit. General Motors Corporation, the nation's largest producer of war matériel, developed specialties for its divisions. From the CADILLAC factory came tanks and howitzer motor carriers; from the Chevrolet plant came aircraft-engines gears and axles for Army vehicles; Fisher Body produced parts for tanks, bombers, and naval gun mounts.

Other GM plants turned out scores of other weapons components, including armor plate and airplane instruments. The Chrysler Corporation made marine engines, ambulances, weapons carriers, antiaircraft guns, antisubmarine nets. Packard built engines for planes and PT-BOATS. At Ford's 1,096-acre Rouge River plant—the largest industrial facility in the world—raw material arrived by ship, and jeeps and trucks were shipped out at the same docks.

But not all of Detroit was breaking records. The government built an aircraft plant for the Ford Motor Company near the village of Willow Run, thirty miles west of Detroit. The plant covered 3,700,000 square feet. HENRY FORD announced that the Willow Run production line would turn out 1,000 planes a day. But the plant—dubbed "Willit Run?"—was a long time getting to work. In Feb. 1943, HARRY S TRUMAN, then chairman of the Senate War Investigating Committee, began an investigation of Willow Run because its production of B-24 LIBERATOR bombers was so low "as to amount to practically none." Under Truman's goading, Ford solved many of Willow Run's production problems, and by the end of 1943 the plant was building an average of 340 planes a month.

Chronic problems plagued war production. In the spring of 1943, reacting both to strikes and to management slowdowns, Under Secretary of War ROBERT P. PATTERSON complained about the "tendency of certain manufacturers to devote too little time, thought, and energy to the design and development of" weapons. Too much energy, Patterson said, was being devoted to the making of "civilian nonessentials" and the planning of postwar products.

In mid-1943, as chaos slowed down assembly lines and threatened even the shipping of munitions to war theaters, the WPB acted. It set up a "controlled materials plan" that compelled manufacturers to report exactly what stocks of critical goods they had and exactly what they needed to meet production quotas. The WPB compared stocks with needs and awarded manufacturers allocations of raw materials.

The plan broke many production bottlenecks, but work stoppages—despite a wartime "no-strike" pledge from labor unions—frequently halted assembly lines. In Dec. 1942, Roosevelt gave the War Manpower Commission authority over SELECTIVE SERVICE, with power to hire and assign jobs in war industries. But Congress stripped the commission of these powers in 1943.

U.S. labor union membership increased from 8,700,000 in 1940 to 14,300,000 in 1945; by 1945 union members made up one third of all nonfarm civilian employment. The National War Labor Board, established in Jan. 1942, held down wage increases but, under intense union pressure, authorized fringe benefits, such as health insurance and work-shift pay differentials.

Strikes had triggered the government's seizure of two aircraft plants and a shipyard in 1941, before U.S. entry into the war. Negotiations soon ended both the strikes and the seizures. Strikes dropped sharply in 1942, probably because of patriotism and steady wages after years of Depression uncertainty. But in 1943 workers were again striking, despite angry editorials and impassioned rhetoric from a relatively powerless government.

YEAR	NUMBER OF STRIKES	WORKERS INVOLVED	WORKER-DAYS LOST	AVG. DAYS LOST PER WORKER
1941	4,288	2,362,620	23,047,556	9.9
1942	2,968	839,961	4,182,557	5.0
1943	3,752	1,981,279	13,500,529	6.8
1944	4,956	2,115,637	8,721,079	4.1
1945	4,616	3,069,300	24,360,000	7.9

An analysis of worker-day losses during 1943, in terms of war production showed:

TYPE OF INDUSTRY	WORKER-DAYS LOST
Mining (primarily coal)	9,370,000
Iron and steel	726,000
Automotive (including tanks, etc.)	441,000
Other transportation equipment	382,000
Textiles	306,000
Construction	140,827

Coal miners, led by United Mine Workers President John L. Lewis, caused most of the labor troubles of 1943. When the miners struck, the government ordered them to go back to work or see the mines seized. They stayed out. On April 29, the government seized the struck mines. Management got the mines working again, but the strike dragged on until the miners got unprecedented "portal-to-portal" pay: compensation for the time it took to get in and out of the mine.

Many workers prospered during the war. In most war plants, production lines hummed twenty-four hours a day. Some workers earned overtime or worked two shifts in two factories. (The "swing shift" was 4 P.M. to midnight; the "graveyard shift" from midnight to 8 A.M.) The average hourly wages of manufacturing production workers rose from 66 cents in 1940 to $1.02 in 1945; for bituminous miners, the rise was from 85 cents to $1.20. Although the cost of living rose during this period, price controls held it low enough to keep most wages ahead of inflation.

The Smith-Connally Act, passed by Congress over Roosevelt's veto in June 1943, empowered the President to seize any property where a labor dispute threatened war production; workers who continued to strike in a seized plant could be fined or jailed. The government seized factories, shipyards, mines, and other production facilities sixty-three times during the war. Most strikes in 1944 were protests over cutbacks in production as the government anticipated the end of the war.

War Relocation Authority,

see JAPANESE-AMERICANS.

War Time

The national standard set for time during the war. War time was declared on Feb. 9, 1942, by an act of Congress advancing the standard time for each U.S. time zone by one hour. Congress had not named the new time; "war time" was suggested by President ROOSEVELT.

The war-time law traced back to World War I, when Congress, concerned about establishing uniform time zones, simultaneously decided to emulate a "daylight saving" scheme tried in Europe as a way to conserve fuel by artificially extending daylight. The Standard Time Act, approved on March 19, 1918, had two purposes: the establishment of five uniform U.S. time zones and, in response to

the war, the advancing of time by one hour in each zone. The new time—"daylight saving time"—was to last for seven months, beginning on the last Sunday in March and ending on the last Sunday in October. After World War I, national daylight saving was dropped, but individual states enacted laws for turning the clocks an hour ahead in spring and an hour back in fall.

The 1942 legislation, which set up war time for *all* the year instead of seven months, was repealed on Sept. 30, 1945. Again, time-setting regulations reverted to individual states. By then, however, the two national wartime experiences with war time had changed enough habits and had enlisted enough advocates for Congress to think again about time. Finally in 1966 Congress passed the Uniform Time Act, which superseded all local laws on time setting.

Warhawk,

see P-40.

Warsaw

Capital of Poland, battered on the first day of the EUROPEAN WAR and again in the final days of liberation. Germany launched the war on Sept. 1, 1939, with an air raid on Warsaw. A few days later, the Germans began pounding the city in a siege that killed tens of thousands, turned historic structures into rubble, and destroyed about 25 percent of the city's homes. Without water, electricity, or food, Warsaw was in flames on Sept. 27, when it finally surrendered.

The Germans' brutal occupation of Poland focused on Warsaw. They herded the city's JEWS into the WARSAW GHETTO and deported about 350,000 other city residents to Germany, where many died. Unknown numbers were shot down in GESTAPO roundups and in reprisal for GUERRILLA actions. Often, the houses of suspects were dynamited and burned. "Warsaw shall not be rebuilt," said RUDOLF HESS, the deputy führer, echoing HITLER'S order. Warsaw suffered for five years.

On Aug. 1, 1944, as advancing Soviet troops reached the outskirts of Warsaw, the underground Polish Home Army led an uprising. While Soviet forces halted outside the ancient capital, German SS troops began a systematic destruction of the city and its people. Using tanks and warplanes against the lightly armed Home Army, the Germans killed more than 55,000 Poles in sixty-six days of fighting. By the time the Soviets finally liberated Warsaw in Jan. 1945, a city with a population of 1,289,000 in 1939 had a ragged, starving population of only 153,000.

Warsaw Ghetto

The largest of the areas where JEWS were herded by SS troops after the German conquest of Poland in 1939. The Germans ordered the building of a 10-foot brick wall around the ghetto, which was 11 miles in circumference. The Germans forced payment for the wall from the *Judenrat,* the Jewish Council that reluctantly administered the ghetto.

In Sept. 1940, the Germans evacuated all non-Jews from the enclosure and moved in Jews living elsewhere in WARSAW. On Nov. 15, when the population was about 360,000, the jammed ghetto was sealed from the rest of the city and the outside world.

Food supplies soon began to run out. Children crawled through sewers to reach the city beyond the ghetto and try to find food. Typhus, a lice-borne disease, reached epidemic intensity. Starvation and disease killed about 5,000 people a month. But the population did not decrease because the Germans continued to pack the ghetto with more Jews from other areas of Poland.

What the Germans called the "resettlement" of the ghetto began on July 22, 1942, in a macabre memorial to REINHARD HEYDRICH, Chief of the REICH CENTRAL SECURITY OFFICE and one of the principal planners of Germany's FINAL SOLUTION. (Heydrich, shot by two Czechs on May 27, had died on June 4.) To commemorate him, HEINRICH HIMMLER, head of the SS and overseer of CONCENTRATION CAMPS, had ordered that all Polish Jews in Polish ghettos and labor camps be sent to their deaths to cleanse Poland of Jews.

Able-bodied Jews selected by their captors had been given permits for working in war plants within the ghetto walls. When the extermination operation began, the workers were exempted. The SS ordered the *Judenrat* to assemble 6,000 Jews a day for "deportation." The first groups included children and elderly people, selected because the *Judenrat* believed that they would do better anywhere

than in the ghetto. But these were exactly the type of "useless eaters" the SS wanted to exterminate.

The deportation was to the DEATH CAMP at TREBLINKA, about 50 miles northeast of Warsaw. In two months, about 300,000 were sent to Treblinka. By Jan. 1943, when Himmler arrived for an inspection, there were only about 60,000 Jews in the ghetto. Disappointed to find the resettlement had not been completed, Himmler ordered that the last Jews be exterminated and the ghetto destroyed by the following month.

Through escapees from Treblinka, word had gotten back to the ghetto about the gas chambers. Knowing they had nothing to lose, Jews in the ghetto began planning a revolt. Leaders of the Jewish Fighting Organization, most of them young Zionists, managed to get some small arms into the ghetto. On Jan. 18, 1943, they fired on SS guards, starting the uprising. By some accounts, snipers killed forty Germans and in response 1,000 Jews were killed.

As in any epic of human valor, legends now eclipse history; no two accounts of the revolt agree on all details. But it is certain that Germans and their Baltic subordinates did temporarily withdraw and the revolt went on.

The ghetto became a honeycomb of passages and tunnels that enabled the organized defenders—about 650 divided into twenty-odd groups—to slip from place to place without risking the heavily patrolled streets. Anti-NAZI Christians outside the wall sold or donated guns (some stripped from the dead on Russian-German battlefields), ammunition, and dynamite.

On April 19, as Passover dawned, a mixed force of about 2,000 men—SS men, German, Baltic, and Ukrainian troops, Polish firemen and policemen—entered the fortress that the shrunken ghetto had become. Defenders threw MOLOTOV COCKTAILS at a TANK, but did not stop it. "Over and over again, new battle groups consisting of twenty to thirty or more Jewish fellows, eighteen to twenty-five years of age, accompanied by a corresponding number of WOMEN, kindled new resistance," *Brigadeführer* Jürgen Stroop, the commander of the German force, later said in a seventy-five page report to Himmler.

After four days of fighting, Stroop decided "to destroy the entire Jewish area by setting every block on fire." Systematically, each building was set on fire or blown up. "Not infrequently," Stroop reported, "the Jews stayed in the burning buildings until, because of the heat and the fear of being burned alive, they preferred to jump from the upper stories after having thrown mattresses and other upholstered articles into the street from the burning buildings. With their bones broken they still tried to crawl across the street into blocks of buildings which had not yet been set on fire."

On May 16 Stroop declared the ghetto "no longer in existence." The number of "Jews dealt with," he said, was 56,065, "including both Jews caught and Jews whose extermination can be proved." He estimated that 5,000 to 6,000 had been killed in the fires. But many had escaped to fight again, some in the Warsaw uprising of Aug. 1944. Stroop, who later served as SS chief in Greece, was sentenced to death by an American WAR CRIMES tribunal and executed on Sept. 8, 1951.

Washington

Washington, although far from the front lines, was unquestionably a wartime capital. The only Allied or AXIS capital unscathed by the war, Washington was the rear-echelon headquarters of the Allied war effort. Like the other capitals, Washington was drastically changed by the war. BOMBS shattered much of LONDON, devastated BERLIN, burned out TOKYO, cratered parts of ROME. What hit Washington was a population explosion.

The 1940 census counted 663,041 people in the District of Columbia's 61 square miles. By the time the war ended in 1945 Washington's population was 926,260 and the 61 square miles were jammed with 66,030 new dwelling places—plus 9,048 dormitories for the men and WOMEN who had come to Washington to help win the war effort and found there was no place to live. In mansions on Massachusetts Avenue as many as six people shared a bedroom that once was a library or reception hall.

Desperate room seekers joined Boarding Clubs. These were usually located in decrepit former stately homes that plywood walls and doors had transformed into warrens. Boarding Club members paid $40 per month for three in a room, $50 for two and $60 for one—in those rare places where single-occupancy rooms could be found. Some clubs had a central dining room where the boarders, for an extra fee, ate breakfast and dinner together.

The clubs were for whites. So were most rooming houses ("residence halls"), which advertised for "white government girls." Washington was very much a southern city divided between the white people and the people then called Negroes or the colored, a substantial, although almost invisible segment of Washington's population. Many of Washington's black families traced their District of Columbia roots to the Civil War. There were newcomers, too—blacks working for the New Deal in unexalted positions.

In those pre-Xerox days, the bureaucracy's mountains of triple or quadruple forms were churned out by pools of typists and reams of carbon paper (despite a wartime typewriter shortage). Among the blacks working for the federal government were young women in typing and stenographic pools; these women were assigned to all-black pools.

Washington was not alone in its policies. America was still a segregated society, and the rules applied to the armed services as well as to civilians. (See SEGREGATION.)

Early in 1941 A. Philip Randolph, the black leader of the Brotherhood of Sleeping Car Porters, put out a call for 100,000 black Americans to march on Washington to present protests about job discrimination to President ROOSEVELT and Congress. In early June, less than a month before the scheduled march, New York City Mayor FIORELLO LA GUARDIA, Mrs. ELEANOR ROOSEVELT, and government representatives met with Randolph and other black leaders. Out of this came, on June 25, a presidential order establishing the Committee on Fair Employment Practice in the Office of Production Management. The executive order guaranteed that discriminatory practices by federal contractors would result in the termination of their contracts.

Washington was beginning to set the agenda for American racial practices. HARRY HOPKINS and the President, touring the nearly completed PENTAGON across the Potomac, found what appeared to be an excessive number of rest rooms. Told that they were to be marked "Colored Men," "Colored Women," "White Men," and "White Women" the President countermanded the order for the signs.

Dec. 7, 1941, there was a Sunday football game

in Washington. At Griffith Stadium, 27,102 fans were watching the Washington Redskins play the Philadelphia Eagles when the loudspeakers began calling ambassadors, high-ranking military officers, and civilian officials to report to their offices. The Japanese had attacked PEARL HARBOR, but the Redskins management decided not to interrupt the game with the news. The Redskins won 20–14, and as the people filed out of the stadium they began to learn what had happened. Thus Redskin fans, one of whom was Navy Ens. JOHN F. KENNEDY, were among the last Americans to learn about the attack.

FEDERAL BUREAU OF INVESTIGATION agents swarmed around the Japanese Embassy. Reporters who managed to get past the FBI agents looked through closed gates into a courtyard where Japanese were burning documents. "Go away! Go away!" a Japanese in a pin-striped suit shouted when some of the newsmen slipped through an unlocked gate.

"What were you burning?" a reporter asked. "Dear sir," a Japanese diplomat said, "those, of course, were my love letters. I hope you will not jump to the hasty conclusion that those were diplomatic documents." Then shooing them out, he added, "Goodbye. I hope that we may meet under more pleasant circumstances the next time."

The United States interned the Japanese diplomats (and, after Dec. 12 declarations of war from Germany and Italy, diplomats from those nations) in West Virginia resorts for eventual repatriation in exchange for U.S. diplomats in Axis countries. When diplomatic relations were resumed after the war, the Japanese diplomatic delegation moved back into the same building.

Washington took on the appearance of a city at war. Olive-green, khaki, and blue uniforms filled the streets. Soldiers bearing arms appeared at the White House and along Constitution Avenue to guard the Munitions Building, where the WAR DEPARTMENT was located, and the next-door NAVY DEPARTMENT building. An arcade connected the two buildings, each of which had its own set of military guards. Until the Army began moving people into the new Pentagon in Nov. 1942, these few buildings would house the top military hierarchy running the war.

In the spring of 1940 the Park and Planning Commission was working to clear the Mall of the ugly wooden "temporary" buildings built in World War I. In the fall of 1940 the War Department said it wanted to keep the "tempos" and had to build even more. The commission chairman resigned. The Navy stayed in the World War I "tempos," and new barracks-like wood and stucco buildings appeared in double lines along the Reflecting Pool from the Washington Monument to the Lincoln Memorial. Secretary of the Interior HAROLD ICKES, whose responsibilities included maintaining the Mall and the monuments, muttered about Army officers who, "by the mere fact of their constantly changing assignments," were not able to appreciate long-range community planning.

Federal employees, who were now working a six-day week, became *personnel*. Into the Washington New Deal LANGUAGE came new vagaries like *priority* and *expedite*. As sharp-tongued Constance McLaughlin Green later wrote in *Washington: A History of the Capital,* "citizens who had never set foot in an industrial plant adopted terms like 'mock-up,' 'stockpile,' and 'tooling up.' . . . The simplicity that had characterized social affairs in New Deal days dropped away. 'Protocol' replaced what Washington for a century had called 'etiquette.'" The staid Mayflower Hotel became known as "The Ammunition Palace" because of the number of war-contractors who stayed there.

Strangers and money brought crime to the wartime boomtown. Washington became the "Murder Capital" of the nation in 1941, with 250 percent more murders, in proportion to population, than New York City and 40 percent more than Chicago. Those who committed felonies, *Newsweek* reported, had a 2-to-1 chance that they would not be arrested and a 15-to-1 chance they would not go to jail.

On the first grim, wartime Christmas Eve, President Roosevelt continued his custom of lighting the "nation's Christmas tree" set up near the White House. He was joined by a distinguished guest, British Prime Minister CHURCHILL. "I spend this anniversary and festival far from my country, far from my family, yet I cannot truthfully say that I feel far from home," Churchill told the crowd gathered at the tree and also a worldwide radio audience. "Here, in the midst of war, raging and roaring over all the lands and seas, creeping nearer to our hearts and homes, here, amid all the tumult, we have tonight the peace of the spirit."

Washington's appetite for ceremony was rarely gratified during the war. The somber inauguration of President Roosevelt for his fourth term in 1945 was the only inaugural ever conducted on the south portico of the White House rather than the Capitol. There was no parade, no inaugural ball. On Sunday Jan. 20, about 2,000 guests watched the President, haggard on the arm of his son James, a Marine colonel in uniform, again take the oath of office. The guests were served a luncheon of chicken salad (which, Mrs. Roosevelt said, had more celery than chicken), rolls without butter, coffee, and unfrosted cake. The guests included fifty wounded soldiers from Walter Reed Army Hospital in Washington and Forest Glen Army Hospital, which had previously been an exclusive Maryland school for girls.

On April 13, the President died in Warm Springs, Ga. His body was brought to Washington on a train that moved slowly through the day and night to Union Station.

David Brinkley, in *Washington Goes to War*, described Washington's saddest day of the war: "A slow funeral cortege—a horse-drawn caisson, a squadron of motorcycle policemen, armored troops, the marine band, the navy band, a battalion of midshipmen from Annapolis, a detachment of service women, a line of black limousines—moved through the streets of Washington between columns of soldiers at attention. Two dozen army fighters roared across the sky in tribute. An elderly black woman sat on the curb in front of the White House, rocked back and force, and cried out as the procession went past her through the gates. 'Oh, he's gone. He's gone forever. I loved him so. He's never coming back.'"

Washington Conferences

Three meetings between President ROOSEVELT and Prime Minister CHURCHILL. In their first wartime conference, the two leaders met quietly in Washington on Dec. 22, 1941 and forged bonds of enduring friendship. The second meeting began on June 18, 1942, after Churchill crossed the Atlantic in a Boeing Clipper flying boat, which landed on the Potomac River after a twenty-seven-hour flight.

At this conference, he and Roosevelt decided on the NORTH AFRICA INVASION of Nov. 1942. A third meeting that became formally known as the "Washington Conference" (code-named Trident) occurred on May 11, 1943, when Churchill arrived to discuss strategy with Roosevelt and U.S. and British military officials. On May 19 Churchill addressed Congress and on May 25 Roosevelt and Churchill held a joint press conference. The leaders agreed on an invasion of France in 1944 and a stepping up of the war against Japan.

WASP

Acronym for the U.S. Women's Airforce Service Pilots. About 1,200 WOMEN pilots served in active, noncombat duty with the Army Air Forces during the war.

JACQUELINE COCHRAN, a famous racing pilot, orginated the WASPs, as they were called. They were on civil service status but they were regarded as officers and wore a WASP version of the standard AAF silver wings. Their principal mission was the ferrying of aircraft from factories to continental bases. They also towed targets and ferried weapons and military personnel. Thirty-eight died in training or on missions.

The Women's Auxiliary Ferrying Squadron, formed separately in 1942, was merged into WASP.

Wasp (CV 7)

U.S. AIRCRAFT CARRIER that "stung" the AXIS several times. Commissioned in April 1940, the *Wasp*'s first operational assignment after training operations in the Caribbean was to take on a load of Army P-40 WARHAWK fighters and other aircraft and fly them off to test the feasibility of launching AAF planes from a carrier. After more training operations in the western Atlantic, she loaded thirty Army P-40C fighters and other aircraft that she launched into Iceland on Aug. 6, 1940.

She then operated on antisubmarine patrols in the North Atlantic. In April 1941, because of the British shortage of aircraft carriers, the *Wasp* was assigned to the British Home Fleet. She unloaded some of her planes ashore and took on forty-seven RAF SPITFIRE fighters. With a British TASK FORCE, she steamed south, past GIBRALTAR, and into the Mediterranean where, on April 20, she launched the "Spits" toward besieged MALTA. The Allied ships then sped westward, to escape attack from German bombers.

Because one-half of the Spitfires were destroyed by German planes shortly after their arrival, the *Wasp* was ordered to make another Malta run. This time, on May 9, she flew off forty-seven Spitfires. One lost its auxiliary fuel tank and returned to land aboard the *Wasp*, which was done successfully despite the pilot never having landed on a carrier and the Spit having no arresting hook. After this second run Prime Minister CHURCHILL signaled "Who said a wasp couldn't sting twice?"

Following this operation the *Wasp* sped back across the Atlantic and on to the South Pacific and in Aug. 1942 supported the U.S. Marine landing on GUADALCANAL. The *Wasp* was in almost constant combat until Sept. 15, 1942, when she was operating with a U.S. force transporting Marine reinforcements to Guadalcanal. That day Comdr. Takaichi Kinashi, commanding officer of the submarine *I-19*, fired the most effective TORPEDO salvo of the war: three torpedoes slammed into the side of the *Wasp*, one struck the BATTLESHIP *North Carolina* (BB 55), and one hit the DESTROYER *O'Brien* (DD 415). The *North Carolina*, the only modern Allied battleship available in the Pacific, was damaged, and the *O'Brien* later foundered.

The *Wasp* erupted in flame. She was abandoned and had to be sunk by a U.S. destroyer. Of 2,247 officers and enlisted men on board when she was torpedoed, 193 were killed and eighty-five were injured. Her career had been brief . . . but active.

The *Wasp* had been launched on April 4, 1939. She displaced 14,700 tons and was 739 feet long. Her steam turbines could drive her at 30 knots. During her Guadalcanal operations she carried seventy aircraft.

Wasserfall (Waterfall)

Antiaircraft ROCKET. This was an unmanned, vertically launched rocket developed by the Germans to intercept Allied bombers. The missile was to be guided by radio commands from the ground and the missile's 518-pound high-explosive warhead would be detonated when near a bomber; the warhead also had a PROXIMITY FUZE. If the missile missed its target it was to self-destruct.

Full-scale development of the *Wasserfall*, based on the aerodynamics of the V-2 MISSILE, was begun at the PEENEMÜNDE research center in Dec. 1942.

The first test flight ended in an explosion; the second, on Feb. 29, 1944, was successful. Up to fifty-one full-scale missiles had been test-fired when the project was abandoned on Feb. 6, 1945. The effort had been hindered by continued parts failures and the need to concentrate available resources on other air-defense projects. An initial production rate of 900 missiles per month at an underground factory was planned.

The *Wasserfall* launch weight was 7,716 pounds; combat ceiling was 58,071 feet.

Watchtower

U.S. code name for the landings on GUADALCANAL and adjacent Tulagi islands in the SOLOMONS, Aug. 8, 1942.

Wavell, Field Marshal Lord Percival (1883–1950)

British officer who began the war as Commander in Chief of British armies in the Middle East and ended it as viceroy of India. Working with limited resources at the end of a long supply line, Wavell was in frequent conflict with Prime Minister CHURCHILL, who wanted a quick success in the Middle East to offset Allied defeats in Europe. Wavell in Dec. 1940 launched his British Western Desert Force against an Italian force that had invaded Egypt. Although outnumbered three-to-one, Wavell's men drove the Italians back into Libya, wiping out ten Italian divisions and taking 130,000 PRISONERS OF WAR. The British then invaded Cyrenaica, the eastern province of Libya.

Wavell's desert victories were eclipsed by disastrous British defeats in Greece and CRETE in the spring of 1941 and his failures at TOBRUK, a key, Italian-developed Libyan port besieged by the Germans. Churchill relieved him of the Middle East command and sent him to India as Commander in Chief. After the Japanese attack on PEARL HARBOR on Dec. 7, 1941, he was made the Supreme Commander of Allied Forces in the Far East. In June 1943 he was made viceroy of India and in July was elevated to Viscount Wavell of Cyrenaica and Win-chester. He was replaced as viceroy by Adm. Lord LOUIS MOUNTBATTEN.

WAVES

The Women's Reserve of the U.S. Navy was established on July 30, 1942, the congressional act permitting Women Accepted for Volunteer Emergency Service (WAVES) to replace men for combat duty. The WAVES grew rapidly, and when the war ended in Aug. 1945 there were 86,000 WOMEN in naval service (not including the Navy Nurse Corps of 11,000 women).

By the end of the war there were WAVES on duty throughout the United States—with almost 20,000 in WASHINGTON—and 4,000 on duty in Hawaii. Capt. Jean T. Palmer commanded the WAVES until Feb. 1946.

The Navy had recruited "Yeomanettes" in World War I.

Weary-Willie,

see APHRODITE.

Webfoot

Code name for Allied rehearsal for Operation Shingle.

Wedemeyer, Lt. Gen. Albert C. (1897—1989)

Successor to Gen. JOSEPH W. STILWELL as commander of U.S. forces in China and Chief of Staff to Generalissimo CHIANG KAI-SHEK. Wedemeyer participated in the AMPHIBIOUS LANDING in SICILY, shifted in Oct. 1943 to the China-India-Burma theater as deputy chief of staff to Adm. Lord LOUIS MOUNTBATTEN, commander of the Southeast Asia Command.

A year later, as a major general, he replaced Stilwell, who had worn out his temper trying to work with Chiang Kai-shek, whom Stilwell despised. Wedemeyer, in contrast, developed a good working relationship with Chiang. He aided Chiang in planning for launching a counteroffensive against Japanese forces in China. The operation was getting under way when the war ended in Aug. 1945. By then Wedemeyer had the temporary rank of lieutenant general. He remained in China until Sept. 1946.

Weimar Republic

The German democracy that began in 1918 and ended when ADOLF HITLER came to power. Goethe's birthplace was the place where the German National Constituent Assembly created the postwar government of Germany, and so it became known as the Weimar Republic. Forged from revolution and war, the republic produced a democratic Germany. But the republic, beset by insoluble economic problems and the rise of Hitler's NATIONAL SOCIALIST GERMAN WORKERS' PARTY, died when he decreed the end of democracy and the beginning of a THIRD REICH that would last a thousand years. (See GERMANY.)

Welles, Sumner (1892–1961)

Wartime under secretary of State. A veteran diplomat, Welles was a specialist on Latin America when President ROOSEVELT, promoting a "Good Neighbor" policy, appointed him assistant secretary of State in 1933.

Roosevelt appointed Welles under secretary of State in 1937, with little enthusiasm from Secretary of State CORDELL HULL, who resented Welles' long working relationship with Roosevelt. Hull was also frustrated by the fact that his ill health forced more responsibilities on Welles, who often served as acting secretary of State.

Early in 1940 Roosevelt sent Welles to Europe to explore the possibility of a U.S.-negotiated end to the EUROPEAN WAR, which was in a quiescent stage called the "phony war."

Welles was at the President's side during his ATLANTIC CONFERENCE at sea off Newfoundland with Prime Minister CHURCHILL. Welles also helped to draw up the ATLANTIC CHARTER, which set the course of Allied war aims, and worked on U.S. plans for the UNITED NATIONS.

In the summer of 1943 Hull learned of reports about a homosexual incident involving Welles, who was married. Hull took the report to President Roosevelt and insisted that Welles be forced to resign. Welles resigned, effective Sept. 30, 1943.

Wellington

An outstanding twin-engine bomber, the Wellington carried the lion's share of the RAF bomber offensive against Germany until the arrival of large numbers of four-engine "heavies." Aviation historian William Green wrote, "Other bombers came forward as the war progressed, but none enjoyed a finer reputation."

Wellingtons flew the first British bombing raid of the EUROPEAN WAR, against the German naval base at Wilhelmshaven on Sept. 4, 1939. They were shifted to night operations after another raid on Wilhelmshaven on Dec. 18, 1939, when ten aircraft were lost and three heavily damaged in a raid of twenty-four—a loss rate of 41 percent. Seventeen Wellingtons participated in the first RAF Bomber Command attack on BERLIN on the night of Aug. 25–26, 1940. Thereafter they flew in combat over Europe (until Oct. 1943), in the Middle East and Far East, and against U-BOATS with RAF Coastal Command.

The historic THOUSAND-PLANE RAID on COLOGNE on the night of May 30–31, 1942, included 599 Wellingtons. A Wellington also dropped the first 4,000-pound "blockbuster" BOMB on a German target, in a strike on Emden, Belgium, on April 1, 1941. Wellingtons were also modified for use as training aircraft, GLIDER tugs, transports, flying ambulances, and aerial minesweepers, with a large number also assigned to experimental work.

Vickers-Armstrong built the prototype Wellington, which first flew on June 15, 1936. The aircraft was redesigned and the first production aircraft flew on Dec. 23, 1937. Multiple production lines were established, and six RAF squadrons flew the Wellington by Sept. 1939. The last of 11,461 Wellingtons was delivered in Oct. 1945. The Mk X was the principal variant, with 3,804 delivered from 1943.

The Wellington had a chunky appearance, with a structure based on a geodetic design developed by Barnes Wallis, inventor of the "bouncing" and "blockbuster" bombs. This design gave the Wellington a remarkable ability to sustain damage and still fly. It was a mid-wing monoplane with a tall tail fin and gun turrets in the nose and tail. Maritime patrol aircraft had surface-search RADAR fitted; minesweeping aircraft had a 48-foot-diameter loop fitted to the plane which, when energized, could explode magnetic MINES.

The Mk X had a top speed of 250 mph and a range of 1,885 miles while carrying a bomb load of 1,500 pounds. The maximum load was 6,000 pounds carried in an internal bomb bay. Defensive armament consisted of two .303-cal. machine guns in a powered nose turret and four .303-cal. guns in a powered tail turret. In the antisubmarine role ROCKETS were fitted to attack surfaced U-boats with DEPTH CHARGES in the bomb bay to strike after they submerged.

Werwolf (Werewolf)

Reputed GUERRILLA operation that was to operate in Germany after the fall of the THIRD REICH. The Werewolves were supposed to put up last-ditch resistance against Allied forces after the German Army was overcome, especially in the Bavarian mountains, possibly operating from a legendary NATIONAL REDOUBT. Gen. Walter Wenck, commander of the German 12th Army, which HITLER had expected to relieve BERLIN from the Soviet siege in April 1945, was to have commanded the Werewolf operation.

A loosely organized Werewolf organization, with an SS general in charge, did exist in the closing weeks of the war. Pamphlets distributed in the organization's name warned that Germans who did not support Werewolves would be killed. But the Werewolves existed more in fiction than fact, being primarily the fictional creation of PROPAGANDA minister JOSEPH GOEBBELS. The ALLIES encountered no organized resistance after the SURRENDER of the German government by Hitler's successor, *Grossadmiral* KARL DÖNITZ.

Werwolf was also the code name for the headquarters near Vinnitsa, in the Ukraine, used by Hitler in 1942.

Weserübüng (Weser Exercise)

Code name for German invasion of Norway, as W. *Nord* (north) and Denmark, W *Sud* (south), April 9, 1944.

West Loch Explosion

Massive detonation of explosives on U.S. Navy landing ships and LANDING CRAFT in the West Loch of PEARL HARBOR. On June 21, 1944, the *LST 353*, in the midst of a cluster of LANDING SHIPS, TANK that were loading munitions at the naval ammunition dept, burst into flame and exploded.

The detonation set off explosives on five other LSTs, some being ignited by red-hot fragments that struck gasoline drums on the decks of the other ships. Fires raged for twenty-four hours, with explosions being heard all over the island of Oahu and far out to sea. Heroic action by harbor tugs that pulled ammunition barges and other ships clear prevented even more disastrous explosions. Six LSTs and three LCTs were destroyed; 163 men were killed and 396 injured.

Navy investigations found no definite reason for the disaster, which was touched off by the detonation of one or more 4.2-inch (106-mm) MORTAR shells. However, after reviewing the investigation, Adm. ERNEST J. KING, the CinC U.S. FLEET, declared that the explosion was caused by the failure of shipboard personnel to comply with safety regulations.

The loss of the LSTs and LCTs did not affect the U.S. schedule for Pacific operations.

West Wall,

see SIEGFRIED LINE.

Whale

Code name for roadway used to form the piers for the Mulberry ARTIFICIAL HARBORS.

Whipcord

Code name for aborted British plan for an invasion of SICILY, Nov. 1941.

White

British code name for reinforcement of MALTA, Nov. 1940.

White Rose

A small organization of students who opposed HITLER. The leaders of the tragically short-lived resistance were Hans Scholl, who had been a medical orderly on the EASTERN FRONT, and his sister Sophie. They were both students at the University of Munich. Their philosophy professor Kurt Huber helped them spread the secret organization to other universities.

The password of the group, begun in 1942, was *Weisse Rose* (White Rose). Members included a young German soldier who had seen the mass murders by ACTION GROUPS operated by the SS in the Soviet Union. In Feb. 1943 Hans and Sophie dropped leaflets from a window of the main university building. "Germany's name will remain disgraced forever," the leaflets said, "unless German youth finally rises up immediately, takes revenge, and atones, smashes its torturers, and builds a new, spiritual Europe."

They were reported to the GESTAPO, arrested, tortured, and sentenced to death by the notorious People's Court. Sophie hobbled to her death on crutches; the Gestapo had broken one of her legs. In keeping with sentences for traitors, she was beheaded on Feb. 22, 1943. Her brother and Professor Huber were also executed. "Somebody, after all, had to make a start," she said before her death. As many as 100 others were arrested at the time; their fate is unknown.

Whitley

One of the first British bombers to fly over BERLIN and the first Allied aircraft to drop BOMBS on both Germany and Italy. The twin-engine Whitley was one of the principal aircraft of the RAF Bomber Command at the beginning of the EUROPEAN WAR. On the first night of the war (Sept. 3–4, 1939) ten Whitleys dropped 13 tons of leaflets (6,000,000 copies) on German cities. These Whitley "paper drops" were extended to Berlin on the night of Oct. 1–2, 1939. Subsequently, Whitleys dropped bombs on German targets, with fourteen joining with HAMPDENs and WELLINGTONs for the first RAF bombing raid on Berlin on the night of Aug. 25–26, 1940. The planes continued to strike targets in Germany and occupied Europe until they were withdrawn from combat at the end of April 1942.

The RAF Coastal Command flew the Whitley on antisubmarine patrol into mid-1942. The Whitley was the first Coastal Command aircraft fitted with surface-search RADAR, the first RAF "radar kill" of a U-BOAT occurring in Nov. 1941, the victim being the *U-206*. Whitleys were also employed for AIRBORNE operations, to deliver parachutists and as GLIDER tugs.

The prototype Whitley flew on March 17, 1936, and was developed by Armstrong Whitworth as the standard RAF heavy bomber. The Whitley entered RAF service in March 1937; the design underwent continued modifications during the war.

The Whitley was a twin-engine, low-wing aircraft with twin rudders set above a large horizontal tail surface. Maximum speed for the Mk I was 192 mph, with the Mk V capable of 222 mph; range of the latter aircraft was 1,650 miles with 3,000 pounds of bombs carried in an internal bomb bay; up to 7,000 pounds could be carried for shorter distances. The standard armament was four .303-cal. machine guns in a powered tail turret and a single machine gun in a nose turret. The crew numbered five.

Widewing

Code name for SUPREME HEADQUARTERS ALLIED EXPEDITIONARY FORCE (SHAEF) at Bushy Park near London.

Wiesengrund (Meadow Land)

German code name for planned occupation of the Rybatchi Peninsula, June 1942.

Wildcat,

see F4F.

Wilfred

Code name for British naval operations in Norwegian waters in support of mining and troop landings, April 1940.

Wilhelm

German code name for a series of planned operations northeast of Kharkov, 1942.

Wilhelm Gustloff

German liner sunk in the worst maritime disaster in history. The *Wilhelm Gustloff* was torpedoed by the Soviet submarine *S-13* off of Pillau (Baltisk), near Danzig, in the eastern Baltic Sea on the night of Jan. 30, 1945. The ship was evacuating Germans from the path of Soviet advances in the eastern Baltic. On board were GESTAPO troops and their families, technicians who had worked at advanced weapon bases along the Baltic, U-BOAT crewmen, 500 female German sailors, the ship's crew, and several thousand refugees—a total of more than 6,100 men, women, and children. Only 904 survived the sinking and the freezing waters of the Baltic.

On Feb. 10 the *S-13* scored again, sinking the liner *General Steuben* off Stolpe Banks in the eastern Baltic. Of some 3,000 wounded and other evacuees on board, only 300 persons survived when that ship sank.

The *S-13* was commanded by Capt. 3rd Rank M. J. Marinesko during these operations.

The *Gustloff*, launched in May 1937, was described by the German military journal *Signal* as being "fitted with every comfort and all the luxuries of the modern passenger steamer—theatre, bathing pool, and sports deck. The accommodation, consisting of outer cabins only, is sufficient for 1500 passengers." The ship was 25,484 gross tons.

Wilkinson, Vice Adm. Theodore S. (1888–1946)

Leading U.S. amphibious force commander in the Pacific. Graduating first in the class of 1909 at the Naval Academy, Wilkinson was awarded the MEDAL OF HONOR for his actions at Veracruz, Mexico, in 1914. He served in PARIS as assistant naval attaché and then in U.S. ships in European waters during World War I.

Before World War II he commanded several DESTROYERS and had duty on seagoing staffs and ashore. As director of naval intelligence from Oct. 1941 he became embroiled in some of the PEARL HARBOR controversies. In Aug. 1942 he became a BATTLESHIP division commander in the Pacific, but saw no action in those ships. After brief service as deputy to Vice Adm. WILLIAM F. HALSEY in the South Pacific, in July 1943 he took command of the Third Amphibious Force, subsequently directing AMPHIBIOUS LANDINGS in the U.S. SOLOMONS-NEW GUINEA CAMPAIGN and then U.S. CENTRAL PACIFIC CAMPAIGN. He was promoted to vice admiral in Aug. 1944 and the following January he flew to Pearl Harbor to begin planning for the invasion of Japan. (See Operation MAJESTIC.) Instead, he took command of the landing of U.S. occupation forces in Sept. 1945.

He then returned to WASHINGTON and in Jan. 1946 was appointed to the STRATEGIC BOMBING SURVEY, but a month later was killed in an automobile accident.

Willi

Code name for the German plan to kidnap the Duke of Windsor from Portugal, July 1940. The Germans hoped to use the Duke for PROPAGANDA purposes and even envisioned putting him on the throne after conquering England. He had abdicated as King Edward VIII in 1936 and was succeeded by his brother, who became King GEORGE VI.

Willkie, Wendell L. (1892–1944)

Presidential candidate. Willkie, Indiana-born and an Army veteran of World War I, combined Hoosier populism with the savvy of a New York–based utilities executive. He fought highly publicized legal battles against the Tennessee Valley Authority public power project and gained famed as a responsible advocate for privately run public utilities. During the 1940 Republican convention he won over isolationists, including Sen. Robert A. Taft of Ohio and THOMAS E. DEWEY of New York.

Willkie appealed to liberal Republicans who saw him as a president who would keep the best of the New Deal while improving the political climate for business and investors. Secretary of the Interior HAROLD L. ICKES called Willkie "a simple barefoot Wall Street lawyer."

President ROOSEVELT, running for an unprecedented third term, easily defeated Willkie, who nevertheless received more votes (22,333,801) than had any presidential candidate other than Roosevelt himself. In 1941–1942 he served as Roosevelt's special emissary and traveled to England, the Middle East, China, and the Soviet Union. His support of Roosevelt's war policies irritated Republican leaders, who did not back his bid for the 1944 presidential nomination.

Wilson, Field Marshal Henry Maitland (1881–1964)

British army commander and, briefly, Supreme Allied Commander in the Mediterranean area. At the beginning of the EUROPEAN WAR Lt. Gen. Wilson became commander of British troops in Egypt—commonly called the Army of the Nile. He directed the highly successful operations against Italian forces in North Africa until Feb. 1941. Wilson led the ill-fated British expeditionary force to Greece in Feb.–April 1941, and then returned to the Middle East as commander of British forces in Palestine and Transjordan. He was responsible for the Anglo-French invasion of Syria in June–July 1941. The following year he served as CinC of the Persia-Iraq Command.

Wilson became the British CinC Middle East in March 1943 and participated in the invasion of SICILY and operations in the Aegean area. In Jan. 1944 he was promoted to field marshal and succeeded Gen. DWIGHT D. EISENHOWER as Supreme Allied Commander in the Mediterranean. He left that post at the end of 1944 to succeed Field Marshal Sir John Dill as head of the British military mission in WASHINGTON and representative of the British CHIEFS OF STAFF to the COMBINED CHIEFS OF STAFF. In that role he was part of the British delegation to the YALTA CONFERENCE in Feb. 1945.

Wilson, whose nickname was "Jumbo," was described as "methodical and unspectacular" by his colleagues.

Winch

British code name for the reinforcement of MALTA, April 1941.

Window

Strips of metallized paper cut to wavelengths used by German RADAR sets. The technique was first used by RAF bombers to confuse German radars during attacks against HAMBURG, July 24 to Aug. 3, 1940. (See ELECTRONIC COUNTERMEASURES.)

Wing

U.S. Army Air Forces organizational structure that had limited use during the war. Before the war the wing had served as the key tactical and administrative organization of the ARMY AIR CORPS. However, during the war its utility was limited, with COMMANDS and GROUPS becoming the principal intermediate commands between AIR FORCES and SQUADRONS.

Within the AAF operational structure, wings ranked between commands and groups.

The wing was the highest aviation organization of the U.S. Marine Corps, with six wings being established by the end of the war (in theory each to support one of the six Marine ground DIVISIONS).

Wingate, Maj. Gen. Orde C. (1903–1944)

A colorful, Bible-quoting British advocate of irregular warfare. Wingate began his career as a commander of GUERRILLA forces when he led Jewish underground forces against Arab bands in British-controlled Palestine. In 1941 in the Sudan he aided Ethiopian guerrillas in their war against the Italians who had invaded their country in 1935.

Posted to India at the beginning of JAPAN'S CHINA-BURMA CAMPAIGN, he organized the CHINDITS, a mixed force of 3,000 GHURKAS, Burmese, and British, and launched raids behind Japanese lines in Burma early in 1943. The raids won him publicity and raised Allied morale but did little to change the military situation. The far-reaching effect was more important: Wingate showed that a force in almost impassable terrain could be supplied by air.

Wingate was a well-publicized hero when he accompanied Prime Minister CHURCHILL to the QUEBEC CONFERENCE, code-named Quadrant, on Aug. 10, 1943. Wingate—Churchill called him "a man of genius"—easily got authorization to go back to the China-Burma-India theater and create an airborne COMMANDO unit, augmented by U.S. air forces.

In March 1944, after launching his expanded force and winning promotion to major general, Wingate was killed in a plane crash.

Winkelried

German code name for the substitute for Operation *Schlingpflanze* (Vine) in the Soviet Union, Oct. 1942.

Wintergewitter (Winter Storm)

German code name for offensive to relieve the Sixth Army at STALINGRAD, Dec. 1942. Also see *DONNERSCHLAG.*

Wirbelwind (Whirlwind)

German code name for operation to pinch off part of the Red Army's Sukhinichi salient on the EASTERN FRONT, Aug. 1942.

Wizard War

British term for electronic developments to increase effectiveness of British forces and to counter German technology developments. (See ELECTRONIC COUNTERMEASURES.)

Wolf Pack

Coordinated attacks against CONVOYS by groups of submarines. The concept was developed by then-*Kommodore* KARL DÖNITZ, head of the German U-BOAT arm, during the winter of 1938–1939. Dönitz conducted an extensive war game to examine the possibility of group tactics in the Atlantic—command, organization, communications, locating convoys, and the massing of U-boats. The conclusions reached in the war game were incorporated into planning for Atlantic operations, when war began *and* when sufficient U-boats were available.

As soon as a chance sighting of a convoy occurred, by an aircraft or submarine—or, more likely, German *B-DIENST* radio intercepts—indicated the presence of a convoy, a scouting line of U-boats would be formed. The first submarine to sight the convoy would not attack, but would drop astern of the ships, maintain contact, and broadcast the location. Other U-boats would concentrate for the attack; depending upon the location and other factors, U-boat headquarters might set up a series of wolf packs to intercept the convoy. Usually the local coordinator would be the senior U-boat captain on the scene.

The wolf pack tactics were highly effective, in part because they concentrated U-boats against the most lucrative target (the convoy) and diffused the efforts of the convoy's escorts. The first wolf pack had been tried in mid-Oct. 1939 when four U-boats attacked a convoy sailing from GIBRALTAR to Britain. In rapid succession, three submarines sank three merchant ships and the convoy scattered. That should have made them more vulnerable to attack, as the few escort ships could not effectively protect them. But on that occasion there were no further convoy losses.

Wolf pack tactics were initiated on a large scale in the spring of 1941, at times involving twenty to thirty submarines. They were highly effective and a major factor in Germany almost winning the BATTLE OF THE ATLANTIC in early 1943.

In the Pacific, the U.S. Navy initiated wolf packs, modeled somewhat on the German tactic, in Sept. 1943. The first American wolf pack consisted of three fleet-type SUBMARINES with Capt. C. B. Momsen riding one of the submarines as pack commander. They did not coordinate their attacks, although two did team up to sink one transport, but exchanged information on contacts by radio. Their achievements were not spectacular—three Japanese ships sunk (23,607 tons) and seven other ships damaged.

Capt. Momsen subsequently recommended that the pack commander be ashore, where he could collect reports, send out information, and coordinate activities by radio. This was the German procedure. The U.S. Navy rejected it mainly because communications facilities were lacking and there was fear that the Japanese could locate submarines by their radio transmissions. U-boat transmissions were carefully controlled, and the risk found worthwhile.

A second three-submarine wolf pack departed in Nov. 1943 and more followed until May 1945. The largest was seven submarines, but two or three was the norm. The tactics added little to the individual effectiveness of U.S. submarines, in part because of American reluctance to inhibit the independent operations of submarines and in part because of the lack of effective Japanese convoy defenses.

Wolf's Lair (Wolfsschanze)

Code name for HITLER's headquarters in a forest near Rastenburg, East Prussia, where he directed Barbarossa, the invasion of the Soviet Union, and made several key decisions about the war. Here he met with Italian leader BENITO MUSSOLINI, learned of the disaster at STALINGRAD, and issued the orders for what would become the battle of the Bulge. His actions here reflected his moods. Jovial and gregarious when the war was going well, with defeats he isolated himself and ate alone, only his dog Blondi at his side.

What had been a field headquarters evolved into a miniature fortress of CAMOUFLAGED concrete bunkers. Hitler's inner lair, where he and his staff worked and lived, was surrounded by a mine field, a perimeter fence of electrified barbed wire, numerous checkpoints, and an inner barbed-wire

fence patrolled by SS troops. In 1944, conspirators planning the JULY 20 PLOT on his life chose this place because they knew how to penetrate its security. Their bomb probably would have been effective in one of the concrete bunkers, but its blast was dispersed in the wooden guest barracks that Hitler used for a conference of his military staff on July 20.

Women

The war effort enlisted American women in unprecedented numbers, both in the armed services (see WAVES, WAC, WAF, SPARs, and WOMEN MARINES) and in the war industry. The U.S. armed services took their lead from England, where women served in the Auxiliary Territorial Service (ATS, renamed the Women's Royal Army Corps in 1949), Women's Auxiliary Air Force (WAAF), and Women's Royal Naval Service (WRNS, nicknamed the "Wrens"). The Soviet Union, alone among the belligerents, allowed women to fight side by side with men in regular military service. (See UNION OF SOVIET SOCIALIST REPUBLICS, AIR FORCE.)

The migration of American women into war plants was ballyhooed by both government PROPAGANDISTS and the media. The mythical worker dubbed "Rosie the Riveter" became a wartime symbol in photographs and posters, a song ("Rosie is . . . working overtime on a riveting machine"), a Norman Rockwell *Saturday Evening Post* cover, a movie, and a *Life* magazine tribute to a real-life Rosie: "neither drudge nor slave but the heroine of a new order."

Anthropologist Margaret Mead estimated that about 3,000,000 women who went to work during the war did so to aid the war effort. Millions more worked because they had to bring in the family's primary paycheck. More than 1,000,000 fathers were drafted, leaving behind young mothers who juggled defense jobs and inadequate day-care facilities. (See CHILDREN.)

On the home front—a term revived from World War I—housewives added RATIONING to the skills needed to run a wartime home. They planted VICTORY GARDENS, ran salvage drives, worked as CIVIL DEFENSE volunteers, and took what the OFFICE OF PRICE ADMINISTRATION called the Home Front Pledge: "I pay no more than top legal prices. I

Men and women of a French medical unit join other troops coming ashore from the U.S. Navy's *LCI(L) 38* during the Aug. 1944 invasion of southern France. These medical personnel have standard U.S. "steel pot" helmets, American-style "webbing," uniforms, and mess gear. *(Imperial War Museum)*

accept no rationed goods without giving up ration stamps."

Women in war plants and shipyards complained of sexual harassment, but the complaints were usually treated lightly, as in signs that warned against wearing tight sweaters because they distracted male workers. One plant laid off a number of women because their sweaters were considered too provocative. In a shipyard studied by sociologist Katharine Archibald, she wrote that the result of such harassment "was to deny the possibility of the establishment of businesslike relationships between men and women on the job and to discredit women as effective workers."

The most dramatic effect of the war on U.S. women was in employment. In 1940 the percentage of women in the U.S. work force was 24.3 percent; by 1945, at the height of wartime employment, the percentage of women in the work force was 34.7 percent. In 1940, most women employed outside the home were in domestic, clerical, or sales jobs; the rest were in "women's jobs": telephone operators, nurses, teachers, social workers. Wartime employment took women for the first time onto production lines in aircraft plants, munitions factories, shipyards, and steel mills. Some unions, such as the boilermakers, tried to keep women out, but the needs of what was still called *man*power forced changes.

The war also introduced the new idea of equal pay for men and women. The National War Labor Board established the principle with a ruling that wage increases that brought women to equal status with men were not truly wage increases in the strict sense of wage control but a way to remove inequities based on sex.

On the basis of this ruling, Congress passed a federal equal pay law in 1946. By then, women had gone to work for good, for, despite the large-scale layoffs that followed the end of the war, the percentage of women in the labor work did not drop to its prewar low but reached 30 percent, a harbinger of the still higher percentages that would come in the future.

Women Marines

The U.S. Marine Corps activated the Women Marines program on Feb. 13, 1943; by the end of the year there were 13,201 distaff Marines, and when the war ended in Aug. 1945 there were 820 WOMEN officers and 17,640 enlisted women. They served throughout the United States and in Hawaii, mostly in administrative, supply, and training assignments, with many serving as photographers, mechanics, control tower operators, and drivers.

Ruth Cheney Streeter was selected to head the Marine program and was commissioned as a major. When she was released from active duty in Dec. 1945 she held the rank of colonel. It was planned to dismiss all female Marines by the end of the following year, but a decision was made to retain a small cadre.

The Marine Corps was the last of the U.S. armed services to have a women's reserve in World War II. There had been 305 Reservists (Female) or "Marinettes" in World War I. The Marines differed from the other armed services as their female branch did not have a "cute" nickname—they were simply Women Marines or Women Reservists (WR). However, according to H. L. Mencken, "Broad-Assed Marine" was the Navy's term for woman Marine. "During the war a naval officer of rank and fancy suggested that *leatherteat* be substituted, but this stroke of genius was frowned upon by the High Command," wrote Mencken in *The American Language*. But "BAM" did catch on.

Woods, Master Sgt. John

U.S. Army sergeant who executed JUSTICE on ten NAZI war criminals convicted at the Nurenburg WAR CRIME trials. Woods, who had previously hanged 347 men during his fifteen-year career as the Army's official hangman, executed the ten Nazi officials and military officers early on the morning of Oct. 16, 1946. (The eleventh sentenced to death, HERMANN GÖRING, had committed suicide the night before the executions.)

Workshop

Code word for early British plans to capture the Italian island of PANTELLERIA, 1940–1941.

Wright, Rear Adm. Jerauld (1898—)

Allied naval planner who participated in several secret missions for Gen. DWIGHT D. EISENHOWER. A 1918 graduate of the Naval Academy, Wright served in surface ships through most of his career. His shore duty included assignment as naval aide to President Herbert Hoover.

When the United States entered the war he was executive officer of the BATTLESHIP *Mississippi* (BB 41) on duty in the North Atlantic. In May 1942 he joined the staff of the CinC U.S. Fleet, Adm. ERNEST J. KING, as an amphibious planner and, with promotion to captain, the following month he joined Gen. Eisenhower's staff in England.

He participated in several clandestine operations, including going ashore in Algeria just before the NORTH AFRICA INVASION to assist Maj. Gen. MARK CLARK in his negotiations with VICHY FRENCH leaders. Wright then took nominal command of the British submarine *SERAPH* to bring French Gen. HENRI GIRAUD out of France to meet with Eisenhower. Wright continued on the staff of Eisenhower and his naval commander, Adm. Sir ANDREW B. CUNNINGHAM, until March 1943, when he became Chief of Staff to the U.S. naval commander for the landings in SICILY and at SALERNO.

Leaving the Mediterranean, in Dec. 1943 he took command of the CRUISER *Santa Fe* (CL 60) in the Pacific, participating in several amphibious operations as well as supporting carrier operations. In Oct. 1944 Wright was promoted to commodore and then rear admiral, taking command of Amphibious GROUP 5 for the OKINAWA landing.

Detached in Aug. 1945, Wright held a number of senior Navy assignments afloat and ashore. In April 1954, as a full admiral, he became CinC of the U.S. Atlantic Command and Atlantic FLEET, and was simultaneously named Supreme Allied Commander Atlantic (NATO). He held those positions until his retirement in May 1960. The following year Wright was recalled to active duty for special service with the Central Intelligence Agency, after which President JOHN F. KENNEDY named him U.S. Ambassador to the Republic of China (Taiwan).

X Report

A secret memorandum, written by Hans von Dohnanyi, an *ABWEHR* official and key player in a plot against HITLER. The X Report told of the activities in Oct. 1939 of Dr. Josef Müller, a prominent German Catholic who secretly tried to get Pope PIUS XII to try to negotiate an end to the EUROPEAN WAR, which had started a month before. The X Report circulated among high-ranking military officers believed to be against Hitler. But none of them was interested in pursuing the report.

Dohnanyi remained involved in anti-Hitler plots and was arrested in April 1943, following an unsuccessful attempt on Hitler's life. Released then but kept under suspicion, Dohnanyi was arrested again after the JULY 20 PLOT in 1944 and is believed to have been executed in April 1945.

X-craft

British MIDGET SUBMARINES. The design for the X-craft came from retired Comdr. Cromwell Varley, a former British submariner, who in the 1930s worked on concepts for midget submarines. The Royal Navy ordered the first such craft to Varley's design—the *X-3*—in 1940 and the craft was delivered in 1942. The 50-foot "midget" was a miniature submarine, with most of the same features of larger undersea craft, only smaller. Also, it had a small floodable chamber so that divers could be "locked out" to place explosives under an enemy ship or cut barrier nets.

A British X-craft midget submarine on the surface. Their gallant crews crippled the German battleship *Tirpitz* in Norwegian waters, and similar XE-craft crippled the Japanese heavy cruiser *Takao* at Singapore, in addition to inflicting other damage on the Axis. *(Royal Navy)*

The craft's armament consisted of two curved two-ton explosive charges carried against the hull; the charges contained the explosive amatol. When carrying two charges the craft weighed 39 tons. (Unlike full-size submarines, an X-craft could be easily lifted out of the water and hence was measured by weight as well as displacement; submerged, the *X-3* displaced 30 tons.)

In combat, a three- or four-man crew would pilot the craft beneath an anchored enemy warship, release the amatol charges under the hull, and slip away before the charges were detonated by a timer.

The initial reaction to the *X-3* by the Admiralty was favorable, and additional craft were ordered. In all, two prototypes were built, followed by five operational X-craft in 1942–1943. Twenty-five larger XE-craft (53-feet long, 34 tons submerged displacement) were completed in 1944–1945 for use in the Pacific, and six similar XT-craft for training were delivered in 1944.

The most famous X-craft operation of the war occurred in Sept. 1943 when six craft were towed by submarines to a position off the Norwegian coast to attack the German battleship *Tirpitz*, at anchor in a small fjord off of Alten Fjord. In Operation Source, three of the six X-craft managed to reach the *Tirpitz*.

The *X-6* and *X-7* each laid two charges of two tons of explosives under the battleship. The *Tirpitz* spotted the midgets, and captured two crewmen. When the charges detonated, they lifted the 52,700-ton battleship about five feet up, inflicted major damage on weapons and equipment, and ruptured her hull; about 5,000 tons of water flooded into her. The battleship was immobile for almost six months until repairs were completed.

In April 1944 the *X-24* penetrated Bergen harbor in Norway and, although intending to sink a German floating dry dock, destroyed a 7,500-ton merchant ship. The *X-24* returned to Bergen harbor on Sept. 10, 1944, and successfully sank the dock. When the NORMANDY INVASION came on June 6, 1944, a pair of X-craft were positioned offshore with special gear to serve as beacons for the assault force (the only contribution of Allied submarines to the Overlord landings).

The larger XE-craft arrived in the Far East in mid-1945. Late on July 30 the *XE-1* and *XE-3*

slipped into SINGAPORE harbor, having been towed to the area by larger submarines. A diver from the *XE-3* attached six limpet MINES to the hull of the Japanese heavy cruiser *Takao*. When the commander attempted to move the submarine away from the cruiser, it was found the XE-craft was stuck fast between the cruiser and the harbor floor. After an hour the midget broke free. The limpet mines had six-hour timers. (The commander and diver were awarded the VICTORIA CROSS for the operation; the two other crewmen received lesser decorations.)

The *XE-1* was unable to reach her cruiser target within the time allotted. This craft then dropped her limpet mines near the *Takao*. All of the mines exploded and the *Takao* sank. Both midgets were able to rendezvous with their larger brethren waiting offshore.

The small craft, manned by intrepid officers and ratings, were relatively fragile and highly susceptible to rough seas (and their crews to seasickness). But they were relatively successful for the investment in resources and crews. In all, seven X-craft were lost during the war: six to enemy action or to unknown causes while operating against the *Tirpitz*, and one was lost (with four crewmen) in a collision with her towing submarine during a storm.

XX Committee

A British intelligence group set up to coordinate information being sent to Germany by German agents under British control. The committee took its name from the "double cross"—*XX*—that involved turning German ESPIONAGE agents in England into agents working for the British. These doubled agents transmitted false information, controlled by the XX Committee, to, in a committee member's words, "influence and perhaps change the operational intentions of an enemy."

"MI5 had developed the necessary skills to run the doubled agents convincingly," wrote espionage authority Nigel West in *Thread of Deceit*, "but their continued performance required a steady flow of plausible high-calibre intelligence."

This was gleaned from real secrets by the committee. One of its most successful British-run agents was DUSKO POPOV.

Yak-1 *Krasavec* (Beauty)

Soviet fighter aircraft that established Alexander Yakovlev as a leading aircraft designer. The Yak-1 entered service late in 1941 as a standard fighter.

Initially designated I-26, the Yak-1 first flew in March 1939 and was judged an immediate success despite shortcomings in firepower, power, and reliability. Yakovlev was awarded the Order of Lenin, a Zis automobile, and a prize of 100,000 rubles for the design. The aircraft entered production during the summer of 1939. More than 8,700 of all Yak-1 variants were produced through mid-1943.

The Yak-1 was a streamlined, low-wing aircraft with a radiator air scoop under the fuselage for its in-line engine (giving it a superficial resemblance to the early P-51 MUSTANG). The aircraft had a wooden wing, a mixed steel-tube and wood fuselage, and a plywood covering with an outer fabric skin coated with thick layers of polish. The main undercarriage fully retracted into the wings. The later Yak-7B production model had an improved, all-round visibility cockpit and an upgraded engine, while the Yak-1U and Yak-7U were two-seat combat conversion trainers.

Maximum speed of the Yak-1 was 364 mph. The standard armament was one 20-mm cannon and two 7.62-mm machine guns; six air-to-ground ROCKETS could be carried. The Yak-9T TANK-busting aircraft had a single 37-mm cannon.

Yak-3

One of the most agile aircraft of the war. Developed by Yakovlev in parallel with the Yak-9, this aircraft was derived from the experimental light-

---

The largest battleships ever built were the Japanese *Yamato,* shown here on sea trials in the fall of 1941, and her sister ship *Musashi.* The only ships they ever fired on in anger were escort carriers and destroyers; both of the superdreadnoughts were sunk by U.S. carrier aircraft. *(Japanese Navy via U.S. Navy)*

weight Yak-1M and was intended specifically for low-level combat and close air support. It was introduced into service in Aug. 1943. The Yak-3 was also employed as fighter escort for Soviet light bombers, sometimes with one fighter section escorting the bombers and another strafing German airfields moments before the arrival of the Soviet attack aircraft.

The Yak-3 first flew late in 1942, and 4,848 are reported to have been produced through May 1945.

The Yak-3 resembled the low-wing Yak-1, with a smaller in-line engine and an increased-visibility cockpit. The aircraft was fabricated of wood and metal with a plywood covering and an outer fabric skin that was highly polished; the landing gear completely retracted (including the tail wheel). Aviation writer William Green observed that pilots who flew both the Yak-3 and early versions of the RAF SPITFIRE claimed that the Soviet fighter was lighter on the ailerons, smoother to fly, and possessed superior speed and initial climb.

The aircraft had a top speed of 403 mph with a range of 500 miles. Armament consisted of one 20-mm cannon and two 12.7-mm machine guns.

Yak-9

One of the most important Soviet fighters of the war, the Yak-9 was produced in vast numbers. The plane made its combat debut at the battle of STALINGRAD in Nov. 1942. Yak-9 fighters served not only with the Red Air Force, but were flown by the French Normandie Squadron, which operated out of Soviet bases, and with Polish units. (See FRANCE, AIR FORCE.)

The Yak-9 was a refinement of A. S. Yakovlev's Yak-7B, entering production in mid-1942. There were several variants, including the Yak-9D, intended for the long-range bomber escort role, and the Yak-9T, which had a 75-mm or 37-mm cannon for use against TANKS. Production through Aug. 1945 totaled a remarkable 16,769 aircraft.

A low-wing aircraft with an in-line engine, the Yak-9 has been characterized as having excellent maneuverability.

The Yak-9T had a maximum speed of 363 mph and a range of 515 miles (the Yak-9D had reduced armament and fuel for 880 miles). Armament consisted of a heavy cannon (see above) and one 12.7-

mm machine gun. Six 82-mm ROCKETS could be fitted, although they were seldom carried. The Yak-9 was a single-seat fighter.

After the war Yak-9s served in Soviet and Eastern Bloc fighter squadrons and were flown by North Korea in the Korean War.

Yalta Conference

Meeting of President ROOSEVELT and Prime Minister CHURCHILL, Feb. 4–11, 1945, with Soviet leader JOSEF STALIN to plan the postwar world. The conference, code-named Argonaut, would not only set the rules for occupation of Germany but would also be the prelude for the Cold War. Just as the prewar MUNICH PACT entered history as a symbol for appeasement, the Yalta Conference in postwar years would symbolize Soviet communism's grasp for European power. Churchill would later say of Yalta, "Our hopeful assumptions were soon to be falsified. Still, they were the only ones possible at the time." At the time, Soviet forces occupied most of Eastern Europe and were showing no signs of leaving.

Although newspapers would headline the conference as a meeting of the BIG THREE, the political reality was Big Two against Big One. Even the site of the conference, a remote Black Sea resort, signaled Stalin's inflexibility; he claimed that his physicians barred him from traveling. Both Churchill and Roosevelt, just inaugurated to his unprecedented fourth term as President, knew they needed a united policy before they met with Stalin. Advisers had mapped their leaders' policies on Europe and the UNITED NATIONS at a Jan. 30–Feb. 2 meeting in MALTA.

On Feb. 11, the Big Three, in a Declaration on Liberated Europe, affirmed the democratic principles of the ATLANTIC CHARTER and United Nations, declaring that membership in the UN would be open only to those governments that had declared war on the AXIS powers. This touched off a flurry of eleventh-hour declarations, particularly by some Latin American nations that had merely professed support to the ALLIES.

The Big Three promised to help "the people in any European liberated state or former Axis satellite state in Europe" in the creation of interim governments "broadly representative of all democratic elements" and pledged to free elections. (In reality, Poland, Czechoslovakia, Hungary, Rumania, and Bulgaria would become the Soviet satellite states of Eastern Europe; free elections would not happen until the peaceful overthrow of Communist governments during the turbulent months of 1989.)

The declaration was specific about Poland: The interim government would be a coalition formed of the non-Communist Polish government-in-exile *and* "democratic leaders from within Poland"—actually a Soviet-created government already in place. The German-Polish border was pushed westward to the Oder-Neisse rivers.

Not in the public declaration were decisions about Germany, then on the verge of defeat. The Big Three agreed that after Germany's UNCONDITIONAL SURRENDER, it would be divided into three occupation zones under "co-ordinated administration" of the Big Three; France could get a fourth zone, which was carved out of the U.S. zone. German reparations, demanded by Stalin, were to be worked out later.

In another secret agreement, Stalin reaffirmed his promise to enter the war against Japan after the defeat of Germany. For this he extracted concessions: return of Russian territory lost to Japan after the Russo-Japanese War of 1904–1905, including what had been the Chinese territory of Port Arthur; and joint Soviet-Chinese administration of the Manchurian railroads. (China and her U.S. supporters would later denounce these decisions made without Chinese participation or assent.)

Secret negotiations also established procedural agreements for the founding of the United Nations and the setting up of the SAN FRANCISCO CONFERENCE on the United Nations.

Yamamoto, Adm. Isoroku (1884–1943)

The Commander in Chief of the Japanese Combined Fleet at the start of the war and key architect of Japan's early successes of the conflict. Yamamoto was a veteran of the Battle of Tsushima in 1905, in which a Japanese battle fleet had wrecked Russian sea power in the Far East, the first such success for a non-European navy.

Of all Japanese military leaders, he was perhaps the most aware of the quality and sheer industrial capacity of the enemy he would face if Japan went

Adm. Isoroku Yamamoto, Commander in Chief of the Japanese Combined Fleet until his death in April 1943. He conceived the attack on Pearl Harbor as a means of giving Japan the time necessary to capture and consolidate the resource-rich areas of the Far East.

to war with the United States. He had formed part of the advisory team that accompanied Navy Minister Tomasaburo Kato to the 1921–1922 WASHINGTON Naval Conference. He had also studied English at Harvard University and later served as Japanese naval attaché in Washington. As a result of his firsthand exposure to the U.S. potential for war, Yamamoto remained a part of the "Treaty Faction" throughout the 1920s and 1930s, believing that Japan could never match the United States in RESOURCES and that it was perilous to underestimate the U.S. willingness to do battle, as many of his peers were prepared to do.

Nevertheless, Yamamoto prepared his Navy well. From 1924, when he took command of the Kasumigaura naval air facility—the Navy's flight school—he pushed the development of Japanese naval aviation. He compared battleships to the ancestral scrolls that upheld a family's prestige, but did little to contribute to current prosperity.

Yamamoto commanded the First Carrier Division in the early 1930s, honing and refining it as the Navy's principal shock weapon, and was the director of the aeronautical branch of the Navy Ministry. He later became vice minister of the Navy, continuing his resistance to the TOTAL WAR school of Japanese militarism. Prime Minister Mitsumasa Yonai appointed him Commander in Chief of the Combined Fleet in Aug. 1939, in part to spare Yamamoto from political ASSASSINATION by getting him out of the fleet.

Yamamoto believed that if "hostilities break out between Japan and the United States, it would not be enough that we take GUAM and the Philippines, nor even Hawaii and San Francisco. To make victory certain, we would have to march into Washington and dictate the terms of peace in the White House." He recognized that as unlikely and believed that any strategy that waited for the Americans to come to him—as had been the Japanese grand strategy—played into U.S. strengths.

Instead, Yamamoto, a well-known gambler, heeded his instinct for high-stakes moves and planned a preemptive attack on the U.S. Pacific Fleet. He studied the successful Nov. 1940 attack on the Italian fleet at TARANTO by a single deckload of British aircraft. Planning the PEARL HARBOR attack, organizing the First Air Fleet, and training for the attack consumed most of 1941 while the United States and Japan moved toward war. When the fleet sailed under Vice Adm. CHUICHI NAGUMO on Nov. 21, Yamamoto awaited results in his flagship in Japanese waters. The attack wrought devastation on the U.S. FLEET, and naval and Army aircraft. Despite the initial success of the JAPANESE CAMPAIGN IN THE CENTRAL PACIFIC, Yamamoto remained uneasy about the failure to sink or damage any U.S. AIRCRAFT CARRIERS and sought a conclusive battle that would further retard the U.S. ability to recover from Pearl Harbor.

When the DOOLITTLE RAID's sixteen B-25 bombers took off from the carrier *HORNET* (CV 8) and bombed Japan in April 1942, Yamamoto became convinced that he had a way to extend Japan's defensive perimeter: take MIDWAY by surprise. He believed that this move offered the best chance to bring the remaining U.S. fleet within range of Japanese aircraft and battleships. His plan was elaborate and included diversionary raids and landings in the ALEUTIAN ISLANDS, the invasion of Midway, and a conclusive naval battle against the U.S. fleet coming to rescue the island. The entire plan depended on Japanese ability to strike by surprise and thus dictate U.S. response.

The outcome was far different from what had been expected. Yamamoto recognized the implications of this defeat. But he still looked for an opportunity to draw the U.S. fleet into battle even as he supported Army operations in the SOLOMONS. That support was exemplified by a series of naval battles near GUADALCANAL that inflicted heavy damage on both fleets, the U.S. Navy generally suffering the heavier losses.

But by Jan. 1943 Yamamoto saw no other option but to withdraw the remaining troops from Guadalcanal. He sought to shore up Japanese defenses farther up the Solomons chain by staging a series of air raids on Allied forces. In the aftermath of these raids, which Yamamoto mistakenly believed to have been successful, he began a tour of forward bases. U.S. intelligence decoded a report of his itinerary. Adm. CHESTER W. NIMITZ, Commander in Chief of the Pacific Fleet, approved an attempt to intercept Yamamoto and shoot him down. This was accomplished on April 18, 1943, by eighteen AAF P-38 LIGHTNING fighters. He was killed when his aircraft crashed into the jungle.

Yamamoto was the most imaginative and skillful Japanese admiral to go to war against the United States. Yet his campaigns had all the merits and faults of a gambler's strategy, especially when their actual execution was left to more cautious men.

Yamashita, Gen. Tomoyuki (1885–1946)

Called the "Tiger of MALAYA," Japanese Gen. Tomoyuki Yamashita was tried after the war in what were hasty, vengeful, and clearly unjust proceedings and was convicted of WAR CRIMES. After appeals failed he was hanged.

Yamashita served on the General Staff in 1916 and then went to the War Ministry in 1919, where he spent the next eighteen years with only brief intermissions. He appears to have supported many of the domestic political aims of the Army intriguers, going so far as to have given tacit support to the attempted coup of Feb. 1936, but also acting as intermediary between the plotters and the imperial government when the coup failed. Yamashita was exiled to a command in North China and later became Chief of Staff of the Northern China Army.

He was less enthusiastic about overseas adventures. Although he agreed in Japan's right to have secure sources for raw materials in other countries, he was doubtful that his country could win and hold such territories against British and American counterstrokes. Yamashita's six-month visit to Germany and Italy in 1941 led him to conclude that Japan could not fight or win a modern war unless it immediately began a substantial modernization program that would require several years. He realized that merely invoking the feudal military code called Bushido—putting honor above life, as the leadership was now promoting—would only kill thousands of soldiers uselessly. Yamashita's report was widely read among Army officers, so arousing Premier HIDEKI TOJO's anger that he again exiled Yamashita to a command in the Kwantung Army in southeast China.

He was recalled from exile in Nov. 1941 to head the invasion of Malaya and the capture of SINGAPORE. Yamashita's forces consisted of three divisions, which consistently outmaneuvered a larger, ill-trained, and very poorly led British-Australian-Indian-Malay force and forced its retreat. Yamashita, recognizing that his 30,000-man force could not win a street-to-street battle with British Gen. Arthur Percival's 100,000 men, demanded an immediate surrender. Percival, bluffed to the last, capitulated on Feb. 15, 1942, capping a brilliantly led campaign for Yamashita. He promised good treatment for soldiers and civilians, but either was not aware or was unable to prevent atrocities by some of his soldiers and by the secret police (KEMPEITAI), who arrived later.

Although lionized in the Japanese press, Yamashita found that Emperor HIROHITO had not forgotten his support of the coup attempt and a jealous Tojo had no interest in rewarding him with new combat commands. In July 1942 Yamashita became 1st area commander in Manchukuo and remained there for more than two years while Japan suffered continuous defeats.

Finally, after the fall of SAIPAN in July 1944 triggered Tojo's fall as premier, the new government conducted a housecleaning. Yamashita was brought out of exile in Sept. 1944 to command the Japanese Fourteenth Army of about 350,000 men on Luzon in the Philippines. Yamashita faced several problems. His predecessor had fatally poisoned relations with the Philippine people and they conducted a GUERRILLA war against Japanese forces. The supply lines from Japan and other Japanese possessions was increasingly tenuous, thanks to U.S. air and SUBMARINE attacks. He was balked in his efforts to provide an effective delaying defense by Field Marshal Count Hisaichi Terauchi, who refused to concede U.S. occupation of Leyte Island. Yamashita did not gain control of air force troops until Jan. 1945, too late to help and after they had committed several atrocious acts against PRISONERS OF WAR.

Yamashita had decided early on that MANILA could not and should not be defended. In early February he ordered a rapid and orderly withdrawal, expressly forbidding unnecessary destruction. His plan was to stage a fighting retreat into Luzon's hills and hold out in the mountain fastness for as long as possible. Unfortunately for the Manilans—and, ultimately, Yamashita—15,000 sailors and marines and 4,000 soldiers under Vice Adm. Sanji Iwabuchi failed to escape U.S. encirclement and turned to slaughter instead. Most of the Japanese, including Iwabuchi, were killed as were about 100,000 Filipino civilians.

The month-long battle for Manila ground much of the city to rubble. Yamashita claimed to have known nothing about the senseless destruction until later. It was certainly beyond his ability to control and directly contrary to his orders. His own troops were gradually worn down by continuing U.S. pressure until he surrendered on Aug. 15 with 50,000 of his men.

On orders of Gen. DOUGLAS MACARTHUR, Yamashita was tried for war crimes in Manila. Found guilty, and with appeals rejected, he was hanged on Feb. 23, 1946.

Yamato

One of the two largest battleships ever built. The Japanese super-dreadnought *Yamato* and her sister ship *Musashi* were armed with nine 18.1-inch (460-mm) guns, the largest ever mounted in a warship. The *Yamato* was completed in Dec. 1941 and became the flagship of Adm. ISOROKU YAMAMOTO in Feb. 1942. She participated in the MIDWAY operation in June 1942, but did not see action, since the loss of four Japanese aircraft carriers in one day aborted the operation.

Following that battle, the Japanese Navy decided to complete the third ship of the class, the *Shinano,* as an aircraft carrier. (A fourth, unfinished ship was broken up on the building ways.) The second ship, the *Musashi,* became operational in Aug. 1942 and early the following year became the flagship for Admiral Yamamoto.

Both battleships were prepared for operations against the advancing U.S. forces, but were not committed because of the need to build up a carrier force to operate with them. The *Yamato* had her baptism of fire late in 1943 off TRUK when a U.S. SUBMARINE scored a single TORPEDO hit on her. She arrived safely in Japan for repairs. Both ships participated in the massive carrier battle of June 1944 off the MARIANAS but saw little action. The loss of several carriers sent the Japanese fleet into retreat.

The *Yamato* and *Musashi* sought to attack U.S. transports off Samar in the Philippines in late Oct. 1944, but U.S. carrier planes struck the Japanese force. The *Musashi* was hit by seventeen BOMBS and twenty aerial TORPEDOES, finally sinking on the night of Oct. 24. Of her crew of 2,399, a reported 1,023 were lost. The *Yamato* and other surface ships broke through to the Samar Gulf and engaged U.S. ESCORT CARRIERS and their screening ships. The *Yamato* fired 104 rounds of 18.1-inch ammunition, contributing to sinking one of the "jeep" carriers and three of their escorting ships. Finally, the Japanese retired.

Returning to Japanese home waters, the *Yamato* next went to sea on April 6, 1945, to attack the U.S. naval forces off OKINAWA. Accompanied by a light cruiser and eight destroyers, the *Yamato* was en route to make a KAMIKAZE attack but before she could reach the U.S. ships, American carrier planes struck. The *Yamato* was hit by at least five bombs and ten torpedoes before she sank on the afternoon of April 7. She went down with all but 269 of her crew of 2,767 men.

The *Yamato* was launched on Aug. 8, 1940, and the *Musashi* on Nov. 1, 1940. The ships had a standard displacement of some 62,315 tons and at full load were 69,990 tons. With an overall length of 862¾ feet, they had steam turbines that could provide a maximum speed of 27 knots. In addition to their nine 18.1-inch guns, the ships carried a secondary battery of twelve 6.1-inch (155-mm) and twelve 5-inch (127-mm) guns plus numerous anti-aircraft guns and ROCKETS.

The third ship of the class, the carrier *Shinano,* was launched on Oct. 8, 1944, but was sunk before becoming operational; she was torpedoed and sunk by the U.S. submarine *Archerfish* (SS 311) in the Inland Sea on Dec. 29, 1944. She was the largest ship ever to be sunk by submarine torpedoes.

Yank Magazine

Like *STARS AND STRIPES, Yank* was a publication for enlisted men and WOMEN, not officers. It was founded in April 1942 by Col. Hyman Munson of the U.S. Army's Special Service Division.

Yank specialized in gripping documentary photography, and was well-printed in one of a dozen plants throughout the world. The reporters and photographers were enlisted men. They wrote and photographed with a soldier's eye for detail.

Yank ended when the war ended. One of the stories in its last year was one by twenty-one-year-old Cpl. Bob Krell, who wrote on March 23, 1945, shortly before jumping with an AIRBORNE unit in Germany: "Tomorrow there will be an early breakfast—0400, the order said. Then we will climb into our parachutes as dawn breaks. . . ."

Twelve hours after writing those words he was dead, killed as a paratrooper near the Rhine.

Yoke

Code name for U.S. organizations in the China-Burma-India theater.

Yugoslavia

Capital: Belgrade, pop. 15,630,000 (est. 1939). Formed of the former Austro-Hungarian kingdoms of the Serbs, Croats, and Slovenes, Yugoslavia was a creation of post–World War I nation-making. At the beginning of the war, Yugoslavia announced a policy of neutrality but, after the fall of France, succumbed to German pressure and on Dec. 11, 1940, signed a treaty of "everlasting friendship" with Germany. On March 25, 1941, Yugoslavia joined the AXIS, signing the TRIPARTITE PACT.

While Serb army officers were organizing opposition to an alliance with Germany, seventeen-year-old King Peter II turned down German demands for collaboration. On April 6, 1941, Germany, moving through Hungary and Bulgaria, invaded an ill-prepared Yugoslavia. Although Belgrade was declared an OPEN CITY, the Luftwaffe repeatedly bombed the city, killing about 17,000 people.

German forces focused on Croatian areas, where Croat army units refused to fight; German PROPAGANDA had promised an independent state, which was later proclaimed. (Some Croatian soldiers later fought side-by-side with Germans against the Soviet Union. Discovery of a mass grave containing as many as 40,000 bodies was reported in 1990. The grave, 45 miles from the Croatian capital of Zagreb, was believed to contain the remains of soldiers and others who collaborated with the NAZIS and were executed by Croatians or Soviets.)

The Yugoslav army, overwhelmed by German land and air power, fell back on all fronts. While many soldiers hid their arms for a potential uprising, Yugoslavia surrendered on April 17. King Peter and his Cabinet fled to LONDON and set up an exile government. Germany handed over large segments of Yugoslavia to Hungary, Bulgaria, and Italy. Serbs and JEWS were massacred. GUERRILLA forces immediately sprang up under Gen. DRAŽA MIHAJLOVIĆ, a Serbian royalist leader, who was recognized by the Yugoslav government-in-exile in London.

"The people just do not recognize authority," a German official complained to Berlin, reporting that the Yugoslavs "follow the Communist bandits blindly." This was a reference to the guerrillas, called partisans, rallying around Josef Brozovich, called TITO. His followers and the Chetniks of Mihajlović fought side by side in a Serbian uprising in 1941, but Tito denounced his rival as pro-German, soon rose as the principal resistance leader, and won British support that augmented aid from his Soviet backers.

British efforts were managed by their SPECIAL OPERATIONS EXECUTIVE, which dropped officers into partisan strongholds by parachute. "I wish I could come myself," British Prime Minister CHURCHILL, an early admirer of Tito, once radioed him, "but I am too old and heavy to jump out on a parachute." Churchill's son, Randolph, a major in the COMMANDOS, did parachute in and served at Tito's headquarters.

Although the ALLIES officially supported the royal government-in-exile, most British supplies and arms going to Yugoslavia were secretly given to Tito, who was openly backed by the Soviet Union. On Dec. 4, 1943, Tito, whose forces held large tracts of territory, declared a provisional government in opposition to the government-in-exile. While political maneuvering gave Tito growing power over royalist supporters in exile, Soviet forces helped his cause even more as they advanced southward in 1944 against weakening German opposition. Tito partisans and Soviet troops joined in the liberation of Belgrade on Oct. 20, 1944. Bulgarian army units began going over to the Tito side, and by the end of 1944 nearly all of Yugoslavia was free.

Tito established an ostensibly coalition cabinet in March 1945, but the following month, when he signed a twenty-year treaty with the Soviet Union, he put his nation firmly in the Communist bloc. In Dec. 1945 the British and U.S. governments recognized Tito's government, but diplomatic wrangling went on over Tito's occupation of TRIESTE.

Z

Z.506B *Airone* (Heron)

Italian floatplane TORPEDO bomber and reconnaissance aircraft. The Cant Z.506 was developed as a commercial transport, with the first military variant being delivered in 1937. The Z.506B was flown on combat missions in the Mediterranean (as well as bombing raids against targets in France) until Italy's capitulation in Sept. 1943, although it was highly vulnerable to Allied fighter attack. Subsequently, they flew for the ALLIES and, after the war the few survivors continued in Italian service. Poland had ordered thirty of these aircraft in 1938 but only one was delivered before the start of the EUROPEAN WAR.

The Cantieri-built, three-engine aircraft had large floats that belied the aircraft's large size. Maximum speed was 217 mph with a range of 1,430 miles. It could carry up to 2,205 pounds of BOMBS or an aerial torpedo in an internal bay. Several machine guns attempted to provide defensive firepower.

Z.1007 *Alcione* (Kingfisher)

Italian medium bomber, second only to the S.M.79 *SPARVIERO* in importance during the war. The aircraft entered service in 1940 but was severely limited by its limited defensive armament, resulting in few successes against Allied forces while fighting on the EASTERN FRONT, in the Mediterranean, and North Africa areas.

The three-engine land plane first flew in late 1937. The Cantieri aircraft was produced in both single and twin tail-fin configurations. The enlarged Z.1007*bis* could internally carry up to 4,410 pounds of BOMBS or two aerial TORPEDOES (a 2,600-pound bomb load was normal). Defensive armament consisted of two 12.7-mm and two 7.7-mm machine guns.

The Japanese A6M Zero fighter was a superior aircraft in terms of speed, maneuverability, and range. Its light construction and limited firepower, however, made it vulnerable to American fighters. (*Courtesy* Aireview)

Z Plan

Plan for reconstruction of the German Navy. Developed and approved by the German Navy in late 1938 for a fleet to be at sea in ten years; it was presented to HITLER in mid-Jan. 1939 by *Grossadmiral* ERICH RAEDER, CinC of the German Navy. This plan marked a shift from a fleet to participate in a planned war against France, Poland, and the Soviet Union, to one in which Britain would also be an enemy. The principal purpose of the planned fleet was to attack British convoys. The Z Plan was to provide a German fleet of some 300 units.

Hitler approved the plan, but declared that it had to be completed within six years (i.e., 1945).

The letter *Z* indicated *Ziel* or "target."

The ships to be built under the plan as amended in early 1939 were:

NO.*	TYPE	STANDARD DISPLACEMENT	NOTES	
6	large battleships	54,000 tons	8 16-inch guns	(1944)
2	aircraft carriers	20,000+ tons	approx. 40 aircraft	(1941)
2	aircraft carriers	20,000+ tons	approx. 40 aircraft	(1947)
4	heavy cruisers	10,000 tons	8 8-inch guns	(1943)
4	heavy cruisers	10,000 tons	8 8-inch guns	(1945)
4	light cruisers			(1944)
13	light cruisers			(1948)
30+	destroyers			
126	U-boats			(1943)
95	U-boats			(1947)

*completed

These were in addition to the following ships in service or under construction that would be completed by 1941:

NO.	TYPE	STANDARD DISPLACEMENT	NOTES
2	battleships	40,000+ tons	15-inch guns
2	battleships	20,000+ tons	11-inch guns
3	POCKET BATTLESHIPS		11-inch guns
2	heavy cruisers		8-inch guns
6	light cruisers		5.9-inch guns
34	destroyers and large TORPEDO boats		
56	submarines (of which only 26 were to be suitable for operation in the Atlantic)		

Z-Day

U.S. code name for AMPHIBIOUS LANDING at Arawe, New Britain, Dec. 15, 1942; the term was used to avoid confusion with the main landing at nearby Cape Gloucester, designated D-Day.

Zacharias, Capt. Ellis M. (1890–1961)

U.S. Navy intelligence officer. A 1912 graduate of the Naval Academy, he served in Japan from 1920 to 1924 to study Japanese language and politics. He subsequently served in a variety of assignments. Zacharias claimed that he had warned Adm. HUSBAND KIMMEL of the coming attack on PEARL HARBOR, but Kimmel later testified that he had no recollection of the conversation.

Early in the war Zacharias commanded the CRUISER *Salt Lake City* (CA 25) in Pacific actions. He served as deputy head of naval intelligence in 1942–1943, then returned to sea in command of the BATTLESHIP *New Mexico* (BB 40), again seeing combat in the Pacific. Late in the war he broadcast messages to the Japanese urging their surrender.

Zacharias retired in 1946 and was promoted to rear admiral on the Retired List. His autobiographical *Secret Missions* was published late that year. He lectured and wrote on international and defense issues. His book *Behind Closed Doors,* a history of the Cold War published in 1950, predicted that World War III between the United States and the Soviet Union would be "likely to materialize some time between the summer of 1952 and the fall of 1956."

Zebra

(1) Code name for U.S.-sponsored Chinese division in eastern China; (2) code name for U.S. AAF mass drop of supplies to the French Marquis by 176 B-17 FLYING FORTRESS bombers dropping 2,077 parachute containers, June 25, 1944; part of Operation Carpetbagger.

Zeke,

see ZERO.

Zeppelin

Code word for part of Jael, the overall Allied deception plan. Zeppelin was designed to convince the Germans that the ALLIES were going to invade Greece and southern France rather than SICILY and Italy. One part of the plan—code-named Mincemeat—involved the use of a deceptive corpse, known as "Major Martin."

Zero

The outstanding Japanese fighter of the war. The A6M Zero demonstrated for the first time that an aircraft could be fully capable of carrier operations (including having folding wing sections) and still have superiority over land-based contemporaries.

Zero designer Jiro Horikoshi wrote that the Japanese Navy's requirements for the plane "seemed impossible to meet. If this airplane could be built, it certainly would be superior to the rest of the world's fighters." Horikoshi's design team met the requirements and for the first two years of the war in the Pacific the Zero was the best fighter in the theater. Not until the appearance of the U.S. Navy's F6F HELLCAT in 1943 did the ALLIES have a fighter that could better the Zero under almost all combat conditions.

The aircraft was formally adopted by the Japanese Navy for carrier service in Aug. 1940 and made its combat debut over China on Sept. 13, 1940, easily shooting down its Chinese opponents, the Soviet-built I-15 and I-16 fighters and a variety of Western aircraft. During a year of combat over China, Zeros destroyed ninety-nine Chinese aircraft for the loss of two aircraft, both of which were shot down by ground fire.

The Zero was the principal Japanese naval fighter throughout the war, participating in all carrier actions, beginning with the PEARL HARBOR attack on Dec. 7, 1941. The first Zero to fall into American hands was a carrier-based plane that crashed on an ALEUTIAN ISLAND on June 3, 1942, the pilot being killed. That plane was later brought back to the United States for detailed examination, making its first flight with U.S. markings in Oct. 1942. During 1945 land-based Zeros were sent aloft primarily to intercept B-29 SUPERFORTRESS bombers attacking Japan.

Produced by the Mitsubishi and, subsequently, Nakajima aircraft companies, the low-wing, single-engine aircraft had excellent maneuverability, speed, and range. However, the lack of armor or bulletproof windscreen for the pilot, and unprotected fuel tanks meant that a Zero that was hit was often killed. During the war the Zero was periodically upgraded with improved engines and other features. (Improved aircraft were given the Allied code names Hap and then Hamp before they were determined to be Zero variants.)

Because of the poor quality of replacement pilots after the carrier battle of MIDWAY and the high losses during the lengthy U.S. SOLOMONS–NEW GUINEA CAMPAIGN, the Zero could never again recapture aerial superiority for the fleet. Beginning in Oct. 1944, land-based Zeros—each generally armed with a 551-pound BOMB—became the first aircraft used in the KAMIKAZE attacks against U.S. ships.

The prototype Zero was first flown on April 1, 1939, and quickly obtained a speed of slightly over 300 mph. By the time of Pearl Harbor there were 521 Zeros in naval service. Production continued until the last day of the war, with 10,938 aircraft being produced. When the war ended 6,300 improved A6M8 variants were on order, but none was completed because of the damage to Japanese industry by U.S. bombing and shortages of raw materials.

The A6M2 variant, in most of the carrier squadrons in Dec. 1941, had a top speed of 331 mph and a normal range of 1,160 miles, which could be extended with a drop tank and careful fuel consumption to an impressive 1,930 miles. The aircraft had two 7.7-mm machine guns in the engine cowling and two wing-mounted 20-mm cannon. Normal bomb load was one 551-pound weapon although the A6M7 and A6M8 models could carry a 1,102-pound bomb in the dive-bomber role.

There was a two-seat trainer derivative (A6M2-K) as well as a floatplane fighter version of the Zero (A6M2-N with the Allied code name RUFE); 327 were built in the latter configuration.

Although given the Allied code name Zeke, the aircraft was invariably known by its Japanese designation Zero for Navy Type 0 fighter, indicating the last digit of the year of issue, i.e., 2600 in the Japanese calendar, corresponding to 1940. Its Japanese service designation was A6M.

Zhukov, Marshal of the Soviet Union G. K. (1896–1974)

The most capable Soviet field commander in the war. Drafted into the czarist CAVALRY in 1915, Georgi Konstantinovich Zhukov became a highly decorated sergeant during World War I. He entered the Red Army in 1918 and joined the Communist Party a year later. Becoming a squadron commander in the civil war, he rose rapidly, mostly in cavalry assignments. In 1939–1940 as commander of the group of forces in the Far East he led the successful Soviet offensive against the Japanese at Khalkhin-Gol in Mongolia in Aug. 1939.

He served as commander of the Kiev Military District in 1940–1941 before moving to the highly important position of chief of the General Staff, where he served from Jan. to July 1941. STALIN then sent him to where the fighting against the Germans was toughest: commanding the reserve army group at the battle for Smolensk in July 1941, organizing the defense of LENINGRAD in Sept. 1941, commanding troops in the defense of MOSCOW in Oct. 1941–Jan. 1942. He had key responsibilities in the pivotal battles for STALINGRAD in 1942 and KURSK in 1943. An official Soviet publication later noted that Zhukov's "great leadership ability and his ability to size up a strategic situation, analyze it thoroughly, and make the correct conclusions" was seen in these battles. He was promoted to the rank of Marshal of the Soviet Union in Jan. 1943.

Subsequently, Zhukov commanded or coordinated Soviet army groups in the 1943–1944 offensives against the Germans. (See SOVIET OFFENSIVE CAMPAIGN.) In the fall of 1944 he briefly commanded the First Polish Army to help plan for the crossing of the Vistula River. For the final assault on Germany he commanded the First Belorussian Front, one of two Soviet army groups that advanced on BERLIN. When Berlin fell, he represented the Soviet Union in the German SURRENDER negotiations.

Zhukov was CinC of the Soviet occupation forces in Germany in 1945–1946 and then became CinC of Soviet Ground Forces. However, Stalin then downgraded him to military district commands until 1953. After Stalin's death he was promoted to first deputy minister of Defense, and from 1955 to 1957 served as minister of Defense. In Feb. 1956 he was elected to candidate membership in the ruling Presidium, the first professional soldier to ever reach that level; he was elected to full membership in June 1957. However, in Oct. 1957 NIKITA KHRUSHCHEV caused him to be removed from all positions and publicly disgraced.

He was awarded the HERO OF THE SOVIET UNION four times.

Zinc Coins

A short-term solution to U.S. wartime metal shortages. The minting of bronze pennies stopped in Dec. 1942. They were replaced by a dull, clunking zinc penny. Production of zinc-coated steel coins began on Feb. 23, 1943. The pennies, which did not jingle, were replaced on Jan. 1, 1944, by a penny that was 95 percent copper and 5 percent zinc. The penny's fate had been foreshadowed by a halt in May 1942 of the minting of the traditionally nickel-copper 5-cent coin. The wartime nickel was made of an alloy that eliminated all the nickel and about 25 percent of the copper. Production of the familiar prewar nickel (75 percent copper, 25 percent nickel) resumed on Jan. 1, 1946.

Zipper

Code name for plan for Allied invasion of Malaya, 1945.

Zitadelle (Citadel)

Code name for German attack on the KURSK salient, July 1943.

Zoot Suiters

Flashily dressed youths wearing pegged trousers with armpit-high waists, thigh-length jackets, and wide-brimmed hats. Zoot suiters in California launched an outlandish fashion that spread across the country in the late 1930s. They wore their hair long and slicked back in "duck tail" style. During World War II many were Mexican-Americans drawn to California as workers on farms and in war plants. Sailors and soldiers on leave, especially in

California, frequently attacked zoot suiters as "draft dodgers" or "foreigners," ripped their clothes, and cut their hair.

Zuckerman, Solly (1904—)

British scientist whose development of OPERATIONS RESEARCH led to scientific work on military problems. Zuckerman, a biologist with a specialty in monkeys, believed that a military operation was "an experiment of a very crude kind." Working from that premise, he advocated operations research: the analysis of military activities through scientific techniques.

He was a scientific adviser to British military organizations throughout the war. He was made an honorary Group Captain by the RAF in gratitude for his work on STRATEGIC BOMBING. He was primarily responsible for working out the "transportation plan," a proposal for selective bombing of French and German railway yards and facilities prior to the NORMANDY INVASION. The plan, opposed by advocates of strategic bombing of Germany, was endorsed by Gen. DWIGHT D. EISENHOWER, the Supreme Allied Commander. The plan was carried out, starting in May 1944, and all railways north of PARIS were cut before the invasion.

Zuckerman, who was made a Baron, wrote *The Social Life of Monkeys and Apes* (1932) near the beginning of his career and *The Scientists and War* (1966) after his wartime career.

Zyklon-B

Chemical used to produce lethal gas in NAZI DEATH CAMPS. The poison gas was produced when prussic acid crystals were exposed to air. The Zyklon gas system was first used at AUSCHWITZ to kill JEWS and Soviet PRISONERS OF WAR. The amethyst-blue crystals were dropped into shafts leading from the surface to underground death chambers disguised as "baths."

Zyklon-B was originally developed commercially by I. G. FARBEN to exterminate vermin and was sold by the German Corporation for Pest Control. As originally produced, Zyklon-B contained an irritating chemical as a warning to people applying it. The irritant eventually was removed because it slowed down the lethal effects of the gas. By the time the chemical was to be used in death camps rights to its patent were obtained from Farben by Tesch and Stebenow of Hamburg and Degesch of Frankfurt am Main. When the irritant-free Zyklon-B was used at Auschwitz, a doctor stood by in case the SS men dropping the crystals into the shafts were accidentally exposed.

Epilogue to War 1946–1990

A s World War II was ending, U.S. and Soviet troops met and shook hands at several locations that symbolized the Allied victories over the AXIS. Official cameras of both countries recorded the historic moments. From Germany to Czechoslovakia to Korea, the handshakes, toasts, smiles, and bear hugs became cliché symbols of the war-winning brotherhood of Yank and Ivan over NAZIS and Japs.

Within a year the sites of those handshakes became symbols of something that had not happened. There had been no brotherhood. The Soviet government told its people that the Red Army had fought its own war against Germany, the *Soviets'* GREAT PATRIOTIC WAR, alone.

Allied help to the Soviet Union—$11,297,883,000

in U.S. LEND-LEASE, the millions of dollars raised for the Russian Relief Organization by private American efforts, the shipments of British war matériel—all this officially did not happen in Soviet accounts of the war. Hundreds of U.S. and British seamen had died running the U-BOAT gauntlet on the deadly RUSSIAN CONVOYS to MURMANSK, but few Soviet people would know of these deaths. There had been only the Great Patriotic War, fought against the Germans from June 1941 to May 1945, and the brief war against an Allied-weakened Japan in the Far East—a campaign measured in days but presented in Soviet PROPAGANDA as the vital effort that beat the Japanese.

The Soviets even changed the history in one place liberated by U.S. forces and then occupied by Soviet troops. On May 5 and 6, 1945, elements of the U.S.

World War II was an atomic war—three atomic bombs were detonated, one at a test range in the United States and two above Japanese cities. Immediately after the war the United States conducted two atomic bomb tests at Bikini atoll to evaluate nuclear effects on ships and military equipment. This is the cloud from the Baker test at Bikini, a bomb detonated under water on July 25, 1946. *(U.S. Navy)*

912

Army's 16th Armored DIVISION and 2nd Infantry Division drove German troops out of Pilsen, Czechoslovakia. At the same time, the Red Army was liberating Czech territory east of Pilsen. When a Soviet-backed Communist government took over Czechoslovakia, the history of liberation was changed. *All* of Czechoslovakia had been freed by the Soviet Union. School children were taught that the Soviets liberated the city. When witnesses recalled seeing U.S. uniforms, they were told that what they really remembered seeing were *Soviet* soldiers in U.S. uniforms.

Not until 1990, when Czechoslovakia ended its decades of Communist control with free elections, was the truth again revealed. "They tried to erase history and create new history," a Pilsen resident said.

Counterfeited history makes the Cold War a story hard to tell. Even the term does not accurately define the realities of the forty-four years between BERNARD BARUCH's first use of the term *Cold War* in 1946 and the unofficial end of the Cold War with the European disarmament agreements of 1989–1990. The Cold War was hot. Men died, unsung, when U.S. reconnaissance planes were shot down over the Soviet Union and China in the 1940s and 1950s. And, when the United States confronted communism in Korea and in Vietnam, tens of thousands of Americans died.

American and British leaders began worrying about the postwar plans of the Soviet Union long before the EUROPEAN WAR was won. HARRY HOPKINS, President ROOSEVELT's special assistant, talking with British Foreign Secretary ANTHONY EDEN in the spring of 1943, said that after the collapse of Germany, "unless we acted promptly and surely" Germany would "go Communist or an out and out anarchic state would set in." The "same kind of thing," Hopkins added, "might happen in any of the countries in Europe and Italy as well."

Go Communist became political shorthand for a phenomenon only dimly understood in 1943: the flight of a country from the ranks of democracy and capitalism to the oppression of dictatorship and collectivism. Western leaders feared the flight, but they did not know how to stop it. Communism was succeeding Nazism as the new enemy. Even as British Prime Minister CHURCHILL watched his jubilant nation celebrate V-E DAY, he later wrote, "The Soviet menace, to my eyes, had already replaced the Nazi foe."

VANNEVAR BUSH, the American scientist who led other scientists in the creation of the ATOMIC BOMB,

saw the Cold War as a form of political aggression that HITLER had "brought . . . into its modern form. Its greatest tool is the threat of war and the spreading of fear to weaken resistance to external demands." The equating of Hitler with communism was made easy by the despotism of STALIN. With Hitler gone, Stalin became, for many in the West, the new Hitler: a tyrant taking over Eastern Europe and, in alliance with what American policymakers called "Communist China," threatening to conquer the world.

No longer did visionaries talk about One World under the blue-and-white banner of the UNITED NATIONS. There were three worlds: the Free World, the Communist World, and the Third World. Western political leaders warned that the Third World's impoverished nations, emerging from colonial rule or plunging into economic chaos, must be kept from going Communist, from entering the Communist World, whatever the cost.

New words and phrases were being added to the political lexicon: Soviet Bloc, Soviet satellites, containment—and, from Churchill, the graphic image that would define the West's view of communism: the Iron Curtain.

On May 12, 1945, a month after the death of Churchill's great comrade in arms, Franklin D. Roosevelt, Churchill sent a top-secret telegram to HARRY S TRUMAN, the new President:

"I have always worked for friendship with Russia," it said in part, "but, like you, I feel deep anxiety because of their misinterpretation of the YALTA decisions, their attitude towards Poland . . . the difficulties they make about Vienna, the combination of Russian power and the territories under their control or occupied, coupled with the Communist technique in so many other countries, and above all their power to maintain very large armies in the field for a long time. What will be the position in a year or two, when the British and American Armies have melted and the French has not yet been formed on any major scale, when we have a handful of divisions, mostly French, and when Russia may choose to keep two or three hundred on active service?

"An iron curtain is drawn upon their front. . . ."

On March 5, 1946, Churchill used the phrase again, this time publicly. "From Stettin in the Baltic to TRIESTE in the Adriatic, an iron curtain has descended across the Continent," he said in an address at Westminster College, in Fulton, Mo. Churchill, no longer prime minister (but destined for the post again), had been invited to Missouri by Truman, the state's most famous son.

Shortly after the Churchill speech at Westminster, Truman wrote to Stalin and invited him to the University of Missouri "to speak your mind." Truman even offered to bring Stalin to America in the BATTLESHIP *MISSOURI* (BB 63)—on whose deck the Japanese SURRENDER had been accepted. Stalin, who called Churchill's speech "a call to war with the Soviet Union," did not accept Truman's invitation.

Truman at first believed that a combination of his political savvy and the atomic bomb would solve U.S. problems with the Soviet Union. In July 1945 at the POTSDAM CONFERENCE, where he had learned of the successful testing of the atomic bomb, Truman wrote in his diary, "I can deal with Stalin. He is honest—but smart as hell."

In the fall of 1945, when Gen. CHARLES DE GAULLE worried aloud to Truman about the continued presence of the Red Army in Europe, Truman told the French leader there was nothing to fear: If the Soviet Union or any other nation threatened the peace, the United States would stop the aggression with the atomic bomb. The United States, Secretary of War HENRY L. STIMSON remarked, was wearing "this weapon rather ostentatiously on our hip."

The atomic bomb did not deter Stalin. His scientists—and spies—were working zealously to get the Soviet Union a bomb of its own. But Stalin was far more influenced by hasty U.S. and British demobilization than by fears of the bomb. He refused to withdraw the Red Army from Eastern Europe and began forcing MOSCOW-controlled Communist governments on Poland, Czechoslovakia, Bulgaria, Rumania, Hungary, and the Soviet occupation zone in Germany. Yugoslavia and Albania also came under Communist governments. U.S. officials, fearing that the same would happen in France and Italy, poured food and billions of dollars into Europe. The architect of the U.S. aid endeavor was GEORGE C. MARSHALL, who had become secretary of State in Feb. 1947. The European recovery effort became known as the Marshall Plan; for it, Marshall received the Nobel Peace Prize in 1953. U.S. aid and covert political operations undoubtedly helped to sway the 1946 parliamentary election in Italy in 1946, but the Communist Party still won 104 of the 556 seats.

Immediately after the war, Stalin reduced the size of the Soviet Army, but he proceeded with its modernization. At the same time, despite the ravaged industry

and devastated shipyards of European Russia, he ordered a massive naval construction program: battle cruisers, aircraft carriers, cruisers, destroyers, and submarines—by some estimates, as many as 1,200. The undersea craft were partly modeled on the technology of the latest German U-boats, which again could threaten to sever the Old World from the RESOURCES of the new world in a future BATTLE OF THE ATLANTIC.

Employing captured German technology, scientists, and engineers, Stalin initiated a missile program that would in 1957, four years after his death, put the world's first artificial satellite—*Sputnik 1*—into orbit. That small, beeping "fellow traveler" would embarrass the United States, touch off a "space race" between the two countries, and inject the "missile gap" controversy in to the U.S. 1960 presidential election.

Since 1942 the Soviet government had been working on ways to build an atomic bomb. The detonation of the first Soviet atomic bomb, announced by President Truman on Sept. 23, 1949, stunned Western intelligence experts who were estimating that the Soviet bomb was one to four years in the future; some Western analysts even believed that the Soviets would *never* be able to develop an atomic bomb.

To deliver this weapon against Western Europe and possibly the United States, Stalin had ordered top priority also be given to copying the three U.S. B-29 SUPERFORTRESS bombers that had come down in Siberia in 1944 during bombing raids against Japan. These four-engine bombers, rapidly duplicated by designer Andrei Tupolev, were given the Soviet designation Tu-4. The first Tu-4 flew in 1947, by which time mass production was already underway. JET-PROPELLED AIRCRAFT were also developed with high priority. Built around a purchased copy of a Rolls-Royce turbojet engine, the MiG-15 became the backbone of the Soviet Air Force of the 1950s and saw extensive combat against American fighters in the Korean War.

The question of Germany's future, which had worried Hopkins in 1943, evolved into a different problem in the postwar world. The worry was less about Germany and more about the Soviet Union in Germany. The four-power arrangement for the occupation of Germany put U.S., British, and French occupation forces in what had been western Germany, and Soviet Forces in eastern Germany, with the western ALLIES retaining rights to BERLIN, in the middle of the Soviet zone.

By June 1948, the governments of the United

States, England, and France were certain that they could not reach an agreement with the Soviet Union about the reestablishment of a unified Germany. The three nations decided to merge their occupied zones and establish that region as an independent nation, which would become West Germany, officially the German Federal Republic. The Soviet Union, which since April 1948 had been harassing Western road and rail movement into Berlin, on June 24 cut off all air, land, and river traffic, besieging more than 2,000,000 residents of West Berlin. The Soviets hoped to force the Western powers to abandon Berlin or scrap their plans for creating an independent republic.

President Truman angrily reacted by ordering a massive expansion of an airlift of military planes established during the April harassment. In what the U.S. pilots called Operation Vittles, the United States supplied food, coal, and other necessities to the encircled city. Some pilots, as they landed and took off, dropped candy on handkerchief parachutes to Berlin children. The Berlin Airlift went on day after day for 321 days—more than 277,000 flights that brought in some 2,500,000 tons.

"Berlin had kept its courage," Gen. LUCIUS D. CLAY, military governor of the U.S. zone, reported. Berliners suffered cold and hunger, but "the determination did not falter. They were proud to carry their burden as the price of their freedom."

The airlift was only the beginning of the West's resistance to Soviet aggression in Europe. By the time the Soviets ended the blockade in May 1949, nine World War II Allies—the United States, England, France, Canada, Belgium, the Netherlands, Luxembourg, Denmark, and Norway—joined with Italy, a former AXIS enemy, and Portugal and Iceland, two nations neutral in the war, to form the North Atlantic Treaty Organization (NATO). The NATO nations set up three major military commands (with two permanently under American officers) and pledged that an attack on any one member nation would be considered an attack on all of them.

Two other Allies, Turkey and Greece, joined NATO in 1952. When a rearmed West Germany joined in 1955, the Soviet Union hastily organized the Warsaw Treaty Organization, whose members—the Soviet Union, Albania, Bulgaria, Czechoslovakia, Hungary, Poland, Rumania, and East Germany—included both former Allies and former Axis partners.

Whatever the conflicts between the Soviets and the other allies of World War II, the victors' occupation of Europe had been easily accomplished. The Allies had little trouble establishing order after the German SURRENDER because they had large formations of troops in Europe who could immediately change roles from fighters to occupiers.

The end of the war in the Pacific, however, meant that Allied occupation forces had to be brought in from elsewhere and placed in Japan and areas in the Far East occupied by Japanese troops. At the time of the Japanese surrender, Japanese troops were scattered from China to NEW GUINEA and the DUTCH EAST INDIES. While postwar Europe was a stage for confrontation and propaganda barrages between Communist and non-Communist nations, four places in the Far East became stages for long and bloody conflict:

China   The end of World War II intensified the civil war between Generalissimo CHIANG KAI-SHEK's nationalist government, supported by the United States, and the Chinese Communists. The Nationalists controlled only southern China; the Communists had about 170,000 regular troops in northern China—a region entered by Soviet forces in the closing days of the war. The Soviets handed key ports over to the Communists and refused entry to the nationalists.

To strengthen Chiang Kai-shek's political position and to supervise the surrender of Japanese troops in China, in Sept.–Oct. 1945 the United States sent some 53,000 Marines into northern China. Communist leader CHOU EN-LAI warned the Marines that his troops would fight if the Marines contested Communist-claimed territory. Some fire fights did flare between the Marines and the Communists as the Marines supervised the disarming of some 326,000 Japanese troops (out of about 1,000,000 in China at the end of the war). Pending repatriation, many of the Japanese troops were allowed to keep some rifles and ammunition to protect themselves amid the civil war. The Nationalists even allowed Japanese troops to protect railways used by the Nationalists from Communist attack.

By mid-1946 it was clear to most Western observers that the Communists would win out over the Nationalists, who had, a U.S. general said, "the world's worst leadership." The United States, tilting toward the Nationalists, tried nevertheless to intercede as a disinterested negotiator. The efforts were in vain. U.S. Ambassador to China PATRICK HURLEY and special presidential envoy George C. Marshall failed in their attempts to end the Chinese civil war.

An ever-dwindling number of Marines remained in

China until the last ones left in May 1949, when SHANGHAI fell to the Communists. Duty in the turmoil of postwar China had cost the Marines ten dead and thirty-three wounded.

Chiang Kai-shek led the remnants of his army from the mainland to the island of Formosa (Taiwan), which the Japanese had occupied during the war. The Communists proclaimed the People's Republic of China on Oct. 1, 1949. The United States did not diplomatically recognize what was called "Communist China" and continued to declare that the Nationalist regime on Formosa was the legal government of China.

The victory of the Communists sent shock waves as far as WASHINGTON, where the complexities of Chinese civil war were reduced to a simplistic question—"Who lost China?"—that haunted U.S. domestic politics for many years. The debate split along party lines, with the Republicans asking the question and the Democrats, rallied around President Truman, trying to answer the question by showing an unrelenting hostility toward communism everywhere in the world.

Korea   On Aug. 12, 1945, four days after entering the war against Japan and two days before the Japanese surrender, the Soviet Union sent troops across the Manchurian border into Korea, which Japan had long considered Japanese territory. Not until Sept. 8 did the United States begin landing occupation troops at the Korean port of Inchon. After the obligatory publicity photos of smiling U.S. and Soviet soldiers, the two wary nations had to decide on an occupation arrangement. The United States proposed the 38th Parallel as a *temporary* line of demarcation between the two occupiers, and the Soviets agreed.

In Dec. 1945 U.S. Secretary of State JAMES BYRNES and Soviet Foreign Minister VYACHESLAV MOLOTOV agreed that Korea would get a provisional government. But the Soviets repeatedly blocked any move to carry out the agreement. In 1948, the United States ended its occupation by establishing the Republic of Korea below the 38th Parallel; in the north, Soviet-backed Korean Communists proclaimed the Democratic People's Republic. Another iron curtain had slammed down.

Two years later, on June 25, 1950, the North Koreans launched a full-scale invasion of South Korea in an effort to unify the country. All U.S. troops, except for a few advisers, by that time had withdrawn from South Korea.

President Truman responded first by ordering U.S.

"air and sea forces to give the Korean Government troops cover and support." Then, on June 30, with the South Korean Army in hasty retreat down the peninsula, Truman sent in ground forces from Japan. The Korean War had begun. It would draw in the People's Republic of China, cost more than 54,000 American lives, and last until July 1953, when President DWIGHT D. EISENHOWER, elected in 1952 after promising to end the war, negotiated a cease-fire. The North Koreans and their Chinese allies were able to sign an armistice, many observers believed, because of the death, on March 5, 1953, of Stalin.

Dutch East Indies   A major objective of the JAPANESE CAMPAIGN IN THE FAR EAST, this Netherlands colony so rich in resources had swiftly fallen to the Japanese—with unexpected results for the Dutch government-in-exile in LONDON. The Japanese conquerors discovered that they could manipulate the incipient independence movement in the Indies. Leaders of the native peoples, who had been clamoring for independence from their white European rulers, watched with grim satisfaction when Japanese occupation forces jailed and humiliated the colonial administrators and other Dutch civilians trapped by the Japanese invasion.

The Japanese, after initially winning over the native peoples, lost their support by shipping thousands of them off to work battalions in New Guinea and elsewhere. But, as Japanese hopes of victory began to fade, the conquerors' policy shifted again and the Japanese rekindled the independence movement. On Aug. 17, 1945, three days after Japan's SURRENDER, nationalists proclaimed the republic of Indonesia and turned against their erstwhile Dutch masters. Instead of joyous liberation from Japanese occupation, many of the internees remained captives under new oppressors.

Dutch officials, whose own country had been liberated only three months before, did not have the means to reinstall a colonial government in the Indies. The mission was given to British forces in the Far East. With great reluctance, British troops finally arrived in Oct. 1945. They found chaos. Japanese soldiers had turned over their arms to the insurgents. Terrorists raided the miserable camps of interned Europeans and PRISONERS OF WAR. Communist workers in Australian ports refused to allow ships to carry Dutch forces to the islands.

Not until Nov. 1946 did military command of the islands pass to Dutch forces. Fighting between nationalists and the Dutch went on for four years until the Netherlands relinquished sovereignty over all but a part of the Indies on New Guinea; that territory subsequently was granted to the republic.

Indochina As in the Dutch East Indies, the Japanese occupation forces in this key French Colony gave support to anti-European nationalists and declared the independence of the "Empire of Vietnam." But in the north, where there were relatively few occupation troops, the Japanese were opposed by a strong Communist movement, known as the Vietminh (formally, the League for the Independence of Vietnam, the eastern portion of Indochina).

During the war the Vietminh, headed by HO CHI MINH, established the Democratic Republic of Vietnam. The United States parachuted arms to the Vietminh GUERRILLAS fighting the Japanese, and U.S. pilots downed in Indochina were rescued by the Vietminh.

When the war ended the Vietminh occupied Hanoi and Haiphong and controlled much of northeast Indochina. France was not immediately able to reinstall itself. As a result, Japanese troops were allowed to remain under arms to maintain order until mid-Sept. 1945 when British and Indian troops began arriving in Saigon to take the surrender of Japanese forces in southern Indochina. Because there were not enough Allied soldiers to police the region, Japanese troops again aided their former enemies in establishing order over the native peoples.

In the north, Chinese troops were given the task of accepting the Japanese surrender. The Chinese officers in the north recognized the Communist-led Vietminh as the region's government and kept troops in the north in support of the Vietminh. In the absence of French forces, the Vietminh solidified their position.

When the French finally made their move to reassume colonial control of Indochina, they began in the south. Then, in Feb. 1946, they moved north, landing 12,100 troops at the port of Haiphong under fire from Chinese troops. (In the summer of 1946 the Chinese withdrew from Indochina.) The French initially recognized the Vietminh government in the north. But the political conflict between European colonialism and Asian communism inevitably erupted into armed conflict.

The cease-fire in Korea allowed China to pour arms into Indochina, building up the military power of the Communist insurgents. The climax of the Indochina war came in Nov. 1953, when the French made a massive parachute drop at Dien Bien Phu, a valley astride the potential Vietminh route to the quasi-independent state of Laos. By March 1954, the French in Dien Bien Phu, surrounded by well-entrenched and well-armed Communist troops, were threatened with annihilation.

The United States had been pouring aircraft and other aid into Vietnam to help the French. With Dien Bien Phu a disaster for an old ally, U.S. officials began to discuss intervention by U.S. troops. On April 3, 1954, Secretary of State John Foster Dulles and Adm. Arthur W. Radford, Chairman of the JOINT CHIEFS OF STAFF, met with congressional leaders and asked for a congressional resolution authorizing U.S. entry into the war to save the French. The leaders, especially Senate Majority Leader LYNDON B. JOHNSON, vehemently rejected the idea.

Two weeks later, Vice President RICHARD M. NIXON publicly raised the issue, saying, "if to avoid further Communist expansion in Asia and Indochina we must take the risk now by putting our boys in, I think the Executive has to take the politically unpopular decision to do it." Public opinion swiftly erupted against the suggestion of another intervention in Asia so soon after the Korean War. But in secrecy military planners still talked about intervention, including use of "small" atomic bombs (which were actually much more powerful than those dropped on Japan).

The fall of Dien Bien Phu on May 7, 1954, essentially ended the war. In July a peace conference put more than half of Indochina under Communist rule. North Vietnam was now a nation of 12,500,000 people. After the agreement, nearly a million people walked, rode, sailed, and swam out of the north and sought refuge in South Vietnam. There U.S. military advisers soon began arming and training what would become the South Vietnamese Army for what, under President Johnson and then-President Nixon, would be the Vietnam War.

The long road to the Vietnam War had begun in the rubble of World War II and had twisted through the occupied zones of Europe and the radioactive wasteland of HIROSHIMA and NAGASAKI. For, in the American crusade against Communism, it was the atomic bomb that had changed the U.S. direction. The turn from negotiations to confrontation was prophetically called Crossroads.

That was the code name for the ATOMIC BOMB TEST at Bikini atoll in July 1946, where history's fourth and fifth atomic bombs were detonated. The targets were ninety-three ships—with weapons, aircraft, and thousands of test animals lashed to their decks. Most of the target ships were U.S. warships, including the venerable AIRCRAFT CARRIER *SARATOGA* (CV 3). The display of American power—the ability not only to blow up warships but also to dispose of them so lavishly—awed the world, especially the Soviet Union. It would be more than three years before the Soviets exploded their first atomic bomb.

In March 1947 President Truman went before a joint session of Congress to seek military aid for Greece, where Soviet-aided Communists were trying to pull down the U.S.-supported government, and Turkey, where the Soviets were making territorial demands. "I believe," Truman said, "that it must be the policy of the United States to support free peoples who are resisting attempted subjugation by armed minorities or by outside pressures." This policy became known as the Truman Doctrine: financial and military assistance to nations threatened with Communist takeover. Truman had only recently clashed with the Soviets over their refusal to leave Iran, which Allied troops had occupied during most of the war. When the Soviets finally began leaving in April 1946, Soviet-backed rebels fomented revolution. Iranian troops drove the rebels across the border into the Soviet Union.

Backing up this public policy was a secret one, the product of two new instruments of statecraft that emerged from World War II: the Central Intelligence Agency (CIA), the successor to the OFFICE OF STRATEGIC SERVICES, and the National Security Council (NSC), a permanent advisory organization of policy, defense, and intelligence officials to counsel the President on national security matters.

On Jan. 30, 1950, Truman secretly asked his advisers for "an over-all review and re-assessment of American foreign and defense policy in the light of the loss of China, the Soviet mastery of atomic energy and the prospect of the fusion bomb"—a reference to what would become the hydrogen bomb, whose power would dwarf that of the atomic bomb.

In early June President Truman received the final draft of the reappraisal of U.S. policy, a National Security Council's top-secret policy paper labeled NSC 68. The document saw the future as "an indefinite period of tension and danger" in which the United States must become the "political and material center with other free nations in variable orbits around it." NSC 68 urged that the United States build up its defenses so as to meet, with force, "each fresh challenge promptly and unequivocally."

The challenge came in only a few days, when North Korean troops crossed over the 38th Parallel. President Truman's reaction to the North Korean invasion drastically changed the course of the U.S. struggle against communism. On June 26, 1950, when he announced plans to aid South Korea, he also expanded the Truman Doctrine to include the Pacific, promising U.S. aid against any nation in Asia fighting communism. He said he was ordering the Seventh FLEET to "prevent any attack on Formosa," was sending more military aid to the French in Indochina, and was stepping up aid to the Philippines, where left-wing Huk guerrillas were threatening the government.

American commitment now was worldwide, and the crossroad had been passed. What had started as a doctrine that pledged American money and munitions had become a doctrine promising American blood, first in the Korean War and then in the Vietnam War.

America intervened in Vietnam with air strikes in 1964, then began sending in troops until in 1969 there were more than 525,000 Americans fighting and dying in Indochina. A long and erratic withdrawal ended in April 1975 with one of the war's many searing images: people struggling to board HELICOPTERS taking off from the roof of the U.S. Embassy in Saigon. Defeated politically and militarily, the nation was shattered by the long and painful ordeal. The United States counted 58,151 deaths—47,752 of them in combat—and 153,303 wounded. Some in sorrow, some in anger, Americans said, "No more Vietnams."

The end of the American war in Vietnam also meant a drastic cutback in defense spending. Social programs demanded that the funds so recently spent for BOMBS and bullets be reallocated to aid the poor, build schools, fight drug addiction, and save inner cities from self-destruction.

Problems also plagued the military. The specter of the unpopular Vietnam War hung over the country while the armed services shifted to an all-volunteer force and WOMEN in the armed forces won *almost* equal status to their male counterparts.

During the presidency of Jimmy Carter (1987–1991) defense planners sought to stress high-tech weapons over traditional ones in the hope that high-tech would be cheaper in the long run because of reduced manpower costs. For the military, these were the lean years.

At the same time, the Soviet Union, under LEONID BREZHNEV, continued a high rate of defense spending. Indeed, as with the perceived bomber and missile gaps of the 1950s, there was again a fear of Soviet military ascendancy, especially since Brezhnev was also showing a propensity to deploy surrogate troops— such as the Cubans in Angola—as well as Soviet troops, who entered Afghanistan in 1979 for what would be a costly nine-year war against steadfast guerrillas. Brezhnev also build up his fleet (including aircraft carriers), and accelerated strategic missile development and production.

President Ronald Reagan entered the White House in 1981, elected in part because of his strong stance on defense issues. His highest priorities went to "rebuilding" Americans defenses, needed, he declared, because the Soviet Union had continually demonstrated itself to be the "Evil Empire," akin to the villainous society in the hit movie *Star Wars*. Reagan's abhorrence of the Soviet Union was demonstrated time and time again, but never so much as it was one day, when, while he was preparing for a radio broadcast and thinking that the microphone was not open, he declared that Congress had voted to destroy the Soviet Union and that the bombers were already en route. This incident, and many others chronicled and unchronicled, made the Soviet political and military leaders in the Kremlin very restless.

Reagan won from Congress higher pay for the men and women of the armed forces, stepped up the production of weapons of all varieties, and deployed a new generation of U.S. theater missiles in Western Europe. His audacious young (thirty-nine-year-old) secretary of the Navy, John F. Lehman, demanded—and largely got—a rejuvenation of American naval power. The Soviets were forced to contend with American political pressure—and, at times, weapons—challenging their incursions in Angola, Afghanistan, and Nicaragua.

Nothing stunned the Soviets more, however, than Reagan's announcement on March 23, 1983, that the United States would develop and deploy a program euphemistically called Strategic Defense Initiative: a ballistic missile defense of the United States. Promptly dubbed *Star Wars* by the press, this missile shield would be an effort with the relative magnitude of the MANHATTAN PROJECT that created the atomic bomb. In the United States, Star Wars was merely highly controversial; in the Kremlin, Star Wars was a nightmare: A Soviet attempt to counter the American defensive plan would mean massive spending from an inferior technological base.

Economically—and probably politically—the Soviet Union could no longer compete. Domestic needs, growing political unrest, and, perhaps most important, the need for technological modernization, led Mikhail Gorbachev, who became head of the ruling Politburo in 1985, to make a dramatic break from the Cold War: *Perestroika* (restructuring) and *glasnost* (openness) became his watchwords as he sought to propel the Soviet Union into the twenty-first century. But such a move could not be made while his nation was engaged in an arms race and a Star Wars race with the United States. In an unprecedented agreement, President Reagan and Party Chairman Gorbachev in Dec. 1987 signed an arms agreement that banned an entire class of nuclear weapons—theater nuclear weapons deployed by both sides in Europe (officially known as Intermediate-range Nuclear Forces).

Disarmament rolled on, gathering momentum at each new conference table. Negotiations were begun to eventually ban all nuclear weapons. In the interim the Conventional Forces in Europe Treaty was signed, causing drastic reductions in conventional combat forces on both sides. Separate and apart from negotiations, Gorbachev began withdrawing combat forces from Eastern Europe. At the same time, he permitted a new awakening of independence in Eastern Europe.

Suddenly there was a crack in the Berlin Wall, and it rapidly spread to Poland, Czechoslovakia, Hungary, and Romania. By 1989 the the Wall was quaking and the borders between East and West were open. The last portions of the Wall fell at midnight on Oct. 3–4, 1990, when the two Germanies were reunited quickly, completely, and without bloodshed. The Wall was gone and, Europe hoped, so was the Iron Curtain that Churchill had watched descend more than forty years before.

APPENDIX A
Military Rank Comparison

GERMAN ARMY	GERMAN NAVY	LUFTWAFFE	U.S. ARMY/ARMY AIR FORCES/MARINE CORPS	U.S. NAVY/COAST GUARD
—	—	Reichsmarschall	—	—
Generalfeld-marschall	Grand Admiral	Generalfeld-marschall	General of the Army*	Fleet Admiral
Generaloberst	Admiral	Generaloberst	General	Admiral
General	Vizeadmiral	General der Flieger	Lieutenant General	Vice Admiral
Generalleutnant	Konteradmiral	Generalleutnant	Major General	Rear Admiral
Generalmajor	Kommodore	Generalmajor	Brigadier General	Commodore
Oberst	Kapitän zur See	Oberst	Colonel	Captain
Oberstleutnant	Fregattenkapitän	Oberstleutnant	Lieutenant Colonel	Commander
Major	Korvettenkapitän	Major	Major	Lieutenant Commander
Hauptmann	Kapitänleutnant	Hauptmann	Captain	Lieutenant
Oberleutnant	Oberleutnant zur See	Oberleutnant	1st Lieutenant	Lieutenant (junior grade)
			2nd Lieutenant	Ensign
Leutnant	Leutnant zur See	Leutnant	Flight Officer (AAF)**	—

*Army and AAF only
**AAF only

BRITISH ARMY	ROYAL AIR FORCE	ROYAL NAVY	SOVIET ARMY/AIR FORCES	SOVIET NAVY*
			Generalissimo	
General of the Army	Marshal of the RAF	Admiral of the Fleet	Glavny Marshal	
General	Air Chief Marshal	Admiral	Marshal	Admiral Flota
Lieutenant General	Air Marshal	Vice Admiral	General-Polkovnik	Admiral
Major General	Air Vice Marshal	Rear Admiral	General-Leitenant	Vitse Admiral
Brigadier	Air Commodore	Commodore	General-Mayor	Kontr Admiral
Colonel	Group Captain	Captain	Polkovnik	Kapitan 1st Ranga
Lieutenant Colonel	Wing Commander	Commander	Podpolkovnik	Kapitan 2nd Ranga
			Mayor	Kapitan 3rd Ranga
Major	Squadron Leader	Lieutenant Commander	Kapitan	Kapitan Leitenant
			Starshy Leitenant	Leitenant
Captain	Flight Lieutenant	Lieutenant	Leitenant	Mladshy
1st Lieutenant	Flying Officer	Sub-Lieutenant	Mladshy Leitenant	
2nd Lieutenant	Pilot Officer			

*This reflects the Soviet Navy rank structure instituted in Dec. 1942. The captain 1st rank had the single broad stripe of a commodore in Western navies. Prior to Dec. 1942 the captain 1st rank was equal to a one-star general (General-Mayor).

APPENDIX B

U.S. Army and Army Air Forces Battle Streamers

American Theater (outside of continental limits of the United States)

antisubmarine   Dec. 7, 1941–Sept. 2, 1945
ground combat   Dec. 7, 1941–Sept. 2, 1945
air combat   Dec. 7, 1941–Sept. 2, 1945

Asiatic-Pacific Theater

antisubmarine   Dec. 7, 1941–Sept. 2, 1945
ground combat   Dec. 7, 1941–Sept. 2, 1945
air combat   Dec. 7, 1941–Sept. 2, 1945
Philippine Islands   Dec. 7, 1941–May 10, 1942
Burma   Dec. 7, 1941–May 26, 1942
Central Pacific   Dec. 7, 1941–Dec. 6, 1943
East Indies   Jan. 1, 1942–July 22, 1942
India-Burma   April 2, 1942–Jan. 28, 1945
air offensive, Japan   April 17, 1942–Sept. 2, 1945
Aleutian Islands   June 3, 1942–Aug. 24, 1943
China defensive   July 4, 1942–May 4, 1945
Papua   July 23, 1942–Jan. 23, 1943
Guadalcanal   Aug. 7, 1942–Feb. 21, 1943
New Guinea   Jan. 24, 1943–Dec. 31, 1944
Northern Solomons   Feb. 22, 1943–Nov. 21, 1944
Eastern Mandates
  air operations   Dec. 7, 1943–April 16, 1944
  ground operations   Jan. 31, 1944–June 14, 1944
Bismarck Archipelago   Dec. 15, 1943–Nov. 27, 1944
Western Pacific
  air operations   April 17, 1944–Sept. 2, 1945
  ground operations   June 15, 1944–Sept. 2, 1945
Leyte   Oct. 17, 1944–July 1, 1945
Luzon   Dec. 15, 1944–July 4, 1945

Central Burma   Jan. 29, 1945–July 15, 1945
Southern Philippines   Feb. 27, 1945–July 4, 1945
Ryukyus (Okinawa)   March 26, 1945–July 2, 1945
China offensive   May 5, 1945–Sept. 2, 1945

European-African-Middle Eastern Theaters

antisubmarine   Dec. 7, 1941–Sept. 2, 1945
ground combat   Dec. 7, 1941–Sept. 2, 1945
air combat   Dec. 7, 1941–Sept. 2, 1945
Egypt-Libya   June 11, 1942–Feb. 13, 1943
air offensive, Europe   July 4, 1942–June 5, 1944
Algeria–French Morocco   Nov. 8–11, 1942
Tunisia
  air operations   Nov. 12, 1942–May 13, 1943
  ground operations   Nov. 17, 1942–May 13, 1943
Sicily
  air operations   May 14, 1943–Aug. 17, 1943
  ground operations   July 9, 1943–Aug. 17, 1943
Naples-Foggia
  air operations   Aug. 18, 1943–Jan. 21, 1944
  ground operations   Sept. 9, 1943–Jan. 21, 1944
Anzio   Jan. 22, 1944–Sept. 9, 1944
Rome-Arno   Jan. 22, 1944–Sept. 9, 1944
Normandy   June 6, 1944–July 24, 1944
Northern France   July 25, 1944–Sept. 14, 1944
Southern France   Aug. 15, 1944–Sept. 14, 1944
Northern Apennines   Sept. 10, 1944–April 4, 1945
Rhineland   Sept. 15, 1944–March 21, 1945
Ardennes-Alsace   Dec. 16, 1944–Jan. 25, 1945
Central Europe   March 22, 1945–May 11, 1945
Po Valley   April 5, 1945–May 8, 1945

APPENDIX C
U.S. Navy Battle Stars

American Area (outside of continental limits of the United States)

Escort, antisubmarine, Armed Guard (specific operations) Feb. 21, 1942–Jan. 31, 1943

Asiatic-Pacific Area

Pearl Harbor–Midway   Dec. 7, 1941
Wake Island   Dec. 8–23, 1941
Philippine Islands*   Dec. 8, 1941–May 6, 1942
Netherlands (Dutch)
   East Indies
     Makassar Strait   Jan. 23–24, 1942
     Badoeng Strait   Feb. 19–20, 1942
     Java Sea   Feb. 27, 1942
Pacific Raids   Feb. 1–March 10, 1942
Coral Sea   May 4–8, 1942
Midway   June 3–6, 1942
Guadalcanal-Tulagi landings (Savo)   Aug. 7–9, 1942
Guadalcanal capture   Aug. 10, 1942–Feb. 8, 1943
Makin Raid   Aug. 17–18, 1942
Eastern Solomons   Aug. 23–25, 1942
Buin-Faisi-Tonoley Raid   Oct. 5, 1942
Cape Esperance (Savo)   Oct. 11–12, 1942
Santa Cruz Islands   Oct. 26, 1942
Guadalcanal (Savo)   Nov. 12–15, 1942
Tassafaronga (Savo)   Nov. 30–Dec. 1, 1942
Eastern New Guinea   Dec. 17, 1942–July 24, 1944
Rennell Island   Jan. 29–30, 1943
Solomons   Feb. 8, 1943–March 15, 1945
Aleutians   March 26–June 2, 1943
New Georgia   June 20–Oct. 16, 1943
Bismarck (Sea) Archipelago   June 25, 1943–May 1, 1944
Pacific Raids   Aug. 31–Oct. 6, 1943
Treasury-Bougainville   Oct. 27–Dec. 15, 1943
Gilbert Islands   Nov. 13–Dec. 8, 1943

Marshall Islands   Nov. 26, 1943–March 2, 1944
Asiatic-Pacific Raids   Feb. 16–Oct. 9, 1944
Western New Guinea   April 21, 1944–Jan. 9, 1945
Marianas operation   June 10–Aug. 27, 1944
Western Caroline Islands   Aug. 31–Oct. 14, 1943
Leyte operation   Oct. 19–Dec. 16, 1944
Luzon operation   Dec. 12, 1944–Jan. 22, 1945
Iwo Jima operation   Feb. 15–March 16, 1945
Okinawa Gunto operation   March 17–June 30, 1945
Third Fleet operations against Japan   July 10–Aug. 15, 1945
Kuril Island operations   Feb. 1, 1944–Aug. 11, 1945
Borneo operations   April 27–July 20, 1945
Tinian operation   July 24–Aug. 1, 1944
Southern Philippines   Feb. 28–July 20, 1945
Hollandia operation   April 21–June 1, 1944
Manila Bay operations   Jan. 29–April 16, 1945
Escort, antisubmarine, Armed Guards, special operations   Aug. 8, 1942–Aug. 9, 1944
Minesweeping (specific operations)   June 23, 1945–March 2, 1946
Submarine War Patrols (specific patrols)   Dec. 7, 1941–Sept. 2, 1945

European-African-Middle Eastern Areas

North African operation   Nov. 8, 1942–July 9, 1943
Sicilian occupation   July 9–Aug. 17, 1943
Salerno landings   Sept. 9–21, 1943
West coast of Italy   Jan. 22–June 17, 1944
Normandy invasion   June 6–25, 1944
Northeast Greenland   July 10–Nov. 17, 1944
Invasion of Southern France   Aug. 15–Sept. 25, 1944
Malta reinforcement   April 14–21, May 3–16, 1942
Escort, antisubmarine, Armed Guards, special operations**   Dec. 16, 1941–July 9, 1944

* Including Guam and concurrent Asiatic Fleet operations.
** Including Russian Convoys.

RECOMMENDED READING

The authors used a variety of sources for this book, especially material researched in U.S., British, German, Japanese, and Soviet libraries and archives. In addition, a number of oral histories were used and many published books and articles were consulted, especially biographical works. The following lists some of the books that were used and that are recommended as worth reading for those who would delve into various aspects of World War II.

In addition, several standard reference books were consulted, especially the various editions of the annuals *Jane's Fighting Ships* and *Jane's All the World's Aircraft*. Also recommended are two encyclopedic works on the war: *The Encyclopedia of 20th Century Warfare* (1989), edited by Dr. Noble Frankland, and the *Simon & Schuster Encyclopedia of World War II*, edited by Thomas Parrish, with S.L.A. Marshall as chief consultant editor (1978). These books suffer from the former being too British in perspective and the latter being dated. Still, they are highly recommended. Also frequently consulted was the long-out-of-print *10 Eventful Years*, a four-volume record of events preceding, including, and following World War II, prepared under the direction of Walter Yust, editor of *Encyclopaedia Britannica* (1947).

Airborne Warfare

John R. Galvin. *Air Assault: The Development of Airmobile Warfare* (1969).
James A. Huston. *Out of the Blue, U.S. Army Airborne Operations in World War II* (1972).
James E. Mrazek. *Fighting Gliders of World War II* (1977).
Cornelius Ryan. *A Bridge too Far* (1974).
Julian Thompson. *Ready for Anything—The Parachute Regiment at War* (1989).
John Weeks. *Assault from the Sky—The History of Airborne Warfare* (1978).

Amphibious Warfare

Harry A. Gailey. *Peleliu 1944* (1983).
Robert Debs Heinel, Jr. *Soldiers of the Sea* (1962).

Jeter Isely and Philip Crowl. *The U.S. Marines and Amphibious War* (1951).
Vice Admiral Lord Louis Mountbatten, [foreword]. *Combined Operations: The Official Story of the Commandos* (1943).
Norman Polmar and Peter Mersky. *Amphibious Warfare* (1988).
Charles L. Updegraph, Jr. *Special Marine Corps Units of World War II* (1972).

Aviation

Alexander Boyd. *The Soviet Air Force Since 1918* (1977).
W. F. Craven and J. L. Cate. *The Army Air Forces in World War II*, 6 vols. (1948–1955).
Noble Frankland. *The Bombing Offensive Against Germany* (1965).
William Green. *Warplanes of the Third Reich* (1970).
Bill Gunston. *Aircraft of the Soviet Union* (1983).
Max Hastings. *Bomber Command* (1989).
Ikuhiko Hata and Yasuho Izawa. *Japanese Naval Aces and Fighter Units in World War II* (1989).
Robert Jackson. *The Red Falcons, The Soviet Air Force in Action, 1919–1969* (1970).
Herbert Molly Mason, Jr. *The Rise of the Luftwaffe, 1918–1940* (1973).
Herbert Molly Mason, Jr. *The United States Air Force* (1976).
Williamson Murray. *Luftwaffe* (1985).
Alfred Price. *Luftwaffe Handbook, 1939–1945* (1977).
J. R. Smith and Antony L. Kay. *German Aircraft of the Second World War* (1972).
F. G. Swanborough. *United States Military Aircraft Since 1909* (1963).
Gordon Swanborough and Peter M. Bowers. *United States Naval Aircraft Since 1911* (1968).
Owen Thetford. *Aircraft of the Royal Air Force, Since 1918* (1957).
Peter Townsend. *Duel of Eagles* (1970).
U.S. Navy. *United States Naval Aviation 1910–1980* (1981).
Ray Wagner (ed.). *The Soviet Air Force in World War II* (1973).
Derek Wood and Derek Dempster. *The Narrow Margin* (1961). [The Battle of Britain.]

Biographical

Stephen Ambrose. *Eisenhower—1890–1952* (1985).

H. H. Arnold. *Global Mission* (1949).

Elyesa Bazna. *I was Cicero* (1962).

Martin Blumenson and James L. Stokesbury. *Masters of the Art of Command* (1975).

Gerhard Boldt. *Hitler: The Last Ten Days* (1973).

Omar Bradley. *A General's Life* (1984).

Omar Bradley. *A Soldier's Story* (1951).

Thomas Buell. *Spruance: The Quiet Warrior* (1987).

Winston S. Churchill. *The Second World War*, 6 vols. (1948–1953).

Ed Cray. *General of the Army George C. Marshall: Soldier and Statesman* (1990).

Viscount Cunningham of Hyndhope. *A Sailor's Odyssey* (1951).

Walter Dornberger. *V-2* (1954).

Dwight D. Eisenhower. *Crusade in Europe* (1948).

Ladislas Farago. *Patton: Ordeal and Triumph* (1964).

Hugh Gibson (ed.). *The Ciano Diaries 1939–1943* (1945).

Martin Gilbert. *Winston S. Churchill, Road to Victory, 1941–1945* (1986).

Joseph Goebbels. *The Diaries of Joseph Goebbels* (1948).

William F. Halsey and J. Bryan III. *Admiral Halsey's Story* (1947).

Hastings L. Ismay. *The Memoirs of General the Lord Ismay* (1960).

Joseph Hobbs (ed.). *Dear General: Eisenhower's Wartime Letters to Marshall* (1971).

Glenn B. Infield. *Skorzeny: Hitler's Commando* (1981).

Albert Kesselring. *Kesselring: A Soldier's Record* (1953).

Ernest J. King and Walter Muir Whitehill. *Fleet Admiral King, A Naval Record* (1952).

Jean Lacouture. *De Gaulle: The Rebel, 1890–1944* (1991).

Eric Larrabee. *Commander in Chief* (1987).

Ronald Lewin. *Churchill as Warlord* (1973).

B. H. Liddell Hart. *The German Generals Talk* (1948).

Douglas MacArthur. *Reminiscences* (1964).

William Manchester. *American Caesar: Douglas MacArthur 1880–1964* (1978).

James P. O'Donnell. *The Bunker* (1978).

Thomas Parrish. *Roosevelt and Marshall* (1989).

George S. Patton. *War As I Knew It* (1947).

Forrest C. Pogue. *George C. Marshall: Ordeal and Hope 1939–1942* (1965).

Forrest C. Pogue. *George C. Marshall: Organizer of Victory 1943–1945* (1973).

Erich Raeder. *My Life* (1960).

Clark G. Reynolds. *Famous American Admirals* (1978).

James O. Richardson and George C. Dyer. *On the Treadmill to Pearl Harbor* (1973).

Matthias Schmidt. *Albert Speer: The End of a Myth* (1984).

Albert Seaton. *Stalin as Military Commander* (1976).

William L. Shirer. *Berlin Diary* (1940).

William L. Shirer. *The Nightmare Years 1930–1940* (1984).

Albert Speer. *Inside the Third Reich, Memoirs* (1970).

Albert Speer. *Spandau: The Secret Diaries* (1976).

Roger Spiller. *American Military Leaders* (1989).

Roger Spiller (ed.). *Dictionary of American Military Biography* (1984).

John Toland. *Adolf Hitler* (1976).

Raymond F. Toliver and Trevor J. Constable. *Fighter Aces* (1965).

Barbara Tuchman. *Stilwell and the American Experience in China* (1970).

Oliver Warner. *Admiral of the Fleet: Cunningham of Hyndhope* (1967).

Georgi Zhukov. *Memoirs* (1971).

The Holocaust and War Crimes

Robert E. Conot. *Justice at Nuremberg* (1983).

Lucy S. Dawidowicz. *The War Against the Jews* (1975).

Martin Gilbert. *The Holocaust* (1985).

Gert Korman (ed.). *Hunter and Hunted: Human History of the Holocaust* (1973).

Robert Jay Lifton. *The Nazi Doctors* (1986).

Benno Müller-Hill. *Murderous Science* (1988).

Richard L. Rubenstein and John K. Roth. *Approaches to Auschwitz* (1987).

Abram L. Sachar. *The Redemption of the Unwanted* (1983).

Jean-François Steiner. *Treblinka* (1967).

David S. Wyman. *The Abandonment of the Jews* (1984).

Intelligence

Pierre Accoce and Pierre Quet. *A Man called Lucy* (1966).

Ralph Bennett. *Ultra in the West* (1979).

Anthony Cave Brown. *Bodyguard of Lies* (1975).

William Casey. *The Secret War Against Hitler* (1988).

Charles P. Curtis. *The Oppenheimer Case: The Trial of a Security System* (1955).

H. Montgomery Hyde. *Room 3603: The Story of the British Intelligence Center in New York during World War II* (1963).

David Kahn. *The Code Breakers: The Story of Secret Writing* (1967).

David Kahn. *Hitler's Spies: German Military Intelligence in World War II* (1978).

Ronald Lewin. *The American Magic: Codes, Ciphers and the Defeat of Japan* (1982).

Ronald Lewin. *Ultra Goes to War* (1978).

J. C. Masterman. *The Double-Cross System* (1972).

Major-General Sir Kenneth Strong. *Intelligence at the Top: The Recollections of a British Intelligence Officer* (1968).

Nigel West. *MI6: British Secret Intelligence Service Operation 1909–45* (1983).

Nigel West. *A Thread of Deceit: Espionage Myths of World War II* (1985).

F. W. Winterbotham. *The Ultra Secret* (1974).

Roberta Wohlstetter. *Pearl Harbor: Warning and Decision* (1962).

Land Combat

The Officer's Guide. 9th edition (1943).

Vasily I. Chuikov. *The Fall of Berlin* (1967).

James F. Dunnigan (ed.). *War in the East* (1977).

George Forty. *U.S. Army Handbook 1939–1945* (1980).

Kent Roberts Greenfield, Robert R. Palmer, and Bell I. Wiley. *The Organization of Ground Combat Troops* (1947).

Max Hastings. *Overlord* (1985).

Alistair Horne. *To Lose a Battle, France 1940* (1969).

Ronald Lewin. *Rommel as Military Commander* (1968).

Kenneth Macksey. *Afrika Korps* (1972).

Kenneth Macksey. *Panzer Division* (1968).

Bill Mauldin. *Up Front* (1945).

F. W. von Mellenthin. *Panzer Battles* (1956).

Charles Messenger. *The Blitzkrieg Story* (1976).

Alan Moorehead. *The March to Tunis* (1943).

Edgar O'Ballance. *The Red Army* (1964).

Hu Pu-yu. *A Brief History of the Sino-Japanese War (1937–1945)* (1974).

Arthur Swinson. *Defeat in Malaya and the Fall of Singapore* (1969).

Telford Taylor. *The Breaking Wave—World War II in the Summer of 1940* (1967).

Jürgen Thorwald. *Flight in the Winter* (1951). [American title: *Defeat in the East.*]

Russell F. Weigley. *Eisenhower's Lieutenants* (1981).

Earl F. Ziemke. *Stalingrad to Berlin: The German Defeat in the East* (1968).

Earl F. Ziemke and Magna E. Bauer. *Moscow to Stalingrad: Decision in the East* (1987).

Marine Corps

John Hersey. *Into the Valley. A Skirmish of the Marines* (1942).

James D. Horan and Gerold Frank. *Out in the Boondocks (Marines in Action in the Pacific)* (1943).

J. Robert Moskin. *The U.S. Marine Corps Story* (1977).

Robert Sherrod. *History of Marine Corps Aviation in World War II* (1952).

Richard Tregaskis. *Guadalcanal Diary* (1943).

Naval Warfare

Paul Auphan and Jacques Mordal. *The French Navy in World War II* (1959).

C. D. Bekker. *Defeat at Sea* (1955).

Clay Blair, Jr. *Silent Victory—The U.S. Submarine War Against Japan* (1975).

Marc' Antonio Bragadin. *The Italian Navy in World War II* (1957).

David Brown. *Warship Losses of World War Two* (1990).

Dorr Carpenter and Norman Polmar. *Submarines of the Imperial Japanese Navy, 1904–1945* (1986).

James C. Fahey. *The Ships and Aircraft of the U.S. Fleet,* 5 editions (1939–1945).

Mitsuo Fuchida and Masatake Okumiya. *Midway, The Battle that Doomed Japan* (1955).

Günter Hessler. *The U-Boat War in the Atlantic, 1939–1945* (1989).

W. J. Holmes. *Undersea Victory—The influence of submarine operations on the war in the Pacific* (1966).

Rikihei Inoguchi, Tadashi Nakajima, and Roger Pineau. *The Divine Wind* (1958).

Masanori Ito with Roger Pineau. *The End of the Imperial Japanese Navy* (1962).

Donald Macintyre. *The Naval War Against Hitler* (1971).

Samuel Eliot Morison. *History of United States Naval Operations in World War II,* 15 vols. (1947–1962).

R. J. Overy. *The Air War: 1939–1945* (1981).

Norman Polmar. *Aircraft Carriers: A History of Carrier Aviation and its Influence on World Events* (1969).

Jürgen Rohwer and G. Hümmelchen. *Chronology of the War at Sea, 1939–1945,* 2 vols. (1974).

S. W. Roskill. *The War at Sea,* 3 vols. (1954–1961).

B. B. Schofield. *The Russian Convoy* (1964).

J. P. Mallman Showell. *U-Boats Under the Swastika* (1973).

John Terraine. *Business in Great Waters—The U-Boat Wars, 1916–1945* (1989).

Kemp Tolley. *Cruise of the Lanikai* (1973).

Dan van der Vat. *The Atlantic Campaign* (1988).

Anthony J. Watts. *The U-Boat Hunters* (1976).

M. J. Whitley. *German Capital Ships of World War Two* (1989).

Strategy and Policy

Kent Roberts Greenfield (ed.). *Command Decisions* (1960).

Maurice Matloff and Edwin M. Snell. *Strategic Planning for Coalition Warfare, 1941–1942* (1953).

Ienaga Saburo. *The Pacific War, 1931–1945* (1978).

Perry McCoy Smith. *The Air Force Plans for Peace, 1943–1945* (1970).

John Toland. *The Rising Sun* (1970).

Weapons and Matériel

John Batchelor and Ian Hogg. *Rail Guns* (1973).

John Campbell. *Naval Weapons of World War Two* (1985).

Leslie R. Groves. *Now it Can be Told: The Story of the Manhattan Project* (1962).

John Hersey. *Hiroshima* (1946).

Alfred Price. *Instruments of Darkness* (1967). [The history of electronic warfare.]

Richard Rhodes. *The Making of the Atomic Bomb* (1986).

Martin J. Sherwin. *A World Destroyed: The Atomic Bomb and the Grand Alliance* (1977).

Also Recommended

Robert H. Adelman and Colonel George Walton. *Rome Fell Today* (1968).

Allan Berube. *Coming Out Under Fire: The History of Gay Men and Women in World War Two* (1990).

Joan and Clay Blair, Jr. *Return from the River Kwai* (1979).

David Brinkley. *Washington Goes to War* (1988).

Arthur Bryant. *Turn of the Tide* and *Triumph in the West* (1959, 1974).

Peter Calvocoressi and Guy Wint. *Total War* (1990).

John Costello. *Love, Sex and War 1939–1945* (1985).

Martin Van Creveld. *Supplying War* (1977).

Cecil B. Currey. *Follow Me and Die* (1984).

Trevor Dupuy and R. Ernest Dupuy. *An Encyclopedia of Military History* (1977).

David Eggenberger. *An Encyclopedia of Battles* (1985).

John S. D. Eisenhower. *The Bitter Woods* (1969).

J. F. C Fuller. *A Military History of the Western World* Vol. 3 (1956).

Oliver Gramling and AP correspondents. *Free Men Are Fighting* (1942).

Neil Grant. *The German-Soviet Pact* (1975).

Tom Harrisson. *Living through the Blitz* (1976).

Edwin Hoyt. *Japan's War* (1985).

James Jones. *World War II* (1975).

John Keegan. *The Second World War* (1989).

Phillip Knightley. *The First Casualty* (1975).

Robert Leckie. *Strong Men Armed: The United States Marines against Japan* (1962).

B. H. Liddell Hart. *History of the Second World War* (1970).

A. J. Liebling. *Mollie & other War Pieces* (1943).

William Manchester. *The Arms of Krupp 1587–1968* (1968).

Roger Manvell. *Films and the Second World War* (1974).

H. G. Nicholas (ed.). *Washington Despatches 1941–45* (1981).

A. W. Palmer. *A Dictionary of Modern History 1789–1945* (1962).

Barrie Pitt (ed.). *The Military History of World War II* (1986).

Gordon Prange. *At Dawn We Slept* (1981).

Edwin O. Reischauer. *Japan: Tradition & Transformation* (1978).

David Roxan and Ken Wanstall. *The Rape of Art* (1964).

William L. Shirer. *The Rise and Fall of the Third Reich* (1959).

Ronald Spector. *Eagle Against the Sun* (1985).

Lawrence Taylor. *A Trial of Generals* (1981).

John Terraine. *The Right of the Line* (1985).

Studs Terkel. *The Good War* (1984).

Russell Weigley. *The American Way of War* (1977).

W. J. West (ed.). *Orwell, The War Commentaries* (1985).

Theodore H. White. *In Search of History* (1978).

Daniel Yergin. *Shattered Peace* (1977).

Personality Index

Code and Project Names Index

*See entries in War Guide.

938